Criminological
Perspectives

Eugene McLaughlin & John Muncie

3rd
EDITION

Criminological Perspectives

SAGE

Los Angeles | London | New Delhi
Singapore | Washington DC

Los Angeles | London | New Delhi
Singapore | Washington DC

SAGE Publications Ltd
1 Oliver's Yard
55 City Road
London EC1Y 1SP

SAGE Publications Inc.
2455 Teller Road
Thousand Oaks, California 91320

SAGE Publications India Pvt Ltd
B 1/I 1 Mohan Cooperative Industrial Area
Mathura Road
New Delhi 110 044

SAGE Publications Asia-Pacific Pte Ltd
3 Church Street
#10-04 Samsung Hub
Singapore 049483

Editor: Natalie Aguilera
Editorial assistant: James Piper
Production editor: Sarah Cooke
Marketing manager: Sally Ransom
Cover design: Francis Kenney
Typeset by: C&M Digitals (P) Ltd, Chennai, India
Printed by: MPG Books Group, Bodmin, Cornwall

This third edition published 2013
Second edition published 2002. Reprinted 2003, 2004,
2005, 2006, 2007, 2008, 2009, 2011
First edition published 1995. Reprinted 1996, 1997, 1998,
1999, 2000, 2001

Library of Congress Control Number: 2012945075

British Library Cataloguing in Publication data

A catalogue record for this book is available from the
British Library

MIX
Paper from
responsible sources
FSC® C018575
www.fsc.org

ISBN 978-1-4462-0785-7
ISBN 978-1-4462-0786-4 (pbk)

Contents

About the Editors

Eugene McLaughlin is Professor of Criminology at the University of Southampton. His first academic post was at the University of Hong Kong and he was at The Open University before moving to City University London. Professor McLaughlin has written extensively on policing and police reform, police–community relations, criminal justice policy reforms and criminological theory. His most recent books are *The Sage Handbook of Criminological Theory* (with Tim Newburn, Sage, 2010) and *The New Policing* (Sage, 2007). His current research concentrates on: the policing of multi-pluralist societies; the mediatization of crime and criminal justice policy; the politics of law and order; and new developments in critical criminological theory. He is an associate editor of *Crime, Media and Culture* and is a former co-editor of *Theoretical Criminology*.

John Muncie is Emeritus Professor of Criminology at the Open University, UK. He is the author of *Youth and Crime* (3rd edition, Sage, 2009), and he has published widely on issues in comparative youth justice and children's rights, including the co-edited companion volumes *Youth Crime and Justice* and *Comparative Youth Justice* (Sage, 2006). He has produced numerous Open University texts and readers, including *Crime: Local and Global* (Willan, 2010), *Criminal Justice: Local and Global* (Willan, 2010), *The Problem of Crime* (2nd edition, Sage, 2001), *Crime Prevention and Community Safety* (Sage, 2001) and *Imprisonment: European Perspectives* (Harvester, 1991). He has also contributed nine volumes to the *The Sage Library of Criminology* (Sage, 2007–2009). He is co-editor of the Sage journal *Youth Justice: An International Journal*.

Preface to the Third Edition

Criminology continues to flourish: important new criminology departments have been established, reflecting the student demand for criminology courses and degrees; national and international criminology conferences of a variety of hues are burgeoning; most academic presses have at least one thriving criminology series and a generation of new journals; and a multitude of sub-specialisms have been established. Criminology also remains an indispensible element of global popular culture and entertainment. There is, however, no one 'Criminology' that is on offer. As ever, the discipline continues to be marked by a series of competing discourses some old, some re-workings, some genuinely new, some reassuring and some troubling, about what criminology is and should be in the twenty-first century. Some believe that we are in need of major criminological reinvention and redrawing of boundaries, yet others are endeavoring to get to grips with various aspects of the archaeology of the criminological and indeed *pre*-criminological knowledge. Yet others seem to have learned to live with or ignore passing fads, and continue to pursue criminology's historical empirical project of 'causes and control'.

This third edition of *Criminological Perspectives* continues to reflect the diverse lines of theoretical enquiry that constitute contemporary criminology. The overall aim of this new edition is two-fold: to provide an accessible set of edited readings which introduces students to the eclectic nature of 'criminological knowledge' and to prompt readers to engage critically with the constituent elements of the unfolding criminological enterprise. In compiling this edition we recognize that we have been unable (not least because of the constraints of space) to cover every aspect of criminology. Like all editors, we have been forced to make some difficult choices and uneasy compromises. But we have remained committed to the importance of our original project to choose and reproduce original readings, rather than to depend on existing textbook summaries, commentaries and reviews. As ever we hope that students will be better able to acquire a critical appreciation of criminology by reading 'in the raw'. As far as possible, we have chosen readings for each part which are to some extent in conversation with each other. To do so, we have concentrated on pieces which provide expositions of key theoretical positions and/or which suggest new lines of departure. It is clear that no one theoretical perspective can lay sole claim to the empirical referents of crime and criminal justice. Criminology in our view is a 'site' of contested meaning where competing theoretical perspectives meet. Sometimes they are able to speak to, listen to and understand each other, at others they appear not to share any common discourse. There is, therefore, no one criminology to be found in this reader but a multitude of often contradictory criminological perspectives which in the main depend and draw upon knowledges generated from elsewhere. To illustrate this point we have included pieces that depart from traditional agendas, and/or offer fruitful avenues for cross-discipline development.

The Reader is in six parts. Part One *Criminological Foundations* focuses on the origins of criminology as expressed through a wide variety of subject positions and theoretical arguments. It reveals a number of 'starting-points' from classicist interpretations of the function of law, positivist interrogations of the causes of crime and quantitative studies of crime statistics, through to Marxist, sociological and anarchist critiques of the problems of crime, law, and the state and social order. We have also included Bentham's 'panopticon', the plan for a 'new model prison' that was to exert such an influence on Foucault's 'discipline and punish' thesis.

Part Two *Causes of Crime* concentrates on criminology's historic obsession with crime causation. Again, a wide variety in type of explanation and level of analysis is notable. The readings illustrate some of the key *contemporary* attempts to tackle the issue of crime causation and include discussion of genetic factors, personality traits, risk factors, illegitimacy and the underclass, relative deprivation, the moral and expressive attractions of the preference for crime over non crime and crime as 'routine activity'. A number of competing theoretical positions and paradigms are at work in these chapters, from individual and sociological variants of positivism to neo-classicism, left realism and cultural criminology. Also included is a feminist critique of criminology's traditional representation of female criminality.

Part Three *Criminalization* reveals that understanding the 'problem of crime' does not simply involve trying to account for why certain individuals transgress moral and legal codes whilst others do not, but also necessitates interrogation of how and why it is that only certain behaviours seem to be subjected to criminal sanction whilst other harmful acts may go unnoticed, un-policed or are even socially approved. Key readings from interactionist, labelling, social reaction, Marxist, cultural and critical criminology perspectives are included to show how the subject matter of criminology has been significantly broadened to encompass issues of social order and power, and the ability of the state and powerful groups in society to confer and enforce the label of criminality on others. Collectively these readings encourage a critical reading and deconstruction of traditional and populist notions of what constitutes 'crime', 'criminality' and 'criminal behaviour'.

Part Four *Criminal Justice and Crime Prevention* examines a number of competing rationales for systems of crime control, from deterrence, just deserts, restoration and rehabilitation through to crime prevention. Critiques of existing crime control systems – emanating from left realist, and abolitionist perspectives – are also included. The part includes readings which explore how far alternative informal systems of control – based on notions such as restorative justice and reintegrative shaming – can offer a more equitable/just and less repressive/punitive vision of the future of social control.

Part Five *Control-ology: Governance and Surveillance* explores how individuals and populations are controlled not simply through the formal processes of criminal justice, but through regulation, surveillance and 'government'. Foucault's vision of a 'carceral society' is used as a starting point to examine the ever-expanding technologies, practices, rationales and strategies that are constitutive of crime governance in what has been defined as a 'post social' moment. The readings explore the dynamics driving the general expansion of post social control; the emergent principles, infrastructures and frameworks of post-social control; and the social, political, legal and ethical implications of post-social control.

Part Six *Global Harms and Risks* poses a number of questions concerning the futures of criminology and its potential for theoretical development particularly in the context of increasing global harms and risks, insecurities and 'unknowns'. A range of perspectives and issues are explored and compared. Some of these appear to herald new openings for the criminological enterprise; others rework more traditional forms of analysis. At one and the same time they underline the past failings of criminology, its continuing diversity and the remaining potential to shed new light on new forms of crime and criminalization, harm and harm reduction and social control. Readers will soon become aware that however well established the debate and however numerous the perspectives, none of the central criminological questions highlighted can stand as resolved. As is nearly always the case in the social sciences all of them constitute perennial problems which are always open to further research and debate.

The history of this text dates back to the early 1990s when we were looking for a collection of original readings to support students studying the Open University third-level course, *Crime, Order and Social Control*. The success of that volume, both within and outside of the Open University, encouraged us to prepare a second edition which was first published in 2003. We were indebted to many people in putting that text together, not least the thousands of students who have studied criminology with The Open University. Their response to, and ability to engage with, previous course materials has been central in our decisions of what to include and in guiding our assessment of what is accessible and appropriate for study. We also then had the benefit of working with an Open University course team who continually reminded us to keep the needs of students in our minds. We have kept these principles uppermost in our thoughts in constructing this third edition.

Over the years we have been indebted to numerous colleagues and commentators. In compiling the first edition informal discussions with Pat Carlen, Stan Cohen, Richard Sparks, Loraine Gelsthorpe and Karim Murji were more influential than they may have realized. In the process of assembling the second edition we benefitted from the advice of John Braithwaite, Lynn Chancer, David Garland, Tony Jefferson, Pat O'Malley, Ken Pease, Joe Sim, Kevin Stenson, Sandra Walklate and Jock Young. For this edition we are indebted to the numerous anonymous

reviewers who kindly submitted enthusiastic reviews and developmental suggestions to Sage. Above all we acknowledge the invaluable work of our co-collaborator
on the first edition, Mary Langan and our co-editor on the second edition, Gordon
Hughes. Their presence is still to be felt in some of the current selection of readings.

For this third edition we are particularly indebted to Caroline Porter and Natalie Aguilera at Sage for agreeing with us that a third edition of *Criminological
Perspectives* is vital for the next generation of criminology students.

Eugene McLaughlin
John Muncie

Acknowledgements

We are grateful for permission to reproduce the following:

CHAPTER 11

Sarnoff A. Mednick, William F. Gabrielli, Jr., and Barry Hutchings, 'Genetic factors in the etiology of criminal behaviour', in Sarnoff A. Mednick, Terrie E. Moffitt and Susan A. Stack (eds), *The Causes of Crime, New Biological Approaches* (1987) © Cambridge University Press, reproduced with permission.

CHAPTER 14

Extract from 'Underclass' by Charles Murray in The Emerging British Underclass (1990) © Civitas: Institute for the Study of Civil Society and reproduced by permission.

CHAPTER 15

John Lea and Jock Young, 'Relative Deprivation' in *What is to be Done about Law and Order?* (1984) pp. 81; 95–101; 218–25, by permission of Penguin Books Ltd.

CHAPTER 17

Travis Hirschi and Michael R. Gottfredson, 'The Generality of Deviance' in *The Generality of Deviance* (1994) pp. 1–23, by permission of Transaction Publishers.

CHAPTER 20

Copyright © 1990 Jack Katz. Reprinted by permission of Basic Books, a member of the Perseus Books Group.

CHAPTER 22

Howard Becker, 'Outsiders' in *Outsiders: Studies in the Sociology of Deviance* (1963) pp. 1–18, by permission of Simon & Schuster, Inc.

CHAPTER 23

Stanley Cohen, 'Mods, Rockers and the Rest: Community Reactions to Juvenile Delinquency' in *The Howard Journal of Criminal Justice* (1967) 12 (2):121–130, by permission of John Wiley and Sons.

CHAPTER 24

William J. Chambliss, 'Toward a political economy of crime' in *Theory and Society* (1975) 2 (1):149–170, with kind permission from Springer Science+Business Media © William J. Chambliss.

CHAPTER 25

Steven Box, 'Crime, power and ideological mystification' in *Power, Crime and Mystification* (1983) Reproduced by permission of Taylor & Francis Books UK. © Tavistock.

CHAPTER 26

Angela Y. Davis, 'Race and Criminalization: Black Americans and the Punishment Industry' in *The House that Race Built* (1997) edited by Wahneema Lubiano. Used by permission of Pantheon Books, a division of Random House, Inc. Any third party use of this material, outside of this publication, is prohibited. Interested parties must apply directly to Random House, Inc. for permission.

CHAPTER 27

Louk H. C. Hulsman, 'Critical criminology and the concept of crime' in *Contemporary Crises* (1986) 10 (1):63–80, with kind permission from Springer Science+Business Media, © Martinus Nijhoff Publishers.

CHAPTER 29

Jeff Ferrell, 'Cultural Criminology' in *Annual Review of Sociology*, (1999) 25:395–418. Republished by permission of Annual Reviews.

CHAPTER 30

Copyright © 1975 JQ Wilson. Reprinted by permission of Basic Books, a member of the Perseus Books Group.

CHAPTER 32

Francis T. Cullen and Karen E. Gilbert 'The value of Rehabilitation' in *Reaffirming Rehabilitation* (2012) © Elsevier.

CHAPTER 33

Ronald V. G. Clarke, '"Situational" Crime Prevention: Theory and Practice' in *The British Journal of Criminology* (1980) 20 (2):136–147, by permission of Oxford University Press.

CHAPTER 35

Nils Christie, 'Conflicts as Property' in *The British Journal of Criminology* (1977) 17 (1):1–15, by permission of Oxford University Press.

CHAPTER 36

John Braithwaite, 'Why and how does shaming work?' in *Crime, Shame and Reintegration*, (1989) © Cambridge University Press, reproduced with permission.

CHAPTER 40

Michel Foucault, *Discipline and Punish* (1977) English Translation copyright © Alan Sheridan (New York: Pantheon). Originally published in French as *Surveiller et Punir*. Copyright © 1975 by Editions Gallimard. Reprinted by permission of Georges Borchardt, Inc., for Editions Gallimard and Penguin Books Ltd.

CHAPTER 41

Stanley Cohen, 'The punitive city: Notes on the dispersal of social control' in *Contemporary Crises* (1979) 3 (4):339–363, with kind permission from Springer Science+Business Media. © Elsevier Scientific Publishing Company.

CHAPTER 42

Clifford D. Shearing and Philip C. Stenning, 'From the Panopticon to Disney World: The Development of Discipline' in *Perspectives in Criminal Law: Essays in Honour of John LL.J. Edwards* (1985) (eds) Anthony N. Doob and Edward L. Greenspan. Reproduced by permission of Canada Law Book, a division of Thomson Reuters Canada Limited.

CHAPTER 45

Copyright © 1997 Lawrence Friedman and George Fisher. Reprinted by permission of Westview Press, a member of the Perseus Books Group.

CHAPTER 48

Loïc Wacquant, 'Ordering Insecurity: Social Polarization and the Punitive Upsurge' in *Radical Philosophy Review* (2008) 11 (1):1–19, by permission of The Philosophy Documentation Center © Radical Philosophy Association.

CHAPTER 55

Jackie Turner and Liz Kelly, 'Intersections between Diasporas and Crime Groups in the Constitution of the Human Trafficking Chain' in *The British Journal of Criminology* (2009) 49 (2):184–201, by permission of Oxford University Press.

Introduction: theorizing crime and criminal justice

Eugene McLaughlin and John Muncie

Whilst the transgression of moral and legal codes has probably always raised concerns for the maintenance of social order, 'crime' and 'criminology' have not always been with us. The first generally recognized school of criminology, the classical school of the eighteenth century, was less concerned with understanding the nature of 'the criminal' and more with developing rational and systematic means of delivering justice. In essence, classicism was, and remains, a plea for the supremacy of law, rather than of religion, superstition and arbitrary justice. Crime is understood as a product of a rational free will; a course of action freely chosen through calculations of the pain and pleasure involved. Its control is assumed to lie in better and more efficient carefully calculated means of punishment. Establishing specific causes of crime or trying to understand its meaning is of little or no concern.

It was not until the early nineteenth century that crime became an object of scientific enquiry in its own right. In important respects, a concept of 'crime' only came to replace a concept of 'sin' when a burgeoning legal apparatus, designed to protect property and the interests of the nation-state, evolved out of the social, economic and cultural transformations of the industrial revolution. As concern over the 'problem of crime' intensified, so crime became the object of more systematic observance and measurement. Analysis of its extent and causes was first made possible through the publication of national criminal statistics in France in the 1820s. Regularities in the occurrence of crime were then explained with reference to such factors as age, sex, climate and economic conditions. If crime rates were regular and predictable, it was assumed that the causes of crime must lie outside of each individual's control. It was not a simple matter of individual choice.

Such was the cornerstone of a positivist criminology which radically proposed that crime was a non-rational and determinate product of undersocialization and could be studied, via clinical and statistical methods, in much the same way as scientists studied the natural world. Typically, positivist conceptions of crime – whether they be individually or socially based – focus on isolating specific causes. The Italian *scuola positiva* of the late nineteenth century maintained that criminality had multi-factor explanations. In its earliest form, biological causes were prioritized. The criminal, it was argued, was a throwback to a more primitive form of human being, distinguishable through such physiological characteristics as large jaw and ears and facial asymmetry. Such a conclusion was based on the painstaking measurement of the skulls and skeletons of 'known criminals'. As a result it has been heralded as the first *scientific* study of crime. And it is probably no coincidence that it is also from this time that the term 'criminology' is widely assumed to have originated.

The impact of positivism on subsequent developments within criminology cannot be overstated. By searching for the causes of *criminal* behaviour as opposed to other human behaviours, positive criminology assumes that such behaviour has its own peculiar set of characteristics. The aim is to isolate key differences between criminals and non-criminals. Some theorists focus on biological and psychological factors, attempt to isolate specific genetic or personality causes or risk factors and thus locate the sources of crime primarily within the individual. Other theorists argue that more insights can be gained by studying the social context external to individuals and maintain that crime is better explained with reference to such factors as levels of economic consumption, sites of social disorganization and types of urban structure. The origins of all such social approaches can be traced to the insistence that social phenomena, such as crime and law, have an objective existence of their own and exist independently of the individuals who experience them.

Positivist criminologies – whether individual or sociological in focus – remain influential because they prolong the modernist concern to account for crime with reference to some quantifiable and objective criteria. They also hold on to the hope that because people are propelled into crime through a range of determining factors, then it will always remain possible to treat or neutralize the underlying causes. Such treatments may range from individual rehabilitation through to social economic and policy reform.

Positivism, however, has always stood uneasily against the key principle of classicism that every individual is, and should be made, responsible for their actions. The development of criminology as governmental practice, for example, has meant that the advocacy of positivist treatment methods has always been contested by dominant classicist assumptions about free will and rationality.

Almost from its inception, scientific positivism was also under attack from radicals for failing to take a more critical stance towards the nature of the social order in which crime and criminality are located. They warned that crime cannot be analysed outside of the social and economic circumstances in which it occurs. The propositions that law is a tool of state repression and that crime is a product of exploitative labour relations challenged the key positivist assumptions that crime is something abnormal and only practised by identifiable, pathological 'others'. Rather, such analyses (with differing ideological and political emphases) maintained that crime was widespread and ubiquitous – a defining characteristic of any social order based on inequality and social division.

Despite pragmatic, theoretical and political misgivings, it was not until the mid-twentieth century that the conventional wisdom of positivism was subjected to sustained intellectual challenge. Whilst positivism tends to deny that criminality involves any element of choice, creativity or meaning, interactionism is more concerned to grant authenticity to deviant actions by recording the motives and meanings of the deviant actors themselves. Interactionism produced an epistemological break by radically shifting the object of criminological inquiry away from trying to isolate the presumed factors propelling a pathological few to break the rules of an assumed social consensus, to an analysis which rested on a conflict or pluralist conception of society in which deviance was ubiquitous and where 'crime' was constructed through the partial and pernicious practices of social reaction and social control. The adages of social reaction theory that 'there can be no crime without law' and that 'social control leads to deviance' effectively turned the time-honoured premises of positivism on their head. By the early 1970s this critical paradigm effectively placed a number of counter propositions on the criminological agenda. Criminology was under challenge from a more comprehensive sociology of crime and deviance. Here questions of social control, rather than crime causation, are the central matters of concern. A determination to 'appreciate' (and some would say 'celebrate') deviance in terms of its subjective meaning for particular actors takes precedence over the scientific assertions that criminal behaviour is determined by a mix of innate, genetic or physiological incapacities (born bad) or instances of ineffective child rearing, family pathology and social disorganization (made bad). By focusing on processes of criminalization and law formation, rather than crime and criminal behaviour, whole new areas of research and empathies have been opened up, in which definitional rather than behavioural issues are central.

It is in this context that we can account for the emergence in the 1970s of 'new criminologies' which were grounded in sociological developments. Their contribution lay not so much in innovation, but in the attempt to synthesize several different old traditions. The concern to respect the authenticity of the diverse and unique worlds of everyday life continued a tradition established by the Chicago School of the 1930s and the social interactionists; whilst dimensions of power and social control were appropriated from social reaction theory. The 'new criminologies', however, attempted to ground this anti-positivist radicalization by taking the world of personal meanings and social reaction back into a critique of the history and structure of society. This was achieved through locating definitions of crime and modes of control in the precise context of the social relationships and institutional arrangements emanating from particular modes of economic production. Clearly what this work was advocating was that the key subject of the criminology was not crime and deviance as behaviours, but a radical analysis of the social order and the power to criminalize and control. When the task of criminology was defined as one of creating a society 'in which the facts of human diversity are not subject to the power to criminalize'(*The New Criminology*), it was clear that the aim was to transform criminology from a science of social control and into a fully politicized struggle for social justice. Part of this also relied on a reworking of the theoretical premises of Marxism. Following the supposition that laws perpetuate a particular mode of economic production, it is argued that bourgeois law not only acts to preserve existing unequal forms of property ownership, but also punishes the property offences of the poor whilst maintaining stable conditions for the exploitation of their labour. The subject matter of criminology has, as a result, been considerably broadened from its previous narrow focus of attempting to discover why those lowest in the social order appeared to exhibit the highest rate of criminality. Investigating the policies and crimes of the powerful and the human rights violations of the state, for example, have become legitimate forms of enquiry. Similarly, it is argued that more can be discovered about crime by examining how certain individuals and communities become subject to processes of criminalization, rather than by trying to identify particular causes.

In this way criminology has also become more critical of the purpose and functioning of the agencies of criminal justice, and suggests that law and its enforcement are the key instruments by which 'race', class and gender power can be 'legitimately' exercised. The scientific objectivity and political neutrality of previous criminology is called into question; and the complex question of the relationship between knowledge and power is posed. Reliance on official statistics as 'real' indicators of where in society crime is committed and the rate at which it is committed is questioned. A critical approach not only argues that a greater number of 'crimes' are committed than official statistics suggest, but also that criminality is to be found at all points in the social formation. The key questions are directed not so much at the criminal act in isolation but at the dynamics of social institutions which construct crime and their ability to convey such social constructions to the public. The study of crime necessitates a much wider study of the agencies, processes and structures of social control.

These theoretical developments, originating from the mid-1970s, however, took place against the political backdrop of a resurgence in popular law and order politics and authoritarianism. In the UK and the United States the rhetoric of a resurgent radical Right revived a neo-classical vision of criminality as voluntaristic – a course of action willingly chosen by calculating individuals, lacking in self-control and with a potential for communal contamination and moral degeneracy. New 'realist' theorists of the Right disengaged from existing criminological agendas – whether they be positivist or critical – by claiming that crime emanates from rationally calculating individuals who are insufficiently deterred from their actions by a criminal justice system deemed to be chaotic and ineffective or lacking in 'just deserts'. Both remind us of the potency and endurance of classicist and neo-classicist formulations of the 'crime problem'. The key concern is with developing efficient means of control rather than with questions of causality. Against a backdrop of perennially growing official statistics of crime and the presumption of increases in a rational public fear, the extension of police powers, the erosion of civil liberties and the expansion of imprisonment to unprecedented levels have all been justified. The public/political debate has come to be dominated by images of violent crime, lawlessness, disorder and declining morality. In the twenty-first century it seems that authoritarianism, and law and order policies have the political potency to undermine welfare and rehabilitation discourses. However, the 'tough on crime' discourse has also been tempered by an apparent failure to prevent escalating crime rates. Within the developing ethos of cost-effectiveness in all public services, it appears to be acknowledged that all that can be realistically hoped for is to implement more pragmatic means of managing crime through situational opportunity preventative measures, and developing ever more cost-effective and efficient methods of managing the criminal justice system.

The New Right colonization of almost the whole terrain of law and order politics in the late 1970s forced sections of the Left to rethink their position and to move closer to the mainstream in a pragmatic attempt to counter some of its more reactionary policies. The self-styled left realists gradually disassociated themselves from the 'new' and 'critical' criminologies in an effort to find a new criminology for new times. Left realism initiated its programme through virulent attacks directed as much to the Left as to the Right. Labelling its former bed fellows as idealist, it argues that the Left has traditionally either romanticized or underestimated the nature and impact of crime and largely 'speaks to itself' through its lack of engagement with the day-to-day issues of crime control and social policy. With empirical support from a series of victim surveys, left realism is able to assert that the fear of crime is indeed growing and that, in particular, property and street crimes are real issues that need to be addressed, rather than dismissed as social constructions. In short it concurs with right realism that people's fear of crime is rational and a reflection of inner city social reality. However, it differs from the Right in its insistence that the causes of crime need to be once more established and theorized; and a social justice and welfare programme should be initiated to tackle social and economic inequalities, under the rubric of 'inclusive citizenship'.

Clearly this marks a distinct break with many critical criminologies. It invokes many themes (such as crime causation) which are grounded in positivist criminology, with, for example, street crime being portrayed as caused by relative deprivation. In this respect it appears to reflect and indeed mirror New Right and media-driven definitions of what constitutes serious crime, and consequently downplays corporate crime and crimes of the state. Analyses of the relationship between the public, criminal justice agencies, offenders and victims are largely restricted to street crime, and fail to capture the harm caused, for example, by workplace injury, occupation-related diseases and environmental pollution. Left realism's dismissal of critical criminology as idealist ignores the interventionist role that critical criminologists have played since the 1970s in developing a politics of support for marginalized groups such as black youth, prisoners, gypsies and women, as well as establishing independent inquiries into aspects of state authoritarianism and monitoring police practices.

Equally, critical criminology has not ignored the necessity of developing new theoretical frameworks in which to further an understanding of processes of criminalization. It believes that the para-Marxist heritage need not be totally abandoned but can be refined and developed; to deliver not a sealed doctrine, but a new set of provisional hypotheses or frames of conceptual resources/ deposits. For example, it has become common to find a more complex set of analyses which move away from a restricted chain of criminological references – state, law, crime, criminals – to the examination of other arenas of social regulation. By recognizing and working within a Foucauldian concept of 'governance' it has become possible to study how networks of power and resistance are diffuse and governed more by their own internal logics and knowledge than by the definite intentions of particular classes or oppressive states. This direction in turn has opened up work on a variety of semi-autonomous realms, such as informal justice, local communities, privatized organizations and families in which notions of policing and control are present, but whose relation to the state is by no means direct and unambiguous. It is in these areas too that interest in the potential of often neglected processes of informal networks of order and control has been awakened, albeit sometimes from different theoretical starting points.

In this context the issue of idealism vs realism becomes something of a red herring. It is surely just as 'real' to unearth the complexities of processes of criminalization, resistance and control, as it is to be bound to public perceptions and victim surveys. Whilst the mainstream of criminology increasingly appears to be simply involved in a technocratic 'what works' exercise to evaluate the effectiveness of criminal justice procedures and practices, the critical paradigm continues to expose the discriminatory powers and outcomes and retains a space in which alternative visions of social justice can be created. Such visions remain important for they enable us to rethink social conditions in terms of them not simply being made bearable (as in left realism or social democratic reformism) but transformed into a vehicle for emancipation.

A key failing of all criminologists up to the 1970s was to acknowledge the 'presence of absence' in the form of critical analysis of gender relations and women and crime. The development of feminist inroads into the male bastion of criminology initially took the form of a comprehensive critique of the discipline, firstly for its neglect even to study women's involvement in crime and criminal justice and, secondly for its distortion of women's experiences as essentially biologically driven. Since the mid-1970s a burgeoning literature has revealed that women's crimes are committed in different circumstances to men's and that the response to women's law breaking is constituted within sexist assumptions of femininity which have only further added to women's oppression. This body of knowledge has now successfully demonstrated how criminology has traditionally been driven by male assumptions and interests, how criminalized women are seen as doubly deviant and how assumptions about appropriate gender roles mean that women are judged less on the nature of their offences and more on their 'deviant' lifestyles. As a result, some feminists have drawn more on sociologies of gender than any pre-existing criminological knowledge, to explore their subject matter, with the important message for male criminology that the object of their enquiry is essentially 'masculine' and that as much can be learned about processes of control and criminalization by focusing on those structures and processes that create conformity and social order, as on a sole concern with those that produce deviance and criminality. Others have gone further by questioning whether the focus on female lawbreakers is a proper concern for feminism, and indeed whether a feminist criminology is theoretically possible or even politically desirable. Latterly this relation between feminism and criminology has been further problematized by a deconstructionist postmodern twist which claims that the signifiers of 'women', 'crime' and 'criminology' trap any investigation in essentialist categories that obstruct the production of new knowledge. It is perhaps no surprise that the deconstruction of criminology has gathered most strength in some feminist perspectives, for it is they that were first alerted to the need for criminology to deconstruct itself if it was to break out of its gender essentialism.

The tendency of the social sciences to deconstruct and question their own internal logic is slowly permeating the discipline of criminology. As some critics have warned, the discipline will remain forever self-justifying unless it is prepared to adopt a more critical stance towards the key referents of 'crime' and 'deviance'. The process of deconstruction also has its origins in the work of Foucault and his location of the discourse of criminology in the combination of knowledge and power that evolved with the modern state and the emergence of the social sciences. Foucault's acknowledgement of a multiplicity of power relations and the diverse settings in which they are activated, in particular, questioned the ability of any total theory (Marxism, for example) to answer all questions. This disenchantment with a priori claims to the 'truth', as represented in stark form by the way criminology has progressed through paradigmatic construction and contestation, is substantiated in the postmodern insistence that we should break with the rational and totalizing (modernist) intellectual movements of the past. Whilst modernism (of which criminology is but one element) attempts to ratify knowledge so that the social can be made an ordered totality, postmodernism views the world as replete with an unlimited number of models of order, each generated by relatively autonomous and localized sets of practices. Modernism strives for universality, postmodernism accepts relativity as a defining feature of the world. In essence postmodernism challenges the logic of 'referential finalities' as the foundation of western social science. Rather it stresses the diversity and particularity of social life and accordingly asserts that no one theoretical paradigm is capable of making sense of the social world.

This post-criminological sensibility implies an abandonment of the concept of crime and its replacement by a new language to designate objects of censure and codes of conduct. By definition this would mean that criminology would lose its very *raison d'être*. Exactly what form such a project might take remains unclear, but the challenge of postmodernism is one that urges us continually to address the limitations of accepted knowledges, to avoid dogmatism and to recognize the existence of a wide variety of subjectivities.

Unsurprisingly, this rejection of totalizing theory and of 'objective' criteria for establishing truth and meaning, can be viewed as intellectually liberating or as intrinsically nihilistic and conservative. For example, at present it is far from clear how a total rejection of established concepts might further an understanding of the relations between criminalization, poverty, inequality, racism, sexual violence and repressive state practices. The failure to replace existing concepts with alternative visions may only leave us with a series of dislocated and fragmented positions. Whilst we may sympathize with the postmodernist objection to the colonization of the intellectual world by a single all-encompassing meta-narrative, does this also mean that we can dispense with the imaginative purchase provided by critical and Utopian visions?

As we noted previously, several principles guided our selection of articles for this book. The first is that within the disciplinary space constituted by and for criminology the intellectual and the political are indivisible. Most obviously, from its origins, for a variety of reasons, criminologists have, despite all claims to neutrality and objectivity, sought to make themselves and their knowledge indispensable to governmental interests. The second is that criminological perspectives are not constructed in a vacuum, but only acquire meaning in specific socio-cultural contexts. Although the basic concepts, methods and concerns have remained more or less the same, the discipline has, often in spite of itself, at key moments experienced a number of important transformations, as the social world that it claims to represent and comprehend has altered. These principles are thrown into stark relief at the beginning of the twenty-first century, and, as a result, sociologically inspired criminologists find themselves working within an unsettled, insecure disciplinary space. Underpinning many of the readings in the last two Parts of this reader is a realization that present conditions pose unprecedented challenges to criminologists who privilege 'the social' as their starting point.

First, there is the need for criminologists of the social to engage in what we might describe as widescreen analysis. A general consensus across the social sciences declares that we are in the midst of unprecedented global transformation defined variously as: post-modernity; late modernity; liquid modernity; disorganized capitalism; turbo-capitalism; the information society; risk society; market society; network society; consumer society, etc. Recently, we have been informed of the need to think about the nature of the new global (dis)order. Such shifts transform the task of all the social sciences. However, a significant part of criminology seems to have been caught unaware of the intellectual requirement to make sense of what is happening, why and with what consequences. In many respects, criminology has yet to face up to the possibility that notions such as fragmentation, difference, plurality and contingency are radically unsettling the established modernist categories, assumptions and models that have served it so well. For sociologically inspired criminology the very idea of 'the social' has been thrown into serious question. To date, sociologists of crime have struggled to articulate visions of this 'post-social' world. Some seem content to either wearily deny that anything really significant is happening, whilst others wish to play the siren role of issuing doom-laden pronouncements about the 'dark' criminogenic side of the changes. There is a flourishing nostalgia-laden social democratic criminological literature that is saturated with images of the disorderly, fragmenting, disintegrating, ungovernable 'social'. Criminologists have engaged in the relatively easy task of narrating the new levels and forms of insecurity and risks and highlighting new modes of soft surveillance and hard control. What we do not have – at least at the moment – is a criminological imagination that provides us with a more nuanced, attuned understanding of the multi-dimensional 'remaking of the social' currently in play. This will require criminologists to overcome their suspiciousness of theoretical developments that originate 'outside' of the discipline and indeed to 'fold' themselves, however uncomfortably, within these scholarly debates.

Second, we are witnessing the latest and perhaps most significant reconstitution of criminology as a self-declared governmental practice. Sociology's hegemony over criminology has been challenged by the demand for an applied criminology that generates 'evidence-based' policy and practice. Across a variety of jurisdictions, we can witness the consolidation of the presence of 'administrative criminology' whose task is to close the gap between theory and criminal justice practice in order to design out crime or to predict and obviate 'risk'. Its practitioners now seem to be in a strategic position to transform themselves into 'crime scientists'. This development heralds the re-emergence of what might be described as 'anti-social criminologies', which: accept dominant definitions of the 'problem of crime'; are seemingly willing participants in any strategy that might control crime; and are resurrecting links with a new wave of socio-biologists and geneticists. We need to not only pay attention to but research how the ideas most closely associated with administrative criminology are implicated in the reordering of core governmental technologies and practices across many jurisdictions.

Third, as a result of the hyper-politicization of law and order and the ratcheting of public fears and anxieties, we have witnessed what might be described as a highly unstable and unpredictable popular criminological imagination. At the same time, paradoxically, sitting alongside what we might define as the 'fear complex' is a popular cultural criminological imagination that is constituted by a mass of hyper-fictional and hyper-real representations of the 'mind of the criminal' and is fascinated by all aspects of law enforcement and criminality. Instead of merely adopting a realist attitude that presents 'fascination' as the antithesis of 'fear' we need to develop a cultural criminology that is able to recognize and explore the interconnectedness and closeness of these two fundamental manifestations of the human/inhuman condition. We also need to examine how and why conventional criminological understandings are in danger of being overwhelmed by (a) images of crime and crime control gleaned from novels, magazines, films, music, cyberspace and computer game simulations, and (b) news media representations that can generate sharp swings in the politics of law and order.

We do not pretend to have a final resolution or even a unanimously held view on how to incorporate these concerns into the criminological agenda. The problem for criminologists is that 'crime' – as social fact, social construct and a multi-media spectacle -- saturates the everyday life of contemporary society. Its sites of production are diverse and multiplying, 'high' and 'low', bizarre and commonplace, local and global, shocking and barely credible, intimate and distant, desperate and exploitative, deeply damaging and potentially progressive. To grasp the complex variety of its subject matter, criminology must remain an intellectual space that rejects a theoretically correct version of itself. It has no choice but to generate reflexive perspectives and practices that are capable of analysing and responding to local, national and global crime and crime control concerns.

Part One

Criminological foundations

INTRODUCTION

This collection of essays is designed to introduce the reader to the diverse origins of the study of crime and the law. It includes some of the now classic formulations of the nature and problem of crime as expressed by such eighteenth-century philosophers as Cesare Beccaria and Jeremy Bentham, early nineteenth-century mathematicians such as Adolphe Quetelet, late nineteenth-century physicians such as Cesare Lombroso, political theorists such as Friedrich Engels and sociological theorists such as Emile Durkheim and Robert Merton. The ten classic readings reproduced here cover a period that stretches from 1764 to 1938. It is a period in which many of the debates about the function of law, the nature of crime, the causes of crime and the extent of crime, with which we are now familiar, were first given intellectual and public expression. The readings are not simply of historical curiosity. Each, in different ways, continues to influence contemporary understandings and formulations of the 'crime problem'.

It is perhaps of some significance that the origins of modern criminological theory can be traced, not to the study of crime and criminals, but to Enlightenment philosophers, particularly in France and Italy, reflecting on the nature and functions of criminal law. Beccaria's *On Crimes and Punishments* (1764) set out a then controversial programme for criminal law reform. Critical of the barbarism, irregularity and ad hoc nature of eighteenth-century criminal justice, he urged that social order be based on law, rather than religion or superstition; that the machinery of justice be answerable to rules of due process; that sentencing policies be formulated to 'fit the crime'; and that punishment be prompt and certain. At the time, Beccaria's work was condemned for its extreme rationalism, but within his recommendations are the seeds of policies present in most criminal justice systems around the world today. Above all he is now recognized as the founding father of a *classical* school of criminology in England (a term he never himself used, but which was used by later theorists), characterized by the key doctrines of rationality, free will and the social contract. Plans for 'the panopticon' were presented by Jeremy Bentham, the founder of English 'utilitarianism' or 'philosophical' radicalism. Bentham's 'new world prison' was designed to ensure that the prisoner could never know when he was being watched. Visibility and surveillance would function as a cost effective instrument of discipline and control. Two ιdred years later, Michel Foucault (see Part Five) would spell out the wider implications of ιtham's utilitarian determination to 'grind rogues honest'.

In contrast a *positivist* criminology, which emerged from the mid-nineteenth century onwards, was concerned less with the content and implementation of criminal law and more with establishing the causes of law breaking. In 1827 the French government published the first national statistical tables of crime, the annual *Compte Général*. Whilst acknowledging the limitations of such statistics in revealing the true extent of crime in society, Quetelet discovered a remarkable constancy in recorded crime in France between 1826 and 1829. He argued that, even if individuals have free will, criminal behaviour appears to obey the same scientific laws that govern the natural world. Of note was the regularity with which young males and those in lowly employment had a greater propensity toward crime. The two factors most strongly associated with criminality were age and sex. Rates of property and personal crime were, however, also found to fluctuate according to the seasons and with the state of the economy. As a result, Quetelet formulated the then remarkable proposition that criminality is not freely chosen or that it is a sign of human wickedness, but that it is an inevitable and resultant feature of social organization. It was thus society that caused crime.

By the 1870s the impact of positivism on the doctrine of free will was underlined in Lombroso's key text *Criminal Man*. After studying anatomy and pathology, Lombroso argued that a significant proportion of criminals had cranial and other physiological defects which suggested that they were born to criminality, and represented a throwback to primitive forms of social evolution. The extract reproduced here from his work with fellow collaborator William Ferrero applies this reasoning to establish a criminal type in women. Although female criminality increases with advances in civilization, most women are deemed non-criminal because biological factors predispose them to be more conservative and socially withdrawn. The physical characteristics of female criminals, such as prostitutes, however, resemble those of male criminals, and their criminality is often more cruel, wicked and vindictive. In an exceptional, and subsequently highly controversial, series of statements Lombroso and Ferrero claimed that the female born criminal, when a complete type, is 'more terrible than the male'.

Lombroso's insistence on the accurate and deliberate measurement of the physical anomalies of known criminals has for many established him as the first 'scientific' criminologist (significantly, the origin of the term 'criminology' is usually attributed to an anthropologist, Paul Topinard, writing in 1890). Whilst Lombroso's particular theory of crime causation was eventually to be discredited through the weight of counter argument, the principles of the Italian school of positivism (of which Lombroso is usually lauded as the founder) were gradually to become influential not only in intellectual circles but in the development of less uniform and more individually oriented forms of penal treatment. By the turn of the century, classicists and positivists were engaged in a series of bitter arguments about the nature of criminal responsibility and the objectives of punishment. The extract from one of three lectures given by Enrico Ferri at the University of Naples in 1901 clearly illustrates the divergencies between these two schools of thought and the depth of feeling by which the exponents of positivism sought to deliver their message.

In contrast the extracts from Engels, Bonger, Durkheim and Merton, whilst sharing some features with the fundamentals of positivism, mark something of a return to the principles of Quetelet in the insistence that the causes of crime lie not in individual abnormalities, but in the nature of economic conditions and social structures. The extract by Friedrich Engels, taken from his classic and vivid description of the brutalizing conditions of working-class life in industrial Manchester in the 1840s, paved the way for a series of Marxist-inspired conflict and critical criminologies which are rooted in the notion that crime is the outcome of conflict, alienation and domination (see Part Three). Crime, of course, was not Engels's (or Marx's) key concern, but the extract reproduced here clearly presents the view that crime is a form of demoralization in which human dignity has been undermined by exploitative working conditions designed solely for capitalist profit. Significantly, Engels stresses that crime, driven by greed and individual competitiveness, is not solely the province of the poor, but is spread throughout the social order; it is endemic to capitalist relations of production and reaches its apogee in the 'murderous' activities of the property-owning class. The Dutch criminologist Willem Bonger, writing in the first decades of the twentieth century, was the first to systematically apply the Marxist-inspired notions of class conflict and capitalist exploitation to the concept of crime. In a scathing attack on the egoistic and competitive tendencies of capitalism, Bonger argued that most crime could be accounted for by a lack of common ownership of property and the brutalized conditions of existence endured by all classes in a society characterized by unfettered forms of capitalist exchange and labour exploitation.

Kropotkin's contribution, originally published in 1898, offers a more strident critique of bourgeois law from an anarchist perspective. In terms echoed some 70 years later by some abolitionist and critical criminologists (see Parts Three and Four), Kropotkin roundly condemns the role of law in facilitating the accumulation of property in the hands of the few and in perpetuating barbaric forms of repression and control. For him the real criminals in society are not those 'unfortunates' who populate the prisons, but those figures of authority who, through their self-interested formulation and implementation of criminal law, have served to put them there.

In contrast, the work of the French sociologist Emile Durkheim in general adopts less of a conflict-based analysis of society, preferring to view the social structure as fundamentally characterized by consensus or a collective conscience. Durkheim, who is lauded as the founder of a sociological criminology, remarked on the regularity and constancy of crime rates in particular societies, and insisted that social phenomena (such as crime and law) have an objective existence irrespective of how they are experienced by individuals. This led to the now famous and perpetually controversial propositions that crime is normal, crime is inevitable and that crime is useful to society. The extract reproduced here from his 1895 work *The Rules of Sociological Method* marks a radical departure from the then prevailing notions of classical free will and positivist ideas of individual abnormality. Rather crime performs a vital function for society in establishing clear moral boundaries and in paving the way for social innovation and change.

The final reading in this Part is from the American sociologist Robert K. Merton. He adopted a key concept from Durkheim – that of anomie – to formulate his own distinctive strain theory.

Merton continues to view crime as normal (in a sociological sense); that is it is a normal response to pathologies generated by the social structure. Criminals are no different to non-criminals. They are simply those that have tried to conform to society's goals but have found their aspirations thwarted. Crime and deviance are normal adaptations to the conflict between the cultural goals associated with the 'American Dream' and the differential availability of institutional means. Thus, as he argues, 'a cardinal American virtue, ambition, promotes a cardinal American vice, deviant behaviour'. Merton's anomie theory defined American criminology in the 1950s and 1960s, generating numerous micro and macro applications, and there continue to be attempts to revise and extend its core principles.

1

On crimes and punishments

Cesare Beccaria

[...]

If we glance at the pages of history, we will find that laws, which surely are, or ought to be, compacts of free men, have been, for the most part, a mere tool of the passions of some, or have arisen from an accidental and temporary need. Never have they been dictated by a dispassionate student of human nature who might, by bringing the actions of a multitude of men into focus, consider them from this single point of view: the *greatest happiness shared by the greatest number.* Happy are those few nations that have not waited for the slow succession of coincidence and human vicissitude to force some little turn for the better after the limit of evil has been reached, but have facilitated the intermediate progress by means of good laws. And humanity owes a debt of gratitude to that philosopher who, from the obscurity of his isolated study, had the courage to scatter among the multitude the first seeds, so long unfruitful, of useful truths.

The true relations between sovereigns and their subjects, and between nations, have been discovered. Commerce has been reanimated by the common knowledge of philosophical truths diffused by the art of printing, and there has sprung up among nations a tacit rivalry of industriousness that is most humane and truly worthy of rational beings. Such good things we owe to the productive enlightenment of this age. But very few persons have studied and fought against the cruelty of punishments and the irregularities of criminal procedures, a part of legislation that is as fundamental as it is widely neglected in almost all of Europe. Very few persons have undertaken to demolish the accumulated errors of centuries by rising to general principles, curbing, at least, with the sole force that acknowledged truths possess, the unbounded course of ill-directed power which has continually produced a long and authorized example of the most

From *On Crimes and Punishments,* pp. 8–19; 55–9; 62–4; 93–9. (New York: Bobbs-Merrill, 1963. First published 1764.)

cold-blooded barbarity. And yet the groans of the weak, sacrificed to cruel ignorance and to opulent indolence; the barbarous torments, multiplied with lavish
and useless severity, for crimes either not proved or wholly imaginary; the filth
and horrors of a prison, intensified by that cruellest tormentor of the miserable,
uncertainty – all these ought to have roused that breed of magistrates who direct
the opinions of men.

The immortal Montesquieu has cursorily touched upon this subject. Truth,
which is one and indivisible, has obliged me to follow the illustrious steps of that
great man, but the thoughtful men for whom I write will easily distinguish
my traces from his. I shall deem myself happy if I can obtain, as he did, the
secret thanks of the unknown and peace-loving disciples of reason, and if I can
inspire that tender thrill with which persons of sensibility respond to one who
upholds the interests of humanity. [...]

THE ORIGIN OF PUNISHMENTS, AND THE RIGHT TO PUNISH
[...]

No man ever freely sacrificed a portion of his personal liberty merely on behalf
of the common good. That chimera exists only in romances. If it were possible,
every one of us would prefer that the compacts binding others did not bind us;
every man tends to make himself the centre of his whole world.

The continuous multiplication of mankind, inconsiderable in itself yet exceeding
by far the means that a sterile and uncultivated nature could offer for the satisfaction of increasingly complex needs, united the earliest savages. These first
communities of necessity caused the formation of others to resist the first, and
the primitive state of warfare thus passed from individuals to nations.

Laws are the conditions under which independent and isolated men united
to form a society. Weary of living in a continual state of war, and of enjoying a
liberty rendered useless by the uncertainty of preserving it, they sacrificed a part
so that they might enjoy the rest of it in peace and safety. The sum of all these
portions of liberty sacrificed by each for his own good constitutes the sovereignty
of a nation, and their legitimate depositary and administrator is the sovereign.
But merely to have established this deposit was not enough; it had to be defended
against private usurpations by individuals each of whom always tries not only
to withdraw his own share but also to usurp for himself that of others. Some
tangible motives had to be introduced, therefore, to prevent the despotic spirit,
which is in every man, from plunging the laws of society into its original chaos.
These tangible motives are the punishments established against infractors of the
laws. I say 'tangible motives' because experience has shown that the multitude
adopt no fixed principles of conduct and will not be released from the sway
of that universal principle of dissolution which is seen to operate both in the
physical and the moral universe, except for motives that directly strike the
senses. These motives, by dint of repeated representation to the mind, counterbalance the powerful impressions of the private passions that oppose the common
good. Not eloquence, not declamations, not even the most sublime truths have

sufficed, for any considerable length of time, to curb passions excited by vivid impressions of present objects.

It was, thus, necessity that forced men to give up part of their personal liberty, and it is certain, therefore, that each is willing to place in the public fund only the least possible portion, no more than suffices to induce others to defend it. The aggregate of these least possible portions constitutes the right to punish; all that exceeds this is abuse and not justice; it is fact but by no means right.

Punishments that exceed what is necessary for protection of the deposit of public security are by their very nature unjust, and punishments are increasingly more just as the safety which the sovereign secures for his subjects is the more sacred and inviolable, and the liberty greater.

CONSEQUENCES

The first consequence of these principles is that only the laws can decree punishments for crimes; authority for this can reside only with the legislator who represents the entire society united by a social contract. No magistrate (who is a part of society) can, with justice, inflict punishments upon another member of the same society. But a punishment that exceeds the limit fixed by the laws is just punishment plus another punishment; a magistrate cannot, therefore, under any pretext of zeal or concern for the public good, augment the punishment established for a delinquent citizen.

The second consequence is that the sovereign, who represents the society itself, can frame only general laws binding all members, but he cannot judge whether someone has violated the social contract, for that would divide the nation into two parts, one represented by the sovereign, who asserts the violation of the contract, and the other by the accused, who denies it. There must, therefore, be a third party to judge the truth of the fact. Hence the need for a magistrate whose decisions, from which there can be no appeal, should consist of mere affirmations or denials of particular facts.

The third consequence is this: even assuming that severity of punishments were not directly contrary to the public good and to the very purpose of preventing crimes, if it were possible to prove merely that such severity is useless, in that case also it would be contrary not only to those beneficent virtues that spring from enlightened reason which would rather rule happy men than a herd of slaves in whom a timid cruelty makes its endless rounds; it would be contrary to justice itself and to the very nature of the social contract.

INTERPRETATIONS OF THE LAWS

A fourth consequence: Judges in criminal cases cannot have the authority to interpret laws, and the reason, again, is that they are not legislators. Such judges have not received the laws from our ancestors as a family tradition or legacy that leaves to posterity only the burden of obeying them, but they receive them, rather, from the living society, or from the sovereign representing it, who is the legitimate depositary of what actually results from the common will of all [. . .]

Nothing can be more dangerous than the popular axiom that it is necessary to consult the spirit of the laws. It is a dam that has given way to a torrent of opinions. This truth, which seems paradoxical to ordinary minds that are struck more by trivial present disorders than by the dangerous but remote effects of false principles rooted in a nation, seems to me to be fully demonstrated. Our understandings and all our ideas have a reciprocal connection; the more complicated they are, the more numerous must the ways be that lead to them and depart from them. Each man has his own point of view, and, at each different time, a different one. Thus the 'spirit' of the law would be the product of a judge's good or bad logic, of his good or bad digestion; it would depend on the violence of his passions, on the weakness of the accused, on the judge's connections with him, and on all those minute factors that alter the appearances of an object in the fluctuating mind of man. Thus we see the lot of a citizen subjected to frequent changes in passing through different courts, and we see the lives of poor wretches become the victims of the false ratiocinations or of the momentary seething ill-humours of a judge who mistakes for a legitimate interpretation that vague product of the jumbled series of notions which his mind stirs up. Thus we see the same crimes differently punished at different times by the same court, for having consulted not the constant fixed voice of the law but the erring instability of interpretation.

The disorder that arises from rigorous observance of the letter of a penal law is hardly comparable to the disorders that arise from interpretations. The temporary inconvenience of the former prompts one to make the rather easy and needed correction in the words of the law which are the source of uncertainty, but it curbs that fatal licence of discussion which gives rise to arbitrary and venal controversies. When a fixed code of laws, which must be observed to the letter, leaves no further care to the judge than to examine the acts of citizens and to decide whether or not they conform to the law as written; when the standard of the just or the unjust, which is to be the norm of conduct for the ignorant as well as for the philosophic citizen, is not a matter of controversy but of fact; then only are citizens not subject to the petty tyrannies of the many which are the more cruel as the distance between the oppressed and the oppressor is less, and which are far more fatal than those of a single man, for the despotism of many can only be corrected by the despotism of one; the cruelty of a single despot is proportioned, not to his might, but to the obstacles he encounters. In this way citizens acquire that sense of security for their own persons which is just, because it is the object of human association, and useful, because it enables them to calculate accurately the inconveniences of a misdeed. It is true, also, that they acquire a spirit of independence, but not one that upsets the laws and resists the chief magistrates; rather one that resists those who have dared to apply the sacred name of virtue to that weakness of theirs which makes them yield to their self-interested and capricious opinions.

These principles will displease those who have assumed for themselves a right to transmit to their inferiors the blows of tyranny that they have received from their superiors. I would, indeed, be most fearful if the spirit of tyranny were in the least compatible with the spirit of literacy.

OBSCURITY OF THE LAWS

If the interpretation of laws is an evil, another evil, evidently, is the obscurity that makes interpretation necessary. And this evil would be very great indeed where the laws are written in a language that is foreign to a people, forcing it to rely on a handful of men because it is unable to judge for itself how its liberty or its members may fare – in a language that transforms a sacred and public book into something very like the private possession of a family. When the number of those who can understand the sacred code of laws and hold it in their hands increases, the frequency of crimes will be found to decrease, for undoubtedly ignorance and uncertainty of punishments add much to the eloquence of the passions. What are we to make of men, therefore, when we reflect that this very evil is the inveterate practice of a large part of cultured and enlightened Europe?

One consequence of this last reflection is that, without writing, a society can never acquire a fixed form of government with power that derives from the whole and not from the parts, in which the laws, which cannot be altered except by the general will, are not corrupted in their passage through the mass of private interests. Experience and reason have shown us that the probability and certainty of human traditions diminish the further removed they are from their source. For, obviously, if there exists no enduring memorial of the social compact, how are the laws to withstand the inevitable pressure of time and of passions? [...]

PROMPTNESS OF PUNISHMENT

The more promptly and the more closely punishment follows upon the commission of a crime, the more just and useful will it be. I say more just, because the criminal is thereby spared the useless and cruel torments of uncertainty, which increase with the vigour of imagination and with the sense of personal weakness; more just, because privation of liberty, being itself a punishment, should not precede the sentence except when necessity requires. Imprisonment of a citizen, then, is simply custody of his person until he be judged guilty; and this custody, being essentially penal, should be of the least possible duration and of the least possible severity. The time limit should be determined both by the anticipated length of the trial and by seniority among those who are entitled to be tried first. The strictness of confinement should be no more than is necessary to prevent him from taking flight or from concealing the proofs of his crimes. The trial itself should be completed in the briefest possible time. What crueller contrast than the indolence of a judge and the anguish of a man under accusation – the comforts and pleasures of an insensitive magistrate on one side, and on the other the tears, the squalor of a prisoner? In general, the weight of punishment and the consequence of a crime should be that which is most efficacious for others, and which inflicts the least possible hardship upon the person who suffers it; one cannot call legitimate any society which does not maintain, as an infallible principle, that men have wished to subject themselves only to the least possible evils.

I have said that the promptness of punishments is more useful because when the length of time that passes between the punishment and the misdeed is less, so much the stronger and more lasting in the human mind is the association of these two ideas, *crime and punishment*; they then come insensibly to be considered, one as the cause, the other as the necessary inevitable effect. It has been demonstrated that the association of ideas is the cement that forms the entire fabric of the human intellect; without this cement pleasure and pain would be isolated sentiments and of no effect. The more men depart from general ideas and universal principles, that is, the more vulgar they are, the more apt are they to act merely on immediate and familiar associations, ignoring the more remote and complex ones that serve only men strongly impassioned for the object of their desires; the light of attention illuminates only a single object, leaving the others dark. They are of service also to more elevated minds, for they have acquired the habit of rapidly surveying many objects at once, and are able with facility to contrast many partial sentiments one with another, so that the result, which is action, is less dangerous and uncertain.

Of utmost importance is it, therefore, that the crime and the punishment be intimately linked together, if it be desirable that, in crude, vulgar minds, the seductive picture of a particularly advantageous crime should immediately call up the associated idea of punishment. Long delay always produces the effect of further separating these two ideas; thus, though punishment of a crime may make an impression, it will be less as a punishment than as a spectacle, and will be felt only after the horror of the particular crime, which should serve to reinforce the feeling of punishment, has been much weakened in the hearts of the spectators.

Another principle serves admirably to draw even closer the important connection between a misdeed and its punishment, namely, that the latter be as much in conformity as possible with the nature of the crime. This analogy facilitates admirably the contrast that ought to exist between the inducement to crime and the counterforce of punishment, so that the latter may deter and lead the mind toward a goal the very opposite of that toward which the seductive idea of breaking the laws seeks to direct it.

Those guilty of lesser crimes are usually punished either in the obscurity of a prison or by transportation, to serve as an example, with a distant and therefore almost useless servitude, to nations which they have not offended. Since men are not induced on the spur of the moment to commit the gravest crimes, public punishment of a great misdeed will be regarded by the majority as something very remote and of improbable occurrence; but public punishment of lesser crimes, which are closer to men's hearts, will make an impression which, while deterring them from these, deters them even further from the graver crimes. A proportioning of punishments to one another and to crimes should comprehend not only their force but also the manner of inflicting them.

THE CERTAINTY OF PUNISHMENT: MERCY

One of the greatest curbs on crimes is not the cruelty of punishments, but their infallibility, and, consequently, the vigilance of magistrates, and that severity of an inexorable judge which, to be a useful virtue, must be accompanied by a mild legislation. The certainty of a punishment, even if it be moderate, will always make a stronger impression than the fear of another which is more terrible but combined with the hope of impunity; even the least evils, when they are certain, always terrify men's minds, and hope, that heavenly gift which is often our sole recompense for everything, tends to keep the thought of greater evils remote from us, especially when its strength is increased by the idea of impunity which avarice and weakness only too often afford.

Sometimes a man is freed from punishment for a lesser crime when the offended party chooses to forgive – an act in accord with beneficence and humanity, but contrary to the public good – as if a private citizen, by an act of remission, could eliminate the need for an example, in the same way that he can waive compensation for the injury. The right to inflict punishment is a right not of an individual, but of all citizens, or of their sovereign. An individual can renounce his own portion of right, but cannot annul that of others.

As punishments become more mild, clemency and pardon become less necessary. Happy the nation in which they might some day be considered pernicious! Clemency, therefore, that virtue which has sometimes been deemed a sufficient substitute in a sovereign for all the duties of the throne, should be excluded from perfect legislation, where the punishments are mild and the method of judgment regular and expeditious. This truth will seem harsh to anyone living in the midst of the disorders of a criminal system, where pardons and mercy are necessary to compensate for the absurdity of the laws and the severity of the sentences. This, which is indeed the noblest prerogative of the throne, the most desirable attribute of sovereignty, is also, however, the tacit disapprobation of the beneficent dispensers of public happiness for a code which, with all its imperfections, has in its favour the prejudice of centuries, the voluminous and imposing dowry of innumerable commentators, the weighty apparatus of endless formalities, and the adherence of the most insinuating and least formidable of the semi-learned. But one ought to consider that clemency is a virtue of the legislators and not of the executors of the laws, that it ought to shine in the code itself rather than in the particular judgments. To make men see that crimes can be pardoned or that punishment is not their necessary consequence foments a flattering hope of impunity and creates a belief that, because they might be remitted, sentences which are not remitted are rather acts of oppressive violence than emanations of justice. What is to be said, then, when the ruler grants pardons, that is, public security to a particular individual, and, with a personal act of unenlightened beneficence, constitutes a public decree of impunity? Let the laws, therefore, be inexorable, and inexorable their executors in particular cases, but let the legislator be tender, indulgent, and humane. Let him, a wise architect, raise his building upon the foundation of self-love and let the general interest be the result of the interests of each; he shall not then be constrained, by partial laws and tumultuous remedies, to separate at every moment the public good from that of individuals, and to build the image of public well-being upon fear and distrust. Wise and compassionate philosopher, let him permit men, his brothers, to enjoy in peace that small portion of happiness which the grand system established by the First Cause, by that *which is*, allows them to enjoy in this corner of the universe.

[...]

PROPORTION BETWEEN CRIMES AND PUNISHMENTS

It is to the common interest not only that crimes not be committed, but also that they be less frequent in proportion to the harm they cause society. Therefore, the obstacles that deter men from committing crimes should be stronger in proportion as they are contrary to the public good, and as the inducements to commit them are stronger. There must, therefore, be a proper proportion between crimes and punishments.

If pleasure and pain are the motives of sensible beings, if, among the motives for even the sublimest acts of men, rewards and punishments were designated by the invisible Legislator, from their inexact distribution arises the contradiction, as little observed as it is common, that the punishments punish crimes which they themselves have occasioned. If an equal punishment be ordained for two crimes that do not equally injure society, men will not be any more deterred from committing the greater crime, if they find a greater advantage associated with it.

Whoever sees the same death penalty, for instance, decreed for the killing of a pheasant and for the assassination of a man or for forgery of an important writing, will make no distinction between such crimes, thereby destroying the moral sentiments, which are the work of many centuries and of much blood, slowly and with great difficulty registered in the human spirit, and impossible to produce, many believe, without the aid of the most sublime of motives and of an enormous apparatus of grave formalities.

It is impossible to prevent all disorders in the universal conflict of human passions. They increase according to a ratio compounded of population and the crossings of particular interests, which cannot be directed with geometric precision to the public utility. For mathematical exactitude we must substitute, in the arithmetic of politics, the calculation of probabilities. A glance at the histories will show that disorders increase with the confines of empires. National sentiment declining in the same proportion, the tendency to commit crimes increases with the increased interest everyone takes in such disorders; thus there is a constantly increasing need to make punishments heavier.

That force, similar to gravity, which impels us to seek our own well-being is restrained in its operation only to the extent that obstacles are set up against it. The effects of this force are the confused series of human actions. If these clash together and disturb one another, punishments, which I would call 'political obstacles', prevent the bad effect without destroying the impelling cause, which is that sensibility inseparable from man. And the legislator acts then like an able architect whose function it is to check the destructive tendencies of gravity and to align correctly those that contribute to the strength of the building.

Given the necessity of human association, given the pacts that result from the very opposition of private interests, a scale of disorders is distinguishable, the first grade consisting of those that are immediately destructive of society, and the last, of those that do the least possible injustice to its individual members. Between these extremes are included all the actions contrary to the public good that are called crimes, and they all descend by insensible gradations from the highest to the lowest. If geometry were applicable to the infinite and obscure combinations of human actions, there ought to be a corresponding scale of punishments, descending from the greatest to the least; if there were an exact and universal scale of punishments and of crimes, we would have a fairly reliable and common measure of the degrees of tyranny and liberty, of the fund of humanity or of malice, of the various nations. But it is enough for the wise legislator to mark the principal points of division without disturbing the order, not assigning to crimes of the first grade the punishments of the last.

[...]

HOW TO PREVENT CRIMES

It is better to prevent crimes than to punish them. This is the ultimate end of every good legislation, which, to use the general terms for assessing the good and evils of life, is the art of leading men to the greatest possible happiness or to the least possible unhappiness.

But heretofore, the means employed have been false and contrary to the end proposed. It is impossible to reduce the turbulent activity of mankind to a geometric order, without any irregularity and confusion. As the constant and very simple laws of nature do not impede the planets from disturbing one another in their movements, so in the infinite and very contrary attractions of pleasure and pain, disturbances and disorder cannot be impeded by human laws. And yet this is the chimera of narrow-minded men when they have power in their grasp. To prohibit a multitude of indifferent acts is not to prevent crimes that might arise from them, but is rather to create new ones; it is to define by whim the ideas of virtue and vice which are preached to us as eternal and immutable. To what should we be reduced if everything were forbidden us that might induce us to crime! It would be necessary to deprive man of the use of his senses. For one motive that drives men to commit a real crime there are a thousand that drive them to commit those indifferent acts which are called crimes by bad laws; and if the probability of crimes is proportionate to the number of motives, to enlarge the sphere of crimes is to increase the probability of their being committed. The majority of the laws are nothing but privileges, that is, a tribute paid by all to the convenience of some few.

Do you want to prevent crimes? See to it that the laws are clear and simple and that the entire force of a nation is united in their defence, and that no part of it is employed to destroy them. See to it that the laws favour not so much classes of men as men themselves. See to it that men fear the laws and fear nothing else. For fear of the laws is salutary, but fatal and fertile for crimes is one man's fear of another. Enslaved men are more voluptuous, more depraved, more cruel than free men. These study the sciences, give thought to the interests of their country, contemplate grand objects and imitate them, while enslaved men, content with the present moment, seek in the excitement of debauchery a distraction from the emptiness of the condition in which they find themselves. Accustomed to an uncertainty of outcome in all things, the outcome of their crimes remains for them problematical, to the advantage of the passions that determine them. If uncertainty regarding the laws befalls a nation which is indolent because of climate, its indolence and stupidity are confirmed and increased; if it befalls a voluptuous but energetic nation, the result is a wasteful diffusion of energy into an infinite number of little cabals and intrigues that sow distrust in every heart, make treachery and dissimulation the foundation of prudence; if it befalls a brave and powerful nation, the uncertainty is removed finally, but only after having caused many oscillations from liberty to slavery and from slavery back to liberty.

Do you want to prevent crimes? See to it that enlightenment accompanies liberty. Knowledge breeds evils in inverse ratio to its diffusion, and benefits in direct ratio. A daring impostor, who is never a common man, is received with adorations by an ignorant people, and with hisses by an enlightened one. Knowledge, by facilitating comparisons and by multiplying points of view, brings on a mutual modification of conflicting feelings, especially when it appears that others hold the same views and face the same difficulties. In the face of enlightenment widely diffused throughout the nation, the calumnies of ignorance are silenced and authority trembles if it be not armed with reason. The vigorous force of the laws, meanwhile, remains immovable, for no enlightened person can fail to approve of the clear and useful public compacts of mutual security when he compares the inconsiderable portion of useless liberty he himself has sacrificed with the sum total of liberties sacrificed by other men, which, except for the laws, might have been turned against him. Any person of sensibility, glancing over a code of well-made laws and observing that he has lost only a baneful liberty to injure others, will feel constrained to bless the throne and its occupant.

[…]

Another way of preventing crimes is to direct the interest of the magistracy as a whole to observance rather than corruption of the laws. The greater the number of magistrates, the less dangerous is the abuse of legal power; venality is more difficult among men who observe one another, and their interest in increasing their personal authority diminishes as the portion that would fall to each is less, especially in comparison with the danger involved in the undertaking. If the sovereign, with his apparatus and pomp, with the severity of his edicts, with the permission he grants for unjust as well as just claims to be advanced by anyone who thinks himself oppressed, accustoms his subjects to fear magistrates more than the laws, [the magistrates] will profit more from this fear than personal and public security will gain from it.

Another way of preventing crimes is to reward virtue. Upon this subject I notice a general silence in the laws of all the nations of our day. If the prizes offered by the academies to discoverers of useful truths have increased our knowledge and have multiplied good books, why should not prizes distributed by the beneficent hand of the sovereign serve in a similar way to multiply virtuous actions? The coin of honour is always inexhaustible and fruitful in the hands of the wise distributor.

Finally, the surest but most difficult way to prevent crimes is by perfecting education – a subject much too vast and exceeding the limits I have prescribed for myself, a subject, I venture also to say, too intimately involved with the nature of government for it ever to be, even in the far-off happy ages of society, anything more than a barren field, only here and there cultivated by a few sages. A great man, who enlightens the world that persecutes him, has indicated plainly and in detail what principal maxims of education are truly useful to men: they are, that it should consist less in a barren multiplicity of things than in a selection and precise definition of them; in substituting originals for the copies of the moral as well as physical phenomena which chance or wilful activity may present to the fresh minds of youths; in leading them toward virtue by the easy way of feeling, and in directing them away from evil by the infallible one of necessity and inconvenience, instead of by the uncertain means of command which obtains only simulated and momentary obedience.

CONCLUSION

From what has thus far been demonstrated, one may deduce a general theorem of considerable utility, though hardly conformable with custom, the usual legislator of nations; it is this: *In order for punishment not to be, in every instance, an act of violence of one or of many against a private citizen, it must be essentially public, prompt, necessary, the least possible in the given circumstances, proportionate to the crimes, dictated by the laws* [original emphasis].

2

Panopticon, or, the inspection-house, & C.

Jeremy Bentham

[…]

LETTER I
Idea of the inspection principle
[…]

    … It will be found applicable, I think, without exception, to all establishments whatsoever, in which, within a space not too large to be covered or commanded by buildings, a number of persons are meant to be kept under inspection. No matter how different, or even opposite the purpose: whether it be that of *punishing the incorrigible, guarding the insane, reforming the vicious, confining the suspected, employing the idle, maintaining the helpless, curing the sick, instructing the willing* in any branch of industry, or *training the rising race* in the path of *education*: in a word, whether it be applied to the purposes of *perpetual prisons* in the room of death, or *prisons for confinement* before trial, or *penitentiary-houses*, or *houses of correction*, or *work-houses*, or *manufactories*, or *mad-houses*, or *hospitals*, or *schools*.

    It is obvious that, in all these instances, the more constantly the persons to be inspected are under the eyes of the persons who should inspect them, the more perfectly will the purpose of the establishment have been attained. Ideal perfection, if that were the object, would require that each person should actually be in that predicament, during every instant of time. This being impossible, the next thing to be wished for is, that, at every instant, seeing reason to believe as much, and not being able to satisfy himself to the contrary, he should *conceive* himself to be so […]

From *The Panopticon Writings*, pp. 29–95. Ed. Miran Bozovic. (London: Verso, 1995. First published 1791.)

LETTER II
Plan for a penitentiary inspection-house

Before you look at the plan, take in words the general idea of it. The building is circular.

The apartments of the prisoners occupy the circumference. You may call them, if you please, the *cells*.

These *cells* are divided from one another, and the prisoners by that means secluded from all communication with each other, by *partitions* in the form of *radii* issuing from the circumference towards the centre, and extending as many feet as shall be thought necessary to form the largest dimension of the cell.

The apartment of the inspector occupies the centre; you may call it if you please the *inspector's lodge.*

It will be convenient in most, if not in all cases, to have a vacant space or *area* all round, between such centre and such circumference. You may call if it you please the *intermediate* or *annular* area.

About the width of a cell may be sufficient for a *passage* from the outside of the building to the lodge.

Each cell has in the outward circumference, a *window*, large enough, not only to light the cell, but, through the cell, to afford light enough to the correspondent part of the lodge.

The inner circumference of the cell is formed by an iron *grating*, so light as not to screen any part of the cell from the inspector's view.

Of this grating, a part sufficiently large opens, in form of a *door*, to admit the prisoner at his first entrance; and to give admission at any time to the inspector or any of his attendants.

To cut off from each prisoner the view of every other, the partitions are carried on a few feet beyond the grating into the intermediate area: such projecting parts I call the *protracted partitions.*

It is conceived, that the light, coming in in this manner through the cells, and so across the intermediate area, will be sufficient for the inspector's lodge. But, for this purpose, both the windows in the cells, and those corresponding to them in the lodge, should be as large as the strength of the building, and what shall be deemed a necessary attention to economy, will permit.

To the windows of the lodge there are *blinds,* as high up as the eyes of the prisoners in their cells can, by any means they can employ, be made to reach.

To prevent *thorough light,* whereby, notwithstanding the blinds, the prisoners would see from the cells whether or not any person was in the lodge, that apartment is divided into quarters, by *partitions* formed by two diameters to the circle, crossing each other at right angles. For these partitions the thinnest materials might serve; and they might be made removable at pleasure; their height, sufficient to prevent the prisoners seeing over them from the cells. Doors to these partitions, if left open at any time, might produce the thorough light. To prevent this, divide each partition into two, at any part required, setting down the one-half at such distance from the other as shall be equal to the aperture of a door.

These windows of the inspector's lodge open into the intermediate area, in the form of *doors*, in as many places as shall be deemed necessary to admit of his communicating readily with any of the cells.

Small *lamps*, in the outside of each window of the lodge, backed by a reflector, to throw the light into the corresponding cells, would extend to the night the security of the day.

To save the troublesome exertion of voice that might otherwise be necessary, and to prevent one prisoner from knowing that the inspector was occupied by another prisoner at a distance, a small *tin tube* might reach from each cell to the inspector's lodge, passing across the area, and so in at the side of the correspondent window of the lodge. By means of this implement, the slightest whisper of the one might be heard by the other, especially if he had proper notice to apply his ear to the tube.

With regard to *instruction*, in cases where it cannot be duly given without the instructor's being close to the work, or without setting his hand to it by way of example before the learner's face, the instructor must indeed here as elsewhere, shift his station as often as there is occasion to visit different workmen; unless he calls the workmen to him, which in some of the instances to which this sort of building is applicable, such as that of imprisoned felons, could not so well be. But in all cases where directions, given verbally and at a distance, are sufficient, these tubes will be found of use. They will save, on the one hand, the exertion of voice it would require, on the part of the instructor, to communicate instruction to the workmen without quitting his central station in the lodge; and, on the other, the confusion which would ensue if different instructors or persons in the lodge were calling to the cells at the same time. And, in the case of hospitals, the quiet that may be insured by this little contrivance, trifling as it may seem at first sight, affords an additional advantage.

A *bell*, appropriated exclusively to the purposes of *alarm*, hangs in a *belfry* with which the building is crowned, communicating by a rope with the inspector's lodge.

The most economical, and perhaps the most convenient, way of *warming* the cells and area, would be by flues surrounding it, upon the principle of those in hothouses. A total want of every means of producing artificial heat might, in such weather as we sometimes have in England, be fatal to the lives of the prisoners; at any rate, it would often times be altogether incompatible with their working at any sedentary employment. The flues, however, and the fire-places belonging to them, instead of being on the outside, as in hothouses, should be in the inside. By this means, there would be less waste of heat, and the current of air that would rush in on all sides through the cells, to supply the draught made by the fires, would answer so far the purpose of ventilation.

[…]

LETTER V
Essential points of the plan

It may be of use, that among all the particulars you have seen, it should be clearly understood what circumstances are, and what are not, essential to the plan. The essence of it consists, then, in the *centrality* of the inspector's situation, combined with the well-known and most effectual contrivances for *seeing without being seen*. As to the *general form* of the building, the most commodious for most purposes seems to be the circular: but this is not an absolutely essential circumstance. Of all figures, however, this, you will observe, is the only one that affords a perfect view, and the same view, of an indefinite number of apartments of the same dimensions: that affords a spot from which, without any change of situation, a man may survey, in the same perfection, the whole number, and without so much as a change of posture, the half of the whole number, at the same time: that, within a boundary of a given extent, contains the greatest quantity of room: – that places the centre at the least distance from the light: – that gives the cells most width, at the part where, on account of the light, most light may, for the purposes of work, be wanted: – and that reduces to the greatest possible shortness the path taken by the inspector, in passing from each part of the field of inspection to every other.

You will please to observe, that though perhaps it is the most important point, that the persons to be inspected should always feel themselves as if under inspection, at least as standing a great chance of being so, yet it is not by any means the *only* one. If it were, the same advantage might be given to buildings of almost any form. What is also of importance is, that for the greatest proportion of time possible, each man should actually *be* under inspection. This is material in *all* cases, that the inspector may have the satisfaction of knowing, that the discipline actually has the effect which it is designed to have: and it is more particularly material in such cases where the inspector, besides seeing that they conform to such standing rules as are prescribed, has more or less frequent occasion to give them such transient and incidental directions as will require to be given and enforced, at the commencement at least of every course of industry. And I think, it needs not much argument to prove, that the business of inspection, like every other, will be performed to a greater degree of perfection, the less trouble the performance of it requires.

Not only so, but the greater chance there is, of a given person's being at a given time actually under inspection, the more strong will be the persuasion – the more *intense*, if I may say so, the *feeling*, he has of his being so. How little turn soever the greater number of persons so circumstanced may be supposed to have for calculation, some rough sort of calculation can scarcely, under such circumstances, avoid forcing itself upon the rudest mind. Experiment, venturing first upon slight transgressions, and so on, in proportion to success, upon more and more considerable ones, will not fail to teach him the difference between a loose inspection and a strict one.

It is for these reasons, that I cannot help looking upon every form as less and less eligible, in proportion as it deviates from the *circular*.

A very material point is, that room be allotted to the lodge, sufficient to adapt it to the purpose of a complete and constant habitation for the principal inspector or head-keeper, and his family. The more numerous also the family, the better; since, by this means, there will in fact be as many inspectors, as the family consists of persons, though only one be paid for it. Neither the orders of the inspector himself, nor any interest which they may feel, or not feel, in the regular performance of his duty, would be requisite to find them motives adequate to the purpose. Secluded oftentimes, by their situation, from every other object, they will naturally, and in a manner unavoidably, give their eyes a direction conformable to that purpose, in every momentary interval of their ordinary occupations. It will supply in their instance the place of that great and constant fund of entertainment to the sedentary and vacant in towns – the looking out of the window. The scene, though a confined, would be a very various, and therefore, perhaps, not altogether an unamusing one.

LETTER VI
Advantages of the plan

I flatter myself there can now be little doubt of the plan's possessing the fundamental advantages I have been attributing to it: I mean, the *apparent omnipresence* of the inspector (if divines will allow me the expression,) combined with the extreme facility of his *real presence*.

A collateral advantage it possesses, and on the score of frugality a very material one, is that which respects the *number* of the inspectors requisite. If this plan required more than another, the additional number would form an objection, which, were the difference to a certain degree considerable, might rise so high as to be conclusive: so far from it, that a greater multitude than ever were yet lodged in one house might be inspected by a single person; for the trouble of inspection is diminished in no less proportion than the strictness of inspection is increased.

Another very important advantage, whatever purposes the plan may be applied to, particularly where it is applied to the severest and most coercive purposes, is, that the *under* keepers or inspectors, the servants and subordinates of every kind, will be under the same irresistible controul with respect to the *head* keeper or inspector, as the prisoners or other persons to be governed are with respect to *them*. On the common plans, what means, what possibility, has the prisoner of appealing to the humanity of the principal for redress against the neglect or oppression of subordinates in that rigid sphere, but the *few* opportunities which, in a crowded prison, the most conscientious keeper *can* afford – but the none at all which many a keeper *thinks* fit to give them? How different would their lot be upon this plan!

In no instance could his subordinates either perform or depart from their duty, but he must know the time and degree and manner of their doing so. It presents an answer, and that a satisfactory one, to one of the most puzzling of political questions – *quis custodiet ipsos custodes?* And, as the fulfilling of his, as well as their, duty would be rendered so much easier, than it can ever have been hitherto, so might, and so should, any departure from it be punished with the more inflexible severity. It is this circumstance that renders the influence of this plan not less beneficial to what is called *liberty*, than to necessary coercion; not less powerful as a controul upon subordinate power, than as a curb to delinquency; as a shield to innocence, than as a scourge to guilt.

Another advantage, still operating to the same ends, is the great load of trouble and disgust which it takes off the shoulders of those occasional inspectors of a high order, such as *judges* and other *magistrates,* who, called down to this irksome task from the superior ranks of life, cannot but feel a proportionable repugnance to the discharge of it. Think how it is with them upon the present plans, and how it still must be upon the best plans that have been hitherto devised! The cells or apartments, however constructed, must, if there be nine hundred of them (as there were to have been upon the penitentiary-house plan,) be opened to the visitors, one by one. To do their business to any purpose, they must approach near to, and come almost in contact with each inhabitant; whose situation being watched over according to no other than the loose methods of inspection at present practicable, will on that account require the more minute and troublesome investigation on the part of these occasional superintendents. By this new plan, the disgust is entirely removed, and the trouble of going into such a room as the lodge, is no more than the trouble of going into any other.

Were *Newgate* upon this plan, all Newgate might be inspected by a quarter of an hour's visit to Mr. Akerman.

Among the other causes of that reluctance, none at present so forcible, none so unhappily well grounded, none which affords so natural an excuse, nor so strong a reason against accepting of any excuse, as the danger of *infection* – a circumstance which carries death, in one of its most tremendous forms, from the seat of guilt to the seat of justice, involving in one common catastrophe the violator and the upholder of the laws. But in a spot so constructed, and under a course of discipline so insured, how should infection ever arise? or how should it continue? Against every danger of this kind, what private house of the poor, one might almost say, or even of the most opulent, can be equally secure?

Nor is the disagreeableness of the task of superintendence diminished by this plan, in a much greater degree than the efficacy of it is increased. On all others, be the superintendent's visit ever so unexpected, and his motions ever so quick, time there must always be for preparations blinding the real state of things. Out of nine hundred cells, he can visit but one at a time, and, in the meanwhile, the worst of the others may be arranged, and the inhabitants threatened, and tutored how to receive him. On this plan, no sooner is the superintendent announced, than the whole scene opens instantaneously to his view.

In mentioning inspectors and superintendents who are such by office, I must not overlook that system of inspection, which, however little heeded, will not be the less useful and efficacious: I mean, the part which individuals may be disposed to take in the business, without intending, perhaps, or even without thinking of, any other effects of their visits, than the gratification of their own particular curiosity. What the inspector's or keeper's family are with respect to *him*, that, and more, will these spontaneous visitors be to the superintendent, – assistants, deputies, in so far as he is faithful, witnesses and judges should he ever be unfaithful, to his trust. So as they are but there, what the motives were that drew them thither is perfectly immaterial; whether the relieving of their anxieties by the affecting prospect of their respective friends and relatives thus detained in durance, or merely the satisfying that general curiosity, which an establishment, on various accounts so interesting to human feelings, may naturally be expected to excite.

You see, I take for granted as a matter of course, that under the necessary regulations for preventing interruption and disturbance, the doors of these establishments will be, as, without very special reasons to the contrary, the doors of all public establishments ought to be, thrown wide open to the body of the curious at large – the great *open committee* of the tribunal of the world. And who ever objects to such publicity, where it is practicable, but those whose motives for objection afford the strongest reasons for it? […]

I hope no critic of more learning than candour will do an inspection-house so much injustice as to compare it to *Dionysius' ear.* The object of that contrivance was, to know what prisoners said without their suspecting any such thing. The object of the inspection principle is directly the reverse: it is to make them not only *suspect*, but be *assured*, that whatever they do is known, even though that should not be the case. Detection is the object of the first: *prevention*, that of the latter. In the former case the ruling person is a spy; in the latter he is a monitor. The object of the first was to pry into the secret recesses of the heart; the latter, confirming its attention to *overt acts*, leaves thoughts and fancies to their proper *ordinary*, the court *above.*

When I consider the extensive variety of purposes to which this principle may be applied, and the certain efficacy which, as far as I can trust my own conceptions, it promises to them all, my wonder is, not only that this plan should never have hitherto been put in practice, but how any other should ever have been thought of . . .

[…]

What would you say, if by the gradual adoption and diversified application of this single principle, you should see a new scene of things spread itself over the face of civilized society? – morals reformed, health preserved, industry invigorated, instruction diffused, public burthens lightened, economy seated as it were upon a rock, the gordian knot of the poor-laws not cut but untied – all by a simple idea in architecture?

3

Of the development of the propensity to crime

Adolphe Quetelet

OF CRIMES IN GENERAL. AND OF THE REPRESSION OF THEM

Supposing men to be placed in similar circumstances, I call the greater or less probability of committing crime, the *propensity to crime*. My object is more especially to investigate the influence of season, climate, sex, and age, on this propensity.

I have said that the circumstances in which men are placed ought to be similar, that is to say, equally favourable, both in the existence of objects likely to excite the propensity and in the facility of committing the crime. It is not enough that a man may merely have the intention to do evil, he must also have the opportunity and the means. Thus the propensity to crime may be the same in France as in England, without, on that account, the *morality* of the nations being the same. I think this distinction of importance.

There is still another important distinction to be made; namely, that two individuals may have the same propensity to crime, without being equally *criminal*, if one, for example, were inclined to theft, and the other to assassination.

Lastly, […] our observations can only refer to a *certain number of known and tried offences, out of the unknown sum total of crimes committed*. Since this sum total of crimes committed will probably ever continue unknown, all the reasoning of which it is the basis will be more or less defective. I do not hesitate to say, that all the knowledge which we possess on the statistics of crimes and offences will be of no utility whatever, unless we admit without question that *there is a ratio, nearly invariably the same, between known and tried offences and the unknown sum total of crimes committed*. This ratio is necessary, and if it did not really exist, every thing which, until the present time, has been said on the statistical documents of crime, would be false and absurd. We are aware, then, how important it is to legitimate such a ratio, and we may be astonished that this has not been done

From *A Treatise on Man*, pp. 82–96; 103–8. (Edinburgh: Chambers, 1842.)

before now. The ratio of which we speak necessarily varies according to the nature and seriousness of the crimes: in a well-organized society, where the police is active and justice is rightly administered, this ratio, for murders and assassinations, will be nearly equal to unity; that is to say, no individual will disappear from the society by murder or assassination, without its being known: this will not be precisely the case with poisonings. When we look to thefts and offences of smaller importance, the ratio will become very small, and a great number of offences will remain unknown, either because those against whom they are committed do not perceive them, or do not wish to prosecute the perpetrators, or because justice itself has not sufficient evidence to act upon. Thus, the greatness of this ratio, which will generally be different for different crimes and offences, will chiefly depend on the activity of justice in reaching the guilty, on the care with which the latter conceal themselves, on the repugnance which the individuals injured may have to complain, or perhaps on their not knowing that any injury has been committed against them. Now, if all the causes which influence the magnitude of the ratio remain the same, we may also assert that the effects will remain invariable. This result is confirmed in a curious manner by induction, and observing the surprising constancy with which the numbers of the statistics of crime are reproduced annually – a constancy which, no doubt, will be also reproduced in the numbers at which we cannot arrive: thus, although we do not know the criminals who escape justice, we very well know that every year between 7,000 and 7,300 persons are brought before the criminal courts, and that 61 are regularly condemned out of every 100; that 170,000 nearly are brought before courts of correction, and that 85 out of 100 are condemned; and that, if we pass to details, we find a no less alarming regularity; thus we find that between 100 and 150 individuals are annually condemned to death, 280 condemned to perpetual hard labour, 1,050 to hard labour for a time, 1,220 to solitary confinement (*à la réclusion*), etc.; so that this budget of the scaffold and the prisons is discharged by the French nation, with much greater regularity, no doubt, than the financial budget; and we might say, that what annually escapes the minister of justice is a more regular sum than the deficiency of revenue to the treasury.

I shall commence by considering, in a general manner, the propensity to crime in France, availing myself of the excellent documents contained in the *Comptes Généraux de l'Administration de la Justice* of this country; I shall afterwards endeavour to establish some comparisons with other countries, but with all the care and reserve which such comparisons require.

During the four years preceding 1830, 28,686 accused persons were set down as appearing before the courts of assize, that is to say, 7,171 individuals annually nearly; which gives 1 accused person to 4,463 inhabitants, taking the population at 32,000,000 souls. Moreover, of 100 accused, 61 persons have been condemned to punishments of greater or less severity. From the remarks made above with respect to the crimes which remain unknown or unpunished, and from mistakes which justice may make, we conceive that these numbers, although they furnish us with curious data for the past, do not give us any thing exact on the propensity to crime. However, if we consider that the two ratios which we have calculated have not sensibly varied from year to year, we shall be led to believe that they will not vary in a sensible manner for the succeeding years; and the probability that this variation will not take place is so much the greater, according as, all things being equal, the mean results of each year do not differ much from the general average, and these results have been taken from a great number of years.

After these remarks, it becomes very probable that, for a Frenchman, there is 1 against 4,462 chances that he will be an accused person during the course of the year; moreover, there are 61 to 39 chances, very nearly, that he will be condemned at the time that he is accused. These results are justified by the numbers of the following table [Table 3.1]:

Table 3.1

Years	Accused persons present	Condemned persons	Inhabitants to one accused person	Condemned in 100 accused persons	Accused of crimes against		Ratio between the numbers of the two kinds of crime
					Persons	Property	
1826	6,988	4,348	4,557	62	1,907	5,081	2.7
1827	6,929	4,236	4,593	61	1,911	5,018	2.6
1828	7,396	4,551	4,307	61	1,844	5,552	3.0
1829	7,373	4,475	4,521	61	1,791	5,582	3.1
Total	28,686	17,610	4,463	61	7,453	21,233	2.8

Thus, although we do not yet know the statistical documents for 1830, it is very probable that we shall again have 1 accused person in 4,463 very nearly, and 61 condemned in 100 accused persons; this probability is somewhat diminished for the year 1831, and still more for the succeeding years. We may, therefore, by the results of the past, estimate what will be realized in the future. This possibility of assigning beforehand the number of accused and condemned persons which any country will present, must give rise to serious reflections, since it concerns the fate of several thousand men, who are driven, as it were, in an irresistible manner, towards the tribunals, and the condemnations which await them.

These conclusions are deduced from the principle […] that effects are proportionate to their causes, and that the effects remain the same, if the causes which have produced them do not vary. If France, then, in the year 1830, had not undergone any apparent change, and if, contrary to my expectation, I found a sensible difference between the two ratios calculated beforehand for this year and the real ratios observed, I should conclude that some alteration had taken place in the causes, which had escaped my attention. On the other hand, if the state of France has changed, and if, consequently, the causes which influence the propensity to crime have also undergone some change, I ought to expect to find an alteration in the two ratios which until that time remained nearly the same.

It is proper to observe, that the preceding numbers only show, strictly speaking, the probability of being accused and afterwards condemned, without rendering us able to determine any thing very precise on the degree of the propensity to crime; at least unless we admit, what is very likely, that justice preserves the same activity, and the number of guilty persons who escape it preserves the same proportion from year to year.

In the latter columns of the preceding table [Table 3.1], is first made the distinction between crimes against persons and crimes against property: it will be remarked, no doubt, that the number of the former has diminished, whilst the latter has increased; however, these variations are so small, that they do not sensibly affect the annual ratio; and we see that we ought to reckon that three persons are accused of crimes against property to one for crimes against person.

[…]

OF THE INFLUENCE OF KNOWLEDGE, OF PROFESSIONS […]
ON THE PROPENSITY TO CRIME

It may be interesting to examine the influence of the intellectual state of the accused on the nature of crimes: the French documents on this subject are such, that I am enabled to form the following table [Table 3.2] for the years 1828 and 1829; to this table I have annexed the results of the years 1830 and 1831, which were not known when the reflections which succeed were written down.

Table 3.2

Intellectual state of the persons accused	1828–9: accused of crimes against		Ratio of crimes against property to crimes against persons	1828–9: accused of crimes against		Ratio of crimes against property to crimes against persons
	Persons	Property		Persons	Property	
Could not read or write	2,072	6,617	3.2	2,134	6,785	3.1
Could read and write but imperfectly	1,001	2,804	2.8	1,033	2,840	2.8
Could read and write well	400	1,109	2.8	408	1,047	2.6
Had received a superior education to this 1st degree	80	206	2.6	135	184	1.4
	3,553	10,736	3.0 aver.	3,710	10,856	2.9 aver.

Thus, all things being equal, the number of crimes against persons, *compared with the number of crimes against property*, during the years 1828 and 1829, was greater according as the intellectual state of the accused was more highly developed; and this difference bore especially on murders, rapes, assassinations, blows, wounds, and other severe crimes. Must we thence conclude that knowledge is injurious to society? I am far from thinking so. To establish such an assertion, it would be necessary to commence by ascertaining how many individuals of the French nation belong to each of the four divisions which we have made above, and to find out if, proportion being considered, the individuals of that one of the divisions commit as many crimes as those of the others. If this were really the case, I should not hesitate to say that, since the most enlightened individuals commit as many crimes as those who have had less education, and since their crimes are more serious, they are necessarily more criminal; but from the little we know of the diffusion of knowledge in France, we cannot state any thing decisively on this point. Indeed, it may so happen, that individuals of the enlightened part of society, while committing fewer murders, assassinations, and other severe crimes, than individuals who have received no education, also commit much fewer crimes against property, and this would explain what we have remarked in the preceding numbers. This conjecture even becomes probable, when we consider that the enlightened classes are presupposed to possess more affluence, and consequently are less frequently under the necessity of having recourse to the different modes of theft, of which crimes against property almost entirely consist; whilst affluence and knowledge have not an equal power in subduing the fire of the passions and sentiments of hatred and vengeance. It must be remarked, on the other hand, that the results contained in the preceding table only belong to two years, and consequently present a smaller probability of expressing what really is the case, especially those results connected with the most enlightened class, and which are based on very small numbers. It seems to me, then, that at the most we can only say that the ratio of the number of crimes against persons to the number of crimes against property varies with the degree of knowledge; and generally, for 100 crimes against persons, we may reckon fewer crimes against property, according as the individuals belong to a class of greater or less enlightenment.

[…]

The following details, which I extract from the *Rapport au Roi* for the year 1829, will serve to illustrate what I advance:

'The new table, which points out the professions of the accused, divides them into nine principal classes, comprising,

The *first*, individuals who work on the land, in vineyards, forests, mines, etc., 2,453.

The *second*, workmen engaged with wood, leather, iron, cotton, etc., 1,932.

The *third*, bakers, butchers, brewers, millers, etc., 253.

The *fourth,* hatters, hairdressers, tailors, upholsterers, etc., 327.

The *fifth,* bankers, agents, wholesale and retail merchants, hawkers, etc., 467.

The *sixth,* contractors, porters, seamen, waggoners, etc., 289.

The *seventh,* innkeepers, lemonade-sellers, servants, etc., 830.

The *eighth,* artists, students, clerks, bailiffs, notaries, advocates, priests, physicians, soldiers, annuitants, etc., 449.

The *ninth,* beggars, smugglers, strumpets, etc., 373.

Women who had no profession have been classed in those which their husbands pursued.

Comparing those who are included in each class with the total number of the accused, we see that the first furnishes 33 out of 100; the second, 26; the third, 4; the fourth, 5; the fifth, 6; the sixth, 4; the seventh, 11; the eighth, 6; the ninth, 5.

If, after that, we point out the accused in each class, according to the nature of their imputed crimes, and compare them with each other, we find the following proportions:

In the first class, 32 of the 100 accused were tried for crimes against persons, and 68 for crimes against property. These numbers are 21 and 79 for the second class; 22 and 78 for the third; 15 and 85 for the fourth and fifth; 26 and 74 for the sixth; 16 and 84 for the seventh; 37 and 63 for the eighth; 13 and 87 for the ninth.

Thus, the accused of the eighth class, who all exercised liberal professions, or enjoyed a fortune which presupposes some education, are those who, relatively, have committed the greatest number of crimes against persons; whilst 87-hundredths of the accused of the ninth class, composed of people without character, have scarcely attacked any thing but property.'

These results, which confirm the remark made before, deserve to be taken into consideration. I shall observe that, when we divide individuals into two classes, the one of liberal professions, and the other composed of journeymen, workmen, and servants, the difference is rendered still more conspicuous.

[…]

ON THE INFLUENCE OF SEASONS ON THE PROPENSITY TO CRIME

The seasons have a well-marked influence in augmenting and diminishing the number of crimes. We may form some idea from the following table [Table 3.3], which contains the number of crimes committed in France against persons and property, during each month, for three years, as well as the ratio of these numbers. We can also compare the numbers of this table with those which I have given to show the influence of seasons on the development of mental alienation, and we shall find the most remarkable coincidences, especially for crimes against persons, which would appear to be most usually dependent on failures of the reasoning powers:

Table 3.3

Months	Crimes against		Ratio: 1827–28	Crimes against		Ratio 1830–31
	Persons	Property		Persons	Property	
January	282	1,095	3.89	189	666	3.52
February	272	910	3.35	194	563	2.90
March	335	968	2.89	205	602	2.94
April	314	841	2.68	197	548	2.78
May	381	844	2.22	213	569	2.67
June	414	850	2.05	208	602	2.90
July	379	828	2.18	188	501	2.66
August	382	934	2.44	247	596	2.41
September	355	896	2.52	176	584	3.32
October	285	926	3.25	207	586	2.83
November	301	961	3.20	223	651	2.95
December	347	1,152	3.33	181	691	3.82
Total	3,847	11,205	2.77	2,428	7,159	2.94

First, the epoch of maximum (June) in respect to the number of crimes against persons, coincides pretty nearly with the epoch of minimum in respect to crimes against property, and this takes place in summer; whilst, on the contrary, the minimum of the number of crimes against persons, and the maximum of the number of crimes against property, takes place in winter. Comparing these two kinds of crimes, we find that in the month of January nearly four crimes take place against property to one against persons, and in the month of June only two to three. These differences are readily explained by considering that during winter misery and want are more especially felt, and cause an increase of the number of crimes against property, whilst the violence of the passions predominating in summer, excites to more frequent personal collisions.

[...]

ON THE INFLUENCE OF SEX ON THE PROPENSITY TO CRIME

At the commencement, we may observe that, out of 28,686 accused, who have appeared before the courts in France, during the four years before 1830, there were found 5,416 women, and 23,270 men, that is to say, 23 women to 100 men. Thus, the propensity to crime in general gives the ratio of 23 to 100 for the sexes.

This estimate supposes that justice exercises its duties as actively with regard to women as to men; and this is rendered probable by the fact, that the severity of repression is nearly the same in the case of both sexes; in other words, that women are treated with much the same severity as men.

We have just seen that, in general, the propensity to crime in men is about four times as great as in women, in France; but it will be important to examine further, if men are four times as criminal, which will be supposing that the crimes committed by the sexes are equally serious. We shall commence by making a distinction between crimes against property and crimes against persons. At the same time, we shall take the numbers obtained for each year, that we may see the limits in which they are comprised [Table 3.4]:

Table 3.4

	Crimes against persons			Crimes against property		
Years	Men	Women	Ratio	Men	Women	Ratio
1826	1,639	268	0.16	4,073	1,008	0.25
1827	1,637	274	0.17	4,020	998	0.25
1828	1,576	270	0.17	4,396	1,156	0.26
1829	1,552	239	0.15	4,379	1,203	0.27
Averages	1,601	263	0.16	4,217	1,091	0.26
1830	1,412	254	0.18	4,196	1,100	0.26
1831	1,813	233	0.13	4,567	993	0.22
Averages	1,612	243	0.15	4,381	1,046	0.24

Although the number of crimes against persons may have diminished slightly, whilst crimes against property have become rather more numerous, yet we see that the variations are not very great; they have but little modified the ratios between the numbers of the accused of the two sexes. We have 26 women to 100 men in the accusations for crimes against property, and for crimes against persons the ratio has been only 16 to 100. In general, crimes against persons are of a more serious nature than those against property, so that our distinction is favourable to the women, and we may affirm that men, in France, are four times as criminal as women. It must be observed, that the ratio 16 to 26 is nearly the same as that of the strength of the two sexes. However, it is proper to examine things more narrowly, and especially to take notice of individual crimes, at least of those which are committed in so great a number, that the inferences drawn from them may possess some degree of probability. For this purpose, in the following table [Table 3.5] I have collected the numbers relating to the four years before 1830, and calculated the different ratios; the crimes are classed according to the degree of magnitude of this ratio. I have also grouped crimes nearly of the same nature together, such as issuing false money, counterfeits, falsehoods in statements or in commercial transactions, etc.

Table 3.5

Nature of crimes	Men	Women	Women to 100 men
Infanticide	30	426	1,320
Miscarriage	15	39	260
Poisoning	77	73	91
House robbery *(vol domestique)*	2,648	1,602	60
Parricide	44	22	50
Incendiarism of buildings and other things	279	94	34
Robbery of churches	176	47	27
Wounding of parents *(blessures envers ascendans)*	292	63	22
Theft	10,677	2,249	21
False evidence and suborning	307	51	17
Fraudulent bankruptcy	353	57	16
Assassination	947	111	12
False coining *(fausse monnaie)*, counterfeit making, false affirmations in deeds etc	1,669	117	11
Rebellion	612	69	10
Highway robbery	648	54	8
Wounds and blows	1,447	78	5
Murder	1,112	44	4
Violation and seduction	685	7	1
Violation on persons under 15 years of age	585	5	1

As we have already observed, to the commission of crime the three following conditions are essential – the will, which depends on the person's morality, the opportunity, and the facility of effecting it. Now, the reason why females have less propensity to crime than males, is accounted for by their being more under the influence of sentiments of shame and modesty, as far as morals are concerned; their dependent state, and retired habits, as far as occasion or opportunity is concerned; and their physical weakness, so far as the facility of acting is concerned. I think we may attribute the differences observed in the degree of criminality to these three principal causes. Sometimes the whole three concur at the same time: we ought, on such occasions, to expect to find their influence very marked, as in rapes and seductions; thus, we have only 1 woman to 100 men in crimes of this nature. In poisoning, on the contrary, the number of accusations for either sex is nearly equal. When force becomes necessary for the destruction of a person, the number of women who are accused becomes much fewer; and their numbers diminish in proportion, according to the necessity of the greater publicity before the crime can be perpetrated: the following crimes also take place in the order in which they are stated – infanticide, miscarriage, parricide, wounding of parents, assassinations, wounds and blows, murder.

With respect to infanticide, woman has not only many more opportunities of committing it than man, but she is in some measure impelled to it, frequently by misery, and almost always from the desire of concealing a fault, and avoiding the shame or scorn of society, which, in such cases, thinks less unfavourably of man. Such is not the case with other crimes involving the destruction of an individual: it is not the degree of the crime which keeps a woman back, since, in the series which we have given, parricides and wounding of parents are more numerous than assassinations, which again are more frequent than murder, and wounds and blows generally; it is not simply weakness, for then the ratio for parricide and wounding of parents should be the same as for murder and wounding of strangers. These differences are more especially owing to the habits and sedentary life of females; they can only conceive and execute guilty projects on individuals with whom they are in the greatest intimacy: thus, compared with man, her assassinations are more often in her family than out of it; and in society she commits assassination rather than murder, which often takes place after excess of drink, and the quarrels to which women are less exposed.

If we now consider the different kinds of theft, we shall find that the ratios of the propensity to crime are arranged in a similar series: thus, we have successively house robbery, robbery in churches, robberies in general, and, lastly, highway robbery, for which strength and audacity are necessary. The less conspicuous propensity to cheating in general, and to fraudulent bankruptcy, again depend on the more secluded life of females, their separation from trade, and that, in some cases, they are less capable than men – for example, in coining false money and issuing counterfeits.

If we attempt to analyse facts, it seems to me that the difference of morality in man and woman is not so great as is generally supposed, excepting only as regards modesty; I do not speak of the timidity arising from this last sentiment, in like manner as it does from the physical weakness and seclusion of females. As to these habits themselves, I think we may form a tolerable estimate of their influence by the ratios which exist between the sexes in crimes of different kinds, where neither strength has to be taken into consideration, nor modesty – as in theft, false witnessing, fraudulent bankruptcy etc.; these ratios are about 100 to 21 or 17, that is to say, about 5 or 6 to 1. As to other modes of cheating, the difference is a little greater, from the reasons already stated. If we try to give a numerical expression of the intensity of the causes by which women are influenced, as, for example, the influence of strength, we may estimate it as being in proportion to the degree of strength itself, or as 1 to 2 nearly; and this is the ratio of the number of parricides for each sex. For crimes where both physical weakness and the retired life of females must be taken into account, as in assassinations and highway robberies, following the same plan in our calculations, it will be necessary to multiply the ratio of power or strength Vi by the degree of dependence 1–5, which gives 1–10, a quantity which really falls between the values 12–100 and 8–100, the ratios given in the table [Table 3.5]. With respect to murder, and blows and wounds, these crimes depend not merely on strength and a more or less sedentary life, but still more on being in the habit of using strong drinks and quarrelling. The influence of this latter cause might almost be considered as 1 to 3 for the sexes. It may be thought that the estimates which I have here pointed out, cannot be of an exact nature, from the impossibility of assigning the share of influence which the greater modesty of woman, her physical weakness, her dependence, or rather her more retired life, and her feebler passions, which are also less frequently excited by liquors, may have respectively on any crime in particular. Yet, if such were the characters in which the sexes more particularly differ from each other, we might, by analyses like those now given, assign their respective influence with some probability of truth, especially if the observations were very numerous.

[...]

OF THE INFLUENCE OF AGE ON THE PROPENSITY TO CRIME
Of all the causes which influence the development of the propensity to crime, or which diminish that propensity, age is unquestionably the most energetic. Indeed, it is through age that the physical powers and passions of man are developed, and their energy afterwards decreases with age. Reason is developed with age, and continues to acquire power even when strength and passion have passed their greatest vigour. Considering only these three elements, strength, passion, and judgment (or reason), we may almost say, a priori, what will be the degree of the propensity to crime at different ages. Indeed, the propensity must be almost nothing at the two extremes of life; since, on the one hand, strength and passion, two powerful instruments of crime, have scarcely begun to exist and, on the other hand, their energy, nearly extinguished, is still further deadened by the influence of reason. On the contrary, the propensity to crime should be at its maximum at the age when strength and passion have attained their maximum, and when reason has not acquired sufficient power to govern their combined influence. Therefore, considering only physical causes, the propensity to crime at different ages will be a property and sequence of the three quantities we have just named, and might be determined by them, if they were sufficiently known. But since these elements are not yet determined, we must confine ourselves to seeking for the degrees of the propensity to crime in an experimental manner; we shall find the means of so doing in the *Comptes Généraux de la Justice*. The following table [Table 3.6] will show the number of crimes against persons and against property, which have been committed in France by each sex during the years 1826, 27, 28, and 29, as well as the ratio of these numbers; the fourth column points out how a population of 10,000 souls is divided in France, according to age; and the last column gives the ratio of the total number of crimes to the corresponding number of the preceding column; thus there is no longer an inequality of number of the individuals of different ages.

Table 3.6

Individuals' age	Crimes against		Crimes against property in 100	Population according to age	Degrees of the propensity to crime
	Persons	Property			
Less than 16 years	80	440	85	3,304	161
16 to 21	904	3,723	80	887	5,217
21 to 25	1,278	3,329	72	673	6,816
25 to 30	1,575	3,702	70	791	6,671
30 to 35	1,153	2,883	71	732	5,514
35 to 40	650	2,076	76	672	4,057
40 to 45	575	1,724	75	612	3,757
45 to 50	445	1,275	74	549	3,133
50 to 55	288	811	74	482	2,280
55 to 60	168	500	75	410	1,629
60 to 65	157	385	71	330	1,642
65 to 70	91	184	70	247	1,113
70 to 80	64	137	68	255	788
80 and upwards	5	14	74	55	345

This table gives us results conformable to those which I have given in my *Recherches Statistique* for the years 1826 and 1827. Since the value obtained for 80 years of age and upwards is based on very small numbers, it is not entitled to much confidence. Moreover, we see that man begins to exercise his propensity to crimes against property at a period antecedent to his pursuit of other crimes. Between his 25th and 30th year, when his powers are developed, he inclines more to crimes against persons. It is near the age of 25 years that the propensity to crime reaches its maximum.

[…]

If, instead of taking crimes collectively, we examine each in particular in proportion to age, we shall have a new proof that the maximum of crimes of different kinds takes place between the 20th and 30th years, and that it is really about that period that the most vicious disposition is manifested. Only the period of maximum will be hastened or retarded some years for some crimes, according to the quicker or slower development of certain qualities of man which are proportioned to those crimes. These results are too curious to be omitted here: I have presented them in the following table [Table 3.7], according to the documents of France, from 1826 to 1829 inclusively, classing them according to the periods of maxima, and taking into account the population of different ages. I have omitted the crimes which are committed in smallest number, because the results from that alone would have been very doubtful.

Table 3.7

Nature of the crimes	Under 16 years	16–21	21–25	25–30	30–35	35–40	40–45	45–50	50–55	55–60	60–65
Violations on children under 15 years	4	120	71	96	73	39	34	45	22	18	26
House robbery	54	965	845	766	528	351	249	207	112	56	61
Other thefts	332	2,479	2,050	2,292	1,716	1,249	1,016	707	433	263	190
Violation and seduction	9	155	156	148	99	38	40	27	9	5	3
Parricide	6	13	12	13	6	3	2	1	4	2	–
Wounds and blows	6	180	300	359	219	129	101	95	55	35	23
Murder	15	139	198	275	172	103	84	49	48	30	25
Infanticide	1	40	99	134	76	44	30	8	7	1	8
Rebellion	5	67	129	156	115	51	51	35	29	16	16
Highway robbery	21	80	111	149	107	60	62	46	22	21	8
Assassination	10	90	144	203	183	100	104	89	53	32	24
Wounding parents	2	47	64	73	72	40	30	16	8	2	1
Poisoning	5	6	17	30	27	15	20	12	6	2	5
False witnessing and suborning	2	23	46	48	44	42	42	35	23	15	15
Various misdemeanours	8	86	202	276	312	244	207	185	129	78	75

Thus the propensity to theft, one of the first to show itself, prevails in some measure throughout our whole existence; we might be led to believe it to be inherent to the weakness of man, who falls into it as if by instinct. It is first exercised by the indulgence of confidence which exists in the interior of families, then it manifests itself out of them, and finally on the public highway, where it terminates by having recourse to violence, when the man has then made the sad essay of the fullness of his strength by committing all the different kinds of homicide. This fatal propensity, however, is not so precocious as that which, near adolescence, arises with the fire of the passions and the disorders which accompany it, and which drives man to violation and seduction, seeking its first victims among beings whose weakness opposes the least resistance. To these first excesses of the passions, of cupidity, and of strength, is soon joined reflection, plotting crime; and man, become more self-possessed and hardened, chooses to destroy his victim by assassination or poisoning. Finally, his last stages in the career of crime are marked by address in deception, which in some measure supplies the place of strength. It is in his decline that the vicious man presents the most hideous spectacle; his cupidity, which nothing can extinguish, is rekindled with fresh ardour, and assumes the mask of swindling; if he still uses the little strength which nature has left to him, it is rather to strike his enemy in the shade; finally, if his depraved passions have not been deadened by age, he prefers to gratify them on feeble children. Thus, his first and his last stages in the career of crime have the same character in this last respect: but what a difference! That which was somewhat excusable in the young man, because of his inexperience, of the violence of his passions, and the similarity of ages, in the old man is the result of the deepest immorality and the most accumulated load of depravity.

[…]

CONCLUSIONS

In making a summary of the principal observations contained in this chapter, we are led to the following conclusions.

1   Age (or the term of life) is undoubtedly the cause which operates with most energy in developing or subduing the propensity to crime.

2   This fatal propensity appears to be developed in proportion to the intensity of the physical power and passions of man: it attains its maximum about the age of 25 years, the period at which the physical development has almost ceased. The intellectual and moral development, which operates more slowly, subsequently weakens the propensity to crime, which, still later, diminishes from the feeble state of the physical powers and passions.

3   Although it is near the age of twenty-five that the maximum in number of crimes of different kinds takes place, yet this maximum advances or recedes some years for certain crimes, according to the quicker or slower development of certain qualities which have a bearing

on those crimes. Thus, man, driven by the violence of his passions, at first commits violation and seduction; almost at the same time he enters on the career of theft, which he seems to follow as if by instinct till the end of life; the development of his strength subsequently leads him to commit every act of violence – homicide, rebellion, highway robbery still later, reflection converts murder into assassination and poisoning. Lastly, man, advancing in the career of crime, substitutes a greater degree of cunning for violence, and becomes more of a forger than at any other period of life.

4   The *difference of sexes* has also a great influence on the propensity to crime: in general, there is only one woman before the courts to four men.

5   The propensity to crime increases and decreases nearly in the same degrees in each sex; yet the period of maximum takes place rather later in women, and is near the thirtieth year.

6   Woman, undoubtedly from her feeling of weakness, rather commits crimes against property than persons; and when she seeks to destroy her kind, she prefers poison. Moreover, when she commits homicide, she does not appear to be proportionally arrested by the enormity of crimes which, in point of frequency, take place in the following order: infanticide, miscarriage, parricide, wounding of parents, assassination, wounds and blows, murder: so that we may affirm that the number of the guilty diminishes in proportion as they have to seek their victim more openly. These differences are no doubt owing to the habits and sedentary life of woman; she can only conceive and execute guilty projects on individuals with whom she is in constant relation.

7   The *seasons,* in their course, exercise a very marked influence on crime: thus, during summer, the greatest number of crimes against persons are committed, and the fewest against property; the contrary takes place during winter.

8   It must be observed that age and the seasons have almost the same influence in increasing or diminishing the number of mental disorders and crimes against persons.

9   *Climate* appears to have some influence, especially on the propensity to crimes against persons: this observation is confirmed at least among the races of southern climates, such as the Pelasgian race, scattered over the shores of the Mediterranean and Corsica, on the one hand; and the Italians, mixed with Dalmatians and Tyrolese, on the other. We observe, also, that severe climates, which give rise to the greatest number of wants, also give rise to the greatest number of crimes against property.

10 The countries where frequent mixture of the people takes place; those in which industry and trade collect many persons and things together, and possess the greatest activity; finally, those where the inequality of fortune is most felt, all things being equal, are those which give rise to the greatest number of crimes.

11 Professions have great influence on the nature of crimes. Individuals of more independent professions are rather given to crimes against persons; and the labouring and domestic classes to crimes against property. Habits of dependence, sedentary life, and also physical weakness in women, produce the same results.

12 *Education* is far from having so much influence on the propensity to crime as is generally supposed. Moreover, moral instruction is very often confounded with instruction in reading and writing alone, and which is most frequently an accessory instrument to crime.

13 It is the same with *poverty;* several of the departments of France, considered to be the poorest, are at the same time the most moral. Man is not driven to crime because he is poor, but more generally because he passes rapidly from a state of comfort to one of misery, and an inadequacy to supply the artificial wants which he has created.

14 The higher we go in the ranks of society, and consequently in the degrees of education, we find a smaller and smaller proportion of guilty women to men; descending to the lowest orders, the habits of both sexes resemble each other more and more.

15 Of 1,129 murders committed in France, during the space of four years, 446 have been in consequence of quarrels and contentions in taverns; which would tend to show the fatal influence of the use of *strong drinks.*

16 In France, as in the Low Countries, we enumerate annually 1 accused person to 4,300 inhabitants nearly; but in the former country, 39 in 100 are acquitted, and in the second only 15; yet the same code was used in both countries, but in the Low Countries the judges performed the duty of the jury. Before correctional courts and simple police courts, where the committed were tried by judges only, the results were nearly the same for both countries.

17 In France, crimes against persons were about one-third of the number of crimes against property, but in the Low Countries they were about one-fourth only. It must be remarked, that the first kind of crimes lead to fewer condemnations than the second, perhaps because there is a greater repugnance to apply punishment as the punishment increases in severity.

I cannot conclude this chapter without again expressing my astonishment at the constancy observed in the results which the documents connected with the administration of justice present each year.

'Thus, as I have already had occasion to repeat several times, we pass from one year to another, with the sad perspective of seeing the same crimes reproduced in the same order, and bringing with them the same punishments in the same proportions.' All observations tend likewise to confirm the truth of this proposition, which I long ago announced, that *every thing which pertains to the human species considered as a whole, belongs to the order of physical facts*: the greater the number of individuals, the more does the influence of individual will disappear, leaving predominance to a series of general facts, dependent on causes by which society exists and is preserved. These causes we now want to ascertain, and as soon as we are acquainted with them, we shall determine their influence on society, just in the same way as we determine effects by their causes in physical sciences.

[…]

[M]an commits crime with at least as much regularity as is observed in births, deaths, or marriages, and with more regularity than the receipts and expenses of the treasury take place. […] since the crimes which are annually committed seem to be a necessary result of our social organization, and since the number of them cannot diminish without the causes which induce them undergoing previous modification, it is the province of legislators to ascertain these causes, and to remove them as far as possible: they have the power of determining the budget of crime, as well as the receipts and expenses of the treasury. Indeed, experience proves as clearly as possible the truth of this opinion, which at first may appear paradoxical, viz., that *society prepares crime, and the guilty are only the instruments by which it is executed.* Hence it happens that the unfortunate person who loses his head on the scaffold, or who ends his life in prison, is in some manner an expiatory victim for society. His crime is the result of the circumstances in which he is found placed: the severity of his chastisement is perhaps another result of it. […]

4

The criminal type in women and its atavistic origin

Cesare Lombroso and Guglielmo Ferrero

[...]

[A] comparison of the criminal skull with the skulls of normal women reveals the fact that female criminals approximate more to males, both criminal and normal, than to normal women, especially in the superciliary arches in the seam of the sutures, in the lower jaw-bones, and in peculiarities of the occipital region. They nearly resemble normal women in their cheek-bones, in the prominence of the crotaphitic line, and in the median occipital fossa. There are also among them a large proportion (9.2 per cent) of virile crania.

The anomalies more frequent in female criminals than in prostitutes are: enormous pterygoid apophisis; cranial depressions; very heavy lower jaw; plagio-cephalia; the soldering of the atlas with the occiput; enormous nasal spine; deep frontal sinuses; absence of sutures; simplicity of sutures; wormian bones.

Fallen women, on the other hand, are distinguished from criminals by the following peculiarities: clinoid apophisis forming a canal; tumefied parietal prominences; median occipital fossa of double size; great occipital irregularity; narrow or receding forehead; abnormal nasal bones; epactal bone; prognathous jaw and alveolar prognathism; cranial sclerosis; a virile type of face; prominent cheek-bones. [...] More instructive than a mere analytical enumeration of the characteristics of degeneration is a synthesis of the different features peculiar to the female criminal type.

We call a *complete type* one wherein exist four or more of the characteristics of degeneration; a *half-type* that which contains at least three of these; and *no type* a countenance possessing only one or two anomalies or none.

From *The Female Offender*, pp. 25; 103–13; 147–52; 190–1. (London: Fisher Unwin, 1895.)

Out of the female delinquents examined 52 were Piedmontese in the prison of Turin, and 234 in the Female House of Correction were natives of different Italian provinces, especially from the South. In these, consequently, we set aside all special characteristics belonging to the ethnological type of the different regions, such as the brachycephali of the Piedmontese, the dolichocephali of the Sardinians, the oxycephali.

We studied also from the point of view of type the 150 prostitutes whom we had previously examined for their several features; as well as another 100 from Moscow whose photographs Madame Tarnowsky sent us.

[…]

The results of the examination may be thus summarized:

1 The rarity of a criminal type in the female as compared with the male delinquent. In our homogeneous group (286) the proportion is 14 per cent, rising, when all other observations are taken into account, to 18 per cent, a figure lower almost by one-half than the average in the male born criminal, namely, 31 per cent.

In normal women this same type is only present in 2 per cent.

[…]

2 Prostitutes differ notably from female criminals in that they offer so much more frequently a special and peculiar type. Grimaldi's figures are 31 per cent (of anomalies), Madame Tarnowsky's 43 per cent, our own 38 per cent; making a mean of 37.1 per cent. These results harmonize with the conclusions to which we had already arrived in our study of particular features, and our survey of the various types of born prostitutes as distinguished from ordinary female offenders.

3 In the differentiation of female criminals, according to their offences, our last observations on the 286 criminals (made first without knowing the nature of their crimes and classified afterwards) give the prevalence of the criminal type among thieves as 15.3 and 16 per cent; among assassins as 13.2 per cent, and as rising to 18.7 per cent in those accused of corruption, among whom were included old prostitutes.

The least frequency was among swindlers, 11 per cent, and infanticides, 8.7 per cent, such women being indeed among the more representative of occasional criminals. […]

Here we see the crescendo of the peculiarities as we rise from moral women, who are most free from anomalies, to prostitutes, who are free from none, and we note how homicides present the highest number of multiple anomalies.

All the same, it is incontestable that female offenders seem almost normal when compared to the male criminal, with his wealth of anomalous features.

[…]

The remarkable rarity of anomalies (already revealed by their crania) is not a new phenomenon in the female, nor is it in contradiction to the undoubted fact that atavistically she is nearer to her origin than the male, and ought consequently to abound more in anomalies.

We saw, indeed, that the crania of male criminals exhibited 78 per cent of anomalies, as against 27 per cent in female delinquents and 51 per cent in prostitutes; but we also saw that the monstrosities in which women abound are forms of disease, consequent on disorder of the ovule. But when a departure from the norm is to be found only in the physiognomy, that is to say, in that portion of the frame where the degenerative stamp, the type declares itself, then even in cases of idiotcy, of madness, and, what is more important for our purpose, of epilepsy, the characteristic face is far less marked and less frequent in the woman. In her, anomalies are extraordinarily rare when compared with man; and this phenomenon, with a few exceptions among lower animals, holds good throughout the whole zoological scale.

[…]

Atavism helps to explain the rarity of the criminal type in woman. The very precocity of prostitutes – the precocity which increases their apparent beauty – is primarily attributable to atavism. Due also to it is the virility underlying the female criminal type; for what we look for most in the female is femininity, and when we find the opposite in her we conclude as a rule that there must be some anomaly. And in order to understand the significance and the atavistic origin of this anomaly, we have only to remember that virility was one of the special features of the savage women.

The criminal being only a reversion to the primitive type of his species, the female criminal necessarily offers the two most salient characteristics of primordial woman, namely, precocity and a minor degree of differentiation from the male – this lesser differentiation manifesting itself in the stature, cranium, brain, and in the muscular strength which she possesses to a degree so far in advance of the modern female.

[…]

The analogy between the anthropology and psychology of the female criminal is perfect.

Just as in the mass of female criminals possessing few or unimportant characteristics of degeneration, we find a group in whom these features are almost more marked and more numerous than in males, so while the majority of female delinquents are led into crime either by the suggestion of a third person or by irresistible temptation, and are not entirely deficient in the moral sense, there is yet to be found among them a small proportion whose criminal propensities are more intense and more perverse than those of their male prototypes.

'No possible punishments,' wrote Corrado Celto, an author of the fifteenth century, 'can deter women from heaping up crime upon crime. Their perversity of mind is more fertile in new crimes than the imagination of a judge in new punishments.'

'Feminine criminality,' writes Rykère, 'is more cynical, more depraved, and more terrible than the criminality of the male.'

'Rarely is a woman wicked, but when she is she surpasses the man' (Italian Proverb).

'The violence of the ocean waves or of devouring flames is terrible. Terrible is poverty, but woman is more terrible than all else' (Euripides).

'The perversity of woman is so great,' says Caro, 'as to be incredible even to its victims.'

[…] Another terrible point of superiority in the female born criminal over the male lies in the refined, diabolical cruelty with which she accomplishes her crime. […] We may assert that if female born criminals are fewer in number than the males, they are often much more ferocious.

What is the explanation? […] [T]he normal woman is naturally less sensitive to pain than a man, and compassion is the offspring of sensitiveness. If the one be wanting, so will the other be.

We also saw that women have many traits in common with children; that their moral sense is deficient; that they are revengeful, jealous, inclined to vengeances of a refined cruelty.

In ordinary cases these defects are neutralized by piety, maternity, want of passion, sexual coldness, by weakness and an undeveloped intelligence. But when a morbid activity of the psychical centres intensifies the bad qualities of women, and induces them to seek relief in evil deeds; when piety and maternal sentiments are wanting, and in their place are strong passions and intensely erotic tendencies, much muscular strength and a superior intelligence for the conception and execution of evil, it is clear that the innocuous semi-criminal present in the normal woman must be transformed into a born criminal more terrible than any man.

What terrific criminals would children be if they had strong passions, muscular strength, and sufficient intelligence; and if, moreover, their evil tendencies were exasperated by a morbid psychical activity! And women are big children; their evil tendencies are more numerous and more varied than men's, but generally remain latent. When they are awakened and excited they produce results proportionately greater.

Moreover, the born female criminal is, so to speak, doubly exceptional, as a woman and as a criminal. For criminals are an exception among civilized people, and women are an exception among criminals, the natural form of retrogression in women being prostitution and not crime. The primitive woman was impure rather than criminal.

As a double exception, the criminal woman is consequently a monster. Her normal sister is kept in the paths of virtue by many causes, such as maternity, piety, weakness, and when these counter influences fail, and a woman commits a crime, we may conclude that her wickedness must have been enormous before it could triumph over so many obstacles.

[…]

M. R., a case described by Ottolenghi, was a thief, a prostitute, a corrupter of youth, a blackmailer, and all this at the age of 17. When only 12 she robbed her father in order to have money to spend among her companions. At 15 she fled from home with a lover, whom she left almost at once for a career of prostitution. With a view to larger gains, when only 16 she organized a vast system of prostitution, by which she provided young girls of 12 and 15 for wealthy men, from whom she exacted large sums, of which only a few sous went to the victims. And by threats of exposure she managed to levy costly blackmail on her clients, one of whom, a highly placed functionary, was dismissed from his post in consequence of her revelations. She was extremely vindictive, and committed two crimes of revenge which serve to show the strange mixture of ferocity and cunning composing her character. One of her companions having spoken evil of her, she (who was then only 16 years of age) let a little time pass, then coaxed her enemy to accompany her outside the gates of the town. They reached a deserted spot as evening fell, and M. R. suddenly threw the other girl on the ground, and while recalling her offence proceeded to beat her violently with a pair of scissors and a key, nor desisted until her victim had fainted; after which she quietly returned to town. 'You might have killed her,' somebody said. 'What did that matter?' she replied; 'there was nobody to see.' 'You might have employed a hired assassin.' 'I am afraid of those,' was the answer. 'Besides, on principle one should do things oneself.' 'But with a key you could never have killed her' (went on the other). 'If one beats the temples well,' M. R. replied, 'it is quite possible to kill a person even with a key.'

She conceived on another occasion such a violent hatred to a brilliant rival that, enticing her into a café, she furtively poisoned her coffee and thus caused her death.

It would be difficult to find greater wickedness at the service of a vindictive disposition and an unbridled greed. We may regard M. R. as an instance in which the two poles of depravity were united. That is to say, she was sanguinary (for she went about always with a dagger in her pocket, and stabbed anybody who offended her in the least) and at the same time inclined to commit the more cautious and insidious crimes, such as poisoning, blackmail, etc. And we consequently find in her an example of the law we have already laid down, to the effect that the female born criminal, when a complete type, is more terrible than the male.

5

Causes of criminal behavior

Enrico Ferri

When a crime is committed in some place, attracting public attention either through the atrocity of the case or the strangeness of the criminal deed – for instance, one that is not connected with bloodshed, but with intellectual fraud – there are at once two tendencies that make themselves felt in the public conscience. One of them, pervading the overwhelming majority of individual consciences, asks: How is this? What for? Why did that man commit such a crime? This question is asked by everybody and occupies mostly the attention of those who do not look upon the case from the point of view of criminology. On the other hand, those who occupy themselves with criminal law represent the other tendency, which manifests itself when acquainted with the news of this crime. This is a limited portion of the public conscience, which tries to study the problem from the standpoint of the technical jurist. The lawyers, the judges, the officials of the police, ask themselves: What is the name of the crime committed by that man under such circumstances? Must it be classed as murder or patricide, attempted or incompleted manslaughter, and, if directed against property, is it theft, or illegal appropriation, or fraud? And the entire apparatus of practical criminal justice forgets at once the first problem, which occupies the majority of the public conscience, the question of the causes that led to this crime, in order to devote itself exclusively to the technical side of the problem, which constitutes the juridical anatomy of the inhuman and antisocial deed perpetrated by the criminal.

In these two tendencies you have a photographic reproduction of the two schools of criminology. The classic school, which looks upon the crime as a juridical problem, occupies itself with its name, its definition, its juridical analysis, leaves the personality of the criminal in the background and remembers it only so far as exceptional circumstances explicitly stated in the law books refer

From *The Positive School of Criminology; Three Lectures by Enrico Ferri* (ed. S.E. Grupp), pp. 70–94. (Pittsburgh, PA: University of Pittsburgh Press, 1968. First published 1901.)

to it: whether he is a minor, a deaf-mute, whether it is a case of insanity, whether he was drunk at the time the crime was committed. Only in these strictly defined cases does the classic school occupy itself theoretically with the personality of the criminal. But ninety times in one hundred these exceptional circumstances do not exist or cannot be shown to exist, and penal justice limits itself to the technical definition of the fact. But when the case comes up in the criminal court, or before the jurors, practice demonstrates that there is seldom a discussion between the lawyers of the defense and the judges for the purpose of ascertaining the most exact definition of the fact, of determining whether it is a case of attempted or merely projected crime, of finding out whether there are any of the juridical elements defined in this or that article of the code. The judge is rather face to face with the problem of ascertaining why, under what conditions, for what reasons, the man has committed the crime. This is the supreme and simple human problem. But hitherto it has been left to a more or less perspicacious, more or less gifted, empiricism, and there have been no scientific standards, no methodical collection of facts, no observations and conclusions, save those of the positive school of criminology. This school alone makes an attempt to solve in every case of crime the problem of its natural origin, of the reasons and conditions that induced a man to commit such and such a crime.

For instance, about 3,000 cases of manslaughter are registered every year in Italy. Now, open any work inspired by the classic school of criminology, and ask the author why 3,000 men are the victims of manslaughter every year in Italy, and how it is that there are not sometimes only as many as, say, 300 cases, the number committed in England, which has nearly the same number of inhabitants as Italy; and how it is that there are not sometimes 300,000 such cases in Italy instead of 3,000?

It is useless to open any work of classical criminology for this purpose, for you will not find an answer to these questions in them. No one, from Beccaria to Carrara, has ever thought of this problem, and they could not have asked it, considering their point of departure and their method. In fact, the classic criminologists accept the phenomenon of criminality as an accomplished fact. They analyze it from the point of view of the technical jurist, without asking how this criminal fact may have been produced, and why it repeats itself in greater or smaller numbers from year to year, in every country. The theory of a free will, which is their foundation, excludes the possibility of this scientific question, for according to it the crime is the product of the fiat of the human will. And if that is admitted as a fact, there is nothing left to account for. The manslaughter was committed, because the criminal wanted to commit it; and that is all there is to it. Once the theory of a free will is accepted as a fact, the deed depends on the fiat, the voluntary determination, of the criminal, and all is said.

But if, on the other hand, the positive school of criminology denies, on the ground of researches in scientific physiological psychology, that the human will is free and does not admit that one is a criminal because he wants to be, but declares that a man commits this or that crime only when he lives in definitely determined conditions of personality and environment which induce him necessarily to act in a certain way, then alone does the problem of the origin of criminality begin to be submitted to a preliminary analysis, and then alone does criminal law step out of the narrow and arid limits of technical jurisprudence and become a true social and human science in the highest and noblest meaning of the word. It is vain to insist with such stubbornness as that of the classic school of criminology on juristic formulae by which the distinction between illegal appropriation and theft, between fraud and other forms of crime against property, and so forth, is determined, when this method does not give to society one single word which would throw light upon the reasons that make a man a criminal and upon the efficacious remedy by which society could protect itself against criminality.

[...]

The method which we, on the other hand, have inaugurated is the following. Before we study crime from the point of view of a juristic phenomenon, we must study the causes to which the annual recurrence of crimes in all countries is due. These are natural causes, which I have classified under the three heads of anthropological, telluric and social. Every crime, from the smallest to the most atrocious, is the result of the interaction of these three causes, the anthropological condition of the criminal, the telluric environment in which he is living, and the social environment in which he is born, living, and operating. It is a vain beginning to separate the meshes of this net of criminality. There are still those who would maintain the onesided standpoint that the origin of crime may be traced to only one of these elements, for instance, to the social element alone. So far as I am concerned, I have combatted this opinion from the very inauguration of the positive school of criminology, and I combat it today. It is certainly easy enough to think that the entire origin of all crime is due to the unfavorable social conditions in which the criminal lives. But an objective, methodical, observation demonstrates that social conditions alone do not suffice to explain the origin of criminality, although it is true that the prevalence of the influence of social conditions is an incontestable fact in the case of the greater number of crimes, especially of the lesser ones. But there are crimes which cannot be explained by the influence of social conditions alone. If you regard the general condition of misery as the sole source of criminality, then you cannot get around the difficulty that out of one thousand individuals living in misery from the day of their birth to that of their death only one hundred or two hundred become criminals, while the other nine hundred or eight hundred either sink into biological weakness, or become harmless maniacs, or commit suicide without perpetrating any crime. If poverty were the sole determining cause, one thousand out of one thousand poor ought to become criminals. If only two hundred become criminals, while one hundred commit suicide, one hundred end as maniacs, and the other six hundred remain honest in their social condition, then poverty alone is not sufficient to explain criminality. We must add the anthropological and telluric factor. Only by means of these three elements of natural influence can criminality be explained. Of course, the influence of either the anthropological or telluric or social element varies from case to case. If you

have a case of simple theft, you may have a far greater influence of the social factor than of the anthropological factor. On the other hand, if you have a case of
murder, the anthropological element will have a far greater influence than the
social. And so on in every case of crime, and every individual that you will have
to judge on the bench of the criminal.

The anthropological factor. It is precisely here that the genius of Cesare
Lombroso established a new science, because in his search after the causes of
crime he studied the anthropological condition of the criminal. This condition
concerns not only the organic and anatomical constitution, but also the psychological, it represents the organic and psychological personality of the criminal.
Every one of us inherits at birth, and personifies in life, a certain organic and
psychological combination. This constitutes the individual factor of human
activity, which either remains normal through life, or becomes criminal or
insane. The anthropological factor, then, must not be restricted, as some laymen
would restrict it, to the study of the form of the skull or the bones of the criminal.
Lombroso had to begin his studies with the anatomical conditions of the criminal, because the skulls may be studied most easily in the museums. But he continued by also studying the brain and the other physiological conditions of the
individual, the state of sensibility, and the circulation of matter. And this entire
series of studies is but a necessary scientific introduction to the study of the psychology of the criminal, which is precisely the one problem that is of direct and
immediate importance. It is this problem which the lawyer and the public prosecutor should solve before discussing the juridical aspect of any crime, for this
reveals the causes which induced the criminal to commit a crime. At present
there is no methodical standard for a psychological investigation, although such
an investigation was introduced into the scope of classic penal law. But for this
reason the results of the positive school penetrate into the lecture rooms of the
universities of jurisprudence, whenever a law is required for the judicial arraign-
ment of the criminal as a living and feeling human being. And even though
the positive school is not mentioned, all profess to be studying the material
furnished by it, for instance, its analyses of the sentiments of the criminal, his
moral sense, his behavior before, during, and after the criminal act, the presence
of remorse which people, judging the criminal after their own feelings, always
suppose the criminal to feel, while, in fact, it is seldom present. This is the anthropological factor, which may assume a pathological form, in which case articles
46 and 47 of the penal code remember that there is such a thing as the personality of the criminal. However, aside from insanity, there are thousands of other
organic and psychological conditions of the personality of criminals, which a
judge might perhaps lump together under the name of extenuating circumstances, but which science desires to have thoroughly investigated. This is not
done today, and for this reason the idea of extenuating circumstances constitutes
a denial of justice.

This same anthropological factor also includes that which each one of us has:
the race character. Nowadays the influence of race on the destinies of peoples
and persons is much discussed in sociology, and there are one-sided schools that

pretend to solve the problems of history and society by means of that racial influence alone, to which they attribute an absolute importance. But while there are some who maintain that the history of peoples is nothing but the exclusive product of racial character, there are others who insist that the social conditions of peoples and individuals are alone determining. The one is as much a one-sided and incomplete theory as the other. The study of collective society or of the single individual has resulted in the understanding that the life of society and of the individual is always the product of the inextricable net of the anthropological, telluric and social elements. Hence the influence of the race cannot be ignored in the study of nations and personalities, although it is not the exclusive factor which would suffice to explain the criminality of a nation or an individual. Study, for instance, manslaughter in Italy, and, although you will find it difficult to isolate one of the factors of criminality from the network of the other circumstances and conditions that produce it, yet there are such eloquent instances of the influence of racial character, that it would be like denying the existence of daylight if one tried to ignore the influence of the ethnical factor on criminality.

In Italy there are two currents of criminality, two tendencies which are almost diametrically opposed to one another. The crimes due to hot blood and muscle grow in intensity from northern to southern Italy, while the crimes against property increase from south to north. In northern Italy, where movable property is more developed, the crime of theft assumes a greater intensity, while crimes due to conditions of the blood are decreasing on account of the lesser poverty and the resulting lesser degeneration of the people. In the south, on the other hand, crimes against property are less frequent and crimes of blood more frequent. Still there also are in southern Italy certain cases where criminality of the blood is less frequent, and you cannot explain this in any other way than by the influence of racial character. If you take a geographical map of manslaughter in Italy, you will see that from the minimum, from Lombardy, Piedmont, and Venice, the intensity increases until it reaches its maximum in the insular and peninsular extreme of the south. […]

Let this be enough so far as the anthropological factor of criminality is concerned. There are, furthermore, the telluric factors, that is to say, the physical environment in which we live and to which we pay no attention. It requires much philosophy, said Rousseau, to note the things with which we are in daily contact, because the habitual influence of a thing makes it more difficult to be aware of it. This applies also to the immediate influence of the physical conditions on human morality, notwithstanding the spiritualist prejudices which still weigh upon our daily lives. For instance, if it is claimed in the name of supernaturalism and psychism that a man is unhappy because he is vicious, it is equivalent to making a one-sided statement. For it is just as true to say that a man becomes vicious because he is unhappy. Want is the strongest poison for the human body and soul. It is the fountain head of all inhuman and antisocial feeling. Where want spreads out its wings, there the sentiments of love, of affection, of brotherhood, are impossible. Take a look at the figures of the peasant in the far-off arid Campagna, the little government employe [sic], the laborer, the little shopkeeper. When work is assured, when living is certain, though poor, then want, cruel want, is in the distance, and every good sentiment can germinate and develop in the human heart. The family then lives in a favorable environment, the parents agree, the children are affectionate. And when the laborer, a bronzed statue of humanity, returns from his smoky shop and meets his white-haired mother, the embodiment of half a century of immaculate virtue and heroic sacrifices, then he can, tired, but assured of his daily bread, give room to feelings of affection, and he will cordially invite his mother to share his frugal meal. But let the same man, in the same environment, be haunted by the spectre of want and lack of employment, and you will see the moral atmosphere in his family changing as from day into night. There is no work, and the laborer comes home without any wages. The wife, who does not know how to feed the children, reproaches her husband with the suffering of his family. The man, having been turned away from the doors of ten offices, feels his dignity as an honest laborer assailed in the very bosom of his own family, because he has vainly asked society for honest employment. And the bonds of affection and union are loosened in that family. Its members no longer agree. There are too many children, and when the poor old mother approaches her son, she reads in his dark and agitated mien the lack of tenderness and feels in her mother [sic] heart that her boy, poisoned by the spectre of want, is perhaps casting evil looks at her and harboring the unfilial thought: 'Better an open grave in the cemetery than one mouth more to feed at home!'

It is true that want alone is not sufficient to prepare the soil in the environment of that suffering family for the roots of real crime and to develop it. Want will weaken the love and mutual respect among the members of that family, but it will not be strong enough alone to arm the hands of the man for a matricidal deed, unless he should get into a pathological mental condition, which is very exceptional and rare. But the conclusions of the positive school are confirmed in this case as in any other. In order that crime may develop, it is necessary that anthropological, social and telluric factors should act together.

[…]

We have now surveyed briefly the natural genesis of crime as a natural social phenomenon, […] which in any determined moment [acts] upon a personality standing on the cross road of vice and virtue, crime and honesty. This scientific deduction gives rise to a series of investigations which satisfy the mind and supply it with a real understanding of things, far better than the theory that a man is a criminal because he wants to be. No, a man commits crime because he finds himself in certain physical and social conditions, from which the evil plant of crime takes life and strength. […]

[…] To sum up, crime is a social phenomenon, due to the interaction of anthropological, telluric, and social factors. This law brings about what I have called criminal saturation, which means that every society has the criminality which it deserves, and which produces by means of its geographical and social conditions such quantities and qualities of crime as correspond to the development of each collective human group.

Thus the old saying of Quetelet is confirmed: 'There is an annual balance of crime, which must be paid and settled with greater regularity than the accounts of the national revenue.' However, we positivists give to this statement a less fatalistic interpretation, since we have demonstrated that crime is not our immutable destiny, even though it is a vain beginning to attempt to attenuate or eliminate crime by mere schemes. The truth is that the balance of crime is determined by the physical and social environment. But by changing the condition of the social environment, which is most easily modified, the legislator may alter the influence of the telluric environment and the organic and psychic conditions of the population, control the greater portion of crimes, and reduce them considerably. It is our firm conviction that a truly civilized legislator can attenuate the plague of criminality, not so much by means of the criminal code, as by means of remedies which are latent in the remainder of the social life and of legislation. And the experience of the most advanced countries confirms this by the beneficent and preventive influence of criminal legislation resting on efficacious social reforms.

We arrive, then, at this scientific conclusion: in the society of the future, the necessity for penal justice will be reduced to the extent that social justice grows intensively and extensively.

6

The condition of the working class in England

Friedrich Engels

RESULTS

[…]

When one individual inflicts bodily injury upon another, such injury that death results, we call the deed manslaughter; when the assailant knew in advance that the injury would be fatal, we call his deed murder. But when society places hundreds of proletarians in such a position that they inevitably meet a too early and an unnatural death, one which is quite as much a death by violence as that by the sword or bullet; when it deprives thousands of the necessaries of life, places them under conditions in which they cannot live – forces them, through the strong arm of the law, to remain in such conditions until that death ensues which is the inevitable consequence – knows that these thousands of victims must perish, and yet permits these conditions to remain, its deed is murder just as surely as the deed of the single individual; disguised, malicious murder, murder against which none can defend himself, which does not seem what it is, because no man sees the murderer, because the death of the victim seems a natural one, since the offence is more one of omission than of commission. But murder it remains.

[...]

That a class which lives under the conditions already sketched and is so ill-provided with the most necessary means of subsistence, cannot be healthy and can reach no advanced age, is self-evident. Let us review the circumstances once more with especial reference to the health of the workers. The centralisation of

From *The Condition of the Working Class in England in 1844* (trans. F.K.Wischnewetzky), pp. 95–133. (London, Allen and Unwin, 1892. First published 1845.)

population in great cities exercises of itself an unfavourable influence; the atmosphere of London can never be so pure, so rich in oxygen, as the air of the country; two and a half million pairs of lungs, two hundred and fifty thousand fires, crowded upon an area three to four miles square, consume an enormous amount of oxygen, which is replaced with difficulty, because the method of building cities in itself impedes ventilation. The carbonic acid gas, engendered by respiration and fire, remains in the streets by reason of its specific gravity, and the chief air current passes over the roofs of the city. The lungs of the inhabitants fail to receive the due supply of oxygen, and the consequence is mental and physical lassitude and low vitality. For this reason, the dwellers in cities are far less exposed to acute, and especially to inflammatory, affections than rural populations, who live in a free, normal atmosphere; but they suffer the more from chronic affections. And if life in large cities is, in itself, injurious to health, how great must be the harmful influence of an abnormal atmosphere in the working-people's quarters, where, as we have seen, everything combines to poison the air. In the country, it may, perhaps, be comparatively innoxious to keep a dung-heap adjoining one's dwelling, because the air has free ingress from all sides; but in the midst of a large town, among closely built lanes and courts that shut out all movement of the atmosphere, the case is different. All putrefying vegetable and animal substances give off gases decidedly injurious to health, and if these gases have no free way of escape, they inevitably poison the atmosphere. The filth and stagnant pools of the working-people's quarters in the great cities have, therefore, the worst effect upon the public health, because they produce precisely those gases which engender disease; so, too, the exhalations from contaminated streams. But this is by no means all. The manner in which the great multitude of the poor is treated by society today is revolting. They are drawn into the large cities where they breathe a poorer atmosphere than in the country; they are relegated to districts which, by reason of the method of construction, are worse ventilated than any others; they are deprived of all means of cleanliness, of water itself, since pipes are laid only when paid for, and the rivers so polluted that they are useless for such purposes; they are obliged to throw all offal and garbage, all dirty water, often all disgusting drainage and excrement into the streets, being without other means of disposing of them; they are thus compelled to infect the region of their own dwellings. Nor is this enough. All conceivable evils are heaped upon the heads of the poor. If the population of great cities is too dense in general, it is they in particular who are packed into the least space. As though the vitiated atmosphere of the streets were not enough, they are penned in dozens into single rooms, so that the air which they breathe at night is enough in itself to stifle them. They are given damp dwellings, cellar dens that are not waterproof from below or garrets that leak from above. Their houses are so built that the clammy air cannot escape. They are supplied bad, tattered, or rotten clothing, adulterated and indigestible food. They are exposed to the most exciting changes of mental condition, the most violent vibrations between hope and fear; they are hunted like game, and not permitted to attain peace of mind and quiet enjoyment of life.

They are deprived of all enjoyments except that of sexual indulgence and drunkenness, are worked every day to the point of complete exhaustion of their mental and physical energies, and are thus constantly spurred on to the maddest excess in the only two enjoyments at their command. And if they surmount all this, they fall victims to want of work in a crisis when all the little is taken from them that had hitherto been vouchsafed them.

[....]

Thus the social order makes family life almost impossible for the worker. In a comfortless, filthy house, hardly good enough for mere nightly shelter, ill-furnished, often neither rain-tight nor warm, a foul atmosphere filling rooms overcrowded with human beings, no domestic comfort is possible. The husband works the whole day through, perhaps the wife also and the elder children, all in different places; they meet night and morning only, all under perpetual temptation to drink; what family life is possible under such conditions? Yet the working-man cannot escape from the family, must live in the family, and the consequence is a perpetual succession of family troubles, domestic quarrels, most demoralising for parents and children alike. Neglect of all domestic duties, neglect of the children, especially, is only too common among the English working-people, and only too vigorously fostered by the existing institutions of society. And children growing up in this savage way, amidst these demoralising influences, are expected to turn out goody-goody and moral in the end! Verily the requirements are naive, which the self-satisfied bourgeois makes upon the working-man!

The contempt for the existing social order is most conspicuous in its extreme form – that of offences against the law. If the influences demoralising to the working-man act more powerfully, more concentratedly than usual, he becomes an offender as certainly as water abandons the fluid for the vaporous state at 80 degrees, Réaumur. Under the brutal and brutalising treatment of the bourgeoisie, the working-man becomes precisely as much a thing without volition as water, and is subject to the laws of Nature with precisely the same necessity; at a certain point all freedom ceases. Hence with the extension of the proletariat, crime has increased in England, and the British nation has become the most criminal in the world. From the annual criminal tables of the Home Secretary, it is evident that the increase of crime in England has proceeded with incomprehensible rapidity. The numbers of arrests for criminal offences reached in the years: 1805, 4,605, 1810, 5,146; 1815, 7,818; 1820, 13,710; 1825, 14,457; 1830, 18,107; 1835, 20,731; 1840, 27,187; 1841, 27,760; 1842, 31,309 in England and Wales alone. That is to say, they increased sevenfold in thirty-seven years. Of these arrests, in 1842, 4,497 were made in Lancashire alone, or more than 14 per cent of the whole; and 4,094 in Middlesex, including London, or more than 13 per cent. So that two districts which include great cities with large proletarian populations, produced one-fourth of the total amount of crime, though their population is far from forming one-fourth of the whole. Moreover, the criminal tables prove directly that nearly all crime arises within the proletariat; for, in 1842, taking the average, out of 100 criminals, 32.35 could neither read nor write; 58.32 read and wrote imperfectly; 6.77 could read and write well; 0.22 had enjoyed a higher education, while the degree of education of 2.34 could not be ascertained. In Scotland, crime has increased yet more rapidly. There were but 89 arrests for criminal offences in 1819, and as early as 1837 the number had risen to 3,126, and in 1842 to 4,189. In Lanarkshire, where Sheriff Alison himself made out the official report, population has doubled once in thirty years, and crime once in five and a half, or six times more rapidly than the population. The offences, as in all civilised countries, are, in the great majority of cases, against property, and have, therefore, arisen from want in some form; for what a man has, he does not steal. The proportion of offences against property to the population, which in the Netherlands is as 1:7,140 and in France, as 1:1,804, was in England, when Gaskell wrote as 1:799. The proportion of offences against persons to the population is, in the Netherlands, 1:28,904; in France, 1:17,573; in England, 1:23,395; that of crimes in general to the population in the agricultural districts, as 1:1,043; in the manufacturing district as 1:840. In the whole of England today the proportion is 1:660; though it is scarcely ten years since Gaskell's book appeared!

These facts are certainly more than sufficient to bring any one, even a bourgeois, to pause and reflect upon the consequences of such a state of things. If demoralisation and crime multiply twenty years longer in this proportion (and if English manufacture in these twenty years should be less prosperous than heretofore, the progressive multiplication of crime can only continue the more rapidly), what will the result be? Society is already in a state of visible dissolution; it is impossible to pick up a newspaper without seeing the most striking evidence of the giving way of all social ties. I look at random into a heap of English journals lying before me; there is the *Manchester Guardian* for October 30, 1844, which reports for three days. It no longer takes the trouble to give exact details as to Manchester, and merely relates the most interesting cases: that the workers in a mill have struck for higher wages without giving notice, and been condemned by a Justice of the Peace to resume work; that in Salford a couple of boys had been caught stealing, and a bankrupt tradesman tried to cheat his creditors. From the neighbouring towns the reports are more detailed: in Ashton, two thefts, one burglary, one suicide; in Bury one theft; in Bolton, two thefts, one revenue fraud; in Leigh, one theft; in Oldham, one strike for wages, one theft, one fight between Irish women, one non-Union hatter assaulted by Union men, one mother beaten by her son, one attack upon the police, one robbery of a church; in Stockport, discontent of working-men with wages, one theft, one fraud, one fight, one wife beaten by her husband; in Warrington, one theft, one fight; in Wigan, one theft, and one robbery of a church. The reports of the London papers are much worse; frauds, thefts, assaults, family quarrels crowd one another. A *Times* of September 12, 1844, falls into my hand, which gives a report of a single day, including a theft, an attack upon the police, a sentence upon a father requiring him to support his illegitimate son, the abandonment of a child by its parents, and the poisoning of a man by his wife. Similar reports are to be found in all the English papers. In this country, social war is under full headway, every one stands for himself, and fights for himself against all comers, and whether or not he shall injure all the others who are his declared foes, depends upon a cynical calculation as to what is most advantageous for himself. It no longer occurs to any one to come to a peaceful understanding with his fellow-man; all differences are settled by threats, violence, or in a law-court. In short, every one sees in his neighbour an enemy to be got out of the way, or, at best, a tool to be used for his own advantage. And this war grows from year to year, as the criminal tables show, more violent, passionate, irreconcilable. The enemies are dividing gradually into two great camps – the bourgeoisie on the one hand, the workers on the other. This war of each against all, of the bourgeoisie against the proletariat, need cause us no surprise, for it is only the logical sequel of the principle involved in free competition. But it may very well surprise us that the bourgeoisie remains so quiet and composed in the face of the rapidly gathering storm-clouds, that it can read all these things daily in the papers without, we will not say indignation at such a social condition, but fear of its consequences, of a universal outburst of that which manifests itself symptomatically from day to day in the form of crime. But then it is the bourgeoisie, and from its standpoint cannot even see the facts, much less perceive their consequences. One thing only is astounding, that class prejudice and preconceived opinions can hold a whole class of human beings in such perfect, I might almost say, such mad blindness. Meanwhile, the development of the nation goes its way whether the bourgeoisie has eyes for it or not, and will surprise the property-holding class one day with things not dreamed of in its philosophy.

7

Criminality and economic conditions

Willem Bonger

[…] [I]t is certain that man is born with social instincts, which, when influenced by a favorable environment can exert a force great enough to prevent egoistic thoughts from leading to egoistic acts. And since crime constitutes a part of the egoistic acts, it is of importance, for the etiology of crime in general, to inquire whether the present method of production and its social consequences are an obstacle to the development of the social instincts, and in what measure. We shall try in the following pages to show the influence of the economic system and of these consequences upon the social instincts of man.

After what we have just said it is almost superfluous to remark that the egoistic tendency does not *by itself* make a man criminal. For this something else is necessary. It is possible for the environment to create a great egoist, but this does not imply that the egoist will necessarily become criminal. For example, a man who is enriched by the exploitation of children may nevertheless remain all his life an honest man from the legal point of view. He does not think of stealing, because he has a surer and more lucrative means of getting wealth, although he lacks the moral sense which would prevent him from committing a crime if the thought of it occurred to him. We shall show that, as a consequence of the present environment, man has become very egoistic and hence more *capable of crime*, than if the environment had developed the germs of altruism.

The present economic system is based upon exchange. […] such a mode of production cannot fail to have an egoistic character. A society based upon exchange isolates the individuals by weakening the bond that unites them. When it is a question of exchange the two parties interested think only of their own advantage even to the detriment of the other party. In the second place the possibility

From *Criminality and Economic Conditions*, pp. 402–5; 667–72. (London: Heinemann, 1916.)

of exchange arouses in a man the thought of the possibility of converting the surplus of his labor into things which increase his well-being in place of giving the benefit of it to those who are deprived of the necessaries of life. Hence the possibility of exchange gives birth to cupidity.

The exchange called simple circulation of commodities is practiced by all men as consumers, and by the workers besides as vendors of their labor power. However, the influence of this simple circulation of commodities is weak compared with that exercised by capitalistic exchange. It is only the exchange of the surplus of labor, by the producer, for other commodities, and hence is for him a secondary matter. As a result he does not exchange with a view to profit (though he tries to make as advantageous a trade as possible), but to get things which he cannot produce himself.

Capitalistic exchange, on the other hand, has another aim – that of making a profit. A merchant, for example, does not buy goods for his own use, but to sell them to advantage. He will, then, always try, on the one hand, to buy the best commodities as cheaply as possible, by depreciating them as much as he can; on the other hand, to make the purchaser pay as high a price as possible, by exaggerating the value of his wares. *By the nature of the mode of production itself* the merchant is therefore forced to make war upon two sides, must maintain his own interests against the interests of those with whom he does business. If he does not injure too greatly the interests of those from whom he buys, and those to whom he sells, it is for the simple reason that these would otherwise do business with those of his competitors who do not find their interest in fleecing their customers. Wherever competition is eliminated for whatever cause the tactics of the merchant are shown in their true light; he thinks only of his own advantage even to the detriment of those with whom he does business. 'No commerce without trickery' is a proverbial expression (among consumers), and with the ancients Mercury, the god of commerce, was also the god of thieves. This is true, that the merchant and the thief are alike in taking account *exclusively* of their own interest to the detriment of those with whom they have to do.

The fact that in our present society production does not take place generally to provide for the needs of men, but for many other reasons, has important effects upon the character of those who possess the means of production. Production is carried on for profit exclusively; if greater profits can be made by stopping production it will be stopped – this is the point of view of the capitalists. The consumers, on the other hand, see in production the means of creating what man has need of. The world likes to be deceived, and does not care to recognize the fact that the producer has only his own profit in view. The latter encourages this notion and poses as a disinterested person. If he reduces the price of his wares, he claims to do it in the interest of the public, and takes care not to admit that it is for the purpose of increasing his own profits. This is the falsity that belongs inevitably to capitalism.

In general this characteristic of capitalism has no importance for the morality of the consumer, who is merely duped, but it is far otherwise with the press, which is almost entirely in the power of the capitalists. The press, which ought to be a guide for the masses, and is so in some few cases, in the main is in the hands of capitalists who use it only as a means of making money. In place of being edited by men who, by their ability and firmness, are capable of enlightening the public, newspapers are carried on by persons who see in their calling only a livelihood, and consider only the proprietor of the sheet. In great part the press is the opposite of what it ought to be; it represents the interests of those who pay for advertisements or for articles; it increases the ignorance and the prejudices of the crowd; in a word, it poisons public opinion.

Besides this general influence upon the public the press has further a special place in the etiology of crime, from the fact that most newspapers, in order to satisfy the morbid curiosity of the public, relate all great crimes in extenso, give portraits of the victims, etc., and are often one of the causes of new crimes, by arousing the imitative instinct to be found in man.

As we have seen above the merchant capitalist makes war in two directions; his interests are against those of the man who sells to him, and of the man who buys from him. This is also true of the industrial capitalist. He buys raw materials and sells what he produces. But to arrive at his product he must buy labor, and this purchase is 'sui generis.'

Deprived as he is of the means of production the working-man sells his labor only in order not to die of hunger. The capitalist takes advantage of this necessitous condition of the worker and exploits him. […] Little by little one class of men has become accustomed to think that the others are destined to amass wealth for them and to be subservient to them in every way. Slavery, like the wage system, demoralizes the servant as well as the master. With the master it develops cupidity and the imperious character which sees in a fellow man only a being fit to satisfy his desires. It is true that the capitalist has not the power over the proletarian that the master has over his slave; he has neither the right of service nor the power of life and death, yet it is none the less true that he has another weapon against the proletarian, a weapon whose effect is no less terrible, namely enforced idleness. The fact that the supply of manual labor always greatly exceeds the demand puts this weapon into the hands of every capitalist. It is not only the capitalists who carry on any business that are subjected to this influence, but also all who are salaried in their service.

Capitalism exercises in still a third manner an egoistic influence upon the capitalistic 'entrepreneur'. Each branch has more producers than are necessary. The interests of the capitalists are, then, opposed not only to those of the men from whom they buy or to whom they sell, but also to those of their fellow producers. It is indeed claimed that competition has the effect simply of making the product better and cheaper, but this is looking at the question from only one point of view. The fact which alone affects criminality is that competition forces the participants, under penalty of succumbing, to be as egoistic as possible. Even the producers who have the means of applying all the technical improvements to perfect their product and make it cheaper, are obliged to have recourse to gross deceits in advertising, etc., in order to injure their competitors. Rejoicing at the evil which befalls another, envy at his good fortune, these forms of egoism are the inevitable consequence of competition.

[…]

What are the conclusions to be drawn from what has gone before? When we sum up the results that we have obtained it becomes plain that economic conditions occupy a much more important place in the etiology of crime than most authors have given them.

First we have seen that the present economic system and its consequences weaken the social feelings. The basis of the economic system of our day being exchange, the economic interests of men are necessarily found to be in opposition. This is a trait that capitalism has in common with other modes of production. But its principal characteristic is that the means of production are in the hands of a few, and most men are altogether deprived of them. Consequently, persons who do not possess the means of production are forced to sell their labor to those who do, and these, in consequence of their economic preponderance, force them to make the exchange for the mere necessaries of life, and to work as much as their strength permits.

This state of things especially stifles men's social instincts; it develops, on the part of those with power, the spirit of domination, and of insensibility to the ills of others, while it awakens jealousy and servility on the part of those who depend upon them. Further the contrary interests of those who have property, and the idle and luxurious life of some of them, also contribute to the weakening of the social instincts.

The material condition, and consequently the intellectual condition, of the proletariat are also a reason why the moral plane of that class is not high. The work of children brings them into contact with persons to associate with whom is fatal to their morals. Long working hours and monotonous labor brutalize those who are forced into them; bad housing conditions contribute also to debase the moral sense, as do the uncertainty of existence, and finally absolute poverty, the frequent consequence of sickness and unemployment. Ignorance and lack of training of any kind also contribute their quota. Most demoralizing of all is the status of the lower proletariat.

The economic position of woman contributes also to the weakening of the social instincts.

The present organization of the family has great importance as regards criminality. It charges the legitimate parents with the care of the education of the child; the community concerns itself with the matter very little. It follows that a great number of children are brought up by persons who are totally incapable of doing it properly. As regards the children of the proletariat, there can be no question of the education properly so-called, on account of the lack of means and the forced absence of one or both of the parents. The school tends to remedy this state of things, but the results do not go far enough. The harmful consequences of the present organization of the family make themselves felt especially in the case of the children of the lower proletariat, orphans, and illegitimate children. For these the community does but little, though their need of adequate help is the greatest.

Prostitution, alcoholism, and militarism, which result, in the last analysis, from the present social order, are phenomena that have demoralizing consequences.

As to the different kinds of crime, [...] the very important group of economic criminality finds its origin on the one side in the absolute poverty and the cupidity brought about by the present economic environment, and on the other in the moral abandonment and bad education of the children of the poorer classes. Then, professional criminals are principally recruited from the class of occasional criminals, who, finding themselves rejected everywhere after their liberation, fall lower and lower. The last group of economic crimes (fraudulent bankruptcy, etc.) is so intimately connected with our present mode of production, that it would not be possible to commit it under another.

The relation between sexual crimes and economic conditions is less direct; nevertheless these also give evidence of the decisive influence of these conditions. We have called attention to the four following points.

First, there is a direct connection between the crime of adultery and the present organization of society, which requires that the legal dissolution of a marriage should be impossible or very difficult.

Second, sexual crimes upon adults are committed especially by unmarried men; and since the number of marriages depends in its turn upon the economic situation, the connection is clear; and those who commit these crimes are further almost exclusively illiterate, coarse, raised in an environment almost without sexual morality, and regard the sexual life from the wholly animal side.

Third, the causes of sexual crime upon children are partly the same as those of which we have been speaking, with the addition of prostitution.

Fourth, alcoholism greatly encourages sexual assaults.

As to the relation between crimes of vengeance and the present constitution of society, [...] it produces conflicts without number; statistics have shown that those who commit them are almost without exception poor and uncivilized, and that alcoholism is among the most important causes of these crimes.

Infanticide is caused in part by poverty, and in part by the opprobrium incurred by the unmarried mother (an opprobrium resulting from the social utility of marriage).

Political criminality comes solely from the economic system and its consequences.

Finally, economic and social conditions are also important factors in the etiology of degeneracy, which is in its turn a cause of crime.

Upon the basis of what has gone before, we have a right to say that the part played by economic conditions in criminality is preponderant, even decisive.

This conclusion is of the highest importance for the prevention of crime. If it were principally the consequence of innate human qualities (atavism, for example), the pessimistic conclusion that crime is a phenomenon inseparably bound up with the social life would be well founded. But the facts show that it is rather the optimistic conclusion that we must draw, that where crime is the consequence of economic and social conditions, we can combat it by changing those conditions.

However important crime may be as a social phenomenon, however terrible may be the injuries and the evil that it brings upon humanity, the development of society will not depend upon the question as to what are the conditions which could restrain crime or make it disappear, if possible; the evolution of society will proceed independently of this question.

What is the direction that society will take under these continual modifications? This is not the place to treat fully of this subject. In my opinion the facts indicate quite clearly what the direction will be. The productivity of labor has increased to an unheard of degree, and will assuredly increase in the future. The concentration of the means of production into the hands of a few progresses continually; in many branches it has reached such a degree that the fundamental principle of the present economic system, competition, is excluded, and has been replaced by monopoly. On the other hand the working class is becoming more and more organized, and the opinion is very generally held among working-men that the causes of material and intellectual poverty can be eliminated only by having the means of production held in common.

Supposing that this were actually realized, what would be the consequences as regards criminality? Let us take up this question for a moment. Although we can give only personal opinions as to the details of such a society, the general outlines can be traced with certainty.

The chief difference between a society based upon the community of the means of production and our own is that material poverty would be no longer known. Thus one great part of economic criminality (as also one part of infanticide) would be rendered impossible, and one of the greatest demoralizing forces of our present society would be eliminated. And then, in this way those social phenomena so productive of crime, prostitution and alcoholism would lose one of their principal factors. Child labor and overdriving would no longer take place, and bad housing, the source of much physical and moral evil, would no longer exist.

With material poverty there would disappear also that intellectual poverty which weighs so heavily upon the proletariat; culture would no longer be the privilege of some, but a possession common to all. The consequences of this upon criminality would be very important, for […] even in our present society with its numerous conflicts, the members of the propertied classes, who have often but a veneer of civilization, are almost never guilty of crimes of vengeance. There is the more reason to admit that in a society where interests were not opposed, and where civilization was universal, these crimes would be no longer present, especially since alcoholism also proceeds in large part from the intellectual poverty of the poorer classes. And what is true of crimes of vengeance, is equally true of sexual crimes in so far as they have the same etiology.

A large part of the economic criminality (and also prostitution to a certain extent) has its origin in the cupidity excited by the present economic environment. In a society based upon the community of the means of production, great contrasts of fortune would, like commercial capital, be lacking, and thus cupidity would find no food. These crimes will not totally disappear so long as there has not been a redistribution of property according to the maxim, 'to each according to his needs', something that will probably be realized, but not in the immediate future.

The changes in the position of woman which are taking place in our present society, will lead, under this future mode of production, to her economic independence, and consequently to her social independence as well. It is accordingly probable that the criminality of woman will increase in comparison with that of man during the transition period. But the final result will be the disappearance of the harmful effects of the economic and social preponderance of man.

As to the education of children under these new conditions it is difficult to be definite. However, it is certain that the community will concern itself seriously with their welfare. It will see to it that the children whose parents cannot or will not be responsible for them, are well cared for. By acting in this way it will remove one of the most important causes of crime. There is no doubt that the community will exercise also a strict control over the education of children; it cannot be affirmed, however, that the time will come when the children of a number of parents will be brought up together by capable persons; this will depend principally upon the intensity that the social sentiments may attain.

As soon as the interests of all are no longer opposed to each other, as they are in our present society, there will no longer be a question either of politics ('a fortiori' of political *crimes*) or of militarism.

Such a society will not only remove the causes which now make men egoistic, but will awaken, on the contrary, a strong feeling of altruism. [...] In a larger measure this will be realized under a mode of production in common, the interests of all being the same.

In such a society there can be no question of crime properly so called. The eminent criminologist, Manouvrier, in treating of the prevention of crime expresses himself thus: 'The maxim to apply is, act so that every man shall always have more interest in being useful to his fellows than in harming them.' It is precisely in a society where the community of the means of production has been realized that this maxim will obtain its complete application. There will be crimes committed by pathological individuals, but this will come rather within the sphere of the physician than that of the judge. And then we may even reach a state where these cases will decrease in large measure, since the social causes of degeneracy will disappear, and procreation by degenerates be checked through the increased knowledge of the laws of heredity and the increasing sense of moral responsibility.

'It is society that prepares the crime', says the true adage of Quetelet. For all those who have reached this conclusion, and are not insensible to the sufferings of humanity, this statement is sad, but contains a ground of hope. It is sad, because society punishes severely those who commit the crime which she has herself prepared. It contains a ground of hope, since it promises to humanity the possibility of some day delivering itself from one of its most terrible scourges.

8

Law and authority

Peter Kropotkin

If one studies the millions of laws that rule humanity, one can see easily that they are divisible into three main categories: protection of property, protection of government, protection of persons. And in analysing these three categories one comes to the same conclusion regarding each of them: *the uselessness and harmfulness of the law.*

As for the protection of property, the socialists know what that means. Laws regarding property are not fashioned to guarantee either individuals or society the fruits of their labour. They are made, on the contrary, to pilfer from the producer part of what he produces and to assure to the few whatever they have pilfered, either from the producers or from society as a whole. When the law established the right of Sir Such-and-Such over a house, for example, it established his right, not over a cabin that he might have built himself, nor over a house he might have erected with the help of a few friends; nobody would dispute his right if such had been the case. The law, on the contrary, established his rights over a mansion that *is not* the product of his labour, first because he has had it built by others, whom he has not paid the true value of their work, and next because his mansion represents a social value he could not produce on his own: the law establishes his rights over a portion of that which belongs to everybody and not to anyone in particular. The same house, built in the beautiful heart of Siberia, would not have the value it has in a large city. Its value derives, as we know, from the works of fifty generations who have built the city, adorned it, provided it with water and gas, with fine boulevards, universities, theatres and shops, with railways and roads radiating in all directions.

Thus in recognizing the rights of Sir Such-and-Such over a house in Paris, in London, in Rouen, the law appropriates to him – unjustly – a certain part of the

From *Words of a Rebel* (trans. G. Woodcock), pp. 159–64. (Montreal/New York: Black Rose Books, 1992. First published 1898.)

products of the work of all humanity. And it is precisely because that appropriation is a crying injustice (all other forms of property have the same character) that it has needed a whole arsenal of laws and a whole army of soldiers, policemen and judges to sustain it, against the good sense and the feeling of justice that is inherent in humanity.

Thus the greater part of our laws – the civil codes of all countries – have no other object than to maintain this appropriation, this monopoly to the profit of a few against the whole of humanity. Three-quarters of the cases judged by the tribunals are merely quarrels that have cropped up among monopolists; two robbers quarrelling over the booty. And a great part of our criminal laws have the same aim, since their object is to keep the worker in a position subordinate to the employer, to assure to one the exploitation of the other.

As to guaranteeing the producer the product of his work, there are not even any laws that provide it. That is so simple and so natural, so much in accordance with human customs and habits that the law has not even dreamed of it. Open brigandage, with arms in hand, no longer exists in our century; a worker need no longer dispute with another worker over the products of their toil; if there is some failure of understanding between them, they deal with it without having recourse to the law, by calling in a third party, and if there is anyone who insists on requiring from another person a part of what he has produced, it can only be the property-owner, coming to claim his lion's share. As to humanity in general, it respects everywhere the right of each person over what he has produced, without the need to have any special laws to cover it.

All these laws about property, which make up the great volumes of codes and are the delight of our lawyers, have no object but that of protecting the unjust appropriation of the work of humanity by certain monopolists, and thus have no reason to exist; and socialist revolutionaries are determined to make them vanish on the day of the revolution. We can, in fact and in full justice, make a great bonfire of *all* the laws that are related to the so-called 'rights of property', of all the property titles, of all the archives – in brief, of all that has reference to an institution which soon will be considered a blot on the history of humanity as humiliating as slavery and serfdom in past centuries.

What we have just said about the laws concerning property applies completely to the second category of laws – the laws that maintain the government – constitutional laws, in other words.

Once again there is a whole arsenal of laws, decrees, or ordinances, this time serving to protect the various forms of representative government – by delegation or usurpation – under which human societies struggle for existence. We know very well – the anarchists have often demonstrated it by their incessant criticism of the various forms of government – that the mission of *all* governments, monarchical, constitutional and republican, is to protect and maintain by force the privileges of the owning classes: aristocracy, priesthood and bourgeoisie. A good third of our laws, the 'fundamental' laws, laws on taxes, customs duties, on the organization of ministries and their chancelleries, on the army, the police, the church, etc. – and there are tens of thousands of them in every country – have no other end but to maintain, keep in repair and develop the governmental machine, which in its turn serves almost entirely to protect the privileges of these possessing classes. Analyse all these laws, observe them in action from day to day, and you will see that there is not a single one worth keeping, beginning with those that bound the communes hand and foot to the parson, the local merchant and the governmental boss, and ending with that famous constitution (the nineteenth or twentieth since 1789), which gives us a chamber of dunces and petty speculators ready for the dictatorship of any adventurer who comes along, for the rule of some crowned cabbage-head.

Briefly, regarding these laws there can be no doubt. Not only the anarchists, but also the more or less revolutionary middle class are in agreement on this: that the best use one can make of the laws concerning the organization of government is to burn them in a bonfire celebrating their end.

There remains the first category of laws, the most important, because most of the prejudices cluster around them; the laws regarding the protection of persons, the punishment and prevention of 'crimes'. If the law enjoys a certain consideration, it is because people believe this category of laws absolutely indispensable for the security of the individual in society. Laws have developed from the nucleus of customs that were useful for human societies and were exploited by the rulers to sanction their domination. The authority of the chiefs of the tribes, of the rich families of the communes, and of the kind, were supported by the function of judges which they exercised, and even to the present, when people talk of the need for government, it is its function of supreme judge that is implied. 'Without government, people would strangle each other', says the village wiseacre. 'The ultimate end of society is to give every accused person twelve honest jurors', said Edmund Burke.

But despite all the presuppositions that exist on this subject, it is high time the anarchists loudly declared that this category of the laws is as useless and harmful as the rest.

First of all, when we consider the so-called 'crimes', the attacks against the persons, it is well known that two-thirds or even three-quarters of them are inspired by the desire to lay hold of somebody's wealth. That immense category of so-called 'crimes and misdemeanours' would disappear on the day private property ceased to exist.

'But', we shall be told, 'there will still be the brutes who make attempts on the lives of citizens, who strike with the knife in every quarrel, who avenge the least offence by a murder, if there are not laws to restrain them and punishments to hold them back.' This is the refrain that has been sung to us ever since we expressed doubt of society's right to punish. Yet one fact has been clearly established: the severity of punishments in no way diminishes the number of crimes. You can hang, draw and quarter the murderers as much as you like, but the number of murders will not diminish. On the other hand, if you abolish the death penalty there will not be a single murder more. Statisticians and legists know that when the severity of the penal code is lessened there is never an increase in the number of attempts against the lives of citizens. On the other hand, when the crops are abundant, when bread is cheap and the weather is good, the number of murders decreases at once. It is proved by statistics that the number of crimes increases and declines in relation to the price of necessities and to good or bad weather. Not that all murders are inspired by hunger. Far from it; but when the harvests are good and necessities are affordably priced, people are happy and less wretched than usual, and they do not let themselves be led away by dark passions that tempt them to stick knives into the chests of their neighbours for futile reasons.

Besides, it is well known that fear of punishment has not halted a single murderer. Whoever is about to kill his neighbour for vengeance or poverty does not reflect a great deal on the consequences; there has never been a murderer who lacked the firm conviction that he would escape from prosecution. Let anyone think about this subject, let him analyse crimes and punishments, their motives and consequences, and if he knows how to reason without letting himself be influenced by preconceived ideas, he is bound to reach this conclusion:

'Without considering a society where people will receive a better education, where the development of all their faculties and the possibility of using them will give men and women so much pleasure that they would not risk it all by indulging in murder, without considering that future society, and taking into account only our present society, with the sad products of poverty we see everywhere in the low taverns of the cities, the number of murders would not increase in any way if one day it were decided that no punishment be inflicted on murderers; indeed it is very likely there would be a fall in the number of cases involving recidivists, brutalized in the prisons.'

We are told constantly of the benefits of the law and of the salutary effects of punishment. But has anyone ever tried to establish a balance between the benefits that are attributed to the law and its penalties, and the degrading effect of those penalties on humanity? One has merely to consider the accumulation of evil passions that are awakened among the spectators by the atrocious punishments inflicted publicly in our streets and squares. Who is it that has thus fostered and developed the instincts of cruelty among humanity (instincts unknown to the animals, man having become the most cruel animal on earth), if it is not the king, the judge and the priest, armed by the law, who had flesh torn away by strips, with burning pitch poured into the wounds, had limbs dislocated, bones broken, men sawn in two, so as to maintain their authority? You need merely consider the torrent of depravity let loose in human societies by spying and informing, encouraged by judges and paid for by the government in hard cash under the pretext of assisting the discovery of crimes. You need only to go into prisons and observe there what the man becomes who is deprived of liberty and thrust among other depraved beings permeated with all the corruption and vice that breed in our prisons today, to realize that the more they are 'reformed', the more detestable the prisons become, our modern and model penitentiaries being a hundred times more corrupting than the dungeons of the Middle Ages. Finally, you need only consider what corruption and deprivation of the mind is generated among humankind by these ideas of *obedience* (essence of the law), of punishment, of

authority having the right to punish and judge apart from the urgings of conscience, by all the functions of executioners, jailers and informers – in brief by all
that immense apparatus of law and authority. You have only to consider all that,
and you will certainly be in agreement with us, when we say that law and its penalties are abominations that should cease to exist.

Meanwhile, people who are not ruled by police, and because of that are less
imbued by authoritarian prejudices, have perfectly understood that someone
called a 'criminal' is simply an unfortunate; that it is not a question of whipping
or chaining him, or causing his death on the scaffold or in prison, but of succour-
ing him by the most brotherly care, by treating him as an equal and taking him
to live among honest people. And we hope the coming revolution will resound
with this call:

'Burn the guillotines, demolish the prisons, drive away the judge, the policeman, the spy – an impure race if ever there was one – but treat as a brother him
who has been led by passion to do ill to his kind; above all deprive the truly great
criminals, those ignoble products of bourgeois idleness, of the possibility of parad-
ing their vices in seductive form, and you can be sure that we shall no longer have
more than a very small number of crimes to point to in our society. Apart from
idleness, what sustains crime is law and authority; the laws on property, the laws
on government, the laws with their penalties and punishments. And Authority,
which takes on itself to make these laws and apply them.

'No more laws! No more judges! Freedom, Brotherhood and the practice of
Solidarity are the only effective bulwark we can raise to the anti-social instincts
of a few among us.'

9

The normal and the pathological

Emile Durkheim

[...]
   If there is any fact whose pathological character appears incontestable, that fact is crime. All criminologists are agreed on this point. Although they explain this pathology differently, they are unanimous in recognizing it. But let us see if this problem does not demand a more extended consideration.

   [...] Crime is present not only in the majority of societies of one particular species but in all societies of all types. There is no society that is not confronted with the problem of criminality. Its form changes; the acts thus characterized are not the same everywhere; but, everywhere and always, there have been men who have behaved in such a way as to draw upon themselves penal repression. If, in proportion as societies pass from the lower to the higher types, the rate of criminality, i.e., the relation between the yearly number of crimes and the population, tended to decline, it might be believed that crime, while still normal, is tending to lose this character of normality. But we have no reason to believe that such a regression is substantiated. Many facts would seem rather to indicate a movement in the opposite direction. From the beginning of the [nineteenth] century, statistics enable us to follow the course of criminality. It has everywhere increased. In France the increase is nearly 300 per cent. There is, then, no phenomenon that presents more indisputably all the symptoms of normality, since it appears closely connected with the conditions of all collective life. To make of crime a form of social morbidity would be to admit that morbidity is not something accidental, but, on the contrary, that in certain cases it grows out of the fundamental constitution of the living organism; it would result in wiping out all distinction between the physiological and the pathological. No doubt it is possible that crime itself will have abnormal

From *The Rules of Sociological Method*, pp. 65–73. (New York: Free Press, 1964. First published 1895.)

forms, as, for example, when its rate is unusually high. This excess is, indeed, undoubtedly morbid in nature. What is normal, simply, is the existence of criminality, provided that it attains and does not exceed, for each social type, a certain level […]

Here we are, then, in the presence of a conclusion in appearance quite paradoxical. Let us make no mistake. To classify crime among the phenomena of normal sociology is not to say merely that it is an inevitable, although regrettable phenomenon, due to the incorrigible wickedness of men; it is to affirm that it is a factor in public health, an integral part of all healthy societies. This result is, at first glance, surprising enough to have puzzled even ourselves for a long time. Once this first surprise has been overcome, however, it is not difficult to find reasons explaining this normality and at the same time confirming it.

In the first place crime is normal because a society exempt from it is utterly impossible. Crime […] consists of an act that offends certain very strong collective sentiments. In a society in which criminal acts are no longer committed, the sentiments they offend would have to be found without exception in all individual consciousnesses, and they must be found to exist with the same degree as sentiments contrary to them. Assuming that this condition could actually be realized, crime would not thereby disappear; it would only change its form, for the very cause which would thus dry up the sources of criminality would immediately open up new ones.

Indeed, for the collective sentiments which are protected by the penal law of a people at a specified moment of its history to take possession of the public conscience or for them to acquire a stronger hold where they have an insufficient grip, they must acquire an intensity greater than that which they had hitherto had. The community as a whole must experience them more vividly, for it can acquire from no other source the greater force necessary to control these individuals who formerly were the most refractory. For murderers to disappear, the horror of bloodshed must become greater in those social strata from which murderers are recruited; but, first it must become greater throughout the entire society. Moreover, the very absence of crime would directly contribute to produce this horror; because any sentiment seems much more respectable when it is always and uniformly respected.

One easily overlooks the consideration that these strong states of the common consciousness cannot be thus reinforced without reinforcing at the same time the more feeble states, whose violation previously gave birth to mere infraction of convention – since the weaker ones are only the prolongation, the attenuated form, of the stronger. Thus robbery and simple bad taste injure the same single altruistic sentiment, the respect for that which is another's. However, this same sentiment is less grievously offended by bad taste than by robbery; and since, in addition, the average consciousness has not sufficient intensity to react keenly to the bad taste, it is treated with greater tolerance. That is why the person guilty of bad taste is merely blamed, whereas the thief is punished. But, if this sentiment grows stronger, to the point of silencing in all consciousnesses the inclination which disposes man to steal, he will become more sensitive to the offenses which, until then, touched him but lightly. He will react against them, then, with more energy; they will be the object of greater opprobrium, which will transform certain of them from the simple moral faults that they were and give them the quality of crimes. For example, improper contracts, or contracts improperly executed, which only incur public blame or civil damages, will become offenses in law.

Imagine a society of saints, a perfect cloister of exemplary individuals. Crimes, properly so called, will there be unknown; but faults which appear venial to the layman will create there the same scandal that the ordinary offense does in ordinary consciousnesses. If, then, this society has the power to judge and punish, it will define these acts as criminal and will treat them as such. For the same reason, the perfect and upright man judges his smallest failings with a severity that the majority reserve for acts more truly in the nature of an offense. Formerly, acts of violence against persons were more frequent than they are today, because respect for individual dignity was less strong. As this has increased, these crimes have become more rare; and also, many acts violating this sentiment have been introduced into the penal law which were not included there in primitive times.

In order to exhaust all the hypotheses logically possible, it will perhaps be asked why this unanimity does not extend to all collective sentiments without exception. Why should not even the most feeble sentiment gather enough energy to prevent all dissent? The moral consciousness of the society would be present in its entirety in all the individuals, with a vitality sufficient to prevent all acts offending it – the purely conventional faults as well as the crimes. But a uniformity so universal and absolute is utterly impossible; for the immediate physical milieu in which each one of us is placed, the hereditary antecedents, and the social influences vary from one individual to the next, and consequently diversify consciousnesses. It is impossible for all to be alike, if only because each one has his own organism and that these organisms occupy different areas in space. That is why, even among the lower peoples, where individual originality is very little developed, it nevertheless does exist.

Thus, since there cannot be a society in which the individuals do not differ more or less from the collective type, it is also inevitable that, among these divergences, there are some with a criminal character. What confers this character upon them is not the intrinsic quality of a given act but that definition which the collective conscience lends them. If the collective conscience is stronger, if it has enough authority practically to suppress these divergences, it will also be more sensitive, more exacting; and, reacting against the slightest deviations with the energy it otherwise displays only against more considerable infractions, it will attribute to them the same gravity as formerly to crimes. In other words, it will designate them as criminal.

Crime is, then, necessary; it is bound up with the fundamental conditions of all social life, and by that very fact it is useful, because these conditions of which it is a part are themselves indispensable to the normal evolution of morality and law.

Indeed, it is no longer possible today to dispute the fact that law and morality vary from one social type to the next, nor that they change within the same type if the conditions of life are modified. But, in order that these transformations may be possible, the collective sentiments at the basis of morality must not be hostile to change, and consequently must have but moderate energy. If they were too strong, they would no longer be plastic. Every pattern is an obstacle to new patterns, to the extent that the first pattern is inflexible. The better a structure is articulated, the more it offers a healthy resistance to all modification; and this is equally true of functional, as of anatomical, organization. If there were no crimes, this condition could not have been fulfilled; for such a hypothesis presupposes that collective sentiments have arrived at a degree of intensity unexampled in history. Nothing is good indefinitely and to an unlimited extent. The authority which the moral conscience enjoys must not be excessive; otherwise no one would dare criticize it, and it would too easily congeal into an immutable form. To make progress, individual originality must be able to express itself. In order that the originality of the idealist whose dreams transcend his century may find expression, it is necessary that the originality of the criminal, who is below the level of his time, shall also be possible. One does not occur without the other.

Nor is this all. Aside from this indirect utility, it happens that crime itself plays a useful role in this evolution. Crime implies not only that the way remains open to necessary changes but that in certain cases it directly prepares these changes. Where crime exists, collective sentiments are sufficiently flexible to take on a new form, and crime sometimes helps to determine the form they will take. How many times, indeed, it is only an anticipation of future morality – a step toward what will be! According to Athenian law, Socrates was a criminal, and his condemnation was no more than just. However, his crime, namely, the independence of his thought, rendered a service not only to humanity but to his country. It served to prepare a new morality and faith which the Athenians needed, since the traditions by which they had lived until then were no longer in harmony with the current conditions of life. Nor is the case of Socrates unique; it is reproduced periodically in history. It would never have been possible to establish the freedom of thought we now enjoy if the regulations prohibiting it had not been violated before being solemnly abrogated. At that time, however, the violation was a crime, since it was an offense against sentiments still very keen in the average conscience. And yet this crime was useful as a prelude to reforms which daily became more necessary. Liberal philosophy had as its precursors the heretics of all kinds who were justly punished by secular authorities during the entire course of the Middle Ages and until the eve of modern times.

From this point of view the fundamental facts of criminality present themselves to us in an entirely new light. Contrary to current ideas, the criminal no longer seems a totally unsociable being, a sort of parasitic element, a strange and unassimilable body, introduced into the midst of society. On the contrary, he plays a definite role in social life. Crime, for its part, must no longer be conceived as an evil that cannot be too much suppressed. There is no occasion for self-congratulation when the crime rate drops noticeably below the average level, for we may be certain that this apparent progress is associated with some social disorder. Thus, the number of assault cases never falls so low as in times of want. With the drop in the crime rate, and as a reaction to it, comes a revision, or the need of a revision in the theory of punishment. If, indeed, crime is a disease, its punishment is its remedy and cannot be otherwise conceived; thus, all the discussions it arouses bear on the point of determining what the punishment must be in order to fulfil this role of remedy. If crime is not pathological at all, the object of punishment cannot be to cure it, and its true function must be sought elsewhere.

[...]

10

Social structure and anomie

Robert K. Merton

There persists a notable tendency in sociological theory to attribute the malfunctioning of social structure primarily to those of man's imperious biological drives which are not adequately restrained by social control. In this view, the social order is solely a device for 'impulse management' and the 'social processing' of tensions. These impulses which break through social control, be it noted, are held to be biologically derived. Nonconformity is assumed to be rooted in original nature.[1] Conformity is by implication the result of an utilitarian calculus or unreasoned conditioning. This point of view, whatever its other deficiences, clearly begs one question. It provides no basis for determining the nonbiological conditions which induce deviations from prescribed patterns of conduct. In this paper, it will be suggested that certain phases of social structure generate the circumstances in which infringement of social codes constitutes a 'normal' response.[2]

The conceptual scheme to be outlined is designed to provide a coherent, systematic approach to the study of socio-cultural sources of deviate behavior. Our primary aim lies in discovering how some social structures *exert a definite pressure* upon certain persons in the society to engage in nonconformist rather than conformist conduct. The many ramifications of the scheme cannot all be discussed; the problems mentioned outnumber those explicitly treated.

Among the elements of social and cultural structure, two are important for our purposes. These are analytically separable although they merge imperceptibly in concrete situations. The first consists of culturally defined goals, purposes, and interests. It comprises a frame of aspirational reference. These goals are more or less integrated and involve varying degrees of prestige and sentiment. They constitute a basic, but not the exclusive, component of what Linton aptly has called 'designs for group living.' Some of these cultural aspirations are related to

From *American Sociological Review*, 1938, 3(5): 672–682.

the original drives of man, but they are not determined by them. The second phase of the social structure defines, regulates, and controls the acceptable modes of achieving these goals. Every social group invariably couples its scale of desired ends with moral or institutional regulation of permissible and required procedures for attaining these ends. These regulatory norms and moral imperatives do not necessarily coincide with technical or efficiency norms. Many procedures which from the standpoint of *particular individuals* would be most efficient in securing desired values, e.g., illicit oil-stock schemes, theft, fraud, are ruled out of the institutional area of permitted conduct. The choice of expedients is limited by the institutional norms.

To say that these two elements, culture goals and institutional norms, operate jointly is not to say that the ranges of alternative behaviors and aims bear some constant relation to one another. The emphasis upon certain goals may vary independently of the degree of emphasis upon institutional means. There may develop a disproportionate, at times, a virtually exclusive, stress upon the value of specific goals, involving relatively slight concern with the institutionally appropriate modes of attaining these goals. The limiting case in this direction is reached when the range of alternative procedures is limited only by technical rather than institutional considerations. Any and all devices which promise attainment of the all important goal would be permitted in this hypothetical polar case.[3] This constitutes one type of cultural malintegration. A second polar type is found in groups where activities originally conceived as instrumental are transmuted into ends in themselves. The original purposes are forgotten and ritualistic adherence to institutionally prescribed conduct becomes virtually obsessive.[4] Stability is largely ensured while change is flouted. The range of alternative behaviors is severely limited. There develops a tradition-bound, sacred society characterized by neophobia. The occupational psychosis of the bureaucrat may be cited as a case in point. Finally, there are the intermediate types of groups where a balance between culture goals and institutional means is maintained. These are the significantly integrated and relatively stable, though changing, groups.

An effective equilibrium between the two phases of the social structure is maintained as long as satisfactions accrue to individuals who conform to both constraints, viz., satisfactions from the achievement of the goals and satisfactions emerging directly from the institutionally canalized modes of striving to attain these ends. Success, in such equilibrated cases, is twofold. Success is reckoned in terms of the product and in terms of the process, in terms of the outcome and in terms of activities. Continuing satisfactions must derive from sheer *participation* in a competitive order as well as from eclipsing one's competitors if the order itself is to be sustained. The occasional sacrifices involved in institutionalized conduct must be compensated by socialized rewards. The distribution of statuses and roles through competition must be so organized that positive incentives for conformity to roles and adherence to status obligations are *provided for every position* within the distributive order. Aberrant conduct, therefore, may be viewed as a symptom of dissociation between culturally defined aspirations and socially structured means.

Of the types of groups which result from the independent variation of the two phases of the social structure, we shall be primarily concerned with the first, namely, that involving a disproportionate accent on goals. This statement must be recast in a proper perspective. In no group is there an absence of regulatory codes governing conduct, yet groups do vary in the degree to which these folkways, mores, and institutional controls are effectively integrated with the more diffuse goals which are part of the culture matrix. Emotional convictions may cluster about the complex of socially acclaimed ends, meanwhile shifting their support from the culturally defined implementation of these ends. As we shall see, certain aspects of the social structure may generate countermores and antisocial behavior precisely because of differential emphases on goals and regulations. In the extreme case, the latter may be so vitiated by the goal-emphasis that the range of behavior is limited only by considerations of technical expediency. The sole significant question then becomes, which available means is most efficient in netting the socially approved value?[5] The technically most feasible procedure, whether legitimate or not, is preferred to the institutionally prescribed conduct. As this process continues, the integration of the society becomes tenuous and anomie ensues.

Thus, in competitive athletics, when the aim of victory is shorn of its institutional trappings and success in contests becomes construed as 'winning the game' rather than 'winning through circumscribed modes of activity,' a premium is implicitly set upon the use of illegitimate but technically efficient means. The star of the opposing football team is surreptitiously slugged; the wrestler furtively incapacitates his opponent through ingenious but illicit techniques; university alumni covertly subsidize 'students' whose talents are largely confined to the athletic field. The emphasis on the goal has so attenuated the satisfactions deriving from sheer participation in the competitive activity that these satisfactions are virtually confined to a successful outcome. Through the same process, tension generated by the desire to win in a poker game is relieved by successfully dealing oneself four aces, or, when the cult of success has become completely dominant, by sagaciously shuffling the cards in a game of solitaire. The faint twinge of uneasiness in the last instance and the surreptitious nature of public delicts indicate clearly that the institutional rules of the game *are known* to those who evade them, but that the emotional supports of these rules are largely vitiated by cultural exaggeration of the success-goal.[6] They are microcosmic images of the social macrocosm.

Of course, this process is not restricted to the realm of sport. The process whereby exaltation of the end generates a *literal demoralization*, i.e., a deinstitutionalization, of the means is one which characterizes many[7] groups in which the two phases of the social structure are not highly integrated. The extreme emphasis upon the accumulation of wealth as a symbol of success[8] in our own society militates against the completely effective control of institutionally regulated modes of acquiring a fortune.[9] Fraud, corruption, vice, crime, in short, the entire catalogue of proscribed behavior, becomes increasingly common when the emphasis on the culturally induced success-goal becomes divorced from a coordinated institutional emphasis. This observation is of crucial theoretical importance in examining the doctrine that antisocial behavior most frequently derives from biological drives breaking through the restraints imposed by society. The difference is one between a strictly utilitarian interpretation which conceives man's ends as random and an analysis which finds these ends deriving from the basic values of the culture.[10]

Our analysis can scarcely stop at this juncture. We must turn to other aspects of the social structure if we are to deal with the social genesis of the varying rates and types of deviate behavior characteristic of different societies. Thus far, we have sketched three ideal types of social orders constituted by distinctive patterns of relations between culture ends and means. Turning from these types of *culture patterning*, we find five logically possible, alternative modes of adjustment or adaptation by *individuals* within the culture-bearing society or group.[11] These are schematically presented in the following table, where (+) signifies 'acceptance,' (−) signifies 'elimination' and (±) signifies 'rejection and substitution of new goals and standards.'

Table 10.1

	Culture Goals	Institutionalized Means
I. Conformity	+	+
II. Innovation	+	−
III. Ritualism	−	+
IV. Retreatism	−	−
V. Rebellion[12]	±	±

Our discussion of the relation between these alternative responses and other phases of the social structure must be prefaced by the observation that persons may shift from one alternative to another as they engage in different social activities. These categories refer to role adjustments in specific situations, not to personality *in toto*. To treat the development of this process in various spheres of conduct would introduce a complexity unmanageable within the confines of this paper. For this reason, we shall be concerned primarily with economic activity in the broad sense, 'the production, exchange, distribution and consumption of goods and services' in our competitive society, wherein wealth has taken on a highly symbolic cast. Our task is to search out some of the factors which exert pressure upon individuals to engage in certain of these logically possible alternative responses. This choice, as we shall see, is far from random.

In every society, Adaptation I (conformity to both culture goals and means) is the most common and widely diffused. Were this not so, the stability and continuity of the society could not be maintained. The mesh of expectancies which constitutes every social order is sustained by the modal behavior of its members falling within the first category. Conventional role behavior oriented toward the basic values of the group is the rule rather than the exception. It is this fact alone which permits us to speak of a human aggregate as comprising a group or society.

Conversely, Adaptation IV (rejection of goals and means) is the least common. Persons who 'adjust' (or maladjust) in this fashion are, strictly speaking, *in* the society but not *of* it. Sociologically, these constitute the true 'aliens.' Not sharing the common frame of orientation, they can be included within the societal population merely in a fictional sense. In this category are *some* of the activities of psychotics, psychoneurotics, chronic autists, pariahs, outcasts, vagrants, vagabonds, tramps, chronic drunkards and drug addicts.[13] These have relinquished, in certain spheres of activity, the culturally defined goals, involving complete aim-inhibition in the polar case, and their adjustments are not in accord with institutional norms. This is not to say that in some cases the source of their behavioral adjustments is not in part the very social structure which they have in effect repudiated nor that their very existence within a social area does not constitute a problem for the socialized population.

This mode of 'adjustment' occurs, as far as structural sources are concerned, when both the culture goals and institutionalized procedures have been assimilated thoroughly by the individual and imbued with affect and high positive value, but where those institutionalized procedures which promise a measure of successful attainment of the goals are not available to the individual. In such instances, there results a twofold mental conflict insofar as the moral obligation for adopting institutional means conflicts with the pressure to resort to illegitimate means (which may attain the goal) and inasmuch as the individual is shut off from means which are both legitimate *and* effective. The competitive order is maintained, but the frustrated and handicapped individual who cannot cope with this order drops out.

Defeatism, quietism and resignation are manifested in escape mechanisms which ultimately lead the individual to 'escape' from the requirements of the society. It is an expedient which arises from continued failure to attain the goal by legitimate measures and from an inability to adopt the illegitimate route because of internalized prohibitions and institutionalized compulsives, *during which process the supreme value of the success-goal has as yet not been renounced*. The conflict is resolved by eliminating both precipitating elements, the goals and means. The escape is complete, the conflict is eliminated and the individual is socialized.

Be it noted that where frustration derives from the inaccessibility of effective institutional means for attaining economic or any other type of highly valued 'success,' that Adaptations II, III and V (innovation, ritualism and rebellion) are also possible. The result will be determined by the particular personality, and thus, the *particular* cultural background, involved. Inadequate socialization will result in the innovation response whereby the conflict and frustration are eliminated by relinquishing the institutional means and retaining the success-aspiration; an extreme assimilation of institutional demands will lead to ritualism wherein the goal is dropped as beyond one's reach but conformity to the mores persists; and rebellion occurs when emancipation from the reigning standards, due to frustration or to marginalist perspectives, leads to the attempt to introduce a 'new social order.'

Our major concern is with the illegitimacy adjustment. This involves the use of conventionally proscribed but frequently effective means of attaining at least the simulacrum of culturally defined success – wealth, power, and the like. As we have seen, this adjustment occurs when the individual has assimilated the cultural emphasis on success without equally internalizing the morally pre-scribed norms governing means for its attainment. The question arises, Which phases of our social structure predispose toward this mode of adjustment? We may examine a concrete instance, effectively analyzed by Lohman,[14] which pro-vides a clue to the answer. Lohman has shown that specialized areas of vice in the near north side of Chicago constitute a 'normal' response to a situation where the cultural emphasis upon pecuniary success has been absorbed, but where there is little access to conventional and legitimate means for attaining such suc-cess. The conventional occupational opportunities of persons in this area are almost completely limited to manual labor. Given our cultural stigmatization of manual labor, and its correlate, the prestige of white collar work, it is clear that the result is a strain toward innovational practices. The limitation of opportunity to unskilled labor and the resultant low income can not compete *in terms of conventional standards of achievement* with the high income from organized vice.

For our purposes, this situation involves two important features. First, such antisocial behavior is in a sense 'called forth' by certain conventional values of the culture *and* by the class structure involving differential access to the approved opportunities for legitimate, prestige-bearing pursuit of the culture goals. The lack of high integration between the means-and-end elements of the cultural pat-tern and the particular class structure combine to favor a heightened frequency of antisocial conduct in such groups. The second consideration is of equal sig-nificance. Recourse to the first of the alternative responses, legitimate effort, is limited by the fact that actual advance toward desired success-symbols through conventional channels is, despite our persisting open-class ideology,[15] relatively rare and difficult for those handicapped by little formal education and few eco-nomic resources. The dominant pressure of group standards of success is, there-fore, on the gradual attenuation of legitimate, but by and large ineffective, strivings and the increasing use of illegitimate, but more or less effective, expe-dients of vice and crime. The cultural demands made on persons in this situation are incompatible. On the one hand, they are asked to orient their conduct toward the prospect of accumulating wealth and on the other, they are largely denied effective opportunities to do so institutionally. The consequences of such structural inconsistency are psycho-pathological personality, and/or antisocial conduct, and/or revolutionary activities. The equilibrium between culturally designated means and ends becomes highly unstable with the progressive emphasis on attaining the prestige-laden ends by any means whatsoever. Within this context, Capone represents the triumph of amoral intelligence over morally prescribed 'failure,' when the channels of vertical mobility are closed or narrowed[16] *in a society which places a high premium on economic affluence and social ascent for all its members.*[17]

This last qualification is of primary importance. It suggests that other phases of the social structure besides the extreme emphasis on pecuniary success, must be considered if we are to understand the social sources of antisocial behavior. A high frequency of deviate behavior is not generated simply by 'lack of opportunity' or by this exaggerated pecuniary emphasis. A comparatively rigidified class structure, a feudalistic or caste order, may limit such opportunities far beyond the point which obtains in our society today. It is only when a system of cultural values extols, virtually above all else, certain *common* symbols of success for the *population at large* while its social structure rigorously restricts or completely eliminates access to approved modes of acquiring these symbols *for a considerable part of the same population*, that antisocial behavior ensues on a considerable scale. In other words, our egalitarian ideology denies by implication the existence of noncompeting groups and individuals in the pursuit of pecuniary success. The same body of success-symbols is held to be desirable for all. These goals are held to *transcend class lines*, not to be bounded by them, yet the actual social organization is such that there exist class differentials in the accessibility of these *common* success-symbols. Frustration and thwarted aspiration lead to the search for avenues of escape from a culturally induced intolerable situation; or unrelieved ambition may eventuate in illicit attempts to acquire the dominant values.[18] The American stress on pecuniary success and ambitiousness for all thus invites exaggerated anxieties, hostilities, neuroses and antisocial behavior.

This theoretical analysis may go far toward explaining the varying correlations between crime and poverty.[19] Poverty is not an isolated variable. It is one in a complex of interdependent social and cultural variables. When viewed in such a context, it represents quite different states of affairs. Poverty as such, and consequent limitation of opportunity, are not sufficient to induce a conspicuously high rate of criminal behavior. Even the often mentioned 'poverty in the midst of plenty' will not necessarily lead to this result. Only insofar as poverty and associated disadvantages in competition for the culture values approved for *all* members of the society is linked with the assimilation of a cultural emphasis on monetary accumulation as a symbol of success is antisocial conduct a 'normal' outcome. Thus, poverty is less highly correlated with crime in southeastern Europe than in the United States. The possibilities of vertical mobility in these European areas would seem to be fewer than in this country, so that neither poverty *per se* nor its association with limited opportunity is sufficient to account for the varying correlations. It is only when the full configuration is considered, poverty, limited opportunity and a commonly shared system of success symbols, that we can explain the higher association between poverty and crime in our society than in others where rigidified class structure is coupled with *differential class symbols of achievement*.

In societies such as our own, then, the pressure of prestige-bearing success tends to eliminate the effective social constraint over means employed to this end. 'The-end-justifies-the-means' doctrine becomes a guiding tenet for action when the cultural structure unduly exalts the end and the social organization unduly limits possible recourse to approved means. Otherwise put, this notion and associated behavior reflect a lack of cultural coordination. In international relations, the effects of this lack of integration are notoriously apparent. An emphasis upon national power is not readily coordinated with an inept organization of legitimate, i.e., internationally defined and accepted, means for attaining this goal. The result is a tendency toward the abrogation of international law, treaties become scraps of paper, 'undeclared warfare' serves as a technical evasion, the bombing of civilian populations is rationalized,[20] just as the same societal situation induces the same sway of illegitimacy among individuals.

The social order we have described necessarily produces this 'strain toward dissolution.' The pressure of such an order is upon outdoing one's competitors. The choice of means within the ambit of institutional control will persist as long as the sentiments supporting a competitive system, i.e., deriving from the possibility of outranking competitors and hence enjoying the favorable response of others, are distributed throughout the entire system of activities and are not confined merely to the final result. A stable social structure demands a balanced distribution of affect among its various segments. When there occurs a shift of emphasis from the satisfactions deriving from competition itself to almost exclusive concern with successful competition, the resultant stress leads to the breakdown of the regulatory structure.[21] With the resulting attenuation of the institutional imperatives, there occurs an approximation of the situation erroneously held by utilitarians to be typical of society generally wherein calculations of advantage and fear of punishment are the sole regulating agencies. In such situations, as Hobbes observed, force and fraud come to constitute the sole virtues in view of their relative efficiency in attaining goals – which were for him, of course, not culturally derived.

It should be apparent that the foregoing discussion is not pitched on a moralistic plane. Whatever the sentiments of the writer or reader concerning the ethical desirability of coordinating the means-and-goals phases of the social structure, one must agree that lack of such coordination leads to anomie. Insofar as one of the most general functions of social organization is to provide a basis for calculability and regularity of behavior, it is increasingly limited in effectiveness as these elements of the structure become dissociated. At the extreme, predictability virtually disappears and what may be properly termed cultural chaos or anomie intervenes.

This statement, being brief, is also incomplete. It has not included an exhaustive treatment of the various structural elements which predispose toward one rather than another of the alternative responses open to individuals; it has neglected, but not denied the relevance of, the factors determining the specific incidence of these responses; it has not enumerated the various concrete responses which are constituted by combinations of specific values of the analytical variables; it has omitted, or included only by implication, any consideration of the social functions performed by illicit responses; it has not tested the full explanatory power of the analytical scheme by examining a large number of group variations in the frequency of deviate and conformist behavior; it has not adequately dealt with rebellious conduct which seeks to refashion the social framework radically; it has not examined the relevance of cultural conflict for an analysis of culture-goal and institutional-means malintegration. It is suggested that these and related problems may be profitably analyzed by this scheme.

NOTES

1   E.g., Ernest Jones, *Social Aspects of Psychoanalysis*, 28, London, 1924. If the Freudian notion is a variety of the 'original sin' dogma, then the interpretation advanced in this paper may be called the doctrine of 'socially derived sin.'

2   'Normal' in the sense of a culturally oriented, if not approved, response. This statement does not deny the relevance of biological and personality differences which may be significantly involved in the *incidence* of deviate conduct. Our focus of interest is the social and cultural matrix; hence we abstract from other factors. It is in this sense, I take it, that James S. Plant speaks of the 'normal reaction of normal people to abnormal conditions.' See his *Personality and the Cultural Pattern*, 248, New York, 1937.

3   Contemporary American culture has been said to tend in this direction. See André Siegfried, *America Comes of Age*, 26–37, New York, 1927. The alleged extreme (?) emphasis on the goals of monetary success and material prosperity leads to dominant concern with technological and social instruments designed to produce the desired result, inasmuch as institutional controls become of secondary importance. In such a situation, innovation flourishes as the *range of means* employed is broadened. In a sense, then, there occurs the paradoxical emergence of 'materialists' from an 'idealistic' orientation. Cf. Durkheim's analysis of the cultural conditions which predispose toward crime and innovation, both of which are aimed toward efficiency, not moral norms. Durkheim was one of the first to see that 'contrairement aux idées courantes, le criminel n'apparait plus comme un être radicalement insociable, comme une sorte d'élément parasitaire, de corps étranger et inassimilable, introduit au sein de la société; c'est un agent régulier de la vie sociale.' See *Les Règles de la Méthode Sociologique*, 86–89, Paris, 1927.

4   Such ritualism may be associated with a mythology which rationalizes these actions so that they appear to retain their status as means, but the dominant pressure is in the direction of strict ritualistic conformity, irrespective of such rationalizations. In this sense, ritual has proceeded farthest when such rationalizations are not even called forth.

5   In this connection, one may see the relevance of Elton Mayo's paraphrase of the title of Tawney's well known book. 'Actually the problem is *not that of the sickness of an acquisitive society; it is that of the acquisitiveness of a sick society.*' *Human Problems of an Industrial Civilization*, 153, New York, 1933. Mayo deals with the process through which wealth comes to be a symbol of social achievement. He sees this as arising from a state of anomie. We are considering the unintegrated monetary-success goal as an element in producing anomie. A complete analysis would involve both phases of this system of interdependent variables.

6   It is unlikely that interiorized norms are completely eliminated. Whatever residuum persists will induce personality tensions and conflict. The process involves a certain degree of ambivalence. A manifest rejection of the institutional norms is coupled with

some latent retention of their emotional correlates. 'Guilt feelings,' 'sense of sin,' 'pangs of conscience' are obvious manifestations of this unrelieved tension; symbolic adherence to the nominally repudiated values or rationalizations constitute a more subtle variety of tensional release.

7   'Many,' and not all, unintegrated groups, for the reason already mentioned. In groups where the primary emphasis shifts to institutional means, i.e., when the range of alternatives is very limited, the outcome is a type of ritualism rather than anomie.

8   Money has several peculiarities which render it particularly apt to become a symbol of prestige divorced from institutional controls. As Simmel emphasized, money is highly abstract and impersonal. However acquired, through fraud or institutionally, it can be used to purchase the same goods and services. The anonymity of metro- politan culture, in conjunction with this peculiarity of money, permits wealth, the sources of which may be unknown to the community in which the plutocrat lives, to serve as a symbol of status.

9   The emphasis upon wealth as a success-symbol is possibly reflected in the use of the term 'fortune' to refer to a stock of accumulated wealth. This meaning becomes com- mon in the late sixteenth century (Spenser and Shakespeare). A similar usage of the Latin *fortuna* comes into prominence during the first century B.C. Both these periods were marked by the rise to prestige and power of the 'bourgeoisie.'

10   See Kingsley Davis, 'Mental Hygiene and the Class Structure,' *Psychiatry*, 1928, I, esp. 62–63; Talcott Parsons, *The Structure of Social Action*, 59–60, New York, 1937.

11   This is a level intermediate between the two planes distinguished by Edward Sapir; namely, culture patterns and personal habit systems. See his 'Contribution of Psychiatry to an Understanding of Behavior in Society,' *Amer. J. Sociol.*, 1937, 42: 862–870.

12   This fifth alternative is on a plane clearly different from that of the others. It repre- sents a *transitional response* which seeks to *institutionalize* new procedures oriented toward revamped cultural goals shared by the members of the society. It thus involves efforts to *change* the existing structure rather than to perform accommoda- tive actions *within* this structure, and introduces additional problems with which we are not at the moment concerned.

13   Obviously, this is an elliptical statement. These individuals may maintain some ori- entation to the values of their particular differentiated groupings within the larger society or, in part, of the conventional society itself. Insofar as they do so, their con- duct cannot be classified in the 'passive rejection' category (IV). Nels Anderson's description of the behavior and attitudes of the bum, for example, can readily be recast in terms of our analytical scheme. See *The Hobo*, 93–98, *et passim*, Chicago, 1923.

14   Joseph D. Lohman, 'The Participant Observer in Community Studies,' *Amer. Sociol. Rev.*, 1937, 2: 890–898.

15   The shifting historical role of this ideology is a profitable subject for exploration. The 'office-boy-to-president' stereotype was once in approximate accord with the facts. Such vertical mobility was probably more common then than now, when the class structure is more rigid. (See the following note.) The ideology largely persists, how- ever, possibly because it still performs a useful function for maintaining the *status quo*. For insofar as it is accepted by the 'masses,' it constitutes a useful sop for those who might rebel against the entire structure, were this consoling hope removed. This ideology now serves to lessen the probability of Adaptation V. In short, the role of this notion has changed from that of an approximately valid empirical theorem to that of an ideology, in Mannheim's sense.

16 There is a growing body of evidence, though none of it is clearly conclusive, to the effect that our class structure is becoming rigidified and that vertical mobility is declining. Taussig and Joslyn found that American business leaders are being *increasingly* recruited from the upper ranks of our society. The Lynds have also found a 'diminished chance to get ahead' for the working classes in Middletown. Manifestly, these objective changes are not alone significant; the individual's subjective evaluation of the situation is a major determinant of the response. The extent to which this change in opportunity for social mobility has been recognized by the least advantaged classes is still conjectural, although the Lynds present some suggestive materials. The writer suggests that a case in point is the increasing frequency of cartoons which observe in a tragi-comic vein that 'my old man says everybody can't be President. He says if ya can get three days a week steady on W.P.A. work ya ain't doin' so bad either.' See F. W. Taussig and C. S. Joslyn, *American Business Leaders*, New York, 1932; R. S. and H. M. Lynd, *Middletown in Transition*, 67 ff., chap. 12, New York, 1937.

17 The role of the Negro in this respect is of considerable theoretical interest. Certain elements of the Negro population have assimilated the dominant caste's values of pecuniary success and social advancement, but they also recognize that social ascent is at present restricted to their own caste almost exclusively. The pressures upon the Negro which would otherwise derive from the structural inconsistencies we have noticed are hence not identical with those upon lower class whites. See Kingsley Davis, *op. cit.*, 63; John Dollard, *Caste and Class in a Southern Town*, 66 ff., New Haven, 1936; Donald Young, *American Minority Peoples*, 581, New York, 1932.

18 The psychical coordinates of these processes have been partly established by the experimental evidence concerning *Anspruchsniveaus* and levels of performance. See Kurt Lewin, *Vorsatz, Wille und Bedurfnis*, Berlin, 1926; N. F. Hoppe, 'Erfolg und Misserfolg,' *Psychol. Forschung*, 1930, 14:1–63; Jerome D. Frank, 'Individual Differences in Certain Aspects of the Level of Aspiration,' *Amer. J. Psychol.*, 1935, 47: 119–128.

19 Standard criminology texts summarize the data in this field. Our scheme of analysis may serve to resolve some of the theoretical contradictions which P. A. Sorokin indicates. For example, 'not everywhere nor always do the poor show a greater proportion of crime … many poorer countries have had less crime than the richer countries … The [economic] improvement in the second half of the nineteenth century, and the beginning of the twentieth, has not been followed by a decrease of crime.' See his *Contemporary Sociological Theories*, 560–561, New York, 1928. The crucial point is, however, that poverty has varying social significance in different social structures, as we shall see. Hence, one would not expect a linear correlation betweem crime and poverty.

20 See M. W. Royse, *Aerial Bombardment and the International Regulation of War*, New York, 1928.

21 Since our primary concern is with the socio-cultural aspects of this problem, the psychological correlates have been only implicitly considered. See Karen Horney, *The Neurotic Personality of Our Time*, New York, 1937, for a psychological discussion of this process.

Part Two

Causes of crime

INTRODUCTION

The search for the causes of crime has formed the bedrock of most criminological studies, at least up to the 1970s. Since then, the question of causation has been critiqued by a variety of radical criminologies more concerned to reveal how 'crime' and 'the criminal' are constructed through processes of law creation and enforcement (see Part Three); and more recently the search for causation has been dismissed as a fruitless and failed exercise which distracts attention away from the more pressing tasks of crime management (see Part Four). It is common for many contemporary criminologists to claim that studies of the aetiology of crime are in terminal decline.

However, this selection of readings should reveal that this is not necessarily the case. The selection has been governed by two main criteria: first, to illustrate the diverse schools of thought which make claim to the theorization of the causes of crime; and secondly, to establish that each of these schools has retained a strong contemporary presence. For this reason, we have chosen to focus upon a body of theoretical work which marks a reworking or critical development of earlier positions.

If Lombroso's work established a need to examine the biological bases of criminality, then the extract reproduced here from Mednick, Gabrielli and Hutchings represents its modern and more sophisticated version. Based on a detailed study of adoptees, their biological parents and adoptive parents, this work claims that some genetic and biological factors are transmitted through the generations of some families, and that these factors must be involved in the aetiology of at least some criminal behaviour. Eysenck's reiteration and reinforcement of his 1964 theory, that certain personality traits are likely to lead to a greater propensity towards anti-social behaviour, shares some of these concerns. However, biology alone, he argues, is an insufficient explanation. Eysenck's work is more concerned to reveal the impact of interrelationships between genetic factors and processes of socialization.

By the 1990s risk factor analysis had become predominant in isolating those aspects of an individual's personal history, personality and biography that appeared capable of predicting future crime. A key part of this evidence has been derived from longitudinal research based at the

Institute of Criminology at the University of Cambridge. Beginning in the 1960s the researchers followed the development of over 400 working-class London boys from the age of eight onwards. By the age of 21, about 30 per cent of the sample had some sort of official record of delinquency. A scale was devised to measure 'anti-social' tendencies, based on attitudinal measures and such activities as smoking, loitering, tattooing, heavy drinking, gambling and promiscuous sex. They found that those who scored high on anti-social attitudes and behaviours were more likely in the future to have criminal records than those who scored low. The researchers concluded that a 'delinquent' way of life – particular attributes of personality and life-style – were clearly connected to officially recorded criminality. The most important indicators included parental criminality as well as marital conflict, large family size, poor parental supervision, and parents' cruel, passive and neglecting attitudes and erratic or harsh discipline. The extract reproduced here by David Farrington, the leader of the Cambridge study, reviews the state of the (now purportedly global) evidence regarding criminal careers, risk factors and protective factors, concluding that the evidence is now strong enough to reliably inform effective strategies of crime prevention. It underlines the growing importance of 'evidence-led' and policy relevant research in some schools of criminology. It is difficult to underestimate its influence, particularly in political and policy circles. Indeed the tendency has grown towards shifting attention away from any one distinct cause (such as a 'criminal personality') to a level of analysis that considers the relevance of family environment and upbringing coupled with motivational states, cognitive processes, situational contexts and latent biological predispositions.

Much public discussion of crime also appears persuaded by the arguments of the American political scientist Charles Murray. He argues forcibly that rising crime rates are caused by the growth of an underclass – identified primarily by illegitimacy, family breakdown and welfare dependence. In his view the growth in crime is directly related to increasing numbers of barbaric young men who have grown up without the civilizing institution of marriage and without the moral awareness brought about through family responsibilities.

If Murray represents one strand of a contemporary conservative or 'right realist' criminology, the extract from Lea and Young represents a political response from some sections of the left. Advocating 'left realism', they argue that the key to crime is not absolute deprivation, or unemployment, but relative deprivation. Crime occurs when there is an excess of expectations over opportunities for fulfilling them. The extract here from *What Is to Be Done about Law and Order?* explores how the Left can regain some of the political initiative on matters of law and order by adopting a middle ground which neither claims that crime is caused by abject poverty nor that it is a freely chosen activity on the part of the wicked. Rather it stems from economic and political discontent and an absence of economic and political opportunities.

The centrality of 'the social' in explanations of crime was established by studies of the criminogenic qualities of city life. In the 1920s and 1930s sociologists at the University of Chicago embarked on a systematic study of all aspects of their local urban environment. Park, a newspaper reporter turned sociologist, and Burgess, his collaborator, were particularly influential in the formulation of a human ecology perspective. They noted that, like any ecological system, the development and organization of the city of Chicago was not random but patterned, and that social relations, including crime, could be understood in terms of such social processes as invasion, conflict, accommodation and assimilation. The reading included here from Rodney Stark reviews the continuing pertinence of such theories, that are based less on identifying 'kinds of people' and more on 'kinds of places', concluding that it is place of residence, location and neighbourhood that matters in the constitution of crime.

In the next reading Hirschi provides a version of control theory – the social bond perspective – which he traces back to Durkheim. Thus, Hirschi is employing a sociological rather than psychological sensibility. Social control theories maintain that each individual is a potential law breaker and that contemporary societies create many criminal/deviant opportunities. The critical question becomes why do people choose to abide by the law? Hirschi's much tested thesis argues that young people who engage in delinquency are free of intimate attachments, aspirations and moral beliefs that bind them to a law-abiding existence. Young people are not forced into a delinquent way of life. They engage in delinquency because they are relatively free from the ties of the conventional social order.

Felson also departs from criminology's traditional focus on identifying the factors causing individuals to commit crime. He addresses the 'other side' of crime causation examining how society encourages or inhibits crime in the routine activities of everyday life. Routine activity theory is an opportunity theory in that it focuses on the convergence in space and time of the elements considered essential for a crime to occur: a motivated offender; a suitable target and the absence of a capable guardian against crime. The attractiveness of routine activity theory for policy makers is that like situational crime prevention it promises to reduce crime through common-sense changes in the physical environment and patterns of everyday activity.

The next selection from Klein is designed to introduce the reader to an even more complex range of issues which are raised through interrogations of the relationship between crime and gender. Klein provides a thorough critique of many of the early criminologies, not only for their relative neglect of the criminality of women but also for their assumptions about the inherent nature of women. Thus, traditionally, female crime has been analysed in terms of sexuality, biological drives, inferiority, deceit and mental instability. Above all, many of the concepts applied to male crime, such as those derived from economic and social determinism, are notably lacking in analyses of female crime. For example, economic offences such as shoplifting have for women been traditionally explained as outlets for sexual frustration. When Klein published her critique in 1973, feminist work on crime and criminality was in its infancy. As she notes in an afterword, published some 20 years after her original work, the field has subsequently burgeoned in a variety of directions.

The final extract from Katz's *Seductions of Crime* eschews all the reference to factors of individual or social structural causation in favour of examination of the situational inducements surrounding crime. This highly controversial criminological text explores (and exposes) what he defines as the unacknowledged 'seductive', 'sensually compelling' lived experience of criminality – what does it mean, feel, sound, taste or look like to commit a crime is the question he poses. Critiqued by the Right for being overly concerned with the criminal's own point of view and by the Left for irresponsibly celebrating the thrill-seeking aspect of crime, Katz's argument is likely to remain influential in his insistence that all of us readily engage in activities which at other times and in other places we would unhesitatingly describe as being 'criminal'.

Collectively these essays reveal that questions of aetiology remain fiercely debated. The issue remains, though, of how far any one theory is capable of providing a comprehensive explanation. It is more likely that *certain* theories will remain better placed to analyse *certain* behaviours and social events, of which some may come to be defined as 'crime'. Numerous 'general theories' of crime causation continue to be advanced which seek to integrate many of the specific propositions raised in these individual chapters. But whatever is gained in generality is certainly lost in an unfettered multi-dimensional eclecticism. Given the widespread nature of crime, it may be that no specific motivational theory is required, or is indeed possible. Crime, as Durkheim (see Part One) argued, is as social fact. It may require no more or less an explanation than is required for any other everyday activity.

11

Genetic factors in the etiology of criminal behavior

Sarnoff A. Mednick, William F. Gabrielli Jr and Barry Hutchings

Human behavior patterns are generally ascribed to an interaction of life experiences and genetic predispositions, but the importance of genetic influences in shaping conduct has often been contested. This debate has been especially intense, and often emotional, in explaining criminal behavior (Sarbin and Miller, 1970). Reluctance to consider genetic factors in crime has had political overtones (Haller, 1968), but it may also reflect the fact that, until recently, the evidence for genetic influences consisted mainly of studies of twins, some of which were methodologically questionable.

Christiansen (1977a) reported on the criminality of a total population of 3,586 twin pairs from a well-defined area of Denmark. He found 52 per cent of the twins concordant for criminal behavior for (male-male) identical twin pairs and 22 per cent concordance for (male-male) fraternal twin pairs. This result suggests that identical twins inherit some biological characteristic (or characteristics) that increases their common risk of being registered for criminal behavior.

It has been pointed out, however, that identical twins are treated more alike than are fraternal twins (Christiansen, 1977b). Thus their greater similarity in criminal behavior may be partly related to their shared experience. This has produced a reluctance to accept in full the genetic implications of twin research. The study of adoptions better separates environmental and genetic effects; if convicted adoptees have a disproportionately high number of convicted biological fathers (given appropriate controls), this would suggest the influence of a genetic factor in criminal behavior. This conclusion is supported by the fact that almost

From *The Causes of Crime: New Biological Approaches* (eds S. Mednick, T. Moffitt and S. Stack), pp. 74–91. (Cambridge: Cambridge University Press, 1987.)

none of the adoptees know their biological parents; adoptees often do not even realize they have been adopted.

Two US adoption studies have produced highly suggestive results. Crowe (1975) found an increased rate of criminality in 37 Iowan adoptees with criminal biological mothers. Cadoret (1978) reported on 246 Iowans adopted at birth. Antisocial behavior in these adoptees was significantly related to antisocial behavior in the biological parents. In a study of Swedish adoptees Bohman, Cloninger, Sigvardsson, and von Knorring (1982) found that criminal behavior in the biological parents was significantly related to criminal behavior in the adoptees. This relationship held only for property crimes.

Table 11.1 Number of adoptions in five-year periods

Years	Male	Female	Total
1924–8	578	1,051	1,629
1929–33	730	1,056	1,786
1934–8	832	1,092	1,924
1939–43	1,650	1,731	3,381
1944–7 (4 years)	2,890	2,782	5,672
Year uncertain	20	15	35
Total	6,700	7,727	14,427

The study to be described in this chapter was based on a register of all 14,427 non-familial adoptions in Denmark in the years 1924–47. This register was established at the Psykologisk Institut in Copenhagen by a group of American and Danish investigators (Kety et al., 1968). The register includes information on the adoptee and his or her adoptive and biological parents. We hypothesized that registered criminality in the biological parents would be associated with an increased risk of registered criminal behavior in the offspring.

PROCEDURES

Information on all non-familial adoptions in the Kingdom of Denmark between 1924 and 1947 (n =14,427) was obtained from records at the Ministry of Justice. The distribution of adoptions by sex of adoptee for five-year periods appears in Table [11.1]. Note the increase in adoptions with increasing population, especially during the war years, and the larger number of females adopted.

Criminality data

Court convictions were used as an index of criminal involvement. Minors (below 15 years of age) cannot receive court convictions. Court convictions information is maintained by the chief of the police district in which an individual is born. The court record (Strafferegister) contains information on the date of the conviction, the paragraphs of the law violated, and the sanction. To obtain access to these records it is necessary to know the place of birth. When subjects' conviction records could not be checked, it was usually because of a lack of information or ambiguity regarding their date and/or place of birth. The court record was obtained for all of the subjects for whom date and place of birth were available ($n = 65,516$).

Information was first recorded from the adoption files of the Ministry of Justice. In these files, birthplace was then available for the biological and adoptive parents but not for the adoptees; birthplace for the adoptees was obtained from the Central Persons Register or the local population registers. The Central Persons Register was established in 1968; adoptees who died or emigrated before 1968 were thus excluded from the study. There were some difficulties in these searches. The criminal records of persons who have died or have reached the age of 80 are *sometimes* removed from the registers and archived in the Central Police Office in Copenhagen. Thus if an individual had a court conviction but had died before our search began, his or her record might have been transferred from the local police district to the Copenhagen Central Police Office. There the record would be maintained in a death register. In view of this, the entire population (adoptees and parents) was checked in the death register. If an adoptee had died or emigrated before the age of 30, the adoptee and parents were dropped from the study since the adoptee had not gone through the entire risk period for criminal conviction. A small section of Denmark in southern Jutland belonged to Germany until 1920. If an individual from this area was registered for criminality before 1920 but not *after* 1920, that individual's record was lost to this study.

Table 11.2 Conviction rates of completely identified members of adoptee families

Family member	Number identified	Number not identified	Number of criminal law court convictions			
			None	One	Two	More than two
Male adoptee	6,129	571	0.841	0.088	0.029	0.040
Female adoptee	7,065	662	0.972	0.020	0.005	0.003
Adoptive father	13,918	509	0.938	0.046	0.008	0.008
Adoptive mother	14,267	160	0.981	0.015	0.002	0.002
Biological father	10,604	3,823	0.714	0.129	0.056	0.102
Biological mother	12,300	2,127	0.911	0.064	0.012	0.013

For each individual we coded the following information: sex, date of birth, address, occupation, place of birth and size of the community into which the child was adopted. The subjects' occupations permitted us to code socio-economic status (Svalastoga, 1959). For the adoptees we also coded marital status in 1976.

Not fully identified cases

It will be recalled that in order to check the court register it was necessary to have name, date and place of birth. A considerable number of cases were lost to this investigation for the following reasons, (a) There was no record of place and/or date of birth, (b) In Denmark the biological mother is required by law to name the biological father. In some few cases she refused, was unsure, or named more than one possible father. These cases were dropped from the population, (c) Among the adoptive parents, 397 were single women. This was because either the adoptive father died just before the formal adoption or the child was adopted by a single woman (not common in this era), (d) Because of additional difficulties involved in checking the criminal registers before 1910, individuals who were born before January 1, 1885, were excluded from the study.

In the case of exclusion of an *adoptee* for any of the above reasons the entire adoptive family was dropped. If a parent was excluded, the remaining subjects were retained for analysis. Table [11.2] presents the number of fully identified individuals in each of the subject categories.

Results

The data to be reported consist of convictions for violation of the Danish Criminal Code (Straffeloven). The levels of court convictions for each of the members of the adoption family are given in Table [11.2]. The biological-father and male-adoptee conviction rates are considerably higher than the rates for the adoptive father. The rate for adoptive fathers is a bit below that (8 per cent) for men of this age group, in this time period (Hurwitz and Christiansen, 1971). Note also that most of the adoptive-father convictions are attributable to one-time offenders. The male adoptees and the biological fathers are more heavily recidivistic.

The rates of conviction for the women are considerably lower and there is considerably less recidivism than there is for men. The biological mothers and female adoptees have higher levels of court convictions than the adoptive mothers. The adoptive mothers are just below the population average for women of this age range and time period, 2.2 per cent. The individuals who gave up their children for adoption, and their biological offspring, show higher rates of court convictions than the general population and the adoptive parents.

In light of current adoption practices one might be surprised that adoptive parents with court convictions were permitted to adopt. It should be recalled, however, that many of these adoptions took place during the Great Depression and World War II. It was more difficult to find willing adoptive homes in these periods owing partly to the relative unavailability of adoptive parents and to the additional number of adoptees available. Adoptive parents were accepted if they had had a 5-year crime-free period before the adoption.

In most of the analyses that follow, we shall consider the relation between parents' criminal convictions and criminal convictions in the adoptees. If either mother or father (biological and/or adoptive) had received a criminal law conviction, the *parents* of that adoptee will be considered criminal. In view of the low level of convictions among the female adoptees, the analyses will concentrate on the criminal behavior of the male adoptees.

Types of crime

Of the adoptive parents, 5.50 per cent were convicted for property crimes; 1.05 per cent committed violent acts; and 0.54 per cent were convicted for sexual offenses. Of the biological parents, 28.12 per cent were responsible for property crimes; 6.51 per cent committed violent crimes; and 3.81 per cent committed sexual offenses. Individuals could be registered for more than one type of crime.

Table 11.3   Cross-fostering analysis: percentage of adoptive sons convicted of criminal law offenses

Have adoptive parents been convicted?	Have biological parents been convicted?	
	Yes	**No**
Yes	24.5 (of 143)	14.7 (of 204)
No	20.0 (of 1,226)	13.5 (of 2,492)

Note: Numbers in parentheses represent the total number for each cell.

Cross-fostering analysis

Because of the size of the population it is possible to segregate subgroups of adoptees who have combinations of convicted and non-convicted biological and adoptive parents. Table [11.3] presents the four groups in a design that is analogous to the cross-fostering paradigm used in behavior genetics. As can be seen in the lower-right-hand cell, if neither the biological nor adoptive parents are convicted, 13.5 per cent of their sons are convicted. If the adoptive parents are convicted and the biological parents are not convicted, this figure rises to only 14.7 per cent. Note that 20.0 per cent of the sons are convicted if the adoptive parents are *not* convicted and the biological parents are convicted. If *both* the biological and adoptive parents are convicted, we observe the highest level of conviction in the sons, 24.5 per cent. The comparison analogous to the cross-fostering paradigm favors a partial genetic etiology. We must caution, however, that simply knowing that an adoptive parent has been convicted of a crime does not tell us how criminogenic the adoptee's environment has been. (Recall the preponderance of one-time offenders in the adoptive parents and the adoptive agency's condition that the adoptive parents not have a conviction for the 5 years preceding the adoption.) On the other hand, at conception, the genetic influence of the biological father is already complete. Thus this analysis does not yield a fair comparison between environmental and genetic influences included in Table [11.3]. However, this initial analysis does indicate that sons with a convicted biological parent have an elevated probability of being convicted. This suggests that some biological characteristic is transmitted from the criminal biological parent that increases the son's risk of obtaining a court conviction for a criminal law offense.

A log-linear analysis of the data in Table [11.3] is presented in Table [11.4]. Adoptive-parent convictions are not associated with a significant increment in the son's level of convictions. The effect of the biological parents' convictions is marked. The model presented in [Table 11.4] reveals that, considering only the *additive* effect of the biological parent and the adoptive parent, the improvement in the chi-square value leaves almost no room for improvement by an interaction effect.

The adoptive parents have a low frequency of court convictions. In order to simplify interpretation of the relations reported below we have excluded cases with adoptive-parent criminality. (Analyses completed that did include adoptive-parent criminality did not alter the nature of the findings to be reported.)

Table 11.4 Log-linear analysis: influences of adoptive-parent and biological-parent convictions on male-adoptee convictions

Model	Model			Improvement		
	X^2	di.	P	X^2	d.f.	P
Baseline (S, AB)	32.91	3	0.001			
Adoptive parent (SA, AB)	30.71	2	0.001	2.20	1	n.s.
Biological parent (SB, AB)	1.76	2	0.415	31.15	1	0.001
Combined influence (SB, SA, AB)	0.30	1	0.585	32.61	2	0.001
Biological parent given adoptive parent (SB/SA, AB)	–	–		28.95	1	0.001
Adoptive parent given biological parent (SA/SB, AB)	–	–		1.46	1	n.s.

Note: S denotes adoptee-son effect; A, adoptive-parent effect; B, biological-parent effect; n.s., not significant.

Figure [11.1] presents the relation between convictions in the sons and degree of recidivism in the biological parents. The relation is positive and relatively monotonic (with the scales utilized on the X and Y axes). Note also that the

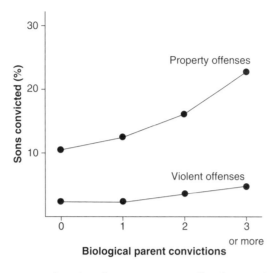

Figure 11.1 Percentage of male adoptee property offenders and violent offenders by biological-parent convictions

relation is highly significant for property crimes and not statistically significant for violent crimes.

The chronic offender

The chronic offender is rare but commits a markedly disproportionate number of criminal offenses. This extremely high rate of offending suggested that genetic predisposition may play an important role in these cases. We examined the relation between convictions of the chronic adoptee offender and his biological parents.

Table 11.5 Proportion of chronic offenders, other offenders, and non-offenders among male adoptees as a function of convictions of biological parents

	Number of biological-parent convictions			
Number of male-adoptee convictions	0	1	2	3 or more
Non-offenders (no convictions)	0.87	0.84	0.80	0.75
Other offenders (1 or 2 convictions)	0.10	0.12	0.15	0.17
Chronic offenders (3 or more convictions)	0.03	0.04	0.05	0.09
Number of adoptees	2,492	547	233	419

Note: Data do not include cases in which adoptive parents were convicted of criminal law violation.

In an important US birth cohort study (Wolfgang et al., 1972), the chronic offender was defined as one who had been arrested five or more times; these chronic offenders comprised 6 per cent of the males and had committed 52 per cent of the offenses. In our adoption cohort we recorded court convictions rather than arrest data. If we select as chronic offenders those with three or more court convictions, this includes 4.09 per cent of the male adoptees. This small group of recidivists accounts for 69.4 per cent of all the court convictions for all the male adoptees. This is a high concentration of crime in a very small fraction of the cohort.

Table [11.5] shows how the chronic offenders, the other offenders (one or two convictions), and the non-offenders are distributed as a function of level of crime in the biological parents. As can be seen, the proportion of chronic adoptee offenders increases as a function of level of recidivism in the biological parents.

Another way of expressing this concentration of crime is to point out that the chronic male adoptee offenders with biological parents with three or more offenses number only 37. Although they comprise only 1 per cent of the 3,691 male adoptees in Table [11.5], they are responsible for 30 per cent of the male adoptee convictions. We should also note that the mean number of convictions for the chronic adoptee offenders increases sharply as a function of biological parent recidivism. The biological parents with zero, one, two, or three or more convictions have male adoptees (i.e., male children who are subsequently adopted by others) averaging 0.30, 0.41, 0.48 and 0.70 convictions, respectively.

We have presented evidence that there is an association between biological parents' convictions and the convictions of their (subsequently) adopted sons. The relation seems stronger for chronic offenders. The sons of chronic offenders account for a disproportionate number of the convictions in the cohort.

Sibling analyses

There are a number of instances in which a biological mother and/or biological father contributed more than one child to this population. These offspring are, of course, full and half-siblings; they were sometimes placed in different adoptive homes. We would predict that the separated full siblings should show more concordance for criminal convictions than the separated half-siblings. Both of these groups should show more concordance than two randomly selected, unrelated, separately reared male adoptees.

Table 11.6 Concordance for criminal law convictions in male siblings placed in separate adoptive homes

Degree of genetic relation	Pairwise concordance (%)
Unrelated, raised apart	8.5
Half-siblings, raised apart	12.9
Full siblings, raised apart	20.0
Half-siblings and full siblings, raised apart, criminal father	30.8
Unrelated 'siblings' raised together in adoptive home	8.5

The probability of any one male adoptee being convicted is 0.159. The probability of drawing a pair of unrelated, separated male adoptees with at least one having a conviction is 0.293. The probability that both of the pair will have been convicted is 0.025. Thus pairwise concordance for unrelated separated male adoptees is 8.5 per cent. This can be seen as a baseline. There were 126 male-male half-sibling pairs placed in separate adoptive homes. Of these, 31 pairs had at least one member of the sibship convicted; of these 31 pairs, 4 pairs were concordant for convictions. This yields a concordance rate for half-siblings of 12.9 per cent. There were 40 male-male full-sibling pairs placed in different adoptive homes. Of these, 15 pairs had at least one member of the sibship convicted; of these 15 pairs, three pairs were concordant for convictions. This yields a concordance rate for full siblings of 20 per cent. These numbers are very small, but the results are in the predicted direction. As the degree of genetic relation increases, the level of concordance increases.

We also considered the level of concordance of the sibling pairs whose biological father was a criminal (had at least one conviction). Of 98 fathers with at least one pair of male-male, separated, adopted-away siblings, 45 had received at least one conviction. (It should be noted that this is a significantly higher rate of convictions (45.9 per cent) than the conviction rate (28.6 per cent) for the total population of biological fathers, $\Psi^2(1) = 14.6, p < 0.01$.)

We combined full- and half-sibling pairs (because of the small number and because the siblings shared criminal biological fathers). Of the 45 sibling pairs, 13 had at least one member with a conviction; of these 13, four pairs were concordant for convictions. This yields a concordance rate of 30.8 per cent. Table [11.6] summarizes these sibling analyses. The pairwise concordance rates can be compared with the male-male rates for twins from a population twin study; Christiansen (1977a) reported 36 per cent pairwise concordance for identical twins and a 13 per cent rate for fraternal twins.

Although these numbers are very small, they represent all of the cases, as defined, in a total cohort of adoptions. The results suggest that a number of these separated, adopted siblings inherited some characteristic that predisposed both of them to being convicted for criminal behavior. As would be expected, in those instances in which the biological father was criminal, the effect was enhanced.

Specificity of a genetic relation

Earlier, we mentioned a study of a small sample of adoptees (Crowe, 1975). Crowe reported the impression that there was some similarity in the types of crime committed by the biological mother and the adoptee. This suggests specific genetic predispositions for different types of crime. In order to explore this possibility, we examined the rates of violent crimes in the adoptees as a function of violent crime in the biological parents. We completed similar analyses for property crimes. We also examined more specific types of crime (theft, fraud, assault, etc.) for similarity in the biological parent and the adoptee.

If the genetic predisposition was specific for type of crime, these 'specificity' analyses should have resulted in our observing a closer relation between adoptee and biological-parent levels of conviction for each of these types of crime. The best predictor of each type of adoptee crime, however, was number of biological-parent convictions rather than type of biological-parent offense. This suggests that the biological predisposition the adoptee inherits must be of a general nature, partly determining the degree of law abidance shown by the adoptee. It is also possible that the data of this study are too gross for the detection of a specificity relation. This may require careful coding of details of the criminal behavior. This was not possible in our study.

Sex differences

As can be seen in Table [11.2], convictions of females for criminal law violations are very infrequent. It might be speculated that those women who do exhibit a level of criminal behavior that prompts a court conviction must have a severe predisposition for such behavior. Criminal involvement of many men, on the other hand, may tend to be more socially or environmentally inspired. These statements suggest that convictions in the biological mother are more closely related to the adoptee's conviction(s) than criminal behavior in the biological father.

In every analysis we conducted, the relation between biological-mother conviction and adoptee conviction is significantly stronger than the relation between biological-father conviction and adoptee conviction. In comparison with the relation between biological-father and adoptee convictions, convictions of the biological mothers are more closely related to convictions of the daughters. This result is statistically significant, but the relatively low frequency of female convictions forces us to interpret these findings with caution.

Historical period

The period of these adoptions (1924–67) spans some important historical changes in Denmark, including a world war, the Great Depression, and industrialization. It is conceivable that the influence of genetic factors might be affected by these social upheavals. It is also possible that changes in level or type of crime during these years might influence the relations observed. Analyses conducted for the entire population were repeated for each of the 5-year periods. The results were virtually identical for all of the periods and virtually identical to the analyses of the total sample. The social changes during these years did not interact with the relation between biological-parent and adoptee crime.

Controlling genetic influence in examining environmental effects

In many social science investigations genetic characteristics are not considered. In some analyses this may contribute error; sometimes omission may lead to incomplete conclusions. For example, separation from a father is associated with an increased level of delinquency in a son. This has been interpreted as a result of failure of identification or lack of consistent discipline. As we can see from Table [11.2], some fathers who permit themselves to be separated from their child have a relatively high level of criminal convictions. The higher level of delinquency found for separated children might be partially due to a genetic transmission of criminogenic predispositional characteristics from antisocial fathers. If this genetic variance were partially accounted for, the environmental hypotheses could be more precisely tested. We utilized such partial genetic control to study an important criminological variable, social status. We separated the variance ascribable to 'genetic' social class and 'rearing' social class (Van Dusen et al., 1983). We examined adoptee convictions as a joint function of biological parents' social class and adoptive parents' social class. It is clear from inspection of Table [11.7] that male-adoptee convictions vary as a function of both genetic and environmental social class; log-linear analyses reveal that both effects are statistically significant. Although the genetic effect is of interest here, we emphasize that, to our knowledge, this is the first controlled demonstration that *environmental* aspects influence the social class–crime relation. This finding suggests that, regardless of genetic background, improved social conditions are likely to lead to a reduction in criminal behavior.

Table [11.7] is of interest in another regard. Careful inspection reveals a correlation between adoptive-parent socioeconomic status (SES) and biological-parent SES. This represents the attempt by the adoptive agency to match certain characteristics of the two sets of parents in order to increase the likelihood that the adoptee will fit into the adoptive home. In terms of the adoption research design, this correlation is undesirable because it reduces the independence of the genetic rearing and environmental influences on the adoptee. Since social class is not independent of convictions (Table [11.7]), it is conceivable that the relation between biological-parent and adoptee convictions is, in part, mediated by social class. Inspection of Table [11.7] reveals, however, that this relation exists at each level of adoptive-parent social class. In addition we have conducted stepwise multiple regression analyses that varied the order of entry of biological-parent convictions and SES and adoptive-parent convictions and SES. These analyses indicate that, independent of SES, biological-parent convictions are significantly related to adoptee convictions.

METHODOLOGICAL ISSUES

Not fully identified subjects

If we are to generalize from the results of this study, it is useful to consider what biases might be introduced by the loss of subjects in specific analyses. Table [11.2] indicates the total number of subjects who could not be fully identified (name, birthday and birthplace). We should note that we know the name, occupation, birthdate and other facts concerning most of the lost subjects; in almost all cases a subject could not be checked in the court conviction register because we were not certain of the subject's place of birth.

Table 11.7 Percentage of male adoptees with criminal convictions as a function of adoptive and biological parents' socioeconomic status

	Biological parents' SES			
Adoptive parents' SES	High	Middle	Low	Total
High	9.30	11.52	12.98	11.58
	(441)	(903)	(775)	(2,099)
Middle	13.44	15.29	16.86	15.62
	(320)	(870)	(795)	(1,985)
Low	13.81	17.25	18.04	17.19
	(210)	(568)	(787)	(1,565)
Total	11.64	14.31	16.00	14.55
	(971)	(2,341)	(2,337)	(5,649)

Note: Numbers in parentheses represent total number for each cell.

The information is relatively complete for the adoptive parents. In contrast, 26.5 per cent of the biological fathers and 14.7 per cent of the biological mothers are not fully identified. These differences probably reflect the relative importance of the adoptive and biological parents to the adoption agency. The agency's chief concern was with the placement and welfare of the adoptee. After the adoption, they had less reason to be concerned with the biological parents.

The most general characteristic of those not fully identified is that they tend *slightly* to come from areas outside Copenhagen. Perhaps the urban adoption offices followed more thorough recording procedures than did offices outside the city. The differences are very small. The sons of the biological fathers not fully identified have a rate of 10.3 per cent criminal law convictions; the identified biological fathers' sons have criminal law convictions in 11.4 per cent of cases. In cases in which the biological mother is not fully identified, slightly fewer of the sons have criminal law convictions (9.6 per cent). The adoptees who were not fully identified have biological mothers and biological fathers with slightly higher SES than those who were fully identified. Their rearing (adoptive) homes were of almost identical SES.

Our consideration of the characteristics of those not fully identified does not suggest that their inclusion would have altered the nature of the results presented above. Perhaps the most critical facts in this judgment are that the adopted-away sons of parents not fully identified have levels of criminal law convictions and rearing social status that are approximately the same as for the sons of those parents fully identified. The differences observed are small; it is difficult to formulate any manner in which the lost subjects might have an impact on the relations reported.

Transfer history

Most of these adoptions were the results of pregnancies of unwed women. The adoptive agency had a policy of taking newborns from their biological mothers and either immediately placing them in a previously arranged adoptive home (25.3 percent of the adoptions) or placing them in an orphanage from which they were available for adoption. Of those placed in an orphanage, 50.6 per cent were placed with an adoptive family in the first year, 12.8 per cent were placed with an adoptive family in the second year, and 11.3 per cent were placed after the age of 2.

Within each of these age-of-transfer groups, analyses were conducted to ascertain whether the biological parents' convictions were related to male-adoptee conviction. Similar significant positive relations were observed at each transfer age. Age of transfer did not interact with genetic influence so as to alter significantly the relations observed with the full population. It should be noted that there was a statistically significant tendency for a high level of adoptee criminality to be associated with more time spent in an orphanage awaiting adoption. This effect was true for males only.

The operational definition of criminal behavior in this study included only court convictions for criminal law offenses. (We completed an analysis of police arrest data using a subsample of this adoption cohort and obtained very similar results; see Hutchings and Mednick, 1977.) Use of the conviction definition has some advantages. We are relatively certain that the individual actually committed the offense recorded. Court convictions imply a high threshold for inclusion; minor offenses are less likely to result in court conviction. There are also disadvantages. The subject's behavior goes through several screening points. Someone must make a complaint to the police, or the police must happen on the scene of the crime. The police must decide that a crime has been committed and apprehend the culprit. The prosecuting attorney must decide that the evidence is sufficient to warrant a court trial. The court must then find the culprit guilty. There are decision points all along the way that may result in the elimination of individuals who have actually committed offenses against the criminal code. Such individuals might then end up among our control subjects (assuming that they do not also commit offenses for which they are convicted). In this case they add error to the analyses. Data comparing self-reports of crimes and official records of crimes suggest, however, that whereas only a fraction of crimes committed by an individual are noted by the police, those who 'self-report' more crimes have more crimes recorded in the official registers. Those offenders who are not found in the official registers have typically committed very few and very minor offenses (Christie et al., 1965).

Labeling of the adoptee

The advantage of the adoption method is the good separation of genetic and rearing contributions to the adoptee's development. But the adoptions were not arranged as controlled experiments. The adoption agency's prime concern was the welfare of the adoptee and the adoptive parents. Prospective adoptive parents were routinely informed about the criminal convictions of the biological parents. This could result in the labeling of the adoptee; this in turn might affect the likelihood that the adoptee would commit criminal acts. Thus the convictions of the biological parents might have had an environmental impact on the adoptee via the reactions of the adoptive parents.

We examined one hypothesis related to this possibility. If the biological parents received a criminal conviction before the adoption, it is likely that the adoptive parents were so informed; if the biological parents' first conviction occurred after the adoption, the adoptive parents could not have been informed. Of the convicted biological parents, 37 per cent had received their first conviction before the adoption took place. In these cases, the adoptive parents were likely to have been informed of this criminal record. In 63 per cent of the cases the first conviction occurred after the adoption; in these cases the conviction information could *not* have been transmitted to the adoptive parents. For all convicted biological parents, the probability of a conviction in their adopted-away son was 15.9 per cent. In cases in which the biological parent was first convicted before adoption, 15.6 per cent of the male adoptees were convicted. In cases in which the biological parent was convicted after the adoption, 16.1 per cent of the male adoptees were convicted. In the case of female adoptees, these figures were 4 per cent and 4 per cent.

These analyses utilized convictions. In a previous analysis with a large subsample of this population a very similar result was obtained by studying the effect of timing of the initial arrest of the biological father (Hutchings and Mednick, 1977). Additional analyses by type or severity of crime revealed no effect of the adoptive parents' having been informed of the convictions of the biological parents. The fact that the adoptive parents had been informed of the biological parents' convictions did not alter the likelihood that the adoptive son would be convicted. This result should not be interpreted as suggesting that labeling (as defined) had no effect on the adoptees' lives. It did not, however, affect the probability that the adoptee would be convicted for a criminal act.

Denmark as a research site

This project was carried out in Denmark; on most crime-related social dimensions, Denmark must rank among the most homogeneous of the Western nations. This fact may have implications for the interpretation of this study. An environment with low variability permits better expression of existing genetic tendencies in individuals living in that environment. This factor probably magnifies the expression of any genetic influence. At the same time, however, the Danish population probably has less genetic variability than some Western nations; this, of course, would minimize the expression of genetic influence in research conducted in Denmark. It is very likely impossible to balance these two considerations quantitatively. We are reassured regarding the generality of our findings by similar results in adoption studies in Sweden and Iowa (Bohman et al., 1982; Cadoret, 1978; Crowe, 1975).

SUMMARY AND CONCLUSIONS

In a total population of adoptions, we noted a relation between biological-parent criminal convictions and criminal convictions in their adopted-away children. The relation is particularly strong for *chronic* adoptee and biological-parent offenders. There was no evidence that the type of biological-parent conviction was related to the type of adoptee conviction. A number of potentially confounding variables were considered; none of these proved sufficient to explain the genetic relation. We conclude that some factor is transmitted by convicted parents that increases the likelihood that their children will be convicted for criminal law offenses. This is especially true of chronic offenders. Because the transmitted factor must be biological, this implies that biological factors are involved in the etiology of at least some criminal behavior.

Biological factors and their interaction with social variables may make useful contributions to our understanding of the causes of criminal behavior.

REFERENCES

Bohman, M., Cloninger, C., Sigvardsson, S. and von Knorring, A.L. (1982) 'Predisposition to petty criminality in Swedish adoptees: genetic and environmental heterogeneity', *Archives of General Psychiatry*, 39(11): 1233–41.

Cadoret, R.J. (1978) 'Psychopathy in adopted away offspring of biological parents with antisocial behavior', *Archives of General Psychiatry*, 35: 176–84.

Christiansen, K.O. (1977a) 'A review of studies of criminality among twins', in S.A. Mednick and K.O. Christiansen (eds), *Biosocial Bases of Criminal Behavior*. New York: Gardner Press, pp. 45–88.

Christiansen, K.O. (1977b) 'A preliminary study of criminality among twins', in S.A. Mednick and K.O. Christiansen (eds), *Biosocial Bases of Criminal Behavior*. New York: Gardner Press, pp. 89–108.

Christie, N., Andenaes, J. and Skerbaekk, S. (1965) 'A study of self-reported crime', *Scandinavian Studies in Criminology*, 1: 86–116.

Crowe, R. (1975) 'Adoptive study of psychopathy: preliminary results from arrest records and psychiatric hospital records', in R. Fieve, D. Rosenthal and H. Brill (eds), *Genetic Research in Psychiatry*. Baltimore, MD: Johns Hopkins University Press.

Haller, M.H. (1968) 'Social science and genetics: a historical perspective', in D. Glass (ed.), *Genetics*. New York: Rockefeller University Press.

Hurwitz, S. and Christiansen, K.O. (1971) *Kriminologi*. Copenhagen: Gyldendal.

Hutchings, B. and Mednick, S.A. (1977) 'Registered criminality in the adoptive and biological parents of registered male criminal adoptees', in S.A. Mednick and K.O. Christiansen (eds), *Biosocial Bases of Criminal Behavior*. New York: Gardner Press. pp. 127–42.

Kety, S.S., Rosenthal, D., Wender, P.H. and Schulsinger, F. (1968) 'The types and prevalence of mental illness in the biological adoptive families of adopted schizophrenics', in D. Rosenthal and S.S. Kety (eds), *The Transmission of Schizophrenia*, Oxford: Pergamon.

Sarbin, T.R. and Miller, J.E. (1970) 'Demonism revisited: the XYY chromosomal anomaly', *Issues in Criminology*, 5: 195–207.

Svalastoga, K. (1959) *Prestige, Class and Mobility*, Copenhagen: Gyldendal.

Van Dusen, K., Mednick, S.A., Gabrielli, W.F. and Hutchings, B. (1983) 'Social class and crime in an adoption cohort', *Journal of Criminal Law and Criminology*, 74(1): 249–69.

Wolfgang, M.E., Figlio, R.M. and Sellin, T. (1972) *Delinquency in a Birth Cohort*. Chicago: University of Chicago Press.

12

Personality theory and the problem of criminality

H.J. Eysenck

INTRODUCTION

In psychiatry generally, the diathesis-stress model is widely accepted; it postulates a *predisposition* to develop certain types of mental illness, such as neurosis or psychosis, which is activated by certain environmental stress factors. A similar conception can be applied to criminality; certain types of personality may be more prone to react with anti-social or criminal behaviour to environmental factors of one kind or another. To say this is not to accept the notion of 'crime as destiny', to quote Lange's famous monograph in which he showed that identical twins are much more alike with respect to criminal conduct than are fraternal twins. There is no predestination about the fact that heredity, mediated through personality, plays some part in predisposing some people to act in an anti-social manner. Environment is equally important, and, as we shall see, it is the interaction between the two which is perhaps the most crucial factor.

   Much of the research in this field has been episodic and following the principles of benevolent eclecticism; in this chapter we will rather adopt the method of looking at a general theory of anti-social behaviour, which makes predictions as to the type of personality expected to indulge in such conduct, and summarize the evidence relating to the theory. Before turning to the evidence, it will therefore be necessary to present in brief outline the theory in question (Eysenck, 1960, 1977). The reason for singling out the theory is, in the first place, that it has attracted far more research than any other, and secondly, that it is the only one which has tried to link together genetic factors, a causal theory, and personality in one general theory.

From *Applying Psychology to Imprisonment* (eds B. McGurk, D. Thornton and M. Williams), pp. 30–1; 34–46. (London: HMSO, 1987.)

STATEMENT OF THEORY

Briefly and concisely, the theory tries to explain the occurrence of socialized behaviour suggesting that anti-social behaviour, being obviously egocentric and orientated towards immediate gratification, needs no explanation. It is suggested that the socialization process is essentially mediated by Pavlovian conditioning, in the sense that anti-social behaviour will be punished by parents, teachers, peers etc., and that such punishment constitutes the *unconditioned stimulus* (US), where the contemplation or execution of such behaviour constitutes the conditioned stimulus. The pain/anxiety properties of the US transfer through conditioning to the CS [conditioned stimulus], and as a consequence the person will desist from committing anti-social acts, or even contemplating them, because of the painful CRs [conditioned responses] which inevitably follow. The theory is elaborated in Eysenck (1977), where supportive evidence will be found.

Individual differences in the speed and strength of formation of conditioned responses would, in terms of the theory, be fundamental in accounting for the observed relations between personality and criminality. As Eysenck (1967, 1980) has shown, there is considerable evidence to suggest that introverts form conditioned responses more quickly and more strongly than extraverts, and accordingly one would expect extraversion to be positively correlated with anti-social conduct. Emotional instability or neuroticism would be expected to multiply with the habits of socialized or anti-social conduct, according to Hull's general theory in which performance is a multiplicative function of habit and drive, with anxiety in this case acting as a drive (Eysenck, 1973). The third major dimension of personality, psychoticism, comes into the picture because of the well-documented relationship between crime and psychosis (Eysenck and Eysenck, 1976), and because the general personality traits subsumed under psychoticism appear clearly related to anti-social and non-conformist conduct. The precise nature of these three major dimensions of personality will be discussed later on in this chapter; here we will only look at one particular problem which is closely related to the general theory of conditioning as a basis for anti-social conduct.

The theory suggests that conditioning produces socialized behaviour, and that introverts will show more socialized behaviour because they condition more readily. The same theory would also imply, however, that if the socialization process were inverted, i.e. if parents, teachers, peers, etc. praised the child for anti-social conduct, and punished him for socialized behaviour, then introverts would be more likely to show anti-social behaviour. Raine and Venables (1981) have shown that this is indeed so; children who showed better conditioning in a laboratory situation than other children were remarkably socialized in their behaviour when brought up in a favourable type of environment, and remarkably anti-social in their behaviour when brought up in a non-favourable type of environment. This experiment shows more clearly than almost any other the inter-relationship between genetic factors on the one hand, and environmental ones on the other.

[…]

DIMENSIONS OF PERSONALITY

We will now turn to personality factors as more narrowly defined. Our discussion will begin with the three major dimensions of personality, which emerge from hundreds of correlational and factor analytic studies in many different countries. Royce and Powell (1983) have summarized and reanalysed these data, and confirm the theory developed by Eysenck and Eysenck (1976) that these three factors deal essentially with social interactions (extraversion–introversion), emotional reactions and anxieties (neuroticism), and aggressive and egocentric impulses and their control (psychoticism). Many different terms are of course used for these dimensions but Eysenck and Eysenck (1985) discuss the experimental literature which suggests the relevance of the terms proposed above.

The nature of these three major dimensions of personality can best be discerned from the data shown in Figures [12.1–12.3]. These list the various traits, correlations between which have generated at the empirical level the three major dimensions of P, E and N. In this section we will simply look at descriptive studies involving the relationship between anti-social and criminal behaviour, on the one hand, and these major dimensions, and the traits relating thereto, on the other. […] Here let us mainly stress that the personality traits and dimensions dealt with here have a strong genetic component […]; this does not prove, but it does suggest that genetic factors may also play an important part in the genesis of anti-social and criminal behaviour.

Much of the early literature has been summarized by Passingham (1972), who found that while a number of studies supported Eysenck's hypothesis of a positive correlation between criminality and P, E and N, there were many exceptions, and occasional reversals. There are of course many reasons why results have not always been positive. Criminals are not a homogeneous group, and different investigators have studied different populations, specializing in different types of crime. Control groups have not always been carefully selected; some investigators, for instance, have used the usual students groups as controls, which is inadvisable. There has been a failure to control for dissimulation; there is evidence that high lie-scorers lower their neuroticism and psychoticism

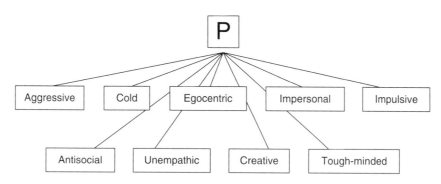

Figure 12.1 Traits characterizing the psychoticism factor

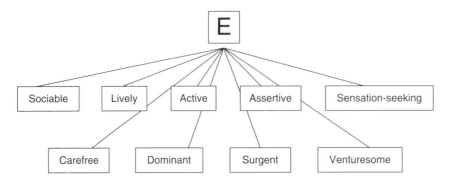

Figure 12.2   Traits characterizing the extraversion factor

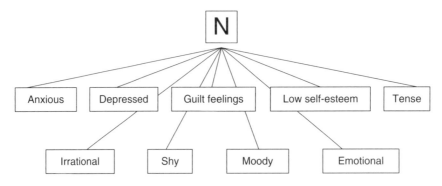

Figure 12.3   Traits characterizing the neuroticism factor

scores, and they seem to do the same for extraversion (McCue et al., 1976) […]
Some of the most negative reports contain evidence of high L scales, and are
hence inadmissible. Other reasons refer to the incarceration of many delinquents; this would interfere with verbal responses on questionnaire items
relating to sociability, and hence lead to an understatement of the delinquent's
degree of extraversion. More important even than any of these reasons is probably the fact that many early investigations were done without any prior
hypothesis being stated, and used questionnaires and other measures which
bear only tangential relation to the Eysenck Questionnaires.

Eysenck (1977) lists many more recent investigations, most done from the point
of view of testing the hypothesis linking criminality and P, E and N; these results
are very much more positive. Some of the studies also strongly support the view
that within the criminal fraternity different types of crimes are related to different
personality patterns. Thus Eysenck, Rust and Eysenck (1977) studied five separate
groups of criminals (conmen, i.e. confidence tricksters; criminals involved with
crime against property; criminals specializing in violence; inadequate criminals,
and a residual group, not specializing in one type of crime). Figure [12.4] shows

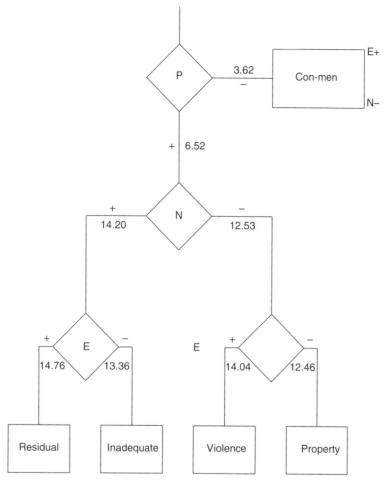

Figure 12.4   P, E and N scores of different types of criminals (Eysenck et al., 1977)

the differential patterns of P, E and N of these various groups, with conmen for instance having a much lower P score than the other groups.

Mitchell et al. (1980) studied the difference between violent and non-violent delinquent behaviour and found that violence was more frequently associated with low trait anxiety than non-violent behaviour; their results agree with the Eysenck, Rust and Eysenck findings. Schwenkmezger (1983) subdivided his sample of delinquents into three major groups, corresponding to conmen, offences against property, and offences involving violence. As in the Eysenck, Rust and Eysenck study, conmen have much lower values on the various measures involved (impulsivity, risk taking, aggressiveness, dominance, and excitement) than the other two groups. Discriminant function analysis showed two significant functions, the first of which separates conmen from the other two groups. The second function involved mainly aggressive, dominant and risk taking behaviour, and has offences involving violence at one extreme.

The most recent study by Wardell and Yeudall (1980), specially concerned with this problem, used ten personality factors derived from an extensive psychological test battery administered to 201 patients on criminal wards at a mental hospital and showed many important differences between patients involved with different types of crime. Other recent studies supporting this view are by McGurk (1978), McGurk and McDougall (1981), McGurk and McEwan (1983), and McGurk, McEwan and Graham (1981). To this list might be added some studies cited by Eysenck (1977) showing that murderers (i.e. mainly the usual type of family murder) tend to be significantly introverted. Professional gunmen, on the other hand, are exceedingly extraverted, thus showing that even a single category (murder) may require subdivision in order to give comprehensible and replicable correlations with personality.

Rahman and Hussain (1984), studying female criminals in Bangladesh, found them to have much higher P and N scores than controls; those engaged in prostitution, fraud, kidnapping and possession of illegal arms also had high E scores. Murderers, on the other hand, were significantly introverted.

Holcomb et al. (1985) have shown how complex motivation and personality even within a single category of crime may be. They studied a sample of 80 male offenders charged with premeditated murder, and found that these could be divided into five personality types using MMPI scores. The results were cross validated using a second sample of 80 premeditated murders. A discriminant analysis resulted in a 96.25 correct classification of subjects from the second sample into the five types. Clinical data from a mental status interview schedule supported the external validity of these types. There were significant differences among the five types in hallucinations, disorientation, hostility, depression and paranoid thinking.

THE EYSENCK STUDIES

We may now turn to the work of the Eysencks in temporal order, as these were the major studies to try to obtain direct empirical evidence regarding the theory under discussion. In the first of these studies (Eysenck and Eysenck, 1970), 603 male prisoners were compared with a control group of over 1,000 males. Results supported strongly the hypothesis that prisoners would have higher P scores, moderately strongly the hypothesis that prisoners would have higher N scores, and rather more weakly the hypothesis that prisoners would have higher E scores. Similar results were found in a later study by Eysenck and Eysenck (1971), contrasting 518 criminals and 606 male trainee railmen. Significant differences were found on P and N, and on E the direction of the prediction was reversed, criminals having lower E scores than controls. In a later study of the personality of female prisoners (Eysenck and Eysenck, 1973) 264 female prisoners were found to be characterized by high P, high N and high E scores; for them therefore E agreed with the predicted direction.

In a study of personality and recidivism in Borstal boys (Eysenck and Eysenck, 1974), recidivists were insignificantly higher than non-recidivists on P and N, but significantly higher on E. In the last of this series of studies (Eysenck and Eysenck, 1977) over 2,000 male prisoners and over 2,400 male controls were given the Eysenck personality questionnaire, and then subdivided into age groups, ranging from 16 to 69 at the extremes. It was found that the lie-scale disclosed little dissimulation in either group. Scores on psychoticism, extraversion and neuroticism fell with age for both prisoners and controls. Prisoners had higher scores than controls, as predicted, on all three scales.

A replication of some of this work was carried out by Sanocki (1969) in Poland, using the short form of the Maudsley Personality Inventory on 84 Polish prisoners and 337 Polish controls, matched for age, education and social class. Criminals were found to be significantly more extraverted, and non-significantly more neurotic. Sanocki also found that different types of prisoners in his study differed significantly with respect to the inventory scores, adding another proof to the hypothesis of criminal heterogeneity. He also showed that a prisoner's behaviour in prison correlated with E, extraverts offending significantly more frequently against prison rules.

Two further points about the Eysenck studies may be of relevance. The first is that Eysenck and Eysenck (1971) constructed an empirical criminality scale by bringing together all those items which showed the greatest differentiation between criminals and normals; this will later on be referred to as the 'C' scale. The other point is made by Burgess (1972), who pointed out that Eysenck's theory implies that criminals and normals would differ on a combination of N and E, not necessarily on one or the other in separation; he was able to show that even in studies which failed to show significance for one or the other variable, the combination did show highly significant differences.

The 'C' scale was constructed for adults; similar scales have been proposed by Allsop and Feldman (1975), and by Saklofske, McKerracher and Eysenck (1978) for children. Like the adult scale they use selected items from the P, E and N scales. The scales have been found to be very useful in discriminating different groups of children. The data demonstrate clearly that delinquent boys have higher extraversion, psychoticism and neuroticism scores, and that the criminal propensity (C) scale discriminates even better between them and non-delinquent boys. Similar differences were also observed between well-behaved and badly behaved non-delinquent boys.

OTHER RECENT STUDIES

Barack and Widom (1978) studied American women awaiting trial. Compared to a heterogeneous control group, these women scored significantly higher on the neuroticism and psychoticism scales, and on Burgess's h scale ($h = E \times N$). Singh (1982) compared 100 Indian female delinquents with 100 female non-delinquents, matched in terms of socioeconomic status, age and urban versus rural place of residence; he found that delinquents had higher scores on extraversion and neuroticism than did non-delinquents. Smith and Smith (1977) looked at the psychoticism variable in relation to reconviction, and found a very highly significant correlation between psychoticism and reconviction. Their finding supported the results obtained by Saunders and Davies (1976), who administered the Jesness Inventory to samples of young male offenders, and concluded that:

> one can … see a picture of the continuing delinquent as being unsocialised, aggressive, anti-authority and unempathic. This appears to present a somewhat similar pattern of characteristics to that described by Eysenck as 'psychotic'.

Of particular interest are some results of a follow-up of an investigation carried out by West and Farrington (1973). (See also Farrington et al., 1982.) In the original study 411 boys, aged 8 to 9, attending six adjacent primary schools in a working class area of London, were given the Junior Maudsley Inventory at age 10 to 11, and again at age 14 to 15; they were also given the Eysenck Personality Inventory at age 16 to 17. The original data did not provide very strong support for the theory, but more interesting are new data relating to delinquency as a young adult, i.e. convictions in court for offences committed between a boy's 17th and 21st birthdays. Eighty-four boys were classified as juvenile delinquents, 94 as young adult delinquents, and 127 as delinquents at any age (up to 21). This study is particularly important because the delinquents were almost all non-institutionalized at the time of testing. (The following data were communicated privately by D.P. Farrington on 10 June 1976.)

Extraversion   As regards juvenile delinquency, E scores were dichotomized into roughly equal halves, and 24 per cent of those with above average scores became juvenile delinquents, in comparison with 16 per cent of those with below average scores; so the lowest quarter of E scores at age 16 included significantly few juvenile delinquents – 12.6 per cent as opposed to 23.4 per cent. The tendency of above average E scorers at age 16 to become young adult delinquents was much clearer (30 per cent as opposed to 16 per cent). Farrington states that: 'Low E scores genuinely predicted a low likelihood of adult delinquency.' The major burden of these and other significant relationships was borne by the lowest quarter of E scorers; introverts were very unlikely to become delinquents.

Neuroticism   There was little overall relationship between neuroticism and criminality except that those on the lowest quarter of N scorers at age 10 tended not to become adult delinquents (12 per cent as opposed to 25 per cent), and not to be delinquents at any age (17 per cent as opposed to 34 per cent). Quadrant analysis, of the kind suggested by Burgess (1972) shows that neurotic extraverts at age 16 included significantly more adult delinquents, and significantly more delinquents at any age, than the remainder.

The data, as Farrington points out, suggest that the personality theory might apply to adult delinquency rather than to juvenile delinquency. It is notable that the adult offences included proportionately more aggressive crimes, more damaging offences and more drug offences than the juvenile offences.

For reasons to be discussed presently, this seems an unlikely hypothesis; in school-boys for instance very clear-cut relationships between personality and anti-social behaviour often of a not very serious kind, have been found. These studies are mainly based on self-reports (Gibson, 1971), a type of study which furnishes the child with a list of minor and not-so-minor misdemeanours frequently committed by school children, and asks him or her anonymously to endorse those items which they have been guilty of. There are two studies which have related self-reported offending to the three major dimensions of personality (Allsop and Feldman, 1975, 1976). In addition, these studies used an outside criterion (teacher's ratings) in order to check on the validity of self ratings; results were very similar for both types of measures. The ratings of the teachers were concerned with school behaviour ('naughtiness'). Scores on the anti-social behaviour scale (ASB) were positively and significantly related to P, E and N in descending order of significance, and 'naughtiness' (Na) scores to P and N, although only the former achieved statistical significance. The P, E and N scores were then divided at the median points and the mean ASB and Na scores plotted for those high (i.e. above the median) on all 3, 2 only, one only, or none out of P, E and N. The results, which are quite striking, are shown in Figure [12.5]. They clearly suggest the usefulness of combining personality scores when analysing self-report data. These data come from the study of secondary schoolgirls (Allsop and Feldman, 1975); a similar study, done on schoolboys, has obtained very similar results (Allsop and Feldman, 1976).

The differential relationship between personality and type of offence has also been studied using self-reports. Hindelang and Weis (1972), using cluster analysis, formed 26 offences self-reported by 245 Los Angeles middle class high-school males into seven groups, and then correlated the scores on each of the seven

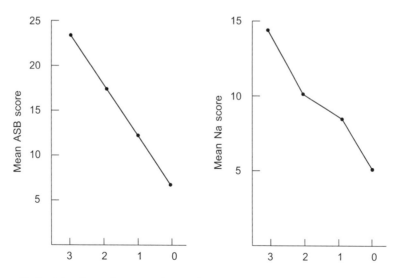

Figure 12.5 Number of personality scales (P, E and N) on which subjects scored highly, as related to anti-social behaviour (ASB) score and naughtiness (Na) score (Allsop and Feldman, 1975)

clusters with the four possible combinations of E and N. They expected a descending order of frequency of offending – EN, either En or eN, and en; this was obtained for 'general deviance' and 'traffic truancy' and partially obtained for two other clusters, concerning 'drug-taking' and 'malicious destruction', respectively. No difference between the combinations of E and N was found for theft and the second of two clusters concerning drugs. For the 'aggressive' clusters the En combination was the highest. These data again show the need to break down criminality into more homogeneous clusters, but of course the sample is a somewhat unusual one.

Allsop (1976) has reported one further study where he used 368 white boys between the ages of 13 and 16. Teachers were asked to rate the behaviour of the boys; on this basis they were divided into well and badly behaved. When these ratings were compared with the personality scale scores, the results indicated that:

> badly behaved boys predominate at the high level of P and at the low level of P where there is a combination of high E/high N scores; well-behaved boys predominate at the low level of P except where E and N are simultaneously high.

Using the ASB, he subdivided the total scale into ten sub-scales according to type of offence; this table sets out the correlations of P, E and N with each of the sub-scales as well as the total scale. It showed that all the correlations are positive, being highest with P and lowest with N.

Among non-incarcerated adolescents the pattern is much the same. R. Foggitt (1976) has studied a non-institutionalized sample of delinquent and non-delinquent adolescents. Factor analysis of the intercorrelations between the crimes and the personality scales of E and N showed that they were all positively intercorrelated and that a single general factor emerged from the analysis on which different crimes had loadings as follows. Truancy, 0.56; poor work history, 0.62; vagrancy, 0.71; attempted suicide, 0.56; frequency of violence, 0.74; destructiveness of violence, 0.72; heavy drinking, 0.45; excessive drugs, 0.52; theft, 0.71; fraud, 0.50; group-delinquency, 0.46; number of convictions, 0.59. For the personality variables the loadings were 0.44 for E and 0.42 for N.

Two interesting recent studies extend the scope of the work so far reviewed. Perez and Torrubia (1985) used Zuckerman's (1979) concept of sensation-seeking defined as the need for varied, novel and complex sensations and experiences, and willingness to take risks for the sake of such experiences. This scale, which is correlated with extraversion and defines one aspect of that dimension of personality (Eysenck and Eysenck, 1985) was measured in a Spanish translation of the scale published by Zuckerman, Eysenck and Eysenck (1978). Three hundred and forty-nine students were tested, using the sensation seeking scale as well as a 37-item Spanish version of a written self-report delinquency (SRD) scale. A correlation of 0.46 was obtained for the total of the sensation seeking scale, with the highest correlations going to the experience seeking (0.45) and disinhibition (0.43) scales. These are the values for males; for females they were 0.49 for the total scale, and 0.43 and 0.45 for the experience seeking and disinhibition scales. Correlations for the other two scales were smaller (in the neighbourhood of 0.20) but still significant.

Also using a self-report format, Rushton and Chrisjohn (1981) tested eight separate samples, obtaining significant positive correlations with extraversion, largely insignificant ones with neuroticism, and very positive and significant ones with psychoticism. Correlations with the lie scale were uniformly negative and mostly significant. Subjects of these experiments were high school and university students, totalling 410 in all. As the authors summarize their findings:

> The evidence showed clear support for a relationship between high delinquency scores and high scores on both extraversion and psychoticism. These relationships held up across diverse samples and different ways of analyzing the data. No support was found for a relationship between delinquency scores and the dimension of neuroticism. (1981: 11)

In another interesting study, Martin (1985) pointed out that:

> Attempts to verify Eysenck's theory of criminality have usually been concerned with the proportion by which delinquents differ from non-delinquents on the dimensions of extraversion, neuroticism and psychoticism. There are very few studies concerned with the proportion in which these dimensions are related to the acquisition of moral social rules, the real core of this theory. The current study examines the theory from a new approach, trying to show in what measures the value priorities of a group of 113 juvenile delinquents are related to the personality dimensions stated by Eysenck. (1985: 549)

It was found that extraversion and psychoticism showed the largest number of significant relationships. The youths who scored high and low on the E scale differed in six terminal values and six instrumental values out of a total of 36 values. Values concerned with morality, and those which imply an acceptance of the social norms, are considered the most important factors for the youths with low E scores.

Those who scored high on the psychoticism dimension consider the following values as the most important: 'An exciting life; pleasure; ability'; all these have clear personal significance. They gave less importance to values related to the social environment, such as 'world peace', 'equality' and 'social recognition'. As far as they go, these results are in good accord with the personality theory under discussion, and they also suggest a new approach to validating the theory.

Drug takers constitute a rather special sample of criminals, although the study just mentioned shows drug taking offences to be highly correlated with other types of criminality. Shanmugan (1979) compared 212 drug users and 222 non-drug users matched with respect to sex, age, educational qualification and socioeconomic status, and found that drug users were high on extraversion and neuroticism; stimulant-depressant drug users were found to be high on psychoticism as well as on the 'C' (criminal propensity) scale. Gossop (1978) studied the personality correlates of female drug addicts convicted of drug-related violent and other offences. Convicted subjects were more extraverted than non-convicted subjects. Another study, Gossop and Kristjansson (1977), investigated 50 drug takers and found that subjects convicted of non-drug offences scored higher on extraversion than subjects not convicted of such offences. Drug-dependent subjects altogether scored extremely highly on the 'C' (criminal propensity) scale. This reflects to some extent their high scores on the P and N dimensions.

SPECIFIC TRAITS AND CRIMINALITY

Before considering the large number of German-speaking studies using inventories derived from and similar to the Eysenck Questionnaires, it may be useful to consider quickly studies involving a number of specific traits which, as Figures [12.1–12.3] show, are involved in the three major dimensions of personality. Most work has been done on such factors as anxiety and depression, sensation-seeking, impulsiveness, impulse control, hostility and aggression, and lack of conformity. Typical and relatively recent studies only will be quoted; these usually have bibliographies referring to earlier studies.

Sensation or stimulation seeking has been studied by Farley and Sewell (1976) and Whitehill, De Myer-Gapin and Scott (1976), the former using a questionnaire, the latter a laboratory experimental technique. They found support for the hypothesis, which was formulated earlier by Quay (1965), that criminals would be sensation seekers. Robins (1972), can also be quoted in support.

Impulsiveness and lack of impulse control has frequently been suggested as a major component of criminality. Hormuth et al. (1977) using both questionnaires and experimental methods, were able to verify the prediction of less impulse control in delinquents with the former. The latter study also found positive results favouring the hypothesis. These data may be considered together with a related concept, namely that of risk-taking, which is often considered almost synonymous with impulsivity or lack of impulse control. A very thorough review of the literature is given by Lösel (1975), who found risk-taking more prominent among delinquents. The best available study on risk-taking, also giving a good summary of the literature, is by Schwenkmezger (1983); his conclusion is that results obtained by various investigators can best be interpreted in the sense that delinquent behaviour is favoured by impulsive, risky decision strategies, influenced more by hope of luck and chance than by realistic estimates of one's own abilities and possibilities.

Hostility and aggression are other traits frequently associated with criminality, and the Foulds scales (Foulds et al., 1960) have often been used as a measuring instrument. Data reported by Blackburn (1968, 1970), and Crawford (1977) suggest that positive relationships exist, with long-term prisoners generally having higher total hostility scores than normals, and violent offenders being more extrapunitive than non-violent offenders. Megargee's (1966) hypothesis contrasting over- and under-control would distinguish between extremely assaultive offenders (over-controlled) who would be expected to express less hostility than only moderately assaultive offenders. This theory was supported by Blackburn (1968) but not by Crawford (1977). Berman and Paisley (1984) compared juveniles convicted of assaultive offences with others convicted of other types of offences, and found that the former exhibited significantly higher psychoticism, extraversion and neuroticism scores; sensation seeking scores were also significantly lower for the non-assaultive group of property offenders.

A French Canadian group was studied by Coté and Leblanc (1982). Using the Jesness Inventory (Jesness, 1972) and the Eysenck Personality Inventory, they studied 825 adolescents from 14 to 19 years old, and correlated personality measures with self-reported indices of delinquency. They found the following traits very significantly correlated with delinquency; psychoticism (0.36), manifest aggressiveness (0.34), extraversion (0.32), bad social adjustment (0.32), alienation (0.25), repression (-0.25), and some traits showing even lower but still significant correlations.

The Jesness Inventory, just mentioned, consists of 155 items, scored on ten subscales (social maladjustment, value orientation, immaturity, alienation, autism, withdrawal, manifest aggression, social anxiety, repression and denial), and a predictive score, the Anti-social index. The relationships between the Eysenck and Jesness Personality Inventories have been explored by Smith (1974). Some of the observed correlations are quite high, e.g. between social maladjustment, autism, manifest aggression, withdrawal, on the one hand, and N and P, on the other. Social anxiety is negatively correlated with E, and highly positively with N. Saunders and Davies (1976) found evidence for the validity of the Jesness Inventory, as did Mott (1969). The scales most diagnostic appeared to be social maladjustment, value orientation, alienation, manifest aggression, and denial. In addition, Davies (1967) found some evidence in his follow-up studies for the validity of the autism, withdrawal and repression scales.

There are many studies using MMPI profiles, such as those of Davies and Sines (1971), and Beck and McIntyre (1977). The scales usually involved are the psychopathic deviate and hysteria scales, hypochondriasis, masculinity/femininity interest patterns, and mania; these suggest neurotic extraversion in the main. A more detailed account of work with the MMPI will be found in Dahlstrom and Dahlstrom (1980). As regards anxiety, a typical report is that by Lidhoo (1971), who studied 200 delinquent and 200 non-delinquent adolescents, matched for age, sex and socioeconomic status; all the subjects were Indian. The main and highly significant differences observed were with respect to emotionality, with the delinquents more tense, more depressed, and more easily provoked, and sexual maladjustment.

With only one or two exceptions, all the studies so far considered have been published in English and relate to English and American populations. It may be useful to summarize the major findings before going on to the large body of German-speaking studies investigating the major theories here considered. Replication is the life-blood of science, and here we would seem to have an ideal opportunity to compare two sets of data, not just collected by different investigators, but collected in different countries and by means of different inventories, although the German inventory used in all these studies was explicitly based on the Eysenck Personality Inventory. Thus we would here seem to have a cross-cultural replication, and if similar results are obtained, we could feel much more secure in regarding these conclusions as being firmly based.

The first conclusion which seems appropriate is that while the earlier studies summarized by Passingham were not theory centred, often used inappropriate questionnaires, and paid little attention to important methodological requirements, later studies summarized in Eysenck (1977), were methodologically much superior, and gave much more definitive and significant support to the personality theory in question. Studies carried out since then have maintained this improvement, and are nearly all equally positive in the outcome. Our first conclusion therefore must be that we now have good evidence for the implication of psychoticism, extraversion and neuroticism as predisposing factors in juvenile and adult criminality, and even in juvenile anti-social behaviour not amounting to legally criminal conduct. These correlations are based both on self-reported anti-social behaviour and criminal activity, and on legally defined criminality.

It would seem that different types of criminal activity may show differential relationships to personality, but too little has been done in that field to be very definitive to one's conclusions. Males and females seem to have similar personality patterns, as far as criminality is concerned, but little seems to have been done in making deliberate gender comparisons.

While P, E and N are related to criminality at all ages, there seem to be definite patterns suggesting that N is more important with older criminals, E with younger criminals. Why this should be so is not clear, but the data definitely tend in that direction. Possibly N, as a multiplicative drive variable, assumes greater importance with older people in whom habits have already been settled more clearly than is the case with younger persons. Another possibility is that the largely incarcerated adult samples cannot properly answer the social activity questions which make up a large part of the extraversion inventory. A study specifically directed to the solution of this problem would seem called for.

SUMMARY OF GERMAN STUDIES

A summary of 15 empirical German studies, using altogether 3,450 delinquents and a rather larger number of controls, has been reported by Steller and Hunze (1984). All these studies used the FPI (Freiburger Persönlichkeits Inventar) of Fahrenberg, Selg and Hampel (1978). In addition, Steiler and Hunze report a study of their own, using a self-report device for the measurement of anti-social conduct. The FPI contains nine traits and three dimensional scales, the latter being extraversion, emotional ability or neuroticism, and masculinity. The nine trait scales relate to nervousness, aggressiveness, depression, excitability, sociability, stability, dominance, inhibition and openness. Typical of the general findings are those of the special study carried out by Steiler and Hunze, where they found that delinquents showed higher scores on nervousness, depression, excitability, sociability, extraversion, and neuroticism. These results appeared separately on two alternative forms of the FPI.

In summarizing the results from all the other German studies, Steiler and Hunze point out that for the trait scales there is a very clear picture. Delinquents are higher on depression, nervousness, excitability and aggression. Regarding the major dimensions, a great majority show excessive degrees of neuroticism, and to a lesser extent extraversion. Sociability, as a major trait involved in extraversion, was significantly elevated in 25 per cent of all the comparisons, with criminals being more sociable. If we can use aggressiveness as an important part of psychoticism, then it is clear that these results agree very well with those of the English-speaking samples.

German studies show a similar differentiation between older and younger subjects, as far as neuroticism and extraversion are concerned. For the younger groups, delinquents are characterized much more clearly by greater sociability, dominance and openness; extraversion is implicated in almost every comparison between young delinquents and non-delinquents. This agrees well with the English-speaking data.

The German data give evidence also for the fact that the different types of criminality may be related differentially to personality, but the data are not extensive enough to make any definitive summary possible. There is, however, an interesting summary of data relating personality to the duration of incarceration, suggesting an increase in emotional instability with incarceration. However, there is also evidence that prisoners on probation showed increases in emotional instability. Clearly a more detailed investigation of this question is in order, particularly as Bolton et al. (1976) report discrepant findings.

It is sometimes suggested that possibly the differences between criminals and non-criminals might be due to the process of incarceration itself. This is unlikely, because several of the studies discussed compared the anti-social and criminal activities of children and juveniles none of whom were incarcerated at any time. Even more relevant and impressive is work showing that long before anti-social acts are committed, children who later on commit them are already differentiated from those who do not. Consider as an example the work of Burt (1965) who reported on the follow-up of children originally studied over 30 years previously. Seven hundred and sixty-three children of whom 15 per cent and 18 per cent respectively later became habitual criminals or neurotics, were rated by the teachers for N and for E. Of those who later became habitual offenders, 63 per cent had been rated as high on N; 54 per cent had been rated as high on E, but only 3 per cent as high on introversion. Of those who later became neurotics, 59 per cent had been rated as high on N, 44 per cent had been rated as high on introversion, but only 1 per cent as high on E. Similar data are reported by Michael (1956), and more recently Taylor and Watt (1977) and Fakouri and Jerse (1976) have published data showing that prediction of future criminal behaviour is possible from early school records. Thus the future criminal, like the future neurotic, is already recognizable in the young child.

Several of the studies summarized by Steller and Hunze used self-reported delinquency, and found, very much as did the English-speaking studies, that very similar personality correlates were observed here as in the case of legally defined delinquency.

The authors conclude that:

> in agreement with Eysenck's hypothesis and findings, it was found that in many samples emotional instability ('neuroticism') and high extraversion were found (in delinquents). The corresponding increases in the FPI dimensional scales were found most clearly in juvenile samples, but for grown-up delinquents were found in the FPI trait scales which represent major components of dimensional scales emotional instability and extraversion. (1984: 107)

We may thus conclude that this essay in replication has been eminently successful, in that identical findings are reported from the German literature as we have found to be representative of the English-speaking literature. There seems to be little doubt, therefore, that personality and anti-social and criminal behaviour are reasonably intimately correlated, and that these correlations can be found in cultures other than the Anglo-American. Eysenck (1977) has reported such confirmatory studies from widely different countries, including India, Hungary, Poland, and others, as well as the German and French-speaking samples mentioned in this chapter. [...]

REFERENCES

Allsop, J.F. (1976) 'Investigations into the applicability of Eysenck's theory of criminality to the anti-social behaviour of schoolchildren'. Unpublished PhD thesis, University of London.

Allsop, J.F. and Feldman, M.P. (1975) 'Extraversion, neuroticism and psychoticism and anti-social behaviour in school girls', *Social Behaviour and Personality*, 2: 184–9.

Allsop, J.F. and Feldman, M.P. (1976) 'Item analyses of questionnaire measures of personality and anti-social behaviour in school girls', *British Journal of Criminology*, 16: 337–51.

Barack, L.I. and Widom, C.S. (1978) 'Eysenck's theory of criminality applied to women awaiting trial', *British Journal of Psychiatry*, 133: 452–6.

Beck, E.A. and McIntyre, C.S. (1977) 'MMPI patterns of shoplifters within a college population', *Psychological Reports*, 41: 1035–40.

Berman, T. and Paisley, T. (1984) 'Personality in assaultive and non-assaultive juvenile male offenders', *Psychological Reports*, 54: 527–30.

Blackburn, R. (1968) 'Personality in relation to extreme aggression in psychiatric offenders', *British Journal of Psychiatry*, 114: 821–8.

Blackburn, R. (1970) 'Personality types among abnormal homicides', *Special Hospital Research*, No. 1, London.

Bolton, N., Smith, F.V., Heskin, K.J. and Barister, P.A. (1976) 'Psychological correlates of long-term imprisonment', *British Journal of Criminology*, 16: 38–47.

Burgess, P.K. (1972) 'Eysenck's theory of criminality: a new approach', *British Journal of Criminology*, 12: 74–82.

Burt, C. (1965) 'Factorial studies of personality and their bearing in the work of the teacher', *British Journal of Educational Psychology*, 35: 308–28.

Coté, G. and Leblanc, M. (1982) 'Aspects de personalité et comportement delinquent', *Bulletin de Psychologique*, 36: 265–71.

Crawford, D.A. (1977) 'The HDHQ results of long-term prisoners: relationships with criminal and institutional behaviour', *British Journal of Social and Clinical Psychology*, 16: 391–4.

Dahlstrom, W.G. and Dahlstrom, L. (eds) (1980) *Basic Readings on the MMPI*. Minneapolis: University of Minnesota Press.

Davies, M.B. (1967) *The Use of the Jesness Inventory in a Sample of British Probationers*. London: HMSO.

Davies, K.R. and Sines, J.O. (1971) 'An anti-social behaviour pattern associated with a specific MMPI profile', *Journal of Consulting and Clinical Psychology*, 36: 229–34.

Eysenck, H.J. (1960) Symposium: 'The development of moral values in children. VII. The contribution of learning theory', *British Journal of Educational Psychology*, 30: 11–21.

Eysenck, H.J. (1967) *The Biological Basis of Personality*. Springfield, Ill.: C.C. Thomas.

Eysenck, H.J. (1970) *The Structures of Human Personality*, 3rd edn. London: Methuen.

Eysenck, H.J. (1973) 'Personality, learning and "anxiety"', in H J. Eysenck (ed.), *Handbook of Abnormal Psychology*, 2nd edn. London: Pitman, pp. 390–419.

Eysenck, H.J. (1976) 'The biology of morality', in T. Lickona (ed.), *Moral Development and Behavior*. New York: Holt, Rinehart and Winston, pp. 108–23.

Eysenck, H.J. (1977) *Crime and Personality*, 3rd edn. London: Routledge and Kegan Paul.

Eysenck, H.J. (ed.) (1980) *A Model for Personality*. New York: Springer.

Eysenck, H.J. and Eysenck, M.W. (1985) *Personality and Individual Differences*. New York: Plenum.

Eysenck, H.J. and Eysenck, S.B.G. (1976) *Psychoticism as a Dimension of Personality*. London: Hodder and Stoughton.

Eysenck, H.J. and Eysenck, S.B.G. (1978) 'Psychopathy, personality and genetics', in R.D. Hare and D. Schalling (eds), *Psychopathic Behaviour*. London: John Wiley, pp. 197–223.

Eysenck, S.B.G. and Eysenck H.J. (1970) 'Crime and personality: an empirical study of the three-factor theory', *British Journal of Criminology*, 10: 225–39.

Eysenck, S.B.G. and Eysenck, H.J. (1971) 'A comparative study of criminals and matched controls on three dimensions of personality', *British Journal of Social and Clinical Psychology*, 10: 362–6.

Eysenck, S.B.G. and Eysenck, H.J. (1971) 'Crime and personality: item analysis of questionnaire responses', British Journal of Criminology, 11: 49-62.

Eysenck, S.B.G. and Eysenck, H.J. (1973) 'The personality of female prisoners', *British Journal of Psychiatry*, 122: 693–8.

Eysenck, S.B.G. and Eysenck, H.J. (1974) 'Personality and recidivism in Borstal boys', *British Journal of Criminology*, 14: 285–7.

Eysenck, S.B.G. and Eysenck, H.J. (1977) 'Personality differences between prisoners and controls', *Psychological Reports*, 40: 1023–8.

Eysenck, S.B.G., Rust, J. and Eysenck, H.J. (1977) 'Personality and the classification of adult offenders', *British Journal of Criminology*, 17: 169–79.

Fahrenberg, J., Selg, H. and Hampel, R. (1978) *Das Freiburger Persönlichkeits-inventar*. Göttingen: Hogrefe.

Fakouri, E. and Jerse, F.W. (1976) 'Unobtrusive detection of potential juvenile delinquency', *Psychological Reports*, 39: 551–8.

Farley, F.H. and Sewell, T. (1976) 'Test of an arousal theory of delinquency', *Criminal Justice and Behaviour*, 3: 315–20.

Farrington, P., Biron, L. and Leblanc, M. (1982) 'Personality and delinquency in London and Madrid', in J. Gunn and D.P. Farrington (eds), *Abnormal Offenders, Delinquency, and the Criminal Justice System*. New York: Wiley.

Foggitt, R. (1976) 'Personality and delinquency'. Unpublished PhD thesis, University of London.

Foulds, G.A., Caine, T.M. and Creasy, M.I. (1960) 'Aspects of extra- and intra-punitive expression in mental illness', *Journal of Mental Science*, 196: 599–610.

Gibson, H.B. (1971) 'The factorial structure of juvenile delinquency: a study of self-reported acts', *British Journal of Social and Clinical Psychology*, 10: 1–9.

Glueck, S. and Glueck, E. (1956) *Physique and Delinquency*. New York: Harper.

Gossop, M. (1978) 'Drug dependence, crime and personality among female addicts', *Drug and Alcohol Dependence*, 3: 359–64.

Gossop, M.R. and Kristjansson, I. (1977) 'Crime and personality', *British Journal of Criminology*, 17: 264–73.

Hindelang, M. and Weis, J.G. (1972) 'Personality and self-reported delinquency: an application of cluster analysis', *Criminology*, 10: 268–76.

Holcomb, W.R., Adam, N.A. and Ponder, H.N. (1985) 'The development and cross-validation upon MMPI typology of murderers', *Journal of Personality Assessment*, 49: 240–4.

Hormuth, S., Lamm, H., Michelitsch, I., Scheuermann, H., Trommsdorf, G. and Vogele, I. (1977) 'Impulskontrolle und einige Persönlichkeitscharakteristika bei delinquenten und nicht-delinquenten Jugendlichen', *Psychologische Beiträge*, 19: 340–59.

Jesness, C.F. (1972) *The Jesness Inventory: Manual*. Palo Alto, CA: Consulting Psychologist Press.

Lidhoo, M.L. (1971) 'An attempt to construct a psycho-diagnostic tool for the detection of potential delinquents among adolescents aged 14–19 years'. Unpublished PhD thesis, University of Panjab.

Lösel, F. (1975) *Handlungskontrolle und Jugend-delinquenz*. Stuttgart: Enke.

McCue, P., Booth, S. and Root, J. (1976) 'Do young prisoners under-state their extraversion on personality inventories?', *British Journal of Criminology*, 16: 282–3.

McGurk, B.J. (1978) 'Personality types among "normal" homicides', *British Journal of Criminology*, 18: 146–61.

McGurk, B.J. and McDougall, C. (1981) 'A new approach to Eysenck's theory of criminality', *Personality and Individual Differences*, 2: 338–40.

McGurk, B.J. and McEwan, A.W. (1983) 'Personality types and recidivism among Borstal trainees', *Personality and Individual Differences*, 4: 165–70.

McGurk, B.J., McEwan, A.W. and Graham, F. (1981) 'Personality types and recidivism among young delinquents', *British Journal of Criminology*, 21: 159–65.

Martin, A.L. (1985) 'Values and personality: a survey of their relationship in the case of juvenile delinquency', *Personality and Individual Differences*, 4: 519–22.

Megargee, E.I. (1966) 'Undercontrolled and overcontrolled personality types in extreme anti-social aggression', *Psychological Monographs*, 80, Whole Number 611.

Michael, C.M. (1956) 'Follow-up studies of introverted children: IV. Relative incidence of criminal behaviour', *Journal of Criminal Law and Criminality*, 47: 414–22.

Mitchell, J., Rogers, R., Cavanaugh, J. and Wasyliw, O. (1980) 'The role of trait anxiety in violent and non-violent delinquent behavior', *American Journal of Forensic Psychiatry*.

Mott, J. (1969) *The Jesness Inventory: An Application to Approved School Boys*. London: HMSO.

Passingham, R.E. (1972) 'Crime and personality: a review of Eysenck's theory', in V.D. Nebylitsyn and J.A. Gray (eds), *Biological Bases of Individual Behaviour*. London: Academic Press.

Perez, J. and Torrubia, R. (1985) 'Sensation seeking and anti-social behaviour in a student sample', *Personality and Individual Differences*, 6: 401–3.

Quay, H.C. (1965) 'Psychopathic personality as pathological stimulation-seeking', *American journal of Psychiatry*, 122: 180–3.

Rahman, A. and Hussain, A. (1984) 'Personality and female criminals in Bangladesh', *Personality and Individual Differences*, 5: 473–4.

Raine, A. and Venables, P. (1981) 'Classical conditioning and socialization – a biosocial interaction', Personality and Individual Differences, 2: 273–83.

Robins, L.N. (1972) 'Follow-up studies of behaviour disorders in children', in H.C. Quay and J.S. Werry (eds), *Psychopathological Disorders of Childhood*. New York: Wiley.

Royce, J.P. and Powell, A. (1983) *Theory of Personality and Individual Differences: Factors, Systems and Processes*. Englewood Cliffs, NJ: Prentice-Hall.

Rushton, J.F. and Chrisjohn, R.D. (1981) 'Extraversion, neuroticism, psychoticism and self-reported delinquency: evidence from eight separate samples', *Personality and Individual Differences*, 2: 11–20.

Saklofske, D.H., McKerracher, D.W. and Eysenck, S.B.G. (1978) 'Eysenck's theory of criminality: a scale of criminal propensity as a measure of anti-social behaviour', *Psychological Reports*, 43: 683–6.

Sanocki, W. (1969) 'The use of Eysenck's inventory for testing young prisoners', *Przeglad Penitencjarny* (Warszawa), 7: 53–68.

Saunders, G.R. and Davies, M.B. (1976) 'The validity of the Jesness Inventory with British delinquents', *British Journal of Social and Clinical Psychology*, 15: 33–9.

Schwenkmezger, P. (1983) 'Risikoverhalten, Risikobereitschaft und Delinquenz: Theoretische Grundlagen und differentialdiagnostische Untersuchungen'. *Zeitschrift für Differentielle und Diagnostische Psychologie*, 4: 223–39.

Shanmugan, T.E. (1979) 'Personality factors underlying drug abuse among college students', *Psychological Studies*, 24–35.

Singh, A. (1982) 'A study of the personality and adjustments of female juvenile delinquents', *Child Psychiatry Quarterly*, 13: 52–9.

Smith, D.E. (1974) 'Relationships between the Eysenck and Jesness Personality Inventories', *British Journal of Criminology*, 14: 376–84.

Smith, D.E. and Smith, D.D. (1977) 'Eysenck's psychoticism scale and reconvictions', *British Journal of Criminology*, 17: 387–8.

Steller, M. and Hunze, D. (1984) 'Zur Selbstbeschreibung von Delinquenten im Freiburger Persönlichkeitsinventar (FPI) – Eine Sekundäranalyse empirischer Untersuchungen', *Zeitschrift für Differentielle und Diagnostische Psychologie*, 5: 87–110.

Taylor, T. and Watt, D.C. (1977) 'The relation of deviant symptoms and behaviour in a normal population to subsequent delinquency and maladjustment', *Psychological Medicine*, 7: 163–9.

Wardell, D. and Yeudall, L.T. (1980) 'A multidimensional approach to criminal disorders: the assessment of impulsivity and its relation to crime', *Advances in Behaviour Research and Therapy*, 2: 159–77.

West, D. and Farrington, D.P. (1973) *Who Becomes Delinquent?* London: Heinemann.

Whitehill, M., De Myer-Gapin, S. and Scott, T.J. (1976) 'Stimulation seeking in anti-social preadolescent children', *Journal of Abnormal Psychology*, 85: 101–4.

Zuckerman, M. (1979) *Sensation Seeking: Beyond the Optimal Level of Arousal*. Hillsdale: NJ: Erlbaum.

Zuckerman, M., Eysenck, S.B.G. and Eysenck, H.J. (1978) 'Sensation seeking in England and America: cross-cultural, age and sex comparisons', *Journal of Consulting and Clinical Psychology*, 1: 139–49.

13

A criminological research agenda for the next millennium

David P. Farrington

[...]

KEY ISSUES IN CRIMINOLOGY

Key criminological issues addressed in this article fall into three categories. First, there are questions of descriptive epidemiology, such as: How do criminal careers develop over time? Second, there are causal questions, such as: What are the most important causes or risk factors for offending? Third, there are intervention questions, such as: What are the best interventions to prevent offending? In each of these categories, key questions that need to be addressed will be discussed, and then what we know, what we need to know, and how we can find out. Finally, an ambitious coordinated program of cross-national comparative longitudinal research will be recommended: a research agenda for the next millennium.

Criminal careers

There are many key questions about criminal careers: What proportion of the population commits offenses at different ages? (What is the prevalence of offending?) What are the characteristics of offenders compared with nonoffenders at different ages? When does offending start? (What is the age of onset?) When does offending stop? (What is the age of desistance?) How long do criminal careers last? (What is their duration?) How frequently do people commit offenses during their criminal careers? These and other questions can also be asked about different populations (e.g., males versus females) and different types of offenses.

From *International Journal of Offender Therapy and Comparative Criminology*, June 1999, 43(2): 154–67.

Other key questions include the following: How far is there escalation or de-escalation in the seriousness of offending during criminal careers? How far is there specialization or versatility in offending? How far is there continuity or stability in offending over time? How far are there different behavioral manifestations of the same underlying construct (e.g., an antisocial personality) at different ages? How far are criminal careers types of more general antisocial careers? How far are there developmental sequences, pathways, or progressions from one type of offending to another, or from childhood antisocial behavior to offending? How far can we predict the later criminal career from the early criminal career? How are different criminal career features (e.g., age of onset, duration, frequency of offending) interrelated?

Conclusions about criminal careers depend on methods of measurement (e.g., official records or self-reports) and types of offenses. One of the early surprising findings was the high prevalence of offending. For example, in the Cambridge Study in Delinquent Development, which is a prospective longitudinal survey of 400 London males, 40% were convicted up to age 40 (Farrington, 1995a; Farrington, Lambert, & West, 1998). According to their self-reports, 96% had committed an offense that could have led to conviction up to age 32. However, even according to self-reports, only a minority had committed more serious offenses such as burglary (14%) or motor vehicle theft (15%) (Farrington, 1989).

According to official records, offending often begins by age 14, has a peak prevalence in the teenage years (ages 15 to 19) and then declines after age 20 (Farrington, 1986). In the Cambridge study, the peak age of increase in the prevalence of offending by study males was about 14, and the peak age of decrease was about 23. However, some criminal careers can persist over many years and others do not begin until later in life. For example, a quarter of convicted fathers in the Cambridge study were not convicted until after age 35, and their average duration of criminal careers was 16 years (for fathers committing more than one offense) (see Farrington et al., 1998).

A small fraction of the population (the 'chronic offenders') account for a substantial fraction of all offenses. In the Cambridge study, about 6% of the males accounted for about half of all the convictions up to age 40 (Farrington et al., 1998). Also, about 6% of the families accounted for half of all the convictions of all family members (Farrington, Barnes, & Lambert, 1996). Most offenses by offenders younger than age 17 were committed with others, but co-offending decreased steadily with age (Reiss & Farrington, 1991).

There is relative stability in offending because the worst offenders at one age tend also to be the worst offenders at other ages. In the Cambridge study, three quarters of those convicted as juveniles at age 10 to 16 were also convicted at age 17 to 24, compared with only 16% of the remainder (Farrington, 1992). There was also significant continuity in self-reported offending (Farrington, 1989). However, there were changes in absolute levels of offending over time. For example, the prevalence of marijuana use decreased significantly between ages 18 and 32 (from 29% to 19%), but there was a significant correlation between use at age 18 and use at age 32 (Farrington, 1990).

Offending is predominantly versatile rather than specialized, particularly at younger ages. In the Cambridge study, the violent offenders committed an average of 1.7 violent offenses each up to age 32, but an average of 5.3 nonviolent offenses each (Farrington, 1991a). Violent offenses seem to occur almost at random in criminal careers. Also, there is versatility in antisocial behavior generally, suggesting that offending is one element of a syndrome of antisocial behavior that arises in childhood and persists into adulthood (Farrington, 1991b). Offenders tend to be multiple-problem youth.

Many other important facts are known about criminal careers, but there is not enough space to review them here (see Farrington, 1997a). Instead, the next section will review what we need to know about criminal careers. Most previous criminal career research has been based on official records of arrests or convictions. More efforts are needed to investigate criminal career questions using repeated self-reports in prospective longitudinal surveys. Ideally, self-report information is needed about the relative timing of offenses. Self-reports would make it possible to study the probability of a (self-reported) offense leading to a conviction, and the characteristics of people with a high likelihood of committing undetected offenses (compared with others who have a high likelihood of being caught). Self-reports would also make it more possible to study criminal career issues for specific types of offenses.

Most prior criminal career research treats offenders as homogeneous, but different types of people may have different types of careers. For example, Moffitt (1993) distinguished between 'adolescence-limited' and 'life-course-persistent' offenders. Research is needed on what are the most useful typologies of offenders, and on their different developmental pathways to criminal careers. Also, more research is needed on female criminal careers; existing studies focus primarily on males.

An important research priority is to investigate stepping stones in developmental pathways leading to serious or chronic offending, to try to determine optimal opportunities for intervention (when there is some predictability but not too much stabilization). More research is also needed on predicting future criminal careers. It is also important to study failures in prediction, for example, why some juvenile offenders do not become adult offenders (Farrington & Hawkins, 1991). This type of research can help to identify protective factors that might form the basis of interventions.

In the past, there has been little contact between developmental and situational researchers (Farrington, 1995b). More criminal career research is needed on situational factors and circumstances influencing criminal acts, so that it is possible to specify not only how and why criminal potential develops over time, but also how and why the potential becomes the actuality of criminal acts. Similarly, more criminal career research is needed that incorporates biological factors (Farrington, 1997b) and community influences (Farrington, 1993a). Another important research priority is to quantify the total burden on society of chronic offenders, specifying their problems in different areas of life (e.g., education, employment, sexual, mental, and physical health). This information is especially needed in assessing the costs and benefits of prevention and intervention programs (Cohen, 1998).

Causes and risk factors

There are many key questions about causes and risk factors. What are the main causes of offending? Why do people commit offenses at different ages? What are the main risk factors for offending at different ages? It is easier to establish risk factors (factors that predict an increased probability of offending) than causes. It is not easy to determine which risk factors have causal effects. Many researchers are doubtful about the value of asking people direct questions about why they committed offenses (Farrington, 1993b).

Other key questions include the following: What is the relative importance of different risk factors? How far do risk factors have independent, interactive, or sequential effects on offending? (For example, do communities influence families, and families influence children, so that communities have only indirect effects on offending?) What are the main protective factors for offending at different ages? How well, and how early, can offending be predicted? What are the main causes or risk factors for different criminal career features such as onset, persistence, escalation, de-escalation, and desistance? (Because they occur at different ages, the causes of some features are likely to be different from the causes of others.) What are the effects of life events (such as getting married, getting divorced, leaving home, parental death, parental divorce) on the course of development of offending? Are there critical periods when effects of specific life events are greatest? What are the most useful theories for explaining onset, persistence, escalation, de-escalation, desistance, and the time course of criminal careers generally?

A great deal is known about the main risk factors or predictors of offending from prospective longitudinal surveys in different countries (Farrington, 1996a, 1997a). To link knowledge about risk factors with prevention methods, the focus will be on risk factors that can be changed rather than fixed risk factors such as gender. The focus will also be on risk factors that might be explanatory or causal rather than risk factors that might be merely symptoms of an underlying antisocial personality (e.g., bullying, heavy drinking, drug use).

Among the most important risk factors are hyperactivity-impulsiveness attention deficit, low intelligence or attainment, convicted parents or siblings, poor parental supervision, harsh or erratic discipline, parental conflict, separation or divorce, low family income, poor housing, large family size, delinquent friends, attending a high delinquency rate school, and living in a high crime neighborhood.

Although these risk factors are well established, there is little hard evidence about which of them are truly causal. The most compelling evidence of causality could be obtained in prevention experiments, but most such experiments are designed to test a technology rather than a theory. Interventions are often heterogeneous, including, for example, individual skills training, parent training, and teacher training (Hawkins, von Cleve, & Catalano, 1991), because multi-modal interventions are more likely to be successful (Wasserman & Miller, 1998). However, unimodal interventions focussing on a single factor, such as poor parental supervision, could be useful in establishing causality. If a multimodal program proved to be effective, follow-up experiments should be carried out to identify its 'active ingredients.'

After experiments, the next most convincing method of establishing causes is through quasi-experimental, within-individual analyses in which each individual is followed up before and after particular life events (Farrington, 1988). Because the same individuals are investigated, many extraneous variables are held constant. In the Cambridge study, the effects of unemployment on offending were established by comparing a person's offending during unemployment periods with the same person's offending during employment periods (Farrington, Gallagher, Morley, St. Ledger, & West, 1986). Crimes of dishonesty were more frequent during periods of unemployment. The effects of getting married and getting divorced were established by comparing a person's offending before and after these life events (Farrington & West, 1995). Offending decreased after getting married and increased after getting divorced. More analyses of this type are needed.

Although a great deal is known about risk factors for offending in general, little is known about risk factors for different criminal career features, such as onset, persistence, escalation, de-escalation, and desistance. In the Cambridge study, a convicted parent was a strong predictor of convictions in general, but predicted later rather than early onset, and a delinquent sibling was a strong predictor of persistence in the adult years as opposed to desistance (Farrington & Hawkins, 1991).

Also, little is known about risk factors for different types of offenders, such as chronic or persistent offenders. More is known about differences between offenders and nonoffenders than about differences between persistent and occasional offenders. In the Cambridge study, a convicted parent was the strongest predictor of occasional young offenders compared with nonoffenders, and low family income was the strongest predictor of persistent compared with occasional young offenders (Farrington, 1999). The extent to which future chronic offenders can be predicted at the time of their first conviction is a question with important practical implications for policy makers and practitioners; Blumstein, Farrington, and Moitra (1985) predicted 25 males to be chronic offenders, of whom 14 actually became chronics (out of 23 chronics altogether).

Little is known about protective factors, or about independent, interactive, or sequential effects of risk and protective factors. Knowledge about protective factors could be practically useful because targeting protective factors could help to prevent onset and foster early desistance. Wide-ranging theories are needed that explain how individual, family, peer, school, and community factors influence the development of long-term criminal potential, how life events and short-term factors (e.g., quarrelling with a spouse, getting drunk) influence short-term criminal potential, and how criminal potential interacts with situational factors to produce criminal acts (see, e.g., Farrington, 1999).

An important issue for theory and practice is how far risk factors are general as opposed to specific for different types of offending and antisocial outcomes. It often seems that multiple overlapping risk factors predict multiple comorbid outcomes, largely because of the influence of multiple-problem people in multiple-problem families. Although it is clear that the likelihood of offending increases with the number of risk factors (Farrington, 1997c), it is unclear how far the specific risk factors matter or are interchangeable. More research is needed on disentangling specific and general effects of risk factors.

Prevention methods

Crime prevention methods can be classified into four categories (Tonry & Farrington, 1995): developmental (designed to inhibit the development of criminal potential in individuals, focusing on risk and protective factors), community (designed to change community institutions such as families, peers, and organizations), situational (designed to reduce criminal opportunities and decrease the risk of offending), and criminal justice (deterrence, incapacitation, and rehabilitation).

There are many key questions about prevention and intervention. What are the most effective and cost-effective methods of preventing the onset of offending? What are the most effective and cost-effective methods of preventing persistence or escalation after onset? What are the most effective and cost-effective methods of fostering de-escalation or desistance from offending?

There are many demonstrations of the effectiveness of developmental prevention methods in well-designed experiments (Farrington, 1996a, 1996b). The most effective techniques include the following: intensive home visiting of women during their pregnancy and the infancy of their children to give advice about child care, infant development, nutrition, and avoiding substance use (Olds et al., 1997); preschool intellectual enrichment programs designed to increase children's thinking and reasoning abilities (Schweinhart, Barnes, & Weikart, 1993); parent management training designed to encourage close monitoring of child behavior and consistent and contingent rewards and punishments (Patterson, Reid, & Dishion, 1992); interpersonal skills training to encourage children to think before they act and to consider the effect of their behavior on others (Ross, 1995); and peer influence resistance training, to encourage children to resist peer pressures to commit deviant acts (Tobler, 1986).

These prevention methods can be implemented within a risk-focused community prevention program such as Communities That Care (Hawkins & Catalano, 1992). In this, risk and protective factors in the community are measured and proven prevention techniques are implemented to tackle the most important risk factors. Unfortunately, most of the existing prevention experiments are based on small samples and have short follow-up periods, so the persistence of effects is unclear. Experiments with larger samples and longer follow-up periods are needed.

Little is known about optimal intervention strategies. In particular, it is unclear whether it is better to target the whole population using public health methods as in Communities That Care or whether it is better to target children at risk or known offenders. Also, little is known about the optimal intervention points in developmental pathways leading to offending or in criminal careers. Research is also needed on what are the best types of interventions for different types of persons and in different contexts (national, community, subculture, etc.).

There is a great need for more information about the cost-effectiveness of interventions. In evaluating developmental prevention techniques, it is important to measure a wide variety of outcomes as well as offending (unemployment, school failure, dependence on welfare benefits, teenage pregnancy, divorce/separation, substance use, etc.). All benefits of an effective program need to be taken into account in weighing costs against benefits. The costs of crime are so enormous (Miller, Cohen, & Wiersema, 1996) that even a small reduction in offending could lead to an impressive benefit: cost ratio, such as the 7:1 ratio of the Perry preschool project (Schweinhart et al., 1993). Situational prevention projects also can be highly cost-effective (Forrester, Frenz, O'Connell, & Pease, 1990).

THE NEED FOR LONGITUDINAL RESEARCH

To answer questions about the development of criminal careers and about risk factors for different criminal career features, prospective longitudinal surveys are needed in which people are followed up from childhood to adulthood using personal interviews (Loeber & Farrington, 1997). Ideally, longitudinal studies of offending should have repeated assessments at frequent intervals (e.g., every year); reliable and valid measures; multiple data sources and informants (e.g., children, parents, teachers, peers, records); numerous measured variables from different domains (e.g., biological, psychological, family, peer, school, neighborhood, socioeconomic); a long duration to measure long developmental pathways and within-individual change; samples of at least several hundreds; and high risk samples drawn from cities to maximize the yield of chronic and serious offenders.

For example, in the Pittsburgh Youth Study (Loeber, Farrington, Stouthamer-Loeber, Moffitt, & Caspi, 1998), three samples, each of 500 inner-city boys, were followed up, with assessments every 6 months from the boy, mother, and teacher. The oldest (age 13) and youngest (age 7) samples have been followed up for 10 years, and attrition rates have been low. Numerous different risk factors and outcomes (offending, substance use, sexual behavior, and mental health problems) have been measured.

Such prospective longitudinal surveys have many advantages over cross-sectional surveys, including: Retrospective bias is avoided because risk factors are measured before outcomes are known; causal order can be established unambiguously; true predictions can be made; offenders and nonoffenders emerge naturally, thus avoiding problems of drawing appropriate control groups as in case-control studies; and within-individual analyses can be carried out, thereby controlling more effectively for extraneous variables.

THE NEED FOR EXPERIMENTAL RESEARCH

To answer questions about the effectiveness of prevention methods, randomized experiments are needed. Such experiments could also help to establish whether risk factors had causal effects, to the extent that the intervention targeted a single risk factor. Ideally, experiments should have large samples, long follow-up periods, and follow-up interviews. For example, in the Montreal Longitudinal-Experimental Study (Tremblay, Pagani-Kurtz, Vitaro, Masse, & Pihl, 1995), about 250 disruptive (aggressive/hyperactive) boys were identified at age 6. Between ages 7 and 9, the experimental group received individual skills training and parent training, and experimental and control boys were then followed up with yearly assessments (which showed that the experimental boys were less antisocial).

The main advantage of a randomized experiment is that it ensures that those who receive an intervention are closely comparable with the control group on all possible extraneous variables (within the limits of statistical fluctuation). A randomized experiment is better than a matching design because it is only possible to match on a limited number of variables (sometimes combined into a prediction score). However, in evaluating community interventions, a matching design is necessary because it is impossible in practice to assign a large number of communities randomly to experimental and control conditions. Ideally, before and after measures should be compared in experimental and control communities (Farrington, 1997d).

MORE COMPLEX DESIGNS

A major problem with long-term prospective longitudinal surveys is that results may be long delayed. By the time crucial outcome results are obtained, instruments, methods, theories, and policy concerns may appear to be outdated. There is also the problem that researchers age at the same rate as the subjects and are mortal. If a principal investigator begins a birth cohort study at age 45, it will probably be necessary to arrange for the direction of the study to be transferred to a younger investigator sooner or later. It is also difficult to secure a long-term guarantee of funding.

The accelerated longitudinal design overcomes some of these problems. For example, four cohorts could be followed up simultaneously: the youngest from birth to age 6, the next from age 6 to age 12, the next from age 12 to age 18, and the oldest from age 18 to age 24 (Farrington, Ohlin, & Wilson, 1986). In principle, this design would enable knowledge about development from birth to age 24 to be obtained in only 6 years. A final outcome measure in one cohort could be an initial measure in the next, such as conduct disorder at age 6 and early delinquency at age 12.

This design has some potential disadvantages, however. In particular, it is unclear how best to link up the cohorts, and it is not possible to study very long within-individual sequences. A period of overlap of the cohorts in age would be desirable to facilitate linking up cohorts and disentangling aging, period, and cohort effects (Tonry, Ohlin, & Farrington, 1991). Nevertheless, the accelerated design is potentially very promising and should be used more often. For example, the original design of the Pittsburgh Youth Study called for three cohorts of boys to be followed up from age 7 to age 10, age 10 to age 13, and age 13 to age 16 (Loeber, Farrington, Stouthamer-Loeber, & van Kammen, 1998). As mentioned earlier, the follow-up periods of the oldest and youngest cohorts have now been extended to a total of 10 years.

There are also advantages in combining longitudinal and experimental methods by including interventions in longitudinal studies (Loeber & Farrington, 1997). The longitudinal-experimental design is more economical, using the same people to study risk factors and developmental pathways as well as the effects of interventions. The longitudinal data before the intervention helps to understand pre existing trends and interactions between types of persons and types of treatments. The longitudinal data after the intervention helps to establish its long-term impact. Of course, there are also potential disadvantages with this design. For example, the experiment may interfere with the longitudinal study, and it may be necessary to restrict analyses of naturalistic development only to the control group.

The accelerated longitudinal and experimental designs could be combined by implementing different interventions in different cohorts. For example, in the four-cohort design of Farrington, Ohlin, and Wilson (1986), each intervention could be implemented halfway through the 6-year follow-up period. A preschool intervention could be implemented at age 3, parent training at age 9, educational skills training at age 15, and employment skills training at age 21.

CROSS-NATIONAL COMPARATIVE LONGITUDINAL STUDIES

Surprisingly, there are few examples of coordinated cross-national comparative longitudinal surveys in the literature. There are good examples of coordinated comparative longitudinal surveys in different cities in the United States. For example, in the Program of Research on the Causes and Correlates of Delinquency, coordinated longitudinal studies have been carried out in Denver, Pittsburgh, and Rochester (Thornberry, Huizinga, & Loeber, 1995). Big efforts were made to use common measures in these surveys, although their designs were different. Many key findings about risk factors and development were replicated in all three sites.

Project Metropolitan was originally planned in 1960 as a cross-national comparative longitudinal survey to be conducted simultaneously in Norway, Denmark, Sweden, and Finland (Janson, 1981). However, the project only got off the ground in Sweden and Denmark, and the Copenhagen project has yielded rather few publications (Hogh & Wolf, 1983). Project Metropolitan in Stockholm is best known internationally, and its delinquency results can be found in Wikström (1990). The time now is surely ripe to mount a major comparative longitudinal study simultaneously in several countries.

An advantage of cross-national comparative studies is that they would help to establish how far criminal careers, risk factors, and intervention effects are the same or different in participating countries. To the extent that results are similar, they might strengthen our confidence in universal findings and theories. To the extent that results are different, the challenge would be to explain the differences, perhaps by reference to features of national contexts.

PREVIOUS CROSS-NATIONAL COMPARATIVE STUDIES

The International Crime Victims Surveys constitute perhaps the best known series of cross-national comparative surveys in criminology (Mayhew & van Dijk, 1997). Similar questions about victimization were asked by telephone in 1989, 1992, and 1996 in a number of different countries in Europe and elsewhere. Another major effort was the International Self-Reported Delinquency Survey (Junger-Tas, Terlouw, & Klein, 1994). Similar self-report questions were asked in 1992–1993 in several different countries. The success of these initiatives suggests that an international comparative longitudinal survey would be feasible.

The classic book on cross-national longitudinal studies in criminology was edited by Weitekamp and Kerner (1994), based on a NATO conference on the same topic. Unfortunately, although the chapters in this book are excellent summaries of longitudinal studies in different countries, they rather serve to highlight the lack of coordinated cross-national longitudinal surveys. The only cross-national comparative chapter is by Farrington and Wikström (1994), comparing criminal careers in the Cambridge study and in Project Metropolitan in Stockholm. Although many aspects of these careers were similar, the peak in the age-crime curve largely reflected a peak in prevalence in London and a peak in frequency in Stockholm. Very few other cross-national comparisons of longitudinal results have been carried out, although Pulkkinen (1988) systematically compared her criminal career findings in Finland with those obtained in the Cambridge study, again reporting many similarities.

One of the few systematic comparisons of risk factors in longitudinal surveys was completed by Farrington and Loeber (1999), comparing results in the Cambridge study and in the middle cohort of the Pittsburgh Youth Study. In both cases, risk factors measured at age 10 were compared with court delinquency for inner-city boys between ages 10 and 16. Generally, the replicability was remarkable. Most significant risk factors in one survey were comparably strong risk factors in the other. There were only two major exceptions: low social class was more important in Pittsburgh (possibly because the measure included parental education), and harsh maternal discipline was more important in London (possibly because the measure included a cold, rejecting maternal attitude).

CONCLUSIONS

To advance knowledge about the development of criminal careers, about the causes of offending, and about the prevention and treatment of offenders, longitudinal and experimental studies are needed. There are advantages in combining a multiple-cohort accelerated longitudinal design with experimental interventions in different cohorts. The longitudinal study advances knowledge about the development of criminal careers and about the importance of numerous risk factors, but has difficulty in unambiguously demonstrating causal effects. The experimental study unambiguously demonstrates causal effects but can only provide information about the importance of a small number of explanatory variables.

The time is ripe to mount a coordinated program of cross-national comparative longitudinal studies, which could lead to great advances in knowledge about universal risk factors and replicable prevention methods. This would be a very ambitious project; as it may perhaps be the equivalent of the American space shuttle, perhaps we should call it the crime shuttle in trying to get it off the ground! It would surely be appropriate to mark the new millennium with a real millennium project.

REFERENCES

Blumstein, A., Farrington, D. P., & Moitra, S. (1985). Delinquency careers: Innocents, desisters and persisters. In M. Tonry & N. Morris (Eds.), *Crime and justice* (Vol. 6, pp. 187–219). Chicago: University of Chicago Press.

Cohen, M. A. (1998). The monetary value of saving a high-risk youth. *Journal of Qualitative Criminology*, 14, 5–33.

Farrington, D. P. (1986). Age and crime. In M. Tonry & N. Morris (Eds.), *Crime and justice* (Vol. 7, pp. 189–250). Chicago: University of Chicago Press.

Farrington, D. P. (1988). Studying changes within individuals: The causes of offending. In M. Rutter (Ed.), *Studies of psychosocial risk* (pp. 158–183). Cambridge: Cambridge University Press.

Farrington, D. P. (1989). Self-reported and official offending from adolescence to adulthood. In M. W. Klein (Ed.), *Cross-national research in self-reported crime and delinquency* (pp. 399–423). Dordrecht, the Netherlands: Kluwer.

Farrington, D. P. (1990). Age, period, cohort, and offending. In D. M. Gottfredson & R. V. Clarke (Eds.), *Policy and theory in criminal justice: Contributions in honor of Leslie T. Wilkins* (pp. 51–75). Aldershot, England: Avebury.

Farrington, D. P. (1991a). Childhood aggression and adult violence: Early precursors and later life outcomes. In D. J. Pepler & K. H. Rubin (Eds.), *The development and treatment of childhood aggression* (pp. 5–29). Hillsdale, NJ: Lawrence Erlbaum.

Farrington, D. P. (1991b). Antisocial personality from childhood to adulthood. *The Psychologist*, 4, 389–394.

Farrington, D. P. (1992). Criminal career research in the United Kingdom. *British Journal of Criminology*, 32, 521–536.

Farrington, D. P. (1993a). Have any individual, family or neighborhood influences on offending been demonstrated conclusively? In D. P. Farrington, R. J. Sampson, & P.-O. H. Wikström (Eds.), *Integrating individual and ecological aspects of crime* (pp. 7–37). Stockholm: National Council for Crime Prevention.

Farrington, D. P. (1993b). Motivations for conduct disorder and delinquency. *Development and Psychopathology*, 5, 225–241.

Farrington, D. P. (1995a). The development of offending and antisocial behavior from childhood: Key findings from the Cambridge Study in Delinquent Development. *Journal of Child Psychology and Psychiatry*, 36, 929–964.

Farrington, D. P. (1995b). Key issues in the integration of motivational and opportunity-reducing crime prevention strategies. In P.-O. H. Wikström, R. V. Clarke, & J. McCord (Eds.), *Integrating crime prevention strategies: Propensity and opportunity* (pp. 333–357). Stockholm: National Council for Crime Prevention.

Farrington, D. P. (1996a). The explanation and prevention of youthful offending. In J. D. Hawkins (Ed.), *Delinquency and crime: Current theories* (pp. 68–148). Cambridge: Cambridge University Press.

Farrington, D. P. (1996b). *Understanding and preventing youth crime*. York, England: Joseph Rowntree Foundation.

Farrington, D. P. (1997a). Human development and criminal careers. In M. Maguire, R. Morgan, & R. Reiner (Eds.) *The Oxford handbook of criminology* (2nd ed., pp. 361–408). Oxford: Clarendon Press.

Farrington, D. P. (1997b). Key issues in studying the biosocial bases of violence. In A. Raine, P. A. Brennan, D. P. Farrington, & S. A. Mednick (Eds.), *Biosocial bases of violence* (pp. 293–300). New York: Plenum.

Farrington, D. P. (1997c). Early prediction of violent and non-violent youthful offending. *European Journal on Criminal Policy and Research, 5,* 51–66.

Farrington, D. P. (1997d). Evaluating a community crime prevention program. *Evaluation, 3,* 157–173.

Farrington, D. P. (1998). Predictors, causes and correlates of male youth violence. In M. Tonry & M. Moore (Eds.), *Youth violence* (pp. 317–371). Chicago: University of Chicago Press.

Farrington, D. P. (1999). Predicting persistent young offenders. In G. McDowell & J. S. Smith (Eds.), *Juvenile delinquency in the United States and the United Kingdom*. London: Macmillan.

Farrington, D. P., Barnes, G., & Lambert, S. (1996). The concentration of offending in families. *Legal and Criminological Psychology, 1,* 47–63.

Farrington, D. P., Gallagher, B., Morley, L., St. Ledger, R. J., & West, D. J. (1986). Unemployment, school leaving and crime. *British Journal of Criminology, 26,* 335–356.

Farrington, D. P., & Hawkins, J. D. (1991). Predicting participation, early onset, and later persistence in officially recorded offending. *Criminal Behavior and Mental Health, 1,* 1–33.

Farrington, D. P., Lambert, S., & West, D. J. (1998). Criminal careers of two generations of family members in the Cambridge Study in Delinquent Development. *Studies on Crime and Crime Prevention, 7,* 85–106.

Farrington, D. P., & Loeber, R. (1999). Transatlantic replicability of risk factors in the development of delinquency. In P. Cohen, C. Slomkowski, & L. N. Robins (Eds.), *Historical and geographical influences on psychopathology* (pp. 299–329). Mahwah, NJ: Lawrence Erlbaum.

Farrington, D. P., Ohlin, L. E., & Wilson, J. Q. (1986). *Understanding and controlling crime*. New York: Springer-Verlag.

Farrington, D. P., & West, D. J. (1995). Effects of marriage, separation and children on offending by adult males. In J. Hagan (Ed.), *Current perspectives on aging and the life cycle. Vol. 4: Delinquency and disrepute in the life course* (pp. 249–281). Greenwich, CT: JAI.

Farrington, D. P., & Wikström, P.-O. H. (1994). Criminal careers in London and Stockholm: A cross-national comparative study. In E. G. M. Weitekamp & H.-J. Kerner (Eds.), *Cross-national longitudinal research on human development and criminal behavior* (pp. 65–89). Dordrecht, the Netherlands: Kluwer.

Forrester, D., Frenz, S., O'Connell, M., & Pease, K. (1990). *The Kirkholt burglary prevention project: Phase 2*. London: Home Office.

Hawkins, J. D., & Catalano, R. F. (1992). *Communities that care*. San Francisco: Jossey-Bass.

Hawkins, J. D., von Cleve, E., & Catalano, R. F. (1991). Reducing early childhood aggression: Results of a primary prevention program. *Journal of the American Academy of Child and Adolescent Psychiatry, 30*, 208–217.

Hogh, E., & Wolf, P. (1983). Violent crime in a birth cohort: Copenhagen 1953–1977. In K. T. van Dusen & S. A. Mednick (Eds.), *Prospective studies of crime and delinquency* (pp. 249–267). Boston: Kluwer-Nijhoff.

Janson, C.-G. (1981). Project Metropolitan: A longitudinal study of a Stockholm cohort (Sweden). In S. A. Mednick & A. E. Baert (Eds.), *Prospective longitudinal research: An empirical basis for the primary prevention of psychosocial disorders* (pp. 93–99). Oxford: Oxford University Press.

Junger-Tas, J., Terlouw, G.-J., & Klein, M. W. (Eds.). (1994). *Delinquent behavior among young people in the Western world*. Amsterdam: Kugler.

Loeber, R., & Farrington, D. P. (1997). Strategies and yields of longitudinal studies on antisocial behavior. In D. M. Stoff, J. Breiling, & J. D. Maser (Eds.), *Handbook of antisocial behavior* (pp. 125–139). New York: John Wiley.

Loeber, R., Farrington, D. P., Stouthamer-Loeber, M., Moffitt, T. E., & Caspi, A. (1998). The development of male offending: Key findings from the first decade of the Pittsburgh Youth Study. *Studies on Crime and Crime Prevention, 7*, 141–171.

Loeber, R., Farrington, D. P., Stouthamer-Loeber, M., & van Kammen, W. B. (1998). *Antisocial behavior and mental health problems: Explanatory factors in childhood and adolescence*. Mahwah, NJ: Lawrence Erlbaum.

Mayhew, P., & van Dijk, J. J. M. (1997). *Criminal victimization in eleven industrialized countries*. The Hague, the Netherlands: Ministry of Justice.

Miller, T. R., Cohen, M. A., & Wiersema, B. (1996). *Victim costs and consequences: A new look*. Washington, DC: U.S. National Institute of Justice.

Moffitt, T. E. (1993). Adolescence-limited and life-course-persistent antisocial behavior: A developmental taxonomy. *Psychological Review, 100*, 674–701.

Olds, D. L., Eckenrode, J., Henderson, C. R., Kitzman, H., Powers, J., Cole, R., Sidora, K., Morris, P., Pettitt, L. M., & Luckey, D. (1997). Long-term effects of home visitation on maternal life course and child abuse and neglect: Fifteen-year follow-up of a randomized trial. *Journal of the American Medical Association, 278*, 637–643.

Patterson, G. R., Reid, J. B., & Dishion, T. J. (1992). *Antisocial boys*. Eugene, OR: Castalia.

Pulkkinen, L. (1988). Delinquent development: Theoretical and empirical considerations. In M. Rutter (Ed.), *Studies of psychosocial risk* (pp. 184–199). Cambridge: Cambridge University Press.

Reiss, A. J., & Farrington, D. P. (1991). Advancing knowledge about co-offending: Results from a prospective longitudinal survey of London males. *Journal of Criminal Law and Criminology, 82*, 360–395.

Ross, R. R. (1995). The reasoning and rehabilitation program for high-risk probationers and prisoners. In R. R. Ross, D. H. Antonowicz, & G. K. Dhaliwal (Eds.), *Going straight: Effective delinquency prevention and offender rehabilitation* (pp. 195–222). Ottawa: Air Training and Publications.

Schweinhart, L. J., Barnes, H. V., & Weikart, D. P. (1993). *Significant benefits*. Ypsilanti, MI: High/Scope.

Thornberry, T. P., Huizinga, D., & Loeber, R. (1995). The prevention of serious delinquency and violence: Implications from the Program of Research on the Causes and Correlates of Delinquency. In J. C. Howell, B. Krisberg, J. D. Hawkins, & J. J. Wilson (Eds.), *Sourcebook on serious, violent and chronic juvenile offenders* (pp. 213–237). Thousand Oaks, CA: Sage.

Tobler, N. S. (1986). Meta-analysis of 143 drug treatment programs: Quantitative outcome results of program participants compared to a control or comparison group. *Journal of Drug Issues, 16,* 537–567.

Tonry, M., & Farrington, D. P. (1995). Strategic approaches to crime prevention. In M. Tonry & D. P. Farrington (Eds.), *Building a safer society: Strategic approaches to crime prevention* (pp. 1–20). Chicago: University of Chicago Press.

Tonry, M., Ohlin, L. E., & Farrington, D. P. (1991). *Human development and criminal behavior.* New York: Springer-Verlag.

Tremblay, R. E., Pagani-Kurtz, L., Vitaro, F., Masse, L. C., & Pihl, R. O. (1995). A bimodal preventive intervention for disruptive kindergarten boys: Its impact through mid-adolescence. *Journal of Consulting and Clinical Psychology, 63,* 560–568.

Wasserman, G. A., & Miller, L. S. (1998). The prevention of serious and violent juvenile offending. In R. Loeber & D. P. Farrington (Eds.), *Serious and violent juvenile offenders: Risk factors and successful interventions* (pp. 197–247). Thousand Oaks, CA: Sage.

Weitekamp, E.G.M., & Kerner, H.-J. (Eds.). (1994). *Cross-national longitudinal research on human development and criminal behavior.* Dordrecht, the Netherlands: Kluwer.

Wikström, P.-O. H. (1990). Age and crime in a Stockholm cohort. *Journal of Quantitative Criminology, 6,* 61–84.

14

The underclass

Charles Murray

THE CONCEPT OF 'UNDERCLASS'

'Underclass' is an ugly word, with its whiff of Marx and the lumpenproletariat. Perhaps because it is ugly, 'underclass' as used in Britain tends to be sanitized, a sort of synonym for people who are not just poor, but especially poor. So let us get it straight from the outset: the 'underclass' does not refer to degree of poverty, but to a type of poverty.

It is not a new concept. I grew up knowing what the underclass was; we just didn't call it that in those days. In the small Iowa town where I lived, I was taught by my middle-class parents that there were two kinds of poor people. One class of poor people was never even called 'poor'. I came to understand that they simply lived with low incomes, as my own parents had done when they were young. Then there was another set of poor people, just a handful of them. These poor people didn't lack just money. They were defined by their behaviour. Their homes were littered and unkempt. The men in the family were unable to hold a job for more than a few weeks at a time. Drunkenness was common. The children grew up ill-schooled and ill-behaved and contributed a disproportionate share of the local juvenile delinquents.

British observers of the nineteenth century knew these people. To Henry Mayhew, whose articles in the *Morning Chronicle* in 1850 drew the Victorians' attention to poverty, they were the 'dishonest poor', a member of which was

> distinguished from the civilised man by his repugnance to regular and continuous labour – by his want of providence in laying up a store for the future – by his inability to perceive consequences ever so slightly removed from immediate apprehensions – by his passion for stupefying herbs and roots and, when possible, for intoxicating fermented liquors. …

From *The Emerging Underclass*, pp. 1–23; 33–5. (London: Institute of Economic Affairs, 1990.)

Other popular labels were 'undeserving', 'unrespectable', 'depraved', 'debased', 'disreputable' or 'feckless' poor.

As Britain entered the 1960s a century later, this distinction between honest and dishonest poor people had been softened. The second kind of poor person was no longer 'undeserving'; rather, he was the product of a 'culture of poverty'. But intellectuals as well as the man in the street continued to accept that poor people were not all alike. Most were doing their best under difficult circumstances; a small number were pretty much as Mayhew had described them. Then came the intellectual reformation that swept both the United States and Britain at about the same time, in the mid-1960s, and with it came a new way of looking at the poor. Henceforth, the poor were to be homogenized. The only difference between poor people and everyone else, we were told, was that the poor had less money. More importantly, the poor were all alike. There was no such thing as the ne'er-do-well poor person – he was the figment of the prejudices of a parochial middle class. Poor people, *all* poor people, were equally victims, and would be equally successful if only society gave them a fair shake.

The difference between the US and the UK

The difference between the United States and Britain was that the United States reached the future first. During the last half of the 1960s and throughout the 1970s something strange and frightening was happening among poor people in the United States. Poor communities that had consisted mostly of hard-working folks began deteriorating, sometimes falling apart altogether. Drugs, crime, illegitimacy, homelessness, drop-out from the job market, drop-out from school, casual violence – all the measures that were available to the social scientists showed large increases, focused in poor communities. As the 1980s began, the growing population of 'the other kind of poor people' could no longer be ignored, and a label for them came into use. In the US, we began to call them the underclass.

For a time, the intellectual conventional wisdom continued to hold that 'underclass' was just another pejorative attempt to label the poor. But the label had come into use because there was no longer any denying reality. What had once been a small fraction of the American poor had become a sizeable and worrisome population. An underclass existed, and none of the ordinary kinds of social policy solutions seemed able to stop its growth. One by one, the American social scientists who had initially rejected the concept of an underclass fell silent, then began to use it themselves.

By and large, British intellectuals still disdain the term. In 1987, the social historian John Macnicol summed up the prevailing view in the *Journal of Social Policy*, [vol. 16, no. 3, pp. 293–318] writing dismissively that underclass was nothing more than a refuted concept periodically resurrected by Conservatives 'who wish to constrain the redistributive potential of state welfare'. But there are beginning to be breaks in the ranks. Frank Field, the prominent Labour MP, has just published a book with 'underclass' in its subtitle. The newspapers, watching the United States and seeing shadows of its problems in Britain, have begun to use the term. As someone who has been analysing this phenomenon in the United States, I arrived in Britain earlier this year, a visitor from a plague area come to see whether the disease is spreading.

With all the reservations that a stranger must feel in passing judgement on an unfamiliar country, I will jump directly to the conclusion: Britain does have an underclass, still largely out of sight and still smaller than the one in the United States. But it is growing rapidly. Within the next decade, it will probably become as large (proportionately) as the United States' underclass. It could easily become larger.

I am not talking here about an unemployment problem that can be solved by more jobs, nor about a poverty problem that can be solved by higher benefits. Britain has a growing population of working-aged healthy people who live in a different world from other Britons, who are raising their children to live in it, and whose values are now contaminating the life of entire neighbourhoods – which is one of the most insidious aspects of the phenomenon, for neighbours who don't share those values cannot isolate themselves.

There are many ways to identify an underclass. I will concentrate on three phenomena that have turned out to be early-warning signals in the United States: illegitimacy, violent crime, and drop-out from the labour force. In each case I will be using the simplest of data, collected and published by Britain's Government Statistical Service. I begin with illegitimacy, which in my view is the best predictor of an underclass in the making.

ILLEGITIMACY AND THE UNDERCLASS

It is a proposition that angers many people. Why should it be a 'problem' that a woman has a child without a husband? Why isn't a single woman perfectly capable of raising a healthy, happy child, if only the state will provide a decent level of support so that she may do so? Why is raising a child without having married any more of a problem than raising a child after a divorce? The very word 'illegitimate' is intellectually illegitimate. Using it in a gathering of academics these days is a *faux pas*, causing pained silence.

I nonetheless focus on illegitimacy rather than on the more general phenomenon of one-parent families because, in a world where all social trends are ambiguous, illegitimacy is less ambiguous than other forms of single parenthood. It is a matter of degree. Of course some unmarried mothers are excellent mothers and some unmarried fathers are excellent fathers. Of course some divorced parents disappear from the children's lives altogether and some divorces have more destructive effects on the children than a failure to marry would have had. Being without two parents is generally worse for the child than having two parents, no matter how it happens. But illegitimacy is the purest form of being without two parents – legally, the child is without a father from day one; he is often without one practically as well. Further, illegitimacy bespeaks an attitude on the part of one or both parents that getting married is not an essential part of siring or giving birth to a child; this in itself distinguishes their mindset from that of people who do feel strongly that getting married is essential.

Call it what you will, illegitimacy has been sky-rocketing since 1979. I use 'sky-rocketing' advisedly. […] From the end of the Second World War until 1960, Britain enjoyed a very low and even slightly declining illegitimacy ratio. From 1960 until 1978 the ratio increased, but remained modest by international standards – as late as 1979, Britain's illegitimacy ratio was only 10.6 per cent, one of the lowest rates in the industrialized West. Then, suddenly, during a period when fertility was steady, the illegitimacy ratio began to rise very rapidly – to 14.1 per cent by 1982, 18.9 per cent by 1985, and finally to 25.6 per cent by 1988. If present trends continue, Britain will pass the United States in this unhappy statistic in 1990.

The sharp rise is only half of the story. The other and equally important half is that illegitimate births are not scattered evenly among the British population. In this, press reports can be misleading. There is much publicity about the member of the royal family who has a child without a husband, or the socially prominent young career woman who deliberately decides to have a baby on her own, but these are comparatively rare events. The increase in illegitimate births is strikingly concentrated among the lowest social class.

Municipal districts

This is especially easy to document in Britain, where one may fit together the Government Statistical Service's birth data on municipal districts with the detailed socioeconomic data from the general census. When one does so for 169 metropolitan districts and boroughs in England and Wales with data from both sources, the relationship between social class and illegitimacy is so obvious that the statistical tests become superfluous. Municipal districts with high concentrations of household heads in Class I (professional persons, by the classification used for many years by the Government Statistical Service) have illegitimacy ratios in the low teens (Wokingham was lowest as of 1987, with only nine of every 100 children born illegitimate) while municipalities like Nottingham and Southwark, with populations most heavily weighted with Class V household heads (unskilled labourers), have illegitimacy ratios of more than 40 per cent (the highest in 1987 was Lambeth, with 46 per cent).

The statistical tests confirm this relationship. The larger the proportion of people who work at unskilled jobs and the larger the proportion who are out of the labour force, the higher the illegitimacy ratio, in a quite specific and regular numeric relationship. The strength of the relationship may be illustrated this way: suppose you were limited to two items of information about a community – the percentage of people in Class V and the percentage of people who are 'economically inactive'. With just these two measures, you could predict the illegitimacy ratio, usually within just three percentage points of the true number. As a statistician might summarize it, these two measures of economic status 'explain 51 per cent of the variance' – an extremely strong relationship by the standards of the social sciences.

In short, the notion that illegitimate births are a general phenomenon, that young career women and girls from middle-class homes are doing it just as much as anyone else, is flatly at odds with the facts. There has been a *proportional* increase in illegitimate births among all communities, but the *prevalence* of illegitimate births is drastically higher among the lower-class communities than among the upper-class ones.

Neighbourhoods

The data I have just described are based on municipal districts. The picture gets worse when we move down to the level of the neighbourhood, though precise numbers are hard to come by. The proportion of illegitimate children in a specific poor neighbourhood can be in the vicinity not of 25 per cent, nor even of 40 per cent, but a hefty majority. And in this concentration of illegitimate births lies a generational catastrophe. Illegitimacy produces an underclass for one compelling practical reason having nothing to do with morality or the sanctity of marriage. Namely: communities need families. Communities need fathers.

This is not an argument that many intellectuals in Britain are ready to accept. I found that discussing the issue was like being in a time warp, hearing in 1989 the same rationalizations about illegitimacy that American experts used in the 1970s and early 1980s. [...]

'Mainly a black problem'?

'It's mainly a black problem'. I heard this everywhere, from political clubs in Westminster to some quite sophisticated demographers in the statistical research offices. The statement is correct in this one, very limited sense: blacks born in the West Indies have much higher illegitimacy ratios – about 48 per cent of live births in the latest numbers – than all whites. But blacks constitute such a tiny proportion of the British population that their contribution to the overall illegitimacy ratio is minuscule. If there had been no blacks whatsoever in Britain (and I am including all blacks in Britain in this statement, not just those who were born abroad), the overall British illegitimacy ratio in 1988 would have dropped by about one percentage point, from 25 per cent to about 24 per cent. Blacks are not causing Britain's illegitimacy problem.

In passing, it is worth adding that the overall effect of ethnic minorities living in the UK is to *reduce* the size of the illegitimacy ratio. The Chinese, Indians, Pakistanis, Arabs and East Africans in Britain have illegitimacy ratios that are tiny compared with those of British whites.

'It's not as bad as it looks'

In the United States, the line used to be that blacks have extended families, with uncles and grandfathers compensating for the lack of a father. In Britain, the counterpart to this cheery optimism is that an increasing number of illegitimate births are jointly registered and that an increasing number of such children are born to people who live together at the time of birth. Both joint registration and living together are quickly called evidence of 'a stable relationship'.

The statements about joint registration and living together are factually correct. Of the 158,500 illegitimate births in England and Wales in 1987, 69 per cent were jointly registered. Of those who jointly registered the birth, 70 per cent gave the same address, suggesting some kind of continuing relationship. Both of these figures have increased – in 1961, for example, only 38 per cent of illegitimate births were jointly registered, suggesting that the nature of illegitimacy in the United Kingdom has changed dramatically.

You may make what you wish of such figures. In the United States, we have stopped talking blithely about the 'extended family' in black culture that would make everything okay. It hasn't. And as the years go on, the extended family argument becomes a cruel joke – for without marriage, grandfathers and uncles too become scarce. In Britain, is it justified to assume that jointly registering a birth, or living together at the time of the birth, means a relationship that is just as stable (or nearly as stable) as a marriage? I pose it as a question because I don't have the empirical answer. But neither did any of the people who kept repeating the joint-registration and living-together numbers so optimistically.

If we can be reasonably confident that the children of never-married women do considerably worse than their peers, it remains to explain why. Progress has been slow. Until recently in the United States, scholars were reluctant to concede that illegitimacy is a legitimate variable for study. Even as that situation changes, they remain slow to leave behind their equations and go out to talk with people who are trying to raise their children in neighbourhoods with high illegitimacy rates. This is how I make sense of the combination of quantitative studies, ethnographic studies and talking-to-folks journalism that bear on the question of illegitimacy, pulling in a few observations from my conversations in Britain.

Clichés about role models are true

It turns out that the clichés about role models are true. Children grow up making sense of the world around them in terms of their own experience. Little boys don't naturally grow up to be responsible fathers and husbands. They don't naturally grow up knowing how to get up every morning at the same time and go to work. They don't naturally grow up thinking that work is not just a way to make money, but a way to hold one's head high in the world. And most emphatically of all, little boys do not reach adolescence naturally wanting to refrain from sex, just as little girls don't become adolescents naturally wanting to refrain from having babies. In all these ways and many more, boys and girls grow into responsible parents and neighbours and workers because they are imitating the adults around them.

That's why single-parenthood is a problem for communities, and that's why illegitimacy is the most worrisome aspect of single-parenthood. Children tend to behave like the adults around them. A child with a mother and no father, living in a neighbourhood of mothers with no fathers, judges by what he sees. You can send in social workers and school teachers and clergy to tell a young male that when he grows up he should be a good father to his children, but he doesn't know what that means unless he's seen it. Fifteen years ago, there was hardly a poor neighbourhood in urban Britain where children did not still see plentiful examples of good fathers around them. Today, the balance has already shifted in many poor neighbourhoods. In a few years, the situation will be much worse, for this is a problem that nurtures itself.

Child-rearing in single-parent communities

Hardly any of this gets into the public dialogue. In the standard newspaper or television story on single-parenthood, the reporter tracks down a struggling single parent and reports her efforts to raise her children under difficult circumstances, ending with an indictment of a stingy social system that doesn't give her enough to get along. The ignored story is what it's like for the two-parent families trying to raise their children in neighbourhoods where they now represent the exception, not the rule. Some of the problems may seem trivial but must be painfully poignant to anyone who is a parent. Take, for example, the story told me by a father who lives in such a neighbourhood in Birkenhead, near Liverpool, about the time he went to his little girl's Christmas play at school. He was the only father there – hardly any of the other children had fathers – and his daughter, embarrassed because she was different, asked him not to come to the school any more.

The lack of fathers is also associated with a level of physical unruliness that makes life difficult. The same Birkenhead father and his wife raised their first daughter as they were raised, to be polite and considerate – and she suffered for it. Put simply, her schoolmates weren't being raised to be polite and considerate – they weren't being 'raised' at all in some respects. We have only a small body of systematic research on child-rearing practices in contemporary low-income, single-parent communities; it's one of those unfashionable topics. But the unsystematic reports I heard in towns like Birkenhead and council estates like Easterhouse in Glasgow are consistent with the reports from inner-city Washington and New York: in communities without fathers, the kids tend to run wild. The fewer the fathers, the greater the tendency. 'Run wild' can mean such simple things as young children having no set bedtime. It can mean their being left alone in the house at night while mummy goes out. It can mean an 18-month-old toddler allowed to play in the street. And, as in the case of the couple trying to raise their children as they had been raised, it can mean children who are inordinately physical and aggressive in their relationships with other children. With their second child, the Birkenhead parents eased up on their requirements for civil behaviour, realizing that their children had to be able to defend themselves against threats that the parents hadn't faced when they were children. The third child is still an infant, and the mother has made a conscious decision. 'I won't knock the aggression out of her,' she said to me. Then she paused, and added angrily, 'It's *wrong* to have to decide that.'

The key to an underclass

I can hear the howls of objection already – lots of families raise children who have those kinds of problems, not just poor single parents. Of course. But this is why it is important to talk to parents who have lived in both kinds of communities. Ask them whether there is any difference in child-raising between a neighbourhood composed mostly of married couples and a neighbourhood composed mostly of single mothers. In Britain as in the United States – conduct the inquiries yourself – the overwhelming response is that the difference is large and palpable. The key to an underclass is not the individual instance but a situation in which a very large proportion of an entire community lacks fathers, and this is far more common in poor communities than in rich ones.

CRIME AND THE UNDERCLASS

Crime is the next place to look for an underclass, for several reasons. First and most obviously, the habitual criminal is the classic member of an underclass. He lives off mainstream society without participating in it. But habitual criminals are only part of the problem. Once again, the key issue in thinking about an underclass is how the community functions, and crime can devastate a community in two especially important ways. To the extent that the members of a community are victimized by crime, the community tends to become fragmented. To the extent that many people in a community engage in crime as a matter of course, all sorts of the socializing norms of the community change, from the kind of men that the younger boys choose as heroes to the standards of morality in general.

Consider first the official crime figures, reported annually for England by the Home Office. As in the case of illegitimacy, I took for granted before I began this exploration that England had much lower crime rates than the United States. It therefore came as a shock to discover that England and Wales (which I will subsequently refer to as England) have a combined property crime rate apparently as high, and probably higher, than that of the United States. (I did not compare rates with Scotland and Northern Ireland, which are reported separately.) I say 'apparently' because Britain and the United States use somewhat different definitions of property crime. But burglaries, which are similarly defined in both countries, provide an example. In 1988, England had 1,623 reported burglaries per 100,000 population compared with 1,309 in the US. Adjusting for the transatlantic differences in definitions, England also appears to have had higher rates of motor vehicle theft than the United States. The rates for other kind of theft seem to have been roughly the same. I wasn't the only one who was surprised at these comparisons. I found that if you want to attract startled and incredulous attention in England, mention casually that England has a higher property crime rate than that notorious crime centre of the western world, the United States. No one will believe you.

Violent crime

The understandable reason why they don't believe you is that *violent* crime in England remains much lower than violent crime in the United States, and it is violent crime that engenders most anxiety and anger. In this regard, Britain still lags far behind the US. This is most conspicuously true for the most violent of all crimes, homicide. In all of 1988, England and Wales recorded just 624 homicides. The United States averaged that many every 11 days – 20,675 for the year.

That's the good news. The bad news is that the violent crime rate in England and Wales has been rising very rapidly. […]

The size of the increase isn't as bad as it first looks, because England began with such a small initial rate (it's easy to double your money if you start with only a few pence – of which, more in a moment). Still, the rise is steep, and it became much steeper in about 1968. Compare the gradual increase from 1955 to 1968 with what happened subsequently. By 1988, England had 314 violent crimes reported per 100,000 people. The really bad news is that you have been experiencing this increase despite demographic trends that should have been working to your advantage. This point is important enough to explain at greater length.

The most frequent offenders, the ones who puff up the violent crime statistics, are males in the second half of their teens. As males get older, they tend to become more civilized. In both England and the United States, the number of males in this troublesome age group increased throughout the 1970s, and this fact was widely used as an explanation for increasing crime. But since the early 1980s, the size of the young male cohort has been decreasing in both countries. In the United Kingdom, for example, the number of males aged 15 to 19 hit its peak in 1982 and has subsequently decreased both as a percentage of the population and in raw numbers (by a little more than 11 per cent in both cases). Ergo, the violent crime rate 'should' have decreased as well. But it didn't. Despite the reduction in the number of males in the highest-offending age group after 1982, the violent crime rate in England from 1982 to 1988 rose by 43 per cent.

Here I must stop and briefly acknowledge a few of the many ways in which people will object that the official crime rates don't mean anything – but only briefly, because this way lies a statistical abyss.

The significance of official crime rates

One common objection is that the increase in the crime rate reflects economic growth (because there are more things to steal, especially cars and the things in them) rather than any real change in criminal behaviour. If so, one has to ask why England enjoyed a steady decline in crime through the last half of the nineteenth century, when economic growth was explosive. But, to avoid argument, let us acknowledge that economic growth does make interpreting the changes in the property crime rate tricky, and focus instead on violent crime, which is not so directly facilitated by economic growth.

Another common objection is that the increase in crime is a mirage. One version of this is that crime just seems to be higher because more crimes are being reported to the police than before (because of greater access to telephones, for example, or because of the greater prevalence of insurance). The brief answer here is that it works both ways. Rape and sexual assault are more likely to be reported now, because of changes in public attitudes and judicial procedures regarding those crimes. An anonymous purse-snatch is less likely to be reported, because the victim doesn't think it will do any good. The aggregate effect of a high crime rate can be to reduce reporting, and this is most true of poor neighbourhoods where attitudes toward the police are ambiguous.

The most outrageously spurious version of the 'crime isn't really getting worse' argument uses *rate* of increase rather than the *magnitude* of increase to make the case. The best example in Britain is the argument that public concern about muggings in the early 1970s was simply an effort to scapegoat young blacks, and resulted in a 'moral panic'. The sociologist Stuart Hall and his colleagues made this case at some length in a book entitled *Policing the Crisis* [London: Macmillan, 1978] in which, among other things, they blithely argued that because the rate of increase in violent crimes was decreasing, the public's concern was unwarranted. It is the familiar problem of low baselines. From 1950 to 1958, violent crime in England rose by 88 per cent (the crime rate began at 14 crimes per 100,000 persons and rose by 13). From 1980 to 1988 violent crime in England rose by only 60 per cent (it began at 196 crimes per 100,000 persons and rose by 118). In other words, by the logic of Hall and his colleagues, things are getting much better, because the rate of increase in the 1980s has been lower than it was during the comparable period of the 1950s. [...]

The intellectual conventional wisdom

The denial by intellectuals that crime really has been getting worse spills over into denial that poor communities are more violent places than affluent communities. To the people who live in poor communities, this doesn't make much sense. One man in a poor, high-crime community told me about his experience in an open university where he had decided to try to improve himself. He took a sociology course about poverty. The professor kept talking about this 'nice little world that the poor live in', the man remembered. The professor scoffed at the reactionary myth that poor communities are violent places. To the man who lived in such a community, it was 'bloody drivel'. A few weeks later, a class exercise called for the students to canvass a poor neighbourhood. The professor went along, but apparently he, too, suspected that some of his pronouncements were bloody drivel – he cautiously stayed in his car and declined to knock on doors himself. And that raises the most interesting question regarding the view that crime has not risen, or that crime is not especially a problem in lower-class communities:

do any of the people who hold this view actually *believe* it, to the extent that they take no more precautions walking in a slum neighbourhood than they do in a middle-class suburb?

These comments will not still the battle over the numbers. But I will venture this prediction, once again drawn from the American experience. After a few more years, quietly and without anyone having to admit he had been wrong, the intellectual conventional wisdom in Britain as in the United States will undergo a gradual transition. After all the statistical artifacts are taken into account and argued over, it will be decided that England is indeed becoming a more danger-ous place in which to live: that this unhappy process is not occurring every-where, but disproportionately in particular types of neighbourhoods; and that those neighbourhoods turn out to be the ones in which an underclass is taking over. Reality will once again force theory to its knees.

UNEMPLOYMENT AND THE UNDERCLASS

If illegitimate births are the leading indicator of an underclass and violent crime a proxy measure of its development, the definitive proof that an underclass has arrived is that large numbers of young, healthy, low-income males choose not to take jobs. (The young idle rich are a separate problem.) The decrease in labour force participation is the most elusive of the trends in the growth of the British underclass.

The main barrier to understanding what's going on is the high unemploy-ment of the 1980s. The official statistics distinguish between 'unemployed' and 'economically inactive', but Britain's unemployment figures (like those in the US) include an unknown but probably considerable number of people who manage to qualify for benefit even if in reality very few job opportunities would tempt them to work.

On the other side of the ledger, over a prolonged period of high unemployment the 'economically inactive' category includes men who would like to work but have given up. To make matters still more complicated, there is the 'black economy' to consider, in which people who are listed as 'economically inactive' are really working for cash, not reporting their income to the authorities. So we are looking through a glass darkly, and I have more questions than answers.

Economic inactivity and social class

The simple relationship of economic inactivity to social class is strong, just as it was for illegitimacy. According to the 1981 census data, the municipal districts with high proportions of household heads who are in Class V (unskilled labour) also tend to have the highest levels of 'economically inactive' persons of working age (statistically, the proportion of Class V households explains more than a third of the variance when inactivity because of retirement is taken into account).

This is another way of saying that you will find many more working-aged people who are neither working nor looking for work in the slums than in the suburbs. Some of these persons are undoubtedly discouraged workers, but two questions need to be asked and answered with far more data than are currently available – specifically, questions about lower-class young males.

Lower-class young males

First, after taking into account Britain's unemployment problems when the 1981 census was taken, were the levels of economic inactivity among young males consistent with the behaviour of their older brothers and fathers during earlier periods? Or were they dropping out more quickly and often than earlier cohorts of young men?

Second, Britain has for the past few years been conducting a natural experiment, with an economic boom in the south and high unemployment in the north. If lack of jobs is the problem, then presumably economic inactivity among lower-class healthy young males in the south has plummeted to insignificant levels. Has it?

The theme that I heard from a variety of people in Birkenhead and Easterhouse was that the youths who came of age in the late 1970s are in danger of being a lost generation. All of them did indeed ascribe the problem to the surge in unemployment at the end of the 1970s. 'They came out of school at the wrong time,' as one older resident of Easterhouse put it, and have never in their lives held a real job. They are now in their late twenties. As economic times improve, they are competing for the same entry-level jobs as people 10 years younger, and employers prefer to hire the youngsters. But it's more complicated than that, he added. 'They've lost the picture of what they're going to be doing.' When he was growing up, he could see himself in his father's job. Not these young men.

The generation gap

This generation gap was portrayed to me as being only a few years wide. A man from Birkenhead in his early thirties who had worked steadily from the time he left school until 1979, when he lost his job as an assembly-line worker, recalled how the humiliation and desperation to work remained even as his unemployment stretched from months into years. He – and the others in their thirties and forties and fifties – were the ones showing up at six in the morning when jobs were advertised. They were the ones who sought jobs even if they paid less than the benefit rate.

'The only income I wanted was enough to be free of the bloody benefit system,' he said. 'It was like a rope around my neck.' The phrase for being on benefit that some of them used, 'on the suck', says a great deal about how little they like their situation.

This attitude is no small asset to Britain. In some inner cities of the US, the slang for robbing someone is 'getting paid'. Compare that inversion of values with the values implied by 'on the suck'. Britain in 1989 has resources that make predicting the course of the underclass on the basis of the US experience very dicey.

But the same men who talk this way often have little in common with their sons and younger brothers. Talking to the boys in their late teens and early twenties about jobs, I heard nothing about the importance of work as a source of self-respect and no talk of just wanting enough income to be free of the benefit system. To make a decent living, a youth of 21 explained to me, you need £200 a week – after taxes. He would accept less if it was all he could get. But he conveyed clearly that he would feel exploited. As for the Government's employment training scheme, YTS, that's 'slave labour'. Why, another young man asked me indignantly, should he and his friends be deprived of their right to a full unemployment benefit just because they haven't reached 18 yet? It sounded strange to my ears – a 'right' to unemployment benefit for a school-age minor who's never held a job. But there is no question in any of their minds that that's exactly what the unemployment benefit is: a right, in every sense of the word. The boys did not mention what they considered to be their part of the bargain.

'I was brought up thinking work is something you are morally obliged to do,' as one older man put it. With the younger generation, he said, 'that culture isn't going to be there at all.' And there are anecdotes to go with these observations. For example, the contractors carrying out the extensive housing refurbishment now going on at Easterhouse are obliged to hire local youths for unskilled labour as part of a work-experience scheme. Thirty Easterhouse young men applied for a recent set of openings. Thirteen were accepted. Ten actually came to work the first day. By the end of the first week, only one was still showing up.

A generation gap by class

My hypothesis – the evidence is too fragmentary to call it more than that – is that Britain is experiencing a generation gap by class. Well-educated young people from affluent homes are working in larger proportions and working longer hours than ever. The attitudes and behaviour of the middle-aged working class haven't changed much. The change in stance toward the labour force is concentrated among lower-class young men in their teens and twenties. It is not a huge change. I am not suggesting that a third or a quarter or even a fifth of lower-class young people are indifferent to work. An underclass doesn't have to be huge to become a problem.

That problem is remarkably difficult to fix. It seems simple – just make decent-paying jobs available. But it doesn't work that way. In the States, we've tried nearly everything – training programmes, guaranteed jobs, special 'socialization' programmes that taught not only job skills but also 'work-readiness skills' such as getting to work on time, 'buddy' systems whereby an experienced older man tried to ease the trainee into the world of work. The results of these strategies, carefully evaluated against control groups, have consistently showed little effect at best, no effect most commonly, and occasionally negative effects.

If this seems too pessimistic for British youth, the Government or some private foundation may easily try this experiment: go down to the Bull Ring near Waterloo Bridge where one of London's largest cardboard cities is located. Pass over the young men who are alcoholics or drug addicts or mentally disturbed, selecting only those who seem clear-headed (there are many). Then offer them jobs at a generous wage for unskilled labour and see what happens. Add in a training component if you wish. Or, if you sympathize with their lack of interest in unskilled jobs, offer them more extensive training that would qualify them for skilled jobs. Carry out your promises to them, spend as much as you wish, and measure the results after 2 years against the experience of similar youths who received no such help. I am betting that you, too, will find 'no effect'. It is an irretrievable disaster for young men to grow up without being socialized into the world of work.

Work is at the centre of life

The reason why it is a disaster is not that these young men cause upright taxpayers to spend too much money supporting them. That is a nuisance. The disaster is to the young men themselves and the communities in which they live. Looking around the inner cities of the United States, a view which has been eloquently voiced in the past by people as disparate as Thomas Carlyle and Karl Marx seems increasingly validated by events: work is at the centre of life. By remaining out of the work force during the crucial formative years, young men aren't just losing a few years of job experience. They are missing out on the time in which they need to have been acquiring the skills and the networks of friends and experiences that enable them to establish a place for themselves – not only in the workplace, but a vantage point from which they can make sense of themselves and their lives.

Furthermore, when large numbers of young men don't work, the communities around them break down, just as they break down when large numbers of young unmarried women have babies. The two phenomena are intimately related. Just as work is more important than merely making a living, getting married and raising a family are more than a way to pass the time. Supporting a family is a central means for a man to prove to himself that he is a 'mensch'. Men who do not support families find other ways to prove that they are men, which tend to take various destructive forms. As many have commented through the centuries, young males are essentially barbarians for whom marriage – meaning not just the wedding vows, but the act of taking responsibility for a wife and children – is an indispensable civilizing force. Young men who don't work don't make good marriage material. Often they don't get married at all; when they do, they haven't the ability to fill their traditional role. In either case, too many of them remain barbarians.

[...]

WHAT CAN BRITAIN LEARN FROM THE AMERICAN EXPERIENCE?

Britain is not the United States, and the most certain of predictions is that the British experience will play out differently from the US experience. At the close of this brief tour of several huge topics, I will be the first to acknowledge that I have skipped over complications and nuances and certainly missed all sorts of special British conditions of which I am ignorant. Still, so much has been the same so far. In both countries, the same humane impulses and the same intellectual fashions drove the reforms in social policy. The attempts to explain away the consequences have been similar, with British intellectuals in the 1980s saying the same things that American intellectuals were saying in the 1970s about how the problems aren't really as bad as they seem.

So if the United States has had so much more experience with a growing underclass, what can Britain learn from it? The sad answer is – not much. The central truth that the politicians in the United States are unwilling to face is our powerlessness to deal with an underclass once it exists. No matter how much money we spend on our cleverest social interventions, we don't know how to turn around the lives of teenagers who have grown up in an underclass culture. Providing educational opportunities or job opportunities doesn't do it. Training programmes don't reach the people who need them most. We don't know how to make up for the lack of good parents – day-care doesn't do it, foster homes don't work very well. Most of all, we don't know how to make up for the lack of a community that rewards responsibility and stigmatizes irresponsibility.

Let me emphasize the words: *we do not know how.* It's not money we lack, but the capability to social-engineer our way out of this situation. Unfortunately, the delusions persist that our social engineering simply hasn't been clever enough, and that we must strive to become more clever.

Authentic self-government is the key

The alternative I advocate is to have the central government stop trying to be clever and instead get out of the way, giving poor communities (and affluent communities, too) a massive dose of self-government, with vastly greater responsibility for the operation of the institutions that affect their lives – including the criminal justice, educational, housing and benefit systems in their localities. My premise is that it is unnatural for a neighbourhood to tolerate high levels of crime or illegitimacy or voluntary idleness among its youth: that, given the chance, poor communities as well as rich ones will run affairs so that such things happen infrequently. And when communities with different values run their affairs differently, I want to make it as easy as possible for people who share values to live together. If people in one neighbourhood think marriage is an outmoded institution, fine; let them run their neighbourhood as they see fit. But make it easy for the couple who thinks otherwise to move into a neighbourhood where two-parent families are valued. There are many ways that current levels of expenditure for public systems could be sustained (if that is thought to be necessary) but control over them decentralized. Money isn't the key. Authentic self-government is.

But this is a radical solution, and the explanation of why it might work took me 300 pages the last time I tried. In any case, no one in either the United States or Britain is seriously contemplating such steps. That leaves both countries with similar arsenals of social programmes which don't work very well, and the prospect of an underclass in both countries that not only continues but grows.

Oddly, this does not necessarily mean that the pressure for major reforms will increase. It is fairly easy to propitiate the consciences of the well-off and pacify rebellion among the poor with a combination of benefits and social programmes that at least employ large numbers of social service professionals. Such is the strategy that the United States has willy-nilly adopted. Even if the underclass is out there and still growing, it needn't bother the rest of us too much as long as it stays in its own part of town. Everybody's happy – or at least not so unhappy that more action has to be taken.

The bleak message

So, Britain, that's the bleak message. Not only do you have an underclass, not only is it growing, but, judging from the American experience, there's not much in either the Conservative or Labour agendas that has a chance of doing anything about it. A few years ago I wrote for an American audience that the real contest about social policy is not between people who want to cut budgets and people who want to help. Watching Britain replay our history, I can do no better than repeat the same conclusion. When meaningful reforms finally do occur, they will happen not because stingy people have won, but because generous people have stopped kidding themselves.

15

Relative deprivation

John Lea and Jock Young

[…]

Discontent is a product of *relative*, not *absolute*, deprivation. […] Sheer poverty, for example, does not necessarily lead to a subculture of discontent; it may, just as easily, lead to quiescence and fatalism. Discontent occurs when comparisons between comparable groups are made which suggest that unnecessary injustices are occurring. If the distribution of wealth is seen as natural and just – however disparate it is – it will be accepted. An objective history of exploitation, or even a history of increased exploitation, does not explain disturbances. Exploitative cultures have existed for generations without friction: it is the perception of injustice – *relative deprivation* – which counts.

[…]

THE CAUSES OF CRIME

For orthodox criminology crime occurs because of a lack of conditioning into values: the criminal, whether because of evil (in the conventional model) or lack of parental training (in the welfare model), lacks the virtues which keep us all honest and upright. In left idealism, crime occurs not because of lack of values but simply because of lack of material goods: economic deprivation drives people into crime. In the conventional viewpoint on crime, the criminal is flawed; he or she lacks human values and cognition. In the radical interpretation of this, the very opposite is true. The criminal, not the honest person, has the superior consciousness: he or she has seen through the foolishness of the straight world. To be well conditioned is to be well deceived. The criminal then enters into a new world of value – a subculture, relieved in part of the mystifications of the conventional world.

From *What is to be Done about Law and Order?*, pp. 81; 95–101; 218–25. (Harmondsworth: Penguin, 1984.)

We reject both these positions. The radical version smacks of theories of absolute deprivation; we would rather put at the centre of our theory notions of relative deprivation. And a major source of one's making comparisons – or indeed the feeling that one should, in the first place, 'naturally' compete and compare oneself with others – is capitalism itself.

We are taught that life is like a racetrack: that merit will find its own reward. This is the central way our system legitimates itself and motivates people to compete. But what a strange racetrack! In reality some people seem to start half-way along the track (the rich), while others are forced to run with a millstone around their necks (for example, women with both domestic and non-domestic employment), while others are not even allowed on to the track at all (the unemployed, the members of the most deprived ethnic groups). The values of an equal or meritocratic society which capitalism inculcates into people are constantly at loggerheads with the actual material inequalities in the world. And, contrary to the conservatives, it is the well-socialized person who is the most liable to crime. Crime is endemic to capitalism because it produces both egalitarian ideals and material shortages. It provides precisely the values which engender criticism of the material shortages which the radicals pinpoint.

A high crime rate occurs in precise conditions: where a group has learnt through its past that it is being dealt with invidiously; where it is possible for it easily to pick up the contradictions just referred to and where there is no political channel for these feelings of discontent to be realized. There must be economic and political discontent and there must be an absence of economic and political opportunities.

THE NATURE OF CRIME AND CRIMINAL VALUES

For conventional criminology, [...] crime is simply antisocial behaviour involving people who lack values. For left idealists it is the reverse: it is proto-revolutionary activity, primitive and individualistic, perhaps, but praiseworthy all the same. It involves, if it is a theft, a redistribution of income, or if it is part of youth culture, symbolic and stylistic awareness of, say, the loss of traditional working-class community or the repressive nature of the system. In either case it involves alternative values.

We would argue that both of these interpretations of crime are superficial. It is true that crime is antisocial – indeed the majority of working-class crime, far from being a prefigurative revolt, is directed against other members of the working class. But it is not antisocial because of lack of conventional values but precisely because of them. For the values of most working-class criminals are overwhelmingly conventional. They involve individualism, competition, desire for material goods and, often, machismo. Such crime could, without exaggeration, be characterized as the behaviour of those suitably motivated people who are too poor to have access to the Stock Exchange. Crime reflects the fact that our own worlds and our own lives are materially and ideologically riddled with the capitalist order within which we live. Street crime is an activity of marginals but its image is that of those right in the centre of convention and of concern. As Jeremy Seabrook puts it:

> What we cannot bear, rich and liberals alike, is to see our own image in actions that are ugly and more stark reflections of transactions in which we are all implicated in our social and economic relationships: the universal marketing, the superstitious faith in money, the instant profit, the rip-off, the easy money, the backhander, the quick fiddle, the comforting illusion that we can all get richer without hurting anyone, the way in which individual salvation through money has become a secularized and man-made substitute for divine grace. (1983: 64)

The radicals are correct when they see crime as a reaction to an unjust society. But they make a crucial mistake: they assume that the reaction to a just cause is necessarily a just one. On the contrary: it is often exactly the opposite. The reaction to poverty among poor whites, for example, may be to parade around waving Union Jacks: it may be the tawdry nationalism of the National Front. The reaction to relative deprivation may, as Paul Willis (1977) has so ably shown, be sexism, racism and anti-intellectualism. Crime is one form of egoistic response to deprivation. Its roots are in justice but its growth often perpetuates injustice.

THE NATURE OF THE CRIME STATISTICS

If we look at the official crime statistics in any Western capitalist country we see a remarkable similarity: the young are consistently seen to offend more than the old, the working class more than the middle class, black more than white, and men more than women. In Figure [13.1] we have constructed a series of Aztec pyramids each representing the likelihood of going to prison dependent on class, age, race and gender. We have used American statistics rather than British, as they are more complete. The British figures, particularly in terms of class and race, are kept much more closely guarded. The shape of these pyramids is, however, constant across cultures and there are close parallels; for example, one British study showed that the chances of going to prison by class were exactly the same as in America.

As can be seen, a labourer is 14 times more likely to go to prison than a professional; someone aged between 20 and 24 is 16 times more likely than a 65-year-old; a black male is 28 times more likely than a white female. If one compounds these figures, of course, one achieves much higher ratios, the most extreme being the contrast between the chances of going to prison of an elderly, white professional woman compared to a young, black, lower-working-class man. This has some very dramatic results; for example, on an average day in the United States one in 450 Americans is in prison, but one black man in 26 between the ages of 25 and 34. Offenders, like victims, are sharply focused in terms of social category; in fact, the same social attributes which tend towards high victimization rates tend also towards high offender rates. [...] Serious crime, according to the official statistics, is a minority phenomenon within which certain social categories most

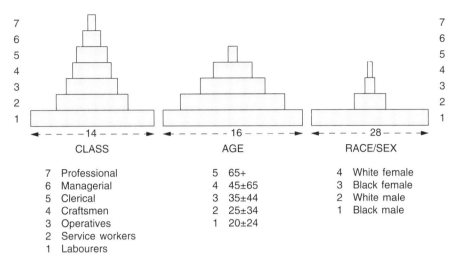

Figure 15.1 Likelihood of going to prison

marginal to society are vastly over-represented. The prisoner is thus on the fringe of the economy (unemployed or a casual labourer), has missed out on the educational system, and belongs to a minority group.

Now, these pyramids illustrate the major empirical problem for understanding crime. For conventional criminology it is scarcely a problem: the lower orders are much more likely to be badly socialized than the middle and upper echelons of society – hence the pyramid. For left idealists, however, this fact poses a considerable quandary. For, on the one hand, gross economic deprivation will surely lead to crime; but on the other, is it not true that the police pick on the poor, ignoring the crimes of the rich? Our response to this contradiction is simply to ask why either/or is a realistic analysis. There is no doubt that different social categories of people behave differently both in their degree of orderliness and criminality and that this relates to their position in the world; but there is also no doubt that the police react differently to different categories of people. If both these points are true, then the official statistics are a product of differences in the 'real' rates of crime between groups and differences in the police predisposition to arrest them. Thus the crime rate of old ladies is no doubt actually very low, but it probably appears *even* lower in the official statistics because of the police disinclination to suspect or arrest elderly persons. And as far as lower-working-class youths are concerned, the exact opposite is true: they commit more crimes and they are excessively harassed, the result being an augmented crime statistic. Moreover, different types of people commit different types of crimes. This point is put particularly well by Reiman. He writes:

> There is evidence suggesting that the particular pressure of poverty leads poor people to commit a higher proportion of the crimes that people fear (such as homicide, burglary,

and assault) than their number in the population. There is no contradiction between this and the recognition that those who are well off commit many more crimes than is generally acknowledged both of the widely feared and of the sort not widely feared (such as 'white-collar' crimes). There is no contradiction here, because, as will be shown, the poor are arrested far more frequently than those who are well off when they have committed the same crimes – and the well-to-do are almost never arrested for white-collar crimes. Thus, if arrest records were brought in line with the real incidence of crime, it is likely that those who are well off would appear in the records far more than they do at present, even though the poor would still probably figure disproportionately in arrests for the crimes people fear. In addition to this ... those who are well off commit acts that are not defined as crimes and yet that are as harmful or more so than the crimes people fear. Thus, if we had an accurate picture of who is really dangerous to society, there is reason to believe that those who are well off would receive still greater representation. (1979: 7–8)

In other words, (a) the pyramids we have constructed with regard to class and crime (and the same is true of race, gender and age) are quantitatively too dramatic: if middle-class people were equally subject to arrest and conviction the contrasts between each level could not be as steep. (b) Qualitatively, given the above provision, they are reasonably correct if one does *not* include white-collar crime and focuses, as Reiman outlines, on the 'normal' crimes which people fear. If people were arrested and imprisoned for white-collar crimes, then the pyramid would remain in shape but its gradient would be lessened even more. (c) To admit to a pyramid of crime by class is not, of course, to believe in a pyramid of impact. That is, the fact that lower-working-class males commit more crime than their upper-class counterparts does not mean that the overall impact of such crimes is necessarily greater. [...] it is probably less, although none of this suggests that we should concentrate on either one or the other, as criminologists, both radical and conventional, have done in the past. Both types of crime create considerable problems for the population. [...]

Relative deprivation

Relative deprivation is the excess of expectations over opportunities. The importance of this concept is that it gets away from simplistic notions that try [to] relate discontent and collective violence to levels of absolute deprivation. The link between relative deprivation and political marginality is crucial for understanding riots and collective violence. Political marginality is unlikely to result in riot unless there is the added sense of frustration stemming from relative deprivation. A social group may be economically and politically marginalized, yet if it has no desire to participate in the structure of opportunities and social rights from which it is excluded, frustration need not occur. For the rioters of the eighteenth century the problem was not the failure to be included in a structure of opportunities stemming from industrial society, so much as the fact that an existing way of life was in the process of being destroyed by industrialization and its opportunity structure. In contemporary industrial societies social groups that have a high degree of economic and political marginality but a low sense of relative deprivation tend to be either deviant subcultures, particularly religious groups oriented to 'other-worldly pursuits', or first-generation immigrant communities. The latter, forced to take the worst jobs and the worst housing that industrial societies have to offer, may still, in the short term, be sheltered from a sense of relative deprivation by virtue of the fact that their standard of comparison is not so much the opportunity structure of the wider society from which they are excluded by racial discrimination or legal barriers, as the societies from which they recently emigrated by comparison with which living standards are higher.

Conversely, of course, a sense of relative deprivation can co-exist with the absence of economic or political marginality. This is the situation with regard to the majority of the organized working class in industrial societies faced with a marked inequality in the distribution of wealth and opportunities. Relative deprivation becomes the driving force of militant trade union and political struggles to increase living standards through the process of political negotiation and compromise. This distinction between relative deprivation combined with political integration and relative deprivation combined with political marginality enables us to understand some of the differences between the 1930s, with their relative absence of riots despite high levels of unemployment, and the present period. During the 1930s the experience of unemployment was not linked as closely as it is today with political marginality. Unemployment was concentrated in the older working-class communities centred in the basic industries of the north, iron and steel, shipbuilding, coal mining, etc. The experience of unemployment was often the collective experience of a whole community related to the slump of the industry around which the community lived and worked. This meant that the institutions of class politics – the trades councils, Labour Party and union branches – appeared to the unemployed as the natural weapons of struggle. The attempt to transfer these traditional methods of struggle *at* work into the arena of the struggle *for* work, such as in the construction of the National Unemployed Workers Movement, was an obvious course of action for the unemployed, most of whom had spent a period of their lives at work. Even the younger unemployed could be drawn into this through the general status and influence of labour-movement institutions in the cohesive working-class community.

The present period presents two contrasts to this. First, the working-class community, particularly in the inner-city areas throughout the country – not just in the older industrial areas – is far less cohesive. The fragmentation of employment between older, industrial employment in decline, newer state employment in the public services, and new small firms relying on cheap labour, combined with a greater cultural and ethnic diversity as older sections of the working class have moved out of the area or just ceased to exist and new immigrant communities have been established, has produced a much greater diversity of levels and types of labour-movement organization. It is not that organization has not emerged in the inner cities, but it no longer constitutes the cohesive and unifying force in the working-class community that it once did. Added to this is the massive growth in the number of young people who have never worked and therefore are not familiar with the organization and attitude of working-class politics. The isolation of youth from work and from class political organizations combines with the reduced hegemony of working-class institutions in the community, by comparison with the 1930s, to produce an acuteness of political marginality probably never previously experienced by any section of British society since industrialization.

But the burden of our argument here is that this acute political marginality is, for the young unemployed, combined with a greater sense of relative deprivation than in the 1930s. It is this volatile combination that underlies the rising street crime and collective violence that we see returning to our cities. This sharp growth of relative deprivation follows from quite fundamental changes, again by contrast with the 1930s, and even more with the nineteenth century, in the mechanisms determining the relationship between expectations and the opportunities for achieving them.

If we define relative deprivation as the excess of expectations over opportunities for fulfilling them, then it is easy to see a situation in which relative deprivation might be kept in check – one which undoubtedly corresponds to the vision of a stable society held by many belonging to what has come to be called the 'new right' in the Conservative Party, in which expectations and opportunities are generally determined by the same mechanism: the free competitive market. Where the competitive market exists not only as a mechanism for the allocation of society's resources but also as a 'moral force' in society, then expectations and opportunities will be brought into some sort of balance. People will not expect a higher income or standard of living than the sale of their particular skill or labour in the market brings, if it is generally considered that the standard of rewards obtaining from the competitive selling of labour or goods in the market is just. Also, in such a competitive society, if an individual does not achieve the same rewards as others from the sale of similar labour or goods, then that individual is likely to blame himself or herself on the grounds that this must be due to offering an inferior product for sale on the market.

Some politicians and academics would like to see this idealized world of *laissez-faire* present in society, in order to solve the problem of relative deprivation, but, to the extent that it actually functioned as a social force in industrial society, it did, and does, provide such a solution only for sections of the middle class. Under nineteenth and early twentieth century capitalism, the fact that the working-class community was insulated by both distance and communication from wealthier sections of society was a far more effective check on relative deprivation, especially coupled with the fact that remnants of pre-industrial religious and customary ways of thinking about society as an inevitable and justifiable hierarchy remained in the popular culture. As the working class became organized and the strength of trade unionism developed, the aims of working-class politics centred not so much around reaching the *same* standards of living as the employers and the ruling class as around the defence of existing working-class living standards, together with modest improvements.

What is even more important about the 1930s is that, despite the depths of the recession, militant discontent was never widespread. Wal Hannington, who led the National Unemployed Workers Movement, had to concede, despite the claims he made for the influence of his organization, that 'at no time has the standing membership approached even 10 per cent of the vast masses of the unemployed'. As Runciman notes:

> The Depression imposed severe and sometimes intolerable hardship on large sections of the working class and many non-manual workers also; but it did not heighten their feelings of relative deprivation in the way that both wars did. Particularly severe wage cuts were, as one would expect, resisted, notably in the textile industry. But the disposition to grin and bear it remained much more widespread than the disposition to storm the barricades. (1966: 64)

Particularly since the last war the growth of the Welfare State has combined with the mass media and mass secondary education to produce a steady growth in relative deprivation. The mass media have disseminated a standardized image of lifestyle particularly in the areas of popular culture and recreation which, for those unemployed and surviving through the dole queue, or only able to obtain employment at very low wages, has accentuated the sense of relative deprivation. The spread of mass state secondary education has had a similar effect, not so much by standardizing expectations of career patterns, living standards, etc., as by raising the minimum expectation. During the period of exceptional economic expansion of the 1950s and 1960s this posed no problems. But now the phenomenon of 'over-education' is beginning to appear. As Cloward and Ohlin (1960: 118–20) have pointed out, the excess of aspirations and opportunities can paradoxically lay the basis for social, racial and other forms of discrimination:

> The democratic ideology of Equality of Opportunity creates constant pressure for formal criteria of evaluation that are universalistic rather than particularistic, achieved rather than ascribed – that is, for a structure of opportunities that are available to all on an open and competitive basis ... However, the democratic society, like other types of society, is characterized by a limited supply of rewards and opportunities. Although many are eligible for success on the basis of formal criteria, relatively few can succeed, even in a rapidly expanding economy. It is therefore necessary to make choices on some basis or other among candidates who are equally eligible on formal grounds ... In this situation, criteria based on race, religion, or class, that have been publicly repudiated in favour of achievement standards, are informally invoked to eliminate the surplus candidates. Thus the democratization of standards of evaluation tends to increase the competition for rewards and opportunities and hence the discrepancy between the formal and the actual criteria of selection for lower-class youngsters.

Finally, the Welfare State has had the same result. New concepts of need and minimum standards of living, coupled with a focus on the poorest sections of society have had the effect of raising the minimum expectation. The *Sunday Telegraph*, comparing the slump of the 1930s with that of today, grasped this well:

> Though unemployment is similar in scale, social security benefits today are not far short of average living standards then. Today's problem, though, is just as acute since expectations, fostered by television and advertising, are high and the frustrations generated by our own slump are vast and dangerous. (*Sunday Telegraph*, 21 February 1982)

The consequence is that expectations have become governed by a set of mechanisms much more loosely, if at all, related to opportunities. The latter are still to a large extent determined by the market mechanism coupled, of course, with the massive growth of state intervention and investment, which itself has had an effect on relative deprivation. As it has become perceived that the state has taken responsibility for major components of the opportunity structure through careers and employment in state services, as well as the general responsibility undertaken by post-war governments, until recently, for maintaining the level of employment, so the discrepancy between expectations and opportunities, now growing as a result of economic recession and cutbacks in state spending, becomes blamed on the 'system' rather than on the individual.

Meanwhile, another quite important change was taking place, the consequences of which are now much clearer. While the tendency, as far as expectations were concerned, was for greater standardization and raising the minimum, the nature of post-war economic expansion was to create a working-class opportunity structure which was increasingly differentiated in terms of wage levels and working conditions. The decline of manufacturing employment in general and the rise of new highly paid white-collar and technical occupations, combined with new sectors of low pay in services (often combining low pay and unsocial hours) and small firms, has produced a more diverse set of opportunities at the same time as expectations have been becoming more standardized. In the short run the solution to this problem in most Western industrial societies was immigrant labour. [...] The passivity of the early, post-war, immigrant communities was based on a combination of a cultural orientation towards the homeland and an expected short stay in Britain. This meant that immigrant workers were prepared to accept working conditions which would not be accepted by native workers, such as low pay and flexible shift systems involving long periods of night work. In addition, the legal barriers of alien status and racial prejudice of the native British population generally excluded immigrants from better paid forms of employment.

This situation has been brought to a conclusion during the 1970s by the growth of a second generation of Britons of immigrant parentage. Going through the same education system (despite various forms of discrimination operating there), the children of immigrant families have grown up with the same spectrum of aspirations and expectations derived from the mass media and the education system as young people in general. Expectations and opportunities, then, have been moving in opposite directions, relative deprivation has been increasing, and, as the state has increasingly been seen as the determinant of opportunities, the resentment of unfulfilled expectations increasingly takes the form of resentment against the state and its manifestations, particularly those, like the police, who are encountered on a day-to-day basis by the young unemployed. [...]

REFERENCES

Cloward, R. and Ohlin, L. (1960) *Delinquency and Opportunity*. New York: The Free Press.
Reiman, J. (1979) *The Rich Get Richer and the Poor Get Prison*. New York: Wiley.
Runciman, W.G. (1966) *Relative Deprivation and Social Justice*. London: Routledge and Kegan Paul.
Seabrook, J. (1983) 'The crime of poverty', *New Society*, 14 (April).
Willis, P. (1977) *Learning to Labour*. London: Saxon House.

16

Deviant places: a theory of the ecology of crime

Rodney Stark

It is well known that high rates of crime and deviance can persist in specific neighborhoods despite repeated, complete turnovers in the composition of their populations. That this occurs suggests that more than 'kinds of people' explanations are needed to account for the ecological concentration of deviance – that we also need to develop 'kinds of places' explanations. This essay attempts to codify more than a century of ecological research on crime and deviance into an integrated set of 30 propositions and offers these as a first approximation of a theory of deviant places.

Norman Hayner, a stalwart of the old Chicago school of human ecology, noted that in the area of Seattle having by far the highest delinquency rate in 1934, 'half the children are Italian.' In vivid language, Hayner described the social and cultural shortcomings of these residents: 'largely illiterate, unskilled workers of Sicilian origin. Fiestas, wine-drinking, raising of goats and gardens ... are characteristic traits.' He also noted that the businesses in this neighborhood were run down and on the wane and that 'a number of dilapidated vacant business buildings and frame apartment houses dot the main street,' while the area has 'the smallest percentage of home-owners and the greatest aggregation of dilapidated dwellings and run-down tenements in the city' (Hayner, 1942: 361–363). Today this district, which makes up the neighborhood surrounding Garfield High School, remains the prime delinquency area. But there are virtually no Italians living there. Instead, this neighborhood is the heart of the Seattle black community.

Thus we come to the point. How is it that neighborhoods can remain the site of high crime and deviance rates *despite a complete turnover in their populations*? If

From *Criminology*, 1987, 25(4): 893–909.

the Garfield district was tough *because* Italians lived there, why did it stay tough after they left? Indeed, why didn't the neighborhoods the Italians departed to become tough? Questions such as these force the perception that the composition of neighborhoods, in terms of characteristics of their populations, cannot provide an adequate explanation of variations in deviance rates. Instead, *there must be something about places as such* that sustains crime.[1]

This paper attempts to fashion an integrated set of propositions to summarize and extend our understanding of ecological sources of deviant behavior. In so doing, the aim is to revive a *sociology* of deviance as an alternative to the social psychological approaches that have dominated for 30 years. That is, the focus is on traits of places and groups rather than on traits of individuals. Indeed, I shall attempt to show that by adopting survey research as the *preferred* method of research, social scientists lost touch with significant aspects of crime and delinquency. Poor neighborhoods disappeared to be replaced by individual kids with various levels of family income, but no detectable environment at all. Moreover, the phenomena themselves became bloodless, sterile, and almost harmless, for questionnaire studies cannot tap homicide, rape, assault, armed robbery, or even significant burglary and fraud – too few people are involved in these activities to turn up in significant numbers in feasible samples, assuming that such people turn up in samples at all. So delinquency, for example, which once had meant offenses serious enough for court referrals, soon meant taking $2 out of mom's purse, having 'banged up something that did not belong to you,' and having a fist fight. This transformation soon led repeatedly to the 'discovery' that poverty is unrelated to delinquency (Tittle, Villemez, and Smith, 1978).

Yet, through it all, social scientists somehow still knew better than to stroll the streets at night in certain parts of town or even to park there. And despite the fact that countless surveys showed that kids from upper and lower income families scored the same on delinquency batteries, even social scientists knew that the parts of town that scared them were not upper-income neighborhoods. In fact, when the literature was examined with sufficient finesse, it was clear that class *does* matter – that serious offenses are very disproportionately committed by a virtual under class (Hindelang, Hirschi, and Weis, 1981).

So, against this backdrop, let us reconsider the human ecology approach to deviance. To begin, there are five aspects of urban neighborhoods which characterize high deviance areas of cities. To my knowledge, no member of the Chicago school ever listed this particular set, but these concepts permeate their whole literature starting with Park, Burgess, and McKenzie's classic, *The City* (1925). And they are especially prominent in the empirical work of the Chicago school (Faris and Dunham, 1939; Shaw and McKay, 1942). Indeed, most of these factors were prominent in the work of 19th-century moral statisticians such as the Englishmen Mayhew and Buchanan, who were doing ecological sociology decades before any member of the Chicago school was born. These essential factors are (1) density; (2) poverty; (3) mixed use; (4) transience; and (5) dilapidation.

Each of the five will be used in specific propositions. However, in addition to these characteristics of places, the theory also will incorporate some specific *impacts* of the five on the moral order as *people respond to them.* Four responses will be assessed: (1) moral cynicism among residents; (2) increased opportunities for crime and deviance; (3) increased motivation to deviate; and (4) diminished social control.

Finally, the theory will sketch how these responses further *amplify* the volume of deviance through the following consequences: (1) by attracting deviant and crime-prone people and deviant and criminal activities to a neighborhood; (2) by driving out the least deviant; and (3) by further reductions in social control.

The remainder of the paper weaves these elements into a set of integrated propositions, clarifying and documenting each as it proceeds. Citations will not be limited to recent work, or even to that of the old Chicago school, but will include samples of the massive 19th-century literature produced by the moral statisticians. The aim is to help contemporary students of crime and deviance rediscover the past and to note the power and realism of its methods, data, and analysis. In Mayhew's (1851) immense volumes, for example, he combines lengthy, first-person narratives of professional criminals with a blizzard of superb statistics on crime and deviance.

Before stating any propositions, one should note the relationship between this essay and ongoing theoretical work, especially my deductive theory of religion (Stark and Bainbridge, 1987). A major impediment to the growth of more formal and fully deductive theories in the social sciences is that usually one lacks the space necessary to work out the links between an initial set of axioms and definitions and the relevant set of propositions (statements deduced from the axioms and definitions). In consequence, it is not shown that the propositions outlined here follow logically from my axiomatic system, but they can be derived. For those interested in these matters, one can refer to the more complete formulation of control theory that was derived in *A Theory of Religion* (Stark and Bainbridge, 1987) to explain the conditions under which people are recruited by deviant religious movements. In any event, logical steps from one proposition to another will be clear in what follows, but the set as a whole must be left without obvious axiomatic ancestry.

> *Proposition 1: The greater the density of a neighborhood, the more association between those most and least predisposed to deviance.*

At issue here is not simply that there will be a higher proportion of deviance-prone persons in dense neighborhoods (although, as will be shown, that is true, too), rather it is proposed that there is a higher average level of interpersonal interactions in such neighborhoods and that individual traits will have less influence on patterns of contact. Consider kids. In low-density neighborhoods – wealthy suburbs, for example – some active effort is required for one 12-year-old to see another (a ride from a parent often is required). In these settings, kids and their parents can easily limit contact with bullies and those in disrepute. Not so in dense urban neighborhoods – the 'bad' kids often live in the same building as the 'good' ones, hang out close by, dominate the nearby playground, and are nearly unavoidable. Hence, peer groups in dense neighborhoods will tend to be inclusive, and all young people living there will face maximum peer pressure to deviate – as differential association theorists have stressed for so long.

> *Proposition 2: The greater the density of a neighborhood, the higher the level of moral cynicism.*

Moral cynicism is the belief that people are much worse than they pretend to be. Indeed, Goffman's use of the dramaturgical model in his social psychology was rooted in the fact that we require ourselves and others to keep up appearances in public. We all, to varying degrees, have secrets, the public airing of which we would find undesirable. So long as our front-stage performances are credible and creditable, and we shield our backstage actions, we serve as good role models (Goffman, 1959, 1963). The trouble is that in dense neighborhoods it is much harder to keep up appearances – whatever morally discreditable information exists about us is likely to leak.

Survey data suggest that upper-income couples may be about as likely as lower-income couples to have physical fights (Stark and McEvoy, 1970). Whether that is true, it surely is the case that upper-income couples are much less likely to be *overheard* by the neighbors when they have such a fight. In dense neighborhoods, where people live in crowded, thin-walled apartments, the neighbors do hear. In these areas teenage peers, for example, will be much more likely to know embarrassing things about one another's parents. This will color their perceptions about what is normal, and their respect for the conventional moral standards will be reduced. Put another way, people in dense neighborhoods will serve as inferior role models for one another – the same people would *appear* to be more respectable in less dense neighborhoods.

> *Proposition 3: To the extent that neighborhoods are dense and poor, homes will be crowded.*

The proposition is obvious, but serves as a necessary step to the next propositions on the effects of crowding, which draw heavily on the fine paper by Gove, Hughes, and Galle (1979).

> *Proposition 4: Where homes are more crowded, there will be a greater tendency to congregate outside the home in places and circumstances that raise levels of temptation and opportunity to deviate.*

Gove and his associates reported that crowded homes caused family members, especially teenagers, to stay away. Since crowded homes will also tend to be located in mixed-use neighborhoods (see Proposition 9), when people stay away from home they will tend to congregate in places conducive to deviance (stores, pool halls, street corners, cafes, taverns, and the like).

> *Proposition 5: Where homes are more crowded, there will be lower levels of supervision of children.*

This follows from the fact that children from crowded homes tend to stay out of the home and that their parents are glad to let them. Moreover, Gove and his associates found strong empirical support for the link between crowding and less supervision of children.

Proposition 6: Reduced levels of child supervision will result in poor school achievement, with a consequent reduction in stakes in conformity and an increase in deviant behavior.

This is one of the most cited and strongly verified causal chains in the literature on delinquency (Thrasher, 1927; Toby and Toby, 1961; Hirschi, 1969; Gold, 1970; Hindelang, 1973). Indeed, Hirschi and Hindelang (1977: 583) claim that the 'school variables' are among the most powerful predictors of delinquency to be found in survey studies: 'Their significance for delinquency is nowhere in dispute and is, in fact, one of the oldest and most consistent findings of delinquency research.'

Here Toby's (1957) vital concept of 'stakes in conformity' enters the propositions. Stakes in conformity are those things that people risk losing by being detected in deviant actions. These may be things we already possess as well as things we can reasonably count on gaining in the future. An important aspect of the school variables is their potential for future rewards, rewards that may be sacrificed by deviance, but only for those whose school performance is promising.

Proposition 7: Where homes are more crowded, there will be higher levels of conflict within families weakening attachments and thereby stakes in conformity.

Gove and his associates found a strong link between crowding and family conflict, confirming Frazier's (1932: 636) observations:

> So far as children are concerned, the house becomes a veritable prison for them. There is no way of knowing how many conflicts in Negro families are set off by the irritations caused by overcrowding people, who come home after a day of frustration and fatigue, to dingy and unhealthy living quarters.

Here we also recognize that stakes in conformity are not merely material.

Indeed, given the effort humans will expend to protect them, our attachments to others are among the most potent stakes in conformity. We risk our closest and most intimate relationships by behavior that violates what others expect of us. People lacking such relationships, of course, do not risk their loss.

Proposition 8: Where homes are crowded, members will be much less able to shield discreditable acts and information from one another, further increasing moral cynicism.

As neighborhood density causes people to be less satisfactory role models for the neighbors, density in the home causes moral cynicism. Crowding makes privacy more difficult. Kids will observe or overhear parental fights, sexual relations, and the like. This is precisely what Buchanan noted about the dense and crowded London slums in 1846 (in Levin and Lindesmith, 1937: 15):

> In the densely crowded lanes and alleys of these areas, wretched tenements are found containing in every cellar and on every floor, men and women, children both male and female, all huddled together, sometimes with strangers, and too frequently standing in

very doubtful consanguinity to each other. In these abodes decency and shame have fled; depravity reigns in all its horrors.

Granted that conditions have changed since then and that dense, poor, crowded areas in the center cities of North America are not nearly so wretched. But the essential point linking 'decency' and 'shame' to lack of privacy retains its force.

Proposition 9: Poor, dense neighborhoods tend to be mixed-use neighborhoods.

Mixed use refers to urban areas where residential and commercial land use coexist, where homes, apartments, retail shops, and even light industry are mixed together. Since much of the residential property in such areas is rental, typically there is much less resistance to commercial use (landlords often welcome it because of the prospects of increased land values). Moreover, the poorest, most dense urban neighborhoods often are adjacent to the commercial sections of cities, forming what the Chicago school called the 'zone of transition' to note the progressive encroachments of commercial uses into a previously residential area. Shaw and McKay (1942: 20) describe the process as follows:

> As the city grows, the areas of commerce and light industry near the center encroach upon areas used for residential purposes. The dwellings in such areas, often already undesirable because of age, are allowed to deteriorate when such invasion threatens or actually occurs, as further investment in them is unprofitable. These residences are permitted to yield whatever return can be secured in their dilapidated condition, often in total disregard for the housing laws. ...

Shaw and McKay were proponents of the outmoded concentric zonal model of cities, hence their assumption that encroachment radiates from the city center. No matter, the important point is that the process of encroachment occurs whatever the underlying shape of cities.

Proposition 10: Mixed use increases familiarity with and easy access to places offering the opportunity for deviance.

A colleague told me he first shoplifted at age eight, but that he had been 'casing the joint for four years.' This particular 'joint' was the small grocery store at the corner of the block where he lived, so he didn't even have to cross a street to get there. In contrast, consider kids in many suburbs. If they wanted to take up shoplifting they would have to ask mom or dad for a ride. In purely residential neighborhoods there simply are far fewer conventional opportunities (such as shops) for deviant behavior.

Proposition 11: Mixed-use neighborhoods offer increased opportunity for congregating outside the home in places conducive to deviance.

It isn't just stores to steal from that the suburbs lack, they also don't abound in places of potential moral marginality where people can congregate. But in dense, poor, mixed-use neighborhoods, when people leave the house they have all sorts of places to go, including the street corner. A frequent activity in such neighborhoods is leaning. A bunch a guys will lean against the front of the corner store, the side of the pool hall, or up against the barber shop. In contrast, out in the suburbs young guys don't gather to lean against one another's houses, and since there is nowhere else for them to lean, whatever deviant leanings they might have go unexpressed. By the same token, in the suburbs, come winter, there is no close, *public* place to congregate indoors.

Thus, we can more easily appreciate some fixtures of the crime and delinquency research literature. When people, especially young males, congregate and have nothing special to do, the incidence of their deviance is increased greatly (Hirschi, 1969). Most delinquency, and a lot of crime, is a social rather than a solitary act (Erickson, 1971).

Proposition 12: Poor, dense, mixed-use neighborhoods have high transience rates.

This aspect of the urban scene has long attracted sociological attention. Thus, McKenzie wrote in 1926 (p. 145): 'Slums are the most mobile ... sections of a city. Their inhabitants come and go in continuous succession.'

Proposition 13: Transience weakens extra-familial attachments.

This is self-evident. The greater the amount of local population turnover, the more difficult it will be for individuals or families to form and retain attachments.

Proposition 14: Transience weakens voluntary organizations, thereby directly reducing both informal and formal sources of social control (see Proposition 25).

Recent studies of population turnover and church membership rates strongly sustain the conclusion that such membership is dependent upon attachments, and hence suffers where transience rates reduce attachments (Wuthnow and Christiano, 1979; Stark, Doyle, and Rushing, 1983; Welch, 1983; Stark and Bainbridge, 1985). In similar fashion, organizations such as PTA or even fraternal organizations must suffer where transience is high. Where these organizations are weak, there will be reduced community resources to launch local, self-help efforts to confront problems such as truancy or burglary. Moreover, neighborhoods deficient in voluntary organizations also will be less able to influence how external forces such as police, zoning boards, and the like act vis-á-vis the community, a point often made by Park (1952) in his discussions of natural areas and by more recent urban sociologists (Suttles, 1972; Lee, Oropesa, Metch, and Guest, 1984; Guest, 1984).

In their important recent study, Simcha-Fagan and Schwartz (1986) found that the association between transience and delinquency disappeared under controls for organizational participation. This is not an example of spuriousness, but of what Lazarsfeld called 'interpretation' (Lazarsfeld, Pasanella, and Rosenberg, 1972). Transience *causes* low levels of participation, which in turn *cause* an increased rate of delinquency. That is, participation is an *intervening variable* or *linking mechanism* between transience and delinquency. When an intervening variable is controlled, the association between X and Y is reduced or vanishes.

Proposition 15: Transience reduces levels of community surveillance.

In areas abounding in newcomers, it will be difficult to know when someone doesn't live in a building he or she is entering. In stable neighborhoods, on the other hand, strangers are easily noticed and remembered.

Proposition 16: Dense, poor, mixed-use, transient neighborhoods will also tend to be dilapidated.

This is evident to anyone who visits these parts of cities. Housing is old and not maintained. Often these neighborhoods are very dirty and littered as a result of density, the predominance of renters, inferior public services, and a demoralized population (see Proposition 22).

Proposition 17: Dilapidation is a social stigma for residents.

It hardly takes a real estate tour of a city to recognize that neighborhoods not only reflect the status or their residents, but confer status upon them. In Chicago, for example, strangers draw favorable inferences about someone who claims to reside in Forest Glen, Beverly, or Norwood Park. But they will be leery of those who admit to living on the Near South Side. Granted, knowledge of other aspects of communities enters into these differential reactions, but simply driving through a neighborhood such as the South Bronx is vivid evidence that very few people would actually *want* to live there. During my days as a newspaper reporter, I discovered that to move just a block North, from West Oakland to Berkeley, greatly increased social assessments of individuals. This was underscored by the frequent number of times people told me they lived in Berkeley although the phone book showed them with an Oakland address. As Goffman (1963) discussed at length, stigmatized people will try to pass when they can.

Proposition 18: High rates of neighborhood deviance are a social stigma for residents.

Beyond dilapidation, neighborhoods abounding in crime and deviance stigmatize the moral standing of all residents. To discover that you are interacting with a person through whose neighborhood you would not drive is apt to influence the subsequent interaction in noticeable ways. Here is a person who lives where homicide, rape, and assault are common, where drug dealers are easy to find, where prostitutes stroll the sidewalks waving to passing cars, where people sell TVs, VCRs, cameras, and other such items out of the trunks of their cars. In this sense, place of residence can be a dirty, discreditable secret.

Proposition 19: Living in stigmatized neighborhoods causes a reduction in an individual's stake in conformity.

This is simply to note that people living in slums will see themselves as having less to risk by being detected in acts of deviance. Moreover, as suggested below in Propositions 25–28, the risks of being detected also are lower in stigmatized neighborhoods.

Proposition 20: The more successful and potentially best role models will flee stigmatized neighborhoods whenever possible.

Goffman (1963) has noted that in the case of physical stigmas, people will exhaust efforts to correct or at least minimize them – from plastic surgery to years of therapy. Presumably it is easier for persons to correct a stigma attached to their neighborhood than one attached to their bodies. Since moving is widely perceived as easy, the stigma of living in particular neighborhoods is magnified. Indeed, as we see below, some people do live in such places because of their involvement in crime and deviance. But, even in the most disorderly neighborhoods, *most* residents observe the laws and norms. Usually they continue to live there simply because they can't afford better. Hence, as people become able to afford to escape, they do. The result is a process of selection whereby the worst role models predominate.

Proposition 21: More successful and conventional people will resist moving into a stigmatized neighborhood.

The same factors that *pull* the more successful and conventional out of stigmatized neighborhoods *push* against the probability that conventional people will move into these neighborhoods. This means that only less successful and less conventional people *will* move there.

Proposition 22: Stigmatized neighborhoods will tend to be overpopulated by the most demoralized kinds of people.

This does not mean the poor or even those engaged in crime or delinquency. The concern is with persons unable to function in reasonably adequate ways. For here will congregate the mentally ill (especially since the closure of mental hospitals), the chronic alcoholics, the retarded, and others with limited capacities to cope (Faris and Dunham, 1939; Jones, 1934).

Proposition 23: The larger the relative number of demoralized residents, the greater the number of available 'victims.'

As mixed use provides targets of opportunity by placing commercial firms within easy reach of neighborhood residents, the demoralized serve as human targets of opportunity. Many muggers begin simply by searching the pockets of drunks passed out in doorways and alleys near their residence.

Proposition 24: The larger the relative number of demoralized residents, the lower will be residents' perception of chances for success, and hence they will have lower perceived stakes in conformity.

Bag ladies on the corner, drunks sitting on the curbs, and schizophrenics muttering in the doorways are not advertisements for the American Dream. Rather, they testify that people in this part of town are losers, going nowhere in the system.

Proposition 25: Stigmatized neighborhoods will suffer from more lenient law enforcement.

This is one of those things that 'everyone knows,' but for which there is no firm evidence. However, evidence may not be needed, given the many obvious reasons why the police would let things pass in these neighborhoods that they would act on in better neighborhoods. First, the police tend to be reactive, to act upon complaints rather than seek out violations. People in stigmatized neighborhoods complain less often. Moreover, people in these neighborhoods frequently are much less willing to testify when the police do act – and the police soon lose interest in futile efforts to find evidence. In addition, it is primarily vice that the police tolerate in these neighborhoods, and the police tend to accept the premise that vice will exist *somewhere*. Therefore, they tend to condone vice in neighborhoods from which they do not receive effective pressures to act against it (see Proposition 14). They may even believe that by having vice limited to a specific area they are better able to regulate it. Finally, the police frequently come to share the outside community's view of stigmatized neighborhoods – as filled with morally disreputable people, who deserve what they get.

Proposition 26: More lenient law enforcement increases moral cynicism.

Where people see the laws being violated with apparent impunity, they will tend to lose their respect for conventional moral standards.

Proposition 27: More lenient law enforcement increases the incidence of crime and deviance.

This is a simple application of deterrence theory. Where the probabilities of being arrested and prosecuted for a crime are lower, the incidence of such crimes will be higher (Gibbs, 1975).

Proposition 28: More lenient law enforcement draws people to a neighborhood on the basis of their involvement in crime and deviance.

Reckless (1926: 165) noted that areas of the city with 'wholesome family and neighborhood life' will not tolerate 'vice,' but that 'the decaying neighborhoods have very little resistance to the invasions of vice.' Thus, stigmatized neighborhoods become the 'soft spot' for drugs, prostitution, gambling, and the like. These are activities that require public awareness of where to find them, for they depend on customers rather than victims. Vice can function only where it is condoned, at least to some degree. In this manner, McKenzie (1926: 146) wrote, the slum 'becomes the hiding-place for many services that are forbidden by the mores but which cater to the wishes of residents scattered throughout the community.'

Proposition 29: When people are drawn to a neighborhood on the basis of their participation in crime and deviance, the visibility of such activities and the opportunity to engage in them increases.

It has already been noted that vice must be relatively visible to outsiders in order to exist. Hence, to residents, it will be obvious. Even children not only will know *about* whores, pimps, drug dealers, and the like, they will *recognize* them. Back in 1840, Allison wrote of the plight of poor rural families migrating to rapidly growing English cities (p. 76):

The extravagant price of lodgings compels them to take refuge in one of the crowded districts of the town, in the midst of thousands in similar necessitous circumstances with themselves. Under the same roof they probably find a nest of prostitutes, in the next door a den of thieves. In the room which they occupy they hear incessantly the revel of intoxication or are compelled to witness the riot of licentiousness.

In fact, Allison suggested that the higher social classes owed their 'exemption from atrocious crime' primarily to the fact that they were not confronted by the temptations and seductions to vice that assail the poor. For it is the 'impossibility of concealing the attractions of vice from the younger part of the poor in the great cities which exposes them to so many causes of demoralization.'

> *Proposition 30: The higher the visibility of crime and deviance, the more it will appear to others that these activities are safe and rewarding.*

There is nothing like having a bunch of pimps and bookies flashing big wads of money and driving expensive cars to convince people in a neighborhood that crime pays. If young girls ask the hookers on the corner why they are doing it, they will reply with tales of expensive clothes and jewelry. Hence, in some neighborhoods, deviants serve as role models that encourage residents to become 'street wise.' This is a form of 'wisdom' about the relative costs and benefits of crime that increases the likelihood that a person will spend time in jail. The extensive recent literature on perceptions of risk and deterrence is pertinent here (Anderson, 1979; Jenson, Erickson, and Gibbs, 1978; Parker and Grasmick, 1979).

CONCLUSION

A common criticism of the ecological approach to deviance has been that although many people live in bad slums, most do not become delinquents, criminals, alcoholics, or addicts. Of course not. For one thing, as Gans (1962), Suttles (1968), and others have recognized, bonds among human beings can endure amazing levels of stress and thus continue to sustain commitment to the moral order even in the slums. Indeed, the larger culture seems able to instill high levels of aspiration in people even in the worst ecological settings. However, the fact that most slum residents aren't criminals is beside the point to claims by human ecologists that aspects of neighborhood structure can sustain high rates of crime and deviance. Such propositions do not imply that residence in such a neighborhood is either a necessary or a sufficient condition for deviant behavior. There is conformity in the slums and deviance in affluent suburbs. All the ecological propositions imply is a substantial correlation between variations in neighborhood character and variations in crime and deviance rates. What an eclogical theory of crime is meant to achieve is an explanation of why crime and deviance are so heavily concentrated in certain areas, and to pose this explanation in terms that do not depend entirely (or even primarily) on *compositional* effects – that is, on answers in terms of 'kinds of people.'

To say that neighborhoods are high in crime because their residents are poor suggests that controls for poverty would expose the spuriousness of the ecological effects. In contrast, the ecological theory would predict that the deviant behavior of the poor would vary as their ecology varied. For example, the theory would predict less deviance in poor families in situations where their neighborhood is less dense and more heterogeneous in terms of income, where their homes are less crowded and dilapidated, where the neighborhood is more fully residential, where the police are not permissive of vice, and where there is no undue concentration of the demoralized.

As reaffirmed in the last paragraphs of this essay, the aim here is not to dismiss 'kinds of people' or compositional factors, but to restore the theoretical power that was lost when the field abandoned human ecology. As a demonstration of what can be regained, let us examine briefly the most serious and painful issue confronting contemporary American criminology – black crime.

It is important to recognize that, for all the pseudo-biological trappings of the Chicago school (especially in Park's work), their primary motivation was to refute 'kinds of people' explanations of slum deviance based on Social Darwinism. They regarded it as their major achievement to have demonstrated that the real cause of slum deviance was social disorganization, not inferior genetic quality (Faris, 1967).

Today Social Darwinism has faded into insignificance, but the questions it addressed remain – especially with the decline of human ecology. For example, like the public at large, when American social scientists talk about poor central city neighborhoods, they mainly mean black neighborhoods. And, since they are not comfortable with racist explanations, social scientists have been almost unwilling to discuss the question of why black crime rates are so high. Nearly everybody knows that in and of itself, poverty offers only a modest part of the answer. So, what else can safely be said about blacks that can add to the explanation? Not much, if one's taste is for answers based on characteristics of persons. A lot, if one turns to ecology.

Briefly, my answer is that high black crime rates are, in large measure, the result of *where* they live.

For several years there has been comment on the strange fact that racial patterns in arrest and imprisonment seem far more equitable in the South than in the North and West. For example, the ratio of black prison inmates per 100,000 to white prison inmates per 100,000 reveals that South Carolina is the most equitable state (with a ratio of 3.2 blacks to 1 white), closely followed by Tennessee, Georgia, North Carolina, Mississippi, and Alabama, while Minnesota (22 blacks to 1 white) is the least equitable, followed by Nebraska, Wisconsin, and Iowa. Black/white arrest ratios, calculated the same way, also show greater equity in the South while Minnesota, Utah, Missouri, Illinois, and Nebraska appear to be least equitable (Stark, 1986). It would be absurd to attribute these variations to racism. Although the South has changed immensely, it is not credible that cops and courts in Minnesota are far more prejudiced than those in South Carolina.

But what *is* true about the circumstance of Southern blacks is that they have a much more normal ecological distribution than do blacks outside the South. For example, only 9% of blacks in South Carolina and 14% in Mississippi live in the central core of cities larger than 100,000, but 80% of blacks in Minnesota live in large center cities and 85% of blacks in Nebraska live in the heart of Omaha. What this means is that large proportions of Southern blacks live in suburbs, small towns, and rural areas where they benefit from factors conducive to low crime rates. Conversely, blacks outside the South are heavily concentrated in precisely the kinds of places explored in this essay – areas where the probabilities of *anyone* committing a crime are high. Indeed, a measure of black center city concentration is correlated .49 with the black/white arrest ratio and accounts for much of the variation between the South and the rest of the nation (Stark, 1986).

'Kinds of people' explanations could not easily have led to this finding, although one might have conceived of 'center city resident' as an individual trait. Even so, it is hard to see how such an individual trait would lead to explanations of why place of residence mattered. Surely it is more efficient and pertinent to see dilapidation, for example, as a trait of a building rather than as a trait of those who live in the building.

Is there any reason why social scientists must cling to individual traits as the *only* variables that count? Do I hear the phrase 'ecological fallacy?' What fallacy? It turns out that examples of this dreaded problem are very hard to find and usually turn out to be transparent examples of spuriousness – a problem to which *all* forms of nonexperimental research are vulnerable (Gove and Hughes, 1980; Stark, 1986; Lieberson, 1985).

Finally, it is not being suggested that we stop seeking and formulating 'kinds of people' explanations. Age and sex, for example, have powerful effects on deviant behavior that are not rooted in ecology (Gove, 1985). What is suggested is that, although males will exceed females in terms of rates of crime and delinquency in all neighborhoods, males in certain neighborhoods will have much higher rates than will males in some other neighborhoods, and female behavior will fluctuate by neighborhood too. Or, to return to the insights on which sociology was founded, social structures are real and cannot be reduced to purely psychological phenomena. Thus, for example, we can be sure that an adult, human male will behave somewhat differently if he is in an all-male group than if he is the only male in a group – and no sex change surgery is required to produce this variation.

NOTE

1   This is *not* to claim that neighborhoods do not change in terms of their levels of crime and deviance. Of course they do, even in Chicago (Bursik and Webb, 1982). It also is clear that such changes in deviance levels often are accompanied by changes in the kinds of people who live there. The so-called gentrification of a former slum area would be expected to reduce crime and deviance there as the decline of a once nicer neighborhood into a slum would be expected to increase it. However, such changes involve much more than changes in the composition of the population. Great physical changes are involved too, and my argument is that these have effects of their own.

REFERENCES

Allison, Archibald 1840 *The Principles of Population and the Connection With Human Happiness*. Edinburgh: Blackwood.

Anderson, L.S. 1979 The deterrent effect of criminal sanctions: Reviewing the evidence. In Paul J. Brantingham and Jack M. Kress (eds.), *Structure, Law and Power*. Beverley Hills: Sage.

Bursik, Robert J., Jr., and Jim Webb 1982 Community change and patterns of delinquency. *American Journal of Sociology* 88: 24–42.

Erickson, Maynard L. 1971 The group context of delinquent behavior. *Social Problems* 19: 114–129.

Faris, Robert E.L. 1967 *Chicago Sociology, 1920–1932*. San Francisco: Chandler.

Faris, Robert E.L. and Warren Dunham 1939 *Mental Disorder in Urban Areas*. Chicago: University of Chicago Press.

Frazier, E. Franklin 1932 *The Negro in the United States*. New York: Macmillan.

Gans, Herbert J. 1962 *The Urban Villagers*. New York: Free Press.

Gibbs, Jack P. 1975 *Crime, Punishment, and Deterrence*. New York: Elsevier.

Goffman, Erving 1959 *Presentation of Self in Everyday Life*. New York: Doubleday.

Goffman, Erving 1963 *Stigma*. Englewood Cliffs, NJ: Prentice-Hall.

Gold, Martin 1970 *Delinquent Behavior in an American City*. Belmont, CA: Brooks/Cole.

Gove, Walter R. 1985 The effect of age and gender on deviant behavior: A biopsychological perspective. In Alice Rossi (ed.), *Gender and the Life Course*. New York: Aldine.

Gove, Walter R. and Michael L. Hughes 1980 Reexamining the ecological fallacy: A study in which aggregate data are critical in investigating the pathological effects of living alone. *Social Forces* 58: 1,157–1,177.

Gove, Walter R., Michael L. Hughes, and Omer R. Galle 1979 Overcrowding in the home. *American Sociological Review* 44: 59–80.

Guest, Avery M. 1984 Robert Park and the natural area: A sentimental review. *Sociology and Social Research* 68: 1–21.

Hayner, Norman S. 1942 Five cities of the Pacific Northwest. In Clifford Shaw and Henry McKay (eds.), *Juvenile Delinquency and Urban Areas*. Chicago: University of Chicago Press.

Hindelang, Michael J. 1973 Causes of delinquency: A partial replication and extension. *Social Problems* 20: 471–478.

Hindelang, Michael J., Travis Hirschi, and Joseph G. Weis 1981 *Measuring Delinquency*. Beverly Hills: Sage.

Hirschi, Travis 1969 *Causes of Delinquency*. Berkeley: University of California Press.

Hirschi, Travis and Michael J. Hindelang 1977 Intelligence and delinquency: A revisionist view. *American Sociological Review* 42: 571–587.

Jensen, Gary F., Maynard L. Erickson, and Jack Gibbs 1978 Perceived risk of punishment and self-reported delinquency. *Social Forces* 57: 57–58.

Jones, D. Caradog 1934 *The Social Survey of Merseyside, Vol. III*. Liverpool: University Press of Liverpool.

Lazarsfeld, Paul F., Ann K. Pasanella, and Morris Rosenberg 1972 *Continuities in the Language of Social Research*. New York: Free Press.

Lee, Barrett A., Ralph S. Oropesa, Barbara J. Metch, and Avery M. Guest 1984 Testing the decline-of-community thesis: Neighborhood organizations in Seattle, 1929 and 1979. *American Journal of Sociology* 89: 1,161–1,188.

Levin, Yale and Alfred Lindesmith 1937 English ecology and criminology of the past century. *Journal of Criminal Law and Criminology* 27: 801–816.

Lieberson, Stanley 1985 *Making It Count: The Impoverishment of Social Research and Theory*. Berkeley: University of California Press.

Mayhew, Henry 1851 *London Labor and the London Poor*. London: Griffin.

McKenzie, Roderick 1926 The scope of human ecology. *Publications of the American Sociological Society* 20: 141–154.

Minor, W. William and Joseph Harry 1982 Deterrent and experimental effects in perceptual deterrence research. *Journal of Research in Crime and Delinquency* 18: 190–203.

Park, Robert E. 1952 *Human Communities: The City and Human Ecology*. New York: The Free Press.

Park, Robert E., Ernest W. Burgess, and Roderick McKenzie 1925 *The City*. Chicago: University of Chicago Press.

Parker, J. and Harold G. Grasmick 1979 Linking actual and perceived certainty of punishment: An exploratory study of an untested proposition in deterrence theory. *Criminology* 17: 366–379.

Reckless, Walter C. 1926 *Publications of the American Sociological Society* 20: 164–176.

Shaw, Clifford R. and Henry D. McKay 1942 *Juvenile Delinquency and Urban Areas*. Chicago: University of Chicago Press.

Simcha-Fagan, Ora and Joseph E. Schwartz 1986 Neighborhood and delinquency: An assessment of contextual effects. *Criminology* 24: 667–699.

Stark, Rodney 1986 *Crime and Deviance in North America: ShowCase*. Seattle: Cognitive Development Company.

Stark, Rodney and William Sims Bainbridge 1985 *The Future of Religion*. Berkeley: University of California Press.

Stark, Rodney and William Sims Bainbridge 1987 *A Theory of Religion*. Bern and New York: Lang.

Stark, Rodney, Daniel P. Doyle, and Jesse Lynn Rushing 1983 Beyond Durkheim: Religion and suicide. *Journal for the Scientific Study of Religion* 22: 120–131.

Stark, Rodney and James McEvoy 1970 Middle class violence. *Psychology Today* 4: 52–54, 110–112.

Suttles, Gerald 1968 *The Social Order of the Slum*. Chicago: University of Chicago Press.

Suttles, Gerald 1972 *The Social Construction of Communities*. Chicago: University of Chicago Press.

Thrasher, Frederick M. 1927 *The Gang*. Chicago: University of Chicago Press.

Tittle, Charles R., Wayne J. Villemez, and Douglas A. Smith 1978 The myth of social class and criminality: An empirical assessment of the empirical evidence. *American Sociological Review* 43: 643–656.

Toby, Jackson 1957 Social disorganization and stake in conformity: Complementary factors in the predatory behavior of hoodlums. *Journal of Criminal Law, Criminology and Police Science* 48: 12–17.

Toby, Jackson and Marcia L. Toby 1961 *Law School Status as a Predisposing Factor in Subcultural Delinquency*. New Brunswick: Rutgers University Press.

Welch, Kevin 1983 Community development and metropolitan religious commitment: A test of two competing models. *Journal for the Scientific Study of Religion* 22: 167–181.

Wuthnow, Robert and Kevin Christiano 1979 The effects of residential migration on church attendance. In Robert Wuthnow (ed.), *The Religious Dimension*. New York: Academic Press.

17

The generality of deviance

Travis Hirschi and
Michael R. Gottfredson

[...]

The theory [of self-control] simply stated, is this: Criminal acts are a subset of acts in which the actor ignores the long-term negative consequences that flow from the act itself (e.g., the health consequences of drug use), from the social or familial environment (e.g., a spouse's reaction to infidelity), or from the state (e.g., the criminal justice response to robbery). All acts that share this feature, including criminal acts, are therefore likely to be engaged in by individuals unusually sensitive to immediate pleasure and insensitive to long-term consequences. The immediacy of the benefits of crime implies that they are obvious to the actor, that no special skill or learning is required. The property of individuals that explains variation in the likelihood of engaging in such acts we call 'self-control.' The evidence suggests to us that variation in self-control is established early in life, and that differences between individuals remain reasonably constant over the life course. It also suggests, consistent with the idea of self-control, that individuals will tend to engage in (or avoid) a wide variety of criminal and analogous behaviors – that they will not specialize in some to the exclusion of others, nor will they 'escalate' into more serious or skillful criminal behavior over time.

Both the stability of differences between individuals and the versatility of offenders can be derived from the fact that all such acts follow a predictable path over the life course, peaking in the middle to late teens, and then declining steadily throughout life. If children who offend by whining and pushing and shoving are the adults who offend by robbing and raping, it must be that whining and pushing and shoving are the theoretical equivalents of robbery and rape. If robbery and rape are theoretical equivalents, they should be engaged in by the same

From *The Generality of Deviance*, pp. 1–23. (New Brunswick: Transaction Publishers, 1994.)

people. They *are* engaged in by the same people (putting the lie to the idea that each of them is peculiarly motivated). If deviant acts at different phases of the life course are engaged in differentially by the same individuals, the underlying trait must be extremely stable over time. If the same individuals tend to engage in serious and trivial acts, these acts must satisfy equivalent desires of the actor.

Evidence for a 'latent trait' that somehow causes deviant behavior thus comes from two primary sources. The first is the statistical association among diverse criminal, deviant, or reckless acts. Because these acts are behaviorally heterogeneous, because they occur in a variety of situations, and because they entail different sets of necessary conditions, it seems reasonable to suppose that what they have in common somehow resides in the person committing them. The second is the stability of differences between individuals over time. Because individuals relatively likely to commit criminal, deviant, or reckless acts at one point in time are also relatively likely to commit such acts at later points in time, it seems reasonable to ascribe these differences to a persistent underlying trait possessed in different degrees by those whose behavior is being compared.

The standards described are well-known as tests of internal consistency and test-retest reliability (or stability). When applied to measures of crime, they offer compelling evidence that a stable trait of personality underlies much criminal, deviant, and reckless behavior (Greenberg 1991; Rowe, Osgood, and Nicewander 1990; Osgood 1990; Osgood et al. 1988; Olweus 1979; Nagin and Farrington 1992).

If the evidence requires that we grant the existence of reliable differences among individuals in the tendency to commit deviant acts, the evidence it seems to us also requires that we conceptualize this 'latent trait' in particular ways. For example, we cannot make it conducive to specialization in some deviant acts rather than others, because that would be contrary to its generality (we cannot easily conceptualize it as 'internalization of norms,' because that would suggest the possibility of internalizing some norms and not others, an idea also contrary to the finding of generality); we cannot make it akin to aggressiveness, because that would be contrary to its often passive, furtive, or retreatist consequences; we cannot make it a positive force requiring for its satisfaction the commission of clearly criminal acts, because it is not conducive to persistence in a course of action but is instead conducive to momentary satisfaction of transient desires. Reasoning in this way, and from examination of the diverse acts produced by or consistent with this 'latent trait,' we concluded that it was best seen as *self-control*, the tendency to avoid acts whose long-term costs exceed their momentary advantages.

NATURAL SANCTIONS

This conception of the trait underlying criminal, deviant, and reckless behavior solves several problems. A persistent problem in this area is extinction, the tendency of responses created and maintained by sanctions to evaporate in the absence of continued reinforcement. How is self-control maintained when there are no obvious social or legal supports for it? It is not hard to find examples of people who continue to 'conform' during very long periods in which their behavior is not observed by other people or subject to the sanctions of the criminal law. In our view, self control is resistent to extinction because its ultimate sources are natural sanctions that by definition do not require continued input from others. Socialization, in this sense, may be seen as a process of educating individuals about the consequences of their behavior. Once they have such knowledge and the habit of acting on it, no further reinforcement is required. In fact in most areas natural sanctions so exceed in strength social or legal sanctions that the latter are not really necessary to explain the conformity of most people. The mystery is, rather, how some people can ignore or misapprehend the automatic consequences of their behavior, both positive and negative, and thus continue to act as though these consequences did not exist.

For example, opportunities to drink are virtually unlimited for all members of the population. Alcohol in one form or another is relatively cheap and is widely available. For many people, normative control is for all intents and purposes absent. They lead essentially private lives, or those around them do not really care about their consumption. The pleasures of alcohol are known and acknowledged by a large majority of the population. Yet self control predicts consumption of alcohol in both public and private settings over the life course. It must be that self-control is maintained by the natural consequences of behavior including but by no means limited to the reactions of others. Consistent with this argument, alcohol consumption also declines with age, suggesting that consumption is governed more by its physiological than by its social consequences.

Self control is highly efficient precisely because it is effective in a variety of settings, many of which lack social or legal surveillance, but few of which lack natural sanctions. People with self control do not risk accidents on lonely mountain roads even though no one is there to see them exceed the speed limit. They do not steal goods belonging to others despite countless opportunities to do so because such actions are inconsistent with prospects for success (prospects that do not allow a record of criminal behavior, but are otherwise independent of social or legal sanctions).

The idea of self control suggests that the origin of all sanctions or norms is to be found in natural sanctions, the rewards and punishments that follow automatically from particular acts or lines of behavior. Many natural sanctions are of course physical or physiological, affecting the health or well-being of the body – producing injury, disease, deterioration, or even death. Excessive use of drugs, interpersonal violence, promiscuous sexual behavior, and theft of all sorts can yield such consequences. As a result, normative and legal systems evolve to draw attention to these consequences (the difficulty we have in saying precisely what these systems are up to suggests that they have many sources and functions). The relation between natural and normative sanctions helps account for the universality of norms governing those behaviors with the most serious consequences, such as interpersonal violence and theft. At the same time, it helps explain society's ambiguous stance toward some norms and their enforcement, such as drug use and sexual promiscuity.

IMPLICATIONS OF SELF-CONTROL

Our conception of the trait underlying criminal, deviant, and reckless behavior is, we believe, consistent with

- research showing the importance of the family in delinquency causation (Glueck and Glueck 1950; Hirschi 1969; Loeber and Stouthamer-Loeber 1986);

- research showing the importance of opportunities to commit criminal acts (Cohen and Felson 1979);

- research showing a sharp decline in all kinds of criminal, deviant, and reckless behavior with age (Hirschi and Gottfredson 1983).

At the same time, this conceptualization of the trait underlying criminal, deviant, and reckless behavior is *in*consistent with

- the idea of a career criminal, an individual who makes a living from well-planned and executed crimes over an extended period of time, or who at least persists in a definite line of criminal activity;

- the idea of organized crime, or organized delinquent gangs engaged in long-term and highly profitable illegal activities, such as gambling, prostitution, and drug trafficking;

- the idea that the causes of 'adolescent delinquency' are different from the causes of 'adult crime' (see Trasler 1991:440);

- the idea that the causes of 'white-collar' crime are different from the causes of 'ordinary' crime; the idea that crime is learned, that it must be acquired from other people.

As might be expected from all this, the idea that low self-control underlies the bulk of criminal and deviant acts has not been greeted with enthusiasm by all segments of the criminological community. On the contrary, the theory has attracted a variety of criticisms. According to the critics, the theory

- is too general. It attempts to encompass too broad a range of deviant behavior. Instrumental and expressive crimes have different causes, as do white-collar and street crimes. Purposive criminal acts have little in common with accidents, bad habits, mental illnesses, or school truancy.

- is tautological. If criminal acts are defined as acts in which the long-term negative consequences for the actor outweigh the short-term gains, it is a matter of definition that those committing such acts tend to ignore or discount long-term consequences.

- is based on an erroneous conception of the relation between age and the various behaviors it attempts to explain, and ignores evidence that the causes of the onset of crime differ from the causes of persistence in and desistence from crime.

- ignores important distinctions between the incidence and prevalence of criminal or deviant behavior.

- fails to distinguish among classes of offenders who differ markedly in the level and variety of their deviant behavior.

- suggests erroneously that the penalties of the criminal justice system are ineffective in crime control. The theory also fails to anticipate important differences among offenders in their sensitivity to institutional experiences or sanctions.

- overstates the importance of self-control, regarding it as the sole cause of crime.

- ignores the fact that self-control is not the stable, general trait the theory claims it to be.

It is not a straightforward matter to respond to critiques of a theory. Such critiques have diverse origins. One ostensibly valid source of criticism is the research literature. But published research may be based on samples or data or interpretations of the theory that are inadequate or inappropriate, and response to research-based criticism therefore requires case-by-case examination of specific studies. Another presumably valid source of criticism is the compatibility between the theory and the rules described by experts in theory construction. But there is in fact considerable disagreement about the logical standards that one can legitimately employ in assessing the adequacy of a theory. Presumably, each theory has its own logic and its own basic assumptions. Adequate response to logic-based criticism would therefore require articulation of the philosophy of science underlying the theory and its competitors, a task that should not be undertaken lightly. Finally, there are the textbooks in a field. These books often provide extensive lists of criticisms of particular theories gathered from a variety of sources. But it is entirely possible that such generic lists of criticisms do more harm than good, suggesting as they do that everything is equally open to doubt, that all research and theory in the field is problematic, that the student is therefore free to believe anything he or she wishes to believe without fear of contradiction.

This is not to say, of course, that theories should be immune from criticism. In fact, in our view, the field suffers from lack of rigorous and persistent criticism of its theories, methods, and assumptions, and too readily accepts the view that all theories contain a grain of truth. (For a recent, excellent review of the field from a critical perspective, see Roshier 1989.) In our view, the primary test of a theory is its ability to organize the data in an area relative to the ability of alternative theories to organize the same data. We recognize that many scholars (e.g., Tittle 1991; Akers 1991) prefer to avoid drawing sharp distinctions between theories, or [...] presenting them in an oppositional mode. But in our view good criticism *must be comparative*, asking how one theory fares relative to its competitors. Our perspective places little value on lists of strengths and weaknesses of theories, and sees little benefit in uncritical 'integrations' of competing theories.

It requires merely a willingness to abide by the dictates of logic and the results of competent research.

One problem with 'criticisms' of theories is that, absent a context of competing theories, they are hard to evaluate. Take the most damning criticism one can allege against a theory (after internal inconsistency): that it is false. The record is reasonably clear that even this criticism will have little impact on the viability of a theory in the absence of a competing theory that claims the same territory.

By the same token, the charge that a theory is 'too general' is hard to evaluate absent a context of competing theory. When specified in the statement 'robbery is not murder' (or, more telling, in the statement 'accidents are not crimes!') this criticism implies that these are such different events that they must have different explanations. But this is tantamount to a critique of the germ theory of disease that asserts that diphtheria is not whooping cough. The theory that diseases are caused by infectious agents is even more general than the germ theory. Is it 'too general' because it includes viruses as well as bacteria? Obviously, a general theory is not damaged by the charge of excess generality.

General theories do not assert that the concrete events or states they explain are identical. They assert only that they have something in common. They assert that robbery and murder have something in common that explains the fact that both are likely to be committed by the same people. It would be a legitimate criticism of such theory if the critic were able to show that people who commit robbery are not more likely than nonrobbers to commit murder, but that would only imply that the theory is wrong, not that it is 'too general.'

Even more curious is the charge that our theory is tautological (Akers 1991). In our view, the charge of tautology is in fact a compliment, an assertion that we followed the path of logic in producing an internally consistent result. Indeed, this is what we set out to do. We started with a conception of crime, and from it attempted to *derive* a conception of the offender. As a result, there should be strict definitional consistency between our image of the actor and our image of the act. What distinguishes our theory from many criminological theories is that we begin with the act, whereas they normally begin with the actor. Theories that start from the causes of crime – for example, economic deprivation – eventually define crime as a response to the causes they invoke. Thus, a theory that sees economic deprivation as the cause of crime will by definition see crime as an attempt to remedy economic deprivation, making the connection between cause and effect tautological.

What makes our theory *peculiarly* vulnerable to complaints about tautology is that we explicitly show the logical connections between our conception of the actor and the act, whereas many theorists leave this task to those interpreting or testing their theory, but again we are not impressed that we are unusual in this regard. One more example: Sutherland's theory of differential association says that offenders have peculiar skills and attitudes toward crime learned from their subcultures. Crime is thus a reflection of those skills and attitudes. In this theory too the connection between the image of the offender and the image of crime (both require particular skills and attitudes) is tautological.

In a comparative framework, the charge of tautology suggests that a theory that is nontautological would be preferable. But what would such a theory look like? It would advance definitions of crime and of criminals that are independent of one another (e.g., crime is a violation of the law; the criminal is a person denied access to legitimate opportunity). Several historically important theories cannot show an empirical connection between their definition of crime and their image of the offender, and must therefore be said to be false [...].

Those charging us with tautology do not see the issue in this light. Thus Akers says,

> It would appear to be tautological to explain the propensity to commit crime by low self-control. They are one and the same, and such assertions about them are true by definition. The assertion means that low self-control causes low self-control. Similarly, since no operational definition of self-control is given, we cannot know that a person has low self-control (stable propensity to commit crime) unless he or she commits crimes or analogous behavior. The statement that low self-control is a cause of crime, then, is also tautological. (1991: 204)

It seems to us that here (and elsewhere) Akers's concept of self-control differs fundamentally from our own. We do not see self-control as the propensity to commit crime, or as the motivating force underlying criminal acts. Rather, we see self-control as the barrier than stands between the actor and the obvious momentary benefits crime provides. We explicitly propose that the link between self-control and crime is *not* deterministic, but probabilistic, affected by opportunities and other constraints. If so, the problem with our conception is more likely to be that it is nonfalsifiable than that it merely definitional.

Fortunately for the theory, Akers himself proposes that the problems he identifies can be resolved by operationalizing the concept of self-control. Thus, following the discussion above, he writes: 'To avoid the tautology problem, independent indicators of self-control are needed' (1991: 204). The question then becomes, can independent indicators of self-control be identified. With respect to crime, we would propose such items as whining, pushing, and shoving (as a child); smoking and drinking and excessive television watching and accident frequency (as a teenager); difficulties in interpersonal relations, employment instability, automobile accidents, drinking, and smoking (as an adult). None of these acts or behaviors is a crime. They are logically independent of crime. Therefore the relation between them and crime is not a matter of definition, and the theory survives the charge that it is mere tautology and that it is nonfalsifiable.

Clearly, our theory cannot be at once nonfalsifiable, true by definition, and false. We know that many readers find that our description of crime rings true, that it corresponds on the whole to what they have seen and heard. Such readers will not understand that our conception is really radically different from the conceptions implicit in the theories that have dominated the field for many years. If they accuse us of being trite or true by definition, we cannot blame them – but we accept their inevitable conclusion that competing theories must be false.

The attractiveness of a theory that identifies commonalities among apparently disparate events is often counterbalanced by the feeling that too much has been sacrificed on the alter of generality. For theorists the problem is made worse by the modern tendency to divide the world into ever more narrow research problems ('homicide among the elderly female population'), each with its own cadre of experts, with the consequence that application of a general theory will be opposed by specialists in each subarea it was intended to subsume […].

As stated, the theory applies to acts that provide immediate benefit at the risk of long-term cost to actors who find opportunities for such acts appealing. Because such acts are injurious to long-term individual and collective interests, they are universally resisted, at least at some level. Confusion arises from the obvious fact that groups vary in their reaction to such events, sometimes dealing with them harshly and formally in the criminal law, sometimes dealing with them as medical problems, sometimes as welfare problems, and sometimes appearing to ignore them altogether. From the point of view of the theory, such reactions are aspects of the long-term costs of the behavior, serving to reduce or intensify them, but never eliminating them altogether. To the extent that alterations in social costs affect the development of self control, they can be important in causing variation in the behaviors in question. Thus, for example, tobacco and alcohol use have natural consequences that to some degree limit their use, but variation in alcohol and tobacco use may also be traced to restrictions on availability and to differences in social and legal sanctions from one group to another. These differences do not negate the conclusion that tobacco and alcohol use fall within the purview of the theory; indeed they show that tobacco and alcohol are in the same class as such currently illegal substances as marijuana and cocaine.

A related source of confusion is the idea that some acts encompassed by the theory have not always been socially condemned, or may not be so condemned in the future. Thus, it is said, cigarette smoking was once actually fashionable, and it is possible to imagine a time when the use of marijuana will be promoted as socially and legally accepted behavior. Does the theory apply equally to both substances when they are legal and illegal? Indeed it does. The only requirement of the theory is that at all times those low in self-control are more likely to engage in the behaviour than those high in self control. In fact, even when smoking was fashionable in the United States delinquents were much more likely than nondelinquents to smoke (Schoff 1915; Glueck and Glueck 1950; Hirschi 1969). We can therefore assume that when or if marijuana is legalized, the correlation between marijuana use and deviant behavior will remain at current levels.

These facts may suggest that self-control inhibits pursuit of immediate pleasure, whatever its long-term consequences – that is, the high self-control people have no fun even when it is free. We think this interpretation is probably incorrect. Knowledge that smoking has long-term harmful effects did not come into the world with the surgeon general's report in 1964. On the contrary, cigarettes were known as 'coffin nails' before the turn of the century. Similarly, it would be unlikely that the deleterious consequences of repeated marijuana use would escape the notice of those concerned with the long term.

The theory thus produces clear expectations about the generality of deviance and the versatility of offenders. […]

REFERENCES

Akers, Ronald L. 1991. 'Self-Control as a General Theory of Crime.' *Journal of Quantitative Criminology* 7: 201–11.

Cohen, Lawrence, and Marcus Felson. 1979. 'Social Change and Crime Rate Trends: A Routine Activity Approach.' *American Sociological Review* 44: 588–608.

Glueck, Sheldon, and Eleanor Glueck. 1950. *Unraveling Juvenile Delinquency*. Cambridge, MA: Harvard University Press.

Greenberg, David. 1991. 'Modeling Criminal Careers.' *Criminology* 25: 17–46.

Hirschi, Travis. 1969. *Causes of Delinquency*. Berkeley: University of California Press.

Hirschi, Travis, and Michael R. Gottfredson. 1983. 'Age and the Explanation of Crime.' *American Journal of Sociology* 89: 552–84.

Loeber, Rolf, and Magda Stouthamer-Loeber. 1986. 'Family Factors as Correlates and Predictors of Juvenile Conduct Problems and Delinquency.' In *Crime and Justice: An Annual Review of Research*, vol. 7, ed. M. Tonry and N. Morris, 29–149. Chicago: University of Chicago Press.

Nagin, Daniel, and David Farrington. 1992. 'The Stability of Criminal Potential from Childhood to Adulthood.' *Criminology* 30: 235–60.

Olweus, Dan. 1979. 'Stability of Aggressive Reaction Patterns in Males: A Review.' *Psychological Bulletin* 86: 852–75.

Osgood, D. Wayne. 1990. 'Covariation and Adolescent Problem Behaviors.' Paper presented at the meetings of the American Society of Criminology, Baltimore, MD.

Osgood, D. Wayne, Lloyd Johnston, Patrick O'Malley, and Jerald Bachman. 1988. 'The Generality of Deviance in Late Adolescence and Early Adulthood.' *American Sociological Review* 53: 81–93.

Roshier, Bob. 1989. *Controlling Crime: The Classical Perspective in Criminology*. Chicago: Lyceum Books.

Rowe, David, D. Wayne Osgood, and W. Alan Nicewander. 1990. 'A Latent Trait Approach to Unifying Criminal Careers.' *Criminology* 28: 237–70.

Schoff, Hannah Kent. 1915. *The Wayward Child*. Indianapolis: Bobbs-Merrill.

Tittle, Charles R. 1991. Review of *A General Theory of Crime*, by Michael Gottfredson and Travis Hirschi. *American Journal of Sociology* 96: 1609–1.

Trasler, Gordon. 1991. Review of *Explaining Criminal Behaviour: Interdisciplinary Approaches*, by Wouter Buikhuisen and Sarnoff A. Mednick. *Contemporary Psychology* 36: 440–41.

18

The routine activity approach as a general crime theory

Marcus Felson

A *paradigm* is a fancy word for a general theory or framework that organizes a field of study (Kuhn 1962). Every science needs one to keep from going to pieces. Criminology lacks one. For example, a recent survey of criminologists found that no more than 17 percent agreed with any one general theory of crime (Ellis 1999). Indeed, criminologists dispersed their votes among 22 general theories. They did not even apply the same theories to serious and persistent offending that they applied to delinquency and minor offending. Some people will insist that criminology is a 'multiple-paradigm' field, but that violates the very idea of a paradigm as a single road map for scientific exploration.[1]

That does not mean that everyone in a discipline needs to agree on every matter, but nearly everyone must agree about the basic concepts and ideas organizing their field of study. Interestingly, criminologists do agree substantially about four basic crime correlations:

1   Family life discourages crime participation.

2   Males commit more crimes than do females.

3   Persons ages 12 to 25 years are disproportionate offenders.

4   As socioeconomic status rises, crime participation declines.

Criminologists disagree about which of these correlations to emphasize and how to put them together into a general theory. Adherents to each theory criticize

From *Of Crime and Criminality* (ed. S.S. Simpson), pp. 205–216. (Thousand Oaks, CA: Pine Forge Press, 2000.)

the competition for neglecting one of the four correlations. A major problem faced by traditional crime theories is that all four of these correlations are overstated. Males commit relatively more crimes, but females are all too active in crime. Youths have no crime monopoly, and those who are older have extra employee theft opportunities. Crime occurs within families, and good parents can have bad kids. The income–crime correlation is not that strong. One never should hitch a paradigm to correlations as weak as these. This is why criminologists need a new general theory. What criteria should we use to develop it?

MAKING CRIME EXPLANATION COHERENT

Criminology already has plenty of facts and ideas. Our problem is to figure out which of these facts and ideas are central and which are peripheral. For example, it is tempting to exaggerate race differences in offending and to forget that nations lacking racial differences still have crime. The race issue, although very important for the operations of the criminal justice system, can become a distraction for studying the origins of crime itself.

Which facts and ideas should we use to forge a general science of crime? To make these difficult decisions, I suggest that we adopt from more successful sciences the following five standards of scientific coherence.

The 'touch-it' standard. Find highly tangible explanations at the outset. Take advantage of the physical world and our five senses to state the first principles in very down-to-earth terms. For example, Harvey figured out the human circulatory system by considering flows of blood among specific organs in a definite order, and Galileo dropped objects from the Tower of Pisa and watched when they hit the ground.

The 'near-and-far' standard. Find explanations that work as well at micro and macro levels, in different settings and eras, internationally, and for all types of crime (Brantingham and Brantingham 1984). A good explanation should help us to understand crime for the individual, neighborhood, town, city, metropolis, and nation as well as for the hour, day, week, month, year, decade, millennium, and epoch. For example, a physiologist can study submicroscopic and microscopic flows of blood as well as those visible with the naked eye. He or she can link capillaries to small blood vessels, to large vessels, to the largest vessel, the aorta. Labs can study blood flows by the second, minute, or hour. Good science is universal for all nations and ethnic groups. This point inspired Gottfredson and Hirschi (1990) to state their 'general theory of crime.' A general theory does not neglect variations among individual cases or localities; it merely puts these variations into a common framework.

The 'few-to-many' standard. Find a few scientific rules with many ramifications. If one's list of first principles gets too long or complex, then he or she is going to get lost. This is why Newton stated only three laws of thermodynamics. Darwin boiled about 1,000 pages of observations down to a single principle of natural selection. Scientists call this process 'Occam's razor,' cutting away at confusion and getting to the point on principles while elaborating on facts and derivations.

The 'exactly how' standard. Find clear *mechanisms*, that is, exactly how something leads to more or less crime (Pawson and Tilley 1997). Scientists want to know the direction in which blood flows, exactly what animals eat, how chlorophyll works, and how organisms live and die. Criminologists must find out exactly what burglars look for and how they break in. Even one's armchair speculations should say exactly how he or she thinks something happens. I would rather be precisely wrong than vaguely right.

The 'fit-the-facts' standard. Learn everything possible about specific crimes, their settings, their modus operandi, and how they are prevented. Make sure that the explanations are consistent with these facts (see, e.g., Clarke 1997). Modify the explanations as more facts come in. If explanations need to be contorted to fit the facts, then it is time for a new paradigm.

We can learn from the more successful sciences how to formulate a general theory for criminology. Fortunately, these five standards for coherent crime explanation apply to one extant general theory of crime: the routine activity approach to crime analysis.

THE ORIGINAL FORMULATION OF THE ROUTINE ACTIVITY APPROACH

The routine activity approach began by describing how a direct contact predatory offense occurred (Cohen and Felson 1979). Such an offense was predatory because it had, at a minimum, one offender and one target of crime. Direct physical contact between the offender and target also was required. The original formulation excluded threats from a distance, suicide, drug sales, and fights in which both participants were offenders. A direct contact predatory offense in the original formulation had three minimal elements:

- a likely offender;

- a suitable target; and

- the absence of a capable guardian against the offense.

During the era of its formulation, the routine activity approach differed greatly from other crime theories because it treated the offender as relatively less significant. The routine activity approach also defined the target of crime distinctly from the victim. The best guardian against a crime is neither a police officer nor a security guard. The best guardian is someone close such as a friend or relative. Guardianship against crime depends on someone's *absence*. Two presences (offender and target) and one absence (guardian) make the best crime setting. The convergence of these three conditions invites a criminal act to occur.

A suitable crime target might include a wallet, a purse, a car, or a human target for personal attack. A target's suitability for attack is determined by four criteria, summed up by the acronym VIVA:

- *Value*

- *Inertia*

- *Visibility*

- *Access*

The value of the target is defined from the offender's viewpoint, depending on what the offender wants. Find out what property someone might like to steal or vandalize or who an offender might prefer to attack or even kidnap. Usually, the offender would be discouraged if a target were high in inertia. For example, a heavy appliance is too difficult to carry out of a home, and a large or muscular person is difficult to outmuscle. Usually, an offender is drawn to a target more visible to him or her such as money flashed in a bar or someone who unwittingly invites an attack. The offender's access to a street or building renders its contents and people more subject to his or her illegal action.

The routine activity approach started with crime conditions right there. It considered how a criminal act occurs or fails to occur at specific times and places. Without the convergence of minimal elements for crime, a direct contact predatory criminal act would be virtually out of the question. Such immediate conditions are set in place from the routine activities of the surrounding community. The transportation system, the structure of work and household, and the technology and production of goods – in short, the everyday *macro-level* organization of the community and society – lead to *micro* convergences of conditions more or less favourable to crime.

Consider how a residential burglary occurs. A burglar tries to find a suitable household that is empty of guardians or within which the guardians are asleep or indisposed. The burglar seeks a place containing valuables easy to remove. Easy access and visibility draw the burglar further. The larger community structure offers the burglar crime opportunities by producing more lightweight but valuable goods and getting people out of their homes for work, school, or leisure. While they are out, the burglar goes in.

APPLYING THE FIVE STANDARDS OF COHERENT SCIENCE TO THE ROUTINE ACTIVITY APPROACH

The routine activities explanation for crime holds up quite well when tested against the five standards of scientific coherence. Following the *touch-it standard*, the routine activity approach is highly tangible, emphasizes the physical world, and considers physical convergences in its core requirements. Its image of the offender takes into account the offender's use of the five senses to carry out crime. Following the *near-and-far standard*, the routine activity approach works at both the micro and macro levels, in different settings and eras, internationally, and for different types of crime (Felson 2000). It shows how offenders, targets, and guardians move into and out of potential crime settings. The routine activity approach also uses a few clear and simple principles. Simplicity is not the same as simple-mindedness. Indeed, very diverse findings, difficult problems, and complex information can be absorbed within its few and simple principles. For example, the many features of home, neighborhood, and household activities could be summed up in one principle: the offender must find the target with nobody there to stop the offender from attacking it. Indeed, routine activity analysis brings forth many nuances of criminal acts, still maintaining coherence by deriving all this from a very few rules, in accordance with the *few-to-many standard*. It starts at a very simple level before it elaborates. If one gets lost, one can just go back to the few fundamentals to find his or her way once more.

The routine activity approach also seeks clear mechanisms, examining which features of daily life lead to more or less crime. Its adherence to the *exactly how standard* is well illustrated elsewhere (Felson 1998). For example, the old theories state vague and inexact hypotheses, for example, 'Social disorganization creates crime.' By contrast, the routine activity approach details mechanisms such as the following:

- Tough guys can seize local abandoned houses for their own illegal uses. For example, they can set up drug houses.

- Failed local businesses leave streets unsupervised and dangerous.

The routine activity approach also helps us to understand why some forms of 'social disorganization' do not give us more crime and might even produce less:

- Shabby paint on buildings might be ugly, but it probably does not itself contribute to more crime.

- Graffiti in subways probably does not lead to more robberies.

- Extreme deterioration of a neighborhood might cause vice crimes to decline by scaring away customers.

The *fit-the-facts standard* of scientific coherence is reflected in the growing convergence between the routine activity approach and several studies of crime specifics, settings, modus operandi, broken windows theory (Kelling and Coles 1996), and prevention. Relatively recent work is devoted to such convergences (Clarke and Felson 1993; Felson 1998; Felson and Clarke 1999).

Burglary offers us many cogent examples of how the routine activity approach follows all five standards of scientific coherence. A burglar follows the touch-it standard using his or her senses to determine crime opportunities and risks and to put criminal acts into motion. In accordance with the near-and-far standard, a burglar responds to specific and local crime opportunities while also benefiting from new transport systems that help the burglar get to additional crime settings.

Specific routine factors assist the burglar (e.g., more lightweight goods, more cash in homes or businesses). The few-to-many standard also is very relevant; the burglar can consider a few aspects of his or her targets, such as VIVA (discussed earlier), to decide whether or not to break in. The burglar might seek easy access and lightweight things to carry away. These minimal elements have elaborate applications when considering what streets lead to a crime target, different types of buildings, the timing of commercial burglary versus residential burglary (weekend for the former and weekday for the latter), and variations among nations varying in how often households are left unsupervised. The exactly how standard demands that criminologists specify how the burglar gets there and chooses that building; what part of a building the burglar enters; where things are kept; lines of sight for guardians and offenders; and why the burglar over- looks other entries, buildings, or booty. For example, middle income areas with small backyards and easy sight lines tend to have low burglary rates; other middle income areas with both spouses working, high bushes, and large back- yards tend to have high burglary rates. Finally, the specific settings and modus operandi of burglary and the details of its prevention become central for routine activity analysis of burglary. To study burglary in scientific terms, we have to consider who, what, where, when, and how. Because the routine activity approach does not try to divide the population into two groups – definite offend- ers and definite nonoffenders – this approach can more readily accommodate the details of crime research. This makes it easier to meet the fit-the-facts standard with the routine activity approach.

EXTENSIONS OF THE ROUTINE ACTIVITY APPROACH

During recent years, I have extended the routine activity approach well beyond direct contact predatory crimes (Felson 1998). Illegal drug sales depend on the physical convergences of buyers and sellers as well as the absence of those who would prevent these sales. Nonpredatory fights involve the convergence of antag- onists with peacemakers absent and provokers present. Even suicides depend on absences of those who would prevent them. This approach now takes into account supervision of youths and offenders in general. The routine activity approach today goes far beyond its original statement. I always am surprised at those who describe the routine activity approach as it was 20 years ago, ignoring its life and growth. The extensions of this approach further demonstrate its adher- ence to the third standard of scientific coherence; it explores numerous ramifica- tions derived from basic principles. [...]

CONCLUSION

Crime is complex, and criminology is difficult. Most theories have not been able to find their way through all this complexity or to find the elusive secret of indi- vidual disposition to commit crime. These theories failed because they tried to predict the unpredictable – what each individual is going to do next. It is much more promising to work with tangible processes and incidents. Five standards of scientific coherence provide us with the tools for progress. The routine activity approach uses these tools well and places the crime incident at the center of inquiry. Crime is a physical act, and we must not forget it.

NOTE

1   During a scientific revolution, two paradigms do battle for a brief period until the new one wins. Criminology today lives in a 'pre-paradigm state,' that is, theoretical chaos. Although many paradigms might exist over the total history of a science, they cannot live together simultaneously. Moreover, an old paradigm might have made good sense in its day given what was then known. But as new information comes along, so does a new and better paradigm. There is no turning back. For example, today's astronomers could not return to Ptolemy's image of the universe even if they wanted to. It just would not work.

REFERENCES

Brantingham, P.J. and P.L. Brantingham. 1984. *Patterns in Crime*. New York: Macmillan.

Clarke, R.V., ed. 1997. *Situational Crime Prevention: Successful Case Studies*. 2nd ed. New York: Harrow & Heston.

Clarke, R.V. and M. Felson. 1993. 'Introduction: Criminology, Routine Activity, and Rational Choice.' In *Routine Activity and Rational Choice: Advances in Criminological Theory*, vol. 5, edited by R.V. Clarke and M. Felson. New Brunswick, NJ: Transaction Books.

Cohen, L.E. and M. Felson. 1979. 'Social Change and Crime Rate Trends: A Routine Activity Approach.' *American Sociological Review* 4:588–608.

Ellis, Lee. 1999. 'Criminologists' Opinions About Causes and Theories of Crime and Delinquency.' *The Criminologist*, July/August, 1, 5.

Felson, M. 1998. *Crime and Everyday Life*. 2nd ed. Thousand Oaks, CA: Pine Forge.

Felson, M. 2000. 'The Routine Activity Approach: A Very Versatile Theory of Crime.' In *Explaining Crime and Criminals*, edited by R. Paternoster. Los Angeles: Roxbury.

Felson, M. and R.V. Clarke, 1999. *Opportunity Makes the Thief: Practical Theory for Crime Prevention*. Police Research Series, No. 98. London: Home Office, Policing and Reducing Crime Unit.

Gottfredson, M. and T. Hirschi. 1990. *A General Theory of Crime*. Stanford, CA: Stanford University Press.

Kelling, G.L. and C. Coles. 1996. *Fixing Broken Windows: Restoring Order and Reducing Crime in Our Communities*. New York: Free Press.

Kuhn, T.S. 1962. *The Structure of Scientific Revolutions*. Chicago: University of Chicago Press.

Pawson, R. and N. Tilley. 1997. *Realistic Evaluation*. Thousand Oaks, CA: Sage.

19

The etiology of female crime

Dorie Klein

INTRODUCTION

The criminality of women has long been a neglected subject area of criminology. Many explanations have been advanced for this, such as women's low official rate of crime and delinquency and the preponderance of male theorists in the field. Female criminality has often ended up as a footnote to works on men that purport to be works on criminality in general.

There has been, however, a small group of writings specifically concerned with women and crime. This paper will explore those works concerned with the etiology of female crime and delinquency, beginning with the turn-of-the-century writing of Lombroso and extending to the present. Writers selected to be included have been chosen either for their influence on the field, such as Lombroso, Thomas, Freud, Davis and Pollak, or because they are representative of the kinds of work being published, such as Konopka, Vedder and Somerville, and Cowie, Cowie and Slater. The emphasis is on the continuity between these works, because it is clear that, despite recognizable differences in analytical approaches and specific theories, the authors represent a tradition to a great extent. It is important to understand, therefore, the shared assumptions made by the writers that are used in laying the groundwork for their theories.

The writers see criminality as the result of *individual* characteristics that are only peripherally affected by economic, social and political forces. These characteristics are of a *physiological* or *psychological* nature and are uniformly based on implicit or explicit assumptions about the *inherent nature of women*. This nature is *universal*, rather than existing within a specific historical framework.

Since criminality is seen as an individual activity, rather than as a condition built into existing structures, the focus is on biological, psychological and social factors that would turn a woman toward criminal activity. To do this, the writers

From *Issues in Criminology*, 1973, 8(2): 3–30.

create two distinct classes of women: good women who are 'normal' non-criminals, and bad women who are criminals, thus taking a moral position that often masquerades as a scientific distinction. The writers, although they may be biological or social determinists to varying degrees, assume that individuals have *choices* between criminal and non-criminal activity. They see persons as atomistically moving about in a social and political vacuum; many writers use marketplace models for human interaction.

Although the theorists may differ on specific remedies for individual criminality, ranging from sterilization to psychoanalysis (but always stopping far short of social change), the basic thrust is toward *individual adjustment*, whether it be physical or mental, and the frequent model is rehabilitative therapy. Widespread environmental alterations are usually included as casual footnotes to specific plans for individual therapy. Most of the writers are concerned with *social harmony* and the welfare of the existing social structure rather than with the women involved or with women's position in general. None of the writers come from anything near a 'feminist' or 'radical' perspective.

In *The Female Offender,* originally published in 1903, Lombroso described female criminality as an inherent tendency produced in individuals that could be regarded as biological atavisms, similar to cranial and facial features, and one could expect a withering away of crime if the atavistic people were prohibited from breeding. At this time criminality was widely regarded as a physical ailment, like epilepsy. Today, Cowie, Cowie and Slater (1968) have identified physical traits in girls who have been classified as delinquent, and have concluded that certain traits, such as bigness, may lead to aggressiveness. This theme of physiological characteristics has been developed by a good number of writers in the last seventy years, such as the Gluecks (Glueck and Glueck, 1934). One sees at the present time a new surge of 'biological' theories of criminality; for example, a study involving 'violence-prone' women and menstrual cycles has recently been proposed at UCLA.[1]

Thomas, to a certain degree, and Freud extend the physiological explanation of criminality to propose a psychological theory. However, it is critical to understand that these psychological notions are based on assumptions of universal *physiological* traits of women, such as their reproductive instinct and passivity, that are seen as invariably producing certain psychological reactions. Women may be viewed as turning to crime as a *perversion of* or *rebellion against* their *natural feminine roles.* Whether their problems are biological, psychological or social-environmental, the point is always to return them to their roles. Thomas (1907, 1923), for example, points out that poverty might prevent a woman from marrying, whereby she would turn to prostitution as an alternative to carry on her feminine service role. In fact, Davis (1961) discusses prostitution as a parallel illegal institution to marriage. Pollak (1950) discusses how women extend their service roles into criminal activity due to inherent tendencies such as deceitfulness. Freud (1933, Jones, 1961) sees any kind of rebellion as the result of a failure to develop healthy feminine attitudes, such as narcissism, and Konopka (1966) and Vedder and Somerville (1970) apply Freudian thought to the problem of female delinquency.

The specific characteristics ascribed to women's nature and those critical to theories of female criminality are uniformly *sexual* in their nature. Sexuality is seen as the root of female behavior and the problem of crime. Women are defined as sexual beings, as sexual capital in many cases, physiologically, psychologically and socially. This definition *reflects* and *reinforces* the economic position of women as reproductive and domestic workers. It is mirrored in the laws themselves and in their enforcement, which penalize sexual deviations for women and may be more lenient with economic offenses committed by them, in contrast to the treatment given men. The theorists accept the sexual double standard inherent in the law, often noting that 'chivalry' protects women, and many of them build notions of the universality of *sex repression* into their explanations of women's position. Women are thus the sexual backbone of civilization.

In setting hegemonic standards of conduct for all women, the theorists define *femininity*, which they equate with healthy femaleness, in classist, racist and sexist terms, using their assumptions of women's nature, specifically their sexuality, to justify what is often in reality merely a defense of the existing order. Lombroso, Thomas and Freud consider the upper-class white woman to be the highest expression of femininity, although she is inferior to the upper-class white man. These standards are adopted by later writers in discussing femininity. To most theorists, women are inherently inferior to men at masculine tasks such as thought and production, and therefore it is logical that their sphere should be reproductive.

Specific characteristics are proposed to bolster this sexual ideology, expressed for example by Freud, such as passivity, emotionalism, narcissism and deceitfulness. In the discussions of criminality, certain theorists, such as Pollak, link female criminality to these traits. Others see criminality as an attempt away from femininity into masculinity, such as Lombroso, although the specifics are often confused. Contradictions can be clearly seen, which are explained by the dual nature of 'good' and 'bad' women and by the fact that this is a mythology attempting to explain real behavior. Many explanations of what are obviously economically motivated offenses, such as prostitution and shoplifting, are explained in sexual terms, such as prostitution being promiscuity, and shoplifting being 'kleptomania' caused by women's inexplicable mental cycles tied to menstruation. Different explanations have to be made for 'masculine' crimes, e.g., burglary, and for 'feminine' crimes, e.g., shoplifting. Although this distinction crops up consistently, the specifics differ wildly.

The problem is complicated by the lack of knowledge of the epidemiology of female crime, which allows such ideas as 'hidden crime', first expressed by Pollak (1950), to take root. The problem must be considered on two levels: women, having been confined to certain tasks and socialized in certain ways, are *in fact* more likely to commit crime related to their lives which are sexually oriented; yet even nonsexual offenses are *explained* in sexual terms by the theorists. The writers ignore the problems of poor and Third World women, concentrating on affluent white standards of femininity. The experiences of these overlooked women, who *in fact* constitute a good percentage of women caught up in the criminal justice system, negate the notions of sexually motivated crime. These women have real economic needs which are not being met, and in many cases engage in illegal activities as a viable economic alternative. Furthermore, chivalry has never been extended to them.

The writers largely ignore the problems of sexism, racism and class, thus their work is sexist, racist and classist in its implications. Their concern is adjustment of the woman to society, not social change. Hence, they represent a tradition in criminology and carry along a host of assumptions about women and humanity in general. It is important to explore these assumptions and traditions in depth in order to understand what kinds of myths have been propagated around women and crime. The discussions of each writer or writers will focus on these assumptions and their relevance to criminological theories. These assumptions of universal, biological/psychological characteristics, of individual responsibility for crime, of the necessity for maintaining social harmony, and of the benevolence of the state link different theories along a continuum, transcending political labels and minor divergences. The road from Lombroso to the present is surprisingly straight.

LOMBROSO: THERE MUST BE SOME ANOMALY

Lombroso's work on female criminality (1920) is important to consider today despite the fact that his methodology and conclusions have long been successfully discredited. Later writings on female crime by Thomas, Davis, Pollak and others use more sophisticated methodologies and may proffer more palatable liberal theories. However, to varying degrees they rely on those sexual ideologies based on *implicit* assumptions about the physiological and psychological nature of women that are *explicit* in Lombroso's work. Reading the work helps to achieve a better understanding of what kinds of myths have been developed for women in general and for female crime and deviance in particular.

One specific notion of women offered by Lombroso is women's physiological immobility and psychological passivity, later elaborated by Thomas, Freud and other writers. Another ascribed characteristic is the Lombrosian notion of women's adaptability to surroundings and their capacity for survival as being superior to that of men. A third idea discussed by Lombroso is women's amorality: they are cold and calculating. This is developed by Thomas (1923), who describes women's manipulation of the male sex urge for ulterior purposes; by Freud (1933), who sees women as avenging their lack of penis on men; and by Pollak (1950), who depicts women as inherently deceitful.

When one looks at these specific traits, one sees contradictions. The myth of compassionate women clashes with their reputed coldness; their frailness belies their capacity to survive. One possible explanation for these contradictions is the duality of sexual ideology with regard to 'good' and 'bad' women.[2] Bad women are whores, driven by lust for money or for men, often essentially *'masculine'* in their orientation, and perhaps afflicted with a touch of penis envy. Good women are chaste, 'feminine', and usually not prone to criminal activity. But when they

are, they commit crime in a most *ladylike* way such as poisoning. In more sophisticated theory, all women are seen as having a bit of both tendencies in them.
Therefore, women can be compassionate *and* cold, frail *and* sturdy, pious *and*
amoral, depending on which path they choose to follow. They are seen as
rational (although they are irrational, too!), atomistic individuals making choices
in a vacuum, prompted only by personal, physiological/psychological factors.
These choices relate only to the *sexual* sphere. Women have no place in any other
sphere. Men, on the other hand, are not held sexually accountable, although, as
Thomas notes (1907), they are held responsible in *economic* matters. Men's sexual
freedom is justified by the myth of masculine, irresistible sex urges. This myth,
still worshipped today, is frequently offered as a rationalization for the existence
of prostitution and the double standard. As Davis maintains, this necessitates the
parallel existence of classes of 'good' and 'bad' women.

These dual moralities for the sexes are outgrowths of the economic, political
and social *realities* for men and women. Women are primarily workers within
the family, a critical institution of reproduction and socialization that services
such basic needs as food and shelter. Laws and codes of behavior for women
thus attempt to maintain the smooth functioning of women in that role, which
requires that women act as a conservative force in the continuation of the
nuclear family. Women's main tasks are sexual, and the law embodies sexual
limitations for women, which do not exist for men, such as the prohibition of
promiscuity for girls. This explains why theorists of female criminality are
not only concerned with sexual violations by female offenders, but attempt
to account for even *non-sexual* offenses, such as prostitution, in sexual terms,
e.g., women enter prostitution for sex rather than for money. Such women are
not only economic offenders but are sexual deviants, falling neatly into the category of 'bad' women.

The works of Lombroso, particularly *The Female Offender* (1920), are a foremost example of the biological explanation of crime. Lombroso deals with crime
as an atavism, or survival of 'primitive' traits in individuals, particularly those
of the female and non-white races. He theorizes that individuals develop differentially within sexual and racial limitations which differ hierarchically from the
most highly developed, the white men, to the most primitive, the non-white
women. Beginning with the assumption that criminals must be atavistic, he
spends a good deal of time comparing the crania, moles, heights etc. of convicted
criminals and prostitutes with those of normal women. Any trait that he finds to
be more common in the 'criminal' group is pronounced an atavistic trait, such as
moles, dark hair, etc., and women with a number of these telltale traits could be
regarded as potentially criminal, since they are of the atavistic type. He specifically rejects the idea that some of these traits, for example obesity in prostitutes,
could be the *result* of their activities rather than an indicator of their propensity to them. Many of the traits depicted as 'anomalies', such as darkness and
shortness, are characteristic of certain racial groups, such as the Sicilians, who
undoubtedly comprise an oppressed group within Italy and form a large part
of the imprisoned population.

Lombroso traces an overall pattern of evolution in the human species that accounts for the uneven development of groups: the white and non-white races, males and females, adults and children. Women, children and non-whites share many traits in common. There are fewer variations in their mental capacities: 'even the female criminal is monotonous and uniform compared with her male companion, just as in general woman is inferior to man' (1920: 122), due to her being 'atavistically nearer to her origin than the male' (1920: 107). The notion of women's mediocrity, or limited range of mental possibilities, is a recurrent one in the writings of the twentieth century. Thomas and others note that women comprise 'fewer geniuses, fewer lunatics and fewer morons' (Thomas, 1907: 45); lacking the imagination to be at either end of the spectrum, they are conformist and dull ... not due to social, political or economic constraints on their activities, but because of their innate physiological limitations as a sex. Lombroso attributes the lower female rate of criminality to their having fewer anomalies, which is one aspect of their closeness to the lower forms of less differentiated life.

Related characteristics of women are their passivity and conservatism. Lombroso admits that women's traditional sex roles in the family bind them to a more sedentary life. However, he insists that women's passivity can be directly traced to the 'immobility of the ovule compared with the zoosperm' (1920: 109), falling back on the sexual act in an interesting anticipation of Freud.

Women, like the lower races, have greater powers of endurance and resistance to mental and physical pain than men. Lombroso states: 'denizens of female prisons ... have reached the age of 90, having lived within those walls since they were 29 without any grave injury to health' (1920: 125). Denying the humanity of women by denying their capability for suffering justifies exploitation of women's energies by arguing for their suitability to hardship. Lombroso remarks that 'a duchess can adapt herself to new surroundings and become a washer-woman much more easily than a man can transform himself under analogous conditions' (1920: 272). The theme of women's adaptability to physical and social surroundings, which are male initiated, male controlled, and often expressed by saying that women are actually the 'stronger' sex, is a persistent thread in writings on women.

Lombroso explains that because women are unable to feel pain, they are insensitive to the pain of others and lack moral refinement. His blunt denial of the age-old myth of women's compassion and sensitivity is modified, however, to take into account women's low crime rate:

Women have many traits in common with children; that their moral sense is deficient; that they are revengeful, jealous ... In ordinary cases these defects are neutralized by piety, maternity, want of passion, sexual coldness, weakness and an undeveloped intelligence. (1920: 151)

Although women lack the higher sensibilities of men, they are thus restrained from criminal activity in most cases by lack of intelligence and passion, qualities which *criminal* women possess as well as all *men*. Within this framework of biological limits of women's nature, the female offender is characterized as *masculine* whereas the normal woman is *feminine*. The anomalies of skull, physiognomy and brain capacity of female criminals, according to Lombroso, more closely approximate that of the man, normal or criminal, than they do those of the normal woman; the female offender often has a 'virile cranium' and considerable body hair. Masculinity in women is an anomaly itself, rather than a sign of development, however. A related notion is developed by Thomas, who notes that in 'civilized' nations the sexes are more physically different.

> What we look for most in the female is femininity, and when we find the opposite in her, we must conclude as a rule that there must be some anomaly ... Virility was one of the special features of the savage woman ... In the portraits of Red Indian and Negro beauties, whom it is difficult to recognize for women, so huge are their jaws and cheekbones, so hard and coarse their features, and the same is often the case in their crania and brains. (1907: 112)

The more highly developed races would therefore have the most feminized women with the requisite passivity, lack of passion, etc. This is a *racist* and *classist* definition of femininity – just as are almost all theories of *femininity* and as, indeed, is the thing itself. The ideal of the lady can only exist in a society built on the exploitation of labor to maintain the woman of leisure who can *be* that ideal lady.

Finally, Lombroso notes women's lack of *property sense*, which contributes to their criminality.

> In their eyes theft is ... an audacity for which account compensation is due to the owner ... as an individual rather than a social crime, just as it was regarded in the primitive periods of human evolution and is still regarded by many uncivilized nations. (1920: 217)

One may question this statement on several levels. Can it be assumed to have any validity at all, or is it false that women have a different sense of property than men? If it is valid to a degree, is it related to women's lack of property ownership and non-participation in the accumulation of capitalist wealth? Indeed, as Thomas (1907) points out, women are considered property themselves. At any rate, it is an interesting point in Lombroso's book that has only been touched on by later writers, and always in a manner supportive of the institution of private property.

THOMAS: 'THE STIMULATION SHE CRAVES'

The works of W.I. Thomas are critical in that they mark a transition from purely physiological explanations such as Lombroso's to more sophisticated theories that embrace physiological, psychological and social-structural factors. However, even the most sophisticated explanations of female crime rely on implicit assumptions about the *biological* nature of women. In Thomas's *Sex and Society*

(1907) and *The Unadjusted Girl* (1923), there are important contradictions in the two approaches that are representative of the movements during that period between publication dates: a departure from biological Social-Darwinian theories to complex analyses of the interaction between society and the individual, i.e., societal repression and manipulation of the 'natural' wishes of persons.

In *Sex and Society* (1907), Thomas poses basic biological differences between the sexes as his starting point. Maleness is 'katabolic', the animal force which is destructive of energy and allows men the possibility of creative work through this outward flow. Femaleness is 'anabolic', analogous to a plant which stores energy, and is motionless and conservative. Here Thomas is offering his own version of the age-old male/female dichotomy expressed by Lombroso and elaborated on in Freud's paradigm, in the structural-functionalist 'instrumental-expressive' duality, and in other analyses of the status quo. According to Thomas, the dichotomy is most highly developed in the more civilized races, due to the greater differentiation of sex roles. This statement ignores the hard physical work done by poor *white* women at home and in the factories and offices in 'civilized' countries, and accepts a *ruling-class* definition of femininity.

The cause of women's relative decline in stature in more 'civilized' countries is a subject on which Thomas is ambivalent. At one point he attributes it to the lack of 'a superior fitness on the motor side' in women (1907: 94); at another point, he regards her loss of *sexual freedom* as critical, with the coming of monogamy and her confinement to sexual tasks such as wifehood and motherhood. He perceptively notes:

> Women were still further degraded by the development of property and its control by man, together with the habit of treating her as a piece of property, whose value was enhanced if its purity was assured. (1907: 297)

However, Thomas's underlying assumptions in his explanations of the inferior status of women are *physiological* ones. He attributes to men high amounts of sexual energy, which lead them to pursue women for their sex, and he attributes to women maternal feelings devoid of sexuality, which lead *them* to exchange sex for domesticity. Thus monogamy, with chastity for women, is the *accommodation* of these basic urges, and women are domesticated while men assume leadership, in a true market exchange.

Why, then, does Thomas see problems in the position of women? It is because modern women are plagued by 'irregularity, pettiness, ill health and inserviceableness' (1907: 245). Change is required to maintain *social harmony*, apart from considerations of women's needs, and women must be educated to make them better wives, a theme reiterated throughout this century by 'liberals' on the subject. Correctly anticipating a threat, Thomas urges that change be made to stabilize the family, and warns that 'no civilization can remain the highest if another civilization adds to the intelligence of its men the intelligence of its women' (1907: 314). Thomas is motivated by considerations of social integration. Of course, one might question how women are to be able to contribute much if they are indeed anabolic. However, due to the transitional nature of Thomas's work, there are immense contradictions in his writing.

Many of Thomas's specific assertions about the nature of women are indistinguishable from Lombroso's; they both delineate a biological hierarchy along race and sex lines.

> Man has, in short, become more somatically specialized an animal than woman, and feels more keenly any disturbance of normal conditions with which he has not the same physiological surplus as woman with which to meet the disturbance ... It is a logical fact, however, that the lower human races, the lower classes of society, women and children show something of the same quality in their superior tolerance of surgical disease. (1907: 36)

Like Lombroso, Thomas is crediting women with superior capabilities of survival because they are further down the scale in terms of evolution. It is significant that Thomas includes the lower classes in his observation; is he implying that the lower classes are in their position *because* of their natural unfitness, or perhaps that their *situation* renders them less sensitive to pain? At different times, Thomas implies both. Furthermore, he agrees with Lombroso that women are more nearly uniform than men, and says that they have a smaller percentage of 'genius, insanity and idiocy' (1907: 45) than men, as well as fewer creative outbursts of energy.

Dealing with female criminality in *Sex and Society* (1907), Thomas begins to address the issue of morality, which he closely links to legality from a standpoint of maintaining social order. He discriminates between male and female morality:

> Morality as applied to men has a larger element of the contractual, representing the adjustment of his activities to those of society at large, or more particularly to the activities of the male members of society; while the morality which we think of in connection with women shows less of the contractual and more of the personal, representing her adjustment to men, more particularly the adjustment of her person to men. (1907: 172)

Whereas Lombroso barely observes women's lack of participation in the institution of private property, Thomas's perception is more profound. He points out that women *are* property of men and that their conduct is subject to different codes.

> Morality, in the most general sense, represents the code under which activities are best carried on and is worked out in the school of experience. It is preeminently an adult and male system, and men are intelligent enough to realize that neither women nor children have passed through this school. It is on this account that man is merciless to woman from the standpoint of personal behavior, yet he exempts her from anything in the way of contractual morality, or views her defections in this regard with allowance and even with amusement. (1907: 234)

Disregarding his remarks about intelligence, one confronts the critical point about women with respect to the law: because they occupy a *marginal* position in the productive sphere of exchange commodities outside the home, they in turn occupy a marginal position in regard to 'contractual' law which regulates relations of property and production. The argument of differential treatment of men and women by the law is developed in later works by Pollak and others, who attribute it to the 'chivalry' of the system which is lenient to women committing offenses. As Thomas notes, however, women are simply not a serious *threat* to property, and are treated more 'leniently' because of this. Certain women do become threats by transcending (or by being denied) their traditional role, particularly many Third World women and political rebels, and they are *not* afforded chivalrous treatment! In fact, chivalry is reserved for the women who are least likely to ever come in contact with the criminal justice system: the ladies, or white middle-class women. In matters of *sexual* conduct, however, which embody the double standard, women are rigorously prosecuted by the law. As Thomas understands, this is the sphere in which women's functions *are* critical. Thus it is not a matter of 'chivalry' how one is handled, but of different forms and thrusts of social control applied to men and women. Men are engaged in productive tasks and their activities in this area *are* strictly curtailed.

In *The Unadjusted Girl* (1923), Thomas deals with female delinquency as a 'normal' response under certain social conditions, using assumptions about the nature of women which he leaves unarticulated in this work. Driven by basic 'wishes', an individual is controlled by society in her activities through institutional transmission of codes and mores. Depending on how they are manipulated, wishes can be made to serve social or antisocial ends. Thomas stresses the institutions that socialize, such as the family, giving people certain 'definitions of the situation'. He confidently – and defiantly – asserts:

> There is no individual energy, no unrest, no type of wish, which cannot be sublimated and made socially useful. From this standpoint, the problem is not the right of society to protect itself from the disorderly and antisocial person, but the right of the disorderly and antisocial person to be made orderly and socially valuable ... The problem of society is to produce the right attitudes in its members. (1923: 232–3)

This is an important shift in perspective, from the traditional libertarian view of protecting society by punishing transgressors, to the *rehabilitative* and *preventive* perspective of crime control that seeks to control *minds* through socialization rather than to merely control behavior through punishment. The autonomy of the individual to choose is seen as the product of his environment which the state can alter. This is an important refutation of the Lombrosian biological perspective, which maintains that there are crime-prone individuals who must be locked up, sterilized or otherwise incapacitated. Today, one can see an amalgamation of the two perspectives in new theories of 'behavior control' that use tactics such as conditioning and brain surgery, combining biological and environmental viewpoints.[3]

Thomas proposes the manipulation of individuals through institutions to prevent antisocial attitudes, and maintains that there is no such person as the 'crime prone' individual. A hegemonic system of belief can be imposed by sublimating natural urges and by correcting the poor socialization of slum families. In this perspective, the *definition* of the situation rather than the situation *itself* is what should be changed; a situation is what someone *thinks* it is. The response to a criminal woman who is dissatisfied with her conventional sexual roles is to change not the roles, which would mean widespread social transformations, but to change her attitudes. This concept of civilization as repressive and the need to adjust is later refined by Freud.

Middle-class women, according to Thomas, commit little crime because they are socialized to sublimate their natural desires and to behave well, treasuring their chastity as an investment. The poor woman, however, 'is not immoral, because this implies a loss of morality, but amoral' (1923: 98). Poor women are not objectively driven to crime; they long for it. Delinquent girls are motivated by the desire for excitement or 'new experience', and forget the repressive urge of 'security'. However, these desires are well within Thomas's conception of *femininity*: delinquents are not rebelling against womanhood, as Lombroso suggests, but merely acting it out illegally. Davis and Pollak agree with this notion that delinquent women are not 'different' from non-delinquent women.

Thomas maintains that it is not sexual desire that motivates delinquent girls, for they are no more passionate than other women, but they are *manipulating* male desires for sex to achieve their own ulterior ends.

> The beginning of delinquency in girls is usually an impulse to get amusement, adventure, pretty clothes, favorable notice, distinction, freedom in the larger world ... The girls have usually become 'wild' before the development of sexual desire, and their casual sex relations do not usually awaken sex feeling. Their sex is used as a condition of the realization of other wishes. It is their capital. (1923: 109)

Here Thomas is expanding on the myth of the manipulative woman, who is cold and scheming and vain. To him, good female sexual behavior is a protective measure –'instinctive, of course' (1907: 241), whereas male behavior is uncontrollable as men are caught by helpless desires. This is the common Victorian notion of the woman as seductress which in turn perpetuates the myth of a lack of real sexuality to justify her responsibility for upholding sexual mores. Thomas uses a market analogy to female virtue: good women *keep* their bodies as capital to sell in matrimony for marriage and security, whereas bad women *trade* their bodies for excitement. One notes, of course, the familiar dichotomy. It is difficult, in this framework, to see how Thomas can make *any* moral distinctions, since morality seems to be merely good business sense. In fact, Thomas's yardstick is social harmony, necessitating *control*.

Thomas shows an insensitivity to real human relationships and needs. He also shows ignorance of economic hardships in his denial of economic factors in delinquency.

> An unattached woman has a tendency to become an adventuress not so much on economic as on psychological grounds. Life is rarely so hard that a young woman cannot earn her bread; but she cannot always live and have the stimulation she craves. (1907: 241)

This is an amazing statement in an era of mass starvation and illness! He rejects economic causes as a possibility at all, denying their importance in criminal activity with as much certainty as Lombroso, Freud, Davis, Pollak and most other writers.

FREUD: 'BEAUTY, CHARM AND SWEETNESS'

The Freudian theory of the position of women is grounded in explicit biological assumptions about their nature, expressed by the famous 'Anatomy is Destiny'. Built upon this foundation is a construction incorporating psychological and social-structural factors.

Freud himself sees women as anatomically inferior; they are destined to be wives and mothers, and this is admittedly an inferior destiny as befits the inferior sex. The root of this inferiority is that women's *sex organs are* inferior to those of men, a fact *universally* recognized by children in the Freudian scheme. The girl assumes that she has lost a penis as punishment, is traumatized, and grows up envious and revengeful. The boy also sees the girl as having lost a penis, fears a similar punishment himself, and dreads the girl's envy and vengeance. Feminine traits can be traced to the inferior genitals themselves, or to women's inferiority complex arising from their response to them: women are exhibitionistic, narcissistic, and attempt to compensate for their lack of a penis by being well dressed and physically beautiful. Women become mothers trying to replace the lost penis with a baby. Women are also masochistic, as Lombroso and Thomas have noted, because their *sexual* role is one of receptor, and their sexual pleasure consists of pain. This woman, Freud notes, is the *healthy* woman. In the familiar dichotomy, the men are aggressive and pain inflicting. Freud comments:

> The male pursues the female for the purposes of sexual union, seizes hold of her, and penetrates into her ... by this you have precisely reduced the characteristic of masculinity to the factor of aggressiveness. (Millett, 1970: 189)

Freud, like Lombroso and Thomas, takes the notion of men's activity and women's inactivity and *reduces* it to the sexual level, seeing the sexual union itself through Victorian eyes: ladies don't move.

Women are also inferior in the sense that they are concerned with personal matters and have little social sense. Freud sees civilization as based on repression of the sex drive, where it is the duty of men to repress their strong instincts in order to get on with the worldly business of civilization. Women, on the other hand,

> have little sense of justice, and this is no doubt connected with the preponderance of envy in their mental life; for the demands of justice are a modification of envy; they lay down the conditions under which one is willing to part with it. We also say of women that their social interests are weaker than those of men and that their capacity for the sublimation of their instincts is less. (1933: 183)

Men are capable of sublimating their individual needs because they rationally perceive the Hobbesian conflict between those urges and social needs. Women are emotional and incapable of such an adjustment because of their innate inability to make such rational judgements. It is only fair then that they should have a marginal relation to production and property.

In this framework, the deviant woman is one who is attempting to be a *man*. She is aggressively rebellious, and her drive to accomplishment is the expression of her longing for a penis; this is a hopeless pursuit, of course, and she will only end up 'neurotic'. Thus the deviant woman should be treated and helped to *adjust* to her sex role. Here again, as in Thomas's writing, is the notion of individual accommodation that repudiates the possibility of social change.

In a Victorian fashion, Freud rationalizes women's oppression by glorifying their duties as wives and mothers:

> It is really a stillborn thought to send women into the struggle for existence exactly the same as men. If, for instance, I imagined my sweet gentle girl as a competitor, it would only end in my telling her, as I did seventeen months ago, that I am fond of her, and I implore her to withdraw from the strife into the calm, uncompetitive activity of my home ... Nature has determined woman's destiny through beauty, charm and sweetness ... in youth an adored darling, in mature years a loved wife. (Jones, 1961: 117–18)

In speaking of femininity, Freud, like his forebears, is speaking along racist and classist lines. Only upper- and middle-class women could possibly enjoy lives as sheltered darlings. Freud sets hegemonic standards of femininity for poor and Third World women.

It is important to understand Freudianism because it reduces categories of sexual ideology to explicit sexuality and makes these categories *scientific*. For the last fifty years, Freudianism has been a mainstay of sexist social theory. Kate Millett notes that Freud himself saw his work as stemming the tide of feminist revolution, which he constantly ridiculed:

> Coming as it did, at the peak of the sexual revolution, Freud's doctrine of penis envy is in fact a superbly timed accusation, enabling masculine sentiment to take the offensive again as it had not since the disappearance of overt misogyny when the pose of chivalry became fashionable. (Millett, 1970: 189)

Freudian notions of the repression of sexual instincts, the sexual passivity of women, and the sanctity of the nuclear family are conservative not only in their contemporary context, but in the context of their own time. Hitler writes:

> For her [woman's] world is her husband, her family, her children and her home ... The man upholds the nation as the woman upholds the family. The equal rights of women consist in the fact that in the realm of life determined for her by nature, she experience the high esteem that is her due. Woman and man represent quite different types of being. Reason is dominant in man ... Feeling, in contrast, is much more stable than reason, and woman is the feeling, and therefore the stable, element. (Millett, 1970: 170)

One can mark the decline in the position of women after the 1920s through the use of various indices: by noting the progressively earlier age of marriage of women in the United States and the steady rise in the number of children born to them, culminating in the birth explosion of the late 1940s and 1950s; by looking at the relative decline in the number of women scholars; and by seeing the failure to liberate women in the Soviet Union and the rise of fascist sexual ideology. Freudianism has had an unparalleled influence in the United States (and came at a key point to help swing the tide against the women's movement) to facilitate the return of women during the depression and postwar years to the home, out of an economy which had no room for them. Freud affected such writers on female deviance as Davis, Pollak and Konopka, who turn to concepts of sexual maladjustment and neurosis to explain women's criminality. Healthy women would now be seen as masochistic, passive and sexually indifferent. Criminal women would be seen as *sexual* misfits. Most importantly, *psychological* factors would be used to explain criminal activity, and social, economic and political factors would be ignored. Explanations would seek to be *universal*, and historical possibilities of change would be refuted.

DAVIS: 'THE MOST CONVENIENT SEXUAL OUTLET FOR ARMIES ... '

Kingsley Davis's work on prostitution (1961) is still considered a classical analysis on the subject with a structural-functionalist perspective. It employs assumptions about 'the organic nature of man' and woman, many of which can be traced to ideas proffered by Thomas and Freud.

Davis sees prostitution as a structural necessity whose roots lie in the *sexual* nature of men and women; for example, female humans, unlike primates, are sexually available year-round. He asserts that prostitution is *universal* in time and place, eliminating the possibilities of historical change and ignoring critical differences in the quality and quantity of prostitution in different societies. He maintains that there will always be a class of women who will be prostitutes, the familiar class of 'bad' women. The reason for the universality of prostitution is that sexual *repression*, a concept stressed by Thomas and Freud, is essential to the functioning of society. Once again there is the notion of sublimating 'natural' sex urges to the overall needs of society, namely social order. Davis notes that in our society sexuality is permitted only within the structure of the nuclear family, which is an institution of stability. He does not, however, analyse in depth the economic and social functions of the family, other than to say it is a bulwark of morality.

> The norms of every society tend to harness and control the sexual appetite, and one of the ways of doing this is to link the sexual act to some stable or potentially stable social relationship ... Men dominate women in economic, sexual and familial relationships and consider them to some extent as sexual property, to be prohibited to other males. They therefore find promiscuity on the part of women repugnant. (1961: 264)

Davis is linking the concept of prostitution to promiscuity, defining it as a *sexual* crime, and calling prostitutes sexual transgressors. Its origins, he claims, lie not in economic hardship, but in the marital restraints on sexuality. As long as men seek women, prostitutes will be in demand. One wonders why sex-seeking women have not created a class of male prostitutes.

Davis sees the only possibility of eliminating prostitution in the liberalization of sexual mores, although he is pessimistic about the likelihood of total elimination. In light of the contemporary American 'sexual revolution' of commercial sex, which has surely created more prostitutes and semi-prostitutes rather than eliminating the phenomenon, and in considering the revolution in China where, despite a 'puritanical' outlook on sexuality, prostitution has largely been eliminated through major economic and social change, the superficiality of Davis's approach becomes evident. Without dealing with root economic, social and political factors, one cannot analyse prostitution.

Davis shows Freudian pessimism about the nature of sexual repression:

> We can imagine a social system in which the motive for prostitution would be completely absent, but we cannot imagine that the system will ever come to pass. It would be a regime of absolute sexual freedom with intercourse practiced solely for pleasure by both parties. There would be no institutional control of sexual expression ... All sexual desire would have to be mutually complementary ... Since the basic causes of prostitution – the institutional control of sex, the unequal scale of attractiveness, and the presence of economic and social inequalities between classes and between males and females – are not likely to disappear, prostitution is not likely to disappear either. (1961: 286)

By talking about 'complementary desire', Davis is using a marketplace notion of sex: two attractive or unattractive people are drawn to each other and exchange sexual favors; people are placed on a scale of attractiveness and may be rejected by people above them on the scale; hence they (*men*) become frustrated and demand prostitutes. Women who become prostitutes do so for good pay *and* sexual pleasure. Thus one has a neat little system in which everyone benefits.

Enabling a small number of women to take care of the needs of a large number of men,
it is the most convenient sexual outlet for armies, for the legions of strangers, perverts
and physically repulsive in our midst. (1961: 288)

Prostitution 'functions', therefore it must be good. Davis, like Thomas, is
motivated by concerns of social order rather than by concerns of what the needs
and desires of the women involved might be. He denies that the women
involved are economically oppressed; they are on the streets through autonomous, *individual* choice.

Some women physically enjoy the intercourse they sell. From a purely economic point of
view, prostitution comes near the situation of getting something for nothing ... Women's
wages could scarcely be raised significantly without also raising men's. Men would then
have more to spend on prostitution. (1961: 277)

It is important to understand that, given a *sexual* interpretation of what is an
economic crime, and given a refusal to consider widespread change (even equali-
zation of wages, hardly a revolutionary act), Davis's conclusion is the logical
technocratic solution.

In this framework, the deviant women are merely adjusting to their feminine
role in an illegitimate fashion, as Thomas has theorized. They are *not* attempting
to be rebels or to be 'men', as Lombroso's and Freud's positions suggest. Although
Davis sees the main difference between wives and prostitutes in a macrosocial
sense as the difference merely between legal and illegal roles, in a personal sense
he sees the women who *choose* prostitution as maladjusted and neurotic. However,
given the universal necessity for prostitution, this analysis implies the necessity
of having a perpetually ill and maladjusted class of women. Thus oppression is
built into the system, and a healthy *system* makes for a sick *individual*. Here Davis
is integrating Thomas's notions of social integration with Freudian perspectives
on neurosis and maladjustment.

POLLAK: 'A DIFFERENT ATTITUDE TOWARD VERACITY'

Otto Pollak's *The Criminality of Women* (1950) has had an outstanding influence on
the field of women and crime, being the major work on the subject in the postwar
years. Pollak advances the theory of 'hidden' female crime to account for what he
considers unreasonably low official rates for women.

A major reason for the existence of hidden crime, as he sees it, lies in the *nature*
of women themselves. They are instigators rather than perpetrators of criminal
activity. While Pollak admits that this role is partly a socially enforced one, he
insists that women are inherently deceitful for *physiological* reasons.

Man must achieve an erection in order to perform the sex act and will not be able to
hide his failure. His lack of positive emotion in the sexual sphere must become overt to
the partner, and pretense of sexual response is impossible for him, if it is lacking.

Woman's body, however, permits such pretense to a certain degree and lack of orgasm does not prevent her ability to participate in the sex act. (1950: 10)

Pollak *reduces* women's nature to the *sex act,* as Freud has done, and finds women inherently more capable of manipulation, accustomed to being sly, passive and passionless. As Thomas suggests, women can use sex for ulterior purposes. Furthermore, Pollak suggests that women are innately deceitful on yet another level:

Our sex mores force women to conceal every four weeks the period of menstruation ... They thus make concealment and misrepresentation in the eyes of women socially required and must condition them to a different attitude toward veracity than men. (1950: 11)

Women's abilities at concealment thus allow them to successfully commit crimes in stealth.

Women are also vengeful. Menstruation, in the classic Freudian sense, seals their doomed hopes to become men and arouses women's desire for vengeance, especially during that time of the month. Thus Pollak offers new rationalizations to bolster old myths.

A second factor in hidden crime is the roles played by women which furnish them with opportunities as domestics, nurses, teachers and housewives to commit undetectable crimes. The *kinds* of crimes women commit reflect their nature: false accusation, for example, is an outgrowth of women's treachery, spite or fear and is a sign of neurosis; shoplifting can be traced in many cases to a special mental disease – kleptomania. Economic factors play a minor role; *sexual-psychological* factors account for female criminality. Crime in women is *personalized* and often accounted for by mental illness.

Pollak notes:

Robbery and burglary ... are considered specifically male offenses since they represent the pursuit of monetary gain by overt action ... Those cases of female robbery which seem to express a tendency toward masculinization come from ... [areas] where social conditions have favored the assumptions of male pursuits by women ... The female offenders usually retain some trace of femininity, however, and even so glaring an example of masculinization as the 'Michigan Babes,' an all woman gang of robbers in Chicago, shows a typically feminine trait in the modus operandi. (1950: 29)

Pollak is defining crimes with economic motives that employ overt action as *masculine*, and defining as *feminine* those crimes for *sexual* activity, such as luring men as baits. Thus he is using circular reasoning by saying that feminine crime is feminine. To fit women into the scheme and justify the statistics, he must invent the notion of hidden crime.

It is important to recognize that, to some extent, women *do* adapt to their enforced sexual roles and may be more likely to instigate, to use sexual traps, and

to conform to all the other feminine role expectations. However, it is not accidental that theorists label women as conforming even when they are *not*; for example,
by inventing sexual motives for what are clearly crimes of economic necessity, or
by invoking 'mental illness' such as kleptomania for shoplifting. It is difficult to
separate the *theory* from the *reality*, since the reality of female crime is largely
unknown. But it is not difficult to see that Pollak is using sexist terms and making sexist assumptions to advance theories of hidden female crime.

Pollak, then, sees criminal women as extending their sexual role, like Davis
and Thomas, by using sexuality for ulterior purposes. He suggests that the condemnation of extramarital sex has 'delivered men who engage in such conduct
as practically helpless victims' (1950: 152) into the hands of women blackmail-
ers, overlooking completely the possibility of men blackmailing women, which
would seem more likely, given the greater taboo on sex for women and their
greater risks of being punished.

The final factor that Pollak advances as a root cause of hidden crime is that of
'chivalry' in the criminal justice system. Pollak uses Thomas's observation that
women are differentially treated by the law, and carries it to a sweeping conclusion based on *cultural* analyses of men's feelings toward women.

> One of the outstanding concomitants of the existing inequality ... is chivalry, and the
> general protective attitude of man toward woman ... Men hate to accuse women and
> thus indirectly to send them to their punishment, police officers dislike to arrest them,
> district attorneys to prosecute them, judges and juries to find them guilty, and so on.
> (1950: 151)

Pollak rejects the possibility of an actual discrepancy between crime rates for
men and women; therefore, he must look for factors to expand the scope of
female crime. He assumes that there is chivalry in the criminal justice system that
is extended to the women who come in contact with it. Yet the women involved
are likely to be poor and Third World women or white middle-class women who
have stepped *outside* the definitions of femininity to become hippies or political
rebels, and chivalry is *not* likely to be extended to them. Chivalry is a racist and
classist concept founded on the notion of women as 'ladies' which applies only
to wealthy white women and ignores the double sexual standard. These 'ladies',
however, are the least likely women to ever come in contact with the criminal
justice system in the first place.[4]

THE LEGACY OF SEXISM

A major purpose in tracing the development and interaction of ideas pertaining to sexual ideology based on implicit assumptions of the inherent nature of
women throughout the works of Lombroso, Thomas, Freud, Davis and Pollak, is
to clarify their positions in relation to writers in the field today. One can see the
influence their ideas still have by looking at a number of contemporary theorists
on female criminality. Illuminating examples can be found in Gisela Konopka's

Adolescent Girl in Conflict (1966), Vedder and Somerville's *The Delinquent Girl* (1970) and Cowie, Cowie and Slater's *Delinquency in Girls* (1968). The ideas in these minor works have direct roots in those already traced in this paper.

Konopka justifies her decision to study delinquency in girls rather than in boys by noting girls' *influence* on boys in gang fights and on future generations as mothers. This is the notion of women as instigators of men and influencers on children.

Konopka's main point is that delinquency in girls can be traced to a specific emotional response: loneliness.

> What I found in the girl in conflict was ... loneliness accompanied by despair. Adolescent boys too often feel lonely and search for understanding and friends. Yet in general this does not seem to be the central core of their problems, not their most outspoken ache. While these girls also strive for independence, their need for dependence is unusually great. (1966: 40)

In this perspective, girls are driven to delinquency by an emotional problem – loneliness and dependency. There are *inherent* emotional differences between the sexes.

> Almost invariably her [the girl's] problems are deeply personalized. Whatever her offense – whether shoplifting, truancy or running away from home – it is usually accompanied by some disturbance or unfavorable behavior in the sexual area. (1966: 4)

Here is the familiar resurrection of female personalism, emotionalism, and above all, *sexuality* – characteristics already described by Lombroso, Thomas and Freud. Konopka maintains:

> The delinquent girl suffers, like many boys, from lack of success, lack of opportunity. But her drive to success is never separated from her need for people, for interpersonal involvement. (1966: 41)

Boys are 'instrumental' and become delinquent if they are deprived of the chance for creative success. However, girls are 'expressive' and happiest dealing with people as wives, mothers, teachers, nurses or psychologists. This perspective is drawn from the theory of delinquency as a result of blocked opportunity and from the instrumental/expressive sexual dualism developed by structural-functionalists. Thus female delinquency must be dealt with on this *psychological* level, using therapy geared to their needs as future wives and mothers. They should be *adjusted* and given *opportunities* to be pretty, sociable women.

The important point is to understand how Konopka analyses the roots of girls' feelings. It is very possible that, given women's position, girls may be in fact more concerned with dependence and sociability. One's understanding of this, however, is based on an understanding of the historical position of women and the nature of their oppression. Konopka says:

> What are the reasons for this essential loneliness in girls? Some will be found in the nature of being an adolescent girl, in her biological make-up and her particular position in her culture and time. (1966: 41)

Coming from a Freudian perspective, Konopka's emphasis on female emotions as cause for delinquency, which ignores economic and social factors, is questionable. She employs assumptions about the *physiological* and *psychological* nature of women that very well may have led her to see only those feelings in the first place. For example, she cites menstruation as a significant event in a girl's development. Thus Konopka is rooted firmly in the tradition of Freud and, apart from sympathy, contributes little that is new to the field.[5]

Vedder and Somerville (1970) account for female delinquency in a manner similar to that of Konopka. They also feel the need to justify their attention to girls by remarking that (while female delinquency may not pose as much of a problem as that of boys) because women raise families and are critical agents of socialization, it is worth taking the time to study and control them. Vedder and Somerville also stress the dependence of girls on boys and the instigatory role girls play in boys' activities.

Like Freud and Konopka, the authors view delinquency as blocked access or maladjustment to the normal feminine role. In a blatant statement that ignores the economic and social factors that result from racism and poverty, they attribute the high rates of delinquency among black girls to their lack of 'healthy' feminine narcissism, *reducing* racism to a psychological problem in totally sexist and racist terms.

> The black girl is, in fact, the antithesis of the American beauty. However loved she may be by her mother, family and community, she has no real basis of female attractiveness on which to build a sound feminine narcissism ... Perhaps the 'black is beautiful' movement will help the Negro girl to increase her femininity and personal satisfaction as a black woman. (1970: 159–60)

Again the focus is on a lack of *sexual* opportunities for women, i.e., the Black woman is not Miss America. *Economic* offenses such as shoplifting are explained as outlets for *sexual* frustration. Since healthy women conform, the individual delinquents should be helped to adjust; the emphasis is on the 'definition of the situation' rather than on the situation.

The answer lies in *therapy*, and racism and sexism become merely psychological problems.

> Special attention should be given to girls, taking into consideration their constitutional biological and psychological differences, and their social position in our male dominated culture. The female offender's goal, as any woman's, is a happy and successful

marriage; therefore her self-image is dependent on the establishment of satisfactory relationships with the opposite sex. The double standard for sexual behavior on the part of the male and female must be recognized. (1970: 153)

Like Konopka, and to some extent drawing on Thomas, the authors see female delinquents as extending femininity in an illegitimate fashion rather than rebelling against it. The assumptions made about women's goals and needs, including *biological* assumptions, lock women into a system from which there is no escape, whereby any behavior will be sexually interpreted and dealt with.

The resurgence of biological or physiological explanations of criminality in general has been noteworthy in the last several years, exemplified by the XYY chromosome controversy and the interest in brain waves in 'violent' individuals.[6] In the case of women, biological explanations have *always* been prevalent; every writer has made assumptions about anatomy as destiny. Women are prey, in the literature, to cycles of reproduction, including menstruation, pregnancy, maternity and menopause; they experience emotional responses to these cycles that make them inclined to irrationality and potentially violent activity.

Cowie, Cowie and Slater (1968) propose a *chromosomal* explanation of female delinquency that hearkens back to the works of Lombroso and others such as Healy (Healy and Bronner, 1926), Edith Spaulding (1923) and the Gluecks (Glueck and Glueck, 1934). They write:

The chromosomal difference between the sexes starts the individual on a divergent path, leading either in a masculine or feminine direction ... It is possible that the methods of upbringing, differing somewhat for the two sexes, may play some part in increasing the angle of this divergence. (Cowie et al., 1968: 171)

This is the healthy, normal divergence for the sexes. The authors equate *masculinity* and *femininity* with *maleness* and *femaleness*, although contemporary feminists point out that the first categories are *social* and the latter ones *physical.*[7] What relationship exists between the two – how femaleness determines femininity – is dependent on the larger social structure. There is no question that a wide range of possibilities exist historically, and in a non-sexist society it is possible that 'masculinity' and 'femininity' would disappear, and that the sexes would differ only biologically, specifically by their sex organs. The authors, however, lack this understanding and assume an ahistorical sexist view of women, stressing the *universality* of femininity in the Freudian tradition, and of women's inferior role in the nuclear family.[8]

In this perspective, the female offender is *different* physiologically and psychologically from the 'normal' girl.

The authors conclude, in the tradition of Lombroso, that female delinquents are *masculine.* Examining girls for physical characteristics, they note:

Markedly masculine traits in girl delinquents have been commented on ... [as well as] the frequency of homosexual tendencies ... Energy, aggressiveness, enterprise and the

> rebelliousness that drives the individual to break through conformist habits are thought
> of as being masculine ... We can be sure that they have some physical basis. (1968: 172)

The authors see crime as a *rebellion* against sex roles rather than as a malad-justed expression of them. By defining rebellion as *masculine*, they are ascribing characteristics of masculinity to any female rebel. Like Lombroso, they spend time measuring heights, weights, and other *biological* features of female delin-quents with other girls.

Crime defined as masculine seems to mean violent, overt crime, whereas 'ladylike' crime usually refers to sexual violations and shoplifting. Women are neatly categorized no matter *which* kind of crime they commit: if they are violent, they are 'masculine' and suffering from chromosomal deficiencies, penis envy, or atavisms. If they conform, they are manipulative, sexually maladjusted and pro-miscuous. The *economic* and *social* realities of crime – the fact that poor women commit crimes, and that most crimes for women are property offenses – are overlooked. Women's behavior must be *sexually* defined before it will be consid-ered, for women count only in the sexual sphere. The theme of sexuality is a unifying thread in the various, often contradictory theories.

CONCLUSION

A good deal of the writing on women and crime being done at the present time is squarely in the tradition of the writers that have been discussed. The basic assumptions and technocratic concerns of these writers have produced work that is sexist, racist and classist; assumptions that have served to maintain a repressive ideology with its extensive apparatus of control. To do a new kind of research on women and crime – one that has feminist roots and a radical orientation – it is necessary to understand the assumptions made by the traditional writers and to break away from them. Work that focuses on human needs, rather than those of the state, will require new definitions of criminality, women, the individual and her/his relation to the state. It is beyond the scope of this paper to develop pos-sible areas of study, but it is none the less imperative that this work be made a priority by women *and* men in the future.

NOTES

1 Quoted from the 1973 proposal for the Center for the Study and Reduction of Violence prepared by Dr Louis J. West, Director, Neuropsychiatric Institute, UCLA: 'The question of violence in females will be examined from the point of view that females are more likely to commit acts of violence during the pre-menstrual and menstrual periods' (1973: 43).

2 I am indebted to Marion Goldman for introducing me to the notion of the dual moral-ity based on assumptions of different sexuality for men and women.

3 For a discussion of the possibilities of psychosurgery in behavior modification for 'violence-prone' individuals, see Frank Ervin and Vernon Mark, *Violence and the Brain*

(1970). For an eclectic view of this perspective on crime, see the proposal for the Center for the Study and Reduction of Violence (note 1).

4   The concept of hidden crime is reiterated in Reckless and Kay's report to the President's Commission on Law Enforcement and the Administration of Justice. They note:

> A large part of the infrequent officially acted upon involvement of women in crime can be traced to the masking effect of women's roles, effective practice on the part of women of deceit and indirection, their instigation of men to commit their crimes (the Lady Macbeth factor), and the unwillingness on the part of the public and law enforcement officials to hold women accountable for their deeds (the chivalry factor). (1967: 13)

5   Bertha Payak in 'Understanding the Female Offender' (1963) stresses that women offenders have poor self-concepts, feelings of insecurity and dependency, are emotionally selfish, and prey to irrationality during menstruation, pregnancy, and menopause (a good deal of their life!).

6   See Theodore R. Sarbin and Jeffrey E. Miller, 'Demonism revisited: the XYY chromosomal anomaly', *Issues in Criminology* 5(2), (1970).

7   Kate Millett notes that 'sex is biological, gender psychological and therefore cultural ... if proper terms for sex are male and female, the corresponding terms for gender are masculine and feminine; these latter may be quite independent of biological sex' (1970: 30).

8   Zelditch (1960), a structural-functionalist, writes that the nuclear family is an inevitability and that within it, women, the 'expressive' sex, will inevitably be the domestics.

REFERENCES

Bishop, C. (1931) *Women and Crime*. London: Chatto and Windus.

Cowie, J., Cowie V. and Slater, E. (1968) *Delinquency in Girls*. London: Heinemann.

Davis, K. (1961) 'Prostitution', in R.K. Merton and R.A. Nisbet (eds), *Contemporary Social Problems*. New York: Harcourt Brace and Jovanovich. Originally published as 'The sociology of prostitution', *American Sociological Review*, 1937, 2(5).

Ervin, F. and Mark, V. (1970) *Violence and the Brain*. New York: Harper and Row.

Freud, S. (1933) *New Introductory Lectures on Psychoanalysis*. New York: W.W. Norton.

Glueck, E. and Glueck, S. (1934) *Four Hundred Delinquent Women*. New York: Alfred A. Knopf.

Healy, W. and Bronner, A. (1926) *Delinquents and Criminals: their Making and Unmaking*. New York: Macmillan and Company.

Jones, E. (1961) *The Life and Works of Sigmund Freud*. New York: Basic Books.

Konopka, G. (1966) *The Adolescent Girl in Conflict*. Englewood Cliffs, NJ: Prentice-Hall.

Lombroso, C. (1920) *The Female Offender* (trans.). New York: Appleton. Originally published in 1903.

Millett, K. (1970) *Sexual Politics*. New York: Doubleday.

Monahan, F. (1941) *Women in Crime*. New York: I. Washburn.

Payak, B. (1963) 'Understanding the female offender', *Federal Probation*, XXVII.

Pollak, O. (1950) *The Criminality of Women*. Philadelphia: University of Pennsylvania Press.

Reckless, W. and Kay, B. (1967) *The Female Offender*. Report to the President's Commission on Law Enforcement and the Administration of Justice. Washington, DC: U.S. Government Printing Office.

Sarbin, T.R. and Miller, J.E. (1970) 'Demonism revisited: the XYY chromosomal anomaly', *Issues in Criminology*, 5(2) (Summer).

Spaulding, E. (1923) *An Experimental Study of Psychopathic Delinquent Women*. New York: Rand McNally.

Thomas, W.I. (1907) *Sex and Society*. Boston: Little, Brown.

Thomas, W.I. (1923) *The Unadjusted Girl*. New York: Harper and Row.

Vedder, C. and Somerville, D. (1970) *The Delinquent Girl*. Springfield, Ill.: Charles C. Thomas.

West, J. (1973) *Proposal for the Center for the Study and Reduction of Violence*. Neuropsychiatric Institute, UCLA (10 April).

Zelditch, M. Jr (1960) 'Role differentiation in the nuclear family: a comparative study', in N. Bell and E. Vogel (eds), *The Family*. Glencoe, Ill.: The Free Press.

Afterword: Twenty years ago ... today*

'The Etiology of Female Crime: a Review of the Literature', written two decades ago, ended in a call for 'a new kind of research on women and crime – one that has feminist roots and a radical orientation ... that focuses on human needs, rather than those of the state, [and that] will require new definitions of criminality, women, the individual and her/his relation to the state.' At that time, in 1973, there was a new women's movement, paralleling other international and domestic liberation movements. It consisted of thousands of women forming groups, reading the few books or articles available, demonstrating, writing, and swapping pamphlets. At the School of Criminology at the University of California, Berkeley, where I was studying, there flourished a radical, oppositional criminology, determined to remake the field in the image of the movements of the time: prisoners' rights, community control of the police, and decriminalization of victimless offenses.

The presence of a critical mass of politically active women graduate students, at a time when few criminologists were female, allowed us to share and build on what little knowledge we had.[1] At that time there were no professional ethnographies of women law-breakers, no recent theoretical readings in criminology that centered on women or gender, no studies of female prisoners that did not focus on their homosexuality or 'affective' needs.

For a term paper, I decided to take what had been written on the causes of women's offenses and scrutinize it for its unexamined assumptions about women offenders.[2] Writing up what I found, I wondered naively, angrily, how, in our era and given the women's movement, such stereotypes about women could be taken seriously. The paper appeared in the special issue devoted to women by the School's journal (*Issues in Criminology*, 1973).

In the years since, the feminist critique of mainstream academic disciplines has exploded in volume and advanced light-years in depth, and interest in the issues of women, crime, victimization and justice has also grown. Today 'Etiology' may strike one as a long-ago first step, the passionate reaction of a beginner armed with the rhetoric of a young movement.

---

* From *The Criminal Justice System and Women* (eds B.R. Price and N.J. Sokoloff), pp. 47–53. (New York: McGraw-Hill, Inc., 1995.)

But have the concerns and hopes voiced in 'Etiology' been met, or vanished with time? I would suggest neither; rather, they have been expressed in numerous ways and in the process gone through sea-changes. In this Afterword, I will pose the challenge for feminist criminology in three areas which trace a common history to 'Etiology' and hold importance for the future: the scientific basis of theories, the gender and racial bias in science, and the definition of crime. The common thread of my discussion is a simple premise: It is time to move away from considering 'the feminist question in criminology' and toward exploring 'the criminology question in feminism' (see Bertrand, 1991, paraphrasing Harding). Specifically, how can feminist insights into gender, power and knowledge help us critically examine our understanding of crime, criminality, and victimization?

1   The debates over the scientific basis of theories of women's and men's behaviors have continued fiercely over two decades, although with new twists and turns around questions of biology and psychology.

Most recently, feminist philosophical and scientific critiques have argued that for many traditional European-identified thinkers, including Lombroso and his followers, femaleness was associated with biology or nature (e.g., primitive, irrational, nurturing), in contrast to male civilization. What is especially radical about these recent critiques is that they do not merely challenge the gender assignment of certain constructs, as earlier feminist work did (e.g., femaleness as a Lombrosian primitive). Rather, they question the very validity of these dichotomies: nature *versus* civilization, emotion *versus* reason, developed *versus* undeveloped world, female *versus* male (see Benhabib and Cornell, 1987; Nicholson, 1990; Sunstein, 1990).

The contemporary feminist argument is this: a quality that appears natural or biological must not be exclusively assigned to a gender; this very quality may be a historical ideological construction rather than an eternal objective truth. Woman herself is a constructed 'Other', in Simone de Beauvoir's classic phrase, who by definition exists only in contrast to man. This is much like the criminal, who cannot exist without the contrast of the law-abiding citizen. Women, like minority-group members, criminals, and other relatively less powerful 'Others', tend to be perceived in the dominant culture more one-dimensionally, more restrictively, than their opposites. Hence one finds the origins of the stereotyping of female offenders in traditional criminology, as discussed in 'Etiology'.

In contemporary criminology, on the other hand, there is now agreement that differences in women's and men's behaviors are social rather than natural, just as there is agreement that the sources of criminality are social rather than natural. Very few criminologists today argue that prostitution or shoplifting emerges out of women's nature or that violence is hormonal. More generally, few theories of criminality are based on nature. To this extent, criminology has moved away from overt biologism.[3] However, criminological work on women continues to focus on their experiences or qualities as they exist in comparison with those of men: in other words, the differences between the genders. Moreover, much work on women focuses uncritically on sexuality: first, as a natural, as opposed to a social, force, and second, as a female, rather than male, concern. Furthermore, in nearly all criminology, maleness remains the universal, femaleness the special case.

During the years, feminists have also wrestled with theoretical psychological perspectives on gender and sexuality, reexamining Freudianism with a far more sophisticated eye (certainly more so than mine in 1973!). One objective, among others, has been to understand how and why women and men are in fact made, as opposed to being born. The spotlight has been on such 'gender factories' as families, although much of the psychoanalytic theorization is limited in its relevance to affluent populations in modern Western societies.

Within feminist and critical criminology, there is much distrust of psychology as the discourse used in 'blaming the victim' and in the practices of social control. Within radical and critical feminism in general, there is similar distrust of psychological approaches to gender domination, such as those that put primacy on sex roles. Structurally oriented and Marxist-influenced feminisms have instead focused on large-scale institutional and cultural aspects of life, such as the division of paid and unpaid labor.

Yet today there is interest in exploring people's personal choices as well as their structural constraints: in other words, in deepening our understanding of the subjective relations between an individual and society. For example, there has been the intriguing and much-debated work of Carol Gilligan (1982) on differences in women's and men's views of morality. One question now being asked of any psychological theory of gender is not so much what is its specific content, but upon what scientific basis is it making psychological claims about gender differences? Is a psychological theory, for example, implicitly biological (e.g., resting on women's childbearing capacity), psychoanalytic, culturally bound (e.g., based on women's childrearing role), or structural?

Much mainstream criminology today, like the positivist correctionalism of the past, is psychological in orientation, focusing on the personal characteristics of known offenders and victims. Only recently has this criminology shown any likelihood of drawing upon feminist work, with recent attention paid to the possibilities of investigating why certain forms of criminality are disproportionately male behaviors.

In the 1970s and early 1980s, many feminist scholars in different fields, abandoning biology and psychology, searched for the social roots of women's oppression, which cuts across many eras and cultures. Most argued that whatever the causes of patriarchy, they were due to the structuring of gender rather than either to the biological fact of sexual difference or to differential psychological development alone.[4]

Some feminist scholars have recently called for abandoning the search for the primary universal social cause of sexism, not because the search has failed but because, they argue, there is no such thing. Rather, they argue, there are diverse, geographically specific, historically varying causes and fragmented standpoints inclusive of gender and other (ethnic, class, sexual) forces (Nicholson, 1990).

This brings us to the contemporary feminist argument I noted at the outset, which states, at its most extreme, that it is not just the dualism of femininity/masculinity that is socially constructed but femaleness/maleness itself. It is not the existence of two genders that generates sexism but the other way around; in other words, women and men are not just made, but made up. Not only is there no essential woman's nature, as traditionalists (and some feminists) have believed. And not only is there no universal female experience, as most feminists have heretofore argued, in their advocacy of sisterhood. That we divide humans into two genders is a social artifact, according to this radical new argument, and the way this division happens differs enormously across eras and societies.

This approach to the study of gender, and hence of sexism with all its institutional and ideological facets, parallels schools of thought that view many taken-for-granted concepts and problems as socially constructed rather than as naturally occurring or arising spontaneously in society. One particular example is race, and another is crime. What this approach suggests is not that real experiences around gender, race, or crime do not exist. It means that how we label and explain these experiences involves fluid choices rather than inevitabilities. There are no essences to such concepts as woman or man, black or white, criminal or victim, other than what we attach to them. What it means to be a woman or man, black or white, a criminal or victim changes dramatically with time and varies tremendously across cultures.

After acknowledging that something is socially constructed, there is still much to be done. Sexism, no more than racism or crime, cannot be 'deconstructed' away by academic analysis such as the aforementioned. We want to know how and, if possible, who and why, and, above all, what to do about it. This practical urgency will require the continuous generation of 'feminist roots and a radical orientation' for criminology as it considers specific victimizations and injustices.

2 A second, related aspect of the feminist critique concerns the question of whether science and expertise are fundamentally gendered and racially based.

Within criminology, the necessary first steps of this critique, including those begun in 'Etiology', were to challenge traditional assumptions about women, redirect the search for the causes of women's behaviors to their circumstances and experiences, and implicitly hold out the desirability of a fuller range of experiences and behaviors open to all, regardless of gender.

But the next steps were to explore whether science and philosophy are masculine in an even more profound sense than merely male-dominated and male-oriented. Only recently has feminism undertaken critiques of both science and law as gendered in method and philosophical base as well as in overt content (Benhabib and Cornell, 1987; Nicholson, 1990; Sunstein, 1990). In other words, the argument is that the fundamental premises of science and law are not neutral with respect to gender or with respect to cultural ethnicity. It has been difficult to see these biases because they are hidden in taken-for-granted ways of conceptualization, often nearly invisible.

One task, along with making visible and depathologizing femaleness in science and law, is to make visible and denormalize maleness. Unfortunately, criminology and criminal law have not yet been subjected to this level of critique, although recent efforts have been made (Daly and Chesney-Lind, 1988; Smart, 1989). As was true 20 years ago, criminology is implicitly about men, unless it is feminist – in which case it is only about women! And much of the latter is restricted to querying which traditional (masculinist) theories may pertain to women's behaviors!

An example of how criminology might conduct this critique of criminology as fundamentally gendered would be to use the problem of women not being taken seriously as victims and witnesses. Alongside the challenges to common negative images of women victims/witnesses (untrustworthy, provocative, complicit), we would analyse for its gendered content the normal or idealized positive image of the victim/witness (uninvolved with the victimizer, randomly chosen, harmed in public). One question would be, Is this an implicitly male victim/witness?

Another undone task is to constitute a feminist epistemology and methodology, and there has been much debate over what these might look like, if grounded in women's experiences. There has been little development of an explicitly feminist criminological methodology, although some recent studies of women offenders and victims attempt to involve them as subjects rather than examine them as objects. There is only a glimmer of understanding of exactly how women are made the objects of knowledge and power, of the unconscious male identification of the omniscient gaze of experts in criminology (see Benhabib and Cornell, 1987; Diamond and Quinby, 1988). To see the nexus of policing and correctional power, one must first transgress the traditional framework of criminology (Cain, 1989).

For those attempting to reorient their gaze from that of the controller to the standpoint of the dominated, the question changes from What should the discipline do with these people? to How can certain groups of people use the discipline?

One aspect of this shift must be the denormalizing and stepping outside of the dominant ethnic perspective. Race, unlike gender, has never been ignored in criminology, but this is not to say that mainstream criminology has sensitively or accurately addressed the deep and complex associations between criminalization and racism, or between violence and inequality.[5]

Critical criminology, from the days of 'Etiology' onward, certainly has perceived the enormous effects of race and class on criminal justice. A basic premise has been that correctionalism serves to shape and control the lives of the lower classes and people of color, incorporating different strategies: sometimes universalizing standards of the affluent, other times applying differential standards for the poor.

None the less, there has been little development of these issues within either the critical or feminist paradigms during the past 20 years. There has been scant in-depth examination of criminal justice in minority communities. Among feminists, there has been infrequent intellectual exchange between those concerned with criminalized women offenders, who emphasize the repressive and racist character of criminal justice, and those supporting victims of violence, who emphasize the protective and potentially reconciliatory aspects (Klein, 1988). Yet feminist criminology has the greatest potential of any discipline to make these connections (Bertrand, Daly and Klein, 1992). Women in minority communities often directly perceive criminal justice as neither simple protector nor mere oppressor but as the hydra-headed hybrid it is (Gordon, 1988; Klein, 1990). Feminist criminology would benefit from a reexamination of criminal justice from these women's view-point, thus addressing 'human needs, rather than those of the state'.

3   A third issue that feminist criminology must tackle is that of the definition of crime. As an applied field, criminology has tended to take its scope of study from government and policy rather than chart its own course. But to say merely that crime is anything that breaks the law, while self-evident, is tautological. Crime certainly has no natural or universal status. In fact, formerly criminalized activities are continually being legalized, such as abortion or (in Nevada) prostitution; and new crimes are continually being politically constructed, as in the case of recent laws on domestic violence (Klein, 1981). To take for granted the official definition of crime is to forgo both an analysis of the roots of law and the penal system and the possibility of developing alternative visions of justice.

Early radical criminologists of the 1970s, while not always explicitly challenging the official definition of crime in every discussion such as 'Etiology', rarely accepted it as given, arguing that it is steeped in racial and class and gender domination. Which activities are legal and which illegal and which laws are enforced are connected to the relative degrees of power of those involved. Many of us were very much aware of the necessity for disaggregating and transforming the suspect category crime (Schwendinger and Schwendinger, 1970). Yet even now this enterprise remains in the formative stages.

The feminist critique has the specific potential to contribute to what could be called the deconstruction of the taken-for-granted concept we call crime, through the prism of gender. Both law and order, on the one hand, and its opposite, criminality, on the other, are very much linked to complex constructions of power, including masculinity. But these possible connections are concealed by layers of rarely debated official morality.

In more practical terms, feminists have wrestled with whether to advocate the enhancement or the abolition of the criminal justice 'apparatus of control'. An example of the dilemma is the feminist debate over criminalizing violent or harmful pornography. Recently there have emerged tentative discussions about what feminist justice might look like (Gilligan, 1982; Daly, 1989; Sunstein, 1990; Bertrand et al., 1992). Despite many disagreements over the potential role of criminal justice, there is consensus that it should not resemble the existing cycles of partial punishment that characterize contemporary US criminal justice, 'partial' referring to the deeply rooted systemic biases (Rafter, 1985).

In conclusion, the current feminist debates relevant to criminology are those concerning defining crime and justice for women and men, gender and racial bias in science, and the validity of fundamental scientific concepts based on nature and dualism. Few of these debates have been concluded, few dilemmas resolved. Yet they have advanced our understanding to the point that today a proposed article titled 'Etiology of Female Crime' would probably be challenged. One would very likely be informed that the scientific concept of etiology is suspect, that the term 'female' must be deconstructed, and that the definition of crime itself should be reexamined.

NOTES

1   One important thing to note in assessing our accomplishments and limits is that most of us were European-American (as distinct from African-, Asian-, or Latino-American), although we did focus on racism as a fundamental issue for feminist criminology.

2   I was inspired to do this by the work then being engaged in by one of my professors, Herman Schwendinger (Schwendinger and Schwendinger, 1974).

3   Ironically, biologism is more influential in feminist theory than in contemporary criminology. Within the movement to end violence against women, influential works have drawn upon implicit assumptions about male biology (e.g., physical strength, sexual aggression) as explaining rape and other victimizations (Brownmiller, 1975; MacKinnon, 1989). Furthermore, feminist legal defenses for accused women have evolved around such controversial conceptualizations as the premenstrual syndrome.

4   Within mainstream criminology, and its ongoing search for the causes of crime, there has been little interest in this search for the roots of patriarchy. Unfortunately, gender issues have largely remained ignored, as in the days of 'Etiology'.

5   Instead, criminologists debate the accuracy and meaning of African-American, Latino, and Anglo/European rates of criminality in an exercise even longer and less productive than the debate over women's and men's rates.

REFERENCES

Benhabib, S. and Cornell, D. (eds) (1987) *Feminism as Critique: On the Politics of Gender.* Minneapolis: University of Minnesota.

Bertrand, M.-A. (1991) 'Advances in feminist epistemology of the social control of women'. Presented at the American Society of Criminology, San Francisco, November.

Bertrand, M.-A., Daly, K. and Klein, D. (eds) (1992) *Proceedings of the International Feminist Conference on Women, Law and Social Control.* Vancouver: International Centre for the Reform of Criminal Law and Criminal Justice Policy.

Brownmiller, S. (1975) *Against Our Will: Men, Women and Rape.* New York: Simon and Schuster.

Cain, M. (ed.) (1989) *Growing Up Good: Policing the Behaviour of Girls in Europe.* Newbury Park, CA: Sage.

Daly, K. (1989) 'New feminist definitions of justice', *Proceedings of the First Annual Women's Policy Research Conference.* Washington, DC: Institute for Women's Policy Research.

Daly, K. and Chesney-Lind, M. (1988) 'Feminism and criminology', *Justice Quarterly,* 5: 4.

Diamond, I. and Quinby, L. (eds) (1988) *Feminism and Foucault: Reflections on Resistance.* Boston, MA: Northeastern University Press.

Gilligan, C. (1982) *In a Different Voice: Psychological Theory and Women's Development.* Cambridge, MA: Harvard University Press.

Gordon, L. (1988) *Heroes of Their Own Lives: the Politics and History of Family Violence.* New York: Viking.

Klein, D. (1981) 'Violence against women: some considerations regarding its causes and its elimination', *Crime and Delinquency*, 27: 1.

Klein, D. (1988) 'Women and criminal justice in the Reagan era'. Presented at the Academy of Criminal Justice Sciences, San Francisco, April.

Klein, D. (1990) 'Losing (the war on) the war on crime', *Critical Criminologist*, 2: 4.

MacKinnon, C. (1989) *Towards a Feminist Theory of the State.* Cambridge, MA: Harvard University Press.

Nicholson, L. (ed.) (1990) *Feminism/Postmodernism.* New York: Routledge.

Rafter, N. (1985) *Partial Justice: Women in State Prisons, 1800–1935.* Boston, MA: Northeastern University Press.

Schwendinger, H. and Schwendinger, J. (1970) 'Defenders of order or guardians of human rights?' *Issues in Criminology*, 5: 1.

Schwendinger, H. and Schwendinger, J. (1974) *The Sociologists of the Chair.* New York: Basic Books.

Smart, C. (1989) *Feminism and the Power of Law.* New York: Routledge.

Sunstein, C. (ed.) (1990) *Feminism and Political Theory.* Chicago: University of Chicago Press.

20

Seductions and repulsions of crime

Jack Katz

In 1835, in a small French village, Pierre Rivière killed half his family: his mother, a sister, and a brother. After his arrest, he wrote a lengthy explanation to the effect that he had killed his mother to protect his father from her ceaseless cruelties, which had frequently become public humiliations, and he had killed two siblings who were living with her because they had sided with her in the family quarrels, either actively or simply through sustained love. In addition, Rivière explained that by killing his young brother, whom he knew his father to love, he would turn his father against him, thus making less burdensome to his father Rivière's legally mandated death, which he expected would result from his crimes.[1] A team of scholars, led by Michel Foucault, traced the ensuing conflicts among the various 'discourses' engaged in by Rivière, the lawyers, doctors, the mayor, the priest, and the villagers, and they added their own.

Rivière wrote a carefully composed, emotionally compelling account of the background to his crime, recounting, as if reconstructing a contemporaneous journal, a long series of deceits and monetary exploitations by his mother against his father. But, although he entitled his account 'Particulars and Explanation of the Occurrence', in the sixty-seven pages his 'memoir' covers (in this translated reproduction), less than a sentence describes the 'particulars of the occurrence'. Rivière gave no specific significance to the aim or the force of the blows he struck with an axlike farm implement (he destroyed the vertebrae that had connected the head of his mother from her body, and he separated brain from skull, convert-ing bone and muscle to mush); to the multiplicity of the blows, which extended far beyond what was necessary to accomplish death; to his mother's advanced state

From *Seductions of Crime: Moral and Sensual Attractions in Doing Evil*, pp. 310–24. (New York: Basic Books, 1988.)

of pregnancy; or to details of the violence suffered by his brother and sister. Instead, he focused exclusively on the background of his family biography. Although Riviere's account was elaborately inculpating in substance, in style, it bespoke a sophisticated rationality, which in many eyes was exculpating. (Some even labeled it 'beautiful'.)

As an author, Pierre Rivière was primarily concerned with the moral power that the narrative could lend to his crime. By glossing over the homicidal event itself, he continued the attack on his mother before a new, larger audience. The state and lay professional interpreters of his crime followed his lead, relying largely on facts he had acknowledged and discounting the situational details in favor of biographical, historical, and social ecological factors. As Foucault suggested, the very barbarity of the attack made it an act of resistance against the forms of civility. But after the fact, Rivière and many powerful groups in his society literally rationalized the event, locating it as the logical outcome of an ongoing family injustice, a form of madness or mental illness, or (in the comments offered later in the book by some of Foucault's colleagues) of the historical and class position of French peasants.[2]

In short, many of the interpreters sought to exploit too much from the murder to dwell on its gruesome lived reality. Rivière was motivated to construct an account that would make his viciously cruel, extremely messy act neatly reappear as a self-sacrificial, efficient blow for justice. The other commentators had general theoretical perspectives at stake: medical-psychological ideology, institutions of religious understanding, and politically significant interpretations (including the emergence of a school of thought around Foucault himself). On all sides, modern forms of civility would govern the posthumous experience of the crime.

Today, the contemporary incarnations of professional, legal-scientific, and civil interpretive spirits are both stronger and more petty than they were 150 years ago. The effective political spectrum for debate still features a Right and a Left, but most of the intellectual action is within a small and relatively tame segment on the left side of the scale. The length of the scale is much narrower than when the Church and tradition, and occasionally even anarchist voices, were powerful in the debate. Now various disciplines in the social sciences have a go at it, but they go at each other more than at 'lay' opinion, and what is at stake is less clearly the institutionalization of a field than the relative popularity of fads in research methodology.

[…] [T]he readily available, detailed meaning of common criminality has been systematically ruled out as ineligible for serious discussion in the conventions of modern sociological and political thought. Something important happened when it became obscenely sensational or damnably insensitive to track the lived experience of criminality in favor of imputing factors to the background of crime that are invisible in its situational manifestation. Somehow in the psychological and sociological disciplines, the lived mysticism and magic in the foreground of criminal experience became unseeable, while the abstractions hypothesized by 'empirical theory' as the determining background causes, especially those conveniently quantified by state agencies, became the stuff of 'scientific' thought and 'rigorous' method.

Whatever the historical causes for treating background factors as the theoretical core for the empirical study of crime, [...] it is not necessary to constitute the field back to front. We may begin with the foreground, attempting to discover common or homogeneous criminal projects and to test explanations of the necessary and sufficient steps through which people construct given forms of crime. If we take as our primary research commitment an exploration of the distinctive phenomena of crime, we may produce not just ad hoc bits of description or a collection of provocative anecdotes but a systematic empirical theory of crime – one that explains at the individual level the causal process of committing a crime and that accounts at the aggregate level for recurrently documented correlations with biographical and ecological background factors.

MORAL EMOTIONS AND CRIME

The closer one looks at crime, at least at the varieties examined here, the more vividly relevant become the moral emotions. Follow vandals and amateur shoplifters as they duck into alleys and dressing rooms and you will be moved by their delight in deviance; observe them under arrest and you may be stunned by their shame. Watch their strutting street display and you will be struck by the awesome fascination that symbols of evil hold for the young men who are linked in the groups we often call gangs. If we specify the opening moves in muggings and stickups, we describe an array of 'games' or tricks that turn victims into fools before their pockets are turned out. The careers of persistent robbers show us, not the increasingly precise calculations and hedged risks of 'professionals', but men for whom gambling and other vices are a way of life, who are 'wise' in the cynical sense of the term, and who take pride in a defiant reputation as 'bad'. And if we examine the lived sensuality behind events of cold-blooded 'senseless' murder, we are compelled to acknowledge the power that may still be created in the modern world through the sensualities of defilement, spiritual chaos, and the apprehension of vengeance.

Running across these experiences of criminality is a process juxtaposed in one manner or another against humiliation. In committing a righteous slaughter, the impassioned assailant takes humiliation and turns it into rage; through laying claim to a moral status of transcendent significance, he tries to burn humiliation up. The badass, with searing purposiveness, tries to scare humiliation off; as one ex-punk explained to me, after years of adolescent anxiety about the ugliness of his complexion and the stupidity of his every word, he found a wonderful calm in making 'them' anxious about *his* perceptions and understandings. Young vandals and shoplifters innovate games with the risks of humiliation, running along the edge of shame for its exciting reverberations. Fashioned as street elites, young men square off against the increasingly humiliating social restrictions of childhood by mythologizing differences with other groups of young men who might be their mirror image. Against the historical background of a collective insistence on the moral nonexistence of their people, 'bad niggers' exploit ethnically unique possibilities for celebrating assertive conduct as 'bad'.

What does the moral fascination in the foreground of criminal experience imply for background factors, particularly poverty and social class? Is crime only the most visible peak of a mountain of shame suffered at the bottom of the social order? Is the vulnerability to humiliation skewed in its distribution through the social structure? To address these questions, we should examine the incidence and motivational qualities of what is usually called 'white-collar' crime. Perhaps we would find a greater level of involvement in criminality, even more closely linked to shameful motivations. But the study of white-collar crime has been largely a muckraking operation from the outside; despite isolated exceptions, we have no general empirical understanding of the incidence or internal feel of white-collar crime. This absence of data makes all the more remarkable the influence, within both academic and lay political thought on crime, of the assumption of materialist causation.

SENTIMENTAL MATERIALISM

> But whatever the differential rates of deviant behavior in the several social strata, and we know from many sources that the official crime statistics uniformly showing higher rates in the lower strata are far from complete or reliable, it appears from our analysis that the greatest pressures toward deviation are exerted upon the lower strata.[3]

Just fifty years ago, Robert K. Merton published his 'Social Structure and Anomie', an article once counted as the single most frequently cited and reprinted paper in the history of American sociology.[4] Arguing against Freud and psychological analysis in general, Merton attributed deviance to a contradiction in the structure of modern society: 'Americans are bombarded on all sides' by the goal of monetary success, but the means or opportunities for achieving it are not as uniformly distributed. A generation later, Richard Cloward and Lloyd Ohlin, with a revised version of 'opportunity' theory, hit perhaps the pinnacle of academic and political success in the history of criminology, winning professional awards and finding their work adopted by the Kennedy administration as part of the intellectual foundations of what later became the War on Poverty.[5] After a hiatus during much of the Republican 1970s and 1980s, materialist theory – the Mertonian ideas now bolstered by rational-economic models of social action that had become academically attractive in the interim – is again promoting the lack of opportunity (unemployment, underemployment, and low 'opportunity cost') to explain crime.[6]

That this materialist perspective is twentieth century sentimentality about crime is indicated by its overwhelming inadequacy for grasping the experiential facts of crime. The 'model' or 'theory' is so persuasive that the observable facts really do not matter, as Merton put it: 'whatever the differential rates of deviant behavior in the several social strata ... it appears from our analysis that the greatest pressures toward deviation are exerted upon the lower strata'.[7] Indeed, the Mertonian framework as originally presented, as elaborated in the 1960s, and as recently paralleled by the economist's perspective, should now be recognized as an institutionalized academic-political sensibility for systematically making literally unthinkable the contemporary horrors of deviance and for sustaining a quietist criminology.

Consider the many sensually explosive, diabolically creative, realities of crime that the materialist sentiment cannot appreciate. Where is the materialism in the experience of the *barrio* 'homeboy', the night before the first day of high school?

> Although I was not going to be alone, I still felt insecure ... my mother, with an accentuated voice, ordered me to go to sleep. Nevertheless, my anxiety did not let my consciousness rest; instead, what I did was look in the mirror, and began practicing the traditional steps that would show my machismo. ... Furthermore, I was nervously thinking about taking a weapon to the school grounds just to show Vatos from other barrios the answer of my holy clique. All kinds of evil thoughts were stirring in me.[8]

The problem for Merton and materialist theory is not simply with some youthful 'gang' activity. There is now strong evidence that a high proportion of those who go on to especially 'serious', 'heavy', 'career' involvements in criminality start in early adolescence, long before job opportunities could or, in a free social order, should become meaningful considerations.[9] Actually, when Albert Cohen pointed out, long ago, the '"versatility" and the "zest" with which some boys are observed to pursue their group-supported deviations', Merton was willing to concede that much of youth crime was beyond his theory of deviance.[10] It was enough if, as Cohen had offered in a conciliatory gesture, Merton's materialism applied to 'professional' or serious adult property criminals.

But if we look at persistent criminals, we see a life of action in which materialism is by no means the god. Instead, material goods are treated more like offerings to be burnt, quickly, lest retention become sacrilege. As suggested by 'dead presidents', a black street term for US cash, there is an aggressive attack on materialism as a potentially misleading, false deity. Robby Wideman seemed to have Merton in mind when he told his brother:

> Straight people don't understand. I mean, they think dudes is after the things straight people got. It ain't that at all. People in the life ain't looking for no home and grass in the yard and shit like that. We the show people. The glamour people. Come on the set with the finest car, the finest woman, the finest vines. Hear people talking about you. Hear the bar get quiet when you walk in the door. Throw down a yard and tell everybody drink up. ... You make something out of nothing.[11]

The aspiration is not to what is advertised on television. Robby Wideman was not incapable of identifying what drove him; it was to be a star – something literally, distinctively transcendent. Street people are not inarticulate when they say that 'the endgame is to *get over*, to *get across*, to *make it*, to *step fast*'.[12] This language is only a 'poetic' indirect reference to aspirations for material status if we refuse to recognize that it directly captures the objective of transcendence.[13]

So, a lot of juvenile forms of violent crime and an important segment of serious adult crime do not fit the sentimentality of materialism. Neither does the central thrust that guides men and women to righteous slaughters, nor the project of primordial evil that makes 'senseless killings' compellingly sensible to their killers, nor the tactics and reverberations of sneaky thrills. None of these fits, in the Mertonian scheme, the actions of 'innovators' who accept the conventional aims but use deviant means. The aims are specifically unconventional: to go beyond the established moral definitions of the situation as it visibly obtains here and now. Nor can we categorize these deviants as 'retreatists' who reject conventional means and ends. For Merton, retreatists were a spiritually dead, socially isolated, lot of psychotics, drunkards, and vagrants; today's 'bag ladies' would fit that category. And, surely, these deviants are not 'rebels' with revolutionary ideas to implement new goals and means.

None of this argument denies the validity of the recurrent correlations between low socioeconomic status or relative lack of economic opportunity, on the one hand, and violent and personal property crime on the other. The issue is the causal significance of this background for deviance. A person's material background will not determine his intent to commit acquisitive crime, but a person, whether or not he is intent on acquisitive crime, is not likely to be unaware of his circumstances.

Instead of reading into ghetto poverty an unusually strong motivation to become deviant, we may understand the concentration of robbery among ghetto residents as being due to the fact that for people in economically more promising circumstances, it would literally make no sense – it would virtually be crazy – to commit robbery. Merton had no basis but the sentiments stirred by his theory to assume that crime, even materially acquisitive crime, was more common in the 'lower strata'. In part, the appeal of his theory was promoted by the obvious significance of material circumstance in the shaping of crime. We need fear only a few exceptions if we claim that lawyers will not stick up banks, 'frequent-flyer' executives will not kill their spouses in passionate rages, and physicians will not punch out their colleagues or that the unemployed will not embezzle, the indigent will not fix prices, and the politically powerless will not commit perjury in congressional testimony. But this is a different matter from claiming that crime or deviance is distributed in the social structure according to the relative lack of opportunity for material gain.

It is not inconsequential that major forms of contemporary criminality cannot simply be fit within the dominant sentimentality for understanding deviance. If it were recognized that changes in material circumstance affect the form more than the drive toward deviance, it would be more difficult to promote publicly financed programs to increase benefits or opportunities where they are most lacking. A revision of the theory of materialism that would limit it to the explanation of the quality, rather than the quantity, of deviance, would be much less palatable across the political spectrum. Such an analytic framework would not serve those on the Right who point to the social distribution of common crime, along with other pathologies, to discount the moral claims of lower-class minorities for governmental outlays. But neither would a comparative theory of the qualities of crime serve well the social-class sympathies that have often been promoted by the study of white-collar crime. For muckrakers, it has been important to depict the prevalence of elite deviance to weaken the moral basis of corporate political power; often they have argued that white-collar crime is every bit as 'real' and destructive a form of deviance as is street crime. But unless one agrees to reduce nonviolent crimes of deception to a less heinous status than violent personal crime, the comparative perspective will undercut traditional policies of social reform to aid the underprivileged. One has to promise more than a trade-off between street crime and administrative fraud to work up moral enthusiasm for job training programs.

More generally, from Marx through Durkheim and Freud to the contemporary sociological materialists, the hallmark of rhetorically successful theory has been its specification of the source of social evil.[14] Without the claim that background conditions breed the motivation to deviance, criminological theory would not serve the high priestly function of transforming diffuse anxiety about chaos into discrete problems that are confined to marginal segments of social life. Indeed, the research agenda implied by a theory that relates material conditions to the form or quality of deviance but not to its incidence or prevalence is profoundly disquieting.

REPULSIONS OF DEVIANCE

Whether their policy implications point toward increasing penalties to decrease crime or toward increasing legitimate opportunities or 'opportunity costs' to decrease crime, modern causal theories have obliterated a natural fascination to follow in detail the lived contours of crime. Perhaps the indecisive battle among competing determinist theories of crime is itself an important aspect of their persistent popularity, inside academia, in columnists' opinions, and in political speech. Methodological innovations, policy experiments, and the latest wave of governmental statistics continually stimulate the ongoing dialogue, with no side ever gaining a decisive advantage but all sharing in an ideological structure that blocks unsettling encounters with the human experience of crime.

What would follow if we stuck with the research tactic of defining the form of deviance to be explained from the inside and searching for explanations by examining how people construct the experience at issue and then, only as a secondary matter, turned to trace connections from the phenomenal foreground to the generational and social ecological background? We would have to acknowledge that just because blacks have been denied fair opportunity for so long, and so often,[15] the criminality of ghetto blacks can no longer be explained by a lack of opportunity. Just because the critique of American racial injustice has been right for so long, as criminological explanation it now is wrong. Even accepting the Mertonian analysis as initially valid, for how many generations can a community maintain a moral independence of means and ends, innovating deviance only to reach conventional goals? How does a people restrict its economic participation only to the stunted spiritual engagement permitted over centuries of racism? By what anthropological theory can one hold his real self somehow outside the cynical hustles he devises day by day, his soul, untouched by a constant pursuit of illicit action, waiting with confident innocence in some purgatory to emerge when a fair opportunity materializes? The realities of ghetto crime are literally too 'bad' to be confined to the role of 'innovative means' for conventional ends. This is not to deny that the history of racial injustice makes a morally convincing case for increasing opportunities for the ghetto poor. It is to say that materialist theories refuse to confront the spiritual challenge represented by contemporary crime.

The profundity of the embrace of deviance in the black ghetto and the tensions that will emerge among us if we discuss the lived details of these phenomena form one set of the contemporary horrors our positivist theories help us avoid facing. Another blindness they sustain is to the lack of any intellectual or political leadership to confront the massive bloodletting of mate against mate and brother against brother that continues to be a daily reality in the inner city. Each time the sentimentality of materialism is trotted out to cover the void of empirically grounded ideas, it seems more transparent and less inspiring; each time the exhortation to positivism carries a more desperate sentiment that it *has* to be right. And, finally, there is the incalculable chaos that would break out if the institutions of social science were to apply the methods of investigation used here to deviance all across the social order.

Theories of background causes lead naturally to a reliance on the state's definition of deviance, especially as assembled in official crime statistics, and they make case studies virtually irrelevant. But the state will never supply data describing white-collar crime that are comparable to the data describing street or common crime. Politically, morally, and logically, it can't.

The problem is due not to political bias in the narrow sense, but to the dialectical character of white-collar crime as a form of deviance that necessarily exists in a moral metaphysical suspense. To assess the incidence and consequences of common crimes like robbery, one can survey victims and count arrests in a research operation that may be conducted independently of the conviction of the offenders. But individual victims generally cannot authoritatively assert the existence of tax cheating, consumer fraud, insider trading, price fixing, and political corruption; when prosecutions of such crimes fail, not only can the defendants protest their personal innocence, but they can deny that *any* crime occurred. We are on especially shaky grounds for asserting with methodological confidence that white-collar crimes exist before the state fully certifies the allegation through a conviction.

On the one hand, then, white-collar crime can exist as a researchable social problem only if the state officially warrants the problem; on the other hand, white-collar crimes will *not* exist if the state gets too serious about them. The existence of prohibitions against white-collar crimes distinctively depends on the prohibitions not being enforced. The strength of public and political support for robbery and murder prosecutions is not weakened with increased enforcement. But if the official system for prosecuting tax cheating, pollution violations, and even immigration fraud becomes too vigorous, pressure will build to reduce the prohibitory reach of the underlying laws.[16] At the extreme, any group that becomes subject to massive state treatment as criminally deviant is either not an elite or is a class engaged in civil war.

Explanatory social research relies on the state's definition of deviance when it statistically manipulates the demographic and ecological variables quantified by the state, rather than documents in detail the experience and circumstances of the actual doings of deviance. So long as this reliance continues, we will be unable intellectually to constitute a field for the study of white-collar crime. Disparate, occasional studies of white-collar crime will continue to emerge from the margins of organization theory, from interests in equal justice that are sustained by the sociology of law, from studies of criminal justice agencies and of the professions, and from the atheoretical moral force generated by recurrent waves of scandal. But a reliance for explanation on background determinism has made twentieth century social theory fundamentally incapable of comprehending the causation of white-collar crime.

Consider how the traditional boundaries of the field of criminology would break down if we were to extend to white-collar crime the strategy taken in this work to explain common crime. [...] [I]n approaching criminal homicide, adolescent theft, gang delinquency and other forms of violent or personal property crime, we would begin, not with the state's official accounting of crime but by looking for lines of action, distinctive to occupants of high social position, that are homogeneously understood by the offenders themselves to enact a variety of deviance. We would quickly arrive at a broad field with vague boundaries between forms of conduct regarded by the offenders as criminal, civilly liable, professionally unethical, and publicly unseemly. Simultaneously, we would follow the logic of analytic induction and search for negative cases, which means that evidence would take the form of qualitative case studies.

Now, where would we get the data? With white-collar crime, we have a special problem in locating facts to demonstrate the lived experience of deviance. Despite their presumably superior capacity to write books and the healthy markets that await their publication efforts, we have virtually no 'how-I-did-it-and-how it-felt-doing-it' autobiographies by corrupted politicians, convicted tax frauds, and chief executive officers who have been deposed by scandals over insider trading. This absence of naturalistic, autobiographical, participant-observational data is itself an important clue to the distinctive emotional quality of white-collar crime. Stickup men, safecrackers, fences, and drug dealers often wear the criminal label with pride, apparently relishing the opportunity to tell their criminal histories in colorful, intimate detail. But white-collar criminals, perhaps from shame or because the ties to those whom they would have to incriminate are so intimate a part of their own identities that they can *never* be broken, rarely publicly confess; when they do confess, they virtually never confess with the sustained attention to detail that characterizes, for example, almost any mugging related by an ordinary, semiliterate hustler like Henry Williamson.[17]

As a result, to obtain data, etiological theorists of white-collar crime would have to join forces with public and private investigators and with enemy constituencies of the elites under focus – hardly a promising tack for winning academic, much less governmental-institutional, support for developing a broad data base. Even more absurd is the suggestion that the researcher take up the data-generating task directly by working from readily accessible gossip and looking around one or another local corner. Depending on time and place, that might mean studying the chancellor's project to remodel his home; the law professor's marijuana smoking; the medical researcher's practice of putting his name on research papers, the data for which he has never seen; the alumni's means of supporting the football team; the professor's management of expenditures and accounting in research grants; the administrator's exploitation through real estate profiteering of inside information about the expansion of the university; the process of defaulting on student loans; and so on. By maintaining background determinism as the dominant framework for the study of crime, the social sciences leave the serious academic investigation of elite deviance to those proper intellectual folk, the ethical philosophers, who exploit qualitative case materials in the innocuous forms of delightful illustrations from literature, lively hypotheticals, and colorful histories documented by others. All who already have them retain their jobs and their sanity.

But is it so absurd to imagine a democratic society that would treat the arrogance, the public frauds, and the self-deceptions of its elites as a field that would be amenable to theoretically guided, empirical investigation? Is it obvious that institutionally supported social research on the etiology of deviance should seek causal drives more in the shame and impotence of poverty than in the hubris of affluence and power?

And we can go one step further. The fear of chaos that blocks a truly empirical study of crime is not just a repulsion for a disquieting process of investigation. There is also a substantive chaos – a crisis of meaning in collective identity – lurking more deeply behind the dogged appeal of traditions that intimidate the contemporary intellectual confrontation with the lived experience of deviance.

If we were to develop a comparative analysis of the crimes committed by ghetto residents and by occupants of high social positions, we would surely not be examining the identical qualities of experience. Where the ghetto resident may be proud of his reputation as a 'bad nigger' at home and on the streets, the governmental leader is likely to be ashamed, at least in some family and community settings, of a breach in his pristine image. Although the stickup man focuses on the simple requirements for instantly and unambiguously conveying to victims the criminal intentions of his actions, organization men will tacitly work out a concerted ignorance that provides each with 'deniability' while they arrange the most complex frauds.[18]

But considering the third causal condition that we have been tracing in the paths toward common crime – emotional processes that seduce people to deviance – it is much less clear that the quality of the dynamic differs by social position. Putting aside differences in the practical means that social position makes available and the different degrees and forms of moral stereotype and prejudice that are attached to social position, there may be a fundamental similarity in the dynamics that people create to seduce themselves toward deviance. Although the means differ, white middle-class youths may as self-destructively pursue spatial mobility, through reckless driving, as do ghetto youths in gang wars. The attractions of sneaky thrills may not disappear with age, but instead may migrate from shoplifting to adultery and embezzlement. And even the bump that the egocentric badass, strutting arrogantly outside his own neighborhood, arranges as an 'accident' compelling him to battle, is not without its analogies to the incidents that have been arranged by ethnocentric nations, provocatively sailing in foreign waters, to escalate wars.[19]

It would appear that, with respect to the moral-emotional dynamics of deviance, we have grounds to pursue a parallel across the social hierarchy. Consider two strong candidates for the status of most awful street and white-collar crimes: the killing of defenseless victims to sustain a career of robberies and the deception of democratic publics to support government-sponsored killings of defenseless foreigners. In both the street and the high-government cases, both the Left and the Right have their favored materialist-background explanations and accusations: poverty and lack of economic opportunity versus a liberal judiciary, 'handcuffed' police, and inadequate deterrents; the value to capitalists of maintaining power in foreign economic spheres versus the need to use military force against non-Russians to maintain a deterrent strength *vis-à-vis* the ever-menacing Soviet Union. For the most part, public discussion of both these lowly and exalted social problems proceeds as a ritualized exchange between two politically opposed materialist interpretations.

But in both forms of deviance the actors are engaged in a transcendent project to exploit the ultimate symbolic value of force to show that one 'means it'. Those who persist in stickups use violence when it is not justified on cost-benefit grounds because *not* to use violence would be to raise chaotic questions about their purpose in life. They understand that to limit their violence by materialist concerns would weaken them in conflicts with other hardmen and would raise a series of questions about their commitment to their careers that is more intimidating than is the prospect of prison. Just because materialist motivations do not control the drive toward doing stickups, the events are rife with foolish risks and fatal bungles.

It is a fair question whether the foreign exercises of Western governments in legally undeclared, surreptitiously instigated, and secretly aided military conflicts less often bungle into pathetic results – the shooting of innocent fishermen, the kidnapping of CIA chiefs, the mechanical surprises from helicopters and explosive devices, the failures to make 'operational' defenses against sea mines and air attacks, the lapses in security that allow massive military casualties from terrorist tactics, and the like. What is more remarkable still, is that utilitarian evaluations of success and failure do not dominate the public discussions of such interventions, any more than they dominate the career considerations of persistent robbers. In public debates, symbolic displays of national will, like the cultural style of the hardman, give cost-benefit analysis a cowardly overtone.

This is not to suggest that some collective machismo is behind the conspiratorial deceptions of domestic publics undertaken to support state killings of foreigners. (At the time of writing, the fresh examples are 'Contragate', the secret, illegal American government program for generating lies to promote the killing of Nicaraguans, and the French government's deceit over homicidal attacks on environmental activists.)[20] Postulated as a determining background factor, personality traits are no more convincing on the state level than on the individual street level. But in both arenas, the use of violence beyond its clear materialist justification is a powerful strategy for *constructing* purposiveness.

The case of Bernhard ('Bernie') Goetz provides us with a bridge between the street experience of the bad nigger and the collective moral perspective that state leaders may rely on in arranging their homicidal deceits. In 1984, Goetz, a white electrical engineer, shot four young 'bad' blacks in a New York City subway train. Acquitted (of all but the weapons charges) in 1987, Goetz became a hero for large segments of the public,[21] essentially because he manipulated to his advantage a detailed understanding of the doings of stickups.

First, Goetz identified a typical opening strategem in street robberies – the use of civility to move into a position of moral dominance. One of his victims approached him and said,

> 'How are you?' just, you know, 'How are you?' . . . that's a meaningless thing, but in certain circumstances that can be, that can be a real threat. You see, there's an implication there … [22]

Next followed a 'request' for money, which Goetz (and one of the victims) recalled as, 'Give me five dollars', Goetz recalled:

> I looked at his eyes and I looked at his face … his eyes were shiny. He was enjoying himself … had this big smile on his face. You know at that point, you're in a bad situation. … I know in my mind they wanted to play with me … like a cat plays with a mouse. … I know my situation. I knew my situation.[23]

Next Goetz seized on this opening ambiguity, which he understood the blacks had created not simply to further their robbery or assault but to ridicule him, as a pause in which he could draw out his gun unopposed.[24] Goetz likewise turned the tightly enclosed space of the subway car to his advantage; now the impossibility of escape was a problem for them, not for him. Goetz was aware of the fantastic moral reversal he had effected: 'It was so crazy … because they had set a trap for me and only they were trapped. … I know this is disgusting to say – but it was so easy. I can't believe it'.

As in many stickups, Goetz's violence was, to a significant degree if not completely, gratuitous within the situational context of his shooting. Since his victims did not have guns, just showing his gun probably would have been enough.

Instead, his five shots continued after the end of any personal threat that may have been present; before the last shot, which was aimed at the fourth, as yet uninjured victim, he announced, 'You seem to be all right; here's another.' After the fact, he recalled, 'My intention was to do anything I could to hurt them ... to murder them, to hurt them, to make them suffer as much as possible.'[25]

Overall, Goetz demonstrated the rational irrationality of violence that characterizes hardened stickup men. Earlier, and independent of this scene, he had arranged to have hollowed-out ('dum-dum') bullets in his gun to enhance destructive consequence should he fire his weapon. Having been victimized in muggings twice before, he found that a readiness to instigate violence had become especially relevant to him for making sense of continuing to travel the streets and subways of New York City. Like the stickup man who routinely keeps a weapon close at hand so he might exploit a fortuitous circumstance, Goetz would not have carried a gun to the scene had he not had this larger, transsituational project.

Beyond practical danger, Goetz was intent on not suffering further humiliation – not simply the humiliations that muggers could inflict, but the humiliation of his own fear, of continuing in the world with the common, cowardly wish to believe that such things would not happen to him. A similar project guides the career of the criminal hardman, whose violence may go beyond what the resistance of a victim may require because he must not only get out of *this* situation but stay 'out there' and be ready to get into *the next*. An inquiry that is limited to the situational reasonableness of violence, which social scientists have often asked in relation to data on robberies in which the offenders harm the victims and that courts must ask of a defendant like Goetz, is, to a great degree, absurd. In both cases, the moral inquiry ignores the transcendent purpose of violent men. Put another way, whether violence was reasonably necessary to escape harm or capture in the situated interaction, the decision to *enter* the situation prepared for violence is not, in itself, a matter for reasonable calculations.

The celebrity that Goetz received was, in significant measure, a celebration by 'good people' of his transcendent meanness. This same spirit more often wreaks devastation through the instrumentality of national foreign policy. Indeed, if youth 'gangs' rely on military metaphors to organize their conflicts, the mobilization of military action in Western democracies also depends, through the chief executive's histrionics and the jingoism of the press, on fashioning international conflicts into dramaturgic lines of street-fighting tactics (showdowns and callings of bluff, ambushes and quick-draw contests, 'bumps' and the issuance of dares to cross lines that have been artificially drawn over international waters).[26] Surely, there are fundamental differences between the processes of using violence to manifest meanness on city streets and to dramatize resolute purposiveness in relations with foreign states. But we will not know just what the spiritual-emotional-moral differences are until we use a comprehensive theoretical approach to analyze and compare the varieties of criminal experience across the social order, including the uses of deceit by elites for conduct they experience as morally significant.

So it is appropriate to begin a study of the seductions of crime with cases of the use of torture by the American military to interrogate Vietnamese peasants and to close this phase of the study by suggesting that, in the late twentieth century, the great powers of the West find themselves in one dubious foreign, militarized situation after another – promoting wars they cannot win, achieving victories that bring them only the prize of emotional domestic support, and entering battles they would lose for winning – all because, at least in the immediate calculations, not to use violence would signal a loss of meaning in national history. Like the bad nigger who, refusing to be a 'chump' like others of his humbled class and ethnicity, draws innocent blood to construct a more self-respecting career that leads predictably to prison confinement, the Western democracies, still seduced by the colonial myth of omnipotence, must again and again strike down thousands so that when the inevitable retreat comes, it will lead over masses of corpses toward 'peace with honor'. Perhaps in the end, what we find so repulsive about studying the reality of crime – the reason we so insistently refuse to look closely at how street criminals destroy others and bungle their way into confinement to save their sense of purposive control over their lives – is the piercing reflection we catch when we steady our glance at those evil men.

NOTES

1 Michel Foucault (ed.), *I, Pierre Rivière, having slaughtered my mother, my sister, and my brother ...* (New York, Pantheon Books, 1975), p. 106.
2 In the short essay he included in the volume, Foucault continued his pioneering emphasis on the unique phenomenon of power/knowledge. Some of his colleagues and students, however, were quick to impute causal force to class formations, the hypocrisies of the Enlightenment, the market economy, the contractual form, and so on. We learn of the situational facts essentially through the initial, brief reports of doctors who performed what we would today recognize as a coroner's investigation.
3 Robert K. Merton, 'Social structure and anomie', in his *Social Theory and Social Structure* (New York, Free Press, 1968), p. 198.
4 Stephen Cole, 'The growth of scientific knowledge', in Lewis A. Coser (ed.), *The Idea of Social Structure*, (New York, Harcourt Brace Jovanovich, 1975), p. 175.
5 Richard A. Cloward and Lloyd E. Ohlin, *Delinquency and Opportunity* (New York, Free Press, 1960).
6 Robert J. Sampson, 'Urban black violence: the effect of male joblessness and family disruption', *American Journal of Sociology* 93 (September, 1987) pp. 348–82; William Julius Wilson, *The Truly Disadvantaged: the Inner City, the Underclass, and Public Policy* (Chicago, University of Chicago Press, 1987); David Rauma and Richard A. Berk, 'Remuneration and recidivism: the long-term impact of unemployment compensation on ex-offenders', *Journal of Quantitative Criminology* 3 (March, 1987), pp. 3–27.
7 Merton, 'Social structure and anomie', p. 198.
8 Gus Frias, *Barrio Warriors: Homeboys of Peace* (n.p., Diaz Publications, 1982), p. 19.
9 Alfred Blumstein et al., *Criminal Careers and 'Career Criminals'* (Washington, DC, National Academy Press, 1986), 1, pp. 46–7; and Christy A. Visher, 'The Rand Inmate Survey: a reanalysis', in ibid., 2, 168. A recent theory sees adolescents as a social class defined – through legal requirements of school attendance, legal restrictions on employing youths, and laws excepting youths from minimum-wage rates – as having a common position in relation to the means of production. Attractive for their historical and theoretical color, these ideas account no more convincingly than do Merton's for

vandalism, the use of dope, intergroup fighting, and the character of initial experiences in property theft as sneaky thrills. David F. Greenberg 'Delinquency and the Age Structure of Society', *Contemporary Crises*, 1 (April 1977), pp. 189–224.

10 Cohen, as quoted in Merton, 'Social structure and anomie', p. 232.

11 John Edgar Wideman, *Brothers and Keepers* (New York, Penguin Books, 1985), p. 131. Recently, the revelations of insider trading in securities markets have produced strikingly similar statements from high-level miscreants. When the take runs into millions of dollars and comes in faster than the criminals can spend it, it is difficult to explain crime with ideas of overly socialized materialistic aspirations. As the offenders themselves put it, at this level, money quickly becomes a way of keeping score.

12 Edith A. Folb, *Running Down Some Lines: the Language and Culture of Black Teenagers* (Cambridge, MA, Harvard University Press, 1980), p. 128 (emphasis in original).

13 Indeed, if we look at what is used to make materialism seductive in advertising, it is not clear that we find the American dream of shiny material success more than a version of 'street culture': soul-wrenching intonations of black music, whorish styles, fleeting images of men shooting craps in alleys and hustling in pool halls, torn shirts and motorcycles, and all the provocatively sensual evils of 'the night'. Judging from Madison Avenue, materialism may be less essential to the motivation to become deviant than an association with deviance is essential to the motivation to be acquisitive.

14 As Davis noted, 'Each classical social theorist shows how their fundamental factor not only undermines the individual's integrity but also saps the society's vitality.' See Murray Davis, '"That's Classic!" The Phenomenology and Rhetoric of Successful Social Theories', *Philosophy of Social Science 16* (1986), p. 290.

15 And here the evidence continues to mount through increasingly sophisticated historical research that demonstrates the many episodes in which more-qualified Northern blacks were pushed aside when jobs were offered to less-qualified white immigrants. See Stanley Lieberson, *A Piece of the Pie* (Berkeley, CA, University of California Press, 1980). Roger Lane, *Roots of Violence in Black Philadelphia, 1860–1900* (Cambridge, MA, Harvard University Press, 1986), is a provocative argument that European ethnic groups who were new to the city in the nineteenth century (the Irish, then the Italians) initially had high rates of violent crime, sometimes higher than the rates for blacks, but the rates for white ethnics declined as these groups were incorporated into the industrial economy, while the rates for blacks, who were excluded from all but servile and dirty-work jobs by discriminatory preferences for less-qualified whites and by public segregation enforced by violence, continually rose.

16 Or when repeal would be too raw politically, the available alternative is to add constraints on the investigative-prosecutorial process. An obvious example from the 1980s is the move to abolish the office of special prosecutor. A less obvious example from the 1970s was built into the Tax Reform Act of 1976. For this and other examples that marked the closing of the Watergate era, see Jack Katz, 'The social movement against white-collar crime', in Egon Bittner and Sheldon Messinger (eds), *Criminology Review Yearbook* (Beverly Hills, CA, Sage, 1980), 2, pp. 161–84. An important appreciation of the distinctively negotiable character of enforcement efforts against white-collar crime in class-related partisan politics is found in Vilhelm Aubert, 'White collar crime and social structure', *American Journal of Sociology*, 58 (November, 1952), pp. 263–71.

17 See Henry Williamson, *Hustler! The Autobiography of a Thief*, ed. R. Lincoln Keiser (New York, Doubleday, 1965). In his encyclopedic study of bribery, Noonan found an admitted awareness of participating in bribery only in the diaries of Samuel Pepys. See John T. Noonan, Jr, *Bribes* (New York, Macmillan, 1984), p. xiv. In relation to differences in the quality of moral autobiographies written by authors of different social classes, we

should consider the differential demands on writing talent. Much more interpersonal insight and attention to subtle interactional detail are required to trace the inside experience of white-collar crimes, given their elaborate diffusion of deceit over long careers and in complex social relations. The extraordinary biographies of Robert Moses and Lyndon Johnson by Robert Caro indicate the dimensions of the task. See Robert A. Caro, *The Power Broker: Robert Moses and the Pall of New York* (New York, Alfred A. Knopf, 1974); and *The Path to Power: the Years of Lyndon Johnson* (New York, Alfred A. Knopf, 1982). Talent aside, we should also consider that, for our deceitful elites, to bare all that was involved might entail unbearable self-disgust. It is notable that our social order is so constructed that it is virtually impossible emotionally for our elites truly to confess.

18 Jack Katz, 'Concerted ignorance: the social construction of cover-up', *Urban Life*, 8 (October, 1979), pp. 295–316; and Jack Katz, 'Cover-up and collective integrity', *Social Problems*, 25 (Fall, 1977), pp. 1–25.

19 See J.C. Goulden, *Truth Is the First Casualty: the Gulf of Tonkin Affair – Illusion and Reality* (Chicago, Rand McNally, 1969); and Anthony Austin, *The President's War* (Philadelphia, J.B. Lippincott, 1971).

20 John Dyson, *Sink the Rainbow! An Inquiry into the 'Greenpeace' Affair* (London, Gollancz, 1986); Leslie Cockburn, *Out of Control* (New York, Atlantic Monthly Press, 1987).

21 Ray Innis of the Congress on Racial Equality stated with regard to Goetz's attack, 'Some black men ought to have done it long before. ... I wish it had been me'. And Geoffrey Alpert, director of the University of Miami's Center for the Study of Law and Society, noted, 'It's something we'd all like to do. We'd all like to think we'd react the way he did'. And Patrick Buchanan, soon to be President Ronald Reagan's press chief, commented, 'The universal rejoicing in New York over the gunman's success is a sign of moral health'. See Lillian Rubin, *Quiet Rage: Bernie Goetz in a Time of Madness* (New York, Farrar, Straus and Giroux, 1986), pp. 10, 11, and 15, respectively.

22 Kirk Johnson, 'Goetz's account of shooting 4 men is given on tape to New York City jury', *New York Times*, April 30, 1987, p. 14, quotes a tape of Goetz's initial interview with the police.

23 Ibid.

24 There was some indecisive evidence that Goetz responded in kind, with an inverted morally aggressive, ambiguity. According to one victim, who recalled saying to Goetz, 'Mister, give me five dollars', Goetz responded with 'You all can have it'. Kirk Johnson, 'Goetz shooting victims say youths weren't threatening', *New York Times*, May 2, 1987, p. 31. Another version by the same victim, reported in Rubin, *Quiet Rage*, p. 7, had Goetz approached with, 'Hey man, you got five dollars for me and my friends to play video games?' and Goetz responding: 'Yeah, sure ... I've got five dollars for each of you'. According to a paramedic, shortly after the shooting another victim commented that Goetz had preceded his attack with a threat: 'The guys I were with were hassling this guy for some money. He threatened us, then he shot us'. Kirk Johnson, 'A reporter's notebook', *New York Times*, June 15, 1987, p. Bl.

25 Johnson, 'Goetz's account of shooting'.

26 And on blocking the public's encounter with the resulting corpses, injuries, and sorrows of relatives, even in popularly supported military conflicts. See Susan Greenberg, *Rejoice! Media Freedom and the Falklands* (London, Campaign for Press and Broadcasting Freedom, 1983), pp. 9–12; and Arthur Gavshon and Desmond Rice, *The Sinking of the Belgrano* (London, Secker and Warburg, 1984).

Part Three

Criminalization

INTRODUCTION

This selection of readings has been chosen to reflect the parameters of a *radical/critical criminology* which first emerged in the 1960s in the USA and the UK. Although the readings reveal the disparate nature of such an enterprise, they all mark a reappraisal of the purpose and function of criminology, in particular by taking to task positivism's obsession with scientifically establishing the causes of crime. Here the key concern is more with definitional questions – why have certain behaviours and situations come to be defined as criminal? – rather than with questions of individual motivation. Collectively, they illustrate how the central problematic of criminology is not simply one of crime causation, but of accounting for particular processes of criminalization.

This part opens with readings from the American criminologists Matza and Sykes, Becker and Chambliss and the British (though born in South Africa) criminologist Stanley Cohen, who have provided classic expressions of these radical principles. Matza and Sykes's contribution not only provides a critique of positivism and its tendency to dehumanize delinquent behaviours, but also contends that most delinquent values are not particularly different from those held by the mainstream. Their work forces us to appreciate the ways in which young people themselves view and justify their actions. Becker's work also adopts a position of anti-positivism by arguing that definitions of crime and deviance will remain forever problematic because deviance only arises through the imposition of social judgements on the behaviour of others. Deviance can never be an absolutely known fact, because it is constructed through a series of transactions between rule makers and rule violators. Deviance only occurs when a particular social group is able to make its own rules and enforce their application onto others. The proposition that the causes of deviance lie in processes of law creation and social control effectively stood the premises of mainstream criminology on their head.

In the past three decades the concept of *moral panic* has been used to describe public, media and political reactions to certain newsworthy events (for example, mugging, soccer violence, social security 'scroungers', child abuse, vandalism, drug use, student militancy, 'spectacular' youth sub-cultures, street crime, permissiveness, 'bail bandits' and lone parents). The first systematic empirical study of a moral panic in the UK was Stanley Cohen's research on the social reaction to the Mods and Rockers disturbances of 1964 and published as *Folk Devils and Moral*

Panics. In 1967 Cohen presaged many of the themes of 'moral panic' (without then using the concept) in an article published in the *Howard Journal of Penology and Crime Prevention.* It is here where he first established that *social reaction* to a social problem is a key element not only in its constitution, but in its future development.

Whilst labelling and social reaction theory opened the way for analyses of how deviance was defined and processed, a Marxist-based analysis furthered that the relations between definer and defined are not simply subjective encounters. Control agencies have an institutional location and function within particular structures of power. Chambliss, for example, contends that processes of criminalization depend not simply on relations of power, but on power derived from particular class and economic positions: thus the propositions that acts are defined as criminal because it is in the interests of a ruling class to define them as such, and that criminal law, in the main, is designed to protect ruling class interests.

In these ways the study of crime was effectively politicized as part of a more comprehensive sociology of the state and political economy, in which questions of political and social control took precedence over behavioural and correctional issues. Criminology's horizons were expanded, whereby the key problematic was no longer to simply account for individual criminal acts, but to reach a critical understanding of the social order and the power to criminalize.

The reading from Box illustrates how 'common sense' assumptions about crime can be effectively challenged once we acknowledge the widespread nature of personal and property crime engaged in by corporate officials, manufacturers, governments and governmental control agencies. The prevalence of a restricted image of 'the crime problem' in public and political discourse, he argues, is but another way in which the social control of the underprivileged and the powerless is maintained.

Such analysis is also reflected in an important body of literature that details how in many societies 'crime' has become a racialized discourse. At certain moments, 'race' coalesces with other key signifiers of crime such as 'the inner city', 'the underclass', 'immigration' etc. We have included a seminal article by Angela Y. Davis that examines the consequences of US government policy shifting from social welfare to crime control mode. She argues that the utilization of mass incarceration to make problem groups 'disappear' has become 'big business'. What Davis defines as a 'prison industrial complex' relies on racialized assumptions of criminality , racialized fear of crime and racist criminal justice practices. She also points to the role that the corporatization of crime control now plays within the US economy. For Davis the only progressive course of action is to mobilize public opinion behind a radical abolitionist project.

The selection from Hulsman takes critical criminology in yet another direction. Again noting that notions of crime depend crucially on formulations of criminal law, he argues that the concept of crime should be abandoned once and for all. The development of a radical and critical understanding of crime, criminalization and criminal justice is continually hampered by the continual return to a state-constructed category as its key empirical referent. Rather he suggests the development of alternative conceptual tools – 'troubles', 'problems', 'harms' – which can be recognized and responded to without recourse to the formal, narrow and inflexible processes of criminal justice.

The next reading is Jock Young's clarion call for a 'radical left realist' criminology that is imaginative, sophisticated and above all policy relevant. The essential requirement for radical criminology is to reorient itself to take crime seriously by addressing the problem of conventional criminality and generating effective crime control policies. To make 'realism' a fundamental marker, Young, however, rejects virtually every aspect of radical criminology's idealist imaginary.

Latterly, Young's work has also been greatly influenced by cultural criminology. As Jeff Ferrell explains in the article included here:

> the study of crime necessitates not simply the examination of individual criminals and criminal events, not even the straightforward examination of media 'coverage' of criminals and criminal events, but rather a journey into the spectacle and carnival of crime, a walk down an infinite hall of mirrors where images created and consumed by criminals, criminal subcultures, control agents, media institutions and audiences bounce endlessly one off the other. (p. 397)

Cultural criminology engages with, if not synthesizes, a disparate series of old and new criminologies, infused with anarchism. Above all it is concerned with unravelling the complex cultural processes through which 'crime' attains meaning. Vital to this is an ethnographic immersion into the cultural and experiential realities of particular events themselves. Cultural criminology advocates a criminology attuned to the emotions of excitement, humour and desire; to the adrenalin rush of crossing boundaries; to the exhilarations of 'living on the edge'; and to the emancipatory power of transgression.

In all of these readings we find a diverse range of critical analyses which turn cases into political issues; which challenge powerful institutions and their regimes of truth; and which advocate campaigns for social reform and political change. Above all they open a door to expose the enormity of harms, violence, discriminations, injustices, corruption and rights violations which are prevalent in control agencies, corporations and the state but which remain noticeably absent from 'everyday' discourses about the problem of crime.

21

Techniques of neutralization

Gresham M. Sykes and David Matza

In attempting to uncover the roots of juvenile delinquency, the social scientist has long since ceased to search for devils in the mind or stigma of the body. It is now largely agreed that delinquent behavior, like most social behavior, is learned and that it is learned in the process of social interaction.

The classic statement of this position is found in Sutherland's theory of differential association, which asserts that criminal or delinquent behavior involves the learning of (a) techniques of committing crimes and (b) motives, drives, rationalizations, and attitudes favorable to the violation of law.[1] Unfortunately, the specific content of what is learned – as opposed to the process by which it is learned – has received relatively little attention in either theory or research. Perhaps the single strongest school of thought on the nature of this content has centered on the idea of a delinquent subculture. The basic characteristic of the delinquent subculture, it is argued, is a system of values that represents an inversion of the values held by respectable, law-abiding society. The world of the delinquent is the world of the law-abiding turned upside down and its norms constitute a countervailing force directed against the conforming social order. Cohen[2] sees the process of developing a delinquent subculture as a matter of building, maintaining, and reinforcing a code for behavior which exists by opposition, which stands in point by point contradiction to dominant values, particularly those of the middle class. Cohen's portrayal of delinquency is executed with a good deal of sophistication, and he carefully avoids overly simple explanations such as those based on the principle of 'follow the leader' or easy generalizations about 'emotional disturbances'. Furthermore, he does not accept the delinquent sub-culture as something given, but instead systematically examines the function of delinquent values as a viable solution to the lower-class, male child's problems

From *American Sociological Review*, 1957, 22: 664–70.

in the area of social status. Yet in spite of its virtues, this image of juvenile delinquency as a form of behavior based on competing or countervailing values and
norms appears to suffer from a number of serious defects. It is the nature of these
defects and a possible alternative or modified explanation for a large portion of
juvenile delinquency with which this paper is concerned.

The difficulties in viewing delinquent behavior as springing from a set of deviant values and norms – as arising, that is to say, from a situation in which the
delinquent defines his delinquency as 'right' – are both empirical and theoretical.
In the first place, if there existed in fact a delinquent subculture such that the
delinquent viewed his illegal behavior as morally correct, we could reasonably
suppose that he would exhibit no feelings of guilt or shame at detection or confinement. Instead, the major reaction would tend in the direction of indignation
or a sense of martyrdom.[3] It is true that some delinquents do react in the latter
fashion, although the sense of martyrdom often seems to be based on the fact that
others 'get away with it' and indignation appears to be directed against the
chance events or lack of skill that led to apprehension. More important, however,
is the fact that there is a good deal of evidence suggesting that many delinquents
do experience a sense of guilt or shame, and its outward expression is not to be
dismissed as a purely manipulative gesture to appease those in authority. Much
of this evidence is, to be sure, of a clinical nature or in the form of impression-
istic judgements of those who must deal first hand with the youthful offender.
Assigning a weight to such evidence calls for caution, but it cannot be ignored if
we are to avoid the gross stereotype of the juvenile delinquent as a hardened
gangster in miniature.

In the second place, observers have noted that the juvenile delinquent frequently accords admiration and respect to law-abiding persons. The 'really
honest' person is often revered, and if the delinquent is sometimes overly keen
to detect hypocrisy in those who conform, unquestioned probity is likely to win
his approval. A fierce attachment to a humble, pious mother or a forgiving,
upright priest (the former, according to many observers, is often encountered in
both juvenile delinquents and adult criminals) might be dismissed as rank sentimentality, but at least it is clear that the delinquent does not necessarily regard
those who abide by the legal rules as immoral. In a similar vein, it can be noted
that the juvenile delinquent may exhibit great resentment if illegal behavior is
imputed to 'significant others' in his immediate social environment or to heroes
in the world of sport and entertainment. In other words, if the delinquent does
hold to a set of values and norms that stand in complete opposition to those of
respectable society, his norm-holding is of a peculiar sort. While supposedly
thoroughly committed to the deviant system of the delinquent subculture, he
would appear to recognize the moral validity of the dominant normative system in many instances.[4]

In the third place, there is much evidence that juvenile delinquents often
draw a sharp line between those who can be victimized and those who cannot.
Certain social groups are not to be viewed as 'fair game' in the performance of
supposedly approved delinquent acts while others warrant a variety of attacks.

In general, the potentiality for victimization would seem to be a function of the social distance between the juvenile delinquent and others and thus we find implicit maxims in the world of the delinquent such as 'don't steal from friends' or 'don't commit vandalism against a church of your own faith'.[5] This is all rather obvious, but the implications have not received sufficient attention. The fact that supposedly valued behavior tends to be directed against disvalued social groups hints that the 'wrongfulness' of such delinquent behavior is more widely recognized by delinquents than the literature has indicated. When the pool of victims is limited by consideration of kinship, friendship, ethnic group, social class, age, sex, etc., we have reason to suspect that the virtue of delinquency is far from unquestioned.

In the fourth place, it is doubtful if many juvenile delinquents are totally immune from the demands for conformity made by the dominant social order. There is a strong likelihood that the family of the delinquent will agree with respectable society that delinquency is wrong, even though the family may be engaged in a variety of illegal activities. That is, the parental posture conducive to delinquency is not apt to be a positive prodding. Whatever may be the influence of parental example, what might be called the 'Fagin' pattern of socialization into delinquency is probably rare. Furthermore, as Redl has indicated, the idea that certain neighborhoods are completely delinquent, offering the child a model for delinquent behavior without reservations, is simply not supported by the data.[6]

The fact that a child is punished by parents, school officials, and agencies of the legal system for his delinquency may, as a number of observers have cynically noted, suggest to the child that he should be more careful not to get caught. There is an equal or greater probability, however, that the child will internalize the demands for conformity. This is not to say that demands for conformity cannot be counteracted. In fact, as we shall see shortly, an understanding of how internal and external demands for conformity are neutralized may be crucial for understanding delinquent behavior. But it is to say that a complete denial of the validity of demands for conformity and the substitution of a new normative system is improbable, in light of the child's or adolescent's dependency on adults and encirclement by adults inherent in his status in the social structure. No matter how deeply enmeshed in patterns of delinquency he may be and no matter how much this involvement may outweigh his associations with the law-abiding, he cannot escape the condemnation of his deviance. Somehow the demands for conformity must be met and answered; they cannot be ignored as part of an alien system of values and norms.

In short, the theoretical viewpoint that sees juvenile delinquency as a form of behavior based on the values and norms of a deviant subculture in precisely the same way as law-abiding behavior is based on the values and norms of the larger society is open to serious doubt. The fact that the world of the delinquent is embedded in the larger world of those who conform cannot be overlooked nor can the delinquent be equated with an adult thoroughly socialized into an alternative way of life. Instead, the juvenile delinquent would appear to be at least partially committed to the dominant social order in that he frequently exhibits guilt or shame when he violates its proscriptions, accords approval to certain conforming figures, and distinguishes between appropriate and inappropriate targets for his deviance. It is to an explanation for the apparently paradoxical fact of his delinquency that we now turn.

As Morris Cohen once said, one of the most fascinating problems about human behavior is why men violate the laws which they believe. This is the problem that confronts us when we attempt to explain why delinquency occurs despite a greater or lesser commitment to the usages of conformity. A basic clue is offered by the fact that social rules or norms calling for valued behavior seldom if ever take the form of categorical imperatives. Rather, values or norms appear as *qualified* guides for action, limited in their applicability in terms of time, place, persons, and social circumstances. The moral injunction against killing, for example, does not apply to the enemy during combat in time of war, although a captured enemy comes once again under the prohibition. Similarly, the taking and distributing of scarce goods in a time of acute social need is felt by many to be right, although under other circumstances private property is held inviolable. The normative system of a society, then, is marked by what Williams has termed *flexibility*; it does not consist of a body of rules held to be binding under all conditions.[7]

This flexibility is, in fact, an integral part of the criminal law in that measures for 'defenses to crimes' are provided in pleas such as nonage, necessity, insanity, drunkenness, compulsion, self-defense, and so on. The individual can avoid moral culpability for his criminal action – and thus avoid the negative sanctions of society – if he can prove that criminal intent was lacking. *It is our argument that much delinquency is based on what is essentially an unrecognized extension of defenses to crimes, in the form of justifications for deviance that are seen as valid by the delinquent but not by the legal system or society at large.*

These justifications are commonly described as rationalizations. They are viewed as following deviant behavior and as protecting the individual from self-blame and the blame of others after the act. But there is also reason to believe that they precede deviant behavior and make deviant behavior possible. It is this possibility that Sutherland mentioned only in passing and that other writers have failed to exploit from the viewpoint of sociological theory. Disapproval flowing from internalized norms and conforming others in the social environment is neutralized, turned back, or deflected in advance. Social controls that serve to check or inhibit deviant motivational patterns are rendered inoperative, and the individual is freed to engage in delinquency without serious damage to his self image. In this sense, the delinquent both has his cake and eats it too, for he remains committed to the dominant normative system and yet so qualifies its imperatives that violations are 'acceptable' if not 'right'. Thus the delinquent represents not a radical opposition to law-abiding society but something more like an apologetic failure, often more sinned against than sinning in his own eyes. We call these justifications of deviant behavior techniques of neutralization; and we believe these techniques make up a crucial component of Sutherland's 'definitions favorable to the violation of law'. It is by learning these techniques that the juvenile becomes delinquent, rather than by learning moral imperatives, values or attitudes standing in direct contradiction to those of the dominant society. In analyzing these techniques, we have found it convenient to divide them into five major types.

The denial of responsibility   In so far as the delinquent can define himself as lacking responsibility for his deviant actions, the disapproval of self or others is sharply reduced in effectiveness as a restraining influence. As Justice Holmes has said, even a dog distinguishes between being stumbled over and being kicked, and modern society is no less careful to draw a line between injuries that are unintentional, i.e., where responsibility is lacking, and those that are intentional. As a technique of neutralization, however, the denial of responsibility extends much further than the claim that deviant acts are an 'accident' or some similar negation of personal accountability. It may also be asserted that delinquent acts are due to forces outside of the individual and beyond his control such as unloving parents, bad companions, or a slum neighborhood. In effect, the delinquent approaches a 'billiard ball' conception of himself in which he sees himself as helplessly propelled into new situations. From a psychodynamic viewpoint, this orientation toward one's own actions may represent a profound alienation from self, but it is important to stress the fact that interpretations of responsibility are cultural constructs and not merely idiosyncratic beliefs. The similarity between this mode of justifying illegal behavior assumed by the delinquent and the implications of a 'sociological' frame of reference or a 'humane' jurisprudence is readily apparent.[8] It is not the validity of this orientation that concerns us here, but its function of deflecting blame attached to violations of social norms and its relative independence of a particular personality structure.[9] By learning to view himself as more acted upon than acting, the delinquent prepares the way for deviance from the dominant normative system without the necessity of a frontal assault on the norms themselves.

The denial of injury   A second major technique of neutralization centers on the injury or harm involved in the delinquent act. The criminal law has long made a distinction between crimes which are *mala in se* and *mala prohibita* – that is between acts that are wrong in themselves and acts that are illegal but not immoral – and the delinquent can make the same kind of distinction in evaluating the wrongfulness of his behavior. For the delinquent, however, wrongfulness may turn on the question of whether or not anyone has clearly been hurt by his deviance, and this matter is open to a variety of interpretations. Vandalism, for example, may be defined by the delinquent simply as 'mischief' – after all, it may be claimed, the persons whose property has been destroyed can well afford it. Similarly, auto theft may be viewed as 'borrowing', and gang fighting may be seen as a private quarrel, an agreed upon duel between two willing parties, and thus of no concern to the community at large. We are not suggesting that this technique of neutralization, labelled the denial of injury, involves an explicit dialectic. Rather, we are arguing that the delinquent frequently, and in a hazy fashion, feels that his behavior does not really cause any great harm despite the fact that it runs counter to law. Just as the link between the individual and his acts may be broken by the denial of responsibility, so may the link between acts and their consequences be broken by the denial of injury. Since society sometimes agrees with the delinquent, e.g., in matters such as truancy, 'pranks', and so on, it merely reaffirms the idea that the delinquent's neutralization of social controls by means of qualifying the norms is an extension of common practice rather than a gesture of complete opposition.

The denial of the victim   Even if the delinquent accepts the responsibility for his deviant actions and is willing to admit that his deviant actions involve an injury or hurt, the moral indignation of self and others may be neutralized by an insistence that the injury is not wrong in light of the circumstances. The injury, it may be claimed, is not really an injury; rather, it is a form of rightful retaliation or punishment. By a subtle alchemy the delinquent moves himself into the position of an avenger and the victim is transformed into a wrong-doer. Assaults on homosexuals or suspected homosexuals, attacks on members of minority groups who are said to have gotten 'out of place', vandalism as revenge on an unfair teacher or school official, thefts from a 'crooked' store owner – all may be hurts inflicted on a transgressor, in the eyes of the delinquent. As Orwell has pointed out, the type of criminal admired by the general public has probably changed over the course of years and Raffles no longer serves as a hero;[10] but Robin Hood, and his latter day derivatives such as the tough detective seeking justice outside the law, still capture the popular imagination, and the delinquent may view his acts as part of a similar role.

To deny the existence of the victim, then, by transforming him into a person deserving injury is an extreme form of a phenomenon we have mentioned before, namely, the delinquent's recognition of appropriate and inappropriate targets for his delinquent acts. In addition, however, the existence of the victim may be denied for the delinquent, in a somewhat different sense, by the circumstances of the delinquent act itself. In so far as the victim is physically absent, unknown or a vague abstraction (as is often the case in delinquent acts committed against property), the awareness of the victim's existence is weakened. Internalized norms and anticipations of the reactions of others must somehow be activated, if they are to serve as guides for behavior; and it is possible that a diminished awareness of the victim plays an important part in determining whether or not this process is set in motion.

The condemnation of the condemners   A fourth technique of neutralization would appear to involve a condemnation of the condemners or, as McCorkle and Korn have phrased it, a rejection of the rejectors.[11] The delinquent shifts the focus of attention from his own deviant acts to the motives of his violations. His condemners, he may claim, are hypocrites, deviants in disguise, or impelled by personal spite. This orientation toward the conforming world may be of particular importance when it hardens into a bitter cynicism directed against those assigned the task of enforcing or expressing the norms of the dominant society. Police, it may be said, are corrupt, stupid and brutal. Teachers always show favoritism and parents always 'take it out' on their children. By a slight extension, the rewards of conformity – such as material success – become a matter of pull or luck, thus decreasing still further the stature of those who stand on the side of the law-abiding. The validity of this jaundiced viewpoint is not so important as its function in turning back or deflecting the negative sanctions attached to violations of the norms. The delinquent, in effect, has changed the subject of the conversation in the dialogue between his own deviant impulses and the reactions of others; and by attacking others, the wrongfulness of his own behavior is more easily repressed or lost to view.

The appeal to higher loyalties   Fifth, and last, internal and external social controls may be neutralized by sacrificing the demands of the larger society for the demands of the smaller social groups to which the delinquent belongs such as the sibling pair, the gang, or the friendship clique. It is important to note that the delinquent does not necessarily repudiate the imperatives of the dominant normative system, despite his failure to follow them. Rather, the delinquent may see himself as caught up in a dilemma that must be resolved, unfortunately, at the cost of violating the law. One aspect of this situation has been studied by Stouffer and Toby in their research on the conflict between particularistic and universalistic demands, between the claims of friendship and general social obligations, and their results suggest that 'it is possible to classify people according to a predisposition to select one or the other horn of a dilemma in role conflict'.[12] For our purposes, however, the most important point is that deviation from certain norms may occur not because the norms are rejected but because other norms, held to be more pressing or involving a higher loyalty, are accorded precedence. Indeed, it is the fact that both sets of norms are believed in that gives meaning to our concepts of dilemma and role conflict.

The conflict between the claims of friendship and the claims of law, or a similar dilemma, has of course long been recognized by the social scientist (and the novelist) as a common human problem. If the juvenile delinquent frequently resolves his dilemma by insisting that he must 'always help a buddy' or 'never squeal on a friend', even when it throws him into serious difficulties with the dominant social order, his choice remains familiar to the supposedly law-abiding. The delinquent is unusual, perhaps, in the extent to which he is able to see the fact that he acts in behalf of the smaller social groups to which he belongs as a justification for violations of society's norms, but it is a matter of degree rather than of kind.

'I didn't mean it.' 'I didn't really hurt anybody.' 'They had it coming to them.' 'Everybody's picking on me.' 'I didn't do it for myself.' These slogans or their variants, we hypothesize, prepare the juvenile for delinquent acts. These 'definitions of the situation' represent tangential or glancing blows at the dominant normative system rather than the creation of an opposing ideology; and they are extensions of patterns of thought prevalent in society rather than something created *de novo.*

Techniques of neutralization may not be powerful enough to fully shield the individual from the force of his own internalized values and the reactions of conforming others, for as we have pointed out, juvenile delinquents often appear to suffer from feelings of guilt and shame when called into account for their deviant behavior. And some delinquents may be so isolated from the world of conformity that techniques of neutralization need not be called into play. None the less, we would argue that techniques of neutralization are critical in lessening the effectiveness of social controls and that they lie behind a large share of delinquent behavior. Empirical research in this area is scattered and fragmentary at the present time, but the work of Redl,[13] Cressey,[14] and others has supplied a body of significant data that has done much to clarify the theoretical issues and enlarge the fund of supporting evidence. Two lines of investigation seem to be critical at this stage. First, there is need for more knowledge concerning the differential distribution of techniques of neutralization, as operative patterns of thought, by age, sex, social class, ethnic groups, etc. On a priori grounds it might be assumed that these justifications for deviance will be more readily seized by segments of society for whom a discrepancy between common social ideals and social practice is most apparent. It is also possible however, that the habit of 'bending' the dominant normative system – if not 'breaking' it – cuts across our cruder social categories and is to be traced primarily to patterns of social interaction within the familial circle. Secondly, there is a need for a greater understanding of the internal structure of techniques of neutralization, as a system of beliefs and attitudes, and its relationship to various types of delinquent behavior. Certain techniques of neutralization would appear to be better adapted to particular deviant acts than to others, as we have suggested, for example, in the case of offenses against property and the denial of the victim. But the issue remains far from clear and stands in need of more information.

In any case, techniques of neutralization appear to offer a promising line of research in enlarging and systematizing the theoretical grasp of juvenile delinquency. As more information is uncovered concerning techniques of neutralization, their origins, and their consequences, both juvenile delinquency in particular, and deviation from normative systems in general may be illuminated.

NOTES

1 E.H. Sutherland, *Principles of Criminology*, revised by D.R. Cressey (Chicago, Lippincott, 1955), pp. 77–80.

2 Albert, K. Cohen, *Delinquent Boys* (Glencoe, Ill., The Free Press, 1955).

3 This form of reaction among the adherents of a deviant subculture who fully believe in the 'rightfulness' of their behavior and who are captured and punished by the agencies of the dominant social order can be illustrated, perhaps, by groups such as Jehovah's Witnesses, early Christian sects, nationalist movements in colonial areas, and conscientious objectors during World Wars I and II.

4 As Weber has pointed out, a thief may recognize the legitimacy of legal rules without accepting their moral validity. Cf. Max Weber, *The Theory of Social and Economic Organization* (translated by A.M. Henderson and Talcott Parsons) (New York, Oxford University Press, 1947), p. 125. We are arguing here, however, that the juvenile delinquent frequently recognizes *both* the legitimacy of the dominant social order and its moral 'rightness'.

5 Thrasher's account of the 'Itschkies' – a juvenile gang composed of Jewish boys –and the immunity from 'rolling' enjoyed by Jewish drunkards is a good illustration. Cf. F. Thrasher, *The Gang* (Chicago, The University of Chicago Press, 1947), p. 315.

6 Cf. Solomon Kobrin, 'The conflict of values in delinquency areas', *American Sociological Review*, 16 (October, 1951), pp. 653–61.

7 Cf. Robin Williams Jr, *American Society* (New York, Knopf, 1951), p. 28.

8 A number of observers have wryly noted that many delinquents seem to show a surprising awareness of sociological and psychological explanations for their behavior and are quick to point out the causal role of their poor environment.

9 It is possible, of course, that certain personality structures can accept some techniques of neutralization more readily than others, but this question remains largely unexplored.

10 George Orwell, *Dickens, Dali, and Others* (New York, Revnal, 1946).

11 Lloyd W. McCorkle and Richard Korn, 'Resocialization within walls', *Annals of the American Academy of Political and Social Science*, 293 (May, 1954), pp. 88–98.

12 See Samuel A. Stouffer and Jackson Toby, 'Role conflict and personality', in T. Parsons and E.A. Shils (eds), *Toward a General Theory of Action* (Cambridge, MA, Harvard University Press, 1951), p. 494.

13 See Fritz Redl and David Wineman, *Children Who Hate* (Glencoe, Ill., The Free Press, 1956).

14 See D.R. Cressey, *Other People's Money* (Glencoe, Ill., The Free Press, 1953).

22

Outsiders

Howard Becker

All social groups make rules and attempt, at some times and under some circumstances, to enforce them. Social rules define situations and the kinds of behavior appropriate to them, specifying some actions as 'right' and forbidding others as 'wrong'. When a rule is enforced, the person who is supposed to have broken it may be seen as a special kind of person, one who cannot be trusted to live by the rules agreed on by the group. He is regarded as an *outsider*.

But the person who is thus labeled an outsider may have a different view of the matter. He may not accept the rule by which he is being judged and may not regard those who judge him as either competent or legitimately entitled to do so. Hence, a second meaning of the term emerges: the rule-breaker may feel his judges are *outsiders*.

In what follows, I will try to clarify the situation and process pointed to by this double-barrelled term: the situations of rule-breaking and rule-enforcement and the processes by which some people come to break rules and others to enforce them.

Some preliminary distinctions are in order. Rules may be of a great many kinds. They may be formally enacted into law, and in this case the police power of the state may be used in enforcing them. In other cases, they represent informal agreements, newly arrived at or encrusted with the sanction of age and tradition; rules of this kind are enforced by informal sanctions of various kinds.

Similarly, whether a rule has the force of law or tradition or is simply the result of consensus, it may be the task of some specialized body, such as the police or the committee on ethics of a professional association, to enforce it; enforcement, on the other hand, may be everyone's job or, at least, the job of everyone in the group to which the rule is meant to apply.

Many rules are not enforced and are not, in any except the most formal sense, the kind of rules with which I am concerned. Blue laws, which remain on

From *Outsiders: Studies in the Sociology of Deviance*, pp. 1–18. (New York: Free Press, 1963.)

the statute books though they have not been enforced for a hundred years, are examples. (It is important to remember, however, that an unenforced law may be reactivated for various reasons and regain all its original force, as recently occurred with respect to the laws governing the opening of commercial establishments on Sunday in Missouri.) Informal rules may similarly die from lack of enforcement. I shall mainly be concerned with what we can call the actual operating rules of groups, those kept alive through attempts at enforcement.

Finally, just how far 'outside' one is, in either of the senses I have mentioned, varies from case to case. We think of the person who commits a traffic violation or gets a little too drunk at a party as being, after all, not very different from the rest of us and treat his infraction tolerantly. We regard the thief as less like us and punish him severely. Crimes such as murder, rape, or treason lead us to view the violator as a true outsider.

In the same way, some rule-breakers do not think they have been unjustly judged. The traffic violator usually subscribes to the very rules he has broken. Alcoholics are often ambivalent, sometimes feeling that those who judge them do not understand them and at other times agreeing that compulsive drinking is a bad thing. At the extreme, some deviants (homosexuals and drug addicts are good examples) develop full-blown ideologies explaining why they are right and why those who disapprove of and punish them are wrong.

DEFINITIONS OF DEVIANCE

The outsider – the deviant from group rules – has been the subject of much speculation, theorizing and scientific study. What laymen want to know about deviants is: why do they do it? How can we account for their rule-breaking? What is there about them that leads them to do forbidden things? Scientific research has tried to find answers to these questions. In doing so it has accepted the common-sense premise that there is something inherently deviant (qualitatively distinct) about acts that break (or seem to break) social rules. It has also accepted the common-sense assumption that the deviant act occurs because some characteristic of the person who commits it makes it necessary or inevitable that he should. Scientists do not ordinarily question the label 'deviant' when it is applied to particular acts or people but rather take it as given. In so doing, they accept the values of the group making the judgment.

It is easily observable that different groups judge different things to be deviant. This should alert us to the possibility that the person making the judgment of deviance, the process by which that judgment is arrived at, and the situation in which it is made may all be intimately involved in the phenomenon of deviance. To the degree that the common-sense view of deviance and the scientific theories that begin with its premises assume that acts that break rules are inherently deviant and thus take for granted the situations and processes of judgment, they may leave out an important variable. If scientists ignore the variable character of the process of judgment, they may by that omission limit the kinds of theories that can be developed and the kind of understanding that can be achieved.[1]

Our first problem, then, is to construct a definition of deviance. Before doing this, let us consider some of the definitions scientists now use, seeing what is left out if we take them as a point of departure for the study of outsiders.

The simplest view of deviance is essentially statistical, defining as deviant anything that varies too widely from the average. When a statistician analyses the results of an agricultural experiment, he describes the stalk of corn that is exceptionally tall and the stalk that is exceptionally short as deviations from the mean or average. Similarly, one can describe anything that differs from what is most common as a deviation. In this view, to be left-handed or redheaded is deviant, because most people are right-handed and brunette.

So stated, the statistical view seems simple-minded, even trivial. Yet it simplifies the problem by doing away with many questions of value that ordinarily arise in discussions of the nature of deviance. In assessing any particular case, all one need do is calculate the distance of the behavior involved from the average. But it is too simple a solution. Hunting with such a definition, we return with a mixed bag – people who are excessively fat or thin, murderers, redheads, homosexuals and traffic violators. The mixture contains some ordinarily thought of as deviants and others who have broken no rule at all. The statistical definition of deviance, in short, is too far removed from the concern with rule-breaking which prompts scientific study of outsiders.

A less simple but much more common view of deviance identifies it as something essentially pathological, revealing the presence of a 'disease'. This view rests, obviously, on a medical analogy. The human organism, when it is working efficiently and experiencing no discomfort, is said to be 'healthy'. When it does not work efficiently, a disease is present. The organ or function that has become deranged is said to be pathological. Of course, there is little disagreement about what constitutes a healthy state of the organism. But there is much less agreement when one uses the notion of pathology analogically, to describe kinds of behavior that are regarded as deviant. For people do not agree on what constitutes healthy behavior. It is difficult to find a definition that will satisfy even such a select and limited group as psychiatrists; it is impossible to find one that people generally accept as they accept criteria of health for the organism.[2]

Sometimes people mean the analogy more strictly, because they think of deviance as the product of mental disease. The behavior of a homosexual or drug addict is regarded as the symptom of a mental disease just as the diabetic's difficulty in getting bruises to heal is regarded as a symptom of his disease. But mental disease resembles physical disease only in metaphor:

Starting with such things as syphilis, tuberculosis, typhoid fever, and carcinomas and fractures, we have created the class 'illness'. At first, this class was composed of only a few items, all of which shared the common feature of reference to a state of disordered structure or function of the human body as a physiochemical machine. As time went on, additional items were added to this class. They were not added, however, because they were newly discovered bodily disorders. The physician's attention had been deflected from this criterion and had become focused instead on disability and suffering as new criteria for selection. Thus, at first slowly, such things as hysteria, hypochondriasis, obsessive-compulsive neurosis, and depression were added to the category of illness. Then, with increasing zeal, physicians and especially psychiatrists began to call 'illness' (that is, of course, 'mental illness') anything and everything in which they could detect any sign of malfunctioning, based on no matter what norm. Hence, agoraphobia is illness because one should not be afraid of open spaces. Homosexuality is illness because heterosexuality is the social norm. Divorce is illness because it signals failure of marriage. Crime, art, undesired political leadership, participation in social affairs, or withdrawal from such participation – all these and many more have been said to be signs of mental illness.[3]

The medical metaphor limits what we can see much as the statistical view does. It accepts the lay judgment of something as deviant and, by use of analogy, locates its source within the individual, thus preventing us from seeing the judgment itself as a crucial part of the phenomenon.

Some sociologists also use a model of deviance based essentially on the medical notions of health and disease. They look at a society, or some part of a society, and ask whether there are any processes going on in it that tend to reduce its stability, thus lessening its chance of survival. They label such processes deviant or identify them as symptoms of social disorganization. They discriminate between those features of society which promote stability (and thus are 'functional') and those which disrupt stability (and thus are 'dysfunctional'). Such a view has the great virtue of pointing to areas of possible trouble in a society of which people may not be aware.[4]

But it is harder in practice than it appears to be in theory to specify what is functional and what dysfunctional for a society or social group. The question of what the purpose or goal (function) of a group is and, consequently, what things will help or hinder the achievement of that purpose, is very often a political question. Factions within the group disagree and maneuver to have their own definition of the group's function accepted. The function of the group or organization, then, is decided in political conflict, not given in the nature of the organization. If this is true, then it is likewise true that the questions of what rules are to be enforced, what behavior regarded as deviant, and which people labeled as outsiders must also be regarded as political.[5] The functional view of deviance, by ignoring the political aspects of the phenomenon, limits our understanding.

Another sociological view is more relativistic. It identifies deviance as the failure to obey group rules. Once we have described the rules a group enforces on its members, we can say with some precision whether or not a person has violated them and is thus, on this view, deviant.

This view is closest to my own, but it fails to give sufficient weight to the ambiguities that arise in deciding which rules are to be taken as the yardstick against which behavior is measured and judged deviant. A society has many groups, each with its own set of rules, and people belong to many groups simultaneously. A person may break the rules of one group by the very act of abiding by the rules of another group. Is he, then, deviant? Proponents of this definition may object that while ambiguity may arise with respect to the rules peculiar to one or another group in society, there are some rules that are very generally agreed to by everyone, in which case the difficulty does not arise. This, of course, is a question of fact, to be settled by empirical research. I doubt there are many such areas of consensus and think it wiser to use a definition that allows us to deal with both ambiguous and unambiguous situations.

DEVIANCE AND THE RESPONSES OF OTHERS

The sociological view I have just discussed defines deviance as the infraction of some agreed-upon rule. It then goes on to ask who breaks rules, and to search for the factors in their personalities and life situations that might account for the infractions. This assumes that those who have broken a rule constitute a homogeneous category, because they have committed the same deviant act.

Such an assumption seems to me to ignore the central fact about deviance: it is created by society. I do not mean this in the way it is ordinarily understood, in which the causes of deviance are located in the social situation of the deviant or in 'social factors' which prompt his action. I mean, rather, that *social groups create deviance by making the rules whose infraction constitutes deviance*, and by applying those rules to particular people and labeling them as outsiders. From this point of view, deviance is *not* a quality of the act the person commits, but rather a consequence of the application by others of rules and sanctions to an 'offender'. The deviant is one to whom that label has successfully been applied; deviant behavior is behavior that people so label.[6]

Since deviance is, among other things, a consequence of the responses of others to a person's act, students of deviance cannot assume that they are dealing with a homogeneous category when they study people who have been labeled deviant. That is, they cannot assume that these people have actually committed a deviant act or broken some rule, because the process of labeling may not be infallible; some people may be labeled deviant who in fact have not broken a rule. Furthermore, they cannot assume that the category of those labeled deviant will contain all those who actually have broken a rule, for many offenders may escape apprehension and thus fail to be included in the population of 'deviants' they study. In so far as the category lacks homogeneity and fails to include all the cases that belong in it, one cannot reasonably expect to find common factors of personality or life situation that will account for the supposed deviance.

What, then, do people who have been labeled deviant have in common? At the least, they share the label and the experience of being labeled as outsiders. I will begin my analysis with this basic similarity and view deviance as the product of a transaction that takes place between some social group and one who is viewed by that group as a rule-breaker. I will be less concerned with the personal and social characteristics of deviants than with the process by which they come to be thought of as outsiders and their reactions to that judgment.

Malinowski discovered the usefulness of this view for understanding the nature of deviance many years ago, in his study of the Trobriand Islands:

One day an outbreak of wailing and a great commotion told me that a death had occurred somewhere in the neighborhood. I was informed that Kima'i, a young lad of my acquaintance, of sixteen or so, had fallen from a coco-nut palm and killed himself. … I found that another youth had been severely wounded by some mysterious coincidence. And at the funeral there was obviously a general feeling of hostility between the village where the boy died and that into which his body was carried for burial.

Only much later was I able to discover the real meaning of these events. The boy had committed suicide. The truth was that he had broken the rules of exogamy, the partner in his crime being his maternal cousin, the daughter of his mother's sister. This had been known and generally disapproved of but nothing was done until the girl's discarded lover, who had wanted to marry her and who felt personally injured, took the initiative. This rival threatened first to use black magic against the guilty youth, but this had not much effect. Then one evening he insulted the culprit in public – accusing him in the hearing of the whole community of incest and hurling at him certain expressions intolerable to a native.

For this there was only one remedy; only one means of escape remained to the unfortunate youth. Next morning he put on festive attire and ornamentation, climbed a coconut palm and addressed the community, speaking from among the palm leaves and bidding them farewell. He explained the reasons for his desperate deed and also launched forth a veiled accusation against the man who had driven him to his death, upon which it became the duty of his clansmen to avenge him. Then he wailed aloud, as is the custom, jumped from a palm some sixty feet high and was killed on the spot. There followed a fight within the village in which the rival was wounded; and the quarrel was repeated during the funeral. …

If you were to inquire into the matter among the Trobrianders, you would find … that the natives show horror at the idea of violating the rules of exogamy and that they believe that sores, disease and even death might follow clan incest. This is the ideal of native law, and in moral matters it is easy and pleasant strictly to adhere to the ideal – when judging the conduct of others or expressing an opinion about conduct in general.

When it comes to the application of morality and ideals to real life, however, things take on a different complexion. In the case described it was obvious that the facts would not tally with the ideal of conduct. Public opinion was neither outraged by the knowledge of the crime to any extent, nor did it react directly – it had to be mobilized by a public statement of the crime and by insults being hurled at the culprit by an interested party. Even then he had to carry out the punishment himself. … Probing further into the matter and collecting concrete information, I found that the breach of exogamy – as regards intercourse and not marriage – is by no means a rare occurrence, and public opinion is lenient, though decidedly hypocritical. If the affair is carried on *sub rosa* with a certain amount of decorum, and if no one in particular stirs up trouble – 'public opinion' will gossip, but not demand any harsh punishment. If, on the contrary, scandal breaks out – everyone turns against the guilty pair and by ostracism and insults one or the other may be driven to suicide.[7]

Whether an act is deviant, then, depends on how other people react to it. You can commit clan incest and suffer from no more than gossip as long as no one makes a public accusation; but you will be driven to your death if the accusation is made. The point is that the response of other people has to be regarded as problematic. Just because one has committed an infraction of a rule does not mean that others will respond as though this had happened. (Conversely, just because one has not violated a rule does not mean that he may not be treated, in some circumstances, as though he had.)

The degree to which other people will respond to a given act as deviant varies greatly. Several kinds of variation seem worth noting. First of all, there is variation over time. A person believed to have committed a given 'deviant' act may at one time be responded to much more leniently than he would be at some other time. The occurrence of 'drives' against various kinds of deviance illustrates this clearly. At various times, enforcement officials may decide to make an all-out attack on some particular kind of deviance, such as gambling, drug addiction, or homosexuality. It is obviously much more dangerous to engage in one of these activities when a drive is on than at any other time. (In a very interesting study of crime news in Colorado newspapers, Davis found that the amount of crime reported in Colorado newspapers showed very little association with actual changes in the amount of crime taking place in Colorado. And, further, that people's estimate of how much increase there had been in crime in Colorado was associated with the increase in the amount of crime news but not with any increase in the amount of crime.)[8]

The degree to which an act will be treated as deviant depends also on who commits the act and who feels he has been harmed by it. Rules tend to be applied more to some persons than others. Studies of juvenile delinquency make the point clearly. Boys from middle-class areas do not get as far in the legal process when they are apprehended as do boys from slum areas. The middle-class boy is less likely, when picked up by the police, to be taken to the station; less likely when taken to the station to be booked; and it is extremely unlikely that he will be convicted and sentenced.[9] This variation occurs even though the original infraction of the rule is the same in the two cases. Similarly, the law is differentially applied to Negroes and whites. It is well known that a Negro believed to have attacked a white woman is much more likely to be punished than a white man who commits the same offense; it is only slightly less well known that a Negro who murders another Negro is much less likely to be punished than a white man who commits murder.[10] This, of course, is one of the main points of Sutherland's analysis of white-collar crime: crimes committed by corporations are almost always prosecuted as civil cases, but the same crime committed by an individual is ordinarily treated as a criminal offense.[11]

Some rules are enforced only when they result in certain consequences. The unmarried mother furnishes a clear example. Vincent[12] points out that illicit sexual relations seldom result in severe punishment or social censure for the offenders. If, however, a girl becomes pregnant as a result of such activities the reaction of others is likely to be severe. (The illicit pregnancy is also an interesting example of the differential enforcement of rules on different categories of people. Vincent notes that unmarried fathers escape the severe censure visited on the mother.)

Why repeat these commonplace observations? Because, taken together, they support the proposition that deviance is not a simple quality, present in some kinds of behavior and absent in others. Rather, it is the product of a process which involves responses of other people to the behavior. The same behavior may be an infraction of the rules at one time and not at another; may be an infraction when committed by one person, but not when committed by another; some rules are broken with impunity, others are not. In short, whether a given act is deviant or not depends in part on the nature of the act (that is, whether or not it violates some rule) and in part on what other people do about it.

Some people may object that this is merely a terminological quibble, that one can, after all, define terms any way he wants to and that if some people want to speak of rule-breaking behavior as deviant without reference to the reactions of others they are free to do so. This, of course, is true. Yet it might be worthwhile to refer to such behavior as *rule-breaking behavior* and reserve the term *deviant* for those labeled as deviant by some segment of society. I do not insist that this usage be followed. But it should be clear that in so far as a scientist uses 'deviant' to refer to any rule-breaking behavior and takes as his subject of study only those who have been *labeled* deviant, he will be hampered by the disparities between the two categories.

If we take as the object of our attention behavior which comes to be labeled as deviant, we must recognize that we cannot know whether a given act will be categorized as deviant until the response of others has occurred. Deviance is not a quality that lies in behavior itself, but in the interaction between the person who commits an act and those who respond to it.

WHOSE RULES?

I have been using the term 'outsiders' to refer to those people who are judged by others to be deviant and thus to stand outside the circle of 'normal' members of the group. But the term contains a second meaning, whose analysis leads to another important set of sociological problems: 'outsiders', from the point of view of the person who is labeled deviant, may be the people who make the rules he had been found guilty of breaking.

Social rules are the creation of specific social groups. Modern societies are not simple organizations in which everyone agrees on what the rules are and how they are to be applied in specific situations. They are, instead, highly differentiated along social class lines, ethnic lines, occupational lines, and cultural lines. These groups need not and, in fact, often do not share the same rules. The problems they face in dealing with their environment, the history and traditions they carry with them, all lead to the evolution of different sets of rules. In so far as the rules of various groups conflict and contradict one another, there will be disagreement about the kind of behavior that is proper in any given situation.

Italian immigrants who went on making wine for themselves and their friends during Prohibition were acting properly by Italian immigrant standards, but were breaking the law of their new country (as, of course, were many of their Old American neighbors). Medical patients who shop around for a doctor may, from the perspective of their own group, be doing what is necessary to protect their health by making sure they get what seems to them the best possible doctor; but, from the perspective of the physician, what they do is wrong because it breaks down the trust the patient ought to put in his physician. The lower-class delinquent who fights for his 'turf' is only doing what he considers necessary and right, but teachers, social workers, and police see it differently.

While it may be argued that many or most rules are generally agreed to by all members of a society, empirical research on a given rule generally reveals variation in people's attitudes. Formal rules, enforced by some specially constituted group, may differ from those actually thought appropriate by most people.[13] Factions in a group may disagree on what I have called actual operating rules. Most important for the study of behavior ordinarily labeled deviant, the perspectives of the people who engage in the behavior are likely to be quite different from those of the people who condemn it. In this latter situation, a person may feel that he is being judged according to rules he has had no hand in making and does not accept, rules forced on him by outsiders.

To what extent and under what circumstances do people attempt to force their rules on others who do not subscribe to them? Let us distinguish two cases. In the first, only those who are actually members of the group have any interest in making and enforcing certain rules. If an orthodox Jew disobeys the laws of kashruth only other orthodox Jews will regard this as a transgression; Christians or non-orthodox Jews will not consider this deviance and would have no interest in interfering. In the second case, members of a group consider it important to their welfare that members of certain other groups obey certain rules. Thus, people consider it extremely important that those who practice the healing arts abide by certain rules; this is the reason the state licenses physicians, nurses, and others, and forbids anyone who is not licensed to engage in healing activities.

To the extent that a group tries to impose its rules on other groups in the society, we are presented with a second question: Who can, in fact, force others to accept their rules and what are the causes of their success? This is, of course, a question of political and economic power. [...] [P]eople are in fact always *forcing* their rules on others, applying them more or less against the will and without the consent of those others. By and large, for example, rules are made for young people by their elders. Though the youth of this country exert a powerful influence culturally – the mass media of communication are tailored to their interests, for instance – many important kinds of rules are made for our youth by adults. Rules regarding school attendance and sex behavior are not drawn up with regard to the problems of adolescence. Rather, adolescents find themselves surrounded by rules about these matters which have been made by older and more settled people. It is considered legitimate to do this, for youngsters are considered neither wise enough nor responsible enough to make proper rules for themselves.

In the same way, it is true in many respects that men make the rules for women in our society (though in America this is changing rapidly). Negroes find themselves subject to rules made for them by whites. The foreign-born and those otherwise ethnically peculiar often have their rules made for them by the Protestant Anglo-Saxon minority. The middle class makes rules the lower class must obey – in the schools, the courts, and elsewhere.

Differences in the ability to make rules and apply them to other people are essentially power differentials (either legal or extralegal). Those groups whose social position gives them weapons and power are best able to enforce their rules. Distinctions of age, sex, ethnicity, and class are all related to differences in power, which accounts for differences in the degree to which groups so distinguished can make rules for others.

In addition to recognizing that deviance is created by the responses of people to particular kinds of behavior, by the labeling of that behavior as deviant, we must also keep in mind that the rules created and maintained by such labeling are not universally agreed to. Instead, they are the object of conflict and disagreement, part of the political process of society.

NOTES

1 Cf. Donald R. Cressey, 'Criminological research and the definition of crimes', *American Journal of Sociology*, LVI (May, 1951), pp. 546–51.

2 See the discussion in C. Wright Mills, 'The professional ideology of social pathologists', *American Journal of Sociology*, XLIX (September, 1942), pp. 165–80.

3 Thomas Szasz, *The Myth of Mental Illness* (New York, Paul B. Hoeber, 1961), pp. 44–5; see also Erving Goffman, 'The medical model and mental hospitalization', in *Asylums: Essays on the Social Situation of Mental Patients and Other Inmates* (Garden City, NY, Anchor Books, 1961), pp. 321–86.

4 See Robert K. Merton, 'Social problems and sociological theory', in Robert K. Merton and Robert A. Nisbet (eds), *Contemporary Social Problems* (New York, Harcourt, Brace and World, 1961), pp. 697–737; and Talcott Parsons, *The Social System* (New York, The Free Press of Glencoe, 1951), pp. 249–325.

5 Howard Brotz similarly identifies the question of what phenomena are 'functional' or 'dysfunctional' as a political one in 'Functionalism and dynamic analysis', *European Journal of Sociology*, II (1961), pp. 170–9.

6 The most important earlier statements of this view can be found in Frank Tannenbaum, *Crime and the Community* (New York, McGraw-Hill, 1951), and E.M. Lemert, *Social Pathology* (New York, McGraw-Hill, 1951). A recent article stating a position very similar to mine is John Kitsuse, 'Societal reaction to deviance: problems of theory and method', *Social Problems*, 9 (Winter, 1962), pp. 247–56.

7   Bronislaw Malinowski, *Crime and Custom in Savage Society* (New York, Humanities Press, 1926), pp. 77–80. Reprinted by permission of Humanities Press and Routledge and Kegan Paul Ltd.

8   F. James Davis, 'Crime news in Colorado newspapers', *American Journal of Sociology*, LVII (January, 1952), pp. 325–30.

9   See Albert K. Cohen and James F. Short Jr, 'Juvenile delinquency', in Merton and Nisbet, *Contemporary Social Problems*, p. 87.

10 See Harold Garfinkel, 'Research notes on inter- and intra-racial homicides', *Social Forces*, 27 (May, 1949), pp. 369–81.

11 Edwin H. Sutherland, 'White Collar Criminality', *American Sociological Review*, V (February, 1940), pp. 1–12.

12 Clark Vincent, *Unmarried Mothers* (New York: The Free Press of Glencoe, 1961), pp. 3–5.

13 Arnold M. Rose and Arthur E. Prell, 'Does the punishment fit the crime? – a study in social valuation', *American Journal of Sociology*, LXI (November, 1955), pp. 247–59.

23

Mods, Rockers and the rest: community reactions to juvenile delinquency*

Stanley Cohen

This paper deals with one part of a research project being carried out within a certain theoretical framework in criminology and the broader field of the sociology of deviance. To understand why certain aspects of the subject matter – the Mods and Rockers phenomenon – are being considered rather than others, it is necessary to provide a brief statement of this framework.

THEORETICAL FRAMEWORK

The main purpose of the research project is to investigate social reaction to deviant behaviour. The rationale behind this approach was first set out in a strangely neglected textbook by Lemert[1] and systematized more recently by Becker.[2] This approach views deviance as a transactional process, the result of interaction between the person who commits an act and those who respond to it. Social reaction to deviance, the crucial variable in this approach, is largely ignored in conventional research in criminology and social deviance. In the field of juvenile delinquency, for example, the bulk of research is directed towards the taxonomic tabulation of the delinquents' traits (or attitudes, or values) in an attempt to see how delinquents differ from non-delinquents.[3] On this basis causal theories are constructed. But the deviant act is not, or not only, deviant *per se*, it has to be defined and treated as such by the community. Social problems are what people think they are – there is an objective and verifiable situation, but also a subjective awareness of it and a definition by certain people that the situation is inimical to

From the *Howard Journal of Criminal Justice*, 1967, 12(2): 121–30.

their interests and that something should be done about it.[4] The damage to art treasures by floods is a 'problem' to those whose commercial or aesthetic values are tied up with the preservation of art treasures. If this group of people didn't exist, there would be no problem. In the same way, the delinquent is a problem, but a problem *for someone.*

So when Becker writes that society creates deviance, he does not mean this in the conventional sense of there being social factors in the individual's situation which prompt his action, but that '… social groups create deviance by making the rules whose infractions constitute deviance, and by applying these rules to particular persons and labelling them as outsiders.' From this point of view, deviance is not a quality of the act the person commits, but rather a consequence of the application by others of rules and sanctions to an 'offender'.[5] The audience, not the actor, is the crucial variable.

One effect of community reaction is to confirm the deviant in his self-identity. When the community reacts negatively to a person's deviation from valued norms, he tends to define his situation largely in terms of the reaction. He takes on a new self-concept, identifies himself in a new light and even begins to act like the stereotype of him. James Baldwin has vividly described the position of many Negroes in these terms: he notes how his father '.. was defeated long before he died because … he really believed what white people said about him' and warned his nephew: 'You can only be destroyed by believing that you really are what the white world calls a nigger'.[6]

This reaction sequence sets into operation what Wilkins calls a 'deviation-amplifying system'[7] and the present research is aimed at observing the workings of this sort of system. The sequence would run something like this:

1   Initial deviation from valued norms, leading to:

2   Punitive reaction by the community (which may lead to the segregation of groups and marking them as deviant):

3   Development of a deviant self-identity and behaviour appropriate to this identity:

4   Further punitive reaction, etc.

Although it is not within the scope of this lecture to develop the theme, it should be pointed out that this sort of analysis is not just a manipulation of theoretical models. As Wilkins himself has made very clear, the implications for social policy, in the fields of both treatment and prevention, are considerable. Schur has recently used this type of model to examine the impact of public policy on abortion, homosexuality and drug addiction.[8] He shows, for example, how policy based often upon vital misconceptions about the nature of the deviant behaviour, may be expressed in legal prescriptions. This 'criminalization' of deviance then forces the individual into reinforcing a criminal self-image that creates problems for himself and society at large. The classic example, of course, is the creation of the addict sub-culture as partly at least a consequence of the public stereotype (the 'dope fiend') and repressive legislation. In the context of compulsory hospitalization, treatment may just reinforce the self-image.

THE PRESENT STUDY

Deviance is not a 'thing' which can be observed and studied. The term is a conceptual category and all we have are types of behaviour that have been classified as deviant. For research purposes we have to choose one of these types and juvenile delinquency is simply one such type that can be studied. Again though, juvenile delinquency is not a concrete enough category for this type of study – the term is a legal definition and not a behavioural syndrome. So, for reasons including its topical importance as a subject in its own right, the unit of study for this section of the project was narrowed down to what is classifiable (for want of a less emotive word) as 'hooliganism'. The Mods and Rockers phenomenon of the last three years, particularly in the form it took of disturbances and so-called riots at English seaside resorts over bank holiday weekends, provides an archetypal example of this behaviour.

Because we are using the transactional framework to explore certain aspects of the community reaction, the study is necessarily self limiting. It does not attempt to provide a comprehensive account of the whole phenomenon e.g. in historical terms or in terms of sub-cultural theory.

METHOD

In an exploratory study of this nature there are few guidelines on which method to use for collecting data. In the event almost all possible methods were tried. These included:– content analysis of all press cuttings covering the period Easter 1963–August 1966 (national as well as relevant local press); 65 interviews carried out with a quota sample of spectators on the Brighton sea-front during Whitsun 1965; various other interviews with local figures, e.g. newspaper editors, local government officials, hotel proprietors, M.P.'s etc., and personal observation of crowd behaviour, police action and court hearings. (The final research report will also use data from 140 intensive interviews carried out in a London Borough on the more general topic of attitudes to delinquency.)

THE INITIAL DEVIATION

Clacton is an East Coast resort not particularly well known for the range of amusements it provides for its younger visitors. Easter 1963 was worse than usual – it was cold and wet, in fact the coldest Easter Sunday for eighty years. The shopkeepers and the stall-owners were irritated by the lack of business and the young people milling around had their own irritation fanned by rumours of cafe owners and barmen refusing to serve some of them. A few groups started roughing around and for the first time the Mods and Rockers factions, a division at that time only vaguely in the air, started separating out. Those on bikes and scooters roared up and down, windows were broken, some beach huts were wrecked, one boy fired a starting pistol in the air. The vast number of young people crowding the streets, the noise, everyone's general irritation and the often panicky actions of an unprepared and undermanned police force, made the two days seem rather frightening.

One of the most significant features about Clacton is that there appear to have been present a number of what the police would call 'troublemakers' – mainly Rockers from the East End or small East Anglian villages. Contrasted with the fringe supporters, these are the same hard core who in race riots and other crowd situations are predisposed to take the initiative and to respond violently to what is perceived as police provocation. All the 24 boys charged in the Clacton court claimed that they had been the unlucky ones, that they had been picked out at random. Yet 23 out of the 24 had previous convictions – the police's chances of picking out 23 previous offenders at random out of a crowd of say a thousand, is one in a couple of million.

As we shall show, many aspects of the Mods and Rockers have parallels in the class of phenomena known as mass delusion. These studies[9] show that the first stage is invariably a real event – the delusion or hysteria is created because the initial event is reported in such a way as to set in motion a cumulative sequence which serves to fulfill the expectations created by the earlier events. In terms of our model this is an amplifying process.

THE PROCESS OF AMPLIFICATION

One of the most important elements in the reaction to deviance is the growth of a generalised set of beliefs to explain the behaviour. Once the first stage of reporting is past, the community feels the need to make sense of what has occurred – this is especially the case when the event is perceived as a dislocation of the smooth running of things: the killing of a policeman, a political assassination, a natural disaster. People look for explanations, self-styled experts proclaim favourite theories, stereotypes are confirmed or new ones are created, words acquire a symbolic meaning – 'Aberfan', 'Dallas', 'Braybrook Street', 'Clacton'.

In the case of deviancy, these generalised beliefs invariably involve spurious attribution; all sorts of traits are attributed to the deviant and, on the basis of little or no evidence, a whole set of misconceptions arise. Let us give a few examples of some of these elements.

'Violence and Damage' – it was widely believed that the Mods and Rockers caused widespread damage and were involved in violent assaults on each other or 'innocent holidaymakers'. In fact the amount of damage done was not excessive – in the three year period there were less than ten cases of malicious damage – in Hastings, August 1964, for example, one of the 'big' events, there were only four charges of malicious damage out of 64 arrests.

During Whitsun 1964, although there were 54 arrests in Bournemouth the damage was £100, in Brighton with 76 arrests the damage was £400, in Margate with 64 arrests the damage was £250. Compare these figures to the *real* cost to the resorts which was in extra police charges: the four successive bank holidays between Easter 1965 and Easter 1966 cost the Brighton Council an extra £13,000. The amount of serious violence similarly was negligible – only one tenth of the original Clacton offenders were charged with offences involving violence. In Margate, Whitsun 1964, supposedly the most violent week-end, where according to the *Daily Express* (19/5/64) 'The 1964 boys smeared the traditional postcard scene with blood and violence', there were two not very serious stabbings and one man dropped onto a flower bed. The typical offence was using threatening behaviour or obstructing the police. Leaving aside the obvious inconvenience caused to adults by crowds of youths milling about on the pavements and beach, few innocent holidaymakers were the victims of violence – the targets were members of a rival group or, more often, the police.

'Loss of trade' – it was widely believed that the troubles scared potential visitors away and the resorts suffered financially. The evidence for this is at best dubious. Papers quoted figures from Brighton for Whitsun 1964 showing that the number of deck-chairs hired had dropped by 8,000 on the previous year's week-end. This drop was attributed to the effects of the Mods and Rockers. Analyses of other figures, however, show that the total number of visitors was probably more – the reason why fewer deckchairs were hired was that Whit Monday was one of the coldest for decades – the temperature had dropped overnight by 14° F. and the beaches were virtually deserted. Interviews and observation suggest that if anything, the Mods and Rockers attracted some visitors and by the end of 1965 certainly, the happenings were part of the Brighton scene – the pier, whelks and the Mods and Rockers could all be taken in on a day trip.

'Affluent Youth' – attitudes and opinions are often shaped and bolstered up by legends and myths. One of the most recurrent of the Mods and Rockers myths was the one about the boy who told the Margate magistrates that he would pay his £75 fine with a cheque. This myth was frequently used to justify the image of the Mods and Rockers as classless, affluent, and scooter or motor-bike owners. The story was in itself true enough – what few papers bothered to publish and what they all knew, was that the boy's offer was a pathetic gesture of bravado. He later admitted that not only did he not have the £75 cheque but did not even have a bank account and had never signed a cheque in his life. The affluence image has very little factual basis. The Clacton offenders had on them an average of 15/- for the whole bank holiday week-end. The best off was a window cleaner earning £15 a week, but more typical were a market assistant earning £7 10s. and a 17-year-old clerk earning £5 14s. The average take home pay in a sample of offenders from Margate, Whitsun 1964, was £11 per week. The classless image is also none too accurate – the typical Rocker was an unskilled manual worker, the typical Mod a semi-skilled manual worker.[10] In all cases, the majority of young people present hitched or came down by train or coach. The scooter and motorbike riders were a minority, albeit a noisy and ubiquitous minority.

A detailed analysis of a number of other such images, shows that a large component of the deviation is, in Lemert's term, 'putative': 'The putative deviation is that portion of the societal definition of the deviant which has no foundation in his objective behaviour.'[11] Why is this sort of belief system important?

In the first place the stereotypes implied in the putative deviation serve to sensitize the community to any sign of incipient deviance. A previously ambiguous situation which may have been 'written off' as a Saturday night brawl now becomes re-interpreted as a 'Mods and Rockers clash'. In the weeks following the first two or three major happenings, a number of such incidents were reported from widely scattered localities. Minor scuffles and fights and increased police vigilance were reported by the Press under such headings as 'Mods and Rockers Strike Again'. There were also numerous false alarms – after Whitsun 1964 for example, the police in Stamford Hill after answering a false alarm stated that 'people are a bit jumpy after the trouble on the coast'. This type of sensitization which turns non-events into events, is exactly the same process noted by students of mass delusion. In a state of hypersuggestibility following the reporting of a 'Mad Bomber' or a 'Phantom Anaesthetist' or a 'Sex Fiend On The Loose' ambiguous events are re-interpreted to fit into the belief. This is made easier when there is a composite stereotype available with readily identifiable symbols such as clothes. To the residents of Brighton, any boy between fourteen and twenty wearing a fur-collared anorak was a Mod. At the end of one Bank Holiday the police stood at the station putting back on the trains all 'suspicious looking' arrivals who could not prove that they were local residents.

Another way in which beliefs are important in amplifying deviance is that they serve to legitimate the action of society's agents of control. *If* you are dealing with a group that is vicious, destructive, causing your community a financial loss, and symbolically repudiating your cherished values, then you are justified to respond punitively. *If* moreover, this is an affluent horde of scooter-riders, then 'fines won't touch them' and you have to propose confiscation of their scooters, forced labour camps, corporal punishment, turning the fire hoses on them. By the logic of their own definitions, the agents of control have to escalate the measures they take and propose to take to deal with the problem. So by Easter 1965 the magistrates in Brighton were employing the highly dubious practice of remanding young people in custody as a form of extra-legal punishment. Bail was refused not on the merits of the individual case but as a matter of principle – the ostensible reason given by the magistrates for remand as being to enable the police to make enquiries, was not in fact the reason given in court when bail was opposed. The police opposed bail on the grounds that if the boys were allowed to go free justice would not be done and that the public would not be protected. On the flimsiest evidence a boy, who by the police's own account had done nothing more than refuse to 'move along', would be certified as an 'unruly person', refused bail and remanded in custody in an adult prison – in some cases for up to three weeks. A test case of this sort when taken before a Judge in Chambers resulted in the immediate release of a 16-year-old boy from prison on bail. Although precise data is difficult to obtain, at least 20 cases have been traced of successful appeals on the grounds of wrongful arrests or disproportionately high sentences. There is no doubt that in certain cases, admittedly under conditions of extreme physical and psychological strain and under direct provocation, arrests were made quite arbitrarily and with unnecessary violence. In one instance, arrested youths were observed being pushed through a gauntlet of police punches before literally being thrown into the van.

Informal agents of social control also took up extreme positions. On the initiative of a group of senior aldermen and councillors, the Brighton Council overwhelmingly passed a resolution calling for the setting up of compulsory labour camps for Mods and Rockers. A group of Great Yarmouth businessmen and hotel-keepers set up a Safeguard Committee which seriously debated a scheme of setting up road blocks outside the town to prevent any invasion.

We have discussed three types of processes indentifiable in the reaction: the growth of generalised beliefs, which contain a putative element, the sensitization to deviance and the escalation of methods of social control. To evaluate the effects of the reaction on the self image we would need a more complicated type of research design than has been used here – a longitudinal study of the impact of community reaction on young people's self concepts. At present we can only use the overt behaviour as the dependent variable and assume that this behaviour is consonant with the actors' self image.

In the first place, as we have seen, the behaviour was often 'created' because of community sensitization. The atmosphere of expectancy present at the seaside resorts resulted in incidents being created out of nothing.

> Two boys stopped to watch a very drunk old tramp dancing about on the beach. They started throwing pennies at his feet. Within 45 seconds there were at least a hundred people gathered round and in 60 seconds the police were there. I turned my back on the crowd to watch the spectators gathering on the promenade above and by the time I turned back, two policemen were leading a boy away from the crowd.
>
> (*Notes*, Brighton, Easter 1965)

Incidents such as these were created by sensitivity on the part of both audience and actors. There was a sense among the young people that they had to play to the gallery; the literal gallery of the adults lining the railing as at a bullfight, and the photographers running around from one event to the other; and the metaphorical gallery of the consumers of the mass media who had read in their morning papers 'Seaside Resorts Prepare for the Hooligans' Invasion'. The control agents, especially the police, created deviance not only in the sense of provoking the more labile members of the crowd into losing their tempers, but in Becker's sense of making the rules whose infraction constituted deviance. So, for example, certain areas were designated in advance as 'trouble spots'. If a number of youths were congregating in one of these trouble spots even for legitimate reasons (such as sheltering from the rain) they could be moved along, because policy was to keep these spots free. If one refused to move along he could be arrested and charged with wilful obstruction. (Under Sec. 51(3) Police Act 1964.)

Another significant effect of the reaction was, in Tannenbaum's phrase, the 'dramatization of evil'. The adult reaction was not only negative – it could hardly have been otherwise – but it was hostile in the melodramatic sense. There was the famous speech by a Margate magistrate about his town being '... polluted by hordes of hooligans ... these long-haired mentally unstable petty little hoodlums, these sawdust Caesars who can only find courage like rats hunting in packs'; there were the newspaper headlines about 'vermin'; there was the show of force on the spot – police dogs, horses, walkie talkies, water board vans converted into squad cars; there were scenes like the police ceremoniously marching a group of youths through a street lined with spectators.

One way in which this hostility was reacted to was by returning it in kind. In the first series of events, the crowd, with the exception of the hard core referred to earlier, maintained fairly good humoured relations with the police. Attacks were disrespectful gestures such as knocking off helmets rather than malicious. In the 1966 incidents, the atmosphere was more tense. The lines had hardened:

> A policeman walked quite peacefully between two rows of boys near the aquarium. Some of them started whistling the Z-car theme and one shouted out 'Sprachen the Deutsch Constable'?
>
> (*Notes*, Brighton, Easter 1966)

Another way in which the conflict was hardened was between the two groups themselves. Although the Mods and Rockers represent two very different consumer styles – the Mods the more glossy fashion-conscious teenager, the Rockers the tougher, reactionary tradition – the antagonism between the two groups is not very deep, they have much more in common, particularly their working class membership. There was initially nothing like the gang rivalry supposed to characterise the American type of conflict gang caricatured in West Side Story, in fact there was nothing like a gang. Commercial and media exploitation of the Mod-Rocker difference, and misguided attempts to explain the whole situation of unrest in terms of this difference, hardened the barriers. The groups were merely loose collectivities or crowds within which there was occasionally some more structured grouping based on territorial loyalty, e.g. 'The Walthamstow Boys', 'The Lot From Eltham'. Constant repetition of the gang image made these collectivities see themselves as gangs and behave in a gang fashion. Yablonsky has noted the same process in his study of delinquent gangs as near groups.[12]

THE ROLE OF THE MASS MEDIA

Without being able to consider here all the mechanisms through which the reaction was amplified, it is necessary to comment on the most important of these, the mass media. One must remember that in mass society one's view of deviance is usually second hand. In the hypothetical village community one might have been able to react to the village idiot in terms of first-hand impressions. In mass society images arrive already processed – policymakers can and do make decisions about say delinquents or drug addicts on the basis of the most crude and misleading images. In the case of the Mods and Rockers the media were responsible to a large extent for the putative deviance. An analysis, for example, of the House of Commons debate on 'Juvenile Delinquency and Hooliganism' (27th April 1964) shows the extent to which the images and stereotypes provided by the media were the basis for theories and policy proposals.

It is not just that the newspapers exaggerated the amount of behaviour – this is more or less inevitable. Estimates in any crowd situation such as a political rally or sporting event are notoriously inaccurate. What was more important was the manner of presentation – the sensational headlines, the interviews with dramatic characters and subtle techniques well known to war correspondents, such as reporting the same incident twice. Another effective technique was the misleading juxtaposition of headlines – on at least three occasions headlines such as 'Mod Found Dead in Sea', 'Boy Falls to Death from Cliff' were used as sub-headings in Mods and Rockers reports. In every case the deaths had no connection at all with the disturbances and were pure accidents.

The chief roles of the media seem to have been in transmitting the stereotypes and creating an expectancy before each event that something was going to happen. This last role was particularly taken by the local press which highlighted reports about local traders arming themselves with tear gas, citizens forming vigilante patrols, etc.

DIFFERENTIAL REACTION

It is, of course, a fallacy to think of the mass media influencing a purely passive audience. Communication is responded to selectively, and the sort of questions we would like to answer are:– To what extent were the stereotypes and images absorbed by the community? How did the reaction crystallize into attitudes and opinions (e.g. about causes and solutions)? How were these attitudes affected by variables such as social class, education, political membership? Why did the reaction take the form it did?

The final research report will attempt to answer these questions. A preliminary analysis of the data from the Brighton sample only, suggests that the following type of generalisations might emerge:—

1 The reaction of the general public is less intense and less stereotypical than the reaction reflected in the mass media.

2 Local residents in the areas affected are more punitive than out of town visitors and the public in general.

3 Little difference between the Labour and Conservative groups were found. Except at the extreme of authoritarianism, political preference does not correlate with attitudes to delinquency.

4   The two most frequent single causes given for the Mods and Rockers events are 'boredom' and 'too much money'.

5   A dimension such as 'punitiveness' is too gross to measure attitudes to deviant behaviour. Certain groups, particularly working class and upper class, can at the same time be 'tolerant' of the behaviour and also devise the most punitive solutions for dealing with the behaviour when it is perceived as 'going too far'. The middle class less often make this distinction.

CONCLUSION

It must be emphasised again that as this is an analysis of the ways in which social reaction impinges upon the genesis and amplification of deviance, little has been said about the behaviour itself. This does not mean that one is trying to deny an objective reality or even less trying to present the Mods and Rockers as innocent victims of conspiracy and discrimination. Social forces work in far more subtle ways. Although people *were* inconvenienced or hurt, and there were fights and vandalism, there is at the very least enough evidence to suggest that the development of this behaviour was not independent of the reaction it provoked. Can one go further and say that the transactional theory is proved?

Clearly the present study is not a complete validation. For one thing, the crucial variable of the deviant self identity has not been measured and it might be a defect of the theory that this type of variable is peculiarly difficult to operationalise. There are problems in the model immediately apparent – for example why does the Wilkins-type of amplification sequence ever stop? Theoretically something like the Teddy Boy movement should have carried on growing. We know that this did not happen and there are already signs that the Mods and Rockers are going the same way. There are obviously factors 'outside' the model to account for these changes. Another problem is why not everybody exposed to the same definitions develops the appropriate self-image.

Until such questions are answered, we can only conclude that transactional theory provides a potentially useful framework for studying deviance. In the case of the Mods and Rockers at least, it gives an additional dimension to any other causal explanation.

NOTES

*   Lecture given to Howard League, 6th December, 1966.
1   Lemert, E. M.: *Social Pathology*, (London: McGraw Hill 1951).
2   Becker, H. S.: *Outsiders, Studies in the Sociology of Deviance*. (New York: Free Press, 1963).
3   Deutscher, I.: 'Some Relevant Directions for Research in Juvenile Delinquency', in Rose, A. R. (Ed.). *Human Behaviour and Social Processes*. (London: Routledge and Kegan Paul, 1962) pp. 468–481.
4   Fuller, R. C, and Meyers, R. R.: 'Some Aspects of a Theory of Social Problems', *Amer. Sociol. Rev.* 6, (February 1941), pp. 24–32.

5   Becker: op. cit. p. 9.
6   Baldwin, J.: *The Fire Next Time.* (Penguin, 1964) p. 13.
7   Wilkins, L.: *Social Deviance*, (London, Tavistock, 1964).
8   Schur, E. M.: *Crimes Without Victims, Deviant Behaviour and Public Policy*, (New Jersey: Prentice Hall, 1965).
9   Johnson, D. M.: The Phantom Anaesthetist of Mattoon', *Journal of Abnormal and Social Psychology*, 40, (1945) pp. 175–186 etc.
10 Barker, P. and Little, A.: The Margate Offenders: A Survey', *New Society*, Vol. 4, No. 96, (30th July 1964), pp. 6–10.
11 Lemert: op. cit. p. 56.
12 Yablonsky, L.: *The Violent Gang*, (New York: Collier MacMillan, 1962).

24

Toward a political economy of crime

William J. Chambliss

In attempting to develop a Marxist theory of crime and criminal law we are handicapped by the fact that Marx did not devote himself very systematically to such a task. There are none the less several places in his analysis of capitalism where Marx did direct his attention to criminality and law.[1] Furthermore, the logic of the Marxian theory makes it possible to extrapolate from the theory to an analysis of crime and criminal law in ways that are extremely useful. Thus, in what follows I will be focusing on the implications of the Marxist paradigm as well as relying heavily on those Marxist writings that directly addressed these issues.

As with the general Marxist theory, the starting-point for the understanding of society is the realization that the most fundamental feature of people's lives is their relationship to the mode of production. The mode of production consists of both the means of production (the technological processes) and the relationship of different classes to the means of production – whether they own them or work for those who do. Since ultimately, the only source of an economic surplus is that amount of goods which is produced beyond what the worker consumes, then the distinction between those who own and those who work for others is crucial to understanding the control of the surplus in the society.

All of this is of course elementary Marxism and was only briefly summarized here to get us started.

We must then speak of historical periods according to the mode of production which characterizes them. The most fundamental distinction would be between those societies where the means of production are owned privately, and societies where the means of production are not. Obviously there are many possible variations on these two ideal types: societies where the means of production are owned by the state (for example, the Soviet Union) as contrasted with societies where the means of production are controlled by small groups of workers (for example, Yugoslavia), or where the means of production are owned by collective units of workers, farmers, peasants and other strata (China, for example). Each of these different modes of production would of course lead to quite different social relations and therefore to different forms of crime and criminal law.

Capitalist societies, where the means of production are in private hands and where there inevitably develops a division between the class that rules (the owners of the means of production) and the class that is ruled (those who work for the ruling class), create substantial amounts of crime, often of the most violent sort, as a result of the contradictions that are inherent in the structure of social relations that emanate from the capitalist system.

The first contradiction is that the capitalist enterprise depends upon creating in the mass of the workers a desire for the consumption of products produced by the system. These products need not contribute to the well-being of the people, nor do they have to represent commodities of any intrinsic value; none the less, for the system to expand and be viable, it is essential that the bulk of the population be oriented to consuming what is produced. However, in order to produce the commodities that are the basis for the accumulation of capital and the maintenance of the ruling class, it is also necessary to get people to work at tedious, alienating and unrewarding tasks. One way to achieve this, of course, is to make the accumulation of commodities dependent on work. Moreover, since the system depends as it does on the desire to possess and consume commodities far beyond what is necessary for survival, there must be an added incentive to perform the dull meaningless tasks that are required to keep the productive process expanding. This is accomplished by keeping a proportion of the labor force impoverished or nearly so.[2] If those who are employed become obstreperous and refuse to perform the tasks required by the productive system, then there is a reserve labor force waiting to take their job. And hanging over the heads of the workers is always the possibility of becoming impoverished should they refuse to do their job.

Thus, at the outset the structure of capitalism creates both the desire to consume and – for a large mass of people – an inability to earn the money necessary to purchase the items they have been taught to want.

A second fundamental contradiction derives from the fact that the division of a society into a ruling class that owns the means of production and a subservient class that works for wages *inevitably* leads to conflict between the two classes. As those conflicts are manifest in rebellions and riots among the proletariat, the state, acting in the interests of the owners of the means of production will pass laws designed to control, through the application of state sanctioned force, those acts of the proletariat which threaten the interests of the bourgeoisie. In this way, then, acts come to be defined as criminal.

It follows that as capitalism develops and conflicts between social classes continue or become more frequent or more violent (as a result, for example, of increasing proletarianization), more and more acts will be defined as criminal.

The criminal law is thus *not* a reflection of custom (as other theorists have argued), but is a set of rules laid down by the state in the interests of the ruling class, and resulting from the conflicts that inhere in class structured societies; criminal behavior is, then, the inevitable expression of class conflict resulting from the inherently exploitative nature of the economic relations. What makes the behavior of some criminal is the coercive power of the state to enforce the will of the ruling class; criminal behavior results from the struggle between classes whereby those who are the subservient classes individually express their alienation from established social relations. Criminal behavior is a product of the economic and political system, and in a capitalist society has as one of its principal consequences the advancement of technology, use of surplus labor and generally the maintenance of the established relationship between the social classes. Marx says, somewhat facetiously, in response to the functionalism of bourgeois sociologists:

> crime takes a part of the superfluous population off the labor market and thus reduces competition among the laborers – up to a certain point preventing wages from falling below the minimum – the struggle against crime absorbs another part of this population. Thus the criminal comes in as one of those natural 'counterweights' which bring about a correct balance and open up a whole perspective of 'useful' occupation … the criminal … produces the whole of the police and of criminal justice, constables, judges, hangmen, juries, etc.; and all these different lines of business, which form equally many categories of the social division of labor, develop different capacities of the human spirit, create new needs and new ways of satisfying them. Torture alone has given rise to the most ingenious mechanical inventions, and employed many honorable craftsmen in the production of its instruments.[3]

Paradigms, as we are all well aware, do much more than supply us with specific causal explanations. They provide us with a whole set of glasses through which we view the world. Most importantly, they lead us to emphasize certain features of the world and to ignore or at least de-emphasize others.

The following propositions highlight the most important implications of a Marxian paradigm of crime and criminal law.[4]

A On the content and operation of criminal law

1 Acts are defined as criminal because it is in the interests of the ruling class to so define them.

2 Members of the ruling class will be able to violate the laws with impunity while members of the subject classes will be punished.

3 As capitalist societies industrialize and the gap between the bourgeoisie and the proletariat widens, penal law will expand in an effort to coerce the proletariat into submission.

B On the consequences of crime for society

1   Crime reduces surplus labor by creating employment not only for the criminals but for law enforcers, locksmiths, welfare workers, professors of criminology and a horde of people who live off the fact that crime exists.

2   Crime diverts the lower classes' attention from the exploitation they experience, and directs it toward other members of their own class rather than towards the capitalist class or the economic system.

3   Crime is a reality which exists only as it is created by those in the society whose interests are served by its presence.

C On the etiology of criminal behavior

1   Criminal and non-criminal behavior stem from people acting rationally in ways that are compatible with their class position. Crime is a reaction to the life conditions of a person's social class.

2   Crime varies from society to society depending on the political and economic structures of society.

3   Socialist societies should have much lower rates of crime because the less intense class struggle should reduce the forces leading to and the functions of crime.

[…]

ON THE CONTENT AND OPERATION OF THE CRIMINAL LAW

The conventional, non-Marxian interpretation of how criminal law comes into being sees the criminal law as a reflection of widely held beliefs which permeate all 'healthy consciences' in the society. This view has been clearly articulated by Jerome Hall:

> The moral judgements represented in the criminal law can be defended on the basis of their derivation from a long historical experience, through open discussion … the process of legislation, viewed broadly to include participation and discussion by the electorate as well as that of the legislature proper, provides additional assurance that the legal valuations are soundly established. … [5]

THE MARXIAN THEORY OF CRIMINAL LAW

There is little evidence to support the view that the criminal law is a body of rules which reflect strongly held moral dictates of the society.[6] Occasionally we find a study on the creation of criminal law which traces legal innovations to the 'moral indignation' of a particular social class.[7] It is significant, however, that the circumstances described are quite different from the situation where laws emerge from community consensus. Rather, the research points up the rule by a small minority which occupies a particular class position and shares a viewpoint and a set of social experiences which brings them together as an active and effective force of social change. For example, Joseph Gusfield's astute analysis of the emergence of prohibition in the United States illustrates how these laws were brought about through the political efforts of a downwardly mobile segment of America's middle class. By effort and some good luck this class was able to impose its will on the majority of the population through rather dramatic changes in the law.[8] Svend Ranulf's more general study of *Moral Indignation and Middle Class Psychology* shows similar results, especially when it is remembered that the lower middle class, whose emergence Ranulf sees as the social force behind legal efforts to legislate morality, was a decided *minority* of the population. In no reasonable way can these inquiries be taken as support for the idea that criminal laws represent *community* sentiments.

By contrast, there is considerable evidence showing the critically important role played by the interests of the ruling class as a major force in the creation of criminal laws. Jerome Hall's analysis of the emergence of the laws of theft and Chambliss's study of vagrancy laws both point up the salience of the economic interests of the ruling class as the fountainhead of legal changes.[9] A more recent analysis of the legislative process behind the creation of laws attempting to control the distribution of amphetamine drugs has also shown how the owners of the means of production (in this case, the large pharmaceutical companies) are involved in writing and lobbying for laws which affect their profits.[10]

The surface appearance of legal innovations often hides the real forces behind legislation. Gabriel Kolko's studies of the creation of laws controlling the meat packing and railroad industries in the United States have shown how the largest corporations in these industries were actively involved in a campaign for federal control of the industries, as this control would mean increased profits for the large manufacturers and industrialists.[11]

Research on criminal law legislation has also shown the substantial role played by state bureaucracies in the legislative process.[12] In some areas of criminal law it seems that the law enforcement agencies are almost solely responsible for the shape and content of the laws. As a matter of fact, drug laws are best understood as laws passed as a result of efforts of law enforcement agencies which managed to create whatever consensus there is. Other inquiries point up the role of conflicting interests between organized groups of moral entrepreneurs, bureaucrats and businessmen.[13]

In all of these studies there is substantial support for the Marxian theory. The single most important force behind criminal law creation is doubtless the economic interest and political power of those social classes which either (1) own or control the resources of the society, or (2) occupy positions of authority in the state bureaucracies. It is also the case that conflicts generated by the class structure of a society act as an important force for legal innovation.

These conflicts may manifest themselves in an incensed group of moral entre-preneurs (such as Gusfield's lower middle class, or the efforts of groups such as the ACLU, NAACP or Policemen's Benevolent Society) who manage to persuade courts or legislatures to create new laws.[14] Or the conflict may mani-fest itself in open riots, rebellions or revolutions which force new criminal law legislation.

There is, then, evidence that the Marxian theory with its emphasis on the role of the ruling classes in creating criminal laws and social class conflict and as the moving force behind legal changes is quite compatible with research findings on this subject. […]

THE ETIOLOGY OF CRIMINAL BEHAVIOR

It is obviously fruitless to join the debate over whether or not contemporary theories of criminal etiology are adequate to the task. The advocates of 'family background', 'differential association', 'cultural deprivation', 'opportunity theory', and a host of other 'theories' have debated the relative merits of their explanations *ad infinitum* (one might even say *ad nauseam)*.

[…] Everyone commits crime. And many, many people whether they are poor, rich or middling are involved in a way of life that is criminal; and furthermore, no one, not even the professional thief or racketeer or corrupt politician commits *crime all the time.* To be sure, it may be politically useful to say that people become crimi-nal through association with 'criminal behavior patterns', and thereby remove the tendency to look at criminals as pathological. But such a view has little scientific value, since it asks the wrong questions. It asks for a psychological cause of what is by its very nature a socio-political event. Criminality is simply *not* something that people have or don't have; crime is not something some people do and others don't. Crime is a matter of who can pin the label on whom, and underlying this socio-political process is the structure of social relations determined by the political economy. […]

The argument that criminal acts, that is, acts which are a violation of criminal law, are more often committed by members of the lower classes is not tenable. Criminal acts are widely distributed throughout the social classes in capitalist societies. The rich, the ruling, the poor, the powerless and the working classes *all* engage in criminal activities on a regular basis. It is in the enforcement of the law that the lower classes are subject to the effects of ruling class domination over the legal system, and which results in the appearance of a concentration of criminal acts among the lower classes in the official records. In actual practice, however, class differences in rates of criminal activity are probably negligible. What differ-ence there is would be a difference in the type of criminal act, not in the preva-lence of criminality.

The argument that the control of the state by the ruling class would lead to a lower propensity for crime among the ruling classes fails to recognize two fun-damental facts. First is the fact that many acts committed by lower classes and which it is in the interests of the ruling class to control (e.g., crimes of violence, bribery of public officials, and crimes of personal choice, such as drug use, alco-holism, driving while intoxicated, homosexuality, etc.) are just as likely – or at least very likely – to be as widespread among the upper classes as the lower classes. Thus, it is crucial that the ruling class be able to control the discretion of the law enforcement agencies in ways that provide them with immunity; for example, having a legal system encumbered with procedural rules which only the wealthy can afford to implement and which, if implemented, nearly guaran-tees immunity from prosecution, not to mention more direct control through bribes, coercion and the use of political influence.

The Marxian paradigm must also account for the fact that the law will also reflect conflict between members of the ruling class (or between members of the ruling class and the upper class 'power elites' who manage the bureaucracies). So, for example, laws restricting the formation of trusts, misrepresentation in advertising, the necessity for obtaining licenses to engage in business practices are all laws which generally serve to reduce competition among the ruling classes and to concentrate capital in a few hands. However, the laws also apply universally, and therefore apply to the ruling class as well. Thus, when they break these laws they are committing criminal acts. Again, the enforcement prac-tices obviate the effectiveness of the laws, and guarantee that the ruling class will rarely feel the sting of the laws, but their violation remains a fact with which we must reckon. […]

SUMMARY AND CONCLUSION

As Gouldner and Friedrichs have recently pointed out, social science generally, and sociology in particular is in the throes of a 'paradigm revolution'.[15] Predictably, criminology is both a reflection of and a force behind this revolution.

The emerging paradigm in criminology is one which emphasizes social conflict – particularly conflicts of social class interests and values. The para-digm which is being replaced is one where the primary emphasis was on consensus, and within which 'deviance' or 'crime' was viewed as an aberra-tion shared by some minority. This group had failed to be properly socialized or adequately integrated into society or, more generally, had suffered from 'social disorganization'.

The shift in paradigm means more than simply a shift from explaining the same facts with new causal models. It means that we stretch our conceptual framework and look to different facets of social experience. Specifically, instead of resort-ing inevitably to the 'normative system', to 'culture' or to socio-psychological experiences of individuals, we look instead to the social relations created by the political and economic structure. Rather than treating 'society' as a full-blown reality (reifying it into an entity with its own life), we seek to understand the pre-sent as a reflection of the economic and political history that has created the social relations which dominate the moment we have selected to study.

The shift means that crime becomes a rational response of some social classes to the realities of their lives. The state becomes an instrument of the ruling class enforcing laws here but not there, according to the realities of political power and economic conditions.

There is much to be gained from this re-focusing of criminological and sociological inquiry. However, if the paradigmatic revolution is to be more than a mere fad, we must be able to show that the new paradigm is in fact superior to its predecessor. In this paper I have tried to develop the theoretical implications of a Marxian model of crime and criminal law [...] The general conclusion is that the Marxian paradigm provides a long neglected but fruitful approach to the study of crime and criminal law.

NOTES

1 Primary source materials for Marx's analysis of crime and criminal law are: *Capital, v. 1* (London, Lawrence and Wishart, 1970), pp. 231–98, 450–503, 556–7, 574, 674–8, 718–25, 734–41; *The Cologne Communist Trial* (London, Lawrence and Wishart, 1971); *The German Ideology (1845–6)* (London, Lawrence and Wishart, 1965), pp. 342–79; *Theories of Surplus Value, v. 1*, pp. 375–6; 'The state and the law', in T.B. Bottomore and Maximilien Rubel (eds), *Karl Marx: Selected Writings in Sociology and Social Philosophy* (New York, McGraw-Hill, 1965), pp. 215–31.

2 In the United Sates the proportion of the population living in poverty is between 15 and 30 per cent of the labor force.

3 Marx, *Theories of Surplus Value*, pp. 375–6.

4 For an excellent statement of differences in 'order and conflict' theories, see John Horton, 'Order and conflict approaches to the study of social problems', *American Journal of Sociology*, May 1966; see also Gerhard Lenski, *Power and Privilege* (New York, McGraw-Hill, 1966); William J. Chambliss, *Sociological Readings in the Conflict Perspective* (Reading, MA, Addison-Wesley, 1973).

5 Jerome Hall, *General Principles of Criminal Law* (Indianapolis, Bobbs-Merrill, 1947), pp. 356–7.

6 For a more thorough analysis of this issue, see William J. Chambliss 'The state, the law and the definition of behavior as criminal or delinquent', in Daniel Glaser (ed.), *Handbook of Criminology* (Chicago, Rand McNally, 1974), ch. 1, pp. 7–43.

7 Svend Ranulf, *The Jealousy of the Gods*, vols 1 and 2 (London, Williams and Northgate, 1932) and *Moral Indignation and Middle Class Psychology* (Copenhagen, Levin and Monkagord, 1938); Joseph Gusfield, *Symbolic Crusade: Status Politics and the American Temperance Movement* (Urbana, Ill., University of Illinois Press, 1963).

8 Gusfield, *Symbolic Crusade*; see also Andrew Sinclair *Era of Excess: A Social History of the Prohibition Movement* (New York, Harper and Row, 1964).

9 Jerome Hall, *Theft, Law and Society* (Indianapolis: Bobbs-Merrill and Co., 1952); William J. Chambliss, 'A sociological analysis of the law of vagrancy', *Social Problems*, Summer (1964), pp. 67–77.

10 James M. Graham, 'Profits at all costs: amphetamine profits on Capitol Hill', *Transaction*, January (1972), pp. 14–23.

11 Gabriel Kolko, *Railroads and Regulations* (Princeton, NJ, Princeton University Press, 1965) and *The Triumph of Conservatism* (New York, The Free Press of Glencoe, 1963).

12 Alfred R. Lindesmith, *The Addict and the Law* (Bloomington, Ind., Indiana University Press, 1965); Edwin M. Lemert, *Social Action and Legal Change: Revolution Within the*

Juvenile Court (Chicago, Aldine, 1964); Troy Duster, *The Legislation of Morality: Law, Drugs and Moral Judgement* (New York, The Free Press, 1970).

13 Pamela A. Roby, 'Politics and criminal law: revision of the New York State Penal Law on Prostitution', *Social Problems*, Summer (1969), pp. 83–109.

14 William J. Chambliss and Robert B. Seidman, *Law, Order and Power* (Reading, MA, Addison-Wesley, 1971).

15 Alvin W. Gouldner, *The Coming Crisis in Western Sociology* (New York, Basic Books, 1970); Robert W. Friedrichs, *A Sociology of Sociology* (New York, The Free Press, 1970). For a more general discussion of paradigm revolution in science, see Thomas S. Kuhn, *The Structure of Scientific Revolutions*, 2nd edn (Chicago, University of Chicago Press, 1970).

25

Crime, power and ideological mystification

Steven Box

Murder! Rape! Robbery! Assault! Wounding! Theft! Burglary! Arson! Vandalism! These form the substance of the annual official criminal statistics on indictable offences (or the Crime Index offences in America). Aggregated, they constitute the major part of 'our' crime problem. Or at least, we are told so daily by politicians, police, judges and journalists who speak to us through the media of newspapers and television. And most of us listen. We don't want to be murdered, raped, robbed, assaulted, or criminally victimized in any other way. Reassured that our political leaders are both aware of the problem's growing dimensions and receptive to our rising anxieties, we wait in optimistic but realistic anticipation for crime to be at least effectively reduced. But apart from the number of police rapidly increasing, their technological and quasi-military capacities shamelessly strengthened, their discretionary powers of apprehension, interrogation, detention and arrest liberally extended, and new prisons built or old ones extensively refurbished (all with money the government claims the country has not got to maintain existing standards of education, health, unemployment welfare, and social services), nothing much justifies the optimism.

The number of recorded serious crimes marches forever upward. During the decade 1970–80, serious crimes recorded by the police increased for nearly every category: violence against the person rose by 136 per cent, burglary by 44 per cent, robbery by 138 per cent, theft and handling by 54 per cent and fraud and forgery by 18 per cent. These increases were not merely artefacts of an increased population available to commit serious crimes. For even when the changing population size is controlled statistically, crimes continue to rise. Thus in 1950, there were 1,094 per 100,000 population. This rose to 1,742 by 1960, then to 3,221 by 1970, and

From *Power, Crime and Mystification*, pp. 1–15. (London: Tavistock, 1983.)

reached 5,119 by 1980. From 1980 to 1981 they rose a further 10 per cent, to reach an all-time record. Ironically, as 'our' crime problem gets worse, the demand for even more 'law and order' policies increases, even though these are blatantly having no effect on the level of serious crimes. At least not on the level recorded by the police.

The result, so we are told, is that the 'fear of crime' has now been elevated into a national problem. Techniques for avoiding victimization have become a serious preoccupation: more locks on doors and windows, fewer visits after dark to family, friends, and places of entertainment, avoidance of underground and empty train carriages, mace sprays or personal alarm sirens held nervously in coat pockets, a growing unwillingness to be neighbourly or engage in local collective enterprises, furtive suspicious glances at any stranger, and attempts to avoid any encounter except with the most trusted and close friends.

Who are these 'villains' driving us into a state of national agoraphobia? We are told a fairly accurate and terrifying glimpse can be obtained of 'our' Public Enemies by examining the convicted and imprisoned population. For every 100 persons convicted of these serious crimes, 85 are male. Amongst this convicted male population, those aged less than 30 years, and particularly those aged between 15 and 21 years are over-represented. Similarly, the educational non-achievers are over-represented – at the other end of the educational achievement ladder there appear to be hardly any criminals, since only 0.05 per cent of people received into prison have obtained a university degree. The unemployed are currently only (*sic*) 14 per cent of the available labour force, but they constitute approximately 40 per cent of those convicted. Only 4 per cent of the general population are black, but nearly one-third of the convicted and imprisoned population are black. Urban dwellers, particularly inner-city residents, are over-represented. Thus the typical people criminally victimizing and forcing us to fear each other and fracture our sense of 'community' are young uneducated males, who are often unemployed, live in a working-class impoverished neighbourhood, and frequently belong to an ethnic minority. These villains deserve, so 'law and order' campaigners tell us ceaselessly in their strident moral rhetoric, either short, sharp, shock treatment, including death by hanging or castration by chemotherapy – 'off with their goolies' – or long, endless, self-destroying stretches as non-paying guests in crumbling, insanitary, overcrowded prisons constructed for the redemption of lost Christian souls by our Victorian ancestors. If only these ideas were pursued vigorously and with a vengeance morally justified by the offender's wickedness, then 'our' society would be relatively crime-free and tranquil. So 'law and order' campaigners tell us.

It is tempting to call all this hype – but that would be extreme! 'Conventional' crimes do have victims whose suffering is real; steps should be taken to understand and control these crimes so that fewer and fewer people are victimized. A radical criminology which appears to deny this will be seen as callous and rightly rejected. Furthermore, those crimes so carefully recorded and graphed in official criminal statistics *are* more likely to be committed by young males, living in poor neighbourhoods and so on. A radical criminology which appears to deny this will be seen as naive and rightly rejected. Finally, there are very good grounds for believing that the rising crime wave is real – material conditions for large sections of the community have deteriorated markedly. A radical criminology which remained insensitive of this would be guilty of forgetting its theoretical roots and rightly rejected. So the official portrait of crime and criminals is not entirely without merit or truth.

None the less, before galloping off down the 'law and order' campaign trail, it might be prudent to consider whether murder, rape, robbery, assault, and other crimes focused on by state officials, politicians, the media, and the criminal justice system do constitute the major part of our real crime problem. Maybe they are only *a* crime problem and not *the* crime problem. Maybe what is stuffed into our consciousness as *the* crime problem is in fact an illusion, a trick to deflect our attention away from other, even more serious crimes and victimizing behaviours, which objectively cause the vast bulk of avoidable death, injury and deprivation.

At the same time, it might be prudent to compare persons who commit other serious but under-emphasized crimes and victimizing behaviours with those who are officially portrayed as 'our' criminal enemies. For if the former, compared to the latter, are indeed quite different types of people, then maybe we should stop looking to our political authorities and criminal justice system for protection from those beneath us in impoverished urban neighbourhoods. Instead maybe we should look up accusingly at our political and judicial 'superiors' for being or for protecting the 'real' culprits.

If we do this, we might also cast a jaundiced eye at the view that serious criminals are 'pathological'. This has been the favourite explanatory imagery of mainstream positivistic criminology. It was, however, an explanation that only remained plausible if crimes were indeed committed by a minority of individuals living in conditions of relative deprivation. For whilst this was true it was obvious, at least to the conservative mind, that 'something must be wrong with them'. However, if we look up rather than down the stratification hierarchy and see serious crimes being committed by the people who are respectable, well-educated, wealthy and socially privileged then the imagery of pathology seems harder to accept. If these upper- and middle-class criminals are also pathological, then what hope is there for any of us! Wanting to avoid this pessimistic conclusion, we might instead entertain the idea that these powerful persons commit crimes for 'rational' – albeit disreputable – motives which emerge under conditions that render conformity a relatively unrewarding activity. Having rescued the powerful from 'abnormality' we might do the same for the powerless. Maybe they too are rational rather than irrational, morally disreputable rather than organically abnormal, overwhelmed by adversity rather than by wickedness.

If these are the lessons of prudence, then standing back from the official portrait of crime and criminals and looking at it critically might be a very beneficial move towards getting our heads straight.

However, there is an agonizing choice to make between at least two pairs of spectacles we might wear to take this critical look. We could wear the liberal 'scientific' pair, as did many young trendy academics during the 1960s and early 1970s when the stars of interactionism and phenomenology were in the ascendant. Or we might wear the radical 'reflexive' pair, whose lenses have been recently polished to a fine smoothness by those same trendy academics who have now entered a middle-age period of intellectual enlightenment! These spectacles do provide quite different views on the official portrait of crime and criminals.

LIBERAL 'SCIENTISM': PARTIALLY BLIND JUSTICE

One way of getting a clear perspective on those crimes and criminals causing us most harm, injury and deprivation is to excavate unreported, unrecorded and non-prosecuted crimes. This can be achieved by sifting evidence from numerous self-reported crime studies and criminal victimization surveys. This is undoubtedly an important exercise for it leads us to reconsider the *validity* of official criminal statistics and the more extreme pronouncements made directly and uncritically from them.

What lessons are there to be learnt from the results of these surveys? First, there is much more serious crime being committed than the official police records indicate. The emerging consensus is that one serious crime in three (excluding burglary and car theft) is reported to the police. This knowledge can and does add fuel to the alarmist 'law and order' fire: 'it's even worse than we imagined!' Second, although the official portrait of criminals is not untrue, it is inaccurate. It is more like a distorting mirror; you immediately recognize yourself, but not quite in a flattering shape and form familiar to you. Thus self-report data indicate that serious crimes are disproportionately committed by the young uneducated males amongst whom the unemployed and ethnically oppressed are over-represented, but the contribution they make is less than the official data implies. There are, it appears, more serious crimes being committed by white, respectable, well-educated, slightly older males and females than we are led to believe (Box, 1981a: 56–93).

To the liberal 'scientific' mind, there are two problems here of 'slippage', one more slight than the other. Too many people fail to report crimes because they consider the police inefficient; we need to restore police efficiency in order to increase the reportage rate and hence obtain a better, more reliable gauge of crime. The second, more important slippage, is that the administration of criminal justice is fine in principle, but is failing slightly in practice. The police pursue policies of *differential deployment* (for example, swamping certain parts of London where the West Indian population is prominent) and *'methodological suspicion'* (that is, routinely suspecting only a limited proportion of the population, particularly those with criminal records or known criminal associates). Coupled with these practices are *plea-bargaining* (negotiating a guilty plea in return for being charged with a less serious offence) and *'judicious' judicial decisions* (which take as much notice of who you are as they do of what you have apparently done). In other words, the police, magistrates, judges, and other court officials have too much discretion.

The result is too much 'street-justice', 'charge-dealing', 'plea-bargaining' and 'disparate sentencing'. In these judicial negotiations and compromises, the wealthy, privileged and powerful are better able to secure favourable outcomes than their less powerful counterparts (Box, 1981a: 157–207). This slippage between ideal and practice reveals a slightly disturbing picture. The process of law enforcement, in its broadest possible interpretation, operates in such a way as to *conceal* crimes of the powerful against the powerless, but to *reveal* and *exaggerate* crimes of the powerless against 'everyone'.

Furthermore, because a substantial section of this criminalized population is stigmatized and discriminated against, particularly in the field of employment, its reproduction is secured; many of them, out of resentment, injustice, or desperation, turn to more persistent and even more serious forms of crime. This vicious circle increases the over-representation of the powerless in the highly publicized 'hardened' criminal prisoner population.

The outcome of these processes is that the official portrait of crime and criminals is highly selective, serving to conceal crimes of the powerful and hence shore up their interests, particularly the need to be legitimated through maintaining the appearance of respectability. At the same time, crimes of the powerless are revealed and exaggerated, and this serves the interests of the powerful because it legitimizes their control agencies, such as the police and prison service, being strengthened materially, technologically and legally, so that their ability to survey, harass, deter, both specifically and generally, actual and potential resisters to political authority is enhanced.

To the liberal 'scientific' mind, a solution of this second and more important slippage would involve a strict limitation on police and judicial discretion and less stigmatization either by decriminalizing some behaviours, or imposing less incarceration (Schur, 1973). The adoption of these policies would narrow the 'official' differential in criminal behaviour between the disreputable poor and the respectable middle class so that it approximated more closely the actual differences in criminal behaviour – at least criminal behaviour as defined by the state.

RADICAL 'REFLEXIVENESS': ARTFUL CRIMINAL DEFINITIONS

Although an enormous amount of carefully buried crime can be unearthed by this liberal 'scientific' excavation work, we will still be denied an adequate view of those whose crimes and victimizing behaviours cause us most harm, injury and deprivation.

Through radical 'reflexive' spectacles, all this excavation work occurs so late in the process of constructing crime and criminals that it never gets to the foundations. Those committed to self-report and victimization surveys do not start off asking the most important question of all: 'what is serious crime?' Instead they take serious crime as a pre- and state-defined phenomenon. But by the time crime categories or definitions have been established, the most important foundation stone of 'our crime problem' has been well and truly buried in cement, beyond the reach of any liberal 'scientific' shovel.

Aware that liberal 'scientists' arrive too late on the scene, radicals resolve to get up earlier in the morning. Instead of merely examining how the law enforcement process in its broadest sense constructs a false image of serious crime and its perpetrators, they suggest we should consider the *social construction of criminal law categories*. This involves not only reflecting on why certain types of behaviours are defined as criminal in some historical periods and not others, but also why a particular criminal law comes to incorporate from relatively homogeneous behaviour patterns only a portion and excludes the remainder, even though each and every instance of this behaviour causes avoidable harm, injury, or deprivation.

Some sociologists have pondered these issues and come to the conclusion that *criminal law categories are ideological constructs* (Sumner, 1976). Rather than being a fair reflection of those behaviours objectively causing us collectively the most avoidable suffering, criminal law categories are artful, creative constructs designed to criminalize only some victimizing behaviours, usually those more frequently committed by the relatively powerless, and to exclude others, usually those frequently committed by the powerful against subordinates.

Numerous researchers (Chambliss 1964; Duster 1970; Graham 1972; Gunningham 1974; Hall 1952; Haskins 1960; Hay 1975; Hopkins 1978; McCaghy and Denisoff 1973; Platt 1969; Thompson 1975) have produced evidence consistent with the view that criminal law categories are ideological reflections of the interests of particular powerful groups. As such, criminal law categories are resources, tools, instruments, designed and then used to criminalize, demoralize, incapacitate, fracture and sometimes eliminate those problem populations perceived by the powerful to be potentially or actually threatening the existing distribution of power, wealth and privilege. They constitute one, and only one way by which social control over subordinate, but 'resisting', populations is exercised. For once behaviour more typically engaged in by subordinate populations has been incorporated into criminal law, then legally sanctioned punishments can be 'justifiably' imposed.

In a society such as ours, populations more likely to be controlled in part through criminalization,

> tend to share a number of social characteristics but most important among these is the fact that their behaviour, personal qualities, and/or position threaten the social relationships of production. … In other words, populations become generally eligible for management as deviant when they disturb, hinder, or call into question … capitalist modes of appropriating the product of human labour … the social conditions under which capitalist production takes place … patterns of distribution and consumption … the process of socialization for productive and non-productive roles … and … the ideology which supports the functioning of capitalist society. (Spitzer, 1975: 642)

However, this argument needs qualification. It does not maintain that all criminal laws directly express the interests of one particular group, such as the ruling class. Clearly some legislation reflects temporary victories of one interest or allied interest groups over others, and none of these may necessarily be identical or coincide with the interests of the ruling class. Yet the above argument does not demand or predict that every criminal law directly represents the interests of the ruling class. It recognizes that some laws are passed purely as symbolic victories which the dominant class grants to inferior interest groups, basically to keep them quiet; once passed, they need never be efficiently or systematically enforced. It also recognizes that occasionally the ruling class is forced into a tactical retreat by organized subordinate groups, and the resulting shifts in criminal law enshrine a broader spectrum of interests. But these victories are short lived. Powerful groups have ways and means of clawing back the spoils of tactical defeats. In the last instance, definitions of crime reflect the interests of those groups who comprise the ruling class. This is not to assume that these interests are homogeneous and without serious contradictions (Chambliss, 1981). Indeed, it is just the space between these contradictions that subordinate groups fill with their demands for legal change.

It might be objected that even though *some* criminal laws are in the interests of the dominant class and that others which are obviously not in these interests are ineffectively enforced, thus making them dead-letter laws, it still remains true that laws proscribing those types of victimizing behaviours of which we are all too aware and which set the nerve-ends of neo-classical/conservative criminologists, such as Wilson (1975) and Morgan (1978) tingling with fear and loathing, *are in all our interests.* None of us wants to be murdered, raped, or robbed; none of us wants our property stolen, smashed, or destroyed, none of us wants our bodies punched, kicked, bitten, or tortured. In that sense, criminal laws against murder, rape, arson, robbery, theft and assault are in all our interests, since in principle we all benefit equally from and are protected by their existence. Without them life would be 'nasty, poor, solitary, brutish, and short'.

This is all true, but it is not all the truth. For some groups of people benefit more than others from these laws. It is not that they are less likely to be murdered, raped, robbed or assaulted – although the best scientific evidence based on victimization surveys shows this to be true (Hindelang et al., 1978) – but that in the criminal law, definitions of murder, rape, robbery, assault, theft and other serious crimes are so constructed as to exclude many similar, and in important respects, identical acts, and these are just the acts likely to be committed more frequently by powerful individuals.

Thus the criminal law defines only some types of avoidable killing as murder: it excludes, for example, deaths resulting from acts of negligence, such as employers' failure to maintain safe working conditions in factories and mines (Swartz, 1975); or deaths resulting from an organization's reluctance to maintain appropriate safety standards (Erickson, 1976); or deaths that result from governmental agencies' giving environmental health risks a low priority (Liazos, 1972); or deaths resulting from drug manufacturers' failure to conduct adequate research on new chemical compounds before embarking on aggressive marketing campaigns (Silverman and Lee, 1974); or deaths from a dangerous drug that was approved by health authorities on the strength of a bribe from a pharmaceutical company (Braithwaite and Geis, 1981); or deaths resulting from car manufacturers refusing to recall and repair thousands of known defective vehicles because they calculate that the costs of meeting civil damages will be less (Swigert and Farrell, 1981); and in most jurisdictions deaths resulting from drunken or reckless people driving cars with total indifference to the potential cost in terms of human lives are also excluded.

The list of avoidable killings not legally construed as murder even in principle could go on and on. But the point should be clear. We are encouraged to see murder as a particular act involving a very limited range of stereotypical actors, instruments, situations and motives. Other types of avoidable killing are either defined as a less serious crime than murder, or as matters more appropriate for administrative or civil proceedings, or as events beyond the justifiable boundaries of state interference. In all instances, the perpetrators of these avoidable 'killings' deserve, so we are told, less harsh community responses than would be made to those committing legally defined murder. The majority of people accept this because the state, by excluding these killings from the murder category, has signified its intention that we should not treat them as capital offenders. As the state can muster a galaxy of skilled machiavellian orators to defend its definitions, and has, beyond these velvet tongues, the iron fist of police and military physical violence, it is able to persuade most people easily and convincingly.

It may be just a strange coincidence, as Vonnegut often suggests, that the social characteristics of those persons more likely to commit these types of avoidable killings differ considerably from those possessed by individuals more likely to commit killings legally construed in principle as murder. That the former are more likely to be relatively more powerful, wealthy and privileged than the latter could be one of nature's accidents. But is it likely?

The criminal law sees only some types of property deprivation as robbery or theft; it excludes, for example, the separation of consumers and part of their money that follows manufacturers' malpractices or advertisers' misrepresentations; it excludes shareholders losing their money because managers behaved in ways which they thought would be to the advantage of shareholders even though the only tangible benefits accrued to the managers (Hopkins, 1980b); it excludes the *extra* tax citizens, in this or other countries, have to pay because: (i) corporations and the very wealthy are able to employ financial experts at discovering legal loopholes through which money can be safely transported to tax havens; (ii) Defence Department officials have been bribed to order more expensive weaponry systems or missiles in 'excess' of those 'needed'; (iii) multinational drug companies charge our National Health Services prices which are estimated to be at least £50 million in excess of alternative supplies. If an employee's hand slips into the governor's pocket and removes any spare cash, that is theft; if the governor puts his hand into employees' pockets and takes their spare cash, i.e. reduces wages, even below the legal minimum, that is the labour market operating reasonably. To end the list prematurely and clarify the point, the law of theft includes, in the words of that anonymous poet particularly loved by teachers of 'A' level economic history, 'the man or woman who steals the goose from off the common, but leaves the greater villain loose who steals the common from the goose'.

The criminal law includes only one type of non-consensual sexual act as rape, namely the insertion of penis in vagina by force or threatened force; it excludes sexual intercourse between husband and wife, no matter how much the latter is beaten by the former to exercise his 'conjugal right'; it excludes most sexual acts achieved by fraud, deceit, or misrepresentation – thus a man may pose as a psychiatrist and prescribe sexual intercourse as therapy to a 'gullible female', because he knows the law will regard this as acceptable seduction rather than rape; it excludes men who use economic, organizational, or social power rather than actual or threatened force to overcome an unwilling but sub-ordinate, and therefore vulnerable female; it excludes the forced insertion of any other instrument, no matter how sharp or dangerous. Thus out of a whole range of 'sexual' acts where the balance of consent versus coercion is at least ambigu-ous, the criminal law draws a line demarcating those where physical force is used or threatened from those where any other kind of power is utilized to overcome a female's resistance. The outcome is that men who have few resources other than physical ones are more likely to commit legally defined rape, whilst those men who possess a whole range of resources from economic patronage to cultural charm are likely to be viewed by the law as 'real men' practising their primeval arts – and that is something the majesty of the law should leave alone!

The criminal law defines only some types of violence as criminal assault; it excludes verbal assaults that can, and sometimes do, break a person's spirit; it excludes forms of assault whose injuries become apparent years later, such as those resulting from working in a polluted factory environment where the health risk was known to the employer but concealed from the employee (Swartz, 1975); it excludes 'compulsory' drug-therapy or electric-shock treatment given to 'mentally disturbed' patients or prisoners who are denied the civilized rights to refuse such beneficial medical help (Mitford, 1977; Szasz, 1970, 1977a, 1977b); it excludes chemotherapy prescribed to control 'naughty' schoolboys, but includes physically hitting teachers (Box, 1981b; Schrag and Divoky, 1981).

The criminal law includes and reflects our proper stance against 'murderous' acts of terrorism conducted by people who are usually exploited or oppressed by forces of occupation. But it had no relevance, and its guardians remained mute ten years ago, when bombs, with the United States' and allied governments' blessing, fell like rain on women and children in Cambodia (Shawcross, 1979), or when the same governments aid and support other political/military regimes exercising mass terror and partial genocide against a subjugated people (Chomsky and Herman, 1979a, 1979b). The criminal law, in other words, condemns the importation of murderous terrorist acts usually against powerful individuals or strategic institutions, but goes all quiet when governments export or support avoidable acts of killing usually against the underdeveloped countries' poor. Of course there are exceptions – the Russian 'invasion' of Afghanistan was a viola-tion of international law and a crime against humanity. It may well have been, but what about Western governments' involvement in Vietnam, Laos, Cambodia, Chile, El Salvador, Nicaragua, Suez, and Northern Ireland? Shouldn't they at least be discussed within the same context of international law and crimes against humanity? And if not, why not?

Thus criminal laws against murder, rape, robbery and assault do protect us all, but they do not protect us all equally. They do not protect the less powerful from being killed, sexually exploited, deprived of what little property they possess, or physically and psychologically damaged through the greed, apathy, negligence, indifference and the unaccountability of the relatively more powerful.

Of course, what constitutes murder, rape, robbery, assault and other forms of serious crime varies over historical periods and between cultural groups, as the changes and contradictions *within* and *between* powerful interest groups, and the shifting alliances of the less powerful bring about slight and not-so-slight tilts of society's power axis (Chambliss, 1981). But it is not justifiable to conclude from this that criminal law reflects a value-consensus or even results from the state's neutral refereeing among competing interest groups. It is, however, plausible to view criminal laws as the outcomes of clashes between groups with structurally generated conflicting interests, and to argue that the legislators' intention, or if that is too conspiratorial, then the law's latent function, is to provide the powerful with a resource to reduce further the ability of some groups to resist domination. Needless to stress the point, it is a resource eagerly used to punish and deter actual and potential resisters and thereby help protect the established social order.

NOTHING BUT MYSTIFICATION

Unfortunately for those committed to the radical 'reflexive' view, there is nothing but mystification. Most people accept the 'official' view. They are very aware and sensitized to muggers, football hooligans, street vandals, housebreakers, thieves, terrorists and scroungers. But few are aware and sensitized to crimes committed by *corporate top and middle management* against stockholders, employees, consumers and the general public. Similarly there is only a fog, when it comes to crimes committed by *governments* (Douglas and Johnson, 1977), particularly when these victimize Third World countries (Shawcross, 1979) or become genocidal (Brown, 1971; Horowitz, 1977), or by *governmental control agencies* such as the police when they assault or use deadly force unwarrantedly against the public or suspected persons, or prison officers (Coggan and Walker, 1982; Thomas and Pooley, 1980), or special prison hospital staff when they brutalize and torture persons in their protective custody.

Few people are aware how men, who on the whole are more socially, economically, politically and physically powerful than women, use these resources frequently to *batter* wives and cohabitees (Dobash and Dobash, 1981), *sexually harass* their female (usually subordinate) co-workers, or *assault/rape* any woman who happens to be in the way. But we are very aware of female shoplifters and prostitutes, and those poor female adolescents who are 'beyond parental control' and in 'need of care and protection', even though this is a gross misrepresentation of female crime and though the relative absence of serious female crime contradicts the orthodox view that crime and powerlessness go hand in hand.

Few people become aware of crimes of the powerful or how serious these are, because their attention is glued to the highly publicized social characteristics of the convicted and imprisoned population. It is not directed to the records, files and occasional publications of those quasi-judicial organizations (such as the Factory Inspectorate in the UK or the Federal Drug Administration in the US) monitoring and regulating corporate and governmental crimes. Because of this, people make the attractive and easy deduction that those behind bars constitute our most serious criminals. As this captive audience is primarily young males amongst whom the unemployed and ethnic minorities are over-represented, it is believed that they, and those like them, constitute our 'public enemies'. Had the results of self-report/victimization surveys and the investigations of quasi-judicial agencies been publicized as much as 'official criminal statistics', and had the radical jaundiced and cynical view of criminal definitions been widely publicized, then the mystification produced by focusing exclusively on the characteristics of the prison population would not be so easily achieved. Instead, there would be a greater awareness of how the social construction of criminal definitions and the criminal justice system operate to bring about this misleading image of serious criminals.

Definitions of serious crime are essentially ideological constructs. They do not refer to those behaviours which objectively and *avoidably* cause us the most harm, injury and suffering. Instead they refer to only a sub-section of these behaviours, a sub-section which is more likely to be committed by young, poorly educated males who are often unemployed, live in working-class impoverished neighbourhoods, and frequently belong to an ethnic minority. Crime and criminalization are therefore *social control strategies*. They:

i render underprivileged and powerless people more likely to be arrested, convicted and sentenced to prison, even though the amount of personal damage and injury they cause may be less than the more powerful and privileged cause;

ii create the illusion that the 'dangerous' class is primarily located at the bottom of various hierarchies by which we 'measure' each other, such as occupational prestige, income level, housing market location, educational achievement, racial attributes – in this illusion it fuses relative poverty and criminal propensities and sees them both as effects of moral inferiority, thus rendering the 'dangerous' class deserving of both poverty and punishment;

iii render invisible the vast amount of avoidable harm, injury and deprivation imposed on the ordinary population by the state, transnational and other corporations, and thereby remove the effects of these 'crimes' from the causal nexus for explaining 'conventional crimes' committed by ordinary people. The conditions of life for the powerless created by the powerful are simply ignored by those who explain crime as a manifestation of individual pathology or local neighbourhood friendship and cultural patterns – yet in many respects the unrecognized victimization of the powerless by the powerful constitutes a part of those conditions under which the powerless choose to commit crimes;

iv elevate the criminal justice into a 'community service' – it is presented as being above politics and dispensing 'justice for all' irrespective of class, race, sex, or religion – this further legitimates the state and those whose interests it wittingly, or otherwise, furthers;

v make ordinary people even more dependent upon the state for protection against 'lawlessness' and the rising tidal wave of crime, even though it is the state and its agents who are often directly and indirectly victimizing ordinary people.

Not only does the state with the help and reinforcement of its control agencies, criminologists and the media conceptualize a particular and partial ideological version of serious crime and who commits it, but it does so by concealing and hence mystifying its own propensity for violence and serious crimes on a much larger scale. Matza captured this sad ironic 'truth' when he wrote:

> in its avid concern for public order and safety, implemented through police force and penal policy, the state is vindicated. By pursuing evil and producing the *appearance* of good, the state reveals its abiding method – the perpetuation of its good name in the face of its own propensity for violence, conquest, and destruction. Guarded by a collective representation in which theft and violence reside in a dangerous class, morally elevated by its correctional quest, the state achieves the legitimacy of its pacific intention and the acceptance of legality – even when it goes to war and massively perpetuates activities it has allegedly banned from the world. But that, the reader may say, is a different matter altogether. So says the state – and that is the final point of the collective representation [i.e. ideological construction – author]. (Matza, 1969: 196)

For too long too many people have been socialized to see crime and criminals through the eyes of the state. There is nothing left, as Matza points out, but mystification. This is clearly revealed in the brick wall of indignation which flattens any suggestion that the crime problem defined by the state is not the only crime problem, or that criminals are not only those processed by the state. There is more to crime and criminals than the state reveals. But most people cannot see it.

REFERENCES

Box, S. (1981a) *Deviance, Reality and Society*, 2nd edn. London: Holt, Rinehart and Winston.
Box, S. (1981b) 'Where have all the naughty children gone?', in National Deviancy Symposium, *Permissiveness and Control*, London: Macmillan.

Braithwaite, J. and Geis, G. (1981) 'On theory and action for corporate crime control'. Unpublished paper.

Brown, D. (1971) *Bury My Heart at Wounded Knee*. New York: Holt, Rinehart and Winston.

Chambliss, W.J. (1964) 'A sociological analysis of the law of vagrancy', *Social Problems*, 12: 46–67.

Chambliss, W.J. (1978) *On The Take: From Petty Crooks to Presidents*. Indiana: Indiana University Press.

Chambliss, W.J. (1981) 'The criminalization of conduct', in H.L. Ross (ed.), *Law and Deviance*. London: Sage.

Chomsky, N. and Herman, E.S. (1979a) *The Washington Connection and Third World Fascism*. Nottingham: Spokesman.

Chomsky, N. and Herman, E.S. (1979b) *After the Cataclysm*. Nottingham: Spokesman.

Coggan, G. and Walker, M. (1982) *Frightened For My Life: An Account of Deaths in British Prisons*. London: Fontana.

Dobash, R.E. and Dobash, R. (1981) *Violence Against Wives*. London: Open Books.

Douglas, J.D. and Johnson, J.M. (eds) (1977) *Official Deviance*. New York: Lippincott.

Duster, T. (1970) *The Legislation of Morality*. New York: Free Press.

Erickson, K.T. (1976) *Everything in its Path*. New York: Simon and Schuster.

Graham, J.M. (1972) 'Amphetamine politics on Capitol Hill', *Society*, 9: 14–23.

Gunningham, N. (1974) *Pollution, Social Interest and the Law*. London: Martin Robertson.

Hall, J. (1952) *Theft, Law and Society*, rev. edn. Indianapolis: Bobbs-Merrill.

Haskins, G. (1960) *Law and Authority in Early Massachusetts*. New York: Macmillan.

Hay, D. (1975) 'Property, authority and criminal law', in D. Hay et al., *Albion's Fatal Tree*. London: Allen Lane.

Hindelang, M.J., Gottfredson, M. and Garofalo, L. (1978) *Victims of Personal Crimes*. Cambridge, MA: Ballinger.

Hopkins, A. (1978) *Crime, Law and Business*. Canberra: Australian Institute of Criminology.

Hopkins, A. (1980a) 'Controlling corporate deviance', *Criminology*, 18: 198–214.

Hopkins, A. (1980b) 'Crimes against capitalism – an Australian case', *Contemporary Crises*, 4: 421–32.

Horowitz, I.L. (1977) *Genocide: State-Power and Mass Murder*, 2nd edn. New Jersey: Transaction Books.

Liazos, A. (1972) 'The poverty of the sociology of deviance: nuts, sluts and perverts', *Social Problems*, 20: 103–20.

Matza, D. (1969) *Becoming Deviant*. Englewood Cliffs, NJ: Prentice-Hall.

Mitford, J. (1977) *The American Prison Business*. London: Penguin.

Morgan, P. (1978) *Delinquent Fantasies*. London: Temple Smith.

McCaghy, C.H. and Denisoff, R.S. (1973) 'Pirates and politics', in R.S. Denisoff and C.H. McCaghy (eds), *Deviance, Conflict and Criminality*. Chicago: Rand-McNally.

Platt, A. (1969) *The Child Savers*. Chicago: Chicago University Press.

Schrag, P. and Divoky, D. (1981) *The Myth of the Hyperactive Child*. Harmondsworth: Penguin.

Schur, E.M. (1973) *Radical Non-Intervention*. Englewood Cliffs, NJ: Spectrum.

Shawcross, W. (1979) *Side Show: Kissinger, Nixon and the Destruction of Cambodia*. London: Andre Deutsch.

Silverman, M. and Lee, P.R. (1974) *Pills, Profits and Politics*. Berkeley, CA: University of California Press.

Smith, D.C. (1974) *'We're Not Mad, We're Angry'*. Vancouver: Women's Press.

Spitzer, S. (1975) 'Towards a Marxian theory of crime', *Social Problems*, 22: 368–401.

Sumner, C. (1976) 'Marxism and deviance theory', in P. Wiles (ed.), *Crime and Delinquency in Britain*, vol. 2. London: Martin Robertson.

Swartz, J. (1975) 'Silent killers at work', *Crime and Social Justice*, 3: 15–20.

Swigert, V. and Farrell, R. (1976) *Murder, Inequality and the Law*. Lexington, MA: Heath.

Swigert, V. and Farrell, R. (1981) 'Corporate homicide: definitional processes in the creation of deviance', *Law and Society Review*, 15: 161–82.

Szasz, T. (1970) *Ideology and Insanity*. New York: Anchor.

Szasz, T. (1977a) *Psychiatric Slavery*. New York: Free Press.

Szasz, T. (1977b) *The Theology of Medicine*. Oxford: Oxford University Press.

Thomas, J.E. and Pooley, R. (1980) *The Exploding Prison*. London: Junction Books.

Thompson, E.P. (1975) *Whigs and Hunters*. London: Allen Lane.

Wilson, J.Q. (1975) *Thinking About Crime*. New York: Basic Books.

26

Race and criminalization: black Americans and the punishment industry

Angela Y. Davis

[...]

When the structural character of racism is ignored in discussions about crime and the rising population of incarcerated people, the racial imbalance in jails and prisons is treated as a contingency, at best as a product of the 'culture of poverty,' and at worst as proof of an assumed black monopoly on criminality. The high proportion of black people in the criminal justice system is thus normalized and neither the state nor the general public is required to talk about and act on the meaning of that racial imbalance. Thus Republican and Democratic elected officials alike have successfully called for laws mandating life sentences for three-time 'criminals,' without having to answer for the racial implications of these laws. By relying on the alleged 'race-blindness' of such laws, black people are surreptitiously constructed as racial subjects, thus manipulated, exploited, and abused, while the structural persistence of racism – albeit in changed forms – in social and economic institutions, and in the national culture as a whole, is adamantly denied.

Crime is thus one of the masquerades behind which 'race,' with all its menacing ideological complexity, mobilizes old public fears *and* creates new ones. The current anticrime debate takes place within a reified mathematical realm – a strategy reminiscent of Malthus's notion of the geometrical increase in population and the arithmetical increase in food source, thus the inevitability of poverty and the means of suppressing it: war, disease, famine, and natural disasters. As a matter of fact, the persisting neo-Malthusian approach to population control, which,

From *The House that Race Built* (ed. W. Lubiano), pp. 264–78. (New York: Vintage Books, 1998.)

instead of seeking to solve those pressing social problems that result in real pain and suffering in people's lives, calls for the elimination of those suffering lives – finds strong resonances in the public discussion about expurgating the 'nation' of crime. These discussions include arguments deployed by those who are leading the call for more prisons and employ statistics in the same fetishistic and misleading way as Malthus did more than two centuries ago. Take for example James Wooten's comments in the *Heritage Foundation State Backgrounder:*

> If the 55% of the estimated 800,000 current state and federal prisoners who are violent offenders were subject to serving 85% of their sentence, and assuming that those violent offenders would have committed 10 violent crimes a year while on the street, then the number of crimes prevented each year by truth in sentencing would be 4,000,000. That would be over 2/3 of the 6,000,000 violent crimes reported.[1]

In *Reader's Digest*, Senior Editor Eugene H. Methvin writes:

> If we again double the present federal and state prison population – to somewhere between 1 million and 1.5 million and leave our city and county jail population at the present 400,000, we will break the back of America's 30 year crime wave.[2]

The real human beings – a vastly disproportionate number of whom are black and Latino/a men and women – designated by these numbers in a seemingly race-neutral way are deemed fetishistically exchangeable with the crimes they have or will allegedly commit. The real impact of imprisonment on their lives never need be examined. The inevitable part played by the punishment industry in the reproduction of crime never need be discussed. The dangerous and indeed fascistic trend toward progressively greater numbers of hidden, incarcerated human populations is itself rendered invisible. All that matters is the elimination of crime – and you get rid of crime by getting rid of people who, according to the prevailing racial common sense, are the most likely people to whom criminal acts will be attributed. Never mind that if this strategy is seriously and consistently pursued, the majority of young black men and fast-growing proportion of young black women will spend a good portion of their lives behind walls and bars in order to serve as a reminder that the state is aggressively confronting its enemy.[3]

While I do not want to locate a response to these arguments on the same level of mathematical abstraction and fetishism I have been problematizing, it is helpful, I think, to consider how many people are presently incarcerated or whose lives are subject to the direct surveillance of the criminal justice system. There are already approximately 1 million people in state and federal prisons in the United States, not counting the 500,000 in city and county jails or the 600,000 on parole or the 3 million people on probation or the 60,000 young people in juvenile facilities. Which is to say that there are presently over 5.1 million people either incarcerated, on parole, or on probation. Many of those presently on probation or parole would be behind bars under the conditions of the recently passed crime bill. According to the Sentencing Project, even before the passage of the crime bill, black people were 7.8 times more likely to be imprisoned that whites.[4] The Sentencing Project's most recent report[5] indicates that 32.2 percent of young black men and 12.3 percent of young Latino men between the ages of twenty and twenty-nine are either in prison, in jail, or on probation or parole. This is in comparison with 6.7 percent of young white men. A total of 827,440 young African-American males are under the supervision of the criminal justice system, at a cost of $6 billion per year. A major strength of the 1995 report, as compared to its predecessor, is its acknowledgement that the racialized impact of the criminal justice system is also gendered and that the relatively smaller number of African-American women drawn into the system should not relieve us of the responsibility of understanding the encounter of gender and race in arrest and incarceration practices. Moreover, the increases in women's contact with the criminal justice system have been even more dramatic than those of men.

> The 78% increase in criminal justice control rates for black women was more than double the increase for black men and for white women, and more than nine times the increase for white men. ... Although research on women of color in the criminal justice system is limited, existing data and research suggest that it is the combination of race and sex effects that is at the root of the trends which appear in our data. For example, while the number of blacks and Hispanics in prison is growing at an alarming rate, the rate of increase for women is even greater. Between 1980 and 1992 the female prison population increased 276%, compared to 163% for men. Unlike men of color, women of color thus belong to two groups that are experiencing particular dramatic growth in their contact with the criminal justice system.[6]

It has been estimated that by the year 2000 the number of people imprisoned will surpass 4 million, a grossly disproportionate number of whom will be black people, and that the cost will be over $40 billion a year,[7] a figure that is reminiscent of the way the military budget devoured – and continues to devour – the country's resources. This out-of-control punishment industry is an extremely effective criminalization industry, for the racial imbalance in incarcerated populations is not recognized as evidence of structural racism, but rather is invoked as a consequence of the assumed criminality of black people. In other words, the criminalization process works so well precisely because of the hidden logic of racism. Racist logic is deeply entrenched in the nation's material and psychic structures. It is something with which we are all very familiar. The logic, in fact, can persist, even when direct allusions to 'race' are removed.

Even those communities that are most deeply injured by this racist logic have learned how to rely upon it, particularly when open allusions to race are not necessary. Thus, in the absence of broad, radical grassroots movements in poor black communities so devastated by new forms of youth-perpetrated violence, the ideological options are extremely sparse. Often there are no other ways to express collective rage and despair but to demand that police sweep the community clean of crack and Uzis, and of the people who use and sell drugs and wield weapons. Ironically, Carol Moseley-Braun, the first black woman senator in our nation's history, was an enthusiastic sponsor of the Senate Anticrime Bill, whose passage in November 1993 paved the way for the August 25, 1994, passage of the bill by the House. Or perhaps there is little irony here. It may be precisely because there is a Carol Moseley-Braun in the Senate and a Clarence Thomas in the Supreme Court – and concomitant class differentiations and other factors responsible for far more heterogeneity in black communities than at any other time in this country's history – that implicit consent to antiblack racist logic (not to speak of racism toward other groups) becomes far more widespread among black people. Wahneema Lubiano's explorations of the complexities of state domination as it operates within and through the subjectivities of those who are the targets of this domination facilitates an understanding of this dilemma.[8]

Borrowing the title of Cornel West's recent work, race *matters*. Moreover, it matters in ways that are far more threatening and simultaneously less discernible than those to which we have grown accustomed. Race matters inform, more than ever, the ideological and material structures of U.S. society. And, as the current discourses on crime, welfare, and immigration reveal, race, gender, and class matter enormously in the continuing elaboration of public policy and its impact on the real lives of human beings.

And how does race matter? Fear has always been an integral component of racism. The ideological reproduction of a fear of black people, whether economically or sexually grounded, is rapidly gravitating toward and being grounded in a fear of crime. A question to be raised in this context is whether and how the increasing fear of crime – this ideologically produced fear of crime – serves to render racism simultaneously more invisible and more virulent. Perhaps one way to approach an answer to this question is to consider how this fear of crime effectively summons black people to imagine black people as the enemy. How many black people present at this conference have successfully extricated ourselves from the ideological power of the figure of the young black male as criminal – or at least seriously confronted it? The lack of a significant black presence in the rather feeble opposition to the 'three strikes, you're out' bills, which have been proposed and/or passed in forty states already, evidences the disarming effect of this ideology.

California is one of the states that has passed the 'three strikes, you're out' bill. Immediately after the passage of that bill, Governor Pete Wilson began to argue for a 'two strikes, you're out' bill. Three, he said, is too many. Soon we will hear calls for 'one strike, you're out.' Following this mathematical regression, we can imagine that at some point the hard-core anticrime advocates will be arguing that to stop the crime wave, we can't wait until even one crime is committed. Their slogan will be: 'Get them before the first strike!' And because certain populations have already been criminalized, there will be those who say, 'We know who the real criminals are – let's get them before they have a chance to act out their criminality.'

The fear of crime has attained a status that bears a sinister similarity to the fear of communism as it came to restructure social perceptions during the fifties and sixties. The figure of the 'criminal' – the racialized figure of the criminal – has come to represent the most menacing enemy of 'American society.' Virtually anything is acceptable – torture, brutality, vast expenditures of public funds – as long as it is done in the name of public safety. Racism has always found an easy route from its embeddedness in social structures to the psyches of collectives and individuals precisely because it mobilizes deep fears. While explicit, old-style racism may be increasingly socially unacceptable – precisely as a result of antiracist movements over the last forty years – this does not mean that U.S. society has been purged of racism. In fact, racism is more deeply embedded in socioeconomic structures, and the vast populations of incarcerated people of color is dramatic evidence of the way racism systematically structures economic relations. At the same time, this structural racism is rarely recognized as 'racism.' What we have come to recognize as open, explicit racism has in many ways begun to be replaced by a secluded, camouflaged kind of racism, whose influence on people's daily lives is as pervasive and systematic as the explicit forms of racism associated with the era of the struggle for civil rights.

The ideological space for the proliferations of this racialized fear of crime has been opened by the transformations in international politics created by the fall of the European socialist countries. Communism is no longer the quintessential enemy against which the nation imagines its identity. This space is now inhabited by ideological constructions of crime, drugs, immigration, and welfare. Of course, the enemy within is far more dangerous than the enemy without, and a black enemy within is the most dangerous of all.

Because of the tendency to view it as an abstract site into which all manner of undesirables are deposited, the prison is the perfect site for the simultaneous production and concealment of racism. The abstract character of the public perception of prisons militates against an engagement with the real issues afflicting the communities from which prisoners are drawn in such disproportionate numbers. This is the ideological work that the prison performs – it relieves us of the responsibility of seriously engaging with the problems of late capitalism, of transnational capitalism. The naturalization of black people as criminals thus also erects ideological barriers to an understanding of the connections between late-twentieth-century structural racism and the globalization of capital.

The vast expansion of the power of capitalist corporations over the lives of people of color and poor people in general has been accompanied by a waning anticapitalist consciousness. As capital moves with ease across national borders, legitimized by recent trade agreements such as NAFTA and GATT, corporations are allowed to close shop in the United States and transfer manufacturing operations to nations providing cheap labor pools. In fleeing organized labor in the U.S. to avoid paying higher wages and benefits, they leave entire communities in shambles, consigning huge numbers of people to joblessness, leaving them prey to the drug trade, destroying the economic base of these communities, thus affecting the education system, social welfare – and turning the people who live in those communities into perfect candidates for prison. At the same time, they create an economic demand for prisons, which stimulates the economy, providing jobs in the correctional industry for people who often come from the very populations that are criminalized by this process. It is a horrifying and self-reproducing cycle.

Ironically, prisons themselves are becoming a source of cheap labor that attracts corporate capitalism – as yet on a relatively small scale – in a way that parallels the attraction unorganized labor in Third World countries exerts. A statement by Michael Lamar Powell, a prisoner in Capshaw, Alabama, dramatically reveals this new development:

> I cannot go on strike, nor can I unionize. I am not covered by workers' compensation of the Fair Labor Standards Act. I agree to work late-night and weekend shifts. I do just what I am told, no matter what it is. I am hired and fired at will, and I am not even paid minimum wage: I earn one dollar a month. I cannot even voice grievances or complaints, except at the risk of incurring arbitrary discipline or some covert retaliation.
>
> You need not worry about NAFTA and your jobs going to Mexico and other Third World countries. I will have at least five percent of your jobs by the end of this decade.
>
> I am called prison labor. I am The New American Worker.[9]

This 'new American worker' will be drawn from the ranks of a racialized population whose historical superexploitation – from the era of slavery to the present – has been legitimized by racism. At the same time, the expansion of convict labor is accompanied in some states by the old paraphernalia of ankle chains that symbolically links convict labor with slave labor. At least three states – Alabama, Florida, and Arizona – have reinstituted the chain gang. Moreover, as Michael Powell so incisively reveals, there is a new dimension to the racism inherent in this process, which structurally links the superexploitation of prison labor to the globalization of capital.

In California, whose prison system is the largest in the country and one of the largest in the world, the passage of an inmate labor initiative in 1990 has presented businesses seeking cheap labor with opportunities uncannily similar to those in Third World countries. As of June 1994, a range of companies were employing prison labor in nine California prisons. Under the auspices of the Joint Venture Program, work now being performed on prison grounds includes computerized telephone messaging, dental apparatus assembly, computer data entry, plastic parts fabrication, electronic component manufacturing at the Central California Women's facility at Chowchilla, security glass manufacturing, swine production, oak furniture manufacturing, and the production of stainless steel tanks and equipment. In a California Corrections Department brochure designed to promote the program, it is described as 'an innovative public-private partnership that makes good business sense.'[10] According to the owner of Tower Communications, whom the brochure quotes,

> The operation is cost effective, dependable and trouble free. ... Tower Communications has successfully operated a message center utilizing inmates on the grounds of a California state prison. If you're in business leader planning expansion, considering relocation because of a deficient labor pool, starting a new enterprise, look into the benefits of using inmate labor.

The employer benefits listed by the brochure include

federal and state tax incentives; no benefit package (retirement pay, vacation pay, sick leave, medical benefits); long term lease agreements at far below market value costs; discount rates on Workers Compensation; build a consistent, qualified work force; on call labor pool (no car breakdowns, no babysitting problems); option of hiring job-ready ex-offenders and minimizing costs; becoming a partner in public safety.

There is a major, yet invisible, racial supposition in such claims about the profitability of a convict labor force. The acceptability of the superexploitation of convict labor is largely based on the historical conjuncture of racism and incarceration practices. The already disproportionately black convict labor force will become increasingly black if the racially imbalanced incarceration practices continue.

The complicated yet unacknowledged structural presence of racism in the U.S. punishment industry also includes the fact that the punishment industry which sequesters ever-larger sectors of the black population attracts vast amounts of capital. Ideologically, as I have argued, the racialized fear of crime has begun to succeed the fear of communism. This corresponds to a structural tendency for capital that previously flowed toward the military industry to now move toward the punishment industry. The ease with which suggestions are made for prison construction costing in the multibillions of dollars is reminiscent of the military buildup: economic mobilization to defeat communism has turned into economic mobilization to defeat crime. The ideological construction of crime is thus complemented and bolstered by the material construction of jails and prisons. The more jails and prisons are constructed, the greater the fear of crime, and the greater the fear of crime, the stronger the cry for more jails and prisons, ad infinitum.

The law enforcement industry bears remarkable parallels to the military industry (just as there are anti-Communist resonances in the anti-crime campaign). This connection between the military industry and the punishment industry is revealed in a *Wall Street Journal* article entitled 'Making Crime Pay: The Cold War of the '90s':

Parts of the defense establishment are cashing in, too, scenting a logical new line of business to help them offset military cutbacks. Westinghouse Electric Corp, Minnesota Mining and Manufacturing Co, GDE Systems (a division of the old General Dynamics) and Alliant Techsystems Inc., for instance, are pushing crime-fighting equipment and have created special divisions to retool their defense technology for America's streets.

According to the article, a conference sponsored by the National Institute of Justice, the research arm of the Justice Department, was organized around the theme 'Law Enforcement Technology in the 21st Century.' The secretary of defense was a major presenter at this conference, which explored topics like 'the role of the defense industry, particularly for dual use and conversion':

Hot topics: defense-industry technology that could lower the level of violence involved in crime fighting. Sandia National Laboratories, for instance, is experimenting with a dense foam that can be sprayed at suspects, temporarily blinding and deafening them under breathable bubbles. Stinger Corporation is working on 'smart guns,' which will fire only for the owner, and retractable spiked barrier strips to unfurl in front of fleeing vehicles. Westinghouse is promoting the 'smart car,' in which mini-computers could be linked up with big mainframes at the police department, allowing for speedy booking of prisoners, as well as quick exchanges of information.[11]

Again, race provides a silent justification for the technological expansion of law enforcement, which, in turn, intensifies racist arrest and incarceration practices. This skyrocketing punishment industry, whose growth is silently but powerfully sustained by the persistence of racism, creates an economic demand for more jails and prisons and thus for similarly spiraling criminalization practices, which, in turn fuels the fear of crime.

Most debates addressing the crisis resulting from overcrowding in prisons and jails focus on male institutions. Meanwhile, women's institutions and jail space for women are proportionately proliferating at an even more astounding rate than men's. If race is largely an absent factor in the discussions about crime and punishment, gender seems not even to merit a place carved out by its absence. Historically, the imprisonment of women has served to criminalize women in a way that is more complicated than is the case with men. This female criminalization process has had more to do with the marking of certain groups of women as undomesticated and hypersexual, as women who refuse to embrace the nuclear family as paradigm. The current liberal-conservative discourse around welfare criminalizes black single mothers, who are represented as deficient, manless, drug-using breeders of children, and as reproducers of an attendant culture of poverty. The woman who does drugs is criminalized both because she is a drug user and because, as a consequence, she cannot be a good mother. In some states, pregnant women are being imprisoned for using crack because of possible damage to the fetus.

According to the U.S. Department of Justice, women are far more likely than men to be imprisoned for a drug conviction.[12] However, if women wish to receive treatment for their drug problems, often their only option, if they cannot pay for a drug program, is to be arrested and sentenced to a drug program via the criminal justice system. Yet when U.S. Surgeon General Joycelyn Elders alluded to the importance of opening discussion on the decriminalization of drugs, the Clinton administration immediately disassociated itself from her remarks. Decriminalization of drugs would greatly reduce the numbers of incarcerated women, for the 278 percent increase in the numbers of black women in state and federal prisons (as compared to the 186 percent increase in the numbers of black men) can be largely attributed to the phenomenal rise in drug-related and specifically crack-related imprisonment. According to the Sentencing Project's 1995 report, the increase amounted to 828 percent.[13]

Official refusals to even consider decriminalization of drugs as a possible strategy that might begin to reverse present incarceration practices further bolsters the ideological staying power of the prison. In his well-known study of the history of the prison and its related technologies of discipline, Michel Foucault pointed out that an evolving contradiction is at the very heart of the historical project of imprisonment.

> For a century and a half, the prison has always been offered as its own remedy: ... the realization of the corrective project as the only method of overcoming the impossibility of implementing it.[14]

As I have attempted to argue, within the U.S. historical context, racism plays a pivotal role in sustaining this contradiction. In fact, Foucault's theory regarding the prison's tendency to serve as its own enduring justification becomes even more compelling if the role of race is also acknowledged. Moreover, moving beyond the parameters of what I consider the double impasse implied by his theory – the discursive impasse his theory discovers and that of the theory itself – I want to conclude by suggesting the possibility of radical race-conscious strategies designed to disrupt the stranglehold of criminalization and incarceration practices.

In the course of a recent collaborative research project with U.C. Santa Barbara sociologist Kum-Kum Bhavnani, in which we interviewed thirty-five women at the San Francisco County Jail, the complex ways in which race and gender help to produce a punishment industry that reproduces the very problems it purports to solve became dramatically apparent. Our interviews focused on the women's ideas about imprisonment and how they themselves imagine alternatives to incarceration. Their various critiques of the prison system and of the existing 'alternatives,' all of which are tied to reimprisonment as a last resort, led us to reflect more deeply about the importance of retrieving, retheorizing, and reactivating the radical abolitionist strategy first proposed in connection with the prison-reform movements of the sixties and seventies.

We are presently attempting to theorize women's imprisonment in ways that allow us to formulate a radical abolitionist strategy departing from, but not restricted in its conclusions to, women's jails and prisons. Our goal is to formulate alternatives to incarceration that substantively reflect the voices and agency of a variety of imprisoned women. We wish to open up channels for their involvement in the current debates around alternatives to incarceration, while not denying our own role as mediators and interpreters and our own political positioning in these debates. We also want to distinguish our explorations of alternatives from the spate of 'alternative punishments' or what are now called 'intermediate sanctions' presently being proposed and/or implemented by and through state and local correctional systems.

This is a long-range project that has three dimensions: academic research, public policy, and community organizing. In other words, for this project to be successful, it must build bridges between academic work, legislative and other policy interventions, and grassroots campaigns calling, for example, for the decriminalization of drugs and prostitution – and for the reversal of the present proliferation of jails and prisons.

Raising the possibility of abolishing jails and prisons as the institutionalized and normalized means of addressing social problems in an era of migrating corporations, unemployment and homelessness, and collapsing public services, from health care to education, can hopefully help to interrupt the current law-and-order discourse that has such a grip on the collective imagination, facilitated as it is by deep and hidden influences of racism. This late-twentieth-century 'abolitionism,' with its nineteenth-century resonances, may also lead to a historical recontextualization of the practice of imprisonment. With the passage of the Thirteenth Amendment, slavery was abolished for all except convicts – and in a sense the exclusion from citizenship accomplished by the slave system has persisted within the U.S. prison system. Only three states allow prisoners to vote, and approximately 4 million people are denied the right to vote because of their present or past incarceration. A radical strategy to abolish jails and prisons as the normal way of dealing with the social problems of late capitalism is not a strategy for abstract abolition. It is designed to force a rethinking of the increasingly repressive role of the state during this era of late capitalism and to carve out a space for resistance.

NOTES

1 Charles S. Clark, 'Prison Overcrowding,' *Congressional Quarterly Researcher* 4, no. 5 (Feb. 4, 1994): 97–119.
2 Ibid.
3 Marc Mauer, 'Young Black Men and the Criminal Justice System: A Growing National Problem,' Washington, D.C.: The Sentencing Project, February 1990.
4 Alexander Cockburn, *Philadelphia Inquirer*, August 29, 1994.
5 Marc Mauer and Tracy Huling, 'Young Black Americans and the Criminal Justice System: Five Years Later,' Washington, D.C.: The Sentencing Project, October 1995.
6 Ibid., 18.
7 *See* Cockburn.
8 *See* Lubiano's essay ... as well as 'Black Ladies, Welfare Queens, and State Minstrels: Ideological War by Narrative Means,' in *Race-ing Justice, En-gendering Power: Essays on Anita Hill, Clarence Thomas, and the Construction of Social Reality*, ed. Toni Morrison (New York: Pantheon, 1992), 323–63.
9 Unpublished essay, 'Modern Slavery American Style,' 1995.
10 I wish to acknowledge Julie Brown, who acquired this brochure from the California Department of Correction in the course of researching the role of convict labor.
11 *Wall Street Journal*, May 12, 1994.
12 Lawrence Rence, A. Greenfield, Stephanie Minor-Harper, *Women in Prison* (Washington, D.C.: U.S. Dept. of Justice, Office of Justice Programs, Bureau of Statistics, 1991).
13 Mauer and Huling, 'Young Black Americans,' 19.
14 Michel Foucault, *Discipline and Punish: The Birth of the Prison*, trans. Alan Sheridan (New York: Vintage, 1979), 395.

27

Critical criminology and the concept of crime

Louk H.C. Hulsman

ARE CRIMINAL EVENTS EXCEPTIONAL? PROBLEMATIZING THE NORMAL OUTLOOK ON CRIME

[...]

People who are involved in 'criminal' events do not appear in themselves to form a special category of people. Those who are officially recorded as 'criminal' constitute only a small part of those involved in events that legally are considered to require criminalization. Among them young men from the most disadvantaged sections of the population are heavily over-represented.

Within the concept of criminality a broad range of situations are linked together. Most of these, however, have separate properties and no common denominator: violence within the family, violence in an anonymous context in the streets, breaking into private dwellings, completely divergent ways of illegal receiving of goods, different types of conduct in traffic, pollution of the environment, some forms of political activities. Neither in the motivation of those who are involved in such events, nor in the nature of the consequences or in the possibilities of dealing with them (be it in a preventive sense, or in the sense of the control of the conflict) is there any common structure to be discovered. All [that] these events have in common is that the CJS [criminal justice system] is authorized to take action against them. Some of these events cause considerable suffering to those involved, quite often affecting both perpetrator and victim. Consider for example traffic accidents and violence within the family. The vast majority of the events which are dealt with within the CJS in the sphere of crime, however, would not score particularly high on an imaginary scale of personal hardship. Matrimonial difficulties, difficulties between

From *Contemporary Crises*, 1986, 10(1): 63–80.

parents and children, serious difficulties at work and housing problems will, as a rule, be experienced as more serious both as to degree and duration. If we compare 'criminal events' with other events, there is – on the level of those directly involved – nothing which distinguishes those 'criminal' events intrinsically from other difficult or unpleasant situations. Nor are they singled out as a rule by those directly involved themselves to be dealt with in a way differing radically from the way other events are dealt with. Last, not least, some of these events are considered by those directly involved (and sometimes also by 'observers') as positive and harmless.

It is therefore not surprising that a considerable proportion of the events which would be defined as serious crime within the context of the CJS remain completely outside that system. They are settled within the social context in which they take place (the family, the trade union, the professional association, the circle of friends, the workplace, the neighbourhood) in a similar way as other non-criminal trouble.

All this means that there is no 'ontological reality' of crime.

CRITICAL CRIMINOLOGY AND THE CONCEPT OF CRIME: WHAT HAS BEEN PROBLEMATIZED AND WHAT NOT?

Critical criminology has naturally problematized and criticized many of the 'normal' notions about crime [...]. The contribution to this form of 'debunking' varies according to the different perspectives of the stream of critical criminology involved. In a certain period, Marxist criminology predominantly took the stand that 'crime' was a product of the capitalistic system, and that crime would disappear if a new society took birth. In this perspective the disappearance of 'crime' was seen as a disappearance of the 'problematic situations' which are supposed to trigger the criminalization processes. Disappearance of crime was not seen as 'the disappearance of criminalization processes *as an answer* to problematic situations'. In a later stage, critical criminology problematized the class-biased and 'irrational' aspects of the processes of primary and secondary criminalization. In those endeavours the 'functionality' as well as the 'legal equality principle', which are so often invoked as legitimation of processes of primary criminalization, were de-mystified. On the basis of such a de-mystification, critical criminology has argued for partial decriminalization, a more restrictive policy with respect to recourse to criminal law, radical non-intervention with respect to certain crimes and certain criminals. It has pointed to the far more weighty crimes of the powerful and asked for a change in criminal justice activities from the weak and the working class towards 'white-collar crime'. It has pictured the war against crime as a sidetrack from the class struggle, at best an illusion invented to sell news, at worst an attempt to make the poor scapegoats. With very few exceptions, however, the concept of crime as such, the ontological reality of crime, has not been challenged. [...]

WHAT DOES IT MEAN WHEN WE DO NOT PROBLEMATIZE (AND REJECT) THE CONCEPT OF CRIME?

When we do not problematize (and reject) the concept of crime it means that we are stuck in a catascopic view on society in which our informational base (as well the 'facts' as their 'interpretational frame') depends mainly on the institutional framework of criminal justice. It means therefore that we do not take effectively into account the critical analyses of this institutional framework by 'critical criminology'. [...] [C]ritical criminology has to abandon a catascopic view on social reality, based on the definitional activities of the system which is the subject of its study, and has instead to take an anascopic stance towards social reality. This makes it necessary to abandon as a tool in the conceptual frame of criminology the notion of 'crime'. Crime has no ontological reality. Crime is not the *object* but the *product* of criminal policy. Criminalization is one of the many ways to construct social reality. In other words, when someone (person or organization) wants to criminalize, this implies that he:

1 deems a certain 'occurrence' or 'situation' as undesirable;

2 attributes that undesirable occurrence to an individual;

3 approaches this particular kind of individual behaviour with a specific style of social control: the style of punishment;

4 applies a very particular style of punishment which is developed in a particular (legal) professional context and which is based on a 'scholastic' (last-judgement) perspective on the world. In this sense the style of punishment used in criminal justice differs profoundly from the styles of punishment in other social contexts;

5 wants to work in a special organizational setting – criminal justice. This organizational setting is characterized by a very developed division of labour, a lack of accountability for the process as a whole and a lack of influence of those directly involved in the 'criminalized' event on the outcome of the process.

[...]

DEVELOPING AN ANASCOPIC VIEW

Defining and dealing with trouble outside a formal context
[...]

The meanings which those directly involved (and observers) bestow upon situations influence how they will deal with them. Laura Nader (1980) distinguishes the following procedures people use in dealing with trouble:

- *Lumping it.* The issue or problem that gave rise to a disagreement is simply ignored and the relationship with the person who is part of the disagreement is continued.

- *Avoidance or exit.* This option entails withdrawing from a situation or curtailing or terminating a relationship by leaving.

- *Coercion.* This involves unilateral action.

- *Negotiation.* The two principal parties are the decision makers, and the settlement of the matter is one to which both parties agree, without the aid of a third party. They do not seek a solution in terms of rules, but try to create the rules by which they can organize their relationship with one another.

- *Mediation.* Mediation, in contrast, involves a third party who intervenes in a dispute to aid the principals in reaching an agreement.

- Other procedural modes that are used in attempts to handle trouble are *arbitration* and *adjudication.* In *arbitration* both principals consent to the intervention of a third party whose judgement they must agree to accept beforehand. When we speak about *adjudication* we refer to the presence of a third party who has the authority to intervene in a dispute whether or not the principals wish it.

The list of ways of dealing with trouble which Nader gives is by no means exhaustive. People can address themselves for help to different professional or nonprofessional settings. They may engage in a 'ritual of reordering' which does not involve the other person earlier implied in the problematic situation (Pfohl, 1981).

People may also engage in collective action to bring about a structural change in the situations which cause them trouble (Abel, 1982).

Which of these many courses of action will an involved person choose?

The meaning which a directly involved person bestows upon a situation will influence [...] his course of action. That course of action will also be influenced by the degree to which different strategies to deal with trouble are available and accessible for him; in other words, the degree to which he has a real possibility of choice. This degree of choice is largely influenced by his place in the network of power which shapes his environment and by his practical possibilities to change the 'tribes' of which he is a part for other ones.

Formal and informal ways of defining trouble and dealing with it compared

The process of bestowing meaning on what is going on in life is flexible in face to face relations in so far as those involved in this process feel relatively 'free' towards each other as equal human beings. In other words, if they feel not constrained by the requirements of organizational or professional roles, and [if] they are not caught in a power relation which prevents some of the parties [from fully taking part] in this process. This flexibility has many advantages. It increases the possibilities to reach by negotiation a common meaning of problematic situations. It provides also possibilities for learning. Experience can teach people that the application of a certain frame of interpretation and a certain focus does not lead very far in certain sectors of life.

This flexibility is often lacking when situations are defined and dealt with in a highly formalized context. The more such a context is specialized, the more the freedom of definition – and thus of reaction – is limited by a high degree of division of labour or by a high degree of professionalization. In such a case it depends on the type of institution which has – fortuitously – taken the case up which definition and which answer will be given. It is improbable that a definition and a reaction provided for in such a context [will correspond] with the definition and reactions of [those directly] involved.

There are, however, important differences in the degree of flexibility which formal institutions involved in a problematic situation show. In many countries we find a high degree of flexibility in parts of the police organization, e.g. the neighbourhood police. The same may be true of the first echelons of the health and social work system. Of all formalized control systems the criminal justice system seems the most inflexible. The organizational context (high division of labour) and the internal logic of its specific frame of interpretation (peculiar style of punishment in which a gravity scale modelled according to the 'last judgement' plays an overriding role) both contribute to this inflexibility. Another factor in the particularly alienating effect of criminal justice involvement in problematic situations is its extremely narrow focus: only very specific events modelled in accordance with a legal incrimination may be taken into account and these may only be considered as they were supposed to be [at] a certain moment in time. The dynamic side of constructing reality [is lacking] completely in this particular system. Thus the construction of reality as it is pursued in criminal justice will practically never coincide with the dynamics of the construction of reality of [those directly] involved. In criminal justice one is generally deciding on a reality which exists only within the system and seldom finds a counterpart in the outside world. [...]

CONCLUSION

What would be the task of a critical criminology which has abandoned, according to the view developed above, 'crime' as a conceptual tool? The main tasks of such a critical criminology can be summarized as follows:

1   Continue to describe, explain and demystify the activities of criminal justice and its adverse social effects. This activity should, however, be more directed than up till now to the defining activities of this system. To do that, it would be necessary to compare in concrete fields of human life the activities of criminal justice (and their social effects) with those of other formal control systems (legal ones, like the civil justice system, and non-legal ones, like the medical and social work systems). The activities of those formal control systems with respect to a

certain area of life should be at the same time compared with informal ways of dealing with such an area of life. In such a task, critical criminology can be stimulated by the developments in (legal) anthropology and in a more general way by sociology in an interpretative paradigm. This implies abandoning 'behaviour' and deviance as a starting-point for analysis and adopting instead a situation-oriented approach, micro and macro.

2   Illustrate – but only as a way of example without pretending to be a 'science of problematic situations' – how in a specific field problematic situations could be addressed at different levels of the societal organization without having recourse to criminal justice.

3   Study strategies [on] how to abolish criminal justice; in other words, how to liberate organizations like the police and the courts [from] a system of reference which turns them away [from] the variety of life and the needs of those directly involved.

4   One of these strategies ought to be to contribute to the development of another overall language in which questions related to criminal justice and to public problems which generate claims to criminalization can be discussed without the bias (Cohen, 1985) of the present 'control babble'.

REFERENCES

Abel, R. (ed.) (1982) *The Politics of Informal Justice*. New York: Academic Press.
Cohen, S. (1985) *Visions of Social Control*. Cambridge: Polity.
Nader, L. (ed.) (1980) *No Access to Law: Alternatives to the American Judicial System*. New York: Academic Press.
Pfohl, S J. (1981) 'Labelling criminals', in H.L. Ross (ed.), *Law and Deviance*, Beverly Hills, CA: Sage.

28

The need for a radical realism

Jock Young

[...]

A silent revolution has occurred in conventional criminology in the United States and in Great Britain. The demise of positivism and social democratic ways of reforming crime has been rapid. A few perceptive commentators have noted the sea-change in the orthodox centre of criminology but the extent of the paradigm shift has been scarcely analysed, or its likely impact understood.

The first sighting of realignment in Western criminology was in a perceptive article written in 1977 by Tony Platt and Paul Takagi entitled 'Intellectuals for law and order' (Platt and Takagi, 1981). They grouped together writers such as Ernest van den Haag, James Q. Wilson and Norval Morris and noted how they represented the demise of 'liberal', social democratic ways of understanding crime and prisons in the United States. 'Intellectuals for law and order are not a criminological fad', they write, but 'a decisive influence in criminology' (Platt and Takagi, 1981: 54). Developing this line of argument, Donald Cressey writes:

> The tragedy is in the tendency of modern criminologists to drop the search for causes and to join the politicians rather than develop better ideas about why crime flourishes, for example, these criminologists Wilson, and van den Haag, Ehrlich, Fogel, Morris and Hawkins – and hundreds of others – seem satisfied with a technological criminology whose main concern is for showing policy-makers how to repress criminals and criminal justice work more efficiently, [and he adds:] If more and more criminologists respond – and they seem to be doing so – criminology will eventually have only 'handcuffs 1a' orientation. (Cressey, 1978)

There is an unfortunate tendency to conflate these various thinkers together as if they were politically similar. But van den Haag is very much a traditional

---

From *Confronting Crime* (eds R. Matthews and J. Young), pp. 9–30. (London: Sage, 1986.)

conservative whereas Morris is a 'J.S. Mill' type of liberal and Wilson differs explicitly from both of them. Such a confusion makes it difficult to understand the particular purchase which writers such as James Q. Wilson in the United States and Ron Clarke in Britain have had on the new administrative criminology and their ability to mobilize writers of various positions in support for a broad policy. The basis of this is what all these writers have in common, namely:

1   An antagonism to the notion of crime being determined by social circumstances – 'the smothering of sociological criminology' as Cressey puts it.

2   A lack of interest in aetiology. As Platt and Takagi note: '[they] are basically uninterested in the causes of crime. For them, it's a side issue, a distraction and a waste of their valuable time' (Platt and Takagi, 1981: 45). The historic research programme of criminology into causes and the possibilities of rehabilitation is thus abandoned.

3   A belief in human choice in the criminal act.

4   An advocacy of deterrence.

The key figure in this shift is James Q. Wilson in his role as a theoretician, as author of the bestselling book *Thinking About Crime* and as an adviser to the Reagan administration. His central problem and starting-point is the aetiological crisis of social democratic positivist theory and practice:

If in 1960 one had been asked what steps society might take to prevent a sharp increase in the crime rate, one might well have answered that crime could best be curtailed by reducing poverty, increasing educational attainment, eliminating dilapidated housing, encouraging community organization, and providing troubled or delinquent youth with counseling services ....

Early in the decade of the 1960s, this country began the longest sustained period of prosperity since World War II, much of it fueled, as we later realized, by a semi-war economy. A great array of programs aimed at the young, the poor, and the deprived were mounted. Though these efforts were not made primarily out of a desire to reduce crime, they were wholly consistent with – indeed, in their aggregate money levels, wildly exceeded – the policy prescription that a thoughtful citizen worried about crime would have offered at the beginning of the decade.

Crime soared. It did not just increase a little; it rose at a faster rate and to higher levels than at any time since the 1930s and, in some categories, to higher levels than any experienced in this century.

It all began in about 1963. That was the year, to over-dramatize a bit, that a decade began to fall apart. (Wilson, 1975: 3–4)

What then can be done about crime? Wilson does not rule out that crime may be caused by psychological factors or by the breakdown of family structure. But he argues that there is little that public policy can do in this region. He adamantly rules out the option of reducing crime by improving social conditions. In terms of this interpretation of the aetiological crises – the amelioration of social conditions has resulted in an exponential rise in crime rather than its decline. Thus reform on any level is discarded and with it the notion that the reduction of crime can be achieved by an increase in social justice. But there are other factors that policy can manipulate and it is to these that Wilson turns his attention.

Although the poor commit crime more than the rich, he notes that only a small minority of the poor ever commit crimes. People obviously, then, have a choice in the matter; furthermore, these moral choices can be affected by the circumstances decreed by governments. And here he focuses in on the jugular of liberal thinking about crime and punishment:

> If objective conditions are used to explain crime, spokesmen who use poverty as an explanation of crime should, by the force of their own logic, be prepared to consider the capacity of society to deter crime by raising the risks of crime. But they rarely do. Indeed, those who use poverty as an explanation are largely among the ranks of those who vehemently deny that crime can be deterred. (Wilson, 1975: xiv. See also Van den Haag, 1975: 84–90.)

The goal of social policy must be to build up effective deterrents to crime. The problem is not to be solved, he argues, by the conservative measures of draconian punishments but rather by an increase of police effectiveness; the certainty of punishment, not its severity, is his key to government action. Thus Wilson differentiates his view from both conservatives and 'liberal'/social democrats. He advocates punishment but punishment which is appropriate and effective. He sees the informal controls of community as eventually more important than the formal, but that in areas where community has broken down and there is a high incidence of crime, formal control through policing can regenerate the natural regulative functions of the community (the influential Wilson-Kelling hypothesis, see Wilson and Kelling, 1982).

This intellectual current is immensely influential on policy-making in the United States. Thus, the working party set up in the United States in the early years of the Reagan administration under the chairmanship of Wilson gave a low priority, amongst other things, to 'the aetiology of delinquency and a high rating to work in the area of the effects of community cohesiveness and policing for controlling crime' (see Trasler, 1984; Wilson, 1982).

A similar 'social control' theory of crime has been dominant in Britain at the Home Office Research Unit in the recent period particularly influenced by their major theoretician Ron Clarke (see Clarke, 1980). Here, as with Wilson, causal theories of crime came under caution as unproven or impractical (Clarke calls them disposition theories). Situational factors, however, are eminently manipulable. The focus should, therefore, be on making the opportunities for crime more difficult through target hardening, reducing the opportunities for crime and increasing the risks of being caught. This represents a major shift in emphasis against the dispositional bias in almost all previous criminologies.

This move to administrative criminology (or varieties of 'control theory' as Downes and Rock, 1982, would have it) represents the re-emergence of neo-classicist theory on a grand scale. The classicist theory of Beccaria and Bentham had many defects, among them a uniform notion of the impact of the various deterrent devices legislated to control crime (see Rutter and Giller, 1983: 261–2). By introducing concepts of differential risk and opportunity as variables which can be varied by policy-makers and police on a territorial basis, they add a considerable refinement to this model of control. [...]

LEFT IDEALISM: THE LOSS OF A CRIMINOLOGY

I have detailed elsewhere the fundamental characteristics of left idealism (Lea and Young, 1984; Young, 1979). Suffice it to say that the tenets of left idealism are simple and familiar to all of us. Crime is seen to occur amongst working-class people as an inevitable result of their poverty, the criminal sees through the inequitable nature of present day society and crime itself is an attempt – however clumsily and ill-thought out – to redress this balance. There is little need to have complex explanations for working-class crime. Its causes are obvious and to blame the poor for their criminality is to blame the victim, to point moral accusations at those whose very actions are a result of their being social casualties. In contrast, the real crime on which we should focus is that of the ruling class: the police, the corporations and the state agencies. This causes real problems for the mass of people, unlike working-class crime which is seen as minor, involving petty theft and occasional violence, of little impact to the working-class community. If the causes of working-class crime are obviously poverty, the causes of upper-class crime are equally obvious: the natural cupidity and power-seeking of the powerful as they enact out the dictates of capital. Criminal law in this context is a direct expression of the ruling class; it is concerned with the protection of their property and the consolidation of their political power. The 'real' function of policing is political rather than the control of crime *per se*; it is social order rather than crime control which is the *raison d'être* of the police.

[...]

THE CONVERGENCE BETWEEN LEFT IDEALISM AND ADMINISTRATIVE CRIMINOLOGY

I have noted that the anomaly which traditional positivist criminology confronted was what I have termed the aetiological crisis; that is, a rapidly rising crime rate despite the increase in all the circumstances which were supposed to decrease crime. This was coupled by a crisis in rehabilitation – the palpable failure of the prison system despite decades of penal 'reform'. With the passing of the 1960s the new administrative criminology concluded that, given that affluence itself had led to crime, it was social control which was the only variable worth focusing upon. On the other hand, left idealism forgot about the affluent period altogether and found the correlation between crime and the recession too obvious to merit a discussion of aetiology. If administrative criminology sidestepped the aetiological crisis, left idealism conveniently forgot about it. Both, from their own political perspective, saw social control as the major focus of the study, both were remarkably unsophisticated in their analysis of control within the wider society – and anyway were attempting the impossible, to explain the crime control whilst ignoring the causes of crime itself – the other half of the equation.

In a way, such a convergence suggests a stasis in criminological theory. And, of course, this is precisely what has occurred over the past ten years. But, as I have tried to indicate, theory is very much influenced by changes in empirical data and in social and political developments. And it is in this direction, particularly in the phenomenal rise of criminal victimization studies, that we must look for the motor forces which begin to force criminology back to theory.

The empirical anomalies arising from both radical and conventional victimology were a major spur to the formation of realist criminology. Paradoxically, findings which nestled so easily with administrative criminology caused conceptual abrasions with left idealism. Thus, as the crisis of aetiology waned, the problem of the victim became predominant.

THE NATURE OF LEFT REALISM

> The basic defect of pathology and of its romantic opposite is that both yield concepts that are untrue to the phenomenon and which thus fail to illuminate it. Pathology reckons without the patent tenability and durability of deviant enterprise, and without the subjective capacity of man to create novelty and manage diversity. Romance, as always, obscures the seamier and more mundane aspects of the world. It obscures the stress that may underlie resilience. (Matza, 1969: 44)

The central tenet of left realism is to reflect the reality of crime, that is in its origins, its nature and its impact. This involves a rejection of tendencies to romanticize crime or to pathologize it, to analyse solely from the point of view of the administration of crime or the criminal actor, to underestimate crime or to exaggerate it. And our understanding of methodology, our interpretation of the statistics, our notions of aetiology follow from this. Most importantly, it is realism which informs our notion of practice: in answering what can be done about the problems of crime and social control.

It is with this in mind that I have mapped out the fundamental principles of left realism […]

It is unrealistic to suggest that the problem of crime like mugging is merely the problem of mis-categorization and concomitant moral panics. If we choose to embrace this liberal position, we leave the political arena open to conservative campaigns for law and order – for, however exaggerated and distorted the arguments conservatives may marshal, the reality of crime in the streets *can be* the reality of human suffering and personal disaster. (Young, 1975: 89)

To be realistic about crime as a problem is not an easy task. We are caught between two currents, one which would grotesquely exaggerate the problems of crime, another covering a wide swathe of political opinion that may seriously underestimate the extent of the problem. Crime is a staple of news in the Western mass media and police fiction a major genre of television drama. We have detailed elsewhere the structured distortion of images of crime, victimization and policing which occur in the mass media (see Cohen and Young, 1981). It is a commonplace of criminological research that most violence is between acquaintances and is intra-class and intra-racial. Yet the media abound with images of the dangerous stranger. On television we see folk monsters who are psychopathic killers or serial murderers yet offenders who even remotely fit these caricatures are extremely rare. The police are portrayed as engaged in an extremely scientific investigative policy with high clear-up rates and exciting denouements although the criminologist knows that this is far from the humdrum nature of reality. Furthermore, it grossly conceals the true relationship between police and public in the process of detection, namely that there is an extremely high degree of dependence of the police on public reporting and witnessing of crime.

The nature of crime, of victimization and of policing is thus systematically distorted in the mass media. And it is undoubtedly true that such a barrage of misinformation has its effect – although perhaps scarcely in such a one-to-one way that is sometimes suggested. For example, a typical category of violence in Britain is a man battering his wife. But this is rarely represented in the mass media – instead we have numerous examples of professional criminals engaged in violent crime – a quantitatively minor problem when compared to domestic violence. So presumably the husband can watch criminal violence on television and not see himself there. His offence does not exist as a category of media censure. People watching depictions of burglary presumably get an impression of threats of violence, sophisticated adult criminals and scenes of desecrated homes. But this is of course not at all the normal burglary – which is typically amateurish and carried out by an adolescent boy. When people come home to find their house broken into there is no one there and their fantasies about the dangerous intruder are left to run riot. Sometimes the consequences of such fantastic images of criminals are tragic. For example, people buy large guard dogs to protect themselves. Yet the one most likely to commit violence is the man of the house against his wife, and there are many more relatives – usually children – killed and injured by dogs than by burglars!

In the recent period there has been an alliance between liberals (often involved in the new administrative criminology) and left idealists which evokes the very mirror image of the mass media. The chance of being criminally injured, however slightly, the British Crime Survey tells us, is once in a hundred years (Hough and Mayhew, 1983) and such a Home Office view is readily echoed by left idealists who inform us that crime is, by and large, a minor problem and indeed the fear of crime is more of a problem than crime itself. Thus, they would argue, undue fear of crime provides popular support for conservative law and order campaigns and allows the build-up of further police powers whose repressive aim is political dissent rather than crime. For radicals to enter into the discourse of law and order is further to legitimize it. Furthermore, such a stance maintains that fear of crime has not only ideological consequences, it has material effects on the community itself. For to give credence to the fear of crime is to divide the community – to encourage racism, fester splits between the 'respectable' and 'non-respectable' working class and between youths and adults. More subtly, by emptying the streets particularly at night, it actually breaks down the system of informal controls which usually discourage crime.

Realism must navigate between these two poles; it must neither succumb to hysteria nor relapse into a critical denial of the severity of crime as a problem. It must be fiercely sceptical of official statistics and control institutions without taking the posture of a blanket rejection of all figures or, indeed, the very possibility of reform.

Realism necessitates an accurate victimology. It must counterpoise this against those liberal and idealist criminologies, on the one side, which play down victimization or even bluntly state that the 'real' victim is the offender and, on the other, those conservatives who celebrate moral panic and see violence and robbery as ubiquitous on our streets.

To do this involves mapping out who is at risk and what precise effect crime has on their lives. This moves beyond the invocation of the global risk rates of the average citizen. All too often this serves to conceal the actual severity of crime amongst significant sections of the population whilst providing a fake statistical backdrop for the discussion of 'irrational' fears.

A radical victimology notes two key elements of criminal victimization. First, that crime is focused both geographically and socially on the most vulnerable sections of the community. Secondly, that the impact of victimization is a product of risk rate and vulnerability. Average risk rates across a city ignore such a focusing and imply that equal crimes impact equally. As it is, the most vulnerable are not only more affected by crime, they also have the highest risk rates.

Realism must also trace accurately the relationship between victim and offender. Crime is not an activity of latter day Robin Hoods – the vast majority of working-class crime is directed within the working class. It is intra-class *not* inter-class in its nature. Similarly, despite the mass media predilection for focusing on inter-racial crime it is overwhelmingly intra-racial. Crimes of violence, for example, are by and large one poor person hitting another poor person – and in almost half of these instances it is a man hitting his wife or lover.

This is not to deny the impact of crimes of the powerful or indeed of the social problems created by capitalism which are perfectly legal. Rather, left realism notes that the working class is a victim of crime from all directions. It notes that the more vulnerable a person is economically and socially the more likely it is that *both* working-class and white-collar crime will occur against them; that one sort of crime tends to compound another, as does one social problem another. Furthermore, it notes that crime is a potent symbol of the antisocial nature of capitalism and is the most immediate way in which people experience other problems, such as unemployment or competitive individualism.

Realism starts from problems as people experience them. It takes seriously the complaints of women [with regard to] the dangers of being in public places at night, it takes note of the fears of the elderly with regard to burglary, it acknowledges the widespread occurrence of domestic violence and racist attacks. It does not ignore the fears of the vulnerable nor recontextualize them out of existence by putting them into a perspective which abounds with abstractions such as the 'average citizen' bereft of class or gender. It is only too aware of the systematic concealment and ignorance of crimes against the least powerful. Yet it does not take these fears at face value – it pinpoints their rational kernel but it is also aware of the forces towards irrationality.

Realism is not empiricism. Crime and deviance are prime sites of moral anxiety and tension in a society which is fraught with real inequalities and injustices. Criminals can quite easily become folk devils onto which are projected such feelings of unfairness. But there is a rational core to the fear of crime just as there is a rational core to the anxieties which distort it. Realism argues with popular consciousness in its attempts to separate out reality from fantasy. But it does not deny that crime is a problem. Indeed, if there were no rational core the media would have no power of leverage to the public consciousness. Crime becomes a metaphor but it is a metaphor rooted in reality.

When one examines anxiety about crime, one often finds a great deal more rationality than is commonly accorded to the public. Thus, frequently a glaring discrepancy has been claimed between the high fear of crime of women and their low risk rates. Recent research, particularly by feminist victimologists, has shown that this is often a mere artefact of a low reporting of sexual attacks to interviewers – a position reversed when sympathetic women are used in the survey team (see Hall, 1985; Hanmer and Saunders, 1984; Russell, 1982). Similarly, it is often suggested that fear of crime is somehow a petit bourgeois or upper middle-class phenomenon despite the lower risk rates of the more wealthy. Yet the Merseyside Crime Survey, for example, showed a close correspondence between risk rate and the prioritization of crime as a problem, with the working class having far higher risk rates *and* estimation of the importance of crime as a problem. Indeed, they saw crime as the second problem after unemployment whereas in the middle-class suburbs only 13 per cent of people rated crime as a major problem (see Kinsey et al., 1986). Similarly, Richard Sparks and his colleagues found that working-class people and blacks rated property crimes more seriously than middle-class people and whites (Sparks et al., 1977). Those affected by crime and those most vulnerable are the most concerned about crime.

Of course, there is a fantastic element in the conception of crime. The images of the identity of the criminal and his mode of operation are, as we have seen, highly distorted. And undoubtedly *fear displacement* occurs, where real anxieties about one type of crime are projected on another, as does *tunnel vision*, where only certain sorts of crime are feared, but the evidence for a substantial infrastructure of rationality is considerable.

The emergence of a left realist position in crime has occurred in the last five years. This has involved criminologists in Britain, Canada, the United States and Australia. In particular, the Crime and Justice Collective in California have devoted a large amount of space in their journal for a far-ranging discussion on the need for a left-wing programme on crime control (see e.g., *Crime and Social Justice*, Summer, 1981). There have been also violent denunciations, as the English journalist Martin Kettle put it:

> For their pains the [realists] have been denounced with extraordinary ferocity from the left, sometimes in an almost paranoid manner. To take crime seriously, to take fear of crime seriously and, worst of all, to take police reform seriously, is seen by the fundamentalists as the ultimate betrayal and deviation. (Kettle, 1984: 367)

This, apart, the basis of a widespread support for a realist position has already been made. What remains now is the task of creating a realist *criminology*. For although the left idealist denial of crime is increasingly being rejected, the tasks of radical criminology still remain. That is, to create an adequate explanation of crime, victimization and the reaction of the state. And this is all the more important given that the new administrative criminology has abdicated all such responsibility and indeed shares some convergence with left idealism.

[...]

CONCLUSION

This article has argued for the need for a systematic programme within radical criminology which should have theoretical, research and policy components. We must develop a realist theory which adequately encompasses the scope of the criminal act. That is, it must deal with both macro- and micro-levels, with the causes of criminal action and social reaction, and with the triangular interrelationship between offender, victim and the state. It must learn from past theory, take up again the debates between the three strands of criminological theory and attempt to bring them together within a radical rubric. It must stand for theory in a time when criminology has all but abandoned theory. It must rescue the action of causality whilst stressing both the specificity of generalization and the existence of human choice and value in any equation of criminality.

On a research level we must develop theoretically grounded empirical work against the current of atheoretical empiricism. The expansion of radical victimology in the area of victimization surveys is paramount but concern should also be made with regard to developments in qualitative research and ethnography (see West, 1984). The development of sophisticated statistical analysis (see for example Box and Hale, 1986; Greenberg, 1984; Melossi, 1985) should not be anathema to the radical criminologist nor should quantitative and qualitative work be seen as alternatives from which the radical must obviously choose. Both methods, as long as they are based in theory, complement and enrich each other.

In terms of practical policy we must combat impossibilism: whether it is the impossibility of reform, the ineluctable nature of a rising crime rate or the inevitable failure of rehabilitation. It is time for us to *compete* in policy terms, to get out of the ghetto of impossibilism. Orthodox criminology with its inability to question the political and its abandonment of aetiology is hopelessly unable to generate workable policies. All commentators are united about the inevitability of a rising crime rate. Left idealists think it cannot be halted because without a profound social transformation nothing can be done; the new administrative criminologists have given up the ghost of doing anything but the most superficial containment job. Let us state quite categorically that the major task of radical criminology is to seek a solution to the problem of crime and that of a socialist policy is substantially to reduce the crime rate. And the same is true of rehabilitation. Left idealists think that it is at best a con-trick, indeed argue that unapologetic punishment would at least be less mystifying to the offender. The new administrative criminologists seek to construct a system of punishment and surveillance which discards rehabilitation and replaces it with a social behaviourism worthy of the management of white rats in laboratory cages. They both deny the moral nature of crime, that choice is always made in varying determining circumstances and that the denial of responsibility fundamentally misunderstands the reality of the criminal act. As socialists it is important to stress that most working class crime is intra-class, that mugging, wife battering, burglary and child abuse are actions which cannot be morally absolved in the flux of determinacy. The offender should be ashamed, he/she should feel morally responsible within the limits of circumstance and rehabilitation is truly *impossible* without this moral dimension.

Crime is of importance politically because unchecked it divides the working class community and is materially and morally the basis of disorganization: the loss of political control. It is also a potential unifier – a realistic issue, *amongst others*, for recreating community.

Bertram Gross, in a perceptive article originally published in the American magazine *The Nation*, wrote: 'on crime, more than on most matters, the left seems bereft of ideas' (Gross, 1982: 51). He is completely correct, of course, in terms of there being a lack of any developed strategy amongst socialists for dealing with crime. I have tried to show, however, that it was the prevalence – though often implicit and frequently ill-thought [out] – of left idealist ideas which, in fact, directly resulted in the neglect of crime. There is now a growing consensus amongst radical criminologists that crime really is a problem for the working class, women, ethnic minorities: for all the most vulnerable members of capitalist societies, and that something must be done about it. But to recognize the reality of crime as a problem is only the first stage of the business. A fully blown theory of crime must relate to the contradictory reality of the phenomenon as must any strategy for combating it. And it must analyse how working class attitudes to crime are not merely the result of false ideas derived from the mass media and such like but have a rational basis in one moment of a contradictory and wrongly contextualized reality.

In a recent diatribe against radical criminology Carl Klockars remarked: 'Imagination is one thing, criminology another' (Klockars, 1980: 93). It is true that recent criminology has been characterized by a chronic lack of imagination – although I scarcely think that this was what Klockars lamented by his disparaging remark. Many of us were attracted to the discipline because of its theoretical verve, because of the centrality of the study of disorder to understanding society, because of the flair of its practitioners and the tremendous human interest of the subject. Indeed many of the major debates in the social sciences in the 1960s and 1970s focused quite naturally around deviance and social control. And this is as it should be – as it has been throughout history both in social science and in literature – both in mass media and the arts. What is needed now is an intellectual and political imagination which can comprehend the way in which we learn about order through the investigation of disorder. The paradox of the textbook in orthodox criminology is that it takes that which is of great human interest and transmits it into the dullest of 'facts'. I challenge anyone to read one of the conventional journals from cover to cover without having a desperate wish to fall asleep. Research grants come and research grants go and people are gainfully employed but crime remains, indeed it grows and nothing they do seems able to do anything about it. But is it so surprising that such a grotesquely eviscerated discipline should be so ineffective? For the one-dimensional discourse that constitutes orthodox criminology does not even know its own name. It is often unaware of the sociological and philosophical assumptions behind it. James Q. Wilson, for example, has become one of the most influential and significant of the new administrative criminologists. Yet his work and its proposals have scarcely been examined outside of the most perfunctory empiricist discussions. The discipline is redolent with a scientism which does not realize that its relationship with its object of study is more metaphysical than realistic, an apolitical recital of facts, more facts and even more facts [and] then does not want to acknowledge that it is profoundly political, a paradigm that sees its salvation in the latest statistical innovation rather than in any ability to engage with the actual reality of the world. It is ironic that it is precisely in orthodox criminology, where practitioners and researchers are extremely politically constrained, that they write as if crime and criminology were little to do with politics. Radical criminology, by stressing the political nature of crime and social censure, and the philosophical and social underpinnings of the various criminologies is able immediately to take such problems aboard. The key virtue of realist criminology is the central weakness of its administrative opponent.

We are privileged to work in one of the most central, exciting and enigmatic fields of study. It is the very staple of the mass media, a major focus of much day to day public gossip, speculation and debate. And this is as it should be. But during the past decade the subject has been eviscerated, talk of theory, causality and justice has all but disappeared and what is central to human concern has been relegated to the margins. It is time for us to go back to the drawing boards, time to regain our acquaintanceship with theory, to dispel amnesia about the past and adequately comprehend the present. This is the central task of left realist criminology: we will need more than a modicum of imagination and scientific ability to achieve it.

REFERENCES

Box, S. and Hale, C. (1986) 'Unemployment, crime and imprisonment, and the enduring problem of prison overcrowding', in R. Matthews and J. Young (eds), *Confronting Crime*. London: Sage.

Clarke, R. (1980) 'Situational crime prevention: theory and practice', *British Journal of Criminology*, 20(2): 136–47.

Cohen, S. and Young, J. (1981) *The Manufacture of News*, rev. edn. London: Constable/ Beverly Hills, CA: Sage.

Cressey, D. (1978) 'Criminological theory, social science, and the repression of crime', *Criminology*, 16: 171–91.

Downes, D. and Rock, P. (1982) *Understanding Deviance*. Oxford: Clarendon Press.

Greenberg, D.F. (1984) 'Age and crime: in search of sociology'. Mimeo.

Gross, B. (1982) 'Some anticrime proposals for Progressives', *Crime and Social Justice*, Summer, 51–4.

Hall, R.E. (1985) *Ask Any Woman – a London Enquiry into Rape and Sexual Assault*. Bristol: Falling Wall Press.

Hanmer, J. and Saunders, S. (1984) *Well-Founded Fears: a Community Study of Violence to Women*. London: Hutchinson.

Hough, M. and Mayhew, P. (1983) *The British Crime Survey: First Report*. London: Home Office Research and Planning Unit.

Kettle, M. (1984) 'The police and the Left', *New Society*, 70(1146): 366–7.

Kinsey, R., Lea, J. and Young, J. (1986) *Losing the Fight Against Crime*. Oxford: Blackwell.

Klockars, C. (1980) 'The contemporary crisis of Marxist criminology', in J. Incardi (ed.), *Radical Criminology: the Coming Crisis*. Beverly Hills, CA: Sage.

Lea, J. and Young, J. (1984) *What is to be Done About Law and Order?* Harmondsworth: Penguin.

Matza, D. (1969) *Becoming Deviant*. Englewood Cliffs, NJ: Prentice Hall.

Melossi, D. (1985) 'Punishment and social action', in S.C. McNall (ed.), *Current Perspectives in Social Theory*. Greenwich, CT: JAI Press.

Platt, T. and Takagi, P. (1981) 'Intellectuals for law and order: a critique of the New Realists', in T. Platt and P. Takagi (eds), *Crime and Social Justice*. London: Macmillan.

Russell, D. (1982) *Rape in Marriage*. New York: Macmillan.

Rutter, M. and Giller, H. (1983) *Juvenile Delinquency*. Harmondsworth: Penguin Books.

Sparks, R., Genn, H. and Dodd, D. (1977) *Surveying Victims: a Study of the Measurement of Criminal Victimisation*. Chichester: Wiley.

Trasler, G. (1984) *Crime and Criminal Justice Research in the United States*, Home Office Research Bulletin, 18, HMSO.

Van den Haag, E. (1975) *Punishing Criminals*. New York: Basic Books.

West, G. (1984) 'Phenomenon and form', in L. Barton and S. Walker (eds), *Educational Research and Social Crisis*. London: Croom Helm.

Wilson, J.Q. (1975) *Thinking About Crime*. New York: Vintage.

Wilson, J.Q. (1982) *Report and Recommendations of the Ad Hoc Committee on the Future of Criminal Justice Research*. Washington, DC: National Institute of Justice.

Wilson, J.Q. and Kelling, G. (1982) 'Broken Windows', *The Atlantic Monthly*, March, pp. 29–38.

Young, J. (1975) 'Working class criminology', in I. Taylor, P. Walton and J. Young (eds), *Critical Criminology*. London: Routledge and Kegan Paul.

Young, J. (1979) 'Left idealism, reformism and beyond: from New Criminology to Marxism', in B. Fine et al. (eds), *Capitalism and the Rule of Law: From Deviancy Theory to Marxism*. London: Hutchinson.

29

Cultural criminology

Jeff Ferrell

INTRODUCTION

[…]

The concept of 'cultural criminology' denotes both specific perspectives and broader orientations that have emerged in criminology, sociology, and criminal justice over the past few years. Most specifically, 'cultural criminology' represents a perspective developed by Ferrell & Sanders (1995), and likewise employed by Redhead (1995) and others (Kane 1998a), that interweaves particular intellectual threads to explore the convergence of cultural and criminal processes in contemporary social life. More broadly, the notion of cultural criminology references the increasing analytic attention that many criminologists now give to popular culture constructions, and especially mass media constructions, of crime and crime control. It in turn highlights the emergence of this general area of media and cultural inquiry as a relatively distinct domain within criminology, as evidenced, for example, by the number of recently published collections undertaking explorations of media, culture and crime (Anderson & Howard 1998, Bailey & Hale 1998, Barak 1994a, Ferrell & Sanders 1995, Ferrell & Websdale 1999, Kidd-Hewitt & Osborne 1995, Potter & Kappeler 1998). Most broadly, the existence of a concept such as cultural criminology underscores the steady seepage in recent years of cultural and media analysis into the traditional domains of criminological inquiry, such that criminological conferences and journals increasingly provide room and legitimacy for such analysis under any number of conventional headings, from juvenile delinquency and corporate crime to policing and domestic violence.

[…]

CONTEMPORARY AREAS OF INQUIRY

[…] Cultural criminological research and analysis have emerged in the past few years within a number of overlapping substantive areas. The first two of these

From *Annual Review of Sociology*, 1999, 25: 395–418.

can be characterized by an overly simple but perhaps informative dichotomy between 'crime as culture' and 'culture as crime.' The third broad area incorporates the variety of ways in which media dynamics construct the reality of crime and crime control; the fourth explores the social politics of crime and culture and the intellectual politics of cultural criminology.

Crime as culture

To speak of crime as culture is to acknowledge at a minimum that much of what we label criminal behavior is at the same time subcultural behavior, collectively organized around networks of symbol, ritual, and shared meaning. Put simply, it is to adopt the subculture as a basic unit of criminological analysis. While this general insight is hardly a new one, cultural criminology develops it in a number of directions. Bringing a postmodern sensibility to their understanding of deviant and criminal subcultures, cultural criminologists argue that such subcultures incorporate – indeed, are defined by – elaborate conventions of argot, appearance, aesthetics, and stylized presentation of self and thus operate as repositories of collective meaning and representation for their members. Within these subcultures as in other arenas of crime, form shapes content, image frames identity. Taken into a mediated world of increasingly dislocated communication and dispersed meaning, this insight further implies that deviant and criminal subcultures may now be exploding into universes of symbolic communication that in many ways transcend time and space. For computer hackers, graffiti writers, drug runners, and others, a mix of widespread spatial dislocation and precise normative organization implies subcultures defined less by face-to-face interaction than by shared, if second-hand, symbolic codes (Gelder & Thornton 1997: 473–550).

Understandably, then, much research in this area of cultural criminology has focused on the dispersed dynamics of subcultural style. Following from Hebdige's (1979) classic exploration of 'subculture: the meaning of style,' cultural criminologists have investigated style as defining both the internal characteristics of deviant and criminal subcultures and external constructions of them. Miller (1995), for example, has documented the many ways in which gang symbolism and style exist as the medium of meaning for both street gang members and the probation officers who attempt to control them. Reading gang styles as emblematic of gang immersion and gang defiance, enforcing court orders prohibiting gang clothing, confiscating gang paraphernalia, and displaying their confiscated collections on their own office walls, the probation officers in Miller's study construct the meanings of gang style as surely as do the gang members themselves. Likewise, Ferrell (1996) has shown how contemporary hip hop graffiti exists essentially as a 'crime of style' for graffiti writers, who operate and evaluate one another within complex stylistic and symbolic conventions, but also for media institutions and legal and political authorities who perceive graffiti as violating the 'aesthetics of authority' essential to their ongoing control of urban environments. More broadly, Ferrell (in Ferrell & Sanders 1995: 169–89) has explored style as the tissue connecting cultural and criminal practices and has examined the ways in which subcultural style shapes not only aesthetic communities, but official and unofficial reactions to subcultural identity. Finally, Lyng & Bracey (1995) have documented the multiply ironic process by which the style of the outlaw biker sub-culture came first to signify class-based cultural resistance, next to elicit the sorts of media reactions and legal controls that in fact amplified and confirmed its meaning, and finally to be appropriated and commodified in such a way as to void its political potential. Significantly, these and other studies (Cosgrove 1984) echo and confirm the integrative methodological framework outlined above by demonstrating that the importance of style resides not within the dynamics of criminal subcultures, nor in media and political constructions of its meaning, but in the contested interplay of the two.

If subcultures of crime and deviance are defined by their aesthetic and symbolic organization, cultural criminology has also begun to show that they are defined by intensities of collective experience and emotion as well. Building on Katz's (1988) wide-ranging exploration of the sensually seductive 'foreground' of criminality, cultural criminologists like Lyng (1990, 1998) and Ferrell (1996) have utilized *verstehen*-oriented methodologies to document the experiences of 'edgework' and 'the adrenalin rush' – immediate, incandescent integrations of risk, danger, and skill – that shape participation and membership in deviant and criminal subcultures. Discovered across a range of illicit subcultures (Presdee 1994, O'Malley & Mugford 1994, Tunnell 1992: 45, Wright & Decker 1994: 117), these intense and often ritualized moments of pleasure and excitement define the experience of subcultural membership and, by members' own accounts, seduce them into continued sub-cultural participation. Significantly for a sociology of these subcultural practices, research (Lyng & Snow 1986) shows that experiences of edgework and adrenalin exist as collectively constructed endeavors, encased in shared vocabularies of motive and meaning (Mills 1940, Cressey 1954). Thus, while these experiences certainly suggest a sociology of the body and the emotions, and further *verstehen*-oriented explorations of deviant and criminal subcultures as 'affectually determined' (Weber 1978: 9) domains, they also reveal the ways in which collective intensities of experience, like collective conventions of style, construct shared subcultural meaning.

Culture as crime

The notion of 'culture as crime' denotes the reconstruction of cultural enterprise as criminal endeavor – through, for example, the public labeling of popular culture products as criminogenic, or the criminalization of cultural producers through media or legal channels. In contemporary society, such reconstructions pervade popular culture and transcend traditional 'high' and 'low' cultural boundaries. Art photographers Robert Mapplethorpe and Jock Sturges, for example, have faced highly orchestrated campaigns accusing them of producing obscene or pornographic images; in addition, an art center exhibiting Mapplethorpe's photographs was indicted on charges of 'pandering obscenity,' and Sturges's studio was raided by local police and the FBI (Dubin 1992). Punk and heavy metal bands, and associated record companies, distributors, and retail outlets, have encountered obscenity rulings, civil and criminal suits, high-profile police raids, and police interference with concerts. Performers, producers, distributors, and retailers of rap and 'gangsta rap' music have likewise faced arrest and conviction on obscenity charges, legal confiscation of albums, highly publicized protests, boycotts, hearings organized by political figures and police officials, and ongoing media campaigns and legal proceedings accusing them of promoting – indeed, directly causing – crime and delinquency (Hamm & Ferrell 1994). More broadly, a variety of television programs, films, and cartoons have been targeted by public campaigns alleging that they incite delinquency, spin off 'copy-cat' crimes, and otherwise serve as criminogenic social forces (Ferrell 1998, Nyberg 1998).

These many cases certainly fall within the purview of cultural criminology because the targets of criminalization – photographers, musicians, television writers, and their products – are 'cultural' in nature, but equally so because their criminalization itself unfolds as a cultural process. When contemporary culture personas and performances are criminalized, they are primarily criminalized through the mass media, through their presentation and re-presentation as criminal in the realm of sound bites, shock images, news conferences, and newspaper headlines. This mediated spiral, in which media-produced popular culture forms and figures are in turn criminalized by means of the media, leads once again into a complex hall of mirrors. It generates not only images, but images of images – that is, attempts by lawyers, police officials, religious leaders, media workers, and others to craft criminalized images of those images previously crafted by artists, musicians, and film makers. Thus, the criminalization of popular culture is itself a popular, and cultural, enterprise, standing in opposition to popular culture less than participating in it, and helping to construct the very meanings and effects to which it allegedly responds. Given this, cultural criminologists have begun to widen the notion of 'criminalization' to include more than the simple creation and application of criminal law. Increasingly, they investigate the larger process of 'cultural criminalization' (Ferrell 1998: 80–82), the mediated reconstruction of meaning and perception around issues of culture and crime. In some cases, this cultural criminalization stands as an end in itself, successfully dehumanizing or delegitimating those targeted, though no formal legal charges are brought against them. In other cases, cultural criminalization helps construct a perceptual context in which direct criminal charges can more easily follow. In either scenario, though, media dynamics drive and define the criminalization of popular culture.

The mediated context of criminalization is a political one as well. The contemporary criminalization of popular culture has emerged as part of larger 'culture wars' (Bolton 1992) waged by political conservatives and cultural reactionaries. Controversies over the criminal or criminogenic characteristics of art photographers and rap musicians have resulted less from spontaneous public concern than from the sorts of well-funded and politically sophisticated campaigns that have similarly targeted the National Endowment for the Arts and its support of feminist/gay/lesbian performance artists and film festivals. In this light it is less than surprising that contemporary cultural criminalization is aimed time and again at marginal(ized) subcultures – radical punk musicians, politically militant black rap groups, lesbian and gay visual and performance artists – whose stylized celebration of and confrontation with their marginality threaten particular patterns of moral and legal control. Cultural criminalization in this sense exposes yet another set of linkages between subcultural styles and symbols and mediated constructions and reconstructions of these as criminal or criminogenic. In addition, as a process conducted largely in the public realm, cultural criminalization contributes to popular perceptions and panics, and thus to the further marginalization of those who are its focus. If successful, it constructs a degree of social discomfort that reflects off the face of popular culture and into the practice of everyday life.

Media constructions of crime and crime control

The mediated criminalization of popular culture exists, of course, as but one of many media processes that construct the meanings of crime and crime control. As noted in earlier discussions of textual methodologies, cultural criminology incorporates a wealth of research on mediated characterizations of crime and crime control, ranging across historical and contemporary texts and investigating images generated in newspaper reporting, popular film, television news and entertainment programming, popular music, comic books, and the cyber-spaces of the Internet. Further, cultural criminologists have begun to explore the complex institutional interconnections between the criminal justice system and the mass media. Researchers like Chermak (1995, 1997, 1998) and Sanders & Lyon (1995) have documented not only the mass media's heavy reliance on criminal justice sources for imagery and information on crime, but more importantly, the reciprocal relationship that undergirds this reliance. Working within organizational imperatives of efficiency and routinization, media institutions regularly rely on data selectively provided by policing and court agencies. In so doing, they highlight for the public issues chosen by criminal justice institutions and framed by criminal justice imperatives, and they in turn contribute to the political agendas of the criminal justice system and to the generation of public support for these agendas. In a relatively nonconspiratorial but nonetheless powerful fashion, media and criminal justice organizations thus coordinate their day-to-day operations and cooperate in constructing circumscribed understandings of crime and crime control.

A large body of research in cultural criminology examines the nature of these understandings and the public dynamics of their production. Like cultural criminology generally, much of the research here (Adler & Adler 1994, Goode & Ben-Yehuda 1994, Hollywood 1997, Jenkins 1992, Sparks 1995, Thornton 1994) builds on the classic analytic models of cultural studies and interactionist sociology, as embodied in concepts such as moral entrepreneurship and moral enterprise in the creation of crime and deviance (Becker 1963), and the invention of folk devils as a means of generating moral panic (Cohen 1972/1980) around issues of crime and deviance. Exploring the epistemic frameworks surrounding everyday understandings of crime controversies, this research (Fishman 1978, Best 1995, Acland 1995, Reinarman 1994, Reinarman & Duskin 1992, Websdale 1996) problematizes and unpacks taken-for-granted assumptions regarding the prevalence of criminality and the particular characteristics of criminals, and the research traces these assumptions to the interrelated workings of interest groups, media institutions, and criminal justice organizations.

Emerging scholarship in cultural criminology also offers useful reconceptualizations and refinements of these analytic models. McRobbie & Thornton (1995), for example, argue that the essential concepts of 'moral panic' and 'folk devils' must be reconsidered in multi-mediated societies; with the proliferation of media channels and the saturation of media markets, moral panics have become both dangerous endeavors and marketable commodities, and folk devils now find themselves both stigmatized and lionized in mainstream media and alternative media alike. Similarly, Jenkins's (1999) recent work has begun to refine understandings of crime and justice issues as social and cultural constructions. Building on his earlier, meticulous deconstructions of drug panics, serial homicide scares, and other constructed crime controversies, Jenkins (1994a, b) argues that attention must be paid to the media and political dynamics underlying 'unconstructed' crime as well. Jenkins explores the failure to frame activities such as anti-abortion violence as criminal terrorism, situates this failure within active media and political processes, and thus questions the meaning of that for which no criminal meaning is provided.

Through all of this, cultural criminologists further emphasize that in the process of constructing crime and crime control as social concerns and political controversies, the media also construct them as entertainment. Revisiting the classic cultural studies/new criminology notion of 'policing the crisis' (Hall et al 1978), Sparks (1995; see 1992), for example, characterizes the production and perception of crime and policing imagery in television crime dramas as a process of 'entertaining the crisis.' Intertwined with mediated moral panic over crime and crime waves, amplified fear of street crime and stranger violence, and politically popular concern for the harm done to crime victims, then, is the pleasure found in consuming mediated crime imagery and crime drama. To the extent that the mass media constructs crime as entertainment, we are thus offered not only selective images and agendas, but the ironic mechanism for amusing ourselves to death (Postman 1986) by way of our own collective pain, misery, and fear. Given this, contemporary media scholarship in cultural criminology focuses as much on popular film, popular music, and television entertainment programming as on the mediated manufacture of news and information, and it investigates the collapsing boundaries between such categories. Recent work in this area targets especially the popularity of 'reality' crime programs (Fishman & Cavender 1998). With their mix of street footage, theatrical staging, and patrol-car sermonizing, reality crime programs such as 'C.O.P.S.,' 'L.A.P.D,' and 'True Stories of the Highway Patrol' generate conventional, though at times contradictory, images of crime and policing. Along with talk shows devoted largely to crime and deviance topics, they in turn spin off secondary merchandising schemes, legal suits over videotaped police chases and televised invasions of privacy, and criminal activities allegedly induced by the programs themselves. Such dynamics demonstrate the entangled reality of crime, crime news, and crime entertainment, and suggest that as mediated crime constructions come to be defined as real, 'they are real in their consequences' (Thomas 1966: 301).

The politics of culture, crime, and cultural criminology

Clearly, a common thread connects the many domains into which cultural criminology inquires: the presence of power relations, and the emergence of social control, at the intersections of culture and crime. The stylistic practices and symbolic codes of illicit subcultures are made the object of legal surveillance and control or, alternatively, are appropriated, commodified, and sanitized within a vast machinery of consumption. Sophisticated media and criminal justice 'culture wars' are launched against alternative forms of art, music, and entertainment, thereby criminalizing the personalities and performances involved, marginalizing them from idealized notions of decency and community and, at the extreme, silencing the political critiques they present. Ongoing media constructions of crime and crime control emerge out of an alliance of convenience between media institutions and criminal justice agencies, serve to promote and legitimate broader political agendas regarding crime control, and in turn function to both trivialize and dramatize the meaning of crime.

Increasingly, then, it is television crime shows and big budget detective movies, nightly newscasts and morning newspaper headlines, recurrent campaigns against the real and imagined crimes of the disenfranchised that constitute Foucault's (in Cohen 1979: 339) 'Hundreds of tiny theatres of punishment' – theatres in which young people, ethnic minorities, lesbians and gays, and others play villains deserving of penalty and public outrage.

At the same time, cultural criminologists emphasize and explore the various forms that resistance to this complex web of social control may take. As Sparks (1992, 1995) and others argue, the audiences for media constructions of crime are diverse in both their composition and their readings of these constructions; they recontextualize, remake, and even reverse mass media meanings as they incorporate them into their daily lives and interactions. Varieties of resistance also emerge among those groups more specifically targeted within the practice of mediated control. Artists and musicians caught up in contemporary 'culture wars' have refused governmental awards, resigned high-profile positions, won legal judgements, organized alternative media outlets and performances, and otherwise produced public counterattacks (Ferrell 1998). Within other marginalized subcultures, personal and group style certainly exists as stigmata, inviting outside surveillance and control, but at the same time is valued as a badge of honor and resistance made all the more meaningful by its enduring defiance of outside authority (Hebdige 1988). Likewise, as Lyng (1990, 1998) and Ferrell (1996) emphasize, those immersed in moments of illicit edgework and adrenalin construct resistance doubly. First, by combining in such moments high levels of risk with precise skills and practiced artistry, those involved invent an identity, a sense of crafted self, that resists the usual degradations of subordinate status and deskilled, alienated labor. Second, as these moments become more dangerous because targeted by campaigns of criminalization and enforcement, participants in them find an enhancement and amplification of the edgy excitement they provide, and in so doing transform political pressure into personal and collective pleasure. In investigating the intersections of culture and crime for power relations and emerging forms of social control, then, cultural criminologists carry on the tradition of cultural studies (Hall & Jefferson 1976) by examining the many forms of resistance that emerge there as well.

Moreover, cultural criminology itself operates as a sort of intellectual resistance, as a diverse counter-reading and counter-discourse on, and critical 'intervention' (Pfohl & Gordon 1986: 94) into, conventional constructions of crime. In deconstructing moments of mediated panic over crime, cultural criminologists work to expose the political processes behind seemingly spontaneous social concerns and to dismantle the recurring and often essentialist metaphors of disease, invasion, and decay on which crime panics are built (Brownstein 1995, 1996, Reinarman 1994, Reinarman & Duskin 1992, Murji 1999). Beyond this, Barak (1988, 1994a) argues for an activist 'newsmaking criminology' in which criminologists integrate themselves into the ongoing mediated construction of crime, develop as part of their role in this process alternative images and understandings of crime issues, and in so doing produce what constitutive criminologists (Henry & Milovanovic 1991, Barak 1995) call a 'replacement discourse' regarding crime and crime control. Much of cultural criminology's ethnographic work in subcultural domains functions similarly, as a critical move away from the 'official definitions of reality' (Hagedorn 1990: 244) produced by the media and the criminal justice system and reproduced by a 'courthouse criminology' (see Polsky 1969) that relies on these sources. By attentively documenting the lived realities of groups whom conventional crime constructions have marginalized, and in turn documenting the situated politics of this marginalization process, cultural criminologists attempt to deconstruct the official demonization of various 'outsiders' (Becker 1963) – from rural domestic violence victims (Websdale 1998) to urban graffiti writers (Ferrell 1996, Sanchez-Tranquilino 1995), gay hustlers (Pettiway 1996), and homeless heroin addicts (Bourgois et al 1997) – and to produce alternative understandings of them. Approaching this task from the other direction, Hamm (1993) and others likewise venture inside the worlds of particularly violent criminals to document dangerous nuances of meaning and style often invisible in official reporting on such groups. In its politics as in its theory and method, then, cultural criminology integrates subcultural ethnography with media and institutional analysis to produce an alternative image of crime.

TRAJECTORIES OF CULTURAL CRIMINOLOGY

In describing an emergent orientation like cultural criminology, it is perhaps appropriate to close with a brief consideration of its unfinished edges. The following short discussions are therefore meant to be neither systematic nor exhaustive; they simply suggest some of what is emerging, and what might productively emerge, as cultural criminology continues to develop.

Situated media, situated audiences

The dynamic integration of subcultural crime constructions and media crime constructions has surfaced time and again in this essay as one of cultural criminology's essential insights. This insight further implies that the everyday notion of 'media' must be expanded to include those media that take shape within and among the various subcultures of crime, deviance, and crime control. As noted in the above methodological discussions, various illicit subcultures certainly come into regular contact with the mass media, but in so doing appropriate and reinvent mass media channels, products, and meanings. Further, illicit subcultures regularly invent their own media of communication; as McRobbie & Thornton (1995: 559) point out, even the interests of 'folk devils' are increasingly 'defended by their own niche and micro-media.' Thus, alternative and marginalized youth subcultures self-produce a wealth of zines (alternative magazines) and websites; street gang members construct elaborate edifices of communication out of particular clothing styles, colors, and hand signs; and graffiti writers develop a continent-wide network of freight train graffiti that mirrors existing hobo train graffiti in its ability to link distant subcultural members within a shared symbolic community. As also suggested in above discussions, multiple, fluid audiences likewise witness efflorescences of crime and crime control in their everyday existence, consume a multitude of crime images packaged as news and entertainment, and in turn remake the meaning of these encounters within the symbolic interaction of their own lives. Investigating the linkages between 'media' and crime, then, means investigating the many situations in which these linkages emerge, and moreover the situated place of media, audience, and meaning within criminal worlds (see Vaughan 1998). Ultimately, perhaps, this investigation suggests blurring the analytic boundary between producer and audience – recognizing, in other words, that a variety of groups both produce and consume contested images of crime – and moving ahead to explore the many microcircuits of meaning that collectively construct the reality of crime.

The media and culture of policing

Increasingly, the production and consumption of mediated meaning frames not only the reality of crime, but of crime control as well. Contemporary policing can in fact hardly be understood apart from its interpenetration with media at all levels. As 'reality' crime and policing television programs shape public perceptions of policing, serve as controversial tools of officer recruitment and suspect apprehension, and engender legal suits over their effects on street-level policing, citizens shoot video footage of police conduct and misconduct – some of which finds its way, full-circle, onto news and 'reality' programs. Meanwhile, within the police subculture itself, surveillance cameras and on-board patrol car cameras capture the practices of police officers and citizens alike and, as Websdale (1999) documents, police crime files themselves take shape as 'situated media substrates' which, like surveillance and patrol car footage, regularly become building blocks for subsequent mass media images of policing. The policing of a postmodern world emerges as a complex set of visual and semiotic practices, an expanding spiral of mediated social control (Manning 1998, 1999a, b).

From the view of cultural criminology, policing must in turn be understood as a set of practices situated, like criminal practices, within subcultural conventions of meaning, symbolism, and style. In this regard, Kraska & Kappeler (1995: 85) integrate perspectives from police studies, feminist literature, and critical theory to explore the subcultural ideologies, situated dynamics, and broader 'cultural and structural context' within which police deviance and police sexual violence against women develop. Perhaps most interesting here, in light of the reflexive methodologies discussed above, is Kraska's (1998) grounded investigation of police paramilitary units. Immersing himself and his emotions in a situation of police paramilitary violence, Kraska details the stylized subcultural status afforded by particular forms of weaponry and clothing, and he documents the deep-seated ideological and affective states that define the collective meaning of such situations. With crime control as with crime, subcultural and media dynamics construct experience and perception.

Crime and cultural space

Many of the everyday situations in which crime and policing are played out, and in fact many of the most visible contemporary controversies surrounding crime and policing issues, involve the contestation of cultural space. Incorporating perspectives from cultural studies, cultural geography, and postmodern geography (Merrifield & Swyngedouw 1997, Scott & Soja 1996, Davis 1992), the notion of cultural space references the process by which meaning is constructed and contested in public domains (Ferrell 1997). This process intertwines with a variety of crime and crime control situations. Homeless populations declare by their public presence the scandal of inequality, and they are in turn hounded and herded by a host of loitering, vagrancy, trespass, public lodging, and public nuisance statutes. 'Gutter punks' invest downtown street corners with disheveled style, 'skate punks' and skateboarders convert walkways and parking garages into playgrounds, Latino/a street 'cruisers' create mobile subcultures out of dropped frames and polished chrome – and face in response aggressive enforcement of laws regarding trespass, curfew, public sleeping, and even car stereo volume. Street gangs carve out collective cultural space from shared styles and public rituals; criminal justice officials prohibit and confiscate stylized clothing, enforce prohibitions against public gatherings by 'known' gang members, and orchestrate public gang 'round-ups.' Graffiti writers remake the visual landscapes and symbolic codes of public life, but they do so in the face of increasing criminal

sanctions, high-tech surveillance systems, and nationally coordinated legal campaigns designed to remove them and their markings from public life.

As with the mediated campaigns of cultural criminalization discussed above,
these conflicts over crime and cultural space regularly emerge around the marginalized subcultures of young people, ethnic minorities, and other groups, and
thus they raise essential issues of identity and authenticity (Sanchez-Tranquilino
1995). Such conflicts in turn incorporate a complex criminalization of these subcultures as part of a systematic effort to erase their self-constructed public
images, to substitute in their place symbols of homogeneity and consensus, and
thereby to restore and expand the 'aesthetics of authority' noted in above discussions. Ultimately, these disparate conflicts over crime and cultural space reveal
the common thread of contested public meaning, and something of the work of
control in the age of cultural reproduction.

Bodies, emotions, and cultural criminology

Perhaps the most critical of situations, the most intimate of cultural spaces in
which crime and crime control intersect are those in and around the physical and
emotional self (Pfohl 1990). Throughout this essay such situations have been seen:
the development of subcultural style as marker of identity and locus of criminalization; the fleeting experience of edgework and adrenalin rushes, heightened by
risk of legal apprehension; the utilization of researchers' own experiences and
emotions in the study of crime and policing. These situations suggest that other
moments merit the attention of cultural criminology as well, from gang girls' construction of identity through hair, makeup, and discourse (Mendoza-Denton 1996)
and phone fantasy workers' invocation of sexuality and emotion (Mattley 1998), to
the contested media and body politics of AIDS (Kane 1998b, Watney 1987, Young
1996: 175–206). Together, these and other situations in turn suggest a criminology
of the skin (see Kushner 1994) – a criminology that can account for crime and crime
control in terms of pleasure, fear, and excitement and that can confront the deform-
ities of sexuality and power, control and resistance that emerge in these inside
spaces. They also demand the ongoing refinement of the reflexive, *verstehen*-oriented
methodologies and epistemologies described above – of ways of investigating and
knowing that are at the same time embodied and affective (Scheper-Hughes 1994),
closer to the intimate meaning of crime and yet never close enough.

CONCLUSIONS

As an emerging perspective within criminology, sociology, and criminal justice, cultural criminology draws from a wide range of intellectual orientations.
Revisiting and perhaps reinventing existing paradigms in cultural studies,
the 'new' criminology, interactionist sociology, and critical theory; integrating
insights from postmodern, feminist, and constructionist thought; and incorporating
aspects of newsmaking, constitutive, and other evolving criminologies, cultural
criminology seek less to synthesize or subsume these various perspectives than to

engage them in a critical, multifaceted exploration of culture and crime. Linking these diverse intellectual dimensions, and their attendant methodologies of ethnography and media/textual analysis, is cultural criminology's overarching concern with the meaning of crime and crime control. Some three decades ago, Cohen (1988: 68, 1971: 19) wrote of 'placing on the agenda' of a culturally informed criminology issues of 'subjective meaning,' and of deviance and crime as 'meaningful action.' Cultural criminology embraces and expands this agenda by exploring the complex construction, attribution, and appropriation of meaning that occurs within and between media and political formations, illicit subcultures, and audiences around matters of crime and crime control. In so doing, cultural criminology likewise highlights the inevitability of the image. Inside the stylized rhythms of a criminal subculture, reading a newspaper crime report or perusing a police file, caught between the panic and pleasure of crime, 'there is no escape from the politics of representation' (Hall 1993: 111). [...]

REFERENCES

Acland C.R. 1995. *Youth, Murder, Spectacle: The Cultural Politics of 'Youth in Crisis'*. Boulder, CO: Westview.

Adler P.A., Adler P. eds. 1994. *Constructions of Deviance: Social Power, Context, and Interaction*. Belmont, CA: Wadsworth.

Anderson S.E, Howard G.J. eds. 1998. *Interrogating Popular Culture: Deviance, Justice, and Social Order*. Guilderland, NY: Harrow & Heston.

Bailey F.Y, Hale D.C. eds. 1998. *Popular Culture, Crime, and Justice*. Belmont, CA: West/Wadsworth.

Barak G. 1988. Newsmaking criminology: reflections on the media, intellectuals, and crime. *Justice Q.* 5: 565–87.

Barak G. ed. 1994a. *Media, Process, and the Social Construction of Crime: Studies in Newsmaking Criminology*. New York: Garland.

Barak G. ed. 1994b. *Varieties of Criminology*. Westport, CT: Praeger

Barak G. 1995. Media, crime, and justice: a case for constitutive criminology. See Ferrell & Sanders 1995, pp. 142–66.

Becker H.S. 1963. *Outsiders: Studies in the Sociology of Deviance*. New York: Free Press.

Best J. ed. 1995. *Images of Issues: Typifying Contemporary Social Problems*. New York: Aldine de Gruyter. 2nd ed.

Bolton R. ed. 1992. Culture Wars: Documents from the Recent Controversies in the Arts. New York: New Press.

Bourgois P, Lettiere M, Quesada J. 1997. Social misery and the sanctions of substance abuse: confronting HIV risk among homeless heroin addicts in San Francisco. *Soc. Probl.* 44: 155-73.

Brownstein H.H. 1995. The media and the construction of random drug violence. See Ferrell & Sanders 1995, pp. 45–65.

Brownstein H.H. 1996. *The Rise and Fall of a Violent Crime Wave: Crack Cocaine and the Social Construction of a Crime Problem*. Guilderland, NY: Harrow & Heston.

Chermak S. 1995. *Victims in the News: Crime and the American News Media*. Boulder, CO: Westview.

Chermak S. 1997. The presentation of drugs in the news media: the news sources involved in the construction of social problems. *Justice Q.* 14: 687–718.

Chermak S.M. 1998. Police, courts, and corrections in the media. See Bailey & Hale 1998, pp. 87–99.

Cohen S. ed. 1971. *Images of Deviance*. Harmondsworth, UK: Penguin.

Cohen S. 1972/1980. *Folk Devils and Moral Panics*. London: Macgibbon & Kee.

Cohen S. 1979. The punitive city: notes on the dispersal of social control. *Contemp. Crises.* 3: 339–63.

Cohen S. 1988. *Against Criminology*. New Brunswick, NJ: Transaction.

Cosgrove S. 1984. The zoot-suit and style warfare. *Radical Am.* 18: 38–51.

Cressey D. 1954. The differential association theory and compulsive crime. *J. Crim. Law Criminol.* 45: 49–64.

Davis M. 1992. *City of Quartz*. New York: Vintage.

Dubin S. 1992. *Arresting Images: Impolitic Art and Uncivil Actions*. London: Routledge.

Ferrell J. 1996. *Crimes of Style: Urban Graffiti and the Politics of Criminality*. Boston: Northeastern Univ. Press.

Ferrell J. 1997. Youth, crime, and cultural space. *Soc. Justice* 24: 21–38.

Ferrell J. 1998. Criminalizing popular culture. See Bailey & Hale 1998, pp. 71–83.

Ferrell J, Hamm M.S. eds. 1998. *Ethnography at the Edge: Crime, Deviance, and Field Research*. Boston: Northeastern Univ. Press

Ferrell J, Sanders C.R. eds. 1995. *Cultural Criminology*. Boston: Northeastern Univ. Press.

Ferrell J, Websdale N. eds. 1999. *Making Trouble: Cultural Constructions of Crime, Deviance, and Control*. Hawthorne, NY: Aldine de Gruyter.

Fishman M. 1978. Crime waves as ideology. *Soc. Probl.* 25: 531–43.

Fishman M, Cavender G. eds. 1998. *Entertaining Crime: Television Reality Programs*. Hawthorne, NY: Aldine de Gruyter.

Gelder K, Thornton S. eds. 1997. *The Subcultures Reader*. London: Routledge.

Goode E, Ben-Yehuda N. 1994. *Moral Panics*. Cambridge, MA: Blackwell.

Hagedorn J.M. 1990. Black in the field again: gang research in the nineties. In *Gangs in America*, ed. CR. Huff, pp. 240–59. Newbury Park, CA: Sage.

Hall S. 1993. What is this 'black' in black popular culture? *Soc. Justice* 20: 104–14.

Hall S, Critcher C, Jefferson T, Clarke J, Roberts B. 1978. *Policing the Crisis: Mugging, the State, and Law and Order*. Houndmills, UK: Macmillan.

Hall S, Jefferson T. eds. 1976. *Resistance Through Rituals: Youth Subcultures in Postwar Britain*. London: Hutchinson.

Hamm M.S. 1993. *American Skinheads: The Criminology and Control of Hate Crime*. Westport, CT: Praeger.

Hamm M.S., Ferrell J. 1994. Rap, cops, and crime: clarifying the 'cop killer' controversy. *ACJS Today* 13: 1, 3, 29.

Hebdige D. 1979. *Subculture: The Meaning of Style*. London: Methuen.

Hebdige D. 1988. *Hiding in the Light*. London: Routledge.

Henry S, Milovanovic D. 1991. Constitutive criminology: the maturation of critical theory. *Criminology* 29: 293–315.

Hollywood B. 1997. Dancing in the dark: ecstasy, the dance culture, and moral panic in post ceasefire Northern Ireland. *Crit. Criminol.* 8: 62–77.

Jenkins P. 1992. *Intimate Enemies: Moral Panics in Contemporary Great Britain*. Hawthorne, NY: Aldine de Gruyter.

Jenkins P. 1994a. *Using Murder: The Social Construction of Serial Homicide*. Hawthorne, NY: Aldine de Gruyter.

Jenkins P. 1994b. 'The Ice Age': the social construction of a drug panic. *Justice Q.* 11: 7–31.

Jenkins P. 1999. Fighting terrorism as if women mattered: anti-abortion violence as unconstructed terrorism. See Ferrell & Websdale 1999, pp. 319–46.

Kane S. 1998a. Reversing the ethnographic gaze: experiments in cultural criminology. See Ferrell & Hamm 1998, pp. 132–45.

Kane S. 1998b. *AIDS Alibis: Sex, Drugs and Crime in the Americas*. Philadelphia: Temple Univ. Press.

Katz J. 1988. *Seductions of Crime: Moral and Sensual Attractions in Doing Evil*. NY: Basic Books.

Kidd-Hewitt D, Osborne R. eds. 1995. *Crime and the Media: The Post-Modern Spectacle*. London: Pluto.

Kraska P.B. 1998. Enjoying militarism: political/personal dilemmas in studying U.S. police paramilitary units. See Ferrell & Hamm 1998, pp. 88–110.

Kraska P.B, Kappeler V.E. 1995. To serve and pursue: exploring police sexual violence against women. *Justice Q.* 12: 85–111.

Kushner T. 1994. A socialism of the skin. *Nation* 259: 9–14.

Lyng S. 1990. Edgework: a social psychological analysis of voluntary risk taking. *Am. J. Sociol.* 95: 851–86.

Lyng S. 1998. Dangerous methods: risk taking and the research process. See Ferrell & Hamm 1998, pp. 221–51.

Lyng S, Bracey M.L. 1995. Squaring the one percent: biker style and the selling of cultural resistance. See Ferrell & Sanders 1995. pp. 235–76.

Lyng S, Snow D. 1986. Vocabularies of motive and high-risk behavior: the case of skydiving. In *Advances in Group Processes*, ed. E. Lawler, pp. 157–79. Greenwich, CT: JAI.

Manning P.K. 1998. Media loops. See Bailey & Hale 1998, pp. 25–39.

Manning P.K. 1999a. Semiotics and social justice. In *Social Justice/Criminal Justice*, ed. B.A. Arrigo, pp. 131–49. Belmont, CA: West/Wadsworth.

Manning P.K. 1999b. Reflections: the visual as a mode of social control. See Ferrell & Websdale 1999, pp. 255–75.

Mattley C. 1998. (Dis)courtesy stigma: fieldwork among phone fantasy workers. See Ferrell & Hamm 1998, pp. 146–58.

McRobbie A, Thornton S.L. 1995. Rethinking 'moral panic' for multi-mediated social worlds. *Br. J. Sociol.* 46: 559–574.

Mendoza-Denton N. 1996. 'Muy macha': gender and ideology in gang-girls' discourse about makeup. *Ethnos* 61: 47–63.

Merrifield A, Swyngedouw E. eds. 1997. *The Urbanization of Injustice*. Washington Square. NY: New York Univ. Press.

Miller J.A. 1995. Struggles over the symbolic: gang style and the meanings of social control. See Ferrell & Sanders 1995, pp. 213–34.

Mills C.W. 1940. Situated actions and vocabularies of motive. *Am. Sociol. Rev.* 5: 904–13.

Murji K. 1999. Wild life: constructions and representations of yardies. See Ferrell & Websdale 1999, pp. 179–201

Nyberg A.K. 1998. Comic books and juvenile delinquency: a historical perspective. See Bailey & Hale 1998, pp. 61–70.

O'Malley P, Mugford S. 1994. Crime, excitement, and modernity. See Barak 1994b, pp.189–211.

Pettiway L.E. 1996. *Honey, Honey, Miss Thang: Being Black, Gay, and on the Streets*. Philadelphia: Temple Univ. Press.

Pfohl S. 1990. Welcome to the Parasite Cafe: postmodernity as a social problem. *Soc. Probl.* 37: 421–42.

Pfohl S, Gordon A. 1986. Criminological displacements: a sociological deconstruction. *Soc. Probl.* 33: 94–113.

Polsky N. 1969. *Hustlers, Beats, and Others*. Garden City, NY: Anchor.

Postman N. 1986. *Amusing Ourselves to Death*. London: Heinemann.

Potter G.W, Kappeler, V.E. eds. 1998. *Constructing Crime: Perspectives on Making News and Social Problems*. Prospect Heights, IL: Waveland.

Presdee M. 1994. Young people, culture, and the construction of crime: doing wrong versus doing crime. See Barak 1994b, pp. 179–87.

Redhead S. 1995. *Unpopular Cultures: The Birth of Law and Popular Culture*. Manchester, UK: Manchester Univ. Press.

Reinarman C. 1994. The social construction of drug scares. See Adler & Adler 1994, pp. 92–104.

Reinarman C, Duskin C. 1992. Dominant ideology and drugs in the media. *Intern. J. Drug Pol.* 3: 6–15.

Sanchez-Tranquilino M. 1995. Space, power, and youth culture: Mexican American graffiti and Chicano murals in East Los Angeles, 1972–1978. In *Looking High and Low: Art and Cultural Identity*, ed. B.J. Bright, L. Bakewell, pp. 55–88. Tucson, AZ: Univ. Ariz. Press.

Sanders CR, Lyon E. 1995. Repetitive retribution: media images and the cultural construction of criminal justice. See Ferrell & Sanders 1995, pp. 25–44.

Scheper-Hughes N. 1994. Embodied knowledge: thinking with the body in critical medical anthropology. In *Assessing Cultural Anthropology*, ed. R. Borofsky, pp. 229–42. New York: McGraw-Hill.

Scott A, Soja E. eds. 1996. *The City: Los Angeles and Urban Theory at the End of the Twentieth Century*. Berkeley: Univ. Calif. Press.

Sparks R. 1992. *Television and the Drama of Crime: Moral Tales and the Place of Crime in Public Life*. Buckingham, UK: Open Univ. Press.

Sparks R. 1995. Entertaining the crisis: television and moral enterprise. See Kidd-Hewitt & Osborne 1995, pp. 49–66.

Thomas W.I. 1966. The relation of research to the social process. In *W.I. Thomas on Social Organization and Social Personality*, ed. M. Janowitz, pp. 289–305. Chicago: Univ. Chicago Press.

Thornton S. 1994. Moral panic, the media, and British rave culture. In *Microphone Fiends: Youth Music and Youth Culture*, eds. A. Ross, T. Rose, pp. 176–92. New York: Routledge.

Tunnell K.D. 1992. *Choosing Crime: The Criminal Calculus of Property Offenders*. Chicago: Nelson-Hall.

Vaughn D. 1998. Rational choice, situated action, and the social control of organizations. *Law Soc. Rev.* 32: 501–39.

Watney S. 1987. *Policing Desire: Pornography, AIDS and the Media*. Minneapolis: Univ. Minn. Press.

Weber M. 1978. *Economy and Society*. Berkeley: Univ. Calif. Press.

Websdale N. 1996. Predators: the social construction of 'stranger-danger' in Washington State as a form of patriarchal ideology. *Women Crim. Justice* 7:43–68.

Websdale N. 1998. *Rural Women Battering and the Justice System: An Ethnography*. Thousand Oaks, CA: Sage.

Websdale N. 1999. Police homicide files as situated media substrates. See Ferrell & Websdale 1999, pp. 277–300.

Wright R, Decker S. 1994. *Burglars on the Job*. Boston: Northeastern Univ. Press.

Young A. 1996. *Imagining Crime: Textual Outlaws and Criminal Conversations*. London: Sage.

Young J. 1971. The role of the police as amplifiers of deviancy, negotiators of reality and translators of fantasy. In *Images of Deviance*, ed. S. Cohen, pp. 27–61. Harmondsworth, UK: Penguin.

Part Four

Criminal justice and crime prevention

INTRODUCTION

In 1974 Robert Martinson declared that '[w]ith few and isolated exceptions, the rehabilitative efforts that have been reported so far have had no appreciable effect on recidivism' ('What works? Questions and answers about penal reform' [*The Public Interest*, no. 35, p. 25]). This 'nothing works' statement heralded the final death knell for those who believed that modern post-war Western societies had the capacity to rehabilitate and/or treat offenders and reduce recidivism. As the readings in this section indicate, it also sparked off a wide-ranging, high profile post-rehabilitation debate about whether and how crime could be controlled/prevented effectively.

James Q. Wilson argues that we need to forget theorizing about the causes of crime and concentrate on the realities and pragmatics of crime and criminality. He stresses that a significant and meaningful reduction can be achieved by recognizing that crime is a quasi-economic endeavour whose occurrence can be made to vary with the costs imposed upon it. By imposing prison sentences swiftly and without exception, society can remove from circulation the most frequently convicted and most active criminals for a significant portion of their criminal careers. The knowledge of swift processing and near certain incarceration, he argues, could, in addition to incapacitating convicted criminals, also intimidate potential offenders. Thus society could, if it chose to, control crime to some degree by recognizing that punishment is a worthy objective of the criminal justice system and by raising the stakes considerably. In the course of the 1990s this perspective coined the populist soundbite 'prison works'.

Andrew von Hirsch proposes what he and the members of the Committee for the Study of Incarceration view as a politically feasible alternative to the populist 'lock 'em up' approach of Wilson. 'Just and commensurate deserts' stressed that punishment rather than rehabilitation or treatment is important because it implies blame and the severity of the punishment symbolizes the degree of blame. Once we have acknowledged that certain forms of action and behaviour are wrong and ought to be punished, we can set reasonable limits on the extent of the punishment and retribution. The severity of the punishment should be proportionate to the gravity of the offence. Stringent punishments should be limited to crimes that inflict serious harm and indicate considerable culpability on the part of the offender. As the magnitude of the crime diminishes so should the nature of the punishment. This theory attempts to centre the question 'What is fair and just?' rather than 'What works?' In doing so, it is not interested in speculating on the motives of offenders or in attempting to socially engineer lower crime rates.

In the next reading, Francis T. Cullen and K.E. Gilbert mount a spirited defence of the rehabilitative ideal against both Wilson and 'just deserts'. They argue that liberals and those on the left should not abandon rehabilitation because it: imposes positive obligations on the state to have regard for the welfare of offenders; can act as a bulwark against the punitive law and order demands of the Right; has considerable support within the criminal justice system; and is essentially humanitarian, compassionate and optimistic in orientation.

Ron Clarke offers another highly pragmatic vision of what effective crime control would entail. If we view crime as being the consequence of immediate choices and decisions by offenders about risks and rewards then a whole series of possibilities for preventing crime situationally present themselves. He argues that it is perfectly possible to reduce substantially the physical opportunities for offending and to increase the chances of a given offender being caught in the act. Despite being initially berated for its rational choice suppositions about human nature and anti-theoretical stance, this approach enjoys remarkable political popularity. Like routine activities theory it carries the positive message that a multitude of crimes can be effectively designed out and eradicated and that all of us can take active collective and individual steps to protect ourselves and our property from the criminal.

Elliott Currie presents us with a left realist social crime prevention programme. For him the transition to a market-based society has had a devastating impact on key areas of social, economic and cultural life. The result is spiralling crime rates, social fragmentation and individual alienation. Currie stresses that effective crime control requires confronting the roots of the problem. To tackle economic and social inequalities we need proactive state coordinated labour market policies and comprehensive welfare strategies which are based on the notion of inclusive citizenship. We also need as a matter of urgency to develop a package of very specific child and family interventions, youth-oriented policies and imaginative drug regulation programmes.

The development of criminal justice has, however, typically witnessed the removal of interpersonal conflict and dispute from the control of those individuals involved and their appropriation by an ever increasing number of state agencies. It was not until the mid twentieth century that this notion of crime, as conflict and dispute, was significantly revived. Writing from an abolitionist perspective, the Norwegian criminologist, Nils Christie, argued that conflicts (now defined as 'crimes' by the state) have been 'stolen' from offenders and victims (who are their rightful 'owners') by the apparatus of criminal justice. In the reading included here Christie maintains that orthodox thinking about crime, criminality and crime control is fundamentally flawed because the harms associated with social life cannot, and should not, be regulated by the criminal justice system. Social problems, conflicts, harms and antagonisms are an inevitable part of everyday life and their ownership is lost if they are delegated to professionals and specialists promising to provide 'expert solutions'. When professionals intervene, the essence of social problems and conflicts is effectively stolen and re-presented in forms that only aid their perpetuation. As such the criminal justice system is overwhelmingly counter-productive in relation to its objectives. It does not function according to the claims made by it, whether these be rehabilitation, retribution, deterrence or prevention.

The Australian criminologist John Braithwaite presents the case for a genuine alternative to carceral and coercive methods of social control: 'Reintegrative shaming'. By this he means dealing with offenders in ways which embody the expression of community and familial disapproval, but also incorporate a process of re-acceptance. Rather than stigmatizing offenders and excluding them from society, this restorative justice approach aims to bring them back into society and thus to enhance social solidarity.

Willem De Haan argues beyond the other approaches by stating that responding positively and constructively requires abandoning the notion of 'crime'. We need to talk and think about diverse troubles, conflicts, harms, damage, conflicting interests, unfortunate events and accidents. We also need to break with the crime control = punishment = imprisonment nexus. It is only then that we will be in a position to construct rational, innovative and constructive redress-based mechanisms for resolving conflicts, settling disputes and preventing social negativity. De Haan does not underestimate the problems that such a radical imaginary will encounter but he argues forcefully that the other proposals have manifestly failed to deliver long-term crime control and should be in fact viewed as part of the problem rather than as part of the solution.

Our next reading is the internationally acclaimed 'Broken windows' thesis of Wilson and Kelling. Although originally published in 1982 it did not really impact upon criminal justice debates until the 1990s when it was repackaged by the NYPD as 'zero tolerance' or 'quality of life' policing and marketed globally as the future of law enforcement. Wilson and Kelling's central thesis is that small signs of disorder in a neighbourhood, like broken windows or graffiti, can encourage more serious forms of criminality by giving the symbolic impression that nobody cares. The 'Broken windows' thesis declares that civility and order are baseline components of society and it both requires and mandates the police to restore and maintain neighbourhood order and civility through proactive, confident street policing.

We conclude this section by acknowledging the increasing influence of scientific approaches to crime investigation and control. In academic and policy circles this has become known as 'crime science'. Crime science is informed not only by environmental criminology, but also forensic science, crime mapping, cost–benefit analysis, DNA identification, genetic and psychological risk identification, offender profiling, computer science and technologies of behavioural control. In the reading reproduced here from Martha Gever, we choose not to reflect on the efficacy of this research per se but to expose how one aspect of it – medico-legal death investigations – has been represented and how it has achieved popular support through dramas such as *Crime Scene Investigation*. The success of CSI's combination of medicine and criminal justice does indeed appear premised on the certainty and assurances of scientific evidence, which in turn also play an important role in informing a public about how individual and social bodies can be made transparently knowable and validated by scientific instruments and procedures. CSI allows viewers to experience criminal investigation as an interactive 3D process. It remains a moot point as to how far the technological 'dehumanization' that lies at the core of CSI is also capable of becoming 'non-fictional'.

30

On deterrence

James Q. Wilson

The average citizen hardly needs to be persuaded of the view that crime will be more frequently committed if, other things being equal, crime becomes more profitable compared to other ways of spending one's time. Accordingly, the average citizen thinks it obvious that one major reason why crime has gone up is that people have discovered it is easier to get away with it; by the same token, the average citizen thinks a good way to reduce crime is to make the consequences of crime to the would-be offender more costly (by making penalties swifter, more certain, or more severe), or to make the value of alternatives to crime more attractive (by increasing the availability and pay of legitimate jobs), or both. Such opinions spring naturally to mind among persons who notice, as a fact of everyday life, that people take their hands off hot stoves, shop around to find the best buy, smack their children to teach them not to run out into a busy street, and change jobs when the opportunity arises to earn more money for the same amount of effort.

These citizens may be surprised to learn that social scientists who study crime are deeply divided over the correctness of such views. To some scholars, especially economists, the popular view is also the scientifically correct one – becoming a criminal can be explained in much the same way we explain becoming a carpenter or buying a car. To other scholars, especially sociologists, the popular view is wrong – crime rates do not go up because people discover they can get away with it and will not come down just because society decides to get tough on criminals.

The debate over the effect on crime rates of changing the costs and benefits of crime is usually referred to as a debate over deterrence – a debate, that is, over the efficacy (and perhaps even the propriety) of trying to prevent crime by making would-be offenders more fearful of committing crime. But that is something of a misnomer, because the theory of human nature on which is erected the idea of

From *Thinking About Crime*, pp. 117–23; 142–4. (New York: Basic Books, 1983, 2nd revised edition. First published 1975.)

deterrence (the theory that people respond to the penalties associated with crime) is also the theory of human nature that supports the idea that people will take jobs in preference to crime if the jobs are more attractive. In both cases, we are saying that would-be offenders are reasonably rational and respond to their perception of the costs and benefits attached to alternative courses of action. When we use the word 'deterrence', we are calling attention only to the cost side of the equation. There is no word in common scientific usage to call attention to the benefit side of the equation; perhaps 'inducement' might serve. To a psychologist, deterring persons from committing crimes or inducing persons to engage in non-criminal activities are but special cases of using 'reinforcements' (or rewards) to alter behavior.

The reason there is a debate among scholars about deterrence is that the socially imposed consequences of committing a crime, unlike the market consequences of shopping around for the best price, are characterized by delay, uncertainty, and ignorance. In addition, some scholars contend that a large fraction of crime is committed by persons who are so impulsive, irrational, or abnormal that even if there were no delay, uncertainty, or ignorance attached to the consequences of criminality, we would still have a lot of crime.

Imagine a young man walking down the street at night with nothing on his mind but a desire for good times and high living. Suddenly he sees a little old lady standing alone on a dark corner stuffing the proceeds of her recently cashed social security check into her purse. There is nobody else in view. If the boy steals the purse, he gets the money immediately. That is a powerful incentive, and it is available immediately and without doubt. The costs of taking it are uncertain; the odds are at least fourteen to one that the police will not catch a given robber, and even if he is caught the odds are very good that he will not go to prison, unless he has a long record. On the average, no more than three felonies out of 100 result in the imprisonment of the offender. In addition to this uncertainty, whatever penalty may come his way will come only after a long delay; in some jurisdictions, it might take a year or more to complete the court disposition of the offender, assuming he is caught in the first place. Moreover, this young man may, in his ignorance of how the world works, think the odds in his favor are even greater and that the delay will be even longer.

Compounding the problems of delay and uncertainty is the fact that society cannot feasibly reduce the uncertainty attached to the chances of being arrested by more than a modest amount and though it can to some degree increase the probability and severity of a prison sentence for those who are caught, it cannot do so drastically by, for example, summarily executing all convicted robbers or even by sending all robbers to 20-year prison terms. Some scholars add a further complication: the young man may be incapable of assessing the risks of crime. How, they ask, is he to know his chances of being caught and punished? And even if he does know, is he perhaps 'driven' by uncontrollable impulses to snatch purses whatever the risks?

As if all this were not bad enough, the principal method by which scholars have attempted to measure the effect on crime of differences in the probability and severity of punishment has involved using data about aggregates of people (entire cities, counties, states, and even nations) rather than about individuals. In a typical study, of which there have been several dozen, the rate at which, say, robbery is committed in each state is 'explained' by means of a statistical procedure in which the analyst takes into account both the socioeconomic features of each state that might affect the supply of robbers (for example, the percentage of persons with low incomes, the unemployment rate, or the population density of the big cities) and the operation of the criminal justice system of each state as it attempts to cope with robbery (for example, the probability of being caught and imprisoned for a given robbery and the length of the average prison term for robbery). Most such studies find, after controlling for socioeconomic differences among the states, that the higher the probability of being imprisoned, the lower the robbery rate. Isaac Ehrlich, an economist, produced the best known of such analyses using data on crime in the United States in 1940, 1950, and 1960. To simplify a complex analysis, he found, after controlling for such factors as the income level and age distribution of the population, that the higher the probability of imprisonment for those convicted of robbery, the lower the robbery rate. Thus, differences in the certainty of punishment seem to make a difference in the level of crime. At the same time, Ehrlich did not find that the severity of punishment (the average time served in prison for robbery) had, independently of certainty, an effect on robbery rates in two of the three time periods (1940 and 1960).[1]

But there are some problems associated with studying the effect of sanctions on crime rates using aggregate data of this sort. One is that many of the most important factors are not known with any accuracy. For example, we are dependent on police reports for our measure of the robbery rate, and these undoubtedly vary in accuracy from place to place. If all police departments were inaccurate to the same degree, this would not be important; unfortunately, some departments are probably much less accurate than others, and this variable error can introduce a serious bias into the statistical estimates of the effect of the criminal justice system.

Moreover, if one omits from the equation some factor that affects the crime rate, then the estimated effect of the factors that are in the equation may be in error because some of the causal power belonging to the omitted factor will be falsely attributed to the included factors. For example, suppose we want to find out whether differences in the number of policemen on patrol among American cities are associated with differences in the rate at which robberies take place in those cities. If we fail to include in our equation a measure of the population density of the city, we may wrongly conclude that the more police there are on the streets, the *higher* the robbery rate and thus give support to the absurd policy proposition that the way to reduce robberies is to fire police officers. Since robberies are more likely to occur in larger, densely settled cities (which also tend to have a higher proportion of police), it would be a grave error to omit such measures of population from the equation. Since we are not certain what causes crime, we always run the risk of inadvertently omitting a key factor from our efforts to see if deterrence works.

Even if we manage to overcome these problems, a final difficulty lies in wait. The observed fact (and it has been observed many times) that states in which the probability of going to prison for robbery is low are also states which have high rates of robbery can be interpreted in one of two ways. It can mean *either* that the higher robbery rates are the results of the lower imprisonment rates (and thus evidence that deterrence works) *or* that the lower imprisonment rates are caused by the higher robbery rates. To see how the latter might be true, imagine a state that is experiencing, for some reason, a rapidly rising robbery rate. It arrests, convicts, and imprisons more and more robbers as more and more robberies are committed, but it cannot quite keep up. The robberies are increasing so fast that they 'swamp' the criminal justice system; prosecutors and judges respond by letting more robbers off without a prison sentence, or perhaps without even a trial, in order to keep the system from becoming hopelessly clogged. As a result, the proportion of arrested robbers who go to prison goes down while the robbery rate goes up. In this case, we ought to conclude, not that prison deters robbers, but that high robbery rates 'deter' prosecutors and judges.

The best analysis of these problems in statistical studies of deterrence is to be found in a report of the Panel on Research on Deterrent and Incapacitative Effects, set up by the National Research Council (an arm of the National Academy of Sciences). That panel, chaired by Alfred Blumstein of Carnegie-Mellon University, concluded that the available statistical evidence (as of 1978) did not warrant reaching any strong conclusions about the deterrent effect of existing differences among states or cities in the probability of punishment. The panel (of which I was a member) noted that 'the evidence certainly favors a proposition supporting deterrence more than it favors one asserting that deterrence is absent' but urged 'scientific caution' in interpreting this evidence.[2]

Subsequently, other criticisms of deterrence research, generally along the same lines as those of the panel, were published by Colin Loftin[3] and by Stephen S. Brier and Stephen E. Feinberg.[4]

Some commentators believe that these criticisms have proved that 'deterrence doesn't work' and thus the decks have now been cleared to get on with the task of investing in those programs, such as job creation and income maintenance, that *will* have an effect on crime. Such a conclusion is, to put it mildly, a bit premature.

REHABILITATING DETERRENCE

People are governed in their daily lives by rewards and penalties of every sort. We shop for bargain prices, praise our children for good behavior and scold them for bad, expect lower interest rates to stimulate home building and fear that higher ones will depress it, and conduct ourselves in public in ways that lead our friends and neighbors to form good opinions of us. To assert that 'deterrence doesn't work' is tantamount to either denying the plainest facts of everyday life or claiming that would-be criminals are utterly different from the rest of us. They may well be different to some degree – they most likely have a weaker conscience, worry less about their reputation in polite society, and find it harder to postpone gratifying their urges – but these differences of degree do not make them indifferent to the risks and gains of crime. If they were truly indifferent, they would scarcely be able to function at all, for their willingness to take risks would be offset by their indifference to loot. Their lives would consist of little more than the erratic display of animal instincts and fleeting impulses.

The question before us is whether feasible changes in the deferred and uncertain penalties of crime […] will affect crime rates in ways that can be detected by the data and statistical methods at our disposal. Though the unreliability of crime data and the limitations of statistical analysis are real enough and are accurately portrayed by the Panel of the National Research Council, there are remedies and rejoinders that, on balance, strengthen the case for the claim that not only does deterrence work (the panel never denied that), it probably works in ways that can be measured, even in the aggregate.

The errors in official statistics about crime rates have been addressed by employing other measures of crime, in particular reports gathered by Census Bureau interviewers from citizens who have been victims of crime. While these victim surveys have problems of their own (such as the forgetfulness of citizens), they are not the same problems as those that affect police reports of crime. Thus, if we obtain essentially the same findings about the effect of sanctions on crime from studies that use victim data as we do from studies using police data, our confidence in these findings is strengthened. Studies of this sort have been done by Itzhak Goldberg at Stanford and by Barbara Boland and myself, and the results are quite consistent with those from research based on police reports.[5] As sanctions become more likely, crime becomes less common.

There is a danger that important factors will be omitted from any statistical study of crime in ways that bias the results, but this problem is no greater in studies of penalties than it is in studies of unemployment rates, voting behavior, or any of a hundred other socially significant topics. Since we can never know with certainty everything that may affect crime (or unemployment, or voting), we must base our conclusions not on any single piece of research, but on the general thrust of a variety of studies analyzing many different causal factors. The Panel of the National Research Council took exactly this position. While noting that 'there is the possibility that as yet unknown and so untested' factors may be affecting crime, 'this is not a sufficient basis for dismissing' the common finding that crime goes up as sanctions become less certain because 'many of the analyses have included some of the more obvious possible third causes and they still find negative associations between sanctions and crimes.'[6]

It is possible that rising crime rates 'swamp' the criminal justice system so that a negative statistical association between, say, rates of theft and the chances of going to prison for theft may mean not that a decline in imprisonment is causing theft to increase, but rather that a rise in theft is causing imprisonment to become less likely. This might occur particularly with respect to less serious crimes, such as shoplifting or petty larceny; indeed, the proportion of prisoners who are shoplifters or petty thieves has gone down over the last two decades. But it is hard to imagine that the criminal justice system would respond to an increase in murder or armed robbery by letting some murderers or armed robbers off with no punishment. There is no evidence that convicted murderers are any less likely to go to prison today than they were 20 years ago. Moreover, the apparent deterrent effect of prison on serious crimes, such as murder and robbery, was apparently as great in 1940 or 1950, when these crimes were much less common, as it is today, suggesting that swamping has not occurred.[7]

The best studies of deterrence that manage to overcome many of these problems provide evidence that deterrence works. Alfred Blumstein and Daniel Nagin studied the relationship between draft evasion and the penalties imposed for evading the draft. After controlling for the socioeconomic characteristics of the states, they found that the higher the probability of conviction for draft evasion, the lower the evasion rates. This is an especially strong finding because it is largely immune to some of the problems of other research. Draft evasion is more accurately measured than street crime, hence errors arising from poor data are not a problem. And draft evasion cases did not swamp the federal courts in which they were tried, in part because such cases (like murder in state courts) make up only a small fraction of the courts' workload (7 per cent in the case of draft evasion) and in part because the attorney general had instructed federal prosecutors to give high priority to these cases. Blumstein and Nagin concluded that draft evasion is deterrable.[8]

Another way of testing whether deterrence works is to look, not at differences among states at one point in time, but at changes in the nation as a whole over a long period of time. Historical data on the criminal justice system in America is so spotty that such research is difficult to do here, but it is not at all difficult in England where the data are excellent. Kenneth I. Wolpin analyzed changes in crime rates and in various parts of the criminal justice system (the chances of being arrested, convicted, and punished) for the period 1894 to 1967, and concluded that changes in the probability of being punished seemed to cause changes in the crime rate. He offers reasons for believing that this causal connection cannot be explained away by the argument that the criminal justice system was being swamped.[9]

Given what we are trying to measure – changes in the behavior of a small number of hard-to-observe persons who are responding to delayed and uncertain penalties – we will never be entirely sure that our statistical manipulations have proved that deterrence works. What is impressive is that so many (but not all) studies using such different methods come to similar conclusions. [...]

The relationship between crime on the one hand and the rewards and penalties at the disposal of society on the other is complicated. It is not complicated, however, in the way some people imagine. It is not the case (except for a tiny handful of pathological personalities) that criminals are so unlike the rest of us as to be indifferent to the costs and benefits of the opportunities open to them. Nor is it the case that criminals have no opportunities. [...]

It is better to think of both people and social controls as arrayed on a continuum. People differ by degrees in the extent to which they are governed by internal restraints on criminal behavior and in the stake they have in conformity;[10] they also differ by degrees in the extent to which they can find, hold, and benefit from a job. Similarly, sanctions and opportunities are changeable only within

modest limits. We want to find out to what extent feasible changes in the certainty, swiftness, or severity of penalties will make a difference in the behavior
of those 'at the margin' – those, that is, who are neither so innocent nor so
depraved as to be prepared to ignore small changes (which are, in fact, the only
feasible changes) in the prospects of punishment. By the same token, we want to
know what feasible (and again, inevitably small) changes in the availability of
jobs will affect those at the margin of the labor market – those, that is, who are
neither so eager for a good job or so contemptuous of 'jerks' who take 'straight
jobs' as to ignore modest changes in job opportunities. I am aware of no evidence
supporting the conventional liberal view that while the number of persons who
will be affected by changing penalties is very small, the number who will be
affected by increasing jobs is very large; nor am I aware of any evidence supporting the conventional conservative view, which is the opposite of this.

I believe that the weight of the evidence – aggregate statistical analyses,
evaluations of experiments and quasi-experiments, and studies of individual
behavior – supports the view that the rate of crime is influenced by its costs.
This influence is greater – or easier to observe – for some crimes and persons
than for others. It is possible to lower the crime rate by increasing the certainty
of sanctions, but inducing the criminal justice system to make those changes is
difficult, especially if committing the offense confers substantial benefits on the
perpetrator, if apprehending and punishing the offender does not provide substantial rewards to members of the criminal justice system, or if the crime itself
lacks the strong moral condemnation of society. In theory, the rate of crime
should also be sensitive to the benefits of non-crime – for example, the value
and availability of jobs – but thus far efforts to show that relationship have led
to inconclusive results.[11] Moreover, the nature of the connection between crime
and legitimate opportunities is complex: unemployment (and prosperity!) can
cause crime, crime can cause unemployment (but probably not prosperity),
and both crime and unemployment may be caused by common third factors.
Economic factors probably have the greatest influence on the behavior of low-
rate, novice offenders and the least on high-rate, experienced ones. Despite the
uncertainty that attaches to the connection between the economy and crime,
I believe the wisest course of action for society is to try simultaneously to increase
both the benefits of non-crime and the costs of crime, all the while bearing in
mind that no feasible changes in either part of the equation are likely to produce
big changes in crime rates.

Some may grant my argument that it makes sense to continue to try to make
those marginal gains that are possible by simultaneously changing in desirable
directions both the costs of crime and benefits of non-crime, but they may still feel
that it is better to spend more heavily on one side or the other of the cost-benefit
equation. I have attended numerous scholarly gatherings where I have heard
learned persons subject to the most searching scrutiny any evidence purporting
to show the deterrent effect of sanctions but accept with scarcely a blink the theory that crime is caused by a 'lack of opportunities.'[12] Perhaps what they mean is
that since the evidence on both propositions is equivocal, then it does less harm

to believe in – and invest in – the 'benign' (that is, job-creation) program. If so, they are surely wrong. If we try to make the penalties for crime swifter and more certain, and it should turn out that deterrence does not work, then all we have done is increase the risks facing persons who commit a crime. If we fail to increase the certainty and swiftness of penalties, and it should turn out that deterrence *does* work, then we have needlessly increased the risk of innocent persons being victimized. [...]

NOTES

1 Isaac Ehrlich, 'Participation in illegitimate activities: a theoretical and empirical investigation', *Journal of Political Economy*, 81 (1973), pp. 521–65.
2 Alfred Blumstein, Jacqueline Cohen and Daniel Nagin (eds.), *Deterrence and Incapacitation: Estimating the Effects of Criminal Sanctions on Crime Rates* (National Academy of Sciences, Washington, DC, 1978). Isaac Ehrlich responds to this report and its criticisms of his work in Ehrlich and Mark Randall, 'Fear of deterrence', *Journal of Legal Studies*, 6 (1977), pp. 293–316.
3 Colin Loftin, 'Alternative estimates of the impact of certainty and severity of punishment on levels of homicide in American states', in Stephen E. Feinberg and Albert J. Reiss (eds), *Indicators of Crime and Criminal Justice: Quantitative Studies*, report number NCJ-62349 of the Bureau of Justice Statistics (US Department of Justice, Washington, DC, 1980), pp. 75–81.
4 Stephen S. Brier and Stephen E. Feinberg, 'Recent econometric modeling of crime and punishment: support for the deterrence hypothesis?' in Feinberg and Reiss, *Indicators of Crime and Criminal Justice*, pp. 82–97.
5 Itzhak Goldberg, 'A note on using victimization rates to test deterrence', Technical Report CERDCR-5-78, Center for Econometric Studies of the Justice System, Stanford University (December 1978); James Q. Wilson and Barbara Boland, 'Crime', in William Gorham and Nathan Glazer (eds), *The Urban Predicament* (Urban Institute, Washington, DC, 1976).
6 Blumstein et al. *Deterrence and Incapacitation*, p. 23.
7 Isaac Ehrlich and Mark Randall, 'Fear of deterrence', *Journal of Legal Studies*, 6 (1977), pp. 304–7.
8 Alfred Blumstein and Daniel Nagin, 'The deterrent effect of legal sanctions on draft evasion', *Stanford Law Review*, 28 (1977), pp. 241–75.
9 Kenneth I. Wolpin, 'An economic analysis of crime and punishment in England and Wales, 1894–1967', *Journal of Political Economy*, 86 (1978), pp. 815–40.
10 The concept of a 'stake in the conformity' is from Jackson Toby, 'Social disorganization and stake in conformity', *Journal of Criminal Law and Criminology*, 48 (1957), pp. 12–17.
11 Cf. Richard B. Freeman, 'Crime and unemployment' in James Q. Wilson (ed.), *Crime and Public Policy* (Institute for Contemporary Studies, San Francisco, 1983), ch. 6.
12 An egregious example of the double standard at work is Charles Silberman, *Criminal Violence, Criminal Justice* (Random House, New York, 1978), wherein the studies on deterrence are closely criticized (pp. 182–95) in a way that leads the author to conclude that 'more punishment is not the answer' (p. 197) but 'community development programs' are found (on the basis of virtually no data whatsoever) to lead to 'community regeneration' and a virtual absence of criminal violence (pp. 430–66).

31

Giving criminals their just deserts

Andrew von Hirsch

The limits on state power over the individual have yet to be charted in the field of criminal sentencing. The state now has virtually untrammeled authority to sentence a convicted criminal for any purpose and with any degree of severity. It is incumbent upon civil libertarians to suggest, in the interest of fairness to those being sentenced, what the constraints on the state's sentencing power should be.

Attitudes about the criminal sentence have changed. Until recently the ideal of treatment dominated: The sentence was supposed to rehabilitate, and sentencing judges and parole boards were supposed to have wide discretion so they could tailor the sentence to the offender's needs. This notion still had sufficient vitality to prompt David J. Rothman to warn of its dangers in his thoughtful article, 'De-carcerating Prisoners and Patients', in the Fall 1973 issue of *Civil Liberties Review*. Is it rational or fair, he asked, to sentence for treatment without good reason to expect that the therapy will work? Might not the rehabilitative ideology give a misleading aura of beneficence to the harsh realities of punishing people – and thus legitimize more intervention in offenders' lives with fewer constraints on official behavior? Since that article was published, there has been a marked decline of faith in rehabilitation.

Although penal reformers have urged the treatment of offenders for over a century, it was not until the 1940s and 1950s that experimental programs were widely tried and evaluated. The results were disappointing: Offenders placed in correctional treatment programs usually returned to crime about as often as those who did not participate. Thus, for example, a survey by Robert Martinson and his collaborators of most of the major experimental programs between 1945 and 1967 concludes that 'with few and isolated exceptions, the rehabilitative efforts that have been reported so far have had no appreciable effect on recidivism'.

From *Civil Liberties Review*, 1976, 3: 23–35.

Since spring 1974, when Martinson published the conclusions of his survey, the thesis that treatment seldom works has become familiar in professional circles, has been mentioned in newspaper articles, and has been noted in several presidential speeches. Now it is the advocates of treatment who are on the defensive – who insist, almost plaintively, that the failure of many treatment programs in the past does not necessarily mean that all treatments are doomed to fail. As doubts about the effectiveness of treatment grow, traditional faith in the rehabilitative sentence – the sentence especially designed to meet the offender's need for correctional therapy – is declining, and may already be moribund.

What has persisted, however, is the idea that the sentence should primarily be a crime control technique. This assumption underlay the rehabilitative sentence: the offender would be less likely to offend again if consigned to the proper treatment. Now, when rehabilitation seemingly has failed, interest has shifted to other sentencing approaches that supposedly will do the crime control job more effectively.

A renewed faith in incapacitation is symptomatic of this continuing search for the sentence that best prevents crime. If offenders cannot be cured of their criminal tendencies, it is argued, they can at least be isolated – placed behind bars where they cannot prey on those outside. Simple restraint replaces therapy, and restraint works: prisons may have few other merits, but they surely can protect the community against offense-prone persons – at least during the period of confinement. As former Attorney General William B. Saxbe put it in a 1974 speech to a convention of police chiefs: 'Too many dangerous convicted offenders are placed back in society ... and that simply must stop.'

Those less conservative than Saxbe have also been attracted to this approach. The National Council on Crime and Delinquency, a vocal critic of American prisons, issued a policy statement that 'prisons are destructive to prisoners and to those charged with holding them', and that the only offenders who should be sentenced to prison are those 'who, if not confined, would be a serious danger to the public'. The prison sanction, in other words, should be a means of restraining those who would harm others if released. The recent National Advisory Commission on crime likewise urged that the prison sentence be used chiefly to isolate the dangerous recidivist. The theory has been embraced even by those who see themselves as radical critics of today's criminal justice system.

[...]
Gary Wills, in an article in the *New York Review of Books*, denounced prisons as 'human sewers' and declared that their supposed justifications – rehabilitation, deterrence, or retribution – have no merit whatever. Conclusion: abolish the prison, right? Wrong. A letter from a prisoner in a subsequent issue of the *New York Review* asked Wills what he proposed to do with 'people who go about chronically molesting children, or continually stealing and burglarizing'. Wills replied: 'once we properly identify the chronic molester he should be removed from society. ... There is an irreducible minimum of people who present an active danger to society whenever they are released into it. They should be sequestered,

in places which have no other aim *except* sequestration.' In plain English, dangerous offenders should be locked up.

Confining the 'dangerous' has its undeniable attractions: low-risk offenders can be decarcerated, and use of the prison can be limited to those who present high risks of returning to crime. But there are hazards. One is the difficulty of distinguishing the dangerous individuals from the non-dangerous. As Leonard Orland pointed out in 'Can we establish the rule of law in prisons?' (*Civil Liberties Review,* Fall 1975), 'our ability to predict *future* criminal behavior is very limited; it may be nonexistent'. When forecasting serious crimes, there is a strong tendency to over-predict; most of those identified as risks will be 'false positives' – persons mistakenly predicted to offend.

Class bias is another problem. If the sole aim of the sentence is to prevent recurrences, its severity will depend on the offender's status. When a public official or corporation executive commits a heinous crime in office, he can be prevented from doing it again simply by depriving him of his position of power. By contrast, the poor person who commits a grave offense has no position of power to lose, and he is sent to prison to keep him from offending again. Finally, there is the potential for escalation. When the sentence is viewed as a means for isolating dangerous convicts, sentencers will be criticized every time they release someone who subsequently commits a crime, and will respond by steadily widening the net – by opting for confinement whenever there is any doubt whether the individual will stay within the law. They will, in other words, adopt the maxim of California's Attorney General Evelle Younger: 'I'd rather run the risk of keeping the wrong man [in prison] a little longer than let the wrong man out too soon.'

Harvard's James Q. Wilson suggests a more sophisticated approach to incapacitating criminals in his thoughtful and widely read book *Thinking About Crime* (whose influence, incidentally, is manifest in President Ford's and Senator Edward Kennedy's proposals for mandatory minimum sentences). Wilson starts with the hypothesis that most serious crimes are committed by a relatively small number of repeaters who, because of the large number of crimes they perpetrate, sooner or later are caught and convicted. Current sentencing policy imposes long prison terms on a few of these individuals, but allows most of them to be released on probation and thus to return to crime if they so choose. (In Los Angeles County, Wilson notes, the proportion of convicted robbers with major prior records who were sent to prison in 1970 was only 27 per cent.)

If prison sentences – even of modest length – were invariably imposed in such cases, the incapacitative payoff would be substantial, Wilson suggests. One would be taking out of circulation most of those responsible for serious crimes, at least for a portion of their criminal careers. (There would be no need to try to predict which individual convicts are dangerous; instead, there would simply be a rule that conviction for certain crimes results in a stated period of imprisonment.) The crime control benefits from such a strategy, he claims, would be very large. 'Were we to devote [our] resources to a strategy [that is] well within our abilities – namely, to incapacitating a larger fraction of the convicted serious robbers,' he says, 'then not only is a 20 per cent reduction [in robbery] possible, but even larger ones are conceivable.'

Wilson's proposals certainly sound appealing: moderate sentences, less disparity (because judges would have less discretion), and huge payoffs in community protection – with 20 per cent fewer robberies. But Wilson does not ask the uncomfortable question: What if the promised crime-control benefits do not materialize? The history of sentencing reform has been characterized by high hopes for reducing crime followed by disappointment. In the 1820s, long sentences to penitentiaries offering inmates 'moral therapy' were supposed to cut the crime rate. They did not. In the 1900s, probation for treatable offenders and lengthy sentences for dangerous ones were supposed to do the job. They did not. In the 1960s, fewer prison sentences and more sentences to treatment in the community were supposed to succeed. They did not. Now Wilson claims that imprisoning a larger proportion of those convicted will do the crime control job where previous strategies failed. But can one really be so sure?

To sustain his claim, Wilson has to assume that relatively few 'habitual criminals' are responsible not only for the crimes for which they are convicted, but also for the bulk of the unsolved crimes as well. While this is a plausible assumption, it is no more than that: the evidence on who is responsible for crimes committed with impunity is, for obvious reasons, sketchy at best. (Wilson cites calculations by Reuel Shinnar of the CCNY School of Engineering that purport to show a large reduction in the crime rate if every person convicted of a serious crime is imprisoned for a stated period. Shinnar's calculations, however, are no more accurate than the postulates he makes about who commits the unsolved crimes. He himself admits that his estimates would be seriously awry if much of unsolved crime were committed either by occasional criminals or by skilled professionals who never are convicted for a serious crime. The estimates would also be in error if such crimes as robbery were economically attractive enough so that the removal of some robbers from circulation would result in newly recruited robbers taking their places.) Were these assumptions mistaken, the incapacitative payoff from Wilson's sentencing strategy could be much smaller than he expects.

One must therefore be prepared for the possibility of disappointing results. As David Rothman has wisely counselled, strategies for sentencing reform should be based on a failure model – of what is minimally acceptable even if the hoped-for crime control benefits do not materialize. Wilson's plan is the archetypal success model, and that is its weakness. Despite the formidable record of past failures and the speculative nature of his own estimates, Wilson does not seriously ask: 'and what if the scheme led to only 1 per cent fewer robberies, or none fewer?'

That question leads to others that are worrisome. For example, how much extra suffering is inflicted in the interest of a crime control strategy that may fail? Wilson's proposals, if implemented, could mean imprisoning many more people than are confined today. Such persons will lose their liberty on the supposition that their loss will protect the rights of others, the potential victims of crime. But to the extent that Wilson's plan fails, that supposition will have been wrong. We will have added to offenders' suffering without gaining the promised protection of the rights of others, scarcely a morally satisfactory outcome. Granted, we are speaking of persons who have already been convicted of crimes. But if such persons are sent to prison when – but for Wilson's incapacitative theories – they would have received lighter punishments, the moral difficulty persists. (Wilson might reply that his program is experimental, that it should be tried and if it does not work we can still go back to incarcerating fewer people. But the question remains: how much added suffering would there be while this experiment was being carried out? An experiment can be ethically unacceptable if it exacts too great a human toll.)

This problem of inflicting unnecessary suffering is highlighted by Wilson's comments about new prison construction. Disagreeing with many reformers who have urged a moratorium on new prisons, Wilson calls for building more facilities to house those whom he would incapacitate. Imagine, then, the following scenario. To accommodate Wilson's sentencing scheme, new prisons go up. Then, contrary to expectation, the promised reduction in the crime rate does not occur. What are we left with? The same old high crime rate, but more prisons with more beds to fill. Experience suggests that once the facilities are built, the pressures to keep them full of inmates are hard to resist. Wilson's experiment, in short, is apt to be irreversible, whether or not it succeeds in reducing crime.

Another danger is the possibility of escalation of sentences. Wilson assumes that prison terms of moderate length, if invariably imposed on those who have been convicted, will interfere sufficiently with most offenders' criminal careers to diminish crime rates. But suppose his 'modest' sentences do not work? Does not his incapacitative rationale point, then, to much longer sentences? After all, the only sure way to prevent criminally inclined persons from offending again is to hold them until they 'burn out' – until aging has depleted their criminal propensities. Wilson argues that the longer sentences are, the more reluctant sentencers will be to impose them. But if those in charge of the sentencing system take his incapacitative aims seriously, and if experience convinces them that shorter sentences are not enough to do the job, that reluctance may disappear. The possibility of escalation raises the issue [of what] *moral* limits [there should] be on the use of very long prison terms to incapacitate, even if such sentences were effective in reducing crime.

Where Wilson goes wrong, I think, is in his underlying assumption: his preoccupation with crime control to the near exclusion of considerations of justice. It has commonly been supposed – and Wilson continues in this tradition – that justice has largely been satisfied once an offender has been tried and convicted with due process. Thereafter, the focus has been almost exclusively on crime prevention – on which sentencing strategies (rehabilitation or incapacitation? long sentences or short?) serve public safety best. Seldom is the word justice found in the sentencing literature.

The emphasis, I am convinced, should be precisely the reverse: primacy should be given to considerations of justice in sentencing. A system of criminal justice can be tolerable in a free society only if we are determined to make it what its name implies: a system of justice, not a social engineering project. In punishing the convicted, the consequences to the individual are too harsh to permit us to act as if we were merely totting up costs and benefits, seeking the maximum efficiency in preventing crime. Concededly, no sentencing system operating in a society as fraught with inequalities as ours can come close to being truly just. But after conviction as before, justice should not be merely a euphemism for law enforcement; it should be an ideal which we should at least try to approximate.

In the [early 1970s] I was involved in an effort to think through a sentencing scheme grounded mainly on ideas about justice. It was undertaken by the Committee for the Study of Incarceration,[1] an interdisciplinary group which included law professors, sociologists, a psychoanalyst, a criminologist, and (atypically for an inquiry about sentencing) a historian and a philosopher. Instead of continuing the debate about what 'works', we decided at the outset to focus on the question: What is the just sentence?

Suppose one begins with a general definition of justice – (Aristotle's) – that like cases should be treated alike and unlike cases should be treated proportionate to their differences. One must then ask what kind of likeness is relevant for purposes of justice. (Is it, for example, the equally deserving or the equally needy who should be treated alike?) That is a hard question when there are no clues: there is nothing about wealth, for example, that suggests on its face whether it should be distributed according to merit or need. In the case of punishments, rewards and grades, however, the answer should be more obvious. Justice requires that they be distributed according to their recipients' deserts, because they *purport* to be deserved.

Academic grades illustrate this point. Suppose a student writes a poor exam paper. Suppose he needs an A to get into law school. Why not give him the grade he needs? The answer is, of course, that an A symbolizes a superior performance; that the student's performance, in fact, was poor; and hence that he simply does not deserve the A, whatever his needs. Desert is the only fair criterion, because that is precisely what a grade connotes. The same is true of punishment. It treats the person as though he deserves the pain inflicted – and does so because of its symbolism, its implicit moral condemnation of the offender. Punishment is not merely disagreeable (so are taxes and conscription); it implies that the person acted wrongfully and is blameworthy for having done so. Where standards of what constitutes criminal behavior are concerned, this point is a familiar one. It was made two decades ago by the late Henry M. Hart of Harvard Law School in his defense of the criminal law's requirements of culpable intent. Since punishment characteristically ascribes blame, he argued, violations should not be punished unless the offender was at fault (i.e., acted intentionally, or negligently). Accidental violations should not be punished because they are not blameworthy.

What is usually overlooked, however, is that the same argument holds after conviction, when sentence is imposed. By then, it has been decided that the offender deserves punishment, but the question of how much he deserves remains. The severity of the punishment connotes the degree of blame: the sterner the penalty, the greater the implicit reproof. Sending someone away to prison for years implies that he is more to be condemned than does jailing him for a few months or putting him on probation. In deciding severity, therefore, the crime must be sufficiently serious to merit the blame.

This means that sentences should, as a matter of justice, be decided according to a principle of *commensurate deserts*. The severity of punishment should comport with the seriousness of the crime. Stringent punishments should be limited to crimes that are serious; as the gravity of the crime diminishes, so should the severity of the punishment. When this principle is not observed, the degree of blame becomes inappropriate. If an offender convicted of a lesser crime is punished severely, the moral obloquy which so drastic a penalty carries will attach to him – and unjustly so, given the not-so-very-wrongful character of his offense. Conversely, giving a mild punishment to someone convicted of a serious crime understates the blame – and thus depreciates the importance of the values at stake. […]

Once it is accepted as a requirement of justice, the commensurate-deserts principle should determine the sentencing structure. The seriousness of the offender's crime – not his need for treatment, his dangerousness, or the deterrence of others – ought to be decisive. Penalties must be scaled in accordance with the gravity of the offense, and departures from the deserved sentence should be impermissible – even if they had some crime-control usefulness.

A sentencing system based on this conception of justice would have the following principal features.

- The degree of likelihood that the offender might return to crime would be irrelevant to the choice of sentence. Even if crime forecasting techniques could be improved, an offender simply doesn't deserve to have his punishment increased on the basis of what he may do rather than on the basis of what he has done.

- Indeterminacy of sentence would be abolished. Since the seriousness of the crime (the only proper basis for the sentence, in our theory) is known at the time of verdict, there would be no need to delay the decision on sentence length to see how well the offender is adjusting. Prisoners would no longer be kept in agonizing suspense for years, waiting for the parole board to make up its mind about discharge.

- Sentencing discretion would be sharply reduced (and hence today's problem of vast disparities among sentences alleviated). The wide leeway which sentencers now enjoy was sustained by the traditional assumption that the sentence was a means for altering the offender's behavior and had to be especially fashioned to his needs. When this assumption is given up, the basis for such broad discretion crumbles. In order for the sentence to be deserved, there must be standards governing how severely offenders should be punished for different crimes. (Otherwise, sentences will not be consistent; one judge could treat an offense as serious and punish accordingly, while another judge, having a different set of values, could treat the same infraction as minor.) The Incarceration Committee's report thus proposes a system of standardized penalties. For each gradation in seriousness of criminal behavior, a definite penalty – the 'presumptive sentence' – would be set. Offenders convicted of crimes of that degree of gravity would normally receive that specific sentence – except when there were unusual circumstances of mitigation or aggravation.

- Imprisonment would be limited to serious offenses. The commensurate-deserts principle allows severe punishments only for serious crimes. Imprisonment is necessarily a severe penalty. (Even if prison conditions are improved, the loss of liberty itself is a great deprivation.) Prison thus should be the sanction only for crimes, which cause or risk grievous harm – such as assault, armed robbery, and rape – and not for most non-violent larcenies of personal belongings. Even for serious crimes, moreover, the length of imprisonment ought to be stringently rationed, given the painfulness of the prison sanction. The Incarceration Committee's report recommends that most prison sentences be kept below three years. (Bear in mind that we are speaking of actual time in prison, not of a purported sentence that can later be cut back by a parole board.)

- Penalties less severe than imprisonment would be for the non-serious offences which constitute the bulk of the criminal justice system's caseload. These milder penalties would not be rehabilitative measures but, simply and explicitly, less severe punishments. Warnings, limited deprivations of leisure time (and perhaps fines) would be used in lieu of imprisonment. Probation would be phased out because of its discretionary and treatment-oriented features.

There is potential for disagreement, of course, about which crimes are serious. Yet assessments of seriousness – of how harmful the conduct is, and how culpable the offender – at least are moral judgments akin to those we make in everyday life. It should be easier (or certainly no harder) to make such judgments than to surmise on slight evidence how a given sentencing policy will affect crime rates. Moreover, the extent of disagreement on questions of seriousness should not be exaggerated. Beginning [...] with the work of the criminologists Thorsten Sellin and Marvin Wolfgang at the University of Pennsylvania, several studies have measured popular perceptions of the gravity of crimes and found a surprising degree of consensus. When asked to rank common acts of theft, fraud and violence on a scale according to their degree of heinousness, people from widely different walks of life tend to make similar ratings.

In this highly compressed description, I have skipped several of the harder (and more interesting) issues. Why should punishment exist at all? (Why shouldn't we, instead, adopt a wholly different kind of social control mechanism?) How can a just deserts model for sentencing be defended in a society that is not itself just? Is one permitted, in a desert-based system, to take an offender's earlier crimes into account? We try to wrestle with these questions in the Incarceration Committee's report.

In sketching this sentencing scheme, I have considered only the requirements of justice. But the system could have some collateral usefulness in controlling crime, even if it is not fashioned with crime control specifically in mind. While sentences would be much shorter, they would be more certain: Anyone convicted of a sufficiently serious crime would face some time in prison – and increasing the certainty of a substantial punishment may be useful as a deterrent. There also could be some incapacitative benefit. Since all offenders convicted of serious crimes would be imprisoned, those who were inclined to offend again would be restrained, at least temporarily. But we would always bear in mind that these benefits might fail to materialize. Perhaps there will not be a sufficiently large increase in certainty of punishment – because too many of those who commit serious crimes do not get caught, or too many of those caught avoid conviction or succeed in bargaining the charges down. But even with such disappointed hopes (even, in fact, if the scheme proves to have no greater efficiency than today's system), it is still defensible because it is a fairer system. Offenders' punishments would more closely approximate what they deserve, and equally blameworthy individuals would receive more nearly similar sentences. Because the scheme is grounded chiefly on equity, a failure in its crime control effectiveness (always a risk to any criminal justice strategy) would not be so devastating as it would be to a scheme such as Wilson's, which relies almost exclusively on the promise that it will work.

A desert-based scheme can serve, moreover, as a baseline – a norm for judging sentencing systems that have been devised with crime control more immediately in mind. Let us suppose that a penologist wants to build an 'efficient' sentencing system and, for the sake of crime-control efficacy, proposes sentences which diverge from those that are deserved. Is it enough for him to show that his system is likely to work? Certainly not, for our desert-based system may work also. Perhaps his system is capable of reducing serious crime by, say, 5 per cent – but our system of deserved sentences might, conceivably, also affect the crime rate by a similar percentage. In that event, his system should be rejected out of hand, for it sacrifices justice while having little or no greater impact on crime than a more just system would. The burden thus falls on him to show not merely how his system will discourage crime, but how it will do so more effectively than a desert-based system would – and that would be no easy matter to establish. Even if this burden were met, a moral decision would have to be made: whether the added crime-control benefits warranted the sacrifice of equity involved. The greater the departure from just (that is, deserved) sentences, the stronger the moral argument for rejecting the proposal, notwithstanding its expected usefulness in curbing crime.

To illustrate this point, let us look once more at Wilson's proposals. Where serious offenses are concerned, his recommended sentences are not dissimilar to the ones we suggest, despite his different rationale. Wilson proposes that anyone convicted of a major offense such as armed robbery (especially when it is a second or third conviction) be sentenced to prison, but that long sentences be avoided. He promises a dramatic (20 per cent or more) reduction in robberies as the result of such a policy. As we have seen, one well might be skeptical that this result will occur. But even if there were no measurable reduction in the robbery rate, Wilson's recommendation could still be defended – but on our grounds of desert: armed robbery is serious, and serious crimes deserve severe punishments.

The conclusion differs, however, with less serious offenses. Wilson proposes that these more venial infractions (unless 'manifestly trivial') be punished by a 'deprivation of liberty' for a few days, weeks, or months. He allows that the deprivation might be something less than full-time imprisonment (confinement only at night, for example, leaving the offender free to go to work during the day), but states that the choice between full and partial restraint should depend on the need to 'protect society'. This leaves open the possibility that lesser offenders could suffer full-time imprisonment if (as is often the case) they seemed likely to return to crime if released. Here, the moral objection is evident: crimes such as shoplifting, passing bad checks, and the like are not serious enough to deserve the harsh sanction of imprisonment.

As this aspect of Wilson's scheme departs from the requirements of justice, one would have to ask, what reason is there to believe that such stiff penalties for lesser offenses would be appreciably more effective than the more modest sanctions of a desert-based system? And even if they were more effective, is the crime-control payoff really worth the sacrifice of fairness? To the second question, my answer would clearly be no, given my philosophical assumption that primacy ought to be accorded the ends of justice. But the answer might still be no, even were one a little readier to compromise ideals of fairness for the sake of crime control – since the suggested severer than just penalties are for crimes which, being less serious, pose no terrible threat to the community's safety.

It may seem strange that the Incarceration Committee's liberal professors and activists, when faced with the choice between rehabilitation and desert, chose desert. Why go back to so ancient a notion? Why not continue to focus on what works best, and leave what is deserved to casuists and theologians? Unfashionable as the idea of desert has been, we found it essential to justice in sentencing. It is crucial to the question that civil libertarians ought to be asking: What are the ethical limits on making convicted individuals suffer for the sake of preventing crime? The point was aptly stated ninety years ago by F.H. Wines, one of the few prison reformers of that age to question the then dominant ideal of rehabilitation, when he said: 'Of the retribution theory, it may at least be said that if it is an assertion of the right to inflict all the pain which a particular criminal act may merit, it is the denial of the right to inflict on any human being any needless and unmerited pain'.

NOTE

1   See A. von Hirsch, *Doing Justice: the Choice of Punishments*. Report of the Committee for the Study of Incarceration (New York, Hill and Wang, 1976).

32

The value of rehabilitation

Francis T. Cullen and
Karen E. Gilbert

[…] [P]reoccupation with the misuses and limitations of treatment programs has perhaps blinded many current-day liberals to the important benefits that have been or can be derived from popular belief in the notion that offenders should be saved and not simply punished. In this respect, the persistence of a strong rehabilitative ideology can be seen to function as a valuable resource for those seeking to move toward the liberal goal of introducing greater benevolence into the criminal justice system. Alternatively, we can begin to question whether the reform movement sponsored by the Left will not be undermined should liberal faith in rehabilitation reach a complete demise. In this context, four major reasons are offered below for why we believe that liberals should reaffirm and not reject the correctional ideology of rehabilitation.

1 Rehabilitation is the only justification of criminal sanctioning that obligates the state to care for an offender's needs or welfare. Admittedly, rehabilitation promises a pay-off to society in the form of offenders transformed into law-abiding, productive citizens who no longer desire to victimize the public. Yet treatment ideology also conveys the strong message that this utilitarian outcome can only be achieved if society is willing to punish its captives humanely and to compensate offenders for the social disadvantages that have constrained them to undertake a life in crime. In contrast, the three competing justifications of criminal sanctioning – deterrence, incapacitation and retribution (or just deserts) – contain not even the pretence that the state has an obligation to do good for its charges. The only responsibility of the state is to inflict the pains that accompany the deprivation of liberty or of material resources (e.g., fines); whatever utility such practices engender flows only to society and not to its captives. Thus, deterrence aims to protect the social order by making offenders suffer sufficiently to dissuade them as well as onlookers

From *Reaffirming Rehabilitation*, pp. 247–63. (Cincinnati, OH: Anderson, 1982.)

entertaining similar criminal notions from venturing outside the law on future occasions. Incapacitation also seeks to preserve the social order but through a surer means; by caging criminals – 'locking 'em up and throwing away the keys' – inmates will no longer be at liberty to prey on law-abiding members of society. The philosophy of retribution, on the other hand, manifests a disinterest in questions of crime control, instead justifying punishment on the grounds that it presumably provides society and crime victims with the psychic satisfaction that justice has been accomplished by harming offenders in doses commensurate with the harms their transgressions have caused. [...]

These considerations lead us to ask whether it is strategically wise for liberals wishing to mitigate existing inhumanities in the criminal justice system to forsake the only prevailing correctional ideology that is expressly benevolent toward offenders. It is difficult to imagine that reform efforts will be more humanizing if liberals willingly accept the premise that the state has no responsibility to do good, only to inflict pain. Notably, Gaylin and Rothman, proponents of the justice model, recognized the dangers of such a choice when they remarked that 'in giving up the rehabilitative model, we abandon not just our innocence but perhaps more. The concept of deserts is intellectual and moralistic; in its devotion to principle, it turns back on such compromising considerations as generosity and charity, compassion and love'.[1] They may have shown even greater hesitation in rejecting rehabilitation and affirming just deserts had they had an opportunity to dwell on the more recent insights of radical thinkers Herman and Julia Schwendinger:

> Nevertheless, whatever the expressed qualifications, the justice model now also justifies objectively retrogressive outcomes because of its insistence that social policies give priority to punishment rather than rehabilitation. Punishment, as we have seen, is classically associated with deprivation of living standards. Rehabilitation, on the other hand, has served as the master symbol in bourgeois ideology that legitimated innumerable reformist struggles against this deprivation. By discrediting rehabilitation as a basic principle of penal practice, the justice modelers have undermined their own support for better standards of living in penal institutions.[2]

Now it might be objected by liberal critics of rehabilitation that favoring desert as the rationale for criminal sanctioning does not mean adopting an uncaring orientation toward the welfare of offenders. The reform agenda of the justice model not only suggests that punishment be fitted to the crime and not the criminal, but also that those sent to prison be accorded an array of rights that will humanize their existence. The rehabilitative ideal, it is countered, justifies the benevolent treatment of the incarcerated but only as a means to achieving another end – the transformation of the criminal into the conforming. In contrast, the justice perspective argues for humanity as an end in and of itself, something that should not in any way be made to seem conditional on accomplishing the difficult task of changing the deep-seated criminogenic inclinations of offenders. As such, liberals should not rely on state enforced rehabilitation to somehow lessen the rigors of imprisonment, but instead should campaign to win legal rights for convicts that directly bind the state to provide its captives with decent living conditions. [...]

It is not with ease that those of us on the political Left can stop short of completely and publically embracing the concept that 'humanity for humanity's sake' is sufficient reason for combating the brutalizing effects of prison life. This value-stance is, after all, fundamental to the logic that informs liberal policies on criminal justice issues. In this light, it should be clear that we applaud attempts to earn inmates human rights [...] and urge their continuance. However, we must stand firm against efforts to promote the position that the justice model with its emphasis on rights should replace the rehabilitative ideal with its emphasis on caring as the major avenue of liberal reform. [...] [S]upport for the principles of just deserts and determinacy has only exacerbated the plight of offenders both before and after their incarceration. But there are additional dangers to undertaking a reform program that abandons rehabilitation and seeks *exclusively* to broaden prisoner rights. Most importantly, the realities of the day furnish little optimism that such a campaign would enjoy success. [...]

Further, the promise of the rights perspective is based on the shaky assumption that more benevolence will occur if the relationship of the state to its deviants is fully adversarial and purged of its paternalistic dimensions. Instead of the government being entrusted to reform its charges through care, now offenders will have the comfort of being equipped with a new weapon – 'rights' – that will serve them well in their battle against the state for a humane and justly administered correctional system. Yet this imagery contains only surface appeal. As David Rothman has warned, 'an adversarial model, setting interest off against interest, does seem to run the clear risk of creating a kind of ultimate shoot-out in which, by definition, the powerless lose and the powerful win. How absurd to push for confrontation when all the advantages are on the other side'.[3] [...]

Moreover, the rights perspective is a two-edged sword. While rights ideally bind the state to abide by standards insuring a certain level of due process protection and acceptable penal living conditions, rights also establish the limits of the good that the state can be expected or obligated to provide. A rehabilitative ideology, in contrast, constantly pricks the conscience of the state with its assertion that the useful and moral goal of offender reformation can only be effected in a truly humane environment. Should treatment ideology be stripped away by liberal activists and the ascendancy of the rights model secured, it would thus create a situation in which criminal justice officials would remain largely immune from criticism as long as they 'gave inmates their rights' – however few they may be at the time. [...]

Even more perversely, the very extension of new rights can also be utilized to legitimate the profound neglect of the welfare of those under state control. The tragic handling of mental patients [...] is instructive in this regard. As it became apparent that many in our asylums were being either unlawfully abused or deprived of their liberty, the 'mentally ill' won the right to be released to or remain in the community if it could be proven that they were of no danger to themselves or others. [...] Yet, what has been the actual result of this 'right' to avoid state enforced therapy? It brought forth not a new era in the humane treatment of the troubled but a new era of state neglect. Instead of brutalizing people within institutional structures, the state now permits the personally disturbed to be brutalized on the streets of our cities. [...]

   2 *The ideology of rehabilitation provides an important rationale for opposing the conservatives' assumption that increased repression will reduce crime.* Those embracing the conservatives' call for 'law and order' place immense faith in the premise that tough rather than humane justice is the answer to society's crime problem. In the political Right's view, unlawful acts occur only when individuals have calculated that they are advantageous, and thus the public's victimization will only subside if criminal choices are made more costly. This can be best accomplished by sending more offenders away to prison for more extended and uncomfortable stays. Indeed, the very existence of high crime rates is prima facie evidence that greater repression is required to insure that lawlessness in our nation no longer pays.

   Liberals have traditionally attacked this logic on the grounds that repressive tactics do not touch upon the real social roots of crime and hence rarely succeed in even marginally reducing criminal involvement. Campaigns to heighten the harshness of existing criminal penalties – already notable for their severity – will only serve to fuel the problem of burgeoning prison populations and result in a further deterioration of penal living standards. The strategy of 'getting tough' thus promises to have substantial costs, both in terms of the money wasted on the excessive use of incarceration and in terms of the inhumanity it shamefully introduces.

   It is clear that proponents of the justice model share these intense liberal concerns over the appealing but illusory claims of those preaching law and order. However, their opposition to repressive crime control policies encounters difficulties because core assumptions of the justice model converge closely with those found in the paradigm for crime control espoused by conservatives. Both perspectives, for instance, argue that (1) offenders are responsible beings who freely choose to engage in crime; (2) regardless of the social injustices that may have prompted an individual to breach the law, the nature of the crime and not the nature of the circumstances surrounding a crime should regulate the severity of the sanction meted out; and (3) the punishment of offenders is deserved – that is, the state's infliction of pain for pain's sake is a positive good to be encouraged and not a likely evil to be discouraged. Admittedly, those wishing to 'do justice' would contend that current sanctions are too harsh and that prison conditions should be made less rigorous. But having already agreed with conservatives that punishing criminals is the fully legitimate purpose of the criminal justice system, they are left with little basis on which to challenge the logic or moral justification of proposals to get tough. Instead, their opposition to such measures is reduced to a debate with conservatives over the exact amount of deprivation of liberty and of living conditions during incarceration that each criminal act 'justly deserves'. [...]

In contrast, the ideology of rehabilitation disputes every facet of the conclusion that the constant escalation of punishment will mitigate the spectre of crime. To say that offenders are in need of rehabilitation is to reject the conservatives' notion that individuals, regardless of their position in the social order – whether black or white, rich or poor – exercise equal freedom in deciding whether to commit a crime. Instead, it is to reason that social and personal circumstances often constrain, if not compel, people to violate the law; and unless efforts are made to enable offenders to escape these criminogenic constraints, little relief in the crime rate can be anticipated. Policies that insist on ignoring these realities by assuming a vengeful posture toward offenders promise to succeed only in fostering hardships that will, if anything, deepen the resentment that many inmates find difficult to suppress upon their release back into society [...]

A rehabilitative stance thus allows us to begin to speak about, in Karl Menninger's words, not the 'punishment of crime' but the 'crime of punishment'.[4] The conservatives' plea for repression is exposed as a 'crime' because it both needlessly dehumanizes society's captives and falsely deceives the public that strict crime control measures will afford citizens greater safety. Drawing on the logic of the Positivist School of criminology while casting aside the classical image of the lawbreaker, the concept of rehabilitation reveals that fundamental changes in offenders will not be realized as long as inflicting deprivation remains the legitimate goal of our system of criminal 'injustice'. [...] [A] treatment ideology prompts us first to appreciate the troubles and disadvantages that drive many into crime and then to reach out and assist offenders to deal with the conditions and needs that have moved them to break the law. The demand is made, in short, that caring rather than hurting be the guiding principle of the correctional process. Moreover, in sensitizing us to the fact that much of the illegality that plagues society is intimately linked to existing social inequalities and injustices, rehabilitative ideology makes clear that a true solution to the crime problem ultimately rests in the support of reform programs that will bring about a more equitable distribution of resources through a broad structural transformation of the social order. This is in notable contrast to the philosophy of just deserts that assumes full individual responsibility, focuses on the culpability of the single perpetrator, and therefore 'acquits the existing social order of any charge of injustice'.[5]

It is apparent, then, that the ideology of rehabilitation is fully oppositional to the conservatives' agenda for the repression of crime. Importantly, it thus furnishes liberals seeking to effect criminal justice reform with a coherent framework with which to argue that benevolence and not brutality should inform society's attempts to control crime. Sharing no assumptions with the Right's paradigm of law and order, it does not, as in the case of the justice model, easily give legitimacy to either repressive punishment policies or the neglect of offender wellbeing. Instead, it remains a distinctly liberal ideology that can be utilized as a resource in the Left's quest to illustrate the futility of policies that increase pain but accomplish little else.

3 Rehabilitation still receives considerable support as a major goal of the correctional system. With prison populations exploding and punitive legislation being passed across the nation, it is of little surprise to find opinion polls indicating a hardening of public attitudes toward crime control [...] In this light, it can be imagined that public opinion would constitute a serious and perhaps insurmountable obstacle to any proposals advocating the treatment rather than the mere punishment of offenders. The viability of liberal reform strategies aimed at reaffirming rehabilitation would thus seem questionable at best.

But this is not the case. While the average citizen clearly wants criminals to be severely sanctioned – in particular, sent to prison for longer stays – survey research consistently reveals that the American public also believes that offenders should be rehabilitated. [...]

[E]xisting survey data suggest that rehabilitation persists as a prevailing ideology within the arena of criminal justice. This does not mean that treatment programs in our prisons are flourishing and remain unthreatened by the pragmatics and punitiveness of our day. But it is to assert that the rehabilitative ideal and the benevolent potential it holds are deeply anchored within our correctional and broader cultural heritage. That is, rehabilitation constitutes an ongoing rationale that is accepted by or 'makes sense to' the electorate as well as to criminal justice interest groups and policy-makers. Consequently, it provides reformers with a valuable vocabulary with which to justify changes in policy and practice aimed at mitigating the harshness of criminal sanctions – such as the diversion of offenders into the community for 'treatment' or the humanization of the prison to develop a more effective 'therapeutic environment'. Unlike direct appeals for inmate rights to humane and just living conditions that can be quickly dismissed as the mere coddling of the dangerous ('Why should we care about their rights when they certainly didn't care about the rights of their innocent victims?'), liberal reforms undertaken in the name of rehabilitation have the advantage of resonating with accepted ideology and hence of retaining an air of legitimacy. [...] If the public is not willing to pay now to facilitate the betterment of those held in captivity, it can be made clear to them that they will be forced to pay in more bothersome, if not tragic, ways at a later date.

Our message here is simple but, in light of the advent of the justice model, telling in its implications: for liberals to argue vehemently against the ideology of rehabilitation – to say that treatment cannot work because the rehabilitative ideal is inherently flawed – is to undermine the potency of one of the few resources that can be mobilized in the Left's pursuit of less repression in the administration of criminal punishments.

4 Rehabilitation has historically been an important motive underlying reform efforts that have increased the humanity of the correctional system. Liberal critics have supplied ample evidence to confirm their suspicions that state enforced therapy has too frequently encouraged the unconscionable exploitation of society's captives. Their chilling accounts of the inhumanities completed under the guise of 'treatment' call forth the compelling conclusion that far greater benevolence would grace the criminal justice system had notions of rehabilitation never taken hold.

However, while the damages permitted by the corruption of the rehabilitative ideal should neither be denied nor casually swept aside, it would be misleading to idealize the 'curious' but brutal punishments of 'bygone days' and to ignore that reforms undertaken in the name of rehabilitation have been a crucial humanizing influence in the darker regions of the sanctioning process. [...] It is instructive as well to contemplate fully the thoughtful observations of Graeme Newman:

> Yet it would seem that to throw out the whole idea of good intentions, because most of the time they do not reach the lofty heights they were supposed to achieve, may be to throw out many other values that have often accompanied them: human values, the wish, at least, to treat people humanely. Some argue that we do not need the medical [rehabilitative model] as an 'excuse' to treat offenders humanely, that we ought to do it for the sake of being humane in and of itself. But this argument, although admirably principled, does not recognize the great cultural difficulties (largely unconscious) that we have had, and continue to have, in acting humanely to those who are society's outcasts. Surely this is the lesson of history. It is only a couple of hundred years since we gave up mutilating, disemboweling, and chopping up criminals, and we still cannot make up our minds whether to stop killing them. It would seem to me, therefore, that while the medical [rehabilitative] model has its own drawbacks, it has brought along with it a useful baggage of humane values that might never have entered the darkness of criminal justice otherwise.[6]

Those who have traditionally sought to treat offenders have also sought to lessen the discomforts convicts are made to suffer. In part, this occurs, as Allen has remarked, because 'the objectives both of fundamental decency in the prisons and the rehabilitation of prisoners . . . appears to require the same measures'.[7] Yet the studies of Torsten Eriksson suggest that it is the case as well that those endeavoring to pioneer 'the more effective treatment of criminals' have commonly been united in their 'indomitable will to help their erring brother'. They stand out as 'beacons in the history of mankind, the part that deals with compassion with one's fellow man'.[8] In this context, we can again question the wisdom of liberal attempts to unmask the rehabilitative ideal as at best a 'noble lie' and at worst an inevitably coercive fraud. For in discrediting rehabilitation, liberal critics may succeed in deterring a generation of potential reformers from attempting to do good in the correctional system by teaching that it is a futile enterprise to show care for offenders by offering to help these people lead less destructive lives. And should rehabilitation be forfeited as the prevailing liberal ideology, what will remain as the medium through which benevolent sentiments will be expressed and instituted into meaningful policy? Will the medium be a justice model that is rooted in despair and not optimism, that embraces punishment and not betterment, that disdains inmate needs and disadvantages in favor of a concern for sterile and limited legal rights, and whose guiding principle of reform is to have the state do less for its captives rather than more? Or will, as we fear, this vacuum remain unfilled and the liberal camp be left without an ideology that possesses the vitality – as has rehabilitation over the past 150 years – to serve as a rallying cry for or motive force behind reforms that will engender lasting humanizing changes?

NOTES

1   Willard Gaylin and David J. Rothman, 'Introduction' in Andrew von Hirsch, *Doing Justice: the Choice of Punishments* (New York, Hill and Wang, 1976), p. xxxix.

2   Herman and Julia Schwendinger, 'The new idealism and penal living standards', in Tony Platt and Paul Takagi (eds), *Punishment and Penal Discipline: Essays on the Prison and the Prisoners' Movement* (Berkeley, CA, Crime and Social Justice Associates, 1980), p. 187.

3   David J. Rothman, 'The state as parent: social policy in the Progressive era', in Willard Gaylin, Ira Classer, Steven Marcus, and David Rothman (eds), *Doing Good: the Limits of Benevolence* (New York, Pantheon, 1978), p. 94.

4   Karl Menninger, *The Crime of Punishment* (New York, Penguin Books, 1966).

5   Jeffrey H. Reiman, *The Rich Get Richer and the Poor Get Prison: Ideology, Class and Criminal Justice* (New York, John Wiley, 1979), p. 144.

6   Graeme Newman, 'Book Review of *Conscience and Convenience: the Asylum and its Alternatives in Progressive America, David J. Rothman'*, *Crime and Delinquency*, 27 (July 1981), p. 426.

7   Francis A. Allen, *The Decline of the Rehabilitative Ideal: Penal Policy and Social Purpose* (New Haven, CT, Yale University Press, 1981), p. 81.

8   Torsten Eriksson, *The Reformers: an Historical Survey of Pioneer Experiments in the Treatment of Criminals* (New York, Elsevier, 1976), p. 252.

33

'Situational' crime prevention: theory and practice

Ronald V.G. Clarke

Conventional wisdom holds that crime prevention needs to be based on a thorough understanding of the causes of crime. Though it may be conceded that preventive measures (such as humps in the road to stop speeding) can sometimes be found without invoking sophisticated causal theory, 'physical' measures which reduce opportunities for crime are often thought to be of limited value. They are said merely to suppress the impulse to offend which will then manifest itself on some other occasion and perhaps in even more harmful form. Much more effective are seen to be 'social' measures (such as the revitalization of communities, the creation of job opportunities for unemployed youth, and the provision of sports and leisure facilities), since these attempt to remove the root motivational causes of offending. These ideas about prevention are not necessarily shared by the man-in-the-street or even by policemen and magistrates, but they have prevailed among academics, administrators and others who contribute to the formulation of criminal policy. They are also consistent with a preoccupation of criminological theory with criminal 'dispositions' (cf. Gibbons, 1971; Jeffery, 1971; Ohlin, 1970) and the purpose of this paper is to argue that an alternative theoretical emphasis on choices and decisions made by the offender leads to a broader and perhaps more realistic approach to crime prevention.

'DISPOSITIONAL' THEORIES AND THEIR PREVENTIVE IMPLICATIONS

With some exceptions noted below, criminological theories have been little concerned with the situational determinants of crime. Instead, the main object of these theories (whether biological, psychological, or sociological in orientation)

From *British Journal of Criminology*, 1980, 20(2): 136–47.

has been to show how some people are born with, or come to acquire, a 'disposition' to behave in a consistently criminal manner. This 'dispositional' bias of theory has been identified as a defining characteristic of 'positivist' criminology, but it is also to be found in 'interactionist' or deviancy theories of crime developed in response to the perceived inadequacies of positivism. Perhaps the best-known tenet of at least the early interactionist theories, which arises out of a concern with the social definition of deviance and the role of law enforcement agencies, is that people who are 'labelled' as criminal are thereby prone to continue in delinquent conduct (see especially Becker, 1962). In fact, as Tizard (1976) and Ross (1977) have pointed out, a dispositional bias is prevalent throughout the social sciences.

The more extreme forms of dispositional theory have moulded thought about crime prevention in two unfortunate ways. First, they have paid little attention to the phenomenological differences between crimes of different kinds, which has meant that preventive measures have been insufficiently tailored to different kinds of offence and of offender; secondly they have tended to reinforce the view of crime as being largely the work of a small number of criminally disposed individuals. But many criminologists are now increasingly agreed that a 'theory of crime' would be almost as crude as a general 'theory of disease'. Many now also believe, on the evidence of self-report studies (see Hood and Sparks, 1970), that the bulk of crime – vandalism, auto-crime, shoplifting, theft by employees – is committed by people who would not ordinarily be thought of as criminal at all.

Nevertheless, the dispositional bias remains and renders criminological theory unproductive in terms of the preventive measures which it generates. People are led to propose methods of preventive intervention precisely where it is most difficult to achieve any effects, i.e. in relation to the psychological events or the social and economic conditions that are supposed to generate criminal dispositions. As James Q. Wilson (1975) has argued, there seem to be no acceptable ways of modifying temperament and other biological variables, and it is difficult to know what can be done to make parents more inclined to love their children or exercise consistent discipline. Eradicating poverty may be no real solution either, in that crime rates have continued to rise since the war despite great improvements in economic conditions. And even if it were possible to provide people with the kinds of jobs and leisure facilities they might want, there is still no guarantee that crime would drop; few crimes require much time or effort, and work and leisure in themselves provide a whole range of criminal opportunities. As for violent crime, there would have to be a much clearer link between this and media portrayals of violence before those who cater to popular taste would be persuaded to change their material. Finally, given public attitudes to offending, which, judging by some opinion surveys, can be quite punitive, there may not be a great deal of additional scope for policies of diversion and decriminalization which are favoured by those who fear the consequences of 'labelling'.

These difficulties are primarily practical, but they also reflect the uncertainties and inconsistencies of treating distant psychological events and social processes as the 'causes' of crime. Given that each event is in turn caused by others, at what point in the infinitely regressive chain should one stop in the search for effective points of intervention? This is an especially pertinent question in that it is invariably found that the majority of individuals exposed to this or that criminogenic influence do not develop into persistent criminals. Moreover, 'dispositions' change so that most 'official' delinquents cease to come to the attention of the police in their late 'teens or early twenties (presumably because their lives change in ways incompatible with their earlier pursuits, cf. Trasler, 1979). Finally, it is worth pointing out that even the most persistently criminal people are probably law-abiding for most of their potentially available time, and this behaviour, too, must equally have been 'caused' by the events and experiences of their past. Some of the above theoretical difficulties could be avoided by conceiving of crime not in dispositional terms, but as being the outcome of immediate choices and decisions made by the offender. This would also have the effect of throwing a different light on preventive options.

An obvious problem is that some impulsive offences, and those committed under the influence of alcohol or strong emotion, may not easily be seen as the result of choices or decisions. Another difficulty is that the notion of 'choice' seems to fit uncomfortably with the fact that criminal behaviour is to some extent predictable from knowledge of a person's history. This difficulty is not properly resolved by the 'soft' determinism of Matza (1964) under which people retain some freedom of action albeit within a range of options constrained by their history and environment. A better formulation would seem to be that recently expounded by Glaser (1977): 'both free will and determinism are socially derived linguistic representations of reality' brought into play for different explanatory purposes at different levels of analysis and they may usefully co-exist in the scientific enterprise.

Whatever the resolution of these difficulties – and this is not the place to discuss them more fully – commonsense as well as the evidence of ethnographic studies of delinquency (e.g. Parker, 1974) strongly suggest that people are usually aware of consciously choosing to commit offences. This does not mean that they are fully aware of all the reasons for their behaviour nor that their own account would necessarily satisfy a criminologically sophisticated observer, who might require information at least about: (i) the offender's motives; (ii) his mood; (iii) his moral judgements concerning the act in question and the 'techniques of moral neutralization' open to him (cf. Matza, 1964; (iv) the extent of his criminal knowledge and his perception of criminal opportunities; (v) his assessment of the risks of being caught as well as the likely consequences; and finally, as well as of a different order, (vi) whether he has been drinking. These separate components of subjective state and thought processes which play a part in the decision to commit a crime will be influenced by immediate situational variables and by highly specific features of the individual's history and present life circumstances in ways that are so varied and countervailing as to render unproductive the notion of a generalized behavioural disposition to offend. Moreover, as will be argued below, the specificity of the influences upon different criminal behaviours gives much less credence to the 'displacement' hypothesis; the idea that reducing opportunities merely results in crime being displaced to some other time or place has been the major argument against situational crime prevention.

In so far as an individual's social and physical environments remain relatively constant and his decisions are much influenced by past experience, this scheme gives ample scope to account not only for occasional offending but also for recidivism; people acquire a repertoire of different responses to meet particular situations and if the circumstances are right they are likely to repeat those responses that have previously been rewarding. The scheme also provides a much richer source of hypotheses than 'dispositional' views of crime for the sex differences in rates of offending: for example, shoplifting may be a 'female' crime simply because women are greater users of shops (Mayhew, 1977). In view of the complexity of the behaviours in question, a further advantage (Atkinson, 1974) is that the scheme gives some accommodation to the variables thought to be important in most existing theories of crime, including those centred on dispositions. It is perhaps closest to a social learning theory of behaviour (Bandura, 1973; Mischel, 1968) though it owes something to the sociological model of crime proposed by the 'new criminologists' (Taylor et al., 1973). There are three features, however, which are particularly worth drawing out for the sake of the ensuing discussion about crime prevention: first, explanation is focused more directly on the criminal event; second, the need to develop explanations for separate categories of crime is made explicit; and, third, the individual's current circumstances and the immediate features of the setting are given considerably more explanatory significance than in 'dispositional' theories.

PREVENTIVE IMPLICATIONS OF A 'CHOICE' MODEL

In fact, just as an understanding of past influences on behaviour may have little preventive pay-off, so too there may be limited benefits in according greater explanatory importance to the individual's current life circumstances. For example, the instrumental attractions of delinquency may always be greater for certain groups of individuals such as young males living in inner-city areas. And nothing can be done about a vast range of misfortunes which continually befall people and which may raise the probability of their behaving criminally while depressed or angry.

Some practicable options for prevention do arise, however, from the greater emphasis upon situational features, especially from the direct and immediate relationship between these and criminal behaviour. By studying the spatial and temporal distribution of specific offences and relating these to measurable aspects of the situation, criminologists have recently begun to concern themselves much more closely with the possibilities of manipulating criminogenic situations in the interests of prevention. To date studies have been undertaken of residential burglary (Brantingham and Brantingham, 1975; Reppetto, 1974; Scarr, 1973; Waller and Okihiro, 1978) shoplifting (Walsh, 1978) and some forms of vandalism (Clarke, 1978; Ley and Cybrinwsky, 1974) and it is easy to foresee an expansion of research along these lines. Since offenders' perceptions of the risks and rewards attaching to different forms of crime cannot safely be inferred from studies of the distribution of offences, there might be additional preventive benefits if research of this kind were more frequently complemented by interviews with offenders (cf. Tuck, 1979; Walker, 1979).

The suggestions for prevention arising out of the 'situational' research that has been done can be conveniently divided into measures which (i) reduce the physical opportunities for offending or (ii) increase the chances of an offender being caught. These categories are discussed separately below though there is some overlap between them; for example, better locks which take longer to overcome also increase the risks of being caught. The division also leaves out some other 'situational' crime prevention measures such as housing allocation policies which avoid high concentrations of children in certain estates or which place families in accommodation that makes it easier for parents to supervise their children's play and leisure activities. Both these measures make it less likely that children will become involved in vandalism and other offences (cf. Wilson, 1978).

REDUCING PHYSICAL OPPORTUNITIES FOR CRIME AND THE PROBLEM OF DISPLACEMENT

Variations in physical opportunities for crime have sometimes been invoked to explain differences in crime rates within particular cities (e.g. Boggs, 1965; Baldwin and Bottoms, 1975) or temporal variations in crime; for example, Wilkins (1964) and Gould and his associates (Gould, 1969; Mansfield et al., 1974) have related levels of car theft to variations in the number of vehicles on the road. But these studies have not generally provided practicable preventive ideas – for example, the number of cars on the road cannot be reduced simply to prevent their theft – and it is only recently that there has been a concerted effort on the part of criminologists to find viable ways of blocking the opportunities for particular crimes.

The potential for controlling behaviour by manipulating opportunities is illustrated vividly by a study of suicide in Birmingham (Hassal and Trethowan, 1972). This showed that a marked drop in the rates of suicide between 1962 and 1970 was the result of a reduction in the poisonous content of the gas supplied to householders for cooking and heating, so that it became much more difficult for people to kill themselves by turning on the gas taps. Like many kinds of crime, suicide is generally regarded as being dictated by strong internal motivation and the fact that its incidence was greatly reduced by a simple (though unintentional) reduction in the opportunities to commit it suggests that it may be possible to achieve similar reductions in crime by 'physical' means. Though suicide by other methods did not increase in Birmingham, the study also leads to direct consideration of the fundamental theoretical problem of 'displacement' which, as Reppetto (1976) has pointed out, can occur in four different ways: time, place, method and type of offence. In other words, does reducing opportunities or increasing the risks result merely in the offender choosing his moment more carefully or in seeking some other, perhaps more harmful method of gaining his ends? Or, alternatively, will he shift his attention to a similar but unprotected target, for example, another house, car or shop? Or, finally, will he turn instead to some other form of crime?

For those who see crime as the outcome of criminal disposition, the answers to these questions would tend to be in the affirmative ('bad will out') but under the alternative view of crime represented above matters are less straightforward. Answers would depend on the nature of the crime, the offender's strength of motivation, knowledge of alternatives, willingness to entertain them, and so forth. In the case of opportunistic crimes (i.e. ones apparently elicited by their very ease of accomplishment such as some forms of shoplifting or vandalism) it would seem that the probability of offending could be reduced markedly by making it more difficult to act. For crimes such as bank robbery, however, which often seem to be the province of those who make a living from crime, reducing opportunities may be less effective. (This may be less true of increasing the risks of being caught except that for many offences the risks may be so low at present that any increase would have to be very marked.) Providing effective protection for a particular bank would almost certainly displace the attention of potential robbers to others, and if all banks were given increased protection many robbers would no doubt consider alternative means of gaining their ends. It is by no means implausible, however, that others – for example, those who do not have the ability to develop more sophisticated methods or who may not be willing to use more violence – may accept their reduced circumstances and may even take legitimate employment.

It is the bulk of offences, however, which are neither 'opportunistic' nor 'professional' that pose the greatest theoretical dilemmas. These offences include many burglaries and instances of auto-crime where the offender, who may merely supplement his normal income through the proceeds of crime, has gone out with the deliberate intention of committing the offence and has sought out the opportunity to do so. The difficulty posed for measures which reduce opportunity is one of the vast number of potential targets combined with the generally low overall level of security. Within easy reach of every house with a burglar alarm, or car with an anti-theft device, are many others without such protection.

In some cases, however, it may be possible to protect a whole class of property, as the Post Office did when they virtually eliminated theft from telephone kiosks by replacing the vulnerable aluminium coin-boxes with much stronger steel ones (cf. Mayhew et al., 1976). A further example is provided by the [UK] law which requires all motor-cyclists to wear crash helmets. This measure was introduced to save lives, but it has also had the unintended effect of reducing thefts of motor-cycles (Mayhew et al., 1976). This is because people are unlikely to take someone else's motorbike on the spur of the moment unless they happen to have a crash helmet with them – otherwise they could easily be spotted by the police. But perhaps the best example comes from West Germany where, in 1963, steering column locks were made compulsory on *all* cars, old and new, with a consequent reduction of more than 60 per cent in levels of taking and driving away (Mayhew et al., 1976). (When steering column locks were introduced in this country in 1971 it was only to new cars and, although these are now at much less risk of being taken, overall levels of car-taking have not yet diminished because the risk to older cars had increased as a result of displacement.)

Instances where criminal opportunities can be reduced for a whole class of property are comparatively few, but this need not always be a fatal difficulty. There must be geographical and temporal limits to displacement so that a town or city may be able to protect itself from some crime without displacing it elsewhere. The less determined the offender, the easier this will be; a simple example is provided by Decker's (1972) evidence that the use of 'slugs' in parking-meters in a New York district was greatly reduced by replacing the meters with ones which incorporated a slug-rejector device and in which the last coin inserted was visible in a plastic window. For most drivers there would be little advantage in parking their cars in some other district just because they could continue to use slugs there.

The question of whether, when stopped from committing a particular offence, people would turn instead to some other quite different form of crime is much more difficult to settle empirically, but many of the same points about motivation, knowledge of alternatives and so forth still apply. Common-sense also suggests, for example, that few of those Germans prevented by steering column locks from taking cars to get home at night are likely to have turned instead to hijacking taxis or to mugging passers-by for the money to get home. More likely, they may have decided that next time they would make sure of catching the last bus home or that it was time to save up for their own car.

INCREASING THE RISKS OF BEING CAUGHT

In practice, increasing the chances of being caught usually means attempting to raise the chances of an offender being seen by someone who is likely to take action. The police are the most obvious group likely to intervene effectively, but studies of the effectiveness of this aspect of their deterrent role are not especially encouraging (Clarke and Hough, 1980; Kelling et al., 1974; Manning, 1977). The reason seems to be that, when set against the vast number of opportunities for offending represented by the activities of a huge population of citizens for the 24 hours of the day, crime is a relatively rare event. The police cannot be everywhere at once and, moreover, much crime takes place in private. Nor is much to be expected from the general public (Mayhew et al., 1979). People in their daily round rarely see crime in progress; if they do they are likely to place some innocent interpretation on what they see; they may be afraid to intervene or they may feel the victims would resent interference; and they may encounter practical difficulties in summoning the police or other help in time. They are much more likely to take effective action to protect their own homes or immediate neighbourhood, but they are often away from these for substantial periods of the day and, moreover, the risks of crime in residential settings, at least in many areas of this country, are not so great as to encourage much vigilance. For instance, assuming that about 50 per cent of burglaries are reported to the police (cf. Home Office, 1979), a house in this country will on average be burgled once every 30 years. Even so, there is evidence (Department of the Environment, 1977; Wilson, 1978) that 'defensible space' designs on housing estates confer some protection from vandalism, if not as much as might have been expected from the results of Newman's (1973) research into crime on public housing projects in the United States (cf. Clarke,1979; Mayhew, 1979).

A recent Home Office Research report (Mayhew et al., 1979) has argued, however, that there is probably a good deal of unrealized potential for making more deliberate use of the surveillance role of employees who come into regular and frequent contact with the public in a semi-official capacity. Research in the United States (Newman, 1973; Reppetto, 1974) and Canada (Waller and Okihiro, 1978) has shown that apartment blocks with doormen are less vulnerable to burglary, while research in [the UK] has shown that vandalism is much less of a problem on buses with conductors (Mayhew et al., 1976) and on estates with resident caretakers (Department of the Environment, 1977). There is also evidence (in Post Office Records) that public telephones in places such as pubs or launderettes, which are given some supervision by staff, suffer almost no vandalism in comparison with those in kiosks; that car parks with attendants in control have lower rates of auto-crime (*The Sunday Times*, 9 April 1978); that football hooliganism on trains has been reduced by a variety of measures including permission for club stewards to travel free of charge; and that shoplifting is discouraged by the presence of assistants who are there to serve the customers (Walsh, 1978). Not everybody employed in a service capacity would be suited or willing to take on additional security duties, but much of their deterrent role may result simply from their being around. Employing more of them, for greater parts of the day, may therefore be all that is needed in most cases. In other cases, it may be necessary to employ people more suited to a surveillance role, train them better to carry it out, or even provide them with surveillance aids. Providing the staff at four London Underground stations with closed circuit television has been shown in a recent Home Office Research Unit study (Mayhew et al., 1979) to have substantially reduced theft and robbery offences at those stations.

SOME OBJECTIONS

Apart from the theoretical and practical difficulties of the approach advocated in this paper, it is in apparent conflict with the 'nothing works' school of criminological thought as given recent expression by Wolfgang (1977): 'the weight of empirical evidence indicates that no current preventative, deterrent, or rehabilitative intervention scheme has the desired effect of reducing crime'. But perhaps a panacea is being sought when all it may be possible to achieve is a reduction in particular forms of crime as a result of specific and sometimes localized measures. Examples of such reductions are given above and, while most of these relate to rather commonplace offences of theft and vandalism, there is no reason why similar measures cannot be successfully applied to other quite different forms of crime. It has been argued by many people (Rhodes, 1977, provides an example) that reducing the availability of hand-guns through gun-control legislation would reduce crimes of violence in the United States and elsewhere. Speeding and drunken driving could probably be reduced by fitting motor vehicles with devices which are now at an experimental stage (Ekblom, 1979). And there is no doubt (Wilkinson, 1977) that the rigorous passenger and baggage screening measures introduced at airports, particularly in the United States, have greatly reduced the incidence of airline hijackings. There are many crimes, however, when the offender is either so determined or so emotionally aroused that they seem to be beyond the scope of this approach. A further constraint will be costs: many shops, for example, which could reduce shoplifting by giving up self-service methods and employing more assistants or even store detectives, have calculated that this would not be worth the expense either in direct costs or in a reduction of turnover. Morally dubious as this policy might at first sight appear, these shops may simply have learned a lesson of more general application, i.e. a certain level of crime may be the inevitable consequence of practices and institutions which we cherish or find convenient and the 'cost' of reducing crime below this level may be unacceptable.

The gradualist approach to crime prevention advocated here might also attract criticism from some social reformers, as well as some deviancy theorists, for being unduly conservative. The former group, imbued with dispositional theory, would see the only effective way of dealing with crime as being to attack its roots through the reduction of inequalities of wealth, class and education – a solution which, as indicated above, has numerous practical and theoretical difficulties. The latter group would criticize the approach, not for its lack of effectiveness but – on the grounds that there is insufficient consensus in society about what behaviour should be treated as crime – for helping to preserve an undesirable status quo. Incremental change, however, may be the most realistic way of achieving consensus as well as a more equitable society. Most criminologists would probably also agree that it would be better for the burden of crime reduction to be gradually shifted away from the criminal justice system, which may be inherently selective and punitive in its operation, to preventive measures whose social costs may be more equitably distributed among all members of society. The danger to be guarded against would be that the attention of offenders might be displaced away from those who can afford to purchase protection to those who cannot. This probably happens already to some extent and perhaps the best way of dealing with the problem would be through codes of security which would be binding on car manufacturers, builders, local transport operators and so forth. Another danger is that those who have purchased protection might become less willing to see additional public expenditure on the law enforcement and criminal justice services – and this is a problem that might only be dealt with through political leadership and public education.

Many members of the general public might also find it objectionable that crime was being stopped, not by punishing wrong-doers, but by inconveniencing the law-abiding. The fact that opportunity-reducing and risk-increasing measures are too readily identified with their more unattractive aspects (barbed wire, heavy padlocks, guard-dogs and private security forces) adds fuel to the fire. And in some of their more sophisticated forms (closed circuit television surveillance and electronic intruder alarms) they provoke fears, on the one hand, of 'big brother' forms of state control and, on the other, of a 'fortress society' in which citizens in perpetual fear of their fellows scuttle from one fortified environment to another.

Expressing these anxieties has a value in checking potential abuses of power, and questioning the means of dealing with crime can also help to keep the problem of crime in perspective. But it should also be said that the kind of measures discussed above need not always be obtrusive (except where it is important to maximize their deterrent effects) and need not in any material way infringe individual liberties or the quality of life. Steel cash compartments in telephone kiosks are indistinguishable from aluminium ones, and vandal-resistant polycarbonate looks just like glass. Steering column locks are automatically brought into operation on removing the ignition key, and many people are quite unaware that their cars are fitted with them. 'Defensible space' designs in housing estates have the additional advantage of promoting feelings of neighbourliness and safety, though perhaps too little attention has been paid to some of their less desirable effects such as possible encroachments on privacy as a result of overlooking. And having more bus conductors, housing estate caretakers, swimming bath attendants and shop assistants means that people benefit from improved services – even if they have to pay for them either directly or through the rates.

Finally, the idea that crime might be most effectively prevented by reducing opportunities and increasing the risks is seen by many as, at best, representing an over-simplified mechanistic view of human behaviour and, at worst, a 'slur on human nature' (cf. Radzinowicz and King, 1977). (When the contents of *Crime as Opportunity* (Mayhew et al., 1976) were reported in the press in advance of publication an irate psychiatrist wrote to the Home Secretary demanding that he should suppress the publication of such manifest nonsense.) As shown above, however, it is entirely compatible with a view of criminal behaviour as predominantly rational and autonomous and as being capable of adjusting and responding to adverse consequences, anticipated or experienced. And as for being a pessimistic view of human behaviour, it might indeed be better if greater compliance with the law could come about simply as a result of people's free moral choice. But apart from being perilously close to the rather unhelpful dispositional view of crime, it is difficult to see this happening. We may therefore be left for the present with the approach advocated [here], time-consuming, laborious and limited as it may be.

SUMMARY

It is argued that the 'dispositional' bias of most current criminological theory has resulted in 'social' crime prevention measures being given undue prominence and 'situational' measures being devalued. An alternative theoretical emphasis on decisions and choices made by the offender (which in turn allows more weight to the circumstances of offending) results in more support for a situational approach to prevention. Examples of the effectiveness of such an approach are provided and some of the criticisms that have been made of it on social and ethical grounds are discussed.

REFERENCES

Atkinson, M. (1974) 'Versions of deviance', Extended review in *Sociological Review*, 22: 616–24.

Baldwin, J. and Bottoms, A.E. (1975) *The Urban Criminal*. London: Tavistock.

Bandura, A. (1973) *Aggression: a Social Learning Analysis*. London: Prentice Hall.

Becker, H.S. (1962) *Outsiders: Studies in the Sociology of Deviance*. Glencoe, Ill.: The Free Press.

Boggs, S.L. (1965) 'Urban crime patterns', *American Sociological Review*, 30: 899–908.

Brantingham, P.J. and Brantingham, P.L. (1975) 'The spatial patterning of burglary', *Howard Journal of Penology and Crime Prevention*, 14: 11–24.

Clarke, R.V.G. (ed.) (1978) *Tackling Vandalism*. Home Office Research Study No. 47. London: HMSO.

Clarke, R.V.G. (1979) 'Defensible space and vandalism: the lessons from some recent British research', *Städtebau und Kriminalamt (Urban planning and Crime)*. Papers of an international symposium, Bundeskriminalamt, Federal Republic of Germany, December, 1978.

Clarke, R.V.G. and Hough, J.M. (eds) (1980) *The Effectiveness of Policing*. Farnborough, Hants: Gower.

Decker, J.F. (1972) 'Curbside deterrence: an analysis of the effect of a slug-rejector device, coin view window and warning labels on slug usage in New York City parking meters', *Criminology*, August, pp. 127–42.

Department of the Environment (1977) *Housing Management and Design*. (Lambeth Inner Area Study). IAS/IA/18. London: Department of the Environment.

Ekblom, P. (1979) 'A crime-free car?', *Research Bulletin No. 7*. Home Office Research Unit. London: Home Office.

Gibbons, D.C. (1971) 'Observations on the study of crime causation', *American Journal of Sociology*, 77: 262–78.

Glaser, D. (1977) 'The compatibility of free will and determinism in criminology: comments on an alleged problem', *Journal of Criminal Law and Criminology* 67: 486–90.

Gould, L.C. (1969) 'The changing structure of property crime in an affluent society', *Social Forces*, 48: 50–9.

Hassal, C. and Trethowan, W.H. (1972) 'Suicide in Birmingham', *British Medical Journal*, 1: 717–18.

Home Office (1979) *Criminal Statistics: England and Wales 1978*. London: HMSO.

Hood, R. and Sparks, R. (1970) *Key Issues in Criminology*. London: Weidenfeld and Nicolson.

Jeffery, C.R. (1971) *Crime Prevention Through Environmental Design*. Beverly Hills, CA: Sage.

Kelling, G.L., Pate, T., Dieckman, D. and Brown C.E. (1974) *The Kansas City Preventive Patrol Experiment*. Washington, DC: Police Foundation.

Ley, D. and Cybrinwsky, R. (1974) 'The spatial ecology of stripped cars', *Environment and Behaviour*, 6: 53–67.

Manning, P. (1977) *Police Work: the Social Organisation of Policing*. London: Massachusetts Institute of Technology Press.

Mansfield, R., Gould, L.C. and Namenwirth, J.Z. (1974) 'A socioeconomic model for the prediction of societal rates of property theft', *Social Forces*, 52: 462–72.

Matza, D. (1964) *Delinquency and Drift*. New York: John Wiley and Sons.

Mayhew, P. (1977) 'Crime in a man's world', *New Society*, 16 June.

Mayhew, P. (1979) 'Defensible space: the current status of a crime prevention theory', *The Howard Journal of Penology and Crime Prevention*, 18: 150–9.

Mayhew, P., Clarke, R.V.G, Sturman, A. and Hough, J.M. (1976) *Crime as Opportunity*. Home Office Research Study No. 34. London: HMSO.

Mayhew, P., Clarke, R.V.G, Burrows, J.N., Hough, J.M. and Winchester, S.W.C. (1979) *Crime in Public View*. Home Office Research Study No. 49. London: HMSO.

Mischel, W. (1968) *Personality and Assessment*. New York: John Wiley and Sons.

Newman, O. (1973) *Defensible Space: People and Design in the Violent City*. London: Architectural Press.

Ohlin, L.E. (1970) *A Situational Approach to Delinquency Prevention*. Youth Development and Delinquency Prevention Administration. US Department of Health, Education and Welfare.

Parker, H. (1974) *View from the Boys*. Newton Abbot: David and Charles.

Radzinowicz, L. and King, J. (1977) *The Growth of Crime*. London: Hamish Hamilton.

Reppetto, T.A. (1974) *Residential Crime*. Cambridge, MA: Ballinger.

Reppetto, T.A. (1976) 'Crime prevention and the displacement phenomenon', *Crime and Delinquency*, April, 166–77.

Rhodes, R.P. (1977) *The Insoluble Problems of Crime*. New York: John Wiley and Sons.

Ross, L. (1977) 'The intuitive psychologist and his shortcomings: distortions in the attribution process', in L. Berkowitz (ed.), *Advances in Experimental Social Psychology*, Vol. 10. New York: Academic Press.

Scarr, H.A. (1973) *Patterns of Burglary*. US Department of Justice, Washington DC: Government Printing Office.

Taylor, I, Walton, P. and Young, J. (1973) *The New Criminology*. London: Routledge and Kegan Paul.

Tizard, J. (1976) 'Psychology and social policy', *Bulletin of the British Psychological Society*, 29: 225–33.

Trasler, G.B. (1979) 'Delinquency, recidivism, and desistance', *British Journal of Criminology*, 19: 314–22.

Tuck, M. (1979) 'Consumer behaviour theory and the criminal justice system: towards a new strategy of research', *Journal of the Market Research Society*, 21: 44–58.

Walker, N.D. (1979) 'The efficacy and morality of deterrents', *Criminal Law Review*, March, 129–44.

Waller, I. and Okihiro, N. (1978) *Burglary: the Victim and the Public*. Toronto: University of Toronto Press.

Walsh, D.P. (1978) *Shoplifting: Controlling a Major Crime*. London: Macmillan.

Wilkins, L.T. (1964) *Social Deviance*. London: Tavistock.

Wilkinson, P. (1977) *Terrorism and the Liberal State*. London: Macmillan.

Wilson, J.Q. (1975) *Thinking About Crime*. New York: Basic Books.

Wilson, S. (1978) 'Vandalism and "defensible space" on London housing estates', in R.V.G. Clarke, (ed.), *Tackling Vandalism*. Home Office Research Study No. 47. London: HMSO.

Wolfgang, M.E. (1977) 'Real and perceived changes in crime', in S.F. Landau and L. Sebba, (eds), *Criminology in Perspective*. Lexington, MA: Lexington Books.

34

Social crime prevention strategies in a market society

Elliott Currie

All societies make some use of market mechanisms to allocate goods and services. And most of us would acknowledge that the exact determination of what the market does better in this regard and what is best accomplished by other means is often an empirical question. The best balance of private and public is not easy to weigh, and it shifts over time as social needs and technological capacities change. But 'market society', as I will use the term, is a different animal altogether. By market society I mean a society in which the pursuit of private gain increasingly becomes the organizing principle for all areas of social life, not simply a mechanism which we use to accomplish certain circumscribed economic ends. The balance between private and public shifts dramatically, so that the public retreats to a minuscule and disempowered part of social and economic life and the idea of common purposes and common responsibility steadily withers as an important social value.

In market society all other principles of social organization become subordinated to the over-reaching one of private gain. Alternative sources of livelihood, of social support and of cultural value, even of personal identity, become increasingly eroded or obliterated. As a result, individuals, families and communities are more and more dependent on what we somewhat misleadingly call the 'free' market to provide for their human needs, not only material needs but also cultural, symbolic and psychic needs. I say 'somewhat misleadingly' because, as critics have often pointed out, this sort of society – as it is increasingly found in the US, for example – isn't really adequately characterized by the notion of the 'free' market. Economic and social power and the expanded life-chances and opportunities that go with them are not 'free' in the classical Adam Smithian

From *International Developments in Crime and Social Policy*, NACRO Crime and Social Policy, pp. 107–20. (London: NACRO, 1991.)

sense of being equally accessible to all who demonstrate sufficient merit, skill and enterprise. Instead, some groups have increasingly been able to protect themselves against the judgement of the economic market and from the need to perform efficiently at all, while others are subjected to the market's mercies at an ever-accelerating pace.

Now, as I'm using the term, 'market society' is an abstraction, an 'ideal type', and it doesn't, yet, exist anywhere in a pure form. But it has approximations in the real world, both developed and developing, and the United States again has proceeded farther down the road towards market society than any other advanced industrial nation. The UK has, of course, made very considerable efforts in that direction over the past 12 years, but there's still a long way to go before arriving at the evolution of market society we've 'attained'. But something like a broad drift towards market society is increasingly apparent in many other countries across the world. And that's troubling for a variety of reasons but, for our purposes here, specifically because market societies are extraordinarily fertile ground for the growth of crime. I stress again that market society is not the same as the mere existence of a market *economy*. The idea that a serious crime problem is an inevitable accompaniment of a vibrant economy or a free political order is both wrong and pernicious. It is, however, a predictable accompaniment of the growth of market *society*. Why?

Well, let me offer you five propositions about market society's impact on several overlapping areas of social, economic and cultural life which in turn strongly influence the shape and dimensions of the crime problem. (That close overlap is, in fact, what makes the concept of market society helpful in understanding the nature of crime in the industrial societies today. It helps, among other things, to explain why some factors taken individually – say, the unemployment rate, or levels of poverty – may not always fit so well as explanations of crime, an issue much seized upon by some of our conservative colleagues. Looking at the role of these factors through the more holistic perspective offered by the idea of 'market society' helps us understand why poverty, for example, is much more salient for understanding crime in some kinds of societies, at some points in their development, than in others.)

[…]

LINKS BETWEEN MARKET SOCIETY AND CRIME

First mechanism
Market society promotes crime by increasing inequality and concentrated economic deprivation. In the US the rise in violent crime has – not at all unexpectedly from the standpoint of several different lines of criminological theory – gone hand-in-hand with the sharpest rise of economic inequality in our postwar history, the attainment of the widest gap in incomes since we began gathering statistics after the Second World War. In turn, that rising economic inequality in the US can be traced to several related trends.

One is the deterioration of the labour market, both private and public. Throughout the economy, vast numbers of 'middle-level' jobs, especially but not exclusively in blue-collar industry, have disappeared to be replaced by a significant rise in extremely well-rewarded jobs at the top, and a much larger increase in poor jobs, including unstable and part-time ones, at the bottom. This downward shift has been especially destructive to the prospects of younger people. According to data from the US Senate Budget Committee, more than four-fifths of the net new jobs available to young men under 35 during the 1980s paid poverty-level wages or below. In the course of that decade there was a net loss of 1.6 million middle-level jobs available to men of that age group.

This shift in the labour market is not, of course, a matter of the mysterious workings of fate or even of politically neutral changes in technology or demography. It has been driven by deliberate social policy in several ways:

- through the continuing flight of capital and jobs to low-wage havens both in parts of the US itself and, increasingly, overseas, especially to Asia and the Caribbean;

- through the lowering of the real value of the minimum wage, which ensures that new job creation has been overwhelmingly concentrated in poverty-level, low productivity jobs;

- and relatedly, by a more or less conscious policy of achieving profits and staying afloat in the face of international economic competition primarily by lowering wages rather than by increasing the productivity of the workforce and the efficiency of management, what some writers in the US call the deliberate 'dumbing-down' of the labour force.

All of this has resulted in a growing tendency toward what has been called an 'hourglass' income distribution. This tendency is compounded by two other important thrusts of the market-driven social policy of the past fifteen years: the erosion of income support benefits for low-income people and the unemployed, and a pattern of systematically regressive taxation [...]

The result of these compounded distributional policies has been to raise the top to unprecedented pinnacles of wealth and of personal consumption, while dropping the poor into a far deeper and more abysmal hole than they were in before, which was already the deepest among advanced industrial societies.

Today we not only have about six million more poor Americans than we did in 1979, but they are much poorer both relative to the affluent and, often, in absolute terms. As the job structure has narrowed and income support shrivelled, it is now far more difficult, as surveys have discovered, for them to get *out*, at least through legitimate means, a fact which is not lost on the urban poor, especially the young.

We are now in real danger of creating something like an economic apartheid and it is by no means just a problem of the so-called, hard-core urban 'underclass', but of an increasingly threatened and declining bottom third of the American population.

Nor are these general trends confined to the US. [...] The trend towards growing inequality is increasingly international in scope and international in its consequences. And it is deeply implicated in the pattern of crime.

Second mechanism

Market society promotes crime by weakening the capacity of local communities for 'informal' support, mutual provision and socialization and supervision of the young. This is closely related to the first link: it is, in part, a function of the declining economic security and rising deprivation in low income communities, as well as the rapid movement of capital and accordingly of opportunities for stable work which are hallmarks of the advance of market society.

Under the sustained impact of market forces, communities suffer not only from the long-term loss of stable livelihoods, but also from the excessive geographic mobility that results from that loss. The process is by no means confined to the US; it is central to the experience of many countries and especially many in the developing world and those on the periphery of European prosperity. It is compounded, in the US, by the crisis in housing for low-income people as market forces drive up the cost of shelter at the same time that they drive down wages. The loss of stability of shelter, in turn, helps destroy the basis of local social cohesion.

Communities suffering these compounded stresses begin to exhibit the phenomenon some researchers call 'drain': as the ability of families to support themselves and care for their children drops below a certain critical point, they can no longer sustain those informal networks of social support and help that can otherwise be a buffer against the impact of the economic grinding of the market. If you're having tough times you can't lean on your neighbours or your cousins, even if they still live in the same community, because they're having tough times too; and there are therefore decreasing resources, both emotional and material, to offer to anyone else.

Third mechanism

Market society promotes crime by stressing and fragmenting the family. Again, this is deeply enmeshed with the first and second mechanisms. The growing economic deprivation and community fragmentation characteristic of market society put enormous pressures on family life, and it is partly through these pressures that the growth of market society generates crime.

These connections are many and complex: let me just mention two of them for now, again using the American experience as an example.

First, the long-term economic marginalization of entire communities which characterizes market society tends to inhibit the formation of stable families in the first place – as the sociologist William J. Wilson has powerfully argued for the US case – by diminishing the 'pool' of marriageable men who are seen as capable of achieving a legitimate livelihood that can support a family. The result is to encourage single parenthood and its associated poverty.

But unemployment itself is only one way in which the deterioration of the labour market has affected families. The flip side is overwork in inadequate jobs. Because so much of the employment recently created pays poverty-level wages, great numbers of families, especially young families, can only stay afloat by drastically increasing their hours of work, often taking on two or even three jobs. This is an increasingly common phenomenon in low-income communities in the US and one I've encountered over and over again in working with delinquent kids. […] This has given us a generation of parents, especially young parents and single parents, who have virtually no leisure time and who are (a) constantly stressed to breaking point and (b) absent from the home and the community for most of the time.

It is important not to only blame parents for this. But the results are very real and very troubling. The socializing and nurturing capacities of many families have been seriously compromised and children in America are too often thrown back on their own resources and their own peer groups for guidance, support and supervision.

Again, these mechanisms overlap. The pressure of market forces on community stability aggravates the strains on families. Once upon a time, families facing adverse economic conditions could look to other families in the community for help; parents burdened by overwork could look to informal networks of relatives and friends to help care for children. As market society advances, families are increasingly severed from these informal connections and forced to struggle against the uncertainties and deprivations of the market economy alone. The resulting 'social impoverishment' fuses with economic deprivation and insecurity to produce overwhelming stresses, domestic violence and child abuse. […]

These adverse impacts on families are all the more severe because of the *fourth* link between market society and crime.

Fourth mechanism

Market society promotes crime by withdrawing public provision of basic services for those it has already stripped of livelihoods, economic security and 'informal' communal support. Once again, this process has been most advanced in the US among industrial societies. But we are not alone. Before the advent of the Reagan Administration, the US already stood lowest among several industrial countries in the rate at which public benefits brought families and children out of poverty. We became much more miserly during the 1980s when, for example, our income benefits lifted one in five families out of poverty in 1979; the figure is less than one in nine today, and falling.

Beyond public income support there have been substantial cuts in those public services which could prevent or repair some of the damages inflicted by the compound impacts of economic deprivation, family stress and community breakdown. That process has accelerated enormously in the current fiscal crisis of the 1990s, leading to huge cuts in the kind of preventative health and mental health care that might help intervene with some of the children most 'at risk' of delinquency and drug abuse; a tragic shortfall of effective intervention for families at high risk of child abuse; and a continuing inability to develop nurturing and accessible child care for low-income families whipsawed by low wages and overwork.

All these impacts also must be understood in the light of the fifth link between market society and crime.

Fifth mechanism

Market society promotes crime by magnifying a culture of Darwinian competition for status and dwindling resources and by urging a level of consumption that it cannot fulfil for everyone through legitimate channels. I won't dwell on this now: it's been a recurrent theme in criminological theory. My own favourite exposition of this point is that of the great Dutch criminologist Willem Bonger.

Bonger believed that, 'To make prosperity and culture as general as possible' was the 'best preventive against crime'. But he stressed that he meant 'prosperity, not luxury': for 'There is not a weaker spot to be found in the social development of our times than the ever-growing and ever-intensifying covetousness, which, in its turn, is the result of powerful social forces.' Bonger wrote in the early 1930s; ... what he would see today in the US and in many parts of the world would surely blow his mind.

A full-blown market culture promotes crime in several ways: by holding out standards of economic status and consumption which increasing numbers of people cannot legitimately meet, and more subtly, by weakening other values more supportive of the intrinsic worth of human life and well-being and of the value of what we might call 'craft', the value of creative work, of productive contribution, of a job well done.

One of the most chilling features of much violent street crime in America today, and also in some developing countries, is how directly it expresses the logic of immediate gratification in the pursuit of consumer goods, or of instant status and recognition. Some of our delinquents will cheerfully acknowledge that they blew someone away for their running shoes or because they made the mistake of looking at them disrespectfully on the street. People who study crime, perhaps especially from a 'progressive' perspective, sometimes shy away from looking hard at these less tangible 'moral' aspects. In the US we are certainly witnessing a kind of demoralization that must be acknowledged and confronted if we wish to understand crime today. [...] The point is not simply to bemoan the ascendancy of those values among some of the urban young, but to recognize that they are, as Bonger said, the 'result of powerful social forces', a direct and unmediated reflection of the inner logic of market society, part of the total package that we must be prepared to accept if we accept that package at all.

There are other links as well between the growth of market society, market culture and crime. A full analysis of those connections would need to consider, for example, the impact on crime of the specifically psychological distortions of market society, its tendency to produce personalities less and less capable of relating to others except as consumer items or as trophies in a quest for recognition among one's peers. And we need also to consider the long-term political impacts of market society that are related to crime, in particular its tendency to weaken and erode the alternative political means by which those who are victimized by destructive social and economic policies might express their frustration and their desperation in transformative rather than predatory ways. And, finally, the ways of market society also magnify the opportunities for white-collar crime and may simultaneously minimize the seriousness of the governmental response to it.

It is not, then, simply by increasing one or another specific social ill that market policies stimulate crime: it's when you put them together that the effects emerge in full force. But that is precisely what market society does. The growth of market society is a multifaceted process which is at its core destructive of the economic, social and cultural requisites of social peace and personal security.

KEY STRATEGIES

To me these developments point directly to some key strategies that ought to be essential parts of our approach to social crime prevention in the 1990s and in the next century. I will only point to three 'macro' and, briefly, three 'micro' strategies which I believe are especially critical in the face of these global transformations.

The three 'macro' policies are central because they directly attack the growing inequality in the emerging market society. There is much we can do by way of crime prevention without them but we will most certainly be swimming upstream.

First, and I believe central to much else, genuinely social crime prevention strategy requires a supportive labour market policy – what in Scandinavia is called an 'active' labour market policy which seeks to provide all citizens with both the competence and skills to participate in the necessary work of the larger society *and* concrete opportunities to put those skills to work. This necessarily involves a substantial role for the public sector – a deliberate and unapologetic use of public resources not merely to train the labour force for hoped-for jobs in the private sector, but also to create dignified public and non-profit jobs in areas of pressing social need.

One of the most wistfully myopic economic ideas of our time is the belief that an adequate supply of such good, stable jobs, of the kind that can provide a sense of membership in a productive community and the livelihood to support a family in dignity and security, will flow automatically from the normal operation of the private market if we just leave that market alone. Our American pundits, in particular, are much given to expressing confidence that the massive levels of unemployment and subemployment in the US, in the Third World and, increasingly, in some countries of Eastern Europe are simply 'transitional', and they will go away once the market has been left alone long enough to work its magic. The trouble is, of course, that we've already been waiting for generations for that transition to be over in Harlem and Appalachia and Detroit, not to mention San Paulo and San Juan.

Now don't get me wrong. The idea that the private market unaided will provide dignified and meaningful employment for all is a delightful and soothing
idea. I too would like to believe it because it would make life, and social policy, a
great deal easier. The hard reality is that the long-term tendency of the unaided
market is to sharply divide societies into those who have and those who do not
have access to stable and rewarding work. The lesson of both historical experience
and careful research is abundantly clear. Those countries that have managed to
maintain full and dignified human resources are those that have taken on a deliberate, active national commitment to full employment and comprehensive training, usually including the strategic use of public sector employment. The countries
that have recently done the worst in this regard, including the US and the UK,
have on the contrary worked to dismantle much of the public employment and
training system they once had. That strategy flies in the face of everything we
know about human resources and economic productivity: it is foolish, self-defeating,
counterproductive, and expensive.

Exactly what such an active labour market policy should look like will vary
in different countries. Some, of course, including Sweden and, in its own way,
Japan, have already committed themselves to remarkably effective full employment strategies. In the US, it translates into the crying need for a national commitment to publicly supported, community-oriented job creation, especially in
the provision of those critical needs of the social and physical infrastructure that
have been sorely neglected or systematically attacked for many years. With that
kind of strategy we will kill several birds with one stone. We rebuild that eroded
social and material infrastructure in health care, housing, community amenities
and we also create an economic base that can serve as the catalyst for overall
economic development in communities that the private market has essentially
abandoned. And we also provide a whole spectrum of new and genuinely challenging opportunities for respected work and community contribution for young
people now lured by the very genuine challenges of high-risk delinquency and the
drug culture.

Secondly, a long-term approach to social crime prevention also requires a
concerted, unapologetic strategy to reduce extremes of social and economic inequality by upgrading earnings and public benefits and services for low-income
people both in and out of the paid labour force. This is complementary to an
active labour market policy and is precisely the opposite of what many governments have lately been doing in the name of freeing the 'free market'.

I've suggested that one of the links between market society and crime lies in
the stripping away of public services and supports which is today routinely
justified in the name of a supposedly beneficial privatization of public functions. But the long-term result, which we see increasingly in the US, is that we
are now perilously close to creating two distinct classes of citizenship. On
one side are those who by virtue of their connection with the stable part of the
labour force can afford what are increasingly private, and increasingly expensive, fundamentals of social life, from health care to housing to education. Those
essentials are today more often tied to high-wage employment and are frequently

part of the fruits of the 'semi-private welfare state' that has grown up to serve the well-employed. But on the other side are those who are condemned to scramble after the shrinking and increasingly inadequate vestiges of public provision for these needs.

In place of that trend toward two classes of citizenship, we need to counterpose what might be thought of as a post-industrial version of the 'basic needs' strategy often advocated for developing countries. We need to insist that it is society's *first* responsibility, not its last and most expendable, to ensure equal access to those institutions which allow for competent, healthy and respected citizenship: and that means an unshakeable national-level commitment to public health care for all, quality public education and the guarantee of dignified shelter as well as adequate and non-demeaning income benefits for those out of the paid labour force. This, of course, requires the existence of an active labour market policy, because without a productive and an employed labour force you cannot support universally accessible, high-quality public services or generous social benefits.

Meanwhile, for those in that paid labour force, we need likewise to reverse the dramatic present trend toward earnings inequality, especially the growth of what the Senate Budget Committee study in the US calls 'wage impoverishment' at the lower end of the scale. This means a commitment to steadily rising minimum wages. But beyond establishing a minimum floor on earnings, we also need to move in the long run toward what the Scandinavians call a 'solidaristic' wage policy, one that is explicitly aimed at reducing earnings inequality throughout the workforce.

This strategy should explicitly include an effort to reduce the gaps in the earnings of men and women. We have not yet talked much about gender issues, but we should. The low earnings of women are deeply implicated in crime in a variety of complex ways of which only the most obvious is the way they encourage violence against women in the home. As long as women's capacity for self-support is compromised by poor wages – and meagre benefits – then they are especially vulnerable to being trapped in abusive and violent relationships with men, as are their children. Increasing women's economic independence would go a very long way toward reducing the massive tragedy of family violence especially in countries like the US and many in the developing world where violence against women and children is very high and women's overall economic condition is very low. Not to mention the benefits of making greater resources available for poor children, great numbers of whom are growing up in families maintained by women.

Measures like these, designed to reduce inequality and promote competent citizenship, have been systematically attacked by conservative governments around the world on the grounds that they interfere with the market and thereby hinder economic efficiency. Yet nothing could be farther from reality. Again, the lessons of both research and experience are crystal clear. Healthy, well-educated, competent and self-confident citizens are what makes an economy work. The state of the United States economy, today, I'm afraid, is a tragic demonstration of what happens when that lesson is ignored.

Thirdly, we should work internationally toward an active, supportive child and family policy, one that firmly and unapologetically puts the needs of families and children for adequate furtherance, time and income above the private pursuit of material gain.

The two strategies I've already suggested – an active labour market policy and a concerted attack on the widening inequalities of wages and benefits – are in themselves two of the most important elements of that kind of supportive family policy.

But more is needed as well. In particular, we need strategies to reduce the sharp and in many countries growing conflicts between family and work. That means (1) freeing up time from work for parents to be with their children through generous family and parental leave policies and (2) putting in place a high-quality accessible child care system for working families.

In the US, both of these have been fought tooth and nail by the private business community. Here we are far behind some European countries like Sweden or France. In the US, our stunningly timid legislative effort to provide six weeks of unpaid parental leave at the birth of a child has been successfully resisted for years by the business community and its political allies. Once again, that resistance has been justified, fantastically, in the name of economic efficiency. But the reality is that our failure to develop policies to reduce the intolerable work-related stresses of families amounts to a massive, covert subsidy to private business in that it requires the rest of us to pay in the long run for the consequences of the resulting economic strains on families; consequences including child abuse, delinquency, mental illness and a mushrooming expenditure for the remedial programmes to contain them.

The long-range vision behind all three proposals and others is to progressively replace what I've called 'market society' with what I'll call a 'sustaining' society.

That kind of vision calls for creative programmes on the 'micro' level as well, on the close-in level of working directly with individuals and families who've been made most vulnerable by the massive changes now reshaping our societies. For now, I'll only mention briefly three kinds of interventions that I think, on the evidence, must be among the most urgent in a truly effective strategy of social crime prevention: (a) comprehensive child and family support programmes; (b) a youth intervention strategy that focuses on the expansion of tangible opportunities; and (c) a 'user-friendly' approach to drug abuse prevention and treatment.

First, [we need] a comprehensive 'package' of child and family interventions that emphasizes (1) the prevention of child abuse, (2) the provision of early childhood education and (3) a wide range of supports for parents in coping with the real-world stresses in their communities. […] Let me focus on child abuse and neglect prevention for a moment. In the US, and I think in many other countries as well, there's been a tendency for the people who deal with child abuse and neglect to be different from, and unconnected with, those who deal with crime policy. Child abuse thus becomes somebody else's problem, and it is not, at least where I come from, taken very seriously, certainly not as an integral part of a strategy of social crime prevention. But that's a mistake. Where serious violent crime is concerned, I'm increasingly convinced of the critical role of abusive, neglectful, harshly punitive childhood experiences. Our experience in the US does not suggest a simple programmatic response that can be replicated in cookie-cutter fashion, but it does point to successful programmes that show promise. One is hands-on work with high-risk parents from [the] pre-natal period, following them up from birth with counselling on child-rearing methods, home visits, and help with day care, health care and transportation. Another is comprehensive family support programmes of a kind now springing up across the US, that offer high-risk families the tangible help they need to take better care of their children: better knowledge about child-rearing, support groups of other parents in similar conditions, and help in securing the necessities – health care for themselves and their children, housing, income support. These are best delivered in a comprehensive setting that is community-based and culturally sensitive.

Secondly, we need a comprehensive youth intervention strategy. Again, many of the disruptive changes now affecting societies across the world are having their most profound and alienating effect on young people. I'm convinced that the single most important part of a youth strategy is the active labour market policy I spoke of already, for without it we are frankly condemning vast numbers of young men and women around the world to a bleak and uncertain life on the periphery of purposive society. But we also need more specific interventions to work with the young at highest risk. But here, perhaps even more than in other areas of social policy, it is terribly important to separate wheat from chaff and there is a great deal of chaff in the world of youth policy, certainly in the US. There is some tendency to see any youth programme that isn't prison as a worthy endeavour and to tout programmes that are poorly evaluated and theoretically weak as saviours of inner-city youth or, at best, to over-promise on the capacity of very minor interventions to make a big difference in the lives of kids who face very real and profound deprivations.

I believe the accumulating evidence strongly suggests that the youth-oriented strategies that work best are those which actually provide changed lives, that offer new and expanded possibilities for young people where few existed before. I think that what our programme experience in the US shows most clearly is that if you simply try to offer social services of various kinds to youth without changing their probable futures, without genuinely altering their realistic trajectory in life, then you are probably not going to make much of a difference. You are not going to wean many kids away from drug and alcohol abuse, away from the distinct and very powerful appeal of some kinds of delinquency, away from the comradeship and satisfaction that they can find in gangs.

But much of our debate on youth policy, such as it is, in the US today is stuck on the level at best of what I'd call a 'service' strategy of the kind we have recurrently tried, without much success, at various periods since the nineteenth century. In turn, this strategy is typically based on what I've called a 'deficiency' model of delinquency. In a nutshell, the deficiency model assumes that the problem is some lack or deficit within the young person which needs fixing, or filling;

we then design some service to patch it. But two years of intensive interviewing of delinquent kids has convinced me that for most American delinquents, extreme cases aside, far more critical than any such internal deficits is the rapidly shrinking opportunity for them to make legitimate use of the strengths and capacities they already have – a problem greatly exacerbated by the 'dumbing-down' of the economy I spoke of earlier. Quite simply, the kids often have far more skill than the increasingly constricted labour markets allow them to use in legitimate ways; delinquency allows them to *be* more than the straight world can.

To me, this suggests the usefulness of what I'd call an 'opportunity model' of intervention in place of the 'deficiency model' and that is supported by my reading of what works best in the youth programmes we've tried in the US – serious and intensive skills training programmes, such as the Job Corps, which actually provide usable formal skills; or the equally tangible opportunities by a programme like Eugene Lang's 'I Have a Dream', which guarantees college tuition for disadvantaged kids who stay in school. These have among the most consistently encouraging evaluations, and I think that's no accident.

Thirdly, similar considerations apply to a third area of priority, what I'd call 'user-friendly' drug and alcohol assistance. Today in the US, where of course the drug-crime problem is worst, the debate about drugs is now mainly between those who continue to push for more incarceration and harsher penalties for drug users and dealers, versus those who push for more conventional 'treatment'. But I don't think *either* path is the right one.

Like our approach to delinquency, our drug intervention strategies are often rooted in a model which is almost schizophrenically divorced from what the evidence tells us about the causes of the problem. In the US, the model typically underlying drug treatment efforts is some version of an individual medical or psychiatric model. Yet the accumulating research tells us over and over again that mass drug abuse of the kind that is now endemic in many American (and some British) communities is driven less by any identifiable pharmacological or psychological needs than by the systematic, long-term blockage of opportunities and the often overwhelmingly stressful and depriving conditions of life in communities suffering from multiple economic and social deprivation. This is a syndrome that is deepening with the advance of market society, here in Britain as in the US. [...]

We need to rethink treatment as well as expand it. Our current models of treatment tend to assume that addiction is a medical condition, rather like a broken leg or a kidney infection; it is not. People don't catch it and then want to come in and fix it. We're learning that addiction has less to do with the physical properties of the drugs themselves than with the barriers to alternative ways of achieving gratification, status, structure and esteem. The lesson too little heeded is that interventions should be tailored accordingly; they should be oriented more closely to the social context of addiction; should help abusers move away successfully from the drug cultures in which they're enmeshed; open realistic opportunities for stable employment, and offer help with starting and maintaining strong relationships and family ties which the research increasingly tells us is key to successfully moving away from drugs.

In turn, this means making drug programmes more 'user-friendly', in particular addressing the specific needs of groups who are now, at least in the US, largely left out or alienated by conventional treatment including teenagers, women and some minority groups. Much of our conventional treatment in the US is actually user-hostile to those critically important potential clients. It is shaped by what are essentially middle-class, male, adult and psychological models and assumptions, often relying on invasive group therapies based on a kind of 'encounter' model that appeals at best to a sliver of the drug-abusing population, which is why the great majority of that population is not in treatment. We especially need youth-supportive drug programmes that are capable of attracting the young rather than alienating them. Ideally, these ought to be part of a broader commitment to community-based, comprehensive adolescent health-care services that also engage problems of risk-taking behaviour, violence and sexually transmitted disease. Similarly, many treatment programmes for women will not even take pregnant women, much less address the crucial real-world issues many addicted women present; issues of child care, housing, poor employment and relationships with abusive men. These are just three specific directions but there are many more.

[…]

What all this means is that real social crime prevention, like the prevention of other social ills, is now more than ever dependent on our capacity to build more effective movements for social action and social change. These movements should challenge effectively those forces dimming the life chances of vast numbers of people in the developed and developing worlds. Building organisations should be committed to the long-range effort to replace a society based increasingly on the least inspiring of human values with one based on the principles of social solidarity and contributive justice.

[…]

35

Conflicts as property

Nils Christie

INTRODUCTION

Maybe we should not have any criminology. Maybe we should rather abolish institutes, not open them. Maybe the social consequences of criminology are more dubious than we like to think.

I think they are. And I think this relates to my topic – conflicts as property. My suspicion is that criminology to some extent has amplified a process where conflicts have been taken away from the parties directly involved and thereby have either disappeared or become other people's property. In both cases a deplorable outcome. Conflicts ought to be used, not only left in erosion. And they ought to be used, and become useful, for those originally involved in the conflict. Conflicts *might* hurt individuals as well as social systems. That is what we learn in school. That is why we have officials. Without them, private vengeance and vendettas will blossom. We have learned this so solidly that we have lost track of the other side of the coin: our industrialised large-scale society is not one with too many internal conflicts. It is one with too little. Conflicts might kill, but too little of them might paralyse. I will use this occasion to give a sketch of this situation. It cannot be more than a sketch. This paper represents the beginning of the development of some ideas, not the polished end-product.

ON HAPPENINGS AND NON-HAPPENINGS

Let us take our point of departure far away. Let us move to Tanzania. Let us approach our problem from the sunny hillside of the Arusha province. Here, inside a relatively large house in a very small village, a sort of happening took place. The house was overcrowded. Most grown-ups from the village and several from adjoining ones were there. It was a happy happening, fast talking, jokes, smiles, eager attention, not a sentence was to be lost. It was circus, it was drama. It was a court case.

From *The British Journal of Criminology*, 1977, 17(1): 1–15.

The conflict this time was between a man and a woman. They had been engaged. He had invested a lot in the relationship through a long period, until she broke it off. Now he wanted it back. Gold and silver and money were easily decided on, but what about utilities already worn, and what about general expenses?

The outcome is of no interest in our context. But the framework for conflict solution is. Five elements ought to be particularly mentioned:

1   The parties, the former lovers, were in *the centre* of the room and in the centre of everyone's attention. They talked often and were eagerly listened to.

2   Close to them were relatives and friends who also took part. But they did not take over.

3   There was also participation from the general audience with short questions, information, or jokes.

4   The judges, three local party secretaries, were extremely inactive. They were obviously ignorant with regard to village matters. All the other people in the room were experts. They were experts on norms as well as actions. And they crystallised norms and clarified what had happened through participation in the procedure.

5   No reporters attended. They were all there.

My personal knowledge when it comes to British courts is limited indeed. I have some vague memories of juvenile courts where I counted some 15 or 20 persons present, mostly social workers using the room for preparatory work or small conferences A child or a young person must have attended, but except for the judge, or maybe it was the clerk, nobody seemed to pay any particular attention. The child or young person was most probably utterly confused as to who was who and for what, a fact confirmed in a small study by Peter Scott (1959). In the United States of America, Martha Baum ([Baum and Wheeler] 1968) has made similar observations. Recently, Bottoms and McClean (1976) have added another important observation: 'There is one truth which is seldom revealed in the literature of the law or in studies of the administration of criminal justice. It is a truth which was made evident to all those involved in this research project as they sat through the cases which made up our sample. The truth is that, for the most part, the business of the criminal courts is dull, commonplace, ordinary and after a while downright tedious'.

But let me keep quiet about your system, and instead concentrate on my own. And let me assure you: what goes on is no happening. It is all a negation of the Tanzanian case. What is striking in nearly all the Scandinavian cases is the greyness, the dullness, and the lack of any important audience. Courts are not central elements in the daily life of our citizens, but peripheral in four major ways:

1   They are situated in the administrative centres of the towns, outside the territories of ordinary people.

2   Within these centres they are often centralised within one or two large buildings of considerable complexity. Lawyers often complain that they need months to find their way within

these buildings. It does not demand much fantasy to imagine the situation of parties or public when they are trapped within these structures. A comparative study of court architecture might become equally relevant for the sociology of law as Oscar Newman's (1972) study of defensible space is for criminology. But even without any study, I feel it safe to say that both physical situation and architectural design are strong indicators that courts in Scandinavia belong to the administrators of law.

This impression is strengthened when you enter the courtroom itself – if you are lucky enough to find your way to it. Here again, the periphery of the parties is the striking observation. The parties are represented, and it is these representatives and the judge or judges who express the little activity that is activated within these rooms. Honore Daumier's famous drawings from the courts are as representative for Scandinavia as they are for France.

3   There are variations. In the small cities, or in the countryside, the courts are more easily reached than in the larger towns. And at the very lowest end of the court system – the so-called arbitration boards – the parties are sometimes less heavily represented through experts in law. But the symbol of the whole system is the Supreme Court where the directly involved parties do not even attend their own court cases.

3   I have not yet made any distinction between civil and criminal conflicts. But it was not by chance that the Tanzania case was a civil one. Full participation in your own conflict presupposes elements of civil law. The key element in a criminal proceeding is that the proceeding is converted from something between the concrete parties into a conflict between one of the parties and the state. So, in a modern criminal trial, two important things have happened. First, the parties are being represented. Secondly, the one party that is represented by the state, namely the victim, is so thoroughly represented that she or he for most of the proceedings is pushed completely out of the arena, reduced to the triggerer-off of the whole thing. She or he is a sort of double loser; first, vis-à-vis the offender, but secondly and often in a more crippling manner by being denied rights to full participation in what might have been one of the more important ritual encounters in life. The victim has lost the case to the state.

PROFESSIONAL THIEVES

As we all know, there are many honourable as well as dishonourable reasons behind this development. The honourable ones have to do with the state's need for conflict reduction and certainly also its wishes for the protection of the victim. It is rather obvious. So is also the less honourable temptation for the state, or Emperor, or whoever is in power, to use the criminal case for personal gain. Offenders might pay for their sins. Authorities have in time past shown considerable willingness, in representing the victim, to act as receivers of the money or other property from the offender. Those days are gone; the crime control system is not run for profit. And yet they are not gone. There are, in all banality, many interests at stake here, most of them related to professionalisation.

Lawyers are particularly good at stealing conflicts. They are trained for it. They are trained to prevent and solve conflicts. They are socialised into a subculture with a surprisingly high agreement concerning interpretation of norms, and regarding what sort of information can be accepted as relevant in each case. Many among us have, as laymen, experienced the sad moments of truth when our lawyers tell us that our best arguments in our fight against our neighbour are without any legal relevance whatsoever and that we for God's sake ought to keep quiet about them in court. Instead they pick out arguments we might find irrelevant or even wrong to use. My favourite example took place just after the war. One of my country's absolutely top defenders told with pride how he had just rescued a poor client. The client had collaborated with the Germans. The prosecutor claimed that the client had been one of the key people in the organisation of the Nazi movement. He had been one of the master-minds behind it all. The defender, however, saved his client. He saved him by pointing out to the jury how weak, how lacking in ability, how obviously deficient his client was, socially as well as organisationally. His client could simply not have been one of the organisers among the collaborators; he was without talents. And he won his case. His client got a very minor sentence as a very minor figure. The defender ended his story by telling me – with some indignation – that neither the accused, nor his wife, had ever thanked him, they had not even talked to him afterwards.

Conflicts become the property of lawyers. But lawyers don't hide that it is conflicts they handle. And the organisational framework of the courts underlines this point. The opposing parties, the judge, the ban against privileged communication within the court system, the lack of encouragement for specialisation – specialists cannot be internally controlled – it all underlines that this is an organisation for the handling of conflicts. *Treatment personnel* are in another position. They are more interested in *converting the image of the case from one of conflict into one of non-conflict.* The basic model of healers is not one of opposing parties, but one where one party has to be helped in the direction of one generally accepted goal – the preservation or restoration of health. They are not trained into a system where it is important that parties can control each other. There is, in the ideal case, nothing to control, because there is only one goal. Specialisation is encouraged. It increases the amount of available knowledge, and the loss of internal control is of no relevance. A conflict perspective creates unpleasant doubts with regard to the healer's suitability for the job. A non-conflict perspective is a precondition for defining crime as a legitimate target for treatment.

One way of reducing attention to the conflict is reduced attention given to the victim. Another is concentrated attention given to those attributes in the criminal's background which the healer is particularly trained to handle. Biological defects are perfect. So also are personality defects when they are established far back in time – far away from the recent conflict. And so are also the whole row of explanatory variables that criminology might offer. We have, in criminology, to a large extent functioned as an auxiliary science for the professionals within the crime control system. We have focused on the offender, made her or him into an object for study, manipulation and control. We have added to all those forces that have reduced the victim to a nonentity and the offender to a thing. And this critique is perhaps not only relevant for the old criminology, but also for the new criminology. While the old one explained crime from personal defects or social handicaps, the new criminology explains crime as the result of broad economic conflicts. The old criminology loses the conflicts, the new one converts them from interpersonal conflicts to class conflicts. And they are. They are class conflicts – also. But, by stressing this, the conflicts are again taken away from the directly involved parties. So, as a preliminary statement: Criminal conflicts have either become *other people's property* – primarily the property of lawyers – or it has been in other people's interests to *define conflicts away.*

STRUCTURAL THIEVES

But there is more to it than professional manipulation of conflicts. Changes in the basic social structure have worked in the same way.

What I particularly have in mind are *two types of segmentation* easily observed in highly industrialised societies. First, there is the question of segmentation *in space.* We function each day, as migrants moving between sets of people which do not need to have any link – except through the mover. Often, therefore, we know our work-mates only as work-mates, neighbours only as neighbours, fellow cross-country skiers only as fellow cross-country skiers. We get to know them as *roles*, not as total persons. This situation is accentuated by the extreme degree of division of labour we accept to live with. Only experts can evaluate each other according to individual – personal – competence. Outside the speciality we have to fall back on a general evaluation of the supposed importance of the work. Except between specialists, we cannot evaluate how good anybody is in his work, only how good, in the sense of important, the role is. Through all this, we get limited possibilities for understanding other people's behaviour. Their behaviour will also get limited relevance for us. Role-players are more easily exchanged than persons.

The second type of segmentation has to do with what I would like to call our re-establishment of caste-society. I am not saying class-society, even though there are obvious tendencies also in that direction. In my framework, however, I find the elements of caste even more important. What I have in mind is the segregation based on biological attributes such as sex, colour, physical handicaps or the number of winters that have passed since birth. Age is particularly important. It is an attribute nearly perfectly synchronised to a modern complex industrialised society. It is a continuous variable where we can introduce as many intervals as we might need. We can split the population in two: children and adults. But we also can split it in ten: babies, pre-school children, school-children, teenagers, older youth, adults, pre-pensioned, pensioned, old people, the senile. And most important: the cutting points can be moved up and down according to social needs. The concept 'teenager' was particularly suitable 10 years ago. It would not have caught on if social realities had not been in accordance with the word. Today the concept is not often used in my country. The condition of youth is not over at 19. Young people have to wait even longer before they are allowed to enter the work force. The caste of those outside the work force has been extended far into the twenties. At the same time departure from the work force – if you ever were admitted, if you were not kept completely out because of race or sex-attributes – is brought forward into the early sixties in a person's life. In my tiny country of four million inhabitants, we have 800,000 persons segregated within the educational system. Increased scarcity of work has immediately led authorities to increase the capacity of educational incarceration. Another 600,000 are pensioners.

Segmentation according to space and according to caste attributes has several consequences. First and foremost it leads into a *depersonalisation* of social life. Individuals are to a smaller extent linked to each other in close social networks where they are confronted with *all* the significant roles of the significant others. This creates a situation with limited amounts of information with regard to each other. We do know less about other people, and get limited possibilities both for understanding and for prediction of their behaviour. If a conflict is created, we are less able to cope with this situation. Not only are professionals there, able and willing to take the conflict away, but we are also more willing to give it away.

Secondly, segmentation leads to destruction of certain conflicts even before they get going. The depersonalisation and mobility within industrial society melt away some essential conditions for living conflicts; those between parties that mean a lot to each other. What I have particularly in mind is crime against other people's honour, libel or defamation of character. All the Scandinavian countries have had a dramatic decrease in this form of crime. In my interpretation, this is not because honour has become more respected, but because there is less honour to respect. The various forms of segmentation mean that human beings are interrelated in ways where they simply mean less to each other. When they are hurt, they are only hurt partially. And if they are troubled, they can easily move away. And after all, who cares? Nobody knows me. In my evaluation, the decrease in the crimes of infamy and libel is one of the most interesting and sad symptoms of dangerous developments within modern industrialised societies. The decrease here is clearly related to social conditions that lead to increase in other forms of crime brought to the attention of the authorities. It is an important goal for crime prevention to re-create social conditions which lead to an increase in the number of crimes against other people's honour.

A third consequence of segmentation according to space and age is that certain conflicts are made completely invisible, and thereby don't get any decent solution whatsoever. I have here in mind conflicts at the two extremes of a continuum. On the one extreme we have the over-privatised ones, those taking place against individuals captured within one of the segments. Wife beating or child battering represent examples. The more isolated a segment is, the more the weakest among parties is alone, open for abuse. Inghe and Riemer ([Kinberg et al.] 1943) made the classical study many years ago of a related phenomenon in their book on incest. Their major point was that the social isolation of certain categories of proletarised Swedish farm-workers was the necessary condition for this type of crime. Poverty meant that the parties within the nuclear family became completely dependent on each other. Isolation meant that the weakest parties within the family had no external network where they could appeal for help. The physical strength of the husband got an undue importance. At the other extreme we have crimes done by large economic organisations against individuals too weak and ignorant to be able even to realise they have been victimised. In both cases the goal for crime prevention might be to re-create social conditions which make the conflicts visible and thereafter manageable.

CONFLICTS AS PROPERTY

Conflicts are taken away, given away, melt away, or are made invisible. Does it matter, does it really matter?

Most of us would probably agree that we ought to protect the invisible victims just mentioned. Many would also nod approvingly to ideas saying that states, or Governments, or other authorities ought to stop stealing fines, and instead let the poor victim receive this money. I at least would approve such an arragement. But I will not go into that problem area here and now. Material compensation is not what I have in mind with the formulation 'conflicts as property'. It is the *conflict itself* that represents the most interesting property taken away, not the goods originally taken away from the victim, or given back to him. In our types of society, conflicts are more scarce than property. And they are immensely more valuable.

They are valuable in several ways. Let me start at the societal level, since here I have already presented the necessary fragments of analysis that might allow us to see what the problem is. Highly industrialised societies face major problems in organising their members in ways such that a decent quota take part in any activity at all. Segmentation according to age and sex can be seen as shrewd methods for segregation. Participation is such a scarcity that insiders create monopolies against outsiders, particularly with regard to work. In this perspective, it will easily be seen that conflicts represent a *potential for activity, for participation.* Modern criminal control systems represent one of the many cases of lost opportunities for involving citizens in tasks that are of immediate importance to them. Ours is a society of task-monopolists.

The victim is a particularly heavy loser in this situation. Not only has he suffered, lost materially or become hurt, physically or otherwise. And not only does the state take the compensation. But above all he has lost participation in his own case. It is the Crown that comes into the spotlight, not the victim. It is the Crown that describes the losses, not the victim. It is the Crown that appears in the newspaper, very seldom the victim. It is the Crown that gets a chance to talk to the offender, and neither the Crown nor the offender are particularly interested in carrying on that conversation. The prosecutor is fed-up long since. The victim would not have been. He might have been scared to death, panic-stricken, or furious. But he would not have been uninvolved. It would have been one of the important days in his life. Something that belonged to him has been taken away from that victim.[1]

But the big loser is us – to the extent that society is us. This loss is first and foremost a loss in *opportunities for norm-clarification.* It is a loss of pedagogical possibilities. It is a loss of opportunities for a continuous discussion of what represents the law of the land. How wrong was the thief, how right was the victim? Lawyers are, as we saw, trained into agreement on what is relevant in a case. But that means a trained incapacity in letting the parties decide what *they* think is relevant. It means that it is difficult to stage what we might call a polit- ical debate in the court. When the victim is small and the offender big – in size or power – how blameworthy then is the crime? And what about the opposite case, the small thief and the big house-owner? If the offender is well educated, ought he then to suffer more or maybe less, for his sins? Or if he is black, or if he is young, or if the other party is an insurance company, or if his wife has just left him, or if his factory will break down if he has to go to jail, or if his daugh- ter will lose her fiancé, or if he was drunk, or if he was sad, or if he was mad? There is no end to it. And maybe there ought to be none. Maybe Barotse law as described by Max Gluckman (1967) is a better instrument for norm-clarification, allowing the conflicting parties to bring in the whole chain of old complaints and arguments each time. Maybe decisions on relevance and on the weight of what is found relevant ought to be taken away from legal scholars, the chief ideologists of crime control systems, and brought back for free decisions in the court-rooms.

A further general loss – both for the victim and for society in general – has to do with anxiety-level and misconceptions. It is again the possibilities for person- alised encounters I have in mind. The victim is so totally out of the case that he has no chance, ever, to come to know the offender. We leave him outside, angry, maybe humiliated through a cross-examination in court, without any human contact with the offender. He has no alternative. He will need all the classical stereotypes around 'the criminal' to get a grasp on the whole thing. He has a need for understanding, but is instead a non-person in a Kafka play. Of course, he will go away more frightened than ever, more in need than ever of an explana- tion of criminals as non-human.

The offender represents a more complicated case. Not much introspection is needed to see that direct victim-participation might be experienced as painful indeed. Most of us would shy away from a confrontation of this character. That is the first reaction. But the second one is slightly more positive. Human beings have reasons for their actions. If the situation is staged so that reasons can be given (reasons as the parties see them, not only the selection lawyers have decided to classify as relevant), in such a case maybe the situation would not be all that humiliating. And, particularly, if the situation was staged in such a manner that the central question was not meting out guilt, but a thorough discussion of what could be done to undo the deed, then the situation might change. And this is exactly what ought to happen when the victim is reintroduced in the case. Serious attention will centre on the victim's losses. That leads to a natural attention as to how they can be softened. It leads into a discussion of restitution. The offender gets a possibility to change his position from being a listener to a discussion – often a highly unintelligible one – of how much pain he ought to receive, into a participant in a discussion of how he could make it good again. The offender has lost the opportunity to explain himself to a person whose evaluation of him might have mattered. He has thereby also lost one of the most important possibilities for being forgiven. Compared to the humiliations in an ordinary court – vividly described by Pat Carlen (1976) in a recent issue of the *British Journal of Criminology* – this is not obviously any bad deal for the criminal.

But let me add that I think we should do it quite independently of his wishes. It is not health-control we are discussing. It is crime control. If criminals are shocked by the initial thought of close confrontation with the victim, preferably a confrontation in the very local neighbourhood of one of the parties, what then? I know from recent conversations on these matters that most people sentenced are shocked. After all, they prefer distance from the victim, from neighbours, from listeners and maybe also from their own court case through the vocabulary and the behavioural science experts who might happen to be present. They are perfectly willing to give away their property right to the conflict. So the question is more: are *we* willing to let them give it away? Are we willing to give them this easy way out?[2]

Let me be quite explicit on one point: I am not suggesting these ideas out of any particular interest in the treatment or improvement of criminals. I am not basing my reasoning on a belief that a more personalised meeting between offender and victim would lead to reduced recidivism. Maybe it would. I think it would. As it is now, the offender has lost the opportunity for participation in a personal confrontation of a very serious nature. He has lost the opportunity to receive a type of blame that it would be very difficult to neutralise. However, I would have suggested these arrangements even if it was absolutely certain they had no effects on recidivism, maybe even if they had a negative effect. I would have done that because of the other, more general gains. And let me also add – it is not much to lose. As we all know today, at least nearly all, we have not been able to invent any cure for crime. Except for execution, castration or incarceration for life, no measure has a proven minimum of efficiency compared to any other measure. We might as well react to crime according to what closely involved parties find is just and in accordance with general values in society.

With this last statement, as with most of the others I have made, I raise many more problems than I answer. Statements on criminal politics, particularly from those with the burden of responsibility, are usually filled with answers. It is questions we need. The gravity of our topic makes us much too pedantic and thereby useless as paradigm-changers.

A VICTIM-ORIENTED COURT

There is clearly a model of neighbourhood courts behind my reasoning. But it is one with some peculiar features, and it is only these I will discuss in what follows.

First and foremost; it is a *victim-oriented* organisation. Not in its initial stage, though. The first stage will be a traditional one where it is established whether it is true that the law has been broken, and whether it was this particular person who broke it.

Then comes the second stage, which in these courts would be of the utmost importance. That would be the stage where the victim's situation was considered, where every detail regarding what had happened – legally relevant or not – was brought to the court's attention. Particularly important here would be detailed consideration regarding what could be done for him, first and foremost by the offender, secondly by the local neighbourhood, thirdly by the state. Could the harm be compensated, the window repaired, the lock replaced, the wall painted, the loss of time because the car was stolen given back through garden work or washing of the car ten Sundays in a row? Or maybe, when this discussion started, the damage was not so important as it looked in documents written to impress insurance companies? Could physical suffering become slightly less painful by any action from the offender, during days, months or years? But, in addition, had the community exhausted all resources that might have offered help? Was it absolutely certain that the local hospital could not do anything? What about a helping hand from the janitor twice a day if the offender took over the cleaning of the basement every Saturday? None of these ideas is unknown or untried, particularly not in England. But we need an organisation for the systematic application of them.

Only after this stage was passed, and it ought to take hours, maybe days, to pass it, only then would come the time for an eventual decision on punishment. Punishment, then, becomes that suffering which the judge found necessary to apply *in addition to* those unintended constructive sufferings the offender would go through in his restitutive actions *vis-à-vis* the victim. Maybe nothing could be done or nothing would be done. But neighbourhoods might find it intolerable that nothing happened. Local courts out of tune with local values are not local courts. That is just the trouble with them, seen from the liberal reformer's point of view.

A fourth stage has to be added. That is the stage for service to the offender. His general social and personal situation is by now well-known to the court. The discussion of his possibilities for restoring the victim's situation cannot be carried out without at the same time giving information about the offender's situation. This might have exposed needs for social, educational, medical or religious action – not to prevent further crime, but because needs ought to be met. Courts are public arenas, needs are made visible. But it is important that this stage comes *after* sentencing. Otherwise we get a re-emergence of the whole array of so-called 'special measures' – compulsory treatments – very often only euphemisms for indeterminate imprisonment.

Through these four stages, these courts would represent a blend of elements from civil and criminal courts, but with a strong emphasis on the civil side.

A LAY-ORIENTED COURT

The second major peculiarity with the court model I have in mind is that it will be one with an extreme degree of lay-orientation. This is essential when conflicts are seen as property that ought to be shared. It is with conflicts as with so many good things: they are in no unlimited supply. Conflicts can be cared for, protected, nurtured. But there are limits. If some are given more access in the disposal of conflicts, others are getting less. It is as simple as that.

Specialisation in conflict solution is the major enemy; specialisation that in due – or undue – time leads to professionalisation. That is when the specialists get sufficient power to claim that they have acquired special gifts, mostly through education, gifts so powerful that it is obvious that they can only be handled by the certified craftsman.

With a clarification of the enemy, we are also able to specify the goal; let us reduce specialisation and particularly our dependence on the professionals within the crime control system to the utmost.

The ideal is clear; it ought to be a court of equals representing themselves. When they are able to find a solution between themselves, no judges are needed. When they are not, the judges ought also to be their equals.

Maybe the judge would be the easiest to replace, if we made a serious attempt to bring our present courts nearer to this model of lay orientation. We have lay judges already, in principle. But that is a far cry from realities. What we have, both in England and in my own country, is a sort of specialised non-specialist. First, they are used *again and again.* Secondly, some are even *trained,* given special courses or sent on excursions to foreign countries to learn about how to behave as a lay judge. Thirdly, most of them do also represent an extremely *biased sample* of the population with regard to sex, age, education, income, class[3] and personal experience as criminals. With real lay judges, I conceive of a system where nobody was given the right to take part in conflict solution more than a few times, and then had to wait until all other community members had had the same experience.

Should lawyers be admitted to court? We had an old law in Norway that forbids them to enter the rural districts. Maybe they should be admitted in stage one where it is decided if the man is guilty. I am not sure. Experts are as cancer to any lay body. It is exactly as Ivan Illich describes for the educational system in general. Each time you increase the length of compulsory education in a society, each time you also decrease the same population's trust in what they have learned and understood quite by themselves.

Behaviour experts represent the same dilemma. Is there a place for them in this model? Ought there to be any place? In stage 1, decisions on facts, certainly not. In stage 3, decisions on eventual punishment, certainly not. It is too obvious to waste words on. We have the painful row of mistakes from Lombroso, through the movement for social defence and up to recent attempts to dispose of suppos-edly dangerous people through predictions of who they are and when they are not dangerous any more. Let these ideas die, without further comments.

The real problem has to do with the service function of behaviour experts. Social scientists can be perceived as functional answers to a segmented society. Most of us have lost the physical possibility to experience the totality, both on the social system level and on the personality level. Psychologists can be seen as historians for the individual; sociologists have much of the same function for the social system. Social workers are oil in the machinery, a sort of security counsel. Can we function without them, would the victim and the offender be worse off?

Maybe. But it would be immensely difficult to get such a court to function if they were all there. Our theme is social conflict. Who is not at least made slightly uneasy in the handling of her or his own social conflicts if we get to know that there is an expert on this very matter at the same table? I have no clear answer, only strong feelings behind a vague conclusion: let us have as few behaviour experts as we dare to. And if we have any, let us for God's sake not have any that specialise in crime and conflict resolution. Let us have generalised experts with a solid base outside the crime control system. And a last point with relevance for both behaviour experts and lawyers: if we find them unavoidable in certain cases or at certain stages, let us try to get across to them the problems they create for broad social participation. Let us try to get them to perceive themselves as resource-persons, answering when asked, but not domineering, not in the centre. They might help to stage conflicts, not take them over.

ROLLING STONES

There are hundreds of blocks against getting such a system to operate within our western culture. Let me only mention three major ones. They are:

1   There is a lack of neighbourhoods.

2   There are too few victims.

3   There are too many professionals around.

With lack of neighbourhoods I have in mind the very same phenomenon I described as a consequence of industrialised living; segmentation according to space and age. Much of our trouble stems from killed neighbourhoods or killed local communities. How can we then thrust towards neighbourhoods a task that presupposes they are highly alive? I have no really good arguments, only two weak ones. First, it is not quite that bad. The death is not complete. Secondly, one of the major ideas behind the formulation 'Conflicts as Property' is that it is neighbourhood-property. It is not private. It belongs to the system. It is intended as a vitaliser for neighbourhoods. The more fainting the neighbourhood is, the more we need neighbourhood courts as one of the many functions any social system needs for not dying through lack of challenge.

Equally bad is the lack of victims. Here I have particularly in mind the lack of personal victims. The problem behind this is again the large units in industrialised society. Woolworth or British Rail are not good victims. But again I will say: there is not a complete lack of personal victims, and their needs ought to get priority. But we should not forget the large organisations. They, or their boards, would certainly prefer not to have to appear as victims in 5000 neighbourhood courts all over the country. But maybe they ought to be compelled to appear. If the complaint is serious enough to bring the offender into the ranks of the criminal, then the victim ought to appear. A related problem has to do with insurance companies – the industrialised alternative to friendship or kinship. Again we have a case where the crutches deteriorate the condition. Insurance takes the consequences of crime away. We will therefore have to take insurance away. Or rather: we will have to keep the possibilities for compensation through the insurance companies back until in the procedure I have described it has been proved beyond all possible doubt that there are no other alternatives left – particularly that the offender has no possibilities whatsoever. Such a solution will create more paper-work, less predictability, more aggression from customers. And the solution will not necessarily be seen as good from the perspective of the policyholder. But it will help to protect conflicts as social fuel.

None of these troubles can, however, compete with the third and last I will comment on: the abundance of professionals. We know it all from our own personal biographies or personal observations. And in addition we get it confirmed from all sorts of social science research: the educational system of any society is not necessarily synchronised with any needs for the product of this system. Once upon a time we thought there was a direct causal relation from the number of highly educated persons in a country to the Gross National Product. Today we suspect the relationship to go the other way, if we are at all willing to use GNP as a meaningful indicator. We also know that most educational systems are extremely class-biased. We know that most academic people have had profitable investments in our education, that we fight for the same for our children, and that we also often have vested interests in making our part of the educational system even bigger. More schools for more lawyers, social workers, sociologists, criminologists. While I am *talking* deprofessionalisation, we are increasing the capacity to be able to fill up the whole world with them.

There is no solid base for optimism. On the other hand insights about the situation, and goal formulation, is a pre-condition for action. Of course, the crime control system is not the domineering one in our type of society. But it has some importance. And occurrences here are unusually well suited as pedagogical illustrations of general trends in society. There is also some room for manoeuvre. And when we hit the limits, or are hit by them, this collision represents in itself a renewed argument for more broadly conceived changes.

Another source for hope: ideas formulated here are not quite so isolated or in dissonance with the mainstream of thinking when we leave our crime control area and enter other institutions. I have already mentioned Ivan Illich with his attempts to get learning away from the teachers and back to active human beings. Compulsory learning, compulsory medication and compulsory consummation of conflict solutions have interesting similarities. When Ivan Illich and Paulo Freire are listened to, and my impression is that they increasingly are, the crime control system will also become more easily influenced.

Another, but related, major shift in paradigm is about to happen within the whole field of technology. Partly, it is the lessons from the third world that now are more easily seen, partly it is the experience from the ecology debate. The globe is obviously suffering from what we, through our technique, are doing to her. Social systems in the third world are equally obviously suffering. So the suspicion starts. Maybe the first world can't take all this technology either. Maybe some of the old social thinkers were not so dumb after all. Maybe social systems can be perceived as biological ones. And maybe there are certain types of large-scale technology that kill social systems, as they kill globes. Schumacher (1973) with his book *Small is Beautiful* and the related Institute for Intermediate Technology come in here. So do also the numerous attempts, particularly by several outstanding Institutes for Peace Research, to show the dangers in the concept of Gross National Product, and replace it with indicators that take care of dignity, equity and justice. The perspective developed in Johan Galtung's research group on World Indicators might prove extremely useful also within our own field of crime control.

There is also a political phenomenon opening vistas. At least in Scandinavia social democrats and related groupings have considerable power, but are without an explicated ideology regarding the goals for a reconstructed society. This vacuum is being felt by many, and creates a willingness to accept and even expect considerable institutional experimentation.

Then to my very last point: what about the universities in this picture? What about the new Centre in Sheffield? The answer has probably to be the old one: universities have to re-emphasise the old tasks of understanding and of criticising. But the task of training professionals ought to be looked into with renewed scepticism. Let us re-establish the credibility of encounters between critical human beings: low-paid, highly regarded, but with no extra power – outside the weight of their good ideas. That is as it ought to be.

NOTES

1 For a preliminary report on victim dissatisfaction, see Vennard (1976).
2 I tend to take the same position with regard to a criminal's property right to his own conflict as John Locke on property rights to one's own life – one has no right to give it away (cf. C. B. MacPherson (1962)).
3 For the most recent documentation, see Baldwin (1976).

REFERENCES

Baldwin, J. (1976). 'The Social Composition of the Magistracy.' *Brit. J Criminol.*, 16, 171–174.
Baum, M. and Wheeler, S. (1968). ' Becoming an Inmate,' Ch. 7, pp. 153–187, in Wheeler, S. (ed.), *Controlling Delinquents*. New York: Wiley.
Bottoms, A. E. and McClean, J. D. (1976). *Defendants in the Criminal Process*. London: Routledge and Kegan Paul.
Carlen, P. (1976). 'The Staging of Magistrates' Justice.' *Brit. J. Criminol.*, 16, 48–55.
Gluckman, M. (1967). *The Judicial Process among the Barotse of Northern Rhodesia*. Manchester: Manchester University Press.

Kinberg, O., Inghe, G., and Riemer, S. (1943). Incest-Problemet i Sverige. Sth.

MacPherson, C. B. (1962). *The Political Theory of Possessive Individualism: Hobbes to Locke*. London: Oxford University Press.

Newman, O. (1972). *Defensible Space: People and Design in the Violent City*. London: Architectural Press.

Schumacher, E. F. (1973). *Small is Beautiful: A Study of Economics as if People Mattered*. London: Blond and Briggs.

Scott, P. D. (1959). 'Juvenile Courts: the Juvenile's Point of View.' *Brit. J. Delinq.*, 9, 200–210.

Vennard, J. (1976). 'Justice and Recompense for Victims of Crime.' *New Society*, 36, 378–380.

36

Reintegrative shaming

John Braithwaite

[...]

It would seem that sanctions imposed by relatives, friends or a personally relevant collectivity have more effect on criminal behavior than sanctions imposed by a remote legal authority. I will argue that this is because repute in the eyes of close acquaintances matters more to people than the opinions or actions of criminal justice officials. As Blau (1964: 20) points out: 'a person who is attracted to others is interested in proving himself attractive to them, for his ability to associate with them and reap the benefits expected from the association is contingent on their finding him an attractive associate and thus wanting to interact with him'.

A British Government Social Survey asked youths to rank what they saw as the most important consequences of arrest. While only 10 per cent said 'the punishment I might get' was the most important consequence of arrest, 55 per cent said either 'What my family' or 'my girlfriend' would think about it. Another 12 per cent ranked 'the publicity or shame of having to appear in court' as the most serious consequence of arrest, and this was ranked as a more serious consequence on average than 'the punishment I might get' (Zimring and Hawkins, 1973: 192). There is clearly a need for more empirical work to ascertain whether the following conclusion is too sweeping, but Tittle would seem to speak for the current state of this literature when he says:

> social control as a general process seems to be rooted almost completely in informal sanctioning. Perceptions of formal sanction probabilities or severities do not appear to have much of an effect, and those effects that are evident turn out to be dependent upon perceptions of informal sanctions. (Tittle, 1980: 214)

Only a small proportion of the informal sanctions which prevent crime are coupled with formal sanctions, so this literature in a sense understates the

From *Crime, Shame and Reintegration*, pp. 69–83. (Cambridge: Cambridge University Press, 1989.)

importance of informal sanctions. These studies are also by no means tests of the theory of reintegrative shaming […] but they certainly suggest that we are looking in the right place for an explanation of crime. To quote Tittle (1980: 198) again, they suggest that 'to the extent that individuals are deterred from deviance by fear, the fear that is relevant is most likely to be that their deviance will evoke some respect or status loss among acquaintances or in the community as a whole'. In the rational weighting of the costs and benefits of crime, loss of respect weighs more heavily for most of us than formal punishment. Yet in learning theory terms this rational weighing results from the operant conditioning part of learning. There is also the much more important effect of consciences which may be classically conditioned by shame […].

A related reading of the deterrence literature is that it shows it is not the formal punitive features of social control that matter, but rather its informal moralizing features. The surprising findings of a classic field experiment by Schwartz and Orleans (1967) has fostered such a reading. Taxpayers were interviewed during the month prior to the filing of income tax returns, with one randomly selected group exposed to an interview stressing the penalties for income tax evasion, the other to an interview stressing the moral reasons for tax compliance. Whereas the moral appeal led to a significant increase in the actual tax paid, the deterrent threat was associated with no significant increase in tax paid compared to a control group.

BEYOND DETERRENCE. BEYOND OPERANT CONDITIONING: CONSCIENCE AND SHAMING

Jackson Toby (1964: 333) suggests that deterrence is irrelevant 'to the bulk of the population who have introjected the moral norms of society'. People comply with the law most of the time not through fear of punishment, or even fear of shaming, but because criminal behavior is simply abhorrent to them. Most serious crimes are unthinkable to most people; these people engage in no rational weighing of the costs and benefits of crime before deciding whether to comply with the law. Shaming, we will argue, is critical to understanding why most serious crime is unthinkable to most of us.

The unthinkableness of crime is a manifestation of our conscience or super-ego, whatever we want to call it depending on our psychological theoretical preferences. […] We will leave it to the psychologists to debate how much the acquisition and generalization of conscience is a conditioning or a cognitive process. The point is that conscience is acquired.

For adolescents and adults, conscience is a much more powerful weapon to control misbehavior than punishment. In the wider society, it is no longer logistically possible, as it is in the nursery, for arrangements to be made for punishment to hang over the heads of persons whenever temptation to break the rules is put in their path. Happily, conscience more than compensates for absence of formal control. For a well-socialized individual, conscience delivers an anxiety response to punish each and every involvement in crime – a more systematic punishment than haphazard enforcement by the police. Unlike any punishment handed down by the courts, the anxiety response happens without delay, indeed punishment by anxiety precedes the rewards obtained from the crime, while any punishment by law will follow long after the reward. For most of us, punishment by our own conscience is therefore a much more potent threat than punishment by the criminal justice system.

Shaming is critical as the societal process that underwrites the family process of building consciences in children. Just as the insurance company cannot do business without the underwriter, the family could not develop young consciences in the cultural vacuum which would be left without societal practices of shaming. Shaming is an important child-rearing practice in itself; it is an extremely valuable tool in the hands of a responsible loving parent. However, as children's morality develops, as socialization moves from building responsiveness to external controls to responsiveness to internal controls, direct forms of shaming become less important than induction: appealing to the child's affection or respect for others, appealing to the child's own standards of right and wrong. […]

However, the external controls must still be there in the background. If the maturation of conscience proceeds as it should, direct forms of shaming, and even more so punishment, are resorted to less and less. But there are times when conscience fails all of us, and we need a refresher course in the consequences of a compromised conscience. In this backstop role, shaming has a great advantage over formal punishment. Shaming is more pregnant with symbolic content than punishment. Punishment is a denial of confidence in the morality of the offender by reducing norm compliance to a crude cost–benefit calculation; shaming can be a reaffirmation of the morality of the offender by expressing personal disappointment that the offender should do something so out of character, and, if the shaming is reintegrative, by expressing personal satisfaction in seeing the character of the offender restored. Punishment erects barriers between the offender and punisher through transforming the relationship into one of power assertion and injury; shaming produces a greater interconnectedness between the parties, albeit a painful one, an interconnectedness which can produce the repulsion of stigmatization or the establishment of a potentially more positive relationship following reintegration. Punishment is often shameful and shaming usually punishes. But whereas punishment gets its symbolic content only from its denunciatory association with shaming, shaming is pure symbolic content.

Nevertheless, just as shaming is needed when conscience fails, punishment is needed when offenders are beyond being shamed. Unfortunately, however, the shameless, the remorseless, those who are beyond conditioning by shame are also likely to be those beyond conditioning by punishment – that is, psychopaths (consider, for example, the work of Mednick on conditionability and psychopathy – which would seem equally relevant to conditioning by fear of shame or fear of formal punishment (Mednick and Christiansen, 1977; Wilson and Herrnstein, 1985: 198–204). The evidence is that punishment is a very ineffective ultimate backstop with people who have developed beyond the control techniques which were effective when they were infants. This is the problem with behavior modification (based on either rewards or punishment) for rehabilitating offenders. Offenders will play the game by reverting to pre-adolescent responsiveness to reward–cost social control because this is the way they can make their life most comfortable. But when they leave the institution they will return to behaving like the adults they are in an adult world in which punishment contingencies for indulging deviant conduct are remote.

The conscience-building effects of shaming that give it superiority over control strategies based simply on changing the rewards and costs of crime are enhanced by the participatory nature of shaming. Whereas an actual punishment will only be administered by one person or a limited number of criminal justice officials, the shaming associated with punishment may involve almost all of the members of a community. Thus, in the following passage, when Znaniecki refers to 'punishment', he really means the denunciation or shaming associated with the punishment:

> Regardless of whether punishment really does deter future violation of the law or not, it seems to significantly reinforce agreement and solidarity among those who actively or vicariously participate in meting it out … Opposing the misdemeanours of other people increases the conformity of those administering the punishment, thus leading to the maintenance of the systems in which they participate. (Znaniecki, 1971: 604)

Participation in expressions of abhorrence toward the criminal acts of others is part of what makes crime an abhorrent choice for us ourselves to make. [...]

When we shame ourselves, that is when we feel pangs of conscience, we take the role of the other, treating ourselves as an object worthy of shame (Mead, 1934; Shott, 1979). We learn to do this by participating with others in shaming criminals and evil-doers. Internal control is a social product of external control. Self-regulation can displace social control by an external agent only when control has been internalized through the prior existence of external control in the culture.

Cultures like that of Japan, which shame reintegratively, follow shaming ceremonies with ceremonies of repentance and reacceptance. The nice advantage such cultures get in conscience building is two ceremonies instead of one, but, more critically, confirmation of the moral order from two very different quarters – both from those affronted and from him who caused the affront. The moral order derives a very special kind of credibility when even he who has breached it openly comes out and affirms the evil of the breach.

This is achieved by what Goffman (1971: 113) calls disassociation:

> An apology is a gesture through which an individual splits himself into two parts, the part that is guilty of an offense and the part that disassociates itself from the delict and affirms a belief in the offended rule.

In cultures like that of Japan which practise disassociation, the vilification of the self that misbehaved by the repentant self can be much more savage than would be safe with vilification by other persons: 'he can overstate or overplay the case against himself, thereby giving others the task of cutting the self-derogation short' (Goffman, 1971: 113). [...]

In summary then, shame operates at two levels to effect social control. First, it deters criminal behavior because social approval of significant others is something we do not like to lose. Second, and more importantly, both shaming and repentance build consciences which internally deter criminal behavior even in the absence of any external shaming associated with an offense. Shaming brings into existence two very different kinds of punishers – social disapproval and pangs of conscience. [...] Community-wide shaming is necessary because most crimes are not experienced within the average household. Children need to learn about the evil of murder, rape, car theft and environmental pollution offenses through condemnation of the local butcher or the far away image on the television screen. But the shaming of the local offender known personally to children in the neighborhood is especially important, because the wrongdoing and the shaming are so vivid as to leave a lasting impression.

Much shaming in the socialization of children is of course vicarious, through stories. Because they are not so vivid as real-life incidents of shaming, they are not so powerful. Yet they are necessary because so many types of misbehavior will not occur in the family or the neighborhood. A culture without stories for children in which morals are clearly drawn and evil deeds clearly identified would be a culture which failed the moral development of its children. Because human beings are story-telling animals, they get much of their identity from answers to the question 'Of what stories do I find myself a part?' 'Deprive children of stories and you leave them unscripted, anxious stutterers in their actions as in their words' (MacIntyre, 1984: 138).

Essentially, societal processes of shaming do three things:

1   They give content to a day-to-day socialization of children which occurs mainly through induction. As we have just seen, shaming supplies the morals which build consciences. The evil of acts beyond the immediate experience of children is more effectively communicated by shaming than by pure reasoning.

2   Societal incidents of shaming remind parents of the wide range of evils about which they must moralize with their children. Parents do not have to keep a checklist of crimes, a curriculum of sins, to discuss with their offspring. In a society where shaming is important, societal incidents of shaming will trigger vicarious shaming within the family so that the criminal code is eventually more or less automatically covered. Thus, the child will one day observe condemnation of someone who has committed rape, and will ask a parent or other older person about the basis of this wrongdoing, or will piece the story together from a series of such incidents. Of course societies which shame only half-heartedly run a risk that the full curriculum of crimes will not be covered. Both this point and the last one could be summarized in another way by saying that public shaming puts pressure on parents,

teachers and neighbors to ensure that they engage in private shaming which is sufficiently systematic.

3 Societal shaming in considerable measure takes over from parental socialization once children move away from the influence of the family and the school. Put another way, shaming generalizes beyond childhood principles learnt during the early years of life.

This third principle is about the 'criminal law as a moral eye-opener' as Andenaes (1974: 116–17) calls it. As a child, I may have learnt the principle that killing is wrong, but when I leave the familiar surroundings of the family to work in the unfamiliar environment of a nuclear power plant, I am taught by a nuclear safety regulatory system that to breach certain safety laws can cost lives, and so persons who breach them are treated with a comparable level of shame. The principle that illegal killing is shameful is generalized. To the extent that genuine shame is not directed against those who defy the safety rules, however, I am liable to take them much less seriously. Unfortunately, societal shaming processes often do fail to generalize to organizational crime.

Recent years in some Western societies have seen more effective shaming directed at certain kinds of offenses – drunk driving, occupational health and safety and environmental offenses, and political corruption. [...] This shaming has for many adults integrated new categories of wrongdoing (for which they had not been socialized as children) into the moral frameworks pre-existing from their childhood.

While most citizens are aware of the content of most criminal laws, knowledge of what the law requires of citizens in detail can be enhanced by cases of public shaming. Through shaming directed at new legal frontiers, feminists in many countries have clarified for citizens just what sexual harassment, rape within marriage, and employment discrimination mean. Social change is increasingly rapid, particularly in the face of burgeoning technologies which require new moralities of nuclear, environmental and consumer safety, responsible use of new technologies of information exchange and electronic funds transfer, ethical exploitation of new institutions such as futures exchanges, and so on. Shaming is thus particularly vital in sustaining a contemporarily relevant legal and moral order. [...]

THE PROBLEM OF DISCONTINUITY IN SOCIALIZATION PRACTICES

The most fundamental problem of socialization in modern societies is that as children mature in the family we gradually wean them from control by punishment to shaming and reasoned appeals to internal controls. The transition from family to school involves a partial reversion back to greater reliance on formal punishment for social control. The further transition to social control on the streets, at discos and pubs by the police is an almost total reversion to the punishment model. A discontinuity with the developmental pattern set in the family is established by the other major socializing institutions for adolescents – the school and the police.

[...] Japanese society handles this discontinuity much better than Western societies by having a criminal justice system (and a school system) much more orientated to catalysing internal controls than ours. Japanese police, prosecutors and courts rely heavily on guilt-induction and shaming as alternatives to punishment. If appeals to shame produce expressions of guilt, repentance and a will to seek reunification and forgiveness from loved ones (and/or the victim), this is regarded as the best result by all actors in the drama of criminal justice. The Japanese phenomena of neighborhood police, reintegrative shaming at work and school as alternatives to formal punishment processes, have two effects. First, they put social control back into the hands of significant others, where it can be most effective. Second, they soften some of the discontinuity between the increasing trust to inner controls of family life and the shock of a reversion to external control in the wide world. Just as the evidence shows that aggression and delinquency is the reaction to excessive use of punishment and power assertion as the control strategy within the family, we might expect rebellion against a demeaning punitiveness on the street to be all the more acute when families have eschewed authoritarianism in favor of authoritativeness. [...]

In short, societies which replace much of their punitive social control with shaming and reintegrative appeals to the better nature of people will be societies with less crime. These societies will do better at easing the crushing discontinuity between the shift away from punitive control in home life and the inevitable reversion to heavier reliance on punitive control in the wider society. [...]

REFERENCES

Andenaes, J. (1974) *Punishment and Deterrence*. Ann Arbor: University of Michigan Press.

Blau, P.M. (1964) *Exchange and Power in Social Life*. New York: Wiley.

Goffman, E. (1971) *Relations in Public*. New York: Basic Books.

MacIntyre, A. (1984) 'The virtues, the unity of a human life and the concept of a tradition', in M. Sandel (ed.), *Liberalism and Its Critics*. Oxford: Basil Blackwell.

Mead, G.H. (1934) *Mind, Self and Society*. Chicago: University of Chicago Press.

Mednick, S. and Christiansen, K.O. (1977) *Biosocial Bases of Criminal Behavior*. New York: Gardner Press.

Schwartz, R.D. and Orleans, S. (1967) 'On legal sanctions', *University of Chicago Law Review*, 34: 274–300.

Shott, S. (1979) 'Emotion and social life: a symbolic interactionist's analysis', *American Journal of Sociology*, 84: 1317–34.

Tittle, C.R. (1980) *Sanctions and Social Deviance*. New York: Praeger.

Toby, J. (1964) 'Is punishment necessary?' *Journal of Criminal Law, Criminology and Political Science*, 55: 332–7.

Wilson, J.Q. and Herrnstein, R. (1985) *Crime and Human Nature*. New York: Simon and Schuster.

Zimring, F.E. and Hawkins, G.J. (1973) *Deterrence: the Legal Threat in Crime Control*. Chicago: University of Chicago Press.

Znaniecki, F. (1971) *Nauki o Kulturze*. Warsaw: PWN.

37

Abolitionism and crime control

Willem de Haan

An abolitionist perspective on crime control might seem like a contradiction in terms not unlike a peace research approach to waging a war. Abolitionism is based on the moral conviction that social life should not and, in fact, cannot be regulated effectively by criminal law and that, therefore, the role of the criminal justice system should be drastically reduced while other ways of dealing with problematic situations, behaviours and events are being developed and put into practice. Abolitionists regard crime primarily as the result of the social order and are convinced that punishment is not the appropriate reaction. Instead a minimum of coercion and interference with the personal lives of those involved and a maximum amount of care and service for all members of society is advocated.

The term 'abolitionism' stands for a social movement, a theoretical perspective and a political strategy. As a social movement committed to the abolition of the prison or even the entire penal system, abolitionism originated in campaigns for prisoners' rights and penal reform. Subsequently, it developed into a critical theory and praxis concerning crime, punishment and penal reform. As a theoretical perspective, abolitionism takes on the two-fold task of providing a radical critique of the criminal justice system while showing that there are other, more rational ways of dealing with crime. As a political strategy, abolitionism is based on an analysis of penal reform and restricted to negative reforms, such as abolishing parts of the prison system, rather than providing concrete alternatives.

[...] [T]he abolitionist perspective will be discussed along the lines of this distinction. First, we will deal with abolitionism as a penal reform movement, then as a theoretical perspective on crime and punishment and, more specifically, the prison. Next, a conceptualization of the notions of crime and punishment will be offered in the form of the concept of redress. At the same time, strategies for penal reform will be examined. Finally, the implications of the abolitionist

From *The Politics of Crime Control* (eds K. Stenson and D. Cowell), pp. 203–17. (London: Sage, 1991.)

perspective for crime control will be discussed. In conclusion, it will be argued that what is needed is a wide variety of social responses rather than a uniform state reaction to the problem of crime. In policy terms it is claimed that social policy instead of crime policy is needed in dealing with the social problems and conflicts that are currently singled out as the problem of crime.

ABOLITIONISM AS A SOCIAL MOVEMENT

Abolitionism emerged as an anti-prison movement when, at the end of the 1960s, a destructuring impulse took hold of thinking about the social control of deviance and crime among other areas (Cohen, 1985). In Western Europe, anti-prison groups aiming at prison abolition were founded in Sweden and Denmark (1967), Finland and Norway (1968), Great Britain (1970), France (1970), and the Netherlands (1971). Their main objective was to soften the suffering which society inflicts on its prisoners. This implied a change in general thinking concerning punishment, humanization of the various forms of imprisonment in the short run and, in the long run, the replacement of the prison system by more adequate and up-to-date measures of crime control.

It has been suggested that abolitionism typically emerged in small countries or countries with little crime and 'would never have been "invented" in a country like the United States of America with its enormous crime rate, violence, and criminal justice apparatus' (Scheerer, 1986: 18). However, in Canada and the United States family members of (ex-)convicts, church groups and individuals were also engaged in prisoners' support work and actively struggling for prison reform. More specifically, these prison abolitionists in the United States considered their struggle for abolition of prisons to be a historical mission, a continuation and fulfilment of the struggle against slavery waged by their forebears. Imprisonment is seen as a form of blasphemy, as morally objectionable and indefensible and, therefore, to be abolished (Morris, 1976: 11). To this aim, a long-term strategy in the form of a three-step 'attrition model' is proposed, consisting of a total freeze on the planning and building of prisons, excarceration of certain categories of lawbreakers by diverting them from the prison system and decarceration, or the release of as many inmates as possible.

Originating in prison reform movements in the 1960s and 1970s in both Western Europe and North America, abolitionism developed as a new paradigm in (critical) criminology and as an alternative approach to crime control. As academic involvement increased and abolitionism became a theoretical perspective, its focus widened from the prison system to the penal system, thereby engaging in critical analyses of penal discourse and, in particular, the concepts of crime and punishment, penal practices, and the penal or criminal justice system.

ABOLITIONISM AS A THEORETICAL PERSPECTIVE

As a theoretical perspective abolitionism has a negative and a positive side. Negatively, abolitionism is deeply rooted in a criticism of the criminal justice system and its 'prison solution' to the problem of crime. Positively, on the basis of this criticism an alternative approach to crime and punishment is offered both in theory and in practice. Thus, the abolitionist approach is essentially reflexive and (de)constructivist. We will first take a look at the negative side of abolitionism which will be followed by a brief exposé of its positive side.

From the abolitionist point of view, the criminal justice system's claim to protect people from being victimized by preventing and controlling crime, seems grossly exaggerated. Moreover, the notion of controlling crime by penal intervention is ethically problematic as people are used for the purpose of 'deterrence', by demonstrating power and domination. Punishment is seen as a self-reproducing form of violence. The penal practice of blaming people for their supposed intentions (for being bad and then punishing and degrading them accordingly) is dangerous because the social conditions for recidivism are thus reproduced. Morally degrading and segregating people is especially risky when the logic of exclusion is reinforced along the lines of differences in sex, race, class, culture or religion.

For the abolitionist, current crime policies are irrational in their assumptions that: crime is caused by individuals who for some reason go wrong; that crime is a problem for the state and its criminal justice system to control; and that criminal law and punishment or treatment of individual wrongdoers are appropriate means of crime control (Steinert, 1986). Crime control is based on the fallacy of taking *pars pro toto* or, as Wilkins (1984) has put it, crime control policy is typically made by reference to the dramatic incident, thereby assuming that all that is necessary is to get the micro-model right in order for the macro-model to follow without further ado. According to Wilkins, we must consider not only the specific criminal act but also the environment in which it is embedded. It could be added that the same argument holds for punishment and, more specifically, for imprisonment as an alleged solution to the problem of crime.

ABOLITIONISM ABOUT PRISON

For abolitionists, the United States is a prime example of a country suffering from the consequences of a punitive obsession. In the course of a 'get tough' policy of crime control, increasing numbers of people are being sent to prison for longer periods of time. As a result, the prison population in the United States has increased dramatically from roughly 350,000 in the 1970s to 850,000 at the end of the 1980s. Almost 80 per cent of the recent increase in prison admissions is accounted for by drugs offenders. By September 1988 about 44 per cent of all federal prisoners were incarcerated for drug law violations. According to the 1989 National Council of Crime and Delinquency Prison Population Forecast the impact of the 'war on drugs' will be yet another increase of the prison population 1989–1994 by over 68 per cent to a total of 1,133,000 prisoners among whom people of colour will remain strongly over-represented. With an incarceration rate of 440 prisoners per 100,000 population, the United States will more than consolidate its top rank position in the world. Even with its incarceration rate increasing from about 30 in 1980 to about 50 in the mid-1990s, the Netherlands will remain at the bottom end of the scale. At the same time, the crime problem in the Netherlands can hardly be considered worse than in the United States.

As in the United States, 'street crime' is also considered a major social problem in the Netherlands. In fact, the first International Crime Survey (van Dijk et al., 1990) showed that overall victimization rates 1983–1988 in the United States and the Netherlands were higher than in any other country in the survey. However, there were considerable differences both in the seriousness of the crime problem and the effectiveness of its control. Whereas overall victimization rates in the Netherlands and the United States were similarly high, in the Dutch case this was strongly influenced by the extraordinarily high prevalence of bicycle theft, whereas victimization rates for homicide, robbery and (sexual) assault were particularly high in the United States.

If anything, this proves that the relationship between crime and crime control by imprisonment is much more complex than proponents of the prison solution seem to assume. In terms of protection the 'get tough' approach to crime control has little to offer, and the 'war on drugs' can never be won but has serious repercussions.

Taken together, the prison system is counter-productive, difficult to control, and itself a major social problem. Therefore, abolitionists have given up entirely on the idea that the criminal justice system has anything to offer in terms of protection. They are also pessimistic about the criminal law's potential for conflict resolution. It is felt that the present penal system is making things worse, not better.

In the course of the 'war against drugs' which is currently being waged in the United States and many other countries around the world, the use of ethically problematic techniques for apprehending suspects is being condoned if not required. As a result various forms of organizational complicity undermine the already waning legitimacy of the criminal justice system even further. According to Roshier (1989), the 'war against drugs' must be seen as a forced attempt to reach efficiency in the field of law enforcement or, at least, the appearance of it by using purely technical or even military means of surveillance and policing. It is the criminal justice system that defines, selects, documents and disposes of crime. As a result, legal definitions of suspicion, criminal offence etc, are being stretched. Thus, the criminal justice system itself increasingly specifies both the nature of the crime problem and what is to be done about it (Roshier, 1989: 128).

Thus, the criminal justice system is part of the crime problem rather than its solution. Not only does it fail to work in terms of its own stated goals and not only are the negative consequences of the infliction of suffering by the state threatening to get out of hand but, more importantly, it is based on a fundamentally flawed way of understanding. Therefore, there is no point in trying to make the criminal justice system more effective or more just. The abolitionist critique of the criminal justice system and its approach to crime control may be summarized by saying that if this is the solution, what is the problem? Or, put differently, crime as a social problem and object of social analysis needs to be rethought.

ABOLITIONISM ABOUT 'CRIME'

The current approach to crime control, the definition of crime and the justification of punishment is 'systemic', that is, based on an instrumentalist point of
view and confined within the limits of the criminal justice system. From an abolitionist point of view, these issues require a fundamental reconceptualization in
a broader social context. This is where the alternative, positive side of abolitionism starts from. Abolitionists argue that there is no such thing as 'crime'. In fact,
'the very form of criminal law, with its conception of "crime" (not just the contents of what is at a given time and place defined into that category, but the
category itself) and the ideas on what is to be done about it, are historical "inventions"' (Steinert, 1986: 26).

'Crime' is a social construction, to be analysed as a myth of everyday life
(Hess, 1986). As a myth, crime serves to maintain political power relations and
lends legitimacy to the expansion of the crime control apparatus and the
intensification of surveillance and control. It justifies inequality and relative
deprivation. Public attention is distracted from more serious problems and injustices. Thus, the bigger the social problems are, the greater the need for the crime
myth (Hess, 1986: 24–5).

However, not only should the concept of crime be discarded (Hulsman, 1986),
but we need to get rid of the theories of crime as well. As Quensel (1987) has
pointed out, theories about 'crime' acquire their plausibility largely by virtue of
their building on and, at the same time, reinforcing an already-present 'deep
structure'. One element of this 'deep structure' is the notion that 'crime' is inherently dangerous and wicked; another is that crime control is a 'value-inspired'
call for action against that evil (p. 129).

Abolitionists argue that the crucial problem is not explaining but rather
understanding crime as a social event. Thus, what we need is not a better theory
of crime, but a more powerful critique of crime. This is not to deny that there are
all sorts of unfortunate events, more or less serious troubles or conflicts which
can result in suffering, harm, or damage to a greater or lesser degree. These troubles are to be taken seriously, of course, but not as 'crimes' and, in any case, they
should not be dealt with by means of criminal law. When we fully appreciate the
complexity of a 'crime' as a socially constructed phenomenon any simplified
reaction to crime in the form of punishment becomes problematic.

Spector (1981) has argued that when a person offends, disturbs, or injures
other people, various forms of social disapproval exist to remedy the situation.
The matter may be treated as a disease, a sin, or, indeed, as a crime. However,
other responses are also feasible, like considering the case as a private conflict
between the offender and the victim or defining the situation in an administrative way and responding, for example by denial of a licence, permit, benefit
or compensation. Our images, language, categories, knowledge, beliefs and
fears of troublemakers are subject to constant changes. Nevertheless, crime
continues to occupy a central place in our thinking about troublesome people
(1981: 154). Spector suggests that, perhaps, 'we pay too much attention to
crime because the disciplines that study trouble and disapprove – sociology

and criminology – were born precisely in the era when crime was at its zenith' (Quensel, 1987; Spector, 1981).

The concept of 'crime' figures prominently in common sense and has definite effects on it. By focusing public attention on a definite class of events, these 'crimes' can then be almost automatically seen as meriting punitive control. 'Punishment' is thereby regarded as the obvious and proper reaction to 'crime'.

ABOLITIONISM ABOUT PUNISHMENT

Abolitionists do not share the current belief in the criminal law's capacity for crime control. They radically deny the utility of punishment and claim that there can be no valid justification for it, particularly since other options are available for law enforcement. They discard criminal justice as an absurd idea. It is ridiculous to claim that one pain can or, indeed, ought to be compensated by another state-inflicted one. According to them, the 'prison solution' affects the moral quality of life in society at large. Therefore, the criminal justice perspective needs to be replaced by an orientation towards all avoidance of harm and pain (Steinert, 1986: 25). Christie (1982), particularly, has attacked the traditional justifications for punishment. He criticizes deterrence theory for its sloppy definitions of concepts, its immunity to challenge, and for the fact that it gives the routine process of punishment a false legitimacy in an epoch where the infliction of pain might otherwise have appeared problematic. The neo-classicism of the justice model is also criticized: punishment is justified and objectified, the criminal is blamed, the victim is ignored, a broad conception of justice is lacking, and a 'hidden message' is transmitted which denies legitimacy to a whole series of alternatives which should, in fact, be taken into consideration. However, Christie not only criticizes the 'supposed justifications' for punishment, but also claims a decidedly moral position with regard to punishment, which is the intentional infliction of pain which he calls 'moral rigorism'. He deliberately co-opts the terms 'moralism' and 'rigorism' associated primarily with protagonists of 'law and order' and more severe penal sanctions. His 'rigorist' position, however, is that there is no reason to believe that the recent level of pain infliction is the right or natural one and that there is no other defensible position than to strive for a reduction of man-inflicted pain on earth. Since punishment is defined as pain, limiting pain means an automatic reduction of punishment.

More recently, Christie and Mathiesen have both suggested that the expansion of the prison system involves general ethical and political questions such as what could be the effects of all the punishments taken together? What would constitute an acceptable level of punishment in society? What would be the right prison population within a country? How should we treat fellow human beings? And, last but not least, how do we want to meet the crime problem (Christie, 1986; Mathiesen, 1986)?

However, in common-sense and legal discourse alike, 'crime' and 'punishment' continue to be seen 'as independent species – without reference to their sameness or how continuity of both depends on the character of dominating institutions'

(Kennedy, 1974: 107). It should be kept in mind, however, that crime comprises but one of several kinds of all norm violations, that punishment is but one of many kinds of reprisals against such violations, that criteria for separating them refer to phenomena external to actual behaviours classed by legal procedure as crime versus punishment, and that even within the criminal law itself, the criteria by which crime is identified procedurally apply with equal validity to punishment (Kennedy, 1974: 108).

Criminology needs to rid itself of those theories of punishment which assume there are universal qualities in forms of punishment or assume a straightforward connection between crime and punishment. Given the perseverance of this conventional notion of 'punishment' as essentially a 'good' against an 'evil', any effort at changing common-sense notions of 'crime' and 'crime control' requires a reconceptualization of both concepts: 'crime' and 'punishment'.

REDRESS

We need to concern ourselves with the interrelationship and combined effects of crime and punishment. Crime and punishment are closely related with 'social negativity' (Baratta, 1986), destructive developments within contemporary society, in particular, as they affect its already most vulnerable members. In order to formulate a convincing politics of penal reform, crime and punishment should not be seen as action and reaction, but as spiralling cycles of harm (Pepinsky, 1986).

Elsewhere, I have introduced the concept of 'redress' as an alternative to both the concepts of 'punishment' and 'crime' (de Haan, 1990). This seemingly 'obsolete' concept carries an elaborate set of different meanings. The *Concise Oxford Dictionary* offers a wide variety of meanings for 'redress': for instance, to put right or in good order again, to remedy or remove trouble of any kind, to set right, repair, rectify something suffered or complained of like a wrong, to correct, amend, reform or do away with a bad or faulty state of things, to repair an action, to atone a misdeed or offence, to save, deliver from misery, to restore or bring back a person to a proper state, to happiness or prosperity, to the right course, to set a person right by obtaining or (more rarely) giving satisfaction or compensation for the wrong or loss sustained, teaching, instructing and redressing the erroneous by reason (Sixth Edition, 1976: 937).

To claim redress is merely to assert that an undesirable event has taken place and that something needs to be done about it. It carries no implications concerning what sort of reaction would be appropriate; nor does it define reflexively the nature of the initial event. Since claiming redress invites an open discussion about how an unfortunate event should be viewed and what the appropriate response ought to be, it can be viewed as a rational response par excellence. It puts forth the claim for a procedure rather than for a specific result. Punitive claims already implied in defining an event as a 'crime' are opened up to rational debate. Thus, to advocate 'redress' is to call for 'real dialogue' (Christie, 1982). Christie has suggested that social systems be constructed in ways that 'crimes' are more easily seen as expressions of conflicting interests, thereby becoming a starting-point for a 'real dialogue' (1982: 11).

The conceptual innovation suggested here offers a perspective for a politics of redress, aimed at the construction and implementation of procedures along the lines of an ethic of practical discourse. As we have seen, the handling of normative conflicts by rational discourse presupposes other procedures than the present criminal ones. In order to increase chances for participation for those involved, procedures based on the rules and preconditions of rational discourse would, therefore, need to be established outside the realm of criminal law; that is in civil law or even in the life world itself. Instead of the panacea which the criminal justice system pretends to provide for problems of crime control, abolitionism seeks to remedy social problems, conflicts, or troubles within the context of the real world, taking seriously the experiences of those directly involved and taking into account too the diversity which is inherent [in] the social world. The aim of a politics of redress would be to 'arrange it so that the conflict settling mechanisms themselves, through their organization reflect the type of society we should like to see reflected and help this type of society come into being' (Christie, 1982: 113). Social problems or conflicts might be absorbed in order to use them as valuable aids to the social integration of real life and the prevention of social harm.

Abolitionism assumes that social problems or conflicts are unavoidable as they are inherent to social life as such. Therefore, they will have to be dealt with in one way or another. Rather than delegating them to professional specialists, however, they should be dealt with under conditions of mutuality and solidarity. These very conditions will have to be created by social and political action.

The urgent question that remains, of course, is how this might be done. To begin with, no single solution to the problem should be expected. Taking into account the diversity of relevant social phenomena requires the development of a wide variety of forms of social regulation which are not located in or defined by the state but operate (semi-)autonomously as alternative, progressive and emancipatory forms of dispute settlement and conflict resolution.

In reaction to the deeply felt dissatisfaction with the present penal system and, more generally, with the legal system, we see an increasing interest in 'autonomous' forms of conflict resolution and dispute settlement. Other 'styles of social control' (Black, 1976: 4–5) are seen as attractive, promising to provide the parties involved with more chances for participation in settling a dispute or problem. The aim is compensation rather than retaliation; reconciliation rather than blame allocation. To this end, the criminal justice system needs to be decentralized and neighbourhood courts established as a complement or substitute.

The development of alternative procedures for conflict resolution and dispute settlement faces some rather ticklish questions which have proved intractable in current debates, questions concerning voluntarism versus determinism, 'accountability', 'responsibility' and 'guilt', that is, the moral evaluation of behaviour, the fair allocation of blame and the proper dissemination of consequences. Emphasis on participatory processes of definition or the contextuality of conflicts may be welcome, but it can also lead to problematic outcomes. Among the wide variety of reactions the notion of redress entails there might be sanctions which need to be subjected to legal principles and restraints. For these reasons, legal form is still required to ensure fairness. Just as we need sociological imagination to ensure an open discussion, we need legal imagination to be able to put an end to potentially endless debates as well as allow for the possibility of appeal.

However, by allowing for more complexity in the interpretation of social behaviour, social situations and events, the simplistic image of human beings and their activities currently employed in criminal law and reproduced in criminal justice could be avoided. Through contextualization, the dichotomized character of criminal justice (Christie, 1986: 96) could be replaced with a continuum. Participants would be urged to confront and grapple with complexities around notions of human 'agency', 'intentionality', 'responsibility' and 'guilt' rather than reducing them to manageable proportions by applying the binary logic of criminal law. By dropping the simplistic dichotomies of the criminal law and allowing for differential meanings, justice might finally be done to the complexity of human actions and social events. Such a discourse would feature a concept of 'social responsibility' allowing for interpretations which primarily blame social systems rather than individuals (Christie, 1986: 97).

ABOLITIONISM AS A POLITICAL STRATEGY

Initially, a political strategy had been developed on the bases of the experiences of prison reform groups in their political struggle for penal and social reform. This 'politics of abolition' (Mathiesen, 1974, 1986) consistently refuses to offer 'positive' alternatives or solutions. It restricts itself to advancing open-ended, 'unfinished', 'negative' reforms, such as abolishing parts of the prison system. This requires that they be conceptualized in terms alien to current criminal justice discourse.

More recently, positive alternatives to punishment are also being considered. Various proposals have been made by abolitionists and others to decentralize or even completely dismantle the present penal system in order to create forms of 'informal justice' as an addition to or replacement of the present criminal justice system.

Their implementation also raises many questions, however, concerning allegations about widening the net of social control and, at the same time, thinning the mesh, extending and blurring the boundaries between formal penal intervention and other, informal forms of social control, thereby masking the coercive character of alternative interventions (Abel, 1982; Cohen, 1985).

Fundamental reform of the penal system requires not only imaginative alternatives but, at the same time, a radical change in the power structure. Thus a 'politics of abolition' aims at a negative strategy for changing the politics of punishment by abolishing not only the criminal justice system but also the repressive capitalist system part by part or step by step (Mathiesen, 1986).

A fundamental reform of the penal system presupposes not only a radical change of the existing power structure but also of the dominant culture. However, currently there is no appropriate social agency for any radical reform of the politics of punishment. There seems no immediate social basis upon which a progressive, let alone an abolitionist, strategy of crime control might be spontaneously constructed (Matthews, 1987: 389). Abolitionists tend to refer to the re-emergence of the subcultures of the new social movements with their own infrastructure of interaction and communication and their new ethics of solidarity, social responsibility, and care (Steinert, 1986: 28–9; see also Christie, 1982: 75–80). As Harris argues, the inadequacy of virtually all existing reform proposals lies in the failure to step outside the traditional and dominant ways of framing the issues. To explore alternative visions of justice we need to consider 'philosophies, paradigms, or models that transcend not only conventional criminological and political lines, but also natural and cultural boundaries and other limiting habits of the mind' (Harris, 1987: 11). According to Harris a wide range of visions of a better world and a better future offer a rich resource for a fundamental rethinking of our approach to crime and justice. The new social movements, in particular the women's movement, have pointed out fundamental weaknesses or biases in criminology's background assumptions, conceptual frameworks, methodology and tacit morality (Gelsthorpe and Morris, 1990). However, the relationship between abolitionism and, for example, feminism is not without stress (van Swaaningen, 1989).

ABOLITIONISM ON CRIME CONTROL

Abolitionism argues for a structural approach to the prevention of 'social negativity', or redressing problematic situations by taking social problems, conflicts and troubles seriously but not as 'crime'. Therefore, abolitionism argues for social policy rather than crime control policy. Examples of this structural approach would be dealing with drug problems in terms of mental health, with violence in terms of social pathology, and with property crime in terms of economy.

Abolitionism calls for decriminalization, depenalization, destigmatization, decentralization and deprofessionalization, as well as the establishment of other, informal, participatory, (semi-)autonomous ways of dealing with social problems.

Problematic events may just as well be defined as social troubles, problems or conflicts due to negligence or caused by 'accident' rather than by purpose or criminal intent. What is needed is a wide variety of possible responses without a priori assuming criminal intent and responsibility.

As we have seen, prison abolition, let alone penal abolition, requires an imaginative rethinking of possible ways of handling problematic situations as social problems, conflicts, troubles, accidents etc, as well as reconceptualizing punishment and developing new ways of managing 'deviance' on the basis of, at least partial, suspension of the logic of guilt and punishment. Without fixation on individual guilt, responsibility and punishment, 'crimes' would appear as 'conflicts', 'accidents' or 'problematic events' to be dealt with in a more reasonable and caring way by using forms of conflict management which are not exclusively geared towards individuals and confined to the limitations of criminal law in the books as well as in action (Steinert, 1986: 30). Therefore, abolitionists focus instead on extra-legal, autonomous ways for dealing with social problems and conflicts involving offences. The abolitionist challenge to abolish the present prison system now is to construct more participatory, popular or socialist forms of penality (Garland and Young, 1983).

This way of looking at crime and crime control is, of course, controversial. The abolitionist perspective is sometimes criticized for being naive and idealistic. In practice, however, the abolitionist approach turns out to be realistic in that social problems and conflicts are seen as inherent to social life. Since it is illusory that the criminal justice system can protect us effectively against such unfortunate events, it seems more reasonable to deal with troubles pragmatically rather than by approaching them in terms of guilt and punishment. Effectively to prevent and control unacceptable situations and behaviours requires a variety of social responses, one and only one of which is the criminal justice system. Its interventions are more of symbolic importance than of practical value. With some social, technical and organizational imagination 'crime' could be coped with in ways much more caring for those immediately involved. A variety of procedures could be established and institutionalized where social problems or conflicts, problematic events or behaviours could be dealt with through negotiation, mediation, arbitration, at intermediate levels. For dealing with the most common or garden varieties of crime, which is in any case the vast bulk of all recorded criminality, criminal prosecutions are simply redundant.

Certainly for those who are most directly concerned there is little or no benefit. Also in such cases as state or corporate crime where a full abolitionist agenda of dispute settlement – like the criminal justice approach – has profound limitations, it does make sense to look for more workable alternatives to the criminal justice system's mechanisms of apprehension, judgment and punishment. Most of these problems could be dealt with by means of economic, administrative, environmental, health or labour law, rather than by criminal law. Even in cases where a person has become an unacceptable burden to his or her relatives or community, imprisonment could be avoided. Agreements might be reached or orders might be given about temporary or permanent limitations in access to certain people, places or situations. The problems of the really bad and the really mad remain. In these relatively few cases and by way of last resort it might be unavoidable to deprive someone of their liberty, at least for the time being. This exceptional decision should be simply in order to incapacitate and be carried out in a humane way, that is as a morally problematic decision in a dilemma. However, even in these cases it would make sense to look for more just and humane alternatives based on mutual aid, good neighbourliness and real community rather than continue to rely on the solutions of bureaucracies, professionals and the centralized state. Criticism of the inhumanity and irrationality of the prison solution is as valid today as it was twenty or seventy years ago. Therefore, Cohen suggests that three interrelated strategies be followed: first, cultivating an experimental and inductive attitude to the actual historical record of alternatives, innovations and experiments; secondly, being sensitive, not just to failures, co-options and con-tricks, but to success stories – the criterion for success should be, and can be noth-ing other than, an approximation to preferred values; and thirdly, escaping the clutches of criminology (radical or realistic) by expanding the subject of social control way beyond the scope of the criminal justice system (for example, to systems of informal justice, Utopian communes and experiments in self-help) (Cohen, 1988: 131).

In countries with an elaborate welfare system like the Scandinavian countries or the Netherlands, these strategies may seem more reasonable given that their crime problem is less dramatic and, traditionally, their crime control policy is already more cautious. In the context of a relatively mild penal climate with a pragmatic and reductionist penal policy already being implemented, even penal abolition may seem realistic as a long-term goal. However, in those countries where prison populations are enormous and penal institutions are simply 'ware-housing' people in order to incapacitate them from reoffending, prison abolition is more acute. When in the early 1970s several commissions and task forces con-cluded that the American prison system is beyond reform and, therefore, other ways of dealing with criminal offenders need to be developed, the prison popu-lation was about one-third of the current one. These criticisms hold true even more under the present conditions of overcrowding in the prisons. Prisons are places where a lot more harm is done than is necessary or legitimate. Moreover, these institutions contribute to a further brutalization of social conditions. Even in the United States where average prison sentences are much longer than for example in the Netherlands, 99 per cent of the prison population will sooner or later hit the streets again. Therefore, there is a definite need not only for prison reform but also for penal reform. Current crime control policy boils down to doing more of the same. In the long run, however, the resulting spiral of harm needs to be reversed in a downward direction. This can only be achieved by doing more rather than less, albeit not more of the same but more of what gener-ally might be called care.

REFERENCES

Abel, R. (ed.) (1982) *The Politics of Informal Justice*, vols 1 and 2. New York: Academic Press.

Baratta, A. (1986) 'Soziale Probleme und Konstruktion der Kriminalität', *Kriminologisches Journal*, 1: 200–18.

Black, D. (1976) *The Behavior of Law*. New York: Academic Press.

Christie, N. (1982) *Limits to Pain*. Oxford: Martin Robertson.

Christie, N. (1986) 'Images of man in modern penal law', *Contemporary Crises*, 10: 95–106.

Cohen, S. (1985) *Visions of Social Control. Crime, Punishment and Classification*. Cambridge: Polity Press.

Cohen, S. (1988) *Against Criminology*. New York: Transaction Books.

Dijk, J. van, Mayhew, P. and Killias, M. (1990) *Experiences of Crime across the World. Key Findings from the 1989 International Crime Survey*. Boston: Kluwer.

Garland, D. and Young, P. (1983) 'Towards a social analysis of penality', in D. Garland and P. Young (eds), *The Power to Punish. Contemporary Penality and Social Analysis*. London: Heinemann, pp. 1–36.

Gelsthorpe, L. and Morris, A. (eds) (1990) *Feminist Perspectives in Criminology*. Milton Keynes: Open University Press.

Haan, W. de (1990) *The Politics of Redress. Crime, Punishment and Penal Abolition*. London: Unwin Hyman.

Harris, K. (1987) 'Moving into the new millennium: toward a feminist vision of justice', *The Prison Journal*, 67: 27–38.

Hess, H. (1986) 'Kriminalität als Alltagsmythos. Ein Plädoyer dafür, Kriminologie als Ideologiekritik zu betreiben', *Kriminologisches Journal*, 18(1): 22–44.

Hulsman, L. (1986) 'Critical criminology and the concept of crime', *Contemporary Crises*, 10: 63–80.

Kennedy, M. (1974) 'Beyond incrimination', in C. Reasons (ed.), *The Criminologist and the Criminal*. Pacific Palisades: Goodyear. pp. 106–35.

Mathiesen, T. (1974) 'The politics of abolition. Essays', in *Political Action Theory*. London: Martin Robertson.

Mathiesen, T. (1986) 'The politics of abolition', *Contemporary Crises*, 10: 81–94.

Matthews, R. (1987) 'Taking realist criminology seriously', *Contemporary Crises*, 11: 371–401.

Morris, M. (ed.) (1976) *Instead of Prisons: a Handbook for Abolitionists*. Syracuse, NY: Prison Research Action Project.

Pepinsky, H. (1986) 'A sociology of justice', *Annual Review for Sociology*, 12: 93–108.

Quensel, S. (1987) 'Let's abolish theories of crime', in J. Blad, H. van Mastrigt and N. Uitdriks (eds), *The Criminal Justice System as a Social Problem: an Abolitionist Perspective*. Rotterdam: Mededelingen can het Juridisch Instituut van de Erasmus Universiteit. pp. 123–32.

Roshier, B. (1989) *Controlling Crime. The Classical Perspective in Criminology*. Milton Keynes: Open University Press.

Scheerer, S. (1986) 'Towards abolitionism', *Contemporary Crises*, 10: 5–20.

Spector, M. (1981) 'Beyond crime: seven methods to control troublesome rascals', in H. Ross (ed.), *Law and Deviance*. Beverly Hills, CA: Sage, pp. 127–57.

Steinert, H. (1986) 'Beyond crime and punishment', *Contemporary Crises*, 10: 21–39.

Swaaningen, R. van (1989) 'Feminism and abolitionism as critiques of criminology', *International Journal of the Sociology of Law*, 17: 287–306.

Wilkins, L. (1984) *Consumerist Criminology*. London: Heinemann.

38

Broken windows: the police and neighborhood safety

James Q. Wilson and George L. Kelling

In the mid-1970s, the state of New Jersey announced a 'Safe and Clean Neighborhoods Program,' designed to improve the quality of community life in twenty-eight cities. As part of that program, the state provided money to help cities take police officers out of their patrol cars and assign them to walking beats. The governor and other state officials were enthusiastic about using foot patrol as a way of cutting crime, but many police chiefs were skeptical. Foot patrol in their eyes, had been pretty much discredited. It reduced the mobility of the police, who thus had difficulty responding to citizen calls for services, and it weakened headquarters control over patrol officers.

Many police officers also disliked foot patrol, but for different reasons: it was hard work, it kept them outside on cold, rainy nights, and it reduced their chances for making a 'good pinch.' In some departments, assigning officers to foot patrol had been used as a form of punishment. And academic experts on policing doubted that foot patrol would have any impact on crime rates; it was, in the opinion of most, little more than a sop to public opinion. But since the state was paying for it, the local authorities were willing to go along.

Five years after the program started, the Police Foundation, in Washington, D.C., published an evaluation of the foot-patrol project. Based on its analysis of a carefully controlled experiment carried out chiefly in Newark, the foundation concluded, to the surprise of hardly anyone, that foot patrol had not reduced crime rates. But residents of the foot-patrolled neighborhoods seemed to feel more secure than persons in other areas, tended to believe that crime had been reduced, and

From *The Atlantic Monthly*, March, 1982, pp. 29–38.

seemed to take fewer steps to protect themselves from crime (staying at home with the doors locked, for example). Moreover, citizens in the foot-patrol areas had a more favourable opinion of the police than did those living elsewhere. And officers walking beats had higher morale, greater job satisfaction, and a more favorable attitude toward citizens in their neighborhoods than did officers assigned to patrol cars.

These findings may be taken as evidence that the skeptics were right – foot patrol has no effect on crime; it merely fools the citizens into thinking that they are safer. But in our view, and in the view of the authors of the Police Foundation study (of whom Kelling was one), the citizens of Newark were not fooled at all. They knew what the foot-patrol officers were doing, they knew it was different from what motorized officers do, and they knew that having officers walk beats did in fact make their neighborhoods safer.

But how can a neighborhood be 'safer' when the crime rate has not gone down – in fact, may have gone up? Finding the answer requires first that we understand what most often frightens people in public places. Many citizens, of course, are primarily frightened by crime, especially crime involving a sudden, violent attack by a stranger. This risk is very real, in Newark as in many large cities. But we tend to overlook or forget another source of fear – the fear of being bothered by disorderly people. Not violent people, nor, necessarily, criminals, but disreputable or obstreperous or unpredictable people: panhandlers, drunks, addicts, rowdy teenagers, prostitutes, loiterers, the mentally disturbed.

What foot-patrol officers did was to elevate, to the extent they could, the level of public order in these neighborhoods. Though the neighborhoods were predominantly black and the foot patrolmen were mostly white, this 'order-maintenance' function of the police was performed to the general satisfaction of both parties.

One of us (Kelling) spent many hours walking with Newark foot-patrol officers to see how they defined 'order' and what they did to maintain it. One beat was typical: a busy but dilapidated area in the heart of Newark, with many abandoned buildings, marginal shops (several of which prominently displayed knives and straight-edged razors in their windows), one large department store, and, most important, a train station and several major bus stops. Though the area was rundown, its streets were filled with people, because it was a major transportation center. The good order of this area was important not only to those who lived and worked there but also to many others, who had to move through it on their way home, to supermarkets, or to factories.

The people on the street were primarily black; the officer who walked the street was white. The people were made up of 'regulars' and 'strangers.' Regulars included both 'decent folk' and some drunks and derelicts who were always there but who 'knew their place.' Strangers were, well, strangers, and viewed suspiciously, sometimes apprehensively. The officer – call him Kelly – knew who the regulars were, and they knew him. As he saw his job, he was to keep an eye on strangers, and make certain that the disreputable regulars observed some informal but widely understood rules. Drunks and addicts could sit on the stoops, but could not lie down. People could drink on side streets, but not at the main inter-section. Bottles had to be in paper bags. Talking to, bothering, or begging from people waiting at the bus stop was strictly forbidden. If a dispute erupted between a businessman and a customer, the businessman was assumed to be right, espe-cially if the customer was a stranger. If a stranger loitered, Kelly would ask him if he had any means of support and what his business was; if he gave unsatisfactory answers, he was sent on his way. Persons who broke the informal rules, especially those who bothered people waiting at bus stops, were arrested for vagrancy. Noisy teenagers were told to keep quiet.

These rules were defined and enforced in collaboration with the 'regulars' on the street. Another neighborhood might have different rules, but these, every-body understood, were the rules for *this* neighborhood. If someone violated them, the regulars not only turned to Kelly for help but also ridiculed the viola-tor. Sometimes what Kelly did could be described as 'enforcing the law,' but just as often it involved taking informal or extralegal steps to help protect what the neighborhood had decided was the appropriate level of public order. Some of the things he did probably would not withstand a legal challenge.

A determined skeptic might acknowledge that a skilled foot-patrol officer can maintain order but still insist that this sort of 'order' has little to do with the real sources of community fear – that is, with violent crime. To a degree, that is true. But two things must be borne in mind. First, outside observers should not assume that they know how much of the anxiety now endemic in many big-city neighborhoods stems from a fear of 'real' crime and how much from a sense that the street is disorderly, a source of distasteful, worrisome encounters. The people of Newark, to judge from their behavior and their remarks to interviewers, apparently assign a high value to public order, and feel relieved and reassured when the police help them maintain that order.

Second, at the community level, disorder and crime are usually inextricably linked, in a kind of developmental sequence. Social psychologists and police offic-ers tend to agree that if a window in a building is broken *and is left unrepaired*, all the rest of the windows will soon be broken. This is as true in nice neighborhoods as in rundown ones. Window-breaking does not necessarily occur on a large scale because some areas are inhabited by determined window-breakers whereas others are populated by window-lovers; rather, one unrepaired broken window is a signal that no one cares, and so breaking more windows costs nothing. (It has always been fun.)

Philip Zimbardo, a Stanford psychologist, reported in 1969 on some experi-ments testing the broken-window theory. He arranged to have an automobile without license plates parked with its hood up on a street in the Bronx and a comparable automobile on a street in Palo Alto, California. The car in the Bronx was attacked by 'vandals' within ten minutes of its 'abandonment.' The first to arrive were a family – father, mother, and young son – who removed the radiator and battery. Within twenty-four hours, virtually everything of value had been removed. Then random destruction began – windows were smashed, parts torn off, upholstery ripped. Children began to use the car as a playground. Most of the adult 'vandals' were well-dressed, apparently clean-cut whites. The car in Palo Alto sat untouched for more than a week. Then Zimbardo smashed part of it with a sledgehammer. Soon, passersby were joining in. Within a few hours, the car had been turned upside down and utterly destroyed. Again, the 'vandals' appeared to be primarily respectable whites.

Untended property becomes fair game for people out for fun or plunder, and even for people who ordinarily would not dream of doing such things and who probably consider themselves law-abiding. Because of the nature of community life in the Bronx – its anonymity, the frequency with which cars are abandoned and things are stolen or broken, the past experience of 'no one caring' – vandalism begins much more quickly than it does in staid Palo Alto, where people have come to believe that private possessions are cared for, and that mischievous behavior is costly. But vandalism can occur anywhere once communal barriers – the sense of mutual regard and the obligations of civility – are lowered by actions that seem to signal that 'no one cares.'

We suggest that 'untended' behavior also leads to the breakdown of community controls. A stable neighborhood of families who care for their homes, mind each other's children, and confidently frown on unwanted intruders can change, in a few years or even a few months, to an inhospitable and frightening jungle. A piece of property is abandoned, weeds grow up, a window is smashed. Adults stop scolding rowdy children; the children, emboldened, become more rowdy. Families move out, unattached adults move in. Teenagers gather in front of the corner store. The merchant asks them to move; they refuse. Fights occur. Litter accumulates. People start drinking in front of the grocery; in time, an inebriate slumps to the sidewalk and is allowed to sleep it off. Pedestrians are approached by panhandlers.

At this point it is not inevitable that serious crime will flourish or violent attacks on strangers will occur. But many residents will think that crime, especially violent crime, is on the rise, and they will modify their behavior accordingly. They will use the streets less often, and when on the streets will stay apart from their fellows, moving with averted eyes, silent lips, and hurried steps. 'Don't get involved.' For some residents, this growing atomization will matter little, because the neighborhood is not their 'home' but 'the place where they live.' Their interests are elsewhere; they are cosmopolitans, but it will matter greatly to other people, whose lives derive meaning and satisfaction from local attachments rather than worldly involvement; for them, the neighborhood will cease to exist except for a few reliable friends whom they arrange to meet.

Such an area is vulnerable to criminal invasion. Though it is not inevitable, it is more likely that here, rather than in places where people are confident they can regulate public behavior by informal controls, drugs will change hands, prostitutes will solicit, and cars will be stripped. That the drunks will be robbed by boys who do it as a lark, and the prostitutes' customers will be robbed by men who do it purposefully and perhaps violently. That muggings will occur.

Among those who often find it difficult to move away from this are the elderly. Surveys of citizens suggest that the elderly are much less likely to be the victims of crime than younger persons, and some have inferred from this that the well-known fear of crime voiced by the elderly is an exaggeration: perhaps we ought not to design special programs to protect older persons; perhaps we should even try to talk them out of their mistaken fears. This argument misses the point. The prospect of a confrontation with an obstreperous teenager or a drunken pan-handler can be as fear-inducing for defenseless persons as the prospect of meeting an actual robber; indeed, to a defenseless person, the two kinds of confrontation are often indistinguishable. Moreover, the lower rate at which the elderly are vic-timized is a measure of the steps they have already taken – chiefly, staying behind locked doors – to minimize the risks they face. Young men are more frequently attacked than older women, not because they are easier or more lucrative targets but because they are on the streets more.

Nor is the connection between disorderliness and fear made only by the elderly. Susan Estrich, of the Harvard Law School, has recently gathered together a number of surveys on the sources of public fear. One, done in Portland, Oregon, indicated that three fourths of the adults interviewed cross to the other side of a street when they see a gang of teenagers; another survey in Baltimore, discovered that nearly half would cross the street to avoid even a single strange youth. When an interviewer asked people in a housing project where the most dangerous spot was, they mentioned a place where young persons gathered to drink and play music, despite the fact that not a single crime had occurred there. In Boston pub-lic housing projects, the greatest fear was expressed by persons living in the build-ings where disorderliness and incivility, not crime, were the greatest. Knowing this helps one understand the significance of such otherwise harmless displays as subway graffiti. As Nathan Glazer has written, the proliferation of graffiti, even when not obscene, confronts the subway rider with the 'inescapable knowledge that the environment he must endure for an hour or more a day is uncontrolled and uncontrollable, and that anyone can invade it to do whatever damage and mischief the mind suggests.'

In response to fear, people avoid one another, weakening controls. Sometimes they call the police. Patrol cars arrive, an occasional arrest occurs, but crime continues and disorder is not abated. Citizens complain to the police chief, but he explains that his department is low on personnel and that the courts do not punish petty or first-time offenders. To the residents, the police who arrive in squad cars are either ineffective or uncaring; to the police, the residents are animals who deserve each other. The citizens may soon stop calling the police, because 'they can't do anything.'

The process we call urban decay has occurred for centuries in every city. But what is happening today is different in at least two important respects. First, in the period before, say, World War II, city dwellers – because of money costs, transportation difficulties, familial and church connections – could rarely move away from neighborhood problems. When movement did occur, it tended to be along public-transit routes. Now mobility has become exceptionally easy for all but the poorest or those who are blocked by racial prejudice. Earlier crime waves had a kind of built-in self-correcting mechanism: the determination of a neighborhood or community to reassert control over its turf. Areas in Chicago, New York, and Boston would experience crime and gang wars, and then normalcy would return, as the families for whom no alternative residences were possible reclaimed their authority over the streets.

Second, the police in this earlier period assisted in that reassertion of authority by acting, sometimes violently, on behalf of the community. Young toughs were roughed up, people were arrested 'on suspicion' or for vagrancy, and prostitutes and petty thieves were routed. 'Rights' were something enjoyed by decent folk, and perhaps also by the serious professional criminal, who avoided violence and could afford a lawyer.

This pattern of policing was not an aberration or the result of occasional excess. From the earliest days of the nation, the police function was seen primarily as that of a night watchman: to maintain order against the chief threats to order – fire, wild animals, and disreputable behavior. Solving crimes was viewed not as a police responsibility but as a private one. In the March, 1969, *Atlantic* one of us (Wilson) wrote a brief account of how the police role had slowly changed from maintaining order to fighting crimes. The change began with the creation of private detectives (often ex-criminals), who worked on a contingency-fee basis for individuals who had suffered losses. In time, the detectives were absorbed into municipal police agencies and paid a regular salary; simultaneously, the responsibility for prosecuting thieves was shifted from the aggrieved private citizen to the professional prosecutor. This process was not complete in most places until the twentieth century.

In the 1960s, when urban riots were a major problem, social scientists began to explore carefully the order-maintenance function of the police, and to suggest ways of improving it – not to make streets safer (its original function) but to reduce the incidence of mass violence. Order-maintenance became, to a degree, coterminous with 'community relations.' But, as the crime wave that began in the early 1960s continued without abatement throughout the decade and into the 1970s, attention shifted to the role of the police as crime-fighters. Studies of police behavior ceased, by and large, to be accounts of the order-maintenance function and became, instead, efforts to propose and test ways whereby the police could solve more crimes, make more arrests, and gather better evidence. If these things could be done, social scientists assumed, citizens would be less fearful.

A great deal was accomplished during this transition, as both police chiefs and outside experts emphasized the crime-fighting function in their plans, in the allocation of resources, and in deployment of personnel. The police may well have become better crime-fighters as a result. And doubtless they remained aware of their responsibility for order. But the link between order-maintenance and crime-prevention, so obvious to earlier generations, was forgotten.

That link is similar to the process whereby one broken window becomes many. The citizen who fears the ill-smelling drunk, the rowdy teenager, or the importuning beggar is not merely expressing his distaste for unseemly behaviour; he is also giving voice to a bit of folk wisdom that happens to be a correct generalization – namely, that serious street crime flourishes in areas in which disorderly behavior goes unchecked. The unchecked panhandler is, in effect, the first broken window. Muggers and robbers, whether opportunistic or professional, believe they reduce their chances of being caught or even identified if they operate on streets where potential victims are already intimidated by prevailing conditions. If the neighborhood cannot keep a bothersome panhandler from annoying passersby, the thief may reason, it is even less likely to call the police to identify a potential mugger or to interfere if the mugging actually takes place.

Some police administrators concede that this process occurs, but argue that motorized-patrol officers can deal with it as effectively as foot-patrol officers. We are not so sure. In theory, an officer in a squad car can observe as much as an officer on foot; in theory, the former can talk to as many people as the latter. But the reality of police–citizen encounters is powerfully altered by the automobile. An officer on foot cannot separate himself from the street people; if he is approached, only his uniform and his personality can help him manage whatever is about to happen. And he can never be certain what that will be – a request for directions, a plea for help, an angry denunciation, a teasing remark, a confused babble, a threatening gesture.

In a car, an officer is more likely to deal with street people by rolling down the window and looking at them. The door and the window exclude the approaching citizen; they are a barrier. Some officers take advantage of this barrier, perhaps unconsciously, by acting differently if in the car than they would on foot. We have seen this countless times. The police car pulls up to a corner where teenagers are gathered. The window is rolled down. The officer stares at the youths. They stare back. The officer says to one, 'C'mere.' He saunters over, conveying to his friends by his elaborately casual style the idea that he is not intimidated by authority. 'What's you name?' 'Chuck.' 'Chuck who?' 'Chuck Jones.' 'What'ya doing, Chuck?' 'Nothin'.' 'Got a P.O. [parole officer]?' 'Nah.' 'Sure?' 'Yeah.' 'Stay out of trouble, Chuckle.' Meanwhile, the other boys laugh and exchange comments among themselves, probably at the officer's expense. The officer stares harder. He cannot be certain what is being said, nor can he join in and, by displaying his own skill at street banter, prove that he cannot be 'put down.' In the process, the officer has learned almost nothing, and the boys have decided the officer is an alien force who can safely be disregarded, even mocked.

Our experience is that most citizens like to talk to a police officer. Such exchanges give them a sense of importance, provide them with the basis for gossip, and allow them to explain to the authorities what is worrying them (whereby they gain a modest but significant sense of having 'done something' about the problem). You approach a person on foot more easily, and talk to him more readily, than you do a person in a car. Moreover, you can more easily retain some anonymity if you draw an officer aside for a private chat. Suppose you want to pass on a tip about who is stealing handbags, or who offered to sell you a stolen TV. In the inner city, the culprit, in all likelihood, lives nearby. To walk up to a marked patrol car and lean in the window is to convey a visible signal that you are a 'fink.'

The essence of the police role in maintaining order is to reinforce the informal control mechanisms of the community itself. The police cannot, without committing extraordinary resources, provide a substitute for that informal control. On the other hand, to reinforce those natural forces the police must accommodate them. And therein lies the problem.

Should police activity on the street be shaped, in important ways, by the standards of the neighborhood rather than by the rules of state? Over the past two decades, the shift of police from order-maintenance to law-enforcement has brought them increasingly under the influence of legal restrictions, provoked by media complaints and enforced by court decisions and departmental orders. As a consequence, the order-maintenance functions of the police are now governed by rules developed to control police relations with suspected criminals. This is, we think, an entirely new development. For centuries, the role of the police as watchmen was judged primarily not in terms of its compliance with appropriate procedures but rather in terms of its attaining a desired objective. The objective was order, an inherently ambiguous term but a condition that people in a given community recognized when they saw it. The means were the same as those the community itself would employ, if its members were sufficiently determined, courageous, and authoritative. Detecting and apprehending criminals, by contrast, was a means to an end, not an end in itself; a judicial determination of guilt or innocence was the hoped-for result of the law-enforcement mode. From the first, the police were expected to follow rules defining that process, though states differed in how stringent the rules should be. The criminal-apprehension process was always understood to involve individual rights, the violation of which was unacceptable because it meant that the violating officer would be acting as a judge and jury – and that was not his job. Guilt or innocence was to be determined by universal standards under special procedures.

Ordinarily, no judge or jury ever sees the persons caught up in a dispute over the appropriate level of neighborhood order. That is true not only because most cases are handled informally on the street but also because no universal standards are available to settle arguments over disorder, and thus a judge may not be any wiser or more effective than a police officer. Until quite recently in many states, and even today in some places, the police make arrests on such charges as 'suspicious person' or 'vagrancy' or 'public drunkenness' – charges with scarcely any legal meaning. These charges exist not because society wants judges to punish vagrants or drunks but because it wants an officer to have the legal tools to remove undesirable persons from a neighborhood when informal efforts to preserve order in the streets have failed.

Once we begin to think of all aspects of police work as involving the application of universal rules under special procedures, we inevitably ask what constitutes an 'undesirable person' and why we should 'criminalize' vagrancy or drunkenness. A strong and commendable desire to see that people are treated fairly makes us worry about allowing the police to rout persons who are undesirable by some vague or parochial standard. A growing and not-so-commendable utilitarianism leads us to doubt that any behavior that does not 'hurt' another person should be made illegal. And thus many of us who watch over the police are reluctant to allow them to perform, in the only way they can, a function that every neighborhood desperately wants them to perform.

This wish to 'decriminalize' disreputable behavior that 'harms no one' – and thus remove the ultimate sanction the police can employ to maintain neighborhood order – is, we think, a mistake. Arresting a single drunk or a single vagrant who has harmed no identifiable person seems unjust, and in a sense it is. But failing to do anything about a score of drunks or a hundred vagrants may destroy an entire community. A particular rule that seems to make sense in the individual case makes no sense when it is made a universal rule and applied to all cases. It makes no sense because it fails to take into account the connection between one broken window left untended and a thousand broken windows. Of course, agencies other than the police could attend to the problems posed by drunks or the mentally ill, but in most communities – especially where the 'deinstitutionalization' movement has been strong – they do not.

The concern about equity is more serious. We might agree that certain behavior makes one person more undesirable than another, but how do we ensure that age or skin color or national origin or harmless mannerisms will not also become the basis for distinguishing the undesirable from the desirable? How do we ensure, in short, that the police do not become the agents of neighborhood bigotry?

We can offer no wholly satisfactory answer to this important question. We are not confident that there *is* a satisfactory answer, except to hope that by their selection, training, and supervision, the police will be inculcated with a clear sense of the outer limit of their discretionary authority. That limit, roughly, is this – the police exist to help regulate behavior, not to maintain the racial or ethnic purity of a neighborhood.

Consider the case of the Robert Taylor Homes in Chicago, one of the largest public-housing projects in the country. It is home for nearly 20,000 people, all black, and extends over ninety-two acres along South State Street. It was named after a distinguished black who had been, during the 1940s, chairman of the Chicago Housing Authority. Not long after it opened, in 1962, relations between project residents and the police deteriorated badly. The citizens felt that the police were insensitive or brutal; the police, in turn, complained of unprovoked attacks on them. Some Chicago officers tell of times when they were afraid to enter the Homes. Crime rates soared.

Today, the atmosphere has changed. Police–citizen relations have improved – apparently, both sides learned something from the earlier experience. Recently, a boy stole a purse and ran off. Several young persons who saw the theft voluntarily passed along to the police information on the identity and residence of the thief, and they did this publicly, with friends and neighbors looking on. But problems persist, chief among them the presence of youth gangs that terrorize residents and recruit members in the project. The people expect the police to 'do something' about this, and the police are determined to do just that.

But do what? Though the police can obviously make arrests whenever a gang member breaks the law, a gang can form, recruit, and congregate without breaking the law. And only a tiny fraction of gang-related crimes can be solved by an arrest; thus, if an arrest is the only recourse for the police, the residents' fears will go unassuaged. The police will soon feel helpless, and the residents will again believe that the police 'do nothing.' What the police in fact do is to chase known gang members out of the project. In the words of one officer, 'We kick ass.' Project residents both know and approve of this. The tacit police–citizen alliance in the project is reinforced by the police view that the cops and the gangs are the two rival sources of power in the area, and that the gangs are not going to win.

None of this is easily reconciled with any conception of due process or fair treatment. Since both residents and gang members are black, race is not a factor. But it could be. Suppose a white project confronted a black gang, or vice versa. We would be apprehensive about the police taking sides. But the substantive problem remains the same: how can the police strengthen the informal social-control mechanisms of natural communities in order to minimize fear in public places? Law enforcement, per se, is no answer. A gang can weaken or destroy a community by standing about in a menacing fashion and speaking rudely to passersby without breaking the law.

We have difficulty thinking about such matters, not simply because the ethical and legal issues are so complex but because we have become accustomed to thinking of the law in essentially individualistic terms. The law defines *my* rights, punishes *his* behavior, and is applied by *that* officer because of *this* harm. We assume, in thinking this way, that what is good for the individual will be good for the community, and what doesn't matter when it happens to one person won't matter if it happens to many. Ordinarily, those are plausible assumptions. But in cases where behavior that is tolerable to one person is intolerable to many others, the reactions of the others – fear, withdrawal, flight – may ultimately make matters worse for everyone, including the individual who first professed his indifference.

It may be their greater sensitivity to communal as opposed to individual needs that helps explain why the residents of small communities are more satisfied with their police than are the residents of similar neighborhoods in big cities. Elinor Ostrom and her co-workers at Indiana University compared the perception of police services in two poor, all-black Illinois towns – Phoenix and East Chicago Heights – with those of three comparable all-black neighborhoods in Chicago. The level of criminal victimization and the quality of police–community relations appeared to be about the same in the towns and the Chicago neighborhoods. But the citizens living in their own villages were much more likely than those living in the Chicago neighborhoods to say that they do not stay at home for fear of crime, to agree that the local police have 'the right to take any action necessary' to deal with problems, and to agree that the police 'look out for the needs of the average citizen.' It is possible that the residents and the police of the small towns saw themselves as engaged in a collaborative effort to maintain a certain standard of communal life, whereas those of the big city felt themselves to be simply requesting and supplying particular services on an individual basis.

If this is true, how should a wise police chief deploy his meager forces? The first answer is that nobody knows for certain, and the most prudent course of action would be to try further variations on the Newark experiment, to see more precisely what works in what kinds of neighborhoods. The second answer is also a hedge – many aspects of order-maintenance in neighborhoods can probably best be handled in ways that involve the police minimally, if at all. A busy, bustling shopping center and a quiet, well-tended suburb may need almost no visible police presence. In both cases, the ratio of respectable to disreputable people is ordinarily so high as to make informal social control effective.

Even in areas that are in jeopardy from disorderly elements, citizen action without substantial police involvement may be sufficient. Meetings between teenagers who like to hang out on a particular corner and adults who want to use that corner might well lead to an amicable agreement on a set of rules about how many people can be allowed to congregate, where, and when.

Where no understanding is possible – or if possible, not observed – citizen patrols may be a sufficient response. There are two traditions of communal involvement in maintaining order. One, that of the 'community watchmen,' is as old as the first settlement of the New World. Until well into the nineteenth century, volunteer watchmen, not policemen, patrolled their communities to keep order. They did so, by and large, without taking the law into their own hands – without, that is, punishing persons or using force. Their presence deterred disorder or alerted the community to disorder that could not be deterred. There are hundreds of such efforts today in communities all across the nation. Perhaps the best known is that of the Guardian Angels, a group of unarmed young persons in distinctive berets and T-shirts, who first came to public attention when they began patrolling the New York City subways but who claim now to have chapters in more than thirty American cities. Unfortunately, we have little information about the effect of these groups on crime. It is possible, however, that whatever their effect on crime, citizens find their presence reassuring, and that they thus contribute to maintaining a sense of order and civility.

The second tradition is that of the 'vigilante.' Rarely a feature of the settled communities of the East, it was primarily to be found in those frontier towns that grew up in advance of the reach of government. More than 350 vigilante groups are known to have existed; their distinctive feature was that their members did take the law into their own hands, by acting as judge, jury, and often executioner as well as policeman. Today, the vigilante movement is conspicuous by its rarity, despite the great fear expressed by citizens that the older cities are becoming 'urban frontiers.' But some community-watchmen groups have skirted the line, and others may cross it in the future. An ambiguous case, reported in *The Wall Street Journal*, involved a citizens' patrol in the Silver Lake area of Belleville, New Jersey. A leader told the reporter, 'We look for outsiders.' If a few teenagers from outside the neighborhood enter it, 'we ask them their business,' he said. 'If they say they're going down the street to see Mrs. Jones, fine, we let them pass, but then we follow them down the block to make sure they're really going to see Mrs. Jones.'

Though citizens can do a great deal, the police are plainly the key to order-maintenance. For one thing, many communities, such as the Robert Taylor Homes, cannot do the job by themselves. For another, no citizen in a neighborhood, even an organized one, is likely to feel the sense of responsibility that wearing a badge confers. Psychologists have done many studies on why people fail to go to the aid of persons being attacked or seeking help, and they have learned that the cause is not 'apathy' or 'selfishness' but the absence of some plausible grounds for feeling that one must personally accept responsibility. Ironically, avoiding responsibility is easier when a lot of people are standing about. On streets and in public places, where order is so important, many people are likely to be 'around,' a fact that reduces the chance of any one person acting as the agent of the community. The police officer's uniform singles him out as a person who must accept responsibility if asked. In addition, officers, more easily than their fellow citizens, can be expected to distinguish between what is necessary to protect the safety of the street and what merely protects its ethnic purity.

But the police forces of America are losing, not gaining, members. Some cities have suffered substantial cuts in the number of officers available for duty. These cuts are not likely to be reversed in the near future. Therefore, each department must assign its existing officers with great care. Some neighborhoods are so demoralized and crime-ridden as to make foot patrol useless; the best the police can do with limited resources is respond to the enormous number of calls for service. Other neighborhoods are so stable and serene as to make foot patrol unnecessary. The key is to identify neighborhoods at the tipping point – where the public order is deteriorating but not unreclaimable, where the streets are used frequently but by apprehensive people, where a window is likely to be broken at any time, and must quickly be fixed if all are not to be shattered.

Most police departments do not have ways of systematically identifying such areas and assigning officers to them. Officers are assigned on the basis of crime rates (meaning that marginally threatened areas are often stripped so that police can investigate crimes in areas where the situation is hopeless) or on the basis of calls for service (despite the fact that most citizens do not call the police when they are merely frightened or annoyed). To allocate patrol wisely, the department must look at the neighborhoods and decide, from first-hand evidence, where an additional officer will make the greatest difference in promoting a sense of safety.

One way to stretch limited police resources is being tried in some public-housing projects. Tenant organizations hire off-duty police officers for patrol work in their buildings. The costs are not high (at least not per resident), the officer likes the additional income, and the residents feel safer. Such arrangements are probably more successful than hiring private watchmen, and the Newark experiment helps us understand why. A private security guard may deter crime or misconduct by his presence, and he may go to the aid of persons needing help, but he may well not intervene – that is, control or drive away – someone challenging community standards. Being a sworn officer – a 'real cop' – seems to give one the confidence, the sense of duty, and the aura of authority necessary to perform this difficult task.

Patrol officers might be encouraged to go to and from duty stations on public transportation and, while on the bus or subway car, enforce rules about smoking, drinking, disorderly conduct, and the like. The enforcement need involve nothing more than ejecting the offender (the offense, after all, is not one with which a booking officer or a judge wishes to be bothered). Perhaps the random but relentless maintenance of standards on buses would lead to conditions on buses that approximate the level of civility we now take for granted on airplanes.

But the most important requirement is to think that to maintain order in precarious situations is a vital job. The police know this is one of their functions, and they also believe, correctly, that it cannot be done to the exclusion of criminal investigation and responding to calls. We may have encouraged them to suppose, however, on the basis of our oft-repeated concerns about serious, violent crime, that they will be judged exclusively on their capacity as crime-fighters. To the extent that this is the case, police administrators will continue to concentrate police personnel in the highest-crime areas (though not necessarily in the areas most vulnerable to criminal invasion), emphasize their training in the law and criminal apprehension (and not their training in managing street life), and join too quickly in campaigns to decriminalize 'harmless' behavior (though public drunkenness, street prostitution, and pornographic displays can destroy a community more quickly than any team of professional burglars).

Above all, we must return to our long-abandoned view that the police ought to protect communities as well as individuals. Our crime statistics and victimization surveys measure individual losses, but they do not measure communal losses. Just as physicians now recognize the importance of fostering health rather than simply treating illness, so the police – and the rest of us – ought to recognize the importance of maintaining, intact, communities without broken windows.

39

The spectacle of crime, digitized: CSI: Crime Scene Investigation and social anatomy

Martha Gever

[...]

The living night is dissipated in the brightness of death. (Michel Foucault, *The Birth of the Clinic*, 1975[1963]: 146)

Newspaper stories, as well as anecdotal reports, tell us that a large number of aspiring police detectives in the United States have set their sights on careers in criminalistics, also known as crime scene investigation (Gross, 2002; personal communication with E. Cohen, Criminal Justice program faculty, Broward Community College, 2005; St John, 2003).[1] The reason for the spike in interest in this field is not surprising. According to all accounts it is attributable to the popularity of the TV series *CSI: Crime Scene Investigation*, which first aired in autumn 2000 and has been ranked at the top of the Nielsen ratings since the beginning of its third season. Recent figures indicate that over 26 million viewers in the US watch each new episode. However, my own interest in the show does not stem from its enormous popularity, although that is a phenomenon worth considering, but from research on what literary theorist and critic Mark Seltzer has called 'the spectacle of crime'. Seltzer (1992) employs this expression in his study of 19th-century realist literature. But I believe that this concept, as well as its connotations, can be usefully updated, amended and applied in a different media environment where televisual dramas take advantage of digital imaging techniques to produce gripping spectacles. *CSI*, in which dramatic developments frequently

From *European Journal of Cultural Studies*, November 2005, 8(4): 445–63.

pause for dazzling displays of computer graphic virtuosity, offers plentiful examples of such applications. However, electronic media do not just play instrumental and performative roles in *CSI*. Scientific inscriptions also appear as important terms in the series' semiotic vocabulary, supplying the most reliable (and often incontrovertible) information used to identify and locate the felons who set the law enforcement apparatus in motion in every episode.

This article explores how the proliferation of digital imagery on television may – or may not – indicate significant shifts in visual culture, signaling the advent of a new way of seeing, a new visual culture. Surely the term 'new media', used to describe digital electronic entertainment of various kinds, holds out this promise. The proliferation of computerized devices used in the production, storage, retrieval and distribution of information and entertainment has generated qualitative transformations in cultural forms and institutions, as well as in economic and political processes. But undertaking this line of enquiry cannot ignore the lineage of current imaging techniques, which can be traced back to 19th-century mechanical and electrical systems such as photography and telegraphy.[2] The grandchildren of these systems can be found both behind the scenes and on screen in many recent TV crime dramas, perhaps most notably in *CSI*. Their status as performers in *and* producers of electronic, digital spectacles calls attention to *CSI*'s incessant referencing of scientific technologies and knowledge pertaining to human life. In short, the program offers weekly demonstrations of the benefits of modern science linked to efforts to ensure public security, as well as suggestions for how to bring this about.

Alongside the flux of visual imagery that harnesses the quest for scientific truths to scenes of very dramatic and always successful criminal detection in *CSI* there emerges a related and perhaps more significant feature of the series' departure from earlier (as well as many current) television police shows – the mobilization of a historically and culturally specific kind of subject. Victims and criminals alike are portrayed as transparent creatures whose every secret is revealed by means of resolute scrutiny. This aspect of *CSI* is not identical to what has become one of the most controversial effects of electronic digital media on social life: the production, performance and inhabitation of 'virtual' identities and communities. Instead, the transparent self produced by *CSI* is neither 'virtual' nor 'real', nor can it be understood solely in terms of embodiment (or disembodiment). What is more intriguing is that the paradigmatic self proposed by *CSI* also entails the *disappearance* of the subject, a self rendered so transparent that it vanishes or remains perceptible only as the sum of inscriptions.[3]

Thus, this study of *CSI* proposes two analytic vectors. First, the program produces an echo chamber effect, where attention-grabbing digital video images are employed to engage viewers in mysteries best solved using hi-tech forensic investigation techniques. Second, the program's dramatic visualization of crime detection maps a social realm conducive to certain kinds of subjectivity that differ substantially from the coherent, sovereign self of modernity. The article will proceed from the first to the second of these concerns by moving through a set of thematic explorations. However, there are a number of points at which any hope for linear logic must be abandoned, since the various motifs are intricately interrelated.

SPECTACLE

To begin a critique of *CSI* with an emphasis on its visual qualities, its spectacular features, may seem to neglect a central concern of much television criticism: the narrative elements of dramatic fiction and the meanings that can be attributed to these. Nevertheless, it is important to recognize that *CSI is* a cop show, even if the main characters are not police officers but the 'civilian' employees of a police department. Another, more significant, difference between the series and its TV crime show precursors is that the primary agents of law enforcement in *CSI* are not uniformed cops, plain clothes detectives or virtuoso private investigators. They are *scientists*. These protagonists care more about the application of scientific technologies to generate and organize knowledge than crime and punishment. The show's main character is Gil Grissom, a nerdy middle-aged, white forensic scientist who is in charge of the crime laboratory. Although Grissom occupies the position of *eminence grise*, the show does not perpetuate traditional notions of science as an exclusive white or masculine preserve. With one exception, his four associates are younger, less experienced and somewhat less nerdy. Warrick Brown is a black man and Catherine Willows and Sara Sidle are white women; Nick Stokes is the only other white man in the group. A hipper young laboratory technician, Greg Sanders, assumes a key role as the operator of the laboratory's hi-tech equipment. The main set is the Las Vegas Police Department crime laboratory – not a squad room as in most police shows, but like a squad room it serves as the primary site where the regular characters interact, the space to which they return after venturing into the world (Sparks, 1992). (At a panel at the Museum of Television and Radio the series' producers noted that their laboratory is better equipped that any real crime laboratory in the country; Museum of Television and Radio, 2001.)

These features of *CSI* suggest a need for critical approaches that differ substantially from the standard questions that have been asked of television programs dealing with crime. Crime drama has been a staple of television in the US since it became the country's most popular form of entertainment in the 1950s (the first major success of this kind was *Dragnet*), and criminologists, sociologists, social psychologists, TV critics and politicians have all scrutinized the knotty relationships between television's depictions of crime, the police, social behavior deemed criminal and attitudes toward public safety. Some critics are interested in the medium's effects on those prone to engage in illegal activities, a position that assumes the probity of police institutions and practices. This approach tries to determine to what degree TV shows (and other popular media) inspire or glamorize crime. Others are suspicious of television's reinforcement of a moral order that favors authoritarian social structures and justification of related methods of social control. Although the latter critical stance is shared by researchers using various methods and emphasizing different analytic elements, the interpretative strategies undertaken from this position all involve unmasking television's ideological complicity with state power (Buxton, 1990; Carlson, 1985; Donovan, 1998; Ericson, 1995; Scheingold, 1997; Sumser, 1996; Surette, 1992).[4] Despite the apparent opposition of the two schools, both study stories about crime and policing on TV to tease out their moral messages.

Compared to earlier television offerings, *CSI* and other recent shows inject a major new ingredient into this particular kind of program, treating crime dramas as occasions for audiences to engage with displays of power presented as technological mastery. In some cases, the police themselves wield the digital tools, such as the Compstat (computer statistics) system featured in *The District*, which allows a fictional Washington, DC police chief to illustrate deficiencies in crime prevention in order to embarrass underperformers in his department as well as to assist in catching crooks. Other shows such as *Law and Order* increasingly include scenes where a detective looks over the shoulder of a fingerprint analyst watching digitized records from the FBI's Automated Fingerprint Identification System (AFIS) database race by on a computer screen. They also consult regularly with medical examiners and ballistics specialists who hover over microscopes and recite the results of scientific tests. The protagonists in the newer program *Las Vegas* (which is not a proper cop show, but a first cousin featuring security officers at a fancy casino hotel) perform their duties in front of an impressive bank of surveillance monitors. But more than any of these shows, *CSI* relies on hi-tech gadgetry as instruments of discovery and discipline.

In addition to placing *CSI* in the context of contemporary TV crime drama, a critique of *CSI* must take into account what John Thornton Caldwell (1995) calls 'televisuality'. According to Caldwell, the aesthetic priorities of television underwent a massive overhaul in the early 1980s, when dependence on sound as the organizing principle was replaced by an emphasis on visual elements. Competition for TV audiences in the US in an era when proliferating cable channels threatened to chip away at the dominance of the big three networks provoked the development of distinct styles that gave each prime-time program a signature 'look' that set it apart from its rivals. *CSI* is no exception. Its style is replete with high-gloss, color-saturated imagery that often flashes on the screen for brief moments, usually accompanied by fast-paced, driving music. The show's Las Vegas setting provides a rationale for lots of neon glitter. The CSI team forming the core of the show's cast works the night shift, which justifies the use of high-contrast lighting and lots of shadowy spaces to produce dramatic tension. In brief, *CSI* shares the ensemble acting, film-style lighting and camerawork, fragmented yet realist narrative and jazzy graphic construction of many contemporary series that appear on US television, with its own aesthetic flourishes intended to generate visual excitement. But *CSI* also displays other characteristics that are rarely seen in other cop shows. Crimes are almost always portrayed as flashbacks, often as imaginary reconstructions, hardly ever as prosaic realism, which continually disrupts the cause–effect logic that is common to visual narratives. At the same time, the series rarely treads upon the supernatural territory occupied by series such as *The X-Files*, *Profiler* or various Stephen

King-inspired (or scripted) series. Several episodes have involved paranormal adepts who seem able to perform detective work without bothering with scientific instruments or methods. Still, these are rare, perhaps because emphasis on the uncanny would signal a retreat from the show's basic commitment to well-supported, objective, deductive reasoning.

However, as a spectacle, *CSI* demands a revision of Caldwell's concept of televisuality. In particular, he insists on the autonomy of visual elements, proposing that '[t]he practice of graphic performance tends ... to resist analysis as content, since it comes across as an autonomous process based on the potentially endless permutation [of] style and form' (1995: 147). As a result, he plays down the social resonance of spectacle. In his study of realist fiction, Seltzer (1992) suggests a more productive approach. In his discussion of a 1895 novel by Stephen Crane, Seltzer remarks that violence is converted into spectacle through the intervention of the police, who are themselves turned into an entertaining spectacle. More than a century later, applications of digital imaging techniques in both law enforcement and television production have aligned televisual style with police practices. And computer science provides both with the tools of power. *CSI* exploits this technical affinity. This is not merely another example of the fluid interchange between digital formats, referred to as convergence in 'new media' studies. Rather, the incommensurability of form and content that has long been an accepted principle for many cultural critics becomes untenable. On *CSI*, and arguably other programs too, televisual style reiterates and reinforces technologies of the social machine (Seltzer, 1992).

PHOTOGRAPHY

CSI has accomplished a rare feat for commercial television: bridging the divide between modern science (not science fiction) and entertainment. Although this may seem an odd coupling, the two cultural fields share one important attribute: both concentrate upon the production of new kinds of knowledge using new kinds of scientific apparatuses and the inscriptions these produce. Of course, empirical science from the 17th century onwards has been premised upon just such developments. And so, too, has plentiful entertainment. Enlightenment culture was the first to bring the two together. Barbara Maria Stafford notes that telescopes and microscopes were popular as home entertainment in 17th-century Europe:

> Until the middle of the nineteenth century, traveling exhibitionists set up raree shows stocked with monsters, magic lanterns and peep boxes. Perspective games such as concertina-folded views, anamorphoses, mirror metamorphoses and polyoptic pictures were both playful and scientific amusements. (1994: 366)

Still, skepticism regarding visual imagery produced with optical devices abounded, informed by fears that appearances would be mistaken for substance.

Another instance of images produced for scientific purposes but also consumed as amusement was X-ray photography, an accidental discovery made in 1895. These apparently non-intrusive vistas of the innards of living beings engendered what was known as 'X-ray mania', until their pathological properties became accepted as a matter of fact (Cartwright, 1995: 107). There were X-ray movies as well. Cinema in general could be described as the most famous example of popular enthusiasm for a new optical technology almost as soon as it made its public debut at the end of the 19th century. Concomitantly, the cinematic apparatus, as well as its progenitor, photography, was recognized and quickly integrated into biological research and medicine (Cartwright, 1995).

In sum, optical apparatuses, cameras and photographic media in particular, occupy a privileged place in the history of the relationship between science and popular culture. The reason is simple: a camera mechanically records an image by means of chemistry or, nowadays, electronics, free from human manipulation. The photographic image, if not intentionally distorted, is intended as a precise record of what is in front of the camera. In the laboratory, the camera has been employed by scientists as a guarantee of objective observation and inscription of experimental phenomena, since a camera has no sentiments, soul, consciousness, politics or biases – or so commonsense wisdom tells us. Cameras in tandem with microscopes – a duet performed almost as soon as the daguerreotype process was made public in 1859 – epitomize the concept of depersonalized vision.

The intimate relationship between photographic imagery and scientific realism in the realm of policing was established on similar grounds. As early as the 1850s, photographic media provided police departments with an invaluable tool (Tagg, 1981). Alphonse Bertillon, chief of the Paris police at the end of the 19th century, was not the first but probably the most famous advocate of police photography for criminal identification. He augmented his system of criminal classification and identification, which consisted of anthropometric measurements of the bodies of criminal suspects, with what became known as 'mugshots' (Sekula, 1986). The information obtained was compared with a huge file comprising cards with the measurements and photos of previously detained criminal suspects, housed at the Paris Department of Judicial Identification. Significantly, Bertillon was among the first police officials to photograph crime scenes in murder cases, sometimes operating the camera himself (Parry, 2000).

The formation and proliferation of police departments in the 19th century came about because of the perceived need for increased knowledge concerning rapidly growing populations of modern cities. A related factor was the reconceptualization of crimes, previously regarded as actions per se but now understood as actions carried out by deviant *individuals* (Foucault, 1979[1975]). Mugshots codified the connection between particular people and criminal behavior and became a mainstay in the project of policing. And around the turn of the century, police photography added another rational system of identification to its repertoire: fingerprints, which until recently were recorded and archived as photographs (Cole, 2001). Not only is photography the medium used to preserve fingerprints; the two can be linked metaphorically In William J. Mitchell's words, a photograph 'is like a direct physical imprint, like a fingerprint left at the scene of a crime or lipstick traces on your collar. A correspondence with reality is thus causally established' (2001: 24).

Therefore, it is not surprising that when the criminalists in *CSI* go to work at a crime scene they methodically take photographs, which presumably will be used when testifying as expert witnesses in court (although we hardly ever see this phase of the process, a point that will be explored later). In addition to portraying an actual police procedure, these scenes present a visual reiteration of the terms upon which the show is premised, reminding viewers that *visual* knowledge is at stake. Even when cameras are absent in the depiction of a particular investigation, every episode offers persistent references to the primacy of vision, most notably when the crime scene investigators (CSIs) brandish what might be considered the program's trademark: sleek Mag-lite high-intensity flashlights. An almost predictable moment in every episode is a close-up of one of the CSIs delicately describing the area where the crime occurred with her or his flashlight, scrutinizing some minutia that will be plucked from the scene and sent to the laboratory for analysis.

Once in the crime laboratory, the opportunities for eye-catching images emphasizing knowledge gained through visual observation expand exponentially. The laboratory is also where the analogy between digital video effects and digital scientific equipment is most pronounced. The typical shots that accomplish this fill the screen with (supposedly) microscopic views, enlarged electronically so the scientists and the audience can examine, for example, a single carpet fiber, a particle of soil or a fragment of broken glass. Computer screens display data of all kinds. Specialized software simulates the process of facial reconstruction. Digital printouts of DNA analyses appear routinely, offering certain proof of guilt or innocence. Computer programs generate floor plans of entire crime scenes.

Curiously, the notorious potential for altering digital photographic imagery is never mentioned. Of course, tampering with photographs was hardly unknown before the introduction of digital cameras and scanners. Many still view digital photographs as ambiguous representations of reality, and there is little doubt that the mirror-of-nature quality of photography has been seriously undermined in recent years as visual culture becomes increasingly digitized. But to acknowledge this would create a contradiction between the certainties of science that television's CSIs depend upon to assert their authority, and the uncertainty produced by pictures of the world composed of something as imperceptible as electrons, organized by something as immaterial as binary code.

VISION

The collection of artefacts of crimes and their translation into evidence is the basic occupation depicted in *CSI*, which gives rise to myriad imaginative puzzles for the scientists to solve. The options seem limitless, ranging from the staples of forensic police work – blood analysis, microscopic examination of spent bullets, impressions of tire tracks and footwear, chemical analyses of paint chips, etc. – to the more esoteric – calculations of the life-cycles of insect larvae, for example. The variety of forensic techniques depicted in the series may attest to the inventiveness of *CSI* scriptwriters, but the series' standbys are fingerprint analyses and X-rays of DNA molecules. Fingerprint identification, which was accepted as legally admissible by a British judge in 1905, is in many respects the classic type of forensic science (Beavan, 2001; Cole, 2001). Surprisingly, a nationwide computerized fingerprint database was not developed in the US until the early 1970s and even then, police departments in various cities and states installed incompatible systems which delayed the possibility of a fully integrated system until the end of the century (Cole, 2001). It is no accident that this achievement practically coincides with the debut of *CSI*, where an array of fingerprints flashing by as a computer performs a search for a match can be seen in just about every episode.

Such scenes not only portray computers augmenting the power of the police. They also imply a hierarchical human–machine dyad, with machines taking command. In actual AFIS searches computers produce only candidates for matching prints, from which a specialist selects the print that she or he deems identical to whatever was collected at the scene. Then the fingerprint expert must defend this decision in court and judges and juries sometimes disagree. In contrast, on *CSI* the machines do all the work and the matching process is represented as definitive. Likewise, DNA analysis is presented on the program as foolproof evidence of guilt (or innocence), ignoring successful challenges to the iron-clad veracity of this method of identification by defense attorneys, most famously in O.J. Simpson's trial for murder (Halfon, 1998; Jasanoff, 1998; Lynch, 1998). If *CSI*'s crime laboratory workers declare a match between two DNA samples, whoever is the source of the genetic material might as well forget about hiring a lawyer.

Computers running the AFIS and CODIS (Combined DNA Identification System) databases, along with all the other extremely complex and efficient equipment in *CSI*'s laboratory, play prominent roles that practically upstage the human technicians who push buttons and brandish documents containing the machines' output. In doing so, the series reiterates increasingly common analogies between computers and neurological processes found in many sectors of contemporary life. Mark Poster (1990: 148) traces this conflation to developments in computer science: '[T]he scientist projects intelligent subjectivity onto the computer and the computer then becomes the criterion by which to define intelligence, judge the scientist, outline the essence of humanity.' This spiral of substitutions and its effect on subjectivity accelerates as the social environment is increasingly visualized as a digital 'grab bag', as it is in *CSI*. The endeavor becomes an even more vertiginous exercise when the realism implicit in scenes of scientific discovery is delivered by means of elaborate, painstakingly crafted videographic effects.

It seems apt to ask at this point whether mastery of various digital imaging apparatuses on *CSI* and the potency of the inscriptions that they generate is indicative of a new visual culture which, as Bruno Latour (1986: 9) says, 'redefines both what it is to see and what there is to see'. He offers several criteria for the proliferation of new forms of inscription, which then inform new visual cultures. According to Latour, the move from instrumental inscription to conventional visual culture is accomplished when the former results in the domination of a given field, as mechanized printing of maps and other geographical information did for navigation in early-modern Europe, enabling economic and political domination. Control of trade routes and colonization are but two examples of the effects of Europeans' development and utilization of printed documents that described the physical world and, as a result, such documents became authoritative representations of that world. Foremost among Latour's ingredients for a new visual culture are portability and speed – not, he insists, perception. 'The main problem to solve,' he contends, 'is that of *mobilization* ... you have to invent objects which have the property of being *mobile* but also *immutable, presentable, readable* and *combinable* with one another' (1986: 7): five check-offs for digital images. Not only are visual displays – diagrams, photographs, graphs and so forth – used by scientists to *represent* data but these inscriptions also *constitute* data in the first place (Lynch, 1985: 44). Moreover, Latour maintains that what these inscriptions look like makes arguments about how the data should be interpreted (Latour, 1986: 5). It is the same on *CSI*. The visualization of social disorder as a series of problems best investigated *and* represented by the latest computer equipment conveys a way of seeing both crime and policing that valorizes the 'machine intelligence' that organizes and describes 'evidence'.

EVIDENCE

The reliance on truths generated and represented by scientific inscriptions in *CSI* produces yet another significant innovation in TV crime drama: its disregard of psychological knowledge. None of the regular characters are endowed with much of what is called an inner life, nor do they exhibit extraordinary psychological awareness like the protagonists in many other TV series about crime detection. No attempt is made to provide them with so-called well-rounded personalities. They rarely lose their tempers or raise their voices or otherwise appear out of control; this is especially true of Grissom, the boss who sets the tone for his underlings. Plot twists involving protagonists' personal problems are rare. When one of them enquires about another's private life, the friendly gesture is usually brushed aside. Most tellingly, scant attention is paid to the main characters' sexual or romantic relationships, although there was some flirtation between Grissom and Sara in several episodes, but nothing beyond an exchange of meaningful looks.[5]

In the same vein, *CSI* plots do not revolve around efforts to understand the motives of those who commit crimes. Overall, there is remarkably little concern with why people kill but a great deal with how people die. Consider, for example, the infrequency of confession scenes in the series (although for the purposes of narrative coherence criminal characters do sometimes confess, but only if they are confronted with the CSIs' forensic data). In other police shows the confession occurs at the moment when the puzzling elements of a particular crime are finally pieced together. Such an enunciation of truth often serves as the resolution of an episode – or at least as the moment of high drama where the lead interrogator gets to demonstrate his (less frequently her) superb understanding of what makes criminal minds tick. In addition to the narrative function of confessions – and arguably more importantly – these scenes produce an illusion of depth in an otherwise two-dimensional medium. As Peter Brooks (2000: 111) comments, 'the practice of confession creates the metaphors of innerness that it claims to explore ... the very notion of inwardness is consubstantial with the requirement to explore and examine it'. However, on *CSI* the search for truth has been relocated, in concert with a more general cultural turn, from reading minds to reading bodies.

The moment when one of the CSIs informs a suspect that his or her confession is not necessary to establish guilt, which happens quite frequently, signals a revision of the traditional TV representation of the police as psychological experts. Laboratory science supersedes self-revelation and eliminates worries about human fallibility – deceit, inaccuracy or ignorance. Brooks interprets the probative power of confessions in law courts (as well as in other disciplinary contexts such as religion) as a 'generalized demand for transparency' (2000: 4). In *CSI* transparency is still in demand, but the conditions for producing it have changed. The impediments to transparency posed by human distortions, which will always plague confession, are overcome deftly by inanimate machinery capable of processing and analyzing information.

As we are reminded in just about every episode, the CSIs differ from other members of the police force not because they possess greater psychological insight, but because they are required to think scientifically. Over and over the CSIs repeat the mantra: 'The evidence doesn't lie.' When one of them loses sight of this maxim, as when Warrick's inaccurate identification of a murderer leads to the downfall of a friend whose daughter was the murder victim, the error seems to bring the vengeance of Francis Bacon down on the lapsed scientist's head. Gaffs by other CSIs have been less serious, but all become object lessons – for the heedless, too emotionally engaged characters and also for viewers – on the importance of abjuring any personal interest while interpreting evidence.

However, what the show fails to acknowledge is that data – which on the program describes all of the material collected as 'evidence' – is not the same as evidence as understood by scientists. The CSIs' routine statements about the need for rigorous adherence to scientific practices seems to promise a new approach to justice, in which outlaws are convicted well before they appear before a judge or a jury is impaneled, well before the evidence is presented in court to be tested by the defense attorney's cross-examination, well before a jury decides whether the evidence presented by the prosecution is indeed credible and relevant and therefore qualifies as evidence at all. Klaus Amann and Karin Knorr

Cetina (1990: 88) make this distinction very clearly: '[D]ata become evidence only after they have undergone elaborate processes of selection and transformation', which is accomplished by discussions among researchers about what inscriptions of data represent. In scientific practice, the ideal sequence goes like this: data collection–inscription–evidence–truth. In legal contexts, inscriptions qualify as evidence only when their validity is considered and accepted by the court.

But on CSI no disputes over what inscriptions mean seem to trouble the course of justice. Indeed, the program implies that judgments of guilt or innocence based on scientific findings will be more even-handed and impartial than those meted out by humans. Culpability is determined in the laboratory, *proven* by its instruments. Accused lawbreakers are indicted and found guilty by scientists before they even get to court. The absence of adjudication by juries and judges is unusual for a crime show and suggests that *CSI* is not really about crime and punishment (although it may suggest a chilling futuristic fantasy where punishment is meted out without due process). Nor is it about eliciting truth by means of a confession. Rather, the locus of truth in *CSI* resides in expert applications of scientific technologies that organize and produce inscriptions, without troubling with problems of interpretation. What allows *CSI* to skip the step of interpretation – to present inscriptions, which on television are *always* presented as photographic images, as irrefutable proof – is a kind of magical property of photography: a visualization technology associated with the idea of unmediated truth, 'not "copies of nature" but portions of nature herself', to quote Samuel Morse, America's first daguerreotypist and telegraph inventor (quoted in Miller, 1998: 5). But when photographic media are conscripted for entertainment, the hedonistic pleasures associated with popular culture threaten to override impersonal objectivity. This is a problem that the producers of *CSI* seem to have taken to heart, counteracting the sensuality of visually compelling digital effects with images that evoke the somber realness of human flesh – *dead*, weighty, inert human flesh.

AUTOPSY

So far, *CSI* has avoided the charge of excessive violence often leveled at other crime shows. Instead, it serves up blood and guts using such a heavy dose of aestheticization that any accusation of authentic brutality would be difficult to sustain. Nevertheless, the most gruesome autopsy scene in almost every episode (sometimes there is more than one) is concocted as another kind of frightful spectacle. Such scenes of methodical disembowelment, glossed by the narration of the resident pathologist, appear near the beginning of just about every episode and provide the foundation for whatever the team will do for the rest of the hour. (In contrast, the first and only 'cop-science' series on American TV before *CSI*, *Quincey, M.E.* (1976–85), never showed the gory labor performed by the eponymous hero.) What can be seen as the 'money shot' in *CSI* occurs when, during the autopsy, the camera appears to penetrate a wound or orifice and produce gushing blood, exploding organs or distressed viscera, simulating the damage inflicted by the fatal weapon or the disintegration of tissue resulting from some sort of toxic substance.

The virtuoso display of digital videographics used in these close-up zooms boring into human bodies, recall the pictures produced by medical endoscopy. But despite their dependence on state-of-the-art special effects – hybrid images made up of photographs and films of props, virtual 5D models, digital 5D animation and photographic texture mapping – these scenes faithfully recapitulate the authority of the medical gaze – that is, knowledge about human life gained through visual perception that date back several centuries. In *The Birth of the Clinic*, Foucault (1975[1963]) describes the dissection of corpses that became commonplace in European hospitals and medical schools during the mid-18th century. He maintains that these autopsies provided epistemological support for the rationalization of knowledge about disease and health. Foucault's *precis* of the lessons learned from autopsies is: 'That which hides and envelops, the curtain of night over truth, is, paradoxically, life; and death, on the contrary, opens up to the light of day the black coffer of the body' (1975 [1963]: 166).

Numerous scholars have elaborated the history of the diffusion of insights gained through applications of the medical gaze that link examination of the insides of human bodies to knowledge. For example, Ludmilla Jordanova (1980: 57) informs us that 'when Jules Michelet wished to comprehend the condition of women in mid-nineteenth-century France, his first port of call was the dissecting room and his reading was anatomy texts'. Mary Poovey (1995) extends the analysis to analogies of social organization and the human body in mid-19th-century British culture, including examples from early sociological studies of urban environments that combined eyewitness accounts with statistical data to produce images of truth akin to what she calls 'anatomical realism' (1995: 74). The analytic techniques used to achieve verisimilitude in these studies, she contends, resembled the realism attempted in pedagogical drawings and three-dimensional models of human anatomy.

Literary texts written during a slightly later period demonstrate what Seltzer (1992: 95) describes as realist insistence on a compulsory and compulsive visibility, which he relates to '[t]he frequent association of later nineteenth-century realism with a sort of dissection, vivisection, or surgical opening of the body'. In addition to work by British and American novelists Seltzer considers publications by Jacob Riis, whose photographic survey of New York City slums is often credited as the founding text of social documentary photography. Riis's reformist texts, like Poovey's examples, include statistics in order to infuse his study with scientific realism alongside the pictorial realism of photography. Returning to the medical arena at the end of the 19th century, Norman Jewson (1976: 251) identifies a transition from what he calls 'Hospital Medicine', which privileged 'anatomical pathology' to 'Laboratory Medicine', where biologists and chemists reigned. The effect of this phase was, as the title of Jewson's article on the topic asserts, 'the disappearance of the sick man' – which could be construed as the disappearance of the human subject.

Such excursions into sociocultural history demonstrate the legacy of the relationship between anatomical imagery and both social science and popular media. Now, however, the translation of visual images into computer code revs up television's mobilized gaze of modernity – as analyzed by Raymond Williams (1975) and Margaret Morse (1998) – allowing the audience to glide seamlessly between the outside and inside of bodies in feats of micro-voyeurism. This triumph of videographic image-making brings to mind non-invasive medical technologies like the magnetic resonance imaging (MRI) used to render internal bodily tissues transparent. Although *CSI* evokes the anatomical textbook of the 18th century and the disappearing sick man of the 19th, the program distances the production of knowledge about life even further from living bodies. Each dead body is represented as a repository of encoded information, not unlike data stored on digital media. The CSIs frequently talk about their responsibility to 'speak for the dead', a cliché heard often on television crime shows these days that seems to honor the particular lives of those who have been killed. But what the CSIs say on their behalf tells little about specific individuals beyond the particular circumstances of their deaths. Doctors once sought new knowledge about disease, and therefore health, in anatomized, anonymous cadavers. *CSI* extends and resituates the knowledge provided by the performance of autopsies as diagnoses of social pathology. But in order to do this the social body must be visualized, constituted as information and made knowable by employing scientific instruments and procedures. Enter, once again, the police wielding gear devised to visualize, and generate knowledge about, the social landscape and those who inhabit it.

CRIME

One of *CSI*'s most curious features is its ambivalent appeal to realism. The series' episodes are narrative dramas with characters who resemble, and are sometimes modeled on, actual forensic scientists; they are also fictions with plots sometimes borrowed from actual cases (Giatto et al., 2002). But the aesthetic style of the program never tries to mimic documentary realism or employ a formal approach akin to the deadpan, no-frills *Dragnet* of the 1950s. To state the obvious, the way in which the *CSI* characters run exemplary investigations, solve all puzzles and always locate and indict the culprits appears far removed from messy, often inconclusive quotidian police work (or laboratory science). Still, in addition to the realist conventions used to present convincing representations of places, people and events, *CSI* benefits from a 'reality effect' in so far as it reiterates recent trends in law enforcement policy that treat crime as a feature of everyday social commerce. According to this approach, crime is neither extraordinary nor particularly remarkable. Therefore, it is best analyzed in terms of 'risks and rewards, rationality, choice, probability, targeting and the demand for supply of opportunities' (Garland, 1997: 186). Similarly, the miscreant is regarded as a rational economic actor who seizes self-serving opportunities that come his or her way. As a result, the criminal's aura of monstrosity becomes difficult to sustain.

In almost every instance, *CSI*'s wrongdoers fit this description. Murderers (the category to which most of the program's felons belong) take advantage of situations but remain invisible to the police as criminals because of their apparent normalcy. Even more difficult to spot are the accidental killers, who are more prosaic characters than the opportunists. Similarly, crimes and their solutions on *CSI* sidestep moral categorization – right or wrong – and are evaluated instead in terms of truth and falsehood. Without invoking the authority of personal or collective values, crimes are deciphered through applications of objective scientific standards. Ultimately, however, *CSI does* involve morality, but not a system concerned with the distinctions between good and bad individuals. The latter, more familiar framework informs narratives where evil, dangerous villains are captured, indicted and punished. In *CSI* morality operates as an expression of scientific truth, equated with the generalized *social* good.

When the forensic scientists in *CSI* use information-processing, image-producing apparatuses, they delve into the nooks and crannies of the social fabric, in many instances without leaving the laboratory. In order to apprehend those who threaten social wellbeing, they capture and study physical remnants – a strand of hair, a toenail clipping, a fleck of dandruff, a drop of saliva or blood, dirt adhering to soles of shoes, insects feasting on a corpse and so on. In order to produce 'evidence' they transform all sorts of objects, including bodies in the morgue, into digital inscriptions. Scenes showing the CSIs at work searching a database, peering through an electron microscope, or skillfully operating all sorts of elaborate equipment, constitute arguments for the advantages of digital computing and communication systems as the most efficient, most effective surrogate police. And *CSI* affirms this achievement in its constant reminders of the electronic underpinnings of the program's existence. Indeed, *CSI* goes to great lengths to reveal the means of production and a curious kind of self-referentiality is built into the series. The discovery of truth – what *really* happened – in any *CSI* episode requires the careful reading of inscriptions, both by the fictional investigators and the audience. At the same time, the program's televisual style inscribes a particular way of seeing. Whenever a character offers a theory or subjective account of a crime, the voiceover is illustrated by stylized, obviously manipulated images. Such scenes underscore the concept of crime-solving as a visual enterprise. But because they also always turn out to be erroneous, these scenes imply that truth is detected best by machines, not mere humans.

A spectator cannot help but gawk. But she may also want to keep in mind that what she sees is an optical game, an entertaining but hardly innocent vision of computer code configured as knowledge, a power play that commends digital technology for its ability to make lives – individual and collective – transparent. This is a world where electronic mastery provides solutions to all mysteries, full disclosure of all secrets, discovery of all truths. Even the tiniest, mundane residues of human life can incriminate. But rather than leading inevitably to paranoia or despondency, *CSI*'s televisual spectacle of crime also calls attention to the imaginary aspects of digital media, which consistently frustrate ambitions for incontestable knowledge. Significantly this goal, shared by Grissom and company, will always remain beyond reach.

NOTES

1   Gross's article appeared in the *New York Times*'s Sunday 'Style' section and was subtitled, 'Thanks to "CSI" Sleuthing Appeals to the Young and Tech-Savvy'.

2   Or much further, if one considers apparatuses used as aids for inscribing realistic images, such as the camera obscura; some credit Aristotle with the first recorded reference to this device.

3   The metaphor of the transparent subject becomes explicit in another successful Jerry Bruckheimer production for CBS, *Without a Trace*. The initial sequence of each episode shows the last known movements of the character whose disappearance occupies the show's FBI team responsible for locating missing persons. Just before the opening credits roll, the week's object of inquiry appears to evaporate while other aspects of the scene remain unchanged.

4   For Carlson, Ericson and Scheingold, the key question involves disparities between actual crime and arrest rates and how these are distorted in television crime fiction. A good example of genre criticism with an emphasis on ideology is Buxton. Surette and Sumser concentrate on analyses of stereotypes as indicators of ideological effects. Donovan also makes ideology the central issue in her critique of television's representation of crime and justice, although her primary interest is 'reality TV' shows such as *Cops*, where stereotypes are less an issue than the moral implications of relationships between cops and criminals.

5   At least this is as far the attraction had progressed as of the time of writing (summer 2004). Whether or not more intimate involvement between the characters will ensue cannot be predicted, since it is always wise to resist the temptation to speculate about future directions taken by any TV series until it has run its course.

REFERENCES

Amann, K. and K. Knorr Cetina (1990) 'The Fixation of (Visible) Evidence', in M. Lynch and S. Woolgar (eds) *Representation in Scientific Practice*, pp. 85–121. Cambridge, MA: MIT Press.

Beavan, C. (2001) *Fingerprints: The Origins of Crime Detection and the Murder Case that Launched Forensic Science*. New York: Hyperion.

Brooks, P. (2000) *Troubling Confessions: Speaking Guilt in Law and Literature*. Chicago, IL: University of Chicago Press.

Buxton, D. (1990) *From The Avengers to Miami Vice: Form and Ideology in Television Series*. Manchester: Manchester University Press.

Caldwell, J.T. (1995) *Televisuality: Style, Crisis and Authority in American Television*. New Brunswick, NJ: Rutgers University Press.

Carlson, J.M. (1985) *Prime Time Law Enforcement: Crime Show Viewing and Attitudes Towards the Criminal Justice System*. New York: Praeger.

Cartwright, L. (1995) *Screening the Body: Tracing Medicine's Visual Culture*. Minneapolis: University of Minnesota Press.

Cole, S.A. (2001) *Suspect Identities: A History of Fingerprinting and Criminal Investigation*. Cambridge, MA: Harvard University Press.

Donovan, P. (1998) 'Armed with the Power of Television: Reality Crime Programming and the Reconstruction of Law and Order,' in M. Fishman and G. Cavender (eds) *Entertaining Crime: Television Reality Programs*, pp. 117–37. New York: Aldine de Gruyter.

Ericson, R.V. (ed.) (1995) *Crime and the Media*. Aldershot: Dartmouth Publishing.

Foucault, M. (1975[1963]) *The Birth of the Clinic: An Archaeology of Medical Perception*. New York: Pantheon.

Foucault, M. (1979[1975]) *Discipline and Punish: The Birth of the Prison*. New York: Vintage.

Garland, D. (1997) '"Governmentality" and the Problem of Crime', *Theoretical Criminology* 1(2): 173–214.

Giatto, T, L. Benet and A. Chiu (2002) 'The Dead Zone'. *People* (14 Oct.): 112–15.

Gross, J. (2002) 'In Latest Science Classes, Dead Men Do Tell Tales', *New York Times* (31 Dec): A1–C22.

Halfon, S. (1998) 'Collecting, Testing and Convincing: Forensic DNA Experts in the Courts', *Social Studies of Science* 28(5–6): 801–28.

Jasanoff, S. (1998) 'The Eye of Witnessing: DNA in the Simpson Trial', *Social Studies of Science* 28(5–6): 713–40.

Jewson, N.D. (1976) 'The Disappearance of the Sick-Man from Medical Cosmology, 1770–1870', *Sociology* 10(2): 225–44.

Jordanova, L. (1980) 'Natural Facts: A Historical Perspective on Science and Sexuality', in C.P. MacCormack and M. Strathern (eds) *Nature, Culture and Gender*, pp. 42–69. Cambridge: Cambridge University Press.

Latour, B. (1986) 'Visualization and Cognition: Thinking with Eyes and Hands', *Knowledge and Society* 6: 1–40.

Lynch, M. (1985) 'Discipline and the Material Form of Images: An Analysis of Scientific Visibility', *Social Studies of Science* 15(1): 37–66.

Lynch, M. (1998) 'The Discursive Production of Uncertainty: The O.J. Simpson "Dream Team" and the Sociology of Knowledge Machine', *Social Studies of Science* 28(5–6): 829–68.

Miller, T. (1998) *Technologies of Truth: Cultural Citizenship and the Popular Media*. Minneapolis: University of Minnesota Press.

Mitchell, W.J. (2001) *The Reconfigured Eye: Visual Truth in the Post-Photographic Era*. Cambridge, MA: MIT Press.

Morse, M. (1998) *Virtualities: Television, Media Art and Cyberculture*. Bloomington: Indiana University Press.

Museum of Television and Radio (2001) Videotaped panel discussion on *CSI*, including cast members, series creator and producer, director and writers, 1 March.

Parry, E. (2000) *Crime Album Stories: Paris, 1886–1902*. Zurich: Scalo.

Poovey, M. (1995) *Making a Social Body: British Cultural Formation, 1830–1864*. Chicago, IL: University of Chicago Press.

Poster, M. (1990) *The Mode of Information: Poststructuralism and Social Context*. Chicago, IL: University of Chicago Press.

Scheingold, S.A. (ed.) (1997) *Politics, Crime Control and Popular Culture*. Aldershot: Dartmouth/Ashgate Publishing.

Sekula, A. (1986) 'The Body and the Archive', *October* 39: 3–64.

Seltzer, M. (1992) *Bodies and Machines*. New York: Routledge.

Sparks, R. (1992) *Television and the Drama of Crime: Moral Tales and the Place of Crime in Public Life*. Buckingham: Open University Press.

St John, W. (2003) 'Here Come the Glamour Gumshoes', *New York Times* (19 Oct., Sunday 'Style' section): 1–2.

Stafford, B.M. (1994) *Body Criticism: Imaging the Unseen in Enlightenment Art and Medicine*. Cambridge, MA: MIT Press.

Sumser, J. (1996) *Morality and Social Order in Television Crime Drama*. Jefferson, NC: McFarland.

Surette, R. (1992) *Media, Crime and Criminal Justice: Images and Realities*. Pacific Grove, CA: Brooks/Cole Publishing.

Tagg, J. (1981) 'Power and Photography – A Means of Surveillance: The Photograph as Evidence in Law', in T. Bennett, G. Martin and J. Woolacott (eds) *Culture, Ideology and Social Process*, pp. 285–307. London: Batsford.

Williams, R. (1975) *Television: Technology and Cultural Form*. New York: Schocken.

Part Five

Control-ology: governance and surveillance

INTRODUCTION

The institutions, authorities and procedures which provide any society with its mechanism for controlling and preventing crime cannot merely be taken at face value as methods of dealing with the particular behaviours of specific individuals. Such measures reflect wider concerns about the existing social order and, as the readings in this Part indicate, they are a crucial part of the processes for exerting control, regulation and discipline over 'society' and for the *governance* and *surveillance* not only of targeted individuals but also whole populations. Control-ology – a term first used by Jason Ditton in a book of the same name from 1979 – captures the view that criminal justice agencies are part of broader social control mechanisms, like welfare, mental health, education, the military, and the mass media: all of which are used by the state to control 'problem populations'. Such a vision of control-ology was first developed by Michel Foucault. It is widely acknowledged that his book *Discipline and Punish* (1977) provided criminology with a new theoretical language with which to analyse practices of control in modernity, as well as providing the discipline with a greater awareness of its own status as a power/knowledge apparatus related to these very practices. According to Foucault, the 'disciplinary society' emerged in Western Europe in the early nineteenth century. The criminal was no longer regarded merely as somebody who had broken the law and had to be punished. Now the criminal/prisoner required close supervision and expert intervention with the view to returning 'him' to normality. According to Foucault, the prison was just one island in a 'carceral archipelago' of disciplinary institutions which included schools, hospitals and asylums, and barracks, and extending through a 'carceral continuum' to the home and the workplace. In this process the traditional disciplinary mechanisms of the law and custom were powerfully supplemented by new fields of knowledge (including medicine, psychiatry, pedagogy, criminology) and new bodies of experts. As Foucault argues in the first reading included here, the crucial role of the modern prison was to pioneer and legitimize a method of dealing with 'deviants' from prescribed norms which could then be generalized to 'the entire social body'.

As technologies of crime reduction and prevention have developed apace since the 1970s, so have attempts to theorize and make criminological sense of what appears a burgeoning, yet dispersed, culture of *social control*. One of the most influential theorists of 'social control' is the sociologist, Stanley Cohen. In a path-breaking article published in 1979 he cast a critical eye on the supposedly benign or progressive movements of the 1960s and 1970s which advocated a shift of the loci of control from institutions to communities. His 'dispersal of discipline' thesis contends that as control mechanisms are dispersed from custody into the community they penetrate deeper into the social fabric. A blurring of boundaries between the deviant and non-deviant; the public and the private occurs. A 'punitive archipelago' is expanded as new resources, technology and professional interests are applied to an increasing number of 'clients' and 'customers'. Entrepreneurs are drawn into the control enterprise in search of profits. Communities are mobilized to act as voluntary control agents in their own right. But, throughout, the growing invisibility and diversification of the state's role does not mean it has withered away. The prison remains at the core of the system. This formulation of social control acknowledges its versatility: infiltrating many levels of discourse and serving and constituting a diversity of interests.

In many respects Cohen's vision has proved to be remarkably prescient: of particular note is how much of this control has become (or is becoming) privatized – that is removed from direct state control and activated not just by communities, but a wide range of voluntary agencies and private security companies. Social control appears progressively more as a commodity: as something to be purchased and sold. This theme was subsequently developed by Clifford Shearing and Philip Stenning's interest in the mechanisms through which the disciplinary society achieves social control. They contrast the essentially *moral* basis of the traditional criminal justice state (including the prison system) with the more *instrumental* and *amoral* character of control methods which operate in the ever growing private sector. Here the aim is not to reform individuals but to restrict the opportunities for crime. Using Disney World as a case-study, they show how such 'non-carceral' but unmistakably 'disciplinary' control measures are embedded in the structures of modern social practice.

The next reading by Malcolm Feeley and Jonathan Simon argues that the last decades of the twentieth century witnessed the emergence of a new penological discourse. This discourse in essence is a managerialist and *actuarialist* approach to the problem of crime and its control. It is not interested in philosophizing about or assessing the respective merits of deterrence, just deserts, and individual rehabilitation; rather it is committed to the effective management of the criminal justice system and its component parts. Cost-effectiveness, efficient forms of custody and control, competition and organizational targets and outputs are the concerns of the new managerial regime. However, Feeley and Simon do recognize that this new systems approach overlaps with more general populist authoritarian discourses on how to manage (and punish) problem populations.

Pat O'Malley's contribution also begins by plotting the rise in recent decades of post-disciplinary risk-based technologies of power and control. However, he also counters overly deterministic readings of the growth of actuarial risk management technologies of governance, and in turn highlights the 'survival' of older punitive and correctional technologies. O'Malley argues against explanations which focus on increased efficiency as an evolutionary criterion for emerging technologies of power. Instead he suggests that the forms taken by such technologies are primarily determined by the character and success of the political programmes with which they are aligned. Situational crime prevention is explored as a prime example of a neo-liberal, *prudentialist* risk management discourse. Throughout O'Malley's analysis emphasis is placed on the primacy of politics: indeed the 'success' of situational crime prevention compared with other criminological technologies is explained in terms of its broader political and ideological effects (and particularly its attraction to rationalist, neo-conservative and New Right programmes).

To make sense of the complex and contradictory means by which order is achieved in demo-cratic societies numerous authors have increasingly turned to the concept of 'governance'. Derived from Foucault's brief writings on 'governmentality', 'governance' (though often used in an eclectic fashion) refers to any act, means or tactic through which conduct is regulated. Governance means something more than state government. It is also concerned with the tactic of using particular knowledges to arrange things in such a way that populations accept being governed and begin to govern themselves through 'the conduct of conduct'. Jonathan Simon clearly illustrates how 'crime' is routinely employed in contemporary modes of governance. The continual reworking and expansion of criminal justice; a never-ending stream of legislation apparently dominating all other government concerns; the political use of crime and disorder as a means to secure electoral gain; the excessive media fascination – both as news and enter-tainment – with all things 'criminal'; and the obsession with regulation, whether through families, schools or training programmes, all attest to the place of 'crime and disorder' as a central motif of modern governance. When crime and punishment become occasions and institutional con-texts in which we undertake to guide the conduct of others (and even of ourselves) we are now governing ourselves through crime.

In the next reading Mike Davis offers us a chilling vision of the possible dystopian future for cities in the twenty-first century, drawing especially on developments in regulation, surveillance and repression in Los Angeles immediately after the urban disorders of 1992. This reading is a telling reminder of the persistence of modes of brutal, coercive control which exist alongside the new, more subtle modes of governance and ordering in contemporary 'cityscapes'. Davis highlights how technologies of regulation, surveillance and repression in 'post'-*Blade Runner* LA are designed to stabilize class, racial and generational relations across the chasm of the new ine-qualities and in the context of accelerating social polarization and spatial apartheid. In particu-lar, Davis highlights the new culture of fear and the obsession with (privatized) safety and security which lies at the heart of the city and of the new modes of governance in contemporary neo-liberal societies. Davis's work represents a productive dialogue between social theory and science fiction and in the course of this dialogue, his analysis opens up a new criminological imaginary, albeit predicated upon a vision of a profoundly dystopian/pessimistic urban future for us all.

All of this of course has the potential to conjure up images of totalitarian states in the image of George Orwell's *Nineteen Eighty-Four*. However, social theorists such as David Lyon also detect ambiguities and paradoxes in the new surveillance infrastructure. He draws upon Foucault's conclusion that there is little risk that panopticism will *only* generate authoritarian forms of social control because strategies of power-knowledge are never complete or determining. Panoptic power is always in a process of becoming – partial, contingent, unevenly developed; enabling as well as constraining; full of specificities, hybridities, subtleties and 'open-ended cosmologies'. By linking the expansion of surveillance to a simultaneous growth in citizenship, Lyon argues that it is improvements in civil rights and political entitlement which have generated demands for a greater documentary identification, which in turn depends on a growing sophistication in methods of regulation, recording and surveillance. But the development of risk technologies also creates its own risks, not least its use to cement social sorting where some people 'know their place' whilst others are forever condemned to be 'out of place'.

In *Discipline and Punish* (1977) Michel Foucault had argued that the late eighteenth century witnessed a radical turn in penal affairs, when arbitrary and brutal justice gave way to new forms of disciplinary power that were more productive (but also insidious) in character. Yet numerous developments since the 1980s, particularly, but not always, originating in the USA, have led some analysts to consider whether penal policy and practice is now reverting back to that of some 200 years ago. In particular, rising rates of imprisonment, chain gangs, supermax prisons, naming and shaming, public humiliation of offenders, three strikes laws, mandatory minimum sentencing, austere prison regimes, zero tolerance, the death penalty – all appear as particularly draconian and disproportionate responses to offending. This 'new punitiveness' appears primarily driven not by any coherent penal philosophy but from vengeance and cruelty, where the primary objective appears to be largely one of taking satisfaction in the pain of others. Our final reading from the sociologist, Loïc Wacquant's account of the 'punitive upsurge' notes six prominent features of the coming together of neo-liberalism as a political project and the deployment of a proactive punitive penality. First, punitiveness is legitimated through a discourse of 'putting an end to leniency' by not only targeting crime but all manner of disorders and nuisances through a remit of zero tolerance. Second, there has been a proliferation of laws, surveillance strategies and technological quick fixes – from watch groups and partnerships to satellite tracking – that have significantly extended the reach of control agencies. Third, the necessity of this 'punitive turn' is everywhere conveyed by an alarmist, catastrophist discourse on 'insecurity' and 'perpetual risk'. Fourth, declining working-class neighbourhoods have become perpetually stigmatized targets for intervention (particularly their ethnic minority, youth and immigrant populations). Fifth, any residual philosophy of 'rehabilitation' has been more or less supplanted by a managerialist approach centred on the cost-driven administration of carceral stocks and flows, paving the way for the privatization of correctional services. Sixth, the implementation of these new punitive policies has invariably resulted in an extension of police powers, a hardening and speeding-up of judicial procedures and, at the end of the penal chain, dramatic increases in the prison population.

40

The carceral

Michel Foucault

[…] [I]n penal justice, the prison transformed the punitive procedure into a penitentiary technique; the carceral archipelago transported this technique from the penal institution to the entire social body. With several important results.

1 This vast mechanism established a slow, continuous, imperceptible gradation that made it possible to pass naturally from disorder to offence and back from a transgression of the law to a slight departure from a rule, an average, a demand, a norm. In the classical period, despite a certain common reference to offence in general, the order of the crime, the order of sin and the order of bad conduct remained separate in so far as they related to separate criteria and authorities (court, penitence, confinement). Incarceration with its mechanisms of surveillance and punishment functioned, on the contrary, according to a principle of relative continuity. The continuity of the institutions themselves, which were linked to one another (public assistance with the orphanage, the reformatory, the penitentiary, the disciplinary battalion, the prison; the school with the charitable society, the workshop, the almshouse, the penitentiary convent; the workers' estate with the hospital and the prison). A continuity of the punitive criteria and mechanisms, which on the basis of a mere deviation gradually strengthened the rules and increased the punishment. A continuous gradation of the established, specialized and competent authorities (in the order of knowledge and in the order of power) which, without resort to arbitrariness, but strictly according to the regulations, by means of observation and assessment hierarchized, dif-ferentiated, judged, punished and moved gradually from the correction of irregularities to the punishment of crime. The 'carceral' with its many diffuse or compact forms, its institutions of supervision or constraint, of discreet surveillance and insistent coercion, assured the communi-cation of punishments according to quality and quantity; it connected in series or disposed according to subtle divisions the minor and the serious penalties, the mild and the strict forms of treatment, bad marks and light sentences. You will end up in the convict-ship, the slightest indiscipline seems to say; and the harshest of prisons says to the prisoners condemned to life: I shall note the slightest irregularity in your conduct. The generality of the punitive function that the

From *Discipline and Punish* (trans. Alan Sheridan), pp. 298–308. (London: Allen Lane, 1977.)

eighteenth century sought in the 'ideological' technique of representations and signs now had as its support the extension, the material framework, complex, dispersed, but coherent, of the various carceral mechanisms. As a result, a certain significant generality moved between the least irregularity and the greatest crime; it was no longer the offence, the attack on the common interest, it was the departure from the norm, the anomaly; it was this that haunted the school, the court, the asylum or the prison. It generalized in the sphere of meaning the function that the carceral generalized in the sphere of tactics. Replacing the adversary of the sovereign, the social enemy was transformed into a deviant, who brought with him the multiple danger of disorder, crime and madness. The carceral network linked, through innumerable relations, the two long, multiple series of the punitive and the abnormal.

2 The carceral, with its far-reaching networks, allows the recruitment of major 'delinquents'. It organizes what might be called 'disciplinary careers' in which, through various exclusions and rejections, a whole process is set in motion. In the classical period, there opened up in the confines or interstices of society the confused, tolerant and dangerous domain of the 'outlaw' or at least of that which eluded the direct hold of power: an uncertain space that was for criminality a training ground and a region of refuge; there poverty, unemployment, pursued innocence, cunning, the struggle against the powerful, the refusal of obligations and laws, and organized crime all came together as chance and fortune would dictate; it was the domain of adventure that Gil Blas, Sheppard or Mandrin, each in his own way, inhabited. Through the play of disciplinary differentiations and divisions, the nineteenth century constructed rigorous channels which, within the system, inculcated docility and produced delinquency by the same mechanisms. There was a sort of disciplinary 'training', continuous and compelling, that had something of the pedagogical curriculum and something of the professional network. Careers emerged from it, as secure, as predictable, as those of public life: assistance associations, residential apprenticeships, penal colonies, disciplinary battalions, prisons, hospitals, almshouses. These networks were already well mapped out at the beginning of the nineteenth century:

> Our benevolent establishments present an admirably coordinated whole by means of which the indigent does not remain a moment without help from the cradle to the grave. Follow the course of the unfortunate man: you will see him born among foundlings; from there he passes to the nursery, then to an orphanage; at the age of six he goes off to primary school and later to adult schools. If he cannot work, he is placed on the list of the charity offices of his district, and if he falls ill he may choose between twelve hospitals … Lastly, when the poor Parisian reaches the end of his career, seven almshouses await his age and often their salubrious régime has prolonged his useless days well beyond those of the rich man. (Moreau de Jonnès, quoted in Touquet)

The carceral network does not cast the unassimilable into a confused hell; there is no outside. It takes back with one hand what it seems to exclude with the other. It saves everything, including what it punishes. It is unwilling to waste even what it has decided to disqualify. In this panoptic society of which incarceration is the omnipresent armature, the delinquent is not outside the law; he is, from the very outset, in the law, at the very heart of the law, or at least in the midst of those mechanisms that transfer the individual imperceptibly from discipline to the law, from deviation to offence. Although it is true that prison punishes delinquency, delinquency is for the most part produced in and by an incarceration which, ultimately, prison perpetuates in its turn. The prison is merely the natural consequence, no more than a higher degree, of that hierarchy laid down step by step. The delinquent is an institutional product. It is no use being surprised, therefore, that in a considerable proportion of cases the biography of convicts passes through all these mechanisms and establishments, whose purpose, it is widely believed, is to lead away from prison. That one should find in them what one might call the index of an irrepressibly delinquent 'character': the prisoner condemned to hard labour was meticulously produced by a childhood spent in a reformatory, according to the lines of force of the generalized carceral system. Conversely, the lyricism of marginality may find inspiration in the image of the 'outlaw', the great social nomad, who prowls on the confines of a docile, frightened order. But it is not on the fringes of society and through successive exiles that criminality is born, but by means of ever more closely placed insertions, under ever more insistent surveillance, by an accumulation of disciplinary coercion. In short, the carceral archipelago assures, in the depths of the social body, the formation of delinquency on the basis of subtle illegalities, the overlapping of the latter by the former and the establishment of a specified criminality.

3 But perhaps the most important effect of the carceral system and of its extension well beyond legal imprisonment is that it succeeds in making the power to punish natural and legitimate, in lowering at least the threshold of tolerance to penality. It tends to efface what may be exorbitant in the exercise of punishment. It does this by playing the two registers in which it is deployed – the legal register of justice and the extra-legal register of discipline – against one another. In effect, the great continuity of the carceral system throughout the law and its sentences gives a sort of legal sanction to the disciplinary mechanisms, to the decisions and judgements that they enforce. Throughout this network, which comprises so many 'regional' institutions, relatively autonomous and independent, is transmitted, with the 'prison-form', the model of justice itself. The regulations of the disciplinary establishments may reproduce the law, the punishments imitate the verdicts and penalties, the surveillance repeat the police model; and, above all these multiple establishments, the prison, which in relation to them is a pure form, unadulterated and unmitigated, gives them a sort of official sanction. The carceral, with its long gradation stretching from the convictship or imprisonment with hard labour to diffuse, slight limitations, communicates a type of power that the law validates and that justice uses as its favourite weapon. How could the disciplines and the power that functions in them appear arbitrary, when they merely operate the mechanisms of justice itself, even with a view to mitigating their intensity? When, by generalizing its effects and transmitting it to every level, it makes it possible to avoid its full rigour? Carceral continuity and the fusion of the prison-form make it possible to legalize, or in any case to legitimate disciplinary power, which thus avoids any element of excess or abuse it may entail.

But, conversely, the carceral pyramid gives to the power to inflict legal punishment a context in which it appears to be free of all excess and all violence. In the subtle gradation of the apparatuses of discipline and of the successive 'embeddings' that they involve, the prison does not at all represent the unleashing of a different kind of power, but simply an additional degree in the intensity of a mechanism that has continued to operate since the earliest forms of legal punishment. Between the latest institution of 'rehabilitation', where one is taken in order to avoid prison, and the prison where one is sent after a definable offence, the difference is (and must be) scarcely perceptible. There is a strict economy that has the effect of rendering as discreet as possible the singular power to punish. There is nothing in it now that recalls the former excess of sovereign power when it revenged its authority on the tortured body of those about to be executed. Prison continues, on those who are entrusted to it, a work begun elsewhere, which the whole of society pursues on each individual through innumerable mechanisms of discipline. By means of a carceral continuum, the authority that sentences infiltrates all those other authorities that supervise, transform, correct, improve. It might even be said that nothing really distinguishes them any more except the singularly 'dangerous' character of the delinquents, the gravity of their departures from normal behaviour and the necessary solemnity of the ritual. But, in its function, the power to punish is not essentially different from that of curing or educating. It receives from them, and from their lesser, smaller task, a sanction from below; but one that is no less important for that, since it is the sanction of technique and rationality. The carceral 'naturalizes' the legal power to punish, as it 'legalizes' the technical power to discipline. In thus homogenizing them, effacing what may be violent in one and arbitrary in the other, attenuating the effects of revolt that they may both arouse, thus depriving excess in either of any purpose, circulating the same calculated, mechanical and discreet methods from one to the other, the carceral makes it possible to carry out that great 'economy' of power whose formula the eighteenth century had sought, when the problem of the accumulation and useful administration of men first emerged.

By operating at every level of the social body and by mingling ceaselessly the art of rectifying and the right to punish, the universality of the carceral lowers the level from which it becomes natural and acceptable to be punished. The question is often posed as to how, before and after the Revolution, a new foundation was given to the right to punish. And no doubt the answer is to be found in the theory of the contract. But it is perhaps more important to ask the reverse question: how were people made to accept the power to punish, or quite simply, when punished, tolerate being so. The theory of the contract can only answer this question by the fiction of a juridical subject giving to others the power to exercise over him the right that he himself possesses over them. It is highly probable that the great carceral continuum, which provides a communication between the power of discipline and the power of the law, and extends without interruption from the smallest coercions to the longest penal detention, constituted the technical and real, immediately material counterpart of that chimerical granting of the right to punish.

4 With this new economy of power, the carceral system, which is its basic instrument, permitted the emergence of a new form of 'law': a mixture of legality and nature, prescription and

constitution, the norm. This had a whole series of effects: the internal dislocation of the judicial power or at least of its functioning; an increasing difficulty in judging, as if one were ashamed to pass sentence; a furious desire on the part of the judges to judge, assess, diagnose, recognize the normal and abnormal and claim the honour of curing or rehabilitating. In view of this, it is useless to believe in the good or bad consciences of judges, or even of their unconscious. Their immense 'appetite for medicine' which is constantly manifested – from their appeal to psychiatric experts, to their attention to the chatter of criminology – expresses the major fact that the power they exercise has been 'denatured'; that it is at a certain level governed by laws; that at another, more fundamental level it functions as a normative power; it is the economy of power that they exercise, and not that of their scruples or their humanism, that makes them pass 'therapeutic' sentences and recommend 'rehabilitating' periods of imprisonment. But, conversely, if the judges accept ever more reluctantly to condemn for the sake of condemning, the activity of judging has increased precisely to the extent that the normalizing power has spread. Borne along by the omnipresence of the mechanisms of discipline, basing itself on all the carceral apparatuses, it has become one of the major functions of our society. The judges of normality are present everywhere. We are in the society of the teacher-judge, the doctor-judge, the educator-judge, the 'social worker'-judge; it is on them that the universal reign of the normative is based; and each individual, wherever he may find himself, subjects to it his body, his gestures, his behaviour, his aptitudes, his achievements. The carceral network, in its compact or disseminated forms, with its systems of insertion, distribution, surveillance, observation, has been the greatest support, in modern society, of the normalizing power.

5 The carceral texture of society assures both the real capture of the body and its perpetual observation; it is, by its very nature, the apparatus of punishment that conforms most completely to the new economy of power and the instrument for the formation of knowledge that this very economy needs. Its panoptic functioning enables it to play this double role. By virtue of its methods of fixing, dividing, recording, it has been one of the simplest, crudest, also most concrete, but perhaps most indispensable conditions for the development of this immense activity of examination that has objectified human behaviour. If, after the age of 'inquisitorial' justice, we have entered the age of 'examinatory' justice, if, in an even more general way, the method of examination has been able to spread so widely throughout society, and to give rise in part to the sciences of man, one of the great instruments for this has been the multiplicity and close overlapping of the various mechanisms of incarceration. I am not saying that the human sciences emerged from the prison. But, if they have been able to be formed and to produce so many profound changes in the episteme, it is because they have been conveyed by a specific and new modality of power: a certain policy of the body, a certain way of rendering the group of men docile and useful. This policy required the involvement of definite relations of knowledge in relations of power; it called for a technique of overlapping subjection and objectification; it brought with it new procedures of individualization. The carceral network constituted one of the armatures of this power-knowledge that has made the human sciences historically possible. Knowable man (soul, individuality, consciousness, conduct, whatever it is called) is the object-effect of this analytical investment, of this domination-observation.

6 This no doubt explains the extreme solidity of the prison, that slight invention that was nevertheless decried from the outset. If it had been no more than an instrument of rejection or

repression in the service of a state apparatus, it would have been easier to alter its more overt forms or to find a more acceptable substitute for it. But, rooted as it was in mechanisms and strategies of power, it could meet any attempt to transform it with a great force of inertia. One fact is characteristic: when it is a question of altering the system of imprisonment, opposition does not come from the judicial institutions alone; resistance is to be found not in the prison as penal sanction, but in the prison with all its determinations, links and extra-judicial results; in the prison as the relay in a general network of disciplines and surveillances; in the prison as it functions in a panoptic regime. This does not mean that it cannot be altered, nor that it is once and for all indispensable to our kind of society. One may, on the contrary, cite the two processes which, in the very continuity of the processes that make the prison function, are capable of exercising considerable restraint on its use and of transforming its internal functioning. And no doubt these processes have already begun to a large degree. The first is that which reduces the utility (or increases its inconveniences) of a delinquency accommodated as a specific illegal-ity, locked up and supervised; thus the growth of great national or international illegalities directly linked to the political and economic apparatuses (financial illegalities, information ser-vices, arms and drugs trafficking, property speculation) makes it clear that the somewhat rustic and conspicuous work force of delinquency is proving ineffective; or again, on a smaller scale, as soon as the economic levy on sexual pleasure is carried out more efficiently by the sale of contraceptives, or obliquely through publications, films or shows, the archaic hierarchy of pros-titution loses much of its former usefulness. The second process is the growth of the disciplinary networks, the multiplication of their exchanges with the penal apparatus, the ever more impor-tant powers that are given them, the ever more massive transference to them of judicial func-tions; now, as medicine, psychology, education, public assistance, 'social work' assume an ever greater share of the powers of supervision and assessment, the penal apparatus will be able, in turn, to become medicalized, psychologized, educationalized; and by the same token that turning-point represented by the prison becomes less useful when, through the gap between its penitentiary discourse and its effect of consolidating delinquency, it articulates the penal power and the disciplinary power. In the midst of all these mechanisms of normalization, which are becoming ever more rigorous in their application, the specificity of the prison and its role as link are losing something of their purpose.

If there is an overall political issue around the prison, it is not therefore whether it is to be corrective or not; whether the judges, the psychiatrists or the sociologists are to exercise more power in it than the administrators or supervi-sors; it is not even whether we should have prison or something other than prison. At present, the problem lies rather in the steep rise in the use of these mechanisms of normalization and the wide-ranging powers which, through the proliferation of new disciplines, they bring with them. In 1836, a correspondent wrote to *La Phalange:*

> Moralists, philosophers, legislators, flatterers of civilization, this is the plan of your Paris, neatly ordered and arranged, here is the improved plan in which all like things are gathered together. At the centre, and within a first enclosure: hospitals for all diseases, almshouses for all types of poverty, madhouses, prisons, convict-prisons for men, women and children. Around the first enclosure, barracks, court-rooms, police stations,

houses for prison warders, scaffolds, houses for the executioner and his assistants. At the four corners, the Chamber of Deputies, the Chamber of Peers, the Institute and the Royal Palace. Outside, there are the various services that supply the central enclosure, commerce, with its swindlers and its bankruptcies; industry and its furious struggles; the press, with its sophisms; the gambling dens; prostitution, the people dying of hunger or wallowing in debauchery, always ready to lend an ear to the voice of the Genius of Revolutions; the heartless rich … Lastly the ruthless war of all against all. (*La Phalange*, 10 August 1836)

I shall stop with this anonymous text. We are now far away from the country of tortures, dotted with wheels, gibbets, gallows, pillories; we are far, too, from that dream of the reformers, less than fifty years before: the city of punishments in which a thousand small theatres would have provided an endless multicoloured representation of justice in which the punishments, meticulously produced on decorative scaffolds, would have constituted the permanent festival of the penal code. The carceral city, with its imaginary 'geo-politics', is governed by quite different principles. The extract from *La Phalange* reminds us of some of the more important ones: that at the centre of this city, and as if to hold it in place, there is, not the 'centre of power', not a network of forces, but a multiple network of diverse elements – walls, space, institution, rules, discourse; that the model of the carceral city is not, therefore, the body of the king, with the powers that emanate from it, nor the contractual meeting of wills from which a body that was both individual and collective was born, but a strategic distribution of elements of different natures and levels. That the prison is not the daughter of laws, codes or the judicial apparatus; that it is not subordinated to the court and the docile or clumsy instrument of the sentences that it hands out and of the results that it would like to achieve; that it is the court that is external and subordinate to the prison. That in the central position that it occupies, it is not alone, but linked to a whole series of 'carceral' mechanisms which seem distinct enough – since they are intended to alleviate pain, to cure, to comfort – but which all tend, like the prison, to exercise a power of normalization. That these mechanisms are applied not to transgressions against a 'central' law, but to the apparatus of production – 'commerce' and 'industry' – to a whole multiplicity of illegalities, in all their diversity of nature and origin, their specific role in profit and the different ways in which they are dealt with by the punitive mechanisms. And that ultimately what presides over all these mechanisms is not the unitary functioning of an apparatus or an institution, but the necessity of combat and the rules of strategy. That, consequently, the notions of institutions of repression, rejection, exclusion, marginalization, are not adequate to describe, at the very centre of the carceral city, the formation of the insidious leniencies, unavowable petty cruelties, small acts of cunning, calculated methods, techniques, 'sciences' that permit the fabrication of the disciplinary individual. In this central and centralized humanity, the effect and instrument of complex power relations, bodies and forces subjected by multiple mechanisms of 'incarceration', objects for discourses that are in themselves elements for this strategy, we must hear the distant roar of battle. […]

41

The punitive city: notes on the dispersal of social control

Stanley Cohen

This, then, is how one must imagine the punitive city. At the crossroads, in the gardens, at the side of roads being repaired or bridges built, in workshops open to all, in the depths of mines that may be visited, will be hundreds of tiny theatres of punishment.

Michel Foucault, *Discipline and Punish*

The study of social control must be one of the more dramatic examples in sociology of the gap between our private sense of what is going on around us and our professional writings about the social world. Our private terrain is inhabited by premonitions of *1984*, *Clockwork Orange* and *Brave New World*, by fears of the increasing intrusion of the state into private lives and by a general unease that more and more of our actions and thoughts are under surveillance and subject to record. Our professional formulations about social control though, reveal little of such nightmares and science-fiction projections. They tend to repeat bland structural-functional explanations about the necessity of social control or else simplistic comparisons of pre-industrial and industrial societies. There are, to be sure, powerful macro theories, especially Marxist, about the apparatus and ideology of state control and a great deal of Marcusean-like rhetoric left over from the sixties about 'repression'. And then there are those exquisite interactional studies about the social control dimensions in talk, gaze and gesture.

But for an overall sense of what the formal social control apparatus of society is actually getting up to we have surprisingly little information. Those sub-fields of sociology most explicitly concerned with all this – criminology and the sociology of deviance – are not as much help as they should be, especially when trying

From *Contemporary Crises* 1979, 3(4): 339–63.

to understand the major shifts in the ideology and apparatus of control over the last few decades. Thus writings about community control – the subject of this paper and, if my argument is correct, the key area in which to find transformations in social control – are usually of a very low level. They are either blandly descriptive or else 'evaluative' only in the sense of using the pseudo scientific language of process, feedback, goals, inputs, systems etc., to decide whether this or that program 'works' or is cost productive. Little of this helps towards understanding basic structural and ideological trends.

Some connecting bridges have, of course, been made somewhere here between private nightmare and sociological work. This is most evident in the current wave of disenchantment about benevolent state intervention in the name of welfare or rehabilitation.[1] The historical work by David Rothman on the origins of the asylum and (from a quite different tradition) Michel Foucault's series of great works on the history of deviance control have marked a major intellectual breakthrough. The extension of this work into the contemporary scene in Scull's analysis of the decarceration movement and in the less theoretically penetrating but polemically equally compelling formulations about the 'Therapeutic State' (Kittrie), 'Psychiatric Despotism' (Szasz) and the 'Psychological Society' (Gross) are also important. But this work is surprisingly sparse and tends anyway to concentrate on psychiatry, only one limited system of social control.

On the whole, the promise of the new sociology of deviance to deal with the 'control' side of the 'deviance and control' equation, has not been fulfilled. Certainly there are enough good studies of specific control agencies such as courts, prisons, police departments, abortion clinics, mental hospitals, and so on. But the problem with this ethnographic work is not so much (as the familiar criticism runs) that a pre-occupation with labelling, stigma and interaction may leave the analysis at the microscopic level. The problem is more that such studies are often curiously fragmented, abstracted from the density of urban life in which social control is embedded. It is not so much that these agencies often have no history: they also have little sense of place. They need locating in the physical space of the city, but more important in the overall social space: the master patterns of social control, the network of other institutions such as school and family, and broader trends in welfare and social services, bureaucracies and professions. This paper is a preface to a grander project of this sort.

What I want to do – largely for a sociological audience outside crime and justice professionals – is sort out some of the implications of the apparent changes in the formal social control apparatus over the last decade or so. I will concentrate on crime and juvenile delinquency though there are important tendencies – some parallel and some quite different – in such areas as drug abuse and mental illness which require altogether separate comment. I will be drawing material mainly from the United States and Britain – countries which have developed a centralized crime control apparatus embedded in a more (Britain) or less (United States) highly developed commitment to welfare and more (United States) or less (Britain) sophisticated ideologies and techniques of treatment and rehabilitation.

This paper, then, is an exercise in classification and projection, rather than explanation.

FROM PRISON TO COMMUNITY

Our current system of deviancy control originated in those great transformations which took place from the end of the 18th to the beginning of the 19th centuries: firstly the development of a centralized state apparatus for the control of crime and the care of dependency; secondly the increasing differentiation of the deviant and dependent into separate types each with its own attendant corpus of 'scientific' knowledge and accredited experts; and finally the increased segregation of deviants and dependents into 'asylums': mental hospitals, prisons, reformatories and other such closed, purpose-built institutions for treatment and punishment. The theorists of these transformations each place a somewhat different emphasis on just what happened and just why it happened, but all are agreed on its essentials.[2]

The most extraordinary of these three features to explain – the other two being, in a sense, self evident in the development of the modern state – is the growth of the asylum and its subsequent survival despite one and a half centuries of failure. Any account of the current and future place of incarceration, must come to terms with that original historical transformation.[3]

We are now living through what *appears* to be a reversal of this first Great Transformation. The ideological consensus about the desirability and necessity of the segregative asylum – questioned before but never really undermined[4] – has been broken. The attack on prisons (and more dramatically and with more obvious results on mental hospitals) became widespread from the mid nineteen-sixties, was found throughout the political spectrum and was partially reflected in such indices as declining rates of imprisonment. At the end of the eighteenth century, asylums and prisons were places of the *last* resort; by the mid-19th century they became places of the *first* resort, the preferred solution to problems of deviancy and dependency. By the end of the 1960s they looked like once again becoming places of the *last* resort. The extraordinary notion of abolition, rather than mere reform became common talk. With varying degrees of enthusiasm and actual measurable consequences, officials in Britain, the United States and some Western European countries, became committed to the policy labelled 'decarceration': the state-sponsored closing down of asylums, prisons and reformatories. This apparent reversal of the Great Incarcerations of the nineteenth century was hailed as the beginning of a golden age – a form of utopianism whose ironies cannot escape anyone with an eye on history: 'There is a curious historical irony here, for the *adoption* of the asylum, whose *abolition* is now supposed to be attended with such universally beneficent consequences, aroused an almost precisely parallel set of millenial expectations among its advocates'.[5]

The irony goes even further. For just at the historical moment when every commonplace critique of 'technological' or 'post-industrial' or 'mass' society mourned the irreplaceable loss of the traditional *Gemeinschaft* community, so a new mode of deviancy control was advocated whose success rested on this very same notion of community. Indeed the decarceration movement derives its rhetoric from a much wider constituency than is implied by limited questions of how far should imprisonment be used. It touches on issues about centralization, professionalization, the rehabilitative ideal, and the limits of state intervention. The current (variously labelled) 'pessimism', 'scepticism', or 'nihilism' about prisons, draws on all these wider themes.[6]

In the literature on community treatment itself,[7] two sets of assumptions are repeated with the regularity of a religious catechism. The first set is seen either as a matter of common sense, 'what everybody knows' or the irrefutable result of empirical research: 1) prisons and juvenile institutions are (in the weak version) simply ineffective: they neither successfully deter nor rehabilitate. In the strong version, they actually make things worse by strengthening criminal commitment; 2) community alternatives are much less costly and 3) they are more humane than any institution can be – prisons are cruel, brutalizing and beyond reform. Their time has come. Therefore: community alternatives 'must obviously be better', 'should at least be given a chance' or 'can't be worse'.

The second set of assumptions appeal to a number of sociological and political beliefs not as self evident as the previous set, but taken by the believer to be just as well established: 1) theories of stigma and labelling have demonstrated that the further the deviant is processed into the system, the harder it is to return him to normal life – 'therefore' measures designed to minimize penetration into the formal system and keep the deviant in the community as long as possible are desirable; 2) the causal processes leading to most forms of deviance originate in society (family, community, school, economic system) – 'therefore' prevention and cure must lie in the community and not in artificially created agencies constructed on a model of individual intervention; 3) liberal measures, such as reformatories, the juvenile court and the whole rehabilitative model are politically suspect, whatever the benevolent motives which lie behind them. The state should be committed to be doing less harm rather than more good – 'therefore' policies such as decriminalization, diversion and decarceration should be supported.

It is the last of these beliefs which must be used to scrutinize them all – for why should community corrections itself, not be subjected to the very same suspicion about benevolent reform? A large dose of such scepticism, together with a much firmer location of the new movement in overall structural and political changes, is needed for a full-scale critique of community corrections. Such a critique – not the object of this paper – would have to note at least the following doubts:[8] 1) it is by no means clear, in regard to crime and delinquency at least, that decarceration has been taking place as rapidly as the ideology would have us believe; 2) it has not been established that any community alternative is more effective in reducing crime (through preventing recidivism) than traditional imprisonment; 3) nor are these new methods always dramatically cheaper and 4) the humanitarian rationale for the move from imprisonment may be unfounded for two (opposite) reasons: a) decarceration may indeed lead to something like non-intervention or benign neglect: services are withdrawn and deviants are left neglected or exploited by private operators; b) alternatively, new forms of intervention result, which are often difficult to distinguish from the old institutions and reproduce in the community the very same coercive features of the system they were designed to replace.

However cogent this emergent critique might be, though, it comes from the margins of contemporary 'corrections'. Perhaps more than in any other area of social policy, crime and delinquency control has always allowed such doubts to be neutralized in the tidal wave of enthusiasm for any new 'reform'. There is little doubt that the rhetoric and ideology of community control is quite secure. And – whatever may be happening to overall rates of incarceration – most industrialized countries will continue to see a proliferation of various schemes in line with this ideology.

I shall take the term 'community control' to cover almost any form of formal social control outside the walls of traditional adult and juvenile institutions. There are two separate, but overlapping strategies: firstly, those various forms of intensive intervention located 'in the community': sentencing options which serve as intermediate alternatives to being sent to an institution or later options to release from institutions and secondly, those programs set up at some preventive, policing or pre-trial stage to divert offenders from initial or further processing by the conventional systems of justice. Behind these specific policies lies an overall commitment to almost anything which sounds like increasing community responsibility for the control of crime and delinquency.

BLURRING THE BOUNDARIES

The segregated and insulated institution made the actual business of deviancy control invisible, but it did make its boundaries obvious enough. Whether prisons were built in the middle of cities, out in the remote countryside or on deserted islands, they had clear spatial boundaries to mark off the normal from the deviant. These spatial boundaries were reinforced by ceremonies of social exclusion. Those outside could wonder what went on behind the walls, those inside could think about the 'outside world'. Inside/outside, guilty/innocent, freedom/captivity, imprisoned/released – these were all meaningful distinctions.

In today's world of community corrections, these boundaries are no longer as clear. There is, we are told, a 'correctional continuum' or a 'correctional spectrum': criminals and delinquents might be found anywhere in these spaces. So fine – and at the same time so indistinct – are the gradations along the continuum, that it is by no means easy to answer such questions as where the prison ends and the community begins or just why any deviant is to be found at any particular point. Even the most dedicated spokesmen for the community treatment have some difficulty in specifying just what 'the community' is; one N.I.M.H. Report confessed that the term community treatment: '. . . has lost all descriptive usefulness except as a code word with connotations of 'advanced correctional thinking' and implied value judgements against the "locking up" and isolation of offenders'.[9]

Even the most cursory examination of the new programs, reveals that many varieties of the more or less intensive and structured 'alternatives' are virtually indistinguishable from the real thing. A great deal of energy and ingenuity is being devoted to this problem of definition: just how isolated and confining does an institution have to be before it is a prison rather than, say a residential community facility? Luckily for us all, criminologists have got this matter well in hand and are spending a great deal of time and money on such questions. They are busy devising quantitative measures of indices such as degree of control, linkages, relationships, support – and we can soon look forward to standardized scales for assigning programs along an institutionalization-normalization continuum.[10]

But, alas, there are not just untidy loose ends which scientific research will one day tie up. The ideology of the new movement quite deliberately and explicitly demands that boundaries should not be made too clear. The metaphor of 'crumbling walls' implies an undifferentiated open space. The main British prison reform group, the Howard League, once called for steps to ' … restore the prison to the community and the community to the prison' and less rhetorically, here is an early enthusiast for a model 'Community Correction Centre':

> The line between being 'locked up' and 'free' is purposely indistinct because it must be drawn differently for each individual. Once the client is out of Phase I, where all clients enter and where they are all under essentially custodial control, he may be 'free' for some activities but still 'locked up' for others.[11]

There is no irony intended in using inverted commas for such words as 'free' and 'locked up' or in using such euphemisms as 'essentially custodial control'. This sort of blurring – deliberate or unintentional – may be found throughout the complicated networks of 'diversion' and 'alternatives' which are now being set up. The half-way house might serve as a good example. These agencies called variously, 'residential treatment centers', 'rehabilitation residences', 'reintegration centers' or (with the less flowery language preferred in Britain) simply 'hostels', invariably become special institutional domains themselves. They might be located in a whole range of odd settings – private houses, converted motels, the grounds of hospitals, the dormitories of university campuses or even within the walls of prisons themselves. Their programs[12] reproduce rules – for example about security, curfew, permitted visitors, drugs – which are close to those of the institution itself. Indeed it becomes difficult to distinguish a very 'open' prison – with liberal provisions for work release, home release, outside educational programs – from a very 'closed' half-way house. The house may be half-way *in* – for those too serious to be left at home, but not serious enough for the institution and hence a form of 'diversion' – or half-way *out* – for those who can be released from the institution but are not yet 'ready' for the open community, hence a form of 'after care'. To confuse the matter even further, the same center is sometimes used for both these purposes, with different rules for the half way in inmates and the half way out inmates.

Even this blurring and confusion is not enough: one advocate[13] draws attention to the advantages of *quarter-way* houses and *three-quarter* way houses. These 'concepts' we are told are already being used in the mental health field, but are not labelled as such in corrections. The quarter-way house deals with people who need supervision on a near permanent basis, while the three-quarter way house is designed to care for persons in an 'acute temporary crisis needing short term residential care and little supervision'. Then – taking the opposite tack from devising finer and finer classification schemes – other innovators argue for a multi-purpose center: some half-way houses already serve as a parolee residence, a drop-in center, a drug treatment program and a non-residential walk in center for after-care.

The fact that many of these multi-purpose centers are directed not just at convicted offenders, but are preventive, diagnostic or screening enterprises aimed at potential, pre-delinquents, or high risk populations, should alert us to the more important forms of blurring behind this administrative surrealism. The ideology of community treatment allows for a facile evasion of the delinquent/non-delinquent distinction. The British system of 'intermediate treatment' for example provides not just an intermediate possibility between sending the child away from home and leaving him in his normal home environment, but also a new way ' … to make use of facilities available to children who have not been before the courts, and so to secure the treatment of "children in trouble" in the company of other children through the sharing of activities and experiences within the community'.[14] There is a deliberate attempt to evade the question of whether a rule has been actually broken. While the traditional screening mechanism of the criminal justice system [has] always been influenced to a greater or lesser degree by non-offense related criteria (race, class, demeanour) the offense was at least considered. Except in the case of wrongful conviction, some law must have been broken. This is no longer clear: a delinquent may find himself in custody ('short term intensive treatment') simply because of program failure: he has violated the norms of some other agency in the continuum – for example, by not turning up to his therapy group, 'acting out', or being uncooperative.

We are seeing, then, not just the proliferation of agencies and services, finely calibrated in terms of degree of coerciveness or intrusion or unpleasantness. The uncertainties are more profound than this: voluntary or coercive, formal or informal, locked up or free, guilty or innocent. Those apparently absurd administrative and research questions – when is a prison a prison or a community a community? is the alternative an alternative? who is half-way in and who is three-quarter way out? – beckon to a future when it will be impossible to determine who exactly is emeshed in the social control system – and hence subject to its jurisdiction and surveillance – at any one time.

THINNING THE MESH AND WIDENING THE NET

On the surface, a major ideological thrust in the move against institutions derives from a desire to limit state intervention. Whether arising from the supposed failures of the treatment model, or the legal argument about the overreach of the law and the necessity to limit the criminal sanction, or the implicit non-interventionism of labelling theory, or a general disenchantment with paternalism, or simply the pragmatic case for easing the burdens on the system – the eventual message looked the same: the state should do less rather than more. It is ironical then – though surely the irony is too obvious even to be called this – that the major results of the new movements towards 'community' and 'diversion' have been to increase rather than decrease the *amount* of intervention directed at many groups of deviants in the system and, probably, to increase rather than decrease the total *number* who get into the system in the first place. In other words: 'alternatives' become not alternatives at all but new progams which supplement the existing system or else expand it by attracting new populations.

I will refer to these two overlapping possibilities as 'thinning the mesh' and 'widening the net' respectively. No one who has studied the results of such historical innovations as probation and parole should be surprised by either of these effects. As Rothman, for example, comments about the early twentieth century impact of the psychiatric ideology on the criminal justice system: ' … rationales and practices that initially promised to be less onerous nevertheless served to encourage the extension of state authority. The impact of the ideology was to expand intervention, not to restrict it'.[15]

The detailed processes through which the new community agencies are generating such expansion are not my concern here.[16] I will merely use the two strategies of 'alternatives' and 'diversion' to suggest how illusory is the notion that the new movement will lead to a lesser degree of formal social control.

Let us first examine community alternatives to incarceration. The key index of 'success' is not simply the proliferation of such programs, but the question of whether they are replacing or merely providing supplementary appendages to the conventional system of incarceration. The statistical evidence is by no means easy to decipher but it is clear, both from Britain and America, that rates of incarceration – particularly in regard to juveniles – are not at all declining as rapidly as one might expect and in some spheres are even increasing. Critically – as one evaluation suggests[17] the 'alternatives' are not, on the whole, being used for juveniles at the 'deep end' of the system, i.e. those who really would have been sent to institutions before. When the strategy is used for 'shallow end' offenders – minor or first offenders whose chances of incarceration would have been slight – then the incarceration rates will not be affected.

The exact proportions of these types are difficult to estimate: one English study of community service orders shows that only half the offenders sent would otherwise have received custodial sentences.[18] Leaving aside the question of the exact effects on the rest of the system, there is little doubt that a substantial number – perhaps the majority – of those subjected to the new programs, will be subjected to a degree of intervention higher than they would have received under previous non-custodial options like fines, conditional discharge or ordinary probation.

What all this means is that as long as the shallow end principle is used and as long as institutions are not literally closed down (as in the much publicized Massachusetts example) there is no guarantee either than incarceration will decrease dramatically or that the system will be less interventionist overall. The conclusion of the recent National Assessment of Juvenile Corrections holds true generally: although there are exceptions, 'in general as the number of community based facilities increases, the total number of youths incarcerated increases'.[19]

The paradox throughout all this that the more benign, attractive and successful the program is defined – especially if it uses the shallow end principle, as most do – the more it will be used and the wider it will cast its net.

Developing and administering community programs can be a source of gratification to sincere correctional administrators and lay volunteers who believe they are 'doing good' by keeping people out of dungeons and helping them obtain social services. Judges, reluctant to send difficult children to a reformatory and equally reluctant to release them without an assurance that something will be done to prevent them from returning may be especially enthusiastic about the development of alternative dispositions.[20]

Turning now to the more explicit forms of diversion, it is once again clear that the term, like the term "alternatives" is not quite what it implies. Diversion has been hailed as the most radical application of the non-intervention principle short of complete decriminalization. The grand rationale is to restrict the full force of the criminal justice process to more serious offences and to either eliminate or substantially minimize penetration for all others.[21] The strategy has received the greatest attention in the juvenile field: a remarkable development, because the central agency here, the juvenile court, was *itself* the product of a reform movement aimed at 'diversion'.

Clearly, all justice systems – particularly juvenile – have always contained a substantial amount of diversion. Police discretion has been widely used to screen juveniles: either right out of the system by dropping charges, informally reprimanding or cautioning, or else informal referral to social services agencies. What has now happened, to a large degree, is that these discretionary and screening powers have been formalized and extended – and in the process, quite transformed. The net widens to include those who, if the program had not been available would either not have been processed at all or would have been placed on options such as traditional probation. Again, the more benevolent the new agencies appear, the more will be diverted there by encouragement or coercion. And – through the blurring provided by the welfare net – this will happen to many not officially adjudicated as delinquent as well. There will be great pressure to work with parts of the population not previously 'reached'.

All this can be most clearly observed in the area of police diversion of juveniles. Where the police used to have two options – screen right out (the route for by far the *majority* of encounters) or process formally – they now have the third option of diversion into a program. Diversion can then be used as an alternative to screening and not an alternative to processing.[22] The proportion selected will vary. British research on police juvenile liaison schemes and similar measures[23] shows a clear widening of the net and one survey of eleven Californian diversion projects suggests that only 51 percent of clients were actually diverted from the system, with the rest receiving more processing than they would have received otherwise.[24] Another evaluation of 35 police departments running diversion programs concludes:

… the meaning of 'diversion' has been shifted from 'diversion from' to 'referral to'. Ironically, one of the ramifications of this is that in contrast to some earlier cited rationales for diversion as reducing costs, caseload and the purview of the criminal justice system, diversion may in fact be extending the costs, caseload and system purview even further than had previously been the case.[25]

The key to understanding this state of affairs lies in the distinction between *traditional* or *true* diversion – removing the juvenile from the system altogether by screening out (no further treatment, no service, no follow up) – and the *new* diversion which entails screening plus program: formal penetration is minimized by referral to programs in the system or related to it.[26] Only traditional diversion is true diversion in the sense of diverting *from*. The new diversion diverts – for better or worse – *into* the system. Cressey and McDermott's laconic conclusion from their evaluation of one such set of programs might apply more generally.

If 'true' diversion occurs, the juvenile is safely out of the official realm of the juvenile justice system and he is immune from incurring the delinquent label or any of its variations – pre-delinquent, delinquent tendencies, bad guy, hard core, unreachable. Further, when he walks out of the door from the person diverting him, he is technically free to tell the diverter to go to hell. We found very little 'true' diversion in the communities studied.[27]

To conclude this section: whatever the eventual pattern of the emergent social control system, it should be clear that such policies as 'alternatives' in no way represent a victory for the anti-treatment lobby or an 'application' of labelling theory. Traditional deviant populations are being processed in a different way or else new populations are being caught up in the machine. For some observers[28] all this is an index of how good theory produces bad practise: each level diverts to the next and at each level vested interests (like job security) ensures that few are diverted right out. And so the justice machine enlarges itself. This looks 'successful' in terms of the machine's own operational definition of success, but is a failure when compared to the theory from which the policy (supposedly) was derived.

Be this as it may, the new movement – in the case of crime and delinquency at least – has led to a more voracious processing of deviant populations, albeit in new settings and by professionals with different names. The machine might in some respects be getting softer, but it is not getting smaller (and probably not more efficient – but that's another story).

MASKING AND DISGUISING

The softness of the machine might also be more apparent than real. It became common place in historical analyses to suggest that the more benign parts of the system such as the juvenile court[29] masked their most coercive intentions and

consequences. This conclusion might apply with equal force to the current strategies of diversion and alternatives. Even more than their historical antecedents,
they employ a social work rather than legalistic rationale; they are committed to
the principle of blurring the boundaries of social control and they use the all-
purpose slogan of 'community' which cannot but sound benign.

There can be little doubt that the intentions behind the new movement
and – more to the point – its end results, are often humane, compassionate and
helpful. Most clients, deviants or offenders would probably prefer this new
variety to the stark option of the prison. But this argument is only valid if the
alternatives are real ones. The net-thinning and mesh-widening effects, though
indicate that the notion of alternatives can be misleading and mystifying. Note,
for example, the curious claim that agencies like half-way houses are justified
because they are just as successful in preventing crime as direct release into the
community. As Greenberg notes, however, when such alternatives are presented
as a condition of release from prison, ' … the contrast between the brutality of
the prison and the alleged humanitarianism of community corrections is
besides the point, because the community institution is not used to replace the
prison; instead the offender is exposed to both the prison and the community
"alternatives"'.[30]

Even when the alternatives *are* real ones, it is not self evident that they are
always more humane and less stigmatizing just because, in some sense they are
'in the community'. Community agencies, for example, might use a considerable
amount of more or less traditional custody and often without legal justification.
As the assessment of one experiment revealed:

> When subjects failed to comply with the norms of the intensive treatment regime, or
> even when a program agent believes subjects might fail to comply, then, as they say in
> the intensive treatment circles, detention may be indicated. Both these features, and the
> extensive use of home placements as well, suggest that the term 'community' like the
> term 'intensive treatment' may come to have a very special meaning in programs
> designed to deliver 'intensive treatment in the community'.[31]

Such disguised detention, though, is probably not a major overall source of
masking. More important is the bureaucratic generation of new treatment criteria which might allow for more unchecked coercion than at first appears. In a
system with low visibility, and low accountability, there is less room for such
niceties as due process and legal rights. Very often, for example, 'new diversion'
(minimization of penetration) occurs by deliberately avoiding due process: the
client proceeds through the system on the assumption or admission of guilt.
Indeed the deliberate conceptual blurring between 'diversion' and 'prevention'
explicitly calls for an increase in this sort of non-legal discretion.

All this, of course, still leaves open the question of whether the end result –
however mystifying some of the routes that led to it – is actually experienced as
more humane and helpful by the offender. There is little evidence either way on
this, beyond the rather bland common sense assumption that most offenders

would prefer not to be 'locked up'. What is likely, is that deep end projects – those that are genuine alternatives to incarceration – have to make a trade-off between treatment goals (which favour the integrated community setting) and security goals which favour isolation. The trade-off under these conditions will tend to favour security – resulting in programs which simulate or mimic the very features of the institution they set out to replace. Let us consider two somewhat different examples.

The first is Fort Des Moines, a 'Community Correctional Facility' which is part of a wider Community Corrections Program.[32] This is a 50 bed non-secure unit, housed in an ex-army base. The clients work in ordinary jobs outside and there is minimal physical security in the shape of bars or fences.

Here, though, are some of the security trade offs: 1) the low 'client-counsellor' ratio – one staff person for every two clients – allows for intensive 'informal observation' of the clients for security purposes. There is, for example, a 'staff desk person' who signs clients in and out, recording their attitudes and activities. There is also a 'floating staff person' who circulates throughout the institution, observing client behaviour, taking a count of all clients each hour (called the 'eye check') and recording the count in the log; 2) the client has to 'contract' to behave well and participate actively in his rehabilitation: the sanction of being returned to prison is always present. From the beginning of his stay (when he has to sign a waiver of privacy granting the program access to information in confidential agency files) he is closely scrutinized. Besides the obvious offences; like using drugs, fighting or trying to escape the failure to maintain 'a significant level of performance' is one of the most serious offenses a client can commit and results in immediate return to jail;[33] 3) the court retains jurisdiction over the client, receiving detailed rosters and program reports and having to authorize internal requests for work, schooling or furloughs. In addition, the local police and sheriffs departments receive weekly listings of the residents, indicating where each has to be at specified hours of each day. This information is available to patrol officers who may see inmates in the community.

These features – especially the complicated compulsory treatment process itself – suggests an intensity of intervention at least as great as that in most maximum security prisons. The commitment to a behaviourist conditioning program – a feature of many American versions of community treatment – is particularly insidious and is illustrated well in my second example, the Urbana-Champaign Adolescent Diversion Project.[34] This – unlike the first example – is genuinely enough in the community: juveniles considered as 'beyond lecture and release and clearly headed for court' are referred by the police to a program of behavioural contracting organized by a university psychology department. The volunteer staff monitor and mediate contractual agreements between the youth and his parents and teachers: privileges in return for complying with curfew, house chores and personal appearance. Here are extracts from a typical day in the life of Joe, a sixteen year old who had come to the attention of the juvenile division for possession of marijuana and violation of the municipal curfew laws:

Joe agrees to:	Joe's parents agree to:
1. Call home by 4:00 p.m. each afternoon and tell his parents his whereabouts and return home by 5:00 p.m.	1. Allow Joe to go out from 7:30 to 9:30 Monday through Thursday evening and ask about his companions without negative comment.
2. Return home by 12:00 mid-night on weekend nights.	2. Allow Joe to go out the subsequent weekend night.
3. Make his bed daily and clean his room daily (spread neat; clothes hung up).	3. Check his room each day and pay him 75 cents when cleaned.
4. Set table for dinner daily.	4. Deposit 75 cents per day in a savings account for Joe.

Bonus
If Joe performs at 80 percent or above of 1 through 4 above, his parents will deposit an additional 3 dollars in his account for each consecutive seven day period.

Sanction
If Joe falls below 60 percent in 1 and 2 above in any consecutive seven day period, he will cut two inches off his hair. Comments about the alleged 'humanitarianism' of this program are redundant.

MERGING PUBLIC AND PRIVATE
The notion that the state should be solely responsible for crime control only developed in England and America in the later part of the nineteenth century.

The key changes, then – the removal of prisons from private to public control and the creation of a uniformed public police force – are taken as the beginning of the continued and voracious absorption of deviancy control into the centralized apparatus of the state. Certainly the political and economic demands of industrial society have led to increasing state control in the form of laws, regulations, administrative and enforcement agencies.

At a somewhat different level, though, there are other developments – in line with the move from concentration to dispersal traced in this paper – which are going in a somewhat different direction. Indeed some observers – particularly in the case of the police, have gone as far as noting a tendency to the 'privatization of social control'.[35] While this might be an exaggeration, it is apparent that along with the other types of blurring, there has been some merging of the obviously public and formal apparatus of control with the private and less formal. The ideology of community implies this: on the one hand, the repressive, interventionist reach of the state should be blunted, on the other, the 'community' should become more involved in the day to day business of prevention and control.

It would be tempting – but too simple – to see this interpenetration of the public and private as going back, full circle to its earlier historical forms. The connections between crime control and contractual or other forms of profit making which emerged at the end of the seventeenth century, are not quite the same as today's versions of private control – nor can they ever be in the rationalized centralized state.

The increasing involvement, though – particularly in the United States – of private enterprise in the public service sector, is noteworthy enough. Indeed in Scull's analysis decarceration itself is attributed to a fiscal crisis: the state divests itself of expensive crime control functions allowing private enterprise to process deviant populations for profit. This is readily observable in the case of private clinics, hospitals or welfare hotels for the old and mentally ill, where private agencies either serve their 'own' clientele or function under licence or contract from the state.

In the areas of crime and delinquency it is not quite as clear how ' … the spheres of public and private actually have become progressively, less distinct'.[36] The term privatization does not fully cover the complicated ways in which the new community alternatives relate to the system from which they are supposedly diverting. In some cases, there *is* clear privatization in the form of half-way houses, hostels, group homes or fostering schemes being run for private profit. But the fate of most private agencies in this area – especially if they prove successful – is to become co-opted and absorbed into the formal state apparatus. This has happened even to radical self-help organizations which originated in an antagonistic relationship to the system. In the case of diversion, the ideal non-legal agency (free from system control, client oriented, with voluntary participation, independent of sponsor's pressure) often becomes like the various 'para-legal' agencies closely connected to the system and dependent on it for space, referrals, accountability and sponsorship.[37] Various compromises on procedure are made as temporary tactics to deflect suspicion and criticism, but are then institutionalized. The private agency expands, for example, by asking for public funding and in turn might change its screening criteria to fit the official system's demands. It becomes increasingly difficult to assign the status of private or public to these agencies.

At the same time as private agencies find it difficult not to be co-opted, the public sector responds to pressures (some fiscal and some sincerely deriving from the community ideology) by using more private resources, especially in the form of volunteers. Ex-offenders treat offenders, indigenous community residents are recruited to probation or voluntary 'big brother' type schemes, family members and teachers are used in behavioural contracting programs or university students take on counselling functions as part of their course work.

All this is a fairly long way removed from the pre-nineteenth century forms of privatization. The closest parallels to this might be in the area of policing. In both Britain and the United States private policing has become a massive industry. In the United States, private police outnumber their counterparts in the public sector – a growth attributed to the increasing involvement of the ordinary police in human services 'dirty work', leaving large corporations dependent on private protective and investigative services in areas such as pilferage, security checks, industrial espionage and credit card scrutiny.

Alongside all this, there have been changes in police methods which have some other curious historical parallels – to the time when the dividing lines between the civilian population and a uniformed, centralized police force were not at all clear. There has been considerable expansion in the use of informers, secret agents, undercover work, agents provocateurs – all those disguised operations in which the police are made to look more like citizens and citizens more like the police. There is a great deal of evidence about the infiltration of social movements by informers and agents provocateurs[38] while undercover work and entrapment in the field of victimless crime or vice (drugs, gambling, prostitution) has become – if this is not a contradiction – open knowledge. Here, police work is less re-active than pro-active: aimed at anticipating and preventing crimes not yet committed through such methods as police posing as criminals (prostitutes, fences, pornographic book dealers) or as victims (for example, as elderly citizens to attract mugging).

Leaving aside the surrealistic possibilities this opens up (agents who are themselves under surveillance selling drugs to and arresting other agents), and the implications for civil liberties and conceptions of trust and privacy[39] it directs attention to further twists and ambiguities in the already complex relationship between deviance and social control. While some parts of police work are becoming more underground and secretive, others are trying to reach out more openly into the wider community. Schemes for 'community based preventive policing' are now well established in Britain and America. Community relations officers, juvenile liaison bureaus, school-linked officers are all involved in establishing closer links with the community, humanizing the face of police work and encouraging early reporting and surveillance. Official law enforcement agencies also actively support various projects aimed at encouraging early reporting of crime through such methods as building up neighbourhood 'whistle alert networks' or citizen band radio reporting. A more obvious form of privatization is the development of unofficial residents patrols to maintain surveillance over neighbourhoods as well as mediating between the police and residents.[40]

It might be premature to cite these developments as heralding a quite new mode of law enforcement. The appeal of the ideology of citizen involvement in crime prevention, though, is strong and shares the very same roots as the broader movement to the community. Here is an official version:

> … Crime prevention as each citizen's duty is not a new idea. In the early days of law enforcement well over a thousand years ago (sic) the peacekeeping system encouraged the concept of mutual responsibility. Each individual was responsible not only for his actions but for those of his neighbours. A citizen observing a crime had the duty to rouse his neighbours and pursue the criminal. Peace was kept for the most part, not by officials but by the whole community.[41]

Needless to say, today's forms of peacekeeping by the community are not quite the same as those golden days of 'mutual responsibility'. Closed circuit television, two way radios, vigilante patrols and police decoys hardly emulate life in a pre-industrial village. This is not for want of trying. In some large stores, private security police are posing as employees. They conspicuously steal and are then conspicuously 'discovered' by the management and ceremonially disciplined, thus deterring the real employees. They then presumably move on to stage somewhere else another such Durkheimian ceremony of social control.

ABSORPTION, PENETRATION, RE-INTEGRATION

The asylum represented not just isolation and confinement – like quarantining the infected – but a ritual of physical exclusion. Without the possibility of actual banishment to another society, the asylum had to serve the classic social function of scapegoating. The scapegoat of ancient legend was an animal driven to the wilderness, bearing away the sins of the community.

In the new ideology of corrections, there is no real or symbolic wilderness – just the omnipresent community into which the deviant has to be unobtrusively 'integrated' or 'reintegrated'. The blurring of social control implies both the deeper penetration of social control into the social body and the easing of any measures of exclusion, or status degradation. For the apologists of the new corrections the word 're-integration' has a magic ring. Thus Empey[42] argues that we are in the middle of a third revolution in corrections: the first from Revenge to Restraint (in the first part of the nineteenth century), the second from Restraint to Reformation (from the late nineteenth to the early twentieth century) – and now from Reformation to Re-integration. Leaving aside the historical inaccuracy of this sequence, it does not actually tell us what this new utopia will look like.

In the most immediate sense, what is being proposed is a greater direct involvement of the family, the school and various community agencies in the day to day business of prevention, treatment, and resocialization. This implies something more profound than simply using more volunteers or increasing reporting rates. It implies some sort of reversal of the presumption in positivist criminology that the delinquent is a different and alien being. Deviance rather is with us, woven into the fabric of social life and it must be 'brought back home'. Parents, peers, schools, the neighbourhood, even the police should dedicate themselves to keeping the deviant out of the formal system. He must be absorbed back into the community and not processed by official agencies.[43]

The central role allocated to the family – part of the broader movement of the rediscovery of the family in sociology and social policy – is a good example of the integration ideology. Well established methods such as foster care, substitute homes and family placements are being extended and one enthusiast looks forward to ' … the day when middle class American families actually wanted in large numbers to bring juvenile and pre-delinquent youths into their homes as a service commitment'.[44] The family having a delinquent living with them is seen as a remarkable correctional resource' for the future. In Britain and Scandinavia a number of alternative systems of family placement besides salaried foster parents have been tried – for example 'together at home', the system of intensive help in Sweden in which social workers spend hours sharing the family's life and tasks. Alongside these diversionary alternatives, parents and schools are also encouraged to react sooner to early signs of trouble.

Going beyond the family setting, the stress on community absorption has found one of its most attractive possibilities in the system of community service orders developed in England. Under this system, offenders are sentenced to useful supervised work in the community: helping in geriatric wards, driving disabled people around, painting and decorating the houses of various handicapped groups, building children's playgrounds, etc. This is a particularly attractive scheme because it appeals not just to the soft ideology of community absorption, but the more punitive objectives of restitution and compensation.

Needless to say, there are profound limits to the whole ideology of integration – as indeed there are to all such similar patterns I have described. The 'community' – as indicated by the standard local reaction to say, half-way houses or day centers being located in their own neighbourhood – is not entirely enthusiastic about such 'integration'. In the immediate future the segregation of the deviant will remain as the central part of the control apparatus. The established professionals, agencies and service bureaucracies are not going to give up so easily their hard won empires of 'expertise' and identity in the name of some vague notion of integration. Nevertheless at the rhetorical and ideological levels, the move to a new model of deviancy control has been signalled. On this level at least, it may not be too dramatic to envisage the distinction between cannibalism and anthropemy becoming less relevant:

> If we studied societies from the outside, it would be tempting to distinguish two contrasting types: those which practise cannibalism – that is which regard the absorption of certain individuals possessing dangerous powers as the only means of neutralising those powers and even of turning them to advantage – and those which, like our own society, adopt what might be called the practice of anthropemy (from the Greek 'èmai', to vomit); faced with the same problem the latter type of society has chosen the opposite solution, which consists of ejecting dangerous individuals from the social body and keeping them temporarily or permanently in isolation, away from all contact with their fellows, in establishments especially intended for this purpose.[45]

CONCLUSION – TOWARDS THE PUNITIVE CITY

These emerging patterns of social control – dispersal, penetration, blurring, absorption, widening – must be seen as no more than patterns: representations or models of what is yet to be fully constructed. Historians of social policy can use the emergent final system to validate their reading of such early, tentative patterns; the student of contemporary policy has no such luxury. The largest question mark must hang over the future role of the prison itself in the total system. The rhetoric of community control is now unassailable, but it is not yet clear how *far* the prison will be supplemented and complemented by these new forms of control.

It is, eventually, the sheer proliferation and elaboration of these other systems of control – rather than the attack on prison itself – which impresses. What is happening is a literal reproduction on a wider societal level of those astonishingly complicated systems of classification – the 'atlases of vice' – inside the nineteenth century prison. New categories and sub-categories of deviance and control are being created under our eyes. All these agencies – legal and quasi-legal, administrative and professional – are marking out their own territories of jurisdiction, competence and referral. Each set of experts produces its own 'scientific' knowledge: screening devices, diagnostic tests, treatment modalities, evaluation scales. All this creates new categories and the typifications which fill them: where there was once talk about the 'typical' prisoner, first offender or hardened recidivist, now there will be typical 'clients' of half-way houses, or community correctional centers, typical divertees or predelinquents. These creatures are then fleshed out – in papers, research proposals, official reports – with sub-systems of knowledge and new vocabularies: locking up becomes 'intensive placement', dossiers become 'anecdotal records', rewards and punishments become 'behavioural contracts'.

The enterprise justifies itself: there is hardly any point in asking about 'success' – this is not the object of the exercise. Research is done on the classification system *itself* – working out a 'continuum of community basedness', prediction tables, screening devices – and one does not ask for a classification system to 'work'. In one massive American enterprise,[46] some 10 Federal agencies, 31 task forces and 93 experts got together simply to study the ways of classifying various problem groups of children.

The overwhelming impression is one of bustling, almost *frenzied* activity: all these wonderful new things are being done to this same old group of trouble-makers (with a few new ones allowed in). It might not be too far fetched to imagine an urban ethnographer of the future, that proverbial Martian anthro-pologist studying a day in the life of this strange new tribe, filing in a report something like this:[47]

Mr. and Mrs. Citizen, their son Joe and daughter Linda, leave their suburban home after breakfast, saying goodbye to Ron, a fifteen year pre-delinquent who is living with them under the LAK (Look After a Kid) scheme. Ron will later take a bus downtown to the Community Correctional Center, where he is to be given two hours of Vocational Guidance and later tested on the Interpersonal Maturity Level Scale. Mr. C. drops Joe off at the School Problems Evaluation Center from where Joe will walk to school. In his class are five children who are bussed from a local Community Home, four from a Pre-Release Facility and three, who, like Ron live with families in the neighbourhood. Linda gets off next – at the GUIDE Center (Girls Unit for Intensive Daytime Education) where she works as a Behavioural Contract Mediator. They drive past a Threequarter-way House, a Rape Crisis Center and then a Drug Addict Cottage, where Mrs. C. waves to a group of boys working in the garden. She knows them from some volunteer work she does in RODEO (Reduction of Delinquency Through Expansion of Opportunities). She gets off at a building which houses the Special Intensive Parole Unit, where she is in charge of a five year evaluation research project on the use of the HIM (Hill Interaction Matrix) in matching group treatment to client. Mr. C. finally arrives at work, but will spend his lunch hour driving around [in] the car again as this is his duty week on patrol with TIPS (Turn in a Pusher).

Meantime, back in the ghetto …

The logic of this master pattern – dispersal, penetration, spreading out – as opposed to its particular current forms, is not at all new. Its antecedents can be traced though, not to the model which its apologists cite – the idyllic preindustrial rural community – but to a somewhat later version of social control, a version which *in theory* was an alternative to the prison. When, from the end of the eighteenth century, punishment started entering deeper into the social body, the alternative vision to the previous great concentrated spectacles of public torture, was of the dispersal of control through 'hundreds of tiny theatres of punishment'.[48] The eighteenth century reformers dreamed of dispersal and diversity but this vision of the punitive city was never to be fully realized. Instead punishment became concentrated in the coercive institution, a single uniform penalty to be varied only in length. The earlier 'projects of docility' which Foucault describes – the techniques of order, discipline and regulation developed in schools, monasteries, workshops, the army – could only serve as models. Panopticism (surveillance, discipline) began to spread: as disciplinary establishments increased, ' … *their* mechanisms have a certain tendency to become 'de-institutionalized', to emerge from the closed fortresses in which they once functioned and to circulate in a "free" state; the massive compact disciplines are broken down into flexible methods of control, which may be transferred and adapted'.[49]

This principle of 'indefinite discipline' – judgements, examinations and observations which would never end – represented the new mode of control as much as the public execution had represented the old. Only in the prison, though, could this utopia be realized in a pure physical form. The 'new" move into the community is merely a continuation of the overall pattern established in the nineteenth century. The proliferation of new experts and professionals, the generation of specialized domains of scientific knowledge, the creation of complicated classification systems, the establishment of a network of agencies surrounding the court and the prison – all these developments marked the beginning a century ago of the widening of the 'carceral circle' or 'carceral archipelago'.

The continuous gradation of institutions then – the 'correctional continuum' – is not new. What is new is the scale of the operation and the technologies (drugs, surveillance and information gathering techniques) which facilitate the blurring and penetration which I described. Systems of medicine, social work, education, welfare take on supervisory and judicial functions, while the penal apparatus itself becomes more influenced by medicine, education, psychology.[50] This new system of subtle gradations in care, control, punishment and treatment is indeed far from the days of public execution and torture – but it is perhaps not quite as far as

Foucault suggests from that early reform vision of the punitive city. The ideology of community is trying once more to increase the visibility – if not the theatricality – of social control. True, we must not know quite what is happening – treatment or punishment, public or private, locked up or free, inside or outside, voluntary or coercive – but we must know that something is happening, here, in our very own community.

An obvious question: is all this good or bad? Most of us – consciously or not – probably hold a rather bleak view of social change. Things must be getting worse. My argument has obviously tilted towards this view of the world by dwelling on the undesirable consequences – some unintended and others not too unintended – of the emerging social control system. The consequent series of all-purpose radical assumptions, though – that things must always be getting worse; that all reforms, however well intentioned ultimately lead to more repression and coercion; that industrial capitalism contains the seeds of its own destruction – need some correction. Undoubtedly some programs of community treatment or diversion are genuine alternatives to incarceration and in addition are more humane and less intrusive. Sometimes the programs might succeed in avoiding the harsh effects of early stigmatization and brutalization. In addition, all these terrible sounding 'agents of social control' instead of being disguised paratroopers of the state, might be able to deploy vastly improved opportunities and resources to offer help and service to groups which desperately need them. These possibilities must not be ignored for a minute, nor should the possibility that from the delinquent or criminal's own subjective personal experience, these new programs might indeed be preferable – whatever the overall consequences as depicted by any outside sociologist.

Many of these possibilities are yet to be resolved by more or less empirical evidence. But in the long run – as they say – social control is in the interests of the collective, not the individual. It could hardly be otherwise.

NOTES

1   In the United States, some recent and explicit versions of this disenchantment – framed in the language of embittered liberalism – may be found in the various essays in Gaylin, W. et al (1978). *Doing Good: The Limits of Benevolence*, New York: Pantheon Books. In Britain, despite the fact that substantial cuts in welfare services have occurred, the commitment to the welfare state is more entrenched and consequently a liberal disenchantment with 'doing good' has not yet surfaced.

2   Rusche, G. and Kircheimer, O. (1938). *Punishment and Social Structure*, New York: Russell and Russell; Foucault, M. (1967). *Madness and Civilisation*, London: Tavistock and (1977). *Discipline and Punish: The Birth of the Prison*, London: Allen Lane; Rothman, D. J. (1971). *The Discovery of the Asylum*, Boston: Little Brown.

3   For various relevant attempts, see Cohen, S. (1977). 'Prisons and the Future of Control Systems' in M. Fitzgerald et al (eds.) *Welfare in Action*, London: Routledge, pp. 217–228; Scull, A. (1977). *Decarceration: Community Treatment and the Deviant*, London: Prentice Hall; and Rothman, D. 'Behavioural Modification in Total Institutions: A Historical Overview', *Hastings Centre Report*, 5: 17–24.

4   Scull, op. cit., documents both the presence at the end of the nineteenth century of the equivalent of today's liberal/social scientific critique of institutions and the reasons for the failure of this earlier attack. For him, the origins of current policy lie in certain changing features of welfare capitalism. Crudely expressed; it no longer 'suits' the state to maintain segregative modes of control based on the asylum. In relative terms (and hence the appeal to fiscal conservatives) such modes become costly, while the alternative of welfare payments allowing subsistence in the community, is easier to justify and can be sold on humanitarian and scientific grounds. Scull's argument is a useful corrective to accounts purely at the level of ideas, but it places too much importance on the supposed fiscal crisis, it is less relevant to Britain and America and far less relevant for crime and delinquency than mental illness. In regard to crime and delinquency the picture is not the non-interventionist one Scull implies but – as this paper suggests – the development of parallel systems of control.

5   Scull, op. cit., p. 42.

6   See Gaylin et al, op. cit. and Von Hirsh, A. (1976). *Doing Justice: The Choice of Punishments*, New York: Hill and Wang.

7   The most informative sources in the United States would be journals such as *Crime and Delinquency* and *Federal Probation* from the mid-sixties onwards and the various publications from bodies such as the National Institute of Mental Health and, later, the Law Enforcement Assistance Administration. A representative collection of such material is Perlstein, G. R. and Phelps, T. R. (eds.) (1975). *Alternatives to Prison: Community Based Corrections*, Pacific Palisades, Calif: Goodyear Pulishing Co., in Britain the ideology of community control has been slower and less obvious in its development, though it can be traced in various Home Office publications from the end of the nineteen sixties. See also Blom-Cooper, L. (ed.) (1974). *Progress in Penal Reform*, Oxford: Oxford University Press and Tutt, N. (ed.) (1978). *Alternative Strategies for Coping with Crime*, Oxford: Basil Blackwell.

8   Some of these may be found in Scull, op. cit. and Greenberg, D. F. (1975). 'Problems in Community Corrections', *Issues in Criminology*, 10: 1–33.

9   National Institute of Mental Health (1971). *Community Based Correctional Programs: Models and Practices*, Washington, D.C.: U.S. Government Printing Office, p.1.

10 Coates, R. B., et al (1976). 'Social Climate, Extent of Community Linkages and Quality of Community Linkages: The Institutionalisation Normalisation Continuum' unpublished Ms., Centre for Criminal Justice, Harvard Law School.

11 Bradley, H. B. (1969). 'Community Based Treatment for Young Adult Offenders', *Crime and Delinquency*, 15 (3): 369.

12 For a survey, see Seiter, R. P. et al (1977). *Halfway House*, Washington, D.C.: National Institute of Law Enforcement and Criminal Justice, L.E.A.A.

13 Fox, V. (1977). *Community Based Corrections*, Englewood Cliffs: Prentice Hall, pp. 62–63.

14 Hinton, N. (1974). 'Intermediate Treatment' in Blom Cooper (ed.) op. cit., p. 239.

15 Rothman (1975), op. cit., p. 19.

16 The most exhaustive research here deals with the two Californian projects – Community Treatment and Probation Subsidy – widely hailed as exemplars of the new strategy. See, especially Lerman, P. (1975). *Community Treatment and Social Control: A Critical Analysis of Juvenile Correctional Policy*, Chicago: University of Chicago Press and Messinger, S. (1976). 'Confinement in the Community: A Selective Assessment of Paul Lerman's "Community Treatment and Social Control"', *Journal of Research in Crime and Delinquency*, 13 (1): 82–92. Another standard Californian study of the diversion strategy is Cressey, D. and McDermott, R. A. (1974). *Diversion from the Juvenile*

Justice System, Washington, D.C.: National Institute of Law Enforcement and Criminal Justice, L.E.A.A. For two useful general evaluations of the field, see Rutherford, A. and Bengur, O. (1976). *Community Based Alternatives to Juvenile Incarceration*, Washington, D.C.: National Institute of Law Enforcement and Criminal Justice, L.E.A.A.; Rutherford, A. and McDermott, R. (1976). *Juvenile Diversion*, Washington, D.C.: National Institute of Law Enforcement and Criminal Justice, L.E.A.A.

17 Rutherford and Bengur, op. cit.

18 Pease, K. (1977). *Community Service Assessed in 1976*, Home Office Research Unit Study No. 39, London: H.M.S.O.

19 Quoted in Rutherford and Bengur, op. cit., p. 30.

20 Greenberg, op. cit., p. 23.

21 A clear statement of this rationale and the legal problems in implementing it, is to be found in Law Reform Commission of Canada (1975). *Working Paper No. 7: Diversion*, Ottawa: Law Reform Commission of Canada.

22 Dunford, F. W. (1977). 'Police Diversion – An Illusion?', *Criminology*, 15 (3): 335–352.

23 Morris, A. (1978). 'Diversion of Juvenile Offenders from the Criminal Justice System' in Tu (ed.), op. cit., pp. 50–54.

24 Bohnstedt, M. (1978). 'Answers to Three Questions about Juvenile Diversion', *Journal of Research in Crime and Delinquency*, 15 (1): 10.

25 Klein, M. W. et al (1976). 'The Explosion in Police Diversion Programmes: Evaluating the Structural Dimensions of a Social Fad', in M. W. Klein (ed.) *The Juvenile Justice System*, Beverly Hills: Sage, p. 10.

26 Rutherford and McDermott, op. cit.

27 Cressey and McDermott, op. cit., pp. 3–4.

28 Rutherford and McDermott, op. cit., pp. 25–26.

29 See, especially, Platt, A. M. (1969). *The Child Savers: The Invention of Delinquency*, Chicago: Chicago University Press.

30 Greenberg, op. cit., p. 8.

31 Messinger, op. cit., pp. 84–85.

32 Boorkman, D. et al (1976). *An Exemplary Project: Community Based Corrections in Des Moines*, Washington, D.C.: National Institute of Law Enforcement and Criminal Justice, L.E.A.A.

33 Ibid., pp. 35–36.

34 Ku, R. and Blew, C. (1977). *A University's Approach to Delinquency Prevention: The Adolescent Diversion Project*, Washington, D.C.: National Institute of Law Enforcement and Criminal Justice, L.E.A.A.

35 Spitzer, S. and Scull, A. T. (1977a). 'Social Control in Historical Perspective: From Private to Public Responses to Crime' in D. F. Greenberg (ed.) *Corrections and Punishment*, Beverley Hills: Sage, pp. 265–286 and Spitzer, S. and Scull, A. T. (1977b), 'Privatisation and Capitalist Development: The Case of the Private Police', *Social Problems*, 25 (1): 18–29.

36 Spitzer and Scull (1977a) op. cit., p. 265.

37 For a description of this process, see Rutherford and McDermott, op. cit.

38 Marx, G. T. (1974). 'Thoughts on a Neglected Category of Social Movement Participant: The Agent Provocateur and Informant', *American Journal of Sociology*, 80 (2): 402–442.

39 Marx, G. T. (1977). 'Undercover Cops: Creative Policing or Constitutional Threat?', *Civil Liberties Review*, pp. 34–44.

40 For approved examples of these new forms of policing, see Bickman, L. et al (1977). *Citizen Crime Reporting Projects*, Washington, D.C.: National Institute of Law

Enforcement and Administration of Justice and Yin, R. K. et al (1977). *Citizen Patrol Projects*, Washington, D.C.: National Institute of Law Enforcement and Criminal Justice, L.E.A.A.

41 National Advisory Commission on Criminal Justice Standards and Goals (1973). *Community Crime Prevention*, Washington, D.C.: U.S. Government Printing Office, p. 7.

42 Empey, L. T. (1967). *Alternatives to Incarceration*, Washington, D.C.: U.S. Government Printing Office.

43 For typical statements about absorption, see Carter, R. M. (1972). 'The Diversion of Offenders', *Federal Probation*, 36 (4): 31–36.

44 Skoler, D. (1975). 'Future Trends in Juvenile and Adult Community Based Corrections' in Perlstein and Phelps (eds.), op. cit., p. 11.

45 Levi Strauss, C. (1977). *Tristes Tropiques*, Harmondsworth: Penguin, p. 508.

46 Hobbs, N. (1975). *Issues in the Classification of Children*, San Francisco: Jossey Bass Publishers.

47 Strangers to the world of community corrections should be informed that all the projects named in this imaginary report are *real* and current.

48 Foucault (1977), op. cit., p. 113.

49 Ibid., p. 211.

50 Ibid., p. 306.

42

From the Panopticon to Disney World: the development of discipline

Clifford D. Shearing and Philip C. Stenning

In the literature on punishment an interesting and important debate has recently surfaced on the question of whether modern penal developments in the criminal justice system represent an extension of discipline (in the sense in which Foucault used the term) or a move away from it. In an influential article published in 1979, Cohen argued that modern penal practices provide evidence of a significant 'dispersal of social control', in which the community is increasingly being involved in its administration. He also claimed, however, that this dispersal of social control is 'merely a continuation of the overall pattern established in the nineteenth century' (p. 359), and described by Foucault, in which corporal punishment (based on the administration of pain and torture to the body) was replaced by carceral punishment (based on the exercise of sustained discipline over the soul).

In an incisive critique of Cohen's thesis, Bottoms has recently sought to show – successfully in our view – that while Cohen's conclusion that modern penal developments represent a significant dispersal of social control is correct, his conclusion that these developments are an extension of disciplinary punishment is not. Specifically, Bottoms argued that the most significant recent developments in penal practice – the greatly increased use of the fine, the growth of community service orders and the modern resort to compensation and related matters – are not essentially disciplinary in character. In making this argument, Bottoms makes the point that these new modes of punishment lack the element of 'soul-training' which is the essential hallmark of disciplinary carceral punishment. He

From *Perspectives in Criminal Law* (eds A. Doob and E. Greenspan), pp. 335–49. (Ontario: Canada Law Book Inc., 1985.)

went on to speculate that this move away from disciplinary punishment within the criminal justice system may have been made possible, and encouraged, because more effective preventative social control measures are being implemented within the general society outside the criminal justice system. This latter system, the argument goes, is increasingly being regarded only as a 'last resort' in social control, and as a result 'juridical' rather than disciplinary carceral punishments are being resorted to within it (Bottoms, 1983: 187–8, 191, 195).

Thus far, Bottoms's argument is entirely consistent with similar arguments we have made in our explanations of the implications for social control of the modern growth of private security and private control systems (Shearing and Stenning, 1983). These, we have contended, are preventative rather than punitive in character, rely heavily on strategies of disciplinary control, and make resort to the more punitively orientated public criminal justice system only as a last resort when their own strategies have failed to achieve their instrumentally conceived objectives.

Bottoms, however, went on to argue that we, too, are wrong to characterize such private control systems as disciplinary in the Foucauldian sense. This, he wrote, was because the systems we described lack the essential ingredient of discipline, which he characterized as '"the mechanics of training" upon the bodies and souls of individuals' (Bottoms, 1983: 182). Work by Mathiesen (1980, 1983), in which he characterized modern trends away from individualism as the organizing focus of social control, and towards 'surveillance of whole categories of people' as 'a change from open to hidden discipline', was criticized by Bottoms for the same reasons (Bottoms, 1983: 181–2). In both cases, he argued that the mere extension of *surveillance*, without the accompanying individualized soul-training, does not constitute 'discipline' as Foucault intended the term.

The explicit assumption which Bottoms makes in thus characterizing modern non-penal systems of social control as not 'disciplinary', is that 'discipline' necessarily involves individualized soul-training. In this essay, we shall seek to argue that the concept of 'discipline', as used by Foucault, is much broader than this, and is appropriate to describe many modern forms of social control which do not apparently have individualized soul-training as their primary organizing focus. More particularly, we shall argue that the identification of discipline with individualized soul-training reflects a failure adequately to distinguish between Foucault's generic concept of discipline and his more historically specific examination of it in the context of carceral punishment. Having made this argument, the essay will conclude with an examination of a popular modern exemplar of non-carceral disciplinary social control which, we believe, represents an important indication of what the 'social control apparatus of society is actually getting up to' (Cohen, 1979: 339).

DISCIPLINE AND CARCERAL PUNISHMENT

Central to Foucault's argument in *Discipline and Punish* is his contention that discipline as a generic form of power should be distinguished from the particular strategies through which it is expressed at any particular time.

'Discipline' may be identified neither with an institution nor with an apparatus; it is a type of power, a modality for its exercise, comprising a whole set of instruments, techniques, procedures, levels of application, targets; it is a 'physics' or anatomy of power, technology. (1977: 215)

This distinction between discipline, as a type of power, and its particular expression, is important for it allows for the possibility of the evolution of discipline through a series of different concrete expressions. Given this distinction it becomes apparent that carceral punishment, as exemplified in Bentham's Panopticon, should be seen as an instance of discipline that seeks compliance through individual soul-training. It is, however, only one possible expression, albeit the one that occupied Foucault's attention.

What, then, are the essential characteristics of 'discipline' as a generic concept? There can be no doubt that training of one sort or another is an objective if not an explicit element of 'discipline'. Indeed, the very derivation of the word (from the Latin *disciplina* = instruction, tuition) confirms this. The nature of such training, however, and the manner in which it is accomplished, will vary accordingly to the context in which discipline is applied. Of this we shall say more in a moment. For Foucault, there was another essential characteristic of discipline – namely, that it is a type of power that is embedded in, and dispersed through, the micro relations that constitute society. Unlike monarchical power (which is expressed through terror and torture) it is not located outside and above the social relations to be controlled but is integrated into them. As it is part of the social fabric it is everywhere, and yet it is nowhere, because it does not have an identifiable locus.

[D]isciplines have to bring into play the power relations, not above but inside the very texture of the multiplicity, as discretely as possible. (1977: 220)

It is this embedded character that defines the Panopticon as an exemplar for discipline.

[The Panopticon] is an important mechanism, for it automizes and disindividualizes power. Power has its principle not so much in a person as in a certain concerted distribution of bodies, surfaces, lights, gazes; in an arrangement whose internal mechanisms produce the relation in which individuals are caught up. The ceremonies, the rituals, the marks by which the sovereign's surplus power was manifested are useless. There is a machinery that assures dissymmetry, disequilibrium, difference. Consequently, it does not matter who exercises power. Any individual taken almost at random, can operate the machine. ... (1977: 202)

The embedded nature of discipline makes it especially suitable as a preventative mode of control, as the surveillance (that is its basis) becomes part of the very relations to be controlled. Foucault illustrates this in discussing discipline in the context of the workshop:

> The discipline of the workshop, while remaining a way of enforcing respect for the regulations and authorities, of preventing thefts and losses, tends to increase aptitudes, speeds, output and therefore profits; it still exerts a moral influence over behavior, but more and more it treats actions in terms of their results, introduces bodies into a machinery, forces into an economy. (1977: 210)

It is precisely because of this embedded character of discipline that its nature varies according to the context in which it is applied, and it is for this reason that, when applied in the context of carceral punishment, one of its distinctive elements is that of individualized soul-training. This is because the context of carceral punishment (unlike that, for instance, of the factory, the hospital or the workshop) is essentially a moral one rather than a primarily instrumental one. It is perhaps because Foucault was primarily concerned to explain 'the birth of the prison' in *Discipline and Punish*, that the elements of carceral discipline have so easily come to be thought to be the fundamental elements of *all* discipline. As we shall try to illustrate, however, when applied in a context which is primarily instrumental rather than moral, the elements of discipline are significantly different.

INSTRUMENTAL AND MORAL DISCIPLINE

The three models of control that Foucault identifies (monarchical, juridical and carceral), while fundamentally different in disciplinary terms, all share a moral foundation that defines them as 'justice' systems. Foucault, in his analysis of these types of control, tended to take this feature for granted as it was common to all three models. As a result, if one works from within Foucault's framework in studying contemporary control, although one's attention will be directed towards discipline, the issue of whether the moral foundation of social control is changing will tend not to be considered. This is evident in the work of all the participants in the debate we have reviewed. Yet if contemporary control, especially as it appears in the private sector, is to be understood, it is precisely this issue (as the quotation above about disciplinary control in the work place suggests) that needs to be addressed. What makes private control different from traditional criminal justice is not its disciplinary character, which it shares with carceral control, but the challenge it offers to the moral foundation of the order-maintenance process (Shearing and Stenning, 1983).

Within criminal justice 'order' is fundamentally a moral phenomenon and its maintenance a moral process. Accordingly, social order (and its enforcement) tends to be defined in absolute terms: one proper order expressing 'natural justice'. Within criminal justice the premise that shapes order maintenance is that order is the expression of a community of morally righteous people. Thus, the criminal process is concerned with the rightness and wrongness of acts and the goodness and badness of people. It defines the boundaries of moral order by stigmatizing certain acts and persons as morally tainted (Durkheim). Its methods are indignation, retribution and redemption. Each of the models of punishment Foucault identified represents a different set of strategies for doing this.

Every aspect of the criminal process is structured and shaped by its moral, absolutist foundation. Within it, discipline is a technology of power used to achieve this moral purpose. There is no better illustration of this than the carceral regime which targets the soul, the moral centre of the human being, so as to provide for its moral reformation. Not surprisingly, therefore, individualized soul-training is the essential hallmark of carceral discipline.

Private control, in sharp contrast, rejects a moral conception of order and the control process. Private security executives, for example, not only reject [...] the present possibility of moral reform but reject the very idea of moral reform as a basis for control. Within private control, order is conceived primarily in instrumental rather than moral terms. Order is simply the set of conditions most conducive to achieving fundamental community objectives. Thus in a business corporation, for instance, order is usually whatever maximizes profit.

In contrasting their definition of order with that of criminal justice, private control systems stress that for them 'theft' is not a moral category and consequently does not deserve, or require, a moral response. Within private control the instrumental language of profit and loss replaces the moral language of criminal justice. This is not merely terminological (different terms for the same objects) but a reconstitution of the social world. 'Loss' refers not simply to theft but includes, among other things, the cost of attempting to control theft. This redefinition has important implications for the way in which control is exercised and thus for order. For example, theft will not be subject to control if the cost of doing so is likely to be greater than the initial loss.

Where moral rhetoric appears in private control it does so not as principles that guide the order-maintenance process (as it does in judicial decision-making) but simply as a control strategy. For example, employees may be given a lecture on morality not because control is conceived of in moral terms but because it creates attitudes that are good for profit. In such a context, training, as an element of discipline, need be neither individualized nor particularly directed at the soul. Indeed, from the point of view of the evolution of discipline, perhaps the most important consequence of the shift to an instrumental focus has been the move away from a concern with individual reformation to the control of the opportunities that permit breaches of order to occur. Accordingly, within private control it is prevention through the reduction of opportunities for disorder that is the primary focus of attention (Shearing and Stenning, 1982). This directs attention away from traditional offenders to a new class of delinquents: those who create opportunities for disorder. It is thus, to use banking as an illustration, not the employee who steals who is the primary focus of the control system's attention but the teller who creates the opportunity for the theft by neglecting to secure his/her cash drawer.

This transformation of the preventative thrust within discipline has important implications for other aspects of disciplinary control. The most visible is the change in the nature of surveillance as attention shifts from the morally culpable individual to the *categories* of people who create opportunities for disorder (Mathiesen, 1983; Rule et al., 1983).

Although this focus on opportunities creates a need for mass surveillance it does not eliminate carefully pinpointed surveillance. Its purpose, however, changes; it is no longer soul-training, as such, but rather 'tuning up the machine' (of which the human operator merely constitutes one part). While such scrutiny may, for this reason, focus on individuals, it is just as likely to target system deficiencies, for instance, in the paper systems that provide for ongoing surveillance, as well as retrospective surveillance, through the paper trails that they create.

In summary, the emergence of an explicitly instrumental focus in control has changed the nature of disciplinary power while reinforcing its embedded features. Thus surveillance, while changing both its focus and its purpose, has become increasingly embedded in other structures and functions. For example, the surveillance which Oscar Newman sought to achieve through 'defensible space' is embedded both in the structure of the physical environment, as well as in the social relations it facilitates.

Finally, we may note that an instrumental focus implies a variety of orders, each reflecting the fact that different communities have different objectives. Thus, within private control systems, we find not one conception of order but many; not one societal order but many community-based orders.

PRIVATE NON-CARCERAL DISCIPLINE

In seeking to identify the carceral model, and in explicating its relationship to disciplinary control, Foucault realized that, at any point in time, the actual control mechanisms in force would reflect the influences of both established and developing forms (1977: 130). Thus in order to identify the nature and direction of these forms he turned to the ideas and projects of influential reformers. Hence his use of the Panopticon as an exemplar of the disciplinary form as expressed through carceral strategies.

This approach suggests that in seeking to understand contemporary control we should direct our attention to strategies in arenas relatively immune from the influence of the carceral model. As public sector control has been dominated over the past century by the soul-training of the carceral model we are likely to find that the control strategies within this arena will reflect a mix of both established and newer forms, so that although it will be possible to identify disciplinary initiatives, we are not likely to find exemplary instances of contemporary embedded control here. The reverse, however, is likely to be true with respect to private control systems which, because they were in decline for most of the nineteenth and the first half of the twentieth centuries, are remarkably free of carceral overtones (Spitzer and Scull, 1977; Shearing and Stenning, 1981, 1983). Their contemporary manifestations, however, display precisely the embedded features that characterize disciplinary control (Shearing and Stenning, 1982: 101). Thus, in seeking an exemplar of contemporary discipline, we turn to the private arena. [...]

DISNEY WORLD: AN EXEMPLAR OF INSTRUMENTAL DISCIPLINE

As the discussion to this point has indicated, research on private security has already confirmed the development of a contemporary form of discipline outside of the moral restraints of criminal justice and begun to identify some of its distinguishing features. To elucidate the notion of instrumental discipline we contrast it with moral discipline by identifying the analytic equivalents of the carceral project and the Panopticon so as to highlight the nature of the changes that have been occurring in the development of discipline. As the identification of order with profit provides the most explicit example of an instrumental order, corporate control is an appropriate equivalent to the carceral model. As the features of corporate control are highly developed in the recreational facilities operated by Disney Productions and as these facilities are so widely known (directly through visits or indirectly through media coverage and Disney advertising), Disney World, in Orlando, Florida, provides a suitable exemplar to set against the Panopticon. In order to avoid lengthy descriptions of security strategies we will draw our illustrations from consumer controls which every visitor to Disney World encounters.

The essential features of Disney's control system become apparent the moment the visitor enters Disney World. As one arrives by car one is greeted by a series of smiling young people who, with the aid of clearly visible road markings, direct one to one's parking spot, remind one to lock one's car and to remember its location and then direct one to await the rubber wheeled train that will convey visitors away from the parking lot. At the boarding location one is directed to stand safely behind guard rails and to board the train in an orderly fashion. While climbing on board one is reminded to remember the name of the parking area and the row number in which one is parked (for instance, 'Donald Duck, 1'). Once on the train one is encouraged to protect oneself from injury by keeping one's body within the bounds of the carriage and to do the same for children in one's care. Before disembarking one is told how to get from the train back to the monorail platform and where to wait for the train to the parking lot on one's return. At each transition from one stage of one's journey to the next one is wished a happy day and a 'good time' at Disney World (this begins as one drives in and is directed by road signs to tune one's car radio to the Disney radio network). [...]

It will be apparent from the above that Disney Productions is able to handle large crowds of visitors in a most orderly fashion. Potential trouble is anticipated and prevented. Opportunities for disorder are minimized by constant instruction, by physical barriers which severely limit the choice of action available and by the surveillance of omnipresent employees who detect and rectify the slightest deviation.

The vehicles that carry people between locations are an important component of the system of physical barriers. Throughout Disney World vehicles are used as barriers. This is particularly apparent in the Epcot Center, the newest Disney facility, where many exhibits are accessible only via special vehicles which automatically secure one once they begin moving.

Control strategies are embedded in both environmental features and structural relations. In both cases control structures and activities have other functions which are highlighted so that the control function is overshadowed. None the less, control is pervasive. For example, virtually every pool, fountain and flower garden serves both as an aesthetic object and to direct visitors away from, or towards, particular locations. Similarly, every Disney Productions employee, while visibly and primarily engaged in other functions, is also engaged in the maintenance of order. This integration of functions is real and not simply an appearance: beauty *is* created, safety *is* protected, employees *are* helpful. The effect is, however, to embed the control function into the 'woodwork' where its presence is unnoticed but its effects are ever present.

A critical consequence of this process of embedding control in other structures is that control becomes consensual. It is effected with the willing cooperation of those being controlled so that the controlled become, as Foucault (1977: 170) has observed, the source of their own control. Thus, for example, the batching that keeps families together provides for family unity while at the same time ensuring that parents will be available to control their children. By seeking a definition of order within Disney World that can convincingly be presented as being in the interest of visitors, order maintenance is established as a voluntary activity which allows coercion to be reduced to a minimum. Thus, adult visitors willingly submit to a variety of devices that increase the flow of consumers through Disney World, such as being corralled on the monorail platform, so as to ensure the safety of their children. Furthermore, while doing so they gratefully acknowledge the concern Disney Productions has for their family, thereby legitimating its authority, not only in the particular situation in question, but in others as well. Thus, while profit ultimately underlies the order Disney Productions seeks to maintain, it is pursued in conjunction with other objectives that will encourage the willing compliance of visitors in maintaining Disney profits. This approach to profit-making, which seeks a coincidence of corporate and individual interests (employee and consumer alike), extends beyond the control function and reflects a business philosophy to be applied to all corporate operations (Peters and Waterman, 1982).

The coercive edge of Disney's control system is seldom far from the surface, however, and becomes visible the moment the Disney–visitor consensus breaks down, that is, when a visitor attempts to exercise a choice that is incompatible with the Disney order. It is apparent in the physical barriers that forcefully prevent certain activities as well as in the action of employees who detect breaches of order. This can be illustrated by an incident that occurred during a visit to Disney World by Shearing and his daughter, during the course of which she developed a blister on her heel. To avoid further irritation she removed her shoes and proceeded to walk barefooted. They had not progressed ten yards before they were approached by a very personable security guard dressed as a Bahamian police officer, with white pith helmet and white gloves that perfectly suited the theme of the area they were moving through (so that he, at first, appeared more like a scenic prop than a security person), who informed them that walking barefoot was, 'for the safety of visitors', not permitted. [After explaining] that, given the blister, the safety of this visitor was likely to be better secured by remaining barefooted, at least on the walkways, they were informed that their safety and how best to protect it was a matter for Disney Productions to determine while they were on Disney property and that unless they complied he would be compelled to escort them out of Disney World. Shearing's daughter, on learning that failure to comply with the security guard's instruction would deprive her of the pleasures of Disney World, quickly decided that she would prefer to further injure her heel and remain on Disney property. As this example illustrates, the source of Disney Productions' power rests both in the physical coercion it can bring to bear and in its capacity to induce cooperation by depriving visitors of a resource that they value. [...]

As we have hinted throughout this discussion, training is a pervasive feature of the control system of Disney Productions. It is not, however, the redemptive soul-training of the carceral project but an ever-present flow of directions for, and definitions of, order directed at every visitor. Unlike carceral training, these messages do not require detailed knowledge of the individual. They are, on the contrary, for anyone and everyone. Messages are, none the less, often conveyed to single individuals or small groups of friends and relatives. For example, in some of the newer exhibits, the vehicles that take one through swivel and turn so that one's gaze can be precisely directed. Similarly, each seat is fitted with individual sets of speakers that talk directly to one, thus permitting a seductive sense of intimacy while simultaneously imparting a uniform message.

In summary, within Disney World control is embedded, preventative, subtle, cooperative and apparently non-coercive and consensual. It focuses on categories, requires no knowledge of the individual and employs pervasive surveillance. Thus, although disciplinary, it is distinctively non-carceral. Its order is instrumental and determined by the interests of Disney Productions rather than moral and absolute. As anyone who has visited Disney World knows, it is extraordinarily effective.

CONCLUSIONS

While this new instrumental discipline is rapidly becoming a dominant force in social control in this year, 1984, it is as different from the Orwellian totalitarian nightmare as it is from the carceral regime. Surveillance is pervasive but it is the antithesis of the blatant control of the Orwellian state: its source is not government and its vehicle is not Big Brother. The order of instrumental discipline is not the unitary order of a central state but diffuse and separate orders defined by private authorities responsible for the feudal-like domains of Disney World, condominium estates, commercial complexes and the like. Within contemporary discipline, control is as fine-grained as Orwell imagined but its features are very different.

In this auspicious year it is thus, paradoxically, not to Orwell's socialist-inspired Utopia that we must look for a picture of contemporary control but to the capitalist-inspired disciplinary model conceived of by Huxley who, in his *Brave New World*, painted a picture of consensually based control that bears a striking resemblance to the disciplinary control of Disney World and other corporate control systems. Within Huxley's imaginary world people are seduced into conformity by the pleasures offered by the drug 'soma' rather than coerced into compliance by threat of Big Brother, just as people are today seduced to conform by the pleasures of consuming the goods that corporate power has to offer.

The contrasts between morally based justice and instrumental control, carceral punishment and corporate control, the Panopticon and Disney World and Orwell's and Huxley's visions [are] succinctly captured by the novelist Beryl Bainbridge's observations about a recent journey she made retracing J.B. Priestley's celebrated trip around Britain. She notes how during his travels in 1933 the centre of the cities and towns he visited were defined by either a church or a centre of government (depicting the coalition between Church and state in the production of order that characterizes morally based regimes).

During her more recent trip one of the changes that struck her most forcibly was the transformation that had taken place in the centre of cities and towns. These were now identified not by churches or town halls, but by shopping centres; often vaulted glass-roofed structures that she found reminiscent of the cathedrals they had replaced both in their awe-inspiring architecture and in the hush that she found they sometimes created. What was worshipped in these contemporary cathedrals, she noted, was not an absolute moral order but something much more mundane: people were 'worshipping shopping' and through it, we would add, the private authorities, the order and the corporate power their worship makes possible.

REFERENCES

Bottoms, A.E. (1983) 'Neglected features of contemporary penal systems', in D. Garland and P. Young (eds), *The Power to Punish: Contemporary Penality and Social Analysis*. Atlantic Highlands, NJ: Humanities, p. 166.

Cohen, S. (1979) 'The punitive city: notes on the dispersal of social control', *Contemporary Crises*, 3(4): 339.

Foucault, M. (1977) *Discipline and Punish: the Birth of the Prison*. New York: Vintage Books.

Mathiesen, T. (1980) 'The future of social control systems – the case of Norway', *International Journal of the Sociology of Law*, 8: 149.

Mathiesen, T. (1983) 'The future of social control systems – the case of Norway', in D. Garland and P. Young (eds), *The Power to Punish: Contemporary Penality and Social Analysis*. Atlantic Highlands, NJ: Humanities, p. 130.

Newman, O. (1972) *Defensible Space: Crime Prevention through Urban Design*. New York: Macmillan.

Peters, T. and Waterman, R.H, Jr. (1982) *In Search of Excellence: Lessons from America's Best-run Companies*. New York: Warner Books.

Priestley, J.B. (1934) *English Journey: Being a Rambling but Truthful Account of What One Man Saw and Heard and Felt During a Journey Through England the Autumn of the Year 1933*. London: Heinemann &c Gollancz.

Rule, J.B, McAdam, D., Stearns, L. and Uglow, D. (1983) 'Documentary identification and mass surveillance in the United States', *Social Problems*, 31(2): 222.

Shearing, C.D. and Stenning, P.C. (1981) 'Private security: its growth and implications', in M. Tonry and N. Morris (eds), *Crime and Justice – an Annual Review of Research*, vol. 3. Chicago: University of Chicago Press, p. 193.

Shearing, C.D. and Stenning, P.C. (1982) 'Snowflakes or good pinches? Private security's contribution to modern policing', in R. Donelan (ed.), *The Maintenance of Order in Society*. Ottawa: Canadian Police College.

Shearing, C.D. and Stenning, P.C. (1983) 'Private security: implications for social control', *Social Problems*, 30(5): 493.

Spitzer, S. and Scull, A. (1977) 'Privatization and capitalist development: the case of the private police', *Social Problems*, 25(1): 18.

43

The new penology

Malcolm M. Feeley and
Jonathan Simon

DISTINGUISHING FEATURES OF THE NEW PENOLOGY

What we call the new penology is not a theory of crime or criminology. Its uniqueness lies less in conceptual integration than in a common focus on certain problems and a shared way of framing issues. This strategic formation of knowledge
and power offers managers of the system a more or less coherent picture of the
challenges they face and the kinds of solutions that are most likely to work. While
we cannot reduce it to a set of principles, we can point to some of its most salient
features.

The new discourse

A central feature of the new discourse is the replacement of a moral or clinical
description of the individual with an actuarial language of probabilistic calculations
and statistical distributions applied to populations. Although social utility analysis
or actuarial thinking is commonplace enough in modern life – it frames policy considerations of all sorts – in recent years this mode of thinking has gained ascendancy in legal discourse, a system of reasoning that traditionally has employed the
language of morality and been focused on individuals (Simon, 1988). For instance,
this new mode of reasoning is found increasingly in tort law, where traditional fault
and negligence standards – which require a focus on the individual and are based
upon notions of individual responsibility – have given way to strict liability and
no-fault. These new doctrines rest upon actuarial ways of thinking about how to
'manage' accidents and public safety. They employ the language of social utility
and management, not individual responsibility (Simon, 1987; Steiner, 1987). [...]

Although crime policy, criminal procedure and criminal sanctioning have
been influenced by such social utility analysis, there is no body of commentary

From *Criminology*, 1992, 30(4): 452–74.

on the criminal law that is equivalent to the body of social utility analysis for tort law doctrine. Nor has strict liability in the criminal law achieved anything like the acceptance of related no-fault principles in tort law. Perhaps because the criminal law is so firmly rooted in a focus on the individual, these developments have come late to criminal law and penology.

Scholars of both European and North American penal strategies have noted the recent and rising trend of the penal system to target categories and subpopulations rather than individuals (Bottoms, 1983; Cohen, 1985; Mathiesen, 1983; Reichman, 1986). This reflects, at least in part, the fact that actuarial forms of representation promote quantification as a way of visualizing populations.

Crime statistics have been a part of the discourse of the state for over 200 years, but the advance of statistical methods permits the formation of concepts and strategies that allow direct relations between penal strategy and the population. Earlier generations used statistics to map the responses of normatively defined groups to punishment; today one talks of 'high-rate offenders', 'career criminals', and other categories defined by the distribution itself. Rather than simply extending the capacity of the system to rehabilitate or control crime, actuarial classification has come increasingly to define the correctional enterprise itself.

The importance of actuarial language in the system will come as no surprise to anyone who has spent time observing it. Its significance, however, is often lost in the more spectacular shift in emphasis from rehabilitation to crime control. No doubt, a new and more punitive attitude toward the proper role of punishment has emerged in recent years, and it is manifest in a shift in the language of statutes, internal procedures and academic scholarship. Yet looking across the past several decades, it appears that the pendulum-like swings of penal attitude moved independently of the actuarial language that has steadily crept into the discourse.

The discourse of the new penology is not simply one of greater quantification; it is also characterized by an emphasis on the systemic and on formal rationality. While the history of systems theory and operations research has yet to be written, their progression from business administration to the military and, in the 1960s, to domestic public policy must be counted as among the most significant of current intellectual trends. […]

Some of the most astute observers identified this change near the outset and understood that it was distinct from the concurrent rightward shift in penal thinking. Jacobs (1977) noted the rise at Stateville Penitentiary of what he called a 'managerial' perspective during the mid-1970s. The regime of Warden Brierton was characterized, according to Jacobs, by a focus on tighter administrative control through the gathering and distribution of statistical information about the functioning of the prison. Throughout the 1980s this perspective grew considerably within the correctional system. Jacobs presciently noted that the managerial perspective might succeed where traditional and reform administrations had failed because it was capable of handling the greatly increased demands for rationality and accountability coming from the courts and the political system.

The new objectives

The new penology is neither about punishing nor about rehabilitating individuals. It is about identifying and managing unruly groups. It is concerned with the rationality not of individual behavior or even community organization, but of managerial processes. Its goal is not to eliminate crime but to make it tolerable through systemic coordination.

One measure of the shift away from trying to normalize offenders and toward trying to manage them is seen in the declining significance of recidivism. Under the old penology, recidivism was a nearly universal criterion for assessing success or failure of penal programs. Under the new penology, recidivism rates continue to be important, but their significance has changed. The word itself seems to be used less often precisely because it carries a normative connotation that reintegrating offenders into the community is the major objective. High rates of parolees being returned to prison once indicated program failure; now they are offered as evidence of efficiency and effectiveness of parole as a control apparatus.

It is possible that recidivism is dropping out of the vocabulary as an adjustment to harsh realities and is a way of avoiding charges of institutional failure. […] However, in shifting to emphasize the virtues of return as an indication of *effective* control, the new penology reshapes one's understanding of the functions of the penal sanction. By emphasizing correctional programs in terms of aggregate control and system management rather than individual success and failure, the new penology lowers one's expectations about the criminal sanction. These redefined objectives are reinforced by the new discourses discussed above which take deviance as a given, mute aspirations for individual reformation, and seek to classify, sort and manage dangerous groups efficiently.

The waning of concern over recidivism reveals fundamental changes in the very penal processes that recidivism once was used to evaluate. For example, although parole and probation have long been justified as means of reintegrating offenders into the community […] increasingly they are being perceived as cost-effective ways of imposing long-term management on the dangerous. Instead of treating revocation of parole and probation as a mechanism to short-circuit the supervision process when the risks to public safety become unacceptable, the system now treats revocation as a cost-effective way to police and sanction a chronically troublesome population. In such an operation, recidivism is either irrelevant or, as suggested above, is stood on its head and transformed into an indicator of success in a new form of law enforcement.

The importance that recidivism once had in evaluating the performance of corrections is now being taken up by measures of system functioning. Heydebrand and Seron (1990) have noted a tendency in courts and other social agencies toward decoupling performance evaluation from external social objectives. Instead of social norms like the elimination of crime, reintegration into the community, or public safety, institutions begin to measure their own outputs as indicators of performance. Thus, courts may look at docket flow. Similarly, parole agencies may shift evaluations of performance to, say the time elapsed between arrests and due process hearings. In much the same way, many schools have come to focus on standardized test performance rather than on reading or mathematics, and some have begun to see teaching itself as the process of teaching students how to take such tests (Heydebrand and Seron, 1990: 190–4; Lipsky, 1980: 4–53).

Such technocratic rationalization tends to insulate institutions from the messy, hard-to-control demands of the social world. By limiting their exposure to indicators that they can control, managers ensure that their problems will have solutions. No doubt this tendency in the new penology is, in part, a response to the acceleration of demands for rationality and accountability in punishment coming from the courts and legislatures during the 1970s (Jacobs, 1977). It also reflects the lowered expectations for the penal system that result from failures to accomplish more ambitious promises of the past. Yet in the end, the inclination of the system to measure its success against its own production processes helps lock the system into a mode of operation that has only an attenuated connection with the *social* purposes of punishment. In the long term it becomes more difficult to evaluate an institution critically if there are no references to substantive social ends.

The new objectives also inevitably permeate through the courts into thinking about rights. The new penology replaces consideration of fault with predictions of dangerousness and safety management and, in so doing, modifies traditional individual-oriented doctrines of criminal procedure. [...]

New techniques

These altered, lowered expectations manifest themselves in the development of more cost-effective forms of custody and control and in new technologies to identify and classify risk. Among them are low frills, no-service custodial centers; various forms of electronic monitoring systems that impose a form of custody without walls; and new statistical techniques for assessing risk and predicting dangerousness. These new forms of control are not anchored in aspirations to rehabilitate, reintegrate, retrain, provide employment, or the like. They are justified in more blunt terms: variable detention depending upon risk assessment.

Perhaps the clearest example of the new penology's method is the theory of incapacitation, which has become the predominant utilitarian model of punishment (Greenwood, 1982; Moore et al., 1984). Incapacitation promises to reduce the effects of crime in society not by altering either offender or social context, but by rearranging the distribution of offenders in society. If the prison can do nothing else, incapacitation theory holds, it can detain offenders for a time and thus delay their resumption of criminal activity. According to the theory, if such delays are sustained for enough time and for enough offenders, significant aggregate effects in crime can take place although individual destinies are only marginally altered.

These aggregate effects can be further intensified, in some accounts, by a strategy of selective incapacitation. This approach proposes a sentencing scheme in which lengths of sentence depend not upon the nature of the criminal offense or upon an assessment of the character of the offender, but upon risk profiles. Its objectives are to identify high-risk offenders and to maintain long-term control over them while investing in shorter terms and less intrusive control over lower risk offenders. [...]

The new penology in perspective

The correctional practices emerging from the shifts we identified above present a kind of 'custodial continuum'. But unlike the 'correctional continuum' discussed in the 1960s, this new custodial continuum does not design penal measures for the particular needs of the individual or the community. Rather, it sorts individuals into groups according to the degree of control warranted by their risk profiles.

At one extreme the prison provides maximum security at a high cost for those who pose the greatest risks, and at the other probation provides low-cost surveillance for low-risk offenders. In between stretches a growing range of intermediate supervisory and surveillance techniques. The management concerns of the new penology – in contrast to the transformative concerns of the old – are displayed especially clearly in justifications for various new intermediate sanctions.

What we call the new penology is only beginning to take coherent shape. Although most of what we have stressed as its central elements – statistical prediction, concern with groups, strategies of management – have a long history in penology, in recent years they have come to the fore, and their functions have coalesced and expanded to form a new strategic approach. Discussing the new penology in terms of discourse, objective and technique risks a certain repetitiveness. Indeed, all three are closely linked, and while none can be assigned priority as the cause of the others, each entails and facilitates the others.

Thus, one can speak of normalizing individuals, but when the emphasis is on separating people into distinct and independent categories the idea of the 'normal' itself becomes obscured if not irrelevant. If the 'norm' can no longer function as a relevant criterion of success for the organizations of criminal justice, it is not surprising that evaluation turns to indicators of internal system performance. The focus of the system on the efficiency of its own outputs, in turn, places a premium on those methods (e.g., risk screening, sorting and monitoring) that fit wholly within the bureaucratic capacities of the apparatus.

But the same story can be told in a different order. The steady bureaucratization of the correctional apparatus during the 1950s and 1960s shifted the target from individuals, who did not fit easily into centralized administration, to categories or classes, which do. But once the focus is on categories of offenders rather than individuals, methods naturally shift toward mechanisms of appraising and arranging groups rather than intervening in the lives of individuals. In the end the search for causal order is at least premature.

In the section below we explore the contours of some of the new patterns represented by these developments, and in so doing suggest that the enterprise is by now relatively well established.

NEW FUNCTIONS AND TRADITIONAL FORMS

Someday, perhaps, the new penology will have its own Jeremy Bentham or Zebulon Brockway [...], some gigantic figure who can stamp his or her own sense of order on the messy results of incremental change. For now it is better not to think of it so much as a theory or program conceived in full by any particular actors in the system, but as an interpretative net that can help reveal in the present some of the directions the future may take. The test of such a net, to which we now turn, is not its elegance as a model but whether it enables one to grasp a wide set of developments in an enlightening way (in short, does it catch fish?). Below we re-examine three of the major features of the contemporary penal landscape in light of our argument – the expansion of the penal sanction, the rise of drug testing and innovation within the criminal process – and relate them to our thesis.

The expansion of penal sanctions

During the past decade the number of people covered by penal sanctions has expanded significantly. Because of its high costs, the growth of prison populations has drawn the greatest attention, but probation and parole have increased at a proportionate or faster rate. The importance of these other sanctions goes beyond their ability to stretch penal resources; they expand and redistribute the use of imprisonment. Probation and parole violations now constitute a major source of prison inmates, and negotiations over probation revocation are replacing plea bargaining as modes of disposition (Greenspan, 1988; Messinger and Berecochea, 1990).

Many probation and parole revocations are triggered by events, like failing a drug test, that are driven by parole procedures themselves (Simon, 1990; Zimring and Hawkins, 1991). The increased flow of probationers and parolees into prisons is expanding the prison population and changing the nature of the prison. Increasingly, prisons are short-term holding pens for violators deemed too dangerous to remain on the streets. To the extent the prison is organized to receive such people, its correctional mission is replaced by a management function, a warehouse for the highest risk classes of offenders.

From the perspective of the new penology, the growth of community corrections in the shadow of imprisonment is not surprising. The new penology does not regard prison as a special institution capable of making a difference in the individuals who pass through it. Rather, it functions as but one of several custodial options. The actuarial logic of the new penology dictates an expansion of the continuum of control for more efficient risk management. [...]

Thus, community-based sanctions can be understood in terms of risk management rather than rehabilitative or correctional aspirations. Rather than instruments of reintegrating offenders into the community, they function as mechanisms to maintain control, often through frequent drug testing, over low-risk offenders for whom the more secure forms of custody are judged too expensive or unnecessary. [...]

Drugs and punishment

Drug use and its detection and control have become central concerns of the penal system. No one observing the system today can fail to be struck by the increasingly tough laws directed against users and traffickers, well-publicized data that suggest that a majority of arrestees are drug users, and the increasing proportion of drug offenders sent to prison.

In one sense, of course, the emphasis on drugs marks a continuity with the past thirty years of correctional history. Drug treatment and drug testing were hallmarks of the rehabilitative model in the 1950s and 1960s. The recent upsurge of concern with drugs may be attributed to the hardening of social attitudes toward drug use (especially in marked contrast to the tolerant 1970s), the introduction of virulent new drug products, like crack cocaine, and the disintegrating social conditions of the urban poor.

Without dismissing the relevance of these continuities and explanations for change, it is important to note that there are distinctive changes in the role of drugs in the current system that reflect the logic of the new penology. In place of the traditional emphasis on treatment and eradication, today's practices track drug use as a kind of risk indicator. The widespread evidence of drug use in the offending population leads not to new theories of crime causation but to more efficient ways of identifying those at highest risk of offending. With drug use so prevalent that it is found in a majority of arrestees in some large cities [...], it can hardly mark a special type of individual deviance. From the perspective of the new penology, drug use is not so much a measure of individual acts of deviance as it is a mechanism for classifying the offender within a risk group.

Thus, one finds in the correctional system today a much greater emphasis on drug testing than on drug treatment. This may reflect the normal kinds of gaps in policy as well as difficulty in treating relatively new forms of drug abuse. Yet, testing serves functions in the new penology even in the absence of a treatment option. By marking the distribution of risk within the offender population under surveillance, testing makes possible greater coordination of scarce penal resources.

Testing also fills the gap left by the decline of traditional intervention strategies. [...] If nothing else, testing provide[s] parole (and probably probation) agents [with] a means to document compliance with their own internal performance requirements. [...] Testing provides both an occasion for requiring the parolee to show up in the parole office and a purpose for meeting. The results of tests have become a network of fact and explanation for use in a decision-making process that requires accountability but provides little substantive basis for distinguishing among offenders.

Innovation

Our description may seem to imply the onset of a reactive age in which penal managers strive to manage populations of marginal citizens with no concomitant effort toward integration into mainstream society. This may seem hard to square with the myriad new and innovative technologies introduced over the past decade. Indeed the media, which for years have portrayed the correctional system as a failure, have recently enthusiastically reported on these innovations: boot camps, electronic surveillance, high security 'campuses' for drug users, house arrest, intensive parole and probation, and drug treatment programs.

Although some of the new proposals are presented in terms of the 'old penology' and emphasize individuals, normalization and rehabilitation, it is risky to come to any firm conviction about how these innovations will turn out. If historians of punishment have provided any clear lessons, it is that reforms evolve in ways quite different from the aims of their proponents (Foucault, 1977; Rothman, 1971). Thus, we wonder if these most recent innovations won't be recast in the terms outlined in this paper. Many of these innovations are compatible with the imperatives of the new penology, that is, managing a permanently dangerous population while maintaining the system at a minimum cost.

One of the current innovations most in vogue with the press and politicians is correctional 'boot camps'. These are minimum security custodial facilities, usually for youthful first offenders, designed on the model of a training center for military personnel, complete with barracks, physical exercise and tough drill sergeants. Boot camps are portrayed as providing discipline and pride to young offenders brought up in the unrestrained culture of poverty (as though physical fitness could fill the gap left by the weakening of families, schools, neighborhoods, and other social organizations in the inner city).

The camps borrow explicitly from a military model of discipline, which has influenced penality from at least the eighteenth century. No doubt the image of inmates smartly dressed in uniforms performing drills and calisthenics appeals to long-standing ideals of order in post-Enlightenment culture. But in its proposed application to correction, the military model is even less appropriate now than when it was rejected in the nineteenth century; indeed, today's boot camps are more a simulation of discipline than the real thing.

In the nineteenth century the military model was superseded by another model of discipline, the factory. Inmates were controlled by making them work at hard industrial labor (Ignatieff, 1978; Rothman, 1971). It was assumed that forced labor would inculcate in offenders the discipline required of factory laborers, so that they might earn their keep while in custody and join the ranks of the usefully employed when released. One can argue that this model did not work very well, but at least it was coherent. The model of discipline through labor suited our capitalist democracy in a way the model of a militarized citizenry did not.

The recent decline of employment opportunities among the populations of urban poor most at risk for conventional crime involvement has left the applicability of industrial discipline in doubt. But the substitution of the boot camp for vocational training is even less plausible. Even if the typical 90-day regime of training envisioned by proponents of boot camps is effective in reorienting its subjects, at best it can only produce soldiers without a company to join. Indeed, the grim vision of the effect of boot camp is that it will be effective for those who will subsequently put their lessons of discipline and organization to use in the street gangs and drug distribution networks. However, despite the earnestness with which the boot camp metaphor is touted, we suspect that the camps will be little more than holding pens for managing a short-term, mid-range risk population.

Drug testing and electronic monitors being tried in experimental 'intensive supervision' and 'house arrest' programs are justified in rehabilitative terms, but both sorts of programs lack a foundation in today's social and economic realities. The drug treatment programs in the 1960s encompassed a regime of coercive treatment: 'inpatient' custody in secured settings followed by community supervision and reintegration […]. The record suggests that these programs had enduring effects for at least some of those who participated in them (Anglin et al., 1990). Today's proposals are similar, but it remains to be seen whether they can be effective in the absence of long-term treatment facilities, community-based follow-up, and prospects for viable conventional lifestyles and employment opportunities. In the meantime it is obvious that they can also serve the imperative of reducing the costs of correctional jurisdiction while maintaining some check on the offender population.

Our point is not to belittle the stated aspirations of current proposals or to argue that drug treatment programs cannot work. Indeed, we anticipate that drug treatment and rehabilitation will become increasingly attractive as the cost of long-term custody increases. However, given the emergence of the management concerns of the new penology, we question whether these innovations will embrace the long-term perspective of earlier successful treatment programs, and we suspect that they will emerge as control processes for managing and recycling selected risk populations. If so, these new programs will extend still further the capacity of the new penology. The undeniable attractiveness of boot camps, house arrest, secure drug 'centers', and the like, is that they promise to provide secure custody in a more flexible format and at less cost than traditional correctional facilities. Indeed, some of them are envisioned as private contract facilities that can be expanded or reduced with relative ease. Further, they hold out the promise of expanding the range of low-and mid-level custodial alternatives, thereby facilitating the transfer of offenders now held in more expensive, higher security facilities that have been so favored in recent years. Tougher eligibility requirements, including job offers, stable residency and promises of sponsorship in the community, can be used to screen out 'higher risk' categories for non-custodial release programs (Petersilia, 1987). Thus, despite the lingering language of rehabilitation and reintegration, the programs generated under the new penology can best be understood in terms of managing costs and controlling dangerous populations rather than social or personal transformation.

SOCIAL BASES OF THE NEW PENOLOGY

The point of these reinterpretations is not to show that shifts in the way the penal enterprise is understood and discussed inexorably determine how the system will take shape. What actually emerges in corrections over the near and distant future will depend on how this understanding itself is shaped by the pressures of demographic, economic and political factors. Still, such factors rarely operate as pure forces. They are filtered through and expressed in terms in which the problems are understood. Thus, the strategic field we call the new penology itself will help shape the future.

The new discourse of crime

Like the old penology, traditional 'sociological' criminology has focused on the relationship between individuals and communities. Its central concerns have been the causes and correlates of delinquent and criminal behavior, and it has sought to develop intervention strategies designed to correct delinquents and decrease the likelihood of deviant behavior. Thus, it has focused on the family and the workplace as important influences of socialization and control.

The new penology has an affinity with a new 'actuarial' criminology, which eschews these traditional concerns of criminology. Instead of training in sociology or social work, increasingly the new criminologists are trained in operations research and systems analysis. This new approach is not a criminology at all, but an applied branch of systems theory. This shift in training and orientation has been accompanied by a shift in interest. A concern with successful intervention strategies, the province of the former, is replaced by models designed to optimize public safety through the management of aggregates, which is the province of the latter.

In one important sense this new criminology is simply a consequence of steady improvements in the quantitative rigor with which crime is studied. No doubt the amassing of a statistical picture of crime and the criminal justice system has improved researchers' ability to speak realistically about the distribution of crimes and the fairness of procedures. But, we submit, it has also contributed to a shift, a reconceptualization, in the way crime is understood as a social problem. The new techniques and the new language have facilitated reconceptualization of the way issues are framed and policies pursued. Sociological criminology tended to emphasize crime as a relationship between the individual and the normative expectations of his or her community (Bennett, 1981). Policies premised on this perspective addressed problems of reintegration, including the mismatch among individual motivation, normative orientation and social opportunity structures. In contrast, actuarial criminology highlights the interaction of criminal justice institutions and specific segments of the population. Policy discussions framed in its terms emphasize the management of high-risk groups and make less salient the qualities of individual delinquents and their communities.

Indeed, even the use of predictive statistics by pioneers like Ernest Burgess (1936) reflected sociological criminology's emphasis on normalization. Burgess's statistics (and those of most other quantitative criminologists before the 1960s) measured the activity of subjects defined by a specifiable set of individual or social factors (e.g., alcoholism, unemployment etc.). In the actuarial criminology of today, by contrast, the numbers generate the subject itself (e.g., the high-rate offender of incapacitation research). In short, criminals are no longer the organizing referent (or logos) of criminology. Instead, criminology has become a subfield of a generalized public policy analysis discourse. This new criminal knowledge aims at rationalizing the operation of the systems that manage criminals, not dealing with criminality. The same techniques that can be used to improve the circulation of baggage in airports or delivery of food to troops can be used to improve the penal system's efficiency.

The discourse of poverty and the underclass

The new penology may also be seen as responsive to the emergence of a new understanding of poverty in America. The term *underclass* is used […] to characterize a segment of society that is viewed as permanently excluded from social mobility and economic integration. The term is used to refer to a largely black and Hispanic population living in concentrated zones of poverty in central cities, separated physically and institutionally from the suburban locus of mainstream social and economic life in America.

In contrast to groups whose members are deemed employable, even if they may be temporarily out of work, the underclass is understood as a permanently marginal population, without literacy, without skills and without hope; a self-perpetuating and pathological segment of society that is not integratable into the larger whole, even as a reserve labor pool (Wilson, 1987). Conceived of this way, the underclass is also a dangerous class, not only for what any particular member may or may not do, but more generally for collective potential misbehavior. It is treated as a high-risk group that must be managed for the protection of the rest of society. Indeed, it is this managerial task that provides one of the most powerful sources for the imperative of preventative management in the new penology. The concept of 'underclass' makes clear why correctional officials increasingly regard as a bad joke the claim that their goal is to reintegrate offenders back into their communities.

Reintegration and rehabilitation inevitably imply a norm against which deviant subjects are evaluated. As Allen (1981) perceived […], rehabilitation as a project can only survive if public confidence in the viability and appropriateness of such norms endures. Allen viewed the decline of the rehabilitative ideal as a result of the cultural revolts of the 1960s, which undermined the capacity of the American middle classes to justify their norms and the imposition of those norms on others. It is this decline in social will, rather than empirical evidence of the failure of penal programs to rehabilitate, that, in Allen's analysis, doomed the rehabilitative ideal.

Whatever significance cultural radicalism may have had in initiating the breakup of the old penology in the mid-1970s, the emergence of the new penology in the 1980s reflects the influence of a more despairing view of poverty and the prospects for achieving equality (views that can hardly be blamed on the Left). Rehabilitating offenders, or any kind of reintegration strategy, can only make sense if the larger community from which offenders come is viewed as sharing a common normative universe with the communities of the middle classes – especially those values and expectations derived from the labor market. The concept of an underclass, with its connotation of a permanent marginality for whole portions of the population, has rendered the old penology incoherent and laid the groundwork for a strategic field that emphasizes low-cost management of a permanent offender population.

The connection between the new penality and the (re)emergent term *underclass* also is illustrated by studies of American jails. For instance, […] Irwin's 1985 book *The Jail*, is subtitled *Managing the Underclass in American Society*. His thesis is that 'prisoners in jails share two essential characteristics: detachment and disrepute' (p. 2). For Irwin, the function of jail is to manage the underclass, which he reports is also referred to as 'rabble', 'disorganized', 'disorderly', and the 'lowest class of people'.

In one rough version of Irwin's analysis, the jail can be viewed as a means of controlling the most disruptive and unsightly members of the underclass. But in another version, it can be conceived of as an emergency service net for those who are in the most desperate straits. As other social services have shrunk, increasingly this task falls on the jail.

Whichever version one selects, few of those familiar with the jails in America's urban centers find it meaningful to characterize them only as facilities for 'pretrial detention' or for serving 'short-term sentences'. Although not literally false, this characterization misses the broader function of the jail. The high rates of those released without charges filed, the turnstile-like frequency with which some people reappear, and the pathological characteristics of a high proportion of the inmates lead many to agree with Irwin that the jail is best understood as a social management instrument rather than an institution for effecting the purported aims of the criminal process.

Social management, not individualized justice, is also emphasized in other discussions of the criminal process. Long-time public defender James M. Doyle (1992) offers the metaphors 'colonial', 'White Man's burden', and 'Third World', in an essay drawing parallels between the careers of criminal justice officials and colonial administrators. Both, he argues,

> are convinced that they are menaced by both inscrutable, malign natives and ignorant, distant, policy-makers. They believe they are hamstrung by crazy legalities. Young Assistant District Attorneys, like young Assistant District Commissioners, hurriedly seize, then vehemently defend, a conventional wisdom as a protection against these threats. They pledge themselves to a professional code that sees the world in which people are divided into various collectives. Where they might have seen individuals, they see races, types and colors instead. Like the colonialists before them, they embrace a 'rigidly binomial opposition of "ours" and "theirs"'. In the criminal justice system as on the frontiers of empire 'the impersonal communal idea of being a White Man' rules; it becomes 'a very concrete way of being-in-the-world, a way of taking hold of reality, language and thought'. (1992: 74)

Sustaining his metaphor, Doyle parallels the corrupting influence of the White Man's effort to 'manage' Third World natives with those of the criminal justice professionals' effort to handle cases. He concludes, 'we have paid too much attention to the superficial exotic charms by which the reports of the colonial and criminal justice White Man entertain us, too little to the darker strains they also share' (1992: 126).

Whether one prefers Irwin's notion of underclass or Doyle's 'colonial' and 'Third World' metaphors, both resonate with our notion of the new penology. They vividly explain who is being managed and why. But in providing an explanation of these relationships, there is a danger that the terms will reify the problem, that they will suggest the problem is inevitable and permanent. Indeed, it is this belief, we maintain, that has contributed to the lowered expectations of the new penology – away from an aspiration to affect individual lives through rehabilitative and transformative efforts and toward the more 'realistic' task of monitoring and managing intractable groups.

The hardening of poverty in contemporary America reinforces this view. When combined with a pessimistic analysis implied by the term *underclass*, the structural barriers that maintain the large islands of Third World misery in America's major cities can lead to the conclusion that such conditions are inevitable and impervious to social policy intervention. This, in turn, can push corrections ever further toward a self-understanding based on the imperative of herding a specific population that cannot be disaggregated and transformed but only maintained – a kind of waste management function. [...]

REFERENCES

Allen, F. (1981) *The Decline of the Rehabilitative Idea*. New Haven, CT: Yale University Press.

Anglin, D., Speckhart, G. and Piper Deschenes, E. (1990) *Examining the Effects of Narcotics Addiction*. Los Angeles: UCLA Neuropsychiatric Institute, Drug Abuse Research Group.

Bennett, J. (1981) *Oral History and Delinquency: the Rhetoric of Criminology*. Chicago: University of Chicago Press.

Bottoms, A. (1983) 'Neglected features of contemporary penal systems', in D. Garland and P. Young (eds), *The Power to Punish*. London: Heinemann.

Burgess, E.W. (1936) 'Protecting the public by parole and parole prediction', *Journal of Criminal Law and Criminology*, 27: 491–502.

Cohen, S. (1985) *Visions of Social Control: Crime, Punishment and Classification*. Cambridge: Polity.

Doyle, J.M. (1992) '"It's the Third World down there": The colonialist vocation and American criminal justice', *Harvard Civil Rights – Civil Liberties Law Review*, 27: 71–126.

Foucault, M. (1977) *Discipline and Punish*. New York: Pantheon.

Greenspan, R. (1988) 'The transformation of criminal due process in the administrative state'. Paper prepared for delivery at the annual meeting of the Law and Society Association, Vail, Colorado, June 1988.

Greenwood, P. (1982) *Selective Incapacitation*. Santa Monica, CA: Rand.

Heydebrand, W. and Seron, C. (1990) *Rationalizing Justice: the Political Economy and Federal District Courts*. New York: State University of New York Press.

Ignatieff, M. (1978) *A Just Measure of Pain: the Penitentiary in the Industrial Revolution, 1750–1850*. London: Macmillan.

Irwin, J. (1985) *The Jail: Managing the Underclass in American Society*. Berkeley, CA: University of California Press.

Jacobs, J.B. (1977) *Stateville: the Penitentiary in Mass Society*. Chicago: University of Chicago Press.

Lipsky, M. (1980) *Street Level Bureaucrats*. New York: Russell Sage Foundation.

Mathiesen, T. (1983) 'The future of control systems – the case of Norway', in D. Garland and P. Young (eds), *The Power to Punish*. London: Heinemann.

Messinger, S. and Berecochea, J. (1990) 'Don't stay too long but do come back soon'. Proceedings, Conference on Growth and Its Influence on Correctional Policy, Center for the Study of Law and Society, University of California at Berkeley.

Moore, M.H, Estrich, S.R., McGillis, D. and Spelman, W. (1984) *Dangerous Offenders: the Elusive Target of Justice*. Cambridge, MA: Harvard University Press.

Petersilia, J. (1987) *Expanding Options for Criminal Sentencing*. Santa Monica, CA: Rand.

Reichman, N. (1986) 'Managing crime risks: toward an insurance-based model of social control', *Research in Law, Deviance and Social Control*, 8: 151–72.

Rothman, D. (1971) *The Discovery of the Asylum: Social Order and Disorder in the New Republic*. Boston, MA: Little, Brown.

Simon, J. (1987) 'The emergence of a risk society: insurance law and the state', *Socialist Review*, 95: 61–89.

Simon, J. (1988) 'The ideological effect of actuarial practices', *Law and Society Review*, 22: 771–800.

Simon, J. (1990) 'From discipline to management: strategies of control in parole supervision, 1890–1900'. PhD dissertation, Jurisprudence and Social Policy Program, University of California at Berkeley.

Steiner, H.J. (1987) *Moral Vision and Social Vision in the Court: a Study of Tort Accident Law*. Madison, WI: University of Wisconsin Press.

Wilson, W.J. (1987) *The Truly Disadvantaged: the Inner City, the Underclass, and Public Policy*. Chicago: University of Chicago Press.

Zimring, F. and Hawkins, G. (1991) *The Scale of Imprisonment*. Chicago: University of Chicago Press.

44

Risk, power and crime prevention

Pat O'Malley

[…]

RISK-BASED SOCIETY

Almost the defining property of Foucault's conception of disciplinary power is
that it works through and upon the individual, and constitutes the individual as
an object of knowledge. In the disciplines, the central technique is that of normalization in the specific sense of creating or specifying a general rule (norm) in
terms of which individual uniqueness can be recognized, characterized and then
standardized. Normalization in the disciplinary sense thus implies 'correction'
of the individual, and the development of a causal knowledge of deviance and
normalization. Thus, in the prison, Foucault (1977) saw discipline as acting
directly and coercively upon the individual, producing thereby 'a biographical
knowledge and a technique for correcting individual lives' which should follow
the delinquent's life course 'back not only to the circumstances but also to the
causes of his crime' (Foucault 1977: 251–2).

Rejection of the focus upon individuals and on causation therefore would
reflect not merely a redirection of particular policies but rather a shift away from
the disciplinary technology of power itself. In the field of crime and crime management, a number of commentators have noted the development of programs
and policies based on the regulation of behaviours and their consequences – in
which 'actuarial' (Cohen 1985) or 'insurance' based (Reichman 1986; Hogg 1989)
assumptions and techniques are brought into play. Perhaps the most striking
statement of the changes implied has been provided by Cohen (1985) who
observes that the conception of a mind-control society envisaged in Orwell's
1984 is mistaken, for although such key Foucauldian elements as surveillance

From *Economy and Society*, 1992, 21(3): 361–74.

continue to develop, there is little or no concern with individuals as such. Thus in situational crime prevention, one of the fastest growing techniques of crime control, concern is with the spatial and temporal aspects of crime, thought out in terms of the opportunities for crime rather than its causal or biographical origins:

> What is being monitored is behaviour (or the physiological correlates of emotion and behaviour). No one is interested in inner thoughts ... 'the game is up' for all policies directed to the criminal as an individual, either in terms of detection (blaming and punishing) or causation (finding motivational or causal chains). ... The talk now is about 'spatial' and 'temporal' aspects of crime, about systems, behaviour sequences, ecology, defensible space ... target hardening ...

> (Cohen 1985:146–8)

[...]

SITUATIONAL CRIME PREVENTION AS RISK MANAGEMENT

[...] Situational crime prevention may be understood as quintessentially 'actuarial'. It deals hardly at all with individual offenders, is uninterested in the causes of crime, and generally is hostile or at best agnostic toward correctionalism. Its concern is with crime control as risk management (Reichman 1986). [...] Situational crime prevention is enjoying a period of extraordinary success in Britain, the United States, Australia and elsewhere – at least in the political sense of its influence as a program of crime control. Certainly it is tempting to follow earlier arguments and regard this as due to the increased efficiency of actuarial techniques. But the rapidity of its rise to prominence can scarcely be attributed to evidence of its superiority over correctionalism and causal/social criminologies. Rather what emerges, as might be expected from Cohen's (1985) original account of the 'politics of failure', is a political struggle over the definition and the criteria of failure and success. [...]

Such debates are endless. They reveal only that the politics of success and failure normally are struggles over the status of criteria, and can rarely be reduced to any universally accepted scale of efficiency. If this is the case, then the question of why situational crime prevention has proven so influential a technique will need to be answered in terms of its relationship to political programs and strategies, and especially to those currently in ascendance. I believe that the broader political and ideological effects of situational crime prevention reveal that its attractions to economic rationalist, neo-conservative and New Right programs provide such an answer (although not unrelated attractions to police forces are also significant). The primary attractions, I will argue, link directly with core ideological assumptions of the New Right, and through these with the two directions of population management – increasing punitiveness with respect to offenders, and with respect to victims, the displacement of socialized risk management with privatized prudentialism. While it is by no means the case that this is the only possible construction of situational crime prevention (others will be discussed briefly toward the end of this paper), for a variety of reasons it is a particularly durable and readily mobilized version under current conditions.

NEO-CONSERVATIVE READING OF CRIME PREVENTION

Situational crime prevention and the offender

Situational crime prevention destroys the disciplines' biographical individual as a category of criminological knowledge, but the criminal does not disappear. Opportunities only exist in relation to potential criminals who convert open windows into windows of opportunity for crime. To install such an agent, situational crime prevention replaces the biographical criminal with a polar opposition – the abstract and universal 'abiographical' individual – the 'rational choice' actor […].

However, while abstract and abiographic, this rational choice individual nevertheless is clearly structured. It thinks in cost-benefit terms – weighing up the risks, potential gains and potential costs, and then committing an offence only when the benefits are perceived to outweigh the losses. This construction may be thought of as having a source very close to the foundations of actuarialism. It is of course the amoral rational choice individual beloved of classical economics, the *homo economicus* which inhabits the world of insurance – the home base of risk management discourses, and an industry closely connected with the promotion of situational crime prevention (O'Malley 1991).

This same being, but invested with additional moral and political characteristics is the denizen of neo-conservative and New Right discourses. It single-mindedly pursues the entrepreneurial ideal, as an atomistic being it is 'naturally free', self-reliant, and responsible (Gamble 1988). It is the underlying form of the human being that the Right would liberate from the debilitating 'public benefit' shackles of the welfare state which have progressively been imposed upon it especially since the end of the Second World War (Levitas 1986). Indeed, the demolition of socialized risk management and the restoration of social conditions approximating 'freedom' of the responsible individual is central to neo-conservative thinking about crime.

> When the traditional family is undermined, as it has been, self reliance tends to be lost and responsibility tends to disappear, both to be replaced by a dependence often long term, on the government and manipulation by social engineers. It also provides the setting which leads young people to the treadmill of drug abuse and crime.
>
> (Liberal Party of Australia 1988:15)

Already it is possible to see how it might be that the neo-conservatives who are concerned to dismantle so much that Simon (1987) understands as actuarialism, might nevertheless embrace and foster the actuarialism of situational crime prevention. But there are other reasons as well.

Situational crime prevention's rejection of concern with biographical-causal approaches to understanding crime, and the focus on the targets of crime rather than on offenders, combine to deflect attention from the social foundations of offending. This effect is achieved in the case of the rational choice model by its rejection of or agnosticism toward conditions which may have given rise to the offenders' action, but also and especially by constructing the offender as abstract, universal and rational. […] Such abstract and universal, equal and voluntary individuals are free to act in a perfectly 'rational' self-interested fashion, maximizing gains and minimizing costs. They are free to commit crime or not to commit crime.

This latter point suggests that not only is the knowledge of the criminal disarticulated from a critique of society, but in turn, both of these may be disarticulated from the reaction to the offender. As Foucault made clear, what he saw as the 'criminological labyrinth' was constructed around the assumption that crime is caused, and that cause reduces responsibility (1977: 252). Elimination of cause from the discourse of crime obviously restores responsibility and this has its effects on punishment. Thus the logical corollary of situational crime prevention from the point of view of a New Right discourse, is a policy of punitive or just deserts sentencing, rather than a program of sentencing for reform. Compatibility of crime prevention thinking with these models is furthered by the argument that salutary punishment in the form of imprisonment incapacitates offenders and thus acts directly as a means of behavioural crime prevention.

Thus the criminal becomes individually responsible for our concern with offenders as such ceases with that knowledge. In consequence, any class, race, gender or similar foundations of crime, especially as identified by causal criminology, are automatically excluded from consideration except in their role as risk-enhancing factors. If bothered with at all they are taken to be predictive of behaviours, not explanatory of meaningful actions.

This shift in understanding eschews also the moral dimensions of the sociological criminologies, condemned to the status of 'failures' by situational crime prevention theorists […]. Out with them go their respective agendas linking crime and social justice – for example that of strain theory and its concerns with relative deprivation and inequality of opportunity, and the appreciative recognition of cultural variability and of the impact of material degradation of the inner city poor that was the hallmark of ecological analysis. Academically as well as politically and administratively, it now becomes respectable to regard criminals as unconstrained agents, and to regard a crime control policy as divorced from questions of social justice.

Finally, the 'politics of failure' provide a technical glass to justify punitiveness. If correction and deterrence do not work, then sanctions based on these ideas must be swept away. What is left for the offender but punishment, retribution and incapacitation?

Situational crime prevention and the victim

If situational crime prevention short-circuits the link between criminality and social justice, then it might be expected that the victim of crime moves more into the centre of concern. In some sense this is undoubtedly the case, as the rhetoric of 'protecting the public' rings loud throughout this program (e.g. Home Office 1990). However, just as the offenders are disconnected from the political dimensions of their existence, so too are the victims, for victims like offenders are to be understood as rational choice actors, responsible and free individuals.

Prevention now becomes the responsibility of the victim. This view is by no means the construct of academic reflection but permeates crime prevention thinking at all levels. At one level, this position emerges no doubt because it reduces pressure on police forces, which have not noticeably reduced crime victimization and which are therefore vulnerable to political pressure for this reason. Thus a senior official of the Australian insurance Council has noted: 'Severely restricted police resources and the sheer frequency of crime, means that any improvement in the situation will rely heavily on property owners accepting responsibility for their own property and valuables' (Hall 1986: 243).

At broader political levels similar arguments are being presented for much the same reasons. Responding to news that crime rates in Britain have reached record levels, 'the Prime Minister, Mrs Thatcher, blamed a large portion of the crimes on the victims' carelessness. "We have to be careful that we ourselves don't make it easy for the criminal" she said' (*Age* 28 September 1990).

Not only does responsibility and thus critique shift, but so too do costs. Privatization of security practice and costs – to be seen in the trend toward private security agencies, security devices, domestic security practices, neighbourhood watch schemes (with attendant insurance underwriting) – generate the rudiments of a user pays system of policing security. Closer to the heart of neoconservatism, the rational choice public will come to see the justice in this:

> The general public's apathy about self-protection arises mainly from ignorance of the means of protection, and a perception that somebody else – 'the Government' or insurance companies – bears most of the cost of theft and vandalism. The community is beginning to realise however that crime rates are rising despite increased penalties, that the judicial system cannot cope, and that it is the individual who eventually foots the bill for crime through increased taxes for expanded police forces and more jails, and through higher insurance premiums.
>
> (Geason and Wilson 1989:9)

In this process, security becomes the responsibility of the private individuals who through the pursuit of self-interest, and liberated from enervating reliance on 'the state' to provide for them will participate in the creation of the new order.

Putting these points together, it can be seen that in this construction of situational crime prevention there is no conflict between risk management *per se* and punitiveness. Quite to the contrary, in the privatization of the actuarial techniques are the same notions of individual responsibility and rational choice that are present in the justification for expanding punitiveness. Reliance on the state, even for protection against crime, is not to be encouraged. Quite literally therefore it represents the expression in one field of the New Right ideal of the Strong

State and the Free Market, combining to provide crime control in a period when the threat of crime generated by the Right's own market oriented practices can be expected to increase.

CRIME PREVENTION AND SOCIAL JUSTICE

The discussion of situational crime prevention thus far has been one-sided, for it has deliberately focused on developments illustrative of the ways in which risk-based and punitive techniques may be rendered compatible and mutually reinforcing under neo-conservatism. It will not have escaped recognition that situational crime prevention is by no means *necessarily* associated with neo-conservatism. The French Bonnemaison program for example incorporates much that is focused on social justice (King 1988). Likewise, in the Australian state of Victoria situational crime prevention is integrated quite explicitly with a government focus on social justice and is shaped accordingly (Sandon 1991a, 1991b; Victoria Police 1991). Thus with respect to the status of women, an issue on which situational crime prevention has been soundly criticized, such policies have extended well beyond narrowly defensive and privatized risk bearing, and have embedded preventative techniques in socializing reforms, being 'concentrated on reducing violence against women by targeting the involvement of the community to change male behaviour and attitudes, empower women in unsafe situations and change community perceptions and understandings about violence toward women' (Thurgood 1991).

Clearly this social justice contextualization of situational crime prevention conflicts considerably with the behavioural regulation model reviewed above and criticized by Cohen. Not only is this because of the focus on changing people's attitudes and 'inner states', but also because it reflects a series of value assertions and policy directions which are remote from rational choice individualism. Such articulation between situational crime prevention and collective responses to crime as an issue of *social justice* of course reflects precisely that social risk-based model actively discarded by conservatives, and which was highlighted by the analyses of Simon *et al.* Articulation of situational crime prevention with social justice is intelligible in terms of the construction of risk as shared among large sectors of the populace – a precondition of socialized actuarialism. Thus with the welfare model, 'The concept of social risk makes it possible for insurance technologies to be applied to social problems in a way which can be presented as creative simultaneously of social justice and social solidarity' (Gordon 1991: 40).

It is therefore intelligible that risk-based techniques may be allied to socializing political programs through their discursive construction in terms of shared risk. Conversely it is equally clear that it may be articulated with a conservative political program through discursive construction in terms of rational choice individuals. As witnessed, this construction fosters the combination of a variety of disciplinary, punitive, and risk-based techniques in order to achieve effects consistent with neo-conservative programs. […]

REFERENCES

Cohen, Stanley (1985) *Visions of Social Control: Crime, Punishment and Classification*, London: Polity Press.

Foucault, Michel (1977) *Discipline and Punish*, London: Peregrine Books.

Gamble, Andrew (1988) *The Free Economy and the Strong State*, London: Macmillan.

Geason, Susan and Wilson, Paul (1989) *Crime Prevention: Theory and Practice*, Canberra: Australian Institute of Criminology.

Gordon, Colin (1991) 'Governmental rationality: An introduction', in G. Burchell, C. Gordon and P. Miller (eds), *The Foucault Effect. Studies in Governmentality*, London: Harvester/Wheatsheaf.

Hall, John (1986) 'Burglary: The insurance industry viewpoint', in S. Mukherjee (ed.), *Burglary. A Social Reality*, Canberra: AIC.

Hogg, Russell (1989) 'Criminal justice and social control: Contemporary development in Australia', *Journal of Studies in Justice* 2: 89–122.

Home Office (1990) *Crime, Justice and Protecting The Public*, London: HMSO.

King, Michael (1988) *How to Make Social Crime Prevention Work: The French Experience*, London: NACRO Occasional Paper.

Levitas, Ruth (1986) 'Introduction. Ideology and the New Right', in Ruth Levitas (ed.), *The Ideology of the New Right*, Oxford: Basil Blackwell.

O'Malley, Pat (1991) 'Legal networks and domestic security', *Studies in Law, Politics and Society* 11: 181–91.

Reichman, Nancy (1986) 'Managing crime risks: Toward an insurance based model of social control', *Research in Law and Social Control* 8: 151–72.

Sandon, Mai (1991a) *Safety and Security*, Melbourne: Ministry of Policy and Emergency Services (Victoria).

Sandon, Mai (1991b) *Ministerial Statement: Safety, Security and Women*, Melbourne: Parliament of Victoria.

Simon, Jonathan (1987) 'The emergence of a risk society: Insurance, law and the state', *Socialist Review* 95: 61–89.

Thurgood, Pat (1991) 'Safety, security and women', Paper Presented at the Crime Prevention seminar, Ministry of Police and Emergency Services, Melbourne, 30 August.

45

Governing through crime

Jonathan Simon

GOVERNMENT, PUNISHMENT, AND MODERNITY

The claim that our society is 'postmodern' depends in the end on what one thinks has changed in the present that requires breaking the useful interpretive frames that have been associated with modernity.[1] This paper proposes that one powerful candidate for such a change is the historic relationship between government, punishment, and modernity. A century ago, Emile Durkheim[2] argued that the form of legal regulation in a society was a telling indicator of its social order. The degree to which a society was governed through penal laws and sanctions, as opposed to civil law and contractual agreements, provided a kind of index to the modernizing process.

Traditional societies, according to Durkheim, were held together by a 'mechanical solidarity,' i.e., a common identification sustained by a limited division of labor. The major symbolic resource of this identification with society and its commonality was the criminal law, which provided occasions to invoke forceful and ritualistic mobilization of the social group as a whole against its internal enemies. Since crime and the opportunity to punish provide a critical platform to govern traditional societies, categories of criminals or crimes that disappear must be replaced by redefining other conduct as criminal.[3]

Modern societies reproduce social order through a much more complicated system of identifications that Durkheim called 'organic solidarity.' These identifications arise from a highly developed division of labor. Governing such societies required a shift from penal laws to those that regulated and validated a more diffuse array of legal relationships between and among individuals and groups, provided by the bodies of civil law including contract, property, and torts. Modern societies, in short, could be recognized in part by the proliferation of regulative over retributive laws. Even the criminal law, in such a society,

---

From *The Crime Conundrum*, pp. 171–89 (eds L. Friedman and G. Fisher, Boulder, CO: Westview, 1997)

increasingly becomes a vehicle for recognizing degrees of deviation and invoking complex webs of social control.[4]

Durkheim's evolutionary claims have been largely debunked. Still, his essential insight that the division of labor makes it possible to coordinate individuals without as much reliance on the heavy hand of state coercion remains viable. Moreover, Durkheim's picture of a society whose very diversity, dynamism, and complexity made it capable of achieving a deeper level of coordination than simpler societies remains an important part of our self identity as moderns. In a number of different ways the long association of modernization with the diminution of crime and punishment as the central features of social order maintenance seems to be undergoing some kind of reversal.

As historians of crime and violence have largely come to agree, urban life in the past was more rather than less violent. While lacking statistical precision, scholars suggest that with scale of population taken into account, cities in Europe and its North American offshoots have experienced declines in violence from the sixteenth century on, and especially after the middle of the nineteenth century, a process that various scholars have credited to work discipline, moral education, and the deepening interiority of the self.[5] This trend began to collapse in the 1940s and reverse itself, rising sharply in the 1950s and 1960s to levels that continue today.

Imprisonment rates in the United States fluctuated within a limited range from the beginning of reliable statistics in the 1920s through the late 1970s. Since then they have experienced an unprecedented upsurge that continues after tripling the portion of the population incarcerated to more than 409 per 100,000.[6] Among African American males the figure is ten times as great.[7] When we look at total correctional supervision the figures are even more dramatic. More than two percent of the total adult population and more than thirty-three percent of young African American male adults are in some form of custody or under some form of penal supervision on any given day.[8]

One penal practice that acts with particular sensitivity as a marker of modernity is the death penalty, or rather its diminution. Limiting or abolishing the death penalty has been associated with the processes of modernization and democratization almost everywhere from the antimonarchical revolutions of the late eighteenth century through contemporary South Africa. Since World War II virtually all European nations have abandoned the practice altogether or reserved it for categories of atrocities that only rarely come to pass. In the United States, however, the practice of the death penalty is undergoing a resurgence. Political support for the death penalty has grown rapidly since the 1970s and now commands an overwhelming majority of virtually every relevant demographic group. Concern with the legislation and administration of the death penalty is an increasing focus of government and election campaigns. Executions themselves have increased much more slowly, but with one state, Texas, now executing several prisoners per month, the death penalty may be on the eve of its rebirth as a conventional punishment in the United States.

Fear of crime has become a dominant theme of political culture. Because the incarcerated population, despite its unprecedented growth, is still small relative to other sites of governance like schools, businesses, and families, it is tempting to view it as a specialized sector. It is easy to show that incorporation into this sector is quite unequally spread and is among the most problematic differences in advanced industrial societies. But governing through crime seems to have a broader purchase in a number of ways that are harder to measure than the formal jurisdictional demography of the criminal justice system: A shift of attention to criminal justice system elements in the business of Congress and state legislatures; a dramatic over-representation of crime and punishment views as issues in election campaigns for all kinds of office, the more so the more central and powerful the position; the reinvigoration in all sorts of institutions, from colleges to businesses to families, of governance by rule and sanction; the obsessive media attention to crime and punishment that has both drawn on crime as the preferred metaphor for all forms of social anxiety and highlighted acts of punishment or retribution as the primary way of resolving disputes of almost any sort.

In summary, a historical diminution in the significance of crime and punishment to governance has ended. Indeed, something like a reversal is taking place. To a degree that would have surprised the sociological observers of modernity in the nineteenth and the first half of the twentieth century, we are governing ourselves through crime.[9]

GOVERNANCE

The central argument of this essay is that advanced industrial societies (particularly the United States) are experiencing not a crisis of crime and punishment but a crisis of governance that has led them to prioritize crime and punishment as the preferred contexts for governance. I want to refer to this phenomenon as 'governing through crime.' By governance I mean not simply the actions of the state but all efforts to guide and direct the conduct of others.

> The exercise of power consists in guiding the possibility of conduct and putting in order the possible outcome. Basically power is less a confrontation between two adversaries or the linking of one to the other than a question of government. ... To govern, in this sense, is to structure the possible field of action of others.[10]

We govern through crime to the extent to which crime and punishment become the occasions and the institutional contexts in which we undertake to guide the conduct of others (or even of ourselves).[11]

It has been obvious for some time that crime was casting a disproportionate shadow over what we primarily identify with governance, i.e., politicians and the electoral process of democracy. Every U.S. presidential campaign since Goldwater-Johnson in 1964 has been fought partly on the turf of crime. Since the reaction to the 'Willie Horton' ad on behalf of George Bush in 1988, the salience of crime and its interconnection with race have been taken as given features of American politics. If crime kept a lower profile in the 1996 campaign, it was only because both candidates wholly gave themselves up to the public fixation on the 'crisis' of crime.

Although crime rates appear to have dropped significantly in recent years, a trend that has been exhaustively covered in the media and that may continue in the short term, a poll taken at the end of May 1996 showed crime as the top issue on the minds of the public.[12] The *New York Times* summarized the message of the Dole campaign: 'Mr. Dole has repeatedly portrayed himself as a friend of victims and Mr. Clinton as a friend to criminals.'[13] Meanwhile, Mr. Clinton traveled the country urging curfews for teenagers, uniforms for school children, and tougher sentences for juvenile offenders.[14]

Less obvious are the ways in which crime has become a linchpin of governance within the less celebrated but more primary settings of governance. In schools, prevention of crime and drug use has arguably been the most significant agenda item for the last two decades (having replaced integration, among other concerns). Even school uniforms, now suddenly back in fashion, are justified in the name of identifying non-students attempting to infiltrate the school for gang or drug sales activities. In the workplace, noncrime themes still predominate, but drugs and crime are moving up on the margins of struggles about how work shall be governed. We see management testing employees for drugs and unions threatening to 'drop a dime' on employers who violate environmental regulations.

Durkheim's basic intuition that his society was one where crime and punishment formed a far less important source of governance than contract, property, family, and other forms of civil association is doubtless still true of ours. Even a crude quantitative analysis of pages in legal codes, case reporters, or administrative reports would doubtless show that we are governed far less by criminal law than by other sources of commands and norms. But trends are important as well. A refined quantitative analysis might in fact be able to capture a distinct tilt in the production of governance back towards crime and punishment over the last two or three decades.

EXPLANATIONS

The priority of governing through crime might sensibly be thought to arise in response to a genuine increase in crime. As I suggested above, the long curve of declining violence in Western societies seems to have ended in the 1940s. But the steepest increases in crime, and violent crime in particular, came in the 1950s and 1960s. Since then, crime rates appear to have fluctuated within a relatively shallow range. The demand for punishment, however, escalated in the midst of this flat period. Even a political lag would not explain why the demand has actually grown stronger throughout the last decade and a half. This late coming fixation on crime may be explained as a response to the selective crime reporting of the media. But while media representation of crime is clearly a major factor in the politics of crime, it provides just as much of a question as an answer. We still need to understand why crime is such a compelling story about ourselves. Its quantitative increase cannot alone explain that.

We might turn instead for an explanation to the resurgence of conservative political forces that began in the late 1970s in the United States and other mature industrial societies, and persisted through the early 1990s (at least). The rhetoric of conservatives suggests they favor the criminal law as a tool of state governance and regard highly punitive private norms to be the preferred strategy in other settings for governance. From this perspective we can see the crime and violence surge of the 1960s as mobilizing support for conservative policies and vindicating the conservative critique of liberal governments as overly 'permissive.'

There is doubtless some link between the conservative ascendancy and the trend toward governing through crime, but there are also reasons to doubt that the former explains the latter. For one thing contemporary liberals also find themselves drawn toward punishment as a locus for governance. Laws and institutional rules punishing racist speech, domestic violence, sexual harassment, and pornography, for example, have become major agenda items for some liberals. Likewise, twentieth century conservatives often embraced noncriminal approaches to governance as an alternative to social instability.[15] It is interesting that in a period of conservative ascendancy during which the right has articulated aspirations to govern through patriotism, work, and family, as well as crime, it is largely with respect to crime and punishment that there has been significant legislative success.[16]

Even if conservative ideology does not drive the trend toward governing through crime, conservatives in virtually all late- or postmodern societies have benefited politically from their ability to articulate the perception, shared by many of their fellow citizens, that traditional and traditionally modernist means of regulating youth – including families, schools, the labor force, churches, the military, etc. – have weakened.[17] Voters in all these societies, but especially the United States, have affirmed the belief that social control is breaking down and that punishment of crime is the most promising strategy for checking that breakdown.[18]

From this perspective it is helpful to recall that crime and punishment issues have long been associated with the difficulties of governing urban populations.[19] Crime had literally mapped and written the cities during the nineteenth century.[20] By the beginning of the twentieth century, however, the singular figures of the criminal and the homogeneous dangerous classes were no longer central targets of social policy because new practices and sciences made it possible to govern cities through new handles on industry, ethnicity and nationality, youthfulness, and ignorance. Even crime and punishment were reconfigured around these agendas.[21] For much of the twentieth century, punishment of crime was displaced as the key to urban governance by a focus on housing, public health, social work, and education.

This family of strategies has been associated with a variety of terms and figures including Keynesianism, Fordism,[22] collectivism,[23] and the social.[24] These new maps depicted social life as distributions of aggregate risks that could be governed by redistributing them. Elsewhere, I, along with others, have described some of the properties of these new governance strategies and of the new political technologies they deployed, including insurance, case work, and social statistics.[25] One of the key elements in constructing this new approach to governing was the social response to industrial accidents and the quasi-industrial consumer accidents that have concerned us for much of the twentieth century.[26] The accident became a model for designing new ways to intervene in power relations. But the accident could play this role only after a long effort, never completed, to be free of the implication of crime.[27]

When President Clinton repeated during his 1996 State of the Union Address that the era of big government was over, he was echoing the call made successfully by the Republican candidates for Congress in 1994 that the size of the federal government should be reduced. But he may also have been adverting to a less visible point. The era is over when it seemed plausible to govern society through 'big-ness.' That sense of scale is exactly what programs like unemployment insurance, worker's compensation, and the like were about: harnessing insurance and related technologies to balance the risks produced by industrial society with the very scale that seemed the source of much of this risk.

The era of 'big government' went well beyond the state. It was a style of private sector organization as well, exemplified by the great unionized industries like automobiles and steel in which the control of large oligopolies over market conditions helped make possible a labor peace based on cooperative shifting of the cost onto the larger structures of consumption and investment.[28] Insurance companies were once a symbol of this era and the sort of governance it promoted. The 'good hands' of Allstate, for example, were giant hands that invited everybody in. Prudential invited Americans to link their precarious individual circumstances to the strength of its collective capital by owning 'a piece of the rock.' Their latest ad advises consumers to 'be your own rock.'[29]

Lately we seem to be experiencing a crisis of these modes of governance. The United States and other advanced industrial societies have found themselves reevaluating systems of collective risk distribution like welfare, public education, unemployment insurance, and worker's compensation. The failure of modest national health insurance in the United States in 1993 was a potent reminder of how muddled the basic narratives and rationalities supporting these governance modalities have become.[30] Governing through crime, at its broadest, might be looked at as a response to this crisis, both a reaching back to real or imagined strategies for maintaining what appears to be a precarious social order, and a reaching forward toward new platforms to govern a social order that truly is undergoing remarkable demographic and economic change.[31]

A number of scholars have begun to describe the emergence of a neo-liberal family of technologies of governing.[32] In place of the great collectivist risk distribution systems, neo-liberal techniques reemphasize the individual as a critical manager of risk, but do so through deliberate steering mechanisms rather than the threats and exhortations of traditional liberalism.[33] Socializing risk inevitably undermined discipline (just as its critics said it would). The new strategies aim to hold individuals more accountable, or to 'responsibilize' them, as some observers have aptly described it.[34] Governing through crime is also a way of imposing this new model of governance on the population.

GOVERNING THROUGH SECURITY

An observer of political discourse in the United States might believe that people were increasingly governed by a logic that left virtually everything important in life to personal choice disciplined only by the fear of unremitting punishment for those who stepped across the lines drawn by the criminal law. What this picture would miss is how intensely we are regulated in the spaces where middle-class people spend most of their time. Spaces of work and consumption, and those hybrids like airports and shopping centers that are spaces of both, have become sites of extensive and detailed management. Private associations have increasingly filled in the regulatory gap left by official government. Some of this takes the shape of quasi-penal norms, like rules against smoking, playing radios, or skate boarding. Much of the new governance takes the shape of highly engineered environments that are designed to avoid recognized hazards and mitigate others without even seeking the compliance of the subject.

What the governments of many of these places share, besides the demands of a market economy, is a focus on the problem of security.[35] They are focused on making people safe, for themselves and for others. Crime, of course, is a primary form of insecurity for these regimes, but one can govern crime without governing through crime. Governing through security focuses on the potential for harm rather than its source or explanations. While everything is open as a possible strategy for such a risk management approach, including punishments, there is no investment in punishment as a political ceremony. A security regime, in the end, is not there to enforce individual adherence to performance norms except where that is an effective way to minimize cost.

These techniques have been most widely adopted by private organizations responsible for maintaining the security of employees and customers. Perhaps the most famous such organization is the Disney Corporation, whose theme parks are world renowned for amusement. These sites also deserve to be seen as exemplars of risk management in which virtually every aspect has been designed to minimize harmful actions (accidental or otherwise) while at the same time minimizing any appearance of coercive social control, which would be highly incompatible with their primary business of selling family fun.[36] Many of the same technologies are deployed in managing quasi-public spaces around and in large residential, commercial, and mixed-use spaces, which Shearing and Stenning call 'mass private property.'[37] Another important site for the development of government through security has been international airports, which have had to create governance systems capable of dealing with multiple levels of hazard (every flight going in or out is a potential mass disaster) and a fluctuating human population with little in common besides the haste and anxiety attendant on air travel.

The implications of these risk management or security approaches to governance are a subject in their own right.[38] They constitute an emerging alternative to the more collectivist risk distribution systems that are now in crisis. There are clear political dangers associated with this approach to governance. These techniques are easily turned toward exclusionary ends, something often demanded by the market. They are generally insensitive to the importance of spaces of deviation around which important forms of personal and political mobilization may take place. Here it is sufficient to note that they offer promising responses to those tendencies, discussed above, that seem to be driving the trend toward governing through crime.

Risk management techniques do not involve explicit pooling of risk and thus avoid the political problems that have beset efforts to extend the old collectivist risk distribution framework. Thus, theme parks and airports are utterly social in the sense that they have been designed with the collectivity of users in mind, but they require, among consumers at least, no formal association or common responsibilities.

Risk management techniques do not rely on inter subjectivity to produce order. These spaces are engineered to be navigable by those who share not even language. Airports and shopping centers have long had to cope with diverse users. Their technologies are spreading fast in societies where immigration and multiculturalism are undermining (or at least are perceived as undermining) traditional and modern sources of integration.

Risk management techniques do not invoke the form of sovereign power linked to the criminal law and its chain of discrediting and disabling experiences and associations.

COMMUNITY POLICING

The idea of replacing strategies based on crime control with strategies based on making people safe has recently emerged in the discourse of policing. While some of the programs have evoked a nostalgia for the classic 'beat cop' of the old urban neighbourhoods, the reality of community policing has more in common with Disney World. The New York Police Department, often hailed today as an exemplar of the potential for community policing, relies heavily on 'CompStat,' a program that utilizes computer technology to integrate decision making and statistical measures of performance. The strategy is to create objective foundations for accountability that allow commanders to regulate themselves as they regulate their line staff. As former NYPD Commissioner William Bratton describes the orientation of community policing on his watch: 'Today's department doesn't just try to solve individual crimes. We counter crime patterns and dismantle criminal enterprises.'[39]

While emphasizing the idea of security and creating structures to help govern communities through hybrid associations of police, insurance, and individual voluntarism,[40] community policing inevitably links these structures to the apparatus of arrest, prosecution, and punishment. Because they are ultimately accountable to democratic forces and are often more representative of their communities than other power centers, police departments offer an attractive counterbalance to the exclusionary tendency of private security. But community policing, so long as it remains basically committed to crime as the central justification for order maintenance, runs the risk of reinforcing the imperative of our societies to govern through crime. Indeed, the NYPD strategy exemplifies this danger by explicitly justifying the arrest and removal of 'squeegee men,' out-of-door marijuana smokers and alcohol drinkers, and other public order violators as measures against violent crime.

AMERICAN EXCEPTIONALISM

Some will argue that governing through crime is largely an American phenomenon. Virtually all of the evidence I have discussed here has been American. Still, for the reasons explored in the section on explanations, we should expect to find governing through crime to be a prominent feature of all societies that are undergoing the process of dismantling the governance strategies of industrial modernity, a process some have connected with the cultural experience of postmodernity.[41]

But even if governing through crime does have corollaries in other societies, the American case is clearly unique in its degree. I can offer two provisional explanations. The first is race. The problem of race has been intertwined in the practices of crime and punishment almost since the beginning of the European settlement of the North American Atlantic coast. Today the real and imaginary links of violence (and street crime generally)[42] with young African American men are helping to drive the imperative of governing through crime. Whether or not voters acknowledge such motives to pollsters, it is hard to ignore the continuities between the present situation and a traditional preference for governing predominantly African American populations in distinct and distinctly less respectable ways.

The second provisional explanation arises from the commitment to democratization for which the United States has been long and justly famous.[43] For centuries, this democratic spirit has had a complex relationship with the program of governing through crime. The revolutionary generation and the next few to follow considered governing through crime in a democratic way to be an important tool in overturning monarchical governance.[44] Certain forms of punishment, like mutilation and transportation, came to be seen as incompatible with republican institutions, as did overuse of the death penalty. The prison, meanwhile, came to be seen as a positive tool of democracy. There is a sense in which our commitment to governing through crime represents a continued commitment to democratic governance. In insisting that we invest in the apparatus that enables us to use punishment to achieve social order, we affirm the sovereignty of each individual. A society with less faith in the capacity of individuals to govern themselves would seek to constrain their behavior – not merely to punish their misbehavior.[45]

A commitment to democracy also exalts the popular basis of justice. Well into the twentieth century we witnessed a form of direct community ratification of governing through crime. Crime and punishment were regulated by elected sheriffs (or patronage-controlled police), by juries drawn from the white male citizenry, and by local judges who were subject to little appellate review. Such direct community involvement in the processes of crime control is much diminished today. Indeed, the growth of massive police and penal apparatuses and of a bureaucratic court system has problematized the relationship between the popular enthusiasm for criminal justice and its practice.

CONCLUSION: CRIME AND THE POLITICS OF GOVERNANCE

[…] [Currently] in the spring of 1997, the United States, at least, seems quite committed to governing through crime. The Republican party has declared itself irrevocably attached to this strategy. Republican policies call for massively enlarging the penal system while emphasizing such archaic punishments as the death penalty and highway chain gangs. So little concerned is the party of Lincoln with the impact of this strategy on the nation's racial politics that its congressional delegation has rejected the considered and conservative judgment of the United States Sentencing Commission that our current policy, which punishes dealers in crack cocaine far more harshly than those who traffic in its powdered form, is unjustified and discriminatory against African Americans.[46] The same party that a century and a quarter ago made unequal punishment, like slavery, an offense against our Constitution, now sneers at the sight of a large portion of the descendants of freedmen locked into a system that directly jeopardizes their ability to participate in a common national economic market and political society.

Impressed by the ability of Republican presidents to reap electoral benefits from governing through crime, the Clinton Administration has followed a one step forward, two steps back approach, in which small gestures in the direction of governing through security are left undefended while the juggernaut toward expensive and crude penal techniques only gathers speed. As mid-term elections approached in August 1994, the President committed himself to campaigning on a record of governing through crime. He failed to defend innovative ideas embraced by that fall's crime bill, such as midnight basketball, that perfectly exemplified good ways to make people secure in more positive, more productive, less stigmatizing, and less expensive settings than courts and prisons.

The President believed he could run on crime, but the November 1994 election gave that strategy an awful blow. One thing governing through crime does not do is mobilize those constituencies that are receptive to progressive strategies for managing social change. That is, the ideological logic of using crime as a rationale of governing may make it more difficult to undertake badly needed reconstruction of government. In the long run the argument against governing through crime must be that it will make us ungovernable, at least by democratic techniques.

Here are what I take to be the strongest reasons for abandoning this strategy:

Governing through crime is too costly

In a world of limited economic growth the explosive expansion of spending on all aspects of the police and penal systems has had a devastating effect on other forms of public spending to govern society. California is a chilling case in point. Twenty years ago, California's booming economy supported and was supported by a world-class educational system that absorbed the academically achieving children of all its high schools into its elite university system at an affordable $1,000 a year. With around 25,000 inmates in the prisons of the California Department of Corrections, the state could afford to spend twice as much on providing higher education as it did on punishing. For the 1996–1997 academic year, undergraduates at the University of California will pay more than $4,000. At the same time, the California Department of Corrections expects to have an average population of around 140,000 prisoners.[47] Twenty years ago corrections received half the budget that higher education received. The two enterprises are now at parity. Recent legislation mandating sentences of twenty-five years to life for a 'third strike' in California is likely to double the corrections budget within a decade. At the same time the state has cut back on welfare benefits and spending on K-12 education, both of which, in their own ways, have provided means for governing populations of young males who are being transferred to the criminal justice system in record numbers.

Governing through crime costs on the supply side of the economy as well. The cost of governing through crime (i.e. the cost of punishing, less whatever punishing does to lower the cost of crime) is a part of the cost of living, working, and consuming in the United States. To the extent that other societies achieve the levels of social order needed for profitable production and consumption without the high social, political, and economic costs of crime control, they enjoy competitive advantages over the United States.

Governing through crime does not work

Strange as it may sound, given the 'common sense' view, there is little evidence to support the proposition that criminal justice system processing reduces the offending rates either of those who pass through it or of the population as a whole. The best study of the state that has invested most heavily in the massive incarceration strategy, California, shows that imprisonment has prevented some crimes but at a cost-effectiveness ratio that few Republicans would defend in their own corporations.[48]

Governing through crime makes communities less governable through alternative strategies

Whatever the precise rationale may be for the massive transfer of lower-class young males from schools and the labor market to the penal system, this phenomenon has enormous consequences for the longer-term governability of this population. It is a transfer to a distinct and isolated institutional space, where they are governed in a distinct way. To live in the criminal justice system is not only to be subject to a somewhat different and far harsher regime of formal law, but in a broader sense to enter a world (that includes the criminal underworld itself) in which the entire economy of power, norms, methods, and forms of solidarity differs from that of the rest of society. In this world violence serves as a tool of government far more readily than it has in the rest of society for a long time.[49]

Incarceration measurably increases the chance that someone will commit another crime and likewise makes it harder for the subject to be absorbed into an alternative economy of power (like work, but also including family and community-building activities). It also produces a powerful set of special interests – correctional officers and managers, companies that service prisons, communities that provide workers to them – that make any effort to adjust, let alone abandon, this strategy politically costly.

Felony convictions blow huge holes in the political and economic status of a person. In most states you lose the right to vote unless it is regranted by a pardons board of some sort. Virtually everywhere you go to the back of the job line. These sanctions reflect our determination to punish. As the war on drugs attaches criminal liability to nearly every household in some parts of our inner cities, it dilutes and squanders the capacity of the criminal law to rouse a common moral solidarity. Just as Prohibition isolated and alienated Irish, Italian, and Jewish communities, the war on drugs threatens to cordon off and criminalize entire urban neighbourhoods.

Governing through crime is corrosive of democracy

Classical theorists recognized that criminal law was intimately related to the larger strategies of governing society. The leaders of our eighteenth century democratic revolutions gave priority to the abolition of monarchical procedures and the formation of new, lighter, more democratic modes of punishment. These leaders believed that free subjects would respond rationally not to the blunt command of the state, but to the incentive structure of its penal laws. The calculus of penalties urged by Beccaria and Bentham was a real alternative to the excessive punishments associated with monarchical codes – codes that, as far as shaping a free and productive society was concerned, were distinctly dysfunctional.[50]

Are the harsher sentences of today meant to send a signal to free men? It would be hard to take this idea seriously. The implausibility of the classical ideal in the real conditions of urban poverty in America is apparent to those on all sides of the political spectrum. But instead of backing away from our commitment to governing through crime, we openly offer punishment for the purposes of warehousing the untrustworthy and creating moral entertainments (like chain gangs) for the virtuous. Whatever the merits of these purposes, neither augurs well for democratic practice.

More ominously, crime and fear of crime continue to drive deeper levels of suburban isolationism. The emerging metropolitan form, with its combination of collapsed urban center and sprawling suburban edge city, with its overlays of race and demonization, constitutes a direct challenge to the ideal of democratic nationhood.[51]

We cannot wish our real urban problems away, but we can make real choices among different orientations toward managing them. Crime will remain an important urban problem for a long time to come no matter what we do about it. But governing through crime reproduces the mentalities and strategies that have helped bring us to this impasse. With the right political choices, we could begin to change those mentalities and strategies tomorrow.

NOTES

1   For a defense of the proposition that the older framework is still a useful one with respect to penal practices, see David Garland, *Punishment and Welfare: A History of Penal Strategies* (Brookfield, Vt.: Gower, 1985), pp. 3–35.

2   *See* Emile Durkheim, *The Division of Labor in Society*, English edition, George Simpson, trans. (New York: Free Press, 1933; originally published 1893).

3   Kai T. Erikson, *Wayward Puritans: A Study in the Sociology of Deviance* (New York: John Wiley and Sons, 1966), pp. 3–5, 8, 26.

4   Michel Foucault, *Discipline and Punish: The Birth of the Prison*, Alan Sheridan, trans. (New York: Vintage, 1979), pp. 73–103.

5   Norbert Elias, *The Civilizing Process: The History of Manners* (New York: Urizen, 1978), pp. 191–205; Roger Lane, *Policing the City: Boston, 1822–1885* (Cambridge: Harvard University Press, 1967), pp. 220–29; Eric H. Monkkonen, 'A Disorderly People? Urban Order in the Nineteenth and Twentieth Centuries' in *Journal of American History*, Vol. 68, No. 3, December 1981, pp. 539–59.

6   Bureau of Justice Statistics, *Sourcebook of Criminal Justice Statistics* (Washington, D.C., 1996), p. 4.

7   Marc Mauer, *Americans Behind Bars: The International Use of Incarceration* (Washington, D.C.: The Sentencing Project, 1995), p. 7.

8   Ibid.

9   It is true that many advanced industrial societies, and not just the United States, have been plagued by crime. What sets the United States apart is the obsessive focus on the problem of *punishment.*

10   Michel Foucault, 'The Subject and Power,' in Hubert L. Dreyfus and Paul Rabinow, eds., *Michel Foucault: Beyond Structuralism and Hermeneutics* (Chicago: University of Chicago Press, 1982), p. 220.

11   Nikolas Rose elaborates on Foucault's definition of government as 'a certain way of striving to reach social and political ends by acting in a calculating manner upon the forces, activities and relations of the individuals that constitute a population.' Nikolas Rose, *Governing the Soul: The Shaping of the Private Self* (London: Routledge, 1990), p. 4. I would differ from Rose slightly and use government for all such calculating actions upon 'forces, activities and relations of individuals,' leaving the priority of the population as a feature of a particular rationality of government that arose in the sixteenth century and remains. The term 'governance' is also beginning to be widely used again in political science and urban studies where the emphasis is on broadening the focus from the government in the sense of the state, to the relationship between government and civil society. *See* Patricia McCarney, Mohammed Halfani, and Alfredo Rodriguez, 'Towards an Understanding of Governance: The Emergence of an Idea and Its Implications for Urban Research in Developing Countries,' in Richard Stren, ed., *Urban Research in the Developing World* (Toronto: Centre for Urban and Community Studies, 1994), p. 95.

12   Richard L. Berke, 'Voter Ratings for President Change Little,' in *New York Times*, June 5, 1996, p. A1.

13   Katharine Q. Seelye, 'Revisiting the Issue of Crime, Dole Offers List of Remedies,' in *New York Times*, May 29, 1996, pp. A1, A12.

14   Berke, 'Voter Ratings,' p. A12.

15   James Gilbert, *Designing the Industrial State: The Intellectual Pursuit of Collectivism in America, 1880–1940* (Chicago: Quadrangle Books, 1972), pp. 5–9.

16   When we look more closely at strategies to govern through patriotism or the family, we find techniques of governing through crime – like laws against flag burning and child sexual abuse. Indeed, when Senator Robert Dole, the Republican nominee for President in 1996, sought to articulate why women should support his candidacy, he listed his support for measures to make it easier to convict rapists and prosecute

domestic violence. Katharine Q. Seelye, 'Dole Says He Has Plan To Win Votes of Women,' in *New York Times*, May 8, 1996, p. A1.

17 Ulrich Beck usefully suggests that modernity developed its own kind of traditional base, the urban and industrial life and culture, which is now waning. Ulrich Beck, *Risk Society: Towards a New Modernity* (London: Sage, 1992).

18 Berke, 'Voter Ratings,' p. A1; Seelye, 'Dole Says He Has Plan,' p. A1.

19 There is, of course, a history of governing cities through the problem of crime and related problems like insurrection, disease, and poverty. Lane, *Policing the City*, pp. 3–25; Louis Chevalier, *Laboring Classes and Dangerous Classes in Paris During the First Half of the Nineteenth Century* (Princeton: Princeton University Press, 1973), pp. 161–254.

20 Marie-Christine Leps, *Apprehending the Criminal: The Production of Deviance in Nineteenth Century Discourse* (Duke: Duke University Press, 1992), pp. 17–31.

21 Garland, *Punishment and Welfare*, pp. 73–158; Jonathan Simon, *Poor Discipline: Parole and the Social Control of the Urban Underclass, 1890–1990* (Chicago: University of Chicago Press, 1993).

22 *See* David Harvey, *The Condition of Postmodernity: An Enquiry into the Origins of Cultural Change* (New York: Blackwell, 1989).

23 Gilbert, *Designing the Industrial State*, pp. 5–9.

24 Jacques Donzelot, *The Policing of Families* (New York: Random House, 1979), pp. 88–89.

25 Garland, *Punishment and Welfare*, pp. 73–158; Rose, *Governing the Soul*, p. 4; Simon, *Poor Discipline*.

26 *See* François Ewald, *L'Etat Providence* (Paris: B. Grasset, 1986).

27 For much of the twentieth century it seemed that tort law would replace criminal law as the major forum for producing governance strategies for assuring order in modern society. We are experiencing not only a renewal of interest in governing through crime, but also a parallel sense of malaise with tort as a source of regulation. *See* Jonathan Simon, *Governing by Accident: Tort Law and the Rationalities of Governance, 1870–1990* (unpublished manuscript).

28 Michael J. Piore and Charles F. Sabel, *The Second Industrial Divide: Possibilities for Prosperity* (New York: Basic Books, 1984), pp. 3–18. One should not overstate the case here. It is difficult to imagine governing industrial and postindustrial societies without continuing reliance on many forms of collectivist risk distribution. Still, both the cultural and the economic trends are away from reliance on these technologies. We can expect to see continued political controversy over those aspects of the system most associated with unpopular groups (like welfare in the U.S.) as well as continued resistance to efforts at expansion (like the Clinton health plan).

29 The Prudential ad aired frequently on NBC during the 1996 NBA play-offs. It is difficult to tell if they are making an offer or a rejection. For the complexity of insurance company narratives generally, see Thomas Baker, 'Constructing the Insurance Relationship: Sales Stories, Claims Stories, and Insurance Contract Damages,' in *Texas Law Review*, Vol. 72, No. 6, May 1994, pp. 1395–1433.

30 Even where these governmental strategies remain strong, as in Germany, there is increasing pressure to change. Klaus Friedrich, 'The End of Germany's Economic Model,' in *New York Times*, June 10, 1996, p. A19.

31 The broadest horizon is not necessarily the deepest. It is clear that other dimensions of late-modern societies, such as renewed ethnic and racial polarization, help to determine the attraction of government through crime as well as the specific shape it takes in specific societies.

32   Andrew Barry, Thomas Osborne, and Nikolas Rose, eds., *Foucault and Political Reason: Liberalism, Neo-liberalism and Rationalities of Government* (Chicago: University of Chicago Press, 1996).

33   Nikolas Rose, 'Governing "Advanced" Liberal Democracies,' in Barry et al., eds., *Foucault and Political Reason*, pp. 37–64.

34   Pat O'Malley, 'Legal Networks and Domestic Security,' in *Studies in Law, Politics, and Society*, Vol. 11, 1991, pp. 171–90.

35   Clifford D. Shearing and Phillip C. Stenning, *Private Policing* (Newbury Park, Calif.: Sage Publications, 1987), pp. 9–18.

36   Clifford D. Shearing and Phillip C. Stenning, 'From the Panopticon to Disney World: The Development of Discipline,' in Anthony N. Doob and E. Greenspan, eds., *Perspectives in Criminal Law* (Aurora, Ont.: Canada Law Books, 1984). Hitherto the Magic Kingdom has claimed a limited jurisdiction since its citizens come for a week or less. In 1995 Disney Corporation began developing a residential community named 'Celebration' near its Orlando, Florida, park. Despite a low-end price of $120,000, nearly 5,000 people attended a lottery for a chance to buy the first 351 lots in November 1995. Joe Blundo, 'Disney's Town Taps Some Talent from Our Town,' in *Columbus Dispatch*, Sunday, March 24, 1996, p. 1K. Clearly, its residents will be paying premium prices at least as much for access to its governance technologies as for access to its amusements.

37   *See* Shearing and Stenning, 'From the Panopticon to Disney World.'

38   Beck, *Risk Society*; Richard Ericson, 'The Division of Expert Knowledge in Policing and Security,' in *British Journal of Sociology*, Vol. 45, No. 2, June 1994, pp. 149–75; Kevin Stenson, 'Community Policing as a Governmental Technology,' in *Economy and Society*, Vol. 22, No. 3, August 1993, pp. 373–89; Pat O'Malley, 'Risk, Power and Crime Prevention,' in *Economy and Society*, Vol. 21, No. 3, August 1992, pp. 252–75; Jonathan Simon, 'In the Place of the Parent: Risk Management and the Government of Campus Life,' *Social and Legal Studies*, Vol. 3, 1994, pp. 15–45; Simon, *Governing By Accident.*

39   William J. Bratton, 'How To Win the War Against Crime,' in *New York Times*, April 5, 1996, p. A17.

40   O'Malley, 'Legal Networks and Domestic Security,' pp. 181–82.

41   Harvey, *The Condition of Postmodernity.*

42   Polls suggest that many U.S. residents view street crime generally as violent even if the particular offense, such as burglary, does not involve assaults or direct threats of bodily harm. Little Hoover Commission, *Putting Violence Behind Bars: Redefining the Role of California's Prisons* (Sacramento: The Commission, 1994), p. 61.

43   David Brion Davis, *The Problem of Slavery in the Age of Revolution, 1770–1823* (Ithaca: Cornell University Press, 1975), pp. 39–83,164–212.

44   David J. Rothman, The *Discovery of the Asylum: Social Order and Disorder in the New Republic* (Boston: Little Brown, 1971), pp. 57–78; Thomas Dumm, *Democracy and Punishment: Disciplinary Origins of the United States* (Madison: University of Wisconsin Press, 1987), pp. 141–54.

45   The classic statement remains Justice Brandeis's condemnation of preventive justification for antisyndicalism laws in his concurrence in *Whitney v. California*, 274 U.S. 357, 378 (1924): 'Among free men, the deterrents ordinarily to be applied to prevent crime are education and punishment for violations of the law … '.

46   U.S. Sentencing Commission, *Executive Summary of Special Report on Cocaine and Federal Sentencing Policy, February 28, 1995*, reprinted in *Criminal Law Reporter*, Vol. 56, No. 21, March 1, 1995, pp. 2159–72.

47   California Department of Corrections, *Fall 1993 Population Projections 1993–1999.*

48   Pete Wilson planned to run for President on the promise that he could do the same for the whole country. His campaign failures, however, should not be taken as a refutation of that political strategy. *See* Franklin E. Zimring and Gordon Hawkins, *Incapacitation: Penal Confinement and the Restraint of Crime* (New York: Oxford University Press, 1995).

49   Matthew Silberman, *A World of Violence: Corrections in America* (Belmont, Calif.: Wadsworth Publishing, 1995), pp. 1–13.

50   Foucault, *Discipline and Punish*, pp. 73–103.

51   The most powerful accounts of this emerging political landscape have come from Mike Davis. Mike Davis, *City of Quartz: Excavating the Future in Los Angeles* (London: Verso, 1991), pp. 101–49.

46

Beyond *Blade Runner*: urban control. The ecology of fear

Mike Davis

1. BEYOND *BLADE RUNNER*

Every American city has its official insignia and slogan, some have municipal mascots, colors, songs, birds, trees, even rocks. But Los Angeles alone has adopted an official Nightmare.

In 1988, after three years of debate, a galaxy of corporate and civic leaders submitted to Mayor Bradley a detailed strategic plan for Southern California's future. Although most of *L.A. 2000: A City for the Future* is devoted to hyperbolic rhetoric about Los Angeles' irresistible rise as a 'world crossroads,' a section in the epilogue (written by historian Kevin Starr) considers what might happen if the city fails to create a new 'dominant establishment' to manage its extraordinary ethnic diversity. 'There is, of course, the *Blade Runner* scenario: the fusion of individual cultures into a demotic poly-glotism ominous with unresolved hostilities.' […]

With Warner Bros.' release of the original (more hard-boiled) director's cut a few months after the 1992 Los Angeles uprising, Ridley Scott's 1982 film version of the Philip K. Dick story ('Do Androids Dream of Electric Sheep?') reasserts its sovereignty over our increasingly troubled sleep. Virtually all ruminations about the future of Los Angeles now take for granted the dark imagery of *Blade Runner* as a possible, if not inevitable, terminal point of the land of sunshine.

Yet for all of *Blade Runner's* glamor as the star of sci-fi dystopias, I find it strangely anachronistic and surprisingly unprescient. […] What remains is recognizably the same vista or urban gigantism that Fritz Lang celebrated in *Metropolis* (1931).

The sinister, man-made Everest of the Tyrell Corporation, as well as all the souped-up rocket-squad-cars darting around the air space, are obvious

From Open Magazine Pamphlet Series, Pamphlet 23 (second printing 1994).

progenies – albeit now swaddled in darkness – of the famous skyscraper city of the bourgeoisie in *Metropolis*. […]

Blade Runner, in other words, remains yet another edition of this core modernist vision –alternately utopia or dystopia, *ville radieuse* or Gotham City – of the future metropolis as Monster Manhattan. […]

Ridley Scott's particular 'gigantesque caricature' may capture ethno-centric anxieties about poly-glottism run amock but it fails to imaginatively engage the real Los Angeles landscape – especially the great unbroken plains of aging bungalows, dingbats and ranch-style homes – as it socially and physically erodes into the twenty-first century.

In my recent book on Los Angeles (*City of Quartz*, 1990) I enumerate various tendencies toward the militarization of this landscape. Events since the uprising of Spring 1992 – including a deepening recession, corporate flight, savage budget cuts, a soaring homicide rate (despite the black gang truce), and a huge spree of gun-buying in the suburbs – only confirm that social polarization and spatial apartheid are accelerating. As the Endless Summer comes to an end, it seems quite possible that Los Angeles 2019 could well stand in a dystopian relationship to any ideal of the democratic city.

But what kind of cityscape, if not *Blade Runner*, would this malign evolution of inequality produce? Instead of seeing the future merely as a grotesque, Wellsian magnification of technology and architecture, I have tried to carefully extrapolate existing spatial tendencies in order to glimpse their emergent pattern. William Gibson, in *Neuromancer* and other novels, has provided stunning examples of how realist, 'extrapolative' science fiction can operate as prefigurative social theory, as well as an anticipatory opposition politics to the cyberfascism lurking over the next horizon.

In what follows, I offer a 'Gibsonian' map to a future Los Angeles that is already half-born. Paradoxically, the literal map itself […], although inspired by a vision of Marxism-for-cyberpunks, looks like nothing so much as that venerable 'combination of half-moon and dart board' that Ernest W. Burgess of the University of Chicago long ago made 'the most famous diagram in social science.'

For those unfamiliar with the legacy of the Chicago School of Sociology and their canonical study of the 'North American city,' let me just say that Burgess' dart board represents the five concentric zones into which the struggle for the survival of the fittest (as imagined by Social Darwinists) supposedly sorts urban social classes and housing types. It portrays a 'human ecology' organized by biological forces of invasion, competition, succession and symbiosis. My remapping of the urban structure takes Burgess back to the future. It preserves such 'ecological' determinants as income, land value, class and race, but adds a decisive new factor: fear.

2. SCANSCAPE

Is there any need to explain *why* fear eats the soul of Los Angeles?

The current obsession with personal safety and social insulation is only exceeded by the middle-class dread of progressive taxation. In the face of unemployment and homelessness on scales not seen since 1938, a bipartisan consensus insists that the budget must be balanced and entitlements reduced. Refusing to make any further public investment in the remediation of underlying social conditions, we are forced instead to make increasing private investments in physical security. The rhetoric of urban reform persists, but the substance is extinct. 'Rebuilding L.A.' simply means padding the bunker.

As city life, in consequence, grows more feral, the different social milieux adopt security strategies and technologies according to their means. Like Burgess' original dart board, the resulting pattern condenses into concentric zones. The bull's eye is Downtown.

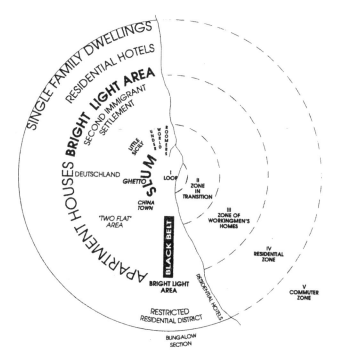

In another essay I have recounted in detail how a secretive, emergency committee of Downtown's leading corporate landowners (the so-called Committee of 25) responded to the perceived threat of the 1965 Watts Rebellion. Warned by law-enforcement authorities that a black 'inundation' of the central city was imminent, the Committee of 25 abandoned redevelopment efforts in the old office and retail core. They then used the city's power of eminent domain to raze neighborhoods and create a new financial core a few blocks further west. The city's redevelopment agency, acting virtually as their private planner, bailed out the Committee of 25's sunk investments in the old business district by offering huge discounts, far below market value, on parcels in the new core.

Key to the success of the entire strategy (celebrated as Downtown L.A.'s 'renaissance') was the physical segregation of the new core and its land values behind a rampart of regarded palisades, concrete pillars and freeway walls. Traditional pedestrian connections between Bunker Hill and the old core were removed, and foot traffic in the new financial district was elevated above the street on pedways whose access was controlled by the security systems of individual skyscrapers. This radical privatization of Downtown public space – with its ominous racial undertones – occurred without significant public debate or protest.

Last year's riots, moreover, have only seemed to vindicate the foresight of Fortress Downtown's designers. While windows were being smashed throughout the old business district along Broadway and Spring streets, Bunker Hill lived up to its name. By flicking a few switches on their command consoles, the security staffs of the great bank towers were able to cut off all access to their expensive real estate. Bulletproof steel doors rolled down over street-level entrances, escalators instantly stopped and electronic locks sealed off pedestrian passageways. As the *Los Angeles Business Journal* recently pointed out in a special report, the riot-tested success of corporate Downtown's defenses has only stimulated demand for new and higher levels of physical security.

In the first place, the boundary between architecture and law enforcement is further eroded. The LAPD have become central players in the Downtown design process. No major project now breaks ground without their participation, and in some cases, like the recent debate over the provision of public toilets in parks and subway stations (which they opposed), they openly exercise veto power.

Secondly, video monitoring of Downtown's redeveloped zones has been extended to parking structures, private sidewalks, plazas, and so on. This comprehensive surveillance constitutes a virtual *scanscape* – a space of protective visibility that increasingly defines where white-collar office workers and middle-class tourists feel safe Downtown. Inevitably the workplace or shopping mall video camera will become linked with home security systems, personal 'panic buttons,' car alarms, cellular phones, and the like, in a seamless continuity of surveillance over daily routine. Indeed, yuppies' lifestyles soon may be defined by the ability to afford *electronic guardian angels* to watch over them. […]

Thirdly, tall buildings are becoming increasingly sentient and packed with deadly firepower. The skyscraper with a computer brain in *Die Hard I* (actually F. Scott Johnson's Fox-Pereira Tower) anticipates a possible genre of architectural anti-heroes as *intelligent buildings* alternately battle evil or become its pawns. The sensory system of the average office tower already includes panoptic vision, smell, sensitivity to temperature and humidity, motion detection, and, in some cases, hearing. Some architects now predict the day when the building's own AI security computer will be able to automatically screen and identify its human population, and, even perhaps, respond to their emotional states (fear, panic, etc.). Without dispatching security personnel, the building itself will manage crises both minor (like ordering street people out of the building or preventing them from using toilets) and major (like trapping burglars in an elevator).

When all else fails, the smart building will become a combination of bunker and fire-base. […]

3. FREE FIRE ZONE

Beyond the scanscape of the fortified core is the halo of barrios and ghettos that surround Downtown Los Angeles. In Burgess' original Chicago-inspired schema this was the 'zone in transition:' the boarding house and tenement streets, inter-mixed with old industry and transportation infrastructure, that sheltered new immigrant families and single male laborers. Los Angeles' inner ring of freeway-sliced Latino neighborhoods still recapitulate these classical functions. Here in Boyle and Lincoln Heights, Central-Vernon and MacArthur Park are the ports of entry for the region's poorest immigrants, as well as the low-wage labor reservoir for Downtown's hotels and garment sweatshops. Residential densities, just as in the Burgess diagram, are the highest in the city. […]

Finally, just as in Chicago in 1927, this tenement zone ('where an inordinately large number of children are crowded into a small area') remains the classic breeding ground of teenage street gangs (over one-hundred according to L.A. school district intelligence). But while 'Gangland' in 1920s Chicago was theorized as essentially *interstitial* to the social organization of the city – 'as better residential districts recede before the encroachments of business and industry, the gang develops as one manifestation of the economic, moral, and cultural frontier which marks the interstice' – a gang map of Los Angeles today is coextensive with the geography of social class. Tribalized teenage violence now spills out of the inner ring into the older suburban zones; the Boyz are now in the 'Hood where Ozzie and Harriet used to live.

For all that, however, the inner ring remains the most dangerous sector of the city. Ramparts Division of the LAPD, which patrols the salient just west of Downtown, regularly investigates more homicides than any other neighborhood police jurisdiction in the nation. Nearby MacArthur Park, once the jewel in the crown of L.A.'s park system, is now a free-fire zone where crack dealers and street gangs settle their scores with shotguns and Uzis. Thirty people were murdered there in 1990.

By their own admission the overwhelmed inner-city detachments of the LAPD are unable to keep track of all the bodies on the street, much less deal with common burglaries, car thefts or gang-organized protection rackets. Lacking the resources or political clout of more affluent neighborhoods, the desperate population of the inner ring is left to its own devices. As a last resort they have turned to Messieurs Smith and Wesson, whose name follows 'protected by … ' on many a porch.

Slumlords, meanwhile, are mounting their own private reign of terror against drug-dealers and petty criminals. Faced with new laws authorizing the seizure of drug-infested properties, they are hiring goon squads and armed mercenaries to 'exterminate' crime in their tenements. […]

Apart from these rent-a-thugs, the Inner City also spawns a vast cottage industry that manufactures bars and grates for home protection. Indeed most of the bungalows in the inner ring now tend to resemble cages in a zoo. As in a George Romero movie, working-class families must now lock themselves in every night from the zombified city outside. One inadvertent consequence has been the terrifying frequency with which fires immolate entire families trapped helpless in their barred homes.

The *prison cell house* has many resonances in the landscape of the inner city. Before the Spring uprising most liquor stores, borrowing from the precedent of pawn-shops, had completely caged in the area behind the counter, with firearms discretely hidden at strategic locations. Even local greasy spoons were beginning to exchange hamburgers for money through bullet-proof acrylic turnstiles. Windowless concrete-block buildings, with rough surfaces exposed to deter graffiti, have spread across the streetscape like acne during the last decade. Now insurance companies may make such *riot-proof bunkers* virtually obligatory in the rebuilding of many districts.

Local intermediate and secondary schools, meanwhile, have become even more indistinguishable from jails. As per capita education spending has plummeted in Los Angeles, scarce resources have been absorbed in fortifying school grounds and hiring armed security police. Teenagers complain bitterly about overcrowded classrooms and demoralized teachers on decaying campuses that have become little more than daytime detention centers for an abandoned generation. The schoolyard, meanwhile, has become a killing field. [...]

Federally subsidized and public housing projects, for their part, are coming to resemble the infamous 'strategic hamlets' that were used to incarcerate the rural population of Vietnam. Although no L.A. housing project is yet as technologically sophisticated as Chicago's Cabrini-Green, where retinal scans (cf., the opening sequence of *Blade Runner*) are used to check i.d.s, police exercise increasing control over freedom of movement. Like peasants in a rebel countryside, public housing residents of every age are stopped and searched at will, and their homes broken into without court warrants. [...]

In a city with the nation's worst housing shortage, project residents, fearful of eviction, are increasingly reluctant to claim any of their constitutional protections against unlawful search or seizure. Meanwhile national guidelines approved by Housing Secretary Jack Kemp (and almost certain to be continued in the Clinton administration) allow housing authorities to evict *families* of alleged drug-dealers or felons. This opens the door to a policy of *collective punishment* as practiced, for example, by the Israelis against Palestinian communities on the West Bank.

4. THE HALF-MOONS OF REPRESSION

In the original Burgess diagram, the 'half-moons' of ethnic enclaves ('Deutschland,' 'Little Sicily,' 'the Black Belt,' etc.) and specialized architectural ecologies ('residential hotels,' 'the two flat area,' etc.) cut across the 'dart board' of the city's fundamental socio-economic patterning. In contemporary metropolitan Los Angeles, a new species of special enclave is emerging in sympathetic synchronization to the militarization of the landscape. For want of a better generic appellation, we might call them 'social control districts' (SCDs). They merge the sanctions of the criminal or civil code with land-use planning to create what Michel Foucault would undoubtedly have recognized as further instances of the evolution of the 'disciplinary order' of the twentieth-century city.

[...]

Currently existing SCDs (simultaneously 'real and ideal') can be distinguished according to their juridical mode of spatial 'discipline.' *Abatement* districts, currently enforced against graffiti and prostitution in sign-posted areas of Los Angeles and West Hollywood, extend the traditional police power over nuisance (the legal fount of all zoning) from noxious industry to noxious behavior. Because they are self-financed by the fines collected or special sales taxes levied (on spray paints, for example), abatement districts allow homeowner or merchant groups to target intensified law enforcement against specific local social problems.

Enhancement districts, represented all over Southern California by the 'drug-free zones' surrounding public schools, add extra federal/state penalties or 'enhancements' to crimes committed within a specified radius of public institutions. *Containment* districts are designed to quarantine potentially epidemic social problems, ranging from the insect illegal immigrant, the Mediterranean

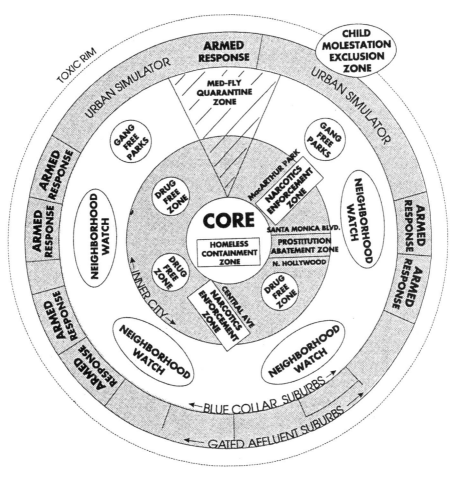

The ecology of fear

fruit fly, to the ever increasing masses of homeless Angelenos. Although Downtown L.A.'s 'homeless containment zone' lacks the precise, if surreal, sign-posting of the state Department of Agriculture's 'Medfly Quarantine Zone,' it is nonetheless one of the most dramatic examples of a SCD. By city policy, the spillover of homeless encampments into surrounding council districts, or into the tonier precincts of the Downtown scanscape, is prevented by their 'contain-ment' (official term) within the over-crowded Skid row area known as Central City East (or the 'Nickle' to its inhabitants). Although the recession-driven explo-sion in the homeless population has inexorably leaked street people into the alleys and vacant lots of nearby inner-ring neighborhoods, the LAPD maintains its pitiless policy of driving them back into the squalor of the Nickle.

The obverse strategy, of course, is the formal *exclusion* of the homeless and other pariah groups from public spaces. A spate of Southland cities, from Orange County to Santa Barbara, and even including the 'Peoples' Republic of Santa Monica,' recently have passed 'anti-camping' ordinances to banish the homeless from their sight. Meanwhile Los Angeles and Pomona are emulating the small city of San Fernando (Richie Valens' hometown) in banning gang members from parks. These 'Gang Free Parks' reinforce non-spatialized sanc-tions against gang membership (especially the recent Street Terrorism Enforcement and Prevention Act or STEP) as examples of 'status criminaliza-tion' where group membership, even in the absence of a specific criminal act, has been outlawed.

Status crime, by its very nature, involves projections of middle-class or con-servative fantasies about the nature of the 'dangerous classes.' Thus in the nine-teenth century the bourgeoisie crusaded against a largely phantasmagorical 'tramp menace,' and, in the twentieth century, against a hallucinatory domestic 'red menace.' In the middle 1980s, however, the ghost of Cotton Mather sud-denly reappeared in suburban Southern California. Allegations that local day-care centers were actually covens of satanic perversion wrenched us back to the seventeenth century and the Salem witch trials. In the course of the McMartin Preschool molestation case – ultimately the longest and most expensive such ordeal in American history – children testified about molester-teachers who flew around on broomsticks and other manifestations of the Evil One.

One legacy of the accompanying collective hysteria, which undoubtedly mined huge veins of displaced parental guilt, was the little city of San Dimas' creation of the nation's first 'child molestation exclusion zone.' This Twin-Peaks-like suburb in the eastern San Gabriel Valley was sign-posted from stem to stern with the warning: 'Hands Off! Our children are photographed and fingerprinted for their own protection.' I don't know if the armies of lurking pedophiles in the mountains above San Dimas were actually deterred by these warnings, but any mapping of contemporary urban space must acknowledge the existence of such dark, Lynchian zones where the *social imaginary* discharges its fantasies.

Meanwhile, post-riot Southern California seems on the verge of creating yet more SCDs. On the one hand, the arrival of the federal 'Weed and Seed' pro-gram, linking community development funds to anti-gang repression, provides a new set of incentives for neighborhoods to adopt exclusion and/or enhancement strategies. As many activists have warned, 'Weed and Seed' is like a police-state caricature of the 1960s War on Poverty, with the Justice Dept. transformed into the manager of urban redevelopment. The poor will be forced to cooperate with their own criminalization as a precondition for urban aid. On the other hand, emerging technologies may give conservatives, and probably neo-liberals as well, a real opportunity to test costsaving proposals for *community imprisonment* as an alternative to expensive programs of prison construction. Led by Heritage Institute ideologue Charles Murray – whose polemic against social spending for the poor, *Losing Ground* (1984), was the most potent manifesto of the Reagan era – conservative theorists are exploring the practicalities of the *carceral city* depicted in sci-fi fantasies like *Escape from New York* [...].

Murray's concept, [...] is that 'drug free zones for the majority' may require social-refuse heaps for the criminalized minority. 'If the result of implementing these policies [landlords' and employers' unrestricted right to discriminate in the selection of tenants and workers] is to concentrate the bad apples into a few hyper-violent, antisocial neighborhoods, so be it.' But how will the underclass be effectively confined to its own 'hyper-violent' super-SCDs and kept out of the drug-free shangri-las of the overclass?

One possibility is the systematic establishment of discrete *security gateways* that will use some bio-metric criterion, universally registered, to screen crowds and bypassers. [...]

Another emerging technology is the police utilization of LANDSAT satellites linked to Geographical Information Systems (GIS). Almost certainly by the end of the decade the largest U.S. metropolitan areas, including Los Angeles, will be using geosynchronous LANDSAT systems to manage traffic congestion and oversee physical planning. The same LANDSAT-GIS capability can be cost-shared and time-shared with police departments to surveil the movements of tens of thousands of electronically tagged individuals and their automobiles.

Although such monitoring is immediately intended to safeguard expensive sports cars and other toys of the rich, it will be entirely possible to use the same technology to put the equivalent of an electronic handcuff on the activities of entire urban social strata. Drug offenders and gang members can be 'bar-coded' and paroled to the omniscient scrutiny of a satellite that will track their 24-hour itineraries and automatically sound an alarm if they stray outside the borders of their *surveillance district*. With such powerful Orwellian technologies for social control, community confinement and the confinement of communities may ultimately mean the same thing.

5. THE NEIGHBORS ARE WATCHING

[...]

The Neighborhood Watch program, comprising more than 5,500 crime-surveillance block clubs from San Pedro to Sylmar, is the LAPD's most important innovation in urban policing. Throughout what Burgess called the 'Zone of

Workingmen's Homes,' which in Los Angeles comprises the owner-occupied neighborhoods of the central city as well as older blue-collar suburbs in the San Fernando and San Gabriel valleys, a huge network of watchful neighbors provides a security system that is midway between the besieged, gun-toting anomie of the inner ring and the private police forces of more affluent, gated suburbs.

Neighborhood Watch, now emulated by hundreds of North American and even European cities, from Rosemead to London, was the brainchild of former police chief Ed Davis. In the aftermath of the 1965–71 cycle of unrest in Southcentral and East L.A, Davis envisioned the program as the anchor of a larger 'Basic Car' strategy designed to rebuild community support for the LAPD by establishing a territorial identity between patrol units and neighborhoods. […]

According to LAPD spokesperson Sgt. Christopher West,

> Neighborhood Watch block clubs are intended to increase local solidarity and self-confidence in the face of crime. Spurred by their block captains, neighbors become more vigilant in the protection of each other's property and well-being. Suspicious behavior is immediately reported and home-owners meet regularly with patrol officers to plan crime prevention tactics.

An off-duty officer in a Winchell's Donut Shop was more picturesque. 'Neighbourhood Watch is supposed to work like a wagon train in an old-fashioned cowboy movie. The neighbors are the settlers, and the goal is to get them to circle their wagons and fight off the Indians until the cavalry – that is to say, the LAPD – can ride to their rescue.'

Needless to say, this Wild West analogy has its dark sides. Who, for example, gets to decide what behavior is 'suspicious' or who looks like an 'Indian'? The obvious danger in any program that conscripts thousands of citizens to become police informers under the official slogan 'Be on the Look Out for Strangers' is that it inevitably stigmatizes innocent groups. Inner-city teenagers are especially vulnerable to this flagrant stereotyping and harassment.

[…]

Critics also worry that Neighborhood Watch does double-duty as a captive constituency for partisan politics. As Sergeant West acknowledged, 'block captains are appointed by patrol officers and the program does obviously tend to attract the most pro-police elements of the population.' These pro-police activists, moreover, tend to be demographically or culturally unrepresentative of their neighborhoods. In poor, young Latino areas, Watch captains are frequently elderly, residual Anglos. In areas where renters are a majority, the pro-police activists are typically homeowners or landlords. […]

6. MINI-CITADELS AND GERONCRATS

When I first began to study gated communities in Southern California in the mid-1980s, it was a trend largely confined to very wealthy neighborhoods or new developments on the distant metropolitan frontier (e.g., the areas Burgess described as the 'restricted residential district' or the 'commuter zone'). Since the Spring 1992 rebellion, however, dozens of ordinary residential neighborhoods in Los Angeles have demanded the right to gate themselves off from the rest of the city. As one newspaper put it, 'The 1980s had their boom in mini-malls; the 1990s may bring a bull market in mini-citadels.'

Although crime and safety are the ostensible issues, increased equity may be the deeper motive. Some realtors have estimated that 'gatedness' can raise home values by as much as 40 percent over ten years. As communities – including black middle-class areas like Windsor Village and Baldwin Hills Estates – race to reap this windfall, Burgess' 'Residential Zone IV begins to look like a fortified honeycomb, with each residential neighborhood now encased in its own walled cell. In most cases, the local homeowners' associations also contract 'armed response' private policing from one of the several multi-national security firms that specialize in residential security. Obviously this only further widens the 'security differential' between the inner city and the suburbs.

'Empty-nest' households are especially passionate advocates of restricted-access neighborhoods, and there is an important sense in which Los Angeles is not merely being polarized between rich and poor, but more specifically between the young poor and the old rich. Furthermore, the 1990 Census showed that metropolitan Los Angeles has the greatest discrepancy in the nation between household size and home size. On the Westside and Hollywood Hills, where 'mansionization' has been in vogue, older, smaller Anglo households occupy ever bigger homes, while in the rest of the city large Latino families are being crammed into diminishing floor-space.

California as a whole is an incipient gerontocracy, and any *post-Blade-Runner* dystopia must take account of the explosive fusion of class, ethnic and generational contradictions. […]

7. PARALLEL UNIVERSES

Burgess and his students, who took 1920s Chicago as a vast research laboratory, never had any doubts about the 'raw reality' of the phenomena that they were systematically studying. Empirical method was matched to empirical reality. The image or mythography of the city did not intervene as a significant stratum in its own right. Nor did the Chicago School pay any attention to the critical role of the Columbian Exposition as an ideal-type for the city's planned development. Although the 1892 and 1933 Chicago World's Fairs were theme parks *avant l'lettre*, urban sociology could not yet make conceptual space for the city as *simulation*.

Today there is no way around the problem. The contemporary city simulates or hallucinates itself in at least two decisive senses. First, in the age of electronic culture and economy, the city redoubles itself through the complex architecture of its information and media networks. […]

If so, *urban cyberspace* – as the simulation of the city's information order – will be experienced as even more segregated, and devoid of true public space, than the traditional built city. Southcentral L.A., for instance, is a data and media black hole, without local cable programming or links to major data systems. Just as it became a housing/jobs ghetto in the early twentieth century industrial city, it is now evolving into an *electronic ghetto* within the emerging *information city.*

Secondly, social fantasy is increasingly embodied in simulacral landscapes – theme parks, 'historic' districts and malls – that are partitioned off from the rest of the metropolis. All the post-modern philosopher kings (Baudrillard, Eco, etc), of course, agree that Los Angeles is the world capital of 'hyper-reality.' Traditionally its major theme parks have been primarily architectural simulations of the movies or television. [...]

Today, however, the city itself – or rather its idealization – has become the subject of simulation. With the recent decline of the military aerospace industry in Southern California, the tourism/hotel/entertainment sector has become the single largest regional employer. But tourists are increasingly reluctant to venture into the perceived dangers of Los Angeles' 'urban jungle.' [...]

MCA and Disney believe the solution is to recreate vital bits of the city within the secure confines of fortress hotels and walled theme parks. As a result, *artificial Los Angeles* is gradually coming into being. In essence, it is an archipelago of well-guarded corporate cashpoints where affluent tourists can relax, spend lots of money, and have 'fun' again. A largely invisible army of low-wage service workers, who themselves live in virtual bantustans like the Santa Ana barrio (Disneyland) or Lennox (LAX) barrios, keep the machinery of simulation running smoothly. [...]

8. HOLLYWOOD(S): POWERS OF SIMULATION

[...]

The HOLLYWOOD in the imagination of the world's movie public, therefore, was kept tenuously anchored to its namesake location by regular rituals (premieres, the Academy Awards, etc.) and the magical investment of a dozen or so places (the Bowl, Graumann's, etc.) as tourist shrines. But over the last generation, as the real Hollywood has become a hyper-violent slum, the rituals have ceased and the magic has waned. As the linkages between historic signifier and its signified decayed, the opportunity arose to resurrect HOLLYWOOD in a safer neighborhood. Thus in Orlando, Disney created a stunning Art Deco mirage of MGM's golden age, while arch-competitor MCA countered with its own idealized versions of Hollywood Boulevard and Rodeo Drive at Universal Studios Florida.

Meanwhile, the elopement of Disney and HOLLYWOOD to Florida further depressed real-estate back in real-time Hollywood. After bitter battles with local home-owners, the major landowners were able to win city authorization for a $1 billion facelift of Hollywood Boulevard. In their scheme, the Boulevard would be transformed into a gated, linear theme park, anchored by mega-entertainment complexes at each end. But while the redevelopers were still negotiating with potential investors, MCA pulled the rug out from under Hollywood Redux with the announcement that its nearby tax-dodge enclave, Universal City, would construct a parallel urban reality called 'CityWalk.'

Designed by master illusionist Jon Jerde, CityWalk is an 'idealized reality,' the best features of Olvera Street, Hollywood and the West side synthesized in 'easy, bite-sized pieces' for consumption by tourists and residents who 'don't need the excitement of dodging bullets … in the Third World country' that Los Angeles has become. […]

Hollywood redevelopers immediately responded to construction of CityWalk with a $4.3 million beautification plan that includes paving Hollywood Blvd. with 'glitz' made from recycled glass. But even spruced up and glitzified there is almost no way that the old Boulevard can compete with the hyper-real perfection on Universal's hill. As its MCA proprietors have taken pains to emphasize, CityWalk is 'not a mall' but a 'revolution in urban design … a new kind of neighborhood' –an urban simulator. Indeed, some critics wonder if it isn't the moral equivalent of the neutron bomb: the city emptied of all lived human experience. With its fake fossil candy wrappers and other deceits, CityWalk sneeringly mocks us as it erases any trace of our real joy, pain or labor.

9. THE TOXIC RIM

Where does the nightmare end? Burgess was not greatly interested in urban boundaries. His Chicago dart board simply fades into the 'commuter zone' and, beyond, into the Corn Belt. The city limits of Dystopia, however, are an intrinsically fascinating problem. In *Blade Runner*, it will be recalled, the dark megalopolis improbably yielded, at its outer edge, to Ecotopia – evergreen forests and boundless wilderness.

No such happy ending will be possible in the coming Los Angeles of 2019. Postmodern geographer Edward Soja has observed that Southern California is already bounded, along an almost unbroken desert perimeter, by huge military air bases, bombing ranges and desert warfare reservations. Now a second, equally ominous circumference clearly is being drawn around this pentagon desert. Choking on its own wastes, with its landfills overflowing and its coastal waters polluted, Los Angeles is preparing to export its garbage and hazardous land-uses to the Eastern Mojave and Baja California. Instead of reducing its production of dangerous waste, the city is simply planning to 'regionalize' their disposal.

This emergent *Toxic Rim* includes giant landfills at Eagle Mountain (the former Kaiser open-pit iron mine) and possibly near Adelanto (defunct Air Force base), the controversial radioactive waste dump in Ward Valley near Needles, and the relocation of such polluting industries as furniture manufacture and metal-plating to Tijuana's *maquiladora* belt. The environmental consequences may be almost catastrophic.

The proposed 300,000 barrels of nuclear waste, for example, in the unlined trenches of the Ward Valley nuclear dump will remain lethal for 10,000 years. They will pose the perennial risk of leaking radioactive tritium into the nearby

Colorado River, thereby poisoning the irreplaceable water source for much of southern California. For its part, the immense landfill at Eagle Mountain – 2.5 miles long, 1 mile wide, and 2,000 feet deep – will not only contaminate the water table but also create a toxic shroud of air pollution over much of eastern Riverside County. Meanwhile, the flight of hazardous industries across the Border, eventually including a large segment of Los Angeles' petrochemical production, will increase the possibility of Bhopal-like catastrophes.

In sum, the formation of this waste-belt will accelerate the environmental degradation of the entire American West (and part of Mexico). Today a third of the trees in Southern California's mountains already have been suffocated by smog, and animal species are rapidly dying off throughout the polluted Mojave Desert. Tomorrow, Los Angeles' radioactive and carcinogenic wastes may be killing life as far away as Utah or Sonora. The Toxic Rim will be a zone of extinction.

10. BEFORE WE WAKE . . .

Finally, leaving behind all the Burgessian diagrams and analogies, what will be the real fate of Los Angeles? Can emergent technologies of surveillance and repression stabilize class and racial relations across the chasm of the new inequality? Will the ecology of fear become the natural order of the twenty-first-century American city? Will razor-wire and security cameras someday be as sentimentally redolent of suburban life as white-picket fences and dogs named Spot?

A global perspective may be useful. Los Angeles in 2019 will be the core of a metro-galaxy of 22–24 million people in Southern and Baja Californias. Together with Tokyo, Sao Paulo, Mexico City, and Shanghai, it will comprise a new evolutionary form: mega-cities of 20–30 million inhabitants. It is important to emphasize that we are not merely talking about larger specimens of an old, familiar type, but an absolutely original, and unexpected, phyla of social life.

No one knows, in fact, whether physical and biological systems of this magnitude and complexity are actually sustainable. Many experts believe that the Third World mega-cities, at least, will eventually precipitate environmental holocausts and/or implode in urban civil wars. Indeed, the contemporary 'New World Order' certainly offers enough grim examples of total societal disintegration – from Bosnia to Somalia – to underscore realistic fears of a mega-city apocalypse.

If Tokyo proves an exception, despite inevitable natural disasters, it will only be by dint of extraordinary levels of public investment, private affluence and social discipline (and because Japan is culturally a highly urban rather than suburban society). In the recent past, however, Los Angeles has begun to resemble Sao Paulo and Mexico City more than post-modern Tokyo-Yokohama.

It may be theoretically possible, of course, for a Democratic administration in Washington over the next decade to begin to reverse American urban decay with massive new public works. But it will remain extraordinarily difficult to secure Congressional support for reinvestment to the Bos-Wash and Southern California urban cores as long as the Reagan-era deficit remains the dominant issue in domestic politics. Indeed the principal legacy of the Perot movement – the most successful electoral insurgency in 75 years – may be precisely the fiscal Gordian knot it has managed to tie around any resolution of the urban crisis.

If hopes of urban reform, now guardedly raised by the Clinton landslide, are once again dashed, it will only accelerate the dystopic tendencies described in this pamphlet. For in the specific case of Los Angeles, where recession has already wiped out a fifth of the region's manufacturing jobs, there is little private-sector help in sight. Even the most traditionally optimistic business-school econometric models now predict a 'Texas-style' regional slump lasting until 1997, while forecasters at the Southern California Association of Governments talk about steady-state unemployment rates of 10–12 percent for the next *twenty years.*

As the golden dream withers, so also may faith in non-violent social reform. If last year's riots set a precedent, anomie neighborhood violence may begin to be transmuted into more organized political violence. Both cops and gangmembers already talk with chilling matter-of-factness about the inevitability of some manner of urban guerrilla warfare. And in spite of all the new residential walls and scan-scapes – even the future police eye in the sky – sprawling Los Angeles is a metropolis uniquely vulnerable to strategic sabotage.

As the examples of Belfast, Beirut and, more recently, Palermo and Lima have demonstrated, the car bomb is the weapon of anonymous urban terror *par excellence* (or, as one counter-insurgency expert once put it, 'the poor man's substitute for an airforce'). Car bombs have reduced half of Beirut to debris, wiped out a neighborhood known as 'Lima's Beverly Hills,' and massacred Italy's most heavily guarded public officials.

If the British Army, uniquely, was finally able to prevent car bombers from entering Belfast, it was only after years of effort and the construction of an immense security cage around the entire city center. A comparable preventative effort in Los Angeles – e.g. closing the freeways and heavily fortifying all the public utilities, oil refineries and pipelines, and commercial centers – would not only cost tens of billions but also dissolve the city as a functioning entity.

The Los Angeles freeway system, in effect, guarantees to the future urban terrorist what the tropical rainforest or Andean Peak offers to the rural *guerrillero:* ideal terrain.

If we continue to allow our central cities to degenerate into criminalized Third Worlds, all the ingenious security technology, present and future, will not safeguard the anxious middle class. The sound of that first car bomb on Rodeo Drive or in front of City Hall will wake us from our mere bad dream and confront us with our real nightmare.

47

Globalizing surveillance: comparative and sociological perspectives

David Lyon

[...]

MODERNITY, SURVEILLANCE AND RISK

Surveillance comes to light, as it were, when people realize that they are being 'watched'. The 'watching' may be almost literal, as in the case of closed circuit television surveillance (CCTV) or much more metaphorical (though no less real) in the case of airport check-ins, supermarket check-outs, Internet cookies, driver's licence production for police, employee cards in the workplace and so on. Surveillance has also become much more visible following the dramatic and disastrous events of 11 September 2001 (hereafter, 9/11). High-tech companies are wooing willing governments with their security and surveillance products, designed to detect 'terrorists' and also other miscreants who may be found in cities or in airports and at borders. In this case, particularly in the USA, much public opinion seems to be tipped in support of surveillance (Lyon, 2003b).

Already, from the reference to 9/11, one may sense the ways that surveillance practices are spreading around the world. If local moral panics produce public interest in video surveillance in streets deemed to be dangerous at night, or on a national level, attacks such as the sarin gas assault on the Tokyo subway in 1995 lead to surveillance crack-downs, then global panic regimes such as that generated by the attacks on the World Trade Center and the Pentagon will have similar effects (Lyon, 2001a). The time-honoured technological fix is invoked once more

From *International Sociology*, 2004, 19(2): 135–49.

to combat guerrilla activities (often called 'terrorism') wherever they may appear. This is not for a moment to deny the understandable desire for safe streets, or to underplay the risks of terrorism in the 21st century. It is simply to acknowledge that where older moral markers have vanished, where nation-states experience a reduction of their role to maintaining law and order, where capitalist restructuring is occurring and where technique has a culturally privileged position (Ellul, 1964), technological solutions will readily be sought. It does not follow, however, that 'technology' is privileged in this account.

Surveillance is not new, or a new technological phenomenon, or a response to external threats, or even a product simply of modernity. In its ancient forms, it was relatively simple, having to do with taxation records or the census, or perhaps with the apprehension of criminals or spies. The 'information state' could be said to have appeared in England, for example, from 1500. Edward Higgs (2001) argues that English central state surveillance arose first as a means of shoring up state power itself, over against other states, and not primarily as a means of social control. The census and civil registration helped to create sets of circumscribed rights but at the same time, it has to be said, provided the means for social control, if circumstances seemed to require or invite it.

This paradox of surveillance is noted by Nicholas Abercrombie et al. (1983), in which the means of granting civil rights was at the same time a potential means for states to gain informational power over citizens. This means, importantly, that at least in this case – and, I would argue, in almost all cases – surveillance is an ambiguous process (Lyon, 1994). Even in a globalizing context, I argue, surveillance retains this paradoxical, ambiguous character. Even though alliances of nation-states now boast tremendous surveillance power, using satellite tracking stations and super-computer message filtering devices, and although corporations also have access to international flows of personal data, this does not translate automatically into crude control.

In its modern forms surveillance is both entwined with capitalist production and consumption as well as state-oriented bureaucracies and international military affairs, and has become highly sophisticated. But surveillance is also routine, an aspect of daily life that increasingly involves everyone. In addition, surveillance has become increasingly bound up with the mediation of risk. For Ulrich Beck, what he calls the risk society appears as an outcome of industrial society when the 'social, political, ecological, and individual risks created by the momentum of innovation increasingly elude the control and protective institutions of industrial society' (Beck, 1996: 27). Beck now argues that 'world risk society' has emerged (Beck, 1999) in which uninsurable risks – including 'terrorism' – have become prominent. In the present case, we could argue that the pace of surveillance growth, enabled by commercial pressure, technological innovation and cultural commitments to 'techniques-as-solutions', far outstrips the capacity of analysis and policy to understand and cope with it. Such surveillance both addresses risks and produces others.

Pre-industrial society had incalculable hazards, in the shape of famine, storms, plagues and wars, but in modernity these became calculable, insurable risks, in which the growing state – and eventually the 'welfare state' – played a large part. But whereas Durkheim, Weber and Simmel saw people being 'released' from corporate transcendental securities into industrial society, now individuals are being 'released' from industrial society into Beck's 'world risk society' (Beck, 1996: 29). Risks, in short, are being individualized, and the old provident state is less and less willing to bear their cost. In order to calculate risks, insurance companies need information, and they need standards of judgement by which to determine insurability (Ericson and Doyle, 2003). That information, as it pertains to individuals, is part of what we know as surveillance today.

But at the same time, risks may be reproduced, in a cycle of risk production. The development of risk technologies, and of their associated surveillance systems, may itself be viewed as risky by those who are its data subjects. Thus a further paradox appears, that in order to cope with the rising tide of risks, practices emerge – processing personal data with inadequate safeguards – that are themselves deemed by many to be risky. This has become increasingly clear since 9/11, as civil liberties groups and privacy lobbies have raised a chorus of complaints about personal data abuses and intrusions resulting from new security laws and 'antiterrorist' measures. Public opinion in the USA may accept in a general sense the surveillance demands of increased security, but opposition groups are becoming increasingly vocal, such that certain measures (air passenger checks, for example; Wald, 2003) are being mitigated.

LATE MODERNITY, SURVEILLANCE AND GLOBALIZATION

Surveillance experienced some important changes during the last part of the 20th century. It began to morph from its erstwhile character as a centralized and hierarchical 'apparatus' of the state or of capitalistic corporations and started to take on a different character as a decentralized and rhizomic 'assemblage' (Haggerty and Ericson, 2000). Fragments of data are extracted from bodies (biometrics does this literally; other forms of surveillance rely on behavioural traces) by a variety of agencies to be processed and often profiled to create data images or 'virtual selves'. These are used as the basis of discrimination between one category and another, and to facilitate differential treatment. While some forms of surveillance retain their face-to-face frame, others have become increasingly dependent on software codes and algorithmic methods (Graham and Marvin, 2001). And as a concomitant of these, surveillance is also being globalized in unprecedented ways. Before examining this more closely, it is worth noting some definitional matters.

Surveillance is here thought of as a product of modernity. That said, it may also display 'postmodern' features. While it is important not to give the impression that somehow modernity has been superseded or left behind, it is of little consequence whether one refers to 'late' or 'post' modernity in this context. The former term is preferred by Anthony Giddens (1990), and many have followed his lead, no doubt because it helps to distinguish sociological analysis from the more cultural studies of postmodernism (Lyon, 1999). The latter term, proposed as a sociological category by Zygmunt Bauman (1992), suggests that in several important ways new social formations appear to be in the making, which may be thought of as having integrity in their own right, and not merely as geriatric stages of some previous form. However these changes are designated, it is important to note that modernity has been undergoing some very significant alterations over the past 30 years. Surveillance is implicated in these changes.

'Late modernity' is used here to refer to the general political, economic and cultural transformations that occurred in the last third of the 20th century. For the purposes of understanding surveillance better, my use of 'late modernity' refers especially to the shift to a *consumer* capitalist phase (this is actually what Bauman emphasizes in his treatment of *post*modernity!), alongside a decided *post-welfarist* tilt in social policy and crime control (Garland, 2001). The kinds of information control involved in consumer data management produce the detailed profiling and data mining on customers that make up commercial surveillance today, while that involved in crime control and security measures contributes to the algorithmic surveillance and actuarial justice that has become equally prevalent. Other sorts of surveillance, notably in government administration and the workplace, continue to be highly significant, but in late modernity they are supplemented, and sometimes interfaced or integrated, with the newer kinds. In all cases, 'social sorting' has become more significant (Lyon, 2002, 2003c).

Another feature or cognate aspect of late modernity is globalization. Again, this term is fraught with controversy. Globalization is characterized by action at a distance, such that social relations and transactions are stretched across time–space (Giddens, 1990); the speed, intensity, reach and impact of communications increase globally; networks and nodes become structurally more important (Castells, 1996) depending on information and generating risks; and the global is mediated by the local, such that it makes sense to talk of 'glocalization' (Robertson, 1992, 1995). Globalization has economic, social, cultural and political dimensions, each of which has ramifications for surveillance. These have to do with the political-economic restructuring that began in earnest in the 1970s.

The globalization of surveillance is directly connected with doing things at a distance. We no longer see, let alone know, many with whom we make exchanges or interact. They are geographically apart from us. As social relations are stretched, courtesy of the new communication technologies, so more and more interactions and transactions become abstract and disembodied, which jeopardizes the sorts of trust that once depended upon the face-to-face and the co-present. Some kinds of trust may be re-established, however, by the use of tokens – such as ID cards, PIN sequences, photo cards, telephone numbers and drivers' licences – all of which now involve searchable databases (see Lessig, 1999). Electronic commerce or air travel are obvious examples of how such systems transcend national boundaries in new nodes and networks, yet different surveillance regimes associated with these have different characteristics in different countries.

In the later 20th century, surveillance underwent certain changes that relate to new technologies. Computers were used to compile personal databases, which became increasingly searchable. As new telecommunications and eventually the Internet and other networks became available, so personal databases became remotely searchable. This is the infrastructural basis of contemporary surveillance, and it also makes it, in principle at least, an international phenomenon. Today's machine-readable passports are a good example of an older administrative scheme that has been upgraded using new technologies (Torpey, 2001; Salter, 2003). Airline passenger data are another example, and in this case, commercial transactions are involved in security surveillance. It is also a case that, like passports, requires some international harmonization. To an extent, what happens in one country has to be matched in others.

As noted already, although technological developments facilitate globalized surveillance, it is a big mistake to imagine that the changes taking place have to do merely with new technologies. Communication and information technologies may *enable* aspects of globalization and global surveillance to occur, but they certainly do not *cause* them to do so. Those new technologies are themselves the product of a quest for ever-increasing mobility and speed dating back before the Second World War, but which was galvanized decisively in the economic and technological boom that followed the war. On the one hand, in the commercial sphere, consumer data were increasingly valued and sought as a means of creating customers for products in the lean, just-in-time approach of the so-called new economy. And on the other hand, in the realm of crime control, *potential* suspect data were sought as a means of anticipating and pre-empting illegal activities, many of which were created by the opportunities appearing in dispersed, mobile, affluent societies.

In the 21st century, it is no accident that some of the key surveillance measures are ones that either relate back to earlier quests for geopolitical power, or to the new contexts created by economic restructuring in the 1980s and 1990s. As to the first, security regimes which since the Second World War have become international alliances now boast complex satellite tracking systems such as 'Echelon'. This spans several continents, although it is the outcome of a so-called UK–USA agreement, and filters messages from many different media – email, telephone, fax and telex – through a device known as a 'dictionary'. Although military concerns prompted this system in the first place, it is also now used for industrial and commercial intelligence as well.

The latter kinds of surveillance, relating to economic restructuring, also require the processing of large amounts of personal data, but this time in the context of either the control of the drug trade, or in electronic commerce transactions. International trade in illicit drugs has spurred extensive policing and surveillance measures in the past 20–30 years. As for electronic commerce, its practices are both for verifying identities but also for profiling consumers, such that their details too can be filtered, sorting them into various categories of consumption. Policing across borders involves cross-border data flow, as does e-commerce across borders.

So far I have commented on the ways that surveillance is similarly enabled by new technologies, wherever it is found, and on some of the social pressures leading to the development of those systems in an international context. But just as technology does not determine outcomes in a single national context, so does it not do so in a global one either. Globalization is often thought of in primarily economic terms, and this dimension of globalization is certainly significant for surveillance. The flexible labour regimes required for contemporary capitalism entail the extensive use of mobile workers, whose activities are tracked across distance and borders. And more and more commercial activity also occurs in direct ways, courtesy of computer networks, such that personal data flow across national divides as well (Bennett and Raab, 2003).

At the same time, globalization also relates to other entities and processes, notably the activities of the nation-state. Personal data have been flowing over national borders for many years in relation to personal travel, in the systems of customs, immigration and citizenship. The passport is a vital document in this regard (Torpey, 2001). Such data also travel courtesy of policing and intelligence services, and this has only intensified since the attacks of 9/11 (Ball and Webster, 2003). Indeed, as guerrilla warfare has grown as a global phenomenon since the last decades of the 20th century so, paradoxically, high technology surveillance methods have been reinforced (Downey and Murdock, 2003). This in turn is not unconnected with the progressive militarization of policing (Haggerty and Ericson, 2001), and of urban life (Graham and Marvin, 2001), again, as globalized phenomena.

Not only are different social sectors drivers of particular kinds of surveillance, but it is also the case that receptivity to surveillance differs depending on cultural and national contexts. New methods may be acceptable in one context and not another. Thus, for instance, national electronic ID card systems may be found already in use in Thailand, Malaysia and Singapore, but they have been rejected in Korea, and are only at a preliminary planning stage in Canada, the UK and the USA. In another example, the electronic monitoring of offenders, which began in the USA, was slow to find such acceptance in Europe. As Gary T. Marx points out in his comparative study of undercover police methods, it is 'premature to conclude that a standard, technocratic, anticipatory, velvet glove, paradigmatic American social control model is taking over the western democratic world' (Marx and Fijnaut, 1995: 324).

It is true that some structural similarities and the common problems facing (late) modern states may produce similar techniques in different places. Airport security systems are an obvious case in point. Equally, the same transnational corporations are trying to sell their equipment across the world, so, again, the chances are strong of similar solutions appearing in quite distant places (see Zureik, 2003). Sun Microsystems, for instance, a US-based company, provides the equipment, software and support for the national electronic ID system of Thailand. Some countries will also want to demonstrate their technical prowess using their surveillance systems – it is arguable that both Spain and Malaysia have developed their new smart ID cards at least in part for this reason (Stalder and Lyon, 2002).

It is also true that local and regional social, political and cultural contexts will experience surveillance in different ways. Some devices with high-level locational surveillance capacities, such as cellphones, are more suited to densely populated areas and thus will increase tracking in cities, but not necessarily in rural areas. Over time, the use of radio-frequency identification devices (RDIFs) and satellite tracking may change this, too. But technological capacities never operate alone. In North America, while commercial interests and government agencies such as the Department of Homeland Security give those technologies their chance, they are also opposed by civil liberties and consumer groups. In South-East Asia, on the other hand, where more authoritarian and less democratic governments are able to mount systems with little public consultation or approval, it is possible to establish large-scale surveillance systems against a backdrop of much more muted dissent.

One of the most striking developments since the 1990s has been that Britain emerged as the clear world leader in CCTV deployment. That country has a far more comprehensive system of urban, public space cameras than any other in the world. This may be explained by the presence of dramatic events (the murder of a small boy whose assailants were caught in the lens of a construction site camera) or long-term problems (such as IRA terrorism) (Norris and Armstrong, 1999). But if one considers the electronic tagging of offenders, it is clear that the USA (where the technique originated) is far more likely to deploy this method than its European counterparts (although there is evidence that this is now changing; Nellis 2000). The mere existence of new technologies is far from a sufficient reason for them to be used.

Wherever they exist, however, and for whatever reasons they have been established, surveillance systems do tend to depend increasingly on searchable databases. This means that they are used for 'social sorting', for the classification of populations as a precursor to differential treatment (Lyon, 2002). In the realm of crime control they display the character of 'categorical suspicion' (Marx, 1988), whereas in the commercial realm they involve 'categorical seduction' (Lyon, 2001b). In the latter case, consumers are sorted and sifted for their relative worth to marketing companies in a form of discrimination that creams some off for special treatment and cuts others off from consuming opportunities altogether (Gandy, 1995).

Social sorting is also a crucially important activity of nation-states, often achieved by means of the census, and of border controls, but also in welfare administration. Comparative studies are very valuable at this level, too. How ID classifications work at borders in Israel is not dissimilar from the ways in which they operated in South Africa under apartheid (Zureik, 2001). Similarly, the categories operated by welfare professionals serve to produce populations for certain purposes, a practice that would bear comparisons across different national jurisdictions (Gilliom, 2001). Beyond this, one could examine fruitfully the ways in which Internet surveillance sorts populations by income, gender, and 'race', how CCTV does something similar with less high-tech methods (Norris, 2002), and how this, too, differs from place to place.

Two things have to be recalled about these social sorting processes, particularly in comparative perspective. One is that the systems themselves are not technically foolproof; they may not function in the ways intended (and of course, they may also have unintended consequences). The other is that the success of surveillance systems always depends upon the collusion (however weak or even unconscious) of their subjects. Some will comply willingly, others will negotiate, and yet others may actively resist. This also means that the same technological systems may be used on occasion for quite varying and even contradictory purposes.

This latter point returns us to a consideration of the inherent ambiguity of surveillance processes. The same technologies may be used for highly repressive surveillance purposes and simultaneously for the purposes of counter-surveillance or resistance. Some interesting comparative work could be done in this area. In China, for instance, western corporations have been sought for advice and equipment to bolster the surveillance capacities of a very undemocratic state (Greg, 2001). At the same time, the Internet and email are used in China as a means of operating beyond the reach of the state, by democratic dissidents, Falun Gong members and so on. In Singapore, too, several 'sites of resistance' may be found on the Internet, despite stringent efforts to circumscribe it (Ho et al., 2001).

One of the most striking events for the globalization of surveillance is the aftermath of the attacks of 9/11. This may be seen in two related surveillance areas. One is the ways in which several governments in different countries have proposed new measures for dealing with the 'terrorist' threat (Ball and Webster, 2003). These include 'smart' ID card systems to try to determine who is and is not a legitimate resident or visitor in a given country, CCTV systems with facial recognition capacities in airports and elsewhere, to check against database images of known terrorists, and various other biometric devices to verify identities more satisfactorily (Lyon, 2003d). A considerable amount of research is called for to determine which country adopts which technologies and why. How far does the experience of one country encourage or discourage another?

The other surveillance consequence of 9/11 is the proliferation of antiterrorist legislation in several countries. These tend to relax the limitations on previously stricter laws, such as those to do with wiretapping or indeed any message interception. Few modern western countries have not altered their laws in some respect, or passed new ones, and in East and South-East Asia, new measures have also been adopted. Already existing systems of cross-border policing have been considerably expanded, with long-term consequences for globalized surveillance (Bigo, 2002). Again, comparative investigation to determine the extent of mutual influence between countries will make a vital contribution to social and political understanding.

GLOBALIZED SURVEILLANCE AND ITS CONSEQUENCES

I have argued that both for ordinary and extraordinary reasons, surveillance is an increasingly globalized phenomenon. The ordinary reasons are that, just as growing surveillance may be explained in terms of the overall structural developments of the western world since the Second World War (and not as sinister attempts at social control), so now, as modernity globalizes, surveillance globalizes along with it. Electronic commerce, increased geographical mobility, the 'war against drugs' and other such processes bring enhanced personal and population surveillance along with them. The extraordinary reasons relate to the events and consequences of 9/11, that are catalyzing surveillance developments in several countries simultaneously, and, importantly, are permitting further convergence of different kinds (state, commercial) of surveillance. Several consequences may be traced from this.

First, whether for the purposes of commerce or policing, networked surveillance blurs the old borders (and the old boundaries) of surveillance. Standards are developed between countries for electronic transactions and identity verification, for example, but also for the detection and apprehension of offenders or suspects. The use of searchable databases and of remote checking makes possible surveillance across borders, as for instance in the case of airline ticketing and security measures. Unfamiliar methods of checking may appear in airports, and some of them – for example biometric checks in Keflavik Airport, Iceland – may appear unusually stringent given the size or remoteness of the country.

Second, certain surveillance trends may be accelerated in a global context in response to 9/11. Policing offers some good examples. Two trends have emerged in greater strength in recent years – the privatization and the militarization of police. More and more private police forces, often referred to as 'security' agencies or similar, complement public policing in the 21st century. But they also seek, and use, the same kinds of personal data as their public counterparts (Ericson and Haggerty, 1997), and they do so according to similar standards (of insurance risk assessment). The other trend is the militarization of the police, which is in one respect a domestication of armed forces once used primarily against external aggressors. Both these trends fit well with the shifts taking place since 9/11, however, in that private police and more military methods are appropriate for the settings in which the new surveillance is required – borders, airports, central urban areas and so on.

Third, in the area of policy, new initiatives are appearing (and others are demanded) in relation to the globalization of surveillance, especially in the commercial realm. As Colin Bennett and Rebecca Grant say, globalization means that personal 'data on individual customers, employees, suppliers, investors, competitors, and so on' are transferred instantaneously around the world, and this traffic 'has the potential to undermine national efforts to protect the privacy of citizens' (Bennett and Grant, 1999: 12). The European Directive on Data Protection has already had extensive influence in Canada and the USA, and this kind of country-to-country or region-to-region transfer of experience on policies and standards is likely to increase. How it occurs, though, is an empirical question, that bears further examination.

Fourth, one can hardly look at the globalization of surveillance, especially within a framework that acknowledges the active role of 'data subjects', without looking at the globalization of resistance. Resistance to surveillance, whether by consumer groups, computer professionals, or civil rights activists (especially after 9/11), is increasingly known about in different countries. Webcams may be used effectively in this regard, for example. The New York Players, who offer dramatic presentations in front of urban video cameras, are known about in other parts of the world. The websites of groups such as Privacy International or the Electronic Privacy Information Center may also be used in a networking fashion for groups that question the existence or extent of surveillance to network with each other. Interestingly, a new body, the Asia-Pacific Privacy Charter Council (www.BakerCyberLawCentre.org/appcc) came into existence in 2003, with the potential to draw many countries beyond Europe and North America into debates over surveillance and privacy.

Fifth, academically, and in relation to policy studies, interest in surveillance and privacy has increased considerably since the 1980s. A number of now classic studies appeared from the mid-1970s (Rule, 1974; Giddens, 1985; Marx, 1988; Flaherty, 1989; Dandeker, 1990; Bennett, 1992; Regan, 1995; inter alia). During the 1990s, a number of more general treatments appeared (e.g. Whitaker, 1999; Staples, 1998), along with further studies of data protection and privacy policy (e.g. Bennett and Grant, 1999; Agre and Rotenberg, 1997) as well as further more theoretically informed studies (e.g. Bogard, 1996; Norris and Armstrong, 1999).

This accounts for the emergence of 'surveillance studies' as a cross-disciplinary field for research. The disciplines represented include geography, history, information and computing sciences, political science, sociology and policy studies. Although this convergence is mainly evident in Europe and North America, interest is also growing in Pacific Asia and elsewhere (Lyon, 2003a). Comparative studies are becoming increasingly important (such as the European Community initiative on closed circuit television in cities, called the 'Urban Eye' project). A new online journal, *Surveillance-and-Society* (www.surveillance-and-society.org), is helping to crystallize some of these strands of interest.

At present, however, there is arguably a lot more interest in the globalization of legislation relating to surveillance (privacy, data protection) than in the globalization of surveillance itself. This represents a major challenge for sociologists and other social scientists, not least because a crucial first step in considering legal changes is to understand analytically the conditions that gave rise to them in the first place. Three items in particular require careful research.

One task is to discover exactly what happens to personal data when they are extracted from or submitted by individuals. All too often, the existence of a personal database (technology) or a data-processing agency (institution) is taken to be evidence of personal data flows of particular kinds, and with predictable effects. But as we have observed, mere software and hardware, or mere institutional resources do not on their own produce specific kinds of surveillance. They may, however, induce certain kinds of determinisms in researchers. Mapping the trajectories of personal data will take place in largely untouched terrain.

A second task is to find out exactly how people respond to and interact with systems that automate their transactions and handle their data. Again, surprisingly little is known in many cases (with some notable exceptions, e.g. Norris and Armstrong, 1999). Yet so-called data-subjects – agents, embodied persons – actually engage extensive repertoires of response, depending on timing, social context, location and so on (Ball, 2002). This may be simple, unthought compliance, through to skilful negotiation and active resistance. Knowing what occurs, in which contexts, and why, will be an immensely constructive task for surveillance studies.

A third task is to explore the consequences of surveillance – especially in its rapidly globalizing varieties – for governance (Rose, 1999). Understanding surveillance in the 21st century also entails an analytic move beyond the conventional loci of power – the state or the corporation – to discover ways in which all sorts of processes, procedures, strategies and tactics help to shape relations and enable or constrain activities touched by globalized flows of personal data, from international to local community levels. Emergent power relationships, relating to surveillance, and within self-organizing networks, cry out for serious and subtle analysis.

REFERENCES

Abercrombie, N. et al. (1983) *Sovereign Individuals of Capitalism*. London: Allen and Unwin.
Agre, P. and Rotenberg, M., eds (1997) *Technology and Privacy: The New Landscape*. Cambridge, MA: MIT Press.
Ball, K. (2002) 'Power, Control, and Computer-based Performance Monitoring: Repertoires, Resistance, and Subjectivities', in D. Lyon (ed.) *Surveillance as Social Sorting: Privacy, Risk, and Digital Discrimination*, pp. 210–25. London and New York: Routledge.
Ball, K. and Webster, F. (2003) *The Intensification of Surveillance*. London: Pluto Press.
Bauman, Z. (1992) *Intimations of Postmodernity*. London and New York: Routledge.
Beck, U. (1996) 'Risk Society and the Provident State', in S. Lash, B. Szerszynski and B. Wynne (eds) *Risk, Environment, and Modernity*. London: Sage.
Beck, U. (1999) *World Risk Society*. Cambridge: Polity Press/Maiden, MA: Blackwell.
Bennett, C. J. (1992) *Regulating Privacy: Data Protection and Public Policy in Europe and the United States*. Ithaca, NY: Cornell University Press.
Bennett, C. J. (1997) 'Convergence Re-Visited: Towards a Global Policy for the Protection of Personal Data?', in P. Agre and M. Rotenberg (eds) *Technology and Privacy: The New Landscape*, pp. 99–123. Cambridge, MA: MIT Press.
Bennett, C. J. and Grant, R., eds (1999) *Visions of Privacy: Policy Choices for the Digital Age*. Toronto: University of Toronto Press.
Bennett, C. J. and Raab, C. (2003) *The Governance of Privacy: Policy Instruments in a Global Perspective*. Aldershot: Ashgate.
Bigo, D. (2002) 'To Reassure and Protect, after September 11', at: www.ssrc.org/september 11/essays/bigo.htm/
Bogard, W. (1996) *The Simulation of Surveillance*. New York: Cambridge University Press.
Castells, M. (1996) *The Rise of the Network Society*. Oxford and Maiden, MA: Blackwell.
Dandeker, C. (1990) *Surveillance, Power, and Modernity*. Cambridge: Polity Press.
Downey, J. and Murdock, G. (2003) 'The Counter-Revolution in Military Affairs: The Globalization of Guerilla Warfare', in D. Thussu and D. Freedman (eds) *War and the Media: Reporting on Conflict*. London: Sage.
Ellul, J. (1964) *The Technological Society*. New York: Vintage.
Ericson, R. and Doyle, A., eds (2003) *Insurance and Morality*. Toronto: University of Toronto Press.

Ericson, R. and Haggerty, K. (1997) *Policing the Risk Society*. Toronto: University of Toronto Press.

Flaherty, D. (1989) *Protecting Privacy in Surveillance Societies*. Chapel Hill: University of North Carolina Press.

Gandy, O. (1995) 'It's Discrimination, Stupid!', in J. Boal and I.A. Brooks (eds) *Resisting the Virtual Life*, pp. 35–48. San Francisco, CA: City Lights.

Garland, D. (2001) *The Culture of Control: Crime and Social Order in Contemporary Society*. Oxford: Oxford University Press/Chicago, IL: University of Chicago Press.

Giddens, A. (1985) *The Nation-State and Violence*. Cambridge: Polity Press.

Giddens, A. (1990) *The Consequences of Modernity*. Cambridge: Polity Press.

Gilliom, J. (2001) *Overseers of the Poor: Surveillance, Resistance, and the Limits of Privacy*. Chicago, IL: University of Chicago Press.

Graham, S. and Marvin, S. (2001) *Splintering Urbanism: Networked Infrastructures, Technological Mobilities, and the Urban Condition*. London and New York: Routledge.

Greg, W. (2001) *The Golden Shield: Corporations and the Development of Surveillance Technology in the People's Republic of China*. Montreal: International Centre for Human Rights and Democratic Development; at: http://go.openflows.org/CGS_ENG.PDF

Haggerty, K. and Ericson, R. V. (2000) 'The Surveillant Assemblage', *British Journal of Sociology* 51(4): 605–22.

Haggerty, K. and Ericson, R. (2001) 'The Militarization of Policing in an Information Age', *Journal of Political and Military Policing* 27: 233–55.

Higgs, E. (2001) 'The Rise of the Information State: The Development of Central State Surveillance of the Citizen in England, 1500–2000', *Journal of Historical Sociology* 14(2): 175–97.

Ho, K. C. and Kluver, R., eds (2003) *Asia.Com*. London and New York: Routledge.

Ho, K. C., Baber, Z. and Khondker, H. (2001) '"Sites" of Resistance: Alternative Websites and State-Society Relations in Singapore', *British Journal of Sociology* 53(1).

Lessig, L. (1999) *Code and other Laws of Cyberspace*. New York: Basic Books.

Lyon, D. (1994) *The Electronic Eye: The Rise of Surveillance Society*. Cambridge: Polity Press/Maiden, MA: Blackwell.

Lyon, D. (1999) *Postmodernity*. Buckingham: Open University Press.

Lyon, D. (2001a) 'Surveillance after September 11', *Sociological Research Online* 6(3); at: www.socresonline.org.uk/6/3/lyon.

Lyon, D. (2001b) *Surveillance Society: Monitoring Everyday Life*. Buckingham: Open University Press.

Lyon, D. (2002) 'Everyday Surveillance: Personal Data and Social Classification', *Information, Communication, and Society* 5(1): 1–16.

Lyon, D. (2003a) 'Cyberspace, Surveillance, and Social Control: The Hidden Face of the Internet in Asia', in K. C. Ho and R. Kluver (eds) *Asia.Com*, pp. 67– 82. London and New York: Routledge.

Lyon, D. (2003b) *Surveillance after September 11*. Cambridge: Polity Press/Malden, MA: Blackwell.

Lyon, D., ed. (2003c) *Surveillance as Social Sorting: Privacy, Risk, and Digital Discrimination*. London and New York: Routledge.

Lyon, D. (2003d) 'Technology vs "Terrorism": ID Cards, Biometric Surveillance and CCTV in the City', paper for RC21,14. ISA World Congress, Brisbane, 12 July 2002, *The International Journal of Urban and Regional Research* 27(3): 666–78.

Marx, G. T. (1988) *Undercover: Police Surveillance in America*. Berkeley: University of California Press.

Marx, G. T. and Fijnaut, C., eds (1995) *Police Surveillance in Comparative Perspective*. The Hague: Kluwer.

Nellis, M. (2000) 'Law and Order: The Electronic Monitoring of Offenders', in D. Dolowitz et al. (eds) *Policy Transfer and British Social Policy: Learning from the USA?* Buckingham: Open University Press.

Norris, C. (2002) 'From Personal to Digital: CCTV, the Panopticon, and the Technological Mediation of Suspicion and Social Control', in D. Lyon (ed.) *Surveillance as Social Sorting: Privacy, Risk, and Digital Discrimination*, pp. 249–81. London and New York: Routledge.

Norris, C. and Armstrong, G. (1999) *The Maximum Surveillance Society: The Rise of CCTV*. Oxford and New York: Berg.

Regan, P. (1993) 'The Globalization of Privacy: Implications of Recent Changes in Europe', *The American Journal of Economics and Sociology* 52(3): 257–74.

Regan, P. (1995) *Legislating Privacy: Technology, Social Values, and Public Policy*. Chapel Hill: University of North Carolina Press.

Robertson, R. (1992) *Globalization: Social Theory and Global Culture*. London: Sage.

Robertson, R. (1995) 'Globalization: Time-Space and Homogeneity-Heterogeneity', in M. Featherstone et al. (eds) *Global Modernities*. London: Sage.

Rose, N. (1999) *Powers of Freedom*. Cambridge: Cambridge University Press.

Rule, J. (1974) *Private Lives and Public Surveillance*. London: Allen-Lane.

Salter, M. (2003) *The Passport in International Relations*. London: Lynne Rienner.

Stalder, F. and Lyon, D. (2002) 'ID Cards and Social Classification', in D. Lyon (ed.) *Surveillance as Social Sorting: Privacy, Risk, and Digital Discrimination*, pp. 77–93. London and New York: Routledge.

Staples, W. (1998) *The Culture of Surveillance*. Boston, MA: Rowman and Littlefield. (Reprinted 2001 as *Everyday Surveillance*.)

Torpey, J. (2001) *The Invention of the Passport: Surveillance, Citizenship and the State*. Cambridge: Cambridge University Press.

Wald, M. (2003) 'US Agency Scales Back Data Required on Air Travel', *The New York Times* 31 July.

Whitaker, J. (1999) *The End of Privacy*. New York: The New Press.

Zureik, E. (2001) 'Constructing Palestine through Surveillance Practices', *British Journal of Middle Eastern Studies* 28(2): 205–27.

Zureik, E. (2003) 'Governance, Security, and Technology: The Case of Biometrics', Surveillance Project/Sociology Department paper, Queen's University, March. (Forthcoming in *Studies in Political Economy*.)

48

Ordering insecurity: social polarization and the punitive upsurge

Loïc Wacquant

[...]

Comparative analysis of penal trends and discourses in the advanced countries over the past decade reveals a close link between the ascendancy of neoliberalism, as ideological project and governmental practice mandating submission to the 'free market' and the celebration of 'individual responsibility' in all realms, on the one hand, and the deployment of punitive and proactive law-enforcement policies targeting street delinquency and the categories trapped in the margins and cracks of the new economic and moral order, on the other hand.[1]

Beyond their national inflections and institutional variations, these policies sport six common features.[2] First, they purport to put an end to the 'era of leniency' and to attack head-on the problem of crime, as well as urban disorders and the public nuisances bordering the confines of penal law, baptized 'incivilities,' while deliberately disregarding their causes. Whence, second, a proliferation of laws and an insatiable craving for bureaucratic innovations and technological gadgets: crime-watch groups and partnerships between the police and other public services (schools, hospitals, social workers, the national tax office, etc.); video surveillance cameras and computerized mapping of offenses; compulsory drug testing, 'tazer' and 'flash-ball' guns; fast-track judicial processing and the extension of the prerogatives of probation and parole officers; criminal profiling, satellite-aided electronic monitoring, and generalized genetic fingerprinting; enlargement and technological modernization of carceral facilities; multiplication of specialized custodial centers (for foreigners awaiting expulsion, recidivist

From *Radical Philosophy Review*, 2008, 11(1): 1–19.

minors, women and the sick, convicts serving community sentences, etc.). Third, the need for this punitive turn is everywhere conveyed by an alarmist, even catastrophist discourse on 'insecurity' animated with martial images and broadcast to saturation by the commercial media, the major political parties, and professionals in the enforcement of order – police officials, magistrates, legal scholars, experts and merchants in 'urban safety' services – who vie to propose remedies as drastic as they are simplistic. Fourth, out of a proclaimed concern for efficiency in the 'war on crime' and solicitude toward this new figure of the deserving citizen that is the crime victim, this discourse openly revalorizes repression and stigmatizes youths from declining working-class neighborhoods, the jobless, homeless, beggars, drug addicts and street prostitutes, and immigrants from the former colonies of the West and from the ruins of the Soviet empire. Fifth, on the carceral front, the therapeutic philosophy of 'rehabilitation' has been more or less supplanted by a managerialist approach centered on the cost-driven administration of carceral stocks and flows, paving the way for the privatization of correctional services. Lastly, the implementation of these new punitive policies have invariably resulted in an extension and tightening of the police dragnet, a hardening and speeding-up of judicial procedures and, at the end of the penal chain, an incongruous increase in the population under lock, without anyone seriously addressing the question of their financial burden, social costs, and civic implications.

These punitive policies are the object of an unprecedented political consensus and enjoy broad public support cutting across class lines, boosted by the blurring of crime, poverty, and immigration in the media as well as by the constant confusion between insecurity and the 'feeling of insecurity.' This confusion is tailor-made to channel towards the (dark-skinned) figure of the street delinquent the diffuse anxiety caused by a string of interrelated social changes: the dislocations of wage work, the crisis of the patriarchal family and the erosion of traditional relations of authority among sex and age categories, the decomposition of established working-class territories and the intensification of school competition as requirement for access to employment. Penal severity is now presented virtually everywhere and by everyone as a healthy necessity, a vital reflex of self-defense by a social body threatened by the gangrene of criminality, no matter how petty. The grand American experiment of the 'war on crime' has also imposed itself as the mandatory reference for the governments of the First World, the theoretical source and practical inspiration for the general hardening of penality that has translated in all advanced countries into a spectacular swelling of the population behind bars.[3] Caught in the vise of the biased alternative between catastrophic and angelic visions, anyone who dares to question the self-evident commonplaces of the *pensée unique* about 'insecurity' that now rules uncontested is irrevocably (dis)qualified as a vain dreamer or an ideologue guilty of ignoring the harsh realities of contemporary urban life.

I. THE GENERALIZATION OF SOCIAL INSECURITY AND ITS EFFECTS

The sudden growth and glorification of the penal state in the United States, starting in the mid-1970s, and then in Western Europe two decades later, does not correspond to a rupture in the evolution of crime and delinquency – the scale and physiognomy of offending did not change abruptly at the start of the two periods in question on either side of the Atlantic. Neither does it translate a leap in the efficiency of the repressive apparatus that would justify its reinforcement, as zealots of the scholarly myth of 'zero tolerance' now spread around the world would have us believe. It is not criminality that has changed here so much as the *gaze that society trains on certain street illegalities*, that is, in the final analysis, *on the dispossessed and dishonored populations* (by status or origin) that are their presumed perpetrators, on the place they occupy in the City, and on the uses to which these populations can be subjected in the political and journalistic fields.

These castaway categories – unemployed youth and the homeless, aimless nomads and drug addicts, postcolonial immigrants without documents or support – have become salient in public space, their presence undesirable and their doings intolerable, because they are the living and threatening incarnation of the generalized social insecurity produced by the erosion of stable and homogenous wage-work (promoted to the rank of paradigm of employment during the decades of Fordist expansion in 1945–1975), and by the decomposition of the solidarities of class and culture it underpinned within a clearly circumscribed national framework.[4] Just as national boundaries have been blurred by the hypermobility of capital, the settlement of migration flows and European integration, the normalization of desocialized labor feeds a powerful current of anxiety in all the societies of the continent. This current mixes the fear of the future, the dread of social decline and degradation, the anguish of not being able to transmit one's status to one's offspring in a competition for credentials and positions that is ever more intense and uncertain. It is this diffuse and multifaceted social and mental insecurity, which (objectively) strikes working-class families shorn of the cultural capital required to accede to the protected sectors of the labor market and (subjectively) haunts large sectors of the middle class, that the new martial discourse of politicians and the media on delinquency has captured, fixating it onto the narrow issue of physical or criminal insecurity.

To understand how the law-and-order upsurge that has swept through postindustrial countries around the close of the century constitutes a *reaction to, a diversion from and a denegation of, the generalization of the social and mental insecurity* produced by the diffusion of desocialized wage labor against the backdrop of increased inequality, one must break with the ritual opposition of intellectual schools and wed the virtues of a *materialist* analysis, inspired by Marx and Engels and elaborated by various strands of radical criminology, attuned to the changing relations that obtain in each epoch between the penal system and the system of production, and the strengths of a *symbolic* approach, initiated by Emile Durkheim and amplified by Pierre Bourdieu, attentive to the capacity that the state has to trace salient social demarcations and to produce social reality through its work of inculcation of efficient categories and classifications.[5] The traditionally hostile separation of these two approaches, the one stressing the instrumental role of penality as a vector of power and the other its expressive mission and integrative capacity, is but an accident of academic history artificially sustained by stale intellectual politics. This separation must imperatively be overcome, for in historical reality penal institutions and policies can and do shoulder both tasks at once: they simultaneously act to enforce hierarchy and control contentious categories, at one level, and to communicate norms and shape collective representations and subjectivities, at another.[6] The police, courts, and prison are not mere technical implements whereby the authorities respond to crime – as in the commonsensical view fostered by law and criminology – but a core political capacity through which the state both produces and manages inequality, identity, and marginality.

Indeed, the generalized hardening of police, judicial, and correctional policies that can be observed in most of the countries of the First World over the past two decades[7] partakes of a *triple transformation of the state*, which it helps simutane-ously accelerate and obfuscate, wedding the amputation of its economic arm, the retraction of its social bosom, and the massive expansion of its penal fist. This transformation is the bureaucratic response of political elites to the mutations of wage work (shift to services and polarization of jobs, flexibilization and intensi-fication of work, individualization of employment contracts, discontinuity and dispersion of occupational paths) and their ravaging effects on the lower tiers of the social and spatial structure. These mutations themselves are the product of a swing in the balance of power between the classes and groups that struggle at every moment for control over the worlds of employment. And in this struggle, it is the transnational business class and the 'modernizing' fractions of the cul-tural bourgeoisie and high state nobility, allied under the banner of neoliberal-ism, that have gained the upper hand and embarked on a sweeping campaign to reconstruct public power in line with their material and symbolic interests.[8]

The commodification of public goods and the rise of underpaid, insecure work against the backdrop of working poverty in the United States and endur-ing mass joblessness in the European Union; the unraveling of social protection schemes leading to the replacement of the collective right to recourse against unemployment and destitution by the individual obligation to take up gainful activity ('workfare' in the U.S. and the UK, ALE jobs in Belgium, PARE and RMA in France, the Hartz reform in Germany, etc.) in order to impose desocialized wage labor as the normal horizon of work for the new proletariat of the urban service sectors;[9] the reinforcement and extension of the punitive apparatus, recentered onto the dispossessed districts of the inner city and the urban periph-ery which concentrate the disorders and despair spawned by the twofold move-ment of retrenchment of the state from the economic and social front: these three trends implicate and intricate with one another in a self-perpetuating causal chain that is redrawing the perimeter and redefining the modalities of govern-ment action.

The Keynesian state, coupled with Fordist wage work operating as a spring of *solidarity*, whose mission was to counter the recessive cycles of the market economy, protect the most vulnerable populations, and curb glaring inequalities, has been succeeded by a state that one might dub neo-Darwinist, in that it erects *competition* to the rank of fetish and celebrates unrestrained individual responsi-bility – whose counterpart is collective and thus political irresponsibility. The

Leviathan withdraws into its regalian functions of law enforcement, themselves hypertrophied and deliberately abstracted from their social environment, and its symbolic mission of reassertion of common values through the public anathematization of deviant categories – chief among them the unemployed 'street thug' and the 'pedophile,' viewed as the walking incarnations of the abject failure to live up to the abstemious ethic of wage work and sexual self-control. Unlike its *belle époque* predecessor, this new-style Darwinism, which praises the 'winners' for their vigor and intelligence and vituperates the 'losers' in the 'struggle for economic life' by pointing to their character flaws and behavioral deficiencies, does not find its model in nature.[10] It is the market that supplies it with its master-metaphor and the mechanism of selection supposed to ensure the 'survival of the fittest.' But only after the market itself has been naturalized, that is to say, depicted under radically dehistoricized trappings which, paradoxically, turn it into a concrete historical realization of the pure and perfect abstractions of the orthodox economic science promoted to the rank of official theodicy of the social order *in statu nascendi.*

Thus the 'invisible hand' of the unskilled labor market, strengthened by the shift from welfare to workfare, finds its ideological extension and institutional complement in the 'iron fist' of the penal state, which grows and redeploys in order to *stem the disorders generated by the diffusion of social insecurity* and by the correlative destabilization of the status hierarchies that formed the traditional framework of the national society (i.e., the division between whites and blacks in the United States and between nationals and colonial immigrants in Western Europe). The regulation of the working classes through what Pierre Bourdieu calls 'the Left hand' of the state,[11] that which protects and expands life chances, represented by labor law, education, health, social assistance, and public housing, is *supplanted* (in the US) or *supplemented* (in the EU) by regulation through its 'Right hand,' that of the police, justice, and correctional administrations, increasingly active and intrusive in the subaltern zones of social and urban space. And, logically, the prison returns to the forefront of the societal stage, when only 30 years ago the most eminent specialists of the penal question were unanimous in predicting its waning, if not its disappearance.[12]

The renewed utility of the penal apparatus in the post-Keynesian era of insecure employment is threefold: (i) it works to bend the fractions of the working-class recalcitrant to the discipline of the new fragmented service wage-labor by increasing the cost of strategies of exit into the informal economy of the street; (ii) it neutralizes and warehouses its most disruptive elements, or those rendered wholly superfluous by the recomposition of the demand for labor; and (iii) it reaffirms the authority of the state in daily life within the restricted domain henceforth assigned to it. The canonization of the 'right to security,' correlative to the dereliction of the 'right to employment' in its old form (that is, full-time and with full benefits, for an indefinite period and for a living wage enabling one to reproduce oneself socially and to project oneself into the future), and the increased interest in and resources granted to the enforcement of order come at just the right time to shore up the deficit of legitimacy suffered by political decision-makers, owing to the very fact that they have abjured the established missions of the state on the social and economic fronts.

Under these conditions, one understands better why, throughout Europe, the parties of the governmental Left smitten with the neoliberal vision have proven so fond of the security thematics incarnated by 'zero tolerance' come from the United States in the past decade, or its British cousins such as 'community policing.' For, in their case, the adoption of policies of economic deregulation and social retrenchment amounts to a political betrayal of the working-class electorate that brought them to power in the hope of receiving stronger state protection against the sanctions and failings of the market. Thus the punitive turn taken by Lionel Jospin in France in the fall of 1997, like those negotiated by Anthony Blair in Britain, Felipe González in Spain, Massimo d'Alema in Italy, and Gerhard Schröder in Germany around the same years, after William Jefferson Clinton had plainly adopted the ultra-punitive agenda of the Republican Party in the U.S. in 1994,[13] has little to do with the alleged 'explosion' in youth delinquency or with the 'urban violence' that have invaded public debate towards the end of the past decade. It has everything to do with the generalization of desocialized wage labor and the establishment of a political regime that will facilitate its imposition. It is a regime that one may call 'liberal-paternalist,' insofar as it is *liberal* and permissive at the top, with regard to corporations and the upper class, and *paternalist* and authoritarian at the bottom, towards those who find themselves caught between the restructuring of employment and the ebbing of social protection or its conversion into an instrument of surveillance and discipline.

II. WHEN PRISONFARE JOINS WELFARE: THE DOUBLE REGULATION OF THE POOR

The resolutely punitive turn taken by penal policies in advanced societies at the close of the twentieth century thus does not pertain to the simple diptych of 'crime and punishment.' It heralds the establishment of a *new government of social insecurity,*' in the expansive sense of techniques and procedures aimed at directing the conduct of the men'[14] and women caught up in the turbulence of economic deregulation and the conversion of welfare into a springboard toward precarious employment, an organizational design within which the prison assumes a major role and which translates, for the categories residing in the nether regions of social space, in the imposition of severe and supercilious supervision. It is the United States that invented this new politics of poverty during the period from 1973 to 1996, in the wake of the social, racial, and anti-statist reaction to the progressive movements of the preceding decade that was to be the crucible of the neoliberal revolution.[15]

The explosive rise of the carceral sector in the United States, where the confined population has quadrupled in two decades to exceed 2.2 million, even as the crime rate stagnated and then declined, partakes of a broader restructuring of the U.S. bureaucratic field tending to criminalize poverty and its consequences so as to anchor precarious wage work as a new norm of citizenship at the bottom of the class structure while remedying the derailing of the traditional mechanisms for maintaining the ethnoracial order. The planned atrophy of the social state, culminating with the 1996 law on 'Personal Responsibility and Work Opportunity,' which replaced the right to 'welfare' with the obligation of 'workfare,' and the sudden hypertrophy of the penal state are two concurrent and complementary developments. Each in its manner, they respond, on the one side, to the forsaking of the Fordist wage–work compact and the Keynesian compromise in the mid-1970s, and, on the other side, to the crisis of the ghetto as a device for the socio-spatial confinement of blacks in the wake of the Civil Rights Revolution and the wave of urban riots of the 1960s. Together, they ensnare the marginal populations of the metropolis in a *carceral-assistential net* that aims either to render them 'useful' by steering them onto the track of deskilled employment through moral retraining and material suasion, or to warehouse them out of reach in the devastated core of the urban 'Black Belt' or in the penitentiaries that have become the latter's distant yet direct satellites.[16]

Social scientists and activists, as well as the politicians, professionals, and activists who wish to reform them, continue to approach social policy and penal policy as separate and isolated domains of public action, whereas in reality they already function in tandem at the bottom of the structure of classes and places. Just as the close of the nineteenth century witnessed the gradual disjunction of the social question from the penal question under the press of working-class mobilization and the reconfiguration of the state it stimulated, the close of the twentieth century has been the theater of a renewed fusion and confusion of these two issues, following the fragmentation of the world of the working class – its industrial dismantlement and the deepening of its internal divisions, its defensive retreat into the private sphere and crushing feeling of downward drift, its loss of a sense of collective dignity, and, lastly, its abandonment by Left parties more concerned with the games internal to their apparatus, leading to its near disappearance from the public scene as a collective actor. It follows that the fight against street delinquency now serves as screen and counterpart to the new social question, namely, the generalization of insecure wage work and its impact on the territories and life strategies of the urban proletariat.

In 1971, Frances Fox Piven and Richard Cloward published their classic book, *Regulating the Poor*, in which they argue that 'relief programs are initiated to deal with dislocations in the work system that lead to mass disorder, and are then retained (in an altered form) to enforce work.'[17] Thirty years later, this cyclical dynamic of expansion and contraction of public aid has been superseded by a new division of the labor of nomination and domination of deviant and dependent populations that couples welfare services and criminal justice administration under the aegis of the same behaviorist and punitive philosophy. The activation of disciplinary programs applied to the unemployed, the indigent, single mothers, and others 'on assistance' so as to push them onto the peripheral sectors of the employment market, on the one side, and the deployment of an extended police and penal net with a reinforced mesh in the dispossessed districts of the metropolis, on the other side, are the two components of a single apparatus for the management of poverty that aims at effecting the authoritarian rectification of the behaviors of populations recalcitrant to the emerging economic and symbolic order. Failing which it aims to ensure the civic or physical expurgation of those who prove to be 'incorrigible' or useless. And, much like the development of modern 'welfare' in the United States from its origins in the New Deal to the contemporary period was decisively shaped by its entailment in a rigid and pervasive structure of racial domination that precluded the deployment of inclusive and universalist programs, the expansion of the penal state after the mid-1970s was both dramatically accelerated and decisively twisted by the revolt and involutive collapse of the dark ghetto as well as by the subsequent ebbing of public support for black demands for civic equality.[18]

In the era of fragmented and discontinuous wage work, the regulation of working-class households is no longer handled solely by the maternal and nurturing social arm of the welfare state; it relies also on the virile and controlling arm of the penal state. The 'dramaturgy of labor' is not played solely on the stages of the public aid office and job-placement bureau, as Piven and Cloward insist in the 1993 revision of their classic analysis of poverty regulation.[19] At century's turn, it also unfolds its stern scenarios in police stations, in the corridors of criminal court, and in the darkness of prison cells.[20] This dynamic coupling of the Left and Right hands of the state operates through a familiar sharing of the roles between the sexes. The public aid bureaucracy, now reconverted into an administrative springboard into poverty-level employment, takes up the mission of inculcating the duty of working for work's sake among poor women (and indirectly their children): 90% of welfare recipients in the U.S. are mothers. The quartet formed by the police, the court, the prison, and the probation or parole officer assumes the task of taming their brothers, their boyfriends or husbands, and their sons: 93% of U.S. inmates are male (men also make up 88% of parolees and 77% of probationers). This suggests, in line with a rich strand of feminist scholarship on public policy, gender, and citizenship,[21] that the invention of the *double regulation of the poor* in America in the closing decades of the twentieth century partakes of an overall *(re)masculinizing of the state* in the neoliberal age, which is in part as an oblique reaction to (or against) the social changes wrought by the women's movement and their reverbations inside the bureaucratic field.

Within this sexual and institutional division in the regulation of the poor, the 'clients' of both the assistential and penitential sectors of the state fall under the same principled suspicion: they are considered morally deficient unless they periodically provide visible proof to the contrary. This is why their behaviors must be supervised and rectified by the imposition of rigid protocols whose violation will expose them to a redoubling of corrective discipline and, if necessary, to sanctions that can result in durable segregation, a manner of social death for moral failing – casting them outside the civic community of those entitled to social rights in the case of public aid recipients, outside the society of 'free' men for convicts. Welfare provision and criminal justice are now animated by the same punitive and paternalist philosophy that stresses the 'individual responsibility' of the 'client,' treated in the manner of a 'subject,' in contraposition to the universal rights and obligations of the citizen,[22] and they reach publics of roughly comparable size. In 2001, the number of households receiving Temporary Assistance to Needy Families, the main assistance program established by the 1996 'welfare reform,' was 2.1 million, corresponding to some 6 million beneficiaries. That same year, the carceral population reached 2.1 million, but the total number of 'beneficiaries' of criminal justice supervision (tallying up inmates, probationers, and parolees) was in the neighborhood of 6.5 million. Moreover, welfare recipients and inmates have germane social profiles and extensive mutual ties that make them the two gendered sides of the same population coin.

III. A 'EUROPEAN ROAD' TO THE PENAL STATE

Excavating the economic underpinnings and the socioracial dynamics of the rise of the penal state in the United States offers indispensable materials for a historical anthropology of the invention of neoliberalism in action. Since the rupture of the mid-1970s, this country has been the theoretical and practical motor for the elaboration and planetary dissemination of a political project that aims to subordinate all human activities to the tutelage of the market. Far from being an incidental or teratological development, the hypertrophic expansion of the penal sector of the bureaucratic field is an essential element of its new anatomy in the age of economic neo-Darwinism. To journey across the U.S. carceral archipelago, then, is not only to travel to the 'extreme limits of European civilization,' to borrow the words of Alexis de Tocqueville. It is also to discover the likely contours of the future landscape of the police, justice, and prison in the European and Latin American countries that have embarked onto the path of 'liberating' the economy and reconstructing the state blazed by the American leader. In this perspective, the United States appears as a sort of historical alembic in which one can observe on a real scale, and anticipate by way of *structural transposition*, the social, political, and cultural consequences of the advent of neoliberal penality in a society submitted to the joint empire of the commodity form and moralizing individualism.

For the United States has not been content to be the forge and locomotive of the neoliberal project on the level of the economy and welfare; over the past decade, it has also become the premier global exporter of 'theories,' slogans, and measures on the crime and safety front.[23] In her panorama of carceral evolution around the planet, Vivien Stern stresses that 'a major influence on penal policy in Britain and other Western European countries has been the policy direction taken in the United States,' an influence to which she attributes 'the complete reversal of the consensus prevailing in the postwar developed world and expressed in UN documents and international conventions' that 'deprivation of liberty should be used sparingly,' and the general discrediting of the ideal of 'the rehabilitation and social reintegration of the offender.'[24] Whether through importation or inspiration, the alignment of penal policies never entails the deployment of identical replicas. In European countries with a strong statist tradition, Catholic or social-democratic, the new politics of poverty does not imply a mechanical duplication of the U.S. pattern, with a clear and brutal swing from the social to the penal treatment of urban marginality leading to hyperincarceration. The deep roots of the social state in the bureaucratic fields and national mental structures, the weaker hold of the individualist and utilitarian ideology that undergirds the sacralization of the market, and the absence of a sharp ethnoracial divide explain that the countries of the European continent are unlikely to shift rapidly to an all-out punitive strategy. Each must clear its own path towards the new government of social insecurity in accordance with its specific national history, social configurations, and political traditions. Nonetheless, one can sketch a provisional characterization of a 'European road' to the penal state (with French, Dutch, Italian, etc., variants) that is gradually coming into being before our eyes through a *double and conjoint accentuation of the social and penal regulation of marginal categories.*

Thus, during the past decade, the French authorities have stepped up both welfare and justice interventions. On the one side, they have multiplied assistance programs (public utility jobs, subsidized youth employment, training schemes, etc.), raised the various 'social minima' (targeted government aid to various destitute categories), established universal medical coverage, and broadened access to the Revenu Minimum d'Insertion (RMI, the guaranteed minimum income grant). On the other, they have created special surveillance units ('*cellules de veille*') and nested emergency riot police squads inside the 'sensitive zones' of the urban periphery; replaced street educators with magistrates to issue warnings to occasional youth delinquents; passed municipal decrees outlawing begging and vagrancy (even though these are patently illegal); multiplied 'crackdown' operations and sweeps inside low-income housing projects and routinized the use of '*comparution immédiate*' (a fast-track judicial procedure whereby an offender caught in the act is deferred before a judge and sentenced within hours); increased penalties for repeated offences; restricted parole release and speeded up the deportation of convicted foreign offenders; threatened the parents of juvenile delinquents or children guilty of school truancy with withholding family benefits, etc.

A second contrast between the United States and the countries of continental Europe is that penalization *à l'européenne* is effected mainly through *the agency of the police and the courts rather than the prison*. It still obeys a predominantly panoptic logic, rather than a segregative and retributive rationale. The correlate is that social services play an active part in this criminalizing process, since they possess the administrative and human means to exercise a close-up supervision of so-called problem populations. But the simultaneous deployment of the social and penal treatment of urban disorders should not hide the fact that the former often functions as a bureaucratic fig-leaf for the latter, and that it is ever more directly subordinated to it in practice. Encouraging state social assistance, health, and education services to collaborate with the police and judicial system turns them into extensions of the penal apparatus, instituting a *social panopticism* which, under cover of promoting the well-being of deprived populations, submits them to an ever-more precise and penetrating form of punitive surveillance.

It remains to be seen whether this 'European road' to liberal paternalism is a genuine alternative to penalization in the mold of the United States or merely an intermediate stage or detour leading, in the end, to carceral hyperinflation. If neighborhoods of relegation are saturated with police without enhancing employment opportunities and life chances in them, and if partnerships between the criminal justice system and other state services are multiplied, there is bound to be an increase in the detection of unlawful conduct and an increased volume of arrests and convictions in criminal court. Who can say today where and when the ballooning of the jails and penitentiaries visible in nearly all the European countries will stop? The case of the Netherlands, which has shifted from a humanist to a managerial penal philosophy and gone from laggard to leader in incarceration among the original 15 members of the European Union is instructive and worrisome in this regard.[25]

IV. THE PENALIZATION OF POVERTY AS PRODUCTION OF REALITY

Just as the emergence of a new government of social insecurity diffused by the neoliberal revolution does not mark a historical reversion to a familiar organizational configuration, but heralds a genuine political innovation, similarly the deployment of the penal state cannot be grasped under the narrow rubric of repression. In point of fact, the repressive trope is a central ingredient in the discursive fog that enshrouds and masks the sweeping makeover of the means, ends, and justifications of public authority at century's close. The leftist activists who rail against the 'punishment machine' on both sides of the Atlantic – castigating the chimerical 'prison-industrial complex' in America and denouncing a diabolical *programme sécuritaire* in France – mistake the wrapping for the package.[26] They fail to see that crime-fighting is but a convenient pretext and propitious platform for a broader redrawing of the perimeter of responsibility of the state operating simultaneously on the economic, social welfare, and penal fronts.

To realize that the rise of the punitive apparatus in advanced society pertains less to crime-fighting than to *state-crafting*, one must reject the conspiratorial view of history that would attribute it to a deliberate plan pursued by omniscient and omnipotent rulers, whether they be political decision-makers, corporate heads, or the gamut of profiteers who benefit from the increased scope and intensity of punishment and related supervisory programs trained on the urban castoffs of deregulation. With Pierre Bourdieu, one must recuse the 'functionalism of the worst case' which casts all historical developments as the work of an omniscient strategist or as automatically beneficial to some abstract machinery of domination and exploitation that would 'reproduce' itself no matter what.[27] Such a vision not only confuses the objective convergence of a welter of disparate public policies, each driven by its own set of protagonists and stakes, with the subjective intentions of state managers. It also fails to heed Foucault's advice that we forsake the 'repressive hypothesis' and treat power as a fertilizing force that remakes the very landscape it traverses.[28] Interestingly, this is an insight that one finds in Karl Marx's erstwhile dispersed remarks on crime, which suggest that

the advent of 'liberal paternalism' is best construed under the generative category of *production*:

> The criminal produces an impression now moral, now tragic, and renders a 'service' by
> arousing the moral and aesthetic sentiments of the public. He produces not only text-
> books on criminal law, the criminal law itself, and thus legislators, but also art, literature,
> novels and the tragic drama. ... The criminal interrupts the monotony and security of
> bourgeois life. Thus he protects it from stagnation and brings forth that restless tension,
> that mobility of spirit without which the stimulus of competition would itself be blunted.[29]

The transition from the social management to the penal treatment of the disorders induced by the fragmentation of wage labor is indeed eminently productive. First, it has spawned new categories of public perception and state action.
Echoing the alleged discovery of 'underclass areas' in the United States, in the
closing decade of the century Europe has witnessed the invention of the '*quartier
sensible*' in France, the 'sink estate' in the United Kingdom, the '*Problemquartier*'
in Germany, the '*krottenwijk*' in the Netherlands, etc., so many bureaucratic
euphemisms to designate the nether sections of the city turned into a social and
economic fallow by the state, and for that very reason subjected to reinforced
police oversight and correctional penetration.[30] The same goes with the bureaucratic notion of '*violences urbaines*' (plural), coined in France by the Minister of
the Interior to amalgamate offensive behaviors of widely divergent nature and
motives – mean looks and rude language, graffiti and low-grade vandalism,
vehicle theft for joy-riding, brawls between youths, threats to teachers, drug-
dealing, and collective confrontations with the police – so as to promote a punitive approach to the social problems besetting declining working-class districts
by depoliticizing them.

New social types are another byproduct of the emerging social-insecurity
regime: the irruption of 'superpredators' in the United States, 'feral youth' and
'yobs' in the United Kingdom, or '*sauvageons*' (wildings, a social-paternalistic
variant of a racial insult scoffing at the alleged deculturation of the lower classes)
in France has been used to justify the reopening or the expansion of detention
centers for juveniles, even though all existing studies deplore their noxious
effects. To these can be added the renovation of classic types such as the 'career
recidivist,' the latest avatar of the *uomo delinquente* invented in 1884 by Cesare
Lombroso, whose distinctive psychophysiological and anthropometric characteristics are now being researched by experts in criminal 'profiling'[31] as well as
guiding the gigantic bureaucratic-cum-scholarly enterprise of 'risk assessment'
for the release of sensitive categories of inmates.

For the policy of penalization of social insecurity is also the bearer of new
knowledges about the city and its troubles, broadcast by an unprecedented range
of 'experts' and, in their wake, journalists, bureaucrats, the managers of activist
organizations, and elected officials perched at the bedside of the 'neighborhoods
of all dangers.'[32] These alleged facts and specialist discourses about criminal insecurity are given form and put into wide circulation by hybrid institutions, situated

at the intersection of the bureaucratic, academic, and journalistic fields, which ape research to provide the appearance of a scientific warrant for lowering the police and penal boom on neighborhoods of relegation. Such is the case, in France, with the Institut des hautes études de la sécurité intérieure, an agency created by the Socialist Minister of the Interior Pierre Joxe in 1989 and then developed by his neo-Gaullist successor Charles Pasqua. This institute, 'placed under the direct authority of the Minister of the Interior' in order to promote 'rational thinking about domestic security,' irrigates the country with the latest novelties in 'crime control' imported from America.[33] It is assisted in this enterprise by the Institut de criminologie de Paris, an *officine* in law-and-order propaganda which is remarkable for not including a single criminologist among its distinguished members.

It would take pages to list the full roster of the agents and devices that contribute to the collective work of material and symbolic construction of the penal state henceforth charged with reestablishing the state's grip over the populations pushed into the cracks and the ditches of urban space, from private firms of 'safety consultants' to '*adjoints de sécurité*' (assistant police officers entrusted with police chores outside of law enforcement), to publishing houses eager to peddle books on this hot topic, '*citoyens relais*' (volunteers who anonymously tip the police about law-enforcement problems in their neighborhoods), and a whole series of judicial innovations (adjunct community judges, neighborhood 'houses of justice,' plea bargaining, etc.), which, on pretext of bureaucratic efficiency, establish a differential justice according to class and place of residence. In sum, *the penalization of precariousness creates new realities*, and realities tailor-made to legitimize the extension of the prerogatives of the punitive state according to the principle of the self-fulfilling prophecy.

A brief illustration: by treating jostling in the school corridors, rudeness in the classroom, or playground ruckus not as matters of discipline pertaining to pedagogical authority in the establishment but as infractions of the law that must be tallied and centrally compiled via a dedicated computer software (the Signa program) and systematically reported to the local police or magistrates; by assigning a 'police correspondent' ('*officier référent*') to every secondary school (rather than a psychologist, nurse, or social worker, who are direly lacking in lower-class districts), the French authorities have redefined ordinary school troubles as matters of law and order and fabricated an epidemic of 'school violence,' even as surveys of students consistently show that over 90% of them feel completely safe at school. With the help of mass-media amplification, this 'explosion' of violence serves in turn to justify the 'school–police partnership' that produced it in the first place, and it validates the enrollment of teaching staff in the declining neighborhoods of the urban periphery in the police missions of surveillance and punishment. Besides, the staging of 'school violence' allows state managers to avoid confronting the professional devaluation and bureaucratic dilemmas created within the educational sphere by the near-universalization of access to secondary schooling, the growing submission of the school system to the logic of competition, and the imperatives of the 'culture of results' imported from the corporate world.[34]

V. CONCLUSION

To understand the fate of the precarious fractions of the working class in their relation to the state, it is no longer possible to limit oneself to studying welfare programs. The sociology of traditional policies of collective 'well-being' – assistance to dispossessed individuals and households, but also education, housing, public health, family allowances, income redistribution, etc. – must be extended to include penal policies. Thus the study of incarceration ceases to be the reserved province of criminologists and penologists to become an *essential chapter in the sociology of the state and social stratification*, and, more specifically, of the (de)composition of the urban proletariat in the era of ascendant neoliberalism. Indeed, the crystallization of a liberal-paternalist political regime, which practices *'laisser-faire et laisser-passer'* toward the top of the class structure, at the level of the mechanisms of production of inequality, and punitive paternalism toward the bottom, at the level of their social and spatial implications, demands that we forsake the traditional definition of 'social welfare' as the product of a political and scholarly common sense overtaken by historical reality. It requires that we adopt an expansive approach encompassing in a single grasp the totality of the actions whereby the state purports to mold, classify, and control the populations deemed deviant, dependent, and dangerous living on its territory.

Linking social and penal policies resolves what would appear to be a doctrinal contradiction, or at least a practical antinomy, of neoliberalism, between the downsizing of public authority on the economic flank and its upsizing on that of the enforcement of social and moral order. If the same who are demanding a minimal state in order to 'free' the 'creative forces' of the market and submit the most dispossessed to the sting of competition do not hesitate to erect a maximal state to ensure everyday 'security,' it is because *the poverty of the social state against the backdrop of deregulation elicits and necessitates the grandeur of the penal state*. And because this causal and functional linkage between the two sectors of the bureaucratic field gets all the stronger as the state more completely sheds all economic responsibility and tolerates a high level of poverty as well as a wide opening of the compass of inequality.

NOTES

1   This article is based on a lecture entitled 'Regulating the Poor in the Neoliberal Age: When Social Policy meets Penal Policy,' delivered to the Workshop on Social Inequality, Kennedy School of Government, Harvard University, on 31 October 2006. It lays out the agenda of my book *Punishing the Poor: The New Government of Social Insecurity* (Durham and London: Duke University Press, forthcoming in 2008), drawing on the Prologue and Chapter 1. I would like to thank William Julius Wilson and the workshop participants for their stimulating comments and critiques.

2   For an overview of the penal scene in the main countries of the First World, see John Pratt et al., eds., *The New Punitiveness: Trends, Theories, and Perspectives* (London: Willan Publishing, 2004); Laurent Mucchielli and Philippe Robert, eds., *Crime et sécurité. L'état des savoirs* (Paris: La Découverte, 2004); Alessandro Dal Lago, *Giovani, stranieri e criminali* (Rome: Manifestolibri, 2001); and Wolfgang Ludwig-Mayerhofer,

ed., *Soziale Ungleichheit, Kriminalität und Kriminalisierung* (Opladen: Leske & Budrich, 2000).

3 I retraced in *Les Prisons de la misère* (Paris: Raisons d'agir Editions, 1999; trans. *Prisons of Poverty*, Minneapolis, University of Minnesota Press, 2008) the three stages in the planetary diffusion of the notions, technologies, and policies of public safety 'made in USA': gestation and implementation (as well as exhibition) in New York City under the tutelage of the neoconservative think tanks that led the campaign against the welfare state; import-export through the agency of the media and of the kindred policy centers that have mushroomed throughout Europe, and particularly in Great Britain, the acclimation chamber of neoliberal penality with a view toward its dissemination on the continent; scholarly 'dressing up' by local *passeurs* who bring the warrant of their academic authority to the adaptation to their countries of theories and techniques of order maintenance come from the United States.

4 Robert Castel, *Les Métamorphoses de la question sociale. Une chronique du salariat* (Paris: Fayard, 1995); Hartmut Häußermann, Martin Kronauer, and Walter Siebel, eds., *An den Rändern der Städte: Armut und Ausgrenzung* (Frankfurt-am-Main: Suhrkamp, 2004); and Loïc Wacquant, *Urban Outcasts: A Comparative Sociology of Advanced Marginality* (Cambridge: Polity Press, 2007).

5 See, in particular, Karl Marx and Friedrich Engels, 'Marx and Engels on Crime and Punishment,' in David Greenberg, ed., *Crime and Capitalism: Readings in Marxist Criminology* (Palo Alto: Mayfield, 1981), 45–56; Stephen Lukes and Andrew Scull, eds., *Durkheim and the Law* (Stanford: Stanford University Press, 1995); and Pierre Bourdieu, 'Rethinking the State: On the Genesis and Structure of the Bureaucratic Field,' in *Practical Reasons* (Cambridge: Polity, 1998 [1994]), 35–63.

6 A forceful argument for recognizing the full 'complexity of structure and density of meaning' of punishment as a multilayered social institution, that skillfully draws on Marx, Durkheim, Elias, and Foucault, is deployed by David Garland, *Punishment and Society: A Study in Social Theory* (Chicago: University of Chicago Press, 1990), esp. 280–92.

7 Norwegian criminologist Thomas Mathiesen detected and denounced it as early as 1990 on the carceral front; see Thomas Mathiesen, *Prison on Trial: A Critical Assessment* (London: Sage, 1990), 11–14.

8 For an analysis of national variations on this common pattern, read Marion Fourcade-Gourinchas and Sarah L. Babb, 'The Rebirth of the Liberal Creed: Paths to Neoliberalism in Four Countries,' *American Journal of Sociology* 108 (November 2002): 533–79.

9 Jamie Peck, *Workfare States* (New York: Guilford, 2001); and Catherine Lévy, *Vivre au minimum. Enquête dans l'Europe de la précarité* (Paris: Editions La Dispute, 2003), ch. 4.

10 Mike Hawkins, *Social Darwinism in European and American Thought, 1860–1945: Nature as Model and Nature as Threat* (Cambridge: Cambridge University Press, 1997).

11 Pierre Bourdieu et al., *La Misère du monde* (Paris: Seuil, 1993), 219–18 (trans. *The Weight of the World*, Cambridge, Polity Press, 1999); and Pierre Bourdieu, *Contre-feux* (Paris: Raisons d'agir, 1997), 9–15 (trans. *Acts of Resistance: Against the Tyranny of the Market*, Cambridge, Polity Press, 1999).

12 In the mid-1970s, the three leading revisionist historians of the prison, David Rothman, Michel Foucault, and Michael Ignatieff agreed to see it as an institution in inevitable decline, destined to be replaced in the medium run by more diffuse, discrete, and diversified instruments of social control; see Franklin E. Zimring and Gordon Hawkins, *The Scale of Imprisonment* (Chicago: University of Chicago Press,

1991), ch. 2. The penal debate then turned on the implications of 'decarceration' and implementation of community sentences. Since this Malthusian prognosis, the evolution of punishment has made an about-face in almost all Western societies: the population behind bars has doubled in France, Belgium, and England; it has tripled in Holland, Spain, and Greece; and it has quintupled in the United States.

13   On Clinton's embrace of traditionally Republican nostrums on crime, see Ann Chih Lin, 'The Troubled Success of Crime Policy,' in Margaret Weir, ed., *The Social Divide: Political Parties and the Future of Activist Government* (Washington, DC: Brookings Institution and Russell Sage Foundation, 1998), 312–57; on the punitive turn of Blair's New Labour, product of a servile imitation of U.S. policies, read Michael Tonry, *Punishment and Politics: Evidence and Emulation in the Making of English Crime Control Policy* (London: Willan, 2004); the *aggiornamento* of the Italian Left in penal matters is described by Salvatore Verde, *Massima sicurezza. Dal carcere speciale allo stato penale* (Rome: Odradek, 2002); the law-and-order conversion of the neo-socialists under Jospin's leadership in France is retraced in Loïc Wacquant, *Les Prisons de la misère*.

14   Michel Foucault, *Résumé des cours, 1970–1982* (Paris: Juillard, 1989), 'Du gouvernement des vivants,' 123. For a historiographic illustration of this notion, read Giovanna Procacci, *Gouverner la misère. La question sociale en France, 1789–1848* (Paris: Seuil, 1993); for a conceptual reconsideration and elaboration, see Nikolas Rose and Mariana Valverde, 'Governed by Law?,' *Social & Legal Studies* 7, no. 4 (December 1998): 541–52.

15   Michael K. Brown, *Race, Money, and the American Welfare State* (Ithaca: Cornell University Press, 1999), 323–53.

16   Loïc Wacquant, 'Deadly Symbiosis: When Ghetto and Prison Meet and Mesh,' *Punishment & Society* 3, no. 1 (Winter 2001): 95–133.

17   Frances Fox Piven and Richard A. Cloward, *Regulating the Poor: The Functions of Public Welfare*, new expanded ed. (New York: Vintage, 1993, orig. 1971), xvii.

18   The Gordian knot of racial division and penality in the United States after the peaking of the Civil Rights movement is untied in my book *Deadly Symbiosis: Race and the Rise of the Penal State* (Cambridge: Polity Press, 2008).

19   Piven and Cloward, *Regulating the Poor*, 381–87, 395–97.

20   Similarities in the culture and organization of the supervision of single mothers who received public aid and convicts behind bars or released on parole are immediately apparent upon the parallel reading of Sharon Hays, *Flat Broke With Children: Women in the Age of Welfare Reform* (New York: Oxford University Press, 2003), and John Irwin, The Warehouse Prison (Los Angeles: Roxbury, 2004).

21   See Ann Orloff, 'Gender in the Welfare State,' *Annual Review of Sociology* 22 (1996): 51–78; and Julia Adams and Tasleem Padamsee, 'Signs and Regimes: Reading Feminist Research on Welfare States,' *Social Politics 8*, no. 1 (Spring 2001): 1–23.

22   Dorothy Roberts, 'Welfare and the Problem of Black Citizenship,' *Yale Law Journal* 105, no. 6 (April 1996): 1563–1602.

23   Loïc Wacquant, 'The Penalisation of Poverty and the Rise of Neoliberalism,' *European Journal of Criminal Policy and Research*, Special issue on "Criminal Justice and Social Policy," 9, no. 4 (Winter 2001): 401-12; and Tim Newburn and Richard Sparks, eds., *Criminal Justice and Political Cultures: National and International Dimensions of Crime Control* (London: Willan, 2004).

24   Vivien Stern, 'Mass Incarceration: "A Sin Against the Future"?,' *European Journal of Criminal Policy and Research* 3 (October 1996): 14.

25   David Downes and René van Swaaningen, 'The Road to Dystopia? Changes in the Penal Climate of the Netherlands,' in Michael Tonry & Catrien Bijleveld (eds.), *Crime and Justice in the Netherlands* (Chicago: The University of Chicago Press, 2006), 31–72.

26 For a critique of the 'demonic myth of the "prison-industrial complex"'in the United States, read Loïc Wacquant, 'The New Mission of the Prison in the Neoliberal Age,' in Willem Schinkel (ed.), *Globalization and the State: Sociological Perspectives on the State of the State* (Basingstoke: Palgrave, 2008).

27 'One of the principles of sociology consists in recusing this negative functionalism: social mechanisms are not the product of a Machiavellian intention. They are much more intelligent than the most intelligent of the dominant.' Pierre Bourdieu, *Questions de sociologie* (Paris: Minuit, 1980), 71, my translation (trans. *Sociology in Question*, London, Sage, 1990).

28 Michel Foucault, 'Two Lectures' (1976), in *Power/Knowledge: Selected Interviews and Other Writings, 1972–1977*, ed. Colin Gordon (New York: Pantheon, 1980), 97.

29 Karl Marx, *Theories of Surplus Value*, cited in Tom Bottomore and Maximilien Rubel, eds., *Karl Marx: Selected Writings in Society and Social Philosophy* (New York: McGraw-Hill, 1958), 159.

30 Wacquant, *Urban Outcasts*, 237–41, 276–79.

31 The 'power-knowledge' constellation that subtends the genesis and success of the biological theory of crime (then and now) is explored by David Horn in *The Criminal Body: Lombroso and the Anatomy of Deviance* (New York: Routledge, 2003).

32 To recall the savorous expression of one of the French prophets of law-and-order doom, former police commissioner Richard Bousquet, author of *Insécurité: nouveaux risques. Les quartiers de tous les dangers* (Paris: L'Harmattan, 1998).

33 In July of 2004, the IHESI was replaced by the INHES (Institut national des hautes études de sécurité), a very similar outfit presented by Interior Minister Nicolas Sarkozy as 'the elite school of security that France needs.' Its board of overseers features not a single researcher. Its work is complemented by the activities of the Observatory on Crime and Delinquency, created by Sarkozy and directed by Alain Bauer, self-proclaimed 'criminologist' and president of Alain Bauer Associates, France's leading consulting firm on 'urban security.'

34 Eric Debardieux, 'Insécurité et clivages sociaux : l'exemple des violences scolaires,' *Les Annales de la recherche urbaine* 75 (June 1997): 43–50; and Franck Poupeau, *Contestations scolaires et ordre social. Les enseignants de Seine-Saint-Denis en grève* (Paris: Syllepse, 2004).

[…]

Part Six

Global harms and risks

INTRODUCTION

Historically, law making and law enforcement have been the prerogative of the nation-state. Policy making and policy analysis in this area have traditionally been framed by a priori assumptions about national sovereignty and nation-state independence. Criminology has long mirrored such parochialism and has been mired in its own methodological nationalism. However, now that it has become commonplace to assume that we live in a world marked by globalization, a more complex and transnational level of analysis is thought necessary. As many of the readings in Part Five of this reader have already indicated, the sheer scale of the transformation of 'the social' currently underway calls into question criminology's traditional assumptions, rationales, ways of thinking and purpose. In particular, our choice of readings in this Part concentrates on the criminological consequences of the extensive globalization of economic, political and cultural activities that is producing new harms across the world. The rapid change accompanying certain globalizations is bringing serious risks of global economic instability as a result of unregulated neo-liberal markets and the equally serious risk of political and social disorder and mounting violence resultant from the decline of traditional forms of governance and the fragmentation of social relations.

Janet Chan argues that in the twenty-first century criminology will be remade by three inter-connected processes: globalization; reflexive modernization and governmentality. Neo-liberal globalization is generating new crime risks and threats as well as the ability to transfer crime control policies and practices. In a sense one provides the justification for the other. Geo-political change and economic shifts have facilitated the emergence of 'joined up' globalized criminal networks and new forms of highly profitable crime. Organized global criminal activity has the potential to corrupt democratic institutions, undermine the rule of law and human rights and embed itself within conventional modes of economic exchange. The challenge for criminologists lies in developing concepts and methods to analyse new forms of globalized crime as well as understanding how crime control policy and practice transfer is taking place and with what consequences. The debate is barely started as to whether we need (a) a globalized criminology (b) a global consciousness and sensibility or (c) a specialist 'global criminology'. For Chan this is further complicated as reflexive modernization demystifies the scientific claims-making of all academic disciplines, including criminology. The robustness of its theories, concepts and practices will be subjected to relentless interrogation. At the same moment the ability of many others to generate criminological knowledge redefines who can claim to be a professional criminologist. And although Chan does not discuss it, criminological knowledge production and dissemination increasingly takes place across a multitude of borderless popular cultural formats and social media websites. Finally, she argues that the changing nature of governmental expectations regarding the relevance of criminology is in danger of narrowing the intellectual horizons of its practitioners at a moment when it needs to be open to new ideas.

Neil Middleton argues that the institutional logics of the global financial and trading system is generating extreme poverty and inequalities and a host of related harms. For him, the physical reality of immiseration is the most widespread and destructive form of crime and, we could argue, cause of crime. What is remarkable is that poverty has fallen off the criminology research agenda.

The reading by Moisés Naím was originally produced for the first meeting of the *Global Commission on Drug Policies* held in Geneva in 2011. In a striking exposé, Naím details the extent of involvement and complicity of some nation states and their leaders in various illegalities such as trade in illegal drugs, arms smuggling and human trafficking, The collusion is such that it is impossible to distinguish between the activities of some governments and that of organized criminal groups. And the fundamental issue then becomes not one of say controlling markets for drugs but of preventing 'criminals from taking over governments around the world'. In this analysis the 'real criminals' are not to be found amongst the impoverished and disadvantaged but are members of their nation's political, military, business, cultural and media elites.

However, criminology's growing fascination with globalization has not simply focused on how the global may have created new avenues and sites for orthodox crime, it has also encouraged the discipline to look beyond its traditionally narrow nation-specific and legally defined contexts and concerns. And, as a result, the gaze of criminology has been considerably broadened. The next reading explores the notion of a 'global risk society' that is claimed to be one of the hallmarks of late/post modernity. Ulrich Beck argues that we are now entering a significant period in human development characterized by a series of uncontrollable and unquantifiable insecurities. Moreover, we do not even have the language to be able to describe what we are facing. The amorphous yet enormous nature of ecological, financial and terrorist crises lies beyond the imaginary of the nation state and largely beyond the (up to now) limited vocabulary of the social sciences. Ultimately, for Beck, the pertinence of 'global risk' requires the abandonment of methodological parochialism and the development of a radical transnational science of cosmopolitanism.

Stanley Cohen in the course of his discussion of human rights abuses and crimes of the state, also questions the core concerns of traditional criminology. He notes how for example criminologists have devoted time and effort to analysing the state of crime and virtually ignored the criminological significance of the crimes of the state. With one or two notable exceptions criminologists have been remarkably silent on the genocide, ethnic cleansing, extra-judicial killings and violations of human rights that are occurring in many parts of the world. Cohen provides us with an important case study of how key criminological concepts can be updated, which he deploys to analyse and explain the state inspired criminal events and actions that are defining the twenty-first century.

The next reading by Rob White explores how criminology can impact on the study of environmental issues, in this case the social, political and economic dynamics surrounding the provision of safe drinking water. In essence, White introduces us to a wide range of issues which may be clustered under the umbrella of an emergent 'green criminology': that is the study by criminologists of environmental harms (that may incorporate wider definitions of crime than that provided in strictly legal definitions), environmental laws (including enforcement, prosecution and sentencing practices); environmental regulation (systems of civil and criminal law that are designed to manage, protect and preserve specified environments and species, and to manage the negative consequences of particular industrial processes); and movements of resistance to such developments.

Jackie Turner and Liz Kelly focus our attention on the complex phenomenon of human trafficking. In particular they note how globalization has not only fuelled the growth of transnational organized criminal groups, but also has encouraged new patterns of migration and increasingly fluid international labour markets. Above all they argue for a gendered perspective on diasporas and transnationalism in a globalized world in order to better understand the 'trade secrets' of traffickers, and how the globalized exploitation of human beings is organized, managed and maintained.

In the final reading Sheila Brown's contribution once more forces us to reconsider the limitations of existing agendas, concepts and languages to be encountered in criminology. In the growing context of ubiquitous virtual technologies, cybernetics, genetic engineering and techno-social networks, Brown queries the continuing relevance of 'thinking crime and criminal justice' through the binary opposites (right/wrong; left/right, science/nature and so on) that typically underpin and inform much criminological study. In all of criminology to date, whether in its positivist, critical, cultural or crime science variants, there is no vision of the world as a 'human/ technical hybrid' or as an 'informational net'. Brown asks the fundamental yet challenging question of exactly what might criminology look like if its analyses began not with pre-formed binary principles but rather with the more fluid and hybrid notions of the cyber, the data-human and the techno-social.

49

Globalisation, reflexivity and the practice of criminology

Janet Chan

This paper examines recent theorising of broader social and political trends in modern societies and discusses their implications for the practice of criminology. Globalisation has facilitated the "free trade" of criminological knowledge and ideologies and accelerated the deterritorialisation of culture and politics. Under "reflexive modernisation", the scientific authority of criminology is being challenged, not only from within the discipline in the form of academic critique, but also from without, in the arena of law and order politics. At the same time, criminologists and criminal justice policies are increasingly being "governed" by "technologies of performance" and the "technologies of agency" as part of "reflexive government" in advanced liberal societies.

THE STATE OF CRIMINOLOGY

The notion that criminology is in crisis is not new. The "failure" of criminology has been a recurrent theme (Hogg, 1996, pp. 43, 47; see also Cohen, 1988; Braithwaite, 1989). This failure is alternately related to criminology's inability to "prescribe policies that will work to reduce crime" (Braithwaite, 1989, p. 133) or the absence of a critical edge among its "mainstream" practitioners (Taylor, Walton & Young, 1973; Cohen, 1981). But the crisis of criminology is not limited to its lack of impact on policy or politics, it relates more crucially to the self-image of the

From *Australian and New Zealand Journal of Criminology*, 2000, 33(2): 118–35.

discipline. Pavarini pronounced some years ago that criminology "is now facing a situation of crisis of identity so profound that we may have serious doubts about its capacity for survival as presently constituted" (1994, p. 43). For Pavarini, part of this identity crisis relates to the repetitive and banal exercise of unmasking the "naturalistic fallacy" of crime and punishment that criminology has engaged in over the past decades. But this "permanent state of precariousness and crisis, this recurrent temptation towards suicide" is also a consequence of criminology's "confused claims to knowledge", its "parasitic" relation to other branches of science and the unregulated fluidity of its disciplinary boundaries (Pavarini, 1994, pp. 50–51).

Another manifestation of this crisis is found in the contradictory nature of criminal justice policy. Garland (1996) has observed in the UK and elsewhere a trend in official criminology[1] which is increasingly dualistic, polarised, and ambivalent: offenders are characterised as rational beings at one end of the spectrum but demonised at the other end. The result of this ambivalence is that strategies aimed at "normalizing crime, responsibilizing others and defining deviance down" coexist with punitive policies, but while the former are based on research results and rational decisions, the latter are driven by political considerations (Garland, 1996, p. 462; cf Chan, 1999).

To explore the challenges facing criminology in the new millennium, this paper examines recent theorising about the broader social and political trends in modern societies. In particular, it focuses on processes of globalisation and reflexive modernisation which have consequences for criminology, criminal justice policies and law-and-order politics. Before studying these broader trends, however, it is important to describe the existing practices of criminology in Australia and other similar countries. One way (see Chan, 1996)[2] of conceptualising the practice of criminology – instead of the usual distinction between "administrative" criminology and "academic" criminology – is to use the Bourdieuian framework of "field" (of power and capital) and "habitus" – those taken-for-granted aspects of practice which "delimit the thinkable and predetermine the thought" (Bourdieu & Wacquant, 1992, pp. 39–40; see also Bourdieu, 1975; Bourdieu, 1988).

Ericson defines a criminologist as "someone who uses abstractions of crime and security to establish institutional and professional jurisdiction over social problems" (1996, p. 19). The field of criminology covers both academic and non-academic sites. The production of academic criminology takes place in a diversity of "university organisation, paradigms, research funding, publication outlets and professional association" (Ericson, 1996, p. 17). Like other academic fields, the field of academic criminology is a space of struggle over "academic capital" (power based on control of appointment, promotion and tenure within universities), and "scientific authority" (intellectual renown and scientific prestige), which may be converted into "symbolic capital" (legitimacy or power to define) or "social capital" (network of influence) (see Bourdieu & Wacquant, 1992, p. 76; Bourdieu, 1988, pp. 78–79). Winners of "criminological jurisdiction" owe much of their success to the strength of their location in academic institutions, the dominance of their theoretical or political paradigms, the access they have to research funding, the prestige of their publishers and the power of their professional associations (Ericson, 1996). Criminologists also occupy a hierarchy of organisations outside the academy. Within government agencies, for example, power and resources are usually more abundant in units connected with criminal law, courts, the judiciary, police or the legal profession, compared with units dealing with community services, juvenile justice or corrective services. Stark differences in status and resources also exist between criminologists who work for private consultancy firms and those who are employed in community organisations. Non-academic criminologists also compete for scientific authority, symbolic and social capital, as well as research funding. Compared with their academic counterparts, non-academic criminologists possess less independence (a form of symbolic capital) from economic and political constraints.

Given the multidisciplinary nature of the field, criminologists do not operate under a single, homogeneous habitus (cf Brubaker, 1993). Criminologists working from different disciplinary bases or institutions (fields) are structured by different sets of dispositions. Those who work under a predominantly positivist tradition, for example, make different assumptions, employ different methods of data collection and analysis, and abide by different criteria of validity from those who work under a social constructionist, feminist or poststructuralist tradition. Variations may also be found among different disciplines: for example, historians, psychologists, economists and lawyers are likely to develop research practices that overlap only minimally. Similarly, the habituses of university researchers do not normally share many common features with those of policy analysts in government agencies. In spite of the heterogeneity of the field, there are some shared aspects of the habitus among practitioners of criminology. As an applied scientific field, criminology primarily draws on developments in mainstream disciplinary theories rather than pursues its own theoretical project. It has a bias towards the generation of policy-relevant knowledge and a tendency towards self-reflection and criticism, especially in relation to its failure (Chan, 1996). These common elements of the habitus explain the enduring popularity of the politically disinterested, methodologically rigorous model of criminological research, usually based on "hard", quantitative data. As Bourdieu (1975, p. 24) observes, the ability to draw on the established legitimacy of the natural science provides strength to social science researchers' own claim to legitimacy.

The field of criminology is not independent of other social fields, even though criminology is not "merely an effect of determining social forces" (O'Malley, 1996, p. 36). It is therefore important to examine the broader social and political trends which may have implications for the practice of criminology. In the following sections I will draw on three major bodies of work that analyse recent trends in modern societies: the literature on globalisation, theories of "reflexive modernisation", and studies of "governmentality". While there have been concerns that these bodies of work are not compatible, I am persuaded by Garland's argument that there is no reason why governmentality studies and sociological theories should be regarded as mutually exclusive, and that much can be gained from encouraging a "more fruitful dialogue … between these forms of work" (Garland, 1997, p. 205).

GLOBALISATION

Globalisation has become, as Bauman suggests, "a fad word fast turning into a shibboleth"(1998, p. 1). It has alternately been depicted as something totally unprecedented or as nothing new (Hirst and Thompson, 1996), but, as Held has argued, it should be recognised that "forms of globalisation have changed over time" (2000, p. 45). Globalisation involves "the intensification of worldwide social relations which link distant localities in such a way that local happenings are shaped by events occurring many miles away and vice versa" (Giddens, 1990, p. 64); it is therefore a two-way process. Tomlinson's (1999, p. 2) notion of "complex connectivity" best captures the condition of globalisation: these connections exist in a variety of modalities – social, institutional, material, symbolic as well as technological, although the most significant and visible developments involve the growth in trade, financial flow, and the general "enmeshment of national economies in global economic transactions" (Held, 2000, p. 47).

When globalisation is mentioned in the context of criminal justice, the usual concern is how to deal with the threat of transnational or organised crimes (Nelken, 1997, p. 253). This paper is, however, more concerned with the extent to which criminology and criminal justice policies have been affected by globalisation. This is not to deny that some connection exists between crime trends and trends in criminal justice policies, but globalisation's effect on criminology and policy is not necessarily related to its effect on crime. It is important, however, to distinguish between two consequences of globalisation – homogenisation and interdependence – since "interdependence does not necessarily presume or produce homogeneity" (Nelken, 1997, pp. 260–261). For example, transnational policing has always been around and it involves both interdependence and homogenisation; nevertheless, more recent developments such as the "opening-up of global markets, the information revolution, and the end of the Cold War" have contributed to an exponential growth of transnational policing (Sheptycki, 1998, pp. 496–7).

Globalisation, criminology and criminal justice

As an "expert system", criminology has always been global in its orientation. As Giddens has argued, expert systems form one type of "disembedding mechanism" in late modernity, that is, a mechanism which "lifts out" social relations from local contexts and then restructures them across "indefinite spans of time-space" (Giddens, 1990, p. 21). Expertise is normally considered to be independent of context, open to all who are interested, and valid regardless of locale (Giddens, 1994, pp. 84–85). While the increased popularity of the English language and advances in modern transport and communication technologies may have made a difference to the extent to which knowledge is globalised, criminology has always had a transnational and even transcontinental existence.[3] Van Swaaningen's (1999) observation that the centre of criminological thinking has shifted from Europe to America since the 1940s is illustrative of this (albeit uni-directional) globalising tendency:

> Since its emergence in the second half of last century until World War II, European criminology was the major source of inspiration for Anglo-American students of crime and crime control. The Belgian Adophe Quetelet, the Italian Enrico Ferri, the Frenchman Gabriel Tarde, the Dutchman Willem Bonger: which self-respecting criminologist would not know them?… After World War II, the dominant stream of influence and inspiration turned around. From now on the wind would blow from the "new" to the "old" world. New developments on the European continent were no longer introduced in the English-speaking world. Now English succeeded French as the academic *lingua franca*, Anglo-American studies became much more widely read in Europe. Which European criminologist would currently not know Shaw and MacKay, Edwin Sutherland, Howard Becker or indeed Travis Hirschi? Many North American scholars have left their traces in continental European criminology and criminal justice policy alike. (van Swaaningen, 1999, pp. 8–9)

Although Giddens maintains that, unlike its earlier phase, today's globalisation is a two-way process, and not synonymous with Western imperialism (1994, p. 96), van Swaaningen's observation is consistent with the general perception that American criminology pays little attention to developments elsewhere, as it sees itself as the centre of globalised knowledge.[4] The global influence of John Braithwaite's work (see Cohn & Farrington, 1998, p. 167 where Braithwaite ranked as the fifth most cited scholar between 1991 and 1995 in the four international criminology journals analysed) is perhaps the exception that proves the rule.

But does the global dominance of Anglo-American criminology necessarily lead to the homogenisation of criminology and criminal justice policy? One view is that the diversity of the scientific field of criminology described earlier is sufficiently entrenched along disciplinary and theoretical lines that globalisation is likely to *reinforce* rather than threaten this diversity through facilitating the formation of virtual communities and networks (cf Elkins, 2000, p. 69). The same may not be true for criminal justice policy where the homogenising influence of globalisation seems plainly evident – from the traditional use of prisons, juvenile courts, fines, probation, parole, to the modern introduction of community service orders, situational crime prevention, community policing, private jails and restorative justice. It is obvious that global exportation of criminal justice policies has been around for a very long time (cf Nelken, 1997, p. 263), but convergence in criminal justice policies and practices is now more likely as a result of "normative convergence" and "technology transfer" flowing from increased economic and cultural interdependency between nations in the developed world:

> What the police and prisons do in Texas or Brisbane to criminals can be a matter of great concern to citizens and government in foreign nations because of high mobility. In the United States, executions in Texas of Latin-American nationals cause riots in Mexico and South America. In Australia, death sentences for drugs in Singapore or Malaysia are a cause celebre when Australian nationals are involved, and American media go into states of high arousal for month[s] when an American teen is sentenced to caning … To the extent that nations group themselves into communities of common interest and function, minimum standards of decency and fairness in policy, in justice system procedures, and in punishment are of increasing importance. (Zimring, 1999, pp. 3–4)

Examples of "normative convergence" cited by Zimring include the abolition of capital punishment and the convergence in national imprisonment rates in many developed countries, except the United States. While technological pressure is not considered to be as strong as normative pressure, Zimring predicts nevertheless that "technology transfer" is an important force behind the convergence of criminal justice policy:

> The other great force for convergence in criminal justice policy is international flow of information and rhetoric. Part of this is technological transfer as the best practices in policing and forensics get known in international circles. DNA is important in Sydney within two years of being important in Los Angeles.[5] Part of this is transmission of trends and styles. This year's fashions in criminal justice travel almost as fast as this year's skirt length does from Paris to Perth. (Zimring, 1999, p. 6)

Convergence of criminal justice policy is, of course, not always seen as a positive development. For example, the "exporting" of inappropriate criminal justice policy from powerful nations to others is a controversial area (see Chan, 1994 in relation to the privatisation of prisons in New South Wales). Nelken points also to the threat of transnational policing to democracy:

> [The fear] is that police forces are in fact using these fears about transnational crime to forge alliances which are not democratically accountable. America has long been in the lead here in exporting abroad its war against drugs and terrorism, but in Europe this is also well illustrated by the inter-state TREVI or EUROPOL policing arrangements; the European Commission itself only has observer status, the European Parliament still less say. Criminal justice is thus globalizing along with everything else (and in the same way) and efforts at transnational police action represent a real danger to democratic structures which themselves presuppose the national state. (Nelken, 1997, p. 254)

Bauman goes as far as to suggest that the escalation of punitive "law and order" policies may be a cultural consequence of globalisation:

> The complex issue of existential insecurity brought about by the process of globalization tends to be reduced to the apparently straightforward issue of "law and order". On the way, concerns with "safety", more often than not trimmed down to the single-issue worry about the safety of the body and personal possessions, are "overloaded", by being charged with anxieties generated by other, crucial dimensions of present-day existence – insecurity and uncertainty. (Bauman, 1998, p. 5)

The "condensation" of the problems of insecurity and uncertainty brought about by (economic) globalisation into anxiety about personal safety is attractive for politicians, who "can be supposed to be doing something about the first two just because being seen to be vociferous and vigorous about the third" (Bauman, 1998, p. 117). Governments are therefore reduced to the role of fighting crime to provide a "safe environment" for market forces to operate in a global economy (Bauman, 1998, p. 120).

Deterritorialisation of culture and politics

The homogenising effect of globalisation should not be exaggerated, especially in relation to cultural practices such as criminological research and criminal justice policy. People still live in physical localities and are concerned about local issues, even if they are connected to global events and actions (Tomlinson, 1999, p. 9). While politicians and policymakers regularly seek the "wisdom" of overseas experts and take advantage of "study tours" on the latest panacea in crime control, the invasion of multinational corporations has so far been restricted to security companies and management consultant firms, most likely because the criminological research market is currently too insignificant for large multinationals to bother investing their resources . What globalisation does, however, is to transform "the relationship between the *places* we inhabit and our cultural practices, experiences and identities" (Tomlinson, 1999, p. 106). In other words, the "local" is transformed as a result of the processes of globalisation, but not in the crude sense of losing its identity totally to the "global". Rather, the major cultural impact of globalisation is *deterritorialisation* – the "local" is losing its capacity to define people's "terms of existence":

> …complex connectivity weakens the ties of culture to place. This is in many ways a troubling phenomenon, involving the simultaneous penetration of local worlds by distant forces, and the dislodging of everyday meanings from their "anchors" in the local environment. (Tomlinson, 1999, p. 29)

Deterritorialisation is, however, not a universal or linear phenomenon – it can be uneven or accompanied by resistance and countervailing tendencies – nor is it necessarily alienating or destructive in its consequences (Tomlinson, 1999). Globalisation can widen people's awareness and experience, from an awareness of how global events can affect their lives to the experience of sampling other cultures through travel, food, entertainment and other consumer products. For most people, this weakening of the tie between everyday culture and location is experienced as a mixed bag "of familiarity and difference, expansion of cultural horizons and the increased perception of vulnerability, access to the 'world out there' accompanied by penetration of our own private worlds, new opportunities and new risks"(Tomlinson, 1999, p. 128). Robertson's (1995) concept of "glocalisation" helps capture the complexity of the relationship between the global and the local. Borrowing the term "glocalisation" from its business origin in micromarketing ("the tailoring and advertising of goods and services on a global or near-global basis to increasingly differentiated local and particular markets"), Robertson does not see the local and the global as oppositional: "globalization has involved the reconstruction, in a sense the production, of 'home', 'community' and 'locality'" (1995, p. 30). Globalisation, then, involves not simply the "linking of localities", but also the "invention" of locality, indeed an institutionalised global creation of locality (Featherstone & Lash, 1995, p. 4).

How does the global construct the local? In spite of the relative ease and affordability of international travel in recent times, most people experience the outside world through the media (Giddens, 1991; Tomlinson, 1999). Mediation, particularly in the form of televisual systems, has the capacity to reproduce local conditions of "intimacy" over distance and involve people "emotionally and morally with distant others, events and social-cultural contexts" (Tomlinson, 1999, p. 151). Mass-mediated "quasi-interaction" (Thompson, 1995) is, however, by its nature a limiting experience because it is essentially a one-way (monological) form of communication and hence the audience are limited in their ability to engage in the events presented. People respond to televisual communications in a variety of ways: some people are "shocked", "emotionally touched", "moved to compassion and even to action", while others turn away (Tomlinson, 1999, p. 176). In effect, people selectively relate to those experiences that matter to them in constituting their self-identity, so that, even though globalisation may have brought remote events closer to home than before, the local, direct experience still predominates (Tomlinson, 1999, pp. 177–178; Thompson, 1995). As it turns out, law and order, to rewrite Nelken's (1997, p. 251) observation about law, is "both the most local and the most universal or globalized of cultural phenomena". In fact, as Garland (1996, p. 446) suggests, "the threat of crime has become a routine part of modern consciousness, an everyday risk to be assessed and managed". The media, then, reinforce the sense of commonality of risk faced by people from different localities and pave the way for apparently successful solutions to be exported from one locality to another.

One example of the "glocalisation" of criminal justice policy relates to the so-called "New York Miracle"– "zero-tolerance" policing strategies which were claimed to have led to a dramatic decline in crime and violence in New York City. Within a short time of its "success story" being known to the world, zero-tolerance had captured the imagination of some Australian politicians who became enthusiastic supporters of such a style of policing (Dixon, 1999). On the surface this looks like a simple case of cultural exportation from America, aided by global communications technology (see, for example, Giuliani, 1997) and the ease of international travel (a number of Australian public officials including police managers have gone on "study tours" to visit New York). However, there has not been a blanket adoption of zero-tolerance policing in any Australian jurisdiction. Rather, elements of the NYPD model (Brereton, 1999; Bowling, 1999) such as Compstat (the use of crime mapping to allocate resources and monitor local police performance) and saturation policing certainly found their way into the operation and management of New South Wales Police Service (see, for example, Chan, Dixon, Maher &. Stubbs, 1998; Darcy, 1999). Globalisation may have resulted in some of the NYPD policing methods becoming disembedded from their original location and re-embedded in New South Wales. In turn, New South Wales' adoption of these strategies played a part in constituting "zero-tolerance policing" as a global trend in policing. What may have been a local policing issue now has its reference point half a world away. Supporters and critics alike can no longer debate policing strategies purely in terms of local issues, in this way the local and the global have penetrated each other. This example illustrates that to the extent that a local or national criminology or criminal justice policy orientation exists, it is increasingly defined in relation to the global.

REFLEXIVE MODERNISATION

The theory of "reflexive modernisation" was developed independently by Giddens (1990) and Beck (1992; see also Beck, Giddens & Lash, 1994). Beck (1992, p. 10) postulates that "we are witnessing not the end but the *beginning* of modernity – that is, of a modernity *beyond* its classical industrial design". He argues that classical (simple) modernisation, which involves the demystification of "privileges of rank and religious world views", is being replaced by reflexive modernisation, which is concerned with the demystification of science and technology and the "modes of existence in work, leisure, the family and sexuality" (1992, p. 10). Giddens, who also theorised a "radicalised" phase of modernity, considers the twin processes of globalisation and the "disinterring and problematizing of tradition" as having become "particularly acute in the current era" (1994, p. 57). For Giddens, reflexivity has become an integral feature of modern social life, as "social practices are constantly examined and reformed in the light of incoming information about those very practices, thus constitutively altering their character" (1990, p. 38).

The word "reflexivity" does not, however, mean the same thing to every writer. For example, Nelken has found at least five different uses of the word "reflexive" in contemporary social theory (Nelken, 1994, p. 9). Nevertheless, reflexivity is usually understood in one of two senses: "the first invites the theorist to be more *reflective* about the point and manner of his or her theorising, the other draws attention to the *recursiveness* which characterises the way contemporary systems, discourses and agents actually reproduce themselves" (Nelken, 1994, p. 9). For Beck, the concept of "reflexive modernisation" does not imply "reflection, but (first) self-confrontation" (1994, p. 5). In other words, it is not a self-conscious, intentional process, but one which "occurs undesired, unseen and compulsively", although he does not rule out reflection as a secondary process (Beck, 1994, pp. 5; 177). Beck insists that this new stage of modernisation, "in which progress can turn into self-destruction" is not related to a crisis or a revolution; rather, it "occurs surreptitiously and unplanned in the wake of normal, autonomized modernization and with an unchanged, intact political and economic order" (1994, pp. 2–3). Reflexive modernisation – the "modernization of modernization" (Beck, 1994, p. 4) – marks the transition from industrial society to risk society, in which the "threats produced so far on the path of industrial society begin to dominate" (Beck, 1994, p. 6).

How does reflexive modernisation affect the practice of criminology? It does so in three ways. First, criminology as a science is demystified or at least its status as an authoritative source of truth is undermined as a result of further scientisation. Second, users of criminological research have become "coproducers" of criminological knowledge and shoppers in the supermarket of ideas and arguments. Third, new forms of law and order politics begin to emerge which defy old political categories.

Demystification of science

Beck postulates that under reflexive modernisation, methodological scepticism – the hallmark of science – is applied to science itself, with the result that "its claims to enlightenment are demystified" (1992, p. 154). Science, which in an earlier modernity functioned as a tradition whose truth was once respected and accepted unquestioningly by non-scientists, is, under reflexive modernity, treated as contestable and open to "discursive articulation" and critique (Giddens, 1994, 1999; Lash, 1994). For Beck, this demystification of science has meant the loss of science's claim to authoritative truth (Beck, 1992, p. 166). The almost universally accepted fallibility of scientific knowledge – "scientific knowledge is always tentative and open to refutation" – has meant that the acceptability of scientific results can only be established by convention: "through a consensus of experts in the field and the fulfilment of certain methodological and professional norms" (Majone, 1989, p. 43). At the same time, the critiques of science have themselves become scientised, so that "alternative" sciences which reflect different principles or interests have begun to emerge. As Ericson and Haggerty observe, "Doubt [about science] becomes institutionalized because knowledge is always under revision in the reflexive practice of science, the reflexive use of expertise, and the reflexive monitoring of everyday life" (1997, p. 98).

It is evident that criminology, in spite of its short history of existence as a "science" (Pavarini, 1994, p. 43), has had its fair share of reflexivity, both in terms of self-confrontation and self-reflection. From the critique of administrative criminology by Taylor, Walton and Young (1973) to the left realist, feminist and postmodern critiques of recent years (see Pavlich, 1999), reflexive criminology may have come perilously close to Beck's (1994) notion of progress turning into self-destruction. Nevertheless, these exercises of self-confrontation were largely restricted to a small section of the practitioners of criminology, and amounted to little more than the usual disagreement or critique among experts.

Such disagreements are not likely to destabilise academic criminology, since critique is in fact the "motor of their enterprise" (Giddens, 1994, p. 86). A more damaging form of reflexivity involves the criminologies of policy, where the initial promise of positive criminology to individualise punishment to prevent crime gave way to the "nothing works" cynicism of the 70s, which was then replaced by the euphoria and subsequent doubts over community corrections in the 80s (Cohen, 1985), and new enthusiasm and controversy in relation to restorative justice in the 90s (Alder & Wundersitz, 1994).There is a growing concern among the public that criminology has not produced policies that control crime. At times like this, the "recourse to scientific results for the socially binding definition of truth is becoming more and more necessary, but at the same time less and less sufficient" (Beck, 1992, p. 167, italics removed). The reaction of mainstream criminology is to salvage this situation by reclaiming scientific authority through experimental research (Strang, Barnes, Braithwaite, & Sherman, 1999), meta-analyses (Sherman, Gottfredson, MacKenzie, Eck, Reuter & Bushway, 1998), and risk management strategies, while seeking "foreground" (Katz, 1988), "opportunity" (Clark, 1983), as well as background (Currie, 1988) explanations. Left realist criminology (Matthews & Young, 1992) was also born out of this desire to redefine criminology and reclaim its authority in law and order politics.

Such efforts may already be too late as the decline of expert authority has already begun. Zimring has provided a remarkable case study in relation to the passage of the "Three Strikes" legislation in California, which represented "an extreme example of populist preemption of criminal justice policy making" (1996, p. 243). The law was rushed through without consulting any criminal justice professionals or experts to assess its likely impact. Although the "Three Strikes" law may have been no more than a "one-time California fiasco", Zimring is concerned that there appears to be a decline of expert authority evident in criminal justice policy making in the United States:

> … the sheer amount of expertise available on questions of crime and punishment has expanded rapidly…. But expert influence on the process and expert involvement in the process has declined… Part of the problem is that most academic lawyers are not much interested in criminal justice policy processes. Most of the problem is that there is no demand for what experts have to offer, which is information about the implications and consequences of policy choices. (Zimring, 1996, p. 253)

This trend can also be found in Australia, a notable example being our Prime Minister's preference to consult an American FBI chief rather than listen to Australian drug research experts on ways to deal with the heroin problem (*Sydney Morning Herald* 22/2/99 "Howard's FBI war on drugs").

Non-experts as coproducers of knowledge

While the demystification of science has its positive side in terms of freeing people from the "'patronizing' cognitive dictates of the experts" (Beck, 1992, p. 168), it can be disturbing since "there are no super-experts to turn to" (Giddens, 1994, p. 87).

The authority of science is increasingly established on the basis of political compatibility, "presentation, personal persuasive power, contacts, access to the media" or other techniques for the "mobilisation of belief" (Beck, 1992, pp. 168–9). Reflexive scientisation challenges the contrast between "lay people" and "experts" (Beck, 1992, p. 154). Users of scientific results – including policymakers, the media and other non-experts – are no longer simply consumers, but "coproducers" of "valid knowledge", while the sciences are "transformed into *self-service shops* for financially well endowed customers in need of arguments" (Beck, 1992, p. 173):

> It is not uncommon for political programs to be decided in advance simply by the choice of what expert representatives are included in the circle of advisers. Not only are practitioners and politicians able to choose between expert groups, but those groups can also be *played off against each other* within and between disciplines, and in this way the autonomy of the customers is increased. (Beck, 1992, p. 173)

Consumers also learn that "unwelcome results can be blocked *professionally* (by methodological criticism, for instance)" (ibid).

This has certainly been the trend in policy-oriented research, including criminology. Social science research is rarely used to fill a "knowledge gap" and provide policymakers with authoritative data to make rational decisions (see Weiss, 1991, 1995; Chan, 1995; Brereton, 1996). At best, it percolates into people's consciousness subtly as ideas and shapes their assumptions and definitions; more often it enters into the policy arena as arguments, often supplied by interest groups or advocates of certain positions (Weiss, 1995). In general, "Political actors select their ideas and arguments from the supply that happens to be available at a given time" (Majone, 1989, p. 164). Policy issues are rarely "purely technical"– they are often "trans-scientific", that is "questions of fact that can be stated in a language of science but are, in principle or in practice, unanswerable by science" (Majone, 1989, p. 3; see also Brereton, 1996). When the issues are "trans-scientific", scientific experts are likely to be questioned by generalists in public debates. Beck even speaks of public discussion as a type of science which is "related to everyday life, drenched with experience and plays with cultural symbols", "media-dependent, manipulable, sometimes hysterical"– as distinct from "standard science" (1994, pp. 30–31). Researchers increasingly have to learn to communicate their findings to a wider audience, including through the media, in order to have impact on policy (Weiss, 1995; Haslam & Bryman, 1995; Daly, 1995).

Emergence of new politics
Reflexive modernisation also leads to a "reinvention of politics" in the sense that "The forms of political involvement, protest and retreat blur together in an ambivalence that defies the old categories of political clarity":

> … a contradictory multiple engagement arises, which mixes and combines the classical poles of politics so that … everyone thinks and acts as a right-winger and left-winger, radically and conservatively, democratically and undemocratically, ecologically and anti-ecologically, politically and unpolitically, all at the same time. Everyone is a pessimist, a passivist, an idealist and an activist in partial aspects of his or her self. That only means, however, that the current clarities of politics – right and left, conservative and socialistic, retreat and participation – are no longer correct or effective. (Beck, 1994, p. 21)

It is likely that with criminal justice issues, the emerging politics is strategic rather than programmatic. For example, Hogg and Brown's (1999) reply to their critics reflects a deliberate lack of political clarity:

> … we resist the idea that there is any useful way in which we may lay down a transformative trail or a political blueprint in relation to a future law and order strategy…The politics of effecting progressive change always involve conditions, possibilities and constraints that are unwarranted and unchosen by their protagonists. Progressive outcomes are never guaranteed; unintended consequences always threaten to thwart the best laid plans and theories. Politics is by its nature a realm of conflict, compromise and contingency… Therefore the actual direction, composition, priorities, strategies and chosen allies in movements, campaigns and projects for progressive reform are likely to vary enormously for different issues and contexts. (Hogg & Brown, 1999, pp. 331–332)

Hogg and Brown (1998) see Hirst's (1994) notion of "associative democracy" as a promising alternative. In the UK, Giddens has advocated "The Third Way", which seeks "the renewal of social democracy" (Giddens, 1998), a political path which is also increasingly being taken seriously in Australia.

REFLEXIVE GOVERNMENT

Beck's account of reflexive modernisation and risk was criticised by Dean (1999) because it rests on totalising and realist assumptions. Nevertheless, Dean suggests that, by "focusing on the concrete and empirical and analysing specific types of risk rationalities and practices", Beck's notion of reflexivity can be useful for analysing the rationality of government in advanced liberal democracies (Dean, 1999, p. 182). Thus Dean introduces the term "reflexive government" to describe the "governmentalisation of government" or the "turning of the state upon itself":

> The imperative of reflexive government is to render governmental institutions and mechanisms, including those of the social itself, efficient, accountable, transparent and democratic by the employment of technologies of performance such as the various forms of auditing and the financial instruments of accounting, by the devolution of budgets, and by the establishment of calculating individuals and calculable spaces… (Dean, 1999, p. 193)

Dean suggests that "reflexive government" is facilitated by "technologies of agency" and "technologies of performance". Technologies of agency include various forms of contracts (e.g., contracting out of public services, performance contracts, learning contracts) and techniques of empowerment, consultation and negotiation (Dean, 1999, pp. 167–8). Technologies of performance are "designed to penetrate the enclosures of expertise fostered under welfare state and to subsume the substantive domains of expertise… to new formal calculative regimes" (Dean, 1999, pp. 168–169). Examples of these are familiar: "the devolution of budgets, the setting of performance indicators, 'benchmarking', the establishment of 'quasi-markets' in expertise and service provision, the 'corporatization' and 'privatization' of formerly public services, and the contracting-out of services" (Dean, 1999, p. 169). These technologies allow for control from "above" by using performance contracts, indicators and audits; they also facilitate regulation from "below" by empowering users and consumers to contest professional practice and knowledge. As part of the neo-liberal political rationality, these technologies seek to govern by combining self-regulation with external accountability (Power, 1997; cf Chan, 1999).

These trends and technologies are evident in the field of criminology (O'Malley, 1996). The move to marketise and contract-out state functions has created a demand for criminological research through consultancy-based work. At the same time, academic criminologists are "propelled" by resource-starved universities to seek consultancies and research grants to satisfy external demands for productivity, accountability and marketability. Funding agencies in turn demand relevance, value for money and contractual accountability. The same logic of performance and contractualism has led to a new emphasis on evaluation of criminal justice programs and policies as part of the policy process (O'Malley, 1996, p. 35; see also Hogg & Brown, 1998, p. 193; Israel, 2000, pp. 10–11). The distinction between "academic" and "administrative" criminologies, once sharply demarcated, is becoming much less clear-cut (O'Malley, 1996). These new techniques of governance – marketisation, consumerism, managerialism and accountability – also raise serious questions in relation to intellectual property, political independence, and the future direction of criminological research (Israel, 2000).

CONCLUSION

The broad social and political trends discussed in this paper – globalisation, reflexive modernisation and reflexive governmentality – are, of course, deeply intertwined. For Giddens, globalisation and reflexivity are both "consequences of modernity", since modernisation involves the "separation of time and space", the "development of disembedding mechanisms" and the "reflexive appropriation of knowledge" (1990, p. 53; see also Tomlinson, 1999, Chapter 2). Though the extent to which globalisation has facilitated the ascendancy of neo-liberal rationalities of governance requires a separate investigation, it is evident that the sensibilities of "new public management" or "economic rationalism" have found their way from the US and Britain to New Zealand and Australia and taken roots. Each of these developments has had some impact on the field of criminology.

Globalisation has brought about economic and cultural interdependence and a sense of commonality of risk faced by people in different locations. It has made the distribution of access to knowledge (information capital) more equitable, and increased the capacity of researchers to communicate and form support networks (social capital), but the flow of knowledge is still predominantly uni-directional, from the centre (mainly the US and to a less extent the UK) to the periphery. Globalisation has led to significant convergences in criminal justice policy, but the globalisation of criminological knowledge is a double-edged sword: on the one hand, it may lead to the importation of inappropriate policies; on the other, it facilitates the communication of information that can be used to contest such importation. Hence the impact of globalisation on the field of criminology may in fact be to reinforce its diversity through the formation of deterritorialised networks and communities. Reflexive modernisation has led to the demystification of science. As a result, criminology has lost some of its scientific authority (symbolic capital). Users of criminological knowledge have become coproducers of knowledge, selecting ideas and arguments from the available stock, while researchers who would like their work to have impact on policy are increasingly required to repackage and communicate their knowledge to a wider audience. Reflexive governmentality, through various technologies of contract, performance management, consumer feedback and market mechanisms, is blurring the boundary between "administrative" criminology and "academic" criminology.

To what extent do these changes in the field affect the habitus of criminologists? I have suggested earlier that the current diversity of disciplinary and theoretical orientations within criminology is unlikely to be threatened by globalisation. In fact, the challenge to criminology's scientific authority in the course of reflexive modernisation is itself the *cause* of theoretical and methodological diversity. The current bias towards the generation of policy-relevant knowledge is not likely to change under reflexive governmentalisation. It remains to be seen whether the changes in funding and accountability mechanisms will affect the independence, reflexivity and intellectual direction of criminological researchers.

It should be clear from the above discussion that the influences of these larger trends are not universal or deterministic. There is much that can be done to reverse any undesirable trends. For criminology and criminal justice, the challenge is to resist the types of interdependence and homogenisation brought about by globalisation that are inappropriate or detrimental to justice (cf Smart, 1999). The debates surrounding zero-tolerance policing in New South Wales, for example, have shown that criminologists do have a role to play in educating policymakers and the general public about the dangers of mindless importation of foreign products (see Dixon, 1999; Brereton, 1999). By studying the particular and the local, criminologists are able to promote the best of the global and contest its less desirable influences. When the best already resides in the local (e.g., Australia's success in harm-reduction strategies against heroin), the challenge is not only to protect it from being invaded by inferior, foreign products, but also to ensure that it becomes globally recognised.

Reflexive modernisation may have been responsible for a decline of authority among criminological experts. The loss of a position of privilege in the politics of knowledge is frustrating but inevitable given that critique is part of the criminological enterprise. The challenge is to find innovative ways of building consensus among scientists, politicians and the general public. For example, the "round table" model (Beck, 1994, pp. 29–30) has found a successful application in the New South Wales Drug Summit which made use of novel procedures and structures to create a dialogue between experts and non-experts, while providing the space for scientific evidence, direct contact with drug users and families, debates and compromises (see NSW Drug Summit 1999 website).

The technologies of reflexive government can be oppressive for criminologists in reinforcing the "iron cage" of administrative rationality (cf Smart, 1999). They may even be detrimental to policies if they are too narrowly evaluated (O'Malley, 1996). The "new accountability" has produced some unintended consequences that are counterproductive (Power, 1997; Ericson & Haggerty, 1997; Chan 1999). The task for criminologists is to relentlessly contest inappropriate performance indicators or evaluative criteria. The proliferation of contract research and the rise of criminologists in the private sector must be subject to close scrutiny, because, more than anything else, there is a distinct danger that the acceleration of these trends will spell the end of critical – reflexive – criminology.

NOTES

1 "Official criminology" denotes the "criminological thinking" that underpins policy.
2 Several excerpts from Chan (1996) are integrated into this text without attribution to avoid the use of cumbersome and extended quotations.
3 A small illustration of this is found, quite by accident, in a second-hand copy of the English translation of Raffaele Garofalo's *Criminology* (published by Heinemann in London in 1914) I picked up in a Sydney bookshop. The book once belonged to the Queensland Parliamentary Library, whose stamp, dated 23 July 1914, was found in several pages of the book. The acquisition of this book by an Australian library within the same year of its publication in England is truly remarkable, something not always achievable even in these days of Amazon.com.
4 Cohn and Farrington (1998) show that the vast majority of "most-cited scholars" cited in the American journal Criminology are American, whereas many more "foreign" scholars appeared in the corresponding lists for the British, Canadian and Australian/ New Zealand journals studied.
5 The implication seems to be that "technology transfer" takes place from the centre (the US) to the periphery (Australia), even though DNA was developed in the UK, and Australia leads the world in some aspects in the use of police technology. I am grateful to David Dixon for this observation.

REFERENCES

Alder, C, & Wundersitz, J. (Eds.). (1994). *Family conferencing and juvenile justice. The way forward or misplaced optimism?* Canberra: Australian Institute of Criminology.

Beck, U. (1992). *Risk society: Toward a new modernity.* London: Sage.

Beck, U. (1994). The reinvention of politics: Towards a theory of reflexive modernization. In U. Beck et al. (Eds.), *Reflexive modernization: Politics, tradition and aesthetics in the modern social order* (pp. 1–55). Cambridge: Polity Press.

Beck, U., Giddens, A., & Lash, S. (1994). *Reflexive modernization: Politics, tradition and aesthetics in the modern social order.* Cambridge: Polity Press.

Bauman, Z. (1998). *Globalization: The human consequences.* Cambridge: Polity Press.

Bourdieu, P. (1975). The specificity of the scientific field and the social conditions of the progress of reason, *Social Science Information* 14(6), 19–47.

Bourdieu, P. (1988). *Homo academicus.* Cambridge: Polity Press.

Bourdieu, P., &. Wacquant, L. (1992). *An invitation to reflexive sociology.* Cambridge: Polity Press.

Bowling, B. (1999). The rise and fall of New York murder: Zero tolerance or crack's decline? *British Journal of Criminology,* 39(4), 531–554.

Braithwaite, J. (1989). The state of criminology: Theoretical decay or renaissance? *Australian and New Zealand Journal of Criminology,* 22,129–135.

Brereton, D. (1996). Does criminology matter: Crime, politics and the policy process [Special issue], *Current Issues in Criminal Justice,* 8(1), 82–87.

Brereton, D. (1999, March). Zero tolerance and the NYPD: Has it worked there and will it work here? Paper to the Australian Institute of Criminology Conference Mapping the Boundaries of Australia's Criminal Justice System, Canberra.

Brubaker, R. (1993). Social theory as habitus. In C. Calhoun, E. LiPuma, &. M. Postone, (Eds.), *Bourdieu: Critical Perspectives.* Cambridge: Polity Press.

Chan, J. (1994). The privatisation of punishment: A review of the key issues. In P. Moyle (Ed.), *Privatisation of prisons and police in Australia and New Zealand.* Sydney: Pluto Press.

Chan, J. (1995). Systematically distorted communication? Criminological knowledge, media representation and public policy [Special supplementary issue], *Australian and New Zealand Journal of Criminology,* 1995, 23–30.

Chan, J. (1996). The future of criminology: An introduction [Special issue], *Current Issues in Criminal Justice,* 8(1), 7–13.

Chan, J., Dixon, D., Maher, L., & Stubbs, J. (1998). *Policing in Cabramatta.* Final report to the New South Wales Police Service. Chan, J. (1999). Governing police practice: Limits of the new accountability, *British Journal of Sociology,* 50(2), 251–70.

Clark, R.V. (1983). Situational crime prevention: Its theoretical basis and practical scope. In M. Tonry & N. Morris (Eds.), *Crime and justice: An annual review of research* (pp. 225–256). Chicago: University of Chicago. Press.

Cohen, S. (1981). Footprints on the sand: A further report on criminology and the sociology of deviance in Britain. In M. Fitzgerald, G. McLennan, & J. Pawson (Eds.), *Crime and society: Readings in history and theory.* London: Routledge.

Cohen, S. (1985). *Visions of social control.* Cambridge: Polity Press.

Cohen, S. (1988). *Against criminology,* New Brunswick: Transaction Books.

Cohn, E.G., & Farrington, D.P (1998). Changes in the most-cited scholars in major international journals between 1986–90 and 1991–95, *British Journal of Criminology,* 38(1), 156–170.

Currie, E. (1988). Two visions of community crime prevention. In Hope, T. & Shaw, M. (Eds.), *Communities and crime reduction* (pp. 280–285.). London: Home Office Research and Planning Unit.

Darcy, D. (1999). Zero tolerance – Not quite the influence on NSW policing some would have you believe, *Current Issues in Criminal Justice*, 10(3), 290.

Daly, K. (1995). Celebrated crime cases and the public's imagination: From bad press to bad policy? [Special supplementary issue], *Australian and New Zealand Journal of Criminology*, 1995, 6–22.

Dean, M. (1999). *Governmentality: Power and rule in modern society*. London: Sage.

Dixon, D. (1999, March). Beyond zero-tolerance. Paper to the Australian Institute of Criminology Conference Mapping the Boundaries of Australia's Criminal Justice System, Canberra.

Elkins, D. (2000). Thinking global governance and enacting local cultures. In R. Ericson, & N. Stehr, (Eds.), *Governing modern societies* (pp. 60–79). Toronto: University of Toronto Press.

Ericson, R. (1996). Making criminology [Special issue], *Current Issues in Criminal Justice*, 8(1), 14–25.

Ericson, R., & Carriere, K. (1994). The fragmentation of criminology. In D. Nelken (Ed.), *The futures of criminology* (pp. 89–109), London: Sage.

Ericson, R., & Haggerty, K. (1997). *Policing the risk society*. Toronto: University of Toronto Press.

Featherstone, M., Lash, S., & Robertson, R. (Eds.). (1995). *Global modernities*. London: Sage.

Garland, D. (1996). The limits of the sovereign state: Strategies of crime control in contemporary society, *British Journal of Criminology*, 36, 445–471.

Garland, D. (1997). "Governmentality" and the problem of crime: Foucault, criminology and sociology, *Theoretical Criminology*, 1(2), 173–214.

Giddens, A. (1990). *The consequences of modernity*. Cambridge: Polity Press.

Giddens, A. (1991). *Modernity and self-identity: Self and society in the late modern age.* Cambridge: Polity Press.

Giddens, A. (1994). Living in a post-traditional society. In U. Beck et al. (Eds.), *Reflexive modernization: Politics, tradition and aesthetics in the modern social order* (pp. 56–109). Cambridge: Polity Press.

Giddens, A. (1998). *The third way: The renewal of social democracy*. Cambridge: Polity Press.

Giuliani, R. (1997). Mayor Rudolph W. Giuliani's testimony before the House Committee on Government Reform, March 13, 1997. [URL: http://www.ci.nyc.ny.us/htm]

Haslam, C. & Bryman, A. (Eds.). (1994). *Social scientists meet the media*. London and New York: Routledge.

Held, D. (2000). The changing contours of political community: Rethinking democracy in the context of globalization. In R. Ericson, & N. Stehr, (Eds.), *Governing modern societies* (pp 42–59). Toronto: University of Toronto Press.

Hirst, P. (1994). *Associative democracy – New forms of economic and social governance.* Cambridge: Polity Press.

Hirst, P. & Thompson, G. (1996). *Globalization in question: The international economy and the possibilities of governance.* Cambridge: Polity Press.

Hogg, R. (1996). Criminological failure and governmental effect [Special issue], *Current issues in Criminal Justice*, 8(1), 43–59.

Hogg, R., & Brown, D. (1998). *Rethinking law and order.* Sydney: Pluto Press.

Hogg, R., & Brown, D. (1999). Rethinking law and order: A rejoinder, *Australian and New Zealand Journal of Criminology*, 32(3), 331–3.

Israel, M. (2000). The commercialisation of university-based criminological research in Australia, *Australian and New Zealand Journal of Criminology,* 33(1), 1–20.

Katz, J. (1998). *Seductions of crime.* New York: Basic Books.

Lash, S. (1994). Reflexivity and its doubles: Structure, aesthetics, community. In U. Beck et al. (Eds.), *Reflexive modernization: Politics, tradition and aesthetics in the modern social order* (pp. 110–73). Cambridge: Polity Press.

Majone, G. (1989). *Evidence, argument, and persuasion in the policy process.* New Haven and London: Yale University Press.

Matthews, R., &. Young, J. (1992). *Issues in realist criminology.* London: Sage.

Nelken, D. (1994). Reflexive criminology? In D. Nelken (Ed.), *The futures of criminology* (pp. 7–42). London: Sage.

Nelken, D. (1997). The globalization of crime and criminal justice: Prospects and problems, *Current Legal Problems,* 50, 251–277.

New South Wales Drug Summit website [http://www.nsw.gov.au/drugsummitl999]

O'Malley, P. (1996). Post-social criminologies: Some implications for current political trends for criminological theory and practice, *Current Issues in Criminal Justice* [Special Issue], "The Future of Criminology", 8(1), 26–38.

Pavarini, M. (1994). Is criminology worth saving? In D. Nelken (Ed.), *The futures of criminology,* (pp. 43–62). London: Sage.

Pavlich, G. (1999). Criticism and criminology: In search of legitimacy, *Theoretical Criminology* 3(1), 29–51.

Power, M. (1997). *The audit society.* Oxford: Oxford University Press.

Robertson, R. (1995). Globalization: Time – space and homogeneity – heterogeneity. In M. Featherstone, S. Lash, &. R. Robertson (Eds.). *Global modernities.* London: Sage.

Sheptycki, J.W.E. (1998). Policing, postmodernism and transnationalization, *British Journal of Criminology,* 38(3), 485–503.

Sherman, L., Gottfredson, D.C., MacKenzie, D.L., Eck, J., Reuter, P., & Bushway, S.D. (1998). *Preventing Crime: What works, What doesn't, What's promising.* Washington DC: US Department of Justice, National Institute of Justice.

Smart, B. (Ed.). (1999). *Resisting McDonaldization.* London: Sage.

Strang, H., Barnes, G.C., Braithwaite, J., & Sherman, L.W. (1999). *Experiments in restorative policing. A* progress report on the Canberra reintegrative shaming experiments (RISE). [http:www.aic.gov.au/rustice/rise/progress/1999.html]

Taylor, I., Walton, P., & Young, J. (1973). *The new criminology.* London: Routledge.

Thompson, J.B. (1995). *The media and modernity.* Cambridge: Polity Press.

Tomlinson, J. (1999). *Globalization and culture.* Cambridge: Polity Press.

Van Swaaningen, R. (1999). Reclaiming critical criminology: Social justice and the European tradition, *Theoretical Criminology,* 3(1), 5–28.

Weiss, C. (1991). Policy research as advocacy: Pro and con, *Knowledge and Policy,* 4(1&2), 37–55.

Weiss, C. (1995). The haphazard connection: Social science and public policy, *International Journal of Educational Research,* 23(2), 137–150.

Zimring, F. (1996). Populism, democratic government, and the decline of expert authority: Some reflections on "Three Strikes" in California, *Pacific Law Journal,* 28(1), 243–256.

Zimring, F. (1999, September). Crime, criminal justice, and criminology for a smaller planet: Some notes on the 21st Century, plenary paper to the ANZ Society of Criminology Annual Conference, Perth.

50

Poverty goes global

Neil Middleton

Poverty is the worst and most widespread of all human rights abuses. The main offenders are the world's trading and financial institutions in pursuit of more and faster returns on capital.

An estimated 1.6 billion people live on incomes at, or below, the level of what the World Bank calls 'absolute poverty' and the number is rising. 'Life expectancy', 'maternal mortality', 'infant mortality' and 'malnutrition', somehow sanitise the reality that women, children and men are dying in huge numbers from being too poor. According to UNICEF's 1998 The State of the Worlds Children, even in years without notable droughts or famines, 12 million children under five die in families in the developing world too poor to afford basic sanitation, adequate diets and minimal health care. Like their elders, they generally die of the preventable diseases of poverty rather than of absolute inanition. This is a litany of woes so often repeated that we no longer hear it.

And almost without exception, poor people are getting poorer. One example, Mexico, will serve for many. The decade 1984–94 was one in which the 'benefits' of the North American Free Trade Association (NAFTA) were supposedly accruing to Mexico. To no-one's surprise, it was its wealthiest 10 per cent whose incomes increased by 20.8 per cent. Everyone else followed a lengthy trend in losing both relatively and absolutely, but the poorest 10 per cent were hit hardest with an absolute income loss of 23.2 per cent.

From *Index on Censorship*, 1998, 27(3): 133–8.

For a variety of reasons, income poverty is only one guide to deprivation. In its 1997 report, the UNDP (United Nations Development Programme) attempts the creation of a Human Poverty Index based on three main criteria: longevity, literacy and 'a decent standard of living'. The first criterion uses a life expectancy of 40 years as an indicator, the third is based on access to clean water, sanitation and health services and on the number of malnourished children. It lists 78 developing countries for which 'adequate data' are available. Of these, 47 have at least a quarter of their populations living in absolute poverty; in eight of them the proportion is half or more. Over 25 per cent of them will die before they reach 40 years of age; 30 per cent of them have no access to safe water or health services; 49 per cent are illiterate; 38 per cent of their children will die before they are five years old; almost 85 million people have been killed or affected by disasters; 6.6 million are refugees; and further untold numbers are displaced.

Enormous numbers of people do not have adequate diets, and malnutrition in its many forms, commonly associated in the public mind with disasters or famines is chronic. Those suffering from it are acutely vulnerable to disease and commonly without even the simplest health care. Many children who do not actually die as a consequence are exposed to numerous other subsequent hazards.

This sketchy and obviously selective recitation of figures is necessary because most of us rarely encounter the physical reality of extreme poverty nor do we easily grasp its scale. Even more important, we tend to give little more than a passing thought to its causes. Susan George has written extensively and impressively about the issue of Third World debt and even the World Bank acknowledges that there is an overall net return of financial resources from the poorest countries to the richest. Despite endless promises, little has been done by the world's banking system to resolve the issue; even when proposals for debt cancellation are advanced their prosecution is at best dilatory and, of course, they are modest – they rarely, if ever amount to more than small percentages of the total. Most important, debt cancellation seems never to be considered in regional, but only in national terms – banks, including the multilaterals, deal piecemeal. As George points out, it is easier to keep individual states in thrall, and it makes the bribery of ruling elites simpler. George also comments that debt cancellation, by itself, may do little to assist the poor, serving only to line, yet further, the pockets of corrupt rulers. Nonetheless, one of the most obvious consequences of the incubus of overwhelming external debt is economic stasis in the countries afflicted by it. Severely indebted countries are compelled, if they want their debts rescheduled or to borrow further, to open their markets to cheap imports, particularly food, from the industrialised world, thus drastically undermining indigenous production and further impoverishing their own workers.

When, a decade or so ago, 'globalisation' was widely discussed, it was equally widely misunderstood; commentators referred to the frightening ability of trans-national corporations (TNCs) to move themselves and their production to wherever it suited them. In practice, TNCs usually stay in their countries, or regions, of origin – the overwhelming majority of them are to be found in the US, Europe and Japan. Production, on the other hand, moved, and still does, in pursuit of low wages and minimal environmental regulation. Notorious examples are to be found in the exploitation of impoverished Mexicans in US *maquiladora* industries, further encouraged by NAFTA; but this process is not new, Marx, for instance, refers to an early version of it in the first volume of *Capital.*

Globalisation consists of two principal elements: the elimination of protectionism of all kinds and the reduction of regulations governing the movement of investment capital. Barriers to 'free' trade were progressively to be dismantled, direct subsidies to production were to be stopped and everyone was thus to trade on supposedly equal terms. All national borders were to be as porous as possible in order to facilitate trade. There was much nauseating rhetoric from supporters of the Bretton Woods triplets (the World bank, the International Monetary Fund and the World Trade Organisation) about the creation of 'level playing fields' which completely ignored, among many other things, the advantages of scale enjoyed by TNCs and the hidden infrastructural subsidies given to producers in the industrialised world. The OECD estimates that every farmer in the USA is indirectly subsidised to the tune of US$29,000, thus creating a 'playing field' in which few, if any, farmers in the Third World are able to compete. The World Trade Organisation (WTO) is an organisation for dumpers with ludicrously minimal safeguards for vulnerable economies.

The second element in globalisation, the reduction of governmental interference in foreign investment, is being negotiated in great secrecy by the industrialised countries within the OECD in the form of an agreement called the Multilateral Agreement on Investment (MAI) that will reduce to almost nothing the power of national governments to regulate investment in the public interest. Oxfam ascribes the origin of this agreement to pressure from business, the EC, the USA and other industrialised nations. Since it will render illegal any national agreements designed to protect workers, the environment or other essential interests which TNCs define as obstacles to investment, it is a devastatingly undemocratic proposal for everyone, but here we are concerned with its effect on the acutely poor. The MAI will achieve for investment capital what the WTO's porous borders achieved for trade. If the MAI becomes, as the OECD expects, the model for a worldwide agreement administered by the Bretton Woods triplets, then it will be illegal for any country to erect protective barriers, including worker and environmental protection, against foreign predatory investment in its resources.

Globalisation is the macro-economic condition within which poverty flourishes. Uncritical worship of free markets – 'free', of course, only to those rich enough to benefit from them – the relentless demand for modernisation in production, the facilitation of the power of TNCs which already control 70 per cent of the world's trade, all conspire to render the poor yet more powerless.

Examples are legion and we need only consider one, the destruction of nomadic pastoralism throughout the Greater Horn of Africa. The final collapse of the Somalian state followed an extensive and bloody campaign by its military ruler, Siad Barre, which, among other things, had the sequestration of productive farmland as its object. Sedentary farmers, holding land by ancient customary laws, and nomadic pastoralists, with whom they had coexisted relatively peacefully, were driven from their land and ranges to make way for plantations controlled by Barre's satraps. These plantations were devoted to the production of crops designed for the international food commodity trade, were environmentally destructive of extremely fragile ecosystems and were financed by international capital. Farmers and pastoralists became refugees and died in appalling numbers in the disaster of 1991–3. That disaster continues, like so many other chronic disasters, and is related to others in the Greater Horn.

In Kenya, President Daniel arap Moi's continued assault on the Kikuyu, together with his less well-known attacks on the vast numbers of refugees along the Somali border, includes similar objectives. The process, aptly described by the campaigning researchers of African Rights as 'land-looting' (they coined the term for Somalia), is part of an overall attempt to incorporate Kenyan agriculture into the world market. Since Kenya, unlike Somalia, still has a government of sorts, it is backed heavily in this programme by the IMF. Similar ambitions drive the racialist government of Sudan in its genocidal wars against the Nubans and the South.

In each of these cases, and in so many more about the world, international 'humanitarian' aid can be relied upon to provide temporary welfare states for the dispossessed for as long as the particular 'emergency' remains in the industrialised world's public consciousness. Indigenous venal governments are often partly responsible for the plight of many of their people, but even relatively honest and progressive governments in the developing world are caught in the toils of the international free market and the global reach of its financial and trading institutions. We must recognise the extent to which globalisation is creating a new geography of poverty. The world's most fundamental abuse of human rights is perpetrated not so much by despotic states, even though they play a part, but by the world's trading and financial institutions. Even Shell's involvement in the exploitation of the Ogoni pales beside the universal and deadly abandonment of the world's poor by all such institutions in their preposterous pursuit of faster and faster returns on capital.

51

The drug trade: the politicization of criminals and the criminalization of politicians

Moisés Naím

INTRODUCTION: MORE THAN DRUGS

Hashim Thaci is the head of a mafia-like Albanian group responsible for smuggling weapons, drugs and human organs through Eastern Europe. He also happens to be the prime minister of Kosovo.[1]

In November 2008 William Klein, then the economic counselor at the U.S. embassy in Kiev, informed Washington that Dmitry Firtash, one of Ukraine's wealthiest oligarchs, was taking over one of the country's largest banks. In his cable, the U.S. diplomat described Firtash's extensive associations with top politicians and government officials. And with Seymon Moglievich, the leader of a well-known Russian criminal organization.[2]

Through another cable obtained by WikiLeaks we learn that Nicaragua's president, Daniel Ortega, funded his electoral campaign with money from international drug traffickers and through suitcases full of cash sent by Venezuela's president Hugo Chavez.[3]

President Chavez is known for the use of his unlimited access to his nation's oil money to support his allies in other countries. In one well documented 2007 incident, a suitcase with US$ 800,000 in cash was accidentally discovered by customs agents in Buenos Aires in a private plane arriving from Caracas with officials close to Argentina's President Nestor Kirchner and Chavez. The cash was either destined to fund the electoral campaign of the president's wife, Cristina Kirchner; a kickback on its way to the pockets of its corrupt beneficiary or a combination of both.[4] According to the testimony in a trial held in the United

Working Paper, Prepared for the First Meeting of the Global Commission on Drug Policies, Geneva, 24–25 January 2011.

States involving some of the participants in this event, one of the key players in the attempt to cover it up was Henry Rangel Silva, a Venezuelan General.[5] In November 2010, President Chavez appointed General Rangel Silva as the top commander of the Venezuelan armed forces.

Two years before, the US Treasury Department had officially designated General Rangel as a 'drug kingpin', accusing him of 'materially assisting narcotic trafficking activities'.[6] According to the United Nations Office on Drugs and Crime, Venezuela now accounts for more than half of all the cocaine shipments to Europe – often via Africa.[7] African countries have become important trans-shipment points for drugs coming from the Andes and parts of Asia on their way to rich and drug-hungry European markets. Inevitably, several African rulers and their families as well as military officers, politicians and members of the judiciary entered the narcotics trafficking business. In Guinea, for example, the country's biggest narcotics kingpin turned out to be the president's son.[8] In South Africa, Jackie Selebi, the former National Police Commissioner, was sentenced in 2010 to 15 years in prison after it was discovered that he was a leader of one of the country' s main criminal syndicates.[9]

Police departments, the military, the courts and the media are increasingly the takeover targets of criminal organizations.

The Venezuelan military, for example, is far from unique in having some of its commanders colluding with drug traffickers. According to secret cables released by WikiLeaks, members of Burma's military junta enrich themselves with drug money.[10] In December 2010, the InterPress Service reported that 'As military-ruled Burma prepares to unveil its new political cast, an enduring link between the junta and the country's notorious drug lords is poised to come under the spotlight. Among the candidates who won in the South-east Asian nation's first election in 20 years on November 7th, six are well known drug barons'.[11]

The intertwining of the state and criminal organizations is also evident in Afghanistan, where top government officials and provincial governors – including President Karzai's own brother – are routinely accused not just of colluding with drug traffickers but of actually leading these organizations.[12] In Bulgaria, Atanas Atanasov, a member of parliament and ex-chief of counterintelligence, observed that 'Other countries have the mafia, in Bulgaria the mafia has the country'.[13]

These are not isolated examples. The point of all these vignettes is to illustrate that they are part of a broader trend whose manifestations are visible from Asia to Africa and from Eurasia to Europe or Latin America. Criminals are in power.

A lucid summary of this global trend was provided by Spain's special prosecutor for corruption and organized crime, Jose Grinda, while presenting a paper about the Spanish case to a meeting of experts convened in Madrid in 2010.[14] Grinda outlined the multifaceted ways in which the Russian Mafia operated in Spain and how, during the decade in which he investigated organized crime in his country, he came to realize that it was often impossible to tell apart the criminal organizations from the governments of the countries in which they were based. According to Grinda, Spain is constantly and severely challenged by criminal networks that often are mere appendices of the governments of Russia, Belarus, Chechnya and Ukraine, nations that he labeled 'virtual mafia states'. Moreover, in these countries the government and the criminal organizations often worked together through 'legal' business conglomerates with close ties to political leaders and top government officials and their families and friends.

After the meeting, the then U.S. Ambassador to Spain sent a secret cable to Washington (now publicly available through WikiLeaks) with the prosecutor's analysis, noting that 'Grinda's main gripe is that the Russian state appears to be protecting or using certain high-level criminals … and that what he has read from 10–12 years' worth of investigations on OC (organized crime) has led him to believe that *whereas terrorists aim to substitute the essence of the state itself, OC seeks to be a complement to state structures* (emphasis added). He summarized his views by asserting that the GOR's [Government of Russia] strategy is to use OC groups to do whatever the GOR cannot acceptably do as a government'.

Two examples (among many offered by Grinda) of the use by the Russian government of criminal syndicates were a gun running operation to the Kurds using a mafia operative controlled by the Russian military intelligence which was aimed at destabilizing Turkey and the mysterious case of a ship [the *Arctic Sea*] believed to have been loaded with a cargo of sophisticated weapons that was 'hijacked' in the high seas and disappeared for several days. Grinda asserts that this was part of a joint operation by Eurasian security services and organized criminal groups.[15]

But the central message of Grinda's analysis is that in the nations that he calls 'mafia states' the interlock of criminals and political leaders is vast, deep and permanent. According to Grinda, 'one cannot differentiate between the activities of the government and OC [organized crime] groups'.[16]

His conclusion is uncannily similar to a report of the Council of Europe: 'The signs of collusion between the criminal class and the highest political and institutional office holders are too numerous and too serious to be ignored'.[17] This report was about Kosovo. Grinda was discussing his experience in Spain. Yet, both conclusions are perfectly – and disturbingly applicable to too many other countries in the five continents.

From this last observation flows a sobering and important corollary: Fighting drug trafficking is no longer about drugs. It is about government. The main focus of the fight should not be about stopping addicts from using drugs. It should be about stopping criminals from taking over governments around the world. Yes, drug use is a problem. But one that pales in comparison to the threat posed by the proliferation of mafia states.

ILLUSION AND REALITY IN GLOBAL CRIME

In my book *Illicit*[18] I alerted the reader to three assumptions that are as common as they are wrong. The first is that with respect to international crime there is nothing new. The assumption is that illicit trades, smuggling, black markets and crime are part of the human experience and, therefore, 'there is nothing new under the sun'. The second mistaken assumption is that smuggling – of drugs, weapons, people, human organs, dirty money or any other contraband – across national borders is a criminal activity that should therefore be conceptualized as such and fought with the usual crime-fighting tools: law enforcement, the courts and punishment through fines or incarceration. The third wrong assumption is that, like crime in general, illicit trade is an 'underground' phenomenon that only involves a small community of deviants that operates at the margins of society.[19]

The reality is very different. There is plenty that is new about crime – not least its ability to seize the opportunities spawned by the technological, economic and political revolutions that exploded in the 1990s and continue today. Criminal networks – especially those which already operated in multiple countries – were 'early adopters' of the innovations in communication and transportation of the 1990s. And they also were the 'first movers' into the new markets opened by the economic and political reforms that many countries implemented after the fall of the Berlin Wall. Criminal networks were – and continue to be – at the forefront of globalization, of technology and politics.

It is, of course, true that criminals, smugglers and black markets have always existed. But never before have criminal organizations had the ability to operate at a global level with such ease and therefore reach a scale and scope in their activities that easily match those of the world's largest multinational corporations. And, if large multinational corporations are politically powerful, why assume that large international criminal organizations will not invest sizable parts of their immense revenues to gain political power? They will – and they do. Yes, crime and politics often go together. But now these associations have an immense capacity to impact business, society, geopolitics, international security and national politics. In the 20th Century the Italian mafia was large and powerful and it then expanded its operations to the United States. But it never acquired the global reach or the political influence, economic might or international diversification now common among some of the largest transnational criminal organizations based in Russia, China, Eastern Europe or Latin America.[20]

One consequence of the criminal organizations' newly acquired potency is that the traditional tools to fight them are no longer adequate. As the opening vignettes to this text make abundantly clear, the leaders of these criminal cartels are not just mere criminals; they are also heads of state, top military officers, politicians, spy chiefs or the owners of some of the world's largest and best endowed business conglomerates. As Grinda, the Spanish prosecutor, explained, he often found himself not just fighting mafias but rather mafia states. And, as he also aptly noted, while terrorists aim to destroy the state, criminal organizations seek to take it over and use its resources and institutions to consolidate their power and expand their activities at home and abroad. The asymmetry of a lone national prosecutor fighting a criminal organization which is not only transnational, wealthy, violent and ruthless, but that can also command the full support of a national government and its diplomats, judges, spies, generals, cabinet ministers and chiefs of police is jarring. Protecting society are overworked courts which have to rely on old legislation, unwieldy international treaties and the usual limitations of slow moving and resource constrained government bureaucracies. Confronting them are fast moving, highly motivated organizations with the money to hire the best legal and financial talent, acquire the most advanced technology and recruit the most powerful allies inside and outside government.

Another asymmetry stems from the fact that law enforcement agencies are inherently national, while the large and most dangerous criminal organizations tend to operate in multiple national jurisdictions. Governments are designed to function inside national borders, whereas smuggling organizations are designed to operate across them. For government agencies, national borders are straightjackets, while for smugglers borders are what allow them to exist, grow and prosper. Without national borders different prices for the same good or service (cocaine or a worker's salary, for example) would not exist. These price differentials are what in turn create the huge profit opportunities seized by the smugglers. In addition, borders also serve to shield criminals from another country's law enforcement agencies.

These asymmetries are very problematic and the tools we have to counter their effects (treaties, multilateral organizations, intergovernmental bodies, law enforcement cooperation, etc) are slow and unwieldy. The idea that progress in the fight against international criminal cartels requires an internationally coordinated response is now widely accepted. But how does a government coordinate its anti-crime efforts with another nation whose government leaders are also the leaders of a state-sponsored mafia? How do you collaborate with another nation's police department when it is headed by a kingpin?

In 2006, the heads of police of 152 nations met in Brazil for the 75th General Assembly of INTERPOL, the multilateral organization whose mission is 'To ensure and promote the widest possible mutual assistance between all criminal police authorities … '. In its opening speech INTERPOL's president exhorted his colleagues 'to find systems to make sure that our borders and border control are on a firm footing … '.[21] A noble cause – except that on that occasion it was being championed by a crime lord. The speaker was Jackie Selebi, then South Africa's Chief of Police, and who, as already noted above, is now in jail serving a 15 years sentence for his role in leading one of his country's criminal organizations.

This complexity is compounded by the reality that, in contrast to another common assumption, in many countries criminals are no longer 'underground', they are not marginal members of society and most are not particularly deviant. In fact, the contrary is all too often the case. The leaders of criminal organizations are frequently well-known to the public and instead of living in hiding or 'underground', they are regularly featured in the newspapers' society pages or in the sports events of the popular teams they own. They are some of their nation's largest philanthropists who also control TV and radio stations as well as influential newspapers. They are members of their nation's political, military, business, cultural and media elites. And the 'foot soldiers', who are not the members of the elite, are average members of society and not necessarily criminal deviants. The millions that are actively involved in China's counterfeit industry, in Afghanistan's drug trade, that smoke marihuana regularly or the hundreds of thousands that every year hire criminals to smuggle them to Europe or the United States or the professional couple in Manhattan or Milan that employs an 'illegal' worker knowingly breaking the law don't fit any of the standard definitions of deviancy found in criminology texts. They are not deviants, but average members of a vast social group.

In the first section, I concluded that the main threat to society stemming from the global narcotics trade is not the health of drug users or the consequences of their individual behavior on others, but the more ominous consequences that result from the widespread capture of governments by criminal organizations. Therefore a main goal of any initiative aimed at curbing the drug trade should not be reduced to containing the production and consumption of narcotics. It should aim at containing the proliferation of mafia states and neutralize those that already exist. What this section highlights is that these criminal organizations have acquired unprecedented power, that they are deeply embedded in their societies and that those who fight them do so with enormous disadvantages. This is an asymmetric war in which honest governments are on the weaker side of the battle.

WHAT TO DO?

The list of policy prescriptions related to the fight against drugs is as well known as it has been hard to transform into an effective global action plan that yields lasting results. The usual recommendations include all or some of the following:

- Approach drug use as a public health issue and not as a 'war' on drug consumers.

- Spend more on prevention and less on interdiction and incarceration. Shift public funds from policing, courts and prisons to clinics, hospitals and education. Make 'harm reduction' the priority.

- Selectively deregulate and decriminalize individual use while attacking the networks that transport and distribute large volumes and the harder drugs.

- Go after the funding and disrupt the finances, logistics and infrastructure of the criminal networks.

- Target the leaders and kingpins as well as the 'facilitators' (lawyers, accountants, and experts in finance, logistics, trade and information technology)

- Unify what continue to be highly fragmented and poorly coordinated national and international anti-drug trafficking efforts.

- Develop more effective multi-country initiatives and invest in multilateral approaches that aim to match the networks' international mobility and scope of operations. Create 'global networks' of anti drug experts, magistrates, law enforcement agencies and policy leaders.

Different countries have adopted these measures with varying degrees of intensity, effectiveness and success. But despite the widely accepted rhetoric that recognizes that a global problem cannot be fought with purely national solutions, the bulk of the efforts continues to have a substantially national orientation. Also, while there is increasing recognition that the global criminal networks now pose threats to the functioning of democracy, to the financial sector, to the survival of entire industries, to citizen safety, human rights or that they can even become dangerous sources of geopolitical instability, the work of police departments and other law enforcement agencies continues to be divorced from the activities of the agencies in charge of national security. Needless to say, in many countries some of the standard prescriptions listed above – especially those in favor of abolishing prohibition – are politically untouchable even by leaders that in private are ready to accept that the current approach is not working and is even harmful to their society.

> But the most dangerous lag in our collective understanding is that criminal enterprises have now become governments and that some governments have taken over criminal organizations not to dismantle them but to use them for their financial, political and military advantage.
>
> Criminals are becoming politicians and government officials. And top government officials and political leaders are doubling as the heads of vast – and often international – criminal enterprises.

This 'inconvenient truth' may lie at the heart of the slow progress and frequent failures that characterize the efforts to contain the growth of international criminal organizations in general and drug trafficking in particular. Progress will require that publics everywhere become more aware of the immense threat posed by the criminalization of governments. But such an awareness will be hard to generate while so many aspects of the approach to curb drug use remain as controversial as they are today. In many countries the mere suggestion of abolishing prohibition in order to reduce incentives, and allow governments to concentrate their limited resources on battling the most harmful aspects of the drug trade elicits accusations of being soft on crime or worse.

Perhaps the way in which the once controversial 'inconvenient truth' regarding global warming became more accepted and eventually found its way into serious debates, public policies and even global treaties may show a possible trajectory that the inconvenient truth regarding the growing criminalization of governments may also follow.[22]

Al Gore's movie and book, his two Oscars and the Nobel Peace prize alone would have not created the groundswell of political support that led governments everywhere – but especially in the United States – to initiate actions to respond to what had been long seen as a highly speculative, ideologically driven and scientifically controversial possibility. New data and better science about global warming and its climatic consequences were the indispensable complements that led to Al Gore's spectacular success at energizing a hitherto lethargic and largely indifferent public. On the other hand, science alone or the consensus among specialists might have also been insufficient to motivate the public to pay attention and governments to act. It was the combination of better data, more science and an effective public campaign that led to shifts in public opinion and eventually – and slowly – to policy changes. These same ingredients are needed to spark the reactions that will lead to more effective initiatives against the threats posed by the criminalization of governments. Stopping the proliferation of criminal governments and not drug consumption per se should be the priority of our efforts.

NOTES

1   This grave accusation is not the gossipy, unfounded assertion of a rogue journalist. It is one of the findings of a December 2010 report of the Council of Europe. *The Guardian*, 'Kosovo PM is head of a human organ and arms ring, Council of Europe reports', December 14, 2010

2   *The Guardian*, 'US embassy cables: Ukranian gas billionaire has close ties to Russian crime boss', December 1, 2010

3   *El Pais*, 'EEUU:Chavez y el Narcotrafico financian la Nicaragua de Ortega', December 6, 2010

4   Hugo Alconada 'Los Secretos de la Valija' Buenos Aires, Editorial Planeta, 2009

5   Ibid.

6   *El Universal* (Venezuela), 'Brand-new General-in-Chief has been accused of drug trafficking', November 15, 2010

7   UNODC 'World Drug Report 2010: drug use is shifting towards new drugs and new markets', June 23, 2010. Also *USA Today*, 'Venezuela drug trade booms', July 21, 2010

8   *The New York Times*, 'Cables Portray Expanded Reach of Drug Agency' by Ginger Thompson and Scott Shane, December 25, 2010

9   BBC, 'South Africa ex-police chief Selebi jailed for 15 years', August 3, 2010

10 *The New York Times*, 'Cables Portray Expanded Reach of Drug Agency' by Ginger Thompson and Scott Shane, December 25, 2010

11 IPS 'Junta's Drug Exports to China test Economic Ties' by Marwaan Macan-Markar, December 31, 2010

12 *The New York Times*, 'Inside Corrupt-istan, a Loss of Faith in Leaders' by Dexter Filkins, September 4, 2010

13 *The New York Times*, 'Mob Muscles its Way into Politics in Bulgaria' by Doreen Carvajal and Stephen Castle, October 16, 2008

14 Jose Grinda Gonzalez, 'The Organized Crime and the Russian Mafia' paper presented at the the US-Spain Counter-Terrorism and Organized Crime Experts Working Group, Madrid, January 13, 2010

15 Ibid. For an interesting analysis of the role of organized crime in Russia and its neighboring countries see also Thomas de Waal: 'Mafiosi in the Caucasus' in *The National Interest* Online, December 22, 2010

16 *The Guardian*, 'WikiLeaks cables: Russian government using mafia for its dirty work', December 1, 2010.

17 *The Guardian*, 'Kosovo PM is head of a human organ and arms ring, Council of Europe reports', December 14, 2010.

18 Moisés Naím, *Illicit: How Smugglers, Traffickers and Copycats are Hijacking the Global Economy*, Doubleday 2005

19 Ibid. Pages 3 to 7

20 See *Illicit* chapters 11 and 13 and Misha Glenny *McMafia: A Journey Through the Global Criminal Underworld*, Vintage 2009

21 INTERPOL: 75th General Assembly, Speech by INTERPOL President Jackie Selebi, Rio de Janeiro, 19 September 2006 http://www.interpol.int/public/ICPO/speeches/75thGASelebi.asp

22 Al Gore, *An Inconvenient Truth: The Planetary Emergency of Global Warming and What We Can Do About It*, Rodale 2006

52

The terrorist threat: world risk society revisited

Ulrich Beck

Does 11th September stand for something new in history? There is one central aspect for which this is true: 11th September stands for the complete collapse of language. Ever since that moment, we've been living and thinking and acting using concepts that are incapable of grasping what happened then. The terrorist attack was not a war, not a crime, and not even terrorism in the familiar sense. It was not a little bit of each of them and it was not all of them at the same time. No one has yet offered a satisfying answer to the simple question of what really happened. The implosion of the Twin Towers has been followed by an explosion of silence. If we don't have the right concepts it might seem that silence is appropriate. But it isn't. Because silence won't stop the self-fulfilling prophecies of false ideas and concepts, for example, war. This is my thesis: the collapse of language that occurred on September 11th expresses our fundamental situation in the 21st century, of living in what I call 'world risk society'.

There are three questions I discuss in this article:

First, what does 'world risk society' mean?

Second, what about the *politics* of world risk society, especially linked to the terrorist threat?

Third, what are the methodological consequences of world risk society for the social sciences?

WHAT DOES WORLD RISK SOCIETY MEAN?

What do events as different as Chernobyl, global warming, mad cow disease, the debate about the human genome, the Asian financial crisis and the September

From *Theory, Culture & Society*, 2002, 19(4): 39–55.

11th terrorist attacks have in common? They signify different dimensions and dynamics of world risk society. Few things explain what I mean by global risk society more convincingly than something that took place in the USA just a few years ago (Benford, 2000). The US Congress appointed a commission with the assignment of developing a system of symbols that could properly express the dangers posed by American nuclear waste-disposal sites. The problem to be solved was: how can we communicate with the future about the dangers we have created? What concepts can we form, and what symbols can we invent to convey a message to people living 10,000 years from now?

The commission was composed of nuclear physicists, anthropologists, linguists, brain researchers, psychologists, molecular biologists, sociologists, artists and others. The immediate question, the unavoidable question was: will there still be a United States of America in 10,000 years time? As far as the government commission was concerned, the answer to that question was obvious: USA forever! But the key problem of how to conduct a conversation with the future turned out to be well nigh insoluble. The commission looked for precedents in the most ancient symbols of humankind. They studied Stonehenge and the pyramids; they studied the history of the diffusion of Homer's epics and the Bible. They had specialists explain to them the life-cycle of documents. But at most these only went back 2000 or 3000 years, never 10,000.

Anthropologists recommended using the symbol of the skull and crossbones. But then a historian remembered that, for alchemists, the skull and bones stood for resurrection. So a psychologist conducted experiments with 3-year-olds to study their reactions. It turns out that if you stick a skull and crossbones on a bottle, children see it and immediately say 'Poison' in a fearful voice. But if you put it on a poster on a wall, they scream 'Pirates!' And they want to go exploring.

Other scientists suggested plastering the disposal sites with plaques made out of ceramic, metal and stone containing many different warnings in a great variety of languages. But the verdict of the linguists was uniformly the same: at best, the longest any of these languages would be understood was 2000 years.

What is remarkable about this commission is not only its research question, that is, how to communicate across 10,000 years, but the scientific precision with which it answered it: it is not possible. This is exactly what world risk society is all about. The speeding up of modernization has produced a gulf between the world of quantifiable risk in which we think and act, and the world of non-quantifiable insecurities that we are creating. Past decisions about nuclear energy and present decisions about the use of gene technology, human genetics, nanotechnology, etc. are unleashing unpredictable, uncontrollable and ultimately incommunicable consequences that might ultimately endanger all life on earth (Adam, 1998, 2002).

'Risk' inherently contains the concept of control. Pre-modern dangers were attributed to nature, gods and demons. Risk is a modern concept. It presumes decision-making. As soon as we speak in terms of 'risk', we are talking about calculating the incalculable, colonizing the future.

In this sense, calculating risks is part of the master narrative of first modernity. In Europe, this victorious march culminates in the development and organization of the welfare state, which bases its legitimacy on its capacity to protect its citizens against dangers of all sorts. But what happens in world risk society is that we enter a world of *uncontrollable risk* and we don't even have a language to describe what we are facing. 'Uncontrollable risk' is a contradiction in terms. And yet it is the only apt description for the second-order, *un*natural, human-made, manufactured uncertainties and hazards beyond boundaries we are confronted with.

It is easy to misconstrue the theory of world risk society as Neo-Spenglerism, a new theory about the decline of the western world, or as an expression of typically German *Angst*. Instead I want to emphasize that world risk society does not arise from the fact that everyday life has generally become more dangerous. It is not a matter of the *increase*, but rather of the *de-bounding* of uncontrollable risks. This de-bounding is three-dimensional: spatial, temporal and social. In the spatial dimension we see ourselves confronted with risks that do not take nation-state boundaries, or any other boundaries for that matter, into account: climate change, air pollution and the ozone hole affect everyone (if not all in the same way). Similarly, in the temporal dimension, the long latency period of dangers, such as, for example, in the elimination of nuclear waste or the consequences of genetically manipulated food, escapes the prevailing procedures used when dealing with industrial dangers. Finally, in the social dimension, the incorporation of both jeopardizing potentials and the related liability question lead to a problem, namely that it is difficult to determine, in a legally relevant manner, who 'causes' environmental pollution or a financial crisis and who is responsible, since these are mainly due to the combined effects of the actions of many individuals. 'Uncontrollable risks' must be understood as not being linked to place, that is they are difficult to impute to a particular agent and can hardly be controlled on the level of the nation state. This then also means that the boundaries of private insurability dissolve, since such insurance is based on the fundamental potential for compensation of damages and on the possibility of estimating their probability by means of quantitative risk calculation. So the hidden central issue in world risk society is *how to feign control over the uncontrollable* – in politics, law, science, technology, economy and everyday life (Adam, 2002; Beck, 1992, 1999; Featherstone, 2000; Giddens, 1994; Latour, 2002; van Loon, 2000).

We can differentiate between at least three different axes of conflict in world risk society. The first axis is that of *ecological* conflicts, which are by their very essence global. The second is *global financial* crises, which, in a first stage, can be individualized and nationalized. And the third, which suddenly broke upon us on September 11th, is the threat of global terror networks, which empower governments and states.

When we say these risks are global, this should not be equated with a homogenization of the world, that is, that all regions and cultures are now equally affected by a uniform set of non-quantifiable, uncontrollable risks in the areas of ecology, economy and power. On the contrary, global risks are per se unequally distributed. They unfold in different ways in every concrete formation, mediated by different historical backgrounds, cultural and political patterns. In the so-called periphery, world risk society appears *not* as an *endogenous* process, which can be fought by means of autonomous national decision-making, but rather as an *exogenous* process that is propelled by decisions made in other countries, especially in the so-called centre. People feel like the helpless hostages of this process insofar as corrections are virtually impossible at the national level. One area in which the difference is especially marked is in the experience of global financial crises, whereby entire regions on the periphery can be plunged into depressions that citizens of the centre do not even register as crises. Moreover, ecological and terrorist-network threats also flourish with particular virulence under the weak states that define the periphery.

There is a dialectical relation between the unequal experience of being victimized by global risks and the transborder nature of the problems. But it is the transnational aspect, which makes cooperation indispensable to their solution, that truly gives them their global nature. The collapse of global financial markets or climatic change affect regions quite differently. But that doesn't change the principle that everyone is affected, and everyone can potentially be affected in a much worse manner. Thus, in a way, these problems endow each country with a common global interest, which means that, to a certain extent, we can already talk about the basis of a global community of fate. Furthermore, it is also intellectually obvious that global problems only have global solutions, and demand global cooperation. So in that sense, we can say the principle of 'globality' (Albrow, 1996; Robertson, 1992), which is a growing consciousness of global interconnections, is gaining ground. But between the potential of global cooperation and its realization lie a host of risk conflicts.

Some of these conflicts arise precisely because of the uneven way in which global risks are experienced. For example, global warming is certainly something that encourages a perception of the earth's inhabitants, both of this and future generations, as a community of fate (Held et al., 1999). But the path to its solution also creates conflicts, as when industrial countries seek to protect the rainforest in developing countries, while at the same time appropriating the lion's share of the world's energy resources for themselves. And yet these conflicts still serve an *integrative* function, because they make it increasingly clear that global solutions must be found, and that these cannot be found through war, but only through negotiation and contract. In the 1970s the slogan was: 'Make love, not war'. What then is the slogan at the beginning of the new century? It certainly sounds more like 'Make *law*, not war' (Mary Kaldor).

The quest for global solutions will in all probability lead to further global institutions and regulations. And it will no doubt achieve its aims through a host of conflicts. The long-term anticipations of unknown, transnational risks call transnational risk communities into existence. But in the whirlpool of their formation, as in the whirlpool of modernity, they will also transform local cultures into new forms, destroying many central institutions that currently exist. But transformation and destruction are two inescapable sides of the necessary political process of experimentation with new solutions.

Ecological threats are only one axis of global risk conflict. Another lies in the risks of globalized financial markets. Crisis fluctuations in the securities and finance markets are as old as the markets themselves. And it was already clear during the world crisis of 1929 that financial upheavals can have catastrophic consequences – and that they can have huge political effects. The post-Second World War institutions of Bretton Woods were global political solutions to global economic problems, and their efficient functioning was an indispensable key to the rise of the Western welfare state. But since the 1970s, those institutions have been largely dismantled and replaced by a series of ad hoc solutions. So we now have the paradoxical situation where global markets are more liberalized and globalized than ever, but the global institutions set up to control them have seen their power drastically reduced. In this context, the possibility of a 1929-size catastrophe certainly cannot be excluded.

Both ecological and financial risks incorporate several of the characteristics we have enumerated that make risks politically explosive. They go beyond rational calculation into the realm of unpredictable turbulence. Moreover, they embody the struggle over the distribution of 'goods' and 'bads', of positive and negative consequences of risky decisions. But above all, what they have in common is that their effects are deterritorialized. That is what makes them *global* risks. And that is what sets in motion the formation of global risk communities – and world risk society.

But while they show similarities, there are also important differences between the various kinds of global risk that significantly influence the resultant conflict. One is that environmental and technological risks come from the 'outside'. They have physical manifestations that then become socially relevant. Financial risks, on the other hand, originate in the heart of the social structure, in its central medium. This then leads to several other differences. Financial risks are more immediately apparent than ecological risks. A consciousness leap is not required to recognize them. By the same token, they are more individualized than ecological risks. A person and her/his next-door neighbour can be affected in very different ways. But, this aspect does not make financial threats potentially less risky. On the contrary, it increases their potential speed and reach. The economy is the central subsystem of modern society. And because all other subsystems depend on it, a failure of this type could be truly disastrous. So there are very compelling reasons to consider the world economy as another central axis of world risk society.

A further distinction can be made, however, between ecological and financial threats on the one hand, and the threat of global terrorist networks on the other. Ecological and financial conflicts fit the model of modernity's self-endangerment. They both clearly result from the accumulation and distribution of 'bads' that are tied up with the production of goods. They result from society's central decisions, but as unintentional side-effects of those decisions. Terrorist activity, on the other hand, is intentionally bad. It aims to produce the effects that the other crises produce unintentionally. Thus the principle of *intention* replaces the principle of *accident*, especially in the field of economics. Much of the literature on risk in economics treats risk as a positive element within investment decisions, and risk-taking as a dynamic aspect linked to the essence of markets. But investing in the face of risk presupposes trust. Trust, in turn, is about the binding of time and space, because trust implies committing to a person, group or institution over time.

This prerequisite of active trust, in the field of economics as well as in everyday life and democracy, is dissolving. The perception of terrorist threats replaces *active trust* with *active mistrust*. It therefore undermines the trust in fellow citizens, foreigners and governments all over the world. Since the dissolution of trust multiplies risks, the terrorist threat triggers a self-multiplication of risks by the de-bounding of risk perceptions and fantasies.

This, of course, has many implications. For example, it contradicts the images of the *homo economicus* as an autarkic human being and of the individual as a decider and risk taker. One of the consequences thereof is that the principle of *private* insurance is partly being replaced by the principle of *state* insurance. In other words, in the terrorist risk society the world of *individual* risk is being challenged by a world of *systemic* risk, which contradicts the logic of economic risk calculation. Simultaneously, this opens up new questions and potential conflicts, namely how to negotiate and distribute the *costs* of terrorist threats and catastrophes between businesses, insurance companies and states.

Therefore, it becomes crucial to distinguish clearly between, on the one hand, the conventional enemy image between conflicting states and, on the other, the 'transnational terrorist enemy', which consists of individuals or groups but not states. It is the very transnational and hybrid character of the latter representation that ultimately reinforces the hegemony of already powerful states.

The main question is: who defines the identity of a 'transnational terrorist'? Neither judges, nor international courts, but powerful governments and states. They empower themselves by defining who is *their* terrorist enemy, *their* bin Laden. The fundamental distinctions between war and peace, attack and self-defence collapse. Terrorist enemy images are *deterritorialized, de-nationalized and flexible state constructions that legitimize the global intervention of military powers as 'self-defence'*. President George W. Bush painted a frightening picture of 'tens of thousands' of al-Qaida-trained terrorists 'in at least a dozen countries'. Bush uses the most expansive interpretation: 'They are to be destroyed.' Bush's alarmism has a paradoxical effect: it gives Islamic terrorists what they want most – a recognition of their power. Bush has encouraged the terrorists to believe that the United States really can be badly hurt by terrorist actions like these. So there is a hidden mutual enforcement between Bush's empowerment and the empowerment of the terrorists.

US intelligence agencies are increasingly concerned that future attempts by terrorists to attack the United States may involve Asian or African al-Qaida members, a tactic intended to elude the racial profiles developed by US security personnel. Thus the internal law enforcement and the external counter-threat of US intervention not only focus on Arab faces, but possibly on Indonesian, Filipino, Malaysian or African faces. In order to broaden terrorist enemy images, which, to a large extent, are a one-sided construction of the powerful US state, expanded parameters are being developed so as to include networks and individuals who may be connected to Asian and African terrorist organizations. This way, Washington constructs the threat as immense. Bush insists that permanent mobilization of the American nation is required, that the military budget be vastly increased, that civil liberties be restricted and that critics be chided as unpatriotic.

So there is another difference: the *pluralization* of experts and expert rationalities, which characterizes ecological and financial risks, is then replaced by the gross *simplification* of enemy images, constructed by governments and intelligence agencies without and beyond public discourse and democratic participation.

So there are huge differences between the external risks of ecological conflicts, the internal risks of financial conflicts and the intentional terrorist threat. Another big difference is the speed of acknowledgement. Global environmental and financial risks are still not truly recognized. But with the horrific images of New York and Washington, terrorist groups *instantly* established themselves as new global players competing with nations, the economy and civil society in the eyes of the world. The terrorist threat, of course, is reproduced by the global media.

To summarize the specific characteristics of terrorist threat: (bad) intention replaces accident, active trust becomes active mistrust, the context of individual risk is replaced by the context of systemic risks, private insurance is (partly) replaced by state insurance, the power of definition of experts has been replaced by that of states and intelligence agencies; and the pluralization of expert rationalities has turned into the simplification of enemy images.[1]

Having outlined their differences, it should be no surprise that the three kinds of global risk, that is ecological, financial and terrorist threat, also interact. And terrorism again is the focal point. On the one hand, the dangers from terrorism increase exponentially with technical progress. Advances in financial and communication technology are what made global terrorism possible in the first place. And the same innovations that have individualized financial risks have also *individualized war*.

But the most horrifying connection is that all the risk conflicts that are stored away as potential could now be intentionally unleashed. Every advance from gene technology to nanotechnology opens a 'Pandora's box' that could be used as a terrorist's toolkit. Thus the terrorist threat has made everyone into a disaster movie scriptwriter, now condemned to imagine the effects of a home-made atomic bomb assembled with the help of gene or nanotechnology; or the collapse of global computer networks by the introduction of squads of viruses and so on.

POLITICS OF WORLD RISK SOCIETY

There is a sinister perspective for the world after September 11th. It is that uncontrollable risk is now irredeemable and deeply engineered into all the processes that sustain life in advanced societies. Pessimism then seems to be the only rational stance. But this is a one-sided and therefore truly misguided view. It ignores the new terrain. It is dwarfed by the sheer scale of the new opportunities opened up by today's threats, that is the axis of conflicts in world risk society.

People have often asked: 'What could unite the world?' And the answer some-times given is: 'An attack from Mars.' In a sense, that was just what happened on September 11th: an attack from our 'inner Mars'. It worked as predicted. For some time, at least, the warring camps and nations of the world united against the common foe of global terrorism. I would like to suggest six lessons that can be drawn from this event.

The first lesson: in an age where trust and faith in God, class, nation and progress have largely disappeared, humanity's common fear has proved the last – ambivalent – resource for making new bonds. In his book *The Public and Its Problems* (1954), John Dewey argues that it is not a decision, but its consequences and risk that create a public in the post-traditional world. So the theory of world risk society is *not* just another kind of 'end-of-history' idea; this time world history does not end with the resolution of political and social tensions, as Marx and Fukuyama believed, but with the end of the world itself. Nevertheless, what the global public discourse on global risks creates is a reason for hope, since the political explosiveness of world risk society displays a potential enlightenment function. The perceived risk of global terrorism has had exactly the opposite effect than that which was intended by the terrorists. It has pushed us into a new phase of globalization, the globalization of politics, the moulding of states into transnational cooperative networks. Once more, the rule has been confirmed that resistance to globalization only accelerates it. Anti-globalization activists operate on the basis of global rights, markets and networks. They both think and act in global terms, and use them to awaken global awareness and a global public. The term 'anti-globalization movement' is misleading. Many fight for an alternative globalization – global justice – rather than anti-globalization.[2]

The second big lesson of the terrorist attack is: national security is no longer national security. Alliances are nothing new, but the decisive difference about this global alliance is that its purpose is to preserve *internal* and not external security. All the distinctions that make up our standard picture of the modern state – the borders that divide domestic from international, the police from the military, crime from war and war from peace – have been overthrown. It was precisely those distinctions that defined the nation state. Without them, it is a zombie idea. It still looks alive, but it is dead.[3]

Foreign and domestic policy, national security and international cooperation are now all interlocked. The only way to deal with global terror is also the only way to deal with global warming, immigration, poison in the food chain, financial risks and organized crime. In all these cases, national security *is* transnational cooperation. Since September 11th, 'terrorist sleepers' have been identified in Hamburg, Germany, and many other places. Thus, German domestic policy is now an important part of US domestic and foreign policy. So are the domestic as well as foreign, security and defence policies of France, Pakistan, Great Britain, Russia and so on.

In the aftermath of the terrorist attack, the state is back, and for the old Hobbesian reason – the provision of security. Around the world we see governments becoming more powerful, and supranational institutions like NATO becoming less powerful.

But at the same time, the two most dominant ideas about the state – the idea of the *national* state, and the idea of the *neoliberal* state – have both lost their reality and their necessity. When asked whether the $40 billion that the US government requested from Congress for the war against terrorism didn't contradict the neoliberal creed to which the Bush administration subscribes, its spokesman replied laconically: 'Security comes first.'

Here is the third lesson: September 11th exposed neoliberalism's shortcomings as a solution to the world's conflicts. The terrorist attacks on America were the Chernobyl of globalization. Just as the Russian disaster undermined our faith in nuclear energy, so September 11th exposed the false promise of neoliberalism.

The suicide bombers not only exposed the vulnerability of western civilization but also gave a foretaste of the conflicts that globalization can bring about. Suddenly, the seemingly irrefutable tenets of neoliberalism – that economics will supersede politics, that the role of the state will diminish – lose their force in a world of global risks.

The privatization of aviation security in the US provides just one example, albeit a highly symbolic one. America's vulnerability is indeed very much related to its political philosophy. It was long suspected that the US could be a possible target for terrorist attacks. But, unlike in Europe, aviation security was privatized and entrusted to highly flexible part-time workers who were paid even less than employees in fast-food restaurants.

It is America's political philosophy and self-image that creates its vulnerability. The horrible pictures of New York contain a message: a state can neoliberalize itself to death. Surprisingly, this has been recognized by the US itself: aviation has been transformed into a federal state service.

Neoliberalism has always been a fair-weather philosophy, one that works only when there are no serious conflicts and crises. It asserts that only globalized markets, freed from regulation and bureaucracy, can remedy the world's ills – unemployment, poverty, economic breakdown and the rest. Today, the capitalist fundamentalists' unswerving faith in the redeeming power of the market has proved to be a dangerous illusion.

This demonstrates that, in times of crises, neoliberalism has no solutions to offer. Fundamental truths that were pushed aside return to the fore. Without taxation, there can be no state. Without a public sphere, democracy and civil society, there can be no legitimacy. And without legitimacy, no security. From these premises, it follows that, without legitimate forums for settling national and global conflicts, there will be no world economy in any form whatsoever.

Neoliberalism insisted that economics should break free from national models and instead impose transnational rules of business conduct. But, at the same time, it assumed that governments would stick to national boundaries and the old way of doing things. Since September 11th, governments have rediscovered the possibilities and power of international cooperation – for example, in maintaining internal security. Suddenly, the necessity of statehood, the counter-principle of neoliberalism, is omnipresent. A European arrest warrant that supersedes national sovereignty in judicial and legal enforcement – unthinkable until recently – has suddenly become a possibility. We may soon see a similar convergence towards shared rules and frameworks in economics.

We need to combine economic integration with cosmopolitan politics. Human dignity, cultural identity and otherness must be taken more seriously in the future (Beck, 2002a, 2002b). Since September 11th, the gulf between the world of those who profit from globalization and the world of those who feel threatened by it has been closed. Helping those who have been excluded is no longer a humanitarian task. It is in the West's own interest: the key to its security. The West can no longer ignore the black holes of collapsed states and situations of despair.

To draw the fourth lesson I pick up my statement again that no nation, not even the most powerful, can ensure its national security by itself. World risk society is forcing the nation-state to admit that it cannot live up to its constitutional promise to protect its citizens' most precious asset, their security. The only solution to the problem of global terror – but also to the problems of financial risk, climate catastrophe and organized crime – is transnational cooperation. This leads to the paradoxical maxim that, in order to pursue their national interest, countries need to denationalize and transnationalize themselves. In other words, they need to surrender parts of their autonomy in order to cope with national problems in a globalized world. The zero-sum logic of mutual deterrence, which held true for both nation-states and empires, is losing its coherence.

In this context, then, a new central distinction emerges between sovereignty and autonomy. The nation-state is built on equating the two. So from the nation-state perspective, economic interdependence, cultural diversification and military, judicial and technological cooperation all lead to a loss of autonomy and thus sovereignty. But if sovereignty is measured in terms of political clout – that is, by the extent to which a country is capable of having an impact on the world stage, and of furthering the security and wellbeing of its people by bringing its judgements to bear – then it is possible to conceive the same situation very differently. In the latter framework, increasing interdependence and cooperation, that is, a *decrease* in autonomy, can lead to an increase in sovereignty. Thus, sharing sovereignty does not reduce it; on the contrary, sharing actually enhances it. This is what cosmopolitan sovereignty means in the era of world risk society.

Fifth lesson: I think it is necessary to distinguish clearly between on the one hand, not national, but *global unilateralism* – meaning the politics of the new American empire: *the Pax Americana* – and on the other hand, two concepts of multilateralism or the multilateral state: namely the *surveillance* state and *cosmopolitan* state. Before and after September 11th, US foreign policy changed rapidly from national unilateralism to the paradox of a 'global unilateralism'. In the aftermath of the Afghanistan war, the idea of a 'new world order' has taken shape in Washington's think-tanks and the US is supposed to both make and enforce its laws. The historian Paul Kennedy believes that the new American empire will be even more powerful than the classical imperial powers like Rome and Britain.

This is America's core problem today: a 'free society' is based on openness and on certain shared ethics and codes to maintain order, and Americans are now intimately connected to many societies that do not have governments that can maintain these ethics and order. Furthermore, America's internal security depends on peoples who are aggressively opposed to the American way of life. For America to stay America, a free and open society, intimately connected to the world, the world has to become – *Americanized*. And there are two ways to go about it: open societies either grow from the bottom up or freedom, democracy and capitalism are imposed from the outside by (the threat of) external intervention. Of course, there is the alternative: to affirm and value real international cooperation. Real cooperation will require the Bush administration to swallow a word that even September 11th didn't quite force down: 'multilateralism'. In effect, the message from Washington to Europe and the other allies is: 'We will do the cooking and prepare what people are going to eat, then you will wash the dirty dishes.'

On the other hand, we have to distinguish between two forms of multilateralism as well: surveillance states and cosmopolitan states. *Surveillance states* threaten to use the new power of cooperation to build themselves into fortress states, in which security and military concerns will loom large and freedom and democracy will shrink. Already we hear about how western societies have become so used to peace and well-being that they lack the necessary vigour to distinguish friends from enemies. And that priorities will have to change. And that some of our precious rights will have to be sacrificed for the sake of security. This attempt to construct a western citadel against the numinous Other has already sprung up in every country and will only increase in the years to come. It is the sort of phenomenon out of which a democratic authoritarianism might arise, a system in which maintaining flexibility towards the world market would be premised on increasing domestic rigidity. Globalization's winners would get neoliberalism, and globalization's losers would get the other side of the coin: a heightened fear of foreigners, born out of the apprehension of terrorism and bristling with the poison of racism.

This is my sixth and final lesson: if the world is to survive this century, it must find a way to civilize world risk society. A new big idea is wanted. I suggest the idea of the *cosmopolitan state*, founded upon the recognition of the otherness of the other (Beck, 2002b).

National states present a threat to the inner complexity, the multiple loyalties, the social flows and fluids of risks and people that world risk society has caused to slosh across national borders. Conversely, nation states cannot but see such a fuzzing of borders as a threat to their existence. Cosmopolitan states, by contrast, emphasize the necessity of solidarity with foreigners both inside and outside the national borders. They do this by connecting self-determination with responsibility for (national and non-national) Others. It is not a matter of limiting or negating self-determination. On the contrary, it is a matter of freeing self-determination from its national cyclopean vision and connecting it to the world's concerns. Cosmopolitan states struggle not only against terror, but against the *causes* of terror. They seek to regain and renew the power of politics to shape and persuade, and they do this by seeking the solution of global problems that are even now burning humanity's fingertips but which cannot be solved by individual nations on their own. When we set out to revitalize and transform the state in a cosmopolitan state, we are laying the groundwork for international cooperation on the basis of human rights and global justice.

Cosmopolitan states can theoretically be founded on the principle of the national indifference of the state. This is a concept that is redolent of the way in which, during the 16th century, the Peace of Westphalia ended the religious civil war we call the '30 years war' through the separation of church and state. In a similar manner, the separation of state and nation could be the solution to some global problems and conflicts of the 21st century. For example: just as the a-religious state finally made possible the peaceful coexistence of multiple religions side by side, the cosmopolitan state could provide the conditions for multiple national and religious identities to coexist through the principle of constitutional tolerance.

We should seize this opportunity to reconceive the European political project as an experiment in the building of cosmopolitan states. And we could envision a cosmopolitan Europe, whose political force would emerge directly not only out of the worldwide struggle against terrorism, ecological and financial risks, but also out of both the affirmation and taming of European national complexity.

METHODOLOGY OF WORLD RISK SOCIETY

The consequences of the theory of world risk society are not only political but also methodological: world risk society questions the mostly non-reflective fundamental premises of social science, that is 'methodological nationalism'. *Methodological nationalism* takes the following ideal premises for granted: it equates societies with nation-state societies, and sees states and their governments as the cornerstones of a social science analysis. It assumes that humanity is naturally divided into a limited number of nations, which, on the inside, organize themselves as nation-states and, on the outside, set boundaries to distinguish themselves from other nation-states. It goes even further: this outer delimitation, as well as the competition between nation-states, represents the most fundamental category of political organization.

A sharp distinction should be made between *methodological* nationalism on the one hand and *normative* nationalism on the other. The former is linked to the social sciences observer perspective whereas the latter refers to the negotiation perspectives of political actors. In a normative sense, nationalism means that every nation has the right to determine itself within the frame of its cultural distinctiveness. Methodological nationalism assumes this normative claim as a socio-ontological given and simultaneously links it with the most important conflict and organization orientations of society and politics. These basic tenets have become the main perception-grid of social science. Indeed the social science stance is rooted in the concept of nation-state. It is a nation-state outlook on society and politics, law, justice and history, which governs the sociological imagination.

These premises also structure empirical research, as in, for example, the choice of statistical indicators, which are almost always exclusively national. A refutation of methodological nationalism from a strictly empirical viewpoint is therefore difficult, nigh impossible, because many statistical categories and investigation processes are based upon it.

The comparative analyses of societies, international relations, political theory, a significant part of history and jurisprudence all essentially function on the basis of methodological nationalism. This is valid to the extent that the majority of positions in the contemporary social and political science debate over globalization can be systematically interpreted as transdisciplinary reflexes linked to methodological nationalism. It is therefore of historical importance for the future development of social science that this methodological nationalism, as well as the categories of perception and disciplinary organization that pertain to it, be theoretically, empirically and organizationally reassessed.

The critique of methodological nationalism should not be mistaken for the thesis of the end of the nation-state – just as, when criticizing methodological individualism, one does not necessarily promote the end of the individual. Nation-states (as all investigations have shown) will continue to thrive or will be transformed into transnational states. At any rate, the decisive point is that *national organization as a structuring principle of societal and political action can no longer serve as a premise for the social science observer perspective*. In this sense, social science can only react to the challenge of globalization adequately if it manages to overcome methodological nationalism, and if it manages to raise empirically and theoretically fundamental questions within specialized fields of research and to thus elaborate the foundations of a *cosmopolitan* social and political science.

Cosmopolitan social science entails the systematic breaking up of the reciprocal confirmation process through which the national perspective of politics and society as well as the methodological nationalism of political science, sociology, history and law approve and strengthen each other in their definitions of reality. It thus also tackles (what had previously been *analytically* excluded as a sort of silent cartel of divided fundamental convictions) the various development versions of de-bounded politics and society, corresponding research questions and research programmes, the strategic expansions of the national and international political field as well as basic transformations in the domain of state, politics and society.

This paradigmatic reconstruction of social science from a national to a cosmopolitan perspective can be understood and explained as a 'positive problem shift' (Lakatos, 1970), that is, in the sense of a broadening of horizons for social science research. 'When politics and society are de-bounded, the consequence is that the labels "national" and "international" can no longer be separated. Considering the fact that, to an increasing extent, governing takes place in de-bounded spaces', the increasingly problematic distinction – though it is a distinction typical of the field – between 'domestic' and 'foreign' politics, as 'national governmental politics' and 'international relations', becomes definitely obsolete. Thus it is not only a matter of integrating national explanation factors in the analysis of international political processes, or of re-evaluating the international determinants of national political processes, as was pursued in numerous approaches over the past years. Rather, it is a matter of questioning the very separation between 'inside' and 'outside' (Grande and Risse, 2000). To sum up, traditional conceptualizations of terms and constructing borders between domestic and foreign politics or society and state are less and less appropriate to tackle the challenges linked to the world risk society.

Therefore, it becomes necessary systematically to raise the question of a paradigmatic change, which is characterized by the conceptual opposition of methodological nationalism and methodological cosmopolitanism (Beck, 2002a, 2002b) (see Table [52.1]). The horizon opened up by this distinction reveals a new configuration of the world. Previously, the national cosmos could be decomposed into a clear distinction between inside and outside. Between the two, the nation-state governed and order was established. In the inner experiential space, the central themes of work, politics, law, social inequality, justice, cultural identity were negotiated against the background of the nation, which was the guarantor of a collective unity of action. In the international realm, that is, in the outer experiential field, the corresponding concept of 'multiculturalism' developed. Multiculturalism, by delimiting and defining the foreign, mirrored and crystallized national self-image. Thus, the national/international distinction always represented more than a distinction, it actually functioned as a permanent self-affirming prophecy.

Against the background of cosmopolitan social science it becomes suddenly obvious that it is neither possible to distinguish clearly between the national and the international, nor, in a similar way, convincingly to contrast homogeneous units. National spaces have become de-nationalized, so that the national is no longer national, just as the international is no longer international. This entails that the foundations of the power of the nation-state are collapsing both from the inside and the outside, and that new realities are arising, a new mapping of space

Table 52.1 Paradigmatic change from a national perspective to a cosmopolitan social science

		Political action	
		National perspective	Cosmopolitan perspective
Political science	*Methodological nationalism*	Nation-state-centred understanding of society and politics both in the political practice and science	Critique of 'zombie categories' of nation-state organized societies, cultures and politics.[4]
	Methodological cosmopolitanism	Opening up of the nation-state-centred society and politics, sociology and political science: New Critical Theory with a cosmopolitan intent	The cosmopolitan society and its enemies: what do a cosmopolitan society, state and regime mean?

and time, new coordinates for the social and the political, coordinates which have to be theoretically and empirically researched and elaborated.[5]

However, the paradigmatic opposition between (inter)nationalism and cosmopolitanism does not establish a logical or temporal exclusivity, but an ambivalent transitional coexistence, a new concurrence of non-concurrents.

Thus world risk society makes heavy demands on social science. Social science must be re-established as a transnational science of the reality of de-nationalization, transnationalization and 're-ethnification' in a global age – and this on the levels of concepts, theories and methodologies as well as organizationally. This entails that the fundamental concepts of 'modern society' must be re-examined. *Household, family, class, social inequality, democracy, power, state, commerce, public, community, justice, law, history, politics* must be released from the fetters of methodological nationalism and must be reconceptualized and empirically established within the framework of a cosmopolitan social and political science which remains to be developed. So this is quite a list of understatements. Nevertheless, it has to be handled and managed if the social sciences are to avoid becoming a museum of antiquated ideas.

NOTES

This article was originally delivered as a public lecture at the London School of Economics and Political Science, February 2002.

1 Of course, September 11th was a moment of decision. This marks the decision the Bush administration took. There are alternatives: for example, strengthening of international law, choosing the 'cosmopolitan alternative' (see later).
2 But, of course, there is a new attraction of nihilism in combination with religious fanaticism, and there are important roots and movements of this violent nihilism in the West as well.
3 This does not imply, of course, that the concept of state is becoming irrelevant. The opposite is true: is has to be redefined in the context of world risk society.
4 For the critique of zombie categories see Beck and Beck-Gernsheim (2002).
5 This is the research agenda of the 'Reflexive Modernization' Research Centre at Munich University; see Beck et al. (2002).

REFERENCES

Adam, B. (1998) *Timescapes of Modernity*. London: Routledge.
Adam, B. (2002) 'Reflexive Modernization Temporized', *Theory, Culture & Society* 20(1) (in press).
Adam, B., U. Beck and J. van Loon (2000) *The Risk Society and Beyond*. London: Sage.
Albrow, M. (1996) *The Global Age*. Cambridge: Polity Press.
Beck, U. (1992) *Risk Society – Towards a New Modernity*. London: Sage (first published in German, 1986).
Beck, U. (1999) *World Risk Society*. Cambridge: Polity Press.
Beck, U. (2002a) 'The Cosmopolitan Society and its Enemies', Special Issue on Cosmopolis, *Theory, Culture & Society* 19(1–2): 17–44.

Beck, U. (2002b) *Macht und Gegenmacht im globalen Zeitalter: Neue weltpolitische Ökonomie.* Frankfurt am Main: Suhrkamp.

Beck, U. and E. Beck-Gernsheim (2002) *Individualization.* London: Sage.

Beck, U., W. Bonß and C. Lau (2002) 'The Theory of Reflexive Modernization', *Theory, Culture & Society* 20(1) (in press).

Benford, G. (2000) *Deep Time – How Humanity Communicates Across Millennia.* New York: Bard (Avon).

Dewey, J. (1954) *The Public and Its Problems.* Denver, CO: Swallow (first published New York, 1927).

Featherstone, M. (2000) 'Technologies of Post-Human Development and Potential for Global Citizenship', pp. 203–32 in J.N. Pieterse (ed.) *Global Futures – Shaping Globalization.* London: Zed.

Giddens, A. (1994) *Beyond Left and Right.* Cambridge: Polity Press.

Grande, E. and T. Risse (2000) 'Bridging the Gap. Konzeptionelle Anforderungen an die politikwissenschaftliche Analyse von Globalisierungsprozessen', *Zeitschrift für Internationale Beziehung* 2: 235–67.

Held, D., A.J. McGrew, D. Goldblatt and J. Perraton (eds) (1999) *Global Transformations.* Cambridge: Polity Press.

Lakatos, I. (1970) 'Falsification and the Methodology of Scientific Research Programmes', pp. 91–6 in I. Lakatos and A. Musgrave (eds) *Criticism and the Growth of Knowledge.* Cambridge: Cambridge University Press.

Latour, B. (2002) 'Is Remodernization Occurring – And If So, How to Prove It?', *Theory, Culture & Society* 20(1) (in press).

Robertson, R. (1992) *Globalization, Social Theory and Global Culture.* London: Sage.

Van Loon, J. (2000) 'Mediating Risks of Virtual Environments', pp. 229–40 in S. Allan, B. Adam and C. Carter (eds) *Environmental Risks and the Media.* London: Routledge.

53

Human rights and crimes of the state: the culture of denial

Stanley Cohen

[...]

It would be ludicrous to claim that Western criminology over the past decades has completely ignored the subject of state crime or the broader discourse of human rights. [...] [T]he subject has often been raised and then its implications conveniently repressed. This is a process strangely reminiscent of my substantive interest in the sociology of denial: how information is known but its implications are not acknowledged.

The first significant confrontation with the subject came in the early phase of radical criminology in the late 1960s. That favourite debate of the times – 'who are the *real* criminals?' – naturally turned attention from street crime to white-collar/corporate crime and then to the wider notion of 'crimes of the powerful'. The particular context of the Vietnam War, pushed our slogans ('Hey, hey LBJ! How many kids have you killed today?') explicitly in the direction of 'crimes of the state'.

In criminology, this sentiment was expressed in the much cited paper by the Schwendingers (1970) entitled 'Defenders of order or guardians of human rights?'. Looking back at this text, it appears a missed opportunity to deal with the core issues of state crime.

Quite rightly, the Schwendingers saw themselves going in the same direction, but a step further than Sutherland by invoking the criterion of *social injury* to define crime. In the case of white-collar crime, this mandated us to go beyond criminal law into the areas of civil and administrative law. The Schwendingers then noted that if Sutherland had consistently followed what they rightly call his 'ethical' rather than legal categorization, he should also have arrived at those

From *Australian and New Zealand Journal of Criminology*, 1993, 26(2): 97–115.

other socially injurious actions which are not defined as either criminal or civil law violations. So far, so good. But their argument then goes awry.

First, they cite as examples of other socially injurious action (their only examples) 'genocide and economic exploitation'. Now, besides the fact that these are hardly morally equivalent categories, genocide is crucially different from economic exploitation. It is recognized in current political discourse as crime by the state; it is clearly illegal by internal state laws; and since the Nuremberg Judgements and the 1948 UN Convention Against Genocide, it is a 'crime' according to international law. Genocide belongs to the same conceptual universe as 'war crimes' and 'crimes against humanity'. By any known criteria, genocide is more self-evidently criminal than economic exploitation.

The Schwendingers make no such distinctions nor try to establish the criminality of human rights violations. Instead they launch into a moral crusade against imperialistic war, racism, sexism and economic exploitation. We might agree with their ideology and we might even use the term 'crime' rhetorically to describe racism, sexism and economic exploitation. This type of 1960s rhetoric indeed anticipates the current third and fourth generation 'social rights'. A more restricted and literal use of the concept 'state crime', however, is both more defensible and useful. If we come from the discourse of human rights, this covers what is known in the jargon (for once, not euphemistic) as 'gross' violations of human rights – genocide, mass political killings, state terrorism, torture, disappearances. If we come from the discourse of criminology, we are talking about clear criminal offences – murder, rape, espionage, kidnapping, assault.

I don't want to get into definitional quibbles. Enough to say that the extension of criminology into the terrain of state crimes can be justified without our object of study becoming simply everything we might not like at the time. Let us see what happened after that mid-1960s to mid-1970s phase when questions about state crimes and human rights were placed on the criminological agenda by the radicals.

What mostly happened was that the human rights connection became lost. In the discourse of critical criminology, the putative connection between crime and politics took two different directions, both quite removed from the idea of state crime.

The first was the short-lived notion of the criminal as proto-revolutionary actor and the extension of this to all forms of deviance. This whole enterprise – referred to as the 'politicization of deviance' – was soon abandoned and eventually denounced as naive, romantic and sentimental. The second connection – which turned out the more productive – was the focus on the criminalizing power of the state. This led to the whole revisionist discourse on the sociology of law, social control and punishment that has remained so salient and powerful.

But neither direction leads anywhere near towards talking about state crimes. The subject simply faded away from criminological view in the mid-1970s to mid-1980s. By the time left realist criminology appeared, we [had moved] entirely from 'crimes of the state' back to the 'state of crime'. Today, the subject has reappeared from two contexts, one *external* to the discipline, the other *internal.*

The *external* context is the incremental growth of the international human rights movement itself. Emerging from the United Nations Charter and the great declarations and conventions of the next decade, from international governmental organizations such as UNESCO and the Council of Europe, from fledgling pressure groups such as Amnesty International to the vast current list of national and international non-governmental organizations, the human rights movement has become a major institutional force. Pushed by the rhetorical use of 'human rights' by the Carter Administration about Latin America and its critique of the Soviet Union, the ideal of human rights took on a powerful life of its own. It has become a secular religion.

This discourse, of course, is very dense, complex and contradictory [...] 'Human Rights' has become a slogan raised from most extraordinary different directions. Progressive forces and organizations like Amnesty can enlist famous rock stars to perform in defence of international human rights. Right wing pressure groups in the USA can unseat politicians and defeat Supreme Court nominations by invoking the human rights of the unborn foetus. Civil liberties groups defend pornography on the grounds of freedom of speech and the women's movement attacks this freedom as an assault on the human rights of women. Nations with the most appalling record of state violence and terror can self-righteously join together in the UN to condemn other nations for their human rights violations. Some human rights activists are awarded the Nobel Peace Prize, others are jailed, tortured, have disappeared or been assassinated. The human rights of one group are held sacred, the rights of another totally ignored ... and so on.

But whatever the concept of human rights means, it has become a dominant narrative. Arguably, with the so-called death of the old meta-narratives of Marxism, liberalism and the Cold War, human rights will become *the* normative political language of the future. I have no time to go into its conceptual ambiguities – the difference between civil and human rights, the relationship between political and human rights work, the tension between universalism and cultural relativism. Nor can I raise the numerous policy issues of policing, enforcement and international law. One of the most salient issues for criminologists, raised dramatically by the current horrors in the former Yugoslavia, is the long-proposed establishment of an international criminal tribunal.

So this is one way – from the outside – that criminologists as citizens who read the news, must have become aware of the subject of human rights violations and crimes of the state. Not that you know about this awareness if you just read criminological texts. There is, however, one *internal* way in which the subject has been registered in criminology. This is through the growth of victimology.

There are many obvious echoes of human rights issues in victimological literature – whether in the feminist debate about female victims of male sexualized violence; in talking about children and children's rights; in the concern about victims of corporate crime, ecological abuse, etc. Some students (Karmen, 1990) find these echoes only in 'radical' rather than 'conservative' or 'liberal' victimology. The conservative tendency is concerned with victims of street crime, making offenders accountable, encouraging self reliance and advocating retributive justice. The liberal tendency includes white-collar crime, is concerned with making the victim 'whole' and advocates restitution and reconciliation. Only the radical tendency extends to all forms of human suffering and sees law and the criminal justice system as implicated in this suffering.

This distinction, though, between conservative, liberal and radical tendencies, is not always clear. And in the context of one crucial subject – what happens to state criminals such as torturers after democratization or a change in regime – the distinction breaks down altogether. Here, it is the 'radicals' who call for punishment and retributive justice, while it is the 'conservatives' who invoke ideals such as reconciliation to call for impunity.

In any event, these external and internal inputs are slowly making their way into criminology. In the mainstream, this can be seen in recent standard textbooks which explicitly deal with the subject of state crime, and others which consider the human rights definition of crime.

In the radical stream, there is Barak's recent (1991) volume *Crimes By the Capitalist State*. The editor makes a strong case for including state criminality in the field of criminology – both on the grounds that the consequences of state crimes are more widespread and destructive than traditional crime and because this would be a logical extension of the already accepted move into the field of white-collar crime. The overall tone of the volume, though, is too redolent of the 1960s debates: general ideas about discrimination and abuse of political and economic power, the focus only on capitalism and the disproportionate attention on worldwide low intensity warfare by the USA (CIA, counter-insurgency etc.).

Despite this recent interest, major gaps in the criminological discourse remain.

a First, there is little understanding that a major source of criminalization at national and international levels draws on the rhetoric of human rights. Significant waves of moral enterprise and criminalization over the last decade are derived not from the old middle-class morality, the Protestant ethic nor the interests of corporate capitalism, but from the feminist, ecological and human rights movements. A major part of criminology is supposed to be the study of law making – criminalization – but we pay little attention to the driving force behind so many new laws: the demand for protection from 'abuses of power'. The radical slogans of the 1960s have become the commonplace of any government and inter-government forum. Alongside our standard research on domestic legislatures and ministries of justice, we should see what our foreign ministries are doing – at the Council of Europe, the United Nations, etc.

b Another important defect in recent literature is its American focus. It is preoccupied with 'exposures' – of the CIA (e.g. drug running in Vietnam), FBI surveillance methods, the global drug wars, international arms dealing, etc. This results in a certain ethnocentrism, but also allows the derivative subjects (political economy, globalization, state propaganda, illegal clandestine operations, counterintelligence) to be denied as being 'normal politics' (like the white-collar crime issue allowed the denial of 'normal business'). For my purposes here, I want to stress not the politicality of the subject but its criminality. For this, we don't need theories of the state, we need merely to pick up the latest Amnesty Annual Report.

c If we have missed something about law making, we have ignored even more the facts of victimization. Again, there is a ritualistic acknowledgement of the damage, harm and violence that are the obvious consequences of state crime – and then we return to easier topics. It is as if we don't want to face these facts; as if – to anticipate the substance of the second part of [this chapter] – we have denied their implications. I am aware that phrases such as 'crimes of the twentieth century' sound bombastic – but for vast populations of the world, this is a fair characterization of those 'gross violations of human rights': genocide, mass political killings, disappearances, torture, rape by agents of state.

This terrible record is known but (as I will show) simultaneously not known. Take genocides and mass political killings only: the Turkish genocide of at least a million Armenians; the Holocaust against six million Jews and the hundreds of thousands of political opponents, gypsies and others; the millions killed under Stalin's regime; the tribal and religious massacres in Burundi, Bengal and Paraguay; the mass political killings in East Timor and Uganda; the 'autogenocide' in Cambodia; the 'ethnic cleansing' in Bosnia; the death squads and disappearances in Argentina, Guatemala, El Salvador. Or take torture – a practice supposedly eradicated from Europe by the beginning of the nineteenth century and now routinely used in two-thirds of the world.

To add up the deaths, injuries and destruction from all these sources and then compare this to the cumulative results of homicide, assault, property crime and sexual crime in even the highest crime countries of the world, is too tendentious an exercise, too insulting to the intelligence. One cannot calibrate human suffering in this way.

But criminologists do, after all, talk about offence 'seriousness'. The standard literature in this area – and allied debates on culpability, harm, responsibility and the 'just deserts' model – already compares street crime with white-collar crime. A current important contribution (von Hirsch and Jareborg, 1991) tries to gauge criminal harm by using a 'living-standard analysis'. Von Hirsch and his colleague have argued ingeniously that criminal acts can be ranked by a complicated scale of 'degrees of intrusion' on different kinds of legally protected interests: physical integrity; material support and amenity; freedom from humiliation; privacy and autonomy.

What von Hirsch calls 'interests' are strikingly close to what are also called 'human rights'. His examples, however, come only from the standard criminological terrain of citizen against citizen. Including corporate crime would extend the list to (business) organizations against citizen. This is certainly an interesting and worthwhile exercise. It allows, for example, the ranking of forcible rape by a stranger as very grave because this is so demeaning and gross an attack against the 'freedom from humiliation' interest; therefore rape at gun point becomes more serious than armed robbery; date rape comes lower on the cumulative scale on grounds that threat to bodily safety is eliminated, and so on.

But neither crimes of state nor the wider category of 'political crime' are mentioned. There is no logical reason why the identity of the offender should be assumed to be fixed as citizen against citizen, rather than state agent against citizen when talking about, say, murder, assault or rape. In fact, there are good *moral* reasons why any grading of seriousness should take this into account – in particular, the fact that the very agent responsible for upholding law, is actually responsible for the crime. And there is a good *empirical* reason: that for large parts of the world's population, state agents (or paramilitary groups, vigilantes or terrorists) are the normal violators of your 'legally protected interests'.

I don't want to oversimplify the many conceptual objections and obstacles that criminologists will legitimately raise to my glib appeal to include state crime in our frame of reference. Most such objections fall under two categories.

First, there are the equivalent arguments to those used in the field of corporate crime – that the state is not an actor and that individual criminal responsibility cannot be identified. For corporate crime, this objection has been disposed of often enough, most recently (and to my mind convincingly) by Braithwaite and Fisse (1990). The corporation engages in rational goal-seeking behaviour; it can act; it can have intentions; it can commit crimes. This is just as (though more complicatedly) true for the state.

The second objection (again paralleled from Sutherland onwards in the case of corporate crime) is that the resultant action is not 'really' crime. Here, the counterarguments are complicated and come from a number of different directions: (i) an appeal to international law and conventions on such concepts as 'war crimes' or 'crimes against humanity'; (ii) a demonstration that these acts are illegal by domestic criminal law and fit all criteria of 'crime'; (iii) and even if the acts in question are legal by internal state jurisdiction, then the question arises of how this legal legitimation occurs. We have to remember (perhaps by inscribing this on our consciousness each morning) that state crimes are not just the unlicensed terror of totalitarian or fascist regimes, police states, dictatorships or military juntas. And in even the most extreme of these regimes, such as Nazi Germany, the discourse of legality is used (Muller, 1991).

One of the clearest and most eloquent texts for understanding these symbiotic issues of responsibility and criminality, is the 1985 trial in Argentina of the former military junta members responsible for the mass killings, atrocities, disappearances of the 'dirty war'. Reports of this trial (e.g. by Amnesty International) should be on all criminology reading lists.

The reasons why we don't make these connections are less logical than epistemological. The political discourse of the atrocity is, as I will soon show, designed to hide its presence from awareness. This is not a matter of secrecy, in the sense of lack of access to information, but an unwillingness to confront anomalous or disturbing information. Take the example of torture. Democratic-type societies – the French in Algeria (Maran, 1989); the British in Northern Ireland; the Israelis in the Occupied Territories (Cohen, 1991) – could all proclaim their adherence to international conventions and domestic laws against torture. This called for a complex discourse of denial that what they were doing constituted torture. No, it was something else, 'special procedures' or 'moderate physical pressure'. So something happened – but it was not illegal. In more totalitarian societies (with no accountability, no free press, no independent judiciary) denial is simpler – you do it, but say you do not. Nothing happened.

The standard vocabulary of official (government) denial weaves its way – at times simultaneously, at times sequentially – through a complete spiral of denial. First you try 'it didn't happen'. There was no massacre, no one was tortured. But then the media, human rights organizations and victims show that it does happen: here are the graves; we have the photos; look at the autopsy reports. So you have to say that what happened was not what it looks to be but really something else: a 'transfer of population', 'collateral damage', 'self-defence'. And then – the crucial subtext – what happened anyway was completely justified – protecting national security, part of the war against terrorism. So:

- It doesn't happen here.

- If it does, 'it' is something else.

- Even if it is what you say it is, it is justified.

Faced with this spiral of denial, criminologists may not be expected to respond very differently from ordinary citizens. But the debate is only a little more complex and dramatic than debates about whether white-collar crime is really crime. I say more 'dramatic' because we are forced back not just to questions about what is normal business, but what is the normal state. Take, for example, the question of jurisdiction and punishment. Precisely because we expect so little from domestic and international law as sanctions against gross state crimes (against our own or other citizens), we seldom frame human rights violations in criminal terms. Talking about the limitations in the 1948 UN Convention Against Genocide and in the UN Charter itself, the anthropologist Leo Kuper remarks with characteristic irony that an unstated assumption of the international discourse is that:

> the sovereign territorial state claims, as an integral part of its sovereignty, the right to commit genocide or engage in genocidal massacres against people under its rule, and that the United Nations for all practical purposes, defends this right. (Kuper, 1981: 161)

Obviously, this is very complex territory – more complex than I can even hint at here – and it is understandable why mainstream criminology is reluctant to become too immersed in these debates. Their absence in 'left realist' criminology is stranger to explain. After all, the ontological base here is a realist philosophy which starts with harm, victimization, seriousness, suffering and supposed indifference to all this by the adolescent left idealism of the 1960s.

I will return to some possible explanations for this blindsight. On one level, this is nothing more sinister than a Western ethnocentrism preoccupied with its own national concerns and secure in the great achievement of liberal capitalism; the separation of crime from the state. On another more interesting level, this stems from the universal tendency to see only what is convenient to see.

THE CULTURE OF DENIAL

Let me now turn to my substantive topic – denial. How did I get to this subject?

During the decade in which I have lived in Israel, but especially the past five years of the *intifada* (the uprising of Palestinians in the Occupied Territories), I have been puzzled by the apparent lack of overt reaction (dissent, criticism, protest) in just those sectors of Israeli society [which] one would expect to be reacting more. In the face of clear information about what's going on – escalating levels of violence and repression, beatings, torture, daily humiliations, collective punishment (curfews, house demolition, deportations), death-squad-type killings by army undercover units – the level of shame, outrage and protest is not psychologically or morally appropriate.

Of course there are no objective scales of psychological or moral 'appropriateness'. But many observers, inside and outside the country, have sensed that this part of the public should find [things] more disturbing and be prepared to act accordingly.

Remember that I am talking not about that clear majority of the population who support these measures and would not object to even more severe repression. My object of study is the minority: the enlightened, educated middle class, responsive to messages of peace and co-existence, first to condemn human rights violations everywhere else in the world.

Note that unlike most societies where gross human rights violations occur, the facts are both private and public knowledge. Nearly everyone has direct personal knowledge, especially from army service. These are not conscripts or mercenary soldiers drawn from the underclass; everybody serves (including the middle class liberals) or has a husband, son, cousin or neighbour in reserve duty. There is a relatively open press, liberal in tone, which regularly and clearly exposes what is happening in the Occupied Territories. No one – least of all the group which interests me – can say those terrible (though, as I will show, complicated) words 'I didn't know'.

It is way beyond my scope to discuss the special reasons in Israel for denial, passivity or indifference. These are part of a complex political history – of being Jewish, of Zionism, of fear and insecurity. I mention this case only because it led me to comparisons, to looking for similarities and differences in other societies. I went back to my experience of growing up in apartheid South Africa. More fatefully, I turned to the emblematic events of this century: the Holocaust 'texts' about the good Germans who knew what was happening; the lawyers and doctors who colluded; the ordinary people who passed by the concentration camps every day and claimed not to know what was happening; the politicians in Europe and America who did not believe what they were told. Then from this one historical event, I went to the contemporary horrors reported every day in the mass media and documented by human rights reports – about Bosnia, Peru, Guatemala, Burma, Uganda …

All this – and the relevant social scientific literature – led me back to versions of the same universal question. This is not Milgram's famous question of how ordinary people will behave in terrible ways, but rather how ordinary, even good people, will not react appropriately to knowledge of the terrible. Why, when faced by knowledge of others' suffering and pain – particularly the suffering and pain result-ing from what are called 'human rights violations' – does 'reaction' so often take the form of denial, avoidance, passivity, indifference, rationalization or collusion?

I have mentioned the official state discourse: the pure denials (it didn't hap-pen, they are lying, the media are biased, the world community is just picking on us) and the pure justifications (deterrence, self-defence, national security, ideol-ogy, information gathering). But my concern is not the actor but rather (back, in a curious way, to labelling theory!) the audience. In the triangle of human suffer-ing so familiar to criminologists – the victim, to whom things are done; the per-petrator, who is actively causing the suffering; the observer who sees and knows – my interest lies in this third corner: the audience, the observers, the bystanders.

For my purposes here, I want to consider a specific group of observers – not those whose avoidance derives from (crudely speaking) their *support* for the action. If they see nothing morally wrong or emotionally disturbing in what is happening, why should they do anything? In this sense, their denial or passivity is 'easy' to explain. My interest is more in the subgroup who are ideologically predisposed to be against what is happening, to be disturbed by what they know. How do they react to their knowledge of the terrible?

Before presenting some lines of enquiry into this subject, let me note an important distinction which I won't have time to follow through. In talking about the denial of atrocities or human rights violations, there is a world of dif-ference between reacting to your own government's actions as distinct from what might be happening in a distant country. My response, say, as an Australian, to newspaper revelations about the treatment of Aborigines in custody, follows different lines from my response to sitting in Melbourne and reading a human rights report about death squads in El Salvador.

[…] First, I will list some of the more useful bodies of literature which deal – directly, but more often obliquely – with the general phenomenon of denial. Then I will give a preliminary classification of the major forms of denial. Finally, I will note a few questions from my fieldwork on human rights organizations. Through interviews, analysis of publications, educational material advertise-ments and campaign evaluations, I am trying to understand how human rights messages are disseminated and received.

This last part of the work is a study in communication. The *sender* is the inter-national human rights community (directly or through the mass media). The *audience* is our real and metaphorical bystanders. The *message* is something like this (to quote from an actual Amnesty International advert in Britain in 1991):

> *Brazil has solved the Problem of how to keep kids off the street. Kill Them.*

What bodies of literature might be of relevance?

1 The psychology of denial

Orthodox psychoanalysis sees denial as an unconscious defence mechanism for coping with guilt and other disturbing psychic realities. Freud originally distinguished between 'repression' which applies to defences against internal instinctual demands and 'denial' (or what he called 'disavowal') which applies to defences against the claims of external reality.

With a few exceptions, pure psychoanalytic theory has paid much less attention to denial in this sense than repression (but see Edelstein, 1989). We have to look in the more applied fields of psychoanalysis (or its derivatives) for studies about the denial of external information. This yields a mass of useful material. There is the rich literature on the denial of knowledge about fatal disease (especially cancer and more recently, AIDS) affecting self or loved ones. More familiar to criminologists, there is the literature on family violence and pathology: spouse abuse, child abuse, incest etc. The concept of denial is standard to describe a mother's reaction on 'discovering' that her husband had been sexually abusing their daughter for many years: 'I didn't notice anything'. In this case, the concept implies that in fact the mother did 'know' – how could she not have? – but that this knowledge was too unbearable to confront.

The subject of denial has also been dealt with by cognitive psychology and information theory. Of particular interest is the 'denial paradox': in order to use the term 'denial' to describe a person's statement 'I didn't know', you have to assume that he or she knew or knows about what it is he or she claims not to know (otherwise the term 'denial' is inappropriate).

Cognitive psychologists have used the language of information processing, selective perception, filtering, attention span etc., to understand the phenomenon of how we notice and simultaneously do not notice (Goleman, 1985). Some have even argued that the neurological phenomenon of 'blindsight' suggests a startling possibility: that one part of the mind may know just what it is doing, while the part that supposedly knows, remains oblivious of this.

We are all familiar, from basic social psychology, with the notion of cognitive bias: the selection of information to fit existing perceptual frames. At the extreme, information which is too threatening to absorb is shut out altogether. The mind somehow grasps what is going on, but rushes a protective filter into place, steering information away from what threatens. Information slips into a kind of 'black hole of the mind' – a blind zone of blocked attention and self-deception. Attention is thus diverted from facts or their meaning. Thus, the 'vital lies' sustained by family members about violence, incest, sexual abuse, infidelity, unhappiness. Lies continue unrevealed, covered up by the family's silence, collusion, alibis and conspiracies (Goleman, 1985).

Similar processes have been well documented outside both the social psychology laboratory and intimate settings like the family. The litany by observers of atrocities is all too familiar: 'we didn't see anything', 'no one told us', 'it looked different at the time'.

In addition to psychoanalytical and cognitive theory, there is also the tradition in philosophical psychology concerned with questions of self-knowledge and self-deception. The Sartrean notion of 'bad faith' is of particular interest in implying – contrary to psychoanalytical theory – that the denial is indeed conscious.

2 Bystanders and rescuers

Another body of literature more obviously relevant (and more familiar to criminologists) derives from the victimological focus on the bystander. The classic
'bystander effect' has become a cliché: how witnesses to a crime will somehow
disassociate themselves from what is happening and not help the victim. The
prototype is the famous Kitty Genovese case. (One night in New York in 1964, a
young woman, Kitty Genovese, was savagely assaulted in the street just before
reaching her apartment. Her assailant attacked her over a period of forty minutes
while she struggled, battered and screaming, to reach her apartment. Her screams
and calls for help were heard by at least 38 neighbours who, from their own
windows saw or heard her struggle. No one intervened directly or by calling the
police. Eventually a patrol car arrived – too late to save her life.)

Studies of the bystander effect (Sheleff, 1978) suggest that intervention is less
likely to occur under three conditions:

1   *Diffusion of responsibility* – so many others are watching, why should I be the one to inter-
    vene? Besides, it's none of my business.

2   *Inability to identify with the victim* – even if I see someone as a victim, I won't act if I cannot
    sympathize or emphathize with their suffering. We help our family, friends, nation, in-group –
    not those excluded from our moral universe (*Journal of Social Issues*, 1990). In fact, those who
    are outside our moral universe may be blamed for their predicament (the common experience
    of women victims of sexual violence). If full responsibility is laid on the political out-group (they
    provoked us, they had it coming), this releases you from your obligation to respond.

3   *Inability to conceive of effective intervention* – even if you do not erect barriers of denial, even
    if you feel genuine moral or psychological unease ('I feel so awful about what's going on in
    Bosnia', 'I just can't get those pictures from Somalia out of my mind'), this will not necessar-
    ily result in intervention. Observers will not act if they do not know what to do, if they feel
    powerless and helpless themselves, if they don't see any reward in helping, or if they fear
    punishment if they help.

These processes are of obvious relevance to my work on human rights violations. There are immediate and literal 'bystanders': all massacres, disappearances and atrocities have their witnesses. And there are also metaphorical
bystanders; remember the reader looking at the Amnesty adverts about street
kids being killed in Brazil or dissidents being tortured in Turkey: Is this really my
problem? Can I identify with these victims? What can I do about it anyway?

The obverse of the bystander effect has generated its own special discourse.
Just as interesting as the social bases of indifference, are the conditions under
which people are aroused to intervene – often at great personal cost and risk.
There is a vast ranging literature here: experimental studies on the social psychology of altruism and pro-social behaviour; the sociology of charity and phi-
lanthropy; philosophical and economic discussions of altruism (notably attempts
to reconcile the phenomenon to rational choice theory); historical studies of

helping, rescuing, altruism, the Good Samaritan. The best known of this work deals with rescuers of Jews in Nazi Europe (Oliner and Oliner, 1988).

3 Neutralization theory

More familiar ground to criminologists is the body of literature known as 'motivational accounts' or 'vocabulary of motives' theory. The application of this theory in Sykes and Matza's (1957) 'techniques of neutralization' paper is a criminological classic. [...]

The theory assumes that motivational accounts which actors (offenders) give of their (deviant) behaviour must be acceptable to their audience (or audiences). Moreover, accounts are not just *post facto* improvisations, but are drawn upon in advance from the cultural pool of motivational vocabularies available to actors and observers (and honoured by systems of legality and morality). Remember Sykes and Matza's original list; each technique of neutralization is a way of denying the moral bind of the law and the blame attached to the offence: denial of injury ('no one got hurt'); denial of victim ('they started it'; 'it's all their fault'); denial of responsibility ('I didn't mean to do it', 'they made me do it'); condemnation of the condemners ('they are just as bad') and appeal to higher loyalties (friends, gang, family, neighbourhood).

Something very strange happens if we apply this list not to the techniques for denying or neutralizing conventional delinquency but to human rights violations and state crimes. For Sykes and Matza's point was precisely that delinquents are *not* 'political' in the sense implied by subcultural theory; that is, they are not committed to an alternative value system nor do they withdraw legitimacy from conventional values. The necessity for verbal neutralization shows precisely the continuing bind of conventional values.

But exactly the same techniques appear in the manifestly political discourse of human rights violations – whether in collective political trials (note, for example, the Nuremberg trials or the Argentinian junta trial) or official government responses to human rights reports (a genre which I am studying) or media debates about war crimes and human rights abuses. I will return soon to 'literal denial', that first twist of the denial spiral which I identified earlier (it didn't happen, it can't happen here, they are all liars). Neutralization comes into play when you acknowledge (admit) that something happened – but either refuse to accept the category of acts to which it is assigned ('crime' or 'massacre') or present it as morally justified. Here are the original neutralization techniques, with corresponding examples from the realm of human rights violations.

- *Denial of injury* – they exaggerate, they don't feel it, they are used to violence, see what they do to each other.

- *Denial of victim* – they started it, look what they've done to us; they are the terrorists, we are just defending ourselves, we are the real victims.

- *Denial of responsibility* – here, instead of the criminal versions of psychological incapacity or diminished responsibility (I didn't know what I was doing. I blacked out, etc.) we find a denial of individual moral responsibility on the grounds of obedience: I was following orders, only doing my duty, just a cog in the machine. (For individual offenders like the ordinary soldier, this is the most pervasive and powerful of all denial systems.)

- *Condemnation of the condemners* – here, the politics are obviously more explicit than in the original delinquency context. Instead of condemning the police for being corrupt and biased or teachers for being hypocrites, we have the vast discourse of official denial used by the modern state to protect its public image: the whole world is picking on us; they are using double standards to judge us; it's worse elsewhere (Syria, Iraq, Guatemala or wherever is convenient to name); they are condemning us only because of their anti-semitism (the Israeli version), their hostility to Islam (the Arab version), their racism and cultural imperialism in imposing Western values (all Third World tyrannies).

- *Appeal to higher loyalty* – the original subdued 'ideology' is now total and self-righteous justification. The appeal to the army, the nation, the volk, the sacred mission, the higher cause – whether the revolution, 'history', the purity of Islam, Zionism, the defence of the free world or state security. As the tragic events of the last few years show, despite the end of the cold war, the end of history and the decline of meta narratives, there is no shortage of 'higher loyalties', old and new.

Let us remember the implications of accounts theory for our subject. Built into the offender's action, is the knowledge that certain accounts will be accepted. Soldiers on trial for, say, killing a peaceful demonstrator, can offer the account of 'obeying orders' because this will be honoured by the legal system and the wider public. This honouring is, of course, not a simple matter: Were the orders clear? Did the soldier suspect that the order was illegal? Where in the chain of command did the order originate from? These, and other ambiguities, make up the stuff of legal, moral and political discourses of denial.

I have no time here to apply each of these theoretical frameworks – psychoanalysis, cognitive psychology, bystander theory, motivational accounts etc. – to my case study of reactions to knowledge of human rights violations and state crimes. (There are obviously also many other relevant fields: political socialization and mobilization, mass media analysis, collective memory.) For illustration only, let me list some elementary forms of denial which these theories might illuminate.

I will distinguish three forms of denial, each of which operates at (i) the individual or psychic level and (ii) at the organized, political, collective or official level.

1 Denial of the past

At the individual level, there are the complex psychic mechanisms which allow us to 'forget' unpleasant, threatening or terrible information. Memories of what we have done or seen or known are selected out and filtered.

At the collective level, there are the organized attempts to cover up the record of past atrocities. The most dramatic and successful example in the modern era is the eighty years of organized denial by successive Turkish governments of the 1915–17 genocide against the Armenians – in which some one and half million people lost their lives (Hovanissian, 1986). This denial has been sustained by deliberate propaganda, lying and cover-ups, forging of documents, suppression of archives and bribing of scholars. The West, especially the USA, has colluded by not referring to the massacres in the UN, ignoring memorial ceremonies and by surrendering to Turkish pressure in NATO and other arenas of strategic cooperation.

The less successful example, of course, is the so-called 'revisionist' history of holocaust of European Jews, dismissed as a 'hoax' or a 'myth'.

At both levels, we can approach the process of denial through its opposite: the attempt to recover or uncover the past. At the individual level, the entire psychoanalytic procedure itself is a massive onslaught on individual denial and self-deception. At the political level, there is the opening of collective memory, the painful coming to terms with the past, the literal and metaphorical digging up of graves when regimes change and try to exorcise their history.

2 Literal denial

Here we enter the grey area sketched out by psychoanalysis and cognitive theory. In what senses can we be said to 'know' about something we profess not to know about? If we do shut something out of knowledge, is this unconscious or conscious? Under what conditions (for example, information overload or desensitization) is such denial likely to take place?

There are many different versions of literal denial, some of which appear to be wholly individual, others which are clearly structured by the massive resources of the state. We didn't know, we didn't see anything, it couldn't have happened without us knowing (or it could have happened without us knowing). Or: things like this can't happen here, people like us don't do things like this. Or: you can't believe the source of your knowledge: – victims, sympathizers, human rights monitors, journalists are biased, partial or ignorant.

The psychological ambiguities of 'literal denial' and their political implications are nicely illustrated by the psychoanalyst John Steiner's re-interpretation of the Oedipus drama (Steiner, 1985, 1990).

The standard version of the legend is a tragedy in which Oedipus is a victim of fate who bravely pursues the truth. At the beginning he does not know the truth (that he has killed his father, that he had sexual relations with his mother); at the end he does. This is taken as a paradigm for the therapeutic process itself: the patient in analysis to whom, gradually and painfully, the secrets of the unconscious are revealed. But alongside this version, Steiner shows, Sophocles also conveys a quite different message in the original drama: the message is that the main characters in the play must have been aware of the identity of Oedipus and realized that he had committed patricide and incest. There is a deliberate ambiguity throughout the text about the nature of this awareness – just how much did each character know? Each of the participants (including Oedipus himself) and especially the various court officials, had (good) different reasons for denying their knowledge, for staging a cover-up. The Oedipus story is not at all about the discovery of truth, but the denial of truth – a cover-up like Watergate, Iran Contra. Thus the question: how much did Nixon or Bush 'know'?

The ambiguity about how conscious or unconscious our knowledge is, how much we are aware of what we say we are unaware, is nicely captured in Steiner's title 'Turning a Blind Eye'. This suggests the possibility of *simultaneously* knowing and not knowing. We are not talking about the simple lie or fraud where facts are accessible but lead to a conclusion which is knowingly evaded. This, of course, is standard in the organized government cover-up: bodies are burnt, evidence is concealed, officials are given detailed instructions on how to lie. Rather, we are talking about the more common situation where 'we are vaguely aware that we choose not to look at the facts without being conscious of what it is we are evading' (Steiner, 1985: 61).

3 Implicatory denial

The forms of denial that we conceptualize as excuses, justifications, rationalizations or neutralizations, do not assert that the event did not happen. They seek to negotiate or impose a different construction of the event from what might appear the case. At the individual level, you know and admit to what you have done, seen or heard about. At the organized level, the event is also registered but is subjected to cultural reconstruction (for example, through euphemistic, technical or legalistic terminology). The point is to deny the implications – psychological and moral – of what is known. The common linguistic structure is 'yes, but'. Yes, detainees are being tortured but there is no other way to obtain information. Yes, Bosnian women are being raped, but what can a mere individual thousands of miles away do about it?

'Denial of Responsibility', as I noted earlier, is one of the most common forms of implicatory denial. The sociology of 'crimes of obedience' has received sustained attention, notably by Kelman and Hamilton (1989). The anatomy of obedience and conformity – the frightening degree to which ordinary people are willing to inflict great psychological and physical harm to others – was originally revealed by Milgram's famous experiment. Kelman and Hamilton begin from history rather than a university laboratory: the famous case of Lieutenant Calley and the My Lai massacre during the Vietnam War in May 1968 when a platoon of American soldiers massacred some 400 civilians. From this case and other 'guilt free' or 'sanctioned' massacres, they extract a rather stable set of conditions under which crimes of obedience will occur.

1 *Authorization*: when acts are ordered, encouraged, or tacitly approved by those in authority, then normal moral principles are replaced by the duty to obey.

2 *Routinization*: the first step is often difficult, but when you pass the initial moral and psychological barrier, then the pressure to continue is powerful. You become involved without considering the implications; it's all in a day's work. This tendency is re-inforced by special vocabularies and euphemisms ('surgical strike') or a simple sense of routine.

(Asked about what he thought he was doing, Calley replied in one of the most chilling sentences of all times: 'It was no big deal'.)

3   *Dehumanization*: when the qualities of being human are deprived from the other, then the usual principles of morality do not apply. The enemy is described as animals, monsters, gooks, sub-humans. A whole language excludes them from your shared moral universe.

The conditions under which perpetrators behave can be translated into the very bystander rationalizations which allow the action in the first place and then deny its implications afterwards. As Kelman and Hamilton show in their analysis of successive public opinion surveys (in which people were asked both to imagine how they would react to a My Lai situation themselves and to judge the actual perpetrators), obedience and authorization are powerful justifications. And observers as well as offenders are subject to desensitization (the bombardment by horror stories from the media to a point that you cannot absorb them any more and they are no longer 'news') and dehumanization.

My research on human rights organizations (national and international) deals with their attempts to overcome these barriers of denial. What is the difference between working in your own country and trying to arouse an international audience in distant and different places? What messages work best in mobilizing public action (whether going to a demonstration, donating money or joining an organization like Amnesty International)? Does focusing on a country work better than raising an issue (such as torture or the death penalty)? And which countries or which issues? Are some techniques of confronting denial – for example, inducing guilt or representing the horrors more vividly – counter-productive? Is there competition for the human rights message within the same audiences (for example, from the environmental movement)? ...

CONCLUSION

[...]

Instead of a conclusion, let me instead end with two footnotes. One raises – dare I say – some meta-theoretical issues; the other introduces a little optimism into an otherwise bleak story.

Meta theory

I mentioned the strange neglect of these issues by new realist criminologists and suggested that what is at stake is their sense of reality. But 'reality' is not a word used too easily these days – or if used, only politically correct in inverted commas. This is the legacy of post-structuralism, deconstructionism and postmodernism. There are a number of trends in postmodernist theory which – usually unwittingly – impinge on the human rights discourse. Let me mention a few such meta issues:

First, there is the question of moral relativism. This is the familiar claim – now supposedly finally vindicated – that if there is no universal, foundational base for morality (the death of meta-narratives), then it is impossible to stake out universal values (such as those enshrined in human rights standards). Then comes the derivative claim that such values and standards are Western, ethno-centric, individualistic, alien and imposed.

Now, whatever the historical record, this claim has some strange political implications. The standard and age-old government denials of the applicability of international human rights norms – we are different, we face special problems, the world doesn't understand us – now acquire a new philosophical dignity. And further, the condemners are condemned for being ethnocentric and imperialist.

A similar problem comes from the assertion that local struggles for human rights lose their meaning because they are informed by the very universal foun-dations and master narratives now so thoroughly discredited or tarnished. This is again a complex debate; I side with those who argue that no amount of decon-structive scepticism should deny the force with which we defend these values. It is surely a bizarre sight for Western progressives to be telling human rights activ-ists from the Third World or Eastern Europe that their struggle is, after all, not worth the candle.

A second problem is posed by the proclaimed end of history. This is the cur-rent round of the old 'end of ideology' game: the collapse of international social-ism finally proving the triumph of Western democratic capitalism. Besides the poverty of the case itself, it can make little sense for those still living between death squads, famine, disease and violence. For them, history is not over. But even if one meta narrative has won and there is nothing left for 'history' in the industrialized world, then how does this world react to what is happening else-where? Why – if not because of racism, selfishness, greed, and the type of denial I've talked about – do the victors not devote more resources to achieve these values elsewhere?

A third postmodernist theme is even more directly relevant to my subject here – and potentially even more destructive. This is the attack on all modes of rational enquiry which work with positivist categories of reality. The human rights movement can live without absolute, foundational values. But it cannot live with a theory which denies any way of knowing what has really happened. All of us who carried the anti-positivist banners of the 1960s are responsible for the emergent epistemological circus.

[…] On 29 March 1991, shortly after the cessation of hostilities in the Gulf War – just as thousands were lying dead and maimed in Iraq, the country's infra-structure deliberately destroyed by savage bombing, the Kurds abandoned to their fate – the high priest of postmodernism, Jean Baudrillard, published an article entitled 'The Gulf War Has Not Taken Place' (Baudrillard, 1991b). The 'true bel-ligerents' he argued, are those who thrive on the ideology of the truth of this war.

He was only being consistent with an article he wrote a few days before the war (Baudrillard, 1991a) in which he predicted that it would never happen. The war existed only as a figment of media simulation, of imaginary scenarios that exceeded all limits of real world facticity. The war, Baudrillard had solemnly declared, was strictly unthinkable except as an exchange of threats so exorbitant that it would guarantee that the event would not take place. The 'thing' would happen only in the minds of its audience, as an extension of the video games imagery which had filled our screens during the long build up. Dependent as we all were – prime time viewers as well as generals – on these computer generated images, we might as well drop all self-deluding distinctions between screen events and 'reality'.

Given this 'prediction', it was unlikely that Baudrillard would be proved wrong if the war really did break out. So indeed the 'war' – a free floating signifier, devoid of referential bearing – did not happen. To complain that he was caught out by events only shows our theoretical naïveté, our nostalgia for the old truth-telling discourses.

What does one make of all this? I take my cue from Christopher Norris (1992), who has devoted a splendid polemical book to attacking Baudrillard's theses on the Gulf War. Norris is by no means a philistine critic or an unregenerated 'positivist'. He is the author of altogether sympathetic studies of Derrida and deconstructionism. And he concedes that Baudrillard makes some shrewd observations about how the war was presented by its managers and the media: the meaningless statistical data to create a illusory sense of factual reporting, the absurd claims about 'precision targeting', and 'clever bombs' to convince us that the mass destruction of civilian lives were either not happening (literal denial) or were accidental (denial of responsibility).

But Norris is now appalled by the precious nonsense to which the fashionable tracks of postmodernism have led. What disturbs him is how seriously these ideas were taken, 'to the point where Baudrillard can deliver his ludicrous theses on the Gulf War without fear of subsequent exposure as a charlatan or of finding these theses resoundingly disconfirmed by the course of real-world events' (Norris, 1992: 17).

It is beyond my scope and competence to consider Norris's explanation for how these ideas emerged and just where they lost their plausibility. He places particular importance on the curious ascendancy of literary theory as a paradigm for other areas of study. There is the bland assumption that because every text involves some kind of narrative interest, therefore there is no way to distinguish factual, historical or documentary material on the one hand from fictive, imaginary or simulated material on the other. With no possible access to truth or historical record, we are asked, Norris shows, to inhabit a realm of unanchored persuasive utterances where rhetoric goes all the way down and where nothing could count as an argument against what the media or governments would have us currently believe.

This re-definition of history finds strange echoes, as Norris notes, among the right wing revisionist historians of the holocaust, 'those for whom it clearly comes as good news that past events can only be interpreted according to present consensus values, or ideas of what currently and contingently counts as "good in the way of belief"' (Norris, 1992: 21). In the case of current events, like the Gulf War, we are left with no resources to deal with the obvious contradictions between official propaganda and personal witness (for example, about the bombing of the Amiriyah civilian air raid shelter). The cult following of these ideas by some intellectuals reflects, as Norris suggests, their lack of desire to make any political judgement, their cynical acquiescence in the war. If the war was so unreal, so completely beyond our competence to judge as informed observers, then we can say nothing to challenge the official (media sponsored) version of events.

My point in raising this example is simple. If the Turkish government can deny that the Armenian genocide happened; if revisionist historians and neo-Nazis deny that the Holocaust took place; if powerful states all around the world today can systematically deny the systematic violations of human rights they are carrying out – then we know that we're in bad shape. But we're in even worse shape when the intellectual *avant garde* invent a form of denial so profound, that serious people – including progressives – will have to debate whether the Gulf War actually took place or not.

Acknowledgement

I promised a more optimistic second footnote. This is not to cheer you up, but just to be honest. Denial has it opposites. What has to be understood are the conditions under which denial does not occur, in which the truth (even if this concept is disappearing down the postmodern black hole) is acknowledged, not just its existence but its moral implications.

After all, in the Milgram experiment, somewhere around 30 per cent of the subjects (depending on the conditions) did not push the button. In Kelman and Hamilton's public opinion surveys, again another 30 per cent would not obey orders to shoot innocent women and children. In the middle of even the most grotesque of state crimes, such as genocide, there are extraordinary tales of courage, rescuing and resistance. Acts of altruism, compassion and pro-social behaviour are woven into the social fabric. Above all, there is the whole human rights movement itself, which over the last three decades has mobilized an extraordinary number of people into wholly selfless behaviour to alleviate the suffering of others – whether by giving money, writing to a prisoner of conscience or joining a campaign.

In my initial interviews with human rights organizations, I was surprised to hear a sense of optimism. Yes, there are some people (referred to in the trade as the 'ostriches') who do not want to know. But most organizations were certain that their potential pool has not been reached. I mentioned to one of my interviewees the cynical notion of 'compassion fatigue' – that people are just too tired to respond, they can't bear seeing any more pictures of the homeless in the streets, victims of AIDS, children starving in Somalia, refugees in Bosnia. Her response was that the concept was a journalistic invention; what there is, is media fatigue.

This is where we return to the state of hyper-reality which postmodernist theories have so well exposed. The question is right open: Will the type of manipulation and simulation seen in the Gulf War dominate, creating indeed a culture of denial? Or can we conceive of a flow of information which will allow people to acknowledge reality and act accordingly?

This might seem a pretentious question for us humble criminologists to consider, but I hope that you will allow me to get away with it.

REFERENCES

Barak, G. (ed.) (1991) *Crimes by the Capitalist State: an Introduction to State Criminality.* Albany: State University of New York Press.

Baudrillard, J. (1991a) 'The Reality Gulf', *Guardian*, 11 January.

Baudrillard, J. (1991b) 'La guerre du Golfe n'a pas eu lieu', *Libération*, 29 March.

Braithwaite, J. and Fisse, B. (1990) 'On the plausibility of corporate crime theory', in W. Laufer and F. Adler (eds), *Advances in Criminological Theory*, vol. II. New Brunswick, NJ: Transaction Books.

Cohen, S. (1991) 'Talking about torture in Israel', *Tikkun*, 6(6): 22–30, 89–90.

Edelstein, E.L. et al. (eds) (1989) *Denial: a Clarification of Concepts and Research*. New York: Plenum Press.

Goleman, D. (1985) *Vital Lies, Simple Truths: On the Psychology of Self Deception*. New York: Simon and Schuster.

Hovanissian, R.G. (ed.) (1986) *The Armenian Genocide in Perspective*. New Brunswick, NJ: Transaction Books.

Karmen, A. (1990) *Crime Victims: an Introduction to Victimology*. Pacific Grove, CA: Brooks Cole.

Kelman, H.C. and Hamilton, V.L. (1989) *Crimes of Obedience*. New Haven, CT: Yale University Press.

Kuper, L. (1981) *Genocide*. Harmondsworth: Penguin Books.

Maran, R. (1989) *Torture: the Role of Ideology in the French-Algerian War*. New York: Praeger.

Muller, I. (1991) *Hitler's Justice: the Courts of the Third Reich*. Cambridge, MA: Harvard University Press.

Norris, C. (1992) *Uncritical Theory: Postmodernism, Intellectuals and the Gulf War*. London: Lawrence and Wishart.

Oliner, S. and Oliner, P. (1988) *The Altruistic Personality: Rescuers of Jews in Nazi Europe*. New York: Free Press.

Schwendinger, H. and Schwendinger, J. (1970) 'Defenders of order or guardians of human rights', *Issues in Criminology*, 7: 72–81.

Sheleff, L. (1978) *The Bystander*, Lexington, MA: Lexington Books.

Steiner, J. (1985) 'Turning a blind eye: the cover up for Oedipus', *International Review of Psycho-Analysis*, 12: 161–72.

Steiner, J. (1990) 'The retreat from truth to omnipotence in Sophocles' Oedipus at Colonus', *International Review of Psycho-Analysis*, 17: 227–37.

Sykes, G. and Matza, D. (1957) 'Techniques of neutralization: a theory of delinquency', *American Sociology Review*, 22: 664–70.

Von Hirsch, A. and Jareborg, N. (1991) 'Gauging criminal harm: a living-standard analysis', *Oxford Journal of Legal Studies*, 11(1): 1–38.

54

Environmental issues and the criminological imagination

Rob White

[...]

BY WAY OF INTRODUCTION: KEY QUESTIONS

Given the pressing nature of many environmental issues, criminologists now view environmental crime and environmental victimization as topics requiring concerted analytic and practical attention (see, for example, Williams, 1996; Halsey, 1997a; South, 1998). Indeed, as a field of sustained research and scholarship, environmental criminology necessarily incorporates a range of theoretical perspectives and strategic emphases. It deals with a wide range of environments (e.g. land, air, water) and issues (e.g. fishing, pollution, toxic waste). It involves conceptual analysis as well as pragmatic intervention on many fronts, and includes multi-disciplinary strategic assessment (e.g. economic, legal, social and ecological evaluations). It involves the undertaking of organizational analysis, as well as the investigation of 'best practice' methods of monitoring, assessment, enforcement and education regarding environmental protection and regulation. Research in this area must also evaluate local, regional, national and global domains and how activities in each overlap.

But environmental criminology also demands more than simply talking about the environment in general and what needs to be done to protect or preserve it. It requires investigating particular trends and issues and, regardless of whether we agree with answers, asking hard questions (see Wright Mills, 1959). More than this, too, investigating environmental issues from a criminological perspective requires an appreciation of how harm is socially and historically constructed. In

From *Theoretical Criminology*, 2003, 7(4): 483–506.

turn, this necessitates understanding and interpreting the structure of a globalizing world; the direction(s) in which this world is heading; and how diverse groups' experiences are shaped by wider social, political and economic processes. Thus this area of criminology is at once basic and exceedingly complex.

On the one hand, what happens in and to our 'natural' and 'built' environments affects us in quite personal ways; what we eat and drink, and the circumstances surrounding how we do so, directly affects our health and well-being. At the same time, far from involving only private matters, these issues raise, in the words of C. Wright Mills questions of 'social structure' (1959: 8). As this article demonstrates through the case study of water, environmental harm occurs on both local and global levels; this harm is linked to major changes now taking place in the international domain. For water, arguably at the centre of life, is at present undergoing social reconstitution, its exchange-value increasingly dominating its use-value; in other words, the commodification of nature needs to be examined (White, 2002). Simultaneously, for criminologists, a critical study of water also raises queries relevant to the larger tasks of criminology itself. First, what exactly is the character, extent and impact of environmental harm? Second, what responses are or should be taken to address such harm? Neither question is simple or straightforward, although this article's goal is to suggest ways of responding to both.

Defining environmental harm

This first question raises problems of definition and explanation. To define what constitutes environmental harm implies a particular philosophical stance on the relationship between human beings and nature. What is 'wrong' or 'right' environmental practice depends on the criteria used to conceptualize the values and interests represented in this relationship, as reflected in anthropocentric, biocentric and ecocentric perspectives (see Halsey and White, 1998). Within the realm of eco-philosophy, numerous competing claims and explanations have been offered about the source of the problem. From overpopulation to industrial model of production, human nature to patriarchy, capitalism to lack of an environmental ethic, myriad reasons have been cited for why environmental degradation occurs.

Meanwhile, in discipline-specific terms, debates still occur about the proper object of criminological attention: how and under what conditions should an act or omission be conceived as environmental 'crime' per se? A strictly legalistic response focuses on the central place of criminal law in defining criminality. Thus, as Situ and Emmons suggest, 'An environmental crime is an unauthorised act or omission that violates the law and is therefore subject to criminal prosecution and criminal sanctions' (2000: 3). However, other writers propose that, as with criminology in general, the concept of 'harm' ought to encapsulate activities that may be legal and 'legitimate' but nonetheless have detrimental impacts on people and environments (Sutherland, 1949; Schwendinger and Schwendinger, 1975).

Within environmental criminology, this broader conceptualization of crime or harm is often deemed essential for evaluating the systemic, as well as particularistic, nature of environmental harm. For example Halsey (1997a, 1997b) identifies social practices that are legal but environmentally disastrous, like the clearfelling of old growth forests. A wider conception of the problem is also vital in developing a critique of existing regulatory measures designed to manage (or, as some argue, to facilitate) harm. For example, Seis (1993) contends that US legislation intended to protect air quality is actually based on counter-ecological principles. As such, this legislation necessarily fails to protect and enhance air quality. The problem is not with the lack of criminal or civil law or enforcement powers, but with anthropocentric assumptions built into the legislation.

Responding to environmental harm

Analysis of responses to environmental harm also takes multiple forms. For instance, one approach is to chart existing environmental legislation and to provide a sustained socio-legal analysis of specific breaches of law, the role of law enforcement agencies and the difficulties and opportunities of using criminal law against environmental offenders (see del Frate and Norberry, 1993; Gunningham et al., 1995; Heine et al., 1997; Situ and Emmons, 2000). For others, the key focus is not criminal sanctions as such, but regulatory strategies that could be utilized to improve environmental performance. Here the main concern is with varying forms of 'responsive regulation' (Ayres and Braithwaite, 1992; Braithwaite, 1993) and 'smart regulation' (Gunningham and Grabosky, 1998). These approaches attempt to recast the state's role by using non-government, and especially private sector, participation and resources in fostering regulatory compliance in relation to the goal of 'sustainable development'. Increasingly important to these discussions is the perceived and potential role of third-party interests, in particular non-government environmental organizations, in influencing policy and practice (Gunningham and Grabosky, 1998; Braithwaite and Drahos, 2000; O'Brien et al., 2000).

Other writers are more sceptical of such perspectives and developments, arguing that key elements of such strategies dovetail with neo-liberal ideologies and practices (especially the trend towards de-regulation of corporate activity) in ways that do not address systemic environmental degradation (White, 1999; Snider, 2000). Furthermore, in terms of restructuring class relationships on a global scale, reforms in environmental management and regulation are perceived as closely linked with efforts made by transnational corporations to further their hegemonic control over the planet's natural resources (see Goldman, 1998a, 1998b; Pearce and Tombs, 1998; White, 2002). In this type of analysis, political struggle and the contest over class power is viewed as central to any discussion of environmental issues. Issues of gender, ethnicity and race are important to these discussions as well, but are incorporated into a specifically ecosocialist understanding of capitalism and nature (see Pepper, 1993; O'Connor, 1994).

Whether at the level of definition or redress, then, discussions of environmental harm have an onion-like character. There are layers of complexity to unpeel, and important ideological differences that emerge over whether the core of the system is worth preserving or beyond redemption. Consequently, themes of analytical complexity and value judgement are central to this discussion. While trying to incorporate these themes, the next section of the article briefly describes recent developments pertaining to the use and management of drinking water. This analysis is by no means definitive or comprehensive. My intention is merely to survey this issue for illustrative purposes, rather than to provide an in-depth investigation. Last, I consider conceptual and political implications arising from these matters. Here, political economy and issues of environmental justice, corporate interests, strategic action and social power are key to showing how harm can be defined in relation to water and struggles over water as a resource.

DRINKING WATER

Water is vital to human life. Yet thousands of human lives are lost each day, week and month due to inadequate supply and the poor quality of drinking water in many parts of the world. Clear social and environmental harms are associated with existing practices related to the production, consumption and management of fresh water reserves. As such, what we drink, and the conditions under which we drink, is a topic deserving the close attention of environmentally oriented criminologists.

The trend towards water market privatization

In recent years, drinking water has been increasingly valued for its 'exchange-value' rather than 'use-value': it is not the usefulness of water that counts but its saleability as a commodity. Key international organizations, including the World Bank, the International Monetary Fund and the World Trade Organization, have fostered this concept of water as an economic resource. More specifically, such thinking has been actively promoted by organizations like the World Water Council (a platform for major water firms), the Global Water Partnership (initiated by senior World Bank staff) and Business Partners for Development (an industry/World Bank promoter of privatization). The protection of this natural resource on behalf of private companies is presently sought through the extension of corporate bill-of-rights protection to water (as well as education, health services and utilities) via the General Agreement on Trade in Services (GATS) currently being negotiated through the World Trade Organization. Such neo-liberal 'free trade' provisions are intended precisely to allow the commodification of an ever-growing range of goods and services (many of which are essential to human well-being) and to facilitate the entry of private sector interests into previously state-owned and state-regulated spheres.

The financial attraction of privatizing and commodifying drinking water is perfectly understandable. First, it is obviously a basic requirement of human life; water is always needed and, therefore, marketable. Second, restricted quantities of clean water make it a particularly valuable property for those who own and control it. For example, the global consumption of water is doubling every 20 years, more than twice the rate of human population growth. According to the United Nations, more than 1 billion people on earth already lack access to fresh drinking water. If the current trends persist, by 2025, the demand for fresh water is expected to rise by 56 per cent more than is available at present (Hausman et al., 2001). The actual scarcity of fresh, clean water means that there are lucrative profits to be made by privatizing water (and water-intensive industries), and delivering it only to those who can pay for it.

The role of the World Bank and the International Monetary Fund has been crucial to the processes of commodification and privatization of drinking water (see South African Municipal Workers Union, 2001). Thus, for example, water privatization and full cost recovery policies have been imposed as conditions for IMF loans in more than 12 African countries (such as Angola, Benin, Guinea-Bissau, Niger, Rwanda, Sao Tome, Senegal and Tanzania). The result has been that water is now less accessible and less affordable and that, in some cases, people are resorting to unsafe water sources. In Ghana, to take one example, 'the results of forcing the poor to pay "market rate tariffs" for water means that most people can no longer afford water at all. Only 36 per cent of the rural population have access to safe water and just 11 per cent have adequate sanitation within the existing system' (SAMWU, 2001: 22). It was the local World Bank resident representative in Ghana who actively pushed for the leasing, over 10–25 years, of two large urban water systems to supply several million residents; five multinational corporations bid for the contracts (Bond, 2001a). Good quality water is consequently being sold on the basis of 'willingness to pay' rather than 'ability to pay'.

Similar stories are told about countries like Angola, where there is an agreement that water prices should rise regularly so that the company delivering water can make a 'reasonable' profit (SAMWU, 2001). Over a two-year period in Chile, the two most important water plants were sold to private interests and then resold at higher prices (Hall, 1999). Closer to home for this author, similar developments regarding water have occurred in Australia. For example, the Sydney Water Board was corporatized by the New South Wales (state) government in the early 1990s. This led to a markedly different environment for water supply and maintenance. As Archer explains:

> The main function of the old Water Board was to manage Sydney's massive water supply system on behalf of its citizens; to make sure there would be enough for the future while keeping a watchful eye on water quality and things of that nature ... Its principal responsibility to the people of Sydney was to provide safe drinking water. The new Sydney Water Corporation [created in 1993] was given more important things to do. Its first priority was not the provision of safe water, its first priority was profit. In common with all corporations its number one objective was to make money. That remains the fundamental operating principle of Sydney Water even after the catastrophe that occurred in July, August, and September of 1998.
>
> (1998: 22)

In order of priority, the duties of the Managing Director are described as being running a successful business, protecting the environment in its operations and promoting public health by supplying safe drinking water.

Corporatization – that is, the management of state agencies and bodies as for-profit institutions – is frequently linked to the future privatization of such bodies or, at the least, to the farming out of selected operational activities to private sector businesses. This is happening with drinking water as it is with other goods and services such as telephone services, electricity grids, banking services, health services and education. For instance, the corporatization of Sydney Water also included the 'out-sourcing' of four water treatment plants to private operators.

Privatized water concessions have sprung up in cities on every continent (see Hall, 1999). In every region of the world, the great majority of these concessions are run by one of the two biggest French groups – Vivendi (previously known as Generales des Eaux) and Suez-Lyonnaise (SLE) – with a smaller number, particularly in Africa, run by the third French group SAUR. SLE is the largest water company in the world outside France, while Vivendi is larger inside France. SLE has bought into US water resources companies, and water treatment companies in the USA, Chile, Italy and Germany. There are a smaller number of water concessions held by one of the UK companies – Thames Water, Anglian Water, United Utilities – but they lag behind the French transnational water companies in market dominance (Hall, 1999). While there are at least nine internationally active water companies in the world market, effectively only four or five control the bulk of water contracts (Public Services Privatization Research Unit, 1996). According to Vivendi projections on the future extent of privatization, the company believes that in 2010, over 80 per cent of water will still be in public sector hands in Asia, the USA and central and eastern Europe, and about 65 per cent of western Europe and Africa. Only in Latin America will the public sector share dip below 50 per cent (Hall, 1999). In Australia, the water corporations recently joined together to form the Water Services Association of Australia in order to consolidate their authority and power. Collectively, the Association members now exercise control over 80 per cent of Australia's water supplies (Archer, 2001). The track record of these transnational water companies is less than impressive. For example, they have been implicated in bribery scandals, price gouging and supply of poor quality water (see Public Services Privatization Research Unit, 1996; Vassilopoulos, 1998a: 13).

Service and quality issues

According to the South African Municipal Workers Union (2001), more than 5 million people, most of them children, die each year from illnesses caused from drinking poor quality water. In many countries around the world, developed and less developed, there have been major outbreaks of disease. A few illustrative examples follow.

South Africa

The impoverished township of Alexandra (near Johannesburg) is home to an estimated 300,000 people crammed into about five square kilometres of mainly squalid housing. In January 2001, there was an outbreak of cholera spread by the

Jukskei River that cuts through the township. As part of a national epidemic, deaths were reported in four of South Africa's nine provinces. The reason for this is that nearly seven years after the formal end of racial apartheid, most South Africans still had to rely upon untreated water. At the epidemic's epicentre in deep rural KwaZulu-Natal, the outbreak was preceded by destitute people, who could not afford the US$7 connection fee, having their piped water cut off. For the 17 years before, water had been supplied free by the apartheid regime (Bond, 2001b).

USA

The US Centre for Disease Control and Prevention revealed that in 1993 more than a million people in the USA became ill and 900 died from drinking contaminated water (Archer, 1998). In April 1993, 400,000 residents of Milwaukee, Wisconsin, fell ill with waterborne cryptosporidiosis, the gastroenteric disorder caused by Cryptosporidium which passed undetected through the city's modern water treatment plant (Archer, 1998). Yet, in 2001, US President George W. Bush cancelled a health regulation that would have reduced allowable levels of arsenic in US drinking water from 50 parts per billion (ppb) to 10 ppb. In 1993, the World Health Organization set 10 ppb as the recommendation limit for arsenic in drinking water. The European Union adopted 10 ppb as a mandatory standard for arsenic in drinking water in 1998. The (US) Environmental Protection Agency estimated that cutting allowable arsenic from 50 to 10 ppb would prevent 1000 bladder cancers and 2000 to 5000 lung cancers during a human lifetime (Massey, 2001).

Canada

In 2000, seven people died and 2700 were poisoned in the town of Walkerton, Ontario. This has been blamed on privatization of testing, in which the town's water testing for Escherichia coli was outsourced to a local firm that failed to do the testing (Bond and Bakker, 2001). What happened in Walkerton has been directly linked to government efforts to slash red tape in areas such as environmental protection through active endorsement of deregulation (see Snider, 2002). In British Columbia, in 1996, there were more than 12,000 cases of water-borne illnesses caused by Cryptosporidium associated with human activities and livestock (Archer, 1998).

Australia

In a report commissioned by Sydney Water in 1992, consultants Dwyer Leslie 'conservatively' estimated that, as a direct result of 'current water quality', Sydney consumers experienced 'continuously occurring events' which caused 'between 4280 and 13,780 illness days per year; and 100 deaths per year' (Archer, 1998: 10). On three separate occasions in 1998, more than 3 million Sydney residents were forced to boil their water before drinking it due to the detection of the parasitic protozoa, Cryptosporidium and Giardia, to levels considered to be a health hazard to whomever drank it (White, 1998). In the state of Victoria, a 1994 government study of country water supplies reported that more than 700,000 consumers were drinking polluted water. 'More than two-thirds of Victorians are supplied with water that does not meet basic health guidelines', the report said (Archer, 1996: 16).

Many of these incidents and events were preventable. In most cases they are attributable to changes in the tariffs placed upon drinking water (issues of access and affordability); changes in the philosophy of water management (from public need to commercial profitability); changes in operational practices (linked to corporatization and privatization, and away from structures that allow greater public scrutiny and accountability); and changes in quality control practices. Privatization is often accompanied by loss of jobs in the water services industry and increases in prices. For example, this is precisely what happened in the case of the corporatization of Sydney Water (see Vassilopoulos, 1998b). Thus the shift in service orientation of the major provider of water (towards commercial interests), coupled with the privatization of specific functions (again, involving commercial considerations), had immediate ramifications on the service produced.

   Another dimension to issues surrounding water supply is that of the relationship of alternative markets to the main water market. For instance, a water crisis may engender a shift among a proportion of the captive market to pursue alternative sources of clean water. For those who have the capacity to pay, it is possible to buy bottled water, another form of water commodity that is itself a source of profit for the companies involved (see Archer, 1996, 2001). Even in relatively advantaged market circumstances, it is therefore possible that a segment of the buying population will turn away from the main provider. The demand in this case is fostered by the lack of apparent quality of the mass-provided commodity. It also hinges on the ability, and perceived necessity, of a substantial number of people to purchase their commodity (which they buy for its use-value) via other means. In this regard, note that Vivendi bought US Filter for over $6 billion in April 1999, giving the former a major presence in water-related products, including bottled water, and also a strong position for expansion into municipal utility services of water supply and sewerage. This also strengthened Vivendi's position in other markets, including bottled water in Latin America (Hall, 1999).

Political resistance

Despite these trends, commodification of drinking water and the privatization of its ownership has encountered resistance. For instance, in the South African township of Mpumalanga, near Durban, local residents engaged in concerted struggles against recent water initiatives. Residents are now required to pay a flat-rate for their water services. Durban UniCity has tried to attach water meters to each private pipe and to charge for water from public taps. In response, 'the Mpumalanga community reacted with a vengeance, ripping up meters and chasing the contractors away. Running battles were fought with police' (Bohmke, 2001: 22). In April 2001 the new UniCity council began installing water meters once more:

> Again residents have resisted fiercely, ripping up the water meters. Ten thousand peo-
> ple have attended rallies; the speeches are hot and the demand steadfast: free essen-
> tial services for the poor. But the repression has also been harsher than ever. The army
> has been called in and meetings have been 'banned'.

> (Bohmke, 2001: 22)

Interestingly, the leaders of this 'resistance' include former foes: a former activist with the ANC and a former member of the Inkatha Freedom Party.

State repression against water protesters has occurred in other parts of South Africa, too. On 26 September 2001, police opened fire on protesting residents in Tafelsig, Cape Town, who had mobilized to prevent 1800 households' water supplies being cut off by the Cape Town UniCity council. Most people affected by the water cuts were unemployed, pensioners or disabled; therefore, they could not afford to pay the more than R400 (A$100) to have their water reconnected. They would have had to pay an additional meter reconnection penalty of R125 (Dixon, 2001).

Resistance in Ghana has grown more organized, surfacing in the formation of the Ghana National Coalition Against the Privatization of Water in 2001. The CAP is campaigning to ensure that the right to water is explicitly guaranteed under the constitution, and that the ownership, control and management of water services stay in public hands (Vanderpuye, 2001). Perhaps they could take heart from events in Bolivia, where consumers and union leaders halted a World Bank-prescribed water privatization project. These protests culminated in an eight-day blockade and state of siege in April 2000 that claimed at least six lives before the Bolivian government was forced to cancel the deal. The protests began in response to stiff price hikes, with families earning the minimum wage of less than US$100 per month faced with water bills of $20 or more (Shallat, 2001).

Public concern about drinking water issues has led some jurisdictions explicitly to consider new regulatory initiatives. For example, in the Canadian province of British Columbia, a recent government report outlines a series of measures meant to reassure the public that something will be done to address public fears (Government of British Columbia, 2001). Among other things, these include the setting of state/region-wide and/or site-specific standards for drinking water sources (e.g. to include maximum allowable levels for specified substances that cannot be readily removed by conventional water treatments), and the stronger enforcement of Safe Drinking Water Regulations (including minimum standards for tap water quality monitoring and public reporting by water providers). It is clear that unease among the public at large over reported incidents of water contamination, with resultant deaths and illness, have forced some governments to reconsider the regulatory and policy framework under which water services are provided. The official inquiry into the contamination of the water supply in Walkerton was followed by a second inquiry into the safety of Ontario's drinking water generally. A key finding of the first inquiry was that re-regulation (but not necessarily public ownership of collective resources) is the remedy, and that deregulation and downsizing had gone too far (see Snider, 2002). In the end the actual extent of government intervention, and the enforcement of quality and service standards, is an empirical question warranting further evaluation. On a conceptual level, though, it is more than apparent that issues of regulation cannot be divorced from the central questions of ownership, control, management and private/public sector involvement.

THEMES AND ISSUES FOR ENVIRONMENTAL CRIMINOLOGY

One cannot take a specific environmental issue and expect that, on its own, it will encapsulate every aspect of criminological theory and practice. Nevertheless the example of drinking water provides an entry point for developing an analytic framework that is conceptually generic, beginning to address trends and issues evident when studying other examples relevant to environmental criminology as well.

Environmental justice

Analysis of environmental issues proceeds from the assumption that, indeed, someone or something has been harmed. In this regard, a distinction is sometimes made between 'environmental justice' and 'ecological justice'. Environmental justice refers to the distribution of environments among peoples (Low and Gleeson, 1998) and the impacts of particular social practices on specific populations. The focus of analysis is on human health and well-being, and on how these are affected by particular types of production and consumption. Here we can distinguish between environmental issues that affect everyone, and those which disproportionately affect specific individuals and groups (see Williams, 1996). Again, water is a basic human requirement; people who have been affected by poor water quality in the advanced capitalist countries represent a broad cross-section of the population. In this sense, the periodic water crises are non-discriminatory in terms of class, gender, ethnicity and other social factors. This creates a basic 'equality of victims' since environmental problems – among them ozone depletion, global warming, air pollution and acid rain (Beck, 1996) – threaten everyone in the same way.

Nevertheless, as discussion of water management in South Africa and other African nation-states demonstrates, some people are more likely than others to be disadvantaged in gaining access to quality water. In this instance, capacity to pay for water services or bottled drinking water creates and reflects significant social differences in how people relate to their environments. Often, particular class differences are intertwined with ethnic or 'race' differences as well. It is poor people of colour, rather than 'white' people (regardless of income), who are likely to suffer from bad water quality and services, in part due to their location in particular 'black' neighbourhoods (as opposed to 'white' suburbs). Thus patterns of 'differential victimization' are evident with respect to the siting of toxic waste dumps, extreme air pollution and access to safe clean drinking water, among other manifestations of this problem.

Another dimension of differential victimization relates to the subjective disposition and consciousness of people involved. Specific groups who experience environmental problems may not always describe or see the issues in strictly environmental terms (see, for examples, Williams, 1996). The unequal distribution of exposure to environmental risks, whether this involves the location of toxic waste sites or proximity to clean drinking water, may not always be conceived as an 'environmental' issue or 'problem'. For instance, Harvey (1996) points out that overlapping poverty, racism and desperation occasionally leads to situations where, for the sake of jobs and economic development, community leaders actively solicit the relocation of hazardous industries or waste sites to their neighbourhoods.

Ecological justice

Ecological justice refers to the relationship of human beings, more generally, to the rest of the natural world. Here, analysis concentrates on the health of the biosphere, especially on plants and creatures that inhabit the biosphere (see Benton, 1998; Franklin, 1999). The main concern is with the quality of the planetary environment (frequently envisioned as having its own intrinsic value) and the rights of other species, particularly animals, to life free from torture, abuse and destruction of habitat. Insofar as poor quality drinking water, and diminished clean water resources, are attributable to social practices like disposal of agricultural, urban and industrial effluents into water catchments and river systems, not only humans are affected. Indeed local natural environments, and non-human inhabitants of both wilderness and built environments, can be harmed by human practices that destroy, re-channel or pollute existing fresh water systems. Thus how humans interact with particular environments presents immediate and potential risks to everything within them. For example, the practice of clear-felling old growth forests directly affects many animal species by destroying their homes (see Halsey, 1997b).

Commodification of nature

None of this is politically neutral: often 'choices' that result in environmental victimization of human beings and animals stem from systemic imperatives to exploit the planetary environment through commodification. In other words, how human beings produce, consume and reproduce themselves is socially patterned in ways that are dominated by global corporate interests (see Athanasiou, 1996; Beder,

1997; White, 2002). And, thus, the privatization of water services illustrated above suggests both the dominance of neo-liberal ideology as a guiding rationale for further commodification of nature, and the concentration of decision making in state bureaucracies and transnational corporate hands. Overseeing this transfer from public to private sectors, and from conceptions of public need and account-ability to notions of commercial viability and confidentiality, are institutions of global capitalist governance like the World Trade Organization, the World Bank and the International Monetary Fund (Goldman, 1998a). Yet not all environmental harm or crime is perpetrated by the 'big players' (corporations, nation-states, mul-tilateral economic institutions). Personal practices at an individual level can also be harmful (such as inappropriate disposal of left-over house paint). But, structurally, the most harmful forms of environmental destruction and degradation are clearly linked to those with the power to generalize such activity across wide geographi-cal expanses and human domains.

The commodification and transformation of nature into a specifically capital-ist nature (O'Connor, 1994) simultaneously involves the exploitation of human beings as workers and consumers. In the example of drinking water, the profit-motive is inextricably linked to preoccupation with ways to make the 'produc-tion' process more efficient. This can be achieved by reducing the size of the water services workforce, increasing its productivity and manipulating wages, conditions and hours of work to best suit companies. It means putting more money into public relations and advertising, and less into maintenance, research and workplace improvements (see Archer, 1998, 2001). Meanwhile, citizens and residents are treated as 'clients' who will only receive the service if they pay for it and accept the terms of the contract underpinning the sale of the commodity. The obligation is on the consumer to adhere to the prescriptions of the provider; the primary accountability of the company is to its shareholders.

Production and consumption practices are socially constructed, and ultimately this occurs through the machinations and lens of the dominant classes. For exam-ple, work- and home-related pressures (both material and cultural) reinforce reli-ance on capitalistically produced consumer goods and services like pre-cooked meals, ready-made clothes, bottled water; in other times, these goods would have been produced by family members themselves (see White, 2002). Thus the power of capitalist hegemony manifests itself through certain forms of production and consumption becoming part of a taken-for-granted commonsense. The transition from one kind of consumption (such as provision of drinking water on the basis of need and use-value) to another kind of consumption (drinking water supplied on the basis of capacity to pay and exchange-value) may involve disruption and social unease since it challenges what came before. Hence, concerted campaigns surface materially to prepare the ground for commodification of water (e.g. by running down state-owned services prior to sale) and ideologically to sell the idea (e.g. through propaganda regarding the advantages of 'free trade' in services, or talk of WTO agreements over which individual nation-states ostensibly have little control). Environmental and ecological injustices are rationalized as the way things have to be in the new globalized system of trade and governance. Dissent may be tolerated, but only insofar as it does not challenge the core imperatives for economic growth, nor the generalized power of transnational capital to set the agenda.

From the point of view of environmental criminology, analysis of the nature of environmental harm has to encompass both objective and subjective dimensions of victimization (see Williams, 1996). It also has to locate the processes of environmental victimization within the context of the wider political economy. That is, the dynamics of environmental harm cannot be understood apart from consideration of who has the power to make decisions, the kinds of decisions that are made, in whose interests they are made and how social practices based on these decisions are materially organized. As demonstrated above, issues of power and control also have to be analysed in light of global economic, social and political developments.

ENVIRONMENTAL REGULATION AND PREVENTION OF HARM

But what is to be done? Writings on this subject have approached environmental regulation, and the prevention of environmental harm, in the following ways. For one thing, interest has burgeoned in the area of corporate regulation (see, for example, Haines, 1997; Braithwaite and Drahos, 2000). At a theoretical level, much of this 'regulation' literature presents regulation on a continuum from direct control by the state through voluntary compliance on the part of companies and individuals. One suggested model of regulation is based on the notion of a regulatory pyramid, with persuasion the favoured approach at the base moving to coercion at the pinnacle (Ayres and Braithwaite, 1992; Grabosky, 1994, 1995). Fundamentally, the argument has been that the most effective regulatory regime is one that combines a range of measures; most of these measures presume that targeted institutions and groups are interested in participating or complying (see Braithwaite, 1993; Gunningham and Grabosky, 1998).

In contrast to approaches that highlight notions like effectiveness, efficiency and 'win/win' regulatory strategies, other writers have examined the nature of regulatory trends in recent decades through the lens of class analysis. For instance, when it comes to corporate harm and wrongdoing, a broad tendency under neo-liberalism towards deregulation (or, as a variation of this, 'self-regulation') has lately been noted. On the other hand, surveillance and use of harsher punitive measures in the case of conventional street crimes have intensified (see White, 1999; Snider, 2000). The first represents a major retreat of the state in the area of corporate regulation, while the second suggests a major offensive against the working class, poor people and people of ethnic minority backgrounds, especially young marginalized people. Importantly, the shift away from use of coercion in the area of corporate regulation has severe ramifications for those touting the pyramid regulatory theories: the pyramid only 'works' if there is the possibility, and reality, of hard-edged sanctions at the top. If these do not exist, by definition, the pyramid loses regulatory effectiveness.

Capitalism, the state and neo-liberalism

When it comes to environmental regulation, and even if only through the absence of state intervention, the role of government remains central. Again, the general trend at present has been away from direct governmental regulation towards 'softer' regulatory approaches. For example, Snider (2000) describes that in Canada, despite policy directives specifying 'strict compliance', a permissive philosophy of 'compliance promotion' has reigned. Given that mainstream regulation literature offers a theoretical justification for enlisting private interests through incentives and inducements, it is not surprising that persuasion is favoured at a practical level. But, more than seeing this as simply a reflection of a new regulatory ideology, it is essential to consider the financial and political environment within which regulators are forced to work. For example, while never before in history have there been so many laws pertaining to the environment, it is rare indeed to find extensive government money, resources and personnel put into enforcement and compliance activities. Rather, such monies are usually put in the service of large corporations as a form of state welfare designed to facilitate and enhance the business climate and specific corporate interests.

The extensive links between capital and the state are manifest in overlapping financial and ideological agendas regarding the privatization and commodification of nature. The translation of social and environmental problems into economic and legal issues has meant that state action depends on a combination of political and jurisprudential considerations. For instance, governments that are materially and ideologically supportive of corporatization and privatization tend to avoid undermining these processes by intervening heavily in private corporate affairs. Neo-liberalism is oriented precisely towards less, rather than more, government regulation of corporate activity. This process has recently accelerated since governments are trying to attract and be on good terms with international capital so as to boost local investment and commodity production.

But what happens when specific cases of environmental harm become so apparent that, politically, they cannot simply be ignored? Once a problem like the Sydney water crisis has been identified, the conditions of privatization themselves can serve to deflect action away from dealing adequately with the problem's source. Thus, for example, appeals to 'commercial confidentiality' may appear as a way to evade close public scrutiny of operational practices and financial arrangements. Moreover, specific contractual conditions may open the door to protracted litigation over who is responsible for which facet of the production process, and who is responsible for the overall maintenance and improvement in water quality (versus those who simply operate the installations). In the end, the prosecution of selected individuals and corporations on specific offences tends to be the exception that makes the rule. Specific instances of environmental harm, as in the case of water quality issues, are subject to myriad legal considerations ranging from the nature of commercial contracts through to criminal responsibility. And, of course, the legal system is a strategic arena in which capital is particularly adept at defending its interests.

Defending corporate interests

The corporate arsenal not only includes positive state action on behalf of selected business interests (via welfare handouts such as tax incentives, and through mobilization of police protection of property that enables profit making to occur, as with the installation of water meters). It also includes particular uses of the law as an offensive weapon. For instance, civil court action by companies in the form of what has been described as 'Strategic Lawsuits Against Public Participation' (SLAPPs) have been directed against environmentalists, individual citizens and community groups. The point of such suits is not to 'win' in the conventional legal sense, but to intimidate those who might be critical of existing or proposed developments (see Beder, 1997). If they cannot be criminalized, at least environmentalists can be sued. Either way, the point is to de-legitimate and to silence the critics of both state and capitalist economic agendas.

At the centre of changes in environmental regulation has been a movement towards 'corporate ownership' of the definitions, and responses to, environmental problems. Again, this has taken different forms. One sort of response has been concerted efforts to 'greenwash' environmental issues. This has involved the spending of billions of dollars on public relations and advertising to portray companies as essentially environmentally benign (see Athanasiou, 1996; Beder, 1997; Hager & Burton, 1999). The activities of international financial institutions like the World Bank (as well as individual firms and companies) are re-dressed in ways that convey the message that 'sustainable development' is happening, and that global power-brokers are doing what needs to be done to protect the environment. This belies actual environmental harms perpetrated by many of these institutions and by specific businesses that, cumulatively, are doing great damage to the global environment. It also ignores the cumulative effect of practices that ensue from the logic of economic growth, expanded consumption of resources and the further commodification of nature (as in the example of drinking water).

Another type of response has been to adopt the language of 'environmental management systems' (EMS) and to assert that regulation is best provided by those industries and companies directly involved in production processes. This occurs at both particular firm levels and when it comes to the setting of international standards for environmental management. EMS has various dimensions including environmental valuation and risk analysis, product design, corporate culture and environmental awareness, and supply and waste chain management (see Kirkland and Thompson, 1999). For my purposes here, though, the crucial point is that, while EMS is seen by some (especially proponents of 'smart regulation' strategies) as progressive and a positive step forward in environmental regulation, embedded in EMS ideology are several assumptions that imply 'more of the same' rather than system transformation. For example, Levy (1997) observes that EMS does address some of the worst environmental excesses (i.e. real material consequences of production practices in specific cases). But he argues that on ideological and symbolic levels, EMS serves primarily to construct products and companies as 'green' and to legitimize corporate management as the primary societal agent responsible for addressing environmental issues. Consequently, decisions to adopt EMS can be seen as part of a political, practical and ideological response to the threat to corporate hegemony posed by environmental movements.

The key message of EMS is that corporations have the 'know-how', through technical means and managerial strategies, best to protect the environment. As Levy (1997) points out, and as echoed in the 'smart regulation' literature (see Gunningham and Grabosky, 1998), EMS is presented as a win–win opportunity in which the potential structural conflicts between profit maximization and environmental goals are avoided. This provides yet another cover to circumvent governmental regulation; at the same time, the supposed benefits of EMS have not been demonstrated empirically. Yet much the same has been argued, optimistically, about the 'standards' put forward by the International Organization for Standardization (ISO). The 'ISO 14000', concerning environmental impacts, is a private sector initiative that allows for the state to divulge itself of regulatory functions; simultaneously, this initiative removes regulation and standards-setting from democratic participation, putting these beyond the reach of citizens and social movements (Wall and Beardwood, 2001). From this, it becomes apparent that issues of who or what regulates, and who controls the process, are central to any discussion of how best to respond to environmental harm.

STRUGGLES OVER THE GLOBAL COMMONS

I have argued that the overall direction of movement on environmental issues requires understanding the strategic location and activities of transnational capital as supported by hegemonic nation-states on a world scale. At the same time, informed analyses of political economy also open the door to identifying strategic sites for protest on the part of those fighting for environmental and ecological justice.

Different levels of analysis

Capitalist globalization, bolstered via neo-liberal state policy, has increased the potential scope of environmentally destructive activities. Nevertheless, different fractions of capital have divergent orientations to the environment depending on their market focus – for example, public relations firms, newly emerging environmental protection industries and/or forestry companies. International competition among capitalist sectors and among communities for access to healthy resources, including clean water, has also intensified because the natural resource base has shrunk. In this competition, the dominance of western capital has been sustained partly through 'environmental regulation' itself; ironically, this has sometimes been used as an entry card to new international markets. For example, markets may be protected through universalizing environmental regulation (developed in and by the private sector, and later enforced by governments in the form of preferred contracts, and business legal requirements) that themselves advantage the high-technology companies of the advanced industrialized countries (Goldman, 1998a, 1998b). The largest companies are most likely to be capable of being environmentally 'virtuous'; they also have disproportionate influence when it comes to redesigning the rules of international standardization through environmental management (see also Haines, 2000).

In addition, it has been argued that the cleaning up of old dirty industries and the re-writing of property laws in accordance with new international standards of environmental management and trade liberalization (particularly in the Third World, and Russia) is a precursor to capitalist penetration and exploitation of nature (Goldman, 1998a). To see environmental regulation in this light is to acknowledge the economic rather than ecological rationale behind the actions of global regulatory bodies like the WTO, IMF and World Bank. The undemocratic character of these institutions stems in part from the fact that 'regulation', in this instance, is about facilitation of the exploitation of nature and human beings, not about human interests and needs. Ultimately the appeal of 'smart regulation', which has found corporate expression in EMS and other global remedies like ISO 14000, lies in adhering to an 'ecological modernization' framework that represents economic and environmental interests as compatible. This is represented as a needed step beyond the 'standard view' of environmental management (see Harvey, 1996) that has proved to be woefully and obviously inadequate to address environmental problems, especially where scientific and popular concerns can no longer be ignored or avoided. But, in practice, the emphasis remains on efficiency and effectiveness and the outcome ensures corporate sector 'ownership' of environmental responses.

In light of these developments, it is important that environmental criminology analyse issues of definition of harm and of regulation at different levels of abstraction. A specific firm, industry or event can be examined relative to various proactive and reactive measures put into place either to forestall environmental harm or to minimize negative publicity in relation to such harm. Investigation also must target broader political economic developments like the appropriation of natural resources and specific market opportunities, and the systemic consequences of neo-liberal policies and practices for environmental protection and preservation.

Both in terms of definitions of harm and responses to harm, then, further critical work is needed to unpack the material and ideological implications of the entrenchment of particular management models like EMS. Specifically, we need to examine their applications at local and global levels and how they serve to reinforce private sector control over regulatory and management processes. We also need to be wary of how the disappearance of criminality and coercion in regard to environmental regulation, and the trend towards favouring persuasive, self-regulating and co-operative strategies, also entails an ideological shift from environmental and social harm to enhanced 'environmentally friendly' production. Such enhancements collectively degrade the global ecological commons.

However, acts of destruction and discourses of absolution themselves generate counter-hegemonic resistance, sometimes in unlikely places. For instance,

Snider (2002) describes how the inquiry into water issues in Ontario gave voice to opposing groups and thus to alternative ways of seeing and understanding the issues. The inquiry strengthened some voices of resistance and exposed the threats to social life posed by neo-liberalism. While not transformative in its recommendations (calls for fundamental change, i.e. public ownership, were not on the agenda), this case did present a progressive opening for reasserting public accountability in relation to essential services.

On another front, it is important to expose the track record of environmental vandals as part of a larger public accountability process. This can be done in relation to specific practices, as in the case of companies supplying poor or contaminated water. It can also be achieved by highlighting the overall negative practices and reputation of a particular company. Thus, for example, shares in Vivendi International plunged on the stock market in July 2002, due to concerns about its accounting practices and the downgrading of its bonds to 'junk' status by the credit-rating agency Moody's. But this downfall itself resulted from exposing efforts made by Vivendi's chief executive to spend US$100 billion transforming a water utility into a rival of huge telecommunications groups like AOL Time Warner.

Different types of strategic action

The quest for environmental and ecological justice requires reacting against undemocratic decision making locally and globally, as well as against the imposition of a global capitalist economic agenda. Of necessity, resistance to the systemic forces that underpin global environmental destruction is fraught with difficulties, tensions and divisions. Furthermore the core philosophies, ideologies, policies and organizational structures of community groups and environmental movements vary greatly. For instance, green movements diverge over choices of tactics and strategies; goals and objectives; key philosophy; and concepts of environmental problems themselves. Simultaneously proposed solutions range from individualistic approaches urging spiritual change through to calls for collective action. Specific group orientations include 'soft green' approaches supportive of sustainable development through 'hard green' approaches calling for ecological sustainability. Thus major political issues divide a broad spectrum of green movements, affecting whether action will be taken in collaboration with or against capitalist institutions (see, for example, Goldman, 1998b). This means that not only capitalist institutions but processes of reform and transformation (involving complicated questions of legislative change, and legal and illegal forms of activism) demand critical investigation by environmental criminologists.

Not coincidentally, those who wish to protest aspects of government policy or companies that do damage to the environment are increasingly likely to be dealt with under state public order provisions that show zero tolerance for street activism as well as street crime. Political dissent itself has been subject to a process of criminalization through myriad laws intended to curb 'anti-social behaviour' in public spaces. As illustrated by the case of South African demonstrators protesting water commodification, the coercive apparatus of the state is frequently directed at those who wish to protect environments, rather than at those who control and degrade them. A major concern for environmental criminologists should be the rise in paramilitary policing directed against popular movements (see, for example, McCulloch, 2001). How and under what circumstances environmental issues are fought often implicates the state in maintaining dominant institutional arrangements. Of course, the criminal justice system has no small role to play in this process (see Haines, 2000).

In the post-11 September 2001 world, is it even possible that the 'war on terrorism' will bring state mobilization against environmental activists? This may happen through granting enhanced police powers for surveillance and intervention, and through renewed political acceptability for closely monitoring 'suspect' individuals. Given that green propaganda and activity is sometimes directed against specific corporations, including transnational water companies, might this, too, become newly defined as somehow 'terrorist'? Meanwhile, wider-ranging questions need to be asked about the state's role in privately owned or run essential services like water utilities that may be the target of future terrorist attempts. In sum, public interest and protection must be linked with public ownership and accountability.

CONCLUSION

This article raised numerous concerns relevant to environmental criminology. Fundamentally, I have been arguing that criminologists need to examine these issues in ways that incorporate the growing complexity and multi-dimensionality of this area. By way of illustration, I used a case in point of drinking water. This is an issue that, while apparently straightforward, actually entails layers of ambiguity and contestation. Thus, water can be used to demonstrate the range of considerations that need to be taken into account when investigating other specific issues, too, that involve defining and responding to environmental harm.

I also reviewed environmental actions and resistance, both from the perspective of corporate and state sectors and from that of green activists. Here, again, it is essential critically to scrutinize developments from multidimensional and often complicated angles to discern when 'reform' means managing rather than redressing problems, and when democratic participation becomes simultaneous occasions for demonization and criminalization.

Finally, despite the use of coercive measures, ideological campaigns and efforts to co-opt and divide environmental movements, it is clear that ordinary people continue to react against environmental degradation in their lives, whether toxic waste, oil spills and/or bad drinking water. Clever corporate greenwashing and the hesitancy of nation-states to limit corporate interests cannot hide the material basis of continuing protests against environmental destruction. Most relevant here, though, is that our criminological imagination contribute to these struggles by rethinking how new global relationships can diagnose, deter, prevent – and indeed, sometimes criminalize – ongoing environmental harms.

REFERENCES

Archer, J. (1996) *The Water You Drink: How Safe Is It?* Sydney: Pure Water Press.

Archer, J. (1998) *Sydney on Tap*. Sydney: Pure Water Press.

Archer, J. (2001) *Australia's Drinking Water: The Coming Crisis*. Sydney: Pure Water Press.

Athanasiou, T. (1996) *Divided Planet: The Ecology of Rich and Poor*. Boston, MA: Little, Brown & Company.

Ayres, I. and J. Braithwaite (1992) *Responsive Regulation: Transcending the Deregulation Debate*. New York: Oxford University Press.

Beck, U. (1996) 'World Risk Society as Cosmopolitan Society? Ecological Questions in a Framework of Manufactured Uncertainties', *Theory, Culture & Society* 13(4): 1–32.

Beder, S. (1997) *Global Spin: The Corporate Assault on Environmentalism*. Melbourne: Scribe Publications.

Benton, T. (1998) 'Rights and Justice on a Shared Planet: More Rights or New Relations?', *Theoretical Criminology* 2(2): 149–75.

Bohmke, H. (2001) 'Former Rivals Unite to Fight ANC Attacks', *Green Left Weekly*, 9 May, p. 22.

Bond, P. (2001a) 'Ghana: Sharpening Hydro-Class Struggles', *Green Left Weekly*, 30 May, pp. 21–22.

Bond, P. (2001b) 'South Africa: Welcome to the "New" Johannesburg', *Green Left Weekly*, 28 February, p. 13.

Bond, P. and K. Bakker (2001) 'Canada: Blue Planet Targets Commodification of World's Water', *Green Left Weekly*, 18 July, p. 22.

Braithwaite, J. (1993) 'Responsive Business Regulatory Institutions', in C. Coady and C. Sampford (eds) *Business Ethics and the Law*. Sydney: Federation Press.

Braithwaite, J. and P. Drahos (2000) *Global Business Regulation*. Cambridge: Cambridge University Press.

Del Frate, A. and J. Norberry (eds) (1993) *Environmental Crime: Sanctioning Strategies and Sustainable Development*. Rome: UNICRI/Sydney: Australian Institute of Criminology.

Dixon, N. (2001) 'South Africa: Anti-Cut Off Activists Shot', *Green Left Weekly*, 10 October, p. 22.

Franklin, A. (1999) *Animals and Modern Cultures: A Sociology of Human–Animal Relations in Modernity*. London: Sage Publications.

Goldman, M. (1998a) 'Introduction: The Political Resurgence of the Commons', in M. Goldman (ed.) *Privatizing Nature: Political Struggles for the Global Commons*, pp. 1–19. London: Pluto Press in association with Transnational Institute.

Goldman, M. (1998b) 'Inventing the Commons: Theories and Practices of the Commons' Professional', in M. Goldman (ed.) *Privatizing Nature: Political Struggles for the Global Commons*, pp. 20–53. London: Pluto Press in association with Transnational Institute.

Government of British Columbia (2001) *Drinking Water Protection Plan: A Discussion Document*. Vancouver: Government of British Columbia.

Grabosky, P. (1994) 'Green Markets: Environmental Regulation by the Private Sector', *Law and Policy* 16(4): 419–48.

Grabosky, P. (1995) 'Regulation by Reward: On the Use of Incentives as Regulatory Instruments', *Law and Policy* 17(3): 256–79.

Gunningham, N. and P. Grabosky (1998) *Smart Regulation: Designing Environmental Policy*. Oxford: Clarendon Press.

Gunningham, N., J. Norberry and S. McKillop (eds) (1995) *Environmental Crime, Conference Proceedings*. Canberra: Australian Institute of Criminology.

Hager, N. and B. Burton (1999) *Secrets and Lies: The Anatomy of an Anti-Environmental PR Campaign*. New Zealand: Craig Potton Publishing.

Haines, F. (1997) *Corporate Regulation: Beyond 'Punish or Persuade'*. Oxford: Clarendon Press.

Haines, F. (2000) 'Towards Understanding Globalisation and Control of Corporate Harm: A Preliminary Criminological Analysis', *Current Issues in Criminal Justice* 12(2): 166–80.

Hall, D. (1999) *The Water Multinationals*. London: Public Services International Research Unit, University of Greenwich.

Halsey, M. (1997a) 'Environmental Crime: Towards an Eco-Human Rights Approach', *Current Issues in Criminal Justice* 8(3): 217–42.

Halsey, M. (1997b) 'The Wood for the Paper: Old-Growth Forest, Hemp and Environmental Harm', *Australian and New Zealand Journal of Criminology* 30(2): 121–48.

Halsey, M. and R. White (1998) 'Crime, Ecophilosophy and Environmental Harm', *Theoretical Criminology* 2(3): 345–71.

Harvey, D. (1996) *Justice, Nature and the Geography of Difference*. Oxford: Blackwell.

Hausman, T., D. Hazen, T. Straus and K. Fish (2001) 'Exposing the News that Didn't Make the News', *Australian Options* 25: 9.

Heine, G., M. Prabhu and A. del Frate (eds) (1997) *Environmental Protection: Potentials and Limits of Criminal Justice*. Rome: UNICRI.

Kirkland, L.-H. and D. Thompson (1999) 'Challenges in Designing, Implementing and Operating an Environmental Management System', *Business Strategy and the Environment* 8: 128–43.

Levy, D. (1997) 'Environmental Management as Political Sustainability', *Organization and Environment* 10(2): 126–47.

Low, N. and B. Gleeson (1998) *Justice, Society and Nature: An Exploration of Political Ecology*. London: Routledge.

McCulloch, J. (2001) *Blue Army: Paramilitary Policing in Australia*. Melbourne: Melbourne University Press.

Massey, R. (2001) 'United States: Arsenic from Your Tap', *Green Left Weekly*, 23 May, p. 24.

O'Brien, R., A. Goetz, J. Scholte and M. Williams (2000) *Contesting Global Governance: Multilateral Economic Institutions and Global Social Movements*. Cambridge: Cambridge University Press.

O'Connor, J. (1994) 'Is Sustainable Capitalism Possible?', in M. O'Connor (ed.) *Is Capitalism Sustainable?: Political Economy and the Politics of Ecology*, pp. 152–75. New York: The Guilford Press.

Pearce, F. and S. Tombs (1998) *Toxic Capitalism: Corporate Crime and the Chemical Industry*. Aldershot: Dartmouth Publishing Company.

Pepper, D. (1993) *Eco-Socialism: From Deep Ecology to Social Justice*. New York: Routledge.

Public Services Privatisation Research Unit (1996) *The Privatisation Network*. London: PSPRU.

Schwendinger, H. and J. Schwendinger (1975) 'Defenders of Order or Guardians of Human Rights?', in I. Taylor, P. Walton and J. Young (eds) *Critical Criminology*, pp. 113–46. London: Routledge & Kegan Paul.

Seis, M. (1993) 'Ecological Blunders in US Clean Air Legislation', *Journal of Human Justice* 5(1): 58–81.

Shallat, L. (2001) 'Consumer Challenges to Corporate Might', in *Corporate Citizenship in the Global Market*. Internet: Consumers International Website [http://www.consumidores-int.cl].

Situ, Y. and D. Emmons (2000) *Environmental Crime: The Criminal Justice System's Role in Protecting the Environment*. Thousand Oaks, CA: Sage Publications.

Snider, L. (2000) 'The Sociology of Corporate Crime: An Obituary (or: Whose Knowledge Claims Have Legs?)', *Theoretical Criminology* 4(2): 169–206.

Snider, L. (2002) 'Zero Tolerance Reversed: Constituting the Non-Culpable Subject in Walkerton', paper presented at Annual Meeting, Canadian Law and Society Association, Vancouver, 31 May.

South, N. (1998) 'A Green Field for Criminology', *Theoretical Criminology* 2(2): 211–34.

South African Municipal Workers Union (SAMWU) (2001) 'Union "Mourns" on World Water Day', SAMWU statement on World Water Day, reprinted in *Green Left Weekly*, 28 March, p. 22.

Sutherland, E. (1949) *White Collar Crime*. New York: Dryden Press.

Vanderpuye, F. (2001) 'Ghana: Campaign Intensifies against Water Privatisation', *Green Left Weekly*, 20 June, p. 20.

Vassilopoulos, J. (1998a) 'Water Companies' Criminal Record', *Green Left Weekly*, 2 September, p. 13.

Vassilopoulos, J. (1998b) 'Sydney Water Crisis due to Corporatisation', *Green Left Weekly*, 12 August, p. 13.

Wall, E. and B. Beardwood (2001) 'Standardizing Globally, Responding Locally: The New Infrastructure, ISO 14000, and Canadian Agriculture', *Studies in Political Economy* 64: 33–58.

White, R. (1998) 'Environmental Criminology and Sydney Water', *Current Issues in Criminal Justice* 10(2): 214–19.

White, R. (1999) 'Criminality, Risk and Environmental Harm', *Griffith Law Review* 8(2): 235–57.

White, R. (2002) 'Environmental Harm and the Political Economy of Consumption', *Social Justice* 29(1–2): 82–102.

Williams, C. (1996) 'An Environmental Victimology', *Social Justice* 23(4): 16–40.

Wright Mills, C. (1959) *The Sociological Imagination*. New York: Oxford University Press.

55

Trade secrets: intersections between diasporas and crime groups in the constitution of the human trafficking chain

Jackie Turner and Liz Kelly

[...]

INTRODUCTION

Trafficking in persons, as the term suggests, involves movement – the movement of persons from one place to another by a variety of means and for a variety of exploitative purposes. Movement, however, is also associated with migration, and the accelerated migratory flows of recent decades and changes in patterns of contemporary migration, fuelled by the forces of globalization, have revitalised interest in diasporas. Globalization, however, has also fuelled the growth of transnational organized crime groups, among them those that engage in human trafficking. And it is this that points to a hitherto under-explored theme in the literature (Kelly 2002; 2005), namely possible intersections between crime networks involved in human trafficking and their respective diasporas.

Members of diasporas are recognized as facilitating much legitimate commerce between home and host countries. They can generate trade, for example, through a demand for home-country products and foods, and the networks they establish can form the basis of new international business connections (Kapur and McHale 2005). Many of their attributes give them an edge in the global economy. As Cohen (1997: 168) suggests, '[i]n the age of globalization, their language skills, familiarity with other cultures and contacts in other countries make them highly competitive'. These same attributes, however, also lend themselves to activities of an illicit nature, to facilitate a different kind of trade, or to create a demand for different home-country commodities. Kapur and McHale (2005: 128–9) go as far as to assert that '[d]iasporas have been a boon to international crime', and suggest that '[m]uch like any international industry, many criminal networks rely on expatriated populations to help facilitate their activities abroad'. The cross-border trade in human beings is an international industry; moreover, it is a low-risk-high-profit enterprise that has the added advantage that, unlike drugs, trafficked people can be sold repeatedly (Shelley 2007: 117). However, also unlike drugs or other inert commodities, the victims of human traffickers must first be recruited, and then controlled during their transportation and subsequent exploitation; to achieve this, traffickers arguably require networks throughout transit and destination countries – connections that will facilitate the movement and control of trafficked persons.

ESTABLISHING THE CONNECTIONS

This paper explores the extent to which, and how, diasporas may play a part in the processes of human trafficking through presenting a typology and drawing on the current, albeit still limited, evidence base on this question.

The proposed typology hypothesizes four possible primary diasporic intersections with trafficking groups.

1 Integrated diasporic model: a fully diasporic closed criminal network across the entire trafficking chain, linked by ethnicity and/or family connections, that engages in the trafficking of own country nationals only and that profits from their exploitation.

2 Partially integrated diasporic model: a fully diasporic closed criminal network across the entire trafficking chain, save that the group's activities end with delivery of trafficked persons to the country of destination and/or the group traffics foreign country nationals.

3 Instrumental diasporic model: a partially open diasporic network that operates in collaboration with other indigenous/foreign crime groups, trafficking and/or exploiting individuals of varying nationality/ethnicity, and that uses diasporas instrumentally, such as to render themselves less visible, to provide a market for trafficked persons, or to provide the means of laundering the proceeds of trafficking operations.

4 Fully open model: the final model comprises a criminal group, engaged in human trafficking and/or exploitation of trafficked persons, but in which any links to diasporas are purely incidental and form no part of the group's structure or modus operandi.

In both the first and second models, it might be anticipated that the success of the group's activities will draw heavily on knowledge, trust and loyalty through links of ethnicity and identity. Additionally, separate variables would be employed to interrogate each model according to the gender composition of the trafficking chain, and the types of exploitation engaged in. For example, (1) single sex for multiple exploitation; (2) single sex for sexual exploitation; (3) mixed sex for multiple exploitation; and (4) mixed sex for sexual exploitation. The purpose of such further disaggregation is to make both women and men more visible within the trafficking process, as perpetrators and as victims, and to pave the way for a more critical approach to both constructs. This is particularly important when considering the systemic and structural inequalities that underpin trafficking in persons, particularly with regard to gender and ethnicity.

The paper explores a number of themes. The first section sets the scene, focusing particularly on the overlap between migration, smuggling and human trafficking, and the conditions, in a global world, that render individuals vulnerable to the deceptive strategies of technology-savvy crime groups, well connected to past and present. The second section examines more closely the role of transnational organized crime in human trafficking operations. It highlights the peculiar absence of a gendered perspective in the discourse on organized crime generally, and explores some of the implications of this with respect to the trade in human beings – a trade rooted in historic traditions and complex interconnections of ethnicity and gender. This is a theme that is explored further in the third section, which, again, argues the need for a gendered perspective on diasporas and transnationalism in a globalized world. Diasporic connections facilitate not only legitimate commercial trade; they may also form the networks of crime groups engaged in human trafficking. As globalization has widened rather than narrowed the inequalities that shape the world's landscape, this has particular implications for women, increasingly forced to migrate but frequently with limited access to legitimate migration channels. The fourth section sets out to examine more specifically how a global trade is managed locally, by considering the intersections between criminal networks and their diasporas, while section five draws on what is known of some crime groups and their activities, and examines this against the proposed typology, emphasizing again the need for a more detailed exploration of gender and ethnicity. The final section then seeks to pull together the arguments and to pave the way for a more rigorous, empirical study of intersections between diasporas and human trafficking networks.

SETTING THE SCENE

The international legal definition of human trafficking can be found in the United Nations (UN) Optional Protocol to Prevent, Suppress and Punish Trafficking in Persons, Especially Women and Children (the Palermo Protocol), which sets out, at Article 3a:

> Trafficking in persons shall mean the recruitment, transportation, transfer, harbouring or receipt of persons, by means of the threat or use of force or other forms of coercion, of the abuse of power or of a position of vulnerability or of the giving or receiving of payments or benefits to achieve the consent of a person having control over another person,

for the purpose of exploitation. Exploitation shall include, at a minimum, the exploitation of the prostitution of others or other forms of sexual exploitation, forced labour or services, slavery or practices akin to slavery, servitude or the removal of organs.

Under the terms of the Palermo Protocol, it is clear that individuals can be trafficked internally within the boundaries of a nation-state. This is a significant problem in parts of the world, and one warranting serious attention, but the focus here is on cross-border human trafficking. The offence itself can be divided into its constituent parts of *action*, *means* and *purpose.* Viewed more succinctly, however, trafficking is better understood as a process, involving *recruitment*, *transportation* and *exploitation*, respectively, in countries of origin and, for these purposes, through countries of transit, to countries of destination, or centres of exploitation, hence reference to the trafficking chain, which comprises and facilitates the trade in human beings. It should, however, be noted that exploitation can, and does, occur at all stages of the human trafficking process (Kelly 2002).

Trafficking is sometimes described as a form of modern-day slavery – an alias that is highly evocative and illustrative of many of the processes and outcomes of trafficking in persons. However, most victims of human traffickers do not begin or end their journeys shackled and chained. Instead, they are drawn into what Salt and Stein (1997) call the 'migration business'. Described variously as a 'continuum of facilitation' (Skeldon 2000), or as a 'trafficking-migration nexus' (Piper 2005), the overlap between trafficking, smuggling and other forms of irregular migration has been well documented (see also Kelly 2002; 2005; Anderson and O'Connell Davidson 2002), and they share many of the same root causes. Wars, conflicts and the social and economic crises generated in some regions of the world by the destabilizing effects of globalization and transition have contributed to large and irregular population flows, creating 'fertile fields for exploitation' (Kelly 2007: 81). Those with limited prospects of security, survival or prosperity at home may see little option but to barter what few resources they, or their families, have and take their chances in the lottery of the assisted migration industry. And lottery it is, for the 'fertile fields' are also the hunting grounds of human traffickers, in their many deceptive guises.

There are few, if any, regions of the world that can be described as human traffic-free zones. According to the United Nations Office on Drugs and Crime (UNODC 2006), virtually all countries are now implicated, as countries of origin, transit or destination, and sometimes as all three. As has already been suggested, intra-country and intra-regional trafficking is a significant problem in parts of South-East Asia and elsewhere, but trafficked individuals are also being found further and further from their home countries, indicating that international trafficking is on the rise. Although reliable estimates of its scale are hard to come by, a well grounded study by the International Labour Organisation (ILO 2005) suggests that, at any given time, a minimum of 2.45 million people are trapped in situations of forced labour throughout the world. Of these, some 43 per cent are believed to have been trafficked for the purposes of commercial sexual exploitation, 32 per cent for other economic exploitation, with the remaining 25 per cent trafficked for unknown reasons or some mix of the other two. The victims of human traffickers are found in the world's sex industries, in construction, agriculture, catering, the clothing and other manufacturing industries, and in private households across the globe in conditions of domestic servitude and bonded labour. This is an illustrative, rather than exhaustive, list. Demand for ever more and ever cheaper goods and services can be met only by ever more and ever cheaper labour. Against this backdrop, the formal economy merges with the informal economy, the licit shades into the illicit, and the margins and grey areas are inhabited by those who traverse both, to control and profit from others whose 'space for action' (Kelly 2007: 89) has been limited by adverse conditions at home, and elsewhere by those who deem their business and household aspirations, or assumed sexual entitlements, are best served by the cheap or unpaid labour of others.

The rise and spread of international human trafficking are linked to the growth of transnational organized crime groups (UNODC 2006), able to take advantage of the new infrastructures and technologies associated with the global age. If globalization can be characterized as the free movement of capital, goods and services across the world, aided by advanced systems of communication and transportation, human traffickers can, and certainly do, corrupt those systems to aid the movement of 'unfree' people. But they still face formidable logistical and other problems. Access to the internet may well mean that 'organized crime groups in India and Russia are able to buy and sell women with the ease of a mouse-click' (Shelley 2007: 119), but the purchase and sale of persons via the worldwide web do not simultaneously beam them from origin to destination. The trade in human beings pre-dates modern communication and transportation systems. Indeed, it is 'as old as trade itself' (Lee 2007: 1). Human traffickers may take advantage of new infrastructures and technologies, but their recruitment, transportation and exploitation practices will vary greatly according to the specific circumstances of their intended victims, as well as the prevailing political, cultural and socio-economic conditions in countries of origin, transit and destination. Indeed, one of the enduring features of human trafficking is the extent to which it is embedded in different cultural and historical contexts (Bales 2005).

Criminal networks will share with their diasporas those historic roots, and can draw on knowledge of patterns of movement and trade that have been in existence for centuries. Simultaneously, through global diasporas, they can access vital information about local conditions, not just to overcome the logistical problems of often clandestine movement, but also to assess conditions of supply and demand. A better understanding of such connections, therefore, will not only add to the knowledge base, it will also contribute to deeper reflections on how cultural traditions and practices may operate, both to sustain and to resist, the continued trade in human beings.

TRAFFICKING IN PERSONS AND TRANSNATIONAL ORGANIZED CRIME

The Palermo Protocol supplements the UN Convention Against Transnational Organised Crime, thereby establishing the link between trafficking in persons and organized crime groups that operate transnationally. Even so, the role of organized crime in human trafficking is a matter of continuing debate. In part, this is due to the diversity of human trafficking operations that defy easy categorization, but it is also due to contested conceptualizations of *organized* crime. Writing of Russian organized crime, Finckenauer (2001) defines true or 'real' organized crime groups as those that possess criminal sophistication, structure and identification with the group. They have a reputation for, and the capacity to use, violence to facilitate or maintain their domination of the criminal underworld, and they have the resources and connections to corrupt legal and political systems at the highest levels. By contrast, Finckenauer argues, human traffickers often comprise smaller, ad hoc groups, loose networks of individuals, more aptly characterized as criminal entrepreneurs who engage in crimes that are organized. In the field of human trafficking, true organized crime may play some role in these activities, such as debt collectors or by demanding a mob tax to permit trafficking through their territory, but to label all human traffickers as organized crime or worse, as mafia, he asserts, is both incorrect and unwise.

For Louise Shelley (1995; 1999; 2007), on the other hand, groups involved in cross-border activities such as human trafficking emerge as clear examples of transnational organized crime. Also writing of organized crime in the former Soviet Union, she attributes its growth to factors such as the technological explosion during the latter part of the last century, as well as the geopolitical situation as it evolved following the dissolution of the Soviet Union. Indeed, according to Shelley, post-Soviet organized crime defies traditional conceptions of organized crime groups in its particular composition of professional criminals and former members of the Party elite and the security apparatus. And, whilst many trafficking groups may be relatively small in size, Shelley (2007: 122–3) challenges the 'erroneous perception that traffickers are only small scale entrepreneurs', who engage exclusively, or primarily, in human trafficking activities, as opposed to the multiplicity of activities identified by Finckenauer (2001) as characteristic of 'real' organized crime groups. Indeed, as UNODC (2006: 68) has noted, whilst some organized crime groups may specialize in human trafficking, others will also simultaneously engage in a range of other forms of illicit activity. In this sense, at least, they cannot be distinguished from 'real' organized crime groups.

What is striking in the debate on organized crime, however, is not the diversity of views as to what it actually is, and how it is to be distinguished from other criminal activity; it is instead the curious neutrality of the discourse with respect to gender. Organized crime is rarely considered to be a gendered issue, although it is very much the territory of men, in which women are at best marginal actors or incidental victims, but are otherwise absent. Moreover, this absence, for the most part, goes entirely unremarked, or is deemed adequately dealt with by way of a passing, or even footnoted, reference (see, e.g. Abadinsky 2007: 4). The point is further demonstrated in the literature on gangs. Although criminological discourse tends to treat organized crime and gangs as separate subjects, 'a distinctive gang culture does underpin many organized crime groups' (Wright 2006: 27); and, as Moore (2007: 187) puts it, 'when they discuss "gangs", most researchers confine themselves to males. As usual, this begs the question of gender'. The consequence of this is that 'criminology, despite the fact that its primary subject matter is male offenders, focuses hardly at all on *men* and *masculinity*. It deals with men without acknowledging this and hence creates theories about criminals without a conceptualization of gender' (Gelsthorpe and Morris 1990: 2–3).

Human trafficking, on the other hand, is very much considered to be a gendered issue, as reflected in the title of the Palermo Protocol itself. Whilst this potentially problematizes complex issues of agency and victimhood, particularly along the continuum of migration, smuggling and trafficking, the focus on gender is generally to be welcomed. However, locating a gendered issue within a context not considered to be gendered presents something of a conundrum. Does it force gender onto the agenda of criminological discourse on organized crime, or does it take organized crime out of criminological approaches to human trafficking? Finckenauer (2001) appears to favour the latter, as is further evident in his analysis of the *impact* of organized crime. Here, he suggests, criminal organizations that qualify as true organized crime groups have the capacity to inflict significant harms of the type identified by Maltz (1990), namely economic, physical, pyschological and societal harms. It is this, he asserts, that singles it out as an instance of sophisticated criminal organization and sets it apart from other groups that lack such harm capacity, although, as he notes, their individual victims are certainly harmed. On this basis, he again concludes, true organized crime has only peripheral, if any, involvement in human trafficking activities.

This not only puts him at odds with the views of Louise Shelley, as has been seen; it also presupposes a particular assessment of what constitutes 'harm'. Certainly, all of the harms outlined above are embodied in trafficking; however, the logical conclusion of the argument is to diminish the significance of the harms when set against the capacity of organized crime groups. In fact, when viewed through the lens of gender, the opposite conclusion is a more accurate one. In the context of the aforementioned ILO study indicating the prevalence worldwide of the trafficking of women into prostitution, or other forced labour, it is arguable, to say the least, that this can be construed as an instance of harm against individuals, namely the women who have the misfortune to be exploited in this manner, as opposed to some greater harm. Indeed, if 'true' organized crime is to be assessed by its capacity to inflict significant harms, human traffickers would certainly seem to fit the bill, as it is difficult to envisage what might constitutute greater 'economic', 'physical', 'psychological' and 'societal' harm, even more so when linked to the root causes of trafficking and the 'fertile field' that renders women especially vulnerable. In downgrading the impact of women trafficked into prostitution or other exploitation to harms affecting predominantly individual women, Finckenauer's argument is revealed as skewed towards the dominant, masculinist discourse on organized crime.

The answer, then, is not to take organized crime out of criminological discourse on human trafficking, but to re-position the discourse on organized crime to recognize it as a gendered issue. This would allow for a much-needed focus on *men* and *masculinity*; it would also pave the way for a more nuanced analysis of the role of organized crime in human trafficking and, specifically, of the ways in which masculinity operates locally to create conditions, not only favourable to the trafficking of women for sexual exploitation, but also those which serve to conceal the trafficking of men and, more particularly, the trafficking of young boys into prostitution – '… thus far a terra incognita in terms of sociological research' (Morawska 2007: 99).

Furthermore, such an approach would raise the profile of women in trafficking operations where they are found not just among the victims, but also figure as traffickers themselves. Indeed, they may occupy key or prominent positions (Shelley 2007), although the majority of women appear to be among the lower ranks, particularly the recruiters, and may, perhaps, be better described as part of a 'second wave' of formerly trafficked women 'who have been offered, or perhaps taken, the option of recruitment rather than continued sexual exploitation' (Kelly 2005: 46). Writing of human trafficking in the Central Asian Republics (CARs), Kelly notes the range of factors that have contributed to a rise in trafficking from the CARs into established sex industries, among them the declining status of women and the re-emergence of traditional cultural beliefs and practices. These not only create conducive contexts for the trafficking and exploitation of women, but also undermine their potential reintegration into families and communities, such that some may choose to stay in countries of destination, whilst others may return to their homes, but do so to recruit from there, and effectively become part of the crime networks by which they were once entrapped.

Shelley (2007) also notes the ways in which different cultural and political contexts impact on the practices of human traffickers. This is particularly important to note in the context of a global era, as it signals the impact of ethnicity within organized crime networks and, like masculinity, points to the ways in which ethnic ties operate locally to facilitate the trade in human beings. Again, to borrow from the sister literature, 'today the keys to understanding gangs are the processes of globalization – the redivision of space, the strengthening of traditional identities, and the underground economy' (Hagedorn 2007: 3). These issues are discussed further below; however, ethnicity is recognized to play a part, particularly at the recruitment stage, when trust might be a critical issue. As Shelley (2007: 126) asserts, '[i]nitial victimisation of the trafficked person is usually by a member of his/her own ethnic group. For example, Chinese, Mexican or Russian groups recruit in their own communities. There are many reasons that recruitment occurs within one's own group. Proximity and access are important. But equally important is trust'. Once recruitment has occurred, differences are then seen to emerge among the various ethnic groups. 'Recruiters, especially those from Slavic countries, the Indian subcontinent and parts of the Middle East often hand over their victims to other ethnic groups subsequently. Other traffickers such as Chinese, African and Latin American tend to retain control past the recruitment stage' (Shelley 2007: 126–7).

Key to understanding the nature of human trafficking and its organization, then, is an appreciation of the different contexts from which it derives, the conditions that enable it to flourish, and the cultural and traditional practices in which it remains embedded and that shape the organizing activities of the crime groups that engage in the cross-border trade in human beings. Again, as Kelly suggests (2007: 85), reflections such as these 'illustrate the necessity of deeper explorations of the many ways in which gender and ethnicity play a part in the complex structuring and diverse consequences of trafficking in persons'. Whilst caution must be urged to avoid the demonization of certain ethnic and cultural groups as representing alien organized crime conspiracies (Woodiwiss 2001), more nuanced considerations of gender and ethnicity will contribute to a deeper understanding of organized crime and its role in transnational human trafficking in a global age.

GLOBALIZATION, DIASPORAS AND TRANSNATIONALISM

Globalization has not only promoted the growth of crime beyond borders; it has also exerted transformative influences on populations and migration flows, and on the world's political, economic and social landscape (UNODC 2002). Like organized crime, it is a contested construct that has attracted many different meanings and interpretations. Kelly *et al.* (2005: 1) suggest it 'may be roughly defined as the emergence of a variety of systems or activities of economic and commercial production, trade and services that are worldwide rather than national or regional in scope and that are generally not controllable by nation-states'. But it is not just the unconstrained movement of goods and services that is so valued. The international mobility of human capital is as prized in the global economy as is the free flow of other capital, trade and commerce. Liberal economic and trade policies, and the new infrastructures and advanced technologies characteristic of globalization, have not only greatly accelerated migration, they have also fuelled changes in patterns of contemporary migration. This has created new opportunities for diasporas to emerge and flourish (Cohen 1997). Traditionally conceived as exilic populations forcibly expelled from their homelands by a traumatic event, diasporas are conventionally characterized by reference to three key features (Butler 2001). In the first instance, there must be dispersal to at least two destinations as a prerequisite to the establishment of internal networks that link various populations in diaspora; secondly, some relationship with the homeland, or the idea of a homeland, must persist as a foundation for the development of diasporan identity; and, finally, diasporan communities are consciously part of an ethno-national group, such that there exists a self-awareness of the group's identity.

The emerging forms of migration associated with the forces of globalization, however, suggest that population movements may no longer be characterized only by outward migratory flows, and diasporas may no longer have as a goal permanent settlement in, or citizenship of, a host country. As Cohen (1997: 170) suggests, '[t]here is no longer any stability in the points of origin, no finality in the points of destination, and no necessary coincidence between social and national identities'. In this sense, the internal networks that link at least some populations in diaspora are, arguably, increasingly coming to resemble the social formations of transnational relations. Although transnationalism remains, for the time being, under-theorized, it can be partly conceived in terms of a restructuring of 'place' or 'locality', in which national borders are crossed, rather than maintained (Vertovec and Cohen 1999). As new or 'emergent' diasporas (Muenz and Ohliger 2003) adapt to the conditions of a globalized world, they share much in common with the transnationalism of migrant communities. If globalization has seen the emergence of supra- or transnational trade and commercial activities unbounded by the borders and controls of nation-states, it has also seen the emergence of new, sojourning diasporas, capable of existing and operating beyond those same borders and controls.

These special attributes of present-day diasporas lend themselves well to life in the global economy. The ease of movement, the ability to 'switch codes' (Woodward 1997) – social, cultural and economic – together with knowledge of home and hostlands, enable members of a diaspora to forge connections between home economies and international businesses that facilitate all manner of economic exchanges. 'Emigration diasporas' (Butler 2001) now co-exist with, or are transformed into, transnational communities, reflecting patterns of migration involving a to-ing and fro-ing across national boundaries, and creating cosmopolitan or transnational identities linked by a sense of 'non-place based solidarity' (Woodward 1997). Permanence gives way to a certain fluidity, a multilocality, unbounded by the nation-state or a given place of residence. Even so, Smith and Guardizo (1998) sound a note of caution. They argue that conceptualizations of place need to take account of the specificities of a given locality. The assumptions inherent in notions of unboundedness are open to challenge precisely because 'the local sites of global processes do matter. The social construction of "place" is still a process of local meaning-making, territorial specificity, juridical control, and economic development, however complexly articulated the localities become in transnational economic, political, and cultural flows' (Smith and Guardizo 1998: 12). Transnationalism, then, does not imply a disconnectedness from the local – far from it. Transnational ties, as those authors suggest, are sustained by the constraints and opportunities found in a given locality, and diasporas, specifically ethnic diasporas, as perhaps the most visible paradigm of transnationalism (Vertovec and Cohen 1999), embody the local and the global through social formations and internal networks that span borders.

Another note of caution must be sounded here. Globalization is said to be frequently discussed in curiously apolitical terms (Cohen 1997: 156), to which might also be added curiously gender-neutral terms, similarly characteristic of much theorizing of transnationalism and diasporas. As with debate on organized crime, apparent gender-neutrality serves to obscure a predominantly masculinist perspective, with ideologies of masculinity masquerading as 'universal'. However, global markets, whether legal, quasi-legal or wholly illicit, operate in a distinctly gendered fashion. The 'invisible hand' is less invisible and more of a sleight of hand when viewed through the lens of gender, since, by every indicator of well-being – income, employment, health, education or other – women fare significantly worse than men (Steiner and Alston 2000). If ideologies of masculinity are peddled through global markets, they flow across borders through global diasporas, linked by transnational ties rooted in the cultures and traditions from which they emanate. Those ties may well be sustained by the specificities of a given locality, but those specificities will include the ways in which masculinities – within diaspora and host communities – operate locally to create conditions conducive to exploitation. And 'however complexly articulated the localities become in transnational economic, political and cultural flows' (Smith and Guardizo 1998: 12), the voices of women are rarely heard, or heeded, in those articulations.

This is particularly relevant in the context of the trafficking of women. As Vertovec and Cohen (1999) suggest, the migratory flows of women have largely been hidden from history. Studies have tended to deal with women as a residual category, those left behind, or those crossing borders as dependent family members. As such, women are likely to experience life in a diaspora very differently, commencing with its very creation. Here, Cohen (1997: 26) lists as a first criterion 'dispersal from an original homeland, often traumatically, to two or more foreign regions'. The traumatic events referred to include slavery, famine and genocide and certainly apply to the African, Irish and Armenian diasporas and, more recently, to those affected by ethnic cleansing and wars in the former Yugoslavia and elsewhere. Such crises invariably disproportionately impact on women, though other events may be more hidden and not recognized as sufficiently traumatic to force mass migration, including domestic violence, child sexual abuse, rape and other forms of violence against women in the community, and discrimination against women in the fields of education, employment and health. Of course, such conditions may be said, in varying degrees, to characterize the lot of women everywhere and, therefore, even if mass migration were an option, it is difficult to see where in the world women might go to escape them. However, although such 'expulsion factors' may go unrecognized, or be subsumed within the dynamics of the 'feminisation of poverty', individual women are nevertheless migrating in ever increasing numbers, and now comprise nearly half the total expatriate population worldwide (Monzini 2005: 58). Despite a 'peculiar blindness to the direct effects of labor market shifts on women' (Moore 2007: 190), their work has increasingly become the primary source of family income (ILO 2004). These pressures arguably lie behind much migration, together with the ever growing demand for women in global service industries, including sex industries. And yet, migration does not in itself diminish the gender-specific risks and dangers to women. The hidden expulsion factors accompany them on their journeys and, if anything, are exacerbated, as regular channels of migration and forms of employment are often denied them, creating further layers of vulnerability and opportunities for exploitation along the murky continuum of migration, smuggling and human trafficking.

Reflections such as these call for a gendered interrogation, not only of conceptualizations of globalization, but also of notions such as the 'ethno-national' consciousness assumed to underpin diasporic identity, or the sense of 'nonplaced based solidarity' of present-day, transnational communities. And, in the world of human trafficking, such an analysis may reveal intersections between old and new to which traffickers are keenly attuned, sharing the historic roots of their respective, stratified diasporas and, through them, access to a detailed knowledge and understanding of local contemporary conditions on a global scale – so essential to the success of their operations.

DIASPORAS AND HUMAN TRAFFICKING: A GLOBAL TRADE UNDER LOCAL MANAGEMENT

In defining the phenomenon of human trafficking in terms of recruitment, transportation and exploitation, the focus has often been on methods of recruitment, modes of transportation and forms of exploitation. Trafficking, however, as has already been indicated, is a process. Moreover, it is a process that is advanced through movement. Cross-border human trafficking involves the movement of persons across state boundaries, inviting consideration of the mechanisms and networks that make such flows possible, particularly those intersecting and crossing two states. Thus, van Schendel (2005: 44) refers to a 'borderland' – an area he describes 'as a zone or region within which lies an international border, [while] a *borderland society* [is] a social and cultural system straddling that border'. Those who inhabit such a borderland will have networks that pre-date the formation of the border, networks that are restrained by the border, and networks that develop as a result of the existence of the border, all of which will incorporate cross-border flows, including those of a clandestine nature. Such 'everyday transnationality', argues van Schendel (2005: 57), means that even those borderlanders not 'involved in illegal trade networks as smugglers, illegal migrants, traffickers of humans, or receivers of migrants' remittances' will be well aware of these activities and their impact on the transnational landscape.

Shifting borders are, of course, nothing new, but, in recent decades, the collapse of the former Soviet Union and the reconfiguration of boundaries there and in Eastern Europe have spawned new borderland societies in which strong and highly meaningful cross-border networks are maintained. Some networks may be constrained by the new border formations, but many old and well established networks will persist, and new networks will develop. However, these border changes may also have created opportunities for a number of networks to extend borderland societies to inland populations established in host societies, through the formation, reinforcement or re-establishment of connections with emigration diasporas. These new forms of international connectivity, or transnationalism, 'could easily yield a diasporan community with a unique level of continuity with the homeland' (Butler 2001: 195), and a unique understanding of the political, cultural and socio-economic systems of their host countries, be they for human trafficking purposes, countries of transit or destination.

For those engaged in cross-border human trafficking, then, such borderland societies may provide vital links in the chain, more so when the connections they encompass extend through diasporic networks and transnational ties to established expatriated populations. Ethnic communities may well provide crime groups with 'recruitment opportunities, cover and support for criminal operations and … serve as a pool of criminal activists prepared to engage in trafficking activities' (Kelly *et al.* 2005: 4), but the spaces in between must be connected to link the chain from recruitment to exploitation. Turning first to recruitment, knowledge of local economic conditions and traditional customs and practices, not to mention a shared language or dialect, all shape the predatory ways in which traffickers target, select and groom their intended victims (UNODC 2006). Where crime groups have their origins in source countries, they may retain members in those countries and/or maintain other connections to ensure a continued supply. Similarly, in destination countries, established communities can prove to be a vital resource. On the one hand, they can be an important source of support and assistance to new arrivals. In illustrating the different ways in which illegal migrants (from Indonesia) enter and remain in West Malaysia, Wong (2005: 87) emphasizes the significance of the presence of friends and relatives already in possession of permanent residence status in that region, many with established homes and businesses. She found that such 'ethnic businesses and settlements were an important focal point for fresh migrants in search of work, residence, and knowledge of survival skills'.

On the other hand, they can also be an important resource for human traffickers, for whom 'survival' consists of remaining undetected and of selling or putting to work those they have trafficked, in order to recoup any costs and maximize their profits. Above all, they must be assured that demand exists to meet supply. Here, too, diasporas may be a pull factor. As has been noted above, they can generate trade by a demand for home-country commodities or food stuffs. Furthermore, by introducing these to host communities, they can greatly expand the market for those products and thereby generate more demand. And it is demand that enables traffickers to accrue considerable wealth from the illicit trade in human beings.

A brief comment on some aspects of the nature of that demand is in order here. It is not suggested that demand exists for the labour or services of *trafficked* persons. Indeed, Anderson and O'Connell Davidson (2003) suggest that an exploiter will be indifferent to the means by which a person comes to be vulnerable to exploitation. On the other hand, they point to evidence that indicates demand exists for 'embodied' labour or service providers from those exhibiting particular qualities pertaining to sex, age, race, caste and ethnicity. A closer examination of the nature of that demand might reveal differences among different crime groups as to how they source and recruit their victims, as well as the markets they create and/or supply. This may have particular relevance to commercial sex industries and the numbers of women trafficked into prostitution in a given destination country, especially one in which the purchase of sexual services is not prohibited by law. A wander through any red-light district will reveal a bewildering array of advertisements for all 'types' of women. And, for anyone with the stomach to do so, even the briefest trawl of the internet will locate websites containing material explicitly promoting women on the basis of ethnic/cultural stereotypes, under the guise of offering 'choice'. Indeed, recent research in the United Kingdom suggests that men who express a preference for women of a specific racial or ethnic background tend to fall into one of two categories: those who prefer women of the same ethnic background, and those seeking the 'exotic other' (Coy *et al.* 2007: 17). That said, such stereotypes are not just exploited in commercial sex industries. They may also influence the purchasers of cheap labour who tend to seek out 'members of groups that not only lack social protection but that are also socially stereotyped as "naturally" servile or otherwise "naturally" suited to working in poor conditions for little recompense' (Anderson and O'Connell Davidson 2002: 25). In this sense, traffickers may exploit existing demand within an established community, as well as exploiting intersecting racial and gender stereotypes to meet, reproduce or, indeed, create a demand for their human commodities.

Human traffickers, then, prey on the vulnerable in source countries, and exploit their vulnerabilities in destination countries, but, to do so, they must first get them there. Where the intended destination country is a long way from the country of origin, journeys can sometimes take months and range across and through several other countries. International trafficking operations, therefore, also depend on access to local knowledge in transit countries. They will need information about routes, safe houses and transportation; they may require the services of document forgers and access to stolen identity papers, and they will need strategies to avoid border controls and police operations. Such information may, of course, be provided to crime groups by locating members along the trafficking routes (Schloenhardt 1999) and in each of the countries concerned but, arguably, the complexities of a global trade require extensive and reliable networks of individuals with a more detailed knowledge of local landscapes. Here, again, members of a group's diaspora can provide the all important links, but not just in terms of information and local services. 'As with any business, international criminal activity requires enforcement mechanisms and trust, which diasporic networks can easily internalize' (Kapur and McHale 2005: 128). And, in a global world, characterized by the more fluid patterns of contemporary migration 'in which individuals come and go but institutions and networks become established in the hostlands' (Butler 2001: 202), be they countries of transit or destination, such diasporic networks may offer unique opportunities to crime groups engaged in human trafficking. They know where the traffic has come from, they know where it is going, and they know how best to get it there. In short, they are uniquely placed to constitute the trafficking chain.

THEORIZING THE CONNECTIONS

It must, of course, be noted that there is no single model of trafficking in persons. So far as the European Union (EU) is concerned, Europol (2004: 7) reports that although traffickers often share the same nationality as their victims, the trend is towards increasing cooperation among networks of different backgrounds. Even so, '[e]thnic organised crime groups are increasingly involving in their activities people of their own social and ethnic environment, living in Member States'. Furthermore, certain ethnic groups have secured strong footholds in a number of destination countries. Albanians, Bulgarians and Lithuanians are among the most frequently reported traffickers of women and children into EU countries (Europol 2004), with significant networks of mutual support in countries of origin, transit and destination and, as with other organized crime groups, their activities appear to be facilitated by the presence of already existing ethnic communities.

Similar links have been noted elsewhere. Research indicates, for example, that, in Israel, much of the sex industry is controlled by Russian organized crime networks, and facilitated, it is suggested, by the presence of a significant Russian diaspora, of which a minority of members are Russian crime bosses (Kelly 2005).

In terms of the proposed typology, then, the first model describes a fully diasporic closed criminal network, which traffics and profits from the exploitation of own-country nationals. This would seem to fit the profile of some Chinese organized crime groups that control the entire process to smuggle large numbers of their own nationals abroad and into Chinese-owned or run businesses. The United Kingdom is a favoured destination in Europe, with so-called 'snakeheads' charging upwards of £20,000 per person to organize the transportation of would-be migrants. Glenny (2008: 368–9) suggests that when Serbia lifted the visa requirements for Chinese citizens in the early 1990s, '[t]he Serbian capital witnessed the fastest growth of any Chinatown during the late 1990s'. That said, New Belgrade was not their intended final destination. It simply hosted planeloads of Chinese migrants and became a friendly staging post for them en route to Western Europe, thereby easing what had previously been a long and often hazardous journey. The arrangement was a gift to the traffickers/smugglers and their human cargo. 'No more dodgy boat trips; no more expensive negotiations with Russian and Ukrainian policemen. No more setting up safe houses in Bucharest or dodging police in Budapest' (Glenny 2008: 369). This arrangement, then, might be indicative of the *integrated diasporic model*, although more recent evidence suggests that the Serbian link failed to endure and/or was not always the preferred route to final destination countries. In addition, instances have been noted of the development of cooperative links between some Chinese and other crime groups. This is discussed further below.

The second model, the *partially integrated diasporic model*, describes a fully closed diasporic crime network that controls and oversees recruitment and transportation of own-country and/or other-country nationals, but that then sells trafficked individuals to other exploiters. This model may be said to characterize some Russian trafficking groups and their operations. Indeed, according to Shelley (2007: 123), Russian traffckers 'sell off human beings as if they were a natural resource like oil or timber'. Such sales may occur at the point of final destination or at some prior point in the process. Although numbers are typically difficult to estimate, it has been suggested that Russian sex trafficking networks have trafficked thousands of women from Asia into and through Eastern Europe (Salt 1998; Finckenauer 2001; Kyle and Koslowski 2001), before either selling them on to other exploiters or placing them within Russian-controlled brothels. In the latter case, of course, the undertaking more closely resembles the *integrated diasporic model*.

Others, again, may conform more to the *instrumental model*, to operate in the shadow of ethnic diasporas and try to both victimize migrants and to involve members of ethnic communities in criminal activities on their behalf (Marshall 1997, cited in Freilich *et al.* 2002: 19). Here, again, the activities of some Chinese crime groups can be seen, not only in their apparent control of the trafficking chain, even when collaborating with other crime groups, but specifically in their use of established communities in destination countries. A police operation reported in January 2008, Operation Greensea (www.eurojust.europa.en), successfully disrupted the activities of two crime groups involved in the smuggling of mainly Chinese nationals across Asia and Europe into France, and from there into the United Kingdom. Those smuggled are believed to have paid up to £21,000 each, and travelled often in extremely cramped conditions in lorries, boats and trains, on a journey that took up to 18 months. The journey to France was organized by the Chinese network, but once in France, the migrants were handed over to a Turkish crime network that facilitated their onward transport to the United Kingdom. On arrival in London and elsewhere, they were handed back to the Chinese network for the purposes of collecting payment. This suggests that the trafficked/smuggled individuals were either kept in conditions of debt bondage and/or some other means were in place to ensure any outstanding sums of money were duly paid over to the network. Typically, this would involve threats or harm to families or friends back home. For our purposes, however, the point to note is that, once in the United Kingdom, the migrants often disappeared into established Chinese communities, making their detection by authorities more difficult. It is, however, not just Chinese crime groups that may operate under cover of, and/or with, the collusion of members of their ethnic constituencies. UNODC (2002: 42) found in a pilot survey of various crime groups that factors contributing to the growth, for example, of West African criminal networks included reliance on 'historic trading networks operating throughout the region and the presence of a significant West African Diaspora in cities around the world'.

Finally, there may be networks that truly have a base in no jurisdiction and that are *fully open* – networks that span continents, and that are bound together by interlinking and overlapping legal and illegal associations. In some instances, crime groups may have evolved and developed cooperative affiliations, as seen above, but in which any diasporic connections are purely incidental. Thus, there is evidence that crime groups 'who previously tended to maintain their own prostitute and brothel networks, often along the lines of nationality, are pooling their resources by advertising women on each other's escort websites and sharing the proceeds when a "booking" is made' (*The Independent*, Monday 22 October 2007). The latter refers to a UK police operation, in which Lithuanian and Chinese criminals were found to be cooperating to traffic women into London from countries as far apart as Malaysia, Lithuania, Brazil and Thailand. Clearly, it is probable that the Lithuanian network maintained good contacts and/or members in Lithuania, but the breadth of the operation, and the likely diversity of routes to the United Kingdom, suggests access to, or collaboration with, wide-ranging criminal networks in a number of source and transit countries. Whether these networks can in fact be said to be *fully open* is not yet clear. They may better be described as a 'criminal diaspora', perhaps more akin to the archetypal transnational corporations (TNCs) that are 'presumed to have jettisoned their national origins' (Vertovec and Cohen 1999: xxi) to operate as fully global organizations.

The 'jettisoning of national origins', however, need not presuppose the dissolution of ethnic ties, or those based on notions of clan, kinship or family. The nodal points in the trafficking chain may still rely on those historic and current connections that have served an ever expanding flow of economic and other transactions between host countries and homelands across the globe. And, indeed, alongside the global flows of finance, goods and services typifying the activities of TNCs is the global flow of human capital and expertise – a flow sometimes described as a 'diaspora by design' (Kotkin 1992). However, this flow and output of TNCs are but a part of the global transactions involving the movement of capital, including human capital. As Cohen (1997: 160) suggests, '[o]ne has to move beneath these visible organizations to glean how a significant chunk of the "real global market works"'. That 'chunk' comprises the multiple transactions among networks of closely integrated co-ethnic members and relationships based on family, clan and kinship ties, which provide a stronger basis for trust, and the more effective enforcement mechanisms identified by Kapur and McHale (2005).

However, the precise mechanisms enabling such cross-border flows remain elusive. The examples cited above may suggest the presence or absence of more or less significant diasporic connections but they are, for now, at best illustrative only in the most general terms; nor, for the time being, do they contribute further vital detail about the gender composition of any of these groups and whether or not they engage in trafficking for single or multiple exploitative purposes.

AN AGENDA FOR RESEARCH

In a post-9/11 world, awash with the rhetoric of terrorism and human security, many governments are quick to invoke the use of a 'Mafia shorthand' (Taylor and Jamieson 1999) to justify ever more muscular responses to threats to national security and territorial sovereignty. Such responses invariably favour traditional conceptualizations of organized crime but, to the extent that these were ever 'true', in the field of human trafficking, at the very least, they serve to camouflage potentially important nodal points of international connectivity. And they do nothing to deal with home-grown demand, which is the primary *raison d'être* of human trafficking, and which itself is rooted in deeply embedded social orders structured by gender and race. Where human traffickers draw on members of ethnic communities to ' serve as a pool of criminal activists prepared to engage in trafficking activities' (Kelly *et al.* 2005: 4), they are able to do so often precisely because of the marginalization of such groups within host communities, even as the vast majority of diaspora populations make rich contributions to the political, cultural and socio-economic life of a country.

However, as migration accelerates in the global economy, and diasporas arguably begin to shed the traditional mantle of exilic populations and don the cloak of transnationalism, they play an ever more critical role in dismantling national barriers and facilitating international commerce. With their superior understanding and knowledge of 'here' and 'there' and, increasingly, of 'everywhere', they form crucial links in the chain of supply and demand in the cross-border, global trade in commodities, goods and services. But their expertise has also contributed to the success of transnational criminal groups, and their role in the chain that constitutes the international trade in human beings warrants closer inspection, even as groups change and evolve to meet new threats and opportunities. Any exploration of such connections must take account of the diverse contexts – the different social and cultural traditions – from which the trade arises, as well as the contemporary conditions in which it is able to prosper. This requires a detailed examination of intersections between gender and ethnicity in specific locations and the multiple ways these shape the networks that form the basis of both old and new forms of international connectivity.

This, then, is the under-explored theme in the literature on human trafficking, the absence of which is readily exploited by traffickers to conceal the tricks of their trade. The social and gendered networks that span continents and bridge the spaces between borderland and inland populations in countries of origin, transit and destination draw both on historic, and on increasingly transnational, diasporic connections. It is through these connections that criminal groups organize the local management of a global trade, and through which they sojourn in the shadows, back and forth, along the highways and through the intersections that map the routes from origin, through transit, to destination countries, and that constitute the embodied networks of transnational organized crime.

The proposed typology is intended to facilitate empirical study of such connections by providing a framework for the collection and analysis of data, and is currently being applied to a sample of UK cases. The suggested models and their variants can be reworked, or even replaced, by more sophisticated formulations as the knowledge base expands and deepens. The intention, however, is to provide a starting point for a closer examination of intersections between crime groups and their diasporas throughout the trafficking chain, and more nuanced considerations of the intersections with gender and ethnicity, to better understand the trade secrets of traffickers, and how the global trade in human beings is organized, managed and maintained.

REFERENCES

Abadinsky, H. (2007), *Organized Crime*. Belmont, CA: Wadsworth Publishing Co.

Anderson, B. and O'Connell Davidson, J. (2002), *Trafficking: A Demand Led Problem?* Save the Children, Stockholm, Sweden.

——— (2003), 'Is Trafficking in Human Beings a Demand Led Problem? A Multi-country Pilot Study', *IOM Migration Research Series*. No. 15. Geneva: IOM.

Bales, K. (2005), *Understanding Global Slavery*. Berkeley: University of California Press.

Butler, K. D. (2001), 'Defining Diasporas, Refining a Discourse', *Diaspora*, 10: 189–219.

Cohen, R. (1997), *Global Diasporas: An Introduction*. London: UCL Press Ltd.

Coy, M., Horvath, M. and Kelly, L. (2007), *'It's Just Like Going to the Supermarket': Men Buying Sex in East London*. Child and Woman Abuse Studies Unit, London Metropolitan University.

Europol (2004), 'European Union Organised Crime Situation Report, Open Version – December 2004', Luxembourg: Office for Official Publications of the European Communities.

Finckenauer, J. O. (2001), 'Russian Transnational Organized Crime and Human Trafficking', in D. Kyle and R. Koslowski, eds, *Global Human Smuggling: Comparative Perspectives*. Baltimore: The Johns Hopkins University Press.

Freilich, J. D., Newman, G., Giorna Shohan, S. and Addad, M., eds (2002), *Migration, Culture, Conflict and Crime*. Aldershot: Ashgate.

Gelsthorpe, L. and Morris, A., eds (1990), *Feminist Perspectives in Criminology*. Milton Keynes: Open University Press.

Glenny, M. (2008), *McMafia, Crime Without Frontiers*. London: The Bodley Head.

Hagedorn, John M., ed. (2007), *Gangs in the Global City*. Urbana and Chicago: University of Illinois Press.

International Labour Organisation (ILO) (2004), *Towards a Fair Deal for Migrant Workers in the Global Economy*. Geneva: ILO.

——— (2005), *A Global Alliance Against Forced Labour*. Geneva: ILO.

Kapur, D. and McHale, J. (2005), *Give Us your Best and Brightest*. Washington, DC: Center for Global Development.

Kelly, L. (2002), 'Journeys of Jeopardy: A Review of Research in Trafficking Women and Children in Europe', *International Organisation for Migration (IOM) Migration Research Series*, No. 11: 6–13, Geneva.

——— (2005), *Fertile Fields: Trafficking in Persons in Central Asia*. Geneva: IOM.

——— (2007), 'A Conducive Context: Trafficking of Persons in Central Asia', in M. Lee, ed., *Human Trafficking*. Uffculme: Willan Publishing.

Kelly, R. J., Maghan, J. and Serio, J. D. (2005), *Illicit Trafficking: A Reference Handbook*. Oxford: ABC-Clio.

Kotkin, J. (1992), *Tribes: How Race, Religion and Identity Determine Success in the New Global Economy*. New York: Random House.

Kyle, D. and Rey Koslowski eds, (2001), *Global Human Smuggling: Comparative Perspective*. Baltimore, London: Johns Hopkins University Press.

Lee, M., ed., (2007), *Human Trafficking*. Uffculme: Willan Publishing.

Maltz, M. (1990), *Measuring the Effectiveness of Organized Crime Control Efforts*. Chicago: Office of International Criminal Justice.

Marshall, W. (1997), cited in Freilich, J. D., Newman, G., Giorna Shoham, S. and Addad, M. (2002). *Migration, Culture, Conflict and Crime*, 19. Aldershot: Ashgate.

Monzini, P. (2005), *Sex Traffic, Prostitution, Crime and Exploitation*. London: Zed Books.

Moore, J. W. (2007), 'Female Gangs: Gender and Globalization', in J. Hagedorn, ed., *Gangs in the Global City*. Urbana and Chicago: University of Illinois Press.

Morawska, E. (2007), 'Trafficking Into and From Eastern Europe', in M. Lee, ed., *Human Trafficking*. Uffculme: Willan Publishing.

Muenz, R. and Ohliger, R., eds, (2003), *Diasporas and Ethnic Migrants: German, Israel and Post-Soviet Successor States in Comparative Perspective*. London: Frank Cass.

'Operation Greensea', available online at http://www.europol.europa.eu/index.asp?page=news&news=pro80131.htm (accessed 6 November 2008).

Piper, N. (2005), 'A Problem by a Different Name? A Review of Research on Trafficking in South-East Asia and Oceania', *International Migration*, 43: 203–33.

Salt, J. and Stein, J. (1997), 'Migration as a Business: The Case of Trafficking', *International Migration*, 35: 467–91.

Schloenhardt, A. (1999), 'The Business of Migration: Organised Crime and Illegal Migration in Australia and the Asia-Pacific Region', in Freilich, J. D., Newman, G., Giorna Shohan, S. and Addad, M., eds (2002), *Migration, Culture Conflict and Crime*. Aldershot: Ashgate.

Shelley, L. (1995), 'Transnational Organized Crime: An Imminent Threat to the Nation State?', *Journal of International Affairs*, 48.

―――― (1999), 'Identifying, Counting and Categorizing Transnational Criminal Organizations', *Transnational Organized Crime*, 5: 1–18.

―――― (2007), 'Human Trafficking as a Form of Transnational Organized Crime', in M. Lee, ed., *Human Trafficking*. Uffculme: Willan Publishing.

Skeldon, R. (2000), 'Trafficking: A Perspective from Asia', *International Migration*, 38: 7–29.

Smith, M. P. and Guardizo, L. E., eds (1998), 'Transnationalism from Below', *Comparative Urban and Community Research*, 6.

Steiner, H. J. and Alston, P. (2000), *International Human Rights in Context*, 2nd edn. Oxford: Oxford University Press.

Taylor, I. and Jamieson, R. (1999), 'Sex Trafficking and the Mainstream of Market Culture', *Crime, Law and Social Change*, 32: 257–78.

The Independent (2007), Monday 22 October.

UNODC (2002), *Results of a Pilot Study of Forty Selected Organized Crime Groups in 16 Countries – September 2002*. Vienna: UNODC.

―――― (2006), *Trafficking in Persons: Global Patterns*. Vienna: UNODC.

Van Schendel, W. (2005), 'Spaces of Engagement; how borderlands, illegal flows and territorial states interlock', in Van Schendel, W. and Abraham, I. (eds), *Illicit Flows and Criminal Things: States, Borders and the Other Side of Globalization*. Bloomington: Indiana University Press.

Vertovec, S. and Cohen, R. eds (1999), *Migration, Diasporas and Transnationalism*. Cheltenham: Edward Elgar, The International Library of Studies on Migration; 9.

Wong, D. (2005), 'The Rumor of Trafficking', in W. van Schendel and I. Abraham, eds, *Illicit Flows and Criminal Things: States, Borders, and the Other Side of Globalization*. Bloomington: Indiana University Press.

Woodiwiss, M. (2001), *Organized Crime and American Power*. Toronto: University of Toronto Press.

Woodward, K., ed. (1997), *Identity and Difference*. London, Thousand Oaks, Calif.: Sage in Association with The Open University.

Wright, A. (2006), *Organised Crime*. Uffculme: Willan Publishing.

56

The criminology of hybrids: rethinking crime and law in technosocial networks

Sheila Brown

[...]

INTRODUCTION: MODERN CRIMINOLOGY AND ITS BINARY DIVISIONS

In the article I am concerned with the way in which criminology as part of a modernist episteme has been largely preoccupied with concepts that depend upon the ability to preserve a number of binary divisions in its conceptions of the world. These concern principally the polarities of science and society, nature and culture and beings and things.[1] In fact, we shall see that these polarities depend upon each other; so that once one polarity is questioned, they all become unclear; moreover, criminology's traditional bifurcatory paradigms are peculiarly unsuited to the analysis of the complex technosocial characteristics of criminological phenomena.

Garland (1997; see also Beirne, 1994) is correct to highlight the dangers of over-simplified characterizations of criminology. Nevertheless it is fair to say that, for the pre-Second World War period, the emphasis on 'science' (as a method) and 'nature' (as its referential point) in criminology remained a constant feature across (western) European societies and the USA (Bianchi et al., 1975; Downes and Rock, 1981; Garland, 1997), reflecting mainstream social theory in general in the West up until the beginning of the 1970s (Giddens, 1987). When the inevitable reaction against 'scientific criminology' came, it emanated (in the USA and the UK at least) most forcibly from interactionism, in a very modified development of a combination of

From *Theoretical Criminology*, 2006, 10(2): 223–44.

Schutzian phenomenology (Schutz, 1962), Chicago sociology deriving from Mead (Mead, 1934; Blumer, 1969), Goffmanesque micro-sociology (Goffman, 1968a, 1968b, 1971) or in Cicourel's case (Cicourel, 1968), ethnomethodology (Garfinkel, 1967; Turner, 1974). Matza's (1964) classic critique of the 'positive delinquent' in fact sought to avoid any overly stark bifurcations, but nevertheless the 'scientific' pretensions of criminology were henceforth to be undermined by uncompromising assertions of the 'social construction' of crime (Lemert, 1967; Schur, 1971) and the 'social interactions' of criminalization (Becker, 1963), both subsequently harnessed to radical and critical criminologies (Taylor et al., 1973, 1975; Quinney, 1974; Chambliss, 1975; Hall et al., 1978).

The European influence of post-structuralism (Boyne, 1990) produced the nearest thing to a break with such dualities, suggesting that the whole nature–culture edifice exists only through the mediation of language, and therefore only the deconstruction of the discursive would reveal the workings of the social 'body deviant'. That is to say, institutional sites of power – notably the carceral – and the discourses surrounding them – notably the medico-scientific complex of knowledge generated by successions of interventions in the minds and bodies of the economically and politically problematic urban poor – spawned a dispersal of power-effects throughout the social body (Foucault, 1977; Cohen, 1985; Boyne, 1990; Garland, 2001). Relatedly, feminist voices in criminology engaged in a critique of 'nature'-bound assumptions (Smart, 1977; Walklate, 1995; Heidensohn, 1996) emphasizing the importance of language and deconstruction in comprehending the regulation of women through knowledge (and indeed through languages of criminology, see Young, 1996). However, poststructuralism and poststructuralist feminisms return one to a polarity. As Lash (2002: 190) notes, words and knowledge in the Foucauldian scheme enter into physiology – and so render the category 'nature' inaccessible to direct, independent observation, leading to the dissolution of the fixed referent. 'Nature' may exist, but it becomes unreachable except through the social.

These polarizations have had a further effect in involving an assumption about the orientation of the human world and the object-world towards each other; of a hierarchical and binary relationship between 'beings' and 'things': 'society' is composed of people, actors, sentient and cognizant beings; de facto it excludes non-human entities which properly belong either to 'nature' – essentially governed by scientific laws – or to the category of 'man-made' – essentially governed by humans within scientific parameters. Writing in 1999, Alex Preda argued for a 'sociological theory of things', claiming that 'things and artefacts are usually treated in sociological theory as marginal, irrelevant, or passive with respect to the production of social order' (1999: 347). Taking issue with this, he concluded that 'social order cannot be conceived of exclusively as a web of intersubjective relationships' (1999: 347).

TECHNOLOGY AND TRANSFORMATION IN CRIMINOLOGY

The polarization within criminology of nature and society, science and society, beings and things, has closed off the very real possibility that the most effective explanations and understandings of crime and control arise at the interstices. The increasing ubiquity and complexity of both material and virtual technologies in the production of social order and control in fact suggest this possibility. Transformational interfacing technologies (cybernetics, genetic engineering, digital visualization, satellite communications, convergent mobile communications, virtual environments) demand a rethinking of our heavily policed criminological boundaries. We need to dissolve the 'scientific' theories and the 'social' theories in order to grasp where we are now; and that is immutably in the technosocial. Above all, this is a world where the 'objects' and the 'subjects', the 'social' and 'scientific', of criminology's purview are co-extensive and symmetrically active.

Has criminology specifically addressed the technosocial at all? The answer is, 'yes', but predominantly from within the ingrained assumptions of the paradigms outlined earlier. True, references to information revolutions, electronic surveillance, transformations in media communications and so on, are everywhere present when criminology discusses globalization, social in/exclusion and governmentality (Loader and Sparks, 2002). Yet the implications of the interfaces remain underexplored, and 'technology' is used in one of two ways: either as the 'technology of social control', or as 'social technologies of control'.

Thus Young (1999) in his influential book on social exclusion and criminology, speaks of technology as though it were a simple instrument in relation to exclusion. 'Let us,' he declares, 'clear up the problem of the technology of social control' (1999: 192). Hence 'CCTV ... is undoubtedly one of the most invidious of inventions. In the wrong hands ... it can invade privacy and make Orwell's 1984 a reality' (Young, 1999: 192). Garland (2001) in a sophisticated piece of work embarks upon a 'genealogical and sociological' attempt to unravel the 'problem of how our contemporary responses to crime came to take the form that they did' (2001: 2); encouragingly, he is concerned to 'avoid the pull towards simple dualisms and the false essentialism they imply', and to map a 'reconfigured complex of interlocking structures and strategies that are themselves composed of old and new elements' (2001: 23). Yet, at the same time, Garland's post- (or as he would have it, 'weak') structuralism, frames all as language, and social practices rest on 'discursive conditions' (Garland, 2001: 25). This is despite the fact that he refers variously to 'advances in technology' (2001: 77) and 'the rise of the electronic mass media' (2001: 78), despite his telling us that television transformed the nature of interaction (2001: 86). It is as if linguistics and purely social arrangements comprehend all of history.

Meanwhile the 'new' cultural criminologists (Ferrell et al., 2004; *Theoretical Criminology*, 2004) continue to portray 'science' as the attaché of administrative criminology, in a critique of 'hard science', 'voodoo numbers' and 'positivism', and consider objects primarily from the point of view of their symbolic or semiotic content (Hayward and Young, 2004; Young, 2004)[2] in everyday life. Contrarily the proponents of the 'new' 'crime science' (http://www.jdi.ucl.ac.uk/about/crime_science/index.php) thrive on the resurgence of fascination with the 'sciencing of crime' (Brown, 2005a; Smith and Tilley, 2005) represented by developments in forensic technologies, biotechnologies and computer simulations and VR. 'Crime Science' 'is a radical way of thinking about the problem of crime in society' (http://www.jdi.ucl.ac.uk/crime_science/index.php) based on 'hard science' (Ekblom, 2005) and allying itself to governance through links with policing strategies and crime and disorder partnerships (Laycock, 2005). Actually there is little new or radical here. An amalgam of quantitative, ICT and design specialisms already firmly grounded in various disciplines and practice areas are deployed in mapping and the creation of statistical prevalence-based predictors and indices, database creation and pre-emptive 'design solutions' (whether in 'gadgets' or building projects).[3] The disappointment in all of this cultural and scientific 'newness' is that the intriguing boundary questions thrown up by phenomena such as DNA testing, databanks, complex computer pattern analysis and surveillance systems are simply sidestepped; likewise, the object creations of architecture, computer science or engineering, are viewed as passive in relation to the human agency of design.

Governmentality theorists have come closest to understanding the significance of technology in crime and control, for 'risk management' and 'government at a distance' are avowedly technical enterprises, and globalization and dispersal are clearly human–technical issues entailing the decline of linear, centralized controls and the dispersal of regulation through networks (O'Malley, 1998; Braithwaite, 2000; Rose, 2000). These theorists, though, over-rely on Foucault's notion of social technology in his deliberations on governmentality (Burchall et al., 1991; Foucault, 1991; Garland, 1997). Thus although a critical rethinking of the 'social' is a feature of such analyses, at least bringing into purview the notion of the post-social (O'Malley, 2001), the latter is seen to centre on modes of the subject, agency and governmentality in human (dis) organization, and has very little to say about 'things' (Preda, 1999; Lash, 2002). The governmentality theorists are primarily concerned with 'social technologies of control'. Nevertheless, the engagement with dispersal and institutions does lever space for a rethinking of the place of non-human entities in the active production of networked 'sociality', as suggested by Haggerty and Ericson's (2000) comments on the 'surveillant assemblage' to both of which I shall return presently.

Otherwise in recent criminological analysis, 'the technical' is seen as a separate specialism set aside from criminology's core; there are important fields in 'cybercrime' (Wall, 2001, 2003), and electronic surveillance (Norris et al., 1998; Coleman and Norris, 2000; McCahill, 2002) but these are presented as *sui generis*, drawing on, rather than building, general theory. In sum, nowhere is captured the vision of the crucial nature of the world as a human/technical hybrid, or as an informational net (Castells, 1996, 2001). Suppose criminology looked outside both the modern 'nature–culture' divide *and* the late modern deconstructionist projects, *and* beyond the governmentalists' highly social notions of technology, towards theories of the technosocial: the cyber, the data-human, the cybernetic and even the a-modern. What sort of contributions, what challenges, might such theorizations make to analyses of crime, law and control?

HYBRID-CULTURE: BEYOND THE NATURAL/SOCIAL BINARY

At this point I would like to invoke an illuminating set of propositions first advanced some years ago by Bruno Latour (1988, 1990, 1993), for in this work may lie the key to addressing some of the problems outlined earlier. For Latour, Modernity itself (and therefore its attendant bifurcatory paradigms) has been an exercise in western epistemological illusion – or delusion; we never *were* modern. 'Moderns', as Latour terms Enlightenment epistemologists, have been distracted by the notion that nature and society, beings and things, were *ever* distinct.

In defence of this proposition, Latour argues thus. 'Science' has 'explained truth through its congruence with natural reality, and falsehood through the constraint of social categories, epistemes, or interests' (1993: 94). Science has concerned itself with the physical world, seen as governed by laws ascertainable only through scientific method. In this type of explanation, the 'social' corrupts 'science'. Science seeks to purge the social from its universe. Positivist *social* scientists may assert the explanatory force of the social – but only when (a staggering contradiction in terms) it is treated 'scientifically'! The constructivist approach meanwhile is concerned with the world of intersubjectivities; and things, objects, the natural world, only of interest as social entities with 'meanings' attached. 'Scientific' categories and taxonomies themselves are neither more nor less than outcomes of socially constructed meanings, open-ended and culturally variable (Douglas, 1973). At the same time it is presumed under constructivism that it is possible to adopt a naturalistic orientation to the social (e.g. Matza, 1964; Hayward and Young, 2004 on naturalism and cultural criminology). Latour boldly washes his hands of this whole business. A *generalized* principle is required in which Nature and Society are to be explained – *equally* – not by each other (Latour, 1993: 95). After all, other (non-western, non-modernist) culture '[C]annot really separate what is knowledge from what is Society, what is sign from what is thing … for Them, Nature and Society, signs and things, are virtually coextensive' (Latour, 1993: 99–100). Latour is reaching for the notion of a seamless connection of beings and things, a melange of human and non-human, a *hybrid*.

Latour expresses the properties of a hybrid thus:

> On page four of my daily newspaper, I learn that the measurements taken above the Antarctic are not good this year: the hole in the ozone layer is growing ominously larger … the same article mixes together chemical reactions and political reactions. A single thread links the most esoteric sciences and the most sordid politics, the most distant sky and some factory in the Lyon suburbs, dangers on a global scale and the impending local elections of the next board meeting. The horizons, the stakes, the time frames, the actors – none of these is commensurable, yet there they are, caught up in the same story.
>
> (1993: 2–3)

It is the 'proliferation of hybrids' (Latour, 1993: 1) that exposes the fault-line in modernist thought. Hybrid – technosocial – culture cannot be accounted for by linear paradigms or causal scientific explanations, nor indeed hierarchies of knowledge concepts. Neither can it be conceived of as merely a constellation of representations. Nor can the answer lie anywhere simply 'in nature' or 'in society'. Yet we are duped by such modern sleights of hand, where the thread which holds the hybrid together, 'will be broken into as many segments as there are pure disciplines. By all means, they seem to say, let us not mix up ... heaven and earth, the global stage and the local scene, the human and the nonhuman' (Latour, 1993: 3).

For Latour, this is to be in denial. For him, the task should be to re-tie the Gordian knot, to *restore* our apprehension of the world as a 'multiply connected network of non-linear forms of life' (1993: 3–5). Moreover, in his use of an extensive epistemic framework, Latour's analysis can take us beyond the 'old wine in new bottles' debates (Wall, 2003) about the 'problem' of technology, presenting us instead with the constitution of the moderns and the status of 'things' (Preda, 1999); it is within *this* problematic that the technology–society question resides. Non-commensurability, in his scheme, is no reason to separate or hierarchize the human/non-human components of a hybrid network; and this is the crucial point to grasp.

BEYOND THE ACTOR: CYBORGS, ASSEMBLAGES AND ACTANTS

Latour's description of the 'incommensurable' elements of the hybrid network above highlights the difficulties experienced by 'social thinkers' in accommodating non-human elements of life. Too often the idea of a 'social theory' has been confused with 'an understanding of society'. The former effectively rules objects out as active co-constituents of the latter (Preda, 1999). The cat is truly among the pigeons in Scott Lash's scenario: for what, asks Lash, 'happens when forms of life become technological?' ... 'in technological forms of life we make sense of the world through technological systems ... we face our environment in our interface with technological systems' (2002: 15).

'Postfeminisms', cybernetic theory and the 'new' sciences of biotechnology have intertwined to generate important questions of technology and virtuality which address the hybrid properties of life forms and have been engaged with in 'social' sciences (for example in the path-breaking post-epistemologies of theorists such as Haraway, 1985, 1991, 1997; Plant, 1996; Soper, 1996; Stone, 1996, 2000; Wolmark, 1999; Waldby, 2000); above all, they have identified the blurring or dissolution of 'the categories of the biological, the technological, the natural, the artificial *and* the human' (Featherstone and Burrows, 1995: 3, emphasis in original).

Such approaches reject the assumption that a 'technology' is an object, a tool, for utilization *by* Man (*sic*). Haraway points out that under such an assumption,

> any status as *agent* in the production of knowledge must be denied the object ... the world must in short be objectified as thing ... matter for the self-formation of the only social being in the production of knowledge, the human knower.
>
> (1991: 198, emphasis in original)

Indeed, patriarchal modernism 'turns everything into a resource for its appropriation, in which an object of knowledge is finally itself only matter for the
seminal power, the act, of the knower' (Haraway, 1991: 197.) What opens up is a
space for a critique that delineates act*ants* rather than *actors*, uniting object and
subject (Akrich, 1992; Latour, 1993) and refiguring the object as active participant.

This approach does not require a virtual environment per se. In the network,
co-extensivity replaces simple co-presence. Actants are simultaneously informational and organic entities in the deepest sense, technology co-extensive with the
human sensorium or self/personhood as McLuhan (1964/1997) and later
Giddens (1991) recognized – but as McLuhan noted, this could equally apply to
light bulbs; or to Dant's (2004) 'driver-car' – 'neither a thing nor a person; it is an
assembled social being that takes on the properties of both and cannot exist without both' (Dant, 2004: 74). It is rather that cybernetic life forms *are* increasingly
pervasive (Featherstone, 2000) and their sophistication makes clearer the
already-existing problem with bifurcatory paradigms. Stone (1996: 4) remarks of
physicist Stephen Hawking that his medical condition makes it impossible to
function unless he is connected to his portable computer system, so 'exactly
where … *is* Hawking? … a serious part of Hawking extends into the box on his
lap … where *does* he stop? Where are his edges?' (Stone, 1996: 5, emphases in
original); similarly Katz and Aakhus (2002) use the notion of 'perpetual contact'
to link a series of fascinating empirical studies which in effect trace mobile
phone-actants in their networks. In other contexts the 'human' being is rendered
as information-actant, as exemplified by the Human Genome Project and the
Virtual Human Project.[4]

As Lash remarks of Haraway's work, 'discourse is no longer King … the
semiotic and the material are … fused' (2002: 191). So, what is important in our
apprehension of this world, within which are inscribed those actions dedicated
as crimes and deemed to be harmful? What is to be regulated? Humans, objects
or information?

HUMAN, OBJECT OR INFORMATION? REAPPRAISING THE BODY IN CRIME AND LAW NETWORKS

In this section I want to consider just some of the transformations and challenges
to law and criminology posed by the technosocial world. I appropriate more
specifically here the work of actor-network theorists (e.g. Callon, 1986a, 1986b;
Latour, 1996, 2002; Law and Hassard, 1999; Dant, 2004) and the ideas of Gabriel
Tarde (1843–1904) the long-buried but currently (slightly) fashionable sociologist
and sometime criminologist (Latour, 2002; Borch, 2005).[5] Technosociality is here
placed centre stage as indicating the combination of materiality and immaterial-
ity, subject and object, sentientism and insentientism and intentionality and
automation in networks of crime and control. The existence of technosociality
implicitly acknowledges that 'monads', to use Tarde's (1999) term for the basic
items of the universe, may possess any property (human or non-human) and be

arranged in any combination, but only some combinations achieve any longevity. Relatively enduring agglomerates of this basic stuff produce 'sociality', a quality that is not inherently defined by humanity or inter-subjectivity (Latour, 2002).

In exploring this I would like to focus on the body, one of the most central ideas in criminal law (Jefferson, 2001) and criminology (Beirne, 1994; Garland, 2002). Social order was framed by Hobbes as directly related to the ordering of bodies, while social control in modernity related to the 'problems of reproduction and restraint from the growth of an urban society in which populations were regulated in social space' (Turner, 1984: 104; see also Foucault, 1977). Equally, the criminal code enshrines the notion of the protection of the body from malicious harm and violation. Moreover, the preservation of conceptions of embodied 'human dignity' in law (Beyleveld and Brownsword, 2001); and the debates over the creation, preservation or ending of physical life, are central to notions of (and heated controversy over) 'rights' (Fukuyama, 2002). Thus, the body-in-law comprises of at least the criminal(ized) body; the culpable (evidential) body, the victim(ized) body; and the ethical body. However, since the body cannot be conceived of as fully 'human' in technosocial networks, it must be thought through here as an actant-body, one node among many in the assemblages of monads (Tarde, 1999; Latour, 2002) constituting the networks of crime and law.

'The criminal body and the culpable body'

Embodied individuals have been required in order to establish guilt, in order to punish; they have been the lynchpin of adversarial justice and symbols of popular vengeance in the ideology of 'laying blame accurately' (Douglas, 1968/1994, 1992; Foucault, 1977; Lacey, 2002). From a technosocial perspective on embodied individuals (Featherstone et al., 1991; Nettleton and Watson, 1998), the criminal body is open to question in all of these aspects.

We are experiencing through the technosocial a realization of the falsity of the concept of purely embodied personhood (Capeller, 2001). The body extends outward into data; it is dis-assembled and re-assembled in networks. A recognition of this quality is implicit in the UK government's imminent introduction of digitized identity cards, part of an ever-more extensive official effort to freeze-frame unique identities as they extend from the corporeal to the digital. Regulation becomes more than the matter of bodies as proposed by Williams and Bendelow (1998: 49); it is to be equally achieved through data policing. Hence we see expansions in body-based regulations of incarceration, curfews, 'intensive community sentences' and so on, *and* expansions in electronic data control; *and* proliferations of hybrid data-body regulations such as electronic tagging.

The co-extensivity of the data/body is abundantly clear in the matter of criminal evidence. Advances in genomic typing diminish the requirement for the body of the victim, or the body of the accused, to be directly visible at all in the establishment of certitude in matters criminal. Criminal investigations arc over the body itself to the informational properties of the crime actants: forensic methodologies seek to prove the existence of a certitude *beyond the substrate of the matter itself.*

Watson (2003) makes the point quite clearly in relation to a number of criminal cases – most notably where American District Attorneys have successfully taken out 'John Doe' arrest warrants against genetic codes despite having no name or embodied person to attach them to (Watson, 2003: 283–4).[6] Similarly, 'evidence' is increasingly rendered as data-human, from DNA profiles to the digitization of other traces from blood spatter patterns to cellphone conversations, to the itinerization of entire investigations on large-scale police computer systems.[7] The digital manipulations of the database 'proves' who 'you' are, that you were there, what you are *in essence*, that you are essentially itinerized.

You are interpellated not as a subject (Althusser, 1977) but as a data-agent, an infinitely re-itinerable entity, subject to all future procedures and competences – if we can't get you now, we will be able to sometime (http://www.ornl.gov/TechResources/Human_Genome/). Criminally speaking, this is the vision of infinite detective work; a case is never closed.[8] This is not tantamount to the 'disappearance of the body-in-law' (Redhead, 1995); but rather to the *expansion* of the data/body. The prosecution process demonstrates this. In the UK, the rules of disclosure under the Criminal Procedures and Investigations Acts 1996 (http://www.hmso.gov.uk/acts/acts1996/96025—a.htm) require the prosecution to retain, and under certain circumstances produce, all 'exhibits' (physical entities) gathered during the course of an investigation. In recent research by this author,[9] examples of murder investigations were encountered that generated between 1500 and 3000 exhibits, all of which must be retained indefinitely in secure storage; the same exhibits were also logged in detail on the virtual enquiry system and, where submitted for forensic analysis, transformed into complex data constructions of DNA databases, molecular compositions, cell-site analysis models and so on. The cumulative effect is mind-boggling.

The victim-body

In similar vein, how embodied does 'real' victimization have to be? How is the actant hurt? Clearly, for example, feminist paradigms successfully offer challenges to merely embodied definitions of violence (Dworkin, 1981; Lacey, 2002). Yet feminism also encounters problems here, because it assumes that the victims of (for example) pornographic misogyny are indeed embodied women. In cyber rape it is the virtual self that is being violated; the 'real' self of which it is an extension, invention or projection, is not necessarily embodied in the gender, sexuality, race or any such dimension of identity of the offline user (Turkle, 1995; Williams, 2001). In cyberhate, textual violence and role-playing stand proxy for embodied race-hate.[10] In cyber porn, simulations are frequently used in place of the digitalized photographic or video footage of 'real' objects of sexual exploitation. This is seen in debates over the status of 'simulated' child pornography. For Carr 'if it looks like child pornography then it should be treated as if it were child pornography' and whether or not an image is real is of 'absolutely no significance'

(Carr, 2002: 2). This of course is highly problematic (Rimm, 1995): does this apply to all simulations, in all contexts? And what is to be counted as a simulation? And simulation of what? Chatterjee (2001) makes a persuasive case for a postmodern/postpostmodern orientation towards pornography in cyberspace, emphasizing fluidity and uncertainty, floating concepts rather than fixed signifiers, and the destabilizing of (gender) representations consequent on the separation of identities from fixed embodied markers: on a theoretical level it is hard to disagree. Yet Williams (2001), from a broadly linguistic perspective, makes a clear case for injuriousness in relation to virtual rape and virtual sexual assault (that they produce responses of fear, anxiety, avoidance, humiliation, withdrawal). Following this logic, it is clear that in the case of paedophilia, child pornography, endlessly circulating, shifting, pixels affect real children's lives and the dignity of children; real humiliations and human pains are generated; and real relations of (patriarchal) power and exploitation are reproduced and reinforced. Power-effects, in other words, are still produced in the network. However, the degree to which we traditionally depend upon a stable and attributable locus of identity for the purposes of moral and legal attribution is brought sharply into focus when the practical harms arising from the disruption of these definitions is considered. This problem can only be addressed when we consider the network as a whole.

The interface between human and machine presents a problem not *because* of the technology nor *because* of the wide (male) cultural support for child sexual abuse practices globally, but precisely because of the interface, the threads linking a complex network of paedophiliac actants of people and things. A delicate thread which might link web-cams to pixels, the pixels to the Internet, the Internet to men, the men to economics, economics to the sex industry, the sex industry to desire, desire to paedophilia, paedophilia to killing, killing to DNA, DNA to men … and so on, has to be apprehended in terms of an immanent and infinitely connected universe of quasi-objects *otherwise it makes no sense*. In this way Lash's (2002) call for a new theory of the sign can be acknowledged, while retaining the ability to comment concretely upon the power-effects traced through the network *and* underline, as Chatterjee correctly does, the inadequacy of law based in 'monistic enlightenment concepts of a unitary self' (2001: 90).

The ethical body

This brings us to the question of sentience and its relationship to ethics and ethical governance in actant-networks. One obvious objection to granting equivalence to things and people is that things are not sentient; however one looks at it, it is the essentially human monad that experiences pain, fear and suffering, not the pixel or the machine. Consequently, the interface between people and things in the essential matters of ethics is particularly problematic, for how is the 'essentially human' to be isolated? Thus, for example, lawyers face the problem of how to maintain notions of ethical governance in the face of 'virtual humanity' (Beyleveld and Brownsword, 2001), which moreover frequently overlaps with criminal law. If 'our posthuman future' (Fukuyama, 2002) leads inexorably towards gene splicing, stem cell technology, body part manufacturing and cloning (and there is no real reason to suggest that it does not), then it also leads to the transformation of embodied law. Border transactions over life and death (when is life 'artificially' created or sustained? When is it 'wilfully' terminated?) intensify, and criminal responsibility becomes increasingly perplexed, involving tortuous processes of referral to alternate jurisdictions and forms of appeal over matters from the use of a dead man's frozen semen to the creation of 'designer babies' or the withdrawal of life support (cybernetic) mechanistics. The genetically engineered baby can neither be described as natural or unnatural; the complexly wired-up PVS patient is neither human nor un(*sic*)human. 'How much' of an actant is human, and therefore subject to deliberations of 'rights' discourses?

Thus the body-in-law, so long a stable point of reference for interpreting and assessing the state of social order, has lost its definition, become blurred, unsteady, unsure, extensive. Is the body human? Is human necessarily embodied? Can control, punishment, compliance, legislature, constitutions, rest on such an unclear and fragile proposition as the 'human being'? It seems doubtful; the briefest of examples reveal multiple ambiguities and the difficulty of severing the reproduction of order from the matter of the machines. How then, can we bring the machines back in? Like it or not, they are here to stay.

ACTANT, ASSEMBLAGE AND NETWORK: THE PRACTICAL ALLIANCES OF SOCIAL ORDER

Haraway writes, 'the world-building alliances of humans and non-humans, in technoscience shape subjects and objects, subjectivity and objectivity, action and passion' (1997: 51); the same can be said of technosociality. If we take the monads and actant-networks pertinent to criminology, it is clear that crime and control, and social order itself, is actively and practically produced precisely through such alliances. Callon (1992) and Preda (1999) argue that 'constellations of hybrid relationships are suffused with social power that cannot be located in any precise object or engine' (Preda, 1999: 360).

Haggerty and Ericson (2000), in an article on the 'surveillant assemblage' make an important point in relation to surveillance technologies. Describing the surveillant assemblage as a convergence of discrete surveillance systems, they note that it is characterized by the transformation of human bodies into abstracted 'data doubles' amenable to almost limitless scrutiny and potential for intervention (2000: 606). Concerned with governance, Haggerty and Ericson focus on the way in which the assemblage transforms the body into pure information so that it may be 'rendered more mobile and comparable' (2000: 613).[11]

These are practical power-effects of the network. Although well delineated, the surveillant assemblage and the 'disappearance of disappearance' (Haggerty and Ericson, 2000: 620) is better accounted for by a comprehension of the actant-network. This reduces the governmentalists' over-reliance on the notion of cognizant drivers of institutions and reframes the 'institution' as a network of actants that is *not* propelled principally by human cognition or social principles such as capital accumulation. In that case, specifying the surveillant assemblage becomes a more complex anthropological matter implying, in Preda's useful scheme, 'complex alignments' of 'actors and artifacts' (i.e. actants), the 'stabilization and maintaining of technological depositives' (better used in the original sense as 'depositifs'), 'the open ended production of knowledge' and 'the co-dependency of humans and networks' (Preda, 1999: 360).

In all this talk of objects, then, it sometimes seems as if sentience and cognizance were being discounted from criminological networks; which clearly would be nonsensical. However, it is apparent that a technosocial analysis *changes* the notion of 'subjectivity' from being a *property of* the person. Lianos with Douglas (2000) go some way towards this approach in their suggestion that Automated Socio-Technical Environments (ASTEs) mark a radical transformation of culture by cutting out negotiation and short-circuiting cognition and human value reproduction; there are then only levels of access in interaction with the system of which one is or is not an authorized user; judgement of right or wrong does not enter into interaction. Neither the human nor the machine 'cause' this situation, for 'the availability of a certain technology is only a prerequisite but not a reason for the applications that it will find' (Lianos with Douglas, 2000: 109). As Dant, following Latour, points out,

> the programme of action of both subject and object is transformed once they come together – combined they may act towards quite a different goal than either could have achieved independently … the assemblage brings about a form of social being and a set of social actions that is different from other forms of being and action.

> (Dant, 2004: 70)

In other words, questions of motivation, morality and responsibility are rendered even more elusive when regarded through a technosocial prism.

CONCLUSION: CRIMINOLOGY, LAW AND TECHNOLOGICAL CULTURE

The above discussion marks only the beginning of what the technosocial might imply for law and criminology. It is not enough to develop 'old law for new technologies' (email interview in Taylor, 1999: 153) or to draw easy analogies between embodied crime and cybercrime (see, for example, Grabowsky and Smith, 1998). There is quite simply no such thing as a 'technological' crime (such as a 'cyber-crime') as distinct from an 'embodied' crime; crimes as network activities only contain varying degrees of virtual or embodied monads. The technosocial notion of the act*ant* re-materializes the virtual world, a 'corrective to those perspectives which seek to privilege the digital or virtual realm over material spaces' (Gandy, 2005: 42), investing the materiality of objects with due significance, but at the same time fully comprehends the inherent virtuality of networks in the so-called 'material' world. At the same time the actant-network cannot be seen as comprised of uniquely cognizant and motivated human beings, since the practical effects of human–non-human alliances include cultural and normative transformations (Bell and Kennedy, 2000; Lianos with Douglas, 2000).

Criminology is faced with a different kind of dilemma for the foreseeable future; including a different kind of 'aetiology' altogether that rests not on whether it is possible to specify motivations, cognition and causes of individual human behaviour; but focuses instead on the explanation of human actions with reference to their simultaneous constitution as informational and technical events. Similarly, analyses of criminal justice can no longer rest at analyses of social interests, and motivations, but must address the technological properties of the body politic, and of the institutional landscape of control, as inseparable from their form. Information theory will increasingly infuse both domains of Law and Criminology, for 'social theory' (despite some significant inroads made by governmentality theorists) is simply not adequate to comprehend contemporary forms of criminality, legality and regulation. As Karnow elegantly puts it, '[computer crime law] follows the general legal presumptions of discrete, separable areas surrounding and defining each legally cognizable entity' (1994: 3). Therefore, to the extent that the technosocial confounds 'legally cognizable entities', it confounds the law.

The kind of perspective advocated in this article is, however, problematic from a political or normative perspective because it cannot easily address questions of moral attribution. Nevertheless, the potentiality for explaining *how* and *why* forms of crime and control come about in the network is much enhanced; and as has been my argument elsewhere 'theory ends where ethics begin' (Brown, 2003: 193): a normative criminology is not precluded, but should rather be encouraged. However, we need to recognize theoretically first, that the moderns have been overly preoccupied with dividing up science and nature, things and society; and second, that crime and control are played out in technosocial networks. The next task is to specify the foundations for a criminology of hybrids (Brown, 2005b) and networks, to abandon our penchant for what Haraway aptly calls 'leaky distinctions' (1991: 193), to engage with technosociality in our methodologies. Or, as Latour puts it, drawing on the very modernist end of the 19th century and the sociology of Gabriel Tarde, 'when you want to understand an actor, go and look through the net at the work it has traced' (2002: 127).

NOTES

1   The usage of 'science' and 'society' here follows Latour (1993) and Robertson et al. (1996) and embraces, but does not solely signify, the disciplines of the natural and social sciences and their respective paradigms. 'Scientific' explanations, however, are taken as referring to the nature pole, and 'social' explanations to the society pole – as in Kant's differentiation between *Naturwissenschaften* and *Geisteswissenschaften*. The question in this article is does anything fit such a polarized distinction?

2   See, for example, the launch of journals such as *Crime, Media, Culture* by Sage; the emphasis of the 2005 British Criminology Conference on cultural criminology; and a general burgeoning of English language publishing in cultural criminology.

3 Apparently devised at a Cambridge afternoon tea-party (Laycock, 2005)!
4 The process of virtualizing the human described by Waldby in the VHP is illuminating, and deserves some attention. The first Visible Human started life (!) as a prisoner on Death Row. Waldby describes how (through intricate processes of advanced scanning technologies) the preserved body of the dead prisoner is literally sliced microscopically and digitalized, the slicing being so thin that the body disintegrates as it is visualized/virtualized. What a precise example of the theoretical point made by Waldby: for where does it leave the 'constructivist' viewpoint or the 'science–nature' viewpoint?
5 Tarde's work contained antecedents of actor-network theory, for he did not see a necessity for the notion of 'society' to be restricted to people; nor did he acknowledge the 'over and aboveness' of an independent social supra-structure. In an attempt at an all-encompassing sociology based on a monadologie (Tarde, 1999), he suggested that various combinations of 'monads' – described by Latour (2002) as the stuff of which the Universe is made – may or may not hold together to create agglomerates, links, which produce (in Latour's terms) action and network. 'Monad' is also used interestingly in the functional programming language Haskell to denote 'a strategy for combining computations into more complex computations', allowing 'the programmer to build up computations using sequential building blocks, which can themselves be sequences of computations' (http://www.nomaware.com/monads/html/introduction.html).
6 For example State of Wisconsin v. John Doe, unknown male with matching deoxyribonucleic acid (DNA) profile at genetic locations D1S7, D2S44, DS5110, D10S28 and D17S79, cited in Watson (2003: 284).
7 E.g. HOLMES II: Home Office Large Major Inquiry System II; Airwave, a system of handset interfacing combining two-way radio, mobile phone and data terminal; NDNAD, the UK National DNA Database currently under rapid expansion. Other systems include satellite tracking and cell-site analysis of mobile phones, numerous digital forensic techniques and virtual imaging and simulation systems.
8 See the increasing number of TV programmes, crime fiction and film centring on cold-case reviews. As one senior police officer told this author in interview, 'X's case will never be closed. We are just waiting for more advances in science.'
9 Brown, S. 'Major Incidents: Cultural Constructions and Crime Processing Realities in Homicide Investigations', and 'The Sciences of Detection: Popular Representation and Crime Processing Realities', research reports in preparation.
10 See Zickmund (1997) on the discursive culture of cyber hate. For a gaming example, see the case of 'Hooligans: Storm over Europe', a pro-Nazi game regarded as too offensive by *PC Gamer* magazine (2002: 16) to be given 'the oxygen of publicity'.
11 This is not new – Michel Callon noted a similar process in the practices of scientific research, where living beings are 'translated' into docile figures through the recording of data (Callon, 1986a; for a rare criminological application see Brown, 1991). However, with highly developed and convergent data capture systems now an integral part of everyday life, the surveillant assemblage is born.

REFERENCES
Akrich, M. (1992) 'The De-scription of Technical Objects', in W. Bijker and J. Law (eds) *Shaping Technology/Building Society: Studies in Socio-Technical Change*. Cambridge, MA: MIT Press.

Althusser, L. (1977) 'Ideology and Ideological State Apparatuses', in *Lenin and Philosophy and Other Essays*, pp. 121–73. London: New Left Books.

Becker, H. (1963) *Outsiders*. Glencoe, IL: Free Press.

Beirne, P. (ed.) (1994) *The Origins and Growth of Criminology: Essays on Intellectual History 1760–1945*. Aldershot: Dartmouth.

Bell, D. and B.M. Kennedy (eds) (2000) *The Cybercultures Reader*. London: Routledge.

Beyleveld, D. and R. Brownsword (2001) *Human Dignity in Bioethics and Biolaw*. Oxford: Oxford University Press.

Bianchi, H., M. Simondi and I. Taylor (eds) (1975) *Deviance and Control in Europe*. London: John Wiley & Sons.

Blumer, H. (1969) *Symbolic Interactionism: Perspectives and Method*. New York: Prentice Hall.

Borch, C. (2005) 'Urban Imitations: Tarde's Sociology Revisited', *Theory, Culture and Society* 22(3): 81–100.

Boyne, R. (1990) *Foucault and Derrida: The Other Side of Reason*. London: Unwin Hyman.

Braithwaite, J. (2000) 'The New Regulatory State and the Transformation of Criminology', in D. Garland and R. Sparks (eds) *Criminology and Social Theory*, pp. 47–70. Oxford: Clarendon.

Brown, S. (1991) *Magistrates at Work: Sentencing and Social Structure*. Milton Keynes: Open University Press.

Brown, S. (2003) *Crime and Law in Media Culture*. Buckingham: Open University Press.

Brown, S. (2005a) 'Major Incidents: Cultural Constructions and Crime Processing Realities in Homicide Investigations', unpublished research report on the 'Sciencing of Crime' research project 2003–4.

Brown, S. (2005b) 'Virtual Criminology', in E. McLaughlin and J. Muncie (eds) *The Sage Dictionary of Criminology*, 2nd edn. London: Sage.

Burchall, G., C. Gordon and P. Miller (eds) (1991) *The Foucault Effect: Studies in Governmentality*. Brighton: Harvester Wheatsheaf.

Callon, M. (1986a) 'Some Elements of a Sociology of Translation: Domestication of Scallops and the Fishermen of St Brieuc Bay', in J. Law (ed.) *Power, Action and Belief: A New Sociology of Knowledge. Sociological Review* Monograph 32, pp. 196–233. University of Keele. London: Routledge & Kegan Paul.

Callon, M. (1986b) 'The Sociology of an Actor-Network: The Case of the Electric Vehicle', in M. Callon, J. Law and A. Rip (eds) *Mapping the Dynamics of Science and Technology: Sociology of Science in the Real World*, pp. 19–34. Basingstoke: Macmillan.

Callon, M. (1992) 'Techno-Economic Networks and Irreversibility', in J. Law (ed.) *A Sociology of Monsters: Essays on Power, Technology, and Domination*, pp. 132–64. London: Routledge.

Capeller, W. (2001) 'Not Such a Neat Net: Some Comments on Virtual Criminality', *Social and Legal Studies* 10(2): 229–42.

Carr, J. (2002) 'Pseudo Pornography and the Freedom of Speech', *Newsletter* 39(April): 2–3.

Castells, M. (1996) *The Rise of the Network Society*. Oxford: Basil Blackwell.

Castells, M. (2001) *The Internet Galaxy*. Oxford: Oxford University Press.

Chambliss, W. (1975) 'Towards a Political Economy of Crime', *Theory and Society* 2: 149–70.

Chatterjee, B. (2001) 'Last of the Rainmacs: Thinking about Pornography in Cyberspace', in D. Wall (ed.) *Crime and the Internet*, pp. 74–99. London: Routledge.

Cicourel, A.V. (1968) *The Social Organization of Juvenile Justice*. London: Heinemann.

Cohen, S. (1985) *Visions of Social Control*. Cambridge: Polity.

Coleman, C. and C. Norris (2000) 'CCTV and Crime Prevention: Questions for Criminology', in *Introducing Criminology*, ch. 6. Cullompton: Willan.

Dant, T. (2004) 'The Driver-Car', *Theory, Culture and Society* 21(4/5): 61–79.

Douglas, M. (1968/1994) *Purity and Danger: An Analysis of the Concepts of Pollution and Taboo*. London: Routledge.

Douglas, M. (ed.) (1973) *Rules and Meanings: The Anthropology of Everyday Knowledge*. Harmondsworth: Penguin.

Douglas, M. (1992) *Risk and Blame: Essays in Cultural Theory*. London: Routledge.

Downes, D. and P. Rock (1981) *Understanding Deviance*. Oxford: Clarendon Press.

Dworkin, A. (1981) *Pornography: Men Possessing Women*. London: Women's Press.

Ekblom, P. (2005) 'How to Police the Future: Scanning for Scientific and Technological Innovations Which Generate Potential Threats and Opportunities in Crime, Policing and Crime Reduction', in M.J. Smith and N. Tilley (eds) *Crime Science: New Approaches to Preventing and Detecting Crime*, pp. 27–55. Cullompton: Willan.

Featherstone, M. (ed.) (2000) *Body Modification*. London: Sage.

Featherstone, M. and R. Burrows (eds) (1995) *Cyberspace, Cyberbodies, Cyberpunk: Cultures of Technological Embodiment*. London: Sage/TCS.

Featherstone, M., M. Hepworth and B.S. Turner (eds) (1991) *The Body: Social Process and Cultural Theory*. London: Sage.

Ferrell, J., K. Hayward, W. Morrison and M. Presdee (eds) (2004) *Cultural Criminology Unleashed*. London: Glasshouse Press.

Foucault, M. (1977) *Discipline and Punish*. Harmondsworth: Penguin.

Foucault, M. (1991) 'Governmentality', in G. Burchall, C. Gordon and P. Miller (eds) *The Foucault Effect: Studies in Governmentality*, pp. 87–104. Brighton: Harvester Wheatsheaf.

Fukuyama, F. (2002) *Our Posthuman Future: Consequences of the Biotechnology Revolution*. London: Profile Books.

Gandy, M. (2005) 'Cyborg Urbanization: Complexity and Monstrosity in the Contemporary City', *International Journal of Urban and Regional Research* 29(1): 26–49.

Garfinkel, H. (1967) *Studies in Ethnomethodology*. Englewood Cliffs, NJ: Prentice-Hall.

Garland, D. (1997) 'Governmentality and the Problem of Crime: Foucault, Criminology, Sociology', *Theoretical Criminology* 1(2): 173–214.

Garland, D. (2001) *The Culture of Control*. Oxford: Oxford University Press.

Garland, D. (2002) 'Of Crimes and Criminals: The Development of Criminology in Britain', in M. Maguire, R. Morgan and R. Reiner (eds) *The Oxford Handbook of Criminology*, 3rd edn, pp. 7–50. Oxford: Oxford University Press.

Giddens, A. (1987) *Social Theory and Modern Sociology*. Cambridge: Polity.

Giddens, A. (1991) *Modernity and Self-Identity*. Cambridge: Polity.

Goffman, E. (1968a) *Asylums*. Harmondsworth: Penguin.

Goffman, E. (1968b) *Stigma: Notes on the Management of a Spoiled Identity*. Harmondsworth: Penguin.

Goffman, E. (1971) *The Management of Self in Everyday Life*. Harmondsworth: Penguin.

Grabosky, P.N. and R.G. Smith (1998) *Crime in the Digital Age*. New Brunswick, NJ: Transaction Publishers.

Haggerty, K.D. and R.V. Ericson (2000) 'The Surveillant Assemblage', *British Journal of Sociology* 51(4): 605–22.

Hall, S., C. Critcher, T. Jefferson, J. Clarke and B. Roberts (1978) *Policing the Crisis: Mugging, the State, and Law and Order*. London: Macmillan.

Haraway, D. (1985) 'A Manifesto for Cyborgs: Science, Technology and Socialist Feminism in the 1980's', *Socialist Review* 15: 65–107.

Haraway, D. (1991) *Simians, Cyborgs and Women: The Reinvention of Nature*. London: Free Association Books.

Haraway, D. (1997) *Modest_Witness@Second_Millennium.FemaleMan_ Meets_OncoMouse*. New York: Routledge.

Hayward, K. and J. Young (2004) 'Cultural Criminology: Some Notes on the Script', *Theoretical Criminology* 8(3): 259–73.

Heidensohn, F. (1996) *Women and Crime*. London: Macmillan.

Karnow, C. (1994) 'Recombinant Culture: Crime in the Digital Network', paper presented at Defcon II, Las Vegas, July. www.defcon.org/html/TEXT/2/KARNOW-2.TXT

Jefferson, M. (2001) *Criminal Law* (5th edn). London: Longman.

Katz, J.E. and M.A. Aakhus (eds) (2002) *Perpetual Contact: Mobile Communication, Private Talk, Public Performance*. Cambridge: Cambridge University Press.

Lacey, N. (2002) 'Legal Constructions of Crime', in M. Maguire, R. Morgan and R. Reiner (eds) *The Oxford Handbook of Criminology*, pp. 264–85. Oxford: Oxford University Press.

Lash, S. (2002) *Critique of Information*. London: Sage.

Latour, B. (1988) *The Pasteurization of France*. Cambridge, MA: Harvard University Press.

Latour, B. (1990) 'Postmodern? No, Simply A-modern! Steps towards an Anthropology of Science', *Studies in the History and Philosophy of Science* 1: 145–71.

Latour, B. (1993) *We Have Never Been Modern*. Cambridge, MA: Harvard University Press.

Latour, B. (1996) *Aramis or the Love of Technology*. Trans. Catherine Porter. London: Harvard University Press.

Latour, B. (2002) 'Gabriel Tarde and the End of the Social', in P. Joyce (ed.) *The Social in Question: New Bearings in History and the Social Sciences*, pp. 117–32. London: Routledge.

Law, J. and J. Hassard (1999) *Actor Network and After*. Oxford: Blackwell.

Laycock, G. (2005) 'Defining Crime Science', in M.J. Smith and N. Tilley (eds) *Crime Science: New Approaches to Preventing and Detecting Crime*, pp. 3–24. Cullompton: Willan.

Lemert, E.M. (1967) *Human Deviance, Social Problems and Social Control*. New York: Prentice-Hall.

Lianos, M. with M. Douglas (2000) 'Dangerization and the End of Deviance', in D. Garland and R. Sparks (eds) *Criminology and Social Theory*, pp. 103–26. Oxford: Clarendon.

Loader, I. and R. Sparks (2002) 'Contemporary Landscapes of Crime, Order, and Control: Governance, Risk and Globalization', in M. Maguire, R. Morgan and R. Reiner (eds) *The Oxford Handbook of Criminology*, 3rd edn, pp. 82–111. Oxford: Clarendon Press.

McCahill, M. (2002) *The Surveillance Web: The Rise of Visual Surveillance in an English City*. Cullompton: Willan.

McLuhan, M. (1964/1997) *Understanding Media: The Extensions of Man*. Cambridge, MA: MIT Press.

Matza, D. (1964) *Delinquency and Drift*. New York: John Wiley.

Mead, G.H. (1934) *Mind, Self and Society*. Chicago, IL: Chicago University Press.

Nettleton, S. and J. Watson (eds) (1998) *The Body in Everyday Life*. London: Routledge.

Norris, C., J. Moran and G. Armstrong (eds) (1998) *Surveillance, Closed Circuit Television and Social Control*. Aldershot: Ashgate.

O'Malley, P. (1998) *Crime and the Risk Society*. Aldershot: Ashgate.

O'Malley, P. (2001) 'Risk, Crime and Prudentialism Revisited', in K. Stenson and R. Sullivan (eds) *Crime, Risk and Justice: The Politics of Crime Control in Liberal Democracies*, pp. 89–103. Cullompton: Willan.

PC Gamer (2002) *PC Gamer Magazine* May: 16. Sittingbourne, Kent: The Magazine Group.

Plant, S. (1996) 'The Virtual Complexity of Culture', in G. Roberston, M. Mash, L. Tickner, J. Bird, B. Curtis and T. Putnam (eds) *FutureNatural: Nature, Science, Culture*, pp. 203–17. London: Routledge.

Preda, A. (1999) 'The Turn to Things: Arguments for a Sociological Theory of Things', *Sociological Quarterly* 40(2): 347–66.

Quinney, R. (1974) *Crime and Justice in America: A Critical Understanding*. Boston, MA: Little, Brown.

Redhead, S. (1995) *Unpopular Cultures: The Birth of Law and Popular Culture*. Manchester: Manchester University Press.

Rimm, M. (1995) 'Marketing Pornography on the Information Superhighway: A Survey of 917,410 Images, Descriptions, Short Stories, and Animations Downloaded 8.5 Million Times by Consumers in Over 2000 Cities in Forty Countries, Provinces and Territories', *Georgetown Law Journal* 83: 1849–915. Reprinted in D.S. Wall (ed.) *Cyberspace Crime*. Aldershot: Dartmouth/Ashgate.

Robertson, G., M. Mash, L. Tickner, J. Bird, B. Curtis and T. Putnam (eds) (1996) *FutureNatural: Nature, Science, Culture*. London: Routledge.

Rose, N. (2000) 'Government and Control', in D. Garland and R. Sparks (eds) *Criminology and Social Theory*, pp. 183–208. Oxford: Clarendon.

Schur, E. (1971) *Labelling Deviant Behaviour: Its Sociological Implications*. New York: Random House.

Schutz, A. (1962) *Collected Papers*. The Hague: Martinus Nijhoff.

Smart, C. (1977) *Women, Crime and Criminology*. London: Routledge & Kegan Paul.

Smith, M. and N. Tilley (eds) (2005) *Crime Science: New Approaches to Preventing and Detecting Crime*. Cullompton: Willan.

Soper, K. (1996) 'Nature/"Nature"', in G. Robertson, M. Mash, L. Tickner, J. Bird, B. Curtis and T. Putnam (eds) *FutureNatural: Nature, Science, Culture*, pp. 22–34. London: Routledge.

Stone, A.R. (1996) *The War of Desire and Technology at the Close of the Mechanical Age*. London: MIT Press.

Stone, A.R. (2000) 'Will the Real Body Please Stand Up? Boundary Stories about Virtual Cultures', in D. Bell and B.M. Kennedy (eds) *The Cyber-cultures Reader*, pp. 504–28. London: Routledge.

Tarde, G. (1999) *Oeuvres de Gabriel Tarde*. Paris: Collection Les Empecheurs de Penser en Rond.

Taylor, I., P. Walton and J. Young (1973) *The New Criminology*. London: Routledge & Kegan Paul.

Taylor, I., P. Walton and J. Young (eds) (1975) *Critical Criminology*. London: Routledge & Kegan Paul.

Taylor, P.A. (1999) *Hackers: Crime in the Digital Sublime*. London: Routledge.

Theoretical Criminology (2004) Special Issue on Cultural Criminology. *Theoretical Criminology* 8(3).

Turkle, S. (1995) *Life on the Screen: Identity in the Age of the Internet*. New York: Simon & Schuster.

Turner, B.S. (1984) *The Body and Society*. Oxford: Basil Blackwell.

Turner, R. (ed.) (1974) *Ethnomethodology*. Harmondsworth: Penguin.

Waldby, C. (2000) *The Visible Human Project: Informatic Bodies and Post-human Medicine*. New York & London: Routledge.

Walklate, S. (1995) *Gender and Crime: An Introduction*. Hemel Hempstead: Prentice Hall/Harvester Wheatsheaf.

Wall, D.S. (ed.) (2001) *Crime and the Internet*. London: Routledge.

Wall, D.S. (2003) 'Cybercrimes: New Wine, No Bottles?', in D.S. Wall (ed.) *Cyberspace Crime*, pp. 3–38. Aldershot: Ashgate.

Watson, J. (2003) *DNA: The Secret of Life*. London: Arrow.

Williams, M. (2001) 'The Language of Cybercrime', in D. Wall (ed.) *Crime and the Internet*, pp. 152–66. London: Routledge.

Williams, S.J. and G. Bendelow (1998) *The Lived Body: Sociological Themes, Embodied Issues*. London: Routledge.

Wolmark, J. (ed.) (1999) *Cybersexualities: A Reader on Feminist Theories, Cyborgs and Cyberspace*. Edinburgh: Edinburgh University Press.

Young, A. (1996) *Imagining Crime: Textual Outlaws and Criminal Conversations*. London: Sage/TCS.

Young, J. (1999) *The Exclusive Society*. London: Sage.

Young, J. (2004) 'Voodoo Criminology and the Numbers Game', in J. Ferrell, K. Hayward, W. Morrison and M. Presdee (eds) *Cultural Criminology Unleashed*, pp. 13–27. London: Glasshouse Press.

Zickmund, S. (1997) 'Approaching the Radical Other: The Discursive Culture of Cyberhate', in S.G. Jones (ed.) *Virtual Culture: Identity and Community in Cybersociety*, pp. 185–205. London: Sage.

Author Index

Subject Index